# Yours truly,

# Jack the Ripper

## The London Newspapers
## The Whitechapel Killer
### and
## The Autumn of 1888

Edited by

## H. L. Hanna
### 2015

AQUILA

Harrisburg, Arkansas

# Introduction

"September 25, 1888.

"Dear Boss—I keep on hearing the police have caught me, but they won't fix me just yet. I have laughed when they look so clever and talk about being on the right track. That joke about Leather Apron gave me rare fits. I am down on whores, and I shan't quit ripping them till I do get buckled. Grand work the last job was. I gave the lady no time to squeal. How can they catch me now? I love my work. I want to start again. You will soon hear from me with my funny little games. I saved some of the proper stuff in a ginger-beer bottle over the last job. I did write with it, but it went thick like glue and I couldn't use it. Red ink is fit enough, ha, ha, ha! The next job I do I shall clip the lady's ears and send them to the police-officers just for folly. Wouldn't you keep this letter back till I do a bit more work; then give it out straight? My knife is so nice and sharp, I want to get to work right away, if I get the chance. Good, luck.

"Yours truly,
"JACK THE RIPPER."

"Don't mind me giving the trade name. Wasn't good enough to post this before I got all the red ink off my hands, curse it. They say I'm a doctor. Ha! ha! ha! ha!

~

With this letter, received by the London Central News Agency on the 27th of September, 1888, the man considered to be the world's first serial killer introduced himself to his horrified public. Although there have been some reservations about the veracity of the letters provenance, there can be no doubt that it truly captures the inner essence of a madman filled with blood-lust.

The fact also that the letter was sent to the Central News Agency, which researched, produced, collected and distributed articles and news stories to newspapers in London and throughout Great Britain, rather than to the police, is an illustration of the growing power of the popular press to influence public opinion.

In this work I am not attempting to give an in-depth analysis of the Whitechapel killings, there are many experts far more knowledgeable on the subject than myself, who have produced excellent historical works detailing facts and joining the pieces of this puzzle in an attempt to discover the identity of Jack the Ripper. What I have done is reproduce, in chronological order, news articles from three leading London newspapers, each of which thoroughly covered the investigations of the slayings from its particular political and social point of view.

Because of some obscurities in the text due to the evolution of the English language over the last century and a quarter, I have added explanatory footnotes identifying people and defining slang words, phrases and technical terms that are no longer commonly used. For this purpose I have consulted various Victorian Era dictionaries, histories, newspapers, magazines, encyclopaedias, government sources and works of literature. I have also utilized modern sources concentrating on the Whitechapel killings and Victorian society in general.

The newspapers I have chosen are:

*The Times*, founded in 1785, was considered the flagship of the Conservative Party.

*The Star* was established in the summer of 1888, only months before the killings began. It can be said that *The Star* made its reputation with lurid headlines and stories showcasing the killings. But it also has to be stated that *The Star* and its Irish nationalist editor, T.P. O'Connor, championed reform and aid for the people of the slums.

*The Evening News*, first published in 1881, priced at ½ penny as opposed to the penny of *The Times*, was the first popular evening paper, with its target audience the middle and lower classes.

Due to the fact that these articles are placed in chronological order, a traditional Table of Contents would be needlessly complicated and confusing.. For this reason I have replaced it with a comprehensive Index divided into 20 distinct categories.

As a final word, I have to state that I am truly grateful for the research done by Casebook.org. This work would not have been possible without their vast collection of newspaper articles, essays, references and photographs covering Whitechapel Jack.

H.L. Hanna
Widener, Arkansas
2015

# Index

~

## VICTIMS
### EMMA SMITH
Brick-lane, 3, 39, 40, 46, 47, 52, 71, 74, 81, 88, 92, 93, 98, 125, 128, 153, 200, 214, 261, 301, 387, 514
Inquest, 544
Emma Elizabeth Smith, 8, 10, 13, 56, 162, 544
Mary Ann Smith, 210

### INQUEST TESTIMONY
Dr. G.H. Hillier, 544
Mary Russell, 544
Chief-Insp. John West, H Div., 544

~

### MARTHA TABRAM
Bryan, 2
George-yard, 1, 2, 3, 4, 5, 6, 7, 8, 10, 17, 18, 22, 56, 63, 68, 92, 133, 162, 227, 261, 263, 457, 460, 464, 498, 500

George-yard Buildings, 2, 3, 5, 8, 162, 454, 464
George-yard murder, 460
Inquest, 3, 8, 9, 25, 29, 31
The "Slaughter-house", 17
Annie Tabram, 211
Martha Tabram, 22, 162, 459, 501
Tabran, 56
Martha Tabran, 8
Martha Turner, 3, 5, 6, 7, 9, 17, 18, 233, 239, 247, 454

### INQUEST TESTIMONY
P.C. Thomas Barrett, 226 H, 3
Mary Bousfield (Bowsfield), 8, 10
Mary Ann (Pearly Poll) Connolly, 8, 9, 10, 11
Alfred George Crow, 3, 4
Dr. T.R. Killeen (Keeling), 3, 4
Elizabeth Mahony, 4
Ann Morris, 8, 10
John Saunders Reeves, 3, 4
Henry Samuel Tabran, 8, 9
Henry Turner, 8, 10
Mr. Weathers, 2

### WITNESSES
Alfred George Crow, 3, 4
Buckle, 2
Mary Ann (Pearly Poll) Connolly, 6, 7, 8, 9, 10, 11
Francis Hewitt, 2
Thomas Hunt, 6

~

### MARY ANN NICHOLS
Mr. Drew, 23
Funeral, 41
Inquest, 18, 25, 29, 34, 130, 160
Lambeth Workhouse, 12, 15, 21, 41, 132, 160
Mary Nichols, 31, 32
Mary Ann Nicholls, 15, 22, 45, 47, 50, 70, 101, 130, 193, 434
Mary Ann Nichols, 21, 23, 34, 54, 57, 58, 59, 60, 75, 83, 92, 102, 160
"Polly", 15, 16, **17, 18**
Mr. Smith, Supplied Coffin, 41
Walker, Father of MN, 28

### INQUEST TESTIMONY
Det.-Insp.Fred.G.Abberline, 130, 132
George Cross, 27, 31, 35
William Eade, 160

Thomas Ede, 130
Det.-Sergt. (Insp.) P. Enright, 25, 34
Emma Green, 130
James Hatfield, 132, 141
Insp. Joseph Henry Helson (Helston), J Div., 26, 30, 34, 35, 132
Dr. Henry Ralph Llewellyn, 24
Mary Ann Monk, 36
Patrick Mulshaw, 131
P.C. George Myzen (Mizen), 27, 31, 35
Robert Mann, 132, 141
P.C. John Neil, 97 J, 23
William Nichols, 35
Jane Oram, 35
Robert Paul, 131
P.C. John Phail, 96 J, 131
Walter Purkiss, 130
Insp. John Spratling (Spratley), 23, 25, 26, 29, 34, 132
Henry Tompkins, 26, 30, 34 (Tomkins)
Edward Walker(Father of M.N.), 22

### WITNESSES
Mrs. Colwell, 19, 20, 39
Mr. Green, 25
Mrs. Green, 25
Green Family, 19
Nelly Holland, 22
Mary Ann Monk, 15, 17, 36
James Mumford, *mentioned* 26, 35
William Nichols, 23, 28, 35
Robert Paul, 29, 131
Walter Perkins, 19, 20
Mr. Purkis, 25, 34
Mrs. Purkiss, 161
Mr. Scorer, 18
Edward Walker(Father of M.N.), 22, 28

~

### ANNIE CHAPMAN
29, Hanbury-street, 59, 82, 83, 113, 115, 119, 153
Alias Sieve, 48
Bright Farthings, 70
Chapman, 56, 59, 69, 77, 80, 82, 84, 97, 102, 105, 113, 114, 115, 117, 118, 124, 126, 127, 128, 152, 162, 167, 168, 169, 170, 171, 173, 174, 175, 181, 182, 183, 212, 213, 222, 233,

# Index

# Index

# Index

# Index

# Index

# Index

# Index

# Index

# Index

# Index

# Index

~

## CORONER'S OFFICE

~

## MORTUARIES

# Index

# Index

Geo. Savage, 241
C. J. Solomons, 235
Spahl, 263
W. H. Spencer-Howell, 235
Mary H. Steer, 368
Success, 307
E. Swabey, 156
C. Thomas, 495
H. Thomas, 307
F. Thornburn, 308
Tie, 234
Trafalgar-square, 308
J.P. Vooght, 307
Joseph Walker, 235
Robert Walker, 307
Frederick Arthur Wellesley, 190
Edwin J. Wells, 307
Whitechapel, 338
Dr. L. Forbes Winslow, 91, 98, 108,
    118, 159, 163, 223, 246, 361, 428,
    448
R. H. Winter, 400

~

## PUBLIC HOUSES
Bee Hive, 251
Bells, 46, 47, 49, 128, 468, 473
Black Swan, 371
Bladebone, 416
Bricklayers' Arms, 212, 213
Britannia, 445, 450, 451, 453, 473
Crown Tavern, 128
Crystal Tavern, 515
Dirty Dick's, 49
Duke of York, 493
Eagle Tavern, 535, 539
East India Arms, 528
Five Bells, 473
Foresters' Arms, 130
George, 588
Goddard's, 552
Horse and Groom, 317
Nelson Tavern, 231, 259
Nuns Head Tavern, 333
Paul's Head Tavern, 438, 451
Pope's Head, 65, 74, 80, 98
Prince Albert "Clean House", 49, 68,
    81, 128, 464
Princess Alice Tavern, 7, 39
Queen's Head, 60, 270, 272
Red Lion, 256
The Ringer's, 79, 85, 152, 164, 438,
    444, 450
Silver Cup Tavern, 554
Ten Bells, 49, 128, 468
Thurlow Arms, 203, 220
White Swan, 10

~

## LODGING HOUSES
A Night in Whitechapel, 88, 363
35, Dorset-street, Spital-fields, 47
No. 55, Flower and Dean-street, 257
Albert-chambers, 184, 220, 230

Buller's, 434, 443, 444
Commercial lodging-house, 455
Common Lodging Houses, 261, 263,
    265, 266, 435, 468
Crossingham's, 10
Dorset-chambers, 50, 115
Doss House, 310
Doss Houses, 356
Gordon-chambers, 418
Lodgings, 69, 73, 78, 82, 84, 86, 93,
    106, 161, 196, 216, 226, 260, 265,
    268, 286, 297, 298, 307, 324, 412,
    420, 437, 438, 444, 452, 460, 462,
    468, 470, 495, 506, 509
Wilmot's, 64

~

## MILITARY
3d Surrey, 566
11th Hussars, 493
18th Royal Irish, 370, 375, 378, 379,
    398, 399, 400
Army Reserve, 280, 308, 420
Pvt. John Carvell, 11th Hussars, 493
Coldstream Guards, 7, 9, 11
Col. Sir Alfred Kirby, Tower Hamlets
    Batt. R. Eng., 232, 365
Quartermaster-sergeant, 370, 379
Royal Irish Artillery, 257
Second Battalion, Scots Guards, 462
Soldier, 6, 7, 9, 59, 77, 79
Soldiers, 2, 5, 6, 7, 8, 9, 10, 17, 134,
    143, 156, 191, 235
Sussex Regiment, 47, 57, 70, 109,
    115, 117, 118, 119, 126
Tower Hamlets Battalion, Royal
    Engineers, 232, 365

~

## MONEY
4d., 15, 16, 40, 60, 261, 263, 270, 302
8d., 78, 85, 190, 261, 263, 302, 507,
    508, 514
Eightpence, 135, 261, 263, 299, 363,
    364
Florin, 67, 84
Fourpence, 244, 261, 263, 294, 295,
    299, 311, 312
Half-a-crown, 8, 259, 269, 280, 286
Halfpenny, 144, 152, 259, 269, 456,
    462, 570
Half-sovereign, 553
Half-sovereigns, 54, 70
Money, 8, 10, 15, 16, 21, 22, 24, 33,
    47, 50, 55, 56, 57, 67, 68, 69, 72,
    78, 79, 82, 84, 85, 91, 114, 127,
    129, 135, 138, 140, 149, 161, 164,
    169, 172, 179, 188, 199, 209, 240,
    241, 253, 258, 263, 265, 270, 271,
    272, 273, 286, 287, 291, 297, 298,
    300, 301, 303, 312, 314, 324, 325,
    336, 360, 363, 364, 370, 371, 375,
    377, 378, 379, 389, 400, 416, 436,
    437, 438, 444, 453, 456, 488, 489,

492, 493, 495, 508, 510, 512, 517,
    521, 526, 527, 535, 539, 544, 578
Penny, 51, 61, 78, 84, 109, 145, 149,
    151, 202, 262, 400, 416, 569, 570,
    579
Shilling, 78, 190, 532, 553, 570
Sixpence, 201, 294, 304, 315, 416,
    488, 489, 492
Sixpenny piece, 111
Two Farthings, 54, 70
Twopence, 84, 312, 332

~

## PLACES
4, Burton-crescent, 554, 556
4, Euston Square, 560
12, Burton-Crescent, 62, 558, 559
12, Great Coram-street, 553
13, Miller's-court (Mary J. Kelly's
    Room), 434, 443, 445, 459, 460,
    470, 472
20, Miller's-court, 443, 461, 473
24 New street, 469
26 Dorset-street, 434, 435, 437, 451,
    465
29, Hanbury-street, 59, 82, 83, 113,
    115, 119, 153
32, Flower and Dean-street, 214, 350
40, Berner-street, 182, 194, 208, 224,
    225, 250, 251, 321, 338, 340, 341
46, Hyde-road, 545
86, George-street, 574
139, Harley-street, 563, 564, 567, 568
Adam and Eve-court, 479
Airdrie, Scotland, 308
Aldgate, 10, 82, 91, 181, 182, 187,
    188, 190, 193, 197, 198, 202, 208,
    210, 217, 228, 230, 231, 238, 246,
    259, 269, 273, 280, 284, 285, 287,
    290, 296, 302, 324, 333, 337, 356,
    365, 369, 371, 376, 377, 378, 379,
    380, 381, 382, 383, 409, 436, 442,
    446, 454, 455, 467
Alhambra, 62, 290
Alsatia, 147, 391
America, 2, 40, 149, 167, 168, 172,
    173, 174, 175, 176, 177, 221, 222,
    259, 269, 284, 310, 338, 366, 392,
    494, 495, 496, 511
Anchor-street, 378
Angel-alley, 8, 332, 511
Alderney street, 348
Arthur-street West, 62
Ashburnham-road, 548
Asia Minor, 90
Austin, Tex., 244, 570, 577, 578, 579,
    580, 581, 582
Australia, 96, 259, 290, 368, 391
Austria, 72, 240, 493
Back Church-lane, 196, 321, 322, 399
Bailey, Packing Case Maker, 66, 76,
    77, 83, 97, 100, 102, 115, 117, 126
Baker's-row, 23, 24, 27, 31, 35, 41,
    43, 57, 116

XV

# Index

# Index

# Index

# Index

# Index

# Index

# Index

~
# GENERAL INDEX

# Index

# Index

# Index

# Index

# Index

# Index

# Index

# Index

# Index

# Index

# Tuesday, 7 August, 1888

## The Star
### FIFTH EDITION.
### A Whitechapel Horror.

A woman, now lying unidentified at the mortuary, Whitechapel, was ferociously stabbed to death this morning, between two and four o'clock, on the landing of a stone staircase in George's-buildings, Whitechapel.

George's-buildings are tenements occupied by the poor labouring class. A lodger going early to his work found the body. Another lodger says the murder was not committed when he returned home about two o'clock. The woman was stabbed in 20 places. No weapon was found near her, and her murderer has left no trace. She is of middle age and height, has black hair and a large, round face, and apparently belonged to the lowest class.

## Evening News
### MURDER IN WHITECHAPEL.
### TWENTY-FOUR STABS.

About four o'clock this morning a woman was found in George-yard, Whitechapel, stabbed to death. There were twenty-four wounds in various parts of the body. The police have not yet discovered the unfortunate woman's name and address, nor is it known who committed the crime.

# Wednesday, 8 August, 1888

## The Times

SUPPOSED MURDER.—The dead body of a young woman, aged about 32, and not yet definitely identified, was early yesterday morning found on some stone steps at 37, George-yard-buildings, a block of model dwellings in Whitechapel. There was one large wound over her heart, while several other injuries of the nature of stabs were on her body. Francis Hewitt, the superintendent of the dwellings, stated that it was believed the deceased was seen in the company of some soldiers who frequented a publichouse on Monday evening. The injuries on the deceased are, it is stated, not unlike bayonet wounds, and the police are now making inquiries into the case.

~

## The Star
### THE WHITECHAPEL HORROR
### Clues to the Identity of the Woman who was Found Foully Murdered.

As announced in our edition of Tuesday, a woman was found murdered at George yard, Whitechapel, early on that morning. The murder—for, undoubtedly, such it is—seems to be one of those mysteries by which the East end and other parts of London have been startled of late.

The body of the deceased lies at the mortuary, a dismal looking old building, surrounded by equally dismal houses in a narrow court off Montague street. Several persons called this morning for the purpose of seeing if they could identify the remains of the unfortunate woman. One person named Weathers is said to have identified her as his cousin, and his story is borne out by a man named Buckle, who keeps a marine store in Thrawl street.

This man stated that 14 or 15 years ago the deceased, whose maiden name was Bryan, occupied with her husband, Mr. Weathers, the premises in which he now carries on business. He knew the woman well, and says there are several marks on the features by which he has been able to identify her, though he could not swear that she is the person to whom he refers. She left her husband, who gave up business in consequence both at Thrawl street and at Bournemouth, where he had another store. He went to America, and the deceased has since been living by working for others at a business similar to that which she once carried on. She was a hard working, industrious woman, Mr. Buckle says, though latterly, he thought, given a little to drink. She seems to be about 50 years of age, and was the mother of five or six children, several of whom are at orphanage schools.

The wounds on the body are frightful. There are about eight on the chest, inflicted in almost circular form, while the probably fatal one—certainly much the largest and deepest of any—is under the heart. The wounds appear to be the result of sword or dagger thrusts, rather than that of a knife. No arrest has yet been made.

~

## Evening News
### THE WHITECHAPEL MURDER.

About four o'clock yesterday morning a woman was found in George-yard, White-chapel, stabbed to death. There were twenty-four wounds in various parts of her body.

It is rumoured that one of the soldiers quartered in the Tower has been arrested on suspicion of being concerned in the murder.

# Friday, 10 August, 1888

## The Times
### THE MURDER IN WHITECHAPEL

Yesterday afternoon Mr. G. Collier, Deputy Coroner for the South-Eastern Division of Middlesex, opened an inquiry at the Working Lads' Institute, Whitechapel-road, respecting the death of the woman who was found on Tuesday last, with 39 stabs on her body, at George-yard-buildings, Whitechapel.

Detective-Inspector Reid, H Division, watched the case on behalf of the Criminal Investigation Department.

Alfred George Crow, cabdriver, 35, George-yard-buildings, deposed that he got home at half-past 3 on Tuesday morning. As he was passing the first-floor landing he saw a body lying on the ground. He took no notice, as he was accustomed to seeing people lying about there. He did not then know whether the person was alive or dead. He got up at half past 9, and when he went down the staircase the body was not there. Witness heard no noise while he was in bed.

John S. Reeves, of 37, George-yard-buildings, a waterside labourer,[1] said that on Tuesday morning he left home at a quarter to 5 to seek for work. When he reached the first-floor landing he found the deceased lying on her back in a pool of blood. He was frightened, and did not examine her, but at once gave information to the police. He did not know the deceased. The deceased's clothes were disarranged, as though she had had a struggle with someone. Witness saw no footmarks on the staircase, nor did he find a knife or other weapon.

Police-constable Thomas Barrett, 226 H, said that the last witness called his attention to the body of the deceased. He sent for a doctor, who pronounced life extinct.

Dr. T.R. Killeen, of 68, Brick-lane, said that he was called to the deceased, and found her dead. She had 39 stabs on the body. She had been dead some three hours. Her age was about 36, and the body was very well nourished.

Witness had since made a post mortem examination of the body. The left lung was penetrated in five places, and the right lung was penetrated in two places. The heart, which was rather fatty, was penetrated in one place, and

that would be sufficient to cause death. The liver was healthy, but was penetrated in five places, the spleen was penetrated in two places, and the stomach, which was perfectly healthy, was penetrated in six places. The witness did not think all the wounds were inflicted with the same instrument. The wounds generally might have been inflicted with a knife, but such an instrument could not have inflicted one of the wounds, which went through the chestbone.

His opinion was that one of the wounds was inflicted by some kind of dagger, and that all of them had been caused during life.

The CORONER said he was in hopes that the body would be identified, but three women had identified it under three different names. He therefore proposed to leave the question open until the next occasion. The case would be left in the hands of Detective-Inspector Reid, who would endeavour to discover the perpetrator of this dreadful murder. It was one of the most dreadful murders any one could imagine. The man must have been a perfect savage to inflict such a number of wounds on a defenceless woman in such a way. The inquiry would be adjourned for a fortnight.

The case was then adjourned.

~

## Evening News
### THE WHITECHAPEL MURDER.
### INQUEST.
### 39 STABS WITH TWO KNIVES.

Yesterday afternoon Mr. G. Collier, the deputy coroner for South-East Middlesex, opened an inquiry at the Working Lad's Institute, Whitechapel, on the body of Martha Turner, aged 35, a single woman, lately living at 4, Star-place, Commercial-road, who was found lying on the landing of Georges-yard-buildings on Tuesday morning last, with over twenty stabs about her person.

Detective-inspector Reid watched the case for the police.

Considerable interest was taken in the proceedings, but owing to the size of the room the public were not overcrowded.

#### INDENTIFIED AS TWO PEOPLE.

Previous to calling the first witness, the coroner said that the body had been identified that morning, but he had just been informed

---

[1] **Waterside Labourer.** A dock labourer who worked on the ships in harbour. (Census1891.com)

# Friday, 10 August, 1888

that two other persons also identified her as quite a different person, and under those circumstances he thought the question of identity had better be left till the last.

Elizabeth Mahony, 47, George-yard-buildings, Whitechapel, the wife of a carman,[2] stated that on the night of Bank Holiday[3] she was out with some friends. She returned shortly before two in the morning. Her husband was with her. She afterwards left the house to try and get some supper at the chandler's shop.[4] The stairs are of stone, and were perfectly clear of any obstacles. She walked down the street, and was not absent more than five minutes and then retired to bed. They heard no noise during the night, but at ten o'clock she was told that a murder had been committed in the building. There is no light on the staircase. The spot where the body was found had been pointed out to her. She was not sure it did not lay there at two o'clock when she went in, as it was in a wide part of the stairs and quite in the dark.

Alfred George Crow, a cab-driver, of 35, George-yard-buildings, deposed that on Tuesday morning he returned home from work at half-past-three. On his way upstairs he saw somebody lying on the first landing. It was not an unusual thing to see, so he passed on, and went to bed. He did not know whether the person was dead or alive when he passed.

## HOW THE MURDER WAS DISCOVERED.

John Saunders Reeves, 37, George-yard-buildings, a waterside labourer, deposed that on Tuesday morning he left home at five o'clock to go in search of work. On the first-floor landing he saw a female lying in a pool of blood. She lay on her back, and seemed dead. He at once gave notice to the police. The woman was a perfect stranger to witness. Her clothes were all disarranged, as if she had had a struggle with someone. Witness did not notice any instrument lying about.

Police-constable Barrett, 226 H, deposed to being called by the last witness to view the body of deceased. She was lying on her back, and before she was moved a doctor was sent for, and on arrival pronounced life extinct. The woman's hands were clenched, but did not contain anything. Her clothes were thrown upwards.

Dr. Keeling stated that he was called to the deceased and found her dead. He examined the body and found 39 punctured wounds on the body and legs. There were no less than nine in the throat and 17 in the breast. She appeared to have been dead about three hours. The body was well nourished. He had since made a post-mortem examination, and found the left lung penetrated in five places, and the right lung in two places. The heart had been penetrated, but only in one place. Otherwise it was quite healthy. The liver was healthy but penetrated in five places, and the spleen was penetrated in two places. The stomach was healthy but penetrated in six places.

In witness's opinion the wounds were not inflicted with the same instrument, there being a deep wound in the breast from some long, strong instrument, while most of the others were done apparently by a penknife. The large wound could be caused by a sword-bayonet or dagger. It was impossible for the whole of the wounds to be self-inflicted. Death was due to loss of blood consequent on the injuries.

At the conclusion of this witness's evidence the inquiry was adjourned.

---

[2] **Carman, Carrier or Carter**. Drove a vehicle used to transport goods. (Census1891.com)

[3] The **Bank Holidays Act 1871** established four official holidays in England, Wales and Ireland. These were, Easter Monday, Whit Monday (the day after Pentecost), the First Monday in August and Boxing (St. Stephen's) Day. Scotland, because of its' unique traditions, celebrated five days, New Year's Day, Good Friday, First Monday in May, First Monday in August and Christmas. Good Friday and Christmas were already traditional days of rest in England, Wales and Ireland. (Encyclopaedia Britannica)

[4] **Chandler**. Dealer in specific supplies, provisions. (Morehead)

# Saturday, 11 August, 1888

## Evening News
### THE WHITECHAPEL MYSTERY.
### NO CLUE YET.

The police have not yet obtained a decisive clue to the murderer of the young woman named Martha Turner, whose body was found in a house in George-yard-buildings in White-chapel-road. It appears that on the night of Bank Holiday several soldiers were seen drinking in a public-house a couple of minutes' walk from George-yard-buildings, and it is said that Turner and another woman well-known in the district were seen in company of these men. It is stated that in consequence of inquiries set on foot by the police and the military authorities two soldiers have been placed under arrest at the Tower.

# Tuesday, 14 August, 1888

Evening News

**THE WHITECHAPEL MYSTERY.**
**THE POLICEMAN'S STATEMENT.**
**ANOTHER PARADE TO BE HELD.**

The Press Association learns that up to the present all attempts on the part of the police to dispel the mystery surrounding the death of the woman Turner, who was found in the George-yard, Whitechapel, under circumstances previously reported, have failed.

Inquiries have brought to light the fact that on the night preceding the murder, the deceased and a woman giving the name of Connolly were in company with two soldiers, and that something was said as to deceased accompanying one of the men to the George-yard.

As bearing on this incident the statement of Police-constable Barrett, 226 H, is important. That officer was on duty in the neighbourhood of the tragedy, and he noticed a soldier loitering. Barrett remarked that it was quite time he was in barracks, and the soldier replied that he was waiting for a comrade who had accompanied a woman to one of the buildings close at hand.

At a parade of soldiers which took place at the Tower, yesterday, Barrett identified the man whom he had accosted as described, but the soldier refused to give any account of himself. A parade will take place at Wellington Barracks, probably to-morrow, and Barrett will then be accompanied by the woman Connolly.

The police state that the mortal wound the woman received in the left breast gave the appearance of having been inflicted by a bayonet, whereas the other wounds were all flesh wounds.

The deceased, who had been known under the name of Martha Turner, is said to have lived apart from her husband for some years, and have latterly got her living as a hawker.[5]

This morning the police received from a man at Guildford a letter of inquiry. The man gives the name of Thomas Hunt, and states that illness had prevented his coming to ascertain if the woman Turner was his own wife.

---

[5] **Hawker, Huckster or Coster.** Peddler—sells things on the streets, matches, laces, etc. (Census1891.com)

# Wednesday, 15 August, 1888

## Evening News
**THE WHITECHAPEL MYSTERY.
WHAT THE MURDERED WOMAN'S
FRIEND SAID.**

Last night, the woman Mary Connolly, who was with the murdered woman, Martha Turner, late on the night of the murder, stated that she and the deceased first met the two soldiers near a public-house in the Whitechapel-road, at about ten o'clock.

They walked up and down the White-chapel-road, backwards and forwards, a considerable time, and called in at several houses in the road. The statement which had appeared that they were in the Princess Alice was not true.

She left the deceased with one of the soldiers at the end of the George-yard, and she and the other soldier went off in another direction. When she left the woman, since murdered, it was about a quarter to twelve o'clock.

It is alleged that the soldiers who were in the neighbourhood at the time were in undress, and had white bands round their caps. As that is part of the uniform of the Coldstream Guards, Connolly and Police-constable Barrett will be taken to their quarters, to see if they can identify any one.

Considering the number of tenements, and the traffic up and down the street where the body was found, together with other circumstances there is a doubt whether the murder was perpetrated where the body was found.

~

# Friday, 24 August, 1888

The Times

## INQUEST.

Yesterday afternoon Mr. George Collier, the Deputy Coroner for the South-Eastern Division of Middlesex, resumed his inquiry at the Working Lads' Institute, White-chapel-road, respecting the death of the woman who was found dead at George-yard-buildings, on the early morning of Tuesday, the 7th inst., with no less than 39 wounds on various parts of her body.

The body has been identified as that of MARTHA TABRAN, aged 39 or 40 years, the wife of a foreman packer at a furniture warehouse.

Henry Samuel Tabran, 6, River-terrace, East Greenwich, husband of the deceased woman, said he last saw her alive about 18 months ago, in the Whitechapel-road. They had been separated for 13 years, owing to her drinking habits. She obtained a warrant against him. For some part of the time witness allowed her 12s. a week, but in consequence of her annoyance he stopped this allowance ten years ago, since which time he had made it half-a-crown a week, as he found she was living with a man.

Henry Turner, a carpenter, staying at the Working Men's Home, Commercial-street, Spitalfields, stated that he had been living with the woman Tabran as his wife for about nine years.

Two or three weeks previously to this occurrence he ceased to do so. He had left her on two or three occasions in consequence of her drinking habits, but they had come together again.

He last saw her alive on Saturday, the 4th inst:, in Leadenhall-street. He then gave her 1s. 6d. to get some stock. When she had money she spent it in drink. While living with witness deceased's usual time for coming home was about 11 o'clock. As far as he knew she had no regular companion and he did not know that she walked the streets. As a rule he was, he said, a man of sober habits, and when the deceased was sober they usually got on well together.

By Inspector Reid—At times the deceased had stopped out all night. After those occasions she told him she had been taken in a fit and was removed to the police-station or somewhere else.

By the Coroner—He knew she suffered from fits, but they were brought on by drink.

Mrs. Mary Bousfield, wife of a wood cutter, residing at 4, Star-place, Commercial-road, knew the deceased by the name of Turner. She was formerly a lodger in her house with the man Turner. Deceased would rather have a glass of ale than a cup of tea, but she was not a woman who got continually drunk, and she never brought home any companions with her. She left without giving notice, and owed two weeks' rent.

Mrs. Ann Morris, a widow, of 23, Lisbon-street, E., said she last saw the deceased, who was her sister-in-law, at about 11 o'clock on Bank Holiday night in the Whitechapel-road. She was then about to enter a publichouse.

Mary Ann Connolly ("Pearly Poll"), who at the suggestion of Inspector Reid was cautioned in the usual manner before being sworn, stated she had been for the last two nights living at a lodging house in Dorset-street, Spitalfields. Witness was a single woman. She had known the woman Tabran for about four or five months. She knew her by the name of Emma. She last saw her alive on Bank Holiday night, when witness was with her about three quarters of an hour, and they separated at a quarter to 12. Witness was with Tabran and two soldiers—one private and one corporal. She did not know what regiment they belonged to, but they had white bands around their caps. After they separated, Tabran went away with the private, and witness accompanied the corporal up Angel-alley. There was no quarrelling between any of them. Witness had been to the barracks to identify the soldiers, and the two men she picked out were, to the best of her belief, the men she and Tabran were with. The men at the Wellington Barracks were paraded before the witness. One of the men picked out by witness turned out not to be a corporal, but he had stripes on his arm.

By Inspector Reid.—Witness heard of the murder on the Tuesday. Since the occurrence witness had threaten to drown herself, but she only said it was for a lark. She stayed away two days and two nights, and she only said that when asked where she was going. She knew the police were looking after her, but she did not let them know her whereabouts.

By a juryman.—The woman Tabran was not drunk. They were, however, drinking at different houses for about an hour and three-quarters. They had ale and rum.

Detective-Inspector Reid made a statement of the efforts made by the police to discover the perpetrator of the murder.

Several persons had stated that they saw the deceased woman on the previous Sunday with a corporal, but when all the corporals and privates at the Tower and Wellington Barracks were paraded before them they failed to identify the man.

The military authorities afforded every facility to the police. "Pearly Poll" picked out two men belonging to the Coldstream Guards at the Wellington Barracks. One of those men had three good conduct stripes, and he was proved beyond doubt to have been with his wife from 8 o'clock on the Monday night until 6 o'clock the following morning. The other man was also proved to have been in barracks at five minutes past 10 on Bank Holiday night.

The police would be pleased if anyone would give them information of having seen anyone with the deceased on the night of Bank Holiday.

The Coroner having summed up, the jury returned a verdict to the effect that the deceased had been murdered by some person or persons unknown.

~

## The Star
### THE WHITECHAPEL TRAGEDY
### VERDICT OF THE CORONER'S JURY ON THE REVOLTING MURDER
**The Husband and Other Relatives Testify to the Character of the Deceased —Her Companion Connolly Relates Her Movements on the Fatal Night— Her Soldier Friends**

The mystery surrounding the murder of Martha Turner in George Yard court, Whitechapel, has not been cleared up. The woman, it may be remembered, was found brutally murdered—no fewer than about 30 stabs having been inflicted on her body. It was thought that the wounds were inflicted with a bayonet, and that the murderer must have been a soldier. The soldiers in several barracks have been paraded before the police and witnesses but with no result. There is no direct evidence to show that the deceased woman ever knew a soldier and nothing yet elucidated to show that jealousy was the cause of the crime. The husband of the woman can only speak of her antecedents and her drunken habits. Inspector Reid is still hard at work following up probable clues.

The inquest was continued yesterday at the Working Lads' Institute by Deputy Coroner Collier.

Henry Samuel Tabran, 6 River Terrace, East Greenwich, husband of the deceased, foreman packer in a furniture store, was the first witness. He said:—"I identify the body of the deceased as that of my wife. Her Christian name was Martha. She was between 39 and 40. I saw her last alive in Whitechapel road, 18 months ago. She was then in her usual state of health as far as I could judge."

"How long have you been separated from her?"

—"About 18 years."

"Was it a legal separation?"

—"No, I refused to live with her."

"What was the cause?"

—"Drink, sir; she drank."

"How has she supported herself since?"

—"I used to give her 12s a week. I did that for three years, and since then I used to allow her a few shillings. As she was living with a man I did not think it was my place to support her. She had been living with a man for the last 10 years. The man is outside now. I have not seen her for the last 18 months."

Henry Turner, a carpenter by trade, but at the present time engaged in business as a street hawker, said—"I have lived with the deceased off and on for the last nine years. I did not live with her for the last three weeks, and I occasionally left her when she took drink. She told me all about her husband. She used to hawk on the streets. I saw her last alive on Saturday, 4 Aug., when I met her in Leadenhall street. I heard of her death first on the day of the inquest. I gave her 1s 6d the last time I saw her, to purchase some stock. When she had money, she always spent it in drink. She was in the habit of staying out late at night."

"Did you know whether she had any companions?"

—"No regular companion that I know of."

"Have you ever been to any public house with her?"

—"Yes, of course we have been to drink like other people." He did not know that she was acquainted with a woman who goes by the name of Pearly Poll.

"We agreed," he said, "pretty well together when she was sober."

"You are a man of sober habits?"

—"Yes, sir, as a rule. She had stayed out all night at times. She was subject to fits, brought on through drink."

Mrs. Bowsfield, wife of a woodcutter, said that the deceased woman formerly lived in her house, but left about three weeks before she was found dead.—She was not a woman to get intoxicated. I have never seen her the worse for drink during the four months she stayed with me. She never brought any female companion home with her. I knew that she lived with Turner before she came to my house. She told me that Turner was very good to her, and helped her support her two children. She left my house without giving any notice. The only furniture she had was two mattresses.

Ann Morris, a widow, 23 Lisbon street, E., stated that she was sister in law to the deceased, and she saw her at about eleven o'clock at night on Bank Holiday. The deceased was standing on the kerb in Whitechapel road when witness first saw her, and she afterwards saw her go into a public house, the White Swan. Deceased did not see her, and she did not wish her to. To the best of her belief the deceased was on the streets.

By Detective Inspector Reid:—Deceased had been charged several times with annoying witness.

By the Coroner:—Deceased had been before the magistrate, and was sentenced to seven days. Deceased thought witness harboured her brother, deceased's husband.

By A Juryman:—Deceased had two children by witness's brother, and one was now 17 years of age.

Mary Ann Connolly was the next witness called, and Inspector Reid said he would like the witness cautioned. The Coroner accordingly cautioned her that she was not bound to answer any of his questions, but if she did her answers would be taken down, and might be used in evidence against her. She was then sworn. She said she was living at Crossingham's lodging house, in Dorset street, Spitalfields. She was an unfortunate,[6] and had known the deceased about four or five months. She knew her by the name of Emma. She last saw her alive on Bank Holiday at the corner of George yard, and was with her about three quarters of an hour. They separated at about a quarter to twelve. Witness was with her and two soldiers, one private and one corporal. She did not know to what regiment they belonged, but they had a white band round their hats. She did not notice whether the corporal had his side arm or not. They were all four together during the hour and three quarters, and drank in a public house ... again see the deceased alive. She had been to Wellington Barracks, and the men were paraded before her. To the best of her belief, the two men she picked out were the men she and the deceased were in company with. She left the soldier about five minutes past 12. She went up Whitechapel and he went Aldgate way.

By Inspector Reid:—She first heard of this occurrence the day after Bank Holiday. She had threatened to drown herself since the occurrence, but only said it for a lark. She

---

[6] **Unfortunate.** A prostitute : spec, a homeless street-walker. (Farmer)

Friday, 24 August, 1888# Friday, 24 August, 1888

stopped away two days and two nights, and she only said that when asked where she was going.

By the Coroner:—She went to her cousin's at No. 4 Feather's court, Drury lane.

By Inspector Reid:—She knew they wanted her, but she did not let them know where she was going.

Inspector Reid:—We wanted her to go to the Tower to see the men on parade, but she did not put in an appearance until we found her.

By a Juryman:—The deceased was not drunk, but they had been drinking. They were drinking at different places for an hour and three quarters.

The Coroner: You could not have been very sober.

This exhausted the witnesses, and Detective Inspector Reid made a statement of the efforts made by the police to trace out the perpetrators of the murder. He said a large number of persons had volunteered statements, and in each case the statement had been thrashed out. The deceased was said to have been seen by several persons with a corporal on the Sunday, and there was a general parade of the men at the Tower by these persons without result.

Constable Barrett was also taken to the Tower, and the men on leave at the time he was aid to have seen the corporal were paraded before him, but he failed to identify anyone.

Pearly Poll spoke of the white band round their hats, which, of course, would be the dress of the Coldstream Guards. She was taken to Wellington Barracks, and picked out two men. One of them was a man with three good conduct stripes. She said she was positive he was the man she went to Angel alley with. But careful inquiry resulted in proof that the man was at home with his wife all night, and the other was in barracks at five minutes past ten.

So the inquiries up to the present had been a failure. The police would be glad if anyone knowing anything of the occurrence would come forward and give any information that would thrown light upon it.

The Coroner, in summing up, said he was bound to acknowledge that the military authorities had rendered every possible assistance. He was sorry for several reasons that the perpetrator of this crime, which was one of the most horrible crimes that had been committed for some time past, the details being so horrible that there was a refinement of brutality about some parts which was nothing less than fiendish, had not been traced.

After a few minutes consultation, the jury returned a verdict to the effect that the murder was committed by some person or persons unknown, and added a rider, in which they stated their opinion that the staircases of these model dwellings, which existed all over London, should be lighted up at night.

~

## Evening News
### THE WHITECHAPEL MURDER.

The evidence given by Mary Ann Connolly (Pearly Poll) at the inquest, yesterday, is considered so unsatisfactory that the detectives engaged in the case are making inquiries as to where she spent the two days immediately following the day of the murder. She says she went to her cousin's in Drury-lane, but this has not yet been verified. Her account of how she spent Bank Holiday night will be inquired into, and a strict watch kept upon her, as it is believed that she anticipates committing suicide.

11

## The Star
### FOURTH EDITION.
### A REVOLTING MURDER.
### ANOTHER WOMAN FOUND HORRIBLY MUTILATED IN WHITECHAPEL.
### GHASTLY CRIMES BY A MANIAC.
### A Policeman Discovers a Woman Lying in the Gutter with Her Throat Cut After She has been Removed to the Hospital She is Found to be Disembowelled.

Scarcely has the horror and sensation caused by the discovery of the murdered woman in Whitechapel recently had time to abate, when another discovery is made, which for the brutality exercised on the victim is even more shocking. As Constable John Neil was walking down Buck's-row, Thomas-street, Whitechapel, about a quarter to four o'clock this morning, he discovered a woman lying at the side of the street with

### HER THROAT CUT FROM EAR TO EAR.

The wound was about two inches wide and blood was flowing profusely. She was immediately conveyed to the Whitechapel mortuary, when it was found that besides the wound in the throat the lower part of the abdomen was completely ripped open and the bowels were protruding. The wound extends nearly to her breast, and must have been effected with a large knife. As the corpse lies in the mortuary, it presents a ghastly sight. The victim seems to be between 35 and 40 years of age, and measures 5ft. 2in. in height. The hands are bruised, and bear evidence of having engaged in

### A SEVERE STRUGGLE.

There is the impression of a ring having been worn on one of deceased's fingers, but there is nothing to show that it had been wrenched from her in a struggle. Some of the front teeth have also been knocked out, and the face is bruised on both cheeks and very much discoloured. Deceased wore a rough brown ulster,[7] with large buttons in front. Her clothes

are torn and cut up in several places, bearing evidence of the ferocity with which the murder was committed.

Several persons in the neighbourhood state that an affray occurred shortly after midnight, but no screams were heard, nor anything beyond what might have been considered evidence of an ordinary brawl.

Writing at half-past eleven a.m., our reporter says:—

The body appeared to be that of a woman of 35. It was 5ft. 3in. in height and fairly plump. The eyes were brown, the hair brown, and the two centre upper front teeth missing, those on either side being widely separated. This peculiarity may serve to identify deceased, of whom at present writing nothing is known. Her clothing consisted of a well-worn brown ulster, a brown linsey[8] skirt, and jacket, a gray linsey petticoat, a flannel petticoat, dark-blue ribbed stockings, braid garters, and side-spring shoes.[9] Her bonnet was black and rusty, and faced with black velvet. Her whole outfit was that of a person in poor circumstances, and this appearance was borne out by the mark

### "LAMBETH WORKHOUSE, P. R.,"

which was found on the petticoat bands. The two marks were cut off and sent to the Lambeth institution to discover if possible the identity of deceased.

The brutality of the murder is beyond conception and beyond description. The throat is cut in two gashes, the instrument having been a sharp one, but used in a most ferocious and reckless way. There is a gash under the left ear, reaching nearly to the centre of the throat. Along half its length, however, it is accompanied by another one which reaches around under the other ear, making a wide and horrible hole, and nearly severing the head from the body.

### THE GHASTLINESS OF THIS CUT,

however, pales into insignificance alongside the other. No murder was ever more

---

[7] **Ulster**. Overcoat, named for the province in Ireland. (Morehead)

[8] **Linsey-Woolsey**. A cloth of wool and linen or cotton. (*Cheap and coarse, clothing made from this was worn by the poor.*) (Morehead)

[9] **Side-Spring Boots** or **Shoes**. Footwear with elastic sides, usually vulcanized India rubber. (Post Magazine and Insurance Monitor)

ferociously and more brutally done. The knife, which must have been a large and sharp one, was jobbed into the deceased at the lower part of the abdomen, and then drawn upward, not once but twice. The first cut veered to the right, slitting up the groin, and passing over the left hip, but the second cut went straight upward, along the centre of the body, and, reaching to the breast-bone. Such horrible work could only be

### THE DEED OF A MANIAC.

The other murder, in which the woman received 30 stabs, must also have been the work of a maniac. This murder occurred on Bank Holiday. On the Bank Holiday preceding another woman was murdered in equally brutal but even more barbarous fashion by being stabbed with a stick. She died without being able to tell anything of her murderer.[10] All this leads to the conclusion, that the police have now formed, that there is a maniac haunting Whitechapel, and that the three woman were all victims of his murderous frenzy.

~

---

[10] See Appendix A, Emma Smith Murder, p. 544.

## Evening News
### ANOTHER WHITECHAPEL MYSTERY.
### HORRIBLE MURDER IN BUCK'S ROW, WHITECHAPEL.

The Central News says: Scarcely has the horror and sensation caused by the discovery of the murdered woman in Whitechapel some short time ago had time to abate when another discovery is made which, for the brutality exercised on the victim, is even more shocking, and will no doubt create as great a sensation in the vicinity as its predecessor. The affair up to the present is enveloped in complete mystery, and the police have as yet no evidence to trace the perpetrators of the horrible deed.

### THE DISCOVERY.

The facts are that Constable John Neil was walking down Bucks-row, Thomas-street, Whitechapel, about a quarter to four o'clock this morning, when he discovered a woman between 35 and 40 years of age lying at the side of the street with her throat cut right open from ear to ear, the instrument with which the deed was done traversing the throat from left to right. The wound was about two inches wide, and blood was flowing profusely. She was discovered to be lying in a pool of blood.

She was immediately conveyed to the Whitechapel mortuary, when it was found that besides the wound in the throat the lower part of the abdomen was completely ripped open, with the bowels protruding. The wound extends nearly to her breast, and must have been effected with a large knife.

### A GHASTLY SIGHT.

As the corpse lies in the mortuary it presents a ghastly sight. The victim seems to be between 35 and 40 years of age and measures five feet two inches in height. The hands are bruised, and bear evidence of having engaged in a severe struggle. There is the impression of a ring having been worn on one of deceased's fingers, but there is nothing to show that it had been wrenched from her in a struggle. Some of the front teeth have also been knocked out, and the face is bruised on both cheeks and very much discoloured.

Deceased wore a rough brown ulster, with large buttons in front. Her clothes are torn and cut up in several places, bearing evidence of the ferocity with which the murder was committed.

The only way by which the police can prosecute an inquiry at present is by finding someone who can identify the deceased, and then, if possible, trace in whose company she was last seen.

In Buck's-row, naturally, the greatest excitement prevails, and several persons in the neighbourhood state that an affray occurred shortly after midnight, but no screams were heard, nor anything beyond what might have been considered evidence of an ordinary brawl. In any case, the police unfortunately will have great difficulty in bringing to justice the murderer or murderers.

The woman murdered in Whitechapel has not yet been identified. She was wearing work-house clothes, and it is supposed she came from Lambeth. A night watchman was in the street where the crime was committed. He heard no screams, and saw no signs of the scuffle. The body was quite warm when brought to the mortuary at half-past four this morning.

### LATER PARTICULARS.

Immediately on the affair being reported at the Bethnal Green Police-station, two inspectors proceeded to the mortuary and examined the clothes in the hope of being able to discover something likely to lead to the murdered woman's identification. In this they were not successful, as the only articles found on the body were a broken comb and a piece of looking glass. This fact leads the police to think that the unfortunate woman belongs to the class known as "unfortunates," and that she spent her nights in common lodging-houses where such articles are necessary.

The wounds, of which there are five, could only have been committed with a dagger or a long sharp knife. The officers engaged in the case are pushing their inquiries in the neighbourhood as to the doings of certain gangs known to frequent these parts, and an opinion is gaining ground amongst them that the murderers are the same who committed the two previous murders near the same spot. It is believed that these gangs, who make their appearance during the early hours of the morning, are in the habit of blackmailing these poor unfortunate creatures, and when their demands are refused, violence follows, and in order to avoid their deeds being brought to light they put away their victims.

They have been under the observation of the police for some time past, and it is believed that with the prospect of a reward and a free pardon, some of them might be persuaded to turn Queen's evidence, when some startling revelations might be expected.

Up till noon Mr. Wynne E. Baxter, the Coroner for the district, had not received any official intimation of the occurrence, but he will probably do so during the day, and the inquest will most likely be held on Monday morning.

~

# Saturday, 1 September, 1888

## The Times

### ANOTHER MURDER IN WHITECHAPEL.

Another murder of the foulest kind was committed in the neighbourhood of White-chapel in the early hours of yesterday morning, but by whom and with what motive is at present a complete mystery.

At a quarter to 4 o'clock Police-constable Neill, 97J, when in Buck's-row, Whitechapel, came upon the body of a woman lying on a part of the footway, and on stooping to raise her up in the belief that she was drunk he discovered that her throat was cut almost from ear to ear. She was dead but still warm.

He procured assistance and at once sent to the station and for a doctor. Dr. Llewellyn, of Whitechapel-road, whose surgery is not above 300 yards from the spot where the woman lay, was aroused, and, at the solicitation of a constable, dressed and went at once to the scene. He inspected the body at the place where it was found and pronounced the woman dead. He made a hasty examination and then discovered that, besides the gash across the throat, the woman had terrible wounds in the abdomen.

The police ambulance from the Bethnal-green Station having arrived, the body was removed there. A further examination showed the horrible nature of the crime, there being other fearful cuts and gashes, and one of which was sufficient to cause death apart from the wounds across the throat.

After the body was removed to the mortuary of the parish, in Old Montague-street, White-chapel, steps were taken to secure, if possible, identification, but at first with little prospect of success. The clothing was of a common description, but the skirt of one petticoat and the band of another article bore the stencil stamp of Lambeth Workhouse. The only articles in the pockets were a comb and a piece of a looking glass.

The latter led the police to conclude that the murdered woman was an inhabitant of the numerous lodging-houses of the neighbourhood, and officers were despatched to make inquiries about, as well as other officers to Lambeth to get the matron of the workhouse to view the body with a view to identification. The latter, how-ever, could not identify, and said that the clothing might have been issued any time during the past two or three years.

As the news of the murder spread, however, first one woman and then another came forward to view the body, and at length it was found that a woman answering the description of the murdered woman had lodged in a common lodging-house, 18, Thrawl-street, Spitalfields.

Women from that place were fetched and they identified the deceased as "Polly," who had shared a room with three other women in the place on the usual terms of such houses —nightly payment of 4d. each, each woman having a separate bed. It was gathered that the deceased had led the life of an "unfortunate" while lodging in the house, which was only for about three weeks past.

Nothing more was known of her by them but that when she presented herself for her lodging on Thursday night she was turned away by the deputy because she had not the money. She was then the worse for drink, but not drunk, and turned away laughing, saying, "I'll soon get my 'doss' money;[11] see what a jolly bonnet I've got now." She was wearing a bonnet which she had not been seen with before, and left the lodging house door.

A woman of the neighbourhood saw her later, she told the police—even as late as 2:30 on Friday morning—in Whitechapel-road, opposite the church and at the corner of Osborne-street, and at a quarter to 4 she was found within 500 yards of the spot, murdered.

The people of the lodging-house knew her as "Polly," but at about half-past 7 last evening a woman named Mary Ann Monk, at present an inmate of Lambeth Workhouse, was taken to the mortuary and identified the body as that of Mary Ann Nicholls, also called "Polly" Nich-olls. She knew her, she said, as they were inmates of the Lambeth Workhouse together in April and May last, the deceased having been passed there from another workhouse.

On the 12th of May, according to Monk, Nicholls left the workhouse to take a situation as servant at Ingleside, Wandsworth-common. It afterwards became known that Nicholls

---

[11] **Doss (or Dorse).** A bed, lodging; also asleep, or lib (q.v.) (1789). As verb, to sleep. **Doss-house (Dossing-crib or ken).** A common lodging-house. **Doss-money.** the price of a night's lodging (1838). (Farmer)

15

betrayed her trust as domestic servant, by stealing £3 from her employer and absconding. From that time she had been wandering about.

Monk met her, she said, about six weeks ago when herself out of the workhouse and drank with her. She was sure the deceased was "Polly" Nicholls, and, having twice viewed the features as the body lay in the shell, maintained her opinion. So far the police have satisfied themselves, but as to getting a clue to her murderer they express little hope.

The matter is being investigated by Detective-inspector Abberline, of Scotland-yard, and Inspector Helson, J Division. The latter states that he walked carefully over the ground soon after 8 o'clock in the morning, and beyond the discolourations ordinarily found on pavements there was no sign of stains. Viewing the spot where the body was found, however, it seemed difficult to believe that the woman received her death wounds there.

The police have no theory with respect to the matter, except that a gang of ruffians exists in the neighbourhood, which, blackmailing women of the "unfortunate" class, takes vengeance on those who do not find money for them. They base that surmise on the fact that within 12 months two other women have been murdered in the district by almost similar means—one as recently as the 6th of August last—and left in the gutter of the street in the early hours of the morning.

If the woman was murdered on the spot where the body was found, it is impossible to believe she would not have aroused the neighbourhood by her screams, Bucks-row being a street tenanted all down one side by a respectable class of people, superior to many of the surrounding streets, the other side having a blank wall bounding a warehouse.

Dr. Llewellyn has called the attention of the police to the smallness of the quantity of blood on the spot where he saw the body, and yet the gashes in the abdomen laid the body right open. The weapon used would scarcely have been a sailor's jack knife, but a pointed weapon with a stout back—such as a cork-cutter's or shoe-maker's knife. In his opinion it was not an exceptionally long-bladed weapon.

He does not believe that the woman was seized from behind and her throat cut, but thinks that a hand was held across her mouth and the knife then used, possibly by a left-handed man, as the bruising on the face of the deceased is such as would result from the mouth being covered with the right hand.

He made a second examination of the body in the mortuary, and on that based his conclusion, but will make no actual post mortem until he receives the Coroner's orders. The inquest is fixed for to-day.

~

## The Star
**SPECIAL EDITION.**
**THE WHITECHAPEL HORROR.**
**THE THIRD CRIME OF A MAN WHO MUST BE A MANIAC.**
**Women Lured to Bye Streets to be Butchered—The Latest Victim Identified—Opening of the Inquest—Great Local Excitement.**

The victim of the latest Whitechapel horror—the woman who was found yesterday morning in Buck's-row completely disembowelled and with her head nearly gashed from her body—was for a time completely unknown. As the news of the murder spread, however, first one woman and then another came forward to view the body, and at length it was found that a woman answering the description of the murdered woman had lodged in a common lodging-house, 18, Thrawl-street, Spitalfields. Women from that place were fetched, and they identified the deceased as

**"POLLY,"**
who had shared a room with three other women in the place on the usual terms of such houses—nightly payment of 4d. each, each woman having a separate bed. It was gathered that the deceased had led the life of an "unfortunate" while lodging in the house, which was only for about three weeks past.

Nothing more was known of her by them but that when she presented herself for her lodging on Thursday night she was turned away by the deputy because she had not the money. She was then the worse for drink, but not drunk, and turned away laughing, saying, "I'll soon get my 'doss' money; see

**WHAT A JOLLY BONNET I'VE GOT NOW."**

She was wearing a bonnet which she had not been seen with before, and left the lodging-house

# Saturday, 1 September, 1888

door. A woman of the neighbourhood saw her later she told the police—even as late as half-past two on Friday morning—in Whitechapel-road, opposite the church and at the corner of Osborne-street, and at a quarter to four she was found within 500 yards of the spot murdered. The people of the lodging-house knew her as "Polly," but at about half-past seven last evening a woman named Mary Ann Monk, at present an inmate of Lambeth Workhouse, was taken to the mortuary and identified the body as that of

**MARY ANN NICHOLLS,**

also called "Polly" Nicholls. She knew her, she said, as they were inmates of the Lambeth Workhouse together in April and May last, the deceased having been passed there from another workhouse. On 12 May, according to Monk, Nicholls left the workhouse to take a situation as servant at Ingleside, Wandsworth-common. It afterwards became known that Nicholls betrayed her trust as domestic servant, by stealing £3 from her employer and absconding. From that time she had been wandering about. Monk met her, she said, about six weeks ago, when herself out of the workhouse, and drank with her. She was sure the deceased was "Polly" Nicholls, and, having twice viewed the features as the body lay in a shell, maintained her opinion.

There is a terribly

**SIGNIFICANT SIMILARITY**

between this ghastly crime and the two mysterious murders of women which have occurred in the same district within the last three months. In each case the victim has been a woman of abandoned character, each crime has been committed in the dark hours of the morning, and more important still as pointing to one man, and that man a maniac, being the culprit, each murder has been accompanied by hideous mutilation.

In the second case, that of the woman Martha Turner, it will be remembered that no fewer than 30 stabs were inflicted. The scene of this murder was George-yard, a place appropriately known locally as "the slaughter-house." As in both other cases there was in this not the slightest clue to the murderer—no one was known to have any motive for causing the woman's death. She was parted from her husband, and had lived with a man named Turner, but the searching coroner's inquiry

revealed nothing connecting either with the crime. It was fancied that some of her many wounds had been caused by a bayonet, and she was said to have been seen with a soldier shortly before her death. Some soldiers were paraded at the Tower, and one was said to have been identified by a policeman as having been waiting about George-yard just about the time of the murder. But nothing came of it.

The first murder, which, strangely enough, did not rouse much interest, was committed in Osborne-street. The woman in that case was alive when discovered, but unconscious, and she died in the hospital without recovering her senses, consequently she was unable to whisper a word to put the police on the track of her fiendish assailant, and her murder has remained a mystery. All three crimes have been committed

**WITHIN A VERY SMALL RADIUS.**

Each of the ill-lighted thoroughfares to which the women were decoyed to be foully butchered are off turnings from Whitechapel-road, and all are within half a mile. The fact that these three tragedies have been committed within such a limited area, and are so strangely alike in their details, is forcing on all minds the conviction that they are the work of some cool, cunning man with a mania for murder.

There was no new light thrown on the case this morning. At nine o'clock the body of deceased was removed from the mortuary to an improvised operating room on the premises, and Dr. Ralph Llewellyn made a post-mortem examination. The object of the examination was to determine if possible, the order in which the various cuts were made. It is evident from the cuts in the throat that the head was bent back by the murderer before the knife was used. Whether the other mutilation took place before or after death remains to be settled, as also the position in which the woman lay when the deed done. There are several questions of this kind which may throw light on the case, notably the small quantity of blood at the place where she was found and the fact that there must have been much of it somewhere else. At present

**CLUES TO THE MURDER**

are entirely lacking, and the location of the place where the deed was done was the first point necessary to establish.

While the medical examination was in progress, an officer arrived from the Bethnal-green Station with two men, who were regarded as possibly able to throw some light on the case. The first was a man who keeps the coffee-stall at the corner of Whitechapel-road and Cambridge-road. He said that at three o'clock yesterday morning a woman answering the description of the deceased came to his stall in company with

### A MAN FIVE FEET THREE OR FOUR INCHES HIGH,

dressed in a dark coat and black Derby hat, apparently about thirty-five years old. He had a black moustache and whiskers, and was fidgety and uneasy. He refused to have anything to eat, but paid for the woman's coffee. He grumbled and kept telling her to hurry, as he wished to get home. The other man was a Mr. Scorer, an assistant salesman in the Smithfield Market. He had been attracted by the report in *The Star* that the dead woman's name might be Scorer, and said that his wife, from whom he separated 11 years ago, had been an inmate of Lambeth Workhouse. He said she had a friend named Polly Nicholls, and that he knew the latter by sight. He did not know the colour of his wife's eyes, but said she had two scars on her body—one on the right thigh and the other on the right forearm.

Both men were allowed to view the remains, but

### NOTHING CAME OF IT.

The coffee-stall keeper said he did not think it was the same woman, but was not sure. The woman, if it was the same, had grown thinner in the face. Scorer said that deceased was neither his wife nor her friend Nicholls, so far as he could remember.

—

### INQUEST THIS AFTERNOON.

This afternoon at the Working Lads' Institute, Whitechapel-road, Mr. Wynne E. Baxter opened the inquest on the body of the unfortunate woman. The desire that no time should be lost in tracing the perpetrator of the atrocity prompted the Coroner to commence his investigation as early as possible, although his arrangements for the day had been fixed before information of the crime reached him. In order, however, that the police should not be in any way trammelled in their duties, and that they should have the advantage of having any information in their possession tested on oath,

he decided to at once get through the preliminary formalities of the inquest. On behalf of the police authorities, Inspectors Helston and Spratling, J division, were present, as well as Inspector Abberline and several members of the detective force. It is needless to say that there was a great amount of morbid interest displayed in the inquiry. The jury, having been sworn, went to view the body.

(Proceeding.)

~

## Evening News
### FIFTH EDITION.
### THE WHITECHAPEL MYSTERY.
### HORRIBLE MURDER IN BUCK'S ROW, WHITECHAPEL.
### IDENTIFICATION OF THE BODY.
### THE DOCTOR'S STATEMENT.

The locality of Whitechapel has long been associated with the committal of crimes of a brutal and at times almost incredible nature, in many of which women have been the victims. Some few months ago a woman was barbarously murdered near Whitechapel Church by being stabbed with a swordstick. On the night of last Bank Holiday a woman named Turner was found dead in George-yard, Whitechapel, with 30 stabs on her body. In both cases no clue to the perpetrators of the deed was discovered, and now even a more ghastly deed has come to light.

### THE BODY DISCOVERED.

At a quarter to four yesterday morning Police-constable Neil was on his beat in Buck's-row, Thomas-street, Whitechapel, when his attention was attracted to the body of a woman lying on the pavement close to the door of the stableyard in connection with Essex Wharf. Buck's-row, like many minor thoroughfares in this and similar neighbourhoods, is not overburdened with gas-lamps, and in the dim light the constable at first thought that the woman had fallen down in a drunken stupor, and was sleeping off the effects of a night's debauch. With the aid of the light from his bullseye lantern[12] Neil at once perceived that

---

[12] The **Bulls-eye Lantern**, also called the **Dark Lantern**, was a cylindrical oil lamp fitted with a shutter, a large convex lens, called a "bulls-eye",

# Saturday, 1 September, 1888

the woman had been the victim of some horrible outrage. Her livid face was stained with blood, and her throat cut from ear to ear. The constable at once alarmed the people living in the house next to the stable-yard, occupied by a carter named Green and his family, and also knocked up Mr. Walter Perkins, the resident manager of the Essex Wharf, on the opposite side of the road, which is very narrow at this point.

## NO ONE HEARD ANYTHING.

Neither Mr. Perkins nor any of the Green family, although the latter were sleeping within a few yards of where the body was discovered, had heard any sound of a struggle. Dr. Llewellyn, who lives only a short distance away in Whitechapel-road, was at once sent for and promptly arrived on the scene. He found the body lying on its back across the gateway, and the briefest possible examination was sufficient to prove that life was extinct. Death had not long ensued, because the extremities were still warm.

## MOST BRUTAL MURDER.

With the assistance of Police-sergeant Kirby and Police-constable Thane, the body was removed to the Whitechapel-road mortuary, and it was not until the unfortunate woman's clothes were removed that the horrible nature of the attack which had been made upon her transpired. It was then discovered that in addition to the gash in her throat, which had nearly severed the head from the body, the lower part of the abdomen had been ripped up, and the bowels were protruding. The abdominal wall, the whole length of the body, had been cut open, and on either side were two incised wounds, almost as severe as the centre one. This reached from the lower part of the abdomen to the breast bone. The instrument with which the wounds were inflicted must have been not only of the sharpness of a razor, but used with considerable ferocity.

---

which concentrated the light from the flame, and a highly polished reflector. This gave the Bulls-eye Lantern a directional beam like a modern electric flashlight, although not nearly as bright. These were standard issue for London policemen in 1888, but were replaced by electric lamps in 1892. (Electricity)

## BLOOD STAINS ON BOTH SIDES OF THE STREET.

A general opinion is now entertained that the spot where the body was found was not the scene of the murder. Buck's-row runs through from Thomas-street to Brady-street, and in the latter street what appeared to be blood stains were, early in the morning, found at irregular distances on the footpaths on either side of the street. Occasionally a larger splash was visible, and from the way in which the marks were scattered it seems as though the person carrying the mutilated body had hesitated where to deposit his ghastly burden, and gone from one side of the road to the other until the obscurity of Buck's-row afforded the shelter sought for. The street had been crossed twice within the space of about 120 yards. The point at which the stains were first visible is in front of the gateway to Honey's-mews, in Brady-street, about 150 yards from the point where Buck's-row commences. Several persons living in Brady-street state that early in the morning they heard screams, but this is a by no means uncommon incident in the neighbourhood, and, with one exception, nobody seems to have paid any particular attention to what was probably the death struggle of the unfortunate woman. The exception referred to was a Mrs. Colwell, who lives only a short distance from the foot of Buck's-row.

## AWAKENED BY THE CHILDREN.

According to her statement she was awakened early in the morning by her children, who said someone was trying to get into the house. She listened, and heard a woman screaming "Murder! Police!" five or six times. The voice faded away, as though the woman was going in the direction of Buck's-row, and all was quiet. She only heard the steps of one person. It is almost needless to point out that a person suffering from such injuries as the deceased had had inflicted upon her would be unable to traverse the distance from Honey's-mews to the gateway in Buck's-row, which is about 120 yards from Brady-street, making a total distance of at least 170 yards.

## SHE MUST HAVE BEEN DRAGGED.

Therefore the woman must have been carried or dragged there, and here the mystery becomes all the more involved. Even supposing that, with the severe abdominal wounds she had sufficient strength left to call out in the tones which Mrs. Colwell asserts she heard the deceased's throat could not have been cut at the spot where she was found lying dead, as that would have caused a considerably heavier flow of blood than was found there. As a matter of fact but a very small quantity of blood was to be seen at this spot, or found in Buck's-row at all, so the murderer could not have waited here to finish his ghastly task. If he had cut her throat on the onset the deceased could not have uttered a single cry afterwards. Mrs. Colwell's statement, looked at in the light of these circumstances, by no means totally clears up the mystery as to the exact locality which the murderer selected for the accomplishment of his foul deed.

### AN UNUSUALLY QUIET NIGHT.

Police-constable Neil traversed Buck's-row about three-quarters of an hour before the body was discovered, so it must have been deposited there soon after he had patrolled that thoroughfare. Mrs. Green, Mr. and Mrs. Perkins, the watchman in Schneider's tar factory, and the watchman in a wool depot, which are both situated in Buck's-row, agree that the night was an unusually quiet one for the neighbourhood.

### TWO SPOTS OF BLOOD.

Shortly after midday some men who were searching the pavement in Buck's-row above the gateway found two spots of blood in the roadway. They were nine feet away from the gate, and they might have dropped from the hands or clothing of the murderer as he fled away. The stablery and the vicinity have been carefully searched in the hope of finding the weapon with which the crime was committed, but so far without success. A bridge over the Great Eastern Railway is close at hand, and the railway line was also fruitlessly searched for some distance.

### THE DOCTOR'S STATEMENT.

Dr. Llewellyn made the following statement yesterday:—I was called to Buck's-row, about five minutes to four this morning by Police-constable Thane, who said a woman had been murdered. I went to the place at once, and found deceased lying on her back with her legs out straight as though she had been laid down. Police-constable Neil told me that the body had not been touched. The throat was cut from ear to ear, and the woman was quite dead. On feeling the extremities of the body, I found that they were still warm, showing that death had not long ensued.[13] A crowd was now gathering, and as it was undesirable to make a further examination in the street I ordered the removal of the body to the mortuary, telling the police to send for me again if anything of importance transpired.

### THE MURDER WAS COMMITTED ELSEWHERE.

There was a very small pool of blood on the pathway, which had trickled from the wound in the throat, not more than would fill two wineglasses, or half a pint at the outside. This fact, and the way in which the deceased was lying, made me think at the time that it was at least probable that the murder was committed elsewhere, and the body conveyed to Buck's-row. There were no marks of blood on deceased's legs, and at the time I had no idea of the fearful abdominal wounds which had been inflicted upon the body. At half-past five I was summoned to the mortuary by the police, and was astonished at finding the other wounds.

### A BRUTAL AFFAIR.

I have seen many horrible cases, but never such a brutal affair as this. From the nature of the cuts on the throat it is probable that they were inflicted with the left hand. There is a mark at the point of the jaw on the right side of deceased's face, as though made by a person's thumb, and a similar bruise on the left side as if the woman's head had been pushed back and her throat then cut. There is a gash under the left ear reaching nearly to the centre of the throat, and another cut apparently starting from the right ear. The neck is severed back to the vertebrae, which is also slightly injured. The abdominal wounds are extraordinary for their length and the severity with which they have been inflicted. One cut extends from the base of the abdomen to the breastbone. Deceased's clothes were loose, and the wounds could have been inflicted while she was dressed.

---

[13] The low temperature on the morning of 31 August was 46.7° F. (Casebook Productions)

# Saturday, 1 September, 1888

**THE THEORY OF THE MURDER.**

Inspector Helson, who has charge of the case, is making every effort to trace the murderer, but there is so little to guide the police that at present there does not seem much likelihood of success. The theory that the murder is the work of a lunatic, who is also the perpetrator of the other two murders of women which have occurred in Whitechapel during the last six months, meets with very general acceptance amongst the inhabitants of the district, the female portion of which is greatly alarmed. The more probable theory is that the murder has been committed by one or more of a gang of men, who are in the habit of frequenting the streets at late hours of the night and levying blackmail on women. No money was found upon deceased, and all she had in the pocket of her dress was a handkerchief, a small comb, and a piece of looking-glass.

**IDENTIFICATION OF THE WOMAN.**

The Central News says: It was not until late in the evening that the first real clue towards the solution of the mystery was found-namely, the identification of the deceased. During the day some half-dozen women who thought that they knew deceased visited the mortuary and viewed the body, but without being able to recognise it.

The energetic efforts of Inspector Helson and Detective-sergeants Enright and Godley were eventually successful in clearing up this point.

It transpires that deceased is a married woman, named Mary Ann Nichols, who has been living apart from her husband for some years. Her real age is 36 years, and she had been an inmate of Lambeth Workhouse, off and on, for the past seven years. She was first admitted to the workhouse seven years ago as a patient into the lying-in ward,[14] and from this point seems to have entered upon a downward career. Some few months ago she left the workhouse, after having temporarily sojourned there, to go into domestic service at Rose-hill-road, Wandsworth. She left suddenly, under suspicious circumstances, and for the last seven weeks or so seems to have been frequenting the neighbourhood of Whitechapel.

She was last seen in the Whitechapel-road at half-past two yesterday morning, and was then under the influence of drink.

The inquest will be held by Mr. Wynne E. Baxter, the coroner for the district, at the Working Lads' Institute, Whitechapel-road, this afternoon.

———

The Exchange Telegraph Company, on inquiry this morning at Scotland Yard, were informed that no arrests had been made in connection with the brutal murder at Whitechapel up to eleven o'clock to-day.

~

---

[14] **Lying-In Ward.** (*Archaic*) A room where women were confined in childbirth. (Collins Dictionary)

# Monday, 3 September, 1888

## The Times

### THE WHITECHAPEL MURDER.

Up to a late hour last evening the police had obtained no clue to the perpetrator of the latest of the three murders which have so recently taken place in Whitechapel, and there is, it must be acknowledged, after their exhaustive investigation of the facts, no ground for blaming the officers in charge should they fail in unravelling the mystery surrounding the crime.

The murder, in the early hours of Friday morning last, of the woman now known as Mary Ann Nicholls, has so many points of similarity with the murder of two other women in the same neighbourhood—one Martha Tabram, as recently as August 7, and the other less than 12 months previously—that the police admit their belief that the three crimes are the work of one individual. All three women were of the class called "unfortunates," each so very poor, that robbery could have formed no motive for the crime, and each was murdered in such a similar fashion, that doubt as to the crime being the work of one and the same villain almost vanishes, particularly when it is remembered that all three murders were committed within a distance of 300 yards from each other.

These facts have led the police to almost abandon the idea of a gang being abroad to wreak vengeance on women of this class for not supplying them with money. Detective Inspectors Abberline, of the Criminal Investigation Department, and Detective Inspector Helson, J Division, are both of opinion that only one person, and that a man, had a hand in the latest murder. It is understood that the investigation into the George-yard mystery is proceeding hand-in-hand with that of Buck's Row. It is considered unlikely that the woman could have entered a house, been murdered, and removed to Buck's Row within a period of one hour and a quarter.

The woman who last saw her alive, and whose name is Nelly Holland, was a fellow-lodger with the deceased in Thrawl Street, and is positive as to the time being 2:30. Police constable Neil, 79 J, who found the body, reports the time as 3:45. Buck's Row is a secluded place, from having tenements on one side only. The constable has been severely questioned as to his "working" of his "beat" on that night, and states that he was last on the spot where he found the body not more than half an hour previously—that is to say, at 3:15.

The beat is a very short one, and quickly walked over would not occupy more than 12 minutes. He neither heard a cry nor saw any one. Moreover, there are three watchmen on duty at night close to the spot, and neither one heard a cry to cause alarm. It is not true, says Constable Neil, who is a man of nearly 20 years' service, that he was called to the body by two men. He came upon it as he walked, and flashing his lantern to examine it, he was answered by the lights from two other constables at either end of the street. These officers had seen no man leaving the spot to attract attention, and the mystery is most complete.

The utmost efforts are being used, a number of plainclothes men being out making inquiries in the neighbourhood, and Sergeants Enright and Godley have interviewed many persons who might, it was thought, assist in giving a clue.

—

On Saturday afternoon Mr. Wynne E. Baxter, coroner for the South-Eastern Division of Middlesex, opened his inquiry at the Working Lads' Institute, Whitechapel Road, respecting the death of MARY ANN NICHOLS, whose dead body was found on the pavement in Buck's-row, Whitechapel, on Friday morning.

Detective Inspectors Abberline and Helston and Sergeants Enright and Godley watched the case on behalf of the Criminal Investigation Department.

The jury having been sworn and having viewed the body of the dead woman, which was lying in a shell in the Whitechapel Mortuary.

Edward Walker, of 16 Maidswood-road, Camberwell, deposed that he was now of no occupation, but had formerly been a smith. He had seen the body in the mortuary, and to the best of his belief it was that of his daughter, whom he had not seen for two years. He recognized the body by its general appearance and by some of the front teeth being missing. Deceased also had a scar on the forehead which was caused by a fall when she was young. There was a scar on the body of the woman then lying in the mortuary.

# Monday, 3 September, 1888

His daughter's name was Mary Ann Nichols, and she had been married quite 22 years. Her husband's name was William Nichols, a printer's machinist, and he was still alive. They had been living apart for seven or eight years. Deceased was about 42 years of age. The last time witness heard of the deceased was about Easter, when she wrote him a letter. He produced the letter, which was in the hand-writing of the deceased. It spoke of a situation she was in, and which, she said, she liked very much. He answered that letter, but had not since heard from the deceased.

The last time he saw deceased was in June, 1886, when she was respectably dressed. That was at the funeral of his son, who was burnt to death through the explosion of a paraffin lamp. Some three or four years previous to that the deceased lived with witness; but he was unable to say what she had since been doing.

Deceased was not a particularly sober woman, and that was the reason why they could not agree. He did not think she was "fast" with men, and she was not in the habit of staying out late at night while she was living with him. He had no idea what deceased had been doing since she left him. He did not turn the deceased out of doors. They simply had a few words, and the following morning she left home.

The reason deceased parted from her husband was that he went and lived with the woman who nursed his wife during her confinement. Witness knew nothing of his daughter's acquaintances, or what she had been doing for a living. Deceased was not 5ft. 4in. in height. She had five children, the eldest of whom was 21 years of age and the youngest eight or nine. She left her husband when the youngest child was only one or two years of age. The eldest was now lodging with witness.

He was unable to say if deceased had recently been living with any one; but some three or four years ago he heard she was living with a man named Drew, who was a house smith by trade and had a shop of his own in York Street, Walworth. Witness believed he was still living there. The husband of the deceased had been summoned for the keep of the children, but the charge was dismissed owing to the fact that she was then living with another man. Deceased was in the Lambeth Workhouse in April last, when she left to go to a situation. Her husband was still living at Coburg-road, Old Kent Road, but witness was not aware if he was acquainted with his wife's death. Witness did not think the deceased had any enemies, as she was too good for that.

Police constable John Neil, 97 J, deposed that on Friday morning he was passing down Buck's Row, Whitechapel, and going in the direction of Brady Street, and he did not notice any one about. He had been round the same place some half an hour previous to that and did not see any one. He was walking along the right-hand side of the street when he noticed a figure lying in the street. It was dark at the time, although a street lamp was shining at the end of the row.

He walked across and found the deceased lying outside a gateway, which was about 9ft. or 10ft. in height and led to some stables, was closed. Houses ran eastward from the gateway, while the Board school was westward of the spot. On the other side of the road was the Essex Wharf. The deceased was lying length-ways, and her left hand touched the gate. With the aid of his lamp he examined the body and saw blood oozing from a wound in the throat. Deceased was lying upon her back with her clothes disarranged. Witness felt her arm, which was quite warm from the joints upwards, while her eyes were wide open.

Her bonnet was off her head and was lying by her right side, close by the left hand. Witness then heard a constable passing Brady Street, and he called to him. Witness said to him, "Run at once for Dr. Llewellyn." Seeing another constable in Baker's Row, witness despatched him for the ambulance. Dr. Llewellyn arrived in a very short time. In the meantime witness had rung the bell of Essex Wharf and inquired if any disturbance had been heard. He was told "No." Sergeant Kerby then came, and he knocked.

The doctor, having looked at the woman, said:—"Move the woman to the mortuary; she is dead. I will make a further examination of her." They then placed deceased on the ambulance and removed her to the mortuary. Inspector Spratley came to the mortuary, and while taking a description of deceased lifted up her clothes and discovered she was disem-bowelled. That had not been noticed before.

On the deceased was found a piece of comb

and a bit of looking glass, but no money was found. In the pocket an unmarked white pocket handkerchief was found. There was a pool of blood where the neck of deceased was lying in Buck's Row.

He had not heard any disturbance that night.

The farthest he had been that night was up Baker's Row to the Whitechapel Road, and was never far away from the spot. The Whitechapel road was a busy thoroughfare in the early morning, and he saw a number of women in that road, apparently on their way home. At that time anyone could have got away. Witness examined the ground while the doctor was being sent for. In answer to a juryman, the witness said he did not see any trap[15] in the road. He examined the road, but could not see any marks of wheels.

The first persons who arrived on the spot after he discovered the body were two men who worked at a slaughterhouse opposite. They stated that they knew nothing of the affair, nor had they heard any screams. Witness had previously seen the men at work. That would be a quarter past 3, or half an hour before he found the body.

Mr. Henry Llewellyn, surgeon, of 152, Whitechapel Road, stated that at 4 o'clock on Friday morning he was called by the last witness to Buck's Row. The officer told him what he was wanted for. On reaching Buck's Row he found deceased lying flat on her back on the pathway, her legs being extended. Deceased was quite dead, and she had severe injuries to her throat. Her hands and wrists were cold, but the lower extremities were quite warm. Witness examined her chest and felt the heart.

It was dark at the time. He should say the deceased had not been dead more than half an hour. He was certain that the injuries to the neck were not self-inflicted. There was very little blood round the neck, and there were no marks of any struggle, or of blood as though the body had been dragged.

Witness gave the police directions to take the body to the mortuary, where he would make another examination. About an hour afterwards he was sent for by the inspector to see the other injuries he had discovered on the body. Witness went, and saw that the abdomen was cut very extensively. That morning he made a post mortem examination of the body.

It was that of a female of about 40 or 45 years. Five of the teeth were missing, and there was a slight laceration of the tongue. There was a bruise running along the lower part of the jaw on the right side of the face. That might have been caused by a blow from a fist or pressure from a thumb. There was a circular bruise on the left side of the face, which also might have been inflicted by the pressure of the fingers. On the left side of the neck, about 1in. below the jaw, there was an incision about 4in. in length, and ran from a point immediately below the ear.

On the same side, but an inch below, and commencing about 1in. in front of it, was a circular incision, which terminated in a point about 3in. below the right jaw. That incision completely severed all the tissues down to the vertebrae. The large vessels of the neck on both sides were severed. The incision was about 8in. in length. The cuts must have been caused by a long-bladed knife, moderately sharp, and used with great violence.

No blood was found on the breast, either of the body or clothes. There were no injuries about the body until just below the lower part of the abdomen. Two or three inches from the left side was a wound running in a jagged manner. The wound was a very deep one, and the tissues were cut through. There were several incisions running across the abdomen. There were also three or four similar cuts, running downwards, on the right side, all of which had been caused by a knife which had been used violently and downwards. The injuries were from left to right, and might have been done by a left-handed person. All the injuries had been caused by the same instrument.

At this stage Mr. Wynne Baxter adjourned the inquiry until this morning.

~

---

[15] **Trap**. 3. A carriage; a fast name for a conveyance of any kind. (Farmer)

24

# Monday, 3 September, 1888

## The Star

### THE WHITECHAPEL CRIME.
### THE INQUEST ON THE WOMAN NICHOLS RESUMED TO-DAY.
### Detailed Evidence of the Circumstances Under Which the Body was Discovered - The Slaughterman Called.

At the Lads' Institute, Whitechapel, this morning Coroner Baxter resumed his inquiry into the mysterious murder of the woman Nicholls, who was found horribly murdered near a gateway in Buck's-row early on Friday morning.

Inspector John Spratling was the first witness—a keen-eyed man with iron-grey hair and beard. He said he was called to where the body was found at half-past four on Friday morning. Two policemen were there. One of them pointed out the spot where the woman was found. The blood was then being washed away, but he noticed stains between the stones. The body had been removed to the mortuary in Old Montague-street. Witness went there and found the body still on the ambulance. It was then in the yard; the keeper had been sent for that it might be placed in the dead-house. During the wait witness took a description, but he did not notice wounds on the body. When the body had been put in the mortuary he made a more extended examination, and then discovered for the first time the injuries to the abdomen. The bowels were exposed. On this discovery he sent for Dr. Llewellyn. There were no blood marks between the groin and the knees—there might have been a spot, but not any noticeable quantity. The skin was clean, but it did not appear to have been washed. Two workhouse men stripped the body.

Inspector Enright said in answer to the Coroner and Inspector Spratling, he gave instructions that

### THE BODY SHOULD NOT BE TOUCHED.

The Coroner didn't seem pleased that the body should have been stripped, apparently without authority.

Inspector Spratling, continuing his evidence, said the principal parts of her attire consisted of an old reddish brown ulster, a comparatively new brown linsey dress, two workhouse petti- coats—the workhouse marks had been cut out of the bands—and a pair of stays.[16]

The Coroner said he was anxious to see these stays, and they were sent for. He wanted to know whether they were injured; he thought they should have protected the body.

A juryman said it was important to know, too, whether they were fastened when found on the body, and the Coroner remarked, "It is the little things that tell the tale. The condition of the clothing is most important."

Witness, continuing, said there was no blood on the petticoats; the chemise, however, was bloodstained on the front; he did not notice that it was on the back. There was blood on the upper part of the dress and on the cloak. He noticed when the doctor examined the body that the injuries commenced just below the breast bone.

The Coroner remarked that the stays would be over this part of the body, and the witness said, "Yes, it would." "Yes, I should understand that from the evidence of the doctor," observed the Coroner, evidently impressed.

Resuming his answers to the Coroner, the witness said that at five or six o'clock he set Police-constable Thain to

### EXAMINE ALL THE PREMISES

in the vicinity of the spot where the body was discovered. Witness looked himself for bloodstains in Buck's-row. That was at 11 or 12 o'clock. He couldn't find any. Subsequently, with Sergeant Godley, he examined the East London and District Railway embankment and lines, and also the Great Eastern Railway yard. He found nothing—no weapon.

"You are looking for the weapon and I am looking for the blood," said the Coroner rather sharply.

"No, no blood," answered witness hastily. Green, a carman working for Mr. Brown, washed away the blood. There were men working at the Great Eastern Railway yard all night. He saw various people who had been in the vicinity—Mrs. Green, who lived close to the gateway, and also a watchman 50 yards from the spot—but none could give him any information whatever. A Mr. Purkis told him

---

[16] **Stays, Pair of Stays.** A corset. Most were reinforced with vertical ribs of whalebone; some also used spring steel ribs. (Cunnington)

his wife had been pacing the room early in the morning about the time the murder must have been committed, but heard nothing. The distance from the spot where the body was found to Barber's slaughter yard was 150 paces —walking round the Board School.

"As the crow flies," remarked the coroner, looking at a plan, "it would not be more than half that distance." It was further noted that between the two spots only the low row of cottages intervened.

In answer to the foreman, Inspector Spratling said the other constable besides Neil, whose beat was near, went down Brady-street. They would be within hearing distance from time to time.

Questioned by jurymen, witness said the impression he formed when he first saw the body was that the woman had been murdered with her clothes on, "of course." The body was not left where the school-children could see it before being placed in the dead-house.

Henry Tompkins said he lived at 12, Coventry-street, Bethnal-green. He was

**A HORSE SLAUGHTERER**

in the employment of Mr. Barber. He spent Thursday night and Friday morning in the slaughterhouse in Winthrop-street. He started at between eight and nine p.m., his usual time. His time for leaving was four in the morning. He left off work at twenty minutes past four on Friday morning. He went for a walk. They generally went home when they left work, but didn't that morning. He went to see "that woman what was murdered." Police-constable Pain was passing, at a quarter-past four, the slaughter-house, and told them a woman had been murdered in Buck's-row. There were three men at work in the slaughter-house—himself, James Mumford, and Charles Britten. At twenty minutes past twelve witness and Britten left the slaughter-house and went back at one. "We didn't go far away, only down the court there."

It was explained that this was Wood's-buildings.

"It was as near four as anything when we was done work." Witness went on. Their work was "wery quiet," but they heard nothing. "The gates was all open; any one could come in."

"No, no," said the Coroner; "I want to know whether you could hear any sound."

"No sir, we heard no sound—no cry. No one passed the slaughter-house except the police-man at a quarter past four."

"Where there any women about?"

"Oh, I don't know anything about them," witness answered, with a shrug of the shoulders.

"Did you see any in your walk?"

"Oh, no; I don't know about that. I don't like them."

Pressed by the Coroner, he said there were men and women of all sorts and sizes in the Whitechapel-road. He volunteered the information that it was

**"A VERY ROUGH NEIGHBORHOOD."**

If anybody had called for help in Buck's-row he didn't think he should have heard it—it was too far away. When told that a woman had been murdered in Buck's-row they all went there. Witness and Mumford went first, and Britten followed after. The doctor and three or four policemen were there. "I don't know whether there was two other men there. I think there was." He didn't know who they were. Witness stopped there till the woman was taken away. Lots of people came in the interval—10 or a dozen. He didn't hear anything said as to how the woman came there or where she came from.

"Are you sure there were not three people there?" asked the Coroner.

"I believe there was two there," answered witness.

"What do you mean by 'believe'?"

"Well, I saw two people there then," said the witness, getting provoked. He had not read the papers, he couldn't read. Standing with his hands in his pockets the witness, a roughly dressed young fellow of low stature, was

**BADGERED BY SEVERAL JURYMEN**

about his midnight ramble. They generally, he said, went out to have a drink. He would swear his usual time of knocking off work was not six o'clock. What time they went home depended on what time they got their work done. The policeman called at the slaughter house at a quarter past four for his cape. Then it was he told them of the murder. He did not call to tell them of the murder, but to get his cape.

"That's all," said the Coroner.

"Thank you, sir," said witness, and he went away rather angry and somewhat relieved.

**INSPECTOR HELSTON**

said he received information of the murder at a quarter to seven. He went to the Bethnal-green station, learned the particulars, and went to the mortuary. He saw the body with all the clothing on, and was present when the clothes were removed. The bodice of the dress was buttoned down to the middle. The stays were fastened up. They were fairly tight, but they were rather short. No blood had soaked through the petticoats or the lower part of the ulster, but the back of the bodice had absorbed a good deal which had apparently come from the neck, and so had the corresponding part of the ulster.

## THE HAIR WAS SOAKED WITH BLOOD.

The skin of the woman's thighs was clean, but not so clean as to suggest that that part of the body had been recently washed. There were discolorations on the cheek and under the jaw bone, probably caused by blows, but there were no bruises on the arms to indicate a struggle. All the wounds on the abdomen were visible with the stays on, showing that they could have been inflicted without the removal of the stays. There were no wounds under the stays. He examined the spot where the body was found, but not until after the blood had been washed off. There were no blood splashes on the gate. He found no blood on the pavement either in Buck's-row or Brady-street, except one spot—"it might have been blood"—in Brady-street.

Replying to the foreman, witness said he did not think it strange that there was so little blood. That from the abdominal wounds had flowed into the body. It was his opinion that

## THE MURDER WAS COMMITTED AT THE SPOT

where the body was found. The clothes had been so little deranged that she could not have been carried any distance.

Policeman George Myzen said that at a quarter to four on Friday morning he was in Hanbury-street, Baker's-row. A man passing said to him, "You're wanted round in Buck's-row." That man was Carman Cross (who came into the Court-room in a coarse sacking apron), and he had come from Buck's-row. He said a woman had been found there. Witness went to the spot, found Policeman Neil there, and by his instruction witness went for the ambulance. He assisted in removing the body. He noticed blood running from the throat to the gutter. There was only one pool; it was somewhat congealed. Cross, when he spoke to witness about the affair, was accompanied by another man. Both

went down Hanbury-street. The witness at the time was in the act of knocking a man up. Cross told him a policeman wanted him. He did not say anything about murder or suicide. It was not true that before he went to Buck's-row, witness continued "knocking people up." He went there immediately.

## CARMAN CROSS

was the next witness. He lived at 22 Doveton street, Cambridge-road. He was employed by Pickfords. He left home on Friday at twenty minutes past three, and got to Pickford's yard at Broad-street at four o'clock. He crossed Bradley-street into Buck's-row. He was alone. He saw something lying in front of the gateway —it looked in the distance like tarpaulin. When he got nearer he found it was a woman. At that time he heard a man coming up the street behind him; he was about 40 yards behind. Witness waited until he came up. He started as though he thought witness was going to knock him down. Witness said to him, "There's a woman." They both went to the body and stooped beside it. Witness took the woman's hand, and finding it cold said, "I believe she's dead." The other man put his hand on the breast outside the clothes—over her heart—and said, "I think she's breathing, but very little." He suggested they should shift her—set her up against the wall—but witness said, "I'm not going to touch her. Let's go on till we see a policeman and tell him." Before they left the body the other man tried to pull the clothes over the woman's knees, but they did not seem as though they would come down. Witness noticed no blood; but it was very dark. He did not see that her throat was cut. They went up Baker's-row, and saw the last witness. Witness said to him, "There's a woman lying down in Buck's-row on the broad of her back. I think she's dead or drunk." The other man said, "I believe she's dead." The policeman said, "All right."

## THE OTHER MAN

left witness at the corner of Hanbury-street, and went down Corbett's-court. He was a stranger to witness, but appeared to be a carman. Witness did not see Police-constable Neil—only the constable he spoke to. The constable and the man were the only people he saw after leaving his home. From the position of the body, he thought the woman had been outraged; he did not suppose at the time she had been murdered.

The other man said he would fetch a policeman, but he was behind time. Witness heard no sounds of a vehicle. He thought that had anyone left the body after he had turned into Buck's-row he would have heard them.

Answering a juryman, witness said he did not tell Constable Mizen that another policeman wanted him. After Mizen had been told there was a woman lying in Buck's-row he went out and knocked at a door. He did not go towards Buck's-row to do this.

(Proceeding.)

~

## Evening News
### FIFTH EDITION.
### THE WHITECHAPEL MYSTERY.
### STILL ENSHROUDED IN MYSTERY.
### THE POLICE AT FAULT.
### RESUMED INQUEST TO-DAY.
### [SPECIAL.]

The police have not yet succeeded in effecting an arrest in connection with the atrocious murder of Mrs. Nichols, whose mutilated body was found in Buck's-row early on Friday morning; nor have any fresh facts come to light which make it probable that the crime will be brought home to the perpetrator or perpetrators. Active attempts are being made to discover the actual scene of the murder, for the theory that the crime was committed in Buck's-row, where the body was found, is generally discredited. The small quantity of blood found at this spot—considerably less than half a pint—is conclusive against the theory.

The wounds in the throat severed both the jugular vein, and the carotid artery, with the result that the body was practically drained of blood. A large quantity of blood must also have flowed from the terrible wounds on the abdomen. Yet very little was found on the clothes of the deceased or on the pavement where she was lying. More than this, the traces of blood which extended for some few yards from yards from Buck's-row, are pretty conclusive evidence that the body was dragged or carried along for some distance after the wounds had been inflicted.

This theory is also borne out by the absence of any sounds of quarrelling in Buck's-row on the Thursday night or Friday morning.

There are two theories which find favour. One is that the deceased woman entered some house in the neighbourhood for an immoral purpose, and was there murdered and mutilated, the body being afterwards carried to Buck's-row. If this theory be the correct one there ought to be no difficulty in finding the house, as the room in which the murder was committed must have subsequently borne the appearance of a slaughter-house. Unless the people of the house were parties to the murder, it seems incredible that they should not have communicated with the police before this. And even if these people are implicated they would probably find great difficulty in removing all traces of their crime.

The other theory is that the crime was committed by one or more of a gang of scoundrels who live by levying blackmail upon unfortunate streetwalkers out late at night, and who make a practice of exacting revenge whenever this blackmail is not forthcoming. It is known that Mrs. Nichols was penniless, as she was refused admission to a common lodging-house on the Thursday night because she could not pay for her bed, and therefore she would be unable to buy off the gang if accosted by them. The weakness of this theory consists in its assumption that the murder took place in the streets, whereas the most careful survey of the neighbourhood has failed to discover such marks of bloodshed as must inevitably have come from the wounds inflicted.

Over and above these two theories there are all sorts of speculations that the murder is a maniac or a Lascar,[17] but none of the known facts lend weight to these suppositions.

The identification of the deceased is now complete, and is confirmed by her father, husband, and son. After the inquest the son visited the corpse with his grandfather, and shortly afterwards the deceased's husband appeared at the mortuary. Father and son did not speak, and evidently did not recognise each other, until old Mr. Walker, the father of the dead woman, said to Nichols, "Well, here is your son." The young man had been brought up by his grandfather and had not seen his father for years. After looking at the deceased, Nichols said, "There is no mistake about it. It has come to a sad end at last."

---

[17] **Lascar**. An East Indian sailor. (Morehead)

# Monday, 3 September, 1888

Yesterday crowds of people visited the scene of the crime, and hung for hours around the two main gates heading to the mortuary. The popular mind insists on associating the crime with the two previous murders of lost women which have occurred in the same neighbourhood during the present year.

Robert Paul, a carman, has made the following remarkable statement:

*He says*: It was exactly a quarter to four when I passed up Buck's-row to my work as a carman for Covent-garden market. It was dark, and I was hurrying along, when I saw a man standing where the woman was. He came a little towards me, but as I knew the dangerous character of the locality I tried to give him a wide berth. Few people like to come up and down here without being on their guard, for there are such terrible gangs about. There have been many knocked down and robbed at that spot. The man, however, came towards me and said, "Come and look at this woman." I went and found the woman lying on her back. I laid hold of her wrist and found that she was dead and the hands cold. It was too dark to see the blood about her. I thought that she had been outraged, and had died in the struggle. I was obliged to be punctual at my work, so I went on and told the other man I would send the first policeman I saw. I saw one in Church-row, just at the top of Buck's-row, who was going round calling people up, and I told him what I had seen, and I asked him to come, but he did not say whether he should come or not. He continued calling the people up, which I thought was a great shame, after I had told him the woman was dead. The woman was so cold that she must have been dead some time, and either she had been lying there, left to die, or she must have been murdered somewhere else and carried there. If she had been lying there long enough to get so cold as she was when I saw her, it shows that no policeman on the test had been down there for a long time. If a policeman had been there he must have seen here, for she was plain enough to see. Her bonnet was lying about two feet from her head.

At the Working Lads' Institute, this morning, the inquest was resumed by Mr. Wynne Baxter.

## POLICE EVIDENCE.
Inspector Spratling, of the J division, said that about 1.30 on Friday, he heard of the murder whilst in the Whitechapel-road. He went first to the police-station and afterwards to the scene of the murder. There was a slight stain of blood between the stones. The body had then been removed to the mortuary. He went there with Police-constable Thain, and saw the deceased upon an ambulance in the yard, and he took a description of the story. He did not at that time notice the abdominal wounds, but subsequently when the body was placed on the floor of the mortuary he took a more accurate description of the undergarments, and they discovered the injuries on the lower part of the body. The flesh was turned over from left to right and the intestines exposed. He covered up the woman and sent for Dr. Llewellyn. There were no blood marks between the groin and the knees, except, perhaps, very slight ones. He did not feel very well at the time and the sight "turned him up," so that he did not make a very precise examination. The skin of the deceased was clean, but he could not say that it bore evidence of blood having been recently washed off from it. The doctor afterwards made a second examination, and to enable him to do so, the body was stripped by two persons from the workhouse.

The Coroner said the people who stripped the deceased ought to be present, as their evidence might be of importance.

Witness, continuing, said on his next visit to the mortuary the body had been stripped, and the clothing placed in the yard. Amongst them was a pair of stays, but he could not say whether they had been injured in any way.

The Coroner said it seemed likely that these stays could have protected the injured part of the abdomen, and therefore it was important to know what condition they were in. In matters like the one under consideration it was the little things that told.

Inspector Spratling said the stays were fastened when he first saw the woman. He did not notice blood upon the petticoats, though he did on the breast part of the dress, and a little on the chemise. Part of the body wounds would be covered by the stays.

The Coroner:—I should think that must be so from the evidence of the doctor.

Witness said the stays were not tight fitting, and by raising them, without using force, the whole of the wounds could be seen.

The Foreman:—Can we see the stays, for that is important.

The Coroner:—We must do so.

Witness continuing, said he had examined Buck's-row carefully, but found no stains of blood or marks of a suspicious character. He afterwards examined the Great Eastern Railway yard and the embankment, and other open spaces, but he found nothing—neither blood nor weapon. A carman named Green had swilled away the blood from the pavement in Buck's-row after the body had been removed. Witness had made further inquiries, but could not find any one who had heard screams.

Henry Tompkins, of 12, Coventry-street, said he was in the employ of Mr. Barr, and he was working all night in the slaughter-house in Buck's-row. He started work between eight and nine, and left off about 4.20 next morning, and had a walk to where the body was lying. A policeman had passed the slaughter-house about 4.15, and said a woman had been found murdered in Buck's-row. I had previously left the slaughter-house with a companion at 12.20, and returned about 1 a.m., or a little later, when I recommenced work. None of us left the place again until 4.20. They were all quiet in the slaughterhouse—say from two o'clock. All the gates were open, but I heard no noise from the streets after I returned at one o'clock. I heard no cries whatever. No one came to the slaughter-house except a policeman, and I saw no one pass.

The Coroner:—Are there many women about at that time?

Witness:—I know nothing about that. (Laughter.) I did not notice any when I left the slaughterhouse at 12.20 until I got into the Whitechapel-road. There were plenty there, of all sorts and sizes-both men and women.

The Coroner:—Supposing any one had called for assistance—"Murder" say—in Buck's-row, would you have heard it?

Witness:—It might have been too far away. I should not hear it from where we saw the body.

Two of us went to the body first, and a mate followed us later on. The doctor was there when I arrived, and also three or four policemen. I believe there were also two men there, but do not know who they were. I waited in Buck's-row until they took the body away. By that time probably ten or a dozen people had come up. I heard no statement as to how the body got there or where it came from.

By a juryman:—The policeman who told us about the murder, came to the slaughter-house for his cape, which he had left there earlier on, because it was a fine night.

Inspector Helston was next examined. He said: I first received information of the murder at 6.45 on Friday morning, and went to the mortuary shortly after eight. The body was then dressed in a brown ulster, which had seven buttons down the front, five of which were fastened. Two or three buttons at the front of the dress near the breast were unfastened. She had a petticoat of coarse grey material, and a flannel petticoat underneath. Her stays were fastened up the front, and there were imitation laces at the back. The stays were fairly tight; but, in my opinion, they were shorter than usual. Underneath the stays she wore a chemise and a piece of coarse flannel. There was no blood on the flannel, but there was on the back of the chemise. There were stains of blood on the abdomen, but not on the thighs. There were no signs of violence below the abdomen, and there were no bloodstains on either of the petticoats. The back of the upper part of the dress near the neck had absorbed a great deal of blood; and the upper part of the ulster was also saturated. The hair was clotted with blood.

The Coroner:—Was the skin of the thighs clean?

Witness:—Yes.

The Coroner:—Did it strike you that they were unusually clean—that they had been recently washed?

Witness:—No; there was nothing to show that. There was a circular bruise on the left cheek, and her left eye was slightly discoloured as if by a blow on the cheek. There was another discolouration under the right jaw. The wounds in the abdomen were fairly visible before the clothes were removed, showing that they might have been inflicted whilst the clothes were on the body. None of the wounds were beneath the stays. They were below the bottom of that garment. I afterwards went to the spot where the body was found in Buck's-row. It had then been recently washed, and there was no sign of blood either on the pavement or the gates close to. I also examined the pavement from Buck's-row to Brady-street. With the exception of one stain at the Brady-street end of the row, which might have been blood, I found nothing that I could connect with the murder.

By a Juryman:—Did it not strike you as very strange that you did not find more blood, considering the nature of the wounds?

Witness:—No; I found enough blood at the back of the dress to account for the blood that flowed from the wound in the throat. The blood from the other wounds probably flowed into the abdominal cavity.

Police-constable Mizen, of the H Division, said on Friday last, about a quarter to four, he was in Baker's-row, at the end of Campbell-street. A man who had the appearance of a carman passed him and said, "You are wanted in Buck's-row."

A man named Cross was here brought into the room and identified by witness as the man to whom he referred.

(Inquest proceeding.)

—

## A SIDE LIGHT FOR AN INQUEST
## A PLEA FOR A
## CENTRAL MORTUARY.

I went to the inquest on the body of the woman murdered in Whitechapel as a matter of curiosity rather than of duty. I wanted to see whether the first act is the attempted unravelling of the mystery was so constructed as to have that desired effect, and I may at once express my disappointment.

The body of Mary Nichols was found at about four o'clock, a.m., and the evidence of Dr. Llewellyn showed that when he arrived on the spot, twenty minutes later, perhaps, the extremities were still warm. Hence we may take it that at about two or a little later Mary Nichols was still alive, a supposition confirmed by the statement of those who saw her, or fancied that they had done so, at that time near Whitechapel Church. It is no injustice, therefore, to the memory of the murdered woman to class her among the lowest category of unfortunates.

This lowest category has in every quarter of the metropolis its haunts, as well as the highest; haunts, admittance to which can be gained at almost any hour in the early morning, haunts which are distinctly known to the police, and if they are not, should be. I am not now speaking of the common lodging-houses to which the like of Mary Nichols repair when their perambulations temporarily cease, either through a "stroke of luck" or from the knowledge that they can be no longer profitable; I am speaking of the most dreadful "dens of assignation and accommodation." That there are such dens about Ready and Thomas streets, about Buck's-row, there can be no doubt.

On the Continent the landladies of any and every such a den would have been summoned to appear before the examining magistrate (juge d' instruction) who had taken the case in hand at the outset-there being no such a functionary as the coroner. They would have been interrogated on the chance that they might have harboured Mary Nichols and her paramour.

Edmond Texier, the eminent French journalist, who died about a twelvemonth ago, said that "respectability" was the most tyrannical word in the English language. English respectability thinks itself obliged to close its eyes to the fact of such places existing, for they exist in contravention of the law instead of with its concurrence, as on the Continent.

Consequently the hags that preside in them being severely and "respectably" left alone, no possible light could be forthcoming from that quarter. Assuredly it was not expected that they should voluntarily reveal the means of their nefarious livelihood and so risk not only losing the latter, but the infliction of a fine and perhaps imprisonment besides for keeping a disorderly house.

"The public should be spared those revelations of social and moral leprosy," say the purists. "The public's morbid curiosity should not be overfed." It is no doubt on this principle that they have tacitly ignored if not discountenanced the claims—in the interests of criminal detection more efficient than we at present possess—of the hugest metropolis of the Western world to a central morgue, such as at least Paris, Vienna, and Berlin can boast. It is on this principle, no doubt, that they would approve the senseless and maybe un-warrantable action of the police inspector of the Bethnal Green division in shutting the door of the Whitechapel mortuary against any and every would-be visitor, "now that the body has been identified," to use the words—probably the inspector's own—as reported by a workhouse inmate and an amateur "chucker-out" left in charge. Identified as what? As the daughter of a working-man, whose husband had deserted her, who lived with another artisan for some time, then returned to her father, eventually quitted his roof to go into service, where she betrayed her trust, and finally took to the streets, to meet with her doom at the hands of some unspeakable ruffian-mentally responsible or not for his act.

Were the police under the impression that the public mistook the murdered woman for a patrician or plebeian Lucrece, a noble or proletarian Dinah, who had strayed or been inveigled to the backslums of Whitechapel by a patrician or plebeian Tarquin, been ravished, and dispatched afterwards?

The identification has brought us no nearer to the solution of the mystery, but the exhibition of the body to all comers for another day or two might have done this. I say might, not would. Among the thousands that would have been attracted thither—for Londoners are not a bit less curious than Parisians or Berliners, and thousands visit their respective morgues when the victim of a mysterious crime is exposed—there might have possibly been one who had seen Mary Nichols in the society of a man in the last hours of her life.

He (the supposed informant) need not necessarily have belonged to Whitechapel. He might have been a tramp,[18] a waggoner,[19] who, wending his way through Whitechapel to the west or south of the capital, had stopped at a coffee-stall and noticed the couple. If under the present circumstances such a person exists, and if he had applied as I did at the mortuary, after the jurymen had viewed the body, he would have met with the same courteous and dunderheaded reply that I got on the authority of the sapient inspector of the Bethnal Green

division. A waggoner or a tramp it should be remembered, is not a regular subscriber to the morning and evening papers; a description of Mary Nichols's appearance, dress, and fate may have reached him yesterday through a Sunday paper.

In Paris or Berlin he would go straight to the morgue and look in at the window behind which both the body and the clothes in which it was found would be shown. Here an application to the police would be necessary, provided Mary Nichols was not already buried. If the applicant were lucky enough to meet a detective alone, he might be listened to, for the would-be Vidocq[20] would smell professional glory. If there happened to be two or three, he would be snubbed and brow-beaten through professional jealousy. I am not inventing, but stating facts which it would not be very difficult to prove.

In Paris, to which city I shall confine myself, seeing that its morgue is virtually administered like those of Vienna and Berlin, the police have little or no control in these matters. The body once admitted to the morgue "on the formal and printed request" of a Commissary of Police, the greffier (secretary) of that establishment becomes its responsible custodian until relieved of the charge by an order for burial from the Procurator of the Republic attached to the Court of First Instance. Immediately after its reception the body is undressed and washed, the clothes are disinfected. In some special cases the body is dressed again; in others it is merely wrapped in a winding sheet, left partially nude, and the clothes suspended in front of one of the dozen black marble slabs on which the corpses are laid out. The three plate glass windows under the portico afford a full view of the whole of the interior; to arrest decomposition the slabs and their contents are constantly besprinkled with ice-cold water.

---

[18] **Tramp**. On the lookout for employment; walking about from place to place. (Farmer)
[19] **Waggoner**. A wagon driver. (Census1891.com)

---

[20] **Eugène François Vidocq** (1775-1857), Famous French criminal turned criminologist. His claimed exploits inspired the writers Honoré de Balzac and Victor Hugo, who based both Jean Valjean and Police Inspector Javert on Vidocq. He is credited with founding the Sûreté National and the first private detective agency.

# Monday, 3 September, 1888

If the body is identified and the cause of death surmised or ascertained to be suicide or accident it is removed at once, but kept in the basement in the tiroirs a froid (a kind of huge chest of drawers lined with zinc, not unlike a refrigerator) until the family can be communicated with.

The ceremony of "confrontation" takes place in an appartement, the description of which merits a whole chapter, for it is perhaps unique in the world's annals of crime. Every chair has its associations.

If after three days no information as to identity be forthcoming, the greffier applies for an order of internment to the above-named Procurator, who, through the intermediary of the Prefect of Police, grants said order, provided there is no cause for doubt. Otherwise the body is kept above earth and decomposition retarded by means of chemical injections.

French criminal jurisprudence being not at all averse to forcing the criminal into a confession of his guilt, "confrontation" is resorted to whenever it becomes possible, such bodies have been kept as long as a fortnight and three weeks.

English justice takes all possible precautions against the criminal betraying himself. But between the criminal betraying himself and the police stupidity suppressing a possible clue from the outside there is a great difference. Experience has taught us by now, and ought to have taught them, that their pretended discoveries were due to accident and to the public.

Where they have had no such windfalls as in the last two Whitechapel murders, the Camden Town murder, the Canonbury affair, they have miserably and disastrously failed. If the inspector of the Bethnal Green division be a sample of the average intelligence of his brethren one cannot wonder at these failures.

But Mr. Matthews is an intelligent man, and Parliament would not refuse him the grant for a Central Morgue if applied for. Such an institution would at any rate import the element of chance into the detection of criminals. The police evidently do not believe in this element, any more than some of the gamblers at Monte Carlo, who generally come away ruined. But the latter are generally staking their own money; the London police are staking the lives of at least five millions of inhabitants on the belief in their own infallibility.

A.D.V.

~

# Tuesday, 4 September, 1888

## The Times

### THE WHITECHAPEL MURDER.

Yesterday morning Mr. Wynne E. Baxter, the Coroner for the South-Eastern Division of Middlesex, resumed his inquiry at the Working Lads' Institute, High-street, Whitechapel, respecting the death of Mary Ann Nichols, whose dead body was found on the pavement in Buck's-row, Whitechapel, on Friday morning.

Detective-inspector Abberline (Scotland-yard), Inspector Helston, and Detective-sergeants P. Enright and Godley watched the case on behalf of the Criminal Investigation Department.

Inspector J. Spratling, J Division, was the first witness called. He deposed that at 4:30 on Friday morning he was called to the spot where the body of the deceased was found lying. On getting there he found two constables, one of whom pointed out the exact spot on which he found the body. At that time the blood was being washed away, but he could see some stains in between the stones. He was told that the body had been removed to the mortuary. On going there he found the body was still on the ambulance in the yard. While waiting for the arrival of the keeper of the dead-house he took a description of the deceased, but at that time did not notice any wounds on the body. On the body being put in the mortuary he made a more careful examination, and then discovered the injuries to the abdomen, and at once sent for Dr. Llewellyn. He saw two workhouse men stripping the body.

At this point, in reply to a question, Detective-sergeant P. Enright said he gave instructions that the body should not be touched.

Witness, continuing his evidence, stated he again went to the mortuary and made an examination of the clothing, taken off the deceased. The principle parts of the clothing consisted of a reddish ulster, somewhat the worse for wear, a new brown linsey dress, two flannel petticoats, having the marks of the Lambeth Workhouse on them, and a pair of stays. The things were fastened, but witness did not remove them himself, so could not say positively that all the clothing was properly fastened.

The Coroner observed it was such matters as these that threw a most important bearing on the subject. The question of the clothing was a most important one. Later on he directed Constable Thain, 96 J, to examine all the premises in the vicinity of the spot where the body was discovered.

Inspector Spratling, continuing, said he and Sergeant Godley examined the East London and District Railway embankments and lines, and also the Great Eastern Railway yard, but they were unable to find anything likely to throw any light on the affair. One of Mr. Brown's men wiped up the blood. A constable was on duty at the gate of the Great Eastern Railway yard, which was about 50 yards from the spot where the body was found. He had questioned this constable, but he had not heard anything. Mrs. Green, who also lived opposite the spot, had been seen, and during the night she had not heard anything, although she was up until 4 30 that morning. Mr. Purkis, who also lived close by, stated his wife had been pacing the room that morning, about the time the murder must have been committed, but she had not heard anything. It was 150 yards from the spot where the body was found to Barber's slaughter-yard. That was by walking round the Board school. During the night Constable Neil and another officer were within hearing distance of the spot. He should think deceased had been murdered while wearing her clothes, and did not think she had been dressed after death.

Henry Tomkins, a horse-slaughterer, living at 12, Coventry-street, Bethnal-green, stated he was in the employ of Mr. Barber. Thursday night and Friday morning he spent in the slaughterhouse in Winthrop-street. Witness commenced about his usual time—between 8 and 9 o'clock p.m. On Friday morning he left off work at 20 minutes past 4 and went for a walk. It was their rule to go home when they did so, but they did not do so that morning. A constable told them of the finding of the murdered woman, and they went to look at her. James Mumford, Charles Brittan, and witness worked together. At 12 o'clock witness and Brittan left the slaughterhouse, and returned about 1 o'clock. They did not again leave the slaughterhouse until they heard of the murder. All the gates were open, and witness during the night did not hear any disturbance; the only person who came to the slaughterhouse was the

# Tuesday, 4 September, 1888

constable. At times women came to the place, but none came that night. Had any one called out "Murder" in Buck's-row he might not have heard it. There were men and women in the Whitechapel-road. Witness and Mumford first went and saw the deceased, and then Brittan followed. At that time a doctor and three or four constables were there, and witness remained there until the body was taken away. At night he and his mates generally went out to have a drink. It depended upon what time their work was done when they went home. The constable was at the slaughterhouse at about a quarter past 4, when he called for his cape. It was then that they heard of the murder.

Inspector Helston, J Division, deposed that it was a quarter to 7 on Friday morning when he received information of the murder. Having learnt full particulars, he proceeded to the mortuary, where he saw deceased, who had her clothing on. He saw the things removed. The bodice of the dress was buttoned down to the middle and the stays were fastened. There was no bruises on the arms to indicate that a struggle had taken place. The wounds on the abdomen were visible with the stays on, and that proved they could have been inflicted while the stays were on the deceased. He did not examine the spot where the body was found until after the blood had been washed away. Witness was of opinion that the murder was committed at the spot where the body was found. The clothes were very little disarranged, thus showing that the body could not have been carried far.

Constable G. Mizen, 56 H, stated that at a quarter past 4 on Friday morning he was in Hanbury-street, Baker's-row, and a man passing said "You are wanted in Baker's-row." The man, named Cross, stated that a woman had been found there. In going to the spot he saw Constable Neil, and by the direction of the latter he went for the ambulance. When Cross spoke to witness he was accompanied by another man, and both of them afterwards went down Hanbury-street. Cross simply said he was wanted by a policeman, and did not say anything about a murder having been committed. He denied that before he went to Buck's-row he continued knocking people up.

George Cross, a carman, stated that he left home on Friday morning at 20 minutes past 3, and he arrived at his work, at Broad-street, at 4

o'clock. Witness walked along Buck's-row, and saw something lying in front of the gateway like a tarpaulin. He then saw it was a woman. A man came along and witness spoke to him. They went and looked at the body. Witness, having felt one of the deceased woman's hands and finding it cold, said "I believe she is dead." The other man, having put his hand over her heart, said "I think she is breathing." He wanted witness to assist in shifting her, but he would not do so. He did not notice any blood, as it was very dark. They went to Baker's-row, saw the last witness, and told him there was a woman lying down in Buck's-row on the broad of her back. Witness also said he believed she was dead or drunk, while the other man stated he believed her to be dead. The constable replied "All right." The other man left witness at the corner of Hanbury-street and turned into Corbett's court. He appeared to be a carman, and was a stranger to the witness. At the time he did not think the woman had been murdered. Witness did not hear any sounds of a vehicle, and believed that had any one left the body after he got into Buck's-row he must have heard him.

William Nichols, a machinist, of Coburg-road, Old Kent-road, stated that the deceased woman was his wife. He had been separated from her for upwards of eight years. The last time he saw her was over three years ago, and he had no idea what she had been doing since that time, nor with whom she had lived. Deceased was much given to drink. They separated several times, and each time he took her back she got drunk, and that was why he had to leave her altogether.

Jane Oram, 18, Thrawl-street, Spital-fields, deposed that deceased had slept at the common lodging-house there for about six weeks. Witness and deceased had occupied the same bed. For eight or ten days she had not been to the lodging-house, but witness saw her on the morning of her death in the Whitechapel-road. Deceased told her she was living where men and women were allowed to sleep, but added she should come back and live with witness. Witness believed deceased stated she had been living in Flower and Dean-street. Deceased was the worse for drink and refused to stay with witness, although she did all she could to persuade her to do so. Witness did not think she was a fast woman. She was a clean woman, but

35

witness had previously seen her the worse for drink.

Mary Ann Monk stated that she was an inmate of the Lambeth Workhouse. She knew the deceased, who had been an inmate of the union, but that was six or seven years ago.

The Coroner here informed the jury that the police did not propose to offer any further evidence that day, and it would be as well to adjourn the inquiry sufficiently long to give them an opportunity of obtaining further evidence.

The inquiry was accordingly adjourned for a fortnight.

—

So many stories of "suspicious" incidents have cropped up since the murder, some of them evidently spontaneously generated by frantic terror, and some, even where credible, pointing in contrary directions, that it would be idle to refer to them. A valuable hint may be found by the detectives in some of these volunteered reminiscences, but there is also danger that they may be diverted from the broad and obvious lines of investigation by distracting suggestions. If the perpetrator of crimes so numerous and so extraordinary is not only humiliating, but also an intolerable perpetuation of the danger. Although the Whitechapel murders are without example, the police have also an unexampled number of data from which to draw their conclusions. The most salient point is the maniacal frenzy with which the victims were slaughtered, and unless we accept, as a possible alternative, the theory that the assassin was actuated by revenge for some real or supposed injury suffered by him at the hands of unfortunate women, we are thrown back upon the belief that these murders were really committed by a madman, or by a man whom a sottish passion interlaced with a lust for blood places too far outside the pale of human feelings to be governed by commonly recognized motives. However, if the police are right in believing that certain flash rings were torn from NICHOLS'S finger, this is a circumstance which slightly disconcerts the idea that the murderer was a simple maniac. But, on the whole, this is the most probable theory, and, without any intention to accentuate alarm, it may be pointed out that, if it is correct, the ordinary motives of prudence which deter

murderers from a speedy repetition of their crime cannot be reckoned upon in aid of the safety of wretched women in Whitechapel.

~

## Evening News
### WHY THE WHITECHAPEL CRIME IS NOT DISCOVERED. A POLICE REASON.

There is a pretty unanimous opinion amongst most of the members of the Metropolitan Police Force that the reason of the want of success, or, as the public have it, the want of energy and intelligence on the part of the detective force, in discovering the perpetrators of great crimes is not far to seek.

According to them, in the first place the order prohibiting a constable to participate in any reward offered by the authorities for the capture of a criminal has worked a twofold evil—it lessens the inducement to extra exertion on the part of the men, and, what is worse, breeds a system of deception, as in many instances a third party is put forward as the giver of the information, and after the conviction of the offender the detective and his friend divide the reward, in the case of a reward offered by a private individual even after permission to receive is granted, toll is taken by the "chiefs" before the remainder is handed over to the recipient.

With regard to the "inquiry" expenses, which come from a secret service fund practically unlimited, the men complain that whilst the heads of the department—who, by the way, pass their own accounts—spend any sum they choose, the expenses of the men are so rigidly cut down that they are compelled to pay the informers out of their own pockets if they wish to gain a clue, or otherwise risk a bullying for their extravagance.

The worst case of all, however, is the cruelly unjust and unfair manner to which divisional (uniform) constables, and more especially young constables, are treated. No matter how cleverly one of them may affect a capture, discover or prevent a robbery, or recover stolen property, the moment the charge is booked at the police-station—that moment the case is taken out of his hands and a detective (plain clothes man) is told off to take charge of the case, find out previous convictions, and, if

# Tuesday, 4 September, 1888

necessary, prove them, and in the end get all the credit and praise for the manner in which the arrest has been made, and whilst the real discoverer has to content himself with a back seat, or if he does, when in the witness box, give a true account of his share in the transaction, receives a severe reprimand—this begets a sense of injustice, followed by inevitable carelessness.

Lastly, of late, fears of the military system of reporting in writing every trivial circumstance, which reports are seldom read, has been insisted on and a fine inflicted for neglect; whilst in many instances such reports have been handed over to favourites, thus depriving men of the credit of their labour. This has begotten a want of confidence, which has been increased by the prohibition of the men taking any particular line of their own without first submitting it to the "chief".

Until these evils are remedied, there is little hope of an intelligent, energetic, and combined action on the part of the Scotland-yard officers—at least, so say the men themselves.

# Wednesday, 5 September, 1888

## The Star
### FIFTH EDITION.
### "LEATHER APRON."
### THE ONLY NAME LINKED WITH THE WHITECHAPEL MURDERS.
### A NOISELESS MIDNIGHT TERROR.
**The Strange Character who Prowls About Whitechapel After Midnight—Universal Fear Among the Women—Slippered Feet and a Sharp Leather-knife.**

The mystery attending the horrible murders in Whitechapel shows no sign of lessening. The detectives at work on the case, who were quick to confess themselves baffled, only continue to make the same confession, and there is every prospect that the last ghastly tragedy will go unpunished like its predecessors. Whitechapel is loud in its indignation over the inefficiency of the detectives, and is asking several questions to which there does not seem to be any satisfactory answer. Among other things the people wish to know why the police do not arrest "Leather Apron."

"Leather Apron" by himself is quite an unpleasant character. If, as many of the people suspect, he is the real author of the three murders which, in everybody's judgement, were done by the same person, he is a more ghoulish and devilish brute than can be found in all the pages of shocking fiction. He has ranged Whitechapel for a long time. He exercises over the unfortunates who ply their trade after twelve o'clock at night, a sway that is

### BASED ON UNIVERSAL TERROR.

He has kicked, injured, bruised, and terrified a hundred of them who are ready to testify to the outrages. He has made a certain threat, his favourite threat, to any number of them, and each of the three dead bodies represents that threat carried out. He carries a razor-like knife, and two weeks ago drew it on a woman called "Widow Annie" as she was crossing the square near London Hospital, threatening at the same time, with his ugly grin and his malignant eyes, to "rip her up." He is a character so much like the invention of a story writer that the accounts of him given by all the street-walkers of the Whitechapel district seem like romances. The remarkable thing is, however, that they all agree in every particular.

Ever since the last murder the name "Leather Apron" has been falling repeatedly on the ears of the reporters. On the afternoon of the day following the murder a group of women in Eagle-place, near the mortuary, were busily discussing something to the detriment of their household duties. The subject was "Leather Apron," and the report had spread that

### "LEATHER APRON"
### HAD BEEN ARRESTED

for the murder. Ever since then women have been shaking their heads and saying that "Leather Apron" did it. The strangest thing about the whole case is that in view of public opinion in Whitechapel, the man has not been arrested on suspicion, and his whereabouts on the night of the murder inquired into.

About 50 of the unfortunates in the Whitechapel district gave a description of "Leather Apron" to a *Star* reporter between midnight and three o'clock this morning. The descriptions all agreed, and most of them added to it a personal experience with the man during the last two years in which they were more or less injured. From all accounts he is five feet four or five inches in height and wears a dark, close-fitting cap. He is thickset, and has an unusually thick neck. His hair is black, and closely clipped, his age being about 38 or 40. He has a small, black moustache. The distinguishing feature of his costume is a leather apron, which he always wears, and from which

### HE GETS HIS NICKNAME.

His expression is sinister, and seems to be full of terror for the women who describe it. His eyes are small and glittering. His lips are usually parted in a grin which is not only not reassuring, but excessively repellent. He is a slipper maker by trade, but does not work. His business is blackmailing women late at night. A number of men in Whitechapel follow this interesting profession. He has never cut anybody so far as known, but always carries a leather knife, presumably as sharp as leather knives are wont to be. This knife a number of the women have seen. His name nobody knows, but all are united in the belief that he is a Jew or of Jewish parentage, his face being of a marked Hebrew type. But the most singular characteristic of the man, and one which tends to identify him closely with last Friday night's work, is the universal statement that in moving about

## HE NEVER MAKES ANY NOISE.

What he wears on his feet the women do not know, but they all agree that he moves noiselessly. His uncanny peculiarity to them is that they never see him or know of his presence until he is close by them. When two of the Philpott-street women directed the *Star* reporter to Commercial-street, opposite the Princess Alice Tavern, as the most likely place to find him, she added that it would be necessary to look into all the shadows, as if he was there he would surely be out of sight. This locality, it may be remarked, is but a few steps from the model dwellinghouse in George's-Yard, where the murdered woman of four weeks ago was found.

The noiselessness of 'Leather Apron's' movements recalls the statement of Mrs. Colwell, of Brady-street. She said that about the time the murder was said to have been committed she heard a woman running up the street shrieking "Murder; Police." "She was running away from somebody," said Mrs. Colwell, "who, from the way she screamed, was hurting her as she ran. And it struck me as very strange that I did

## NOT HEAR THE SOUND OF ANY FOOTSTEPS

whatever except hers. This took place where the bloodstains were found, and where the woman evidently received her death cuts. Taken together with the absolutely noiseless way in which she was carried up Brady-street; so noiselessly that three people wide awake and only a few feet distant heard no sound, this looks as though "Leather-Apron" was worth interviewing, to say the least.

"Leather-Apron" never by any chance attacks a man. He runs away on the slightest appearance of rescue. One woman whom he assailed some time ago boldly prosecuted him

for it, and he was sent up for seven days. He has no settled place of residence, but has slept oftenest in a fourpenny lodging-house of the lowest kind in a disreputable lane leading from Brick-lane. The people at this lodging-house denied that he had been there, and appeared disposed to shield him.

## "LEATHER-APRON'S" PAL, "MICKELDY JOE,"

was in the house at the time, and his presence doubtless had something to do with the unwillingness to give information. "Leather-Apron" was last at this house some weeks ago, though this account may be untrue. He ranges all over London, and rarely assails the same woman twice. He has lately been seen in Leather-lane, which is in the Holborn district. There is no question, considering his general character and the certainty that the murders were done by some unsettled character of this kind but that he should be taken into custody and investigated.

There is one point in connection with the murder which has not yet been brought out. This is the certainty that the abdominal mutilation was done not only after death, but after the woman was laid down at the gateway in Buck's-row. She was so horribly cut that anybody who viewed the body will admit that she could not have stood erect with her clothes on, and remained as she was when found. Furthermore,

## THE TWO LARGE DROPS OF BLOOD,

clear and undeniable, which were visible on the Buck's-row pavement, 25 and 35 feet above the place where the body lay, were made by fresh thick blood, and were probably caused by something in the hands of the murderer as he walked away. Added to this is the slight abdominal haemorrhage, such as would be the case if the cutting were done after death.

~

## The Star

### WHAT WE THINK.

DURING the Reign of Terror, death became so familiar to the Parisians that the inmates of the prisons amused themselves with farcical rehearsals of the scenes on the scaffold. They played at guillotining much as Mr. Mould's infants played at "berryin's."[21] We shall soon be in much the same condition in this country. The Whitechapel murders, though quite as horrible as the celebrated Ratcliff Highway murders which drove St. George's-in-the-East almost wild with excitement and terror, have positively fallen flat. We are becoming blasé, like Macbeth: "Direness, familiar to our slaughterous thoughts, cannot once fright us."[22] Men can no longer attract notice by mere murder and suicide. They despatch their wives with rifles, and make the slumbers of their children eternal with a saw, only to be arrested by one bored policeman and put off with four lines in the newspapers headed simply "Another Murder." A lady has cut a child's feet off, and a gentleman has gouged out his eyes; but we do not seem to mind. It is not midsummer madness; for there has been no summer. It is not the ugliness of London; for London was just as ugly last year. It is not "Dr. Jekyll and Mr. Hyde"; for America has not caught the infection, though it has read the novel. Whatever it is, it is not one of the successes of nineteenth century civilisation. Perhaps the British Association will devote a sitting to a discussion of the causes of the growth of despair in England.

—

### "LEATHER-APRON."
### More About His Career—His Latest Movements—In the Borough.

The sense of fear which the murder of the unfortunate woman Nicholls has thrown over the neighbourhood, and especially over her companions, shows no sign of decreasing. A number of the street wanderers are in nightly terror of "Leather-Apron."

One of our reporters visited one of the single women's lodging-houses last night. It is in Thrawl-street, one of the darkest and most terrible-looking spots in Whitechapel. The house keeps open till one o'clock in the morning, and reopens again at five. In the house nightly are 66 women, who get their bed for 4d. The proprietor of the place, who is also owner of several other houses of a similar character in the neighbourhood, told some gruesome stories of the man who has now come to be regarded as the terror of the East-end. Night after night, he said, had women come in in a fainting condition after being knocked about by "Leather-Apron." He himself would never be out in the neighbourhood after twelve o'clock at night except with a loaded revolver. The "terror," he said, would go to a public-house or coffee-room, and peep in through the window to see if a particular woman was there. He would then vanish, lying in wait for his victim at some convenient corner, hidden from the view of everybody.

The police are making efforts to arrest him, but he constantly changes his quarters. Some of the unfortunate women state that he is now in one of the low slums in the Borough. One of them said she saw him crossing London-bridge as stealthily as usual, with head bent, his skimpy coat turned up about his ears, and looking as if he were in a desperate hurry.

The hunt for "Leather Apron" began in earnest last evening. Constables 43 and 173, J Division, into whose hands "Leather-Apron" fell on Sunday afternoon, were detailed to accompany Detective Enright, of the J Division, in a search through all the quarters where the crazy Jew was likely to be. They began at half-past ten in Church-street, in Shoreditch, rumour having located the suspected man there. They went through lodging-houses, into "pubs," down side streets, threw their bull's-eyes into every shadow, and searched the quarter thoroughly, but without result.

### THE HUNT CONTINUED

later down in the Brick-lane neighbourhood, Flower and Dean-lane being "Leather Apron's" preferred lodging place lately. He was not found here, however, and the search, which then took the direction of the London Hospital, resulted in nothing. It is the general belief that the man has left the district.

---

[21] **Mr. Mould the undertaker**, and these "infants" that played in his funeral parlour, are characters from the Charles Dickens novel <u>Martin Chuzzlewit</u>.

[22] **MacBeth**, Act V, Scene 5, "Direness, familiar to our slaughterous thoughts, cannot once start me."

# Thursday, 6 September, 1888

The clue furnished by the woman who denounced the man on Sunday is a very unfortunate one. Her offer to prove by two women that "Leather Apron" was seen walking with the murdered woman in Baker's-row at two o'clock last Friday morning, is the most direct bit of evidence that yet has appeared. The belief in "Leather Apron's" guilt, whether it be well or ill founded, is general, and the instant he is recognised by any one he is sure to be reported and arrested.

His conduct on Sunday was as usual. He never answers a question when it is put to him, and only speaks under strong compulsion. Mike — , the grocer in George's-yard, dwelt a long time last evening on this peculiarity. He knows "Leather Apron" very well, and has known him for six years. He says that **THE MAN IS UNQUESTIONABLY MAD,** and that anybody who met him face to face would know it. That his eyes are never still, but are always shifting uneasily, and he never looks anybody in the eye. "Leather Apron" used to live in the lodging-house around the corner from the grocery, and was turned out of there some months ago with an order not to return. The lodging-house is a few doors below the "model" doorway in which the Turner woman was found with 39 stabs.

Great activity prevails among the police all through Whitechapel. All are sharply on the look-out for "Leather Apron," though many of them, strangely enough, do not know him by sight, and have only his description to go by.

Meanwhile other clues are not neglected. Inspector Hellson has the case in his charge, and is aided by the full division force, by Detective Abberlene, and others from Scotland-yard who are familiar with East-end work. Quite a number of men are necessary, for several parties are under constant supervision. "Leather Apron" is not the only possibility, but he is the only one suspected whom the police cannot lay their hands on at a moment's notice.

—

## THE FUNERAL.

The funeral arrangements were carried out with secrecy. The police knew nothing whatever of the burial; while the old man at the mortuary must have been guilty of at least a score of fibs in order to prevent the annoying inquiries of the morbid crowd. "Has the body been taken away yet?" asked one of our reporters yesterday. "Didn't I tell you it was taken away three nights ago," was the gruff reply. As a matter of fact the body lay all the time at the mortuary. On Saturday it was removed from the dead-house shell into a neat plain coffin supplied by Mr. Smith, of Hanbury-street, and paid for by the friends of the deceased. The father, the husband, and the unfortunate woman's son all came to see that she got a decent burial.

~

## Evening News
### THE WHITECHAPEL MURDER.
### LATEST PARTICULARS.

It is stated by some of the jury who inquired into the death of the mutilated woman found in Buck's-row that they intend to impress upon the Scotland Yard authorities the necessity of further precautions being taken at the common lodging-houses in the metropolis for the purpose of ascertaining the names, and, if possible, the previous address of every lodger, male and female, who enters these houses, together with the time of entry.

This course they hold to be quite necessary, as it appears that all the worst characters in London can dodge from house to house practically unknown, and any inquiries as to their whereabouts at a given time be absolutely nugatory.

At a recent inquest on the body of a man found dead in the Thames, with marks of violence upon him Mr. Barnes, the Westminster coroner, expressed the same opinion as the jurymen in the Whitechapel murder case; and the late Sir John Humphreys held very strong views on the same point.

### STARTLING SUGGESTIONS.

There cannot be the shadow of a doubt that, had it not been for the band of the petticoat of the deceased woman bearing the Lambeth Workhouse marks no identification of the body would have been forthcoming, and thus the chief link in a possible chain of evidence would have been missing. This want of identity was painfully apparent in the horrible murder of the woman in Whitechapel some months ago, when precisely similar injuries were inflicted as in the present case. Dr. Haslip

# Thursday, 6 September, 1888

stated to our reporter that most fiendish brutality had been used in that case, and there seems to be very little question that both the murders were committed by the same person. In the Rainham murder last year, where a woman had been murdered and dismembered, and the different parts of the body thrown in the river and the canal, there were precisely similar injuries to the abdominal walls as in the foregoing cases, and just the same evidences of a familiarity with the vital parts of the body, and skill in the use of the weapon used, and this fact, taken in connection with other murders all over London, leads the police to think it highly probable that all these cases are the work of one hand practised in murder in its most horrible form.

## A DISGRACE TO OUR
## POLICE ORGANISATION.

Dr. Hammerton, the divisional surgeon of the Bow-street Police, stated last night to our correspondent that he considered the recent murders and their non-solution a perfect disgrace to our boasted police organisation, and there appears to be little room for doubt that the detective system in regard to murder is not at all a good one, looking at the great number of murders, mostly of women, that are continually occurring and never detected.

—

## THE EDITOR'S DRAWER.
## THE WHITECHAPEL MURDER.
## TO THE EDITOR OF
## "THE EVENING NEWS."

SIR—Permit me, as an inhabitant of twenty years in Whitechapel, to express on behalf of a number of tradesmen and shopkeepers in Whitechapel our deepest regret and indignation at the shocking and revolting murders which have further disgraced the unfortunate district of Whitechapel of late. The question that now arises is what is to be done, and what can be done to check and prevent the further spreading of such dastardly crimes. In the first place I would suggest that the police force should be strengthened in the East End, and secondly that there should be more gas lights in our back streets, courts, and alleys. There is no doubt but that these unfortunate women were butchered by their bullies[23] (men who gain their livelihood from these unfortunates) and were the police to watch the haunts and dens of these villains and thieves, no doubt in a short time we should have a decrease of these crimes which have disgraced the capital of England. There are several supposed clubs in Whitechapel which these villains frequent, which are open all night for the sale of wines, spirits, and beer, and where any non-member can be admitted and served with as much drink as he or she can pay for. It is in these vile dens that the seed of immorality and crime is sown which brings forth the fruits we have just witnessed. The police must know of these places; if not, I am prepared, if required, to give the names of these places to any person in authority. The East End police are, with a few exceptions, a good and noble body of men who at all times have a hard and difficult duty to perform, and I feel sure that the heads of these police, such gentlemen as Arnold, Final, and West will do their uttermost to stop the breeding of further crimes by these ruffians. In the second place I suggest more gas lights in our bye-streets, courts, and alleys. We pay rates and taxes, and have a right to have our district properly lighted. Only a little while back a City manufacturer living opposite me was knocked down, beaten, and robbed of a valuable gold chain within a few yards of his own street door, the villains escaping because the spot is dark. My sister also a short time ago was knocked down by some cowards. They also got away, the place being dark. Now, Sir, I hope and trust that the Whitechapel Board of Works and the Commercial Gas Company will awake to their duty, and do their best to have this grievance removed. Apologising for trespassing upon your valuable space, I am, &c.,

ALBERT BACHERT.
Gordon House,
Newnham-street, Whitechapel,
September 5.

---

[23] **Bully**. 4. A weapon formed by tying a stone or a piece of lead in a handkerchief: used knuckleduster fashion. 5. A bravo, hector, swashbuckler; now spec, a tyrannical coward.
**Bully-boss**. The landlord of a brothel or thieves' den. (Farmer)

# Friday, 7 September, 1888

## The Star

### THE PEOPLE'S POST BOX.
### Crime in Whitechapel.

SIR,—As a resident in the neighbour-hood of Whitechapel for the last 25 years, I wish to express my opinion as regards the terrible crimes of late at the East-end. I have had it brought under my notice several times. No later than a month back a female friend of mine was attacked by ruffians outside her own residence, a burglary taking place the same night a few doors off. A week later an elderly male friend was knocked down, assaulted, and robbed at the corner of the same street. In neither case has any clue yet been found. Last week myself and a colonial friend were passing through Commercial-street when we were assailed by a gang of six ruffians, but succeeded in getting away without injury. The robberies with violence are so frequent in the district in broad daylight, as well as night time, that it makes you ask the question, "Where are our police?"

Yours, &c.,
A WORKING MAN.

3 Sept.

~

## Evening News

### FIFTH EDITION.
### THE WHITECHAPEL MURDER.
### WATCHING BUCK'S ROW.

This morning, at one o'clock, two reporters commenced a watch in Buck's-row, which terminated at eleven o'clock, and from what they then observed, coupled with the evidence already given, they came to the conclusion that the police are altogether wrong in their assumption that the murder was committed on the spot where the body was found. This seems to be absolutely impossible, for the following reasons.

In the first place, Buck's-row is a decently wide thoroughfare, running at right angles from Baker's-row to Brady-street. Buck's-row is in every sense thoroughly respectable, every tenant being an old inhabitant, and of good class. In addition to well-to-do artisans, the row contains a mission hall, the factor of Messrs. Schneider and Sons, and the factories and warehouses of Messrs. Torr, and Browne and Eagle, together with the private residence of the Rev. Henry North Hall, the curate of St. Mary, Whitechapel. There are watchmen at night at these factories, and many of the private residents were awake at the time the deceased was murdered, but none heard any cries for help on Friday morning.

It has been stated that the street is a dark one, but this is altogether wrong, for it is well lighted at all hours of the night by the great lamps outside the brewery of Messrs. Mann and Crossman, in addition to the ordinary street lamps, and it seems inconceivable that such a well-lighted street would be selected for the crime.

#### WINTHROP STREET.

Winthrop-street, on the other hand, is very narrow and very dark, and tenanted by many of the worst characters in London, and there seems to be no doubt whatever that the murder was committed there, and the body brought round the corner and left a few yards up Buck's-row. The extensive nature of the injuries and the absence of blood in Buck's-row, as proved by the police, also goes to show that the murder was not committed there, and if this be so there was probably a second party

43

cognisant of the murder, if not a participator in it. It may be stated that a thorough search of the houses in Winthrop-street, has not been made by the police yet, and there is good reason to believe that had this been done at the outset a clue to the murder and the actual spot where it took place would have been discovered.

## POLICE BEATS.

The police system of particular beats and regular time for certain constables to be upon those beats is thoroughly well-known by the criminal classes, and the medical evidence gives colour to the theory that Constable Neil was watched, and the moment he had passed through Buck's-row the body was carried there and left where he found it half an hour afterwards on his return along that beat; and as the body was not cold the murder was committed perhaps three-quarters of an hour before the discovery of the victim.

The whole of the inhabitants of Buck's-row are of one opinion, viz., that the murder was not done there, and as many of them know the locality well, having lived there for 20 or 30 years (the youngest inhabitant three years), some respect might, it is thought, be shown to their knowledge.

## SOME SUGGESTIONS FOR SIR CHARLES WARREN.

The inhabitants of Buck's-row are about to suggest to Sir Charles Warren that had the police been smarter in their action the murderer might have been traced at once, and the terrible scandal of three undiscovered murders in Whitechapel within a few months avoided. It will also be urged upon him the necessity of augmenting the police force, for it appears that the whole neighbourhood of the London Hospital is infested by bands of thieves who daily commit robberies in broad daylight with impunity, the courts and alleys in the locality giving them ready means of escape.

# Saturday, 8 September, 1888

## The Star

### HORROR UPON HORROR.
### WHITECHAPEL IS PANIC-STRICKEN AT ANOTHER FIENDISH CRIME.
### A FOURTH VICTIM OF THE MANIAC.

**A Woman is Found Murdered Under Circumstances Exceeding in Brutality the Three Other Whitechapel Crimes.**

London lies to-day under the spell of a great terror. A nameless reprobate—half beast, half man—is at large, who is daily gratifying his murderous instincts on the most miserable and defenceless classes of the community. There can be no shadow of a doubt now that our original theory was correct, and that the White-chapel murderer, who has now four, if not five, victims to his knife, is one man, and that man a murderous maniac. There is another Williams[24] in our midst. Hideous malice, deadly cunning, insatiable thirst for blood—all these are the marks of the mad homicide. The ghoul-like creature who stalks through the streets of London, stalking down his victim like a Pawnee Indian, is simply drunk with blood, and he will have more. The question is, what are the people of London to do? Whitechapel is garrisoned with police and stocked with plain-clothes men. Nothing comes of it. The police have not even a clue. They are in despair at their utter failure to get so much as a scent of the criminal.

Now we have a moral to draw and a proposal to make. We have carefully investi-gated the causes of the miserable and calamitous breakdown of the police system. They are chiefly two: (1) the inefficiency and timidity of the detective service, owing to the manner in which Sir Charles has placed it in leading strings and forbidden it to move except under instructions; (2) the inadequate local knowledge of the police.

Our reporters have discovered that the Whitechapel force knows little of the criminal haunts of the neighbourhood. Now, this is a state of things which obtains in no other great

city in the world but London, and is entirely due to our centralised system. In New York the local police know almost every brick in every den in the district, and every felon or would-be felon who skulks behind it. In Whitechapel many of the men are new to their work, and others who have two or three years' local experience have not been trained to the special work of vigilant and ceaseless inspection of criminal quarters.

Now there is only one thing to be done at this moment, and we can talk of larger reforms when we do away with the centralised non-efficient military system which Sir Charles Warren has brought to perfection. The people of the East-end must become their own police. They must form themselves at once into Vigilance Committees. There should be a central committee, which should map out the neighbourhood into districts, and appoint the smaller committees. These again should at once devote themselves to volunteer patrol work at night, as well as to general detective service. The unfortunates who are the objects of the man-monster's malignity should be shadowed by one or two of the amateur patrols. They should be cautioned to walk in couples. Whistles and a signalling system should be provided, and means of summoning a rescue force should be at hand. We are not sure that every London district should not make some effort of the kind, for the murderer may choose a fresh quarter now that Whitechapel is being made too hot to hold him.

We do not think that the police will put any obstacle in the way of this volunteer assistance. They will probably be only too glad to have their efforts supplemented by the spontaneous action of the inhabitants. But in any case, London must rouse itself. No woman is safe while this ghoul is abroad. Up, citizens, then, and do your own police work!

### "Horror on horrors head accumulates" in Whitechapel.

This morning the district was thrown into a panic by a fourth murder committed in an exactly similar manner to the three mysterious and unpunished crimes which have preceded it. The scene of this latest horror is Hanbury-street, hardly a stone's throw from Osborne-street and Buck's-row, where the two other victims were butchered. Indeed, through Hanbury-street on Thursday Mary Ann Nicholls' terribly-mutilated

---

[24] **John Williams**, suspected to be the Ratcliff High-way murderer, was accused of killing seven people in two separate attacks in December, 1811. Committed suicide, or was suicided, in his cell before he could be brought to trial.

body was carried on the way to its place of burial. The fourth victim to what must be a madman's insatiable thirst for blood, is, like the other three, a poor defenceless walker of the streets. A companion identified her soon after she had been taken to the mortuary as "Dark Annie," and as she came from the mortuary gate bitterly crying said between her tears, "I knowed her; I kissed her poor cold face."

**29, HANBURY STREET**

The scene of the murder is the house 29, Hanbury-street—a packing-case maker's. The body was actually found in the back yard, just behind the back door, mutilated in an even more ghastly manner than the woman Nicholls. As in her case, the throat was cut, and the body ripped open, but the horror was intensified by the fact that

### THE HEART AND LIVER WERE OVER HER HEAD.

It seems that the crime was committed soon after five. At that hour the woman and the man, who in all probability was her murderer, were seen drinking together in the Bells, Brick-lane. But though the murder was committed at this late hour, the murderer—acting, as in the other cases, silently and stealthily—managed to make his escape.

The horror and alarm this fourth crime—following so quickly on the others—has excited in the neighbourhood is inexpressible. Women and men, too, with frightened whitened faces,

are congregated at all corners of the streets, so panic-stricken that they hardly dare to speak above a whisper.

The first discovery of the body was made by John Davis, living on the top floor of 29, Hanbury-street, in the yard of which the body was found. Mr. Davis was crossing the yard at a quarter to six when he saw a horrible-looking mass lying in the corner, partly concealed by the steps. He instantly made for the station and notified the police without touching the body.

Meantime Mrs. Richardson, an old lady sleeping on the first floor front, was aroused by her grandson Charles Cooksley, who looked out of one of the back windows and screamed that there was a dead body in the corner.

### MRS. RICHARDSON'S DESCRIPTION OF THE SIGHT

makes this murder even more horrible than any of its predecessors. She was lying on her back with her legs outstretched. Her throat was cut from ear to ear. Her clothes were pushed up above her waist and her legs bare. The abdomen was exposed, the woman having been ripped up from groin to breast-bone as before. Not only this, but the viscera had been pulled out and scattered in all directions, the heart and liver being placed behind her head, and the remainder along her side. No more horrible sight ever met a human eye, for she was covered with blood, and lying in a pool of it, which hours afterwards had not soaked into the ground.

The yard is a small one, square in shape, with a 4ft. fence on either side. The fence is old and rotten. There is a woodshed at the back. The yard is roughly and irregularly paved with stones of all sizes and shapes rammed into the ground. The back door of the house which leads into the yard is a plain board frame, with no lock on it. Two stone steps are just outside, and in the narrow space between these steps and the fence the body lay. It was evident at a glance that the murder had been

### DONE WHERE THE BODY LAY.

The enormous quantity of blood and the splash on the fence, coupled with the total absence of stains elsewhere, made this clear. It was also clear that the man had decoyed the poor woman into the yard, and murdered her as she lay where she was found. The passage through the house by which the yard was reached is 25ft. long and 3ft. wide. Its floor is bare, and nobody can pass along it without making some noise. The murderer and his victim failed to awaken anybody, however, though people were sleeping only a few feet away. Both front and back door are open all night, and there was no difficulty in reaching the yard. There was a story that a bloody knife had been found in the yard, but this was not true. The only unusual thing about the yard excepting the dead woman was the fact that

**THE RUSTY PADLOCK ON THE DOOR**

of the shed had been broken.

Not a sound seems to have been made by the woman when attacked. Mrs. Bell, an old lady who lives next door, sleeps by an open window, not 20ft. from the spot, and is certain that no noise was made as she sleeps very lightly. The probability is that the woman by five o'clock was stupidly drunk, as she was well on when Donovan, the deputy, last saw her. In this state she could have been easily kept silent until she was unable from loss of blood to speak.

The people, and even the police, were so excited that all sorts of rumours were flying about. The woman living next door declared that this morning there was written on the door of No. 29, "This is the fourth, I will murder sixteen more and then give myself up." There was no basis for this story, however, there being no chalk mark on the door except "29."

As soon as the murder was known there came a rush of people from the market and the houses, and in charge of an inspector the body was removed to the mortuary.

The murder is certainly the fourth of a series by the same fiendish hand. The blood-crazy man or beast that haunts Whitechapel has done his latest work on the same line as its predecessors. Mystery of the deepest kind envelopes it. At a quarter to five the body was not in the yard, Mrs. Richardson's son John, a man of 33, having passed through the yard at that time to see if the cellar door was safe.

**BETWEEN THAT TIME AND A
QUARTER TO SIX**

the woman was murdered in open daylight. She was murdered where she was found, because she could not have been carried into the yard except by the passage-way from the street which is open all night, but the street at that time was filled with market people. There is no blood except in the yard corner, and a huge splash on the fence, like the spurt from an artery.

Chief Inspector West and Inspector Chandler courteously gave a *Star* reporter the meagre particulars of which the police are in possession. The woman's name, as far as they can gather, is Annie Siffey, and her age is about 45. She is five feet high, has fair brown wavy hair, blue eyes, and strangely enough, like Mary Ann Nicholls, has two teeth missing. One peculiarity of her features by which the police hope to get a more positive and complete identity, is a large flat kind of nose. Her clothing, like that of most of her class who ply their trade in this quarter of London, was old and dirty, and nothing was found in her pockets except part of an envelope bearing

**THE SEAL OF THE SUSSEX REGIMENT.**

For the last nine months she has been sleeping at night, or early in the morning rather, at a common lodging-house at 35, Dorset-street, Spitalfields, and she was there as recently as two o'clock this morning eating some potatoes. She had not, however, the money to pay for her bed, and at two o'clock she left with the remark to the keeper of the place, "I'll soon be back again; I'll soon get the money for my doss," almost the very words Mary Ann Nicholls used to the companion she met in Whitechapel-road, at half-past two last Friday morning.

Our representative went to the Bell, in Brick-lane, where, as gossip goes, "Dark Annie" was seen with the man supposed to be her murderer. The barmaid said she opened the place at five o'clock, as is customary on a Saturday morning, as Spitalfields Market is in the near vicinity. She was too busy almost to notice whom she served. She might have served the woman; indeed she had been told by those who knew her that she had, but she had no recollection of it, and certainly could not say whether the unfortunate creature was accompanied by a man.

Another report says:—The victim in this case was discovered about a quarter to four o'clock this morning lying in a backyard at the foot of a passage leading into the lodging-house, 29, Hanbury-street, formerly Old Brown's-lane, Spitalfields. The house is occupied by a Mrs. Emilia Richardson, who lets it out to various lodgers, and it seems that the door which admits into this passage, at the foot of which lies the

# Saturday, 8 September, 1888

yard where the body was found, is always open for the convenience of the lodgers. A Mr. and Mrs. Davis occupy the upper story (the house consisting of three stories) and as Mr. Davis was going down to work at the time mentioned he found a woman lying on her back close up to the flight of steps leading into the yard. Her throat was cut open in a fearful manner, so deep, in fact, that the murderer, evidently

## THINKING THAT HE HAD SEVERED THE HEAD

from the body, tied a handkerchief round it so as to keep it on. It was also found that her stomach had been completely ripped open, and her bowels, heart, and other entrails were lying at her side. The fiendish work was completed by the murderer tying part of the entrails round the poor victim's neck and head. The place on which she was lying was found covered with clots of thick blood. Davis, the lodger, who found the body, immediately communicated with the police at Commercial-street Station, and Inspector Chandler and several constables arrived on the scene in a short time, when they found the woman in the condition described.

## THE SCENE OF THE FOUR CRIMES.

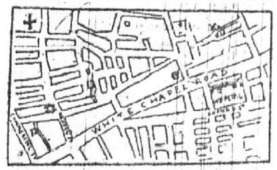

The above sketch shows the localities of the four murders. No. 1 shown in the bottom left hand corner indicates the spot where a woman unidentified was found murdered by having a stick or iron instrument thrust into her body. The crime passed off very quietly. It was put down as a drunken freath[25] of some of the nameless ruffians who swarm about Whitechapel.

No. 2 was the crime of Osborne-street. The scene was laid near the first murder, and a woman was found stabbed in 36 places, lying outside George's-buildings. The impression made by this affair soon died away. The crime was a horrible one, but not a witness was called

---
[25] **Freath**, Scots. Froth. (Jamieson)

at the inquest who could throw any light on the matter. The excitement died from sheer lack of fact to support any theory.

No. 3, the Buck's-row Murder, the scene of which is indicated by a cross in the top right-hand corner, is still too fresh in its horrid details in the public mind to need recapitulation. It has been closely followed by

No. 4, shown by the cross at the top left-hand corner is the crime which has shocked all London to-day.

—

### SPECIAL EDITION.
### WHITECHAPEL.
### (continued from Page 2.)
### FACTS ABOUT THE VICTIM.

The woman's name is Annie Chapman, alias Sieve. She comes from Windsor, and has friends residing at Vauxhall. Her home was a lodging-house at 35, Dorset-street, in White-chapel. Her husband was a pensioner, who allowed her 10s. per week, but he died a twelve-month ago, and, the pension ceasing, she has since earned her living in the streets. She lived for a time with a man named Sieve. She was identified at the mortuary at half-past seven this morning by Frederick Simmons, a young man living in the same house with her. She lay on an operating table exactly as she had been brought in, the hands of one of the constables being dyed with blood. Simmons identified her without difficulty, first by her handkerchief and then by her face, and said that

### SHE HAD THREE RINGS ON

when she left the house, one a wedding ring and the other two chased. These had disappeared, having evidently been mistaken for gold and stolen by the assassin.

Frederick Stevens, another young man living at 35, Dorset-street, states that deceased did not leave the house until one o'clock. He had drunk a pint of beer with her at half-past twelve. She was not very well, having been in the casual ward of the Whitechapel Infirmary from Wednesday night till Friday morning. Her injuries were due to a quarrel last Monday with another woman, who kicked her in the breast, making a painful wound. As she lay in the dead-house, where Simmons identified her, she was a stout woman of fair complexion. Her age is forty-eight. She wore a white handkerchief

48

# Saturday, 8 September, 1888

bordered with red, a black jacket, an old black hat, and old laced-up boots.

## A CLUE TO THE MURDERER.

The only clue of any value thus far is furnished by Mrs. Fiddymont, wife of the proprietor of the Prince Albert publichouse, better known as the "Clean House," at the corner of Brushfield and Stewart streets, half a mile from the scene of the murder. Mrs. Fiddymont states that at seven o'clock this morning she was standing in the bar talking with another woman, a friend, in the first compartment. Suddenly there came into the middle compartment a man whose rough appearance frightened her. He had on a brown stiff hat, a dark coat and no waistcoat. He came in with his hat down over his eyes, and with his face partly concealed, asked for half a pint of four ale. She drew the ale, and meanwhile looked at him through the mirror at the back of the bar. As soon as he saw the woman in the other compartment watching him he turned his back, and got the partition between himself and her. The thing that struck Mrs. Fiddymont particularly was the fact that there were

## BLOOD SPOTS ON THE BACK OF HIS RIGHT HAND.

This, taken in conjunction with his appearance, caused her uneasiness. She also noticed that his shirt was torn. As soon as he had drunk the ale, which he swallowed at a gulp, he went out. Her friend went out also to watch him.

Her friend is Mrs. Mary Chappell, who lives at 28, Stewart-street, near by.

## HER STORY CORROBORATES MRS. FIDDYMONT'S

and is more particular. When the man came in the expression of his eyes caught her attention, his look was so startling and terrifying. It frightened Mrs. Fiddymont so that she requested her to stay. He wore a light blue check shirt, which was torn badly, into rags in fact, on the right shoulder. There was a narrow streak of blood under his right ear, parallel with the edge of his shirt. There was also dried blood between the fingers of his hand. When he went out she slipped out the other door, and watched him as he went towards Bishopsgate-street. She called

Joseph Taylor's attention to him, and Joseph Taylor followed him.

Joseph Taylor is a builder at 22, Stewart-street. He states that as soon as his attention was attracted to the man

## HE FOLLOWED HIM.

He walked rapidly, and came alongside him, but did not speak to him. The man was rather thin, about 5ft. 8in. high, and apparently between 40 and 50 years of age. He had a shabby genteel look, pepper and salt trousers which fitted badly, and dark coat. When Taylor came alongside him the man glanced at him, and Taylor's description of the look was, "His eyes were as wild as a hawk's." Taylor is a perfectly reliable man, well-known throughout the neighbourhood.

The man walked, he says, holding his coat together at the top. He had a nervous and frightened way about him. He wore a ginger-coloured moustache and had short sandy hair. Taylor ceased to follow him, but watched him as far as "Dirty Dick's," in Halfmoon-street, where he became lost to view. Taylor says he has seen this man coming out of a lodging-house in Thrall-street. He thinks that he is a foreigner.

## AT THE TEN BELLS.

The proprietor of the Ten Bells is Mr. E. Waldron. The house stands on the corner of Spitalfields Market, and opens early for the convenience of those who bring their goods from the country. One of the assistants gave some information to our reporter with reference to the rumour that the murdered woman was seen there this morning. He said: A woman did call in here about five o'clock. She was poorly dressed, having no bodice to her skirt. She was middle-aged. She just had something to drink, when a man called for her. He just popped his head in the door and retired immediately afterwards. He had on a little skull cap, and was, as far as I could see, without a coat. But he gave me no opportunity of seeing him. I think, however, I should know his face again, and I think I would also know the woman. The description of the woman corresponds to a certain extent, especially with regard to age, hair, and clothing, with that of the victim of to-day.

49

# Saturday, 8 September, 1888

## AT THE LODGING HOUSE.

Timothy Donovan, deputy at the lodging-house, 35, Dorset-street, interviewed by a *Star* reporter, said the woman came to the place at between half-past one and a quarter to two this morning the worse for drink—in fact, she was "very drunk." She went downstairs to the common kitchen, and when the deputy went down and asked for the money for her bed, she said she had not sufficient. She came upstairs and said, "Jim, I've been in the infirmary. I'm going out. I sha'n't be long." John Edwards, the watchman, went out after her and saw her go in the direction of Brush-field.

Before she went to the lodging-house last night she had not been seen there since the Sunday before.

Last Saturday afternoon she came to the lodging-house with a man about 5ft. 6in., with a dark moustache and short beard, and dressed in the clothes of a labouring man. "He was not 'Leather Apron,' the deputy said."Do you know him?" asked the *Star* man. "Yes, I ought to," was the answer; "I chucked him down the stairs; he tried to murder a woman here."

Coming back to the new horror, Donovan said the man who came to the place with the woman Sivvey on Saturday had come with her to the lodging-house every Saturday for the last six weeks. He used to stop with her at the lodging-house till Monday morning. The woman had spoken about him, and said he was a pensioner.

The other women in the lodging-house say that from what she had said at different times Dark Annie was well connected. She used to do crochet work, and, from her conversation it was evident she was a woman of some education. Her husband seems to have been a soldier; but is now dead, and until lately the woman was in receipt of 10s. a week, which the other women supposed was a pension. But lately this allowance has been stopped, and since then she has been more frequently in want of money.

## RUMOUR OF ANOTHER MURDER.

The air of Whitechapel is thick with murders and rumours of murder. One rumour, which was very general, and which in the prevailing terror found ready acceptance, was that another woman had this morning been found murdered at the back of the London Hospital, but happily it proved to be unfounded.

It being almost positively certain that the murderer of Dark Annie is the murderer of Mary Ann Nicholls, a *Star* reporter went to the Bethnal-green police-station to inquire whether the new murder threw any light on the other. Inspector Helston was "very busy," but Sergeant Godley showed himself. All the information that could be got, however, was that the scene of the new crime "is just out of our district." Our representative suggested that, as a matter of course, the two cases would be investigated together, but the Inspector didn't seem at all sure about this.

## A FELLOW LODGER OF THE VICTIM'S.

Frederick Simpson, who lived at the lodging-house, 35, Dorset-street, says he has known the woman well for two years. She parted from her husband (who died a year since) about two years and a half ago, and since that time has got a living by walking the streets. In conversation with Simpson she had mentioned the fact that she had a son—little boy—in a school at Windsor, and a daughter 14 years old travelling with some performing troupe in France. She has relatives at Vauxhall, where she went last night, "to get some money," as she told the other lodgers at "Dorset-chambers." "They gave me 5d.," she said.

## FALSE REPORTS OF ARRESTS.

The excitement in Spitalfields is now rendering the people almost frantic. Two men were arrested for trifling offences this morning, and on each occasion a maddened crowd ran after the police shouting, "The murderer's caught!" Another man, injured in a quarrel and carried to the police-station on a stretcher, received similar attention, the crowd fairly mobbing the station and declining to disperse.

A man for whom there has been a warrant out for some time was arrested. In an instant the news spread like wild-fire. From every street, from every court, from the market stands, from the public-houses, rushed forth men and women, all trying to get at the unfortunate captive, declaring he was "one of the gang," and they meant to lynch him. Thousands gathered, and the police and a private detective had all their work to prevent the man being torn to pieces. The police barrack doors were closed the moment their prisoner had been brought in, and a number

# Saturday, 8 September, 1888

of constables did duty outside to prevent the mad onrush of the furious crowd. The inspector in charge informed our reporter the man was arrested for an assault on the police. The crowd sighed at hearing the news, but were not persuaded that the person in question had not something to do with the murder.

### TWO MEN DETAINED.

At half-past twelve there was a rumour that an arrest had been made, and that the prisoner had been taken to the Bethnal-green police-station. A *Star* reporter drove at once to the police-office, and a large and excited crowd lent confirmation to the report. The inspector on duty, however, stated in answer to inquiries that two men had been brought there "merely for their own protection." A "hue and cry," he said, had been raised in Whitechapel-road, and the mob which quickly gathered threatened to lynch the men, who to escape violence got on a tram. For their protection, however, it had been necessary to bring them to the police-station.

"Is there any suspicion against the men?" our reporter asked.

The answer was a negative shake of the head.

"Can I see the men?" asked our representative.

"Oh, dear, no!" answered the inspector.

"But then," our reporter expostulated, "if the men are merely brought here for their own protection, they are not prisoners, and if they are not prisoners surely I can see them."

"You can't see them," was the inspector's emphatic answer.

"Well, are they prisoners?" persisted the *Star* man.

"I have told you, sir, all I can tell you," was the curt reply, which left our reporter to draw his own conclusion.

### THE LEATHER APRON AND KNIFE.

John Richardson, of 2, John-street, E.C., said to a *Star* reporter:—I am a porter in Spitalfields Market. I always go round to mother's (Mrs. Richardson, 29, Hanbury-street) on market mornings just to see that everything is right in the back-yard, where her underground packing-case workshops are. The place was burgled a short time back. This morning, as near as I know, it was ten minutes to five o'clock when I entered the backyard of 29. There was nobody there. Of that I am sure. I heard in the market at

6.20 a woman had been found murdered at mother's, and went round and saw the body. The police, by the doctor's order, took possession on my leather apron and knife that were on the premises, and also a box of nails, as well as three pills found near the body.

### BARBER'S SLAUGHTERHOUSE.

It is a singular fact that only a few steps from the house where the woman was found is—as in the Buck's-row case—one of Barber's slaughterhouses.

### PAYING TO VIEW THE SCENE.

For several hours past the occupants of the adjoining house have been charging an admission fee of one penny to people anxious to view the spot where the body was found. Several hundreds of people have availed themselves of this opportunity, though all that can be seen are a couple of packing cases from beneath which is the stain of a blood track.

—

### WHY NOT TRY BLOODHOUNDS?

"A Whitechapel Workman" writes:— Why do the police not employ bloodhounds to trace the murderer? He could not commit such a crime without being covered with the blood of his victim, and this would help the dogs to trace him. Bloodhounds were used to trace out Fish, the murderer, some years ago with success; but that, of course, was before our police force was presided over by Sir Charles Warren.

~

# Saturday, 8 September, 1888

## Evening News

Another brutal case of murder and mutilation in the East-end! That is the intelligence with which we are greeted this morning, and, so far as can be ascertained at this moment, the particulars are very much the same in their revolting character as those which accompanied the slaughter of the poor creature in Buck's-row, Whitechapel, a week ago. This time the scene of the discovery is Brown's-lane (formerly Hambro-street), Spitalfields, sufficiently near to the locality of the late crime to give colour to the theory that these horrors are the work of the same gang of ruffians.

The tragedy discovered at six o'clock this morning makes the third case of murder and hideous mutilation of defenceless women within the last month, and in a comparatively narrow area. But the most significant feature of these butcheries, so far at least as the public is concerned, has been the utter inability of the police to find any clue to the perpetrators of them. There is, however, a gleam of hope now that the murderer or murderers may be brought to justice, for it is stated that near the body of the woman done to death with such inhuman ferocity this morning was discovered a large knife stained with blood and a leather apron. With such a clue in their hands the detectives of the Metropolis ought surely to be able to run the murderer to earth. They are now placed on their mettle with a fair chance of removing from the public mind the feeling of alarm and insecurity which naturally arises where a number of undiscovered atrocities of this nature exist. It is to be hoped they will be speedily successful.

---

**FIFTH EDITION.
ANOTHER EAST END MURDER
EARLY THIS MORNING IN
SPITALFIELDS.
A WOMAN'S THROAT CUT AND
HER BODY RIPPED OPEN.
THE LEATHER APRON FOUND.
TERRIBLE DETAILS.
THE ENTRAILS AND THE
HEART CUT OUT.**

About a quarter to six this morning the body of a woman was found behind a door in a backyard in Brown's-lane (late Hambro-street) Brick-lane, Spitalfields. Her throat, as in the Whitechapel murder, was cut, and her body ripped down the front. The similarity of this to the preceding murders leads us to believe they are all the work of one man. The affair has created immense excitement in the district.

The house at the door of which the body was found is occupied by a Mrs. Emilia Richardson, who lets it out to various lodgers, and it seems that the door which admits into this passage, at the foot of which lies the yard where the body was found, is always open for the convenience of the lodgers. A Mr. and Mrs. Davis occupy the upper storey (the house consisting of three storeys), and as Mr. Davis was going down to work, at the time already mentioned, he found a woman lying on her back, close up to the flight of steps leading into the yard. Her throat was cut open in a fearful manner—so deep, in fact, that the murderer, evidently thinking that he had severed the head from the body, tied a handkerchief round it, so as to keep it on. It was also found that her abdomen had been completely ripped open, and her bowels, heart, and other entrails were lying at her side. The fiendish work was completed by the murderer tying part of the entrails round the poor woman's neck and head. The place on which she was lying was found covered with clots of thick blood, most horrible to look at. The supposition finds ready acceptance that the poor woman was murdered outside and taken into this yard, by those who knew the place well. This is upheld by the fact that spots of blood are lying thick in the narrow passage leading from the street into the yard, and the blood marks where the body was found must have been caused by its being deposited there, there being no signs of any struggle having taken place in the vicinity. Davis, the lodger who found the body, immediately communicated with the police at the Commercial-street Station, and Inspector Chandler and several constables arrived on the scene in a short time when they found the woman in the condition described.

Even at this early hour the news spread quickly, and great excitement prevailed among the occupants of the adjoining houses. An excited crowd gathered in front of Mrs. Richardson's house, and also around the mortuary in Old Montagu-street, to which the body was quickly removed.

# Saturday, 8 September, 1888

As the corpse lies in the rough coffin in which it has been placed in the mortuary, the same coffin in which the unfortunate Mrs. Nicholls was put, it presents an appearance which cannot but evoke pity for the victim and indignation at the brutal murder to an extreme degree.

## DESCRIPTION OF THE BODY.

The body is that of a woman evidently of about 45 years of age. The height is five feet exactly. The complexion is fair with wavy dark brown hair. The eyes are blue, and two teeth have been knocked out in the lower jaw. The nose is rather large and prominent. The third finger of the left hand bore signs of rings having been wrenched off it, and the hands and arms were considerably bruised.

Emilia Richardson, the woman who rents the house, stated in an interview that the murder was beyond all description in its horrible details. The abdomen had been fairly ripped open, it seemed to her, by the hand of some fiend or maniac, who gloated in the horribleness of the deed. Deceased had laced-up boots on, and striped stockings. She had on two cotton petticoats, and was otherwise respectably dressed. Nothing was found in her pockets but a handkerchief and two small combs.

The excitement in the vicinity is intense, and innumerable rumours are flying about. One report has it that a leather apron and a long knife have been found near the place where the body lay, belonging, it is said, to a man whose name is unknown, but who is surnamed "Leather Apron," and evidently known in the district.

A further report states that another woman was nearly murdered early in the morning, and was taken to the hospital in a dying condition. Several persons who were lodging in the house, and who were found in the vicinity where the body was found, were taken to the Commercial-street Station, and are now being closely examined, especially the women who were last with deceased. The police authorities are extremely reticent owing to the fact that any statement might get about which would help the murderer to elude detection. There can be little doubt now that this latest murder is one of the series of fiendish atrocities on women which have been going on for the past few months, this making the fourth case in this short time, all in the same district. It is thought that in this case the victim must have been murdered outside, or in a neighbouring house, and carried into this dark yard, where the murderer evidently thought it was safe from discovery for some time. There is little evidence to show that the murder was committed on the premises where the body was found, as the marks of blood were all found in one place, viz., where the police discovered the body. The only other marks are those found in the passage close to the flight of steps, and these may have been caused in removing the body to the mortuary. The police, however, in this case, have more facts and evidence to go on, and they are sanguine that the murderer will soon be found out. Looking at the corpse no one could think otherwise than that the murder had been committed by a maniac or wretch of the lowest type of humanity.

## LATER.

The murdered woman was known among her companions as "Dark Annie," and gave her name as Annie Sievey, but it is not yet known whether this was her correct name. She was a prostitute and had been recently living at a common lodging-house at Dorset-street, which is near by the scene of last night's atrocious crime. Deceased formerly lived with a sieve-maker in the East-end of London as his wife. The excitement in the district grows in intensity as the day draws on. Crowds have gathered at various points in the vicinity, and the prevalent feeling is one bordering on panic. Rumours are plentiful, but the report of a second murder this morning is entirely unfounded.

---

## SPECIAL ACCOUNT.

The East-end of London has again been the scene of a most atrocious murder, which in its leading features is almost identical with that committed in Buck's-row a few days ago. The victim is a woman, evidently belonging to a low class of prostitute, and aged about 40. Her throat is cut clean to the vertebra, just as was that of the unfortunate Mrs. Nicholls, and her abdomen is ripped and gashed in an almost precisely similar to that of the previous unfortunate victim.

The scene of the murder is the backyard of a lodging house kept by a Mrs. Richardson, at 28, Hanbury-street, Spitalfields.

53

# Saturday, 8 September, 1888

At six o'clock this morning one of the lodgers, named Davis, a porter at Leadenhall Market, had occasion to go into the back yard, and there found the unfortunate woman lying quite dead. Her throat was cut in the manner we have described, and she was lying on her back in a great pool of blood. Her clothes were turned up above her knees, and her entrails were protruding through most horrible wounds in the abdomen. Davis at once gave information to the police, who quickly appeared, and removed the body.

The most intense excitement prevails in the neighbourhood, and it is the universal opinion that the murderer of this latest victim is the same man who murdered Mrs. Nicholls, if not also of the two other women who were murdered earlier in the year.

As the morning wore on, and the news of the terrible tragedy spread over the neighbourhood, Hanbury-street, which is perhaps, better known by its old name of Brown's-lane, became densely crowded by excited and eager people. At every court end, and almost at every door, knots of people were gathered discussing the all-absorbing topic, and Mrs. Richardson's house, where the murder was committed, was simply besieged; so also was the mortuary in which the dead woman is now lying.

The latest information goes to show quite clearly that the murder was actually committed in the back-yard of No. 18, Hanbury-street. The front door of this house is never locked at night, as some of the lodgers come home very late at night, and others have to go to their work early in the morning; and for their convenience the door is always left on the latch. The passage from the front door to the yard is perfectly straight and no one who was at all acquainted with the configuration of the house would have any difficulty in walking straight into the yard at any hour. The probability is the murderer met the woman in the streets at an early hour in the morning, and induced her to go with him into the yard for an immoral purpose, and that as she was lying on the ground the murderer with one gash of a heavy knife inflicted the fearful wound on the throat, which must have proved almost immediately fatal, as both the jugular vein and the carotid artery were completely severed.

The other theory, that the murder was committed in the street, and then concealed in the yard of No. 18, is disproved by the fact that, whereas there is a horrible mass of clotted blood lying on the spot where the body was found there are no blood-stains whatever, either in the passage of the house or anywhere else in the neighbourhood. In the dress of the dead woman two farthings were found, so brightly polished as to lead to the belief that they were intended to be passed as half-sovereigns, and it is probable that they were given to her by the murderer as an inducement for her to accompany him.

## INTERVIEW WITH THE MAN WHO FOUND THE BODY.

This morning our representative interviewed the man Davis, by whom the body was discovered. He is a carman, employed by Mr. Wisdom, a fruiterer and greengrocer in Leadenhall Market. His story is that shortly before six a.m. he had occasion to go into the back, and as soon as he opened the door he saw the woman's body lying on the ground. The face was deluged with blood to such an extent that he did not notice the wound in the throat. Her petticoats were turned up, and the lower portion of her body was quite visible. Davis, who is an old and somewhat feeble-looking man, says he only stayed to notice that her bowels were protruding, and that then he dashed straight away to the police-station, about a couple of hundred yards from the scene of the murder, and there gave information to the police. He did not even wait to arouse any of the other inmates of the house, who only became acquainted with the fact that the ghastly tragedy had been committed after the arrival of the police.

The deceased woman used to live with a sieve maker in Dorset-street, and was known to her acquaintances as "Annie Sievey," a nickname derived from her paramour's trade.

—

## RUMOURED IDENTIFICATION.

It is reported that two men have identified the body found in Spitalfields as that of a woman named Ellen Clarke, with whom they were drinking last night.

The Scotland-yard authorities state that the circumstances in connection with the murder justify the police in believing that it has been committed by the same person or persons who murdered Mary Ann Nichols. The matter, however, is surrounded with mystery, and the police have had but little time to make inquiries. The police at Commercial-street Station are in charge of the inquiry, but a large body of detectives are scouring the district.

## AN ARREST.

At about 11.45 a man was arrested near the City-road, and was taken to Kingsland-road Police-station by six policemen. It was reported that he was the murderer.

## PANIC IN SPITALFIELDS.

The excitement in Spitalfields is now rendering the people almost frantic. Two ordinary prisoners were arrested for trifling offences this morning, and on each occasion a maddened crowd ran after police shouting "The murderer's caught." Another man injured in a quarrel and carried to the police station on a stretcher received similar attention, the crowd fairly mobbing the station, and declining to disperse. As a matter of fact no arrests have been made up to noon though the police are more hopeful on this than on the last occasion. Deceased, it transpires, was unable to pay her lodging money last night, and went on to the streets again to get it. She was then under the influence of liquor, and was seen drinking again in the early hours of the morning.

—

## RUMOUR OF ANOTHER MURDER.

Shortly after ten o'clock, this morning, a rumour was current in the East-end, that the body of a young woman, with her throat cut, had been found in the graveyard attached to St. Philip's Church, at the back of the London Hospital. A representative of *The Evening News* was dispatched to make inquiries in the neighbourhood and was assured by the police that there was no foundation for this extra-ordinary story. It probably had its origin in the panic which had seized the district upon the discovery of the atrocious butchery of the unfortunate creature who was found in Brown's-lane this morning. So quickly, however, had this second rumour spread that before eleven o'clock a large number of inquiries as to its veracity had been made both at the London Hospital and the Whitechapel Mortuary in Old Montague-street.

~

# Monday, 10 September, 1888

## The Times

The series of shocking crimes perpetrated in Whitechapel, which on Saturday culminated in the murder of the woman Chapman, is something so distinctly outside the ordinary range of human experience that it has created a kind of stupor extending far beyond the district where the murders were committed. One may search the ghastliest efforts of fiction and fail to find anything to surpass these crimes in diabolical audacity. The mind travels back to the pages of De Quincey[26] for an equal display of scientific delight in the details of butchery; or Edgar Allan Poe's "Murders in the Rue Morgue" recur in the endeavour to conjure up some parallel for this murderer's brutish savagery. But, so far as we know, nothing in fact or fiction equals these outrages at once in their horrible nature and in the effect which they have produced upon the popular imagination.

The circumstances that the murders seem to be the work of one individual, that his blows fall exclusively upon wretched wanderers of the night, and that each successive crime has gained something in atrocity upon, and has followed closer on the heels of, its predecessor—these things mark out the Whitechapel murders, even before their true history is unravelled, as unique in the annals of crime. All ordinary experiences of motive leave us at a loss to comprehend the fury which has prompted the cruel slaughter of at least three, and possibly four, women, each unconnected with the other by any tie except that of their miserable mode of livelihood. Human nature would not be itself if these shocking occurrences, all taking place within a short distance of one another, and all bearing a ghastly resemblance, had not thrown the inhabitants into a state of panic—a panic, it must be feared, as favourable to the escape of the assassin as it is dangerous to innocent persons whose appearance or conduct is sufficiently irregular to excite suspicion.

The details of Chapman's murder need not be referred to here at length. It is enough to say that she was found, early on Saturday morning, lying,

with her head nearly severed from her body, and mutilated in a most revolting way, in the backyard of No. 29, Hanbury-street, Spitalfields. She was not an occupant of the house, which is a tenement let out to many families of lodgers. It is nearly certain that she made her way into the yard, which is easily accessible through the house at all hours of the night, in company with her murderer, for the purpose of privacy, and that she was not killed in another place and then carried to the spot where she was found. The fact that no cry from the poor woman reached any of the inmates of the house shows that the assassin knew his business well.

The wounds inflicted by him were exactly similar to those which caused the death of the woman Nichols eight days before. Nichols, it will be remembered, was found with her throat cut, and frightfully mutilated, upon the pavement of Buck's-row. Rather more than three weeks previously Martha Tabran was picked up dead on the stairs of George-yard-buildings, Whitechapel, with 39 stabs on her body. It is important to notice that, although some of the stabs might have been inflicted by an ordinary knife, others, according to the medical evidence, were far too formidable to have been produced by anything but "some kind of a dagger."

The case of Emma Smith, who died from the effects of a barbarous assault in the early morning of Easter Tuesday last, is different, and possibly it ought to be entirely dissociated from the murders of last month. Smith lived long enough to describe the outrage, and her account was that at half-past one in the morning she was passing near Whitechapel Church when some men set upon her, took all the money she had, and then inflicted the most revolting injuries upon her. If this murder is to be classed with the three recent ones, then the theory that they were the work of a gang of blackmailers is more than tenable.

But the crimes of August and September naturally separate themselves from the other, both by reason of the considerable interval which elapsed and by the more determined method of the later assassin or assassins.

Probably SMITH'S assailants did not mean to kill her outright. But there is no room for doubt that the slayer of TABRAN, NICHOLS, and CHAPMAN meant murder, and nothing else but murder.

---

[26] **Thomas De Quincey** (1785-1859), English essayist best known for his works <u>Confessions of an English Opium Eater</u> and <u>On Murder Considered as One of the Fine Arts</u>.

# Monday, 10 September, 1888

## ANOTHER MURDER AT THE EAST-END.

Whitechapel and the whole of the East of London have again been thrown into a state of intense excitement by the discovery early on Saturday morning of the body of a woman who had been murdered in a similar way to Mary Ann Nichols at Buck's-row on Friday week. In fact the similarity in the two cases is startling, as the victim of the outrage had her head almost severed from her body, and was completely disembowelled. This latest crime, however, even surpasses the others in ferocity.

The scene of the murder, which makes the fourth in the same neighbourhood within the past few weeks, is at the back of the house, 29, Hanbury-street, Spitalfields. This street runs from Commercial-street to Baker's-row, the end of which is close to Buck's-row.

The house, which is rented by a Mrs. Emilia Richardson, is let out to various lodgers, all of the poorer class. In consequence, the front door is open both day and night, so that no difficulty would be experienced by any one in gaining admission to the back portion of the premises.

Shortly before 6 o'clock on Saturday morning John Davis, who lives with his wife at the top portion of No. 29, and is a porter engaged in Spitalfields Market, went down into the back yard, where a horrible sight presented itself to him. Lying close up against the wall, with her head touching the other side wall, was the body of a woman.

Davis could see that her throat was severed in a terrible manner, and that she had other wounds of a nature too shocking to be described. The deceased was lying flat on her back, with her clothes disarranged. Without nearer approaching the body, but telling his wife what he had seen, Davis ran to the Commercial-street Police-station, which is only a short distance away, and gave information to Inspector Chandler, H Division, who was in charge of the station at the time.

That officer, having despatched a constable for Dr. Baxter Phillips, Spital-square, the divisional surgeon, repaired to the house, accompanied by several other policemen. The body was still in the same position, and there were large clots of blood all round it. It is evident that the murderer thought that he had completely cut the head off, as a handkerchief was found wrapped round the neck, as though to hold it together. There were spots and stains of blood on the wall. One or more rings seem to have been torn from the middle finger of the left hand.

After being inspected by Dr. Baxter Phillips and his assistant, the remains were removed, on an ambulance, to the mortuary in Old Montagu-street. By this time the news had quickly spread that another diabolical murder had been committed, and when the police came out of the house with the body, a large crowd, consisting of some hundreds of persons, had assembled. The excitement became very great, and loud were the expressions of terror heard on all sides.

At the mortuary the doctors made a more minute examination of the body, after which the clothes were taken off. The deceased was laid in the same shell in which Mary Ann Nichols was placed.

Detective-sergeant Thicke, Sergeant Leach, and other detective officers were soon on the spot, while a telegram was sent to Inspector Abberline, at Scotland-yard, apprising him of what had happened. It will be recollected that this officer assisted in the inquiry concerning the murder in Buck's-row. A minute search being made of the yard, a portion of an envelope, stained with blood, was found. It had the crest of the Sussex Regiment on it, and the date "London, August 20;" but the address portion, with the exception of one letter, "M," was torn off. In addition, two pills were also picked up.

Inquiries were quickly set on foot with a view to having the woman identified, and persons of both sexes were taken out of the neighbouring common lodging-houses, which abound in this district, to the mortuary. One of these, Timothy Donovan, the deputy of a common lodging-house, 35, Dorset-street, recognized the body as that of a woman whom he knew by the name of Annie Siffey. He had seen her in the kitchen of the lodging-house as late as half-past 1 or 2 o'clock that morning. He knew her as an unfortunate, and that she generally frequented Stratford for a living.

He asked her for her lodging money, when she said, "I have not got it. I am weak and ill, and have been in the infirmary." Donovan told her she knew the rules, when she went out to get some money. Although there are various statements that she was seen with a man in a publichouse at 5 o'clock, the police have no authentic information respecting that point.

Donovan did not turn the woman out of the lodging-house; he simply did his duty by telling her that she knew the rules of the establishment —that the price of the lodging had to be paid beforehand. At that time she was wearing three brass rings.

Other inquiries soon established that the woman's real name was Annie Chapman, and that she was known by the nickname of "Dark Annie." She was the widow of a pensioner, and had formerly lived at Windsor. Some few years since she separated from her husband, who made her a weekly allowance of 10s. At his death she had to do the best she could for a living. There were two children—a boy and a girl—of the marriage. The former, who is deformed, is at the present time an inmate of the Cripples' Home, while the girl is away in some institution in France.

For some months past the deceased had been living in common lodging-houses in Spitalfields, and when in good health used to frequent the streets of Stratford for a living. It is also known that formerly she lived with a sievemaker in the neighbourhood, and on account of that got the nickname of "Siffey." Only on Monday last she had a quarrel with another woman of her acquaintance, and during a fight and struggle got severely mauled and kicked.

On Saturday afternoon Dr. Baxter Phillips, assisted by his assistant, made a most exhaustive post-mortem examination, lasting upwards of two hours. Although, of course, the exact details have not been made public, it is known that Dr. Phillips was unable to find any trace of alcohol in the stomach of the deceased, thus disproving many reports that when the woman was last seen alive she was the worse for drink. The deceased was a little over 5ft. in height, and of fair complexion, with blue eyes, and dark brown wavy hair. A singular coincidence about the corpse was that there were two front teeth missing, as in the case of Mary Ann Nichols. On the right side of the head was a large bruise, showing that the deceased woman must have been dealt a heavy blow at that spot. There were also other bruises about the face and finger marks were discernible. The

latter indicate that the murderer must first have grasped his victim by the throat, probably in order to prevent her crying out.

The police believe that the murder has been committed by the same person who perpetrated the three previous ones in the district, and that only one person is concerned in it. This person, whoever he might be, is doubtless labouring under some terrible form of insanity, as each of the crimes has been of a most fiendish character; and it is feared that unless he can speedily be captured more outrages of a similar class will be committed.

During the whole of Saturday and yesterday a large crowd congregated in front of the house in Hanbury-street, and the neighbours on either side did much business by making a small charge to persons who were willing to pay it to view from windows the yard in which the murder was committed.

On Saturday a rumour got about that the murderer had been caught, but the only ground for such a statement was that a blind man had been arrested in Spitalfields Market on a warrant to answer a charge of stabbing. Later in the day this man was charged at the Worship-street Police-court, and sentenced to three months' hard labour.

Great complaints are made concerning the inadequate police protection at the East-end, and this want is even admitted by the local police authorities themselves, but they are unable to alter the existing state of affairs. Outrages and acts of lawlessness daily occur in broad daylight in the principal thoroughfares of the East-end, and the offenders are seldom brought to justice, owing to the inability of the police to properly cover the whole of the ground within their jurisdiction.

During Saturday and yesterday several persons were detained at the various police stations in the district, but were liberated after proper inquiries had been made; and up to the present time the police have no clue to the murderer, and lament that they have no good ground to work upon.

An inquest on the body of the murdered woman will be opened to-day.

—

# Monday, 10 September, 1888

**ANOTHER ACCOUNT.**

At five minutes to 6 o'clock on Saturday morning a man named John Davis, living at 29, Hanbury-street, Spitalfields, discovered that a woman had been murdered in the yard at the rear of that house. It was abundantly clear that she was another victim of the miscreant who had murdered Mary Ann Nichols, in Buck's-row, Whitechapel, only a week previously. The same horrible ferocity had been exhibited in the commission of the crime, and the victim was again one of the class called unfortunates, and so poor that robbery could scarcely be suggested as a motive for the murder.

The house, 29, Hanbury-street, which is not half a mile from Buck's-row, is tenanted by a man named Clark, a packing-case-maker, and is let out by rooms to several poor people. The front parlour is in the occupation of a Mrs. Hardiman, who uses it as a shop for the sale of cats' meat. She and her son also sleep in the room. The back parlour is a sort of sitting-room for the landlady and her family, and looks out upon a yard, at the further side of which stands a shed where the packing-case work is done. The passage of the house leads directly to the yard, passing the door of the front parlour. The yard is about four feet below the level of the passage and is reached by two stone steps. The position of the steps creates a recess on their left, the fence between the yard and the next house being about three feet from the steps.

In this recess John Davis, as he crossed the yard at five minutes to 6 o'clock, saw the body of a woman, with the lower part of her body horribly mutilated, and her throat so terribly gashed that the head was almost severed from the trunk. Davis seems at once to have run out and called in Police-constable Pinnock, 238 H, and that constable sent information to the station in Commercial-street.

Inspector Chandler, on duty, with others hurried to the place, and before the body was removed from its position the divisional surgeon, Mr. George Bagster Phillips, of Spital-square, was called to examine it. The fiendish character of the mutilation then became manifest. There was no doubt, he said, that the throat was first cut and the stomach subsequently mutilated.

The body was removed as soon as possible to the mortuary of the parishes of Whitechapel and Spitalfields in Old Montague-street, and placed in a shell—the same in which a week before the hacked body of the previous victim had been placed.

The police description of the body was quickly made out, and before 10 o'clock it was identified as that of Annie Chapman, alias "Sivvey"—a name by which she had become known in consequence of living with a sievemaker. The police satisfied themselves that Chapman was the correct name of the deceased, and that she was the widow of a man who had been a soldier, and from whom, until about 12 months ago, when he died, she had been receiving 10s. a week. She was one of the same class as Mary Ann Nichols, her usual places of abode being also in the common lodging-houses of Spitalfields and Whitechapel. She is described as a stout, well-proportioned woman, of about 5ft. in height, as quiet, and as one who had "seen better days."

Detective Inspector Abberline, of Scotland-yard, who had been detailed to make special inquiries as to the murder of Mary Ann Nichols, at once took up the inquiries with regard to the new crime, the two being obviously the work of the same hands. He held a consultation with Detective Inspector Helson, J Division, in whose district the murder in Buck's-row was committed, and with Acting Superintendent West, in charge of the H Division.

The result of that consultation was an agreement in the belief that the crimes were the work of one man only, and that, not-withstanding many misleading statements and rumours—the majority of which in the excitement of the time had been printed as facts—the murders were committed where the bodies had been found, and that no gang were the perpetrators. It having been stated that the woman must have been murdered elsewhere and her body deposited in the yard—the house-door giving access to the passage, and the yard being never locked—the most careful examination was made of the flooring of the passage and the walls, but not a trace of blood was found to support such a theory. It is, moreover, considered impossible that a body could have been carried in, supposing no blood had dropped, without arousing from their sleep Mrs. Hardiman and her son, past whose bed-room door the murderer had to go.

There is no doubt that the deceased was

acquainted with the fact that the house-door was always open or ajar, and that she and her murderer stealthily passed into the yard.

Although, as in the case of Mary Ann Nichols, a very small quantity of blood was found on the ground (leading to the supposition that the murder was committed elsewhere), its absence is accounted for by the quantity the clothes would absorb.

The deceased had no time to raise a cry, and the tenants of the house agree that nothing was heard to create alarm. The back room of the first-floor, which has an uninterrupted view of all the yard, is a bed-room, and was tenanted by a man named Alfred Walker and his father, neither of whom "heard a sound."

John Richardson, son of a woman living in the house, stated that he entered the place when on his way to work at Leadenhall Market, and at that time—4:50—he was certain no one was in the yard.

The police, however, have been unable to discover any person who saw the deceased alive after 2 a.m., about which time she left the lodging-house, 35, Dorset-street, because she had not 4d. to pay for her bed. No corroboration of the reported statement that she was served in a publichouse at Spitalfields Market on its opening at 5 a.m. could be gained, nor of the sensational report that the murderer left a message on the wall in the yard, which was made out to read, "Five; 15 more, and then I give myself up." Nevertheless, the police express a strong opinion that more murders of the kind will be committed before the miscreant is apprehended.

Soon after the murder was discovered, a woman of the same class reported to the police that a man had accosted her in the streets of Spitalfields at an early hour that morning, but that she tried to avoid him. Thereupon he began to knock her about; she screamed, and he ran off. He gave her two brass medals for half sovereigns. She was asked to describe the man, but her description of him was not considered clear. Still the police determined to follow up the matter, more particularly because the woman states that the man seemed ready to kill her.

The woman's description did not answer the description of a man for whom they have been searching in connexion with the murder of Mary Ann Nichols—a man known as "Leather Apron"—and they incline to the opinion that, after the hue and cry raised about him during the past few days, he would not have ventured into the neighbourhood of Spitalfields, where he is so well known.

It seems certain that the deceased was robbed of three rings she wore on the left hand, which the murderer mistook for gold, though it is said that to a woman in the lodging-house she admitted they were only brass.

—

A young woman named Lyons stated that at 3 o'clock yesterday afternoon she met a strange man in Flower and Dean-street. He asked her to come to the Queen's Head publichouse at half-past 6 and drink with him. Having obtained from her a promise that she would do so he disappeared, and was at the house named at the appointed time.

While they were conversing Lyons noticed a large knife in the man's right-hand trousers pocket, and called another woman's attention to the fact. A moment later Lyons was startled by a remark which the stranger addressed to her. "You are about the same style of woman as the one that's murdered," he said. "What do you know about her?" asked the woman, to which the man replied, "You are beginning to smell a rat. Foxes hunt geese, but they don't always find 'em." Having uttered these words the man hurriedly left.

Lyons followed until near Spitalfields Church, when, turning round at this spot and noticing that the woman was behind him, the stranger ran at a swifter pace into Church-street and was at once lost to view.

One noteworthy fact in this story is that the description of the man's appearance is in all material points identical with the published descriptions of the unknown, and up to the present untracked, "Leather Apron." Over 200 common lodging-houses have been visited by the police in the hope of finding some trace of the mysterious and much talked-of person, but he has succeeded in evading arrest.

On Saturday evening a somewhat suspicious incident occurred at Deptford. About 7 o'clock a man in a hurried manner entered the shop of a newsagent in Grove-street, near the entrance to the Foreign Cattle Market, and in an excited tone asked for a copy of the special *Star* containing an account of the Whitechapel murder. The newsagent replied that he had not one left. The man then asked for a special *Evening News*, and received the same reply. "Then," said the man, "let me have a special anything." The newsagent was at the time reading the special *Standard*, and told him he could have that if he liked. The man snatched the open paper from his hand, threw a penny down upon the counter, rushed out of the shop, and, by the light of the gas in the shop window, appeared to eagerly and excitedly read the account of the tragedy.

Indeed, his manner and appearance were so remarkable, that the newsagent suspected that he might be in some way connected with the murder, and leaving the shop, told a boy who was passing to hurry away for a policeman and bring one back to the shop immediately. The boy started off, and the newsagent returned to his shop, and on doing so was observed by the man, who appeared to become alarmed at the circumstance, for he crushed up the newspaper in his hand, started across the road, ran down Emily-place, and disappeared.

The newsagent is of opinion that he probably ran that way towards a car on the Deptford and Southwark Tramway which runs to Tooley-street, and would take him out of the neighbourhood in a few minutes.

The man wore an old felt hat pulled well forward over his eyes, and his coat collar being up, the impression of the newsagent is that he was endeavouring to conceal his features. He was of stout build, full-chested, rather ruddy complexion, slight moustache, a beard scrubby or of several days' growth, and looked, to use the newsagent's words, "as if a little soap would have done him good." He was wearing an old brown overcoat, well worn and greasy at the pockets.

He stood about two minutes outside the shop reading the paper, and was watched by the newsagent through the window. A constable afterwards came to the shop and took down in writing the statement of the newsagent.

—

A man was arrested at Deptford yesterday afternoon on suspicion of being connected with the East-end tragedy, but there is reason to believe that he will be able to establish his innocence and will soon be released.

—

So many stories of "suspicious" incidents have cropped up since the murder, some of them evidently spontaneously generated by frantic terror, and some, even where credible, pointing in contrary directions, what it would be idle to refer to them. A valuable hint may be found by the detectives in some of these volunteered reminiscences, but there is also danger that they may be diverted from the broad and obvious lines of investigation by distracting suggestions. If the perpetrator of crimes so numerous and so extraordinary is not speedily brought to justice, it will be not only humiliating, but also an intolerable perpetuation of the danger.

Although the Whitechapel murders are without example, the police have also an unexampled number of data from which to draw their conclusions. The most salient point is the maniacal frenzy with which the victims were slaughtered, and unless we accept, as a possible alternative, the theory that the assassin was actuated by revenge for some real or supposed injury suffered by him at the hands of unfortunate women, we are thrown back upon the belief that these murders were really committed by a madman, or by a man whom a sottish passion interlaced with a lust for blood places too far outside the pale of human feelings to be governed by commonly recognized motives.

However, if the police are right in believing that certain flash rings were torn from Nichols's fingers, this is a circumstance which slightly disconcerts the idea that the murderer was a simple maniac. But, on the whole, this is the most probable theory, and, without any intention to accentuate alarm, it may be pointed out that, if it is correct, the ordinary motives of prudence which deter murderers from a speedy repetition of their crime cannot be reckoned upon in aid of the safety of the wretched women of Whitechapel.

~

## The Star

### UNDISCOVERED CRIMES.
### A List of Some London Murders which Have Gone Unavenged.

It was the boast of Mr. Howard Vincent,[27] at the time he was head of the Criminal Investigation Department, that London is the safest city in the world; and so it would seem to be—for the assassin. The undiscovered murders of recent years make a long list.

Passing over the murder of Mrs. Squires and her daughter in their shop at Hoxton in broad daylight;[28] the killing of Jane Maria Clousen in Kidbrook-lane, near Eltham;[29] the murder of the housekeeper to Bevingtons, of Cannon-street,[30] we come to, perhaps, the best remembered and most sensational of the mysterious crimes of the past.

On the morning of Christmas-day, 1872, Harriet Buswell[31] was discovered with her throat cut. She was a ballet-girl, employed at the Alhambra, and had been accompanied to her home, 12, Great Coram-street, by a "gentleman," supposed to have been a German, who on the way purchased some apples, one of which was left in the room, and bore the impression of his teeth. This half-eaten apple was the sole clue to the murderer, who was never found. A German clergyman named Hessel was arrested at Ramsgate on suspicion three weeks after the murder, but a protracted magisterial investigation resulted in his complete acquittal.

Mrs. Samuel was brutally done to death at her house in Burton-crescent,[32] and a few doors further up Annie Yeats was murdered under precisely similar circumstances to those attending the death of Harriet Buswell.[33]

Miss Hacker was found dead in a coal-cellar in the house of one Sebastian Bashendorff, in Euston-square, and Hannah Dobbs was tried, but acquitted.[34] An almost identical case happened in Harley-street. In this case the victim was unknown.[35]

Another unknown woman was discovered lying in Burdett-road, Bow, murdered.

Mrs. Reville, a butcher's wife, of Slough, was found sitting in a chair with her throat cut, I'm sorry but no one was apprehended.[36]

Then there was the murder of an unfortunate in her home near Pye-street, Westminster. A rough fellow was known to have gone home with her, and he left an old and dirty neckerchief behind, but he was never found.

Mrs. Samuel was killed with impunity in the Kentish Town Dairy.[37]

The murderer of Miss Clark, who was found at the foot of the stairs in her house, George-street, Marylebone, has gone unpunished.[38]

Besides these there are the cases in which the victims have been men.

A grocer's assistant was stabbed to death in the Walworth-road by a man who was stealing a pound of tea from a cart. The act was committed in the sight of a number of people, but the man got away, and to this day has not been captured.

Mr. Tower, returning from midnight service on New Year's eve was found in the Stoke Newington reservoir. The police failing to get the faintest clue adopted the theory of suicide, but could get nothing to substantiate it.

On 29 March 1884, E. J. Perkins, a clerk in a City office at 2, Arthur-street West, was murdered and from Saturday till Monday his body lay in a cellar in the basement of the building.

Lieutenant Roper was shot at the top of the barrack stairs at Chatham, and, though Percy Lefroy Mapleton, who was hanged for the murder of Mr. Gould on the Brighton Railway, accused himself of the murder, it was proved that he could have had no connection with the lieutenant's death.

Urban Napoleon Stanger, the baker, of Whitechapel, who vanished so mysteriously, we

---

[27] **Colonel Sir Charles Edward Howard Vincent KCMG CB DL** (1849-1908). First Director of the Criminal Investigation Department (1878-1884). Commanded Queen's Westminster Volunteers 1884-1904. M.P. 1885-1908.

[28] See App. B, Hoxton Murders, p. 545.

[29] See App. C, Eltham Murder, p. 548.

[30] See App. D, Cannon St. Murder, p. 551.

[31] See App. E, Great Coram St. Murder, p. 553.

[32] See App. F, 4, Burton-Crescent Murder, p. 554.

[33] See App. G, 12, Burton-Crescent Murder, p. 558.

[34] See App. H, Euston Square Murder, p. 560.

[35] See App. I, Harley St. Murder, p. 563.

[36] See App. J, Slough Murder, p. 569.

[37] See App. K, Kentish Town Dairy Murder, p. 573

[38] See App. L, George St. Murder, p. 574.

# Monday, 10 September, 1888

pass over. The list, though incomplete, is ghastly enough.

—

## THE POLICE AND THE PRESS.

The police, justly or unjustly, come in for a large share of the blame of these undiscovered crimes. It is true that Whitechapel is densely populated and difficult to cover, but it is also true that under anything like intelligent police management such a quartette of openly committed murders could hardly have occurred.

One thing is absolutely certain, and that is that murderers will always escape with the ease that now characterises their escape in London until the police authorities adopt a different attitude towards the Press. They treat the reporters of the newspapers, who are simply news-gatherers for the great mass of the people, with a snobbery that would be beneath contempt were it not senseless to an almost criminal degree.

On Saturday they shut the reporters out of the mortuary; they shut them out of the house where the murder was done; the constable at the mortuary door lied to them; some of the inspectors at the offices seemed to wilfully mislead them; they denied information which would have done no harm to make public, and the withholding of which only tended to increase the public uneasiness over the affair.

Now if the people of London wish murderers detected they must have all this changed. In New York, where the escape of a murderer is as rare as it is common here, the

## REPORTERS ARE FAR MORE ACTIVE

agents in ferreting out crime than the detectives. They are no more numerous or more intelligent than the reporters of London, but they are given every facility and opportunity to get all the facts, and no part of any case is hidden from them unless the detectives' plan makes it necessary to keep it a secret.

The consequence is that a large number of sharp and experienced eyes are focussed upon every point of a case, a number of different theories develop which the reporters themselves follow up, and instances in which the detection of a criminal is due to a newspaper reporter are simply too common to create any particular comment.

Reporters are not prying individuals simply endeavouring to gratify their own curiosity.

They are direct agents of the people who have a right to the news and a right to know what their paid servants the police and detectives are doing to earn the bread and butter for which the people are taxed. No properly accredited reporter ever wishes to know or print anything that will thwart the ends of justice, but he does desire and is fully entitled to the fullest scope in examining all the details of the case.

The sooner the police authorities appreciate and act on this the sooner the Whitechapel fiend will be captured and human life in London rendered a little more safe.

—

## A NEW SUGGESTION.

"T.C.M." writes:—May not the horrible murders of Whitechapel be the act of some insane butcher or dissecting-room porter? Mrs. Richardson's account of the ghastly sight of the last poor victim seems to bear out my theory of the crime being the deed of some miscreant who has been accustomed to some such work on the dead subject.

As a medical man I am struck by the fact of the viscera being taken out and placed alongside of the unfortunate victim, as if for inspection by the demonstrator at a post-mortem examination.

Anyhow, I think all dissecting room or post-mortem porters of the hospitals or mortuaries and even veterinary assistants should be scrutinised as to their state of mind also, and especially should some account be ascertained of all such persons who have lately left such situations, either of their own free will or by dismissal.

—

## VIGILANCE COMMITTEES.

The Secretary of the St. Jude's District Committee writes:—A few days after the murder of the woman in George-yard, last month, a meeting of about 70 men, residing in the buildings in the immediate neighbourhood, was held, and after discussion a committee of twelve was appointed to act as watchers. We wish to suggest that other committees should be formed without loss of time. If some communication could be set up between these committees, when constituted, our powers would be strengthened, and our opportunities improved.

—

# Monday, 10 September, 1888

**A Man Thought to be "Leather Apron"
Arrested and Released—A Man who
Admits He Quarrelled with a Woman in the
Neighbourhood of Hanbury-street Captured
at Gravesend—Opening of the Inquest on
the Victim.**

The Press Association says:—About nine o'clock this morning a detective arrested a man as "Leather Apron," who was wanted in connection with the Whitechapel murder, at 22, Mulberry-street, Commercial-street. The real name of the man arrested is John Piser, but his friends deny that he has ever been known under the nickname of "Leather Apron." When the detective called at the house the door was opened by Piser himself.

**"JUST THE MAN I WANT,"**

said the detective, who charged him on suspicion of being connected with the murder of the woman Sivvy. The detective searched the house, and took away some finishing tools which Piser is in the habit of using in his work.

By trade he is a boot finisher, and for some time has been living at Mulberry-street with his stepmother (Mrs. Piser) and a married brother, who works as a cabinet-maker.

When he was arrested by the detective this morning his brother was at work, and the only inmates of the house were the prisoner's stepmother, his sister-in-law, and a Mr. Nathan, for whom he has worked.

His mother and his sister-in-law declared positively to a representative of the Press Association that Piser came home at half-past ten on Thursday night, and

**HAS NOT LEFT THE HOUSE SINCE.**

They further stated that Piser is unable to do much on account of ill-health, and that he is by no means a strong person, as some time ago he was seriously injured in a vital part. About six weeks ago he left a convalescent home, in which he had been an inmate on account of a carbuncle on his neck. He is about 35 years of age, and since he was three years old has been brought up by Mrs. Piser. He lost his father some 16 years ago. At the Leman-street Police-station, to which station Piser was taken, a large

force of police were kept in readiness with drawn staves. Only a few people amongst the crowd outside seemed aware that an arrest had been made, and so quietly did the police act in Mulberry-street that few even in the neighbourhood connected the arrest with the murder. The police at Leman-street refuse to give any information, and some officials who had come from Scotland-yard

**DENIED THAT SUCH AN ARREST HAD
BEEN MADE,**

but this statement was, of course, incorrect, seeing that the arrest is admitted by the prisoner's relatives. The prisoner is a Jew.

Our reporter writes:—The man arrested by Detective-Sergeant Thicke is now at Leman-street Station. He fits the description of "Leather Apron" exactly, and this similarity is the cause of his arrest. He denies, however, that he is the man wanted, and says he never wore a leather apron in the streets. He is waiting, however, to be recognised, or the contrary, by some people from Wilmot's Lodging House who know "Leather Apron" well. He went along submissively with Detective-Sergeant Thicke. His stepmother and his stepsister deny in the strongest terms that he is "Leather Apron." They say that he has been steady

**AT WORK FOR THE PAST SIX WEEKS**

for his stepbrother, Piser, who is a boot manufacturer. Before that time he was ill with a carbuncle on his neck, and confined for some time in a hospital.

The women were in great trouble over the arrest, but assured a *Star* reporter that he was never out late at night while living at home, and that assaults on street-women and the robbing of them was simply impossible, as he was a sober, industrious, and kind-hearted man.

Piser was kept for about two hours at Leman-street Station, and then taken up to Commercial-street. At half-past twelve he was ushered into the main office of the station, half a dozen policemen guarding the doors. Piser sat down on the seat next the outside wall. He looked

**PALE AND RATHER DEJECTED.**

No questions were asked him, the only ceremony being that a woman sitting in the corner behind the table was told to look sharp. She had been sitting there all the forenoon, doubtless for the purpose of identification. Then Piser was taken into the inner office, the

64

doors were closed, and the further ceremonies were known only to the detectives.

A later dispatch says: The man arrested by the police this morning and erroneously described as "Leather Apron" was able to satisfy the authorities of Bethnal-green Station of his identity and of his absolute innocence of anything connected with the Spitalfields tragedy. Consequently he was immediately discharged. The police, however, attach far more importance to the arrest which has been made at Gravesend, but will not express an opinion until witnesses who have been sent for have seen him.

Reports are constantly arriving at head-quarters of men whose descriptions resemble that of the supposed murderer being arrested. At noon there were no fewer than seven persons in custody in different parts of the East-end on suspicion. The police at the various centres have, however, received strict instructions from Scotland-yard not to communicate details to the press. Several of those detained have been released.

—

## AN ARREST AT GRAVESEND.

A correspondent telegraphs this morning that a man has been arrested at Gravesend in connection with the murder. Between eight and nine o'clock last night Superintendent Berry, of Gravesend, had a communication made to him that there was a suspicious-looking individual at the Pope's Head Public-house, West-street, and at once despatched a sergeant to the house, and the man was arrested, and taken to the police station. It was noticed that one of his hands was bad, and on examining it the superintendent said it had evidently been bitten. When asked how he accounted for his hand being in this condition, the man said he was

## GOING DOWN BRICK-LANE, WHITECHAPEL,

at half-past four o'clock on Saturday morning last, and a woman fell down in a fit. He stooped to pick her up, when she bit him. He then hit her, and as two policemen came up he ran away. Having examined the man's clothing very carefully, Dr. Whitcombe, the police-surgeon, was sent for, and the doctor discovered blood spots on two shirts, which the man was carrying in a bundle. The doctor also expressed an opinion that blood had been wiped from off his boots. After being cautioned the man is alleged to have stated that the woman who bit him was at the back of a lodging-house at the time. He also said that on Thursday night he slept

## AT A LODGING-HOUSE IN OSBORNE-STREET,

Whitechapel; but that on Friday he was walking about Whitechapel all night, and that he came from London to Gravesend by road yesterday.

This morning he states that his name is William Henry Piggott, and that he is 52 years of age. He further said that some years ago he lived at Gravesend, his father having at one time held a position there connected with a friendly society. The man appears to be in a very nervous state. Detective-Sergeant Abberline has arrived at Gravesend from Scotland-yard.

Pigott was brought up this morning to London-bridge by the eighteen minutes past ten train, in charge of Detective Abberline, who was met at the station by Detective Stacy from Scotland-yard. The prisoner was not handcuffed, and was smoking a clay pipe and carrying a white cloth bundle. He passed quickly out of the station, no one among the public apparently noticing him, and was driven in a four-wheeled cab to the police-station in Commercial-street. He has not yet been charged.

The prisoner stands barely 5ft. high. He has a long dark beard, and he wears dark clothes. He is without a waistcoat, and there are several bloodstains on his clothes. Apparently he has been drinking heavily, his condition indicating a recent recovery from delirium tremens. He still maintains that his hand was bitten by a woman whom he knocked down. The prisoner is now locked up in the cells awaiting the arrival of witnesses with a view to identification.

—

## THE INQUEST.

This morning at the Working Lads' Institute, Whitechapel, Coroner Baxter opened the inquest on the mutilated body of Annie Chapman, alias Sivvy, the woman who was found murdered in the backyard of 29, Hanbury-street, Spitalfields, on Saturday morning.

A more commodious room than that in which the grim inquiry was held could not be desired, ample space being left after the jury had been arranged on the coroner's left. Very few of the general public were admitted,

# Monday, 10 September, 1888

however, but during the proceedings knots of gossips stood in front of the Home discussing the repulsive details of the series of crimes of which this is the latest. Inspector Helson, of the Criminal Investigation Department, watched the proceedings on behalf of the police, and Coroner Baxter had associated with him Mr. Collyer, his deputy. There was only one Jew on the jury, a rather curious circumstance considering to what extent Hebrews compose the local population.

That unpleasant necessity, the viewing of the body, having been duly performed by the jury,

**JOHN DAVIES,**

of 29, Hanbury-street, was called.

He said:—I am a carman, and I have lived at 29, Hanbury-street, for a fortnight, occupying one room at the top of the house with my wife and three sons. My window was closed during the night. I was awake from three to five on Saturday morning, but fell off to sleep at five till a quarter to six. Then I got up, had a cup of tea, and went downstairs to the backyard. The yard door was shut, but I do not know whether it was latched, for I was too upset at what I saw to remember. The yard is a large one, separated from the yards on both sides by close wooden fences about 5ft. 6in. in height.

The Coroner: I hope the police will have a plan ready for me by the next time. I may say that in the country the police always used to give me a little plan in cases of any importance at all, and certainly this is of sufficient importance to warrant the taking of that trouble.

One of the inspectors present informed the Coroner that a plan would be ready by the time to which the inquest was adjourned.

Witness, proceeding, said:—Directly I opened the back door leading into the yard I saw a woman lying near the fence. She was lying flat on her back, with her clothes up above her knees. I ran back along the passage to the front door, and

**CALLED TWO MEN,**

whose names I don't know, but whom I know by sight.

The Coroner: Have the names of those men been ascertained?

Inspector Chandler: I have made inquiries, but I cannot find the men.

The Coroner: They must be found.

Witness:—They work at Bailey's, the packing-case maker's, but I could not find them on Saturday as I had my work to do.

The Coroner: Your work is of no consequence compared with this inquiry.

Witness:—I am giving all the information I can.

The Coroner: You must find these men, either by the assistance of the police or my officer. Now, did these men come when called?

Witness:—Yes, sir; they came, and then we all went and fetched the police. I informed the inspector at the Commercial-street station, and he sent some constables.

Had you ever seen the woman before?

—No, sir.

Were you the first down that day, as far as you know?

—No; because a man named Thompson had to get up to go to work at about half-past three, but I don't suppose he went into the yard.

Have you ever seen women in that yard who don't belong to the house?

—Mrs. Richardson says that women do go there, but I have never seen any, having only been there a fortnight.

Did you hear any noise this Saturday morning before you saw the body lying in the yard.?

—No, sir.

**AMELIA PALMER,**

of 30, Dorset-street, the common lodging-house in which the deceased frequently slept, said:—I am a married woman, but my husband, who was formerly a soldier and then a dock labourer, had an accident, and so I go out to do work for the Jews, washing, charing,[39] & c. I knew the deceased well, and have done for quite five years. I have seen the body, and am quite sure it is the body of Annie Chapman. She was the widow of Frederick Chapman, who was a veterinary surgeon at Windsor, and who died about 18 months ago.

Deceased had lived apart from him for the last four years. She was without any settled home, and lived chiefly in the common lodging-houses of the East-end. Two years ago she lived at 30, Dorset-street, with a man who made wire sieves, and at that time she was

---

[39] **Char/Charwoman/Char Woman.** Cleaning woman. (Census1891.com)

66

receiving 10s. a week from her husband. I do not know the sievemaker's name (proceeded the witness), but I know him well by sight. I saw him last about eighteen months ago, when he had left deceased.

I saw the deceased several times last week. Last Monday she had a bruise on one of her temples and also a bruise on her chest, both of which, she said, had been caused by a woman who was acquainted with a man known as "Harry the hawker." Deceased added that she was with a man named Ted Stanley, a very respectable man, and she went into a public-house in which "Harry the hawker" was present in a drunken state. She prevented the woman with Harry the hawker from besting him of a florin, and that caused the ill feeling which led to the fight. The next time I met deceased she said she did not feel well, so she should go into the casual ward and try and pull round. I gave her 2d. to get a cup of tea, telling her not to get any rum, as I had frequently seen her

### THE WORSE FOR LIQUOR.

I am afraid deceased used to earn her living partly on the streets. She was a very straightforward woman when she was sober, clever and industrious with her needle; but she could not take much drink without getting intoxicated. She had been living a very irregular life all the time I've known her.

The Coroner here perused a letter handed to him by the police. It was a communication from the Windsor police, and the Coroner's remark to the jury after reading it was that it appeared to be very doubtful whether deceased's husband was not a coachman instead of a veterinary surgeon as had been stated.

### TIMOTHY DONOVAN,

of 35, Dorset-street, Spitalfields, the deputy of the lodging-house there, said:—Deceased has lodged at my place for the last four months, but was not there last week. She said she had been in the infirmary. On Friday she asked me not to let her bed, because, although she did not then have the money, she would get it. That was the last I saw of her till I identified her body.

The Coroner: Was she the worse for drink when you saw her last?

—Well, she had had enough, sir, and I remarked to her that it was rather remarkablethat she could find money for beer and not for her bed.

**THE SCENE OF THE MURDER.**
1. Passage to street.
2. Cellar.
3. Where the body lay.

Did you see her with any man that night? —No, sir.

She was going to get money, so where do you think was going to get it?

—I could not say. She used to come and stay at the lodging-house with a man whose name I do not know, but who was said to be a pensioner. He had a soldier-like appearance. She has come at other times with other men, but I have refused her.

The Coroner: You only allow the women at your lodging-house to have one husband then?

—Well, her husband told me not to let the bed to her if she had any other man with her. As a rule she occupied a double bed by herself.

The Coroner: Is anything known of this pensioner by the police?

An Inspector: No, sir.

Witness:—Sometimes he was dressed like a dock labourer, while at other times he was gentlemanly attired. I do not know his Christian name. He was rather dark, and she used to meet him always at the top of the street, I believe.

Do you know anything more about deceased?

—No, except that she was on very good terms with the other lodgers, and we never had any trouble with her. During last week she had a black eye, but she did not say how she got it. All she said was, "Tim, this is lovely, ain't it?"

## JOHN EVANS,

the watchman at 35, Dorset-street, said deceased was the worse for drink when she went away on Friday night to get money for her lodging. Witness knew she was on the streets, but knew of no man with whom she associated except the pensioner. After the body had been found the pensioner called to know if it was true that she was dead, and on being answered in the affirmative, he went straight off, without saying a word.

By the jury: Have you ever heard any one threaten deceased, or heard her express any fear of any one?

—No, sir.

The inquest was then adjourned till Wednesday.

—

There are two general clues to the murderer at the present time. The first deals with the famous, or infamous "Leather Apron," whose name is on everybody's lips in the Whitechapel district.

The case against "Leather Apron," briefly summed up, is as follows:—That the murders are evidently the work of a maniac, and this man is quite crazy enough to fall within that class. His beastly brutality, manifested in his attacks on Whitechapel street-walkers are quite in keeping with the late fiendish deeds. He disappeared from his accustomed haunts just about the time of the George-yard murder, has not been in any of the lodging-houses in which he has slept for years, and since that murder has been seen only once or twice in a district in which he is known by sight to many.

Furthermore a man exactly answering his description was found one night sleeping on the steps in the very house and in the very passage through which the victim of Saturday was led to her death. Jews who are driven to sleep in passage ways are not common even in White-chapel, and there is little question that the party with the Hebrew face who was found asleep in

the passage at 29, Hanbury-street, was the redoubtable "Leather Apron."

## THE OTHER CLUE

is that of the man who went into the Prince Albert public-house with bloody hands, a torn shirt, and a bloodstreak on his neck. Mrs. Chappell, who saw the man along with Mrs. Fiddymont, was a customer, not friend of the latter, and the two stories of the man, which were independent of each other, agreed perfectly. Mrs. Fiddymont yesterday added to her previous statement the fact that the back of the man's head was grimy, as if it had been bloody, and had been dampened or spit upon in the endeavour to rub the blood off instead of washing it. The dried blood between the fingers was thus clear, though the back of the hand held only three or four small distinct spots. The man did not look in the least like a butcher, and no theory born of his appearance could account for his bloody hands at seven a.m.

Joseph Taylor also had some facts to add to his account of Saturday. Mr. Taylor is a cautious and entirely reliable man, and freely told all he knew to two detectives on Saturday. He says that as he entered the public-house Mrs. Fiddymont said that a man had just left whom she would like to give in charge on suspicion of the murder. Taylor went out a moment later without any particular intention of

## FOLLOWING THE MAN,

whom Mrs. Chappell pointed out to him. The man was going towards Bishopsgate, however, and, as this was Taylor's direction, he increased his pace.

"It was all I could do to overtake him," he said yesterday, "and I am not a bad walker my-self. The man walked very rapidly, how-ever, with a peculiar springy walk that I would recognise again. He carried himself very erect, like a horse soldier. He had a ginger-coloured moustache, longer than mine and curling a little at the ends. His shoulders were very square and his neck rather long. He was neither stout nor thin, and seemed between 30 and 40 years old. His face was medium in stoutness. There were faint hollows under the cheekbones.

One thing that impressed me was that the man

## SEEMED BEWILDERED.

He crossed Brushfield-street three times in going from the Prince Albert to the next street, which was Bishopsgate. He clearly did not know where he was going. When he reached Bishopsgate, he stood at the corner and looked up and down the street undecided. Then he made up his mind and started across Brushfield-street rapidly, and kept on down Bishopsgate towards Liverpool-street. I followed as far as Half-Moon street, where my work was, and watched him for some time from the corner, but he kept straight on.

I assure you that when I came alongside of him his look was enough to frighten any woman. His eyes were wild-looking and staring. He held his coat together at the chin with both hands, the collar being buttoned up, and everything about his appearance was exceedingly strange.

—

## DESCRIPTION OF A MAN "WANTED."

The series of murders which now even the police believe to be the work of one man, is engaging the attention of a large force of plain clothes detectives. At eight o'clock last night the Scotland-yard authorities circulated a description of a man who, they say, "entered the passage of the house, 29, Hanbury-street, at which the murder was committed with a prostitute, at two a.m., the 8th." They give his age as 37, height 5ft. 7in., and add that he is rather dark, had a beard and moustache; was dressed in a short dark jacket, dark vest and trousers, black scarf and black felt hat; and spoke with a foreign accent.

—

## FRESH FACTS ABOUT THE VICTIM.

Some more reliable particulars concerning the woman last murdered have been furnished by Amelia Farmer, who had occupied the next bed to her in a lodging-house in Dorset-street.

She says Annie Chapman was the wife of a veterinary surgeon at Windsor, had for a long time been separated from her husband by mutual agreement, and had been allowed 10s. a week by him for her maintenance. About 18 months ago the instalments ceased, because the husband died.

Farmer had been in the habit of writing letters for her friend. She could not remember the exact address of the mother or sister, but thought it was near the Brompton Hospital.

Last Monday Chapman had intimated her intention of communicating with her sister,

saying, "If I can get a pair of boots from my sister I shall go hop-picking." Another relative, a brother-in-law of the deceased, lived somewhere in or near Oxford-street.

For some time past the murdered woman had been living occasionally with a man named Ted Stanley, who had been in the militia, but was now working at some neighbouring brewery.

Ted Stanley was a good-tempered man, rather tall, about 5ft. 10in., fair, and of florid complexion. He was the last man in the world to have quarrelled with Chapman, nor would he have injured her in any way.

At the beginning of the week the deceased had been rather severely knocked about in the breast and face by another woman of the locality through jealousy in connection with Ted Stanley, and had been obliged to go to the casual ward or infirmary.

As a regular means of livelihood she had not been in the habit of frequenting the streets, but had made antimacassars[40] for sale. Sometimes she would buy flowers or matches with which to pick up a living.

## TWO BRASS RINGS.

Farmer was perfectly certain that on Friday night the murdered woman had worn three rings which were not genuine, but were imitations, otherwise she would not have troubled to go out and find money for her lodgings. It has been definitely ascertained that the woman did wear two rings at the time of her death. They were of brass. One was a wedding ring, and the other a keeper of fancy pattern. Both are missing, and the police are still searching for them. It was believed on Saturday night that an important clue had been obtained, a pawnbroker having detained rings of the same description which were offered in pledge, but investigation showed they were not the murdered woman's.

## THE TIME OF THE MURDER.

In order not to lose any evidence of value, the post-mortem examination was conducted without delay at the mortuary, to which the

---

[40] **Antimacassar.** Ornamental protective covering for the arm or back of a chair, sofa, etc. (Name derived from Macassar, a popular hair oil. These cloths protected the upholstery from oil stains.) (Morehead)

body had been removed by the police divisional surgeon, who, upon advice, reserves his description of the injuries until the inquest. It is, however, this gentleman's opinion, as communicated to his chiefs, that death had taken place some two or three hours prior to the first examination of the corpse, shortly after its discovery.

If that view of the medical aspect of the case be correctly stated, the time of the murder must have been earlier than four in the morning. Not a sound was heard to fix the time by. On Saturday the sun rose at twenty-three minutes past five; for half an hour previously the light would be such as to render it difficult for anyone to distinguish even near objects.

At a quarter before five o'clock John Richardson, son of the landlady, of 29, Hanbury-street, as usual, went to his mother's to see if everything was right in the back yard. Richardson sat down on the steps to cut a piece of leather from his boot. The door would then partially hide the corner between the house and the fence. This man is quite clear that he saw nothing to attract his attention before he left.

About twenty-five minutes past five Albert Cadosch, living at No. 31, the next house on the left-hand side, entered the yard adjoining that of No. 29. He states that he heard some talking on the other side of the palings, and he distinguished the word "No." There was then, he fancied, a slight scuffle, with the noise of something falling, but he took no notice, thinking that it was from his neighbours.

It was half an hour later, at six o'clock, that John Davis, before going to his work, walked along the passage into the yard, and made the horrifying discovery of the mutilated body.

There are several reports of deceased having been seen in the company of a man early on Saturday morning, but little reliance is placed upon them. In one case, a man employed at a public-house, who gave information, failed to identify the deceased as the woman he believed to have been called out of the place at five a.m. by a man in a skull cap.

## TELL-TALE BRUISES.

Although, of course, the exact details of the post mortem have not been made public, it is known that Dr. Phillips was unable to find any trace of alcohol in the stomach of the deceased,

thus disproving many reports that when the woman was last seen alive she was the worse for drink. On the right side of the head was a large bruise, showing that the deceased woman must have been dealt a heavy blow at that spot. There were also other bruises about the face, and finger-marks were discernible. The latter indicate that the murderer must first have grasped his victim by the throat, probably in order to prevent her crying out.

From the third finger of the left hand rings, it was seen, had been wrenched off, and the hands and arms were much bruised. Deceased wore lace-up boots and striped stockings, two cotton petticoats, and was otherwise res-pectably, though poorly dressed. In the pockets there were a handkerchief, two small combs, and an envelope with the seal of the Sussex Regiment. There were also found two farthings polished brightly, and, according to some, these coins had been passed off as half-sovereigns upon the deceased by her murderer.

## BRIGHT FARTHINGS AND BRASS MEDALS.

With regard to the bright farthings, a woman has stated that a man accosted her on Saturday morning and gave her two "half-sovereigns," but that, when he became violent, she screamed and he ran off. She discovered afterwards that the "half-sovereigns" were two brass medals.

It is said that this woman did accompany the man, who seemed as if he would kill her, to a house in Hanbury-street, possibly No. 29, at half-past two a.m. This woman, Emily Walter, a lodger in one of the common lodging-houses of Spitalfields, was asked to describe the man, but her description of him was not considered clear. Still the police determined to follow up the matter, more particularly because the woman states that the man seemed ready to kill her.

The woman's description did not answer the description of the man "Leather Apron," for whom they have been searching in connection with the murder of Mary Ann Nicholls.

~

# Monday, 10 September, 1888

## 𝕰𝖛𝖊𝖓𝖎𝖓𝖌 𝕹𝖊𝖜𝖘
## THE WHITECHAPEL HORRORS.

The series of atrocious murders in the East-end of London is a fresh and terrible reminder of the capacity of humanity for evil, and of the facilities which our congested centres of population offer to the commission of the wildest crimes. In ordinary cases the ordinary methods of detection suffice, or approximately suffice, to unearth the authors of crime. When cupidity or revenge actuate the murderer some expression of feeling or some exhibition of stolen goods give the police a clue by which to disentangle the skein of motives and to lead to the individual upon whom they worked. In the problem now presented to Londoners the common data of guidance are lacking. Revenge against the class of street-walkers does not appear a sufficient incentive, and cupidity of any intense nature can scarcely be gratified with the spoils of a woman whose purse prevents her from obtaining the squalid shelter of a Whitechapel lodging-house.

It is clear that inquiry into the extraordinary must not be controlled by the ordinary. Search for the criminal or criminals who have perpetrated the demoniacal outrages now afflicting the public mind must take unusual lines. The police believe, we are told, that some madman at large is the murderer of the four women who have recently been hacked into death in the very thickest centre of our population. It may be so; there are many indications to justify the assumption. Yet, with probability on that side, we must not allow ourselves to be rashly dominated by a theory however simple it seems.

There is a contagion in murder as there is in suicide, and every student of psychology knows how some strange and impressive self-immolation draws behind it a train of imitative crimes. A man hangs himself at Peckham, and boys emulate the action on the lamp-posts of Camberwell. It is, therefore, within the range of possibility that the first morbid genius of Whitechapel has his methods adopted and his schemes worked out by another or other less imaginative followers. A trust in the not too utter depravity of human nature would induce us, however, to accept temporarily the theory that one monster only is responsible for the horrors with which London is now surfeited. It behoves every man, then, to consider in what direction discovery of the savage is to be attained, and we believe that a consideration of some medical and physiological facts relating to the ways of demented persons might not be altogether futile.

The broad data are these: 1st. Women of a certain unfortunate class are the victims; 2nd. The character of the crimes is maintained throughout; 3rd. The operator shows considerable facility in the use of the weapon.

He makes his war only against the class euphemistically denominated unfortunate. We are here confronted with the possibility of monomania, directed for one reason or another against street-walkers. The kind of journalism which has recently been popularised in London by a certain newspaper has tended to concentrate on the sexual relations an utterly unhealthy attention which cannot have failed to have its aberrant effect on badly balanced minds. A man so constituted as to be capable of imagining that humanity, however unwillingly, would benefit by his purificative efforts may as well feel compelled to exercise his calling in Brick-lane as in Northumberland-street. On the other hand, the man may, instead of a fully developed monomaniac,[41] be a mere epileptic subject, in whom every sexual consideration arouses homicidal impulses.

Although medical jurisprudence tells of no cases analogous to those which have now shocked humanity, it is a well known fact to students of insanity that epilepsy is often induced by amatory desires of an inordinate nature. During the epileptic seizure the whole nervous system is thrown out of gear as our telegraphic apparatus is disordered in a thunderstorm, and the subject becomes not only irresponsible for his acts, but practically unconscious of them. The fit, which is usually a series of convulsions, may be replaced by an impulse towards murder or suicide which springs involuntarily into the mind, and is irresistible. Neither in the case of the woman Nichols nor in the more recent and even more painful case is there any medical statement to indicate whether the pretended purpose of the murderer's

---

[41] **Monomania**. Psychosis on a single subject or class of subjects. (Miller)

interview with his victims had reached a consummation; but this is not absolutely necessary to account for the nerve-storm which deranges the faculties. It is therefore possible that the murderer is an epileptic.

In the second place, the character of the crime, while it points, though not indubitably, to one man, is consistent with the supposition that he is dominated by one idea, and therefore a monomaniac; or that he is epileptic, and that the direction of his recurrent fits of madness is continuous.

The last consideration that seems to suggest a clue is the facility with which the murderer uses his weapon. Few men habitually carry with them knives capable of inflicting the wounds these unhappy women bear. If a man un-accustomed to the possession of a large and exceedingly sharp knife did take to wearing one on his person there are many chances that it would be discovered by somebody acquainted with him or thrown into his company. He might even, coward as we might assume him to be, so overcome his timidity as to exhibit it and procure his apprehension. Such a man, how-ever, would scarcely have the skill to employ the knife in the scientific manner of the Whitechapel murderer.

From these considerations we should deduce the belief that the murderer is accustomed to wear a great knife and that he is expert in its use. Even murderers of the wholesale kind of the East-end one do not obtain all their experience in the cutting of human flesh, so that on this point the police may be able to found some intelligible theory which might put them on the right path.

In what seems to be the methods likely to be crowned with success it is not the part of a journalist to instruct the men trained in the discovery of criminals, but we certainly do no harm in suggesting that an inquiry as to the epileptic patients in Whitechapel and Spital-fields might afford more fruitful results than are to be attained by a mere wandering up and down streets, and asking householders whether they have heard unwonted noises.

There are other aspects of the case besides the medical ones which are not altogether pleasant; and here we cannot help entering a word of protest against the morbid excitability which leads people to pay and receive money,

for the privilege of seeing the spot where a dead body was first observed. Another thing which our fellow-citizens in the East-end must guard against is ignorant incitement of racial feeling.

There is absolutely no reason for blaming the Hebrews of the East-end because murders have been committed in a place where they abound. In Russia and some parts of Austria many crimes are charged against the Jewish people, but in England we ought to have passed beyond that stage. In the time of Henry II, Jews were sometimes killed by the hundred in the streets of London for their imaginary sins;[42] but that, as well as the burning of Christian heretics, has gone like a bad dream. Let the mental attitudes not be resumed. It is not more probable that a Jew, rather than a Christian, is the maniac, and the dwellers in the East would do well to suspend their suspicions until there are some grounds for them.

———

The police are coming in for some severe criticism over those horrible murders in Whitechapel, the prevalent opinion in the locality being that, in spite of three of these atrocities having been committed, no extra precautions were taken by Sir Charles Warren to have the neighbourhood watched.

On Saturday morning the police were as completely at sea when the fourth murder was discovered as they were on the first occasion, and the natural feeling among the dwellers in Whitechapel and Spitalfields is one of extreme alarm, almost amounting to panic. Some of these people, however, appear to be unpleasantly cynical in the midst of their fright.

———

A group of working-men were discussing the details of the hideous crime when one of their number not unnaturally remarked, "But I want to know what the police is about?" This was met with the sneering observation of a companion, "Well, you must be a fool to ask a question of that sort. Why, the perlice is too

---

[42] For an in-depth study of Jewish ritual human sacrifice during the Middle Ages see the website for Blood Passover: The Jews of Europe and Ritual Murder. The author, Dr. Ariel Toaff, is the son of the former Chief Rabbi of Rome and professor of Jewish Renaissance and Medieval History at Tel Aviv University. http://bloodpassover.com

busy looking arter the changing of bus hosses in the West-end, and a-watchin' o' Trafalgar Square, to care what becomes of poor devils like us." The murmurs of approval which greeted this homely satire showed that the feeling towards the guardians of the peace is one of distrust, which it is to be hoped will be removed by the discovery of the inhuman assassin who has made life a terror in the East-end.

—

## SECOND FIFTH.
## THE WHITECHAPEL HORROR.
## CAPTURE OF "LEATHER APRON."
## INTERVIEW WITH THE STEPMOTHER & SISTER-IN-LAW OF THE ALLEGED "LEATHER APRON."
## A MAN ARRESTED AT GRAVESEND.
## FULL DETAILS.
## INQUEST ON THE VICTIM.
## SPECIAL REPORT.

This forenoon Mulberry-street, a little alley off Commercial-road, is in a state of great excitement; everybody is at his street door, and crowds of men and women are excitedly discussing the latest development of the case. The dwellings in Mulberry-street are not of a high order, and the house No. 22 in which the person called "Leather Apron" was captured is a little two-storey erection of white bricks, in no way different from the others, and is let out in small rooms as lodgings.

On knocking at the door our reporter was admitted by a lady of tawny colour, and of distinctively Hebrew race. She had a great objection to the answering of queries, a diffidence which he understood when he learned that she was the stepmother of the person apprehended.

### THE STEPMOTHER'S STORY.

The captured man, John Piser, is my stepson. He is a Jew, but I don't know where he was born. I'm sure he was born in England, but I came here too late to know. He is 35 or 36 years of age, and is a boot finisher by trade. He has lived here since Thursday. He is unmarried, and a very simple man. He was never very bright here (touching her forehead), but he could not do such things as spoken about. I never ask him where he has been when he comes in. Though he does not live here constantly the door is always opened to him when he comes. He has been here since Thursday.

### THE SISTER-IN-LAW'S STORY.

Mrs. Piser, jun., is a pleasant woman of about 30, speaking English with more fluency than the older lady. She also naturally did not wish to speak much on the subject, but made the following statement to our reporter:

My brother is not the man to commit a murder. He is an easy-going man. Why I trust him with all my children here. He has been ill, and was treated at some hospital. I don't know which it was, but they afterwards sent him to a convalescent home. He has only come back here since the end of the Jewish holidays. I know nothing about the affair except that a policeman came here this morning and asked for my brother-in-law. When he was brought the policeman said, "I want you, sir," and Piser answered, "What do you want me for?" The policeman said, "I want you for the murder of a woman in Hanbury-street," and Piser went with him without saying anything. As for the name of Leather Apron, I never heard it before. Piser, of course, had a leather apron. He worked some time for my father, Mr. Nathan.

—

The Press Association says: About nine o'clock this morning a detective arrested the man known as "Leather Apron," who was wanted in connection with the Whitechapel murder, at 22, Mulberry-street, Commercial-road.

The real name of the man arrested is John Piser, but his friends deny that he has ever been known by the nick-name of "Leather Apron."

When the detective called at the house the door was opened by Piser himself. "Just the man I want," said the detective, who charged him on suspicion of being connected with the murder of the woman Sievey.

The detective searched the house, and took away some finishing tools which Piser is in the habit of using in his work. By trade he is a boot-finisher, and for some time has been living at Mulberry-street with his step-mother (Mrs. Piser) and a married brother who works as a cabinet-maker.

When he was arrested by the detective, this morning, his brother was at work and the only inmates of the house were the prisoner's step-mother, his sister-in-law, and a Mr. Nathan for whom he has worked. His mother and his sister-in-law declare positively that Piser came home at half-past ten on Thursday night, and has not left the house since. They further state that Piser is unable to do much work on account of ill health, and that he is by no means a strong person, as some time ago he was seriously injured in a vital part. About six weeks ago he left a convalescent home, of which he had been an inmate on account of a carbuncle in his back.

He is about 35 years of age, and since he was three years old has been brought up by Mrs. Piser. He lost his father some 16 years ago. At Leman-street Police-station, to which station Piser was taken, a large force of police was kept in readiness with drawn staves. Only a few people amongst the crowd outside seemed aware that an arrest had been made, and so quietly did the police act in Mulberry-street that few, even in that neighbourhood, connected the arrest with the murder.

The police at Leman-street refuse to give any information, and some officials who have come from Scotland-yard denied that such an arrest had been made, but this statement was, of course, incorrect, seeing that the arrest is admitted by the prisoner's relatives. The prisoner is a Jew.

The excitement in Whitechapel on it becoming known that a man alleged to be "Leather Apron" had been arrested was intense. The police-station was surrounded by a numerous crowd, and all over the neighbourhood the one topic of conversation was that "Leather Apron" was caught. The police, however, refuse to give any details about the matter.

The man apparently has not yet been definitely charged with any offence, but is detained on suspicion. Detective Thicke, who arrested Piser (the alleged "Leather Apron"), in company with another officer, visited the house, 22, Mulberry-street, where the prisoner was found, after he had been removed to the station. They proceeded to closely question the man's relatives and friends in the house as to his antecedents and whereabouts during the last few weeks.

Interviews with several residents in Mulberry-street, which is a narrow thoroughfare off Commercial-road East, ellicit the information that they all give the man who has been arrested a good character, and speak of him as being a harmless sort of person. A young woman residing next door said she had known Piser as a next-door neighbour for many years, and had never heard of his bearing the name of "Leather Apron." He had always seemed a quiet man and unlikely to do such a crime as that of which the police suspect him. She says she heard him about the yard a day or two back, but had not seen him in the street the last few days.

Whitechapel literally swarms with policemen and detectives to-day. Some of them brought in a powerful man to Leman-street soon after twelve o'clock. A large crowd followed, and it was rumoured that his arrest had something to do with the recent tragedies. As to this the police were quite reticent, and all that could be ascertained was that the man was apparently in drink, and strongly resented his detention by the police.

## WHAT DETECTIVE THICKE SAYS.

A representative of *The Evening News* had a brief interview with Detective-Sergeant Thicke at noon to-day, and was informed by that officer that when he captured "Leather Apron" the accused turned pale and trembled, but made no resistance to his capture. Sergeant Thicke and Inspector Helston are now busily engaged in procuring all the evidence they can as regards the recent movements of the accused man.

## ANOTHER ARREST.

A correspondent telegraphs this morning that a man has been arrested at Gravesend in connection with the murder. Between eight and nine o'clock last night Superintendent Berry, of Gravesend, had a communication made to him that there was a suspicious looking individual at the Pope's Head public-house, West-street, and at once despatched a sergeant to the house, and the man was arrested and taken to the police-station.

It was noticed that one of his hands was bad, and on examining it, the superintendent said it had evidently been bitten. When asked how he accounted for his hand being in this condition, the man said he was going down Brick-lane, Whitechapel, at half-past four o'clock on Saturday morning last, and a woman fell down in a fit. He stooped to pick her up when she bit him. He then hit her, and as two policemen came up he ran away.

Having examined the man's clothing very carefully, Dr. Whitcombe, the police surgeon, was sent for, and the doctor discovered blood spots on two shirts which the man was carrying in a bundle. The doctor also expressed an opinion that blood had been wiped from off his boots.

After being cautioned, the man is alleged to have stated that the woman who bit him was at the back of a lodging-house at the time. He also said that on Thursday night he slept at a lodging-house in Osborne-street, Whitechapel, but that on Friday he was walking about Whitechapel all night, and that he came from London to Gravesend by road, yesterday.

This morning he states that his name is William Henry Pigott, and that he is 52 years of age. He further said that some years ago he lived at Gravesend, his father having at one time held a position there connected with a friendly society. The man appears to be in a very nervous state.

Detective-inspector Abberline has arrived at Gravesend from Scotland-yard.

## LATER.

The statement made by the man Pigott, who has been arrested at Gravesend, on suspicion of being the Whitechapel murderer, is considered to be of such a character as to warrant Detective-inspector Abberline conveying the man to London by the 11.13 train on the South Eastern Railway. He will be formally charged before the magistrates at Worship-street, to-day, with the murder.

The Central News says: Detective-inspector Abberline arrived at Commercial-street Police-station at a quarter to one this afternoon, in a four-wheeled cab, having in his custody William Henry Pigott, the man arrested at Gravesend on suspicion of being concerned in the murder at the Spitalfields.

The prisoner stands barely 5ft. high. He has a long, dark beard, and he wears dark clothes. He is without a waistcoat, and there are several bloodstains on his clothes.

Apparently he has been drinking heavily, his condition indicating a recent recovery from delirium tremens. He still maintains that his hand was bitten by a woman whom he knocked down.

The prisoner is now locked up in the cells awaiting the arrival of witnesses with a view to identification.

## SEVEN MORE ARRESTS.

The Press Association, telegraphing at noon, says Reports are constantly arriving at head-quarters of men whose description resembles that of the supposed murderer being arrested. At present no fewer than seven persons are in custody, in different parts of the East-end, on suspicion. The police at the various centres had, however, received strict instructions from Scotland-yard not to communicate details to the Press, and it has not yet transpired whether either of the arrests is likely to lead to the identification of the culprit.

The Press Association has been informed that in more than one case a brief investigation has proved that the person suspected could have no connection with the outrage, and has accordingly immediately been released.

## RETICENCE OF THE POLICE.

As a strongly-marked feature of the hue and cry after the murderer, we feel bound to mention the almost insuperable difficulty there is in obtaining any information from the police. For instance, one of our representatives inquiring at the Commercial-street Police-station at half-past twelve, to-day, as to the arrest of "Leather Apron," he was informed by the inspector on duty that no official information of the capture had reached the station up to that hour.

—

## INQUEST THIS DAY.

The inquest on the body of the unfortunate woman, Annie Chapman, otherwise known as Annie Sievey, who was so brutally murdered and mutilated in Hanbury-street, on Saturday morning, was opened this morning at the Working Lads' Institute, Whitechapel-road, before Mr. Wynne Baxter. The inquiry was held in the same room as that upon the body of Mary Ann Nichols only a week previously.

Very few members of the general public were present, the great bulk of those in the room being jurymen, of whom 18 were sworn, and representatives of the Press. But this was not due to lack of public interest in the inquiry so much as to the rigour with which the attendants excluded all people who would not give a good reason for being admitted.

# Monday, 10 September, 1888

After being sworn in, the jury viewed the body, which was lying in the mortuary in the same shell as had contained the body of Mrs. Nichols. It was laid out in a white shroud, and all traces of the terrible mutilations that had been inflicted were carefully concealed. The jury also inspected the clothing worn by the deceased when her body was found.

Inspectors Helson and Chandler appeared on behalf of the police.

The first witness called, was John Davies, the carman, who first found the body. He is a man apparently about 60 years of age, with a slightly humped back. He said:—I have lived at 29, Hanbury-street for about a fortnight, and am a carman for Mr. Wisdom, of Leadenhall-market. I occupy the top room in front. I have a wife and three sons, and they all occupy the same room as myself. It is a large room. On Friday night I went to bed about eight o'clock, and my wife followed me in about half an hour. My sons came to bed at different times, the last one at about a quarter to eleven. The window of the room is a large one, and it was closed. I was awake from three a.m. to five a.m. on Saturday morning, and then fell asleep again for about half an hour. I am confident about the time, as I looked at the clock. I heard the quarter to six bell at Spitalfields Church and got up and had a cup of tea which my missus made. I then went downstairs to the back-yard. The house faces in Hanbury-street, where there is a window on the ground floor, and next to it is the front door leading into a passage which runs right through into the yard, where there is a door.

The Coroner:—Are either of these doors ever locked?

Witness:—Sometimes they are wide open.

(The Coroner:)—Have you ever found them locked?

(John Davies)—No.

(The Coroner:)—Neither of the doors is ever locked?

(John Davies)—No. I do not think I ever saw a lock or bolt on the doors since I have been there.

(The Coroner:)—Can any one who knows that there is a latch to the door open it, and go through the passage into the yard?

(John Davies)—Yes.

(The Coroner:)—When you went into the yard did you notice whether the back door was shut?

(John Davies)—It was shut, but I cannot say whether it was latched.

(The Coroner:)—Was the front door open?

(John Davies)—Yes, it was wide open.

(The Coroner:)—Did you go into the back yard?

(John Davies)—No; I stopped on the steps.

(The Coroner:)—What size is the yard?

(John Davies)—It is a largish yard, but I cannot say its size. Facing you on the opposite side of the yard, as you stand on the steps, is a shed in which Mrs. Richardson keeps her wood. The yard is separated on both sides from the neighbouring yards by a close fence about 5ft. 6in. high.

The Coroner:—I trust the police will supply me with a plan before the next occasion.

Witness continuing.—Between the steps and fence on the left hand side is a fence about three feet wide. The yard is lower than the passage.

(The Coroner:)—What did you see?

(John Davies)—I saw a woman lying down, directly I got to the yard. She was between the stone steps and the fence.

(The Coroner:)—Did you stay to examine her?

(John Davies)—No.

(The Coroner:)—Where was her head?

(John Davies)—She was laid flat on her back, with her head towards the house and her legs towards the wood shed. Her clothes were up to her groin.

(The Coroner:)—Did you touch her?

(John Davies)—No; I did not go into yard.

(The Coroner:)—What did you do?

(John Davies)—Do? As soon as I saw that I went to the front door, and there saw two men who work at Mr. Bailey's, packing case maker, in Hanbury-street. I do not know their names, although I know them by sight.

The Coroner (to Inspector Chandler):—Do you know those men have not been seen?

Inspector Chandler:—They have not yet been found.

The Coroner (to witness):—You must find them, either with the assistance of the police, or of my officer if the police cannot do it.

Witness:—I have to attend to my work.

The Coroner:—Your work is not of the slightest importance compared with this inquiry.

Witness:—Bailey's place is about three doors from my lodging, and the two men were waiting outside there before commencing work. They came in, saw the sight, did not go into the yard, but ran away to see if they could find a policeman. I went away at the same time to the Commercial-road police-station to give information. I did not inform anyone in the house what I had discovered. The inspector sent off some constables whilst I remained at the station. I afterwards returned to the house and saw the constables there. I had never seen the woman before.

(The Coroner:)—Have you ever seen any women in the passage who do not belong to the house?

(John Davies)—Mrs. Richardson says they come sometimes, but I have never seen them.

(The Coroner:)—Did you hear any noise that Saturday morning?

(John Davies)—No.

(The Coroner:)—Were you the first to get up that morning?

(John Davies)—I do not think so. There is a porter who lodges there and who generally leaves home about half-past three.

At the conclusion of witness's evidence, he said he had lost a day's work, and wished to know who would pay for him.

The Coroner:—I am afraid you will lose a great many days before this inquiry is over. The Treasury may do something for you, but I cannot.

Amelia Palmer said:—I live at 30, Dorset-street, Spitalfields, at a common lodging-house. I have lived there for about four years. I have worked for the Jews generally since my husband, who was formerly a dock labourer, met with a severe accident at the beginning of the year. My husband has been a soldier, and has a pension of 8 1/2d. a day. I do not sew for the Jews, but go out charing for them.

(The Coroner:)—Do you know the deceased?

(Amelia Palmer)—Yes, sir; well.

(The Coroner:)—For how long?

(Amelia Palmer)—For quite five years, I should think.

(The Coroner:) You have seen the body?

(Amelia Palmer)—I saw it on Saturday at the mortuary.

(The Coroner:)—And you are quite sure whose body it is?

(Amelia Palmer)—I am quite sure it is the body of Annie Chapman.

(The Coroner:)—She was a widow?

(Amelia Palmer)—Yes. Her late husband was called Fred Chapman, and lived at Windsor. He was a veterinary surgeon. I did not know his address. He died about 18 months ago. Deceased had lived apart from him for four years or more.

(The Coroner:)—Where did she live?

(Amelia Palmer)—In various places, principally in common lodging-houses in the neighbourhood of Spitalfields.

(The Coroner:)—Has she lived at 30, Dorset-street?

(Amelia Palmer)—Yes; she lived there about two years ago with a man who made wire sieves, and at that time she was receiving 10s. a week from her husband. She always received it by post-office order, payable at Commercial-road. That payment stopped about 18 months ago. I met her about that time, and she said that her husband was dead. She said she had ascertained this fact from a brother or sister of her husband who lived in Oxford-street, Whitechapel. She was nicknamed Mrs. Sievey from her living with a sieve-maker.

(The Coroner:)—Do you know the sieve-maker's name?

(Amelia Palmer)—No, but I know him very well by sight, and last saw him about 18 months ago in the City. He then told me he had left Mrs. Chapman and was living in the neighbourhood of Notting Hill. He only lived with Mrs. Chapman two or three months. I saw deceased two or three times last week. I saw her on Monday, standing outside 35, Dorset-street, where she was living. She was without bonnet or shawl. She had a bruise on the right temple. I asked her how she got it, and he opened her dress and said, "Look at my chest." There was a bruise on it. She said, "You know the woman," and called her a name, which I do not remember. She made me understand that it was a woman who goes out selling books. Both this woman and the deceased were acquainted with a man called "Harry the Hawker." Deceased told me that on Saturday week she was with a man called Ted Stanley, a very respectable man, in a beer shop in Dorset-street. "Harry the Hawker" was also there, and was also under the influence of drink. "Harry the Hawker" put

# Monday, 10 September, 1888

down a two-shilling piece to pay for some drink, and the bookselling woman picked it up and put down a penny. There was ill-feeling in consequence, and the same evening the bookselling woman met deceased, and struck her in the face and chest. I saw deceased again on the following Tuesday near Spitalfields Church. She said she felt no better, and should go into the casual ward until she had pulled herself round. She said she had had nothing to eat. I gave her 2d., and advised her to get a cup of tea, and not to spend the money in rum.

(The Coroner:)—Have you ever seen her the worse for drink?

(Amelia Palmer)—Yes, many times.

(The Coroner:)—What did she do for a living?

(Amelia Palmer)—She used to make crochet work and antimacassars, and sell flowers.

(The Coroner:)—Is it correct to say that she used to get money on the streets?

(Amelia Palmer)—I cannot say. I am afraid she is not particular. She was out late at night at times. She has told me so. On Fridays she had to go to Stratford to sell lace, or flowers, or anything she had to sell. I saw her in Dorset-street on the Friday afternoon about five o'clock. She appeared perfectly sober. I said, "Ain't you going to Stratford to-day?" and she said, "I feel too ill to do anything." I left her, and returned to the same street about ten minutes afterwards, and found her standing in the same place. She said, "It is no use my giving way. I must pull myself together and get some money, or I shall have no lodgings." She said no more, and that is the last time I ever saw her alive or spoke to her. She told me she had been in the casual ward, but she did not say which one. She never said she had been refused in any ward.

(The Coroner:)—Do you consider her a drunken woman?

(Amelia Palmer)—She was a very civil and industrious woman when she was sober. I have often seen her the worse for drink. I do not think she could take much without its making her drunk. She's been living a very irregular life during the whole time I have known her, more especially since the death of her husband. I never knew her to have a settled home. She told me she had a sister and mother living in Brompton, but I do not think they were on friendly terms. I never knew her to stay with her relatives even for a night. When I saw her on Monday she said, "If my sister sends me the boots I will go hopping." She often appeared downhearted, especially about her boy and girl. The boy is in a charity school at Windsor. She was ordinarily a very respectable woman, and I never heard her make use of bad language.

(The Coroner:)—Do you know anyone who would be likely to injure her?

(Amelia Palmer)—No; I only know one man, Stanley, and I do not think he would hurt her.

Timothy Donovan said:—I live at 35, Dorset-street, Spitalfields. I am the deputy of the lodging-house there. I have seen the body, and identify it as that of Annie Chapman, who has lodged at my house for this last four months. She was not there last week till Friday, when she asked me to allow her down into the kitchen. This was about two o'clock in the afternoon. I let her go into the kitchen, and asked her where she had been all the week. She said she had been in the infirmary. I did not see her again until about half-past one on Saturday morning. At that time I was sitting in the office and saw her come in at the front door and go down into the kitchen. I sent the watchman's "missus" downstairs to ask her husband about the bed. Annie Sievey came upstairs and said, "I have not sufficient money for my bed. Don't let it. I shant be long before I am in. Her bed would be 8d. She was then eating potatoes, and after standing at the office windows for about three minutes, she went out saying, "Never mind, Tim; I shall soon be back; don't let it." This might have been 1.45 or 1.50 a.m. She then left the house, and the watchman saw her go down Paternoster-row, in the direction of Brushfield-street. I never saw her alive again.

(The Coroner:)—Was she the worse for drink?

(Timothy Donovan)—Well, she had had enough.

(The Coroner:)—Could she walk straight?

(Timothy Donovan)—As straight as I can.

(The Coroner:)—Was she often the worse for drink?

(Timothy Donovan)—Generally on Saturdays, but not other days.

(The Coroner:)—Did you consider her the worse for drink on this occasion?

(Timothy Donovan)—Yes, I passed the remark, "You can find money for beer when you cannot find money for your bed." She said she had only been at the top of the street at a beer-house called the "Ringers."

(The Coroner:)—Did you see her with any man that night?

(Timothy Donovan)—No, sir.

(The Coroner:)—Where did you think she was going to get money from?

(Timothy Donovan)—I cannot say.

(The Coroner:)—Did you know that she walked the streets?

(Timothy Donovan)—I do not know. She used to come to the lodging house on Saturdays with a man whose name I do not know. She said he was a pensioner, and he had a soldier-like appearance.

(The Coroner:)—Have you seen her with other men?

(Timothy Donovan)—She has come at other times with other men, and I refused her.

(The Coroner:)—You only allow each woman to have one husband at your house?

(Timothy Donovan)—Well, her husband told me not to let her have a bed with any other man but himself. She did not come with any man that night. I never saw her with a man that week. The last time the pensioner and deceased were together at the lodging-house was Sunday week, I do not know whether they left together. The man appeared to be about 40 or 45 years of age, and was 5ft. 6in. or 5ft. 8in. in height. Sometimes he was dressed like a dock labourer, and at other times he had a gentlemanly appearance. He was rather dark. I believe she always used to find him at the top of the street. She was always on good terms with the other lodgers, and I never had any trouble with her until the week before last, when she had a bit of a row with a woman in the kitchen before I was up. I afterwards saw the two women outside the house quarrelling. On Thursday, August 30, I noticed that deceased had a slight touch of a black eye, and she said, "Tim, this is lovely ain't it?" She did not say how she got it.

John Evans, watchman at 35, Dorset-street, deposed that he had identified the body of the deceased as a woman he had known as Annie Sievey from her coming to the lodging-house. He last saw her on Saturday morning last. She left at about a quarter to two, and witness followed her to the door and saw her go through Paternoster-row into Brushfield-street. She then turned to the right towards Spitalfields Church, and never returned. She was the worse for drink, but not badly so. She used to be out on the streets every night; but witness only knew of one man, the pensioner, who used to stay with her. He called at the lodging-house on Saturday about 2.30 p.m., and inquired about deceased. He had heard something about the death, and came down to see if it was true. Witness told him it was, and he then went straight away without saying a word. He had never heard any man threaten her.

The inquiry was then adjourned until two o'clock on Wednesday.

# Tuesday, 11 September, 1888

## The Times

### "The Whitechapel Murders"

Two arrests were made yesterday, but it is very doubtful whether the murderer is in the hands of the police. The members of the Criminal Investigation Department are assisting the divisional police at the East-end in their endeavours to elucidate the mystery in which these crimes are involved.

Yesterday morning Detective-sergeant Thicke, of the H Division, who has been indefatigable in his inquiries respecting the murder of Annie Chapman at 29, Hanbury-street, Spitalfields, on Saturday morning, succeeded in capturing a man whom he believed to be "Leather Apron."

It will be recollected that this person obtained an evil notoriety during the inquiries respecting this and the recent murders committed in Whitechapel, owing to the startling reports that had been freely circulated by many of the women living in the district as to outrages alleged to have been committed by him.

Sergeant Thicke, who has had much experience of the thieves and their haunts in this portion of the metropolis, has, since he has been engaged in the present inquiry, been repeatedly assured by some of the most well-known characters of their abhorrence of the fiend-ishness of the crime, and they have further stated that if they could only lay hands on the murderer they would hand him over to justice. These and other circumstances convinced the officer and those associated with him that the deed was in no way traceable to any of the regular thieves or desperadoes at the East-end.

At the same time a sharp look-out was kept on the common lodginghouses, not only in this district, but in other portions of the metropolis. Several persons bearing a resemblance to the description of the person in question have been arrested, but, being able to render a satisfactory account of themselves, were allowed to go away.

Shortly after 8 o'clock yesterday morning Sergeant Thicke, accompanied by two or three other officers, proceeded to 22, Mulberry-street and knocked at the door. It was opened by a Polish Jew named Pizer, supposed to be "Leather Apron." Thicke at once took hold of the man, saying, "You are just the man I want." He then charged Pizer with being concerned in the murder of the woman Chapman, and to this he made no reply. The accused man, who is a boot finisher by trade, was then handed over to other officers and the house was searched.

Thicke took possession of five sharp long-bladed knives—which, however, are used by men in Pizer's trade—and also several old hats. With reference to the latter, several women who stated they were acquainted with the prisoner, alleged he has been in the habit of wearing different hats. Pizer, who is about 33, was then quietly removed to the Leman-street Police-station, his friends protesting that he knew nothing of the affair, that he had not been out of the house since Thursday night, and is of a very delicate constitution. The friends of the man were subjected to a close questioning by the police. It was still uncertain, late last night, whether this man remained in custody or had been liberated. He strongly denies that he is known by the name of "Leather Apron."

———

The following official notice has been circulated throughout the metropolitan police district and all police-stations throughout the country:—"Description of a man who entered a passage of the house at which the murder was committed of a prostitute at 2 a.m. on the 8th.—Age 37; height, 5ft. 7in.; rather dark beard and moustache. Dress-shirt, dark vest and trousers, black scarf, and black felt hat. Spoke with a foreign accent."

Great excitement was caused in the neighbourhood of Commercial-street Police-station during the afternoon on account of the arrival from Gravesend of a suspect whose appearance resembled in some respects that of "Leather Apron." This man, whose name is William Henry Pigott, was taken into custody on Sunday night at the Pope's Head public-house, Gravesend. Attention was first attracted to Pigott because he had some bloodstains on his clothes. Superintendent Berry, the chief of the local police, was communicated with, and a sergeant was sent to the Pope's Head to investigate the case.

On approaching the man, who seemed in a somewhat dazed condition, the sergeant saw that one of his hands bore several recently-made wounds. Being interrogated as to the cause of this Pigott made a somewhat rambling state-ment to the effect that while going down Brick-

# Tuesday, 11 September, 1888

lane, Whitechapel, at half-past 4 on Saturday morning he saw a woman fall in a fit. He stooped to pick her up, and she bit his hand. Exasperated at this he struck her, but seeing two policemen coming up he then ran away.

The sergeant, deeming the explanation unsatisfactory, took Pigott to the police-station, where his clothing was carefully examined by Dr. Whitcombe, the divisional surgeon. The result of the scrutiny was an announcement that two shirts which Pigott carried in a bundle were stained with blood, and also that blood appeared to have been recently wiped off his boots.

After the usual caution the prisoner made a further statement to the effect that the woman who bit him was in the street at the back of a lodging-house when seized with the fit. He added that he slept at a lodging-house in Osborne-street on Thursday night, but on Friday was walking the streets of Whitechapel all night. He tramped from London to Gravesend on Saturday.

He gave his age as 52, and stated he was a native of Gravesend, his father having some years ago had a position there in connexion with the Royal Liver Society. Subsequently Pigott told the police that he had been keeping several publichouses in London.

As the prisoner's description tallied in some respects with that furnished by headquarters of the man wanted, Superintendent Berry decided to detain him until the morning. In response to a telegram apprising him of the arrest Inspector Abberline proceeded to Gravesend yesterday morning, and after hearing the circumstances of the case decided to bring the prisoner at once to Whitechapel, so that he could be confronted with the women who had furnished the description of "Leather Apron."

A large crowd had gathered at Gravesend railway station to witness the departure of the detective and his prisoner, but his arrival at London-bridge was almost unnoticed, the only persons apprised beforehand of the journey being the police, a small party of whom in plain clothes were in attendance. Inspector Abberline and Pigott went off in a four-wheeled cab to Commercial-street where from early morning groups of idlers had hung about in anticipation of an arrest.

The news of Pigott's arrival, which took place at 12:48, at once spread, and in a few

seconds the police-station was surrounded by an excited crowd anxious to get a glimpse of the supposed murderer. Finding that no opportunity was likely to occur of seeing the prisoner, the mob after a time melted away, but the police had trouble for some hours in keeping the thoroughfare free for traffic.

Pigott arrived at Commercial-street in much the same condition as he was when taken into custody. He wore no vest, had on a battered felt hat, and appeared to be in a state of high nervous excitement. Mrs. Fiddymont, who is responsible for the statement respecting a man resembling "Leather Apron" being at the Prince Albert publichouse on Saturday, was sent for, as were also other witnesses likely to be able to identify the prisoner; but after a very brief scrutiny it was the unanimous opinion that Pigott was not "Leather Apron."

Nevertheless, looking to his condition of mind and body, it was decided to detain him until he could give a somewhat more satisfactory explanation of himself and his movements. After an interval of a couple of hours, the man's manner becoming more strange and his speech more incoherent, the divisional surgeon was called in, and he gave it as his opinion that the prisoner's mind was unhinged. A medical certificate to this effect was made out, and Pigott will, for the present, remain in custody.

———

Intelligent observers who have visited the locality express the upmost astonishment that the murderer could have reached a hiding place after committing such a crime. He must have left the yard in Hanbury-street reeking with blood, and yet, if the theory that the murder took place between 5 and 6 be accepted, he must have walked in almost broad daylight along streets comparatively well frequented, even at that early hour, without his startling appearance attracting the slightest attention.

Consideration of this point has led many to the conclusion that the murderer came not from the wretched class from which the inmates of common lodging-houses are drawn. More probably, it is argued, he is a man lodging in a comparatively decent house in the district, to which he would be able to retire quickly, and in which, once it was reached, he would be able at his leisure to remove from his person all traces of his hideous crime. It is at any rate practically certain that the murderer would not have ventured to return to a common lodging-house smeared with blood as he must have been.

The police are therefore exhorted not to confine their investigations, as they are accused of doing, to common lodging-houses and other resorts of the criminal and outcast, but to extend their inquiries to the class of householders, exceedingly numerous in the East-end of London, who are in the habit of letting furnished lodgings without particular inquiry into the character or antecedents of those who apply for them.

A visit to Dorset-street, which runs parellel with Spitalfields Market from Commercial-street, reveals the fact that nearly every house in the street is a common lodging-house, in which wretched human beings are, at certain seasons of the year, crammed from cellar to roof. The streets leading into Dorset-street, where the woman was last seen alive, are also occupied by lodging-houses. In Hanbury-street, Deal-street, Great Garden-street, and several smaller thoroughfares houses of the same sort are located and are frequented by the poorest class of the "casual" community.

Some of these places have been searched and inquiries made as to their recent inhabitants, but so far nothing has been discovered to lead to the supposition that any regular frequenter of these establishments committed the murder. The woman Chapman was known by appearance to the policemen on the night beats in the neighbourhood, but none of those who were on duty between 12 and 6 on Saturday morning recollect having seen her.

It is ascertained that several men left their lodgings after midnight with the expressed intention of returning who have not returned. Some men went to their lodgings after 3 o'clock, and left again before 6 in the morning, which is not an unfrequent occurrence in those houses. None of the deputies or watchmen at the houses have any have any memory of any person stained with blood entering their premises, but at that hour of the morning little or no notice is taken of persons inquiring for beds. They are simply asked for the money, and shown up dark stairways with a bad light to their rooms. When they leave early, they are seldom noticed in their egress.

It is then considered quite probable that the murderer may have found a refuge for a few hours in one of these places, and even washed away the signs of his guilt. The men in these houses use a common washing place, and water once used is thrown down the sink by the lodger using it. All this might happen in a common lodging-house in the early morning without the bloodstained murderer being noticed particularly.

The conviction is growing even, that taking for granted that one man committed all the recent murders of women in the Whitechapel district, he might in this fashion, by changing his common lodging-house, evade detection for a considerable time. Whoever the man may be—if the same person committed the last three murders—he must on each occasion have been bespattered profusely with bloodstains. He could not well get rid of them in any ordinary dwelling-house or public place. Therefore it is supposed he must have done so in the lodging-houses. The murderer must have known the neighbourhood, which is provided with no fewer than four police stations, and is well watched nightly, on account of the character of many of the inhabitants.

On Saturday morning, between half past 4 o'clock and 6, several carts must have passed through Hanbury-street, and at 5 o'clock, on the opening of the Spitalfields Market, the end of which the murder occurred was blocked with market vehicles, and the market attendants were busy regulating the traffic. In the midst of the bustle it is admitted that two persons might have passed through the hall of 29, Hanbury-street, and in consequence of the noise of passing vehicles, any slight altercation might have occurred without being overheard.

Although at first, from the contiguity of Buck's-row to a slaughter-house and the neighbourhood of the Aldgate Shambles, suspicion fell on the butchers employed in those establishments during the night, the suspicion is disappearing, inasmuch as the names and addresses and the movements of all those engaged in the occupation are known.

A meeting of the chief local tradesmen was held yesterday, at which an influential committee was appointed, consisting of 16 well-known gentlemen, with Mr. J. Aarons as the secretary. The committee issued last evening a notice stating that they will give a substantial reward for the capture of the murderer or for information leading thereto. The movement has been warmly taken up by the inhabitants, and it is thought certain that a large sum will be subscribed within the next few days. The proposal to form district vigilance committees also meets with great popular favour and is assuming practical form. Meetings were held at the various working men's clubs and other organizations, political and social, in the districts, at most of which the proposed scheme was heartily approved.

From inquiries which have been made in Windsor, it seems that the deceased was the widow of a coachman in service at Clewer. While the deceased lived at Clewer she was in custody for drunkenness, but had not been charged before the magistrates.

—

### The Inquest

Yesterday morning Mr. Wynne E. Baxter, the Coroner for the North-Eastern Division of Middlesex, who was accompanied by Mr. George Collier, the Deputy Coroner, opened his inquiry in the Alexandra-room of the Working Lads' Institute, Whitechapel-road, respecting the death of Annie Chapman, who was found murdered in the back yard of 29, Hanbury-street, Spitalfields, on Saturday morning.

Detective-Inspectors Abberline (Scotland-yard), Helson, and Chandler, and Detective-Sergeants Thicke and Leach watched the case on behalf of the Criminal Investigation Department and Commissioners of Police.

The court-room was crowded, and, owing to the number of persons assembled outside the building, the approaches had to be guarded by a number of police-constables.

The jury having been impanelled, proceeded to the mortuary to view the body of the deceased, which was lying in the same shell as that occupied a short time since by the unfortunate Mary Ann Nichols.

John Davis, a carman, of 29, Hanbury-street, Spitalfields, deposed that he occupied the front room, which was shared by his wife and three sons. About 8 o'clock on Friday night he went to bed, and his sons came in at different times. The last one arrived home about a quarter to 11. Witness was awake from 3 to about 5 o'clock, when he fell off to sleep for about half an hour. He got up about a quarter to 6. Soon afterwards

he went across the yard. The front portion of the house faced Hanbury-street. On the ground floor there was a front door, with a passage running through to the back yard. He was certain of the time, because he heard the bell of Spitalfields Church strike. The front door and the one leading into the yard were never locked, and at times were left open at nights. Since he had lived in the house witness had never known the doors to be locked; and when the doors were shut any person could open them and pass into the yard. When he went into the yard on Saturday morning the back door was shut; but he was unable to say whether it was latched. The front door was wide open, and he was not surprised at finding it so, as it was frequently left open all night. Between the yard of 29, Hanbury-street, and the next house there was a fence about 5ft. high. When witness went down the steps he saw the deceased woman lying flat on her back.

The CORONER here observed that in similar inquiries in the country the police always assisted him by preparing a plan of the locality which happened to be the subject of investigation. He thought the present case was one of sufficient importance for the production of such a plan, and he hoped that in future a plan would be laid before him.

Inspector Chandler told the Coroner a plan would be prepared.

The CORONER replied it might then be too late to be of any service.

Witness, continuing, said the deceased was lying between the steps and the fence, with her head towards the house. He could see that her clothes were disarranged. Witness did not go further into the yard, but at once called two men, who worked for Mr. Bailey, a packing-case maker, of Hanbury-street, whose place was three doors off. These men entered the passage and looked at the woman, but did not go into the yard. He was unable to give the names of these two men, but knew them well by sight. Witness had not since seen the men, who went away to fetch the police. Witness also left the house with them.

In answer to the Coroner, Inspector Chandler said these men were not known to the police.

The CORONER remarked that they would have to be found, either by the police or by his

# Tuesday, 11 September, 1888

own officer.

Witness further stated that on leaving the house he went direct to the Commercial-street Police-station, and reported what he had seen. Previous to that he had not informed anyone living in the house of the discovery. After that he went back to Hanbury-street, but did not enter his house. He had never previously seen the deceased.

In cross-examination, the witness said he was not the first person down that morning, as a man, named Thompson, who also lived in the house, was called about half-past 3. He had never seen women who did not live in the house in the passage since he had lived there, which was only a fortnight. He did not hear any strange noises before getting up on Saturday morning.

Amelia Farmer stated that she lived at a common lodginghouse at 30, Dorset-street, Spitalfields, and had lived there for the past four years. She had identified the body of the deceased in the mortuary, and was sure it was that of Annie Chapman. The deceased formerly lived at Windsor, and was the widow of Frederick Chapman, a veterinary surgeon, who died about 18 months ago.

For four years, or more, the deceased had lived apart from her husband, and during that period had principally resided in common lodginghouses in the neighbourhoods of Whitechapel and Spital-fields. About two years since the deceased lived at 30, Dorset-street, and was then living with a man who made iron sieves. She was then receiving an allowance of 10s. a week from her husband. Some 18 months since the payments stopped, and it was then that she found her husband was dead. That fact was also ascertained from a relative of the deceased, who used to live in Oxford-street, Whitechapel.

The deceased went by the name of Sievey, on account of the man with whom she had cohabited being a sieve maker. This man left her some time ago.

During the past week witness had seen the deceased some two or three times. On Monday, in Dorset-street, she complained of feeling unwell. At that time she had a bruise on one of her temples. Witness inquiring how she got it, the deceased told her to look at her breast, which was also bruised. The deceased said, "You know the woman," and she mentioned a name which

witness did not remember. Both the deceased and the woman referred to were acquainted with a man called "Harry the Hawker."

In giving an account of the bruises, the deceased told witness that on the 1st inst. she went into a publichouse with a young man named Ted Stanley in Commercial-street. "Harry the Hawker" and the other woman were also there. The former, who was drunk, put down a florin, which was picked up by the latter, who replaced it with a penny. Some words passed between the deceased and the woman, and in the evening the latter struck her and inflicted the bruises.

Witness again saw the deceased on Tuesday by the side of Spitalfields Church. The deceased again complained of feeling unwell, and said she thought she would go into the casual ward for day or two. She mentioned that she had had nothing to eat or drink that day, not even a cup of tea. Witness gave deceased twopence saying, "Here is twopence to have a cup of tea, but don't have rum." She knew that deceased was given to drinking that spirit.

The deceased, who frequently got the worse for drink, used at times to earn money by doing crochet work, and at others by selling flowers. Witness believed she was not very particular what she did to earn a living and at times used to remain out very late at night. She was in the habit of going to Stratford.

Witness did not again see the deceased until Friday afternoon, and about 5 o'clock on that day she met her in Dorset-street. The deceased, who was sober, in answer to a question from witness as to whether she was going to Stratford, said she felt too ill to do anything. A few minutes afterwards witness again saw the deceased, who had not moved, and she said, "It's no use my giving way. I must pull myself together and go out and get some money, or I shall have no lodgings." That was the last time witness saw her.

She mentioned that she had been an inmate of the casual ward. Deceased was generally an industrial woman, and witness considered her clever. For the last five years she had been living an irregular life, more especially since her husband died. She had two children, and on the death of her husband they were sent away to school. The deceased had a sister and mother, but witness believed they were not on

# Tuesday, 11 September, 1888

friendly terms.

Timothy Donovan stated he was the deputy of a common lodginghouse at 35, Dorset-street, Spitalfields. He had seen the body in the mortuary, and identified it as that of a woman who had lodged at his place. She had been living there for about four months, but was not there any day last week until Friday. About 7 o'clock that day she came to the lodginghouse and asked him to allow her to go down into the kitchen. He asked where she had been all the week, and she replied, "In the infirmary." He then allowed her to go down into the kitchen. She remained there until shortly before 2 o'clock the next morning. When she went out she said, "I have not any money now, but don't let the bed; I will be back soon." At that time there was a vacant bed, and it was the one she generally occupied. She then left the house, but witness did not see which way she turned.

She had had enough to drink when he last saw her, but she was well able to walk straight. The deceased generally got the worse for drink on Saturdays, but not on the other days of the week. He told her that she could find money for drink but not for her bed, and she replied that she had only been to the top of the street as far as the Ringers' publichouse.

He did not see her with any one that night. On Saturday night deceased used to stay at the lodginghouse with a man of military appearance, and witness had heard he was a pensioner. She had brought other men to the lodginghouse. On the 2d inst. deceased paid 8d. a night for her bed. The pensioner was about 45 years of age and about 5ft. 8in. in height. At times he had the appearance of something better. Witness had never had any trouble with the deceased, who was always very friendly with the other lodgers.

John Evans, night watchman at the lodginghouse, also identified the body of deceased. He saw her leave the house at about a quarter to 2 on Saturday morning. Just before he had asked her whether she had not sufficient, and then told the last witness she would not be long before she got it. Witness saw her enter a court called Paternoster-row and walk in the direction of Brushfield-street. Witness should say she was the worse for drink. She told him she had that night been to see one of her sisters who lived at Vauxhall. Before he spoke to her about her lodging money she had been out for a pint of beer. He knew that she had been living a rough life, but only knew one man with whom she associated. That man used to come and see her on Saturdays. He called about half-past 2 on Saturday afternoon to make inquiries about the deceased. He said he had heard of her death. Witness did not know his name or address. After hearing an account of the death of the deceased he went out without saying a word. Witness had never heard any person threaten the deceased, and she had never stated she was afraid of any one. He did not see the deceased leave the lodginghouse with the pensioner on Sunday week. On Thursday the deceased and a woman called Eliza had a fight in the kitchen, during which she got a blow on the chest and a black eye.

The CORONER here intimated that that was as far as he proposed to carry the inquiry at present, and it was adjourned until to-morrow afternoon.

~

## The Star

**FIFTH EDITION.**
**WHITECHAPEL.**
**PISER IDENTIFIED THIS MORNING**
**AT LEMAN-STREET.**
**£100 REWARD OFFERED BY AN M.P.**
**No Further Arrests—Pigott Still**
**Unidentified, and Pronounced**
**Insane—The Identification of Piser with**
**"Leather Apron" Doubtful.**

This morning there are two men detained on suspicion in connection with the Whitechapel crimes. One is the man Piggott, arrested at Gravesend, and supposed to be the man who went into Fiddymont's public-house at seven on the morning of the murder with blood upon his hands.

He was brought to Commercial-street Police Station yesterday afternoon, and placed among a number of other men taken from the street, in order that the builder Taylor, Mrs. Fiddymont, and Mrs. Chappell, the three people who saw the man with the blood-stained hands, might, if possible, identify the captured one. Taylor and Mrs. Fiddymont declared the man at the station not the one they saw, and Mrs. Chappell, though she picked the right man out, failed to positively identify him. This morning, however, Piggot was still in the infirmary recovering slowly from an attack of delirium tremens.

The other man in custody is

**JOHN PISER,**

who was arrested yesterday morning at 22, Mulberry-street, Commercial-road, by Sergeant Thicke. There were reports yesterday afternoon that Piser had been released but, as stated in our extra special edition of last night, these were untrue. At nine o'clock this morning Piser was still comfortably quartered in a room at Leman-street Police Station, and there he is likely to remain until the detectives have cleared up the strong suspicion there is against him.

No one is allowed to see the prisoner but his brother this morning called at the police-station and left both food and drink, which was afterwards given to the prisoner. Piser asked to be allowed to see his brother, but was refused.

The police have made a thorough search again at Piser's lodgings, but beyond the buffers or kind of knife used for scraping leather they have found nothing. The vexed question—owing to conflicting reports, it is vexing to the public at any rate—is whether John Piser is the much-talked-of "Leather Apron." John Piser, John Piser's step-mother, step-brother, step-sister, and neighbors all say "No;" Sergeant Thicke, who is an officer of high reputation, and who knows, perhaps, more of the East-end and its rough denizens than any other man in the force, says almost positively that Piser is "Leather Apron."

In view of the conflict of testimony on this point a *Star* reporter went to Mulberry-street yesterday morning and interrogated the neighbours standing in little crowds at the doorways. The man who seemed

**TO KNOW THE SUSPECT**

best was a tall man leaning against the doorpost without coat or waistcoat. He, like the Pisers, is a German Jew, and, like the man in custody, is a shoemaker; indeed, John Piser, he said, had worked for him. The Pisers have lived for 20 years in the neighbourhood—the arrested man's father died in the very house the son was taken from.

"Has Piser been about this neighbourhood during the last few weeks?" our reporter asked.

"Yes," said the man. "I have seen him in this street five or six times during the last few weeks. He has been in and out in his ordinary manner—he has not been hiding."

In answer to further inquiries, the man said the knives which had been found in the house proved nothing. In fact at that moment he had in his own house knives nearly half as long as his arm—he and Piser used them in their business.

"Is this the man known as 'Leather Apron'?" asked the reporter.

"No, no, I don't know—I don't know him as

'Leather Apron,' said the man, hastily.

After a little further conversation, however, *The Star* reporter innocently asked him to describe the man he had seen taken. This he did readily, and gave a strikingly faithful description of the man whom everybody has been talking of since *The Star* first described him.

The man's identity was borne out by what a *Star* reporter subsequently gleaned from

## SERGEANT THICKE,

a stout-built, keen, but pleasant-faced man, with thick, drooping, yellowish moustache, dressed in a light check suit.

The Sergeant who, by the rough characters among whom his profession takes him, is better known as Johnny Upright, had just been deep in consultation in the station yard with a crowd of detectives, when our representative had the good fortune to get an introduction.

"Of course, you've come about the Whitechapel murder," he said, when a *Star* card was handed to him. "Now, you know as well as I do that I cannot tell you anything."

Our representative urged that he might be able to say something without damaging the public interest, and with a little questioning a few facts were obtained. The sergeant emphatically denied that, as the neighbours had said, "Leather Apron" had for the last six weeks been going about his business in an ordinary manner. "He's been in hiding safe enough, and it's my opinion his friends have been screening him. He has not been in lodging houses; he is too well known there and the people who frequent them would have been ready to lynch him. Why the other day a woman told me plainly that if she saw him she would kill him, and I could do what I liked with her afterwards. No," keen Johnny Upright continued, "'Leather Apron' has not been into a lodging-house since the Sunday

## THE WOMAN DENOUNCED HIM IN WHITECHAPEL,

and the police were bamboozled into letting him go." The Sergeant modestly disclaimed any great deal of credit in making the capture. "I've known him for years," he said. "I didn't take him on the strength of any published descriptions of him. It was not, however, till the early hours of this morning I was told where I could put my hands on him."

*The Star* reporter mentioned that the people in Mulberry-street discounted the importance of the finding of knives. But the Sergeant was not to be trapped into saying anything about the knives—whether there were any bloodstains on them. "I don't mean to say anything to prejudice the case against the man. We are still making inquiry, and in the present stage of the case I can't say any more."

The report yesterday afternoon that a second "Leather Apron"—"the real man"—had been arrested and taken to the Bethnal-green Police-station was quite without foundation; nobody was detained there at all yesterday.

From inquiries at all the police stations this morning it seems that the police are in possession of no further clue.

## PISER PICKED OUT.

Just before one o'clock this afternoon 11 men passing by Leman-street Police-station were asked and consented to go into the station-yard for a few minutes. Piser was brought out, and put amongst them. A middle-aged man, with a face of negro cast, but not black, was then asked whether he could "identify the man," and unhesitatingly he picked out Piser.

"What," said Piser, "you know me?"

But an inspector raised a warning hand, and without anything else being said the men dispersed and Piser was led back to his room.

It has been asserted by one witness that two men were with deceased in Hanbury-street at an early hour on the morning of the murder. These two men have not yet been traced, and the authorities are anxious to know whether one of these was Piser before releasing or charging him. The police say they do not believe "Leather Apron" the guilty man, and point out that the public and the newspapers have accused him—not they.

Although Pigott has been declared to be of unsound mind the police are by no means relaxing their inquiries concerning him.

No more arrests in connection with the murder at Whitechapel had been made up to one o'clock to-day.

—

## REWARDS OFFERED.

Mr. S. Montagu, M.P., has offered £100 as a reward for the capture of the Whitechapel murderer, and has asked Superintendent Arnold to issue notices to that effect.

This morning posters are being posted up all

# Tuesday, 11 September, 1888

over Whitechapel, offering a reward in these terms:—

"Finding that, in spite of murders being committed in our midst, our police force are still inadequate to discover the author or authors of the late atrocities, we, the undersigned, have formed ourselves into a committee and intend offering a substantial reward to anyone, citizen or otherwise, who shall give such information that will bring the murderer or murderers to justice." The committee meets every evening at nine o'clock at the Crown, 74, Mile-end-road.

—

### A NIGHT IN WHITECHAPEL.

A representative of the Central News patrolled the streets and alleys of Whitechapel during last night and the early hours of this morning. The scare (he writes) has considerably subsided. People have become familiar with the tragedy, and are calmed by the knowledge of the active measures adopted for their protection by the police. This is plainly evidenced by the aspect which Whitechapel-road presented last night and up to an early hour of the morning.

On Sunday night the pavements were almost deserted. Twenty-four hours later groups of men and women chatted, joked, and boisterously laughed upon the flagstones until long after St. Mary's clock struck one. "Leather Apron" has already become a by-word of the pavement and gutter. Many members of the police force firmly believe in the existence and

### ALMOST CERTAIN GUILT

of "Leather Apron." The talk of the footways convinces the passer-by that the inhabitants of the East-end are sceptical as to his personality. There was the usual percentage of gaudily dressed, loudmouthed, and vulgar women strutting or standing at the brightly-lighted crossways last night, and the still larger proportion of miserable, half-fed, dejected creatures of the same sex upon which hard life, unhealthy habits, and bad spirits have set their stamp.

Soon after one o'clock the better-dressed members of the motley company disappeared, but the poverty-stricken drabs crawled about from lamp to lamp, or from one dark alley's mouth to another, until faint signs of dawn appeared. Off the main road—in such thoroughfares as Commercial-street and Brick-lane—

there was little to attract attention. Constables passed silently by the knots of homeless vagabonds huddled in the recess of some big doorway; other constables, whose "plain clothes" could not prevent their

### STALWART, WELL-DRILLED FIGURES

from betraying their calling, paraded in couples, now and again emerging from some dimly lighted lane, and passing their uniformed comrades with an air of conscious ignorance.

The streets inclusively referred to by the constables on beat duty in the main thorough-fare as "round at the back" presented a dismal appearance indeed, the dim yellow flames of the not too numerous lamps only rendering the darkness of night more gloomy.

Such passages as Edward-street, connecting Hanbury and Princes-streets, Flower and Dean-street, between Brick-lane and Commercial-street, which, in daylight only strike one as very unwholesome and dirty thoroughfares, appear unutterably forlorn and dismal in the darkness of night. From an alley in one of these, leading to uninviting recesses, a miserable specimen of a man—hollow-chested, haggard, and dirty—shuffled hurriedly into the wider street and, crossing to the opposite pavement, dived into another recess and was instantly lost to view. No constable would have thought of interfering with him had he met him, nor would there have been any excuse for accosting him; and yet his ragged clothes, of some dark hue, might have been saturated with blood, invisible in the depressing yellow shade of the flickering gas jets.

In any one of these dark and filthy passages a human being's life

### MIGHT BE EVERY NIGHT SACRIFICED

were the blow dealt with the terrible sudden-ness and precision which characterised those of the two last homicides, and a police force of double the strength of that now employed and organised under the best possible conditions, might well be baffled in its efforts to capture the slayers.

In the immediate neighbourhood of St. Mary's Church a wide entry presented a deep cavern of Stygian blackness, into which no lamp shone, and where, for aught a passer-by at that hour could discover, a corpse might lie, and from which—such is its position—a murderer might, if possessed of coolness, easily pass unobserved.

In a squalid thoroughfare between Hanbury-street and Whitechapel-road some houses have

# Tuesday, 11 September, 1888

apparently been pulled down, the space being now waste ground enclosed by wooden pailings. This unilluminated spot is separated by a house or two from an alley which, at a point some yards from the street, turns at right angles apparently towards the unoccupied space mentioned.

Into the mouth of this passage, a slatternly woman, her face half hidden in a shawl which formed her only head dress, thrust her head, and in a shrill and angry voice shrieked "Tuppy!" The cry was answered in a few seconds by the appearance of an evil-looking man, with a ragged black beard, who, in reply to an impatient question of

**"WHERE IS SHE?"**

muttered in a surly tone, "Round there," at the same time jerking his thumb backwards towards the alley. "Well, come 'long 'ome, then. I aint agoin' to wait for she," replied the woman, who, with the dark man limping after her, soon disappeared round the corner of the street.

There was no subsequent indication of the presence of a third person. The light from the street was so dim that there was no possibility of recognising the features of the man and woman; and certainly either might have borne traces of crime which would have attracted no attention.

—

### THE SLAUGHTERMAN THEORY.
#### A Correspondent Examines How Far the Facts Support It.

While the police are pursuing the empirical method in their investigation into the White-chapel murders, and apparently looking out for persons who had blood upon them on the days of the crimes (as though at any given time in such a district as Whitechapel there are not any number of people who have just been engaged in personal and pugilistic encounters), it may be well in the columns of a newspaper to follow another method, perhaps more suited to a philosopher's study than a detective's office. To this end let us start with a theory, and then by the light of it look at the facts.

The theory. That the four women were killed by someone to whom bloodshed and slaughter is an everyday affair—*e.g.*, a knacker or slaughter-man. Such a man would have the skill, acquired by practice, necessary to do the work silently, swiftly, and with the minimum of bloodiness. He would have by him, without fear of thereby

attracting suspicion, the kind of weapon exactly suited to the purpose. He would be the only man in all London who could walk along the streets in the early daylight with blood on his hands and clothes without exciting undue notice or remark. He would have the needful anatomical know-ledge by which he would be able to find quickly such internal organs as the heart and liver, supposing he desired to add horror to horror by placing them outside the victim's body.

He would commit the murders within a reasonable distance of his place of trade, so as to be able to reach it at the usual time for beginning work or not to be absent from it long enough to excite notice if the crime were committed during work hours. On Bank-holidays our hypothetical murderer would not be in workaday clothes or have his tools about him, but he would be armed with a stick, which is part of the holiday paraphernalia, or with a bayonet, supposing he were a Volunteer, and in the early hours of the morning after Bank holidays he would be in the immediate vicinity of his workshop.

He would strike with a heavy, swift hand, and not with the light swift stroke of the surgeon or anatomical demonstrator.

In mutilating he would strike downwards in the same way as though he were disembowelling a sheep. Now what are the facts?

The woman Nicholls was discovered in the immediate vicinity of a slaughter-house—and of her Dr. Ralph Llewellyn said, "She was ripped open just as you see a dead calf in a butcher's shop. The murder was done by someone very handy with the knife." The throat was cut, as a calf's or pig's is cut, with one hard blow from left to right. It was not sawn asunder, and there was very little blood on the clothes or on the ground. She was killed in the early morning.

Annie Chapman was found also not far from a slaughter-house. Her throat was cut in precisely the same way, and with the same sort of weapon as Nicholls's. She was ripped up as a calf is ripped up. Some of her internal organs were taken out of her body, and there was very little blood on the spot where she lay. She was found in the rear of premises inhabited by a seller of cat's-meat—a place which would be known by a knacker or slaughterman. She was killed early in the morning.

The other and earlier victims were killed on the mornings after Bank holidays. One was wounded with a stick and the other with some weapon like a bayonet.

Question for the police and the public—Is there a slaughterman or knacker living in Whitechapel who cannot account for his whereabouts on the mornings of these murders, and is he in the Volunteers, or has he a pal a Volunteer who is given to heavy drinking?

—

## THE JEWS AND THE MURDERS.
### What a Jewish Correspondent says of Their Horror of Blood.

If the panic-stricken people who cry "Down with the Jews" because they imagine that a Jew has committed the horrible and revolting crimes which have made Whitechapel a place to be dreaded know anything at all of the Jewish horror of blood itself, they would pause before they invoked destruction on the head of a peaceful and law-abiding people.

Of course, there is little danger of our having in civilised London a recurrence of scenes enacted in the East—in Greece, in Turkey, and in Asia Minor! It is only in recent years that the scandalous superstition known as the "blood accusation" has been exploded by the light of inquiry.

Some years ago, in the countries mentioned, many a Jewish Community was plundered, outraged, and massacred to satisfy a blood-thirsty mob eager for revenge, because a Christian had been discovered dead in a field or on the banks of a river. It was thought by the rude population that the Jewish festival of Passover necessitated

### A HUMAN SACRIFICE,

and that in order to propitiate their God the Jews seized a Christian and put him to death.[43]

Greedy Turkish officials, it was proved on inquiry, fostered this remarkable theory in order that they might share in the general plunder, and that they did so is without doubt.

That they connived at and even instigated the death of Christians in order that the hue and cry might be raised, is not without the range of possibilities. The Turk, in his rapacious moments—and they are not few—is not over-conscientious as to the means he employs to gratify his passions.

The murder record of all countries has but to be examined to demonstrate here how

remarkably exempt from the crime of homicide are the Jewish people. The horror of even the sight of blood may be traced throughout ages, and its origin may be found in the Bible itself. That "The blood is the life" is so perfectly and persistently before the Jews that they soak their butcher-meat in water before they will prepare it for cooking, and Jews have been seen to shrink from tasting the red juice that runs from a succulent beef-steak in process of cutting it. Since the return of Jews to England in 1649, only

### TWO JEWS HAVE BEEN HANGED

for murder, Marks and Lipski, and taking into consideration the origin of many of the poor wretches who fly to this country from foreign persecution, this is a very remarkable record.

That the beast who has made East London a terror is not a Jew I feel assured. There is something too horrible, too unnatural, too un-Jewish I would say, in the terrible series of murders for an Israelite to be the monster. There never was a Jew yet who could have steeped himself in such loathsome horrors as those to which publicity has been given in *The Star*. His nature revolts at blood-guiltiness, and the whole theory and practical working of the Whitechapel butchery are opposed to Jewish character.[44]

~

---

[43] See footnote #42, page 72.

[44] In 2004 Haaretz, the Israeli newspaper, ran the article World of our (God)fathers, by Coby Ben-Simhon, dealing with 19th and early 20th Century Jewish organized crime, which included kidnapping, extortion, robbery and murder. (Ben-Simhon)

# Tuesday, 11 September, 1888

## Evening News
### FIFTH EDITION.
### THE WHITECHAPEL TRAGEDIES.
#### IS THE MURDERER A MANIAC?
#### THE MEANS SUGGESTED FOR HIS CAPTURE.
#### AN INTERVIEW WITH DR. FORBES WINSLOW.

The statement of a morning contemporary about Dr. Forbes Winslow being in communication with Scotland-yard is virtually correct. It should be said, however, that Dr. Winslow made to a certain extent the first advances yesterday morning on the advice of a friend. It is gratifying to know that in a far more generous meaning of the word than that employed by Eccles in "Caste,"[45] there is no pride about our most eminent physicians, and the great specialist is no exception to the rule.

He is convinced that, given the facilities, he could lay hands on the homicidal maniac who is spreading terror through London in a fortnight, if not in less time. For he is equally convinced that one, and only one man has committed the murder of the three, if not of the four, women who have been so mercilessly dispatched since last Christmas in the purlieus[46] of Aldgate.

### THE FIRST AND FOREMOST CONDITION OF THE PROPOSED CAPTURE

"The first and foremost condition of the proposed capture" said Dr. Forbes Winslow this morning to the representative of *The Evening News*, "is the matter being left entirely under my control and an implicit compliance with my demands, however strange these demands might appear. I say this advisedly because there is no doubt that these requests would appear strange.

I have not thought out the plan very carefully as yet, but your surmise as to the employ of a decoy is right, only I should not want one, but a dozen decoys, distributed throughout the whole

---

[45] **Caste.** Popular play by T. W. Robertson, first performed in 1867. Eccles was the drunken father of Esther, a ballerina that married the son of a French nobleman, Captain George d'Alroy, an officer in the British army. After d'Alroy is posted to India, Eccles gambles away at the racetrack the money left to care for Esther and her baby. Captain d'Alroy is mistakenly reported dead and Esther and her baby are poverty stricken until his return.

[46] **Purlieus.** Outskirts, environs. (Morehead)

---

of London. I am not so certain that if the right men for this purpose were found they would, as you express it, be risking their lives with 999 chances in 1,000 against them. They might be hampered by their adoption of female attire, but men used to deal with homicidal maniacs, would not let it come to the bitter end. Their presence of mind—for that more than physical strength would be essential—would save them.

As an instance of this I may tell you a story for the truth of which I can vouch. Not long ago, a professional friend, a doctor in a lunatic asylum, entered the room of a patient known to suffer from homicidal mania.

#### 'I AM GOING TO KILL YOU,'

said the patient on seeing him. Thereupon he took from his waistcoat pocket a flint stone with a very sharp edge. The patient, I should have told you, was a very powerful muscular fellow. My friend is quite the converse. In a struggle, the latter would not have had the least chance. Nevertheless the physician stood his ground without budging, looking his would-be assailant straight in the eyes. 'I don't mind being killed; but don't you think that the blood would make a terrible mess and had not I better fetch a bucket first" said the doctor.

Though the whole of this conversation could have scarcely lasted a minute, it was sufficient to calm the fit, the stupor, or whatever you may choose to call it.

"Are there many such maniacs in England? you ask. Yes, thousands, and the suicides and homicides committed by those at large amount to no less than 50 a week. Of course the homicides are not even all apprehended, and their trial is often a matter of fate, like the case I was lately engaged in with Dr. Crichton-Browne. The culprit had murdered his own sister. Larceny was too evident on the face of it, and the young man is detained during Her Majesty's pleasure. But there are other instances in which it becomes impossible for a jury to detect this lunacy, and then the unhappy sufferer goes to his doom. The judge thinks that because the prisoner sees the culpability of his act, after he has committed it, he is a responsible person, and sums up accordingly.

"My father tried to reform this but was unsuccessful."

"Homicidal mania is absolutely incurable, however long a time may elapse between the recurrent attacks of it. As such, I repeat to you what I said yesterday at Scotland-Yard. I should begin by communicating with the authorities not only of every public and private lunatic asylum round and in London but throughout the length and breadth of the land. I should want not only a list of all those who have escaped, but also of those who have been discharged as 'quasi-cured.' You may give it as my firm opinion that the murderer of Mary Ann Nichols, Annie Chapman and the woman in George-yard is a lunatic at large—and, what is more, a well-to-do lunatic, probably living in the West-end. All the ordinary means of detection will fail, because, once more, the moment his fit of mania is passed, he becomes quite rational. He may, as your leader of yesterday suggests, not even be aware of having committed the murder. That would be what we denominate epileptic stupor.

Such a man would, if caught and tried, sell his own life in the dock for the mere hint that he is a maniac would evoke a storm of indignation on his part. If, on the other hand he is aware of having committed this deed, his position in life will enable him to keep coy during the day. The only way to capture him would be with the fit strong upon him. For this a decoy, and nothing but a decoy, would be effectual. The decoy is merely one part of my programme. I have not thought out the matter fully, but will communicate with you again."

## SCENE OF THE MURDERS BY NIGHT.

The scare which the disclosure of the fourth and most horrible of the murders occasioned in the district has considerably subsided. People have become familiar with the details of the tragedy, and being calmed by the knowledge of the active measures adopted for their protection by the police, are returning to their normal condition of mind. This is plainly evidenced by the aspect which Whitechapel-road presented last night and up to an early hour of the morning—a very different one from that of the corresponding period of the previous day.

## "LEATHER APRON."

On Sunday night the pavements were almost deserted, but 24 hours later groups of men and women chatted, joked and boisterously laughed upon the flagstones, until long after St. Mary's clock struck one. In passing through the groups of people the words most frequently heard in their conversation were "Leather Apron". The term has become already a by-word of the pavement and gutter, and one more often hears it accompanied by a vacant guffaw than whispered in a tone which would indicate any fear of the mysterious individual who is supposed to live under that sobriquet. Whilst a number of persons, including many members of the police force, firmly believe in the existence and almost certain guilt of the aproned one, the talk of the footways convinces the passer-by that a large number of other inhabitants of the East-end are sceptical as to his personality.

So it may be said with truth that the thoroughfares last night presented their customary appearance. There was the usual percentage of gaudily-dressed, loud-mouthed, and vulgar women, strutting or standing at the brightly-lighted cross ways; and the still larger proportion of miserable, half-fed, dejected creatures of the same sex upon whom hard life, unhealthy habits and bad spirits have too plainly set their stamp.

## THE NIGHT PROWLERS
## AND THE PATROL.

Soon after one o'clock these better dressed members of the motley company disappeared by ones and twos, but the poor poverty-stricken drabs, to whom it would appear fortune is less kind; crawled about from lamp to lamp, or from one dark alley's mouth to another, until faint signs of dawn appeared.

Off the main road, in such thoroughfares as Commercial-street and Brick-lane there was little to attract attention. Constables passed silently by the knots of homeless vagabonds huddled in the recess of some big doorway. Other constables, whose "plain clothes" could not prevent their stalwart, well-drilled figures from betraying their calling, paraded in couples, now and again emerging from some dimly-lighted lane, and passing their uniformed comrades with an air of profound ignorance; and ill-fed cats crouched in the gutters or preyed upon some offal rejected by their hardly more fortunate human owners.

## ROUND AT THE BACK.

The streets inclusively referred to by the constables on duty in the main thoroughfare as "round at the back" presented a dismal appearance indeed, the dim yellow flames of the not too numerous public lamps only rendered the darkness of night more gloomy. Such passages as Edward-street connecting Hanbury and Princes-streets, Flower and Dean-street, between Brick-lane and Commercial-street, which in daylight only strike one as very unwholesome and dirty thoroughfares appear utterly forlorn and dismal in the darkness of night.

## MURDER IS EASY HERE.

From an alley in one of these, leading to uninviting recesses, a miserable specimen of a man—hollow-chested, haggard, and dirty—shuffled hurriedly into the wider street and crossing to the opposite pavement, dived into another recess, and was instantly lost to view. No constable would have thought of interfering with him had he met him, nor would there have been any excuse for accosting him; and yet his ragged clothes, of some dark hue, might have been saturated with blood of a murdered victim, which would not have been visible in the depressing yellow shade of the flickering gas jets. In almost any one of these dark and filthy passages a human being's life might be every night sacrificed were the blow dealt with the terrible suddenness and precision which evidently characterised those of the last two homicides; and a police force of double the strength of that now employed, and organised under the best possible conditions, might well be baffled in its efforts to capture the slayers.

In the immediate neighbourhood of St. Mary's Church, a wide entry presented a deep cavern of Stygian blackness, into which no lamp shone, and where, for aught a passer-by at that hour could discover, a corpse might lie, and from which—such is its position—a murderer might, if possessed of coolness, easily pass unobserved.

In a squalid thoroughfare between Hanbury-street and Whitechapel-road some houses have apparently been pulled down, the space being now waste ground, enclosed by wooden palings. This unilluminated spot is separated by a house or two from an alley which, at a point some yards from the street, turns at right angles apparently towards the unoccupied space mentioned.

## A MYSTERIOUS INCIDENT.

Into the mouth of this passage a slatternly woman, her face half hidden in a shawl, which formed her only headdress, thrust her head, and in a shrill and angry voice shrieked the word, "Tuppy!" The cry was answered in a few seconds by the appearance of an evil looking man with a ragged black beard, who, in reply to an impatient question of "Where is she?" muttered in a surly tone, "Round there," at the same time jerking his thumb backwards towards the alley. "Well come 'long 'ome then—I ain't agoin' to wait for she," replied the woman, who, with the dark man limping after her soon disappeared round the corner of the street. There was no subsequent indication of the presence of a third person.

The light from the street was so dim that there was no possibility of recognising the features of the man and woman, and certainly either might have born traces of crime which would have attracted no attention.

Such occurrences as the above are, the police say, quite usual, and they neither have, nor wish to have, authority to question any individual whose conduct may attract attention without exciting suspicion.

## PISER AND PIGOTT

John Piser, the man who was, yesterday, erroneously described as "Leather Apron," is still detained by the police at Leman-street Police-station, although the evidence against the man is absolutely nil. No one is allowed to see the prisoner, but his brother, this morning, called at the police-station and left both food and drink which was afterwards given to the prisoner. Piser asked to be allowed to see his brother but was refused.

The police have made a thorough search again at Piser's lodgings but beyond the buffers, or kind of knife used for scraping leather, they have found nothing. There is no evidence against the man at present; not sufficient even to warrant a magistrate in granting a remand, and it is consequently altogether improbable that he will be charged with complicity in the crime. It is expected that he will be released during the day.

No further arrests have been made up to eleven o'clock to-day, and apparently the police are as far off as ever from unravelling the mystery connected with this appalling crime.

A number of police are engaged in investigating any plausible evidence offered to them, but beyond the suspicious personage described by Mrs. Fiddymont and a girl who states that a man answering his description had assaulted her, the police have literally nothing to go upon. The prospects, therefore, of bringing the wretch to justice are at the present moment far from bright.

The man Pigott arrested at Gravesend is now at the Whitechapel Infirmary, where he will remain for the next 48 hours, and if the authorities there then decide to release him due notice will be given to the police. It is most likely that his friends will take charge of him.

This morning Whitechapel and Spitalfields have settled down to the usual state of affairs. The excitement has altogether abated. There is no crowd around either of the police stations, and very few persons have assembled at the scene of the murder, and these have passed away again after a brief glance at the place.

It has been asserted by one witness that two men were with deceased in Hanbury-street at an early hour on the morning of the murder. These two men have not yet been traced, and the authorities are anxious to know whether one of these was Piser, before releasing or charging him. The police do not believe "Leather Apron" the guilty man, and point out that the public and the newspapers have accused him—not they.

### A REWARD OFFERED.

Mr. S. Montague, M.P., has offered £100 as a reward for the capture of the Whitechapel murderer, and has asked Superintendent Arnold to issue notices to that effect.

### THE POLICE AT FAULT.

Although the utmost vigilance was kept by the large force of detectives around the district in which the murders took place, no further arrests have been made either in connection with the Buck's-row or Hanbury-street tragedies up to eight o'clock this morning. The search, which has now extended over the greater part of East London, has been, as far as the attainment of any real evidence is concerned, futile. There is only one man under detention at Leman-street Station, and all those who were brought to Commercial-street and Bethnal Green Stations have been released.

---

### THE WHITECHAPEL HORRORS
### TO THE EDITOR OF
### "THE EVENING NEWS,"

SIR—I have read your leader of to-day with great interest, especially the portion of it suggesting that the crimes were possibly committed by an epileptic, whose seizures take the form of homicidal impulses. There are many circumstances connected with these murders which support this hypothesis.

With the ordinary criminal it may be assumed that the police are quite capable of dealing; for in the cases of murder which run on general lines, some motive for their commission can be found, and a clue, of course, to the perpetrator may, in consequence, be discovered. Avarice, revenge, jealousy, and so forth, are instances of average motives for murder. Acting on the assumption of the existence of any of these, the police can almost always trace the crime to the criminal. Where, however, superior intelligence is possessed by the murderer, detection, of course, becomes, as a rule, more difficult. The ingenuity in the planning and executing of murder by a person of this class may occasionally baffle the skill of experts in crime investigation. But it may be generally assumed that the accumulated experience of our detectives is equal to the cunning of the most intelligent criminal.

In the case of the Whitechapel murders, however; the police are evidently at fault, since no intelligible motive can be ascribed to the perpetration of any of these crimes. It is well, therefore, to consider them as absolutely with-out motive.

Taking it for granted that they are the work of one man—and many circumstances point to this—then, on the assumption that they are motiveless, it is clear that they are the deeds of a lunatic. In support of this conclusion, the frenzied manner of the slaying and mutilation of the victim will go far. That the murderer is not a furious homicidal maniac, whose mania is continuous, may be assumed, else he would have betrayed himself before this. And the fact that his butcheries were restricted to a certain class would put out of question homicidal mania pure and simple.

Let us consider the question of monomania. It is quite possible that monomania could be directed towards the commission of such crimes as we are considering. But here, again, the monomaniac would be almost certain to betray himself. Both in furious homicidal mania and monomania it is in the highest degree probable that the murderer's plans would be abortive because in the chaotic condition of mind which is the invariable attendant on both these manias, he would be unable to construct any consecutive course of conduct that would ensure success.

The third consideration is that of recurrent mania. What I have said above will dispose of this in so far as it is connected with the two

# Tuesday, 11 September, 1888

manias I have been discussing. But a recurrent mania in the form of epileptic mania will account most adequately for the known facts relating to these crimes.

You have pointed out, Sir, that a homicidal impulse may take the place of the ordinary epileptic seizure, and the connection of epilepsy with erotic excitation is too well known for me to discuss at length here.

Now, it may be assumed that the same privacy would be required for the commission of an immoral act as for the commission of a deed of blood. A homicidal maniac would not seek privacy. He would, of course, slay, whenever he happened to find his victim. In the Whitechapel case there is, to my mind, no doubt that complete seclusion was a necessary condition for the purposes, whatever they may have been of the murderer.

act, his excitement became epileptic with homicidal impulses.

I am therefore convinced of the excellence of your suggestion that "an inquiry as to the epileptic patients in Whitechapel and Spital-fields might afford more fruitful results than are to be attained by a mere wandering up and down streets, and asking householders whether they have heard "unwanted noises".

There are many thinks I might add in support of this deeply interesting theory, but I feel that I have already encroached too largely on your space.

I am &c., MEDICUS.

[We shall be glad to open our columns to correspondence from other medical experts in elucidation of the maniacal theory.—Ed. E. N.]

~

Now, it is quite probable that the murderer's intentions in seeking an out-of-the-way place were nothing else than to commit an immoral act, and being on the point of committing this

# Wednesday, 12 September, 1888

## The Times

### THE WHITECHAPEL MURDER.

The latest reports as to the search for the murderer are not of a hopeful character. On Monday evening it was stated that John Pizer, the man who was detained on suspicion of being concerned in causing the death of the woman Annie Chapman, was still in custody at the Leman-street Police-station. Last night it was decided to release him.

Many reports of a startling character have been circulated respecting the acts of violence committed by a man wearing a leather apron. No doubt many of the accounts of assaults committed on women in this district have been greatly exaggerated, yet so many versions have been related that the police give credit to at least a portion of them. They have, therefore, been keeping a sharp lookout for "leather apron," but nothing has been heard of his whereabouts.

The friends of Pizer stoutly denied that he was known by that name; but on the other hand Sergeant Thicke, who has an intimate know-ledge of the neighbourhood in which the murder was committed, affirms that he knew Pizer well by sight, and always knew him by the nickname spoken of. Sergeant Thicke also knew that he was in the habit of wearing a leather apron after the news of the murder was circulated.

A half-Spaniard and half-Bulgarian, who gave the name of Emanuel Delbast Violenia, waited on the police with respect to this inquiry. He stated that he, his wife, and two children tramped from Manchester to London with the view of being able to emigrate to Australia, and took up their abode in one of the lodging-houses in Hanbury-street.

Early last Saturday morning, walking alone along Hanbury-street, he noticed a man and woman quarrelling in a very excited manner. Violenia distinctly heard the man threaten to kill the woman by sticking a knife into her. They passed on, and Violenia went to his lodging. After the murder he communicated what he had seen to the police.

At 1 o'clock yesterday afternoon Sergeant Thicke, assisted by Inspector Canaby, placed about a dozen men, the greater portion of whom were Jews, in the yard of the Leman-street Police-station. Pizer was then brought out and allowed to place himself where he thought proper among the assembled men. He is a man of short stature, with black whiskers and shaven chin. Violenia, who had been accommodated in one of the lower rooms of the station-house, was then brought up into the yard. Having keenly scrutinized all the faces before him, he at once, without any hesitation or doubt whatever, went up to Pizer and identified him as the man whom he heard threaten a woman on the night of the murder.

Pizer, who has not been allowed to have communication with any of his friends, was then taken back to the station-house. It was then decided, with the approval of Detective-Inspector Abberline, that Violenia should be taken to the Whitechapel mortuary to see whether he could identify the deceased woman as the one he had seen in Pizer's company early on Saturday morning. The result is not announced, but it is believed that he was unable to identify her. Subsequently, cross-examination so discredited Violenia's evidence that it was wholly distrusted by the police, and Pizer was set at liberty.

An important discovery, however, which throws considerable light upon the movements of the murderer immediately after the committal of the crime, was made yesterday afternoon.

In the back yard of the house 25, Hanbury-street, the next house but one to the scene of the murder, a little girl noticed peculiar marks on the wall and on the ground. She communicated the discovery to Detective-Inspector Chandler, who had just called at the house in order to make a plan of the back premises of the three houses for the use of the Coroner at the inquest, which will be resumed to-day. The whole of the yard was then carefully examined, with the result that a bloody trail was found distinctly marked for a distance of five or six feet in the direction of the back door of the house.

Further investigation left no doubt that the trail was that of the murderer, who, it was evident, after finishing his work had passed through or over the dividing fence between Nos. 29 and 27, and thence into the garden of No. 25.

On the wall of the last house there was found a curious mark, between a smear and a sprinkle, which had probably been made by the murderer, who, alarmed by the blood-soaked state of his coat, took off that garment and knocked it against the wall.

Abutting on the end of the yard of No. 25 are

# Wednesday, 12 September, 1888

the works of Mr. Bailey, a packing-case maker. In the yard of this establishment, in an out-of-the-way corner, the police yesterday afternoon found some crumpled paper almost saturated with blood. It was evident that the murderer had found the paper in the yard of 25 and had wiped his hands with it, afterwards throwing it over the wall into Bailey's premises.

The house No. 25, like most of the dwellings in the street, is let out in tenements direct from the owner, who does not live on the premises, and has no direct representative therein. The back and front doors are therefore always left either on the latch or wide open, the tenant of each room looking after the safety of his own particular premises.

The general appearance of the bloody trail and other circumstances seem to show that the murderer intended to make his way as rapidly as possible into the street through the house next door but one, being frightened by some noise or light in No. 29 from retreating by the way by which he came.

A number of tradesmen in the neighbourhood in which the murder was committed have organized a vigilance committee, and yesterday morning the following notice was published:—

"Finding that, in spite of murders being committed in our midst our police force is inadequate to discover the author or authors of the late atrocities, we the undersigned have formed ourselves into a committee and intend offering a substantial reward to anyone, citizens or otherwise, who shall give such information as will be the means of bringing the murderer or murderers to justice."

The names of a large number of tradesmen are appended to the notices. Mr. S. Montagu, M.P., has offered a reward of £100 for the capture of the authors of the outrage. The police have received some hundreds of letters from all parts of the country offering suggestions of various kinds for the discovery of the person or persons concerned in the death of the poor woman. It is almost needless to say that none of the communications help in any way to elucidate the mystery.

A number of persons have also written offering their services, for certain pecuniary considerations, as "special detectives," and give glowing accounts, notwithstanding their previous inexperience in these matters, of their fitness to undertake the office they seek.

Last evening Timothy Donovan, the deputy of the lodging-house in Dorset-street, at which the woman Chapman formerly lived, made a statement to a representative of a news agency. He says he knows "Leather Apron" well. Some months ago he ejected him from the lodging-house, and that was for offering violence to a woman who was staying there. Donovan is surprised that the police have not called on him to go to Leman-street Police-station, as he would have no difficulty in deciding whether the prisoner there is "Leather Apron."

Yesterday morning two police-constables visited Donovan and showed him two rings, one a half-worn out "engaged" ring, the other appearing to be a wedding ring, which they stated had been discovered at a pawnbroker's. Donovan did not think they were the rings he had seen Mrs. Chapman wearing. The policemen then left, and Donovan heard no more of the incident.

Both Donovan and a former watcher at the lodging-house named West say that when they last saw "Leather Apron" he was wearing a kind of deerstalker hat, double peaked. West describes him as a man not more than 5ft. 4in. in height. Mrs. Fiddyman, the landlady of the house into which it was stated a blood-stained and wild-looking man entered shortly after the hour at which the murder was probably committed on Saturday morning, has been taken to Leman-street Station, and on seeing Pizer she expressed herself as quite certain that he was not the man who came into her house on the occasion spoken of.

Pigott, the other man arrested, whose father was well known in Gravesend for many years as an insurance agent, was first seen in Gravesend on Sunday afternoon about 4 o'clock. He then asked four young men, who were standing in the London-road, near Princes-street, where he could get a glass of beer, he having walked from Whitechapel. The young men told him.

Following their directions he jumped into a tramcar going towards Northfleet. The young men noticed that he had a bad hand, and that he carried a black bag. He was without this bag when subsequently seen. He left a paper parcel at a fish shop, kept by Mrs. Beitchteller, stating he was going across the water to Tilbury.

Instead of doing so he went to the Pope's Head publichouse, where his conversation about his hatred of women aroused suspicion, and led to his being detained by the police authorities.

Superintendent Berry, who is making most active and exhaustive inquiries, found the paper parcel at the fish shop to contain two shirts and a pair of stockings, one of the shirts, a blue-striped one, being torn about the breast, and having marks of blood upon it.

At the police-station, Pigott first said he knocked down the woman who had bitten his hand in a yard at the back of a lodging-house in Whitechapel, but he subsequently said the occurrence took place in Brick-lane. What has become of the black bag which Pigott was seen to have in Gravesend on Sunday afternoon is not known.

It appears that Pigott of late years has followed the business of a publican, and that seven or eight years ago he was in a good position, giving £8,000 to go into a house at Hoxton. Some question having arisen as to Pigott's mental condition, it may be added that he appeared perfectly rational during his detention at Gravesend.

—

## TO THE EDITOR OF THE TIMES.

Sir,—My theory having been circulated far and wide with reference to an opinion given to the authorities of the Criminal Investigation Department, I would like to qualify such statements in your columns.

That the murderer of the three victims in Whitechapel is one and the same person I have no doubt.

The whole affair is that of a lunatic, and as there is "method in madness," so there was method shown in the crime and in the gradual dissection of the body of the latest victim. It is not the work of a responsible person. It is a well-known and accepted fact that homicidal mania is incurable, but difficult of detection, as it frequently lies latent. It is incurable, and those who have been the subject of it should never be let loose on society.

I think that the murderer is not of the class of which "Leather Apron" belongs, but is of the upper class of society, and I still think that my opinion given to the authorities is the correct one—viz., that the murders have been committed by a lunatic lately discharged from some asylum, or by one who has escaped. If the former, doubtless one who, though suffering from the effects of homicidal mania, is apparently sane on the surface, and consquently has been liberated, and is following out the inclinations of his morbid imaginations by wholesale homicide. I think the advice given by me a sound one—to apply for an immediate return from all asylums who have discharged such individuals, with a view of ascertaining their whereabouts.

I am your obedient servant,
L. FORBES WINSLOW,
M.B. Camb., D.C.L. Oxon.
70, Wimpole-street,
Cavendish-square, W.,
Sept. 11.

~

# Wednesday, 12 September, 1888

The Star
FIFTH EDITION.

## WHITECHAPEL.
## PISER RELEASED IN THE ABSENCE OF ALL EVIDENCE AGAINST HIM.
### He is Very Candid to an Interviewer—A Pretty Theory of Blood Traces Turns Out a Mare's Nest—The Real Fact—A New Witness Volunteers a Statement.

John Piser was released last evening at eight o'clock, and was received by his friends and neighbours in Mulberry-street, with enthusiastic shouts of welcome. Some East-end Liberals to whom it now appears he is well known, and among whom he has been an active worker, have also called to sympathise with the family in the trouble apparently brought upon them by a police blunder, and also to congratulate John Piser on his release with unstained character.

The detectives searched with unusual diligence, but could find positively nothing against him. And this is not surprising considering that he is not "Leather Apron," at least not the "Leather Apron" who has been the terror and blackmailer of the women of Whitechapel.

John Piser, as the suspected "Leather Apron," was kept at Leman-street Police Station for 36 hours, but so far as we can learn he does not seem to have been done the justice of being confronted with any of the women who describe a man named "Leather Apron" as their terror, and who could immediately have put John Piser's identity to a conclusive test.

We shall probably have some more to say about this.

—

### PISER INTERVIEWED.

A Press Association reporter interviewed Piser at 22, Mulberry-street, Whitechapel, this morning. He was released from Leman-street at half-past eight o'clock last evening.

The ex-prisoner, in reply to questions put to him, said:—"Whatever particulars the world at large, the police authorities, and the public wish to know as to my whereabouts, and as to where I was staying when these atrocious and horrible crimes were committed I am quite willing to give.

I came into this house at a quarter to eleven o'clock on Thursday night last. I knocked at the door. My sister opened it. She was rather surprised to see me, but it is usual at Jewish holiday times to pay visits to friends. My sister's young man was present. I shook hands with him. We had some conversation about work. My sister first went to bed and put the bolt in the latch. Anybody that goes out of the house after the door is latched cannot get in again.

From Thursday night until I was arrested
### I NEVER LEFT THE HOUSE
except to go into the yard. I was several times seen going into the yard by a next door neighbour.

On Monday morning last Sergeant Thicke came here. I opened the door. He said I was wanted, and I asked what for. He replied, 'You know what for. You will have to come with me.' I said, 'Very well, sir. I'll go down to the station with you with the greatest of pleasure.'"

"Did he charge you?" asked the reporter, "or tell you what you were wanted for?"

He said, "You know you are 'Leather Apron,' or words to that effect. Up to that moment I did not know that I was called by that name. I have been in the habit of wearing an apron. I have worn it coming from my employment, but not recently. I was quite surprised when Sergeant Thicke called me by
### THE NAME OF LEATHER APRON.

When I arrived at the police-station the police searched me, naturally I suppose, and in the usual way. They took everything from me, which I suppose is according to the customs and laws of the country. They found nothing in my possession that would incriminate me, thank God. I know of no crime, I have been connected with no crime, and my character will bear the strictest investigation, both by my co-religionists, and Gentiles whom I have worked for. I occasionally stayed at a lodging-house—chambers—but not in Dorset-street."

"Before you came to 22, Mulberry-street, on Thursday night, where had you been staying?"

"In the early part of last week I was at Holloway, and it was from Holloway that I came on Thursday. Last Sunday week I was accosted in Church-street by two females unknown to me. One asked me

99

# Wednesday, 12 September, 1888

**'ARE YOU THE MAN?'**

(Presumably referring to the Buck's-row murder.)

I said, 'God forbid, my good woman.' A stalwart man then came up and said, 'Come in, man, and treat me to half a pint." I went on. I was not the man who is said to have been seen in a publichouse on Saturday morning. I don't know Mrs. Fiddymont's public-house. I was totally ignorant of such a name as "Mrs. Sievey," until it was published, and don't know such a woman.

Between eleven and twelve o'clock yesterday a man came to Leman-street Police-station. One of the authorities asked me if I had any objection to go out to see if I could be identified. I at once went into the station yard. There were several men there. One of them I know to be a boot finisher. He is a stout, stalwart man, of negro caste. He came towards me, and without saying a word he deliberately placed his hand on my shoulder. I promptly replied, "I don't know you; you are mistaken."

His statement that he saw me threaten a woman in Hanbury-street is false, for I can prove, as I have already said, that I never left the place from Thursday night until the time I was arrested.

*The Star* has published a portrait intended to represent me, but it has no more resemblance to me than it has to the man in the moon. I have been told that I shall be wanted at the inquest this afternoon. I am quite ready to go and to make a full statement as to my whereabouts.

I shall see if I cannot legally proceed against those who have made statements about me. The charges made against me have quite broken my spirits, and I am afraid I shall have to place myself under medical treatment for some time."

Piser is a man of medium height, with florid complexion, and wears a moustache and side whiskers.

For a man of his class he displays more than an ordinary amount of intelligence. He was perfectly at ease while making his statement, and more than once appealed to his brother, who was present, for confirmation of his story.

—

In this morning's papers there is a pretty story for the lovers of the sensational. We print it

**ONLY TO CONTRADICT IT**

and show how some of our contemporaries swallow statements without the least attempt to prove them.

The story goes that a little girl happened to be walking in the back garden, or yard, of the house 25, Hanbury-street, the next house but one to the scene of the murder, when her attention was attracted to peculiar marks on the wall and on the garden path.

The yard was carefully examined, with the result that a bloody trail was found distinctly marked for a distance of five or six feet in the direction of the back door of the house. The appearances, it is said, suggested that the murderer had passed through or over the dividing fence between Nos. 29 and 27, and thence into the garden of No. 25.

On the wall of the last house was a curious mark, between a smear and a sprinkle, as if the murderer, alarmed by the bloodsoaked state of his coat, had taken it off, and knocked it against the wall. Abutting on the end of the yard at No. 25, are the works of Mr. Bailey, a packing-case maker. In the yard of this establishment, in an out-of-the-way corner, the police found some crumpled paper, stained, almost

**SATURATED WITH BLOOD.**

On this a nice little theory is built up. The murderer is said to have intended to make his way into the street through the house next door but one, being frightened by some noise or light in No. 29 from retreating by the way which he came. On reaching the yard of No. 25, he made for the back door, and then suddenly remembering his bloodstained appearance, he stopped, and, catching sight of the pieces of paper lying about, he

**RETRACED HIS STEPS**

to the end of the yard, and then performed his gruesome toilet.

A *Star* reporter called on Inspector Chandler this morning to know whether this startling story had any basis in fact. The inspector hadn't seen the statement, and when it was read to him he nearly laughed. And no wonder; the supposed bloodstains are only the discolorations on the mortar caused by urine! As for blood on the bricks, and the bloodstained paper, nothing of the kind had been found.

# Wednesday, 12 September, 1888

—

## A WITNESS OF MURDERER AND VICTIM.

A woman named Durrell, who minds carts on market morning in Spitalfields Market, stated yesterday that, about half-past five o'clock on Saturday morning, she was passing the front door of No. 29, Hanbury-street, when she saw a man and a woman standing on the pavement. She heard the man say, "Will you?" and the woman replied, "Yes." They then disappeared. Mrs. Durrell does not think she could identify the couple.

—

## THE ST. JUDE'S VIGILANCE ASSOCIATION

has only been in existence about four weeks. It is largely composed of working men, assisted by some of the members belonging to Toynbee Hall, its operations being confined to that neighbourhood. A member of the committee stated yesterday that rows are constantly occurring in the district, and that the police force is too small to deal with the disturbers of the peace. The night after the murder in Buck's-row, a man and woman disturbed Wentworth-street for more than half an hour. Two members of the committee were present, but no policeman could be found. Another brawl took place yesterday in the same thoroughfare, and one of the committee, who became aware of it, looked for a constable for twenty minutes before one was found.

—

## ANOTHER ARREST.

A man has been arrested at Holloway on suspicion of being concerned in the Whitechapel murderer. He is believed to be insane.

The Exchange Telegraph Company learns that the police have full knowledge of the whereabouts of the man whose description has been circulated as that of the alleged Whitechapel murderer, and his identity is spoken to by several witnesses. Although not actually under arrest he is carefully watched, and his arrest is said to be only a question of time.

The belief is steadily gaining ground that the man who was seen in a passage with a woman who is supposed to have been Mary Ann Nicholls on the morning of 8 Aug., and who spoke with a foreign accent, is the murderer of both Mary Ann Nicholls and Annie Chapman; and in the event of his arrest strong primâ facie evidence will be forthcoming to connect him with the crimes.

The police have keenly followed up the clue which was given them about this man.

—

## The Slaughterman Theory.

"An Old Butcher" writes:—The supposition that the Whitechapel murderer is a butcher may be correct—very possibly so—but when Dr. Ralph Llewellyn says, "The throat was cut as a calf's or pig's is cut, with one hard blow from left to right," he is talking that which is sheer nonsense, and shows he doesn't know what he is talking about.

A calf is drawn up by its hind legs, and then the butcher, holding its left ear with his left hand, thrusts the knife in the side of the neck just under the ear, drawing it carefully towards the windpipe, but not cutting it.

A pig, on the contrary, is thrown on its side, a small cut is then made laterally just above the breastbone towards the neck, and the knife then thrust into the animal towards the lungs, cutting a main artery, when the blood rushes out.

Neither animal is killed by "one hard blow from left to right," and neither is killed in the same way as this poor woman was killed—consequently, she could not have been killed as they are killed. Again, a butcher does not strike downward to disembowel, and he doesn't "rip a calf up." He makes a slight incision in the animal when skinned, or partially skinned, as it is hanging up, when he very carefully draws down the knife with his fingers inserted inside.

I take it that a butcher would be a far better authority to tell whether done by a butcher than Dr. Llewellyn would. Any practical butcher who was shown the intestines would see at a glance.

~

# Wednesday, 12 September, 1888

## Evening News
### FIFTH EDITION.
### THE WHITECHAPEL TRAGEDIES.
#### ON THE MURDERER'S TRACK.
#### PISER RELEASED.
#### WHAT HE HAS TO SAY ABOUT HIS ARREST.
#### ANOTHER CAPTURE.

The Press Association says that John Piser will, in all probability, be called as a witness at the inquest on the woman Chapman, which is to be held to-day. His brother Samuel Piser, informed a representative of the Press Association that the police had advised him meanwhile to refuse to be interviewed. His brother states that Piser was treated well while in custody, and had every attention shown to him. Piser was released from Leman-street Police-station at 8.30 last night, and left in company with his brother Samuel, and was received by a large and enthusiastic crowd in Mulberry-street, who clapped their hands and cheered repeatedly.

Scotland-yard has been following up, with praiseworthy perseverance, the supposed clue afforded by the discovery of blood trails in the yard used by Mr. Bailey, packing-case maker, at No. 25, Hanbury-street, a few doors from the scene of the Chapman-murder.

The occupiers of the houses near this, through one of which the murderer must have escaped, have been subjected to a minute examination, but the discovery made by the girl Laura Sickings has led to nothing substantial as yet.

It is thought by many in the ill-fated district that the reward offered by Mr. Montagu, M.P., will bring forward some evidence which may convict the murderer, as it is generally believed his whereabouts must be known to somebody. The excitement is gradually toning down, partly because of the belief that the place has got too hot for the murderer, and also by the fact that a large detective force is keeping watch day and night over it.

### THE ALLEGED MURDERER ALLEGED TO BE KNOWN AND WATCHED.

The Exchange Telegraph Company learns that the police have full knowledge of the whereabouts of the man whose description has been circulated as that of the alleged White-chapel murderer, and his identity is spoken to by several witnesses. Although not actually under arrest he is carefully watched, and his arrest is said to be only a question of time.

The belief is steadily gaining ground that the man who was seen in a passage with a woman who is supposed to have been Mary Ann Nichols, on the morning of August 8, and who spoke with a foreign accent, is the murderer of both Mary Ann Nichols and Annie Chapman, and in the event of his arrest, strong prima facie evidence will be forthcoming to connect him with the crimes. The police have keenly followed up the clue which was given to them about the man.

The pensioner who kept company with Annie Chapman, will, it is said, be forth-coming, and also the two men who were tailed by the witness Davis when he found the body in Hanbury-street, but whose names were not then known to the police. They are employed at the works of Mr. Bailey, packing case maker.

There is now said to be no truth in the statement that blood stains were found on the walls of an adjoining house.

### INTERVIEW WITH PISER.

A Press Association reporter interviewed Piser, otherwise, "Leather Apron," at 22, Mulberry-street, Whitechapel, this morning. He was released from Leman-street at half-past eight last evening.

The ex-prisoner, in reply to questions put to him, said: Whatever particulars the world at large, the police authorities, and the public wish to know as to my whereabouts, and as to where I was staying when these atrocious and horrible crimes were committed I am quite willing to give. I came into this house at a quarter to eleven o'clock on Thursday night last. I knocked at the door. My sister opened it. She was rather surprised to see me, but it is usual at Jewish holiday times to pay visits to friends. My sister's young man was present. I shook hands with him. We had some conversation about work.

My sister first went to bed and put the bolt in the latch. Anybody that goes out of the house after the door is latched cannot get in again. From Thursday night until I was arrested, I never left the house except to go into the yard. I was several times seen going into the yard by a next-door neighbour.

On Monday morning last, Sergeant Thicke came here. I opened the door. He said I was wanted, and I asked what for. He replied, "You know what for. You will have to come with me." I said, "Very well, sir. I'll go down to the station with you with the greatest of pleasure."

"Did he charge you?" said the reporter; "or tell you what you were wanted for?"

He said, "You know you are "Leather Apron," or words to that effect. Up to that moment I did not know that I was called by that name. I have been in the habit of wearing an apron. I have worn it coming from my employment, but not recently. I was quite surprised when Sergeant Thicke called me by the name of "Leather Apron."

When I arrived at the police-station the police searched me—naturally, I suppose, and in the usual way. They took everything from me, which, I suppose, is according to the custom and laws of the country. They found nothing in my possession that would incriminate me, thank God, or connect me with the crime that I have unfortunately been placed in custody upon. I know of no crime.

I have been connected with no crime, and my character will bear the strictest investigation, both by my co-religionists and Gentiles whom I have worked for.

I am generally most of my time here, except when I go away to get anything that might be beneficial to me. I occasionally stayed at a lodging-house—chambers—but not in Dorset-street.

Before you came to 22, Mulberry-street, on Thursday night, where had you been staying?

In the early part of last week I was at Holloway, and it was from Holloway that I came on Thursday. Last Sunday week I was approached in Church-street by two females unknown to me. One asked me, "Are you the man?" presumably referring to the Buck's-row murder. I said "God forbid, my good woman." A stalwart man then came up and said "Come in, man, and treat me to half a pint." I went on.

I was not the man who is said to have been seen in a public-house on Saturday morning. I don't know Mrs. Fiddyman's public house. I was totally ignorant of such a name as "Mrs.

Sievey" until it was published. I don't know such a woman.

Between eleven and twelve o'clock yesterday, a man came to Leman-street police station. One of the authorities asked me if I had any objection to go out to see if I could be identified. I at once went into the station yard. There were several men there. One of them I know to be a boot finisher. He is a stout, stalwart man of negro caste. He came towards me, and without saying a word he deliberately placed his hand on my shoulder. I promptly replied, "I don't know you. You are mistaken."

His statement that he saw me threaten a woman in Hanbury-street is false, for I can prove, as I have already said, that I never left this place from Thursday night until the time I was arrested.

One of the evening newspapers has published a portrait intended to represent me, but it has no more resemblance to me than it has to the man in the moon. I have been told that I shall be wanted at the inquest this afternoon. I am quite willing to go, and to make a full statement as to my whereabouts.

I shall see if I cannot legally proceed against those who have made statements about me. The charges made against me have quite broken my spirits, and I am afraid I shall have to place myself under medical treatment for some time.

Piser is a man of medium height, with florid complexion and wears a moustache and side whiskers. For a man of his class he displays more than an ordinary amount of intelligence. He was perfectly at ease while making his statement, and more than once appealed to his brother, who was present, for confirmation of his story.

### THE VICTIM'S FUNERAL.

Annie Chapman, the woman murdered in Spitalfields, has been identified by her brother. Her relatives will take the body away to-day on getting the order from the coroner. The date and place of the funeral will be kept a secret, the friends objecting to any demonstrations.

A man has been arrested at Holloway on suspicion of being concerned in the Spitalfields murder. He is believed to be insane.

—

# Wednesday, 12 September, 1888

**THE EDITOR'S DRAWER.**
**THE EAST END HORRORS.**
**To the Editor of "The Evening News."**

Sir—As a tradesman of many years standing in Whitechapel High-street, one of the finest thoroughfares in London, I protest (and I am sure I am expressing the feelings of my fellow-tradesmen) against the Press placarding the reporting in their various editions of Saturday and Monday (to-day) "Horrible murder in Whitechapel," when in reality it took place in the parish of Christ Church, Spitalfields.

As about half the trade is done with persons residing out of the district, such misrepresentations are very misleading, and persons, especially females, are afraid of coming into Whitechapel to shop, thereby ensuring a very serious loss to traders.

Whitechapel by many persons resident in the country and West-end, is looked upon as being a horrible place. I would advise such ladies and gentlemen to pay a visit to the parish: I think they would then come to a very different conclusion.

I might say to those ladies and gentlemen who do not, or cannot, pay a visit to Whitechapel, that we have a fine, wide, handsome thoroughfare one mile in length, and that during the last seven years upwards of one million pounds has been spent in improvements for the benefit of the working classes.

The whole of the houses surrounding and formerly known as Petticoat-lane have been pulled down and fine blocks of buildings for the artisan have erected in their place. Much remains to be done in the neighbouring parish of Spitalfields, when, I am assured, the new London Council will do justice to that long-neglected parish.

I am, &c.,
REFORMER.
September 10.

~

# Thursday, 13 September, 1888

## The Star
### WHAT WE THINK.

IT looks very much as if the police had entirely lost the scent of the Whitechapel murderer, if, indeed, they ever found it. They made a mistake from the beginning; they took no plan of the house, and they took no steps for following the trail of the murderer. The blood stains story proved to be a mare's-nest,[47] but with bloodhounds put on while the scent was hot, and in the early morning when conflicting trails would not puzzle the dogs, the criminal might have been tracked.

Compare the proceedings of the police in this case with those of Lecoq, Gaboriau's detective hero—the manner in which the young detective tracked the steps in the snow, got the size of the boots of the person who had just left the hovel where the murder had taken place, and sniffed round every square inch of ground both in the house itself and in the yard at the back. There is nothing improbable in this; it is the ordinary proceeding of a French detective, but it does not seem to have been dreamed of by our police. The whole story in Gaboriau's novel might be printed as a leaflet and distributed among Sir Charles Warren's detectives.

MEANWHILE the *Daily Telegraph* is for throwing Mr. Matthews to the lions, and probably every other editor in his heart thinks Sir Charles Warren ought to go too. Of course he, and not Mr. Matthews, is really to blame. A feeble, forcible red-tapeist,[48] with the mind of a dancing master and the statesmanship of an attorney's clerk, like Mr. Matthews, is, of course, unsuitable for his position; but with a just and really strong man at Scotland-yard, Mr. Matthews could have done little harm.

It is Sir Charles Warren who has militarised the force when he ought to have spiritualised—in the French sense—and trained it. Less drill and more brains, less of the "Prepare to meet cavalry" and more of the "Prepare to catch criminals" is what is wanted in our police.

UNHAPPILY the Whitechapel case is being mismanaged from top to bottom. The man Piser has been released; but why was not he confronted with the women who spoke to him and could have identified him, or the contrary? Was he the Leather Apron—the terror of Whitechapel unfortunates—or was he not? If the man is innocent, as he appears to be, the neglect of the police is grossly unfair to him; and in any case the interests of the public are being shamefully neglected.

—

### THE WHITECHAPEL CRIMES.
### Mrs. Durrell Identifies Chapman as the Woman She Saw with a Man.

The police continue their investigations into the Whitechapel crimes, but they seem very unlikely to discover the culprit. The only chance of his detection is the possibility that he may commit another crime and be caught in the act. The man Pigott is still an inmate of the workhouse infirmary, and it is stated that his mental condition has not materially improved. The idea that he was connected in some way with the recent crimes has not been entirely abandoned, and he is still kept under surveillance, while inquiries are being made into his antecedents.

Another arrest on suspicion was made at Holloway yesterday, but it was speedily ascertained that the man was a harmless lunatic, and he was sent to the workhouse infirmary.

A woman named Mrs. Durrell made a statement yesterday to the effect that at about half-past five o'clock on the morning of the murder of Mrs. Chapman she saw a man and a woman conversing outside No. 29, Hanbury-street, the scene of the murder, and that they disappeared very suddenly.

Mrs. Durrell was taken to the mortuary yesterday, and identified the body of Chapman as that of the woman whom she saw in Hanbury-street. If this identification can be relied upon, it is obviously an important piece of evidence, as it fixes with precision

### THE TIME OF THE MURDER,

and corroborates the statement of John Richardson, who went into the yard at a quarter to five, and has consistently and persistently declared that the body was not then on the

---

[47] **Mare's-nest.** A supposed discovery, hoax, delusion: also *to find a mare's nest and laugh at the eggs* (1647). (Farmer)

[48] **Red-Tapist.** (a) A government clerk; (b) a precisian. (ibid)

**Precisian.** Stickler for the rules. (Morehead)

premises. Davis, the man who first saw the corpse, went into the yard shortly after six o'clock.

Assuming, therefore, that the various witnesses have spoken the truth, the murder must have been committed between half-past five and six o'clock, and the murderer must have walked through the streets in almost broad daylight without attracting attention, although he must have been at the time more or less stained with blood.

This seems incredible, and it has certainly strengthened the belief of many of those engaged in the case that the murderer had not far to go to reach his lodgings in a private house.

Among the many suggestions made to the police is one urging that the pupils of the murdered woman's eyes should be photographed, on the chance of the retina retaining an image of the murderer capable of reproduction.[49]

—

### Police Meet and are Mysterious.

The detectives from Scotland-yard and those belonging to the Bethnal-green division who are engaged in the Buck's-row murder met at the Commercial-street Station to-day to make arrangements for certain low quarters to be particularly watched during the night. The police say they believe they are on the track of the murderer. This individual is being carefully looked after, but they cannot arrest him until they have more definite information to act upon.

Considerable doubt is being thrown on the evidence of John Richardson, who stated that he was almost on the exact spot where the body was found at a quarter to five on Satur-

day morning, and no signs of the murder were then apparent. It is now beginning to be believed that the woman was brought to the backyard in Hanbury-street some time earlier. Another link in the chain of evidence which the police are trying to establish is as to the whereabouts of the murdered woman between the time when she was last seen and when she was found murdered. There are at least

### NEARLY FOUR HOURS TO BE ACCOUNTED FOR.

The search of the police is being thorough and systematic. They have accounted for a vast number of the frequenters of the common lodging-houses in the neighbourhood, but some few men are still unaccounted for. There are a large number of the pedlar class who leave the neighbourhood on periodical journeys, and these on their return will be asked whether they saw Annie, the murdered woman, in the vicinity of the Spitalfields Market on Saturday morning last, and who were her companions. It is considered difficult to believe that a woman who was so well known in the district cannot be traced for four hours, and if her whereabouts during the time in question can be ascertained a very tangible piece of evidence will have been attained. Evidence is being withheld from the police by some women who were associates of the two last murdered women because of their terror of sharing a like fate, and several of them have left the neighbourhood.

—

### THE PEOPLE'S POST BOX.
### The Whitechapel Murders.

SIR,—It may interest your readers to learn in connection with the Whitechapel murders that a number of parallel cases occurred some seven years ago near Bochum in Westphalia. The murderer was in the habit of lassoing women, and treating them in exactly the same manner as his confrère[50] of Spitalfields. After many fruitless efforts on the part of the police to catch the perpetrator of the outrages, they at last arrested a gipsy, who was duly sentenced to death and beheaded. Unfortunately, a few days after his execution the murders recommenced! The assassin had the impudence to write to the magistrate of the district that he meant to kill a

---

[49] **Optogram.** The retinal image formed by the bleaching of visual purple under the influence of light. (Miller)
It was believed that the last thing seen before death would be temporarily imprinted on the retina and could be photographed. There have been experiments that proved images can be reproduced from the eyes of the dead, if the eyes are retrieved within a short time post mortem, but these optograms are vague and basically useless.
See Optography and optograms, http://college-optometrists.org/en/college/museyeum/online_exhibitions/eye/optography.cfm

---

[50] **Confrère.** Comrade. (Dubois)

# Thursday, 13 September, 1888

certain number of victims and would then give himself up. The papers applied to such a murder the expressive term of *lustmörd* (pleasure murder).[51]

My German friend, who reminds me of this case would not feel astonished to hear that the Bochum *lustmörder*[52] has put in an appearance at Whitechapel.—Yours, &c.,

S.

London, 10 Sept.

~

---

[51] **Lustmord**. Rape and murder. (Glucksman)

[52] Between 30 December, 1878 and 21 May, 1882 eight women and girls were murdered in the area surrounding the city of Bochum, Westphalia. These women were strangled, sexually violated and at least some were mutilated. For example, the fourth victim, nineteen-year-old Wilhelmine Pott, was reported to have had her eyes gouged out, and the sixth victim, eleven-year-old Christine Hämelmann, was discovered "torn limb from limb in a horrible way." A convicted sex criminal named Wilhelm Schiff was arrested in April, 1881, and was duly executed after being charged with, and convicted of, the first three murders. However, three more murders were committed after his arrest, two of these after his execution. No one else was ever charged for these crimes. (Aragon-Yoshida)

## Evening News
### THE EAST-END MURDER
### THE POLICE ON THE TRACK
### WHITECHAPEL ROUGHS AT WORK

The Exchange Telegraph Company learns with regard to the Whitechapel murder that up to an early hour this morning the police had made no other arrests, nor had they gained any clue which would give hopes of a speedy capture of the murderer. The detectives from Scotland Yard, as well as those belonging to the Bethnal Green Division which has charge of the Buck's-row murder, met at the Commercial-street Station to make arrangements with the police as to certain low quarters which were to be particularly watched during the night. The police still adhere to the statement that they believe they are on the track of the murderer, this individual being carefully looked after, but they cannot arrest him until they have more definite information to act upon.

As evidence of the insecurity prevailing in certain parts of the East-end, notably, Hanbury-street and vicinity about five persons were accosted, yesterday, by a gang of roughs who, amongst other misdeeds, deprived an old man, aged 80, of his gold watch and chain. The Exchange Telegraph Company learns that vital evidence is being withheld from the police by some women who were associates of the two last murdered women because of their terror of sharing a like fate, and several of them have left the neighbourhood.

---

### THE CHARACTER OF
### WINTHROP-STREET

A few days ago one of the news agencies made some remarks respecting the character of Winthrop-street (near Buck's-row) which the inhabitants much resent. The acting trustee of the Torr estate, which includes one side of the street, informs us that the inhabitants are all respectable, hard-working people, many having been tenants for 25 years, and Mr. Hoyle, the collector, says the street does certainly not bear a bad reputation. As the publication of such prejudicial statements regarding the respectability of the street is likely to do harm to honest people whose sons and daughters have to make their way in the world, we have much pleasure in thus authoritatively contradicting the report.

—

## A NOVEL SUGGESTION.

Among the many suggestions made to the police is one arguing that the pupils of murdered woman's eyes should be photographed on the chance of the retina retaining an image of the murderer capable of reproduction.

—

## TO THE EDITOR OF THE "EVENING NEWS."

SIR—I have read with great interest your article, and the letter of Dr. Forbes Winslow, on the Whitechapel murders; and as far as I can judge, the opinions therein expressed have met with the approbation of the great majority of newspaper readers—viz., that the murders are the work of one man, and he epileptic or a homicidal maniac. In the East-end, however, the scene of these tragic mysteries, the majority of the population are not newspaper readers. At least, there is a very large class who cannot, or at any rate do not, read the newspapers, and whose opinions are to a very large extent formed independently of newspapers. Moreover, those people of whom I speak have the advantage of the profoundest and most accurate local knowledge. They know the scene of the crimes intimately, and they know all the characters who frequent the neighbourhood. Now, amongst those people the opinion is general that the murders are not the work of one man, but of several, acting probably, more or less in concert. Those people assert that in that neighbourhood there is, notoriously, a set of low fellows-whom they could point out-who systematically live on the earnings of the poor unfortunates who there ply their wretched trade, one man levying blackmail from several women, and affording them in return his "protection." And those people believe that the murders are the work of some of these "bullies," acting probably, more or less, in concert.

According to this theory, the murders were deliberately planned and executed; what led to them was the inability or unwillingness of the poor women to continue to satisfy the incessant demands of these blood-suckers-the women, it may be, acting more or less in concert; and the motive for the crimes is to be found in, first, a desire for revenge, and, second, a determination to read a terrible lesson to the others. The disembowelling and the other diabolical accompaniments were (according to this theory) dictated by the second part of the motive. If this should prove to be the true theory of the crimes, it would indicate a very serious state of things-far more serious, from one point of view, than even the presence among us of a lunatic at large, homicidal mania in his head, and a butcher's knife in his hand. I express no opinion upon the theory. I merely state it for the consideration of those who have not the same opportunities as myself of hearing it.

I am, P.Q.R.S.

## The Times

### THE WHITECHAPEL MURDER.

Yesterday Mr. Wynne E. Baxter, Coroner for the South-Eastern Division of Middlesex, resumed his inquiry at the Working Lads' Institute, Whitechapel-road respecting the death of Annie Chapman, who was found murdered in the back yard of 29, Hanbury-street, Spital-fields; last Saturday morning.

Detective-inspectors Abberline (Scotland-yard), Helson, Chandler, Beck, and Detective-sergeant W. Thicke, H Division, again represented the Criminal Investigation Department.

Inspector Joseph Chandler, H Division, said that about two minutes past 6 on Saturday morning he was on duty in Commercial-street. He saw several men running up Hanbury-street, and he beckoned to them. One of them said, "Another woman has been murdered."

Witness at once went with him to 29, Hanbury-street, and passed through the passage into the yard. There were several people in the passage, but no one was in the yard. He saw the body of the deceased lying on the ground on her back. Her head was towards the back wall of the house, but it was some 2ft. from the wall, and the body was not more than 6in. or 9in. from the steps. The face was turned on the right side, and the left hand rested on the left breast. The right hand was lying down by the left side, and the legs were drawn up. The body was lying parallel with the fencing, and was about two yards distant.

Witness, remaining there, sent for the divisional surgeon; Dr. Phillips, and also to the station for the ambulance and further assistance. When the constables arrived he removed all persons from the passage, and saw that no one touched the body till the doctor arrived. He obtained some sacking from one of the neighbours to cover the body pending the arrival of the doctor.

Dr. Phillips arrived about half-past 6 and examined the body. He then directed the body to be removed to the mortuary, which was done on the police ambulance.

After the body had been removed a piece of coarse muslin and a small pocket haircomb case were found. A portion of an envelope was found lying near where her head had been, and a piece of paper containing two pills. He had not the pills there, as inquiries were being made about them. On the back of the envelope was the seal of the Sussex Regiment. The other portion of the writing was torn away. On the other side of the envelope was the letter "M" in a man's handwriting. There was also a post-office stamp, "London, 28 Aug., 1888," with a stamp that was indistinct. There was no postage stamp on that portion. On the front side of the envelope were the letters "Sp." in writing.

He also found a leather apron lying in the yard saturated with wet and it was about 2ft. from the water tap. A box, commonly used by packing-case makers, a piece of flat steel that had a since been identified by Mrs. Richardson, and also a spring were found lying close to where the body was found.

By the CORONER.—Some portions of the yard were composed of earth and others of stones. It had not been properly paved. Some of the stones were flat while others were round. He could not detect any appearance of a struggle having taken place. The palings were only temporarily erected, although they might support the weight of a man while he was getting over them. There was no evidence of any one having recently got over them, and there was no breakage. Witness examined the adjoining yard. None of the palings had been broken, although they had since been broken. The palings near the body were stained with blood.

In the wall of No. 27 marks were discovered on Tuesday last, and they had been seen by Dr. Phillips. There were no drops of blood in the passage or outside, and the bloodstains were only found in the immediate neighbourhood of the body. There were also a few spots of blood on the back wall at the head of the body and some 2ft. or 3ft. from the ground. The largest spot was about the size of a six-penny piece. They were all within a small compass. Witness assisted in drawing out a plan of the place, and the plan produced was a correct one.

Witness searched the clothing of the deceased after the body was removed to the mortuary. The outside jacket, which was a long black one and reached to the knees, had bloodstains around the neck, both on the inside and out, and two or three spots on the left arm. The jacket was hooked at the top and buttoned down. There did not appear to have been any struggle with the jacket. The pocket produced

# Friday, 14 September, 1888

was found worn under the skirt. It was torn down the front and also at the side and did not contain anything. The deceased had on a black shirt, on which was a little blood at the back. There was no damage to the lower portion of the clothing. The boots were on her feet, while the stockings were bloodstained. None of the clothing was torn.

Witness saw young John Richardson a little before 7 o'clock in the passage of the house. He told witness he had been to the house about a quarter to 5 that morning, that he went to the back door and looked down at the cellar to see that all was right. He then went away to his work in the market. He did not say anything to witness about cutting his boot, but said he was sure the woman was not there at the time.

By the Foreman.—The back door opened outwards into the yard, on the left-hand side. That was the side on which the body was lying. Richardson might not have seen the body if he did not go into the yard. If he went down the steps and the body was there at the time he was bound to see it. Richardson told witness he did not go down the steps, and did not mention the fact that he sat down on the steps and cut his boots.

The Foreman.—Are you going to produce the pensioner we have heard so much about?

Witness.—We have not been able to find him. No one can give us the least idea who he is. We have instructed the deputy of the lodging-house to let us know at once if he again goes there.

The CORONER. —I should think that if the pensioner knows his own business he would come forward himself.

The Foreman.—It is important he should be here, as he was in the habit of spending Saturday nights with the deceased.

Sergeant Edmund Barry, 31H, stated that on Saturday last he conveyed the body of the deceased from 29, Hanbury-street, to the Whitechapel mortuary on the police ambulance. Detective-Sergeant Thicke examined the body and gave out a description of it to witness. In doing this that sergeant moved the clothing about. Two females from 35, Dorset-street, were also present, and described the clothing to witness. They did not touch the clothing or the body. Inspector Chandler then came.

Inspector Chandler, recalled, said he reached

the mortuary a few minutes after 7 o'clock, and the body, which was lying on the ambulance, did not appear to have been disturbed. He did not remain until the doctor arrived, but left a constable in charge. It was Constable Barnes, 376H.

Robert Mann, an inmate of the Whitechapel Union, stated that he had charge of the mortuary. At 7 o'clock on Saturday morning he received the body of the deceased, and remained with it until the doctor arrived at 2 o'clock. Two nurses from the infirmary came and undressed the body. He was not in the shed when that was done.

The CORONER.—This is not a mortuary, but simply a shed. Bodies ought not to be taken there. In the East-end, where mortuaries are required more than anywhere else, there are no mortuaries. When bodies are thrown up from the river off Wapping they have to be put in boxes, as there is no mortuary.

The Foreman agreed that one was necessary. He added that a reward should be offered in this case by the Government. Some gentlemen were forming a fund to offer a reward, and Mr. Montagu, M.P., had offered £100.

The witness, in further examination, said he was present when Dr. Phillips made his post-mortem examination. While he was doing so witness picked up the handkerchief produced from off the clothing, which was lying in a corner of the room. He gave the handkerchief to Dr. Phillips, who told him to put it in some water. Witness did not see the handkerchief across the throat of the deceased. It had blood on it as though it had been across her throat.

Timothy Donovan, 35, Dorset-street, recalled, identified the handkerchief produced, which deceased generally wore round her throat. She bought it off another lodger at the lodging-house a week or a fortnight before she met with her death. She was wearing it when she left the lodging-house on Saturday morning and had under it a piece of black woollen scarf. It was tied in the front in one knot.

By the Foreman.—He would recognize the pensioner if he saw him again, and he knew "Harry the hawker." He had not seen the pensioner since Saturday. On that day, when he came to the lodging-house, witness sent for the police, but before they came he went away. He was a man of soldierly appearance, and at times

110

# Friday, 14 September, 1888

used to come differently attired.

Mr. George Bagster Phillips, 2, Spital-square, stated he was a divisional surgeon of police, and had been for 23 years. At 6:20 on Saturday morning he was called by the police to 29, Hanbury-street, and he arrived there at 6:30.

He found the dead body of a female in the possession of the police, lying in the back yard, on her back and on the left hand of the steps. The head was about 6in. in front of the level of the bottom step, and her feet were towards a shed, which proved to contain wood, at the bottom of the yard. The left arm was placed across the left breast. The legs were drawn up, the feet resting on the ground, and the knees turned outwards. The face was swollen and turned on the right side. The tongue protruded between the front teeth, but not beyond the lips. The tongue was evidently much swollen. The front teeth were perfect, so far as the first molar, top and bottom, and very fine teeth they were. The body was terribly mutilated.

He searched the yard, and in doing so found a small piece of coarse muslin and a pocket comb in a paper case lying at the feet of the woman near the paling; and they apparently had been placed there in order or arranged there. He also found and delivered to the police other articles, including the leather apron.

The stiffness of the limbs was not marked, but was evidently commencing. He noticed that the throat was dissevered deeply; that the incisions through the skin were jagged, and reached right round the neck.

On the back wall of the house between the steps and the paling which bounded the yard on the left side, about 18in. from the ground, were about six patches of blood varying in size from a sixpenny piece to a small point. On the wooden paling, between the yard in question and the next, smears of blood, corresponding to where the head of the deceased lay, were to be seen. These were about 14in. from the ground, and immediately above the part where the blood lay that had flowed from the neck.

Soon after 2 o'clock on Saturday he went to the labour yard of the Whitechapel Union for the purpose of further examining the body. He was surprised to find that the body had been stripped, and was lying ready on the table for his examination. It was under great difficulty he could make his examination, and, as on many

occasions he had met with similar difficulties, he now raised his protest, as he had previously done, that members in his profession should be called upon to perform their duties in these inadequate circumstances. There were no adequate conveniences for a post-mortem examination; and at particular seasons of the year it was dangerous to the operator.

The CORONER.—As a matter of fact there is no public mortuary in the City of London up to Bow.

Witness, continuing, said,—The body had evidently been attended to since the removal to the mortuary, probably to be washed. He noticed the same protrusion of the tongue. There was a bruise over the right temple. On the upper eyelid there was a bruise, and there were two distinct bruises, each of the size of the top of a man's thumb, on the forepart of the top of the chest. The stiffness of the limbs was now well marked. There was a bruise over the middle part of the bone of the right hand. There was an old scar on the left of the frontal bone. The stiffness was more noticeable on the left side, especially in the fingers, which were partly closed. There was an abrasion over the ring finger, with distinct markings of a ring or rings. The throat had been severed as before described. The incisions into the skin indicated that they had been made from the left side of the neck. There were two distinct, clean cuts on the left side of the spine. They were parallel from each other and separated by about half an inch. The muscular structures appeared as though an attempt had been made to separate the bones of the neck. There were various other mutilations of the body, but he was of opinion that they occurred subsequent to the death of the woman, and to the large escape of blood from the division of the neck.

At this point Dr. Phillips said that, as from these injuries he was satisfied as to the cause of death, he thought that he had better not go into further details of the mutilations, which could only be painful to the feelings of the jury and the public. The Coroner decided to allow that course to be adopted.

Witness, continuing, said,—The cause of death was visible from the injuries he had described. From these appearances he was of opinion that the breathing was interfered with previous to death, and that death arose from syncope, or failure of the heart's action in consequence of loss of blood caused by the severance of the throat.

By the CORONER.—He should say that the instrument used at the throat and the abdomen was the same. It must have been a very sharp knife, with a thin, narrow blade, and must have been at least 6in. to 8in. in length, probably longer. He should say that the injuries could not have been inflicted by a bayonet or sword bayonet. They could have been done by such an instrument as a medical man used for *post mortem* purposes, but the ordinary surgical cases might not contain such an instrument. Those used by slaughtermen, well ground down, might have caused them. He thought the knives used by those in the leather trade would not be long enough in the blade.

There were indications of anatomical knowledge, which were only less indicated in consequence of haste. The whole of the body was not present, the absent portions being from the abdomen. The mode in which these portions were extracted showed some anatomical knowledge. He did not think these portions were lost in the transit of the body.

He should say that the deceased had been dead at least two hours, and probably more, when he first saw her; but it was right to mention that it was a fairly cool morning, and that the body would be more apt to cool rapidly from its having lost a great quantity of blood.

There was not evidence about the body of the woman of a struggle having taken place. He was positive that the deceased entered the yard alive. He made a practical search of the passage and the approach to the house and he saw no trace of blood. There was no blood on the apron, which had the appearance of not having been recently unfolded. He was shown some staining on the wall of No. 25. To the eye of a novice it looked like blood, but it was not so.

The deceased was far advanced in disease of the lungs and membranes of the brain, but they had nothing to do with the cause of death.

The stomach contained a little food, but there was not any sign of fluid. There was no appearance of the deceased having taken alcohol, but there were signs of great deprivation, and he should say she had been badly fed. He was convinced she had not taken any strong alcohol for some hours before her death.

The injuries were certainly not self-inflicted. The bruises on the face were evidently recent, especially about the chin and the sides of the jaw, but the bruises in front of the chest and temple were of longer standing—probably of days. He was of opinion that the person who cut the deceased's throat took hold of her by the chin, and then commenced the incision from left to right.

He thought it was highly probably that a person could call out, but with regard to an idea that she might have been gagged he could only point to the swollen face and protruding tongue, both of which were signs of suffocation.

The handkerchief produced, together with the pocket, he separated from the rest of some articles said to be taken from the body of deceased at the Whitechapel mortuary, and not then in the custody of the mortuary keeper. A handkerchief was round the throat of the deceased when he saw her early in the morning. He should say it was not tied on after the throat was cut.

Mary Elizabeth Simonds, nurse at the Whitechapel Infirmary, said on Saturday morning she and a nurse named Frances Wright were instructed to go to the mortuary. The body was lying on the ambulance. They were directed by Inspector Chandler to undress the deceased. Witness took the clothes off and placed them in a corner of the shed. They left the handkerchief round the neck of deceased. They washed the blood off the body. There was blood on the chest, as if it had run down from the throat. She found the pocket, the strings of which were not broken.

Inspector Chandler stated he did not instruct the nurses to undress and wash the body.

The Coroner's officer said it was done by order of the clerk to the guardians.

At this point the inquiry was adjourned until Wednesday next.

———

Up to the present time the police have not succeeded in connecting any person with the crime.

Dr. Phillips's positive opinion that the woman had been dead quite two hours when he first saw the body at half-past 6, throws serious doubt upon the accuracy of at least two important witnesses, and considerably adds to the prevailing confusion.

The man arrested at Holloway has for some

reason been removed to the asylum at Bow. His own friends give him an indifferent character. He has been missing from home for nearly two months, and it is known that he has been in the habit of carrying several large butcher's knives about his person. Inquiries are now being made with a view to tracing his movements during the past two months.

The principal officers engaged in investigating the Whitechapel murders were summoned to Scotland-yard yesterday. Later in the day Mr. Bruce, Assistant Commissioner, and Colonel Monsell, Chief Constable, paid a private visit to the Whitechapel district without notifying the local officials of their intention to do so. They visited the scene of the Buck's-row murder as well as Hanbury-street, and made many inquiries. They spent nearly a quarter of an hour at No. 29, Hanbury-street, and minutely inspected the house and the yard in which were found the mutilated body of Mrs. Chapman.

The police have satisfied themselves that the man Pigott could have had nothing to do with the murders. His movements have been fully accounted for, and he is no longer under surveillance.

*The Lancet* says:—"The theory that the succession of murders which have lately been committed in Whitechapel are the work of a lunatic appears to us to be by no means at present well established. We can quite understand the necessity for any murderer endeavouring to obliterate by the death of his victim his future identification as a burglar. Moreover, as far as we are aware, homicidal mania is generally characterized by the one single and fatal act, although we grant this may have been led up to by a deep-rooted series of delusions. It is most unusual for a lunatic to plan any complicated crime of this kind. Neither, as a rule, does a lunatic take precautions to escape from the consequences of his act; which data are most conspicuous in these now too celebrated cases."

~

## The Star
### WHAT WE THINK.

THERE will be a perceptible tightening of public interest in the Whitechapel tragedies to-day. Nearly a week has passed since the final crime in the series, and still the police are at fault. Meanwhile, the epidemic of lawlessness continues. Three violent robberies have taken place within a hundred yards of each other, and midway between the scenes of the last two crimes. There has been one more mysterious crime in the West of London, to which again the police have no clue. The evidence at the inquest is bad—bad as can be. Mysterious personages flit through it like the shadowy and awful figures in POE'S and STEVENSON'S novels, or the stealthy and cunning assassins of GABORIAU and DU BOISGOBEY.[53] The body of the woman is washed at the mortuary—nobody knows by whom. A ghostly pensioner starts into view and disappears again. Every new turn of this bewildering labyrinth reveals some fresh depth of social blackness, some strange and repulsive curiosity of human nature.

What are we to do? Where are we to turn? The foreman of the jury indignantly echoes our demand for a large reward by the Government. The reply is that the Government have ceased to issue rewards. The local ignorance of the detectives, the glib carelessness of their methods, illustrate the absolute necessity for forming Vigilant Committees, which we recommended from the first, and which might have saved the neighbourhood from the fresh spurt of criminal energy we record to-day. Neighbourhoods go mad like individuals, and, while the West sits discussing the Whitechapel horrors over its wine, the East is seething with impatience, distrust, horror. What a situation!

Meanwhile, theories as to the crime are setting steadily in one direction. The carefully evolved solution which we advanced in these columns some days ago evidently finds favour with the doctor and the coroner. This is the slaughterman theory. The most startling facts in its favour are these:

---

[53] **Émile Gaboriau** (1832-1873), **Fortuné du Boisgobey** (1821-1891), noted French writers of crime fiction. Most of their works were translated into English and were popular in Britain and the United States.

# Friday, 14 September, 1888

(1) The knowledge of rough anatomy shown by the murderer, who was able to remove vital organs whole.

(2) The resemblance between the method employed, and the manner of slaughtering a sheep.

(3) The probability that the knife employed was larger than a leather-cutter's weapon, and not larger than a slaughterman's.

(4) The extreme rapidity with which the crime was accomplished, and the rude violence of the cuts.

(5) The near neighbourhood of slaughter-houses to the scenes of the last two crimes.

(6) The fact that no other workman but a slaughterman could walk through the streets of London in the early morning be-dabbled with blood without attracting suspicion.

(7) The comparatively small effusion of blood.

Now, here, at all events, is a connected theory. There may be a link wanting here and there, but it stands four-square with some rude facts of East-end life, and it does not leave us a prey to the wild nightmare of delirious fancies into which the more fantastic theorists have plunged us. We don't ask the police to accept it; we only suggest to them, in the mere panic of guessing which seems to have overtaken them, to follow up such clues as it suggests.

But, after all, what is the use of blaming men who are but the victims of a cruel piece of blundering by our Maladroit Martinet? The offenders in this business are three. There is, first, Mr. HOWARD VINCENT, who did away with the old detectives of the Inspector BUCKET[54] type, and substituted a whole squad of novices—a good many of them, it is said, of the decayed valet class. Then there is Mr. MATTHEWS, a feeble mountebank,[55] who would pose and simper over the brink of a volcano. And, worst of all, there is Sir CHARLES WARREN, who finding the police force out of hand, disorganised it utterly, and thinking he had a genius for stamping out dangerous social tendencies, left the social facts at his feet—let the rank crop of crime and misery grow untouched and uncared-for. Property shaking in its shoes because of one wild outburst of the dangerous classes which our wicked system fosters—statesmen pursuing an insensate policy, and fearing for lives which in all probability were never threatened—these became the objects of Sir CHARLES'S tender solicitude. Instead of giving us sturdy constables and smart detectives, Sir CHARLES has naturalised the *mouchard*[56] and the Government reporter. With all his soldierly strictness, the force is far more undisciplined, far more lax in its conduct, than in Sir EDMUND HENDERSON'S days.

Unfortunately we can't impeach Sir CHARLES WARREN. He stands rooted in his self-conceit and fanaticism. But we can reach Mr. MATTHEWS, and every London newspaper but the *Times* is for getting rid of our never-at-home Secretary. The sooner, therefore, he is attacked in Parliament the better. The indirect consequences of this are obvious. Mr. MATTHEWS, after the habits of his kind, will come to the conclusion that if it is a question either of his retirement or of Sir CHARLES WARREN'S he much prefers that the CHIEF COMMISSIONER should go. Rid of one failure, we may be rid of another; and Trafalgar-square will be avenged in the person of one, if not two, of the men who struck down the rights of free speech in London, but could not lay a finger on its criminals.

—

## WHITECHAPEL.
## POINTS ABOUT WHICH THE POLICE ARE INQUIRING TO-DAY.
### A Girl's Statement of a Man with a Knife —Scotland-yard Waking Up.

The police to-day are making inquiries as to the whereabouts of the pensioner who was said to have kept company with the murdered woman Chapman. All traces have been lost of him since Saturday last. Tim Donovan, who gave evidence at the inquest which connected this man with the deceased, says he is known by the name of Ted Stanley, but he does not know his occupation. The watchman at the lodging-house says that when the pensioner went to the lodging-house on Saturday last, and was told

---

[54] **Inspector Bucket** ferreted out the murderer in Charles Dickens 1853 novel <u>Bleak House</u>.

[55] **Montebank**. A person who deceives others, most especially in order to trick them out of their money; a charlatan, swindler, fraud. (Morehead)

[56] **Mouchard**. Sneak, informer, police spy, stool-pigeon. (Dubois)

that Chapman had been murdered he nearly fainted. The police think that he is keeping out of the way more from shame in having been associated with the woman than from any fear that he has of being connected with the murder. It is probable also that he may be one of those who come from the country to the Spitalfields Market on Saturday, and will put in his appearance to-morrow.

Special inquiries, the Exchange Telegraph Company says, are being directed by the police to ascertain who was the writer of the envelope bearing the embossed stamp of the Sussex Regiment, a portion of which envelope was found on Chapman. It has just been ascertained that she had been in the habit of receiving similar letters.

A *Star* reporter has learned, however, that this piece of an envelope was casually picked up somewhere by a man who lodged at Dorset-chambers, and was given by him to Chapman to wrap some pills in. Two pills it will be remembered were found near the body.

The Central News says:—The blood-stained newspapers which were found in Bailey's-yard, close to Hanbury-street, and upon which it is conjectured the murderer wiped his hands after committing his fearful crime, have been subjected to analysis, and the stains this morning are **CERTIFIED TO BE HUMAN BLOOD.**

The police who made the search state distinctly that the paper was not there when they made the search on Saturday, and though they have been closely cross-examined on this point they adhere to their statement. It is not clear that the murderer could have thrown the newspapers on the spot where they were found from the backyard in Hanbury-street, but if he threw the paper, which was rolled up into a round mass, over the wall it might easily have been blown or kicked into the corner in which it was discovered.

To-day the police precautions are even stronger than before, the murderer hitherto having selected Friday or Saturday for the commission of his crimes.

A statement was made last night to a reporter by a young person named Lloyd, living in Heath-street, Commercial-road, E., which may possibly prove of some importance. While standing outside a neighbour's door about half-past ten on Monday night she heard her daughter, who was sitting on the doorstep, scream, and on looking round saw a man walk hurriedly away. Her daughter states that the man peered into her face and she perceived a large knife at his side. A lady living opposite stated that a similar incident took place outside her house. The man was short of stature, with a sandy beard, and wore a cloth cap. The woman drew the attention of some men who were passing to the strange man, and they pursued him some distance, until he turned up a by street, and, after assuming a threatening attitude, he suddenly disappeared.

The principal officers engaged in investigating the Whitechapel murders were summoned to Scotland-yard yesterday. Later in the day Mr. Bruce, Assistant Commissioner, and Colonel Monsell, Chief Constable, paid a private visit to the Whitechapel district without notifying the local officials of their intention to do so. They visited the scene of the Buck's-row murder as well as Hanbury-street, and made many inquiries. They spent nearly a quarter of an hour at No. 29, Hanbury-street, and minutely inspected the house and the yard in which were found the mutilated body of Mrs. Chapman.

The police have satisfied themselves that the man Pigott could have had nothing to do with the murders. His movements have been fully accounted for, and he is no longer under surveillance.

The man arrested at Holloway has for some reason been removed to the asylum at Bow. His own friends give him an indifferent character. He has been missing from home for nearly two months, and it is known that he has been in the habit of carrying several large butchers' knives about his person. Inquiries are now being made with a view to tracing his movements during the past two months.

—

## CRIME IN WHITECHAPEL.
### A Series of Outrages Which Have Just Been Committed with Impunity.

The people of Whitechapel—the respectable people of Whitechapel that is—want more policemen. And not without reason. Wherever you inquire you get some fresh story of robbery and outrage, committed often in broad daylight. A *Star* reporter this morning made some inquiries in the streets lying **BETWEEN THE SCENES OF THE LAST**

# Friday, 14 September, 1888

**TWO MURDERS,**

and found that since the Buck's-row crime hardly a day has passed unmarked by some brutal assault and robbery by a gang. Several such offences have happened during the last few days, while the place has been swarming with plain-clothes policemen.

Last Saturday afternoon in the Whitechapel-road, while the murder excitement was at its height, a cripple was attacked and robbed of his watch.

On Wednesday a gentleman was robbed in Hanbury-street at eleven o'clock in the morning.

In the afternoon of the same day, in the same street, another old gentleman was hustled and robbed of part of his watch-chain, luckily not losing his watch.

In Chicksand-street, not 50 yards away, an old man of seventy was robbed and ill used in a similar manner.

In Baker's-row, within a stone's throw, a feeble old man was badly beaten with the stick he was walking with; and at night, at ten o'clock, in Baker's-row, at the corner of Hanbury-street, a young man was the victim of a brutal onslaught because he looked respectable and worth robbing.

Yesterday morning a baker named Barnett, who keeps a shop in Hanbury-street, was robbed of £19 in a till in which a key had been left only for a few seconds. He followed the thief, but couldn't catch him, and a policeman was nowhere to be seen.

Whitechapel always has been a rough and not a particularly honest neighbourhood. Every respectable inhabitant seems to have been robbed at one time or the other, but the unanimous testimony is that every day

**WHITECHAPEL IS GETTING WORSE.**

It has come to such a pass that a tobacconist in Baker's-row, who recently has been a frequent victim, has had to screw everything he possibly can to the counter.

Opinions about the police vary. Some folks say that when told of a bother they go another way. But the most common view is that there are not enough policemen to cope with the gangs that swarm from the slums. One shopkeeper in Baker's-row, who not long ago was relieved of a carpet, says a word for the too few policemen at the expense of the magistrates. The constables, he says, are discouraged by the frequent airy dismissal of the men they capture. But after all

**WHAT SEEMS MOST AT FAULT**

—much more at fault than the men—is the system they have to work on. They go on beats it takes them more than half an hour to cover, and their regular movements are so well known that the roughs can do their work with a fine feeling of security. And often a drunken man who needs to be carried to the station deprives the inhabitants and way-farers of all protection.

Immunity of punishment for the rough is not without its effect on the law-abiding and would-be law-enforcing citizen. The inefficiency of the protection afforded by the police has given Whitechapel over to a reign of terror, and men look on at daylight misdeeds and are afraid to interfere.

A police inspector who was asked for his opinion on the subject said that to prevent crime in Whitechapel it would be necessary to put a policeman in every street. This only shows more forcibly, perhaps, than anything else how inadequately White-chapel is protected at present. What, however, makes not only Whitechapel, but all London, uneasy is the stupidity of the "heads" of the force.

A characteristic display of it is seen in the experiment being made with the American signal-posts. Innocent Islington has been chosen for this experiment. Why wasn't it tried in wicked Whitechapel, where it seems to be just the thing needed?[57]

---

[57] These telephone units were manufactured by the Gamewell Fire Alarm Telegraph Company of Newton Upper Falls, Massachusetts. Founded in 1879, Gamewell installed their systems in more than 250 U.S. and Canadian cities and municipalities by 1886. Two types of telephone units were developed for police use. The Street Station was described as "octagonal in shape, with pointed top, two feet four inches in diameter, and about eight feet in height. The top being made of glass and iron, it takes the place of a lamp post, and the gas or other lamp is placed upon the top, serving not only as a street light, but to light the interior of the station at night." There were also standalone Call Boxes that could be mounted to poles, post or walls.
Gamewell sales publications stated that if these units were "Placed at the outset in the most turbulent district of the city, it so speedily increased the

# Friday, 14 September, 1888

## Evening News
### THE WHITECHAPEL MURDER.
### IMPORTANT STATEMENT.
### A MAN WITH A KNIFE SEEN
### IN HEATH STREET.

The Press Associations says: A statement was made last night to a reporter by a young person named Lloyd, living in Heath-street, Commercial-road, which may possibly prove of some importance. While standing outside a neighbour's door, about 10.30 on Monday night, she heard her daughter, who was sitting on the doorstep, scream, and on looking round saw a man walk hurriedly away. The daughter states that the man peered into her face and she perceived a large knife at his side. A lady being opposite stated that a similar incident took place outside her house. The man was short of stature, with a sandy beard, and wore a cloth cap. The woman drew the attention of some men who were passing to the strange man and they pursued him some distance, until he turned up a bye street, and, assuming a threatening attitude, he suddenly disappeared.

### THE BLOOD STAINED NEWSPAPERS.

The Central News Agency says: The blood-stained newspapers which were found in Bailey's yard, close to Hanbury-street, and upon which it is conjectured the Spitalfields murderer wiped his hands after committing his fearful crime, have been subjected to analysis and the stains this morning are certified to be those of human blood. The police who made the search

state distinctly that the paper was not there when they made the search on Saturday, and though they have been closely cross-examined on this point, they adhere to their statement. It's not clear moreover that the murderer could have thrown the newspapers in the spot where they were found from the backyard in Hanbury-street, but if he threw the paper, which was rolled up into a round mass, over the wall, it might easily have been blown or kicked into the corner in which it was found.

To-day the police precautions are even stronger than before, the murderer hitherto having selected Friday or Saturday for the commission of his crimes

Our Maidstone correspondent states that a Scotland-yard detective has arrived there and interviewed the commander of the Sussex Regiment, with a view to identifying the writing found on the envelope found on the murdered woman.

### THE HUNT FOR THE SUSPECTED MAN.

Inspector Chandler states that up to noon to-day no arrest had been made in connection with the Whitechapel murders. The expectation of an early arrest entertained by the police yesterday is somewhat less sanguine to-day.

The police to-day are making enquiries as to the whereabouts of the pensioner who was said to have kept company with the murdered woman Chapman. All traces have been lost of him since Saturday last.

Tim Donavan, who gave evidence at the inquest which connected this man with the deceased, says he is known by the name of Ted Stanley, but he does not know his occupation, while the watchman at the lodging-house in Dorset-street whence Chapman left on Saturday morning last and was not afterwards seen alive, assets that the pensioner went to the lodging-house on Saturday last as usual, and on being informed that Chapman had been murdered nearly fainted.

The police think that he is keeping out of the way more from shame in having been associated with the deceased than from any fear that he has of being connected with the murder. It is more than probable also that he may be one of the regular attenders from the country at the Spitalfields Market, and will put in his usual appearance on Saturday.

---

efficiency of the "force," by enabling them to concentrate promptly at any needed point, that, within a few months, the district was as easily cared for and protected as the average districts of the city. Patrolmen soon learned that in case of necessity they, or someone for them, could literally, with the rapidity of lightning, summons assistance from the nearest station, and that they could reckon with certainty on a response. And the criminal and riotous discovered that there was little chance for them where electricity was utilized so successfully in aid of law and its agents."....."The telegraph is the one thing that the criminals dread. It circumvents all their skill and their cunning; and this application of it is certain to prove as valuable in municipalities as it has heretofore proved in securing arrests at distant points." (Bachman)

# Friday, 14 September, 1888

It is regarded as of considerable importance that Dr. Phillips, yesterday, established the fact that the deceased must have been lying in the back yard in Hanbury-street at least upwards of two hours before her body was found, and that young Richardson's evidence cannot, therefore, be relied on, this gives the police only about two hours to account for in connection with the disappearance of Chapman, and evidence is being sought as to her whereabouts during that time.

Special inquiries are being directed by the police to ascertain who was the writer of the envelope bearing the embossed stamp of the Sussex Regiment, a portion of which envelope was found on Chapman. It has just been ascertained that she had been in the habit of receiving similar letters.

—

## ARMED WOMEN AT THE EAST-END. MEETINGS OF THE VIGILANCE COMMITTEES.

A great deal of dissatisfaction exists in the whole district owing to the manner in which the coroner's inquest has been conducted. At a meeting of one of the local vigilance committees last night every member present expressed a decided opinion that the result of Mr. Phillips's post-mortem should have been given to the public at the earliest opportunity, so that his evidences to the character of the murder, the possible calling of the murderer, the kind of weapon used, and, more especially, the probable time at which the assassination took place and the assassin escaped, should have been subjected to thorough scrutiny by the best reasoning brains throughout the kingdom, in addition to giving other person a chance to exercise their vigilance.

It is pointed out now that the murder was committed at 4.30 on Saturday morning, and this is in all probability the exact time when the murderer, covered from head to foot with blood, left 29, Hanbury-street. Everyone in the district is, therefore, appealed to try and remember if such a man was seen round about there at the time mentioned. Dr. Phillips's evidence effectively disposed of the statement of Mr. Richardson, who said that the deceased was not in the yard at 5.15, for the doctor is absolutely certain that the murder was done in the yard, and about 4.30. The fact, therefore, is certain that Mr. Richardson, not suspecting the presence of the dead body, failed to notice it.

Dr. Forbes Winslow's suggestion of male decoys for the assassin has it is stated been acted upon extensively; it is quite certain that for two nights past three medical students have been out armed with revolver and dagger concealed in the dresses worn by them.

In addition to this the hapless women of the streets are themselves armed with knives, and two poor creatures this morning showed a reporter two formidable bowie-knives, which they would unquestionably use upon any man who attempted violence of a deadly character. A thin woman, pale, thin, and starving, said with evident sincerity, "Well, suppose I do get killed, it will be a good thing for me, for the winter is coming on, and the life is awful. I can't leave it; nobody would employ me." She had been 20 years on the streets of the East-end. She is well acquainted with the whole of the lower classes and their habits, and in common with many others of her class and the denizens of the lodging-houses generally feel certain that the murderer "does not belong to them."

## VIGILANCE COMMITTEES.

It has been stated that the excitement is dying out in the district, but this is not by any means a fact, for it is hourly increasing although the indignation is of a quieter and more concentrated kind. This is evidenced by the great number of Vigilance Committees which are being daily inaugurated, and one of the largest holds its meetings nightly and receives dozens of members at every sitting. Money is no object whatever, and is cheerfully subscribed for the purpose of hunting down the murderer.

The following is a copy of one of the many notices issued by the Jewish section of inhabitants, the Jews in particular being thoroughly determined in the matter, owing to the dread engendered in the breasts of their wives of the criminal exercising his horrible proclivities upon them:

"Finding that in spite of murders being committed in our midst, our police force is still inadequate to discover the author or authors of the late atrocities, we, the undersigned have formed ourselves into a committee, and intend offering a substantial reward to anyone, citizen or otherwise, who shall give such information as will bring the murderer or murderers to justice."

The statement by Piser, on Thursday, that had he been caught in Whitechapel on Saturday he would have been "torn to pieces" is perfectly true, and the same state of feeling exists in Whitechapel now as it did then. There is a general opinion that another murder is in store for the district, and should it be detected before the perpetrator can get away, the police will never be troubled with a "charge," for he will be rent limb from limb.

———

## THE WHITECHAPEL TRAGEDIES.
## RESUMED INQUEST.

The inquest on the body of the unfortunate woman, Annie Chapman, otherwise known as Annie Sievey, who was so brutally murdered and mutilated in Hanbury-street, on Saturday morning, the 8th inst., was resumed yesterday, at the Working Lads' Institute, Whitechapel-road, by Mr. Wynne Baxter.

The inquiry took place in the reading-room of the Institute, a spacious room with a moderate book-case at one end, under the care of a librarian, who keeps his post during the whole time ready to carry out his business of giving out books. A couple of tables at one side are placed for the use of the Coroner, and on his left-hand are the jurymen. The rest of the room is nearly filled with witnesses and reporters and their messengers. In this same room the inquiry on Mary Ann Nichols was held a week or two ago.

## POLICE EVIDENCE.

Inspector Chandler, of the H division of the police, said:—On Saturday morning about ten minutes past six I was on duty in Commercial-street. At the corner of Hanbury-street I saw several men running up that street, and I beckoned to them. One of them said, "Another woman has been murdered." I at once went with him to 29, Hanbury-street. I went through the passage into the yard. There were several people in the passage, but not in the yard.

I saw the body of the deceased lying on the ground on her back. Her head was towards the back wall of the house about two feet from the wall at the bottom of the steps. The face was turned on to the right side, and the left hand was resting on the left breast. The breast was not exposed. The right hand was by her side. The legs were drawn up, and the clothing was above the knees. Part of the intestines still connected with the body were lying above the right shoulder with some pieces of skin and flesh. There were also some pieces of skin over the left shoulder and a pool of blood. The body was lying parallel with the fencing.

I remained there and sent for the divisional surgeon, Mr. Phillips, and to the police-station for the ambulance and other assistance. When the constables arrived I removed the people from the passage, and saw that no one touched the body until the doctor arrived. I obtained some sacking to cover the body.

## THE DOCTOR EXAMINED THE BODY.

The doctor arrived about half-past six, examined the body, and directed it to be removed to the mortuary. It was removed on the ambulance.

After the body had been removed I found this piece of coarse muslin, a small-tooth comb, and a small comb in a paper case (produced). They were lying near the feet of the body. A small piece of paper—a portion of an envelope—was found near. It contained two pills. On the back of the envelope there was an embossed seal with the words "Sussex Regiment." On the other side there was the letter "M" in a man's handwriting. There was a postal mark on it, "London, Aug. 3, 1888." There was also another, but that was indistinct. There was no postage stamp.

## THE LEATHER APRON WAS THERE.

Was there anything else in the yard?

—There was a leather apron saturated with wet. It was about two feet from the tap.

Did you show it to the doctor?

—Yes.

Anything else?

—There was a box commonly used to hold nails. There were no nails in it. I also saw some flat steel bands. They have since been identified as part of the springs of a pair of leggings. The yard was partly earth and partly rough stones. It has never been properly paved.

Was there any appearance of a struggle?

—No.

The palings in the yard—are they strongly erected?

—No; quite the contrary. They may be strong enough to support the weight of a man getting over them.

## STAINS OF BLOOD ON THE PALINGS

There were stains of blood on the palings near the body. There were marks discovered on the wall of No. 25. They were noticed on Tuesday. Dr. Phillips has seen them. There were no marks of blood outside the yard or the passage. The others in the yard were only in the immediate neighbourhood of the body. There were a few spots of blood on the wall at the head of the body.

Did you search the clothes of the deceased?

—Yes, at the mortuary. The outside jacket, which was a long black one, had blood-stains around the neck. By the appearance of the jacket there did not seem to have been a struggle. The deceased wore two bodices, both of which were stained round the neck. A large pocket worn under the skirt was torn and empty. The two petticoats were stained very much, but not torn. I saw John Richardson in the course of the morning. He told me he had been at the house that morning about a quarter to five. He had looked into the yard to see if the cellar was all right. He said he was sure the deceased was not there at that time.

By a juryman:—If Richardson went down the steps he must have seen the body. He told me he did not go down the steps at all. I heard him mention cutting his boot here. He said nothing to me about it.

Are you going to produce the man Stanley-the pensioner who used to visit the deceased woman every week? He is a most important witness.

—We can't find him yet, but we are trying.

The Coroner:—If the pensioner knows his own business I should think he would come forward himself.

Police-sergeant Vanner said he removed the body to the mortuary on the police ambulance.

Are you sure you took every piece of the body with you?

—Yes, sir. I placed the body in the mortuary shed. I left it on the stretcher of the ambulance. Two females from 35, Dorset-street came to identify the body. Sergeant Thicke touched the clothing, and the women described it for me to write down. I did not see Sergeant Thicke touch the body.

Inspector Chandler, recalled:—I reached the mortuary a few minutes after seven. The body did not appear to have been disturbed.

## THE MORTUARY KEEPER.

Robert Mansel:—I have charge of the Whitechapel mortuary. On Saturday last I received the body of the deceased at the mortuary about seven o'clock. I was there most of the day. No one touched the body until the nurses came over and undressed it. I remained at the mortuary until the doctor arrived, and the door was locked. The police were in charge of it. No one touched the body except the nurses. I was not present when they laid the corpse out.

The Coroner:—The fact is, gentleman, Whitechapel has no mortuary, and the body ought not to have been taken to this shed, which is a building attached to the work-house. There is a great want of mortuaries in the East-end; and at Wapping, where bodies are thrown up from the river, they have to be put up in boxes. With reference to a reward, I cannot speak officially, but I understand the Government have determined not to offer any more rewards, but to leave these cases in the hands of the police. That applies generally, and not specially to this case.

Witness continued:—I was present when the doctor made the post-mortem examination. I found a handkerchief in the corner of the shed. The nurses must have taken it off the woman's throat.

The Coroner:—How do you know? Are you guessing?

—Yes.

The Coroner:—Well, but you may guess all wrong.

Timothy Donovan, the deputy of the lodging-house at 35 Dorset-street, recalled said:—I recognize the handkerchief (produced) found by the last witness as the property of the deceased. She bought it off another lodger. She was wearing it on Saturday morning. She was wearing it round her neck three-cornerwise, and tied in front with one knot.

A Juryman:—Would you recognize this man Stanley—the pensioner?

—Yes. I don't know what his name is. I know Harry the hawker.

# Friday, 14 September, 1888

The Coroner:—There is no actual evidence that the pensioner's name is Stanley.

(To witness):—When did you see him last?

—On last Saturday. I did not hand him over to the police because he would not stay. I sent a man for the police, but the pensioner went away before the constable came.

## STARTLING STATEMENTS—MEDICAL EVIDENCE.

Mr. George Baxter Phillips, divisional surgeon of the police, said:—On Saturday morning I was sent for at 6.20 to go to 29, Hanbury-street, I found the dead body of a female in the possession of the police lying in the back yard on the left hand of the steps leading into the yard.

The legs were brought up, the feet resting on the ground and the knees turned outwards. The face was swollen and turned on the right side, the tongue protruded between the front teeth, but not beyond the lips. The tongue was evidently much swollen. The small intestines and other portions of the stomach were lying on the right side on the ground above the right shoulder, attached by a coil of intestine to the rest of the stomach. There was a large quantity of blood, with a part of the stomach over the left shoulder. The body was cold except there was some remaining heat under the intestines left in the body. The stiffness of the body was not marked, but it had commenced. The throat was deeply cut. I noticed that the incision of the skin was ragged, and reached right round the neck.

There were about six patches of blood on the back wall of the house, and on the wooden paling there were smears of blood corresponding to where the head lay. These were about 14 inches from the ground, clotted blood was near the severed throat of the deceased.

At two o'clock of the same day I went to the labour yard of the Whitechapel Union for the purpose of further examining the body. I was surprised to find that the body had been stripped and was laying on the table ready for me. I made the post-mortem under great difficulties, and I now raise my protest, as I have done before, that members of the medical profession should be called upon to perform their duties under these inadequate circumstances. The place is only a shed, and quite unfitted for making post-mortem examinations.

The Coroner:—There is no mortuary from the City right up to Bow.

Mr. Phillips continuing:—The body had probably been partially washed. There was a bruise over the right temple and on the upper eyelid. There were other bruises on the chest. The stiffness of the limbs is now well marked. The finger nails were turgid. There were abrasions on the ring finger. On the head being opened, the membranes of the brain were found to be opaque, and the veins loaded with blood of a dark character. There was a large quantity of fluid between the membranes and the substance of the brain. The throat had been cut from the left side. The cause of death arose from the throat being cut.

(The Coroner:—)What sort of instrument had been used?

—I should say that the same instrument for the cutting the throat as for the after mutilations. It must have been a very sharp knife with a thin blade, from six to eight inches in length-probably longer. It could not have been a bayonet or a sword bayonet. The knife may have been one such as a slaughterer uses, well ground down. I think the knives used by cobblers would not have been long enough. There were indications of anatomical knowledge displayed by the person who mutilated the corpse.

The Coroner:—Is there anything missing?

—Yes, a portion of the body from the abdomen.

(The Coroner:—)You say anatomical knowledge was displayed?

—Yes: the mode in which the intestines were abstracted showed some anatomical knowledge, but there was also evidence of haste.

(The Coroner:—)How long do you think the deceased had been dead?

—At least two hours-probably more.

## PARTS OF THE BODY WERE NOT THERE.

(The Coroner:—)Was the whole of the body there?

—No. The absent portions were from the abdomen. I think the mode in which they were extracted did show some anatomical knowledge. I am positive there were indications of a struggle in the yard. The deceased had disease of the lungs of long standing and of the membranes of the brain. There was a full meal in the stomach. Although the deceased was fatty there were signs of great deprivation. I am convinced there had been no strong alcohol taken immediately before death. The marks of bruises on the face were evidently recent, especially about the chin and the sides of the jaws. The bruises about the chest were of long standing, probably of days. I am of opinion that the person who cut the deceased's throat took hold of the chin, and then commenced the incision from left to right.

## THE NURSE GIVES EVIDENCE.

The nurse from the workhouse was now in attendance and was called. Previously to her being sworn, Dr. Phillips identified the deceased's handkerchief, which had been found round her neck, and had afterwards been washed.

Mary Elizabeth Simonds said:—I am a nurse at the Whitechapel Union Infirmary. On September 8 I was requested to attend the mortuary with the senior nurse, whose name I think is Francis Wright. I first saw the body on the ambulance in the yard. It was afterwards taken to the shed and placed on a table.

(The Coroner:—)Were you directed to undress it?

—Yes; by the Inspector, I think. (Inspector Chandler was identified as the officer who gave the instruction.) I took the clothes off. I left the handkerchief round the neck.

(The Coroner:—)Did you wash the body at all?

—Yes, we washed the stains of blood from the body. There were stains over the lower part of the body and the legs. There was blood about the chest which seemed to have run down from the throat. I found the pocket tied round the deceased's waist.

Inspector Chandler stated that he did not instruct the witness to wash the body, which was done at the direction of the clerk of the Board of Guardians.

The inquiry was then further adjourned to Wednesday next.

~

# Saturday, 15 September, 1888

## The Times

### THE WHITECHAPEL MURDERS.

The police at the Commercial-street station have made another arrest on suspicion in connection with the recent murders. It appears that among the numerous statements and descriptions of suspected persons are several tallying with that of the man in custody, but beyond this the police know nothing at present against him. His apprehension was of a singular character. Throughout yesterday his movements are stated to have created suspicion among various persons, and last night he was handed over to a uniform constable doing duty in the neighbourhood of Flower and Dean-street on suspicion in connection with the crime. On his arrival at the police station in Commercial-street the detective officers and Mr. Abberline were communicated with, and an inquiry concerning him was at once opened. On being searched perhaps one of the most extraordinary accumulation of articles were discovered—a heap of rags, comprising pieces of dress fabrics, old and dirty linen, two purses of a kind usually used by women, two or three pocket handker-chiefs, one a comparatively clean white one, and a white one with a red spotted border; two small tin boxes, a small cardboard box, a small leather strap, which might serve the purpose of a garterstring, and one spring onion. The person to whom this curious assortment belongs is slightly built, about 5ft. 7in. or 5ft. 8in. in height, and dressed shabbily. He has a very careworn look. Covering a head of hair, inclined somewhat to be sandy, with beard and moustache to match, was a cloth skull cap, which did not improve his appearance. Suspicion is the sole motive for his temporary detention, for the police, although making every possible inquiry about him, do not believe his apprehension to be of any importance.

Regarding the man Pigott, who was captured at Gravesend, nothing whatever has been discovered by the detectives in the course of their inquiries which can in any way connect him with the crimes, and his release, at all events, from the custody of the police is expected shortly.

In connexion with the arrest of a lunatic at Holloway, it appears that he has been missing from his friends for some time now. The detectives have been very active in prosecuting their inquiries concerning him, and it is believed the result, so far, increases their suspicion. He is at present confined in the asylum at Grove-road, Bow.

All inquiries have failed to elicit anything as to the whereabouts of the missing pensioner who is wanted in connexion with the recent murder.

On the question as to the time when the crime was committed, concerning which there was a difference between the evidence of the man Richardson and the opinion of Dr. Phillips, a correspondent yesterday elicited that Mr. Cadoche, who lives in the next house to No. 29, Hanbury-street, where the murder was committed, went to the back of the premises at half-past 5 a.m. As he passed the wooden partition he heard a woman say "No, no." On returning he heard a scuffle and then someone fell heavily against the fence. He heard no cry for help, and so he went into his house. Some surprise is felt that this statement was not made in evidence at the inquest. There is a very strong feeling in the district and large numbers of persons continue to visit the locality.

Annie Chapman, the victim of the crime, was buried early yesterday morning at Manor Park Cemetery. Some of her relatives attended the funeral.

~

# Saturday, 15 September, 1888

## The Star

SPECIAL EDITION.
LATEST DESPATCHES.
WHITECHAPEL.

### THE TRUTH ABOUT THE HEATH-STREET INCIDENT.

#### A Man Arrested, but Mrs. Lloyd Says She Can't Identify Him—The Pensioner Makes a Satisfactory Statement—Bogus Bloodstains.

The police were yesterday in communication with the pensioner Edward Stanley, who is known to have been frequently in the company of the murdered woman, Chapman. Last night Stanley, who is a man of 47 years of age, attended at the Commercial-street Police-station, and made a statement, which was taken down by Inspector Helson. His explanation of his proceedings is regarded as perfectly satisfactory, and as affording no possible ground for associating him in any way with the recent outrage. In view of his relations with the deceased woman, Stanley felt considerable diffidence in coming forward, but after the expressions of opinion by the coroner at the inquest on Thursday he placed himself in indirect communication with the police. In was by arrangement that he subsequently proceeded to Commercial-street Police Station. Stanley has given the police

#### A FULL ACCOUNT OF HIS WHEREABOUTS

since he last saw the deceased woman, which was on the Sunday preceding the murder. Since then he has been following his usual employment, and has taken no steps to conceal his movements. The man is described as superior to the ordinary run of those who frequent the lodging-houses of Spitalfields. He states that he has known Chapman for about two years, and denies that she was of a quarrelsome disposition. So far as he is aware, there was no man with whom she was on bad terms, or who would have any reason for seeking her life. Stanley will attend the inquest when the proceedings are resumed, though his evidence is not expected to throw much light on the tragedy.

In respect to the pieces of newspaper discovered in Bayley's yard on Tuesday afternoon, where they had been, it was supposed, thrown by the murderer, who had first wiped his hands upon them when standing in the yard of No. 25, Hanbury-street, it has been alleged that they have been subjected to analysis, and the stains upon them proved to be those of human blood. On inquiry at the surgery of Mr. Phillips it was stated that these pieces of paper have not been examined as reported, and the doctor was so satisfied of the real nature of

#### THE OTHER SO-CALLED BLOODSTAINS

upon the wall that he has not thought it necessary to analyse the matter submitted to him. Mr. Phillips personally has hitherto withheld information from reporters upon conscientious grounds, and Inspector Abberline himself says that the surgeon has not told him what portions of the body were missing. From independent testimony it has been gathered that the description of them would enable the jury, if not the public, to form some idea of the motive of the singular crime, and at the same time it would perhaps enable the police to pursue their investigations on a wider basis, and probably with the object of showing that the guilty man moves in a more respectable rank of life than that to which the larger proportion of the inhabitants of Spitalfields and Whitechapel belong.

The police at the Commercial-street police-station have made another arrest on suspicion. It appears that among the numerous statements and descriptions of suspected persons are several tallying with that of the man in custody, but beyond this the police know nothing at present against him. Throughout Thursday his movements are stated to have created suspicion amongst various persons, but it was not until last night he was handed over to a uniform constable doing duty in the neighbourhood of Flower and Dean-street, on suspicion, in connection with the crime. When searched

#### AN ODD ACCUMULATION OF ARTICLES

was found—things only found on tramps, frequenters of common lodging-houses or casual wards. There were pieces of dress fabrics, old and dirty linen, two or three pocket-handkerchiefs, two small tin boxes, a small cardboard box, a small leather strap, some string, one spring onion, two purses with several compartments, usually carried by females, and somewhat worn. There is also said to have been found a small tableknife.

# Saturday, 15 September, 1888

The person to whom this curious assortment belonged is slightly built, about 5ft. 7in. or 5ft. 8in. in height, and, as may be imagined, dressed in very shabby attire. He has a very careworn look. Covering a head of hair somewhat inclined to be sandy, with beard and moustache to match, was a cloth skull cap. His name is Edward M'Kenna, and he gives an address at 15, Brick-lane, Whitechapel. He says the table-knife, which is rather the worse for wear, he uses

## FOR CUTTING HIS FOOD.

According to his own statement, which is fairly detailed, he has recently been on tramp in Kent, and has only just returned to London. He gains a living by peddling laces and other small articles. The police do not attach great importance to the arrest, but have detained him for inquiries, as he answers the description of a man who acted in a suspicious manner in Heath-street on Monday night.

This morning a *Star* reporter saw Mrs. Lloyd and her daughter, of Heath-street, Commercial-road, to whom has been attributed a sensational story about a man with a knife. Mrs. Lloyd says the statement which has been printed in the newspapers has been very much exaggerated, and she herself attaches no importance whatever to the incident. "What has been put into the papers," she said, "was put in without my consent. If anything serious or important had happened I should, of course, have immediately gone to the police. The truth is this. At eleven o'clock I was standing near my front door, and my daughter was sitting on the steps. Some boys chased a man up the street. The man crossed the road and went up to my daughter, looked in her face, and ran away without saying a word."

## "DID HE HAVE A KNIFE?"

asked our reporter.

"That I couldn't say," replied Mrs. Lloyd, "as he ran, he had one hand behind him, and seemed to be holding something in it, but what it was, I don't know. I didn't see anything glittering, and couldn't say whether it was a weapon at all."

"Did he make any attempt to stab your daughter?"

"Not at all. I have been told the police have taken into custody and have got at Commercial-street Station a man who answers the published description of the man I saw, and I have been asked to go to the station and see whether I can identify him. But I know I

## CAN'T SWEAR TO ANY MAN.

I can only say that the man I saw was short in stature, and I think he had a sandy beard. But all I could say positively on this point is that the man wasn't dark. As for the statement that he was mad, he might very likely have only had something to drink. The boy ran after him in Commercial-road, and I saw no more of him."

Regarding the man Pigott, who was captured at Gravesend, nothing whatever has been discovered by the detectives in the course of their inquiries which can in any way identify him with the crime or crimes; and his release, at all events from the custody of the police, is expected shortly.

—

## A HUNT FOR A FRESH MAN.

The attention of the police is being directed to the elucidation of a suspicious incident which occurred yesterday. About ten o'clock in the evening a man passed through the Tower subway from the Surrey to the Middlesex side, and said to the caretaker, "Have you caught any of the Whitechapel murderers yet?" He then produced a knife, about a foot in length, with a curved blade, and remarked, "This will do for them." He was followed, but ran away, and was lost sight of near Tooley-street.

The following is the description of the man:—Age about 30; height 5ft. 3in.; complexion and hair dark, with moustache and false whiskers, which he pulled off while running away. Dress, new black diagonal suit and light dust-coat, and dark cloth double-peak hat.

~

# Saturday, 15 September, 1888

## Evening News
FIFTH EDITION.
## THE WHITECHAPEL MURDER.
### IMPORTANT STATEMENT.
### ANOTHER MAN SEEN WITH A KNIFE.

The attention of the police is being directed to the elucidation of a suspicious incident which occurred yesterday. About ten o'clock in the evening a man passed through the Tower Subway from the Surrey to the Middlesex side, and said to the caretaker, "Have you caught any of the Whitechapel murderers yet?" He then produced a knife, about a foot in length, with a curved blade, and remarked "This will do for them." He was followed, but ran away, and was lost sight of near Torby-street.

The following is a description of the man. Age, about 30, height, 5ft, 3in. Complexion and hair dark, with moustache and false whiskers, which he pulled off while running away. Dress, new black dress suit and light dust-coat, and dark cloth double peak hat.

### THE BLOODSTAINED NEWSPAPERS.

The Central News says: "The blood-stained newspapers which were found in Bailey's yard, close to Hanbury-street, and upon which it is conjectured the Spitalfields murderer wiped his hands after committing his fearful crime, have been subjected to analysis and the stains are certified to be those of human blood. The police who made the search state distinctly that the paper was not there when they made the search on Saturday and though they have been closely cross-examined on this point they adhere to their statement. It is not clear moreover that the murderer could have thrown the newspapers in the spot where they were found from the backyard in Hanbury-street; but if he threw the paper, which was rolled up into a round mass over the wall, it might easily have been blown or kicked into the corner in which it was found. Yesterday the police precautions were even stronger than before, the murderer hitherto having selected Friday or Saturday for the commission of his crimes.

Our Maidstone correspondent states that a Scotland-yard detective has arrived there and interviewed the commander of the Sussex Regiment, with a view to identifying the writing on the envelope found on the murdered woman.

### THE HUNT FOR THE SUSPECTED MAN.

Inspector Chandler states that up to noon yesterday no arrest had been made in connection with the Whitechapel murders. The expectation of an early arrest entertained by the police on Thursday was somewhat less sanguine yesterday.

The police are making enquiries as to the whereabouts of the pensioner who was said to have kept company with the murdered woman Chapman. All traces have been lost of him since Saturday last. Tim Donovan, who gave evidence at the inquest which connected this man with the deceased says he is known by the name of Ted Stanley, but he does not know his occupation, while the watchman at the lodging-house in Dorset-street whence Chapman left on Saturday morning last, and was not afterwards seen alive, asserts that the pensioner went to the lodging-house on Saturday last as usual, and on being informed that Chapman had been murdered nearly fainted.

The police think that he is keeping out of the way more from shame in having been associated with the deceased than from any fear that he has of being connected with the murder. It more than probable also that he may be one of the regular attenders from the country at the Spitalfields market, and will put in his usual appearance on Saturday.

It is regarded as of considerable importance that Dr. Philips, on Thursday, established the fact that the deceased must have been lying in the back yard in Hanbury-street at least upwards of two hours before her body was found, and that young Richardson's evidence cannot, therefore, be relied on, this gives the police only about two hours to account for in connection with the disappearance of Chapman, and evidence is being sought as to her whereabouts during this time.

Special enquiries are being directed by the police to ascertain who was the writer of the envelope bearing the embossed stamp of the Sussex Regiment, a portion of which envelope was found on Chapman. It has just been ascertained that she had been in the habit of receiving similar letters.

No further arrests had been made up to two o'clock yesterday, nor have the police made any enquiries in Heate-street regarding information given to a reporter by the young woman Lloyd. It is significant that the description of the man who

# Saturday, 15 September, 1888

was chased into a bye-street exactly agrees with the description of a strange man seen in Flower and Dean-street on Sunday afternoon, with whom a woman, named Lyons, went into a neighbouring house, and whose suspicious behaviour, coupled with the fact that he carried a large knife, led the woman to communicate with the Commercial-street police.

## THE PENSIONER EXPLAINS.

The police were, yesterday, in communication with the pensioner who was said to have been seen in the company of the murdered woman Chapman. He had voluntarily explained his connections with the deceased and his antecedents. His statements are, it is understood, entirely satisfactory, and he will be produced as a witness when the inquest is resumed.

## AN ARREST LAST NIGHT.

A man was arrested in Whitechapel last night on a charge of threatening to stab people in the neighbourhood of the Tower. A roughly sharpened knife was found upon him. He is a short, stout man, with a sandy beard, and wears a dark cap.

## THE QUESTION OF THE TIME OF THE MURDER.

On the question as to the time when the crime was committed, concerning which there was a difference between the evidence of the man Richardson and the opinion of Dr. Philips, a correspondent yesterday elicited that Mr. Cadoche, who lives in the next house to No. 29, Hanbury-street, where the murder was committed, went to the back of the premises at half-past five a.m. As he passed the wooden partition he heard a woman say. "No, no." On returning he heard a scuffle, and then someone fell heavily against the fence. He heard no cry for help, and so he went into his house. Some surprise is felt that this statement was not made in evidence at the inquest. There is a very strong feeling in the district, and large numbers of persons continue to visit the locality.

—

Mr. John Hay writes to us: About 12 years ago a man was hung at Cambridge for murdering a young girl by cutting her throat. The motive for committing the crime was the girl had caused the man to suffer from a certain illness. In reading the paper about this late murder I noticed the woman was an out-patient of St. Bartholomew's Hospital. If so—if she was suffering from a certain illness—it would be a motive for committing the crime. The man might have contracted the disease from one of the women, and, not knowing which, murdered several. Should the cowardly wretch be arrested, and found to be suffering from the loathsome disease, it would be a link towards bringing the crime home to him. If an Act of Parliament were passed that any woman well knowing her condition were found guilty of this offence and sent to prison, we should not see so many poor wretches crawling about the streets all hours of the night trying to get money for their "doss."

## ANNIE CHAPMAN'S FUNERAL.

The funeral of Annie Chapman, the last victim of the Whitechapel murderer, took place yesterday morning. The utmost secrecy was observed in the arrangements, and none but the undertaker, police, and relatives of the deceased knew anything about it. Shortly after seven o'clock a hearse drew up outside the mortuary in Montagu-street and the body was quickly removed. At nine o'clock, a start was made for Manor Park Cemetery; the place selected by the friends of the deceased for the interment but no coaches followed as it was desired that public attention should not be attracted. Mr. Smith and other relatives met the body at the cemetery, and the service was duly performed in the ordinary manner. The remains of the deceased were enclosed in a black-covered elm coffin, which bore the words, "Annie Chapman, died September 8, 1888. Aged 48 years."

~

## The Times
### THE WHITECHAPEL MURDERS.

The detective officers continued their investigations yesterday, but up to a late hour last night no arrest had been made, neither is there any prospect of an arrest being effected. The public of the neighbourhood continue to make statements, which are committed to writing at Commercial street station, and in several instances the police have been made cognisant of what the informants consider to be suspicious movements of individuals whose appearance is supposed to tall with that of the man wanted. Every clue given by the public in their zeal to assist the police has been followed up, but without success, and the lapse of time, it is feared, will lessen the chances of discovering the perpetrator of the crime.

—

### ONE HUNDRED POUNDS REWARD
### The Whitechapel Murder

The proprietor of the *Illustrated Police News* offers the above reward to any person who will give information as to the perpetrator of the crime of the murder of Mrs. Chapman. The above reward will be paid upon conviction of the murderer. Office, No. 286, Strand.

~

## The Star
### THE WHITECHAPEL CRIMES.
### The Holloway Lunatic said to be a German Porkbutcher Who Carried Knives.

The detective officers who are engaged in the Whitechapel case are said to be more hopeful now than they have been before. It is stated they have some fresh information which encourages them to hope that before the week is over they will be able to solve the mystery.

Considerable excitement existed at Holloway on Saturday, when it was reported that the police had obtained some important information in reference to the lunatic arrested there. He is said to be a master German pork-butcher, and has been in the habit of carrying large sharp knives. He has been absent from home frequently during the past 10 weeks.

The man Edward M'Kenna, who was taken to Commercial-street Police Station on Friday night, and there detained, was on Saturday confronted by several witnesses, who failed to recognise him, and he was in consequence liberated. It was ascertained that he had slept at a common lodging house in Brick-lane on the night of the murder of Annie Chapman. Mrs. Lloyd and her daughter came from Heath-street. They were not able to identify the man as the person who had been chased in their neighbourhood by some boys, and who was alleged to have held a knife behind his back. A Mrs. Lyons was also called, and in her opinion M'Kenna was not the individual she had seen in Flower and Dean-street on the Sunday following the Hanbury-street tragedy.

Similarly the potman[58] from the Ten Bells public-house could not identify him as the man who had angrily called a woman out of the bar on the morning of the murder; and Mr. Taylor, who on the same day had watched a man of suspicious appearance leave the Prince Albert and go into Bishopsgate-street, also could not say that M'Kenna was the same. In each case, it is said, the description given resembled that of the man who was temporarily detained.

One of the Vigilance Committees formed in the East-end held a meeting at the Crown Tavern, Mile-end-road, on Saturday. It was stated that persons who were known to be liberal in public contributions declined to give towards the fund on the ground that it was the duty of the Home Secretary to offer a reward.

~

## Evening News
### WHITECHAPEL MURDERS.
### MEETING LAST NIGHT.
### MEMORIAL TO THE HOME OFFICE.

Last night a large meeting of the Mile End Vigilance Committee took place at the Crown Tavern, Mile End-road, for the purpose of considering the best means for preventing a repetition of the late dreadful outrages, and securing the detection of the murderers.

The chair was taken by Mr. George Lusk, the well-known contractor, who was supported by Messrs. Cohen (vice-president) Aarons, Houghton, H. A. Harris, Laughton, Lord, Isaacs, Rogers, Mitchell, Barnett, Hodgins, Lindsay, Burgess, Jacobs, Reeves, B. Harris

---

[58] **Potman** or **Potboy**. Public house employee that collected and washed dirty pots and glasses. (Census1891.com)

(hon. sec.), and others.

In the course of the proceedings, a long list of subscriptions towards a reward fund for the apprehension of the murderer was read, including £5 from Mr. Spencer Charrington, the well known brewer, and the chairman said that so soon as £100 had been subscribed the reward bills would be sent out. It was stated on all hands, and especially by Mr. Aarons and Mr. Rogers, that there was a consensus of opinion amongst the donees and others that the Home Office authorities were very unwise in withholding a Government reward for the detection of the murderers. A golden key usually opened all doors, and as no means should be left untried to discover and bring to justice escaped murderers, such rewards should always be offered. The Press and the public had over and over again expressed their views on the subject, and the Home Office were bound to give effect to those views in the interests of possible individual victims and of the community at large.

A resolution was put and carried that it was advisable to memorialise the Government in the matter, and in the course of the sitting a letter was drawn out, signed, and there and then despatched to the Home Secretary, embodying the views of the Committee and the meeting, and asking what Her Majesty's Government intended doing for the further protection of defenceless people from the knife of the murderer. Letters were also sent to Mr. W. Isaacson and others on the subject, and the proceedings were adjourned until Wednesday next, when sufficient money will probably be in hand for the offer of the reward.

It was stated that in the event of the definite escape of the murderer, the funds would be given to the London Hospital or some other charitable institution.

—

### THE EDITOR'S DRAWER.
### THE WHITECHAPEL MURDERS.
### TO THE EDITOR OF
### "THE EVENING NEWS."

SIR—I want to say a few words on the all-absorbing topic of the day, viz., the East-end murders. I am afraid you will think this the suggestion of a lunatic, but I cannot help thinking for a week past of what may prove an almost improbable solution of the mystery which has, perhaps, hitherto escaped notice.

Is it possible for a medical maniac in the cause of science to commit them? That there are such is beyond a doubt. Was not M. Pasteur deemed such? Is it a case of human vivisection? And are the unfortunate victims hitherto selected as those to whom a release from their wretched life would be rather a blessing than otherwise? Or, put it in another way, who could be best spared, as he would seem to think?

Is it or is it not possible that there are problems yet unsolved even by the keenest medical expert relative to the mysterious changes that take place in the female sex at about the ages of these poor women?

I am far from wishing to disparage the medical profession, but some time minute research into the mysteries of our being will degenerate into a craze. On that point, and on that point only, I have an opinion that in general my theory will not hold water.

Still, in referring it to a public-spirited paper like *The Evening News* I shall feel somewhat relieved at getting rid of it, knowing it will receive the courteous attention accorded to all readers of that popular halfpennyworth.

I am, &c.,
EX-MEDICO'S DAUGHTER.
September 14.

~

## The Times

### THE WHITECHAPEL MURDERS.

Yesterday Mr. Wynne E. Baxter, Coroner for the North-Eastern Division of Middlesex, resumed his adjourned inquiry at the Working Lads' Institute, Buck's-row, Whitechapel, respecting the death of Mary Ann Nicholls, who was found brutally murdered in Buck's-row, Whitechapel, on the morning of Friday, the 31st ult.

Detective-Inspectors Abberline (Scotland-yard) and Helson, and Inspectors Spratling and Chandler watched the case on behalf of the Criminal Investigation Department and Commissioners of Police.

Mr. Llewellyn, surgeon, recalled, said that since the last inquiry he had been to the mortuary and again examined deceased. She had an old scar on the forehead. No part of the viscera was missing. He had nothing to add to his previous evidence.

Mrs. Emma Green, living at New-cottage, Buck's-row, stated that she was a widow, and occupied the cottage next to where the deceased was found. Her daughter and two sons lived with her. Witness went to bed about 11 o'clock on the night of Thursday, August 30, and one of her sons went to bed at 9 o'clock and the other one at a quarter to 10. Her daughter went to bed when she did, and they occupied the same room. It was a front room on the first floor. Witness did not remember waking up until she heard a knock at the front door about 4 o'clock in the morning. She opened the window and saw three or four constables and two or three other men. She saw the body of deceased lying on the ground, but it was still too dark to clearly distinguish what had happened. Witness heard nothing unusual during the night, and neither her sons or daughter awoke.

By the Jury.—She was a light sleeper, and had a scream been given she would have heard it, though people often went through Buck's-row, and there was often a great noise in it. She did not believe there was any disorderly house in Buck's-row. She knew of no disorderly house in the immediate neighbourhood.

By the CORONER.—She saw her son go out, directly the body was removed, with a pail of water to wash the stains of blood away. A constable was with him.

Thomas Ede, a signalman in the employ of the East London Railway Company, said he saw a man on the line on the morning of the 8th.

The CORONER observed that had no reference to this inquiry. The 8th was the morning of the other murder. It was decided to take the witness's evidence.

Witness, continuing, said on Saturday morning, the 8th inst., he was coming down the Cambridge-heath-road, and when just opposite the Foresters' Arms saw a man on the opposite side of the street. His peculiar appearance made witness look at him. He appeared to have a wooden arm, as it was hanging at his side. Witness watched him until he got level with the Foresters' Arms. He then put his hand down, and witness saw about 4 in. of the blade of a long knife sticking out of his trousers pocket. Three other men were also looking at him and witness spoke to them. Witness followed him, and as soon as he saw he was followed he quickened his pace. Witness lost sight of him under some railway arches. He was about 5ft. 8 in. high, about 35 years of age, with dark moustache and whiskers. He wore a double peak cap, dark brown jacket, and a pair of overalls over a pair of dark trousers. He walked as though he had a stiff knee, and he had a fearful look about the eyes.

By the CORONER.—Witness should say the man was a mechanic. The overalls were perfectly clean. He could not see what kind of a knife it was. He was not a muscular man.

Inspector Helson said they had been unable to trace the man.

Walter Purkiss stated he lived at Essex Wharf, Buck's-row, and was manager there. His house was in Buck's-row and fronted the street. It was nearly opposite to where the deceased was found. His wife, children, and servant occupied the house with him. Witness and his wife slept in the front portion of the house—the room on the second floor. On the night of the occurrence, he went to bed at 11 o'clock or a quarter past 11. Witness awoke at various times during the night and was awake between 1 and 2 o'clock. He did not hear anything until he was called up by the police about 4 o'clock. His wife was awake the greater portion of the night. Neither of them heard a sound during the night, and it was unusually quiet. When the police called him he opened the landing window. He could see the deceased, and there were two or three men there besides three or four constables. Had there been any quarrelling in the row during the night witness would certainly have heard it.

Patrick Mulshaw, a night porter in the employ of the Whitechapel District Board of Works, living at 3, Rupert-street, Whitechapel, said on the night of this occurrence he was at the back of the Working Lads' Institute in Winthorpe-street.[59] He went on duty about a quarter to 5 in the afternoon, and remained until about five minutes to 6 the next morning, when he was relieved. He was watching some sewage works. He dozed at times during the night, but was not asleep between 3 and 4 o'clock. He did not see any one about during that period, and did not hear any cries for assistance, or any other noise. The slaughterhouse was about 70 yards away from where he was. Another man then passed by, and said, "Watchman, old man, I believe somebody is murdered down the street." Witness then went to Buck's-row, and saw the body of deceased lying on the ground. Three or four policemen and five or six working men were there.

By the CORONER.—If any one had called out for assistance from the spot where the body was he might have heard it. Nothing suspicious occurred during the time he was watching, and he saw no person running away. There was no one about after 11 and 12 o'clock, and the inhabitants of the street appeared to be very orderly persons. He did not often see the police there. During the night he saw two constables, including Constable Neil. He was unable to say what time he saw that officer.

Constable John Phail,[60] 96 J, said he was not brought any closer to Buck's-row in his beat than Brady-street, but he passed the end of it. He passed the end of Buck's-row every 30 minutes. Nothing attracted his attention until about 3:45 a.m., when he was signalled by a brother constable flashing his lamp some way down Buck's-row. Witness went to him, and found Constable Neil standing by the body of the deceased. Neil was by himself. Witness ran for the doctor, and having called Dr. Llewellyn, accompanied him to the spot where deceased

was lying. On his return with the doctor, Neil and two workmen were standing by the body. He did not know the workmen. The body was then taken to the mortuary by Sergeant Kerby, Constable Neil, and an officer of the H division. Witness, acting under orders, waited at the spot for Inspector Spratling. He was present when the spots of blood were washed away. On the spot where the deceased had been lying was a mass of congealed blood. He should say it was about 6 in. in diameter, and had run towards the gutter. It appeared to him to be a large quantity of blood.

By the CORONER.—He helped to put the body on the ambulance, and the back appeared to be covered with blood, which, he thought, had run from the neck as far as the waist. He got blood on to his hands. There was also blood on the ground where the deceased's legs had been. Witness afterwards searched Essex Wharf, the Great Eastern Railway, the East London Railway, and the District railway, as far as Thomas-street, but could find no knife, marks of blood, or anything suspicious. He did not make inquiries at the houses in Buck's-row.

By the Jury.—He did not pass the end of Buck's-row exactly at the end of each half-hour. It was a quarter to 4 when he was first called by the constable. It was a quarter-past 3 when he was round there before. He did not take his cape to the slaughterers, but sent it by a brother constable. When he was sent for the doctor he did not first go to the horse-slaughterers and say that as a murder had been committed he had better fetch his cape. He was not supposed to leave his beat. Shortly before he was called by Constable Neil he saw one or two men going to work in the direction of Whitechapel-road. When he was signalled by Neil he was coming up Brady-street, from the direction of Whitechapel-road.

Robert Paul, a carman, of 30, Foster-street, Whitechapel, stated he went to work at Cobbett's-court, Spitalfields. He left home about a quarter to 4 on the Friday morning and as he was passing up Buck's-row he saw a man standing in the middle of the road. As witness approached him he walked towards the pavement, and witness stepped on to the roadway in order to pass him. He then touched witness on the shoulder, and said, "Come and look at this woman here." Witness went with

# Tuesday, 18 September, 1888

him, and saw a woman lying right across the gateway. Her clothes were raised almost up to her stomach. Witness felt her hands and face, and they were cold. He knelt down to see if he could hear her breathe, but could not, and he thought she was dead. It was very dark, and he did not notice any blood. They agreed that the best thing they could do would be to tell the first policeman they met. He could not see whether the clothes were torn, and did not feel any other part of her body except the hands and face. They looked to see if there was a constable, but one was not to be seen. While he was pulling the clothes down he touched the breast, and then fancied he felt a slight movement.

By the CORONER.—The morning was rather a chilly one. Witness and the other man walked on together until they met a policeman at the corner of Old Montagu-street, and told him what they had seen. Up to that time not more than four minutes had elapsed from the time he saw the body. He had not met any one before he reached Buck's-row, and did not see any one running away.

Robert Mann, a pauper inmate of the White-chapel Workhouse, stated he had charge of the mortuary. On the morning in question the police came to the workhouse and told him there was a body at the mortuary. Witness went there about 5 o'clock, and remained there until the body was placed inside the mortuary. He then locked the mortuary door, and went to breakfast. After breakfast witness and Hatfield, another inmate of the workhouse, undressed the body. No police or anyone else was present when that was done. Inspector Helson was not there.

By the CORONER.—He had not been told that he must not touch the body. He could not remember Inspector Helson being present, as he was confused. He was sure the clothing was not torn or cut; but could not describe where the blood was. To get off the clothes Hatfield had to cut them down the front.

By the Jury.—The body was undressed in the mortuary, and was not taken out after it was brought in.

The CORONER said the witness was subject to fits, and his statements were hardly reliable.

James Hatfield said he assisted the last witness in undressing the deceased. Inspector Helson was not there. They first took off the

ulster, and put it on the ground. Witness then took the jacket off and put it in the same place. He did not have to cut the dress to get it off, but cut the bands of the two petticoats, and then tore them down with his hands. Deceased was wearing a chemise, and he tore it right down the front. She was not wearing any stays. No one gave them any instructions to strip the body. They did it so as to have the body ready for the doctor. He had heard something about a doctor coming; and he was not aware that anyone was present while they were stripping the deceased. Afterwards the police came, and examined the clothing. They found the words "Lambeth Workhouse" on the band of one of the petti-coats. Witness cut that portion out by direction of Inspector Helson. That was the first time he had seen Inspector Helson that morning. It was about 6:30 when witness first arrived at the mortuary. Although he had said deceased wore no stays he would not be surprised to find she had stays on.

The Foreman.—Why, you tried the stays on the body of the deceased in my presence at the mortuary, and you said they were short.

Witness admitted his memory was bad.

In answer to the CORONER, Inspector Abberline said they were unable to find the man who passed down Buck's-row while the doctor was examining the body.

Inspector Spratling, J Division, said he had made inquiries at several of the houses in Buck's-row, but not at all of them.

The CORONER.—Then that will have to be done.

Witness further said he had made inquiries at Mrs. Green's, the wharf, at Sneider's Factory, and also at the Great Eastern Wharf, but no one at those places had heard anything unusual during the morning in question. He had seen the Board school keeper, but he had not heard anything. Had the other inhabitants heard a disturbance of any kind they would, no doubt, have communicated with the police. There was a gateman at the Great Eastern Railway, but he was stationed inside the gates, and had not heard anything. There was a watchman employed at Sneider's factory. He distinctly told the mortuary-keeper not to touch the body.

Inspector Helson said he knew of no other evidence.

In answer to a juryman, the officer said the

murderer would have no occasion to get on to the Great Eastern Railway, as he could pass along the street.

The Foreman thought that if a substantial reward had been offered by the Home Secretary in the case of the murder in George-yard, these two horrible murders would not have happened. Mr. Matthews thought that rewards got into wrong hands, but if they did, what did it matter so long as the perpetrator was brought to justice?

The CORONER understood there was a regulation that no reward should be offered in the case of the murder of either a rich or a poor person.

The Foreman believed a substantial one would have been offered had a rich person been murdered. He would be glad to give £5 himself for the capture of the murderer.

The inquiry was then adjourned until Saturday.

—

## POLICE ORGANIZATION.
## TO THE EDITOR OF THE TIMES.

Sir,—The occurrences in Whitechapel are being made the opportunity for the raising a cry against the metropolitan police. This is on every account to be regretted, for whatever imperfections there may be in the administration of that force a cry by people who know nothing about administration is not a good means whereby to reach its reform. Neither is a cry directed against its chief.

Sir Charles Warren is not to be blamed for those alterations in general management which were initiated, I believe, as long ago as 25 or 30 years before the present time. He has carried out, with some additions of detail, a system that began under Colonel Henderson. That system differs from what preceded it in two particulars chiefly. My opinion, which I have formed from practical experience of police government in a large town during several years, is that both deviations from the old system have impaired the efficiency of the metropolitan force, and that from their nature they could not do otherwise than impair it.

It was formerly the practice to keep a well-behaved policeman—and nearly all policemen are well-behaved—on the same beat, without shifting, for a very long time; and a man was seldom or never removed from his beat without some reason. It is now the practice to shift men sometimes once a month, sometimes at the end of two months, and nearly always at the end of three months. I may be told that there is no rule or order on the subject. I have no means of knowing what the rule, if any, may be, but I know what the practice is, about which any Londoner may satisfy himself by asking any policeman that he may have acquaintance with, or, indeed, any policeman whom he may address civilly. Sir Edward Henderson's other innovation was to separate, far more than had been before, the police on ordinary duty from the detective police in as it were two departments. I do not know the particulars, I only know the heads, of this change; and I strongly suspect, though I cannot prove from facts, what its working has been. The two alterations are based it will be evident to all acquainted with police management on the idea of treating the force as a machine. Many minor details that have arisen under the same idea look like militarism. While I do not want to impute militarism to either the late or the present chief, I am of the belief that what I would prefer to call the mechanical idea has dominated both of them too much.

A policeman who knows his beat—being not merely a beat the duty of which is attending to traffic—is worth three who do not know the beat. This applies to the whole of a city, and it applies with double force to such parts as Whitechapel. A man will know the streets of his beat in a day—or may do so if he chooses; although I have asked my way to a street, naming it, which was part of a man's beat, without his having heard of it. But a man will not, till after a very considerable time, know the people who live in a beat; nor will he know, as an old hand will, every house and its doors and windows. A policeman who has attained thorough knowledge, who knows the people, and is known to them, becomes a kind of referee, especially in the poorer neighbourhoods. Knowledge of him produces confidence in him; and he becomes without his knowing it an embryo detective. He is able to put down street rows with a mere glance when a stranger would be unheeded. I need not enumerate the particulars in which the old policeman is and must be the superior of the stranger. If it be said that he will become too intimate with the population, it is not so; he cannot be too intimate. He may abuse his intimacy, which is another thing. Last year, there was much talk of blackmail in connexion with the Regent-street affair. I believe perhaps one-hundredth part of it. But it would be a more difficult thing for a policeman, known by hundreds of neighbours, to pursue a system of blackmail, such as was imputed, than for a man transferred once a month from one beat to another.

The school of detectives, which the metropolitan police was till recently, is now not in existence. Hence I believe the practical separation of the two departments of the force, a separation that tends to the efficiency of neither.

If I be thought to be giving my unsupported opinion, I have authority, the very highest, for my views; indeed, I think the following two authorities amount to proof. Every one that I know holds that the City police is superior in effectiveness to the metropolitan. The only difference, but the slightest, in their organisation is that the City men are kept without a break on the same beats for a *minimum* period of three years; never being removed during those three years except for misconduct; and often, at the end of the term, being placed on day duty instead of night duty on their old beats. My other authority is Paris, the best policed city in the world. There the *Regents de ville* are never removed. I knew one who had been in the same district for 30 years. He knew every man, woman, and child, dog and cat, door, window, shutter and spout in his six or seven streets; and burglary and disorder were most difficult.

Sir Charles Warren inherited the traditions of his predecessor. It is not, as I said, so much the military as the mechanical conception of the force that is erroneous, though these two ideas may have something in common. The military idea is that soldiers, to be effective, must act as bodies; the policeman must nearly always act alone. Such occasions as occurred last winter in Trafalgar-square are quite exceptional.

Yours truly,
EDMUND LAWRENCE.

———

At Woolwich Police Court yesterday, a labourer named Edward Quinn, aged 35, was placed in the dock before Mr. Fenwick, charged nominally with being drunk at the police station. His face and hands were much bruised, and when charged he was much blood stained.

The magistrates were about disposing of the case briefly when the prisoner remarked that he had a complaint to make and stated as follows:—On Saturday I was at a bar down by the arsenal at Woolwich having a drink. I had stumbled over something in the street just before, and had cut my face and knuckles as you see and I had bled a good deal. While at the bat a big, tall man came in and stood beside me and looked at me. He got me in tow, and gave me some beer and tobacco, and then he said, "I mean to charge you with the Whitechapel murders." I thought it was a joke and laughed, but he said he was serious, and pointed to the blood about me. I said, "Nonsense, is that all the clue you have got?" He then dropped the subject and took me for a walk until we got to the police station, where he charged me with the Whitechapel murders."

Mr. Fenwick—Were you not drunk?

Quinn—Certainly not, sir.

Mr. Fenwick—You will be remanded until tomorrow.

Quinn—This is rather rough. I am dragged a mile to the station and locked up, and now I am to wait another day with all this suspicion of murder hanging over my head.

Mr. Fenwick—I will take your own bail in £5 for your reappearance.

Quinn—I object to the whole thing. Me murder a woman! I could not murder a cat. (Laughter.)

The prisoner was then released on his own recognizances.

~

## AT LAST.
## TO THE EDITOR OF THE TIMES.

Sir,—The tilled garden is fast producing the crop sown; it is ripening, it affords ample evidence of the nature of the seed, its fruit is just that which such seed, under such tillage, was certain to produce.

However abhorrent in all cruel, filthy detail are the murders to which public attention is now so painfully called, however hard it may be to believe that they could occur in any civilized community, the fact remains that they have been so committed. Whatever the theories to account for them, whether or no the perpetrators may be yet discovered, they have been the means of affording to us a warning it will be at our extreme peril to neglect.

We have far too long been content to know that within a walk of palaces and mansions, where all that money can obtain secures whatever can contribute to make human life one of luxury and ease within homes, from infancy to old age, surrounded with all that can promote civilized life, there have existed tens of thousands of our fellow creatures begotten and reared in an atmosphere of godless brutality, a species of human sewage, the very drainage of the vilest production of ordinary vice, such sewage ever on the increase, and in its increase for ever developing fresh depths of degradation.

What pen can describe, what mental power can realize the nature of the surroundings of child life under these conditions? Begotten amid all that is devoid of the commonest decency, reared in an atmosphere in which blasphemy and obscenity are the ordinary language, where all exists that can familiarize the child with scenes bestial—thus reared in home life, it can scarcely itself walk or talk, when first introduced to outside life, the street life, such as it is, where these tens of thousands have to dwell. It is already so far morally corrupted that it is hard to conceive that this in itself can be in any way repulsive to it, for to it the home has been a school in all things preparatory; it is the seedling thus transplanted to grow to adolescence as it grew from infancy; be the growth that of male or female, so far as any one feature moral of sex obtains, there is no one distinguishing characteristic; as is the boy so is the girl, what the one has witnessed and heard within the home has been objectively and orally familiar to the other. We may choose to ignore the fact, but there is not a shadow of doubt in the minds of those who have made this deprived race a study, that of both sexes it may be said they scarce have passed childhood before they fall into the grosser sins of that adult life which is their daily street example.

We hear much of the sufferings of those who come under what is called the "sweating" system of employment, and we are told that it is the fierce competition in the labour field that has produced it. What about competition in harlotry? What a text has been given us from which we may draw a sermon, which should go home to every Christian heart, in the evidence of that "unfortunate" who desired a bed to be kept for her, for she would go at once to earn the eightpence! If the wages of such sin have fallen so low we have proof afforded us of the competition in this foul market; can human nature find a greater depth of degradation? But, further, where such competition thus exists, can we be surprised that in this bestial life the jealousies which surely will be begotten of it beget murders, outrages of a character such as scarce the most heathen nation could find in its category of crime, and this in the metropolis of a land ever boastful of its Christian creed.

I believe nearly half a million pounds is yearly raised in this country by societies having their headquarters in London to propagate the Gospel in foreign parts, to support our Established Church system, to send missions to convert the heathen in other lands, to bring the Bible cheaply in all sorts of languages within reach of people of other nationalities; the Nonconformists on their own lines acting in the same spirit. We are raising large sums for a Church Institute to be a rallying-point for Church work; very lately we have had a conference of bishops of the Established Church, at which a large number of the colonial bishops were present and the greatest zeal was shown in regard to the spiritual life and working of the Church Episcopate; and all this within cheap cab hire of that portion of eastern London which for many years has been known to have been in a social condition utterly devoid of the commonest attributes of civilization, so saturated with all that can contribute to heathenize as to be a standing shame to the nation.

We seem to have needed at last some home stroke to awaken us to the fact that we have at our very doors an element of danger threatening consequences which may prove, but too late, that we have suffered, with little attempt to arrest it, the growth of a large and increasing portion of our population to live, move, and have their being under a condition of things tending to the utter subversion of the very commonest principles of civilization; leading to the commission of crimes which hitherto would have been held to have been so abhorrent as to be inconceivable even where all ordinary crime had full sway. I am quite prepared to give all praise to the efforts of the very many excellent,

# Tuesday, 18 September, 1888

pious, hard-working volunteers of both sexes who for years have quietly and earnestly devoted themselves to the work of Christian salvage amid this wreckage of our common humanity; they will have their reward where alone they so devotedly seek it. But although they may here and there rescue a few of those wretched beings and bring them into the habits of civilized life, the masses to whom they owe their existence, the homes in which they were reared remain untouched; and, such as the homes are, so will from them filter forth into street life the same race of beings, bred and reared in all that can make them ignorant of God, defiant of all law, revellers in the profligacy which taints the scenes where they congregate with crimes which, however repulsive to the ordinary mind, are in their own estimation just the issues of the life they best enjoy.

As far as I can see, the great object of the philanthropist of the day is to create a multitude of institutions, societies &c., as a sort of hospitals in which morally-maimed humanity is to be treated, as if these soul and body poisoned beings were merely under some mental and physical disease, for which we had a Pharmacopoeia with prescriptions for each form of it, treating the disease with educational and religious formulae, but ignoring, as far as they can, the fact that much of it is hereditary, the patients so treated healthy as regards their race, only diseased as judged by the ideas regarding health entertained by those who thus seek their cure.

Just so long as the dwellings of this race continue in their present condition, their whole surroundings a sort of warren of foul alleys garnished with the flaring lamps of the gin shops, and offering to all sorts of lodgers, for all conceivable wicked purposes, every possible accommodation to further brutalize, we shall have still to go on - affecting astonishment that in such a state of things we have outbreaks from time to time of the horrors of the present day.

All strange, Sir, as it may appear to you and the generality of your readers, it is within the range of my belief that one or both these Whitechapel murders may have been committed by female hands. There are details in both cases which fit in well with language for ever used where two of these unfortunates are in violent strife; there is far more jealousy, as is well known, between such women in regard to those with whom they cohabit than is the case with married people where one may suspect the other of sin against the marriage vow.

There are, I have no doubt, plenty of women of this class known for their violent temper, with physical power to commit such a deed. As to the nature of their sex forbidding belief that they could so act, how many of them are altogether unsexed, have no one element in character with female feeling? It is now many years ago; when writing in your columns on these guilt gardens, I had procured for me some specimens of the kind of printed matter circulated among this class. From the nature of much which is now open to readers of a very different class, I can well conjecture what manner of cheap reading is open to the poorest class in the present day. The first of these murders was, I have no doubt, served up after a fashion with every horrible detail exaggerated, and may well have had the suggestive effect to produce others.

I can only hope that "at last" we may awaken to the fact that, quite outside the political arena which seems to absorb all our interest, there are causes at work, close at hand, which undealt with may develop into a form of danger far more serious than any political disturbance. Sewer gas will sometimes explode, but this work of hand can remedy. Where will be found the remedy when this moral sewage attains the full development of which these murders are a mere passing sample?

S.G.O.[61]

---

[61] **OSBORNE, Lord SIDNEY GODOLPHIN** (1808–1889), philanthropist, third son of Francis Godolphin Osborne, baron Godolphin (1777–1850), by Elizabeth Charlotte Eden, daughter of William, first baron Auckland, was born at Stapleford in Cambridgeshire on 5 Feb. 1808. He was a direct descendant of Godolphin, the fellow-minister of the Duke of Marlborough, and when in 1859 his elder brother, George Godolphin, succeeded his cousin, Francis Godolphin D'Arcy Osborne, as eighth Duke of Leeds, he obtained the rank of a duke's son. He was educated at Rugby and at Brasenose College, Oxford, whence he graduated B.A. in 1830, and, having taken orders, was appointed rector of Stoke-Poges in Buckinghamshire in 1832. In 1841 he accepted the living of Durweston in Dorset, which was in the gift of Lord Portman, and he occupied that incumbency until 1875. He then resigned the benefice and retired to Lewes, where he died on 9

# Tuesday, 18 September, 1888

## 𝕿𝖍𝖊 𝕾𝖙𝖆𝖗
### WHAT WE THINK.

WE are glad that the jury investigating the murder of Mary Anne Nicholls have spoken out strongly on the failure of the authorities to offer a reward. We have said from the first that this thing ought to have been done. Another thing which ought equally to have been done was to offer a pardon for information from any accomplice. We do not say that either step would have been effectual; but we say that the thing ought to have been done as a matter of principle. It is possible that the murderer may have had accomplices. If he had, it is probable that the offer of a reward or a pardon would have had some effect. In a case of such grave emergency no stone should be left unturned, no avenue open. At the least the offer of a reward would have done something to allay panic by

---

May 1889. He married in 1834 Emily, daughter of Pascoe Grenfell of Taplow Court, Buckinghamshire, and was thus brother-in-law of Charles Kingsley and James Anthony Froude. His wife died on 19 Dec. 1875, leaving two sons and two daughters.

Osborne is chiefly known in connection with the series of 'lay sermons' delivered from the pulpit of the 'Times' newspaper under the signature 'S. G. O.' A philanthropist of a militant and almost ferocious type, he was always lashing abuses and provoking controversy. But the value of much that he wrote is attested by the fact that it has gained in historical that which it has lost in controversial interest. In matters so diverse as free trade, education, sanitation, women's rights, cattle plague, and cholera, he was equally at home, and, generally speaking, in advance of his time. During the Crimean war he journeyed to the East, made an unofficial inspection of the hospitals under Miss Florence Nightingale's care, and published the results in 'Scutari and its Hospitals,' 1855. He was publicly thanked in parliament for his self-appointed task. On the Irish question, in which he took a special interest in consequence of his visit to the west of Ireland during the famine of 1849, he was a strong unionist, and in church matters he regarded sacerdotal claims with frank and cynical dislike. But his special interest was perhaps the agricultural labourer, of whom his knowledge was unrivalled, while his forecast of the villager's social and political emancipation and its results was remarkable for its acumen. The last letters of the series addressed to the 'Times,' extending from 1844 to 1888, were on the subject of the Whitechapel murders. A selection from the letters, which were justly said to be equally a profit and a credit to the writer and to the paper in which they appeared, was published, with a brief introduction, by Mr. Arnold White. 2 vols. London, 1888. (Seccombe)

showing that Mr. Matthews and the police were awake to their responsibilities. It will be difficult to convince anyone of that now.

—

### FIFTH EDITION.
### WHITECHAPEL.
### A MAD BUTCHER AT LARGE FOR TEN WEEKS.
### He Carried a Knife and Steel and Resembles a Man Seen with Blood-stained Hands Soon After the Murder—A Knife Found in a Hampstead Pond.

The Holloway lunatic, who is detained on suspicion in connection with the Whitechapel murders, is not a German, as stated yesterday, but a Swiss, named Isenschmid. A *Star* reporter made inquiries about him last night. Some time ago he kept a pork butcher's shop in Elthorne-road, Holloway, and he is what is known in the trade as a "cutter-up." Some years ago, it seems, he had a sunstroke, and since then he has been subject to yearly fits of madness. These fits have usually come on in the latter part of the summer, and on several occasions his conduct has been so alarming that he has been carried off to Colney Hatch. It is a fact of some significance that he was last released

### JUST BEFORE CHRISTMAS.

One of his delusions is that everything belongs to him—he has called himself the King of Elthorne-road. On several occasions he has threatened to put certain people's lights out, as he has expressed it, and more than once the landlord of the shop in Elthorne-road, a gentleman named Allan, has been warned not to approach his lunatic tenant. One of the alarming practices of Isenschmid when he is mad is his continual sharpening of a long knife, and his disappearance from home for a few days has not been unusual. He went mad some weeks ago, and his frightened wife got an order for his detention in a lunatic asylum, but Isenschmid could not be caught. The police have been looking for him for some little time, and

### HIS HOUSE HAS BEEN WATCHED

in the expectation that he would go there. It may be only a curious coincidence, but the mad pork butcher very closely answers the description of the man who was seen on the morning of the murder near the scene of the crime with bloodstains on his hands. He is about 38 years of age, about 5ft. 7in. in height, of rather stout build, and has hair on his head and face of a ginger colour. George Pigott, arrested at Graves-end, was taken for the man who went with bloody hands into Mrs. Fiddymont's public-house, but three people failed to identify him as the man they saw on the morning of the murder. Can the mad Swiss butcher be the man who behaved so strangely that Joseph Taylor followed him into Shoreditch?

A *Star* reporter had an interview this morning with Mrs. Isenschmid. She said, "Five or six years ago my husband had some sort of a fit, and he has never been right in his head since. About this time of the year he gets much worse. He has been in the asylum once before, but he was not quite right in his mind when they let him out. Since Whitsuntide[62] he has become worse than he has ever been. He got so bad that I got an order to have him put in the asylum again. A doctor came to see him and then he got suspicious. I told him the doctor was only the broker's man, but he said the broker's man wouldn't ask him how he was. He got afraid that he would be put in the asylum again, and

**TEN WEEKS AGO HE RAN AWAY.**

Since that time he has been home five or six times, generally in the night, but he never stopped long and never said where he had been to. On one occasion he came home at six o'clock in the morning with a big grey dog. He walks about till he's nearly starved, when he goes away and he has got pinched in his appearance and much thinner. When he was in a torpid sullen mood he couldn't be got to do anything, not even wash his face, but would sometimes sit and

**READ THE BIBLE FOR 24 HOURS**

straight off and sometimes would fling the book to the other side of the room. 'I must be a very wicked man if all the Bible says is true,' he would sometimes say. When his violent fits came on he became very dangerous. I believe he hates me,' Mrs. Isenschmid said, "and I feel sure he would kill me if he caught me alone."

The poor woman's position is a pitiful one. Her husband's friends are in Switzerland, and unknown to her, and some money her husband had left her has been lost through his madness. She has several little children, is entirely with-

out any means of support, and is even homeless, since all her goods have been taken by the brokers for rent.

The man who now has the shop where Isenschmid formerly carried on business has seen the maniac several times since 10 weeks ago he took flight from his home. Once he went to the shop with his butcher's apron on and

**HIS KNIFE AND STEEL**

hanging by his side, and showing a bullock's tail he said he had slaughtered 40 bullocks. Last week a load of bullocks' entrails were brought to the shop, and the order that they should be sent there had been given by Isenschmid at three o'clock that morning. Where they had been brought from the man at the shop doesn't know, but one of the men, he says, "looked like a Jew."

This morning a knife with a white bone handle and

**A BLADE ABOUT TEN INCHES LONG,**

which appeared to have been much worn, and had dark stains upon it, was found in one of the Hampstead ponds, and was handed over to the police.

At present the police are engaged in tracking Isenschmid's mysterious movements during his 10 weeks' absence from home.

—

**Capture of a Man With a Knife.**

Charles Ludwig, 40, a decently dressed German, of 1, The Minories, at the Thames Police-court to-day, was charged with being drunk and threatening to stab Alexander Finlay, of 51, Leman-street, Whitechapel.

Prosecutor said at three o'clock this morning prisoner came up to a coffee-stall in White-chapel, pulled out a knife and tried to stab witness. Ludwig followed him round the stall, and made several attempts to stab him.

Constable 221 H, who arrested the prisoner, said On the way to the station, he dropped a long-bladed penknife, and on him was found a razor and a long-bladed pair of scissors.

City-constable Johnson, 866, stated early that morning he heard loud screams of "Murder" proceeding from a dark court in the Minories in which there were no lights. The court led to some railway arches, and was a well-known dangerous locality. On going into the court he found the prisoner with a prostitute. The former appeared to be under the influence of drink. The woman, who appeared to be in a

---

[62] **Whitsuntide.** The eighth Sunday after Easter, beginning with Whitsunday. (Morehead)

very agitated condition, said, "Oh, policeman,

**DO TAKE ME OUT OF THIS."**

The woman was so frightened that she could then make no further explanation. He got her and the accused out of the court, and sent the latter off. He walked with the woman to the end of his beat, when she said, "Dear me; he frightened me very much when he pulled a big knife out." Witness said, "Why didn't you all me that at the time?" and she said "I was too much frightened." He then went and looked for the prisoner, but could not find him, and therefore warned several other constables what he had seen. Witness had been out till the morning trying to find the woman, but up to the present time had not been able to do so. He should know her again. He believed the prisoner worked in the neighbourhood.

It has been ascertained that Ludwig, who now professes he is not able to speak English, has been in this country for about three months. He accounts for his time during the last three weeks.

Mr. Saunders ordered prisoner to be remanded.

—

### A Woman May be the Murderer.

"S.G.O." takes up the parable of the Whitechapel murders in a long letter printed in the *Times* in big type. We seem (he says) to have needed at last some home stroke to awaken us to the fact that we have at our very doors an element of danger threatening consequences which may prove, but too late, that we have suffered, with little attempt to arrest it, the growth of a large and increasing portion of our population to live, move, and have their being under a condition of things tending to

**THE UTTER SUBVERSION**

of the very commonest principles of civilisation; leading to the commission of crimes which hitherto would have been held to have been so abhorrent as to be inconceivable even where all ordinary crime had full sway.

Just so long as the dwellings of this race continue in their present condition, their whole surroundings a sort of warren of foul alleys garnished with the flaring lamps of the ginshops, and offering to all sorts of lodgers, for all conceivable wicked purposes, every possible accommodation to further brutalise, we shall have still to go on —affecting astonishment that

in such a state of things we have outbreaks from time to time of the horrors of the present day.

All strange, sir, as it may appear to you and the generality of your readers, it is within the range of my belief that one or both these Whitechapel murders may have been

**COMMITTED BY FEMALE HANDS.**

There are details in both cases which fit in well with language for ever used where two of these unfortunates are in violent strife; there is far more jealousy, as is well known, between such women in regard to those with whom they cohabit than is the case with married people where one may suspect the other of sin against the marriage vow.

—

### Another Theory.

With reference to the missing parts of Annie Chapman's body, Thomas Bolas writes:—"That biologists have been so infatuated by their pursuits as to cause murder to be committed in aid of their researches is a matter of history, and to my mind there is quite enough evidence of the last murder being the work of some half-mad physiologist in search of living tissues or organs from a healthy subject, for experiments on graftation, to justify certain investigations by the police."

~

# Tuesday, 18 September, 1888

## Evening News

**THE WHITECHAPEL MURDER.**
**A SUGGESTION.**
**TO THE EDITOR OF**
**"THE EVENING NEWS."**

SIR—It has been suggested by a correspondent in a contemporary of yours, that the unfortunate woman, Annie Chapman, was murdered by a left-handed person, his reason for thinking so being the fact of the victim's throat being cut from left to right. He says: "Now, from the position of the body, the purpose, presumably, of her visit to the yard, is it not most likely the victim was attacked from the front, in which case, judging from the force of the blow, it would appear to be the work of some left-handed person." I cannot agree with the reasoning of this correspondent.

He presumes that the woman entered the yard for an immoral purpose; with this view I beg to differ. I believe the woman entered this yard, which was known to her, by herself, with the object of finding a quiet resting place. Donovan, the "deputy" at the lodging-house where the deceased frequently stayed, has stated that when he last saw the woman alive at twenty minutes to two on the morning of her death she was the worse for drink, and that she said, "I haven't enough money now, but keep my bed for me. I shan't be long."

From this it is evident she intended returning to the lodging-house; but, presuming she did not get any money, might she not have entered the yard in Hanbury-street, knowing there was little likelihood of her there being disturbed by the police? And I believe the assassin saw and murdered the woman while asleep.

Even if brawls and cries of murder are so frequent in the early hours of the morning in Whitechapel, that little or no notice is taken of them, still at the hour at which the murder is supposed to have been committed quietness would almost reign supreme. And if the woman had been attacked from the front, and while awake, however suddenly, she would at least have uttered one piecing shriek, which in the prevailing stillness could not have failed to have been heard by some light sleeper near. But if the woman was sleeping the heavy sleep of the drunkard, the murderer could stoop over her and pass the cold blade across her neck before she awoke.

Perhaps the murderer had been sleeping in the yard himself, or perhaps he had followed his victim and bided his opportunity to commit his diabolical crime. And now I would modestly offer an opinion as to the motive of the crime.

It has been noticed that all the victims have been women of the "unfortunate" class. Therefore, let us suppose that the murderer has at some time contracted a loathsome disease from one of these women—not necessarily from any of the victims—and that, finding his life a life of misery and suffering, he has allowed his mind to dwell with thoughts of vengeance on the class of women that gave him this disease. This vengeance, growing with a rapid growth in his enfeebled mind, he determines to exterminate as many of these women as he can. He then commences his ghastly work.

If this theory of mine should be considered feasible, I would suggest that a visit be paid to all the hospitals in the neighbourhood of Whitechapel, and inquiries made of them as to out-patients attending now or lately for a certain disease. I believe all hospitals keep books, in which the name, address, and occupation of the patient are entered. Therefore, with a little trouble, it could be found what patients by their trade were likely to be skilled in the handling of a knife, and secret inquiries made as to their past and present life.

I am, &e.,
A. W. HUX.
September 16.

### TO THE EDITOR OF
### "THE EVENING NEWS."

SIR—Amid all the many suggestions for the best means of trying to discover the fiend-ish perpetrator of the Whitechapel murders no mention has been made of one obvious to all, and most simple—namely, a large compensating reward.

For any likelihood of success the reward must be both one and the other. It must be large in proportion to the diabolic ferocity of the crimes, to their unusual and quickly recurring number, and to mark the sense of their hideousness by a feeling that scarcely any amount can be thought too great to prevent their repetition, if, indeed, you cannot punish and avenge their brutality.

# Tuesday, 18 September, 1888

And it must be compensating enough to make it worthwhile for the informer to get out of the reach and power of a bloody vengeance, one that may carry him away to a home beyond the seas, safe from the grip or grasp of any of the friends who may have haunted his old associations and neighbourhoods.

If it was only an ordinary case no one would ask the Government to go out of their way to break their general rule. But these murders have startled and staggered the whole country. A thickly populated district lives in abject fear — almost paralyzed. Is there to be no end to this torture? Is it not the duty of a paternal Government to protect those in whom they must take some faint interest? Or will they permit all that has passed to die out unnoticed and forgotten?

JOHN BULL.

## NOTES.

As a system of criminal inquiry, public investigation before a coroner is an anachronism; but it is not entirely useless, even as that, if it is able to show up the absurdity of other ancient institutions. The inquiry before Mr. Wynne Baxter yesterday into the cause of the death of Mary Ann Nichols is fruitful in again demonstrating to the people of London the entire fatuity of their police arrangements.

On the morning of her murder this poor woman's body was taken to the mortuary attached to the Whitechapel Workhouse, and there undressed and washed *by two men*, pauper inmates of the workhouse. Decency might have found two women paupers, but idiocy could not have supplied two more incapable men.

Robert Mann and James Hatfield, unprovided with material in the shape of body or brains to gain subsistence in the great world, are consigned to a workhouse, and there given power to interfere with the investigations of men with whom brains is a necessity, or their existence is a failure.

Robert Mann yesterday did not know exactly what had happened on the morning of the murder, and the coroner explained that "the witness was subject to fits," and "that his statements are hardly reliable." James Hatfield was even less reliable. He cut off some of the woman's clothes, and tore down her chemise, but he swore she wore no stays. Upon this, the foreman exclaimed, "Why, you tried the stays

on the body of the deceased in my presence at the mortuary."

That two such men should have been allowed without instructions from the police to proceed to cut the clothes, wash the body, and possibly destroy traces that would have aided in the detection of the criminal is so preposterously stupid that it could not exist anywhere but in London.

The time has surely come when the police stations of the metropolis shall have proper mortuaries attached to them so that the help of epileptic paupers warranted to forget what they have done shall not be brought into requisition.

—

## CHIT-CHAT.

Is the following incident a sample of our "detective" work? Yesterday, at Woolwich Police-court, a labourer, named Edward Quinn, was charged with being drunk at the police-station. His face and hands were bruised, and it was deposed that when arrested he was much blood-stained.

Quinn stated that on Saturday afternoon, having stumbled in the street and cut his face and hands, he went into a bar at Woolwich for a drink. "While at the bar," he said, "a big tall man came in and stood beside me and looked at me. He got me in tow, and gave me some beer and tobacco, and then he said 'I mean to charge you with the Whitechapel murders.'" This seems rather like the ingenious *coup de main*[63] that would suggest itself to our average British policeman.

The man's face and hands were bloody, and there had been a murder in Whitechapel only seven days before. What more likely than that the murderer should have forgotten to wash himself for a week? To Quinn, however, it did not seem probable that such astute calculation would be made, for he says, "I thought it was a joke, and laughed, but he said he was serious, and pointed to the blood about me. I said, 'Nonsense, is that all the clue you have got?' He then dropped the subject, and took me for a walk until we got to the police-station, where he charged me with the Whitechapel murders."

Quinn was subsequently released on his own recognisances. But we should like to know if his tale is true, and, if so, who was the big stout man?

---

[63] **Coup de main**. Surprise attack, raid. (Dubois)

# Tuesday, 18 September, 1888

## THE WHITECHAPEL MURDER.
## A POSSIBLE CLUE.

The following facts, which have just come to hand, may furnish a clue by which the Hanbury-street murderer may be traced:

On the day of the murder (the 8th inst.), a man was seen in the lavatory of the City News Rooms, 4, Ludgate-circus-buildings, changing his clothes. He departed hurriedly, leaving behind him a pair of trousers, a shirt, and a pair of socks. Unfortunately, no one connected with the establishment saw the man, or he would certainly have been stopped and questioned as to why he was changing his clothes there and leaving the old ones behind.

Mr. Walker, the proprietor of the News Rooms, states that he did not hear of the occurrence until late in the afternoon, when his attention was called to the clothes in the lavatory. He did not at the time attach any importance to the fact, and the clothes were thrown into the dust-box and placed outside, being carted away in the City Sewers cart on the Monday.

On the following Tuesday, however, he received a visit from a man who said he was a police officer, and asked for the clothes which had been left there on Saturday. Mr. Walker replied that if he wanted them he would have to go to the Commissioners of the City Sewers, telling him at the same time what he had done with them. Two detectives called on Thursday last, and had an interview with Mr. Walker, and they succeeded in finding a man who saw the party changing his clothes in the lavatory, and he has given the police a description of him.

He is described as a man of respectable appearance, about 30 years of age, and wearing a dark moustache, but the police are very reticent about the matter, and decline to give any information on the subject. They evidently attach some importance to the affair, as Mr. Walker again received a visit from two detectives yesterday morning.

The police are now trying to trace the clothes, as it is hoped that they will furnish some clue to lead to the identity of the man whom they are searching for.

## THE EAST END MURDERS AND
## POLICE ORGANISATION.

Under the above heading a letter appears in to-day's Times, from which we make the following extracts:

The occurrences in Whitechapel are being made the opportunity for raising a cry against the metropolitan police. This is on every account to be regretted, for whatever imperfections there may be in the administration of that force a cry by people who know nothing about administration is not a good means whereby to reach its reform. Neither is a cry directed against its chief.

Sir Charles Warren is not to be blamed for those alterations in general management which were initiated, I believe, as long ago as 25 or 30 years before the present time. He has carried out, with some additions of detail, a system that began under Colonel Henderson. That system differs from what preceded it in two particulars chiefly.

### FORMERLY KEPT ON THE SAME BEAT.

It was formerly the practice to keep a well-behaved policeman—and nearly all policemen are well-behaved—on the same beat, without shifting, for a very long time; and a man was seldom or never removed from his beat without some reason. It is now the practice to shift men sometimes once a month, sometimes at the end of two months, and nearly always at the end of three months. I may be told that there is no rule or order on the subject. I have no means of knowing what the rule, if any, may be, but I know what the practice is, about which any Londoner may satisfy himself by asking any policeman that he may have acquaintance with, or, indeed, any policeman whom he may address civilly.

### CONSTABLES AND DETECTIVES KEPT
### MORE SEPARATE.

Sir Edward Henderson's other innovation was to separate, far more than had been before, the police on ordinary duty from the detective police in as it were two departments. I do not know the particulars, I only know the heads, of this change; and I strongly suspect, though I cannot prove from facts, what its working has been. The two alterations are based, it will be evident to all acquainted with police management, on the idea of treating the force as a machine. Many minor details that have arisen

# Tuesday, 18 September, 1888

under the same idea look like militarism. While I do not want to impute militarism to either the late or the present chief, I am of the belief that what I would prefer to call the mechanical idea has dominated both of them too much.

### MEN WHO KNOW THEIR BEATS.

A policeman who knows his beat—being not merely a beat the duty of which is attending to traffic—is worth three who do not know the beat. This applies to the whole of a city, and it applies with double force to such parts as Whitechapel. A man will know the streets of his beat in a day—or may do so if he chooses; although I have asked my way to a street, naming it, which was part of a man's beat, without his having heard of it. But a man will not, till after a very considerable time, know the people who live in a beat; nor will he know, as an old hand will, every house and its doors and windows. A policeman who has attained thorough knowledge, who knows the people, and is known to them, becomes a kind of referee, especially in the poorer neighbour-hoods. Knowledge of him produces confidence in him; and he becomes without his knowing it an embryo detective. He is able to put down street rows with a mere glance when a stranger would be unheeded. I need not enumerate the particulars in which the old policeman is and must be the superior of the stranger. If it be said that he will become too intimate with the population, it is not so; he cannot be too intimate. He may abuse his intimacy, which is another thing. Last year there was much talk of blackmail in connection with the Regent-street affair. I believe, perhaps, one-hundredth part of it. But it would be a more difficult thing for a policeman, known by hundreds of the neighbours, to pursue a system of blackmail, such as was imputed, than for a man transferred once a month from one beat to another.

### CITY POLICE V. METROPOLITAN.

If I be thought to be giving my unsupported opinion, I have authority, the very highest, for my views; indeed, I think the following two authorities amount to proof. Every one that I know holds that the City police is superior in effectiveness to the metropolitan. The only difference, but the slightest, in their organisation is that the City men are kept without a break on the same beats for a minimum period of three

years, never being removed during those three years except for misconduct; and often, at the end of the term, being placed on day duty instead of night duty on their old beats.

### PARIS POLICE.

My other authority is Paris, the best policed city in the world. There the sergents de ville[64] are never removed. I knew one who had been in the same district for 30 years. He knew every man, woman, and child, dog, and cat, door, win-dow, shutter, and spout in his six or seven streets; and burglary and disorder were most difficult.

### THE MECHANICAL CONCEPTION OF THE FORCE.

Sir Charles Warren inherited the traditions of his predecessor. It is not, as I said, so much the military as the mechanical conception of the force that is erroneous, though these two ideas may have something in common. The military idea is that soldiers, to be effective, must act in bodies; the policeman must nearly always act alone. Such occasions as occurred last winter in Trafalgar-square are quite exceptional.

### THE M.P.'S £100 REWARD.

Last evening, at a meeting held in the large hall at the Working Lads' Institute, Whitechapel-road, Mr. S. Montagu, in addressing his constituents, referred to the recent murders in Whitechapel, and said that the crimes had sent a shudder of horror throughout the whole of England.

Mr. Montagu proceeded to explain why he had offered a reward of £100 for the detection of the murderer, and said that after he had heard of the murders he drove to Leman-street Police-station, and he was not then aware that the Government had abandoned the system of offering rewards. He found that Superintendent Arnold was out of town, and knowing the Home Secretary was also out of town, and that some delay might result, he offered Inspector West a written undertaking to pay £100 for the apprehension of the murderer. He was told that the offer would be communicated to the Commissioners of Police and to the Home Office.

This he believed had been done; and that morning he had written to the police authorities begging that they would at once have printed and posted at his expense a sufficient number of placards to give publicity to his offer.

---

[64] **Sergents de ville**. Policemen. (Dubois)

143

# Wednesday, 19 September, 1888

## The Times

### THE WHITECHAPEL MURDERS.

Several reports were current in London yesterday as to discoveries by the police in connexion with the Hanbury-street murder; but the value of the clues said to have been obtained is extremely doubtful. One statement is to the effect that on the day of the murder a man changed his clothes in the lavatory of the City News Rooms, Ludgate-circus, and left hurriedly, leaving behind him a shirt, a pair of trousers, and a pair of socks. The attendant threw the discarded clothes into the dustbin, and they were carted off in the City Sewers cart on the following Monday. The police are said to be endeavouring to trace these clothes, but decline to give information on the subject. It is obviously difficult to conceive why the murderer, having possessed himself of a change of clothes, should pass from Whitechapel to Ludgate-circus and change his dress in a *quasi*-public place such as the City News Rooms. The police, however, will thoroughly sift the matter.

Charles Ludwig, the German charged yesterday at the Thames Police-court with being drunk and threatening to stab, was at once connected by popular imagination with the murder. Our police report will show that some of the circumstances of the case seem to support such an hypothesis.

The youth who was threatened early yesterday morning stated to a correspondent that the first he saw of Ludwig, as he calls him, was about a quarter to 4 o'clock.

The prisoner was then at the top of Commercial-street, in company with a woman, whom he was conducting in the direction of the Minories. "I took no notice of this at the time," added the witness, "except to make a remark to a coffee-stall keeper. In about a quarter of an hour the woman ran back in a state of fright, as it seemed. At any rate she was screaming and exclaiming, "You can't do that to me."

Again I thought little of it, as I only fancied she had had some drink, but within five minutes the prisoner came up and asked for a cup of coffee at the stall where I was standing. He, at all events, was drunk, and would only produce a halfpenny in payment for the coffee which was given him. I suppose he noticed me looking at him, for he suddenly turned round and asked in broken English, "What you looking at?" I replied that I was doing no harm, but he said, 'Oh, you want something,' and pulled out a long penknife, with which he made a dash at me.

I eluded him and snatched from the stall a dish, which I prepared to throw at his head, but as he retreated after making the first dash I only called to a policeman who was nearby and had him arrested.

He is slightly built, and perhaps about 5ft. 6in. in height, dark complexioned, and wearing a grizzled beard and moustache. I should think he is about 40 years of age. There is something the matter with one of his legs, and he walks stiffly.

I heard that at the police-court this morning he pretended not to understand English, but his English when he addressed me was plain enough, though broken; and besides, when the officer who had him in charge told me on the way to Leman-street to see that he did not throw anything away, he at once dropped the penknife—which had till then been in his possession—as if the idea of getting rid of it had only just occurred to him. I have never seen him before."

Ludwig entered the employment of Mr. C. A. Partridge, hairdresser, the Minories, a fortnight ago last Saturday.

On Monday night last he went to an hotel in Finsbury, where he had previously lodged, and remained there until about 1 o'clock in the morning. He produced a number of razors, and acted in such a manner that some of the inmates were quite frightened.

The landlady of this hotel states that on the day after the last murder in Whitechapel Ludwig called early in the morning and washed his hands, stating that he had been injured. Another person has alleged that there was blood on the man's hands, but as to this the landlady cannot speak.

—

### TO THE EDITOR OF THE TIMES.

Sir,—Is it not time that the inquest on Annie Chapman should close, and a verdict of "Wilful Murder against some person or persons unknown " be given?

The question which the jury are soon to determine—viz., how, when, and where the deceased met with her death, and who she was—is virtually solved.

# Wednesday, 19 September, 1888

The discovery of the murderer or murderers is the duty of the police, and if it is to be accomplished it is not desirable that the information they obtain should be announced publicly in the newspapers day by day through the medium of the coroner's inquiry.

J.P.

—

## AT LAST.
## TO THE EDITOR OF THE TIMES.

Sir,—Whitechapel horrors will not be in vain if "at last" the public conscience awakes to consider the life which these horrors reveal. The murders were, it may almost be said, bound to come; generation could not follow generation in lawless intercourse, children could not be familiarized with scenes of degradation, community in crime could not be the bond of society and the end of all be peace.

Some of us who, during many years, have known the life of our neighbours do not think the murders to be the worst fact in our experience, and published evidence now gives material for forming a picture of daily or nightly life such as no one has imagined.

It is for those who, like ourselves, have for years known these things to be ready with practical suggestions, and I would now put some forward as the best outcome of the thought of my wife and myself. Before doing so, it is necessary to remind the public that these criminal haunts are of limited extent. The greater part of Whitechapel is as orderly as any part of London, and the life of most of its inhabitants is more moral than that of many whose vices are hidden by greater wealth. Within the area of a quarter of a mile most of the evil may be found concentrated, and it ought not to be impossible to deal with it strongly and adequately. We would submit four practical suggestions:—

1. Efficient police supervision. In criminal haunts a license has been allowed which would not be endured in other quarters. Rows, fights, and thefts have been permitted, while the police have only been able to keep the main thoroughfares quiet for the passage of respectable people. The Home Office has never authorized the employment of a sufficient force to keep decent order inside the criminal quarters.

2. Adequate lighting and cleaning. It is no blame to our local authority that the back streets are gloomy and ill-cleaned. A penny rate here produces but a small sum, and the ratepayers are often poor. Without doubt, though, dark passages lend themselves to evil deeds. It would not be unwise, and it certainly would be a humane outlay, if some of the unproductive expenditure of the rich were used to make the streets of the poor as light and as clean as the streets of the City.

3. The removal of the slaughter-houses. At present animals are daily slaughtered in the midst of Whitechapel, the butchers with their blood stains are familiar among the street passengers, and sights are common which tend to brutalize ignorant natures. For the sake of both health and morals the slaughtering should be done outside the town.

4. The control of tenement houses by responsible landlords. At present there is lease under lease, and the acting landlord is probably one who encourages vice to pay his rent. Vice can afford to pay more than honesty, but its profits at last go to landlords. If rich men would come forward and buy up this bad property they might not secure great interest, but they would clear away evil not again to be suffered to accumulate. Such properties have been bought with results morally most satisfactory and economically not unsatisfactory. Some of that which remains might now be bought, some of the worst is at present in the market, and I should be glad, indeed, to hear of purchasers.

Far be it from any one to say that even such radical changes as these would do away with evil. When, however, such changes have been effected it will be more possible to develop character, and one by one lead the people to face their highest. Only personal service, the care of individual by individual, can be powerful to keep down evil, and only the knowledge of God is sufficient to give the individual faith to work and see little result of his work. For men and women who will give such service there is a crying demand.

I am, truly yours,
SAMUEL A. BARNETT.
St. Jude's Vicarage, Whitechapel, Sept. 18.

—

# Wednesday, 19 September, 1888

At the Thames Police Court, Charles Ludwig, 40, a decently attired German, who professed not to understand English and gave an address at the Minories, was charged with being drunk and threatening to stab Alexander Finlay, of 51 Leman street, Whitechapel.

Prosecutor said at 3 o'clock on Tuesday morning he was standing at a coffee stall in the Whitechapel road when Ludwig came up in a drunken condition. The person in charge of the stall refused to serve him. Ludwig seemed much annoyed and said to witness, "What are you looking at?" He then pulled out a long bladed knife and tried to stab witness with it. Ludwig followed him round the stall and made several attempts to stab him, until witness threatened to knock a dish on his head. A constable came up and he was then given into custody.

Constable 221 H said that when he was called to take the prisoner into custody he found him in a very excited condition. Witness had previously received information that Ludwig was wanted in the City for attempting to cut a woman's throat with a razor. On the way to the station the prisoner dropped a long bladed knife, which was open, and when he was searched a razor and a long bladed pair of scissors were found on him.

Constable John Johnson, 866 City, deposed that early on Tuesday morning he was on duty in the Minories when he heard loud screams of "Murder" proceeding from a dark court. The court led to some railway arches and was a well known dangerous locality. Witness went down the court and found the prisoner with a prostitute. The prisoner appeared to be under the influence of drink. When asked what he was doing there, he replied, "Nothing." The woman, who appeared to be in a very agitated and frightened condition, said, "Oh, policeman, do take me out of this." The woman was so frightened that she could then make no further explanation. Witness got her and the accused out of the court, and sent the latter off. He walked with the woman to the end of his beat, when she said, "Dear me, he frightened me very much when he pulled a big knife out." Witness said, "Why did you not tell me that at the time?" and she replied, "I was too much frightened." He then went and looked for the prisoner, but could not find him, and therefore warned several other constables of what he had seen and also gave a description of the prisoner. Witness had been out all the morning to find the woman, but up to the present time had not been able to do so. He believed the prisoner worked in the neighbourhood.

Mr. Saunders remanded the prisoner for a week. Considerable excitement prevailed in the neighbourhood owing to the rumour that the prisoner was connected with the recent murders in Whitechapel, and that some important discoveries would result from his capture.

~

146

# Wednesday, 19 September, 1888

## The Star
### WHAT WE THINK.

AT length the tide of talk on the Whitechapel horrors is taking a direction which we thoroughly approve.

To begin with, the London press is waking up to the discovery that the WARREN-MATTHEWS regime has been a mistake. Trafalgar-square was all very well when no one suffered from it but a few Radical processionists, whose broken heads made an excellent object-lesson for enforcing the great moral of law and order. But now that it is seen that a police force, too small to begin with and disorganised by a long course of laxity on the part of the late CHIEF COMMISSIONER, cannot be suddenly turned from a civil to a semi-military body without leaving London a prey to the criminal classes, the note is changed.

The law-and-order school has got its soul's price. Trafalgar-square was put down; the Alsatias[65] of Whitechapel were forgotten. At the first savage epidemic of crime Scotland-yard broke down with so complete, so piteous a display of incompetence as to arouse the compassion of its foes. Of course, the danger now is that the true offenders will not be sacrificed, but that a holocaust of subordinates will be offered up as a vicarious sacrifice for the sins of WARREN and the follies of MATT-

HEWS. The *Daily Telegraph* therefore is quite right in insisting that "MATTHEWS must go." "We have had enough of Mr. Home Secretary MATTHEWS, who knows nothing, has heard nothing, and does not intend to do anything in matters concerning which he ought to be fully informed, and prepared to act with energy and despatch."

And not only must Mr. MATTHEWS go, but Scotland-yard must be reorganised and the detective department freed from the octopus clutch which Sir CHARLES WARREN has laid upon every branch of the force. The subordination of the detectives is part of Sir CHARLES'S "system." Stop that, and our Prefect resigns. And as that is the only alternative between a new outbreak of lawlessness, helplessly watched by the public and police, it is probable that the days of King STORK at Scotland-yard and King LOG at the Home Office are both numbered.

This is good news; but there is better in reserve. Nothing can have been more short-sighted than the callous indifference which the Government have shown towards these Whitechapel murders. If Mr. MATTHEWS had read his *Star* he would have been told in time that Whitechapel was furious at the refusal to grant a reward, and was very significantly saying that if the murders had happened in Mayfair we should have had rewards fast enough. But something better has happened even than the prospect of the Government waking up to its duties towards its poor subjects. The West-end is waking up.

The Rev. Lord SIDNEY GODOLPHIN OSBORNE, an eccentric but kindly clergyman, with a passion for writing letters to the *Times*, has pointed the true moral of the tragedies; and Mr. BARNETT has driven it home. Our social critics are finding that as we have sowed we have reaped. We have given the people moral sewage and poison to drink, and we have got a residuum as foul, as dangerous, as loathly as any that haunted the back streets of Rome in old Imperial days. "S. G. O." says in the *Times*:—

"What pen can describe, what mental power can realise the nature of the surroundings of child life under these conditions? Begotten amid all that is devoid of the commonest decency, reared in an atmosphere in which blasphemy

---

[65] **Alsatia**. 1. Whitefriars: a district adjoining the Temple, between the Thames and Fleet Street. [Formerly the site of a Carmelite convent (founded 1241)] and possessing certain privileges of sanctuary. These were confirmed by a charter of James I. in 1608, where after the district speedily became a haunt of rascality in general, a Latinised form of Alsace having been jocularly conferred on it as a debateable land. Abuses, outrage, and riot led to the abolition of its right of sanctuary in 1697. Also Alsatia the higher. Whence Alsatia the lower, the liberties of the Mint in Southwark; Alsatian, a rogue, debtor, or debauchee ; a resident in Alsatia: also, roguish, debauched; Alsatia phrase, a canting term (B.E. and Grose). [See Fortunes of Nigel, chaps, xvi. and xvii.]. (1688). 2. Hence any rendezvous or asylum for loose characters or criminals, where immunity from arrest is tolerably certain; a disreputable locality: the term has sometimes been applied (venomously) to the Stock Exchange. Alsatian, an adventurer; a Bohemian. (1834.) (Farmer)

and obscenity are the ordinary language, where all exists that can familiarise the child with scenes bestial—thus reared in home life, it can scarcely itself walk or talk, when first introduced to outside life, the street life, such as it is, where these tens of thousands have to dwell."

It is a petrifying thought that the White-chapel murders may have been committed by such an one as this. Why not? Surely the savage incontinence of life, the awful promiscuity of intercourse, the utter absence of moral, of religious, of prudential restraints are equal to the production of such monstrous growths as the Whitechapel murders. Look at the first of the series, unquestionably committed by a gang; look at the Regent's-park murder; look at scores of deeds of insane violence, committed daily and nightly in the loathsome dens where our London lazzaroni[66] herd, and from which they will one day swarm, in our time of trouble, and smash our civilisation like so much pie-crust.

That is a pretty result of eighteen centuries of Christianity, and one of science and the reign of enlightened social law. That is a charming text for discourses by kid-gloved preachers of the Democratic creed. "London at large," the *Times* admits to-day, "is responsible for Whitechapel and its dens of crime."

Responsible! Why, the East-end with its squalor is made by the West End with its luxury; is essential to it; is the necessary corollary of the delightful problem that the earth is not the LORD'S but the landlord's and the capitalist's. In the East a thousand slaves —as ignorant, as hopeless, as corrupt as were the slave-rowers in a Spanish galleon—toil to keep the West in all the trappings of finery, to make Jubilee dresses, ball-room costumes, and all the rest of the "property" for the great sensual show we call "society." Of course "society" does not know the cost at which its Juggernaut is kept up. It is only idly and stupidly selfish, with a cotton-wool kind of callousness, out of which it will only awake by the help of such a thund-erous sermon as the Whitechapel murders.

Well, is the sermon going to have effect? Will the West conclude that all its mad pursuit of wealth, its senseless craving after luxury, its ennui, its cruel indifference to the gospel of the religion it patronises, its neglect of all the teachings of history—is a mistake, and a fatal one? A State built on such miseries, such terrors, as the glimpse into our Whitechapel Alsatias reveals can't last. It is rotten to the core. GOD'S and man's hands are against it.

All our Church Congresses, Church Houses, Westminster Abbeys—all the pretty glamour which art and culture throw round life among the upper and upper middle classes—are so many deceitful veils of the truth. It is on the condition of its poor, and particularly of the poorest of its poor, and not on new ironclads, or pattern armies, or big commercial deals, that the fate of England, of modern civilisation, depends. The great master question of the age is—"What have we done with our neighbour?"

Is Christian England to hear the answer addressed to the Jewish Pharisee of old— "Inasmuch as ye did it not to one of the least of these, ye did it not to Me?"[67]

BY the way, the methods suggested by Mr. Barnett for clearing out our Alsatias might, at all events, be at once put in practice. These are—

1. Efficient police supervision (utterly broken down by Sir Charles Warren's repeated shifting of detectives and constables who knew their ground).

2. Adequate lighting and cleaning. To be paid for by a rate levied on the ground landlords.

3. The removal of the slaughter-houses, with their odious look and suggestions of blood.

4. The control of tenement houses by responsible landlords.

5. Practically, indeed, this comes to what we have been contending for all along—a good grip on the vampire classes —i.e., the landlords.

WE hope Sir Charles Warren will keep his eye on the editor of the *Standard*. Shoe-lane is evidently a centre of the most dangerous form of the social revolution. Mr. Mudford is for confiscation pure and simple, without compen-sation, without a time limit, with none of the safeguards and barriers which prudent and moderate Reformers like Mr. George Bernard

---

[66] **Lazzaroni**. The homeless idlers of Naples who live by chance work or begging; so called from the Hospital of St. Lazarus, which serves as their refuge. (Webster's Revised Unabridged Dictionary)

---

[67] Matthew 25:45. King James Version.

# Wednesday, 19 September, 1888

Shaw, for instance, are for erecting. For it says of the new Trust or monopoly system which is springing up all over England and America:—

> If anything could lend weight to the theories of the dreamers who want to see all private property destroyed, it would be the selfish and criminal co-operation of these syndicates to make their millions out of the difficulties and embarrassments and ruin of a whole trade. For such greedy wretches there should be no mercy. They live by the spoiling of the community. If, in return, they could be stripped of their last farthing by the action of the community, we should rejoice at the administration of so wholesome a lesson.

WELL, this is good high doctrine for a Tory print, but the line of reasoning is one which the community is sure to adopt. If monopoly trading is going to smash free trade in the interest of the capitalist, and dock wages in order to enhance profits, the people, helpless in face of these monster combinations, will very soon inquire why the monopoly principle should not be a trifle extended.

We shall, in fact, get to the state of things which Mr. George foreshadows in his picture of the whole land of the country being owned by one man, who only allows the rest of the community to live on it on his own terms. Supposing all the capital of the country got into the hands of half a dozen trusts? Well, all one can say is that the chance of effecting an easy transfer from the individual to the community would be far too tempting for any democratic State to resist.

SEVERAL journals have been attracted by the details we have recently been giving as to the falling off in the advertising of the *Times*. The *Liverpool Mercury* a day or two ago had a column leader on the decay of the *Times*, and the *Pall Mall* of yesterday devoted its first article to a forecast of the dreadful state we should all be in when the *Times* had ceased to exist. We don't think things have gone so far as that just yet; but no doubt the *Times* is in a very bad way. We are quite sure that for some months in every year the paper is published at a considerable loss every day, and we have heard that as a consequence the shareholders have had occasionally to do without their yearly dividend.

WE cannot entirely agree with the *Pall Mall Gazette* that the death of the *Times* would be a great national loss. On the contrary, we are disposed to believe that it would be a great national gain. The paper has been on the wrong side in all the great controversies that have arisen since its foundation; has opposed every reform with obstinate dullness and malice; and has thrown at every reformer every kind of filth that unscrupulousness could suggest. It would be a due Nemesis to all the good it has delayed and all the honesty it has reviled that it should be snuffed out of existence.

AS to the features by which the *Times* is distinguished from its contemporaries, there would be no fear that some other journal would not be ready to supply us with them. Indeed, it reflects little credit on the enterprise of this country that no serious effort has been made to compete with the *Times*.

London is probably the only really great metropolis in the world in which one journal would be allowed to remain without serious rival for a century. Look at New York. Some years ago the *Herald* was unquestionably as much ahead of all the other journals as the *Times* used to be of its rivals in London. But this was not a state of things which was allowed to last. Other journals spent money freely, bought splendid machinery, and now the *Herald* is only one of many great journals.

We have little doubt that if half as much money were raised as can be got for almost any company with lofty promises that a paper could be published in London at a penny that would have every good feature of the *Times* and pay its proprietors at the same time a princely income. There seems little chance of such a paper being started, and it almost looks as if the Times would die, not from the enterprise of its rivals, but from its own sheer stupidity.

~

# Wednesday, 19 September, 1888

## Evening News
### THE WHITECHAPEL MURDERS
### MEETINGS OF THE
### VIGILANCE COMMITTEE
### LETTER FROM THE
### HOME SECRETARY

No further arrest has been made, and the police are still are fault. The indignation at the East end owing to the attitude of Home Office is hourly increasing, and this morning a meeting of the Vigilance Committee, of which Mr. Lusk is president, met again at 74 Mile End road, for the purpose of receiving the reports of their honorary officers in the matter. From the statements of Mr. Aarons, Mr. Cohen and the president himself there appeared to be some thousands of the better classes at the East end who believed that a substantial Government reward would bring about the apprehension of the murderer, and all donors or non donors to the reward fund, now steadily increasing, were loud in denunciation of the police authorities and the Home Office for declining to offer a reward.

The Secretary said that on the 15th inst. the Committee sent a letter to the Home Secretary on the subject, which was to the following effect:

"At a meeting of the committee of gentlemen, held at 74 Mile End road, E., it was resolved to approach you upon the subject of the reward we are about to issue for the discovery of the author or authors of the late atrocities in the East end of London, and to ask you, Sir, to augment our fund for the said purpose, or kindly state your reasons for refusing."

To this letter he had received the following communication:

"Sir—I am directed by the Secretary of State to acknowledge the receipt of your letter of the 16th inst. with reference to the question of the offer of a reward for the discovery of the perpetrators of the recent murders in Whitechapel, and I am to inform you that had the Secretary of State considered the case a proper one for the offer of a reward he would at once have offered one on behalf of the Government, but that the practice of offering rewards for the discovery of criminals was discontinued some years ago, because experience showed that such offers of rewards tend to produce more harm than good, and the Secretary of State is satisfied that there is nothing in the circumstances of the present case to justify a departure from this rule.

I am, Sir, your obedient servant,
G. Leigh Pemberton."

—

The landlord of the hotel in Finsbury where the man Weitzel, now in custody charged with attempting to stab a youth in Whitechapel, stayed at various times, made the following statement to a representative of the Press Association this morning:

"I must say I have been very suspicious of the man since the last murder in Whitechapel. On the day after that event, that is Sunday, he called here about nine o'clock in a very dirty state, and asked to be allowed to wash. He said he had been out all night, and began to talk to me about the Spitalfields affair. He wore a felt hat, a dirty greyish coat, and yellow seaside slippers. He brought with him a case of razors and a large pair of scissors, and after a time he wanted to shave me. I did not like the way he went on and refused. Previous to this I had not seen him for about 18 months, and he had made most contradictory statements as to where he had been. I did not see whether he had any blood on his hands, as has been said, for I did not watch him very closely, and wanted to get him out of the place as soon as possible. He is a most extraordinary man, and is always in a bad temper, and grinds his teeth in rage at any little thing which puts him out. I believe he has some knowledge of anatomy, as he was for some time an assistant to some doctors in the German army, and helped to dissect bodies. He always carries some razors and a pair of scissors with him, and when he came here again on Monday night last he produced them. He was annoyed because I would not let him sleep here, and threw down the razors in a passion, swearing at the same time. If there had been a policeman near I should have given him into custody. I noticed on this occasion a great change in his dress. Whereas on the former visit he looked very untidy, he was this time wearing a top hat and looked rather smart. He has told me that he has

# Wednesday, 19 September, 1888

been living in the West end, but I believe he is well known at the cheap lodging houses in Whitechapel. From what he has said to me, I know he was in the habit of associating with low women. On Monday last he remained here till about one o'clock, and I than turned him out, as he is a very disagreeable fellow, and very dirty in his habits. The police have not been to see me yet about him."

———

Whitechapel horrors will not be in vain, writes the vicar of St. Jude's, Whitechapel, to *The Times*, if "at last" the public conscience awakes to consider the life which these horrors reveal. The murders were, it may almost be said, bound to come; generation could not follow generation in lawless intercourse, children could not be familiarised with scenes of degradation, community in crime could not be the bond of society, and the end of all be peace.

Some of us who, during many years, have known the life of our neighbours, do not think the murders to be the worst fact in our experience, and published evidence now gives material for forming a picture of daily or nightly life such as no one has imagined. It is for those who, like ourselves, have for years known these things, to be ready with practical suggestions, and I now put some forward as the best outcome of the thought of my wife and myself. Before doing so, it is necessary to remind the public that these criminal haunts are of limited extent. The greater part of Whitechapel is as orderly as any part of London, and the life of most of its inhabitants is more moral than of many whose vices are hidden by greater wealth. Within the area of a quarter of a mile most of the evil may be found concealed, and it ought not to be impossible to deal with it strongly and adequately. We would submit four practical suggestions:

1. Efficient police supervision. In criminal haunts a licence has been allowed which would not be endured in other quarters. Rows, fights, and thefts have been permitted while the police have only been able to keep the main thoroughfares quiet for the passage of respectable people. The Home Office has never authorised the employment of a sufficient force to keep decent order inside the criminal quarters.

2. Adequate lighting and cleaning. It is no blame to our local authority that the back streets are gloomy and ill cleaned. A penny rate here produces but a small sum, and the ratepayers are often poor. Without doubt, though, dark passages lend themselves to evil deeds. It would not be unwise, and it certainly would be a humane outlay, if some of the unproductive expenditure of the rich were used to make the streets of the poor as light and as clean as the streets of the City.

3. The removal of the slaughter houses. At present animals are daily slaughtered in the midst of Whitechapel, the butchers with their blood stained stains are familiar among the street passengers, and sights are common which tend to brutalise ignorant natures. For the sake of both health and morals the slaughtering should be done outside the town.

4. The control of tenement houses by responsible landlords. At present there is lease under lease, and the acting landlord is probably one who encourages vice to pay his rent. Vice can afford to pay more than honesty, but its profits at last go to landlords. If rich men would come forward and buy up this bad property they might not secure great interest, but they would clear away evil not again to be suffered to accumulate. Such properties have been bought with results morally most satisfactory and economically not unsatisfactory. Some of that which remains might now be bought, some of the worst is at present in the market, and I should be glad, indeed, to hear of purchasers.

Far be it from you any one to say even such radical changes as these would do away with evil. When, however, such changes have been effected it will be more possible to develop character, and one by one lead the people to face their highest. Only personal service, the care of individual by individual, can be powerful to keep down evil, and only the knowledge of God is sufficient to give the individual faith to work and see little result for his work. For men and women who will give such service there is a crying demand.

~

## The Times
### THE WHITECHAPEL MURDER.

Yesterday Mr. Wynne E. Baxter, Coroner for the South-Eastern Division of Middlesex, resumed his inquiry, at the Working Lads' Institute, Whitechapel-road, respecting the death of Mary Ann Chapman, who was found murdered in the back yard of No. 29, Hanbury-Street, Spitalfields, on the morning of the 8th inst.

Detective-inspectors Helson and Chandler and Detective-sergeant Thicke, H Division, watched the case on behalf of the Criminal Investigation Department.

Eliza Cooper stated that she lived at 35, Dorset-street, Spitalfields, and had done so for the last five months. Witness knew the deceased, and had a quarrel with her on the Tuesday before she was murdered. On the previous Saturday deceased came in and asked the people there to give her a piece of soap. She was told to ask "Liza." Deceased then came to witness, who opened the locker and gave her a piece of soap. Deceased then handed the soap to Stanley, who went and washed himself. Deceased also went out, and when she came back witness asked her for the soap, which, however, she did not return, but said "I will see you by and by." Stanley gave deceased 2s., and she paid for the bed for two nights. Witness saw no more of deceased that night.

By the CORONER.—Witness was treated by Stanley. On the following Wednesday witness met deceased in the kitchen and asked her to return the piece of soap. Deceased threw a halfpenny on the table and said "Go and get a halfpennyworth of soap." They then began to quarrel, and afterwards went to the Ringers public-house, where the quarrel was continued. Deceased slapped her face and said "Think yourself lucky I did not do more." Witness believed she then struck deceased in the left eye and then on the chest. She could afterwards see that the blow had marked deceased's face.

By the jury.—That was the last time she saw deceased alive. At that time she was wearing three rings on the third finger of the left hand. Deceased bought the rings, which were brass ones, of a black man. Deceased had never possessed a gold wedding ring since witness had become acquainted with her. She had known deceased for about 15 years, and knew that she

associated with Stanley, "Harry the Hawker," and other men. Witness could not say whether any of these persons were missing. With the exception of Stanley, deceased used only casually to bring other men to the lodging-house.

Dr. George Bagster Phillips was recalled. Before he was examined, the CORONER said it was necessary that all the evidence the doctor had obtained from his post-mortem examination should be on the records of the Court for various reasons which he need not then enumerate, however painful it might be.

Dr. Phillips said that had notice been given him he should have been better prepared with the evidence, but he had his original notes with him. While bowing to the Coroner's decision, he still thought it a great pity that he should have to give this evidence, as matters which had since come to light had shown the wisdom of the course pursued on the last occasion, and he could not help reiterating his regret that the Coroner had come to a different conclusion.

On the last occasion he mentioned that there were reasons why he thought that the person who inflicted the cut on the woman's throat had caught hold of her chin. He came to that conclusion because on the left side, on the lower jaw, were scratches one and a half to two inches below the lobe of the ear, and going in a contrary direction to the incision in the throat. They were of recent date.

The abrasions on the left side and on the right side were corresponding bruises. He washed them, when they became more distinct, whereas the bruises mentioned in his last evidence remained the same. The deceased had been seized by the throat while the incision into the throat had been perpetrated. The witness here stated that in the interests of justice he thought it would be better not to give more details.

The CORONER.—We are here to decide the cause of death, and therefore have a right to hear all particulars. Whether that evidence is made public or not rests with the Press. I might add I have never before heard of any evidence being kept back from a coroner.

Dr. Phillips.—I am in the hands of the Court, and what I was going to detail took place after death.

The CORONER.—That is a matter of opinion. You know that medical men often differ.

Dr Phillips repeated that he did not think the details should be given.

The court having been cleared of all women and boys, the witness proceeded to give medical and surgical evidence, totally unfit for publication, of the deliberate, successful, and apparently scientific manner in which the poor woman had been mutilated, and expressed his opinion that the length of the weapon was at least five to six inches, probably more, and the appearance of the cuts confirmed him in the opinion that the instrument, like the one which divided the neck, had been of a very sharp character. The mode in which the knife had been used seem to indicate great anatomical knowledge.

By the CORONER.—He though he himself could not have performed all the injuries he described, even without a struggle, under a quarter of an hour. If he had done it in a deliberate way such as would fall to the duties of a surgeon, it probably would have taken him the best part of an hour. He had not been able to discover any trace of blood on the walls of the next house.

In answer to the jury, the witness said that he had no practical opinion about a person's eyes being photographed, but his opinion would be useless; also with regard to employing blood-hounds. In the latter case they would more probably scent the blood of the murdered woman. The injuries to the body would produce at once partial insensibility.

Elizabeth Long, 198, Church-row, White-chapel, stated that she was the wife of James Long, a park-keeper.[68] On Saturday morning the 8th inst., she was passing down Hanbury-street from home and going to Spitalfields Market. It was about 5:30. She was certain of the time, as the brewers' clock had just struck that time when she passed 29, Hanbury-street. Witness was on the right-hand side of the street—the same side as No. 29. She saw a man and woman on the pavement talking. The man's back was turned towards Brick-lane, while the woman's was towards the Spitalfields Market. They were talking together, and were close against the shutters of No. 29. Witness saw the woman's

face. She had since seen the deceased in the mortuary, and was sure it was the face of the same person she saw in Hanbury-street. She did not see the man's face, except to notice that he was dark. He wore a brown deer stalker hat, and she thought he had on a dark coat, but was not quite certain of that. She could not say what the age of the man was, but he looked to be over 40, and appeared to be a little taller than deceased. He appeared to be a foreigner, and had a shabby genteel appearance. Witness could hear them talking loudly, and she overheard him say to deceased, "Will you?" She replied, "Yes." They still stood there as witness passed, and she went on to her work without looking back.

By the CORONER.—She saw nothing to indicate they were not sober. It was not an unusual thing to see men and women talking together at that hour in that locality.

The Foreman remarked that the time stated by the witness was not consistent with that stated by the doctor.

The CORONER observed that Dr. Phillips had since qualified his statement.

Edward Stanley stated the he lived at 1, Osborne-place, Osborne-street, Whitechapel. He was a bricklayer's labourer, and was known by the name of "The Pensioner." He knew the deceased, and he sometimes visited her at 35, Dorset-street. He was not there with her more than once or twice, but had been elsewhere with her at times. He last saw her alive on Sunday, the 2nd inst., between 1 and 3 o'clock in the afternoon. At that time she was wearing two rings on one of her fingers. One was a flat ring and the other oval. He should think they were brass ones. Witness did not know of anyone with whom deceased was on bad terms.

By the CORONER.—When he last saw deceased her eye was slightly blackened. His memory might be confused, and it was possible he might have seen deceased after the time he had stated, for when he did see her she certainly had a black eye, and spoke to him about it.

The Foreman.—A previous witness had stated that the blows were not inflicted on deceased's face until the Tuesday.

In answer to the jury, the witness denied that he was in the habit of spending Saturdays and Sundays with the deceased.

The CORONER.—Are you a pensioner?

Witness.—Am I bound to answer this question?

---

[68] **Park-keeper**. In Britain, an official employed by a local authority to patrol and supervise a public park. (Collins English Dictionary-Complete and Unabridged)

# Thursday, 20 September, 1888

The CORONER.—You have to answer all questions affecting this case that are put to you.

Witness.—I am not a pensioner, and have not been in the Essex Regiment. What I say will be published all over Europe. I have lost five hours in coming here.

The deputy of 35, Dorset-street, was here called into the room and said Stanley was the person they called "The Pensioner." He was the man who used to come to the lodging-house with the deceased on Saturday and stay till the Monday. Stanley had been to the lodging-house six or seven times. The last time he was there was the Saturday before the woman's death, and he stayed till the Monday. Stanley paid for one night, and deceased afterwards paid for Sunday night.

The CORONER.—What do you think of that Stanley?

Stanley.—The evidence given by Donovan is incorrect. When you talk to me, Sir, you talk to an honest man. I was at Gosport from the 6th of August up to the 1st of September. The deceased met me at the corner of Brushfield-street that night.

The Foreman.—Did you see any quarrel?

Witness.—I saw no quarrel, only the effects of it. I have known the deceased about two years, when she was living at Windsor. I was told by a shoeblack that deceased had been murdered, and I then went to the lodging-house and inquired whether it was correct. After I saw the Coroner's observations in the newspapers, I went to the Commercial-street Police-station.

In further examination the witness said he was told the police wanted him.

The CORONER thought the lodging-house keeper had made a mistake in the man.

Albert Cadosch, a carpenter, stated that he resided at No. 27, Hanbury-street. That was next door to No. 29. On Saturday, the 8th inst. he got up at about 5:15 and went out into the yard of his house. As he returned across the yard, to the back door of his house, he heard a voice say quite close to him, "No." He believed it came from No. 29. He went into the house, and returned to the yard three or four minutes afterwards. He then heard a sort of a fall against the fence, which divided his yard from No. 29. Something seemed suddenly to touch the fence. He did not look to see what it was. He did not hear any other noise.

By the CORONER.—He did not hear the rustling of any clothes. Witness then left the house and went to his work. When he passed Spitalfields Church it was about 32 minutes past 5. He did not hear people in the yard as a rule, but had now and then heard them at that time in the morning.

By the jury.—He did not go into the yard twice out of curiosity. He had been under an operation at the hospital. He informed the police the same day of what he had heard. The palings were about 5ft. 6in. in height. He had not the curiosity to look over the fence, as at times the next door people were early risers. When he left the house he did not see any man or woman in Hanbury-street. He did not see Mrs. Long.

William Stevens, a painter, of 35, Dorset-street, deposed that he knew the deceased, whom he last saw alive about 12 minutes past 12 on the early morning of her death. She was then in the kitchen of the lodging-house, and was not the worse for drink. At that time she had rings on her fingers. Witness believed the piece of envelope produced was the one he saw deceased pick up by the fireplace. He noticed it was about the size of the piece produced, and he saw it had a red post mark on it. Deceased then pulled out a box containing pills from her pocket, and the box breaking she put the pills into the piece of paper, and put it into her pocket. He saw deceased leave the kitchen, and thought she was going to bed, as she said she would not be long out of bed.

By the CORONER.—He did not know of any one with whom the deceased was on bad terms.

The CORONER said that was all the evidence forthcoming. It was a question for the jury whether they would adjourn the case or return their verdict.

The Foreman stated that the reward of Mr. S. Montagu, M.P., of £100 had been posted about, but the Government did not, as the Coroner had previously stated, now offer rewards. At the same time, if the Government had offered a reward, it would have looked more official.

After some further conversation, the inquiry was adjourned until Wednesday next, when it will be completed.

~

# Thursday, 20 September, 1888

## Evening News
### THE EDITOR'S DRAWER
### THE EAST END ATROCITY
### To the Editor of "The Evening News"

Sir—I am glad you have raised your voice against the senseless abuse of the police. As well blame the murderer or murderers for not having left a good clue. A reward, however, should have been offered ere now by the Government, and the police allowed to earn it. Also it is very doubtful whether the force is really strong enough for its duties; and the gait and bearing of detectives drawn from it must often tell against them.

There is, moreover, one fact which should not be lost sight of in connection with the horrible butchery of the last two unfortunate women. Both were homeless. They had not sufficient to pay for a night's lodging, and rather than have recourse to some casual ward or charitable institution they wandered about the streets until they fell into the fangs of some human tiger or tigress. Had they gone to some charitable institution they would probably have been tortured with questions relating to their past. Had they gone to the workhouse for a night's shelter they would have been kept prisoners the following day until they had more than paid with their labour for what they had received.

If that is relief, every employer relieves, and his belief does not taint and degrade the recipient. But the employer does not profess to relieve, nor does he tax the ratepayer. A few days ago a poor old soldier (who, it may be supposed, had risked his life over and over again for his country) was brought before a magistrate for having refused to break 12 cwt.[69] of stone! This was the price exacted for his night's shelter. He very naturally refused to submit to this extortion, and his grateful country made him a criminal.

Depend upon it, Sir, the Poor Law system is largely responsible not only for the late shocking crimes but for many others.

I am, &c.
ONLOOKER
September 18.

---

[69] The Hundredweight in Britain is 112 lbs., in the US 100. 12 British cwt.=1344 lbs.

---

### To the Editor of "The Evening News"

Sir—May I be permitted to add a few lines to those already appearing in your columns with regard to the Whitechapel murders? I do not suppose those in charge of the case would for one moment tolerate the interference or advice of the outside public in the mode of procedure, but if some more feasible theory or suggestion than that hitherto advanced were to be the means of aiding the course of the law, I believe it would not be the first time the community at large were indebted to a private individual for help in unravelling a seemingly complicated and brutal crime.

I believe the suggestion put forward by your correspondent of Saturday last, that the same cause may furnish the motive as in that of the Cambridge murderer, to be very probable, and a clue. But I cannot by any means agree with your correspondent (A.W. Hux) as to his theory that searching inquiry in that direction might lead to a possible way in which the deed was carried out. To carry any practical weight, we should have to assume that the murderer also found the other unfortunate victims under similar circumstances, or, supposing the deed to be the work of a wretch who had no hand in the previous crimes, that he had studies the means and methods to such perfection as to utterly mislead the judgement of medical and criminal detective experts, who I believe unhesitatingly describe the three crimes as the work of one hand, or rather one fiend.

With regard to supposition that the murdered woman, if in company with the man, being able to give some outcry, how would it be possible, unaware of her danger, no doubt in a perfectly helpless position, in the back yard of a house, without the slightest glimmer of light, to warn her of the terrible end in store? One slash of the deadly instrument carried by the cunning imp from hell, and the victim past all outcry. My opinion is that in the event of any crime, such as that under discussion, all supposed unoccupied houses, tenements, and ruins, such as are to be found where buildings have been pulled down for improvements, and vaults left standing, and where it well known hundreds of outcasts slink away during the night for shelter, should be surprised and all those found therein be called upon to give account of themselves.

155

# Thursday, 20 September, 1888

Supposing the man wanted to be of the vagrant class, sane in all things but that of the fearful desire to shed blood for some real or fancied wrong, what is more probable than that he is in hiding during daylight, and stealing out for two or three hours during the night seeking fresh victims, or, failing that, to procure the means to prolong a terrible existence? For I feel positive that no one would shelter a man who must carry such unmistakable signs of bloodshed upon his person as the one wanted must do. Yet another theory and I have done. If the crime has been committed by a man, who, after accomplishing his fearful work, there can be only one or two classes of men who would be able to escape detection in the manner that has been done in the present instance, and they are either meat market porters or slaughtermen, who would be able by means of their ordinary trade garb to walk away right under the nose of a policeman without arousing suspicion.

I sincerely hope that no one following the above callings will feel unnecessarily hurt at the above suggestion, and, to give them credit, I do not believe they would for a moment hesitate to place information in the hands of the police if they had reason to suspect any of their calling of the crime.

Apologising for troubling you, I am, &c.
E.SWABEY
September 18.

—

## SOLDIERS AS POLICEMEN
### To the editor of "The Evening News"

Sir—Will you allow me a small space in your paper with reference to a letter in Friday's Evening News, a Valuable Suggestion, signed "B.F." I don't think "B.F." can know very much about a soldier's duties or he would not make such a suggestion.

It is not because a soldier is taking a walk of an afternoon that he has nothing to do. It's very probable that that soldier was on duty all the previous night, and very likely the twenty four hours previous, as soldiers that do day guards do twenty four hours before being relieved. I don't mean to say that they are walking sentry all that time, but they have to keep on all their clothes and accoutrements that time, and in many instances where duty is heavy a man has to go on guard, with, what is termed in the army, only two or three nights in bed, that means two or three nights between coming off guard and going on again. I have never done duty in London, but in Dublin I have often gone with only two or three nights in bed, and I should think duty is quite as heavy in London as there, and much more so than in a good many places.

Then again there is the patrol duty to do; that means marching about the streets preventing soldiers creating disturbances and running in absentees, &c., that is from about 7 p.m. till midnight. That does not count a turn of duty at all, only a fatigue. If it was a man's turn to go on guard the next day, he would have to go; so I consider a soldier gets plenty of night duty without doing police duty. It could be done by knocking off some of the guards and sentries; but then a soldier should do soldier's duty, and a policeman do policeman's duty. If there are not enough who not get more?

I am, &c.
A Time Expired
September 15.

—

The Home Secretary is probably quite right in one of the reasons which he gives the Whitechapel Vigilance Committee for refusing to offer a reward for the apprehension of the author of the recent horrors, that reason being that "experience showed that such offers of reward tended to do more harm then good." It is unquestionably demoralising to a community to make a practice of holding out a bribe for the trapping of criminals, and as the Home Office only discontinued the practice after much deliberation, no honest citizen will question the dictum of Mr. Matthews on the point.

On the other hand, it does seem remarkable that, under the circumstances, the following expression should have crept into the letter in question. "The Secretary of State is satisfied that there is nothing in the circumstances of the present case to justify a departure from this rule." Now that is just the point on which the respectable inhabitants of Whitechapel (and a good many people outside) will never be able to agree with the Home Secretary. If there ever was a case where departure from the rule was advisable this is surely the one, and for this simple reason—the police have completely broken down as far as detective efficiency is concerned. They are utterly at fault, and the

# Thursday, 20 September, 1888

only apparent hope of securing the assassin is the offering of a substantial reward. It is a pity that the Home Office, in its anxiety to screen the police, refuses to see this.

—

## THE EAST END MURDERS
## EXCITEMENT IN WHITECHAPEL
## HOW THE NEWS OF THE HOME
## SECRETARY'S DECISION WAS
## RECEIVED
## ANOTHER REWARD OFFERED

So far as is known, the police are without any definite clue to the murderer, and the greater part of the force holds a decided opinion that he will only be caught in flagrante delicto, and that another murder or murders must take place before the public are gratified with the news of his apprehension. The writer has now interviewed many inspectors, sergeants, and constables in the matter, and they all hold the opinion that the present regulations at Scotland yard do not give proper facilities for guarding the public, and that there are too few men. They hold that a large Government reward would probably bring about the capture of the man wanted, and express a hope that it will be granted in the present case, at least, even though it may not be taken as a precedent. Last night the writer ascertained that, notwithstanding the succession of murders in one district, all of the same character and evidently by the same hand, not one single extra policeman or plain clothes detective was added to that district until the fourth woman had been butchered.

The moment the newspapers containing the letter of the Home Secretary were read, last evening, a tremendous storm of indignation was roused in the breasts of the people, and a fierce denunciation of the Home Office authorities was heard at every house and street corner. Meetings were held at over 40 places for the one purpose of denouncing the letter, which was described by one speaker as the "lamest piece of officialism ever issued from a Government office."

A great meeting took place last night at 74 Mile End road, for the purpose of discussing the letter of the Home Secretary, and taking measures for the offer of a public reward for the apprehension of the murderer.

The chair was taken by Mr. George Lusk, the president of the Vigilance Committee, and

he was supported by several of the most prominent inhabitants of the district.

He said that it seemed to be a most extraordinary circumstance that the Home Secretary should have written such a letter as the one his committee had received, for in his opinion it bore its own reputation. Any one reading such a letter must believe that the Government would not offer a reward if twenty or even fifty murders took place—(hear, hear)—which was a most terrible thing to contemplate. However, the citizens of London were not going to bow to the decision of the Home Secretary, now would they accept his ideas that rewards did more harm than good. If the Home Secretary declined to offer a reward for preventing further murders of Her Majesty's subjects, his committee and those who supported that committee, were prepared to do so, and there were sufficient funds now in hand to enable them to commence operations. (Cheers.)

Mr. Aarons, the treasurer, announced that he had a tolerably large sum in hand, and he moved that bills should be distributed and advertisements sent to the papers offer a preliminary reward of £50, which would be increased as the funds came in.

The motion was carried unanimously amid much cheering, Mr. Aarons subsequently expressing his conviction that the funds would no doubt flow in steadily now that the people of Whitechapel knew for certain that they could not rely upon the Home Office for help.

Mr. Laughton said that he was sorry to find the Home Secretary so apathetic in the matter, for he felt sure that had a substantial reward been offered in the first place the murderer would have been discovered, and that was the decided opinion of hundreds of people to whom he had mentioned the matter. (A voice: It is the opinion of a million people in East London.)

Mr. B. Harris (Hon. Sec.) announced that the reward bills would be out tomorrow, and several hundreds of letters would at the same time be sent to prominent citizens, asking their help in making the reward fund large enough to convince the Home Secretary that he was wrong.

Mr. Reeves said that, looking at the way in which the murderer had committed the deed, the time he was about it, and consequently the

# Thursday, 20 September, 1888

awful state in which his clothes must have been, he felt positively certain that someone besides the murderer knew of the fact; and a heavy reward would, he thought, be the only inducement for that person to speak out. (Hear, hear.)

Mr. Lusk said that the members of the committee had, like himself, made up their minds to find out the murderer if possible, and nothing would be wanting on their parts to further the ends of justice, looking at the fact that the police were powerless and the Home Office dilatory.

A vote of thanks was accorded Mr. Aarons for the unremitting attention he had given the matter and the kind way in which he had placed his house at the disposal of the public, and the proceedings were adjourned until Saturday.

# Friday, 21 September, 1888

## The Star

### FIFTH EDITION.
### WHITECHAPEL.
### The Police are Satisfied of the Innocence of the Holloway Butcher.

The man who was arrested at Holloway on suspicion of being concerned in the White-chapel murder, and subsequently removed and detained at Bow Asylum, will shortly be released. His brother has given satisfactory explanation as to his whereabouts on the morning of the murder. It has transpired that the authorities of the asylum would not allow the police to interrogate the patient whilst there, as it is against the rules laid down by the Lunacy Commissioners.

—

### The Maniac Theory.

With reference to the statement contained in last week's *Lancet* to the effect that to the editor's mind the lunacy of the murderer was not yet clearly established, and that homicidal tendency in lunatics was confined to the desire to kill one individual, Dr. Forbes Winslow has replied in their columns:—

Having had extensive experience in cases of homicidal insanity, and having been retained in the chief cases during the past 20 years, I speak as an authority on this part of the subject. I cannot agree with your statement. I will give one case which recalls itself to my recollection. A gentleman entered my consulting-room. He took his seat, and on my asking what it was he complained of, replied, "I have a desire to kill everyone I meet." I then asked him for further illustration of his meaning. He then said, "As I walk along the street I say to myself as I pass anyone, 'I should like to kill you;' I don't know why at all." Upon my further pressing him on the matter, he jumped up and

### ATTEMPTED TO SEIZE A WEAPON

from his pocket, and to give me a further, more practicable, and more realistic illustration. I was enabled, however, to frustrate him in this desire. Another case in which I was retained as expert was that of Mr. Richardson, who committed murder at Ramsgate (his homicidal tendency was not confined to one individual), and was tried at Maidstone this year, and there are many others that I could mention. Homicidal lunatics are cunning, deceptive, plausible, and, on the surface, to all outward appearance, sane; but there is contained within their innermost nature a dangerous thirsting after blood, which, though at all times latent, will develop when the opportunity arises.

Although (says the *Photographic News*) we may pretty confidently say that photography of the eyes of the murdered woman would have been useless, there can be no doubt whatever that a series of photographs of the body and of the mutilations ought to have been taken, and in the face of these it would have been far more difficult to conceal essential facts. It is to be hoped that even now the camera will be brought into requisition, especially as there are several experienced anatomists who are also competent photographers. Perhaps a carefully-made series of photographs, and the calling of such scientific experts as have distinguished them-selves in the new art of abdominal surgery, might throw light on the extraordinary action of the authorities in neglecting the most obvious means of getting information or of recording facts, and also on the strange action of Dr. Phillips.

~

## The Times

### THE WHITECHAPEL MURDERS.

On Saturday, Mr. Wynne E. Baxter, coroner for the South-Eastern division of Middlesex, resumed his adjourned inquiry at the Working Lads' Institute, Whitechapel-road, respecting the death of Mary Ann Nichols, who was found brutally murdered in Buck's-row, Whitechapel.

William Eade, recalled, stated he had since seen the man whom he saw with the knife near the Foresters'-hall. He had ascertained that his name was Henry James, and that he did not possess a wooden arm.

The CORONER said the man James had been seen, and been proved to be a well-known harmless lunatic.

As there was no further evidence forthcoming he would proceed to sum up.

Before commencing the few remarks that he proposed to make to the jury, he should, he was sure, be only reflecting their feelings if he first returned his thanks to the committee of the Working Lads' Institute for the use of such a convenient room for the purposes of this inquest.

Without their assistance, they would have been compelled to conduct this inquiry in a publichouse parlour—inconvenient and out of harmony with their functions, for Whitechapel not only did not possess any coroner's court, such as have been erected in St. Luke's, Clerkenwell, the City, and most of the West-end parishes, but it was without any town-hall or vestry-hall, such as were used for inquests at St. George's, Shadwell, Limehouse, and Poplar. To the Working Lads' Institute committee, therefore, he felt they were under obligations deserving of public recognition.

The jury would probably have been surprised to find there was no public mortuary in Whitechapel. He had been informed that there was formerly one, but that it was demolished by Metropolitan Board of Works when making a new street, and that compensation was paid to the local authorities, who have never yet expended it on the object of the trust. Perhaps he had been misinformed, but this he did know, that jury after jury had requested the coroner to draw attention of the sanitary authorities to the deficiency, and, hitherto, without success. They deemed it essential for the health of the neighbourhood; and surely if mortuaries were found necessary at the West-end, there must be stronger reasons for them here, in the midst of so much squalid crowding. But this inconvenience had been felt in other ways in this inquiry.

In the absence of a public mortuary, the police carried the body of the deceased to the deadhouse belonging to the workhouse infirmary. It was admittedly not ornate in appearance, and was not altogether suited for the purpose to which it had been applied; but they must not forget that such mortuary was a private structure, intended solely for use by the Union authorities, and that its use on other occasions had been allowed only by the courtesy of the guardians, but that only proved the necessity for a public mortuary.

Had there been a public mortuary there would also have been a keeper, whose experience would have shown the advisability of the body being attended to only in the presence of the medical witness. He himself trusted now that the attention of the authorities had again been called to this pressing matter, the subject would be taken into serious consideration, and the deficiency supplied.

Referring to the facts in the case before him, the Coroner said the deceased had been identified by her father and her husband to have been Mary Ann Nichols, a married woman with five children, and about 42 years of age.

She was of intemperate habits, and left her husband eight years ago on account of drink. The husband had not seen or heard of her for three years. She had evidently formed irregular connexions, but still lived under her father's roof for three or four years, and then either to avoid the restraints of a settled home, or in consequence of her own misconduct, she left her father, who had not seen her for more than two years.

She was in the Lambeth Workhouse on several occasions, at Christmas last and again in April. While there last she was fortunate enough to find a lady in Wandsworth willing to take her into her house as a domestic servant and at the time she wrote her father a letter, which held out some promise of reform; but her fresh start did not appear to have lasted long, for she soon afterwards left her situation in great disgrace.

From that time until her death it was pretty clear that she had been living an intemperate, irregular, and vicious life, mostly in the common lodging-houses in that neighbourhood.

There was nothing in the evidence as to the movements of the deceased on the day before her death, except a statement by herself that she was

# Monday, 24 September, 1888

living in a common lodginghouse, called the White House, in Flower and Dean-street, Spitalfields; but he believed her movements had been traced by the police, and were not considered to have any connexion with her death.

On Friday evening, the 31st of August, she was seen by Mrs. Holland—who knew her well—at the corner of Osborn-street and White-chapel-road, nearly opposite the parish church. The deceased woman was then much the worse for drink and was staggering against the wall. Her friend endeavoured to persuade her to come home with her, but she declined, and was last seen endeavouring to walk eastward down Whitechapel.

She said she had had her lodging money three times that day, but that she had spent it, that she was going about to get some money to pay her lodgings, and she would soon be back. In less than an hour and a quarter after this she was found dead at a spot rather under three-quarters of a mile distant.

The deceased was first discovered by a carman on his way to work, who passed down Buck's-row, on the opposite side of the road. Immediately after he had ascertained that the dark object in the gateway was the figure of a woman he heard the approaching footsteps of a man. This proved to be Paul, another carman. Together they went to the woman.

The condition of her clothing suggested to them that she had been outraged and had fainted. She was only just dead, if life were really extinct. Paul says he felt a slight movement of her breast, and thought she was breathing. Neither of the carmen appeared to have realized the condition of the woman, and no injuries were noticed by them; but that, no doubt, was accounted for by the early hour of the morning and the darkness of the spot.

The carmen reported the circumstances to a constable at the corner of Hanbury-street, 300 yards distant, but although he appeared to have started without delay, he found another constable was already there. In fact, Constable Neil must independently have found the body within a few minutes of the finding of it by the two carmen.

The condition in which the body was found appeared to prove conclusively that the deceased was killed on the exact spot in which she was found.

There was not a trace of blood anywhere, except at the spot where her neck was lying. That

appeared to him sufficient to justify the assumption that the injuries to the throat were inflicted when the woman was on the ground, while the state of her clothing and the absence of any blood about her legs equally proved that the abdominal injuries were inflicted while she was still in the same position.

Nor did there appear any grounds for doubt that, if deceased was killed where she was found, she met her death without a cry of any kind. The spot was almost under the windows of Mrs. Green, a light sleeper. It was opposite the bedroom of Mrs. Purkiss, who was awake at the time. Then there were watchmen at various spots within very short distances. Not a sound was heard by any.

Nor was there evidence of any struggle. This might have arisen from her intoxication, or from being stunned by a blow.

Again, the deceased could not have been killed long before she was found. Constable Neil was positive that he was at the spot half an hour before, and then neither the body was there nor was any one about. Even if Paul were mistaken in the movement of the chest, Neil found her right arm still warm, and even Dr. Llewellyn, who saw the body about a quarter of an hour afterwards, found the body and lower extremities still warm, notwithstanding the loss of blood and abdominal injuries and that those extremities had been uncovered.

It seemed astonishing, at first thought, that the culprit should escape detection, for there must surely have been marks of blood about his person. If, however, blood was principally on his hands, the presence of so many slaughter-houses in the neighbourhood would make the frequenters of that spot familiar with blood-stained clothes and hands, and his appearance might in that way have failed to attract attention while he passed from Buck's-row in the twilight into Whitechapel-road and was lost sight of in the morning's market traffic.

He himself thought they could not altogether leave unnoticed the fact that the death the jury had been investigating was one of four presenting many points of similarity, all of which had occurred within the space of about five months, and all within a very short distance of the place where they were sitting.

All four victims were women of middle age; all were married and had lived apart from their

161

# Monday, 24 September, 1888

husbands in consequence of intemperate habits, and were at the time of their death leading irregular lives and eking out a miserable and precarious existence in common lodging-houses.

In each case there were abdominal as well as other injuries.

In each case the injuries were inflicted after midnight, and in places of public resort where it would appear impossible but that almost immediate detection would follow the crime, and in each case the inhuman and dastardly criminals were at large in society.

Emma Elizabeth Smith, who received her injuries in Osborn-street on the early morning of Easter Tuesday, the 3rd of April, survived in the London Hospital for upwards of 24 hours, and was able to state that she had been followed by some men, robbed and mutilated, and even to describe imperfectly one of them.

Martha Tabram was found at 3 a.m. on Tuesday, the 7th of August, on the first-floor landing of George-yard-buildings, with 39 punctured wounds on her body.

In addition to these and the case under the consideration of the jury there was the case of Annie Chapman, still in the hands of another jury.

The instruments used in the two earlier cases were dissimilar. In the first it was a blunt instrument, such as a walking stick; in the second some of the wounds were thought to have been made by a dagger, but in the two recent cases the instruments suggested by the medical witnesses were not so different.

Dr. Llewellyn said that the injuries on Nichols could have been produced by a long-bladed instrument moderately sharp. Dr. Phillips was of opinion that those on Chapman were by a very sharp knife, probably with a thin, narrow blade, at least 6in. to 8in. in length, probably longer. The similarity of the injuries in the two cases was considerable.

There were bruises about the face in both cases, the head was nearly severed from the body in both cases, and those injuries, again, had in each case been performed with anatomical knowledge.

Dr. Llewellyn seemed to incline to the opinion that the abdominal injuries were inflicted first, and caused instantaneous death; but, if so, it seemed difficult to understand the object of such desperate injuries to the throat, or how it came about there was so little bleeding from the several arteries, that

the clothing on the upper surface was not stained and the legs not soiled, and that there was very much less bleeding from the abdomen than from the neck. Surely it might well be that, as in the case of Chapman, the dreadful wounds to the throat were first inflicted and the abdominal afterwards.

That was a matter of some importance when they came to consider what possible motive there could be for all this ferocity. Robbery was out of the question, and there was nothing to suggest jealousy. There could not have been any quarrel, or it would have been heard.

The taking of some of the abdominal viscera from the body of Chapman suggested that that may have been the object of her death. Was it not possible that this may also have been the motive in the case they had under consideration?

He suggested to the jury as a possibility that these two women might have been murdered by the same man with the same object, and that in the case of Nichols the wretch was disturbed before he had accomplished his object, and, having failed in the open street, he tried again, within a week of his failure, in a more secluded place.

If this was correct, the audacity and daring was equal to its maniacal fanaticism and abhorrent wickedness.

But that surmise might or might not be correct; the suggested motive might be the wrong one; but one thing was very clear—that the injuries were of such a nature that they could not have been self-inflicted, that no imaginable facts could reduce that to evidence of manslaughter, and that a murder of a most atrocious character had been committed.

The jury, having considered in private, returned a verdict of "Wilful murder against some person or persons unknown."

They also thanked the Coroner for the remarks made with reference to the mortuary and for the very able way in which he had conducted the case.

# Tuesday, 25 September, 1888

## Evening News
### THE CHARGE AGAINST THE MAN LUDWIG.
### THE ACCUSED AGAIN BEFORE THE MAGISTRATE.

Before Mr. Saunders, at the Thames Police-court, today, Charles Ludwig, 40, a decently-attired German, who professed not to understand English, and giving an address in the Minories, was brought up on remand charged with being drunk and threatening to stab Alexander Finley, of 51, Leman-street, Whitechapel.

The evidence of prosecutor showed that at about three o'clock on the morning of that day week he was standing at a coffee-stall in the Whitechapel-road when Ludwig came up in a state of intoxication. The person in charge of the stall refused to serve him. Ludwig seemed much annoyed, and said to witness, "What are you looking at?" He than pulled out a long bladed knife and threatened to stab witness with it. Ludwig followed him round the stall, and made several attempts to stab him, until witness threatened to knock a dish on his head. A constable came up and he was then given into custody.

Constable 221 H said when he was called to take the prisoner into custody he found him in a very excited condition. "Witness had previously received information that Ludwig was wanted in the City jurisdiction for attempting to cut a woman's throat with a razor. On the way to the station, prisoner dropped a long-bladed knife, which was open, and when he was searched a razor and a long-bladed pair of scissors were found on him.

Constable John Johnson, 866 City, deposed that early on the morning of Tuesday week he was on duty in the Minories, when he heard loud scream of "Murder" proceeding from a dark court. The court in question leads to some railway arches, and is a well-known dangerous locality. Witness went down the court, and found the prisoner with a prostitute, The accused appeared to be under the influence of drink. Witness asked what he was doing there, and he replied "Nothing." The woman, who appeared to be in a very agitated and frightened condition, said, "Oh, policeman, do take me out of this." The woman was so frightened that she could then make no further explanation.

Witness got her and the accused out of the court, and sent the latter off. He walked with the woman to the end of his beat, when she said, "Dear me! He frightened me very much when he pulled a big knife out." Witness said, "Why didn't you tell me that at the time?" and she replied, "I was too much frightened." He then went to look for the prisoner, but could not find him, and therefore warned several other constables of what he had seen, and also gave a description of the prisoner. On the last occasion witness was unable to procure the attendance of the woman.

On the application of Detective-Inspector Abberline, of Scotland-yard, Mr. Saunders again remanded the accused for full inquiries to be made. He also allowed Inspector Abberline to interview the accused with the interpreter, Mr. Smaje, to ascertain if he would give any information as to where he was on certain dates.

---

### SHARPENING HIS BOWIE ON THE PAVEMENT

Dr. Forbes Winslow writes from 70, Wimpole-street, Cavendish-square, Sept. 24: "Sir—Will you allow me to draw your attention to rather a peculiar circumstance which occurred at Brighton yesterday afternoon at 4:30. My sister-in-law and her daughter were walking up Norton-road, when a strange-looking man, dressed in a brown pea jacket and cap, about the medium height, suddenly fell down on his knees right in front of them and produced from his pocket a large bowie knife, which he commenced sharpening on the flagstone before them. Naturally alarmed, they hurried home and informed me what had happened. It was too late, however, to capture the man, who hurried down Western-road. I immediately gave information to the police. The circumstance to my mind is of sufficient significance at the present time to draw public attention to it."

## The Times

### THE WHITECHAPEL MURDER.

Yesterday afternoon Mr. Wynne E. Baxter, the coroner for the South-Eastern Division of Middlesex, resumed his adjourned inquiry at the Working Lads' Institute, Whitechapel, respecting the death of Annie Chapman, aged 47, a widow, who was found brutally murdered in the back yard of 29, Hanbury-street, Whitechapel, on the early morning of Saturday, the 8th inst.

Inspectors Helson, Chandler, and Bannister watched the case on behalf of the Commissioners of Police.

Having been informed there was no further evidence forthcoming, The CORONER proceeded to sum up. He congratulated the jury that their labours were then nearly completed. Although up to the present they had not resulted in the detection of the criminal, he had no doubt that if the perpetrator of this foul murder were eventually discovered, their efforts would not have been useless. The evidence given was on the records of that Court, and could be used even if the witnesses were not forthcoming; while the publicity given had already elicited further information, which he would later on have to mention, and which he hoped was not sanguine in believing might perhaps be of the utmost importance.

The deceased was a widow, 47 years of age, named Annie Chapman. Her husband was a coachman living at Windsor. For three or four years before his death she had lived apart from her husband, who allowed her 10s. a week until his death at Christmas, 1886. She had evidently lived an immoral life for some time, and her habits and surroundings had become worse since her means had failed. She no longer visited her relations, and her brother had not seen her for five months, when she borrowed a small sum from him. She lived principally in the common lodginghouses in the neighbourhood of Spitalfields, where such as she herded like cattle. She showed signs of deprivation, as if she had been badly fed.

The glimpse of life in those dens which the evidence in this case disclosed was sufficient to make them feel there was much in the 19th century civilization of which they had small reason to be proud; but the jury, who were constantly called together to hear the sad tale of starvation, or semi-starvation, of misery, immorality, and wickedness which some of the occupants of the 5,000 beds in that district had every week to relate at coroner's inquests, did not require to be reminded of what life in a Spitalfields lodginghouse meant.

It was in one of those that the older bruises found on the temple and in front of the chest of the deceased were received, in a trumpery quarrel, a week before her death. It was in one of those that she was seen a few hours before her mangled remains were discovered.

On the afternoon and evening of Friday, the 7th of September, also spent her time partly in such a place, at 35, Dorset-street, and partly in the Ringers publichouse, where she spent whatever money she had; so that between 1 and 2 o'clock on the morning of Saturday, when the money for her bed was demanded, she was obliged to admit that she was without means, and at once turned out into the street to find it. She left there at 1 45 a.m. She was seen off the premises by the night watchman, and was observed to turn down Little Paternoster-row into Brushfield-street, and not in the more direct direction of Hanbury-street.

On her wedding finger she was wearing two or three rings, which appeared to have been palpably of base metal, as the witnesses were all clear about their material and value.

They now lost sight of her for about four hours, but at half-past 5 o'clock, Mrs. Long was in Hanbury-street, on the way from her home in Church-street, Whitechapel, to Spitalfields Market. She walked on the northern side of the road, going westward, and remembered having seen a man and woman standing a few yards from the place where the deceased was afterwards found, and, although she did not know Annie Chapman, she was positive that the woman was the deceased. The two were talking loudly, but not sufficiently so to arouse her suspicions that there was anything wrong. The words she overheard were not calculated to do so. The laconic inquiry of the man, "Will you?" and the simple assent of the woman, viewed in the light of the subsequent events, could be easily translated and explained. Mrs. Long passed on her way, and neither saw nor heard anything more of her, and that was the last time she was known to have been alive.

There was some conflict in the evidence

# Thursday, 27 September, 1888

about the time at which the deceased was dispatched. It was not unusual to find inaccuracy in such details, but that variation was not very great or very important.

She was found dead about 6 o'clock. She was not in the yard when Richardson was there at 4 50 a.m. She was talking outside the house at half-past 5, when Mrs. Long passed them.

Cadosh said it was about 5:20 when he was in the back yard of the adjoining house and heard a voice say "No," and three or four minutes afterwards a fall against the fence; but if he was out of his reckoning but a quarter of an hour the discrepancy in the evidence of fact vanished; and he might be mistaken, for he admitted that he did not get up until a quarter past 5, and that it was after the half-hour when he passed the Spitalfields clock.

It was true that Dr. Phillips thought that when he saw the body at 6:30 the deceased had been dead at least two hours, but he admitted that the coldness of the morning and the great loss of blood might affect his opinion, and if the evidence of the other witnesses was correct, Dr. Phillips had miscalculated the effect of those forces. But many minutes after Mrs. Long passed them could not have elapsed before the deceased became a mutilated corpse in the yard of No. 29, Hanbury-street, close by where she was last seen by any witness.

That place was a fair example of a large number of houses in the neighbourhood. It was built, like hundreds of others, for the Spitalfields weavers, and when hand looms were driven out by steam and power they were converted into dwellings for the poor. Its size was about such as a superior artisan would occupy in the country, but its condition was such as would to a certainty leave it without a tenant.

In that place 17 persons were living, from a woman and her son, sleeping in a cats' meat shop on the ground floor, to Davis and his wife and their three grown up sons, all sleeping together in an attic. The street door and the yard door were never locked, and the passage and yard appeared to have been constantly used by persons who had no legitimate business there.

There was little doubt that deceased knew the place, for it was only 300 or 400 yards from where she lodged. If so, it was quite unnecessary to assume that her companion had any knowledge—in fact, it was easier to believe that

he was ignorant both of the nest of living beings by whom he was surrounded, and of their occupations and habits. Some were on the move late at night, some were up long before the sun.

A carman named Thompson left the house as early as 3:50 a.m.; an hour later John Richardson was paying the house a visit of inspection; shortly after 5:15 Cadosh, who lived in the next house, was in the adjoining yard twice. Davis, the carman who occupied the third floor front, heard the church clock strike a quarter to 6, got up, had a cup of tea, and went into the back yard, and was horrified to find the mangled body of the deceased. It was then a little after 6 a.m.—a very little, for at ten minutes past the hour Inspector Chandler had been informed of the discovery while on duty in Commercial-street.

There was nothing to suggest that the deceased was not fully conscious of what she was doing. It was true that she had passed through some stages of intoxication, for although she appeared perfectly sober to her friend who met her in Dorset-street at 5 o'clock the previous evening, she had been drinking afterwards; and when she left the lodginghouse shortly after 2 o'clock, the night watchman noticed that she was the worse for drink, but not badly so, while the deputy asserts that, though she had been evidently drinking, she could walk straight, and it was probably only malt liquor that she had taken, and its effects would pass off quicker than if she had taken spirits.

The post-mortem examination showed that while the stomach contained a meal of food, there was no sign of fluid and no appearance of her having taken alcohol, and Dr. Phillips was convinced that she had not taken any alcohol for some time. The deceased, therefore, entered the house in full possession of her faculties, although with a very different object to her companion's.

From the evidence which the condition of the yard afforded and the medical examination disclosed, it appeared that after the two had passed through the passage and opened the swing door at the end, they descended the three steps into the yard. On their left-hand side there was a recess between those steps and the palings. Here, a few feet from the house and a less distance from the palings, they must have stood.

The wretch must have then seized the deceased, perhaps with Judas-like approaches.

165

He seized her by the chin. He pressed her throat, and while thus preventing the slightest cry, he at the same time produced insensibility and suffocation. There was no evidence of any struggle. The clothes were not torn.

Even in those preliminaries, the wretch seems to have known how to carry out efficiently his nefarious work. The deceased was then lowered to the ground, and laid on her back; and although in doing so she may have fallen slightly against the fence, the movement was probably effected with care.

Her throat was then cut in two places with savage determination, and the injuries to the abdomen commenced. All was done with cool impudence and reckless daring; but perhaps nothing was more noticeable than the emptying of her pockets, and the arrangement of their contents with business-like precision in order near her feet.

The murder seemed, like the Buck's-row case, to have been carried out without any cry. None of the occupants of the houses by which the spot was surrounded heard anything suspicious.

The brute who committed the offence did not even take the trouble to cover up his ghastly work, but left the body exposed to the view of the first comer. That accorded but little with the trouble taken with the rings, and suggested either that he had at length been disturbed, or that, as daylight broke, a sudden fear suggested the danger of detection that he was running.

There were two things missing. Her rings had been wrenched from her fingers and had not since been found, and the uterus had been taken from the abdomen.

The body had not been dissected, but the injuries had been made by someone who had considerable anatomical skill and knowledge. There were no meaningless cuts. The organ had been taken by one who knew where to find it, what difficulties he would have to contend against, and how he should used his knife so as to abstract the organ without injury to it.

No unskilled person could have known where to find it or have recognized it when it was found. For instance, no mere slaughterer of animals could have carried out these operations. It must have been some one accustomed to the post mortem room.

The conclusion that the desire was to possess the missing abdominal organ seemed over-whelming. If the object were robbery, the injuries to the viscera were meaningless, for death had previously resulted from the loss of blood at the neck. Moreover, when they found an easily accomplished theft of some paltry brass rings and an internal organ taken, after at least a quarter of an hour's work and by a skilled person, they were driven to the deduction that the abstraction of the missing portion of abdominal viscera was the object, and the theft of the rings was only a thin-veiled blind, an attempt to prevent the real intention being discovered.

The amount missing would go into a breakfast cup, and had not the medical examination been of a thorough and searching character it might easily have been left unnoticed that there was any portion of the body which had been taken.

The difficulty in believing that the purport of the murderer was the possession of the missing abdominal organ was natural. It was abhorrent to their feelings to conclude that a life should be taken for so slight an object; but when rightly considered the reasons for most murders were altogether out of proportion to their guilt.

It had been suggested that the criminal was a lunatic with morbid feelings. That might or might not be the case, but the object of the murderer appeared palpably shown by the facts, and it was not necessary to assume lunacy, for it was clear there was a market for the missing organ. To show the jury that, he (the coroner) must mention a fact which at the same time proved the assistance which publicity and the newspaper Press afforded in the detection of crime.

Within a few hours of the issue of the morning papers containing a report of the medical evidence given at the last sitting of the Court he received a communication from an officer of one of our great medical schools that they had information which might or might not have a distinct bearing on that inquiry.

He attended at the first opportunity, and was informed by the sub-curator of the Pathological Museum that some months ago an American had called on him and asked him to procure a number of specimens of the organ that was missing in the deceased. He stated his willingness to give £20 apiece for each specimen. He stated that his object was to issue an actual specimen with each copy of a publication on which he was then engaged. He was told that his request was impossible to be complied with, but he still urged his request. He wished them preserved, not in spirits of wine, the usual medium, but glycerin, in order to preserve them in a flaccid condition, and he wished them sent to America direct. It was known that this request was repeated to another institution of similar character.

Now was it not possible that the knowledge of this demand might have incited some abandoned wretch to possess himself of a specimen? It seemed beyond belief that such inhuman wickedness could enter into the mind of any man; but, unfortunately, our criminal annals proved that every crime was possible. He need hardly say that he at once communicated his information to the Detective Department at Scotland-yard. Of course he did know what use had been made of it, but he believed that publicity might possibly further elucidate this fact, and therefore he had not withheld the information. By means of the Press some further explanation might be forthcoming from America, if not from here.

He had endeavoured to suggest to the jury the object with which this crime was committed and the class of person who must have committed it. The greatest deterrent from crime was the conviction that detection and punishment would follow with rapidity and certainty, and it might be that the impunity with which Mary Anne Smith and Ann Tabram were murdered suggested the possibility of such horrid crimes as those which the jury and another jury had been considering.

It was therefore a great misfortune that nearly three weeks had already elapsed without the chief actor in this awful tragedy having been discovered. Surely it was not too much even yet to hope that the ingenuity of our detective force would succeed in unearthing this monster.

It was not as if there were no clue to the character of the criminal or the cause of his crime. His object was clearly divulged. His anatomical knowledge carried him out of the category of a common criminal, for that knowledge could only have been obtained by assisting at post mortems or by frequenting the post mortem room. Thus the class in which

search must be made, although a large one, was limited.

In addition to the former description of the man Mrs. Long saw, they should know that he was a foreigner, of dark complexion, over 40 years of age, a little taller than deceased, of shabby genteel appearance, with a brown deerstalker hat on his head and a dark coat on his back.

If the jury's views accorded with his, they would be of opinion that they were confronted with a murder of no ordinary character, committed not from jealousy, revenge, or robbery, but from motives less adequate than many which still disgraced our civilization, marred our progress, and blotted the pages of our Christianity.

The jury returned a verdict of "Wilful murder against some person or persons unknown," the Foreman remarking that they were going to add a rider with respect to the mortuary accommodation, but as that had already been done by another jury they would let it stand. The Foreman then said that, as the jury had been there on five occasions, the majority thought they should be excused from further attendance for at least two years.

The CORONER said if possible that would be done.

———

The lucid statement by the CORONER, which yesterday preceded the verdict of the jury in the inquest held upon the death of the woman CHAPMAN, throws an altogether different light upon the recent murders in Whitechapel, and attributes an appalling motive to what must be in any event a terrible crime. If the CORONER is right,—and his opinion is formed upon no fanciful conjecture,—we must reject all the theories which have been ventured by society in its gropings for an adequate motive.

We have been schooled to believe that a maniac was indulging a craze for human blood, or that the criminal was a creature whom constant practice at the shambles[70] had hardened to habits of slaughter, or that the crimes were perpetrated by some jealous woman, the companion in vice of the victims, and the police were even advised to search for some heathen sect which practised barbarous rites.

---

[70] **Shamble**. A slaughterhouse. (Morehead)

# Thursday, 27 September, 1888

The evidence given by DR. PHILLIPS, after making a *post mortem* examination of the body, first gave the case another complexion. The CORONER now drives that evidence home, and adds to it startling information which is entirely new to the public.

It will be remembered that DR. PHILLIPS's evidence as to the nature of the wounds was given with some reluctance—a reluctance probably dictated at once by disinclination to shock the public with revolting details, and by a desire to keep secret the fact that the police were in possession of a valuable clue. Both these motives were theoretically laudable, and we are not prepared to say that in the majority of cases the course adopted by the CORONER, of insisting upon publicity, might not have turned out injudicious. But in the case before us the publication of the evidence of DR. PHILLIPS by the Press elicited a communication of the highest importance, which, if the secret had remained locked up in the breasts of the police, would, in all probability, never have been made at all.

Upon the nature of the communication made to the CORONER from the Pathological Museum of one of the great medical schools we shall not dwell in detail. It is enough to say that, taken in connexion with the actual nature of the mutilation, it points strongly to the probability that the murder of CHAPMAN belongs to an unspeakable class of crimes which are committed in order to secure the premium offered by certain anatomists and pathologists for the possession of human bodies and human organs.

After carefully reviewing the evidence concerning the injuries inflicted upon CHAPMAN, the CORONER pronounces his deliberate judgement that "no mere slaughterer of animals could have carried out these operations. It must have been some one accustomed to the *post mortem* room." In support of this opinion, another circumstance suggests itself, which, though slight, is by no means unimportant when marshalled in company with the rest of the evidence.

It is a singular fact, which goes to show that the murderer had some special knowledge of the method of suddenly arresting consciousness in his victim, that not a single cry was heard to escape CHAPMAN by the sixteen persons who were sleeping within a few yards of her. The same thing is to be noted in the case of the woman NICHOLLS. The general conclusion is that the murderer must have possessed surgical skill quite unusual in one who had not received professional training.

It is when we come to place this conclusion by the side of the startling information received by the CORONER that we see the immense value of the clue. The field of search is at once vastly narrowed, and various, but precise, channels of inquiry must force themselves upon the attention of the directors of the Criminal Investigation Department.

The "shabby genteel" man who was seen talking to CHAPMAN at an early hour in the morning, close to the place where she was murdered, must be, in point of station and education, considerably superior to the people upon whom the police at first concentrated their attention. He must be some one with anatomical knowledge. If we assume the CORONER's diagnosis of his motive to be correct, he must have had the pecuniary offer referred to, or some similar offer, brought to his notice. There is a perfect abundance of clues, provided that they are followed up.

Nothing conflicts with the CORONER's theory except the robbery of the rings, which may have been a mere blind—here, again, the deliberation and intelligence of the murderer come in—and the fact that, so far as the public is aware, the same form of mutilation was not accomplished in the case of NICHOLLS; but it is hardly necessary to point out that it may have been unsuccessfully attempted.

The CORONER hopes that the publicity which has, so far, served the inquiry so well will elicit fresh evidence, from America or elsewhere. We echo his hope, which is not unlikely to be realized; but at the same time it is just as well to remark that publicity is a double-edged weapon, and that while it enlists the whole of society in the detection of the crime, it simultaneously advertises the murderer of every step which is taken in his pursuit, and warns him against attempting to reap the reward of his atrocious crime.

Atrocious and infamous, indeed, is such a crime, and yet, to the disgrace of humanity, it is not without precedent. Sixty years ago the BURKE and HARE murders showed that, for the sake of the few pounds which careless

# Thursday, 27 September, 1888

anatomists would give for a body, two creatures in the guise of humanity could commit 14 murders one after the other. Two or three years after BURKE was executed, another monster named BISHOP was convicted of a similar offence. In the time of BURKE and HARE and BISHOP the price current for a human body was from £7 to £10, which, even allowing for the depreciation in the value of money, is less than the reward referred to in the CORONER's statement as having been offered by an American.

Hardly different in principle are the murders, which are now becoming so frequent, of children for the sake of the sums for which they are insured in burial clubs. But it would be idle to deny that this murder—or this series of murders, for it is impossible to dissociate one from the others—has elements of atrocity which distinguish it from all previous efforts in crime. Society must perforce stand breathless and expectant while this latest phase of criminality is being hunted down and stamped out. The whole civilized world is concerned in bringing the murderer to justice, and it cannot afford to be beaten in the attempt.

The police will be expected to follow up with the keenest vigilance the valuable clue elicited through the CORONER's inquest, and, since the lines of their investigation are plainly chalked out by information which they themselves failed to collect, it will be a signal disgrace if they do not succeed.

~

## The Star
### WHAT WE THINK.

THE public are greatly indebted to Mr. WYNNE BAXTER, the Coroner for the South-Eastern Division of Middlesex, for his able and lucid, and in many respects startling, summing-up at the inquest on ANNIE CHAPMAN, the last victim of the Whitechapel murderer. On reading the remarks of the Coroner, terse though they be, one gets strange and instructive glimpses of the life lived by the unhappy class to which ANNIE CHAPMAN belonged, and one also finds a clear picture of the circum-stances under which she met her death.

It throws, as the Coroner suggests, a ghastly light on our civilisation in the greatest metropolis of the world, to learn from the details given at the inquest the kind of existence which tens of thousands of people endure at the East-end of London. We see houses occupied from basement to attic with a population crowded together in disregard, not merely of every dictate of decency and mortality, but also of cleanliness and health.

We are able to see the kind of existence that women of CHAPMAN'S unfortunate class are compelled to live. She slept in common lodging-houses, sometimes at one, sometimes in another. Probably she did not rise until the shades of night enabled her to ply her hideous trade, and she then seems to have spent her time in passing from liquor shop to liquor shop with the fitting companions, male and female, of such orgies. Finally, on the night of the murder, she is traced to one of these lodging-houses at between one and two o'clock in the morning. She has by this time spent all the few pence she had, and accordingly she is refused admission; and at that hour she, who had perhaps a happy and innocent girlhood, and was once a wife, had to turn out and seek through the sale of her body the price of a bed. A few hours afterwards, she was found a corpse.

We have already dealt with the questions — searching and discomforting—which such stories of how human beings live, suggest to the minds of all of us. We have also pointed out that even the journals of reaction have been shocked or terrified into a change of tune; and that those who, but a few months ago, had no better remedy for the anguish-cry of hunger and despair than Mr. MATTHEWS'S philanderings and Sir

169

# Thursday, 27 September, 1888

CHARLES WARREN'S batons, have come to declare that these things require consideration and treatment.

We do not mean to again denounce the unreal gush and the resourceless confusion of mind which are for the moment the only real products of this newly-awakened sympathy. For the Coroner has given us in his summing-up matter for more immediate and more startled consideration. For the first time in the history of the case we are presented with something that has the resemblance to a clue to a murder, as remarkable for its apparent want of motive as for its boldness and its savagery.

The Coroner tells us that some time ago an American came to one of our medical schools and asked for specimens of a uterus, offering for each the sum of £20. This is an amount, unfortunately, high enough to tempt the greed of many people living in a great city like this. It would not have suited the purpose of this strange specialist if the uterus were not removed from the body while still living or immediately after death.

The next step in the Coroner's reasoning is that the particular portion of the body which this enterprising American specialist sought, was taken from ANNIE CHAPMAN. It was taken out, also, the Coroner is convinced, by a man who must have had a very intimate acquaintance with anatomy, and must have been accustomed to do the work of dissection, not merely with rapidity, but also with great skill.

As to the skill with which the work was done, the evidence of the Coroner and of the Doctor must be held to be conclusive, and the rapidity with which the foul murderer carried on his operations is proved by the comparative shortness of the time which the murder must have occupied. We have here, therefore, at last something like an adequate motive, and one that fits well in with all the facts of the case.

Unfortunately, we are not able to dismiss this theory because we shrink back in natural and instinctive horror from the idea that any human being could be found base enough to commit a crime for so small a motive. The case of BURKE and HARE will occur to everyone as almost identical in the motive which the Coroner suggests in the Whitechapel case.

If then, we find the theory of the Coroner difficult to accept, it is not because we can't believe there are creatures capable of acting on the motives he suggests; it is rather from the inherent improbability of the story. For the theory implies not one, but two murderers; and two murderers, equally savage, equally callous; equally reckless in daring.

If ANNIE CHAPMAN were murdered to supply a special organ, the receiver placed himself in a position almost equally criminal with that of the murderer. The purchaser and the seller were equally guilty. This necessitates several conditions, the existence of which is extremely improbable.

First you require a communication between the two, a communication which placed in equal peril the neck of both the one and the other, for it was perfectly impossible that with all the details of the murder scattered throughout the civilised world, anybody who received the organ, could be ignorant as to the manner in which it had been obtained. It requires a great stretch of imagination to realise persons carrying on this fiend's traffic, each conscious that he was entrusting his life to the safe keeping of the other.

Then you have to further picture the murderer, fresh from his ghastly work, with possibly the tell-tale stains of guilt upon his clothes, passing through the streets with his hideous burden concealed about him; and you have to imagine his guilty accomplice receiving it with the perfect knowledge that his prize came from a woman on whose mangled remains the attention of the whole world was at that moment focussed.

The person on whom the Coroner throws suspicion, was in a position that makes his detection at least a certainty. He was publishing, or about to publish, a medical work. He thus placed himself in a category comparatively small. He further identified himself from the ranks of a small class, by the special and peculiar nature of the work which he was publishing. Then this person had already made himself known to one, if not more, of our medical schools. In short, he had marked himself out so plainly as to be unmistakable. It is impossible to conceive that any man who intended to murder, or to profit by murder, would be guilty of such folly.

While, then, the public has a right to be thankful to the Coroner for suggesting something like an intelligible clue where the Police authorities seem hopelessly and wildly at sea, we cannot, for our own part, accept the clue as satisfactory. The Whitechapel mystery remains, in our judgement, as much a mystery as ever.

—

## THE MURDER OF ANNIE CHAPMAN.
### A Man Makes a "Confession," but Doesn't Know the Date of the Crime.

A man giving the name of John Fitzgerald gave himself up at Wandsworth Police-station last night and made a statement to the effect that he was the murderer of Annie Chapman in Hanbury-street. He was taken to Leman-street Police-station, where he is now detained. He is a plasterer or a bricklayer's labourer, and is believed to have been more or less under the influence of drink. In appearance he does not tally with the description given of a man seen with the woman on the morning of the murder.

From later inquiries it seems Fitzgerald first "confessed" to a private individual, who gave information to the police. A search was made, and the man was discovered in a common lodging-house at Wandsworth. He is known to have been living recently at Hammersmith. His self-accusation is said to be not altogether clear, and it is even reported that he cannot give the date of the murder, so the authorities do not place much reliance on his statements. The police are nevertheless making inquiries.

It will be seen from the above that there is not the slightest importance to be attached to this "confession."

—

## THE AMERICAN'S OFFER.

From inquiries made at some of the great medical institutions it has been ascertained that requests similar to that of the American gentleman have before been made, but the peculiar conditions attaching to the request could not possibly be complied with unless the operation were performed before or immediately after death. Ever since the Coroner communicated the facts to the police authorities no stone has been left unturned to follow up the clue, and active inquiries are still proceeding.

—

The blood-stained clothing found in Great Portland-street, and believed to be connected in some way or other with the Whitechapel murder, has been examined and found to have no bearing whatever on the crime.

~

## Evening News
### "HORROR ON HORROR'S HEAD"

The theory which Mr. Wayne E. Baxter, the coroner, put forward yesterday respecting the motives which probably prompted the murderer of Annie Chapman, in Hanbury-street, a few weeks ago, adds an even deeper tinge of horror to what was already on e of the most atrocious crimes that has ever shocked a civilized community.

At the first blush the crime itself and the subsequent mutilations appeared to be so absolutely meaningless that it was possible to believe them to be the work of an irresponsible maniac; and, out of regard to our common humanity, this theory became the generally accepted one. Furthermore, although the cuts on the body showed that the murderer must possess a certain amount of anatomical skill, it seemed not improbable that they might have been committed by some butcher or other slaughterer of animals; and colour was lent to this theory by the fact that many such men are engaged in the immediate neighbourhood of the murder, and also by the consideration that the murderer, who must have been stained with blood in a most marked degree, would, if a butcher, be much less likely to attract attention as he passed through the streets than an ordinary individual.

Unfortunately, it now appears that these considerations, and the theories built upon them, must give place to the still weightier considerations which Mr. Baxter puts before us. He tells us that the cuts, none of which are meaningless, must have been made by some person who possessed a high degree of anatomical skill and knowledge; and one of the organs of the body, which has been taken away, must have been cut on by someone who knew exactly where to find it, what difficulties he would have to contend against, and how he should use his knife so as to extract the organ without injury to it.

He declares that no unskilled person could have known where to find it, or have recognized it when found, and he is positive that no mere slaughterer of animals could have carried out the operations. His conclusion is, therefore, that they must have been performed by someone familiar with post-mortem dissection—in other words, by a man of education, skill, and professional position.

This conclusion is of itself repugnant to the commonly-accepted notion that education and a knowledge of the arts have a softening and humanising tendency, but all experience teaches us that no amount of education of the mind will ever make a fundamental change in the nature of a man who is innately a brute. Many doctors have been hanged for murder before to-day, but usually, as in the case of Palmer and Pritchard, their crimes take the less revolting though essentially treacherous form of poisoning, and we cannot call to mind an instance of a surgeon who wanted to commit murder preferring to utilize the knowledge he has gained in the dissecting room.

But revolting as is the suspicion that the terrible crime under notice was the work of an educated man, and not that of one of the ignorant wild beasts of the East-end, it pales altogether before the lurid horror of the coroner's other suggestion that there is a market for organs such as that which was taken away from the body of the unfortunate Annie Chapman, and that the murderer's object was to make money in that market. And yet the facts which the coroner disclosed for the first time yesterday point almost irresistibly to this conclusion.

After the publication of the medical evidence the coroner received a communication that the officials of one of our great medical schools could give him information which might have a distinct bearing on the case. He in consequence went to the Pathological Museum, and was there told by the curator that some months ago an American had called on him, and asked him to procure a number of specimens of the organ that was missing in the deceased.

He stated his willingness to give £20 apiece for each specimen. He stated that his object was to issue an actual specimen with each copy of a publication on which he was then engaged. He was told that his request was impossible to be complied with, but he still urged his request. He wished them preserved, not in spirits of wine, the usual medium, but in glycerine, in order to preserve them in a flaccid condition, and he wished them sent to America direct. The coroner adds that it is known that this demand was repeated to another institution of a similar character.

These facts give an exceedingly probable explanation of the murderer's motive—inhuman and fiend-like though that motive be. He could not have been actuated by ordinary motives of revenge, jealousy, or robbery. The wretched position of the woman precludes any such supposition. But the facts that a particular portion of a woman's body has a market value of £20, and that it is this particular portion which is missing, lead to a conclusion which horrible as it is, we are almost bound to accept.

The other fact, that a man accustomed to dissecting-rooms would be more likely than an ordinary man to hear of the American's offer, coupled with the surgical skill shown in the mutilations, points to the further conclusion that the wretch who committed the murder must have been a medical man or a medical student. These facts and conclusions ought to receive the greatest consideration from our detective force, for they point out very plainly the direction in which the murderer is to be sought, and supply, if possible, even stronger reasons for bringing him to justice than have hitherto existed.

—

## THE WHITECHAPEL MURDER.
### A CONFESSION

The Central News understands that a man, giving the name of John Fitzgerald, gave himself up at Wandsworth Police-station last night, and made a statement to the inspector on duty to the effect that he committed the murder in Hanbury-street. He was afterwards conveyed to the Leman-street Police-station, where he is now detained.

The Central News, in a later dispatch, says:

The man in custody at Leman-street is a plasterer or a bricklayer's labourer. He says he has been wandering from place to place, and he is believed to have been more or less under the influence of drink lately. He has not yet been formally charged with the crime, but is merely detained pending further inquiries.

His description does not tally with that given at the inquest by witnesses of a certain man seen on the morning of the murder. It seems that Fitzgerald first communicated the intelligence to a private individual, who subsequently gave its purport to the police. A search was made, and the man was discovered in a common lodging house at Wandsworth. He is known to have been living recently at Hammersmith.

# Thursday, 27 September, 1888

His self-accusation is said to be not altogether clear, and it is even reported that he cannot give the date of the murder, so that the authorities are disinclined to place much reliance on his statements. The police are, nevertheless pursuing vigilant inquiries and if the confession be found to contain any semblance of truth, the prisoner will be formally charged before a magistrate at Worship-street.

———

As a consequence of the startling statement made by the coroner, yesterday, public interest in the fate of the unfortunate Annie Chapman has been stimulated afresh, and, to-day, the subject again occupies the foremost place in conversation. The clue afforded by the coroner is, of course, being followed up by the police, who have now had the information in their possession for a week, but it has not transpired whether it has yet led to any tangible result. The inquires of the police would necessarily extend to America, and on that account it may be some time before fresh facts could be in the hands of the public.

An important point yet to be made clear is as to whether the object of the murderer was the same in the cases of the women Nichols and of Annie Chapman. The coroner, in the former case, when he summed up last Saturday, appeared to think that it was, and at the time of expressing that opinion he must have been in receipt of an important communication from the sub-curator of the Pathological Museum attached to one of the metropolitan hospitals, to which he referred in his summing-up on the body of Annie Chapman.

The opinion he expressed last Saturday regarding Nichols' case thus carries weight. The "shabby genteel" man who was seen in Chapman's company shortly before her murder is being sought for, but up to the present it would appear without success.

From inquiries made at some of the great medical institutions, it has been ascertained that requests similar to that of the American gentlemen have before been made, but the peculiar conditions attaching to the requests could not possibly be complied with unless the operation were performed before or immediately after death. Ever since the Coroner communicated the facts to the police authorities, no stone has been left unturned to follow up the clue, and active inquiries are still proceeding.

~

# Friday, 28 September, 1888

## The Times

### THE WHITECHAPEL MURDERS.

A man, giving the name of John Fitzgerald, gave himself up at Wandsworth Police-station on Wednesday night and made a statement to the inspector on duty to the effect that he committed the murder in Hanbury-street. He was conveyed to Leman-street Police station, where he is now detained. The officers engaged in the case were yesterday tracing his movements about the time of the murder, but their inquiries are not yet complete. It is believed that the man had been drinking to excess for some days past.

—

### TO THE EDITOR OF THE TIMES.

Sir,—The statement made by the coroner to the jury in the inquest on the death of the woman Chapman and your comments thereon induce me, in the interests of humanity as well as of justice, to request your serious attention to the injurious influence which the theory referred to in your article of this morning is calculated to exert on the public mind.

I will, for the sake of argument, assume that the information given to the coroner by the officer of one of the medical schools is correct, and that Dr. Phillips is right in considering that the character of the mutilation in question justifies the assumption that the perpetrator was probably one who possessed some knowledge of anatomy.

But that the inference which has been deduced is warranted, anyone who is the least acquainted with medical science and practice will unhesitatingly deny and indignantly repudiate. That a lunatic may have desired to obtain possession of certain organs for some insane purpose is very possible, and the theory of the murdering fiend being a madman only derives confirmation from the information obtained by the coroner.

But that the parts of the body carried off were wanted for any quasi-scientific publication or any other more or less legitimate purpose no one having any knowledge of medical science will for a moment believe. To say nothing of the utterly absurd notion of the part, or organ, being preserved in a particular way to accompany each copy of an intended publication, the facilities for obtaining such objects for any purpose of legitimate research, in any number, either here or in America, without having recourse to crime of any kind are such as to render the suggestion made utterly untenable.

There can be no analogy whatever with the atrocious crimes of Burke and Hare, the merest insinuation of which is a gross and unjustifiable calumny on the medical profession and is calculated both to exert an injurious influence on the public mind and defeat the ends of justice.

If I have expressed myself strongly you will, I trust, ascribe it to my anxiety that neither you nor the officers of justice should be misled, and not to any mere feeling that discredit has unjustly been thrown on the medical profession.

Your obedient servant,
JAS. RISDON BENNETT.[71]
22, Cavendish-square, Sept 27.

~

---

[71] **Sir James Risdon Bennett** (1809-1891). President of the Royal College of Physicians from 1876.

174

# Friday, 28 September, 1888

## The Star

### WHAT WE THINK.

SIR JAMES RISDON BENNETT'S letter to the *Times* must be held to give the Burke and Hare theory of the Whitechapel murder its quietus. From the first we threw doubt on it; and we are now convinced of its utter untrustworthiness. Sir James points out (1) that no scientific end would be answered by the collection of specimens of the uterus in order to illustrate a medical book; (2) that such specimens are attainable in any quantity either here or in America without the payment of such a preposterous sum as £20 apiece; (3) that the man who proposed such terms must have known that he was inciting to the commission of horrible crime.

NOW let us see where these statements and admissions land us. We must either (*a*) dismiss the American as a myth, and the story of his applications to the Pathological Museum as a hoax; or (*b*) we must regard him as a medical maniac, who (and not any supposed emissary of his) is the real murderer. Reverting to *a*, we must confess our astonishment that the matter has not already been cleared up. What is the American's name? Did he leave an address? What is the nature of the work to illustrate (!) which he is prepared, should he print 1,000 copies, to pay £20,000 for "specimens?" Did the authorities of the Pathological Museum or any other institution (what institution?) treat him seriously, or did they not at once see that he must be either a madman or a practical joker of an uncommonly grim kind? All these are questions to which we expect a definite and a rational answer.

WE come now to *b*. If the American exists, he is a maniac, and is the probable murderer. But then he is a foolish murderer as well, and has put his neck into the noose. According to the Burke and Hare theory, he has been roving about London, applying for specimens of the uterus, offering large sums for them, and, apparently failing to get amateur murders done on a sufficiently large scale, has gone into business on his own account. If so, the scent must be hot indeed, and there is no need of bloodhounds, human or other, to run down our mad "Experimentalist Abroad."

BUT then why adopt this theory at all? In the first place, it destroys the sequence of the murders. It compels us to suppose that the first two—or at least the second—which resembled the others in a startling fashion, were entirely dissociated from the later crimes. Nor is it at all clear that the vital point of the Burke and Hare theory—viz., that the mutilations in the third murder were made for the purpose of extracting the uterus—has been made out. We come back therefore to the theory we ourselves prefer—viz., that of the slaughterman. We are not convinced that a slaughterman's anatomical skill is not fully equal to such operations as were conducted on the bodies of these poor victims of a terrible fate. Similar operations are, we know, performed by slaughtermen with vast celerity.

WE invite our readers' attention to the fact that slaughtermen are in the habit of working till between four and five on Friday and till between five and six on Saturday mornings, that the woman Nicholls was murdered about four on Friday morning, and that the woman Chapman was murdered at a later hour on Saturday morning. There are other facts within our knowledge, which we reserve. But for the present we are content to repudiate the Burke and Hare theory, and to insist that a more rational explanation lies much nearer at hand.

MEANWHILE, it is of the utmost importance that the true moral of the murders should be kept steadily in view. Lord William Compton is very far from being an extreme man, but he sees that until Whitechapel is looked to, we may give up the problem of governing London, or England either. "The homes of the working classes," says Lord William, "are a disgrace to working-class London. Rents are exorbitant, and the tenement rooms scarcely fit for habitation."

THIS is the heart of the matter. Landlordism is the enemy in Whitechapel as elsewhere, and no candidate for the County Council— especially East-end candidates—ought to obtain the support of Radical electors unless he pledges himself to strong measures against the men who rob it of light, air, work, land, and house-room. That should be the principle; and meanwhile candidates should be asked to pledge themselves (1) to as heavy a tax on ground rents as possible; (2) to the provision of model lodging-houses; (3) to sweeping out of the rookeries,[72] and replacing

---

[72] **Rook, Rookery**. (1) A gambling hell; and (2) any place of ill-repute; e.g. (a) a brothel, (b) subalterns'

them by model dwellings, facilities for acquiring which will be placed in the hands of the Council; (4) to better lighting and draining, and better sanitary inspection, both of sweating dens[73] and rookeries.

All this will help us on to *the* Whitechapel we wish to see—in which the fruits of Whitechapel's labour will be available for purifying and beautifying it, and not for piling up senseless luxury for Belgravia.

—

### FOURTH EDITION.
### LATEST DESPATCHES.
### The Whitechapel Murders.

It has been ascertained that the incident to which Mr. Wynne Baxter, coroner for East Middlesex, so emphatically referred in his summing up of the evidence given at the inquest concerning the death of Annie Chapman, occurred some months since, towards the close of last year. The person who made the singular application, as described, at one of the great London hospitals, and which he repeated at a scientific institution, was for some time a student at the hospital in question, and it is stated he would have been able to procure what he required without incurring any risk. Inquiry at the London Hospital, Whitechapel-road, the nearest institution to the scene of the murder, elicited the fact that

### NO APPLICATIONS OF THE KIND

indicated have recently been made to the warden or curator of the pathological museum. Although many hospital authorities do not attach very great importance to the story, the police have given due attention to the matter. In their view, however, it does not provide a clue which will facilitate the identification of the murderer.

~

---

barrack quarters, and (c) a neighbourhood occupied by a criminal or squalid population, a slum (q.v.) (1590). (Farmer)

[73] **Sweating Den**. One definition of **Sweat** was "To work for (or employ labour at) starvation wages; ...hence sweater, an employer of underpaid labour: usually a middleman between the actual employer and employed; a grinding taskmaster; whence sweating-system, sweater, sweated, etc. (1850)." A Sweating Den is analogous to a Sweat Shop. (ibid)

## Evening News
### NOTES.

Sir James Risdon Bennett is very much exercised at the theory which Mr. Wynne Baxter, the Whitechapel Coroner, recently put forward in connection with the murder of Annie Chapman. He declares that no one having any knowledge of medical science will for a moment believe that the parts of the body carried off were wanted for any quasi-scientific publication or any more or less legitimate purpose, and further that the facilities for obtaining such objects for any purpose of legitimate research, in any number, either here or in America, without having recourse to any crime, are such as to render the suggestion of the coroner utterly untenable. But how does Sir James know that the American who made the extraordinary offer to one of our medical schools wanted the particular organ in question for any legitimate purpose? There is no evidence that he did so; whilst the condition he is said to have made that the organ must be extracted from the body either before or immediately after death, would assuredly render it extremely difficult to obtain specimens. Sir James, in his anxiety to defend his own profession, seems not to have taken as calm a view of the facts as he might have done.

—

### THE WHITECHAPEL MURDER.

An extraordinary story was current at Portsmouth, yesterday morning, to the effect that the police the previous night had effected the capture of the perpetrator of the White-chapel murders. The authorities were very reticent about the affair, but the inquiry resulted in the prisoner being merely bound over to keep the peace for assaulting a woman.

The *Law Journal* says: The summing-up of the coroner in the Whitechapel case, although at certain points, particularly when he communicated the information given to himself personally, somewhat sensational, on the whole promoted the true function of a coroner's inquest, which is as near to an approach to a proceeding *in rein* as is known to common law. The regular course would have been to have summoned the person who gave the information as a witness, and the coroner's own evidence, not on oath, of what was told him was technically out of order.

Possibly to summon the witness would not have encouraged the production of further evidence, and no doubt the able exposition of the coroner of the case as it now stands is a valuable contribution towards justice, and from one point of view a relief to the public mind.

Everyone will be glad to know that Whitechapel, whatever its shortcomings, cannot be held in any sense responsible for this murder, except in so far as it happened to afford conveniences for the execution of its horrible motive.

—

The theory of the coroner is too horrible; but those of us who remember the days of Burke and his pitch plaister[74] murder of poor boys for the sake of their bodies may well accept it. Have the remains of the other murdered woman been exhumed to confirm the suggestion, and to connect the three murders with the same diabolical trade?

C.H. Bromby, Bishop.[75]

It has been ascertained that the incident to which Mr. Wynne Baxter, coroner for East Middlesex, so emphatically referred in his summing up of the evidence given at the inquest concerning the death of Annie Chapman, occurred some months since, towards the close of last year.

The person who made the singular application as described, at one of the great London hospitals, and which he repeated at a scientific institution, was for some time a student at the hospital in question, and it is stated he would have been able to procure what he required without incurring any risk.

As a matter of fact, according to the experience of demonstrators of anatomy, there is no such value to be attached to what was mentioned by the coroner, who was informed that £20 would be given by the American in every case. In a pecuniary sense there would be no value attaching at all. As a student the applicant must have been conversant with the rules of the dissecting room and with the very strict regulations of the Government in regard to the disposal of post-mortem subjects. He certainly would have excited suspicion by pressing a demand with unusual conditions, the more especially as under proper treatment glycerine, as the medium of preservation, would have been totally unnecessary.

This at all events is the view taken by some experts, while others state that the use of glycerine, as opposed to spirits of wine, as a preserving agent would depend to a great extent upon the experiment subsequently intended to be made.

Inquiry at the London Hospital, Whitechapel-road, the nearest institution to the scene of the murder, elicited the fact that no applications of the kind indicated have recently been made to the warden or curator of the pathological museum. An opinion was expressed that an American pathologist would scarcely endeavour to obtain his specimens from London, when the less stringent laws prevailing on the Continent would render his task comparatively easy there.

It was stated, however, that a considerable number of Americans, holding medical degrees of more or less value, were in the habit of studying at London pathological museums. On the other hand, if the real object was to add to the practical value of a technical publication in preparation, as alleged, the purposes in view could have been easily attained in America, without the necessity of committing murder.

It is the theory, however, of some among those who are well acquainted with the medical details of the recent mysterious deaths in Whitechapel that the offer of £20 must have become known to someone in the habit of frequenting dissecting rooms, and that, under

---

[74] **Pitch Plaister.** A sticky plaster made of nine parts of Burgundy Pitch melted and mixed with one part of molten yellow wax. This was smeared onto a cloth and used for medicinal purposes, such as to cover a wound. It was said that Burke and Hare, the Irish immigrants that murdered 16 people in Edinburgh to sell their corpses to medical schools in 1828, would seize a victim and slap one of these across their nose and mouth, smothering them. (Thomas)

[75] **Charles Henry Bromby** (1814-1907). Anglican Bishop of Tasmania 1864-1882. Born in Hull, he was the last bishop for Australia that was nominated by the crown. Returned to England after resigning his see in 1882. Rector of Shrawardine-cum-Montford 1882-1887, assistant bishop of Lichfield 1882-1891, warden of St. John's Hospital, Lichfield 1887-1891, assistant bishop of Bath and Wells from 1891 until he retired in 1900.

temptation, this individual had yielded to the impulse of taking life.

The circumstances that two murders had been perpetrated in the streets of Whitechapel within a short period without causing much comment would have led, it is supposed, the miscreant to assume that the police protection in the neighbourhood was so insufficient that he might commit a third murder with impunity.

Upon the body of Mary Anne Nichols, the Buck's-row victim, there were indications that the murderer had entertained, but not fully carried out his project, and had had to hurry away to evade discovery. In the case of Annie Chapman, the opportunity was more favourable and the object was attained. Both women had had their throats cut by a left-handed assailant.

Although many hospital authorities do not attach very great importance to the story, the police have given due attention to the matter. In their view, however, it does not provide a clue which will facilitate the identification of the murderer.—*Daily Telegraph*

—

## "HORRORS," AND THE LANCET.

*The Lancet*, in discussing "murder-culture by the pictorial art," says, while we empower the police to put down with a strong hand the exhibition in shop windows, and the censor of stage plays and spectacles to interdict the parade in theatres of pictures and scenes of an "immoral character," because it is recognized that these have a tendency to corrupt the mind of youth, and age too, nothing whatever is done to restrain the daily increasing evil of pictorial placards displayed on every hoarding, and of highly-wrought scenes produced at nearly all the theatres, which not only direct the thoughts but actively stir the passions of the people in such a way as to familiarize the average mind with murder in all its forms, and to break down that protective sense of "horror" which nature has given us with the express purpose, doubtless, of opposing an obstacle to the evil influence of the exemplification of homicide.

The educationary use of the pictorial art has not been checked by public authority. We have no wish to make wild affirmations, but knowing what we do as observers of development, we can have no hesitation in saying that the increasing frequency of horribly brutal outrages is by no means unaccountable. It is high time that this ingenious and persistent murder-culture should cease.

# Saturday, 29 September, 1888

## The Times

### THE EAST-END.
### TO THE EDITOR OF THE TIMES.

Sir,—Your correspondent "Gamma" proposes that a number of philanthropic gentlemen should float a company for the purpose of buying up and improving the houses at present dedicated to vice and crime, and suggests that such a company would have every prospect of paying a good dividend.

Permit one who is well acquainted with the East-end slums to point out that the first step needful is the prosecution of the landlords of these rookeries of crime for keeping disorderly houses.

When the houses shall have been closed in consequence of such prosecutions, they will be purchasable at a fair price that would, after improvement and reletting under conditions compatible with decency, yield a fair return to the philanthropic investor. If bought as "going concerns", the price would be simply prohibitive; for vice pays a higher rent then virtue, and the purchase money would be proportionate to the rental; while the large figure that would be paid by the philanthropist would only encourage the formation of new rookeries of vice to take the place of those suppressed.

The fact remains that the police must act before the philanthropist can step in.

Let an experiment be made in Dorset-street, Flower-and-Dean-street, and Thrawl-street, places made notorious in connexion with the recent Whitechapel murders. In these streets, literally within a stone's-throw of Toynbee-hall and the Rev. S.A. Barnett's Vicarage, are whole rows of so-called "registered" lodging-houses, each of which is practically a brothel and a focus of crime. The police authorities uniformly refuse to prosecute the owners of such places as keepers of disorderly houses, although the fullest evidence is in their possession to insure conviction, and they always throw the odious duty of prosecution on the neighbours who may feel aggrieved. These cannot prosecute in the cases of the Whitechapel rookeries without risking their lives; for such is the lawless nature of the denizens of these places that they would certainly, and probably with impunity, wreak their vengeance on any private individual who would dare to disturb them.

If the Home Secretary would give instructions for the simultaneous prosecution of the keepers of these nests of crime, the houses would be closed within a few weeks, and the owners would then gladly part with their bad bargains at a fair price to the philanthropic investor.

The suppression of these haunts of crime and the dispersion of their lawless population should be the watchword and cry—the *Carthago delenda est* of every social reformer. That such a seething mass of moral filth and corruption should exist in our midst is a disgrace to our much-vaunted civilization, and a danger to the State.

For obvious reasons I suppress my name and prefer to subscribe myself

ONE WHO KNOWS.

—

### THE WHITECHAPEL MURDER

The man John Fitzgerald, who was arrested at Wandsworth and who has been detained at the Leman street Police Station on his own confession, with having murdered Annie Chapman in Hanbury street on the 8th inst., has been liberated, exhaustive inquiries having proved his statement to be entirely unfounded.

~

179

# Saturday, 29 September, 1888

## The Star

### WHAT WE THINK.

DR. SAVAGE, the mania specialist, in his interesting article on "Homicidal Mania" in the *Fortnightly Review*, inclines to the belief that the Whitechapel murders are the work of a butcher, stimulated either by religious mania or some fiendish plan of revenge. The opinion is important, and it shows again that the slaughter-man theory holds the field. All the local facts favour it; and no other explanation fits in with the escape of the murderer and the diabolical certitude with which the victims were tracked down and massacred. "To suppose the murders to be the work of a medical man," says Dr. Savage, "is, to my thinking, going too far." Yes; and it is going unnecessarily afield when simpler material for discovering the culprit lies at our very doors.

MEANWHILE, the Burke theory is already fading into very dim and distant perspective.

A little investigation at the hospitals has shown—

(1) That no such application as that referred to by Mr. Baxter was made at any hospital or medical school, with the possible exceptions of the schools of University College and Middle-sex Hospital.

(2) That at these institutions the authorities declare that they have "no information," or say that the story has been "mixed with error" or grossly exaggerated.

(3) That the whole business seems to be traceable to a rumour arising from the students' gossip.

All we can say is that if this is correct, the medical officer who made himself the mouth-piece of sensational gossip and misled the coroner and the public ought to be ashamed of himself. There is quite enough highly-coloured falsehood about the Whitechapel business without piling up sham mysteries.

~

# Monday, 1 October, 1888

## The Times

Two more murders must now be added to the black list of similar crimes of which the East-end of London has very lately been the scene. The circumstances of both of them bear a close resemblance to those of the former atrocities. The victim in both has been a woman. In neither can robbery have been the motive, nor can the deed be set down as the outcome of an ordinary street brawl. Both have unquestionably been murders deliberately planed, and carried out by the hand of someone who has been no novice to the work.

It was early yesterday morning that the bodies of the two women were discovered, at places within a quarter of an hour's walk of one another, and at intervals of somewhat less than an hour. The first body was found lying in a yard in Berner-street, a low thoroughfare running out of the Commercial-road. The discovery was made about 1 o'clock in the early morning by a carter, who was entering the yard to put up his cart.

The body was that of a woman with a deep gash on the throat, running almost from ear to ear. She was quite dead, but the corpse was still warm, and in the opinion of the medical experts, who were promptly summoned to the place, the deed of blood must have been done not many minutes before. The probability seems to be that the murderer was interrupted by the arrival of the carter, and that he made his escape unobserved, under the shelter of the darkness, which was almost total at the spot.

The efforts of the police to trace the murderer have been without result as yet. They set to work without delay. Their first attention was directed to the inmates of a Socialist International Club, close to the place at which the body had been found, but there was nothing to give ground for a reasonable suspicion about any of them; nor was there any one in the neighbourhood of the locality on whom the guilt could be presumed to rest.

The body has been identified as that of ELIZABETH STRIDE, a widow according to one account, according to another a woman living apart from her husband, and by all accounts belonging to the "unfortunate" class.

Her movements have been traced up to a certain point. She left her house in Dean-street, Spitalfields, between 6 and 7 o'clock on Saturday evening, saying that she was not going to meet any one in particular. From that hour there is nothing certainly known about her up to the time at which her body was found, lifeless indeed, but not otherwise mutilated than by the gash in the throat, which had severed the jugular vein and must have caused instantaneous death.

Not so the corpse of the second victim. In this case the purpose of the murderer had been fulfilled, and a mutilation inflicted of the same nature as that upon the body of ANNIE CHAPMAN.

It was in the south-western corner of Mitre-square, in Aldgate, that the second body was found. It was again the body of a woman, and again had death resulted from a deep wound across the throat. But in this instance, the face had also been so slashed as to render it hard for the remains to be identified, and the abdomen had been ripped up, and a portion of the intestines had been dragged out and left lying about the neck.

The time of the murder can be approximately fixed. The policeman in whose beat Mitre-square lies had passed the spot at which the body was found a little before half-past one. On his return beat, at about a quarter to two, he found the body lying as we have said, so cut about as almost to defy recognition.

The deed of blood had been the work of a practised hand. The body bore clear proof of some anatomical skill, but the murderer had been in a hurry, and had carried out his design in a more rough fashion than that with which ANNIE CHAPMAN'S body had been mutilated.

The best chance of identification seems to be from the victim's dress, of which a minute description had been put out.

The inference is clear as to the agency in these two almost concurrent murders. They are the work of the same hand. The murderer in ELIZABETH STRIDE'S case had no more than time to inflict the fatal wound. He was then interrupted, but he was not so to be put off from the completion of his abominable design. The opportunity soon offered itself.

A second woman of the unfortunate class was accosted, was lured off into a quiet corner, and time was found for the hurried accomplishment of the full deed of brutality. Beyond this we are unable at present to go.

# Monday, 1 October, 1888

We are once again in the presence of mysterious crimes, for which no adequate motive has been assigned. The object was not plunder—in neither case did the wretched woman offer any temptation for this. The circumstances are such as to forbid the idea of revenge. The victims seem almost certainly to have been mere casual street acquaintances, picked up by the murderer at the moment, and not known to him before.

Have these been the freaks of a madman or the deliberate acts of a sane man who takes delight in murder on its own account, and who selects his victims by preference from the weaker sex, either as the safer and easier to deal with or as giving him the means of gratifying some horrid instinct of cruelty and perverted lust?

The explanation offered by the Coroner in ANNIE CHAPMAN'S case is equally applicable in these, but there has been so much uncertainty thrown upon it, and the facts on which it rests are so far unestablished, that it is impossible to accept it as proved.

The recurrence of these several murders at brief intervals of time, and with details more or less closely resembling one another, makes it more than likely that the two murders of Sunday morning will not be the last of their kind. There has been too much system and method, and too obvious a brutal daring which cares little for the chance of detection. But if this is so, it becomes morally certain that the murderer must be found out. He had a near escape from the unlighted yard in Berners-street. At Mitre-square the police must have been close upon his heels.

The fact that he gives proof of the possession of anatomical skill does much to narrow the inquiry. Not one man in a thousand could have played the part of ANNIE CHAPMAN'S murderer. In one of these new cases, if not in both, we have evidence of a similar kind. Meanwhile no means of detection should be left untried.

Twelve years ago a murder at Blackburn was traced out by the help of a bloodhound, and, thanks to the sagacious instinct of the dog, the murderer was convicted and hanged. The experiment which was successful at Blackburn might once more be of avail.

If any facts could be ascertained about the murderer's movements there would be, at least, a clue which the police might be successful in following up. As the matter stands, they are at fault, and must apparently await helplessly the perpetration of some fresh outrage to give them a renewed chance of getting on the right track.

—

## MORE MURDERS AT THE EAST-END.

In the early hours of yesterday morning two more horrible murders were committed in the East-end of London, the victim in both cases belonging, it is believed, to the same unfortunate class. No doubt seems to be entertained by the police that these terrible crimes were the work of the same fiendish hands which committed the outrages which had already made Whitechapel so painfully notorious.

The scenes of the two murders just brought to light are within a quarter of an hour's walk of each other, the earlier-discovered crime having been committed in a yard in Berner-street, a low thoroughfare out of the Commercial-road, while the second outrage was perpetrated within the city boundary, in Mitre-square, Aldgate.

In the first mentioned case the body was found in a gateway leading to a factory, and although the murder, compared with the other, may be regarded as of an almost ordinary character—the unfortunate woman only having her throat cut—little doubt is felt, from the position of the corpse, that the assassin had intended to mutilate it. He seems, however, to have been interrupted by the arrival of a cart, which drew up close to the spot, and it is believed to be possible that he may have escaped behind this vehicle.

Conflicting statements are made as to the way in which the body was found, but according to one account a lad first made the discovery and gave information to a man named Costa, who proceeded to the spot, where almost immediately afterwards a constable arrived. The body was then removed to No. 40, Berner-street, which is very near to the now notorious Hanbury-street. These premises are occupied by the International Workmen's Club.

The victim, according to the official details, appears to have been a woman of low character, aged about 35. Her height is 5ft. 5in., and her complexion and hair are dark. She wore a jacket made of black diagonal cloth, feather trimmings, a black skirt, velveteen bodice, crape bonnet, spring-side boots, and white stockings.

# Monday, 1 October, 1888

The murder in the City was committed in circumstances which show that the assassin, if not suffering from insanity, appears to be free from any fear of interruption, while at his dreadful work. Mitre-square is entered from three places—Mitre-street, and passages from Duke-street and St. James's-place—through any of which he might have been interrupted by the arrival either of ordinary pedestrians or the police, although the square is lonely at night-time, being occupied chiefly for business purposes.

The constable's beat, moreover is patrolled in between 15 and 20 minutes, and within this short space of time, apparently, the murderer and his victim must have arrived and the crime been committed. The beat is in the charge of a man who is regarded by his superiors as thoroughly trustworthy, who has discharged his duties efficiently for several years, and who reports that when he went through the square at about half-past 1 he noticed nothing unusual and no one about. Plain-clothes constables also occasionally patrol the square, which is a place of irregular form, about 77ft. by 80ft.

On two sides of the square are the ware-houses of Messrs. Kearney and Tonge, and adjoining them are two old houses, which exactly face the scene of the murder—the wide pavement opposite, where, it is stated, there was some deficiency of light from the gas-lamp.

The square is occupied by business firms, excepting the two old houses already referred to, one of which, curiously enough, is tenanted by a police-constable, the other being uninhabited. The corner house of Mitre-square and Mitre-street is held by a picture-frame maker, who, however, does not reside on the premises; and the adjoining three houses in Mitre-street, backing on to the square are unoccupied.

According to the report of Police-constable Watkins, 881, in passing through the square at a quarter to 2 a.m. he found the murdered woman, lying in the south-western corner, with her throat cut and her intestines protruding.

He immediately sent Police-constable Holl-and, 814, for Dr. Sequeira, of Jewry-street, who arrived ten minutes later. Inspector Collard was also communicated with, and telegrams were dispatched which at once brought Major Henry Smith (the acting Commissioner), Mr. M'William (the Inspector of the City Detective Department), and Superintendent Foster to the spot. Dr. Gordon Brown (the surgeon to the City Police), who had also been informed of the discovery, was also present.

The deceased was found lying on her back, with her head inclined to her left side. Her left leg was extended, her right being bent, and both her arms were extended. The throat was terribly cut; there was a large gash across the face from the nose to the right angle of the cheek, and part of the right ear had been cut off. There were also other indescribable mutilations. It is stated that some anatomical skill seems to have been displayed in the way in which the lower part of the body was mutilated, but the ghastly work appears to have been done more rapidly and roughly than in the cases of the women Nicholls and Chapman.

The body was removed as soon as possible to the mortuary in Golden-lane, where it was examined in the presence of Dr. Brown and Dr. Sequeira. Dr. Phillips, of Spital-square, the surgeon of the H Division of Metropolitan Police, arrived shortly afterwards, and assisted in the preliminary examination of the body.

The woman is described as being about 40 years of age and 5ft. in height. She has hazel eyes—the right one having been apparently smashed in, and the left one being also injured—and dark auburn hair.

She wore a black cloth jacket, with imitation fur collar and three large metal buttons. Her dress is of dark green print, the pattern consisting of Michaelmas daisies and golden lilies. She also wore a thin white vest, a drab linsey skirt, and a very old dark green alpaca petticoat, white chemise, and brown ribbed stockings, mended at the feet with white material. Her bonnet was black straw, trimmed with black beads and green and black velvet. She wore a pair of men's laced-boots; and a piece of old white coarse apron and a piece of riband were tied loosely around the neck.

There were also found upon her a piece of string, a common white handkerchief with a red border, a match box with cotton in it, a white linen pocket containing a white bone handle table knife, very blunt (with no blood on it), two short clay pipes, a red cigarette case with white metal fittings, a printed handbill with the name "Frank Cater, 405, Bethnal-green-road," upon it, a check pocket containing five pieces of soap, a small tin box containing tea and sugar, a portion of a pair of spectacles, a three-cornered check handkerchief, and a large white linen pocket containing a small comb, a red mitten, and a ball of worsted.

In the afternoon a post-mortem examination of the body was made by Dr. Brown, assisted by Dr. Sequeira, Dr. Phillips, and Dr. M'Kellar (the chief surgeon of the Metropolitan Police). Dr. Yarrow (H Division Metropolitan Police) and Dr. Sedgwick Saunders were also present at the examination. It may be stated that up to a late hour last night the body had not been identified.

Plans and perspective sketches of the scene of the City murder were prepared for the use of the coroner and the police by Mr. F. W. Foster, of Old Jewry.

Crowds of persons yesterday visited the localities where the murders were committed. The entrances to Mitre-square were, however, closed by order of the police authorities, and a large body of constables, under Inspector Izzard, was kept on the spot to preserve order.

Late last night the woman murdered in Berner-street was identified by a sister as Elizabeth Stride, who, it seems, had resided latterly in Flower and Dean-street. A correspondent, when he was shown the body of the deceased, recognized her by the name of Annie Fitzgerald as having been charged and convicted a great number of times at the Thames Police-court of drunkenness. Whenever so charged she always denied having been drunk, and gave as an excuse that she suffered from fits. This statement, although not strictly true in connexion with her special visits to the Thames Police-court, was partly correct, for while evidence was being adduced against her she had fallen to the floor of the dock in a fit and had to be carried from the court to the cell in an insensible condition. When the body was found it presented no marks of a struggle having taken place.

Last night, shortly before midnight, a man, whose name has not yet transpired, was arrested in the Borough on suspicion of being the perpetrator of the murders in the East-end.

Yesterday morning a tall dark man wearing an American hat entered a lodging-house in Union-street known as Albert-chambers. He stayed there throughout the day, and his peculiar manner drew upon him the attention of his fellow lodgers. Certain observations which he made regarding the topic of the day aroused their suspicions. He attracted the notice of the deputy keeper of the lodging-house, whose suspicions became so strong that he sent for a policeman. On the arrival of the officer the stranger was questioned as to his recent wanderings, but he could give no intelligible account of them, though he said he had spent the previous night on Blackfriars-bridge. He was conveyed to Stones-end Police-station, Blackman-street, Borough.

The inquest in the Berner-street case is fixed for today at 11 a.m., at the Vestry-hall, Cable-street, St. George's.

The Whitechapel Vigilance Committee have addressed to the Queen a petition praying that, in the interests of the public at large, Her Majesty will direct an immediate offer of a large reward for the capture of the murderer.

At 3 o'clock yesterday afternoon a meeting of nearly 1,000 persons took place in Victoria Park, under the chairmanship of Mr. Edward Barrow, of the Bethnal-green-road. After several speeches upon the conduct of the Home Secretary and Sir Charles Warren, a resolution was unanimously passed that it was high time both officers should resign and make way for some officers who would leave no stone unturned for the purpose of bringing the murderers to justice, instead of allowing them to run riot in a civilized city like London. On Mile-end-waste during the day four meetings of the same kind were held and similar resolutions passed.

---

## ANOTHER ACCOUNT.

The scene of the first crime is a narrow court in Berners-street, a quiet thoroughfare running from Commercial-road down to the London, Tilbury, and Southend Railway.

At the entrance to the court are a pair of large wooden gates, in one of which is a small wicket for use when the gates are closed. At the hour when the murderer accomplished his purpose these gates were open; indeed, according to the testimony of those living near, the entrance to the court is seldom closed.

For a distance of 18ft. or 20ft. from the street there is a dead wall on each side of the court, the effect of which is to enshroud the intervening space in absolute darkness after

# Monday, 1 October, 1888

sunset. Further back some light is thrown into the court from the windows of a workmen's club, which occupies the whole length of the court on the right, and from a number of cottages occupied mainly by tailors and cigarette makers on the left.

At the time when the murder was committed, however, the lights in all of the dwelling-houses in question had been extinguished, while such illumination as came from the club, being from the upper story, would fall on the cottages opposite, and would only serve to intensify the gloom of the rest of the court.

From the position in which the body was found it is believed that the moment the murderer had got his victim in the dark shadow near the entrance to the court he threw her to the ground, and with one gash severed her throat from ear to ear. The hypothesis that the wound was inflicted after, and not before, the woman fell is supported by the fact that there are severe bruises on her left temple and left cheek, showing that force must have been used to prostrate her, which would not have been necessary had her throat been already cut.

When discovered the body was lying as if the woman had fallen forward, her feet being about a couple of yards from the street and her head in a gutter which runs down the right-hand side of the court close to the wall. The woman lay on her left side, face downwards, her position being such that although the court at that part is only 9ft. wide, a person walking up the middle might have passed the recumbent body without notice.

The condition of the corpse, however, and several circumstances which have since come to light prove pretty conclusively that no considerable period elapsed between the committal of the murder and the discovery of the body. In fact, it is generally conjectured that the assassin was disturbed while at his ghastly work, and made off before he had completed his design. All the features of the case go to connect the tragedy with that which took place three-quarters of an hour later a few streets distant.

The obvious poverty of the woman is entirely opposed to the theory that robbery could have been the motive, and the secrecy and despatch with which the crime was effected are equally good evidence that the murder was not the result of an ordinary street brawl.

At the club referred to above—the International Workmen's Educational Club—which is an off-shoot of the Socialist League and a rendezvous of a number of foreign residents, chiefly Russians, Poles, and Continental Jews of various nationalities, it is customary on Saturday nights to have friendly discussions of topics of mutual interest and to wind up the evening's entertainment with songs, &c.

The proceedings commenced on Saturday about 8:30 with a discussion on the necessity for Socialism among Jews. This was kept up until about 11 o'clock, when a considerable portion of the company left. Between 20 and 30 people remained behind, however, and the usual concert which followed was not concluded when the intelligence was brought in by the steward of the club that a woman had been murdered within a few yards of the house.

The people residing in the cottages on the other side of the court were all indoors and most of them in bed by midnight. Several of these persons remember lying awake and listening to the singing in the club, and they also remember the concert coming to an abrupt termination; but during the whole of the time between the hour of their retiring to rest and the moment when the body was discovered no one heard anything in the nature of a scream or a woman's cry of distress.

It was Louis Diemsschütz, the steward of the club who found the body. Diemsschütz, who is a traveller[76] in cheap jewellery, had spent the day at Westow-hill, near the Crystal Palace, on business, and had driven home at his usual hour, reaching Berner-street at 1 o'clock.

On turning into the gateway he had some difficulty with his pony, the animal being apparently determined to avoid the right-hand wall. For the moment Diemsschütz did not think much of the occurrence, because he knew the pony was given to shying, and he thought, perhaps, some mud or refuse was in the way. The pony, however, obstinately refused to go straight; so the driver pulled him up to see what was in the way. Failing to discover anything in the darkness, Diemsschütz poked about with the handle of his whip, and then discovered the body.

---

[76] **Traveller.** Travelling salesman. (Census1891.com)

# Monday, 1 October, 1888

He entered the club by the side door higher up the court, and informed those in the concert-room upstairs that something had happened in the yard. A member of the club named Kozebrodski returned with Diemsschütz into the court, and the former struck a match while the latter lifted the body up. It was at once apparent that the woman was dead. The body was still warm, and the clothes enveloping it were wet from the recent rain. The heart had ceased to beat.

Both men ran off without delay to find a policeman. After some search a constable 252 H, was found in Commercial-road. With the aid of the policeman's whistle[77] more constables were quickly on the spot, and the gates at the entrance to the court having been closed and a guard set on all the exits of the club and the cottages, the superintendent of the district and the divisional surgeon were sent for.

In a few minutes Dr. Phillips was at the scene of the murder, and a brief examination sufficed to show that life had been extinct some minutes. Careful note having been taken of the position of the body, it was removed to the parish mortuary of St. George's-in-the-East, Cable-street, to await identification.

The woman appears to be about 30 years of age. Her hair is very dark, with a tendency to curl, and her complexion is also dark. Her features are sharp and somewhat pinched, as though she had endured considerable privations recently. She wore a rusty black dress of a cheap kind of sateen with a velveteen bodice, over which was a black diagonal worsted jacket, with fur trimming. Her bonnet, which had fallen from her head when she was found in the yard, was of black crape. In her right hand were tightly clasped some grapes, and in her left she held a number of sweetmeats. Both the jacket and the bodice were open towards the top, but in other respects the clothes were not dis-arranged. The linen was clean and in tolerably

---

[77] In 1884 the Metropolitan Police Force adopted the whistle developed by Joseph Hudson of Birmingham to replace the wooden rattles that had been been standard since the inception of the organization. This was done for two reasons:
1. The whistle was smaller and easier to carry.
2. The whisle could be heard 1,000 yards away, twice as far as the rattle. (Dibley)

good repair.

The cut in the woman's throat, which was the cause of death, had evidently been effected with a very sharp instrument. The weapon had apparently been drawn across the throat obliquely from left to right, and it had severed both the windpipe and the jugular vein. As the body lies in the mortuary the head seems to be almost severed, the gash being about three inches long, and nearly the same depth.

In the pocket of the woman's dress were discovered two pocket-handkerchiefs, a brass thimble, and a skein of black darning worsted.

In addition to the examination by Dr. Phillips, the body was examined both before and after removal to the mortuary by Dr. Kaye and Dr. Blackwell, both of whom reside in the vicinity of Berner-street.

On the arrival of the superintendent from Leman-street police-station, steps were imme-diately taken to ascertain whether the members of the club were in any way connected with the murder. The names and addresses of all the men present were taken, and a rigorous search of the premises was instituted, much to the annoyance of the members.

The residents in the court had to submit to a similar scrutiny. In neither case, however, was any incriminating evidence discovered.

It was 5 o'clock before the police had finished their investigations at the club for, in addition to the search referred to above, inquiries were made which resulted in a number of written statements which had to be signed.

The fact that another murder had been committed soon became known in the neigh-bourhood, and long before daybreak the usually quiet thoroughfare was the scene of great excitement. Extra police had to be posted right along the street, and even with this precaution, locomotion from an early hour was a matter of extreme difficulty. A large crowd followed the body to the mortuary, and here again it was found necessary to take unusual precautions to keep back the crowd.

Several matters have come to light which tend to fix precisely the time at which the unfortunate woman was murdered.

Morris Eagle, one of the members of the club, left Berner-street at about 12 o'clock and after taking a friend home returned to the club at 20 minutes to 1 with the intention of having supper. He walked up the yard and entered the club by the side entrance, but neither saw nor heard anything to make him suspect any foul play.

Another member of the club, a Russian named Joseph Lave, went down into the court about 20 minutes before the body was discovered. He strolled into the street and returned to the concert room without having encountered anything unusual.

During the day there were many persons at the mortuary, but up to 3 o'clock, none had succeeded in identifying the body.

Mr. Wynne Baxter, the Coroner of the district, was communicated with as soon as the details were ascertained, and he has fixed the inquest for to-day at 11 o'clock at the Vestry-hall, Cable-street.

It is believed in police circles that the murderer was disturbed at his work by the arrival of Diemschütz, and that he made off as soon as he heard the cart at the top of the street.

Sir Charles Warren, and Major Smith, of the City Police, visited the scene of the murder in the course of the morning.

The following description has been circulated by the police of a man said to have been seen with the deceased during Saturday evening:—"Age 28. Slight. Height 5ft. 8in. Complexion dark. No whiskers. Black diagonal coat. Hard felt hat. Collar and tie. Carried newspaper parcel. Respectable appearance."

Mrs. Mortimer, living at 36, Berners-street, four doors from the scene of the tragedy, has made the following statement:—"I was standing at the door of my house nearly the whole time between half-past 12 and 1 o'clock on Sunday morning, and did not notice anything unusual. I had just gone indoors and was preparing to go to bed when I heard a commotion outside, and immediately ran out, thinking that there was a row at the Socialists' club close by. I went to see what was the matter, and was informed that another dreadful murder had been committed in the yard adjoining the club-house, and on going inside I saw the body of a woman lying huddled up just inside the gates with her throat cut from ear to ear. A man touched her face and said it was quite warm, so that the deed must have been done while I was standing at the door of my house. There was certainly no noise made, and I did not observe any one enter the gates. It

was just after 1 o'clock when I went out, and the only man I had seen pass through the street previously was a young man carrying a black, shiny bag, who walked very fast down the street from the Commercial-road. He looked up at the club and then went round the corner by the Board school."

Charles Letchford, living at 30, Berners-street, says:—"I passed through the street at half-past 12 o'clock, and everything seemed to me to be going on as usual, and my sister was standing at the door at ten minutes to 1, but did not see any one pass by. I heard the commotion when the body was found."

Dr. Blackwell made a statement yesterday in which he said that about ten minutes past 1 in the morning he was called by a policeman to 40, Berners-street, where he found the body of the murdered woman. Her head had almost been severed from the body; the body was perfectly warm, and life could not have been extinct for more than 20 minutes. He had no doubt the same man committed both the murders. In his opinion the man is a maniac. His belief was that as the woman held the sweets in her left hand, her head was dragged back by means of a silk handkerchief which she wore round her neck, and that her throat was then cut. One of the woman's hands was smeared with blood, and this was evidently done in the struggle. He had, however, no doubt that the woman's windpipe being completely cut through, she was thus rendered unable to make a sound.

Shortly before 1 o'clock yesterday morning, or about three-quarters of an hour after the crime described above, it was discovered that a second woman had been horribly murdered and mutilated, this being in Mitre-square, Aldgate, within the City boundaries, but on the confines of the now notorious district.

It appears that Police-constable Watkins (No. 881), of the City Police, was going round his beat when, turning his lantern upon the darkest corner of Mitre-square, he saw the body of a woman, apparently lifeless, in a pool of blood. He at once blew his whistle, and several persons being attracted to the spot he despatched messengers for medical and police aid.

Inspector Collard, who was in command at the time at Bishopsgate Police-station, but a short distance off, quickly arrived, followed a few moments after by Mr. G. W. Sequeira, surgeon, of 34, Jewry-street, and Dr. Gordon Brown, the divisional police doctor, of Finsbury-circus.

The scene then disclosed was a most horrible one. The woman, who was apparently about 40 years of age, was lying on her back quite dead, although the body was still warm. Following the plan in the Whitechapel murders, the miscreant was not content with merely killing his victim, but had dreadfully mutilated her.

The officer who found the body is positive that it could not have been there more than a quarter of an hour before he discovered it. He is timed to "work his beat," as it is called, in from ten to 15 minutes. The police theory is that the man and woman who had met in Aldgate watched the policeman pass round the square, and then entered it for an immoral purpose.

The throat of the woman having been cut the murderer hurriedly proceeded to mutilate the body. The wounds do not appear to have been caused so skilfully and deliberately as in the case of the murder of Annie Chapman in Hanbury-street. Five minutes, some of the doctors think, would have sufficed for the completion of the murderer's work, and he was thus enabled to leave the ground before the return of the policeman on duty.

None of the police on duty early yesterday morning appear to have had particular attention drawn to the man and woman together, and this appears strange at first when it is remarked that within the last few weeks the police have been keeping a particularly keen watch upon suspicious couples. The murderer probably avoided much blood-staining on account of the woman being on the ground at the time of the outrage; and leaving the square by either of the courts, he would be able to pass quickly away through the many narrow thoroughfares without exciting observation.

But one of the most extraordinary incidents in connexion with the crime is that not the slightest scream or noise was heard. A watchman is employed at one of the warehouses in the square, and in a direct line, but a few yards away, on the other side of the square, a City policeman was sleeping. Many people would be about in the immediate neigh-bourhood even at this early hour making preparations for the market which takes place every Sunday in Middlesex-street (formerly Petticoat-lane) and the adjacent thoroughfares.

Taking everything into account, therefore, the murder must be pronounced one of extraordinary daring and brutality. The effect it has had upon the residents in the east of London is extraordinary.

A man named Albert Barkert[78] has made the following statement:—"I was in the Three Nuns Hotel, Aldgate, on Saturday night, when a man got into conversation with me. He asked me questions which now appear to me to have some bearing upon the recent murders. He wanted to know whether I knew what sort of loose women used the public bar at that house, when they usually left the street outside, and where they were in the habit of going. He asked further questions, and from his manner seemed to be up to no good purpose. He appeared to be a shabby genteel sort of man, and was dressed in black clothes. He wore a black felt hat and carried a black bag. We came out together at closing time (12 o'clock), and I left him outside Aldgate Railway Station."

—

Messrs. George Lusk and Joseph Aarons, writing from 1, 2, and 3, Alderney-road, Mile-end, September 29, on behalf of the Whitechapel Vigilance Committee, who comm-unicated without result with the Home Secretary with the view of obtaining, on behalf of the public at large, the offer of a Government reward for the apprehension and conviction of the assassin or assassins in the recent East-end atrocities, say:—

"We shall be glad if you will allow us to state that the committee do not for one moment doubt the sincerity of the Home Secretary in refusing the said offer, as he apparently believes that it would not meet with a successful result. If he would, however, consider that in the case of the Phoenix Park murders the man Carey, who was surrounded by, we may say, a whole society steeped in crime, the money tempted him to betray his associates, in our opinion, if Mr. Matthews could see his way clear to coincide with our views, the Government offer would be successful.

---

[78] Albert Bachert.

# Monday, 1 October, 1888

The reward should be ample for securing the informer from revenge, which would be a very great inducement in the matter, in addition to which such offer would convince the poor and humble residents of our East-end that the Government authorities are as much anxious to avenge the blood of these unfortunate victims as they were the assassination of Lord F. Cavendish and Mr. Burke."[79]

---

### THE EAST-END.
### TO THE EDITOR OF THE TIMES.

Sir,—"One Who Knows" is perfectly right when he tells your readers that the police must act before the philanthropist can step in. But in my humble opinion he might with equal justice go a little further and say that the House of Commons should act besides, and that quickly.

It is an acknowledged fact that wherever overcrowding exists it is the origin of all evil. Crime, misery, filth, and degradation are the outcome, and we well know that the sweating system fattens on this wretched fabric. Why can we not grapple with it successfully? The answer to this is, vested interests forbid it. A lodging-house in a congested district to these house-jobbers is a sure fortune. Shylock has but to send his collector round (and the more hardened is the man's conscience the better business man is he considered), and sums like 5s. 6d. a week for each room in a house, and 3s. 6d. a week for the cellar den in it, are wrung out of England's white slaves.

To make the lot of the latter more bitter still, Bismark's destitute Polish Jews have been flung in broadcast to fight the battle of life out with them. It is a positive fact that members of local authorities who have self-interest in this slave trade serve on the local boards, lending no doubt an *otium cum dignitate*[80] to their proceedings. But, I ask, was there ever such a shameless farce played out on those least able to protect themselves? Why should overcrowding be allowed to put a premium on property?

But such is the state of the law at present. I maintain that compensation should only be calculated on the base of the capacity of a house and not on the numbers actually living in it. It was to meet this glaring fraud on the public (for it prevents better houses from being built and lower rents charged) that I brought in a Bill at the commencement of this Session to further amend the law relating to the dwellings of the working classes.

The Government, I regret to say, still hold their hand, although I have received from all sides of the House of Commons the greatest sympathy and support. I have not withdrawn this Bill, and I do not mean to; but if the public would only come forward and give me their support I feel confident that the best part of my Bill would be on the Statute-book by Christmas.

As I plead for a population in our midst as large as Wales and as loyal too, and whose only crime is their poverty, I trust it will not be considered that I have said anything on their behalf one whit too strong.

I remain, Sir, your obedient servant,
HENRY BRUDENELL BRUCE.[81]
September 29.

---

### TO THE EDITOR OF THE TIMES.

Sir,—Will you allow me to ask a question of your correspondents who want to disperse the vicious inhabitants of Dorset-street and Flower and Dean-street? There are no lower streets in London, and, if they are driven out of these, to what streets are they to go?

The horror and excitement caused by the murder of the four Whitechapel outcasts imply a universal belief that they had a right to life. If they had, then they had the further right to hire shelter from the bitterness of the English night. If they had no such right, then it was, on the whole, a good thing that they fell in with unknown surgical genius. He, at all events, has made his contribution towards solving, "the problem of clearing the East-end of its vicious inhabitants."

---

[79] 6 May, 1882, Lord Frederick Cavendish, newly appointed Chief Secretary for Ireland, and Permanent Under-Secretary Thomas Henry Burke were knifed to death in Phoenix Park, Dublin by members of the Irish National Invincibles.

[80] **Otium cum dignitate.** Lat. Leisure with dignity, i.e., useful retirement. Cicero, Pro Sestio (For Sestius).

[81] **Henry Augustus Brudenell-Bruce, 5th Marquess of Ailesbury** (1842-1911). 3rd son of Ernest Brudenell-Bruce, 3rd Marquess of Ailesbury in Buckingham. MP for Chippenham 1886-1892. Inherited the title after the death of his nephew in 1894.

# Monday, 1 October, 1888

The typical "Annie Chapman" will always find someone in London town to let her have a "doss" for a consideration. If she is systematically "dispersed," two results will follow. She will carry her taint to streets hitherto untainted, and she herself will be mulcted[82] in larger sums than before for the accommodation. The price of a doss will rise from 8d. to 10d. or a shilling, the extra pennies representing an insurance fund against prosecution and disturbance. Are these the sort of results that the Rev. Samuel Barnett is working for?

If vestries seem apathetic in the matter of systematic dispersal, it often is because they know that the demand for action is nothing but an astute manoeuvre on the part of a house monger, who is anxious (to use the words of one of your correspondents) that the property should become "purchasable at a fair price."

I am, Sir, your obedient servant,
E. FAIRFIELD.
64, South Eaton-place, S.W.

—

**TO THE EDITOR OF THE TIMES.**

Sir,—I beg to suggest the organization of a small force of plain-clothes constables mounted on bicycles for the rapid and noiseless patrolling of streets and roads by night.

Your obedient servant,
FRED WELLESLEY.[83]
Merton Abbey, Merton, Surrey, Sept. 30.

—

At Lambeth during the week many applications have been made to the magistrate with regard to threats used by husbands against their wives. In the majority of these cases the complainants said the threats used by the husbands were, "I'll Whitechapel you," and in some cases the words uttered were, "Look out for Leather Apron." Mr. Chance remarked on Saturday that such observations were becoming very common and granted in several cases summonses against offenders.

~

---

[82] **Mulct**. Deprive of something by penalty or trickery. (Morehead)

[83] **Frederick Arthur Wellesley** (b. 1844). His father, Henry Wellesley, 1st Earl Cowley, was the nephew of Arthur Wellesley, 1st Duke of Wellington.

## The Star
### WHAT WE THINK.

THE terror of Whitechapel has walked again, and this time has marked down two victims, one hacked and disfigured beyond discovery, the other with her throat cut and torn. Again he has got away clear; and again the police, with wonderful frankness, confess that they have not a clue. They are waiting for a seventh and an eighth murder, just as they waited for a fifth, to help them to it.

Meanwhile, Whitechapel is half mad with fear. The people are afraid even to talk with a stranger. Notwithstanding the repeated proofs that the murderer has but one aim, and seeks but one class in the community, the spirit of terror has got fairly abroad, and no one knows what steps a practically defenceless community may take to protect itself or avenge itself on any luckless wight[84] who may be taken for the enemy. It is the duty of journalists to keep their heads cool, and not inflame men's passions when what is wanted is cool temper and clear thinking; and we shall try and write calmly about this new atrocity.

And, first, let us examine the facts, and the light they throw on any previous theories. To begin with it is clear that the BURKE and HARE theory is all but destroyed. There is no suggestion of surgical neatness, or of the removal of any organ, about the Mitre-square murder. It is a ghastly butchery—done with insane ruthlessness and violence.

The gang theory is also weakened, and the story of a man who is said to have seen the Berner-street tragedy, and declares that one man butchered and another man watched, is, we think, *a priori* incredible.

The theory of madness is on the other hand enormously strengthened. Crafty blood-thirst is written on every line of Sunday morning's doings, the rapid walk from Berner-street to Aldgate, to find a fresh victim, the reckless daring of the deed—in itself the most dangerous and cunning of all the murderer's resources—these all point to some epileptic outbreak of homicidal mania. The immediate motive need not trouble us now, except so far as it suggests the invariable choice of the poor street-

---

[84] **Wight**. (Archaic) A person. (Morehead)

# Monday, 1 October, 1888

wanderers of the East-end.

It may be, as Dr. SAVAGE supposes, a plan of fiendish revenge for fancied wrongs, or the deed of some modern Thug[85] or Sicarius,[86] with a confused idea of putting down vice by picking off unfortunates in detail. A slaughterer or a butcher who has been in a lunatic asylum, a mad medical student with a bad history behind him or a tendency to religious mania—these are obviously classes on which the detective sense which all of us possess in some measure should be kept. Finally, there is the off-chance—too horrible almost to contemplate—that we have a social experimentalist abroad determined to make the classes see and feel how the masses live.

More important is the discussion as to the possible methods of the murderer. Granting that he has some rough knowledge of anatomy, it is probable that his hands only would be smeared by his bloody work, and that after doing the deed he would put on gloves. He must have done so in order to ensnare the second woman—if, indeed, the two deeds were the work of one hand. As a further precaution there might be the donning of an overcoat after the deed. As he nowhere stays to wash his hands,

he probably does not inhabit lodging-houses or hotels, but a private house where he has special facilities—perhaps chemicals and a wash-hand stand communicating directly with a pipe—for get-ting rid of bloody hands and clothes. He must be inoffensive, probably respectable in manner and appearance, or else after the murderous warnings of last week, woman after woman could not have been decoyed by him. Two theories are suggested to us—that he may wear woman's clothes, or may be a policeman.

And now for the remedies. The police, of course, are helpless. We expect nothing of them. The metropolitan force is rotten to the core, and it is a mildly farcical comment on the hopeless unfitness of Sir CHARLES WARREN that when red-handed crime is stalking the streets he has assigned his men the fresh duty of sharing with providence the looking after drunken men.

But there is one scandal about this business so gross as to cry to Heaven. Mr. MATT-HEWS—"helpless, heedless, useless" Mr. MATTHEWS as the *Telegraph* calls him to-day—is philandering with pot-house[87] Tories at Birmingham while GOD'S poor are being slaughtered wholesale in London. Where is this man, and what is he doing? He must be sternly interpellated[88] in Parliament.

As to the men under him and Sir CHARLES WARREN'S directions, they could have done one thing which might even now have caught the murderer. They might yesterday morning have drawn a cordon round the Hanbury-street district—which is plainly the Thug's head-quarters—searched every nook and cranny, and examined every suspicious character.

Meanwhile, we suggest (1) more Vigilance Committees, (2) the shadowing of East-end unfortunates, (3) further rewards. Further, there must be an agitation against Sir CHARLES WARREN, who is now beginning his old bad

---

[85] **Thug**. From the Hindi *Thag* (thief). The Thuggee were originally a sect of professional assassins in India. Followers of the Hindu goddess Kali, they would move around in bands, joining caravans and groups of travellers and pretend to befriend them. After gaining their companions trust, the Thugs would strike. Taking them by surprise, the Thugs would throw a noose or knotted handkerchief around their necks and strangle them, then secretly bury the bodies or toss them in a nearby well. In the 1830's the British began a maximum effort to eradicate the Thugs. It is believed that the Thuggee, as an organized entity, were wiped out by the 1870's. It has been estimated that over their 150 year history the Thugs may have murdered more than a million people. One interesting fact about this organization is that many of the members were Muslims. The plot of the 1939 movie version of Kipling's poem Gunga Din revolves around an expedition against the Thugs.

[86] **Sicarius**. Pl. **Sicarii**. Lat. Dagger-man, from **Sica** (dagger, Knife) assassin, murderer. In the years leading up to the Great Jewish Revolt (66-73 AD) against Rome, the Sicarii were a Judaean resistance group that assassinated Roman civilians, soldiers and officials using concealed sicae.

[87] **Pot-House (or Shop)**. A beer-shop, a Lush-crib (q.v.); pot-house (or coffee-house) politician, an ignorant, irresponsible spouter of politics (Farmer)

[88] **Interpellate**. To question (a member of the government) on a point of government policy, often interrupting the business of the day. 1590s, from Latin interpellatus, past participle of interpellare "to interrupt by speaking" (Collins English Dictionary-Complete and Unabridged)

191

work of breaking up, or allowing paid Tory roughs to break up, the meetings of the unemployed in Hyde-park, and detaching more men from regular police and detective duty to political work.

Above all, let us impress the moral of this awful business on the consciences and the fears of the West-end. The cry of the East-end is for light—the electric light to flash into the dark corners of its streets and alleys, the magic light of sympathy and hope to flash into the dark corners of wrecked and marred lives.

Unless these and other things come, White-chapel will smash the Empire, and the best thing that can happen to us is for some purified Republic of the West to step in and look after the fragments.

—

## THE CONDUCT OF THE POLICE.
### What the Public May Fairly Expect of Them.

We have dealt in our leader columns with some aspects of the Whitechapel tragedies. There are others which command attention. It is necessary that when the conduct of the police comes in question we should know precisely what steps have hitherto been taken to detect the murderer. The carelessness of the police in neglecting some obvious precautions is marked. Bloodhounds ought to have been kept in readiness after the first two or three crimes, and should certainly have been used yesterday morning. No attempt was made to employ them, or to draw a cordon of police around the Hanbury-street district, which seems to be the habitat of the murderer.

There are several questions pressing themselves to the front: (1) whether extra patrol work has been really undertaken; (2) whether the senseless system of "fixed points," by which constables instead of ranging over a given area are kept at certain stations, has been modified in view of the special circumstances of the case; (3) whether any efficient detective work of the higher order has been set on foot; (4) whether the advice of French and American detectives, who are far better organised and trained for the detection of crime than our own, has been taken.

It is obvious that the danger in Whitechapel is on the increase every day. It is already more than probable that the murderer has found imitators. The manner of the deed at Gateshead, if not the actual murder, was probably suggested by the Whitechapel horrors. As the nights grow darker and longer the facilities for murderous action will become enormously increased, and it is only fair to the police to say that their difficulties will grow also. The question to which the citizens of London will expect an answer is, whether steps are being taken to cope with so serious a problem.

Meanwhile another suggestion presents itself. Our reporters testify that the conduct of the City police offers the most marked and welcome contrast to that of the Metropolitan force. The men of the latter body are churlish, uncommunicative, and in some cases deliberately deceitful. The City force, which is in some shadowy form under popular control is civil, communicative, and helpful to the press. The question is whether some steps cannot be taken to give effect to the almost unanimous voice of public opinion against the management of the Metropolitan Police. The outcry against the Warren *regime* will gain a sensible volume this morning. The *Daily Telegraph* renews its pressing call on Lord Salisbury to force on the resignation of Mr. Matthews; and the *Observer*, another Unionist organ, remarked yesterday, *apropos* of Sir Charles Warren's new instructions to the police to keep a sharp look out on drunken people in order to find out the publicans who served them with drink, that "the goose-step, a mongrel military drill, and prayer meetings, under the new *regime*, exhaust the leisure of the most vigorous and versatile constable." The fact is, of course, that the policeman on his beat has really too much to do, and is taken up with a variety of duties which have nothing to do with the detection and pursuit of crime. It is time that these duties should be taken off the hands of constables, and the men set free for police work pure and simple.

The agitation against the heads of the Metropolitan Police, therefore, is growing, and the question is whether some means cannot be taken to give it shape. A rough plébiscite of the people of London, taken on the question whether or not Sir Charles Warren should be dismissed, might possibly be organised. We throw out the suggestion, and shall be glad to have developments of the idea.

Meanwhile, another question presents itself. With the failure of the Detective Department one naturally asks whether, in addition to the

# Monday, 1 October, 1888

protection of unfortunates by Vigilance Committees, some superior detective work cannot be undertaken by a few men of leisure, of education, and with some innate aptitude for the work. Surely some call of the kind might be responded to. The work done by Vigilance Committees in regard to the social evil suggests a machinery at hand, and possibly a fit *personnel* for the task.

### A Contrast.

As illustrating the different treatment extended to the Press by the City and the Metropolitan Police—the obliging courtesy on the one hand, and the insulting curtness on the other—we give the following two little interviews.

| | |
|---|---|
| Our reporter asked the inspector in charge of the men guarding 40, Berner-street, a few simple questions:— | Our reporter called along with a colleague at Bishops-gate Police Station, in order to get a description of the other murdered woman. |
| "Can you tell me the exact time that the police first heard of the murder?" | "Gentlemen of the Press, I presume" said Inspector Izzard, as he entered. |
| Inspector: "No." | "Yes, they have |
| "Do you know whether the constable on the beat looks down the yard as he passes?" | called to ask if they may have a description of the body," explained the |
| Inspector: "I don't know." | Sergeant on duty. |
| "Do you know where the body was taken?" | "By all means," said the Inspector, "we shall be only too pleased to give them any information." |
| Inspector: "To the mortuary, I suppose." | |
| And so on. The intelligent Inspector actually knew where the body was taken— or rather supposed he did. | |

Every facility is afforded the pressmen at Bishopsgate-street Station, and scant courtesy shown them at Leman-street.

—

## WHITECHAPEL.
## THE MURDER MANIC SACRIFICES MORE WOMEN TO HIS THIRST FOR BLOOD.
## TWO VICTIMS THIS TIME.
## BOTH WOMEN SWIFTLY AND SILENTLY BUTCHERED IN LESS THAN AN HOUR.
### One Woman's Throat Cut and the Other Victim Disfigured and Disembowelled —Interviews with the Men who Found the Murdered Women—Sketches and Scenes in the Streets—Descriptions of the Victims —Supposed Clues and Arrests.

The series of blood-chilling tragedies which have shocked the public mind and sent a thrill of horror throughout the land, have been crowned by murder more foul than any of the former crimes. Two more poor unfortunate and degraded women have fallen victims to the knife of the hellish fiend who stalks abroad in Whitechapel leaving a track of blood behind him.

At one o'clock on Sunday morning the body of a woman is found with her throat cut in a yard in Berner-street, Commercial-road. At a quarter to two a second victim is found hacked, mutilated, and disembowelled in Mitre-square, Aldgate. Everything points to the fact that both murders were the work of the same hand—that fiendishly cunning hand, which not many weeks since struck down a woman in Osborne-street, inflicted 36 stabs on the body of another unknown and unfortunate female in George Yard, massacred Mary Ann Nicholls in Buck's-row, and butchered Annie Chapman in Hanbury-street.

And the present crimes only differ from the preceding in the more daring and damnable manner in which they were committed, and in the more atrocious way in which one woman has been mutilated. Here in Berner-street, in a yard through which people were passing every few minutes, close to the door of a room where a dance is taking place, a woman is found almost decapitated. Prevented from completing his hideous work of mutilation the murderer, before the blood had ceased to trickle from the throat of his first victim strikes down another in a spot where a policeman passes every twelve minutes, and goes away unseen, unheard, and unknown, thwarting the efforts of the police and the vigilance of the panic-stricken inhabitants.

Below we give full descriptions of the two tragedies, sketches of the scenes, interviews with persons who found the bodies, and all other information obtainable yesterday and this morning.

## SCENE OF THE FIRST MURDER.
### Description of the Spot—How the Murder was Committed—Identification of the Woman—Conduct of the Police.

Berner-street branches off Commercial-road a little way down on the right. It is inhabited almost entirely by Jews. It is not five minutes' walk from Hanbury-street, where the fifth victim was found. It is but two minutes' walk from Batty-street, where Mrs. Angel was murdered by Lipski last year, and in the adjoining street a few months since a man murdered a woman and then cut his own throat in the open street.

The scene of the murder was within the gateway at No. 40, which is occupied by a Jewish working men's club under the name of the International Men's Education Society. It is a building of two stories. A passage wide enough to admit a cart separates it from the next house. The members of this club are either secularists or are indifferent to the Jewish religion and

### HOWLS OF INDIGNATION
were raised against them by the faithful a fortnight ago when they held a banquet on the evening of the Day of Atonement.

There is an entrance to the club from the street, and also one from the court. The court is very small. The club building occupies one side and three dwelling-houses the other, and there are premises belonging to Walter H. Hindley and Co., sack manufacturers, and Arthur Dutfield, van and cart builder, at the further end of the court.

At night this courtyard is dark except for the light from the house windows. At the street entrance there is a large folding door, on the right half of which there is a small panel door. The large gate is supposed to be shut every night, but the small door is left open for the use of persons living in the court. It was in the passage leading to the court proper, and only three feet from the side entrance to the club that the body of the murdered woman was found.

There is a good deal of movement in this court at one o'clock in the morning, but no one seems to have heard or seen anything. Besides the club, there are three dwelling houses in the court, and the inhabitants of these were not in bed at one o'clock. A debate takes place at the club every Saturday evening, followed by a dance, and

### THE DANCE WAS IN FULL SWING
on the first floor when the murder was committed. There was a woman in the kitchen —which is only a few feet from the spot where the body was found, and several other people downstairs, but they heard nothing.

The precise spot where the woman was found lying is marked by a small splash of blood. She lay on her back, her head was near the grating of the cellar, and her body stretched across the passage. There is a severe bruise on the cheek of the unfortunate woman, which may be explained by the theory that the throat was cut while she was standing, and the body allowed to fall heavily upon its side, bringing the cheek into contact with a stone that abuts from the wall just at this point.

### THE MAN WHO FOUND THE BODY INTERVIEWED.
The first to find the body was Mr. Diemshitz, steward of the club. Interviewed by a *Star* reporter, Mr. Diemshitz said:—"I was coming home from market at one o'clock on Sunday morning. I am a traveller by trade, and go to different markets to sell my goods.

Yesterday I went to Westow-hill. As the night was so wet I did not stay quite so late as usual. After I had passed through the gate which had been left open on driving into the yard my donkey shied a little in consequence of my cart coming in contact with something on the ground. On looking down I saw the ground was not level, so I took the butt end of my whip and touched what appeared to me in the dark to be a heap of dirt lately placed there, a thing I was not accustomed to see. Not being able to move it, I struck a match and

### FOUND IT WAS A WOMAN.
First of all I thought it was my wife, but I found her inside the club enjoying herself with the others. I said to some of the members there is a woman lying in the yard, and I think she is drunk. Young Isaacs, a tailor machinist, went to the door and struck a match, and to our horror

# Monday, 1 October, 1888

we saw blood trickling down the gutter almost from the gate to the club. The dance was immediately stopped. I and Isaacs ran out for a policeman, but could not find one after traversing several streets, but in the meantime another man from the Club, Eagle, ran to the Leman-street police-station and fetched two policemen, who arrived about seven minutes after the discovery.

### The Unfortunate Victim.

The woman was about 30 years of age. Her hair is very dark, with a tendency to curl, and her complexion is also dark. Her features are sharp and somewhat pinched, as though she had endured considerable privations recently—an impression confirmed by the entire absence of the kind of ornaments commonly affected by women of her station.

She wore a rusty black dress of a cheap kind of satteen, with a velveteen bodice, over which was a black diagonal worsted jacket with fur trimming. Her bonnet, which had fallen from her head when she was found in the yard, was of black crape, and inside, apparently with the object of making the article fit close to the head, was folded a copy of a newspaper.

In her right hand were tightly clasped some grapes, and in her left she held a number of sweetmeats.

Both the jacket and the bodice were open towards the top, but in other respects the clothes were not disarranged. The linen was clean and in tolerably good repair, but some articles were missing.

The cut in the woman's throat which was the cause of death was evidently effected with a very sharp instrument, and was made with

### ONE SHARP INCISION.

The weapon was apparently drawn across the throat rather obliquely from left to right, and in its passage it severed both the windpipe and jugular vein. As the body lies in the mortuary the head seems to be almost severed, the gash being about 3in. long and nearly the same depth.

In the pocket of the woman's dress were discovered two pocket-handkerchiefs, a gentleman's and a lady's, a brass thimble, and a skein of black darning worsted.

Dr. Blackwell, the first medical man called, says,—"At about ten minutes past one I was called to 40, Berner-street by a policeman, where I found a woman who had been murdered. Her head had been almost severed from her body. She could not have been dead more than twenty minutes, the body being perfectly warm. The woman did not appear to be a Jewess, but more like an Irishwoman. I roughly examined her, and found no other injuries, but this I cannot definitely state until I have made a further investigation of the body. She had on a black velvet jacket and black dress of different material. In her hand she held a box of cachous, whilst pinned in her dress was a flower. I should say that as the woman had held sweets in her left hand that her head was dragged back by means of a silk handkerchief she wore round her neck, and her throat was then cut. One of her hands, too, was smeared with blood, so she may have used this in her rapid struggle. I have no doubt that, the woman's windpipe being completely cut through, she was unable to make any sound. I might say it does not follow that the murderer would be bespattered with blood, for as he is sufficiently cunning in other things he could contrive to avoid coming in contact with the blood by reaching well forward."

M. Rombrow is the editor of *The Worker's Friend*,[89] whose printing office is in the yard. It was just outside the door of this office that the body was found. M. Rombrow says that he was in this office all the time, and had there been the noise of any struggle, however slight, he should have heard it. He heard nothing, however, until the steward's coming into the yard.

A woman living just opposite says that she was waiting up for her husband and listening for his coming, and she heard nothing to arouse her suspicion.

Mr. Wess, a member of the club, says:—"I was in the printing office of *The Worker's Friend*, and crossed the yard to the club at a quarter-past twelve. There was nothing whatever in the yard then. I saw that the gates were open, and thought about closing them, but, remembering that our steward was out with his cart, I left them still open to allow him to come in easily."

---

[89] ***The Worker's Friend*** (Der Arbeter Fraint). Yiddish language anarchist weekly newspaper founded in 1885. Associated with the International Workers Educational Club from 1886.

# Monday, 1 October, 1888

## THE POLICEMAN UPON DUTY

in the street states that as he passed along he noticed a man and a woman talking together not far from the yard, but as that was no unusual sight at that hour took no particular notice.

The police examined everyone who was in the club. They also made a careful search of the club and took away a knife which was found in the kitchen, but which had no marks of blood on it. They then guarded the premises with their usual vigilance and would allow no one to go out or into the yard.

## INFORMATION WHICH MAY BE IMPORTANT

was given to the Leman-street police late yesterday afternoon by an Hungarian[90] concerning this murder. This foreigner was well dressed, and had the appearance of being in the theatrical line. He could not speak a word of English, but came to the police-station accompanied by a friend, who acted as an interpreter. He gave his name and address, but the police have not disclosed them.

A *Star* man, however, got wind of his call, and ran him to earth in Backchurch-lane. The reporter's Hungarian was quite as imperfect as the foreigner's English, but an interpreter was at hand, and the man's story was retold just as he had given it to the police. It is, in fact, to the effect that he

## SAW THE WHOLE THING.

It seems that he had gone out for the day, and his wife had expected to move, during his absence, from their lodgings in Berner-street to others in Backchurch-lane. When he came homewards about a quarter before one he first walked down Berner-street to see if his wife had moved. As he turned the corner from Commercial-road he noticed some distance in front of him a man walking as if partially intoxicated. He walked on behind him, and presently he noticed a woman standing in the entrance to the alley way where the body was afterwards found.

The half-tipsy man halted and spoke to her. The Hungarian saw him put his hand on her shoulder and push her back into the passage, but, feeling rather timid of getting mixed up in quarrels, he crossed to the other side of the street. Before he had gone many yards, how-

ever, he heard the sound of a quarrel, and turned back to learn what was the matter, but just as he stepped from the kerb

## A SECOND MAN CAME OUT

of the doorway of the public-house a few doors off, and shouting out some sort of warning to the man who was with the woman, rushed forward as if to attack the intruder. The Hungarian states positively that he saw a knife in this second man's hand, but he waited to see no more. He fled incontinently, to his new lodgings.

He described

## THE MAN WITH THE WOMAN

as about 30 years of age, rather stoutly built, and wearing a brown moustache. He was dressed respectably in dark clothes and felt hat.

The man who came at him with a knife he also describes, but not in detail. He says he was taller than the other, but not so stout, and that his moustaches were red. Both men seem to belong to the same grade of society.

The police have arrested one man answering the description the Hungarian furnishes. This prisoner has not been charged, but is held for inquiries to be made. The truth of the man's statement is not wholly accepted.

### Description of a Suspect.

Another man was, however, seen in the company of a woman by someone only a short time before the commission of the crime, and this is the description which the police have of him:—Aged about 28, and in height 5ft. 8in. or thereabouts; complexion dark, and wearing a black diagonal coat and hard felt hat, collar and tie. He was of respectable appearance, and was carrying a newspaper parcel.

### The Identification.

Late last night a well-known character, known as "One-armed Liz," recognised the woman as a frequenter of the Flower and Dean-street lodging-houses. She was also identified by John Arundell and Charles Preston, who knew her as lodging at No. 32 in that street. She was known by more names than one, but commonly as "Long Liz," though her true name is said to be Elizabeth Stride.

She left Flower and Dean-street between six and seven o'clock on Saturday night. She then said she was not going to meet anyone in particular.

---

[90] Israel Schwartz.

Stride is believed to be a Swedish woman from Stockholm. According to her associates, she was of calm temperament, rarely quarrelling with anyone; in fact, she was so good-natured that she would "do a good turn for any one." Her occupation was that of a charwoman. She had the misfortune to lose her husband in the Princess Alice disaster[91] on the Thames some years ago. She had lost her teeth, and suffered from a throat infection.

—

## THE SECOND TRAGEDY.
### Ghastly Mutilation—A Sickening Sight—Interviews with Doctors and the Policeman who found the Body.

Mitre-square, the scene of the second tragedy, is off Mitre-street. It is approachable by three thoroughfares—by narrow entrances from St. James's-place, Duke-street, and by Mitre-street, and in the daytime is the scene of much commercial activity. There are two dwelling-houses in the square, one of which is occupied by a day policeman. He was in bed at the time.

It was in this square, and in the darkest corner of it, that the second outrage was perpetrated. And it must have been done quickly, as it was done surely, for a policeman passes through the square every quarter of an hour. Police-constable Watkins, the man in question, was on duty there, and no more conscientious officer is in the force. His inspector speaks of him in the highest terms.

He was on duty on the same beat last night, and a *Star* man went carefully over the same ground covered by him on the preceding night. "I was working left-handed last night," said the police officer. "Sometimes I go into Mitre-square through the Church-passage, but last night I entered from Mitre-street. It was just half-past one when I turned out of Aldgate and passed round the next corner into the square. At that time there was nothing unusual to be seen." I looked carefully in all the corners, as I always do,

---

[91] **Princess Alice Disaster.** (3 Sept., 1878) The Thames excursion steamer SS *Princess Alice* was rammed by the collier *Bywell Castle* while returning to London from a day trip to Gravesend. As children were not required to have tickets, the exact number of people aboard that day is unknown, but it is thought that there were between 750 and 800 passengers. At least 600 were killed. (Gilpin)

## TURNING MY LANTERN

light in every direction. I am positive there was nothing wrong at that time."

"And when did you pass through the square again?" asked the reporter.

"At about a quarter before two."

"Had you met any person on your rounds?"

"Not a soul."

"Nor heard any noise?"

"Not a sound, but the echo of my own footsteps."

"You entered the square the same way?"

"Just the same. Here we are now at the entrance to the square. I came this way, stopped at this corner to look up and down the street, and then turned in. As I came to the back of this picture frame maker's I turned my light into the corner, and there lay the woman."

"Did you recognise the situation at once?"

"Well, I can tell you it didn't take me a moment to see that the Whitechapel murderer had been our way. Her head lay here on this coal-hole," said he, throwing the light of his lantern on it, "and her clothes were thrown up breast-high. But the first thing I noticed was that she was ripped up like a pig in the market. There was the big gash up the stomach, the entrails torn out and flung in a heap about her neck; some of them appeared to be lying in the ugly cut at the throat, and the face—well, there was no face. Anyone who knew the woman alive would never recognise her by her face. I have been in the force a long while, but I never saw such a sight. I went at once to Dr. Sequeira and some of the others rushed off to the station house."

"Were there any signs of a struggle?"

"None at all. There was perhaps a quart of blood on the stones, but there were no footprints or finger marks, except where the woman's chemise had been caught hold of as if it had fallen down in the way. Her clothing was filthy."

### The Night Watchman's Story.

The *Star* man next got hold of Morris, the watchman at Kearley and Tonge's. He was standing at the door, and said, first, that he had just been through the warehouse and had gone to the front door to look out into the square two moments before Watkins called to him last night.

"Do you always take a look out into the square?"

"Every night in the week, barring Saturday night, I stand at this door and smoke my pipe from one till two o'clock. It is a habit with me, and the police on the beat know it well, but on Saturday nights I have some work to do inside that interferes with it."

"Did you see anything lying about that indicated what sort of man the murderer might be?"

"I saw the doctor pick up two studs out of the pool of blood and put them in the shell."

"But are there any signs of a struggle having taken place?"

"No, but the studs might have been worked out by the man's own exertions in using the knife."

### Other Statements by Neighbours.

P.C. Pearce, who lives at No. 3, opposite where the body was found, slept the while calmly, and his wife shared both his bed and his composure. She had left a light burning in the first floor front, and the blind was halfway up, a fact that could hardly have escaped the notice of anyone entering the square. "I only wish it had been my luck to have dropped on that chap," was the way Pearce put it to the *Star* man, "but, to tell you the truth, I knew nothing about it till I was waked up this morning."

Just through the north-east passage is the fire brigade station, and none of those on duty saw or heard anything unusual, so quietly was the deed committed, and so carefully did the man make his exit.

Mr. Klapp is a caretaker of the business premises, which are approached from the court where the body was found by a wooden gateway. The lower portion of the premises are used for business purposes, but the second floor back rooms contain three windows looking down over the low wall and palisade upon the scene of the murder.

Mrs. Lindsay, who occupies the two front rooms of 11, Duke-street—almost opposite Church-passage, leading to the court —records a strange circumstance, which may or may not have a direct bearing upon the murder. She says that she is a very light sleeper, and is easily awakened by hearing any unusual noise. Early on Sunday morning she says—at what hour she could not specify—she heard the sound of one or two voices in the street below. Prompted by curiosity she looked out of the window just in time to hear a man's voice say, "I am

### NOT THE MURDERER,"

uttered apparently in a tone of anger. Surprised on hearing the words, she called her husband, who, with her, saw a man disappearing down the street towards Aldgate. As he passed beneath a lamp she was able to discern that he was a man of average height, dressed in dark clothes, and carrying in his hand an umbrella and a small parcel.

### A Couple Asked After.

James Blenkingsop, who was on duty as a watchman in St. James's-place (leading to the square), where some street improvements are taking place, states that about half-past one a respectably-dressed man came up to him and said, "Have you seen a man and a woman go through here?" "I didn't take any notice," returned Blenkingsop. "I have seen some people pass." The murdered woman was found lying on her back, and presented

### A HORRIBLE AND SICKENING SIGHT.

Her head was lying on the right side. He left leg was extended and her right doubled up. Both arms were extended. The throat was cut half round. There was a large gash running from the nose on a right angle to the right cheek, the bone of which was bare. The other cheek was also cut. The nose was hacked off and only hung by a shred of skin. The right ear was likewise cut off. There was a cut underneath each eye and the lips were cut. The clothes had been pulled up, the abdomen ripped open, and the puberic bone left completely bare. As in the case of Annie Chapman part of the intestines were pulled out and thrown over the woman's neck.

### NO PART OF THE BODY WAS MISSING.

The following is a description of the murdered woman—Age 40, hazel eyes, auburn hair; dressed in a black jacket, with fur trimming and large metal buttons, dark green chintz with Michaelmas daisies[92] and golden lily pattern skirt, drab linsey underskirt, blue-

---

[92] **Michaelmas Daisy.** The blue European Aster *Amellus* gets its name because it blooms at about the time of the Catholic feast of Saint Michael the Archangel, Sept. 29.

ribbed stockings, mended white; black straw bonnet trimmed with black beads and green and black velvet.

### A Bloody Apron Found.

After committing the second murder, the man seems to have gone back towards the scene of the former. An apron, which is thought by the police to belong to the woman found in Mitre-square, as it was the same material as part of her dress was found in Goldstar-street. It was smeared with blood, and had been evidently carried away by the murderer to wipe his hands with.

One of the doctors in an interview with a *Star* reporter, after describing the various wounds, said the woman belonged to the very poorest class. She appeared to be an outcast, and carried her tea and sugar about with her. She was very thin. "I should say, from the fact that her hands were brown, that she had just come from the country—had been hop picking, perhaps. I think she was an Irish woman."

"Does the form of her features make you think so?"

"No, but because

### SHE CARRIED A PIPE."

"The woman's throat," continued the doctor, "had first been cut, and it had been cut while the woman was on the ground."

"How do I know that?"

"Because there was no blood in front."

"Do you think that the murderer was a skilled man?"

"He had some knowledge of how to use a knife. The knife which he used must have been very sharp."

"How long would it have taken him to mutilate the body as you found it?"

"At least five minutes."

The murderer must have, therefore, entered the square about five minutes after the policeman had passed through, and left it five minutes before he returned.

The clothing of the woman was very thin and bare. No money was found upon her, but the following articles were in the pockets of her dress:—A short clay pipe and an old cigarette case; a matchbox, an old pocket handkerchief, a knife which bore no traces of blood, and a small packet of tea and sugar, such as poor people who frequent common lodging-houses are in the habit of carrying.

A *Star* reporter saw Dr. J. G. Sequiera, 34, Jewry-street, who was the first medical man on the spot. "I was there," he said, "about 10 minutes after the policeman found the body. The woman could not have been dead more than a quarter of an hour. The work had been quickly done."

"By an expert, do you think?"

"No, not by an expert, but by a man who was not altogether ignorant of the use of the knife. It would have taken about three minutes."

—

### The Action of the Police.

Policemen and detectives swarmed in every corner of Whitechapel yesterday. Intelligence of the first murder was telegraphed to Scotland-yard. Chief Inspector Swanson and Inspector Abberline at once commenced investigations. **SIR CHARLES WARREN HIMSELF** visited Whitechapel early in the forenoon. The other murder was committed within the jurisdiction of the City Police, and Acting-Commissioner Major Henry Smith was soon on the scene. He was directing the investigations by Inspector Tizzard, Inspector Collard, and Superintendent Foster. The City police, from the Major downwards, try to oblige the representatives of the Press rather than to frustrate them in their inquiries, like Sir Charles Warren's.

—

### The Vigilance Committee.

The Vigilance Committee which was recently formed to try and hunt down the murderer, have gathered a great deal of information which may be useful to the police. The greatest indignation prevails amongst the Committee at what they regard as the apathy of the Home Secretary in face of these appalling outrages. When, after the fourth murder, Mr. Matthews was asked to offer a reward for the apprehension of the criminal, he replied, through his secretary, that the "Secretary of State is satisfied that there is nothing in the present case to justify a departure from the rule" not to offer any reward as from the Government.

The committee have now subscriptions amounting to £300, and in addition to this Mr. Montagu, M.P., has offered £100 as a reward and the same sum has been offered by the *Police News*. Mr. Lusk, the chairman of the committee, has sent a petition to the Queen calling Her Majesty's attention to the fact that the Home Secretary has refused to offer a reward, and asking her to "direct that a Government reward, sufficient in amount to meet the peculiar exigencies of the case, may immediately be offered."

—

## FIFTH EDITION.
## SCENES IN THE STREET.

Never did ill news travel faster than yesterday. While dwellers in other parts of the metropolis were enjoying a Sunday morning's license for lying abed, the entire East-end was in a furore of excitement. By eleven o'clock it seemed as if the entire population of the East-end was out of doors. Streams of all sorts and conditions of men poured incessantly in the direction of Berner-street and of Mitre-square. Cordons of police blocked the three entrances to the latter, but the sensation-seeking crowds seemed to gather some satisfaction from mere proximity to the spot where the curtain had last been raised on the terrible series of tragedies. The police kept up a continuous chorus of "Move on!" but no serious trouble occurred in the vicinity of Mitre-square. The greater crowd was down Berner-street way. Luckily there was an outlet at either end of this street, so the pent-up feelings of the jostled and the jostlers had time only for vent in an occasional paliasage at arms before the "move on" tactics of the police began to take effect. No one could say there were not enough police in the East-end to-day. The

**BLUE HELMETS WERE THICK AS BEES**

in a clover field, and there was a detective to about every three uniformed men on duty as well. Well known figures from Scotland-yard moved with ostensible ease in the midst of the throngs, and the heavy swells of the force were not unrepresented. Prominent among those on the spot, however, was Superintendent Foster, of the City Police. He personally superintended the preparation of the measurements and drawings of Mitre-square, which were necessary for purposes of investigation, and even paid a visit to the scene of the Berner-street tragedy, to compare the two cases. Coming back from this errand, the superintendent was the victim of

**A VERY ANNOYING CIRCUMSTANCE,**

which severely tried his stock of good humour. As he came out of Berner-street, a man in a tweed suit was seen walking by his side, and

someone in the crowd shouted out: "There they go. The super's got him. I told you he was a toff."[93] This silly remark was enough to turn the tide of attention in the direction of the officer and his companion.

The City chief and the superintendent would not take a cab, so their unsought retinue followed on till they met the tide from the other direction, and then the side streets swallowed up the surplus and the officials escaped. All day long the streets in that vicinity were full, and sunset did not find the numbers diminished.

The *Star* man started from the Bishopsgate Police-station soon after eight o'clock to make a comprehensive tour of the disturbed territory. Wending his way through the labyrinth of narrow bye-ways that leads into Spitalfields, he found himself in Hanbury-street, the scene of the most revolting of the series of crimes until Mitre-court was heard from.

Here in the midst of scenes made familiar to the readers of *The Star* were little groups of ill-clad women standing under the glare of a street lamp or huddling in a doorway talking about the all-absorbing topic of the hour. "He'll be coming through the houses and pulling us out of our beds next," says one. "Not he," says another; "he's too clever for that.

**HE CATCHES THE LATE BIRDS,**

he does." "Then he won't catch me," says the first. "I don't leave my doorway after dark." It was worthy of notice that the dark corners and gloomy passages, and they are not few in that neighbourhood, were utterly deserted last night. Here and there one encountered a company jabbering in some outlandish tongue, and a little later on there would be overheard an expression of opinion in the better-known vernacular that is more universally employed in Whitechapel.

Such a group secured the attention of a policeman on the corner while the *Star* man was there, and kept the representative of law and order unsuccessfully employed for full 15 minutes in

**GETTING A CLUE**

from a triangular statement of some home-hatched theory. Out in Brick-lane the *Star* man began to pay the penalty of having his Sunday coat on his back. Every third man he met whined out the pitiful

---

[93] **Toff**. 1. A gentleman, a fop, a swell. (Farmer)

appeal, "Give us the price of a doss, guv'nor," and followed it up with an assiduity which, if employed by the police, must long ago have resulted in the capture of the murder-master. The *Star* man was just reflecting how well this persistent begging illustrated the desperate straits these people sometimes reach, when a police officer who knew him volunteered the tip that someone in Flower and Dean-street had just been down to

### IDENTIFY THE WOMAN,

who had been murdered in Berner-street.

Down into that highly-flavoured lane went the reporter, and found no trouble in locating the identifier. The air was full of the subject, for was not the murdered woman a dweller in that very street, and was it not

### "ONE-ARMED LIZ,"

that had just given the police all necessary information? To be sure, "One-armed Liz" had good reason to be kind to the police. She occasionally fell into their hands, and needed all the mercy she could get laid up in her favour, but she had done her duty to-night, and was the heroine of the hour. "Did you want to see her? Here she is, in here."

**"ONE-ARMED LIZ,"**

The speaker led the way to one of the barrack-like lodging-houses half way down the street. "Can't you get her to step out?" asked the reporter. "Oh, you walk right in; you needn't be afraid. They are all ladies and gentlemen in there." Thus encouraged the *Star* man entered.

The door opened into a large room, of which the ceiling was so low that a Guardsman who rose from a seat between two girls to see what was to do couldn't stand upright, and the walls were black as grime and filth could make them. The floor was inches deep with dirt, and the atmosphere could have been served up with a spoon. On the benches and tables sat or squatted some half a hundred of men and women of all ages and degrees of poverty. A huge fireplace at the end of the room held a cooking apparatus, on which were displayed a score of suppers in course of preparation.

And there, in a halo of vile vapour and amid an incense of fried fish stood "One-armed Liz." She had the air of a queen as she bowed in deference to the greeting of the scribe, and she had an answer of some sort to every question. She had known Liz Stride well. She was sorry she was dead, but she would be glad if Liz's death would lead to the capture of that butcher. "One-armed Liz" made use of certain adjectives

### SUFFICIENTLY EXPRESSIVE

of how deeply she felt on the subject, but the reporter omitted to take a note of them. She did not refuse the price of her bed, nor yet did the unkempt personage who had shown the way to the house. He was outside waiting, and a character he was too. "I'm all right, guv'nor," said he; none of your "Leather Apron" style. Everybody about here knows.

While Toby was speaking a woman came along with an armful of walking sticks, each one showing that they were swordsticks of a cheap but dangerous pattern. "Here you are, now," she cried, "sixpence for a swordstick. That's the sort to do for 'em." The man of news was astounded, but Toby only smiled. "Oh!" said he; "she does a good business, she do. She's been down in Berner-street all day, and sold a lot of 'em."

Presently this good-natured native got back to the subject of his murdered neighbour.

"I didn't know this woman to talk to," continued Toby, "but I had seen her in a lodging-house where I had been at work."

"Did she have any particular follower, Toby?"

# Monday, 1 October, 1888

TOBY.

"Not her," was the answer, "she wasn't particular. I wasn't a bit surprised when I heard it was her. That sort of women are sure to get done by him."

"Then you think there is someone on the look-out for that sort?"

"Don't it look like it?" queried he.

**"WELL, WHAT SORT OF A MAN**
do you think it is?"

"Well, now, I'll tell you," said Toby, with a wise look. "It waren't none of the kind that puts up at a six-penny doss. That chap's got a room to wash himself in.

He don't live far off neither. I shouldn't be surprised if he was walking up and down in the crowd out there now. He's a cool one he is, and it would be just like him to call and see if he could identify the bodies."

Before midnight there was scarcely a woman to be seen on the streets, though the reporter found half-a-dozen taking a good night look at the dark corner in Mitre-square just before the Aldgate clock struck the hour. By this time the police cordon had been withdrawn, and a score of people only remained loitering in the square.

A keen-eyed little Jew was explaining to the half-dozen women the position the body had occupied, and was pointing out some water marks as blood stains, when the baby of one of the women began to cry. The mother, ever thoughtful of her offspring, drew the child

from beneath her shawl and brought it forward a step or two.

**"DOES IT WANT TO SEE THE BLOOD,**
bless its heart? So it shall. Take a good look at it, my pet. You may see enough of it if this sort of thing keeps up." Thus comforted, the child quieted down, and the mother walked away with her companions with an air that suggested an idea of duty performed being like a rainbow in the soul.

But the *Star* man's duty was not yet done. He wanted to see the streets of Whitechapel and Aldgate when cats and policemen ought to have them all to themselves. He wandered back toward Spitalfields, and stopped a few moments to look at the spot where the first of these terrible crimes was committed. Then he passed by the house immortalised by the arrest of Leather Apron, and finally found himself walking down Berner-street at the very moment the murderer must have covered the same ground early on Sunday morning. There was not a person in sight at the moment he passed the corner of Commercial-road.

The *Star* man had little difficulty in imagining that there was no one but a dead woman in the alley-way, and that there was a clear coast for anyone to get away from the spot without being observed. He walked briskly up to Commercial-road. A policeman across the way paid no attention to him, but two squares nearer Aldgate two officers scrutinised him closely as if to show that now at least they were wide awake. Just then a man came by with a great comforter about his neck and shoulders and his hands wrapped up in the ends. "Nobody would notice if that chap's hands were bloody—now, would they?" sagely remarked one of the officers, and the scribe made note of how safely

**THE MUFFLED INDIVIDUAL**
went on. From there to Aldgate no one was met but two cabdrivers at a coffee stall.

If the Star man had been in search of gore instead of news he need not have feared molestation as he went on to Duke-street. There was not even a policeman in sight, notwithstanding the extra force. When he had turned down through Church-passage into the square, however, he found four. He recalled the old proverb about locking the barn after the horse had been stolen. Certainly the red-hand would get a warm grip if it was stretched out there again this morning. It was now just five-and-twenty minutes of two. There were six people in the square all told, but no one was making any noise. Presently footsteps were heard coming along the narrow passage leading from the other square, and when the newcomers appeared, their blue jackets and white aprons discovered their calling at once, and one could not escape thought that here was evidence that

### SLAUGHTERERS

were not strangers to Mitre-square. Then arose a train of reasoning that might have led back to *The Star's* original theory of a slaughterman having to do with some of the earlier murders, but just then the crescent moon sailed up above the surrounding buildings, and the *Star* man resigned into her hands the duty of throwing light upon the mystery of the dark corner.

—

### More about "Long Liz."

Thomas Bates, a watchman, told a reporter that "Long Liz" had lived with them for five or six years, but her real name he never knew. She was a Swede by birth. Her husband was shipwrecked and drowned. She was a clean and hardworking woman. Her usual occupation was that of a charwoman, and it was only when driven to extremities that she walked the streets. She would at times disappear for a month or so—even as much as three months.

She returned to the house on Tuesday last, after a prolonged absence, and remained there until Saturday night. That evening she went out about seven o'clock, and she appeared to be in cheery spirits. The fact of her not returning that night was not taken any particular notice of. Their apprehensions, however, were aroused when rumours of the murders reached them.

While narrating these facts the watchman was affected, and wound up his statement by exclaiming, "Lor' bless you, when she could get no work she had to do the best she could for her living, but a neater and a cleaner woman never lived."

—

### ARRESTS AND POSSIBLE CLUES.

A little after ten o'clock last night a man whose behaviour was suspicious was arrested by a police-constable in the neighbourhood of Commercial-street, and at once taken to the police-station in that thoroughfare, where he was questioned by the inspector on duty respecting his whereabouts on Saturday night and the early hours of Sunday morning. The prisoner, however, readily furnished his name and address, and apparently had no knowledge whatever of the details of the murders. He was discharged upon his statement being verified.

At a late hour last night an arrest was made in the neighbourhood of Whitechapel, and the man taken to Leman-street, where he is still detained. At a quarter past three this morning a second man was arrested and likewise brought to Leman-street Police-station. He remains under detention. The police, presumably acting under instructions from head-quarters, decline to state either the names given by the prisoners or the circumstances which led to their arrests. There is, however, good reason to believe that so far not the slightest tangible clue has been obtained.

A man was arrested last night at a coffee shop opposite the Thurlow Arms public-house at West Norwood on suspicion of being concerned with the Whitechapel murders. Suspicion appears to have been excited by his face being much scratched, and by marks apparently of blood upon his clothes.

Just before daylight an arrest was made between Cannon-street-road and Back Church-lane, the person taken into custody being apparently a woman. On being taken to Leman-street Station it was found that the prisoner was a well-known local reporter, who had dressed in female attire, and had walked over from Leytonstone in the hope that in this disguise he might gather some important information. He was shortly released from custody.

The police have been told that a man, aged between 35 and 40 years of age, and of fair complexion, was seen to throw the woman murdered in Berner-street to the ground. Those who saw it thought that it was a man and his wife quarrelling, and no notice was taken of it.

The police have also received information that about half past ten on Saturday night, a man, aged about 35 years, entered a public-house in Batty-street, Whitechapel, and whilst the customers in the house were in conversation about the Whitechapel murders he stated that he knew the Whitechapel murderer, and that they would hear about him in the morning. After which he left.

# Monday, 1 October, 1888

Near the spot where the woman lay two pawn tickets were picked up. It is not known whether they belong to the deceased or to her murderer. The tickets were in a small tin mustard box. One was for 6d., and dated August last; the other was for 1s., and dated the 28 Aug. They were for a pair of boots and a man's shirt, and in the name of Emily Birrell and Anne Kelly. They were pawned with Jones, Church-street, and if they belong to the man may form important clues.

From two different sources we have the story that a man when passing through Church-lane at about half-past one, saw a man sitting on a door-step and wiping his hands. As everyone is on the lookout for the murderer the man looked at the stranger with a certain amount of suspicion, whereupon he tried to conceal his face. He is described as a man who wore a short jacket and a sailor's hat.

—

### What the Police were Doing.

In the midst of the excitement following on the Berner-street murder, some of the police were mean enough to try to purchase tobacco and drink from some of the members of the Jewish club. Money was tendered when request was made, but was, of course, refused. The police were not so entirely absorbed in endeavouring to catch the criminal but that they could attempt to inveigle innocent persons into committing a petty crime for the sake of securing a paltry conviction.

—

### THE BERNER-STREET INQUEST.

The inquest on Elizabeth Stride, the victim of the Berner-street atrocity was opened shortly after eleven o'clock this morning by Coroner Baxter, in the large upper room at the Vestry Hall, Cable-street, St. George's-in-the-East.

The few additional facts which have come to light concerning the deceased corroborate the fact that it was a miserable and depraved life from which she was released by the murderer's hand. She was a familiar figure at the Thames Police-court, where she occasionally fell down in the dock in one of the epileptic fits to which she was subject.

She sometimes went in the name of Fitzgerald, and was known, in the expressive nomenclature of her frail sisterhood as "Epileptic Annie," or "Long Liz."

The jury having been sworn, they at once proceeded to view the body, which was laid out in the mortuary attached to the parish church. They had to pass through the graveyard for that purpose, and to elbow their way through a motley crowd of morbid onlookers who had been allowed to collect.

The woman's body was laid upon the slab exactly as it had been found. None of her clothing had been removed or interfered with. The dress was partially opened and the left side of the face was covered with mud. The wound in the neck did not extend all the way round, as in the Hanbury-street murder, but was very deep and completely severed the windpipe.

It was particularly noticeable that the expression on the face was not one of pain, but of complete repose.

### WILLIAM WEST,

of 40, Berner-street, said:—I am a printer, and live just at the back of the International Working Men's Constitutional Club. On the ground floor of the club there is a window and a door leading into a passage, and at the side there is a passage into a yard. The entrance to the yard is through two wooden gates, which are mostly closed at night; and there is also a small door, which is locked after the tenants have retired for the night. No particular person looks after the locking of the gates or door. There is only one other house in the yard, but it is arranged in three or four tenements, and has three or four doors leading into the yard. There is no other way out of the yard except through the gates. Opposite there is a stable, which, I believe, is unoccupied. The ground floor front of the club is used as a dining room, and in the middle of the passage there is a staircase leading to the first floor. At the back of the dining room is a kitchen.

The Coroner:That has a window looking out into the yard, has it not?

—No; there is a passage between the kitchen and the yard, so the window looks out into the passage. At the back of this kitchen, but in no way connected with it, there is a printing office, consisting of two rooms.

# Monday, 1 October, 1888

Do you know when the compositors left on Saturday?

—Two o'clock in the day, so far as I remember. The editor was on the premises **ALL DAY,** being a member of the club. He was there until the discovery.

How many members of the club are there?

—From 75 to 80. Any working man, of any nationality, can be a member. It is a Socialist Club. I was in the club myself on Saturday from two in the afternoon till within an hour of the discovery of the deceased, with the exception of an hour and a half, from eight till half-past nine. When I returned at half-past nine I went in through the street door, and there was then a discussion on upstairs. There were in the upstairs hall two or three windows looking into the yard, and there were 90 or 100 persons present. The discussion closed between half-past eleven and twelve, when the bulk of the people left the premises, going through the street door. A number of people, about 25 or 30, remained behind in this upper hall, some conversing and others singing. The windows were partly open. I left at about a quarter-past twelve, having five minutes before then been into the printing office in the yard. I then noticed that the yard gates were open, but did not go towards them. There is no light at all in the yard, which is only lit by the lights from the windows. The editor was in the printing office reading. The singing in the club could be heard in the yard, but there was not much noise.

The Coroner: You looked towards the gates, but did you look sufficiently to see if there was anything on the ground?

—There was nothing unusual to attract my attention, and I did not look sufficiently closely to say there was **NOTHING ON THE GROUND.**

What made you look towards the gates at all?

—Because they were open. I then went into the club, called my brother, and went away with him to where I sleep in William-street.

Did you see anyone in the yard before?

—No.

Did you meet anyone in Berner-street?

—Not that I remember.

You often go home late?

—Generally between twelve and one.

Do you ever see low women about?

—Sometimes I see men and women standing about in Fairclough-street.

Have you ever seen a man and woman in the yard of your club?

—About a twelvemonth ago I happened to go into the yard, and heard some chatting near the gate, when I at once went to shut it. I then noticed a man and woman go out. That is the only occasion I ever noticed such a thing.

**MORRIS EAGLE,**

of 4, New-road, Commercial-road, a jewellery traveller, said:—I am a member of the International Working Men's Club, and I was there on Saturday evening occupying the chair during the discussion. I left the club between half-past eleven and a quarter to twelve. I did not go through the yard, but out of the front door. I returned at about twenty minutes to one. The front door being closed, I went through the gateway into the yard, and thus into the club.

Did you notice anything lying on the ground?

—I did not notice anything coming in. It was rather dark, and I cannot say for certain whether there was anything there or not.

You have formed no opinion?

—No.

Did you see anyone about in Berner-street?

—I cannot remember.

Supposing there had been a man and woman in the yard then, **WOULD YOU HAVE SEEN THEM?**

—I am sure I would.

(Proceeding.)

—

### "Jack the Ripper's" Joke.

A practical joker, who signed himself "Jack the Ripper," wrote to the Central News last week, intimating with laboured flippancy that he was going to commence operations again in Whitechapel shortly. He said he would cut the woman's ears off to send to the police. This morning the same agency received a postcard smeared apparently with dirty blood. It was written with red chalk. It says:—

"I was not codding[94] dear old Boss

---

[94] **Codding**. Nonsense, humbug, chaff: see Cod.
**Cod**. 2. A fool, a humbug, an imposition, and as verb, to hoax, chaff, take a rise out of. (Farmer)

# Monday, 1 October, 1888

when I gave you the tip. You'll hear about saucy Jacky's[95] work to-morrow. Double event this time. Number one squealed a bit. Couldn't finish straight off. Had not time to get ears for police. Thanks for keeping back last letter till I got to work again.

JACK THE RIPPER."

—

### Worth Inquiry.

A reporter heard a strange story this morning that may be connected with the murders. A gentleman living not far from the British Museum says:—In the room above mine there is an American lodging. He professes to be a doctor, but does not look like one. In fact, if one judged by his looks, he might be—well, a perfect ruffian. No one knows anything about him. He never does any work, and always seems rather hard up, although he pays his rent regularly. He must wear something over his boots that enables him to walk silently, for no one ever hears him come in. At intervals he disappears for a time. On Saturday he went out, and has not been back since.

—

### A Word For the Police.
### TO THE EDITOR OF "THE STAR."

SIR,—There is one thing to be said for the police in defence of their failure to catch the murderer. His victim, it must be remembered, is in a conspiracy to escape the eye of the constable. She, as well as he, watches him out of sight and hearing, and waits to put herself every minute more completely in the power of her destroyer.—Yours, &c.,

FAIR PLAY.
London, 1 Oct.

~

---

95 **Saucy Jack, Jack-sauce.** An impudent fellow, sauce-box (q.v.) (1571). (ibid)

## Evening News
### THE REIGN OF TERROR IN WHITECHAPEL.
### AT THE SCENE OF THE CRIMES ON SUNDAY.
### SPECIAL.

It would be impossible for any pen to do justice to a description of the excitement which prevailed in Whitechapel and its immediate neighbourhood all yesterday, from the time that the first news of these fresh horrors was bruited about until long after midnight. Terror and amazement were depicted in almost every face that one met in the streets of that now notorious district. I moved about the dense throngs which had grown to enormous proportions as the day wore on and whose numbers seemed to culminate in the afternoon, when people came trooping in from distant parts athirst for the latest news bearing upon these awful tragedies. Trains, trams, and omnibuses disgorged their hundreds of passengers, who wended their way to the two localities, which have, for the moment, put Buck's-row and Hanbury-street into the shade.

### A TERRIBLE PANIC

Has taken possession of the entire district, and its effects are to be seen in the wild, terrified faces of the women, and heard in the muttered imprecations of the men who have their homes in the densely populated streets of the East End. The very lads, ready at all times for ribald jest, and noisy horse-play, stood around in awe-struck groups, whispering to each other of the fiendish things that were happening, just as one could have supposed the people stood and talked in Goodman's Fields, near by, more than two centuries ago when the Black Death claimed some of its first victims.

"God help us," exclaimed a poor creature, whose tawdry dress and hardened countenance indicated all too clearly the wretched calling she pursued. "If the human devil who murdered all these women isn't caught, and that pretty soon, too? Why, *I* might be next! It makes my blood run cold."

She was standing, as she spoke, gazing down the alley leading into Mitre-square, and from whence could be seen the corner where the policeman had stumbled upon the body of the

206

# Monday, 1 October, 1888

murdered woman, and at her words other women drew their shawls closer around them with a shudder at the thought of the hideous vendetta which is being waged upon their sex and class.

### WHERE WERE THE POLICE?

That was the question that assailed one's ears on every hand. It seems incredible that, within the short space of twelve minutes, a man and woman should have entered the deserted precincts of Mitre-square, that the man should have murdered his victim, disembowelled her with the same unerring skill and a precisely similar result to that achieved in the case of Annie Chapman, and should have made his escape from the scene, without being seen at all.

He must, when he hurried away after accomplishing his devilish purpose, have been reeking with blood. And yet the policeman on the beat is positive that he saw nothing of either the man or the woman within those twelve short minutes until he came upon the latter weltering in her blood.

### A FIENDING CUNNING.

After having seen all that was to be seen in and around Mitre-square, I came away more than ever impressed with the deliberate, inhuman cunning of the monster who is still abroad in our midst, and who has added those two latest horrors to the ghastly record of his crimes.

Mitre-square is quite out of the beaten track, is surrounded by warehouses and shops, and would be as deserted at midnight as though it lay in the centre of Salisbury Plain. No safer place, apparently, could possibly have been selected for the commission of such an awful crime, and the murderer, whoever he is, must have been familiar with that fact.

It does not seem possible that accident could have led him to a spot so pre-eminently suited to his deadly purpose. The police, moreover, declare that they have never known the place used for the purposes for which these wretched women court secrecy.

### THE CROWD IN BERNER-STREET.

Making the best of my way through the dense mass of people wedged in the narrow space of Duke-street, Houndsditch, I strolled along to Berner-street.

I found the street literally packed with people of both sexes, all ages, and nearly all classes. Clubmen from the West-end rubbed shoulders with the grimy denizens of St. George's-in-the-East: daintily dressed ladies, whom a wondering curiosity had drawn to the spot, elbowed their way amid knots of their less favoured sisters, whose dirty and ragged apparel betokened the misery of their daily surround-dings. Policemen were there in great numbers, jealously guarding the approach to the yard in which the murdered women was found. I may mention that the same thing (the number of police on duty) struck me in passing Mitre-square, reminding one irresistibly of the old adage about locking the stable door after the steed has been stolen.

"It's a pity some of you fine chappies wasn't about 'ere larst night," said a morose individual who had been ordered to move on. "You'd a-done a deal more good than shovin' innercent folks hoff the pavement this arternoon." Then, in a jeering tone, "When do you expect you'll ketch the murderer, sonny?"

"Ketch the murderer?" laughed another dilapidated onlooker. "Not till they puts a "bobby"[96] to sit upon hevery doorstep in Vitechapel. And then 'alf on 'em will be asleep."

These taunts, and the manner in which they were received by the crowd, show how utterly the poor creatures in that neighbourhood have lost confidence in police protection. I shall never forget the aspect of that street, yesterday afternoon. The intense excitement, the vast swaying throng of eager, and, for the most part, terrified faces, the murmur of the hundreds of voices, the frantic struggles to get as near as possible to the scene of the sickening tragedy, all made it utterly impossible for one to realize that it was the afternoon of a Christian sabbath in the capital of the most civilized and religious country in the world.

---

[96] **Bobby**. A policeman: this nickname, though possibly not derived from, was certainly popularised by the fact that the Metropolitan Police Act of 1828 was mainly the work of Mr., afterwards Sir, Robert Peel. Long before that statesman remodelled the police, however, the term Bobby the beadle was in use to signify a guardian of a public square or other open space. There seems, however, a lack of evidence, and examples of its literary use prior to 1851 have not been discovered. At the Universities the Proctors are, or used to be called, bobbies. (Farmer)

207

# Monday, 1 October, 1888

## INTERVIEW WITH A NEIGHBOUR.

Some three doors from the gateway where the body of the first victim was discovered, I saw a clean, respectable-looking woman chatting with one or two neighbours. She was apparently the wife of a well-to-do artisan, and formed a strong contrast to many of those around her. I got into conversation with her and found that she was one of the first on the spot.

## TEN INCHES OF COLD STEEL.

"I was just about going to bed, sir, when I heard a call for the police. I ran to the door, and before I could open it I heard somebody say, 'Come out quick; there's a poor woman here that's had ten inches of cold steel in her.' I hurried out, and saw some two or three people standing in the gateway. Lewis, the man who looks after the Socialist Club at No. 40, was there, and his wife.

"Then I see a sight that turned me all sick and cold. There was the murdered woman a-lying on her side, with her throat cut across till her head seemed to be hanging by a bit of skin. Her legs was drawn up under her, and her head and the upper part of her body was soaked in blood. She was dressed in black as if she was in mourning for somebody.

## MURDERED WITHIN SOUND OF MUSIC AND DANCING.

"Did you hear no sound of quarrelling, no cry for help?" I asked.

"Nothing of the sort, sir. I should think I must have heard it if the poor creature screamed at all, for I hadn't long come in from the door when I was roused, as I tell you, by that call for the police. But that was from the people as found the body. Mr. Lewis, who travels in cheap drapery things a bit now and again, had just drove into the yard when his horse shied at something that was lying in the corner. He thought 'twas a bundle of some kind till he got down from his cart and struck a light. Then he saw what it was and gave the alarm."

"Was the street quiet at the time?"

"Yes, there was hardly anybody moving about, except at the club. There was music and dancing going on there at the very time that that poor creature was being murdered at their very door, as one may say."

## A MAN WITH A BLACK BAG!

"I suppose you did not notice a man and woman pass down the street while you were at the door?"

"No, sir. I think I should have noticed them if they had. Particularly if they'd been strangers, at that time o' night. I only noticed one person passing, just before I turned in. That was a young man walking up Berner-street, carrying a black bag in his hand."

"Did you observe him closely, or notice anything in his appearance?"

"No, I didn't pay particular attention to him. He was respectably dressed, but was a stranger to me. He might ha' been coming from the Socialist Club., A good many young men goes there, of a Saturday night especially."

That was all that my informant had to tell me. I wonder will the detectives think it worth while to satisfy themselves about that black bag?

—

## THE WHITECHAPEL HORRORS.

The East-end fiend is still abroad and two other victims have become his prey. On Sunday morning a woman was found with her throat cut and her body partially mutilated in a court in Berner-street, Whitechapel, close by the International Club situated in that locality.

The discovery seems to have been made at one in the morning by Lewis Diemschitz, the steward of the club. Another member of the club, Mr. Morris Eagle, had passed through the court at twenty minutes to one, and had not seen anything unusual near the premises. Even if it was too dark to see the body of this woman it is impossible to suppose that Morris Eagle would not have tripped over it had it been there when he went into the club.

The inference is therefore this: if the woman was murdered and mutilated where she was found, the deed was done in the short period of twenty minutes—the deed was done in the time which the police surgeon said a medical expert would take to do it. The residents in the court know nothing about the murder. Neither they nor the people in the club heard or had seen anything that led them to suspect that foul play was going on around them.

About three-quarters of an hour after this corpse was found, another was discovered in Mitre-square, Aldgate. It was that of a woman with her throat cut, but in her case the inevitable

# Monday, 1 October, 1888

abdominal mutilation had been accomplished.

A watchman was on duty in a counting-house in the square at the time the assassin was operating. Firemen were also on duty at a station close by. Yet nobody heard or saw anything likely to rouse suspicion. The silence and secrecy in which the atrocities were perpetrated wrap them in an impenetrable veil of mystery for the moment.

As in former cases the murderer seems to have been almost miraculously successful in securing his retreat. His success in this respect seems to indicate a wonderful power of combination and organisation—an amazing gift for calculating the chances against the success of his schemes or purposes. In fact, the similarity of the murders leads to the conclusion that they have been committed by the one man or the one gang. The worst of it is that we do not know what a "gang" may mean. It might mean an organisation of great extent, or only the partnership between a criminal and his "pal." Recent events seem to suggest that there is more than one individual in the horrid business.

The public cannot fail to be impressed with one fact-the apparent bravado of the assassin. He seems to revel in brutality—and the more energetic the police become in tracking him, the more contemptuously does he defy their efforts. At first he seems to have lost nerve at the critical part of his operation. Now he holds the fancied interruptions of the police patrol in contempt, and commits his murder, and hacks his victim's body, almost within their sight and hearing. Nay, he does this in spite of the fact that Sir Charles Warren has trebled his patrols in the region of the murders, and that it is under the close supervision of a vigilance committee. *Cui bono?*[97]

The assassin it is clear can baffle all ordinary means of detection, and till he commits a singular act of indiscretion—which murderers usually do sooner or later—it appears to use very unlikely that he will ever be discovered. If he has a "pal" that will increase the chance of detection. If he has many and is a member of a gang, his secret will probably be betrayed when a suitable reward is offered as "blood money." The revolting details of the last murders need not be specified here.

We need not say that no plausible explanation of these crimes is as yet forthcoming. The new feature in them is the fact that one followed the other within the space of three-quarters of an hour. All the old features are present.

The victims are women of the same class. As women of this sort are now on the alert in Whitechapel, we may infer that the assassin must appeal to them in some way that disarms suspicion. In other words, he cannot suggest by his appearance that he is a bloodthirsty mis-creant. Hence the police are justified in coming to the conclusion that whoever he may be, he is not a person of the "Leather Apron" class.

For the rest, all that we know about him is that for some reason he selects one locality as his hunting-ground, that his fixed idea is to obtain possession of a certain portion of a woman's body, and that he perpetrates his atrocities at the end of the week, sometime between Friday night and Sunday morning.

Here we see a curious element of periodicity in the crime. This suggests the idea that if the murderer be a maniac at once lustful and bloodthirsty, he is a homicidal maniac of the type whose attacks only recur at regular intervals. The idea that he is a medical man, who for scientific purposes wants to obtain certain portions of the human body under unique conditions, is not quite compatible with the facts.

Why should he want an indefinite number of specimens? Why should he want them at the end of each week? The notion that he means to sell or issue them as illustrations to a book seems now to be abandoned even by the police. And rightly; for to sell the specimens would be to lose the market for them, and inevitably lead to suspicion being concentrated on the murderer.

Sexual insanity, however, is, on the face of the facts, the only intelligible motive of the murder—but then the facts essential for the formation of a sound judgment are at present wanting. There are so few available facts that it is impossible to arrive at a very definite opinion as to the cause of these murders.

Meantime the people of the East end are again becoming angry, first, because the police are unable to protect them, and, second, because the Government does not offer a reward for the discovery of the murderer.

—

---

[97] **Cui bono?** Lat. To whose benefit?

# Monday, 1 October, 1888

FIFTH EDITION.
THE WHITECHAPEL HORRORS.
HORRIBLE MURDER OF A WOMAN NEAR
COMMERCIAL ROAD.
ANOTHER WOMAN MURDERED AND
MUTILATED IN ALDGATE.
ONE VICTIM IDENTIFIED.
BLOOD STAINED POST CARD FROM
"JACK THE RIPPER."
SPECIAL ACCOUNTS.
A HOMICIDAL MANIAC
OR
HEAVEN'S SCOURGE FOR PROSTITUTION.

Two more ghastly tragedies were, yesterday, added to the appalling list of crimes with which the East-end of London has been associated during the last few months; and there is every reason to believe that the whole series is the work of one man.

The first of the two murders was committed in a yard turning out of Berner-street. The body was discovered by a Russian Jew named Diem-schitz, about one o'clock yesterday morning, on his return from the neighbourhood of Sydenham, where he had been selling cheap jewellery. He drove into the yard, which is situate next to a working man's club, of which he is steward, and noticed that his pony shied at something which was lying in a heap in a corner of the yard. Having fetched out a friend from the club, he looked more closely into the matter, and then found a woman lying on the ground, dead, with her throat cut clean to the vertebrae.

The body was quite warm, and blood was still flowing freely from the throat, so it is pretty certain that the murder must have been committed within a very few minutes of the time when Diemschitz discovered the body. Indeed, all the facts go to show that it was the arrival of Diemschitz in his trap which disturbed the murderer, and we may safely assume that, but for this disturbance, the miscreant would have proceeded to mutilate the body in a similar way to that in which he mutilated the bodies of the two unfortunate women, Mary Anne Nichols and Annie Chapman.

The wound in the throat is almost identical with the throat wounds of the other victims—a savage cut severing the jugular and carotids, and going clean down to the vertebrae. It bears, if we may be permitted to use the phrase, the trade-mark of the man who has so infamously distinguished himself before, and leaves no room for doubt that the three murders were committed by one and the same person.

Having been disturbed in his first attempt, yesterday morning, the murderer seems to have made his way towards the City, and to have met another "unfortunate," whom he induced to go with him to Mitre-square, a secluded spot, lying off Aldgate, and principally occupied by warehouses. He took her to the south-western corner of the square, and there cut her throat, quite in his horribly regulative way, and then proceeded to disembowel her.

He must have been extremely quick at his work, for every portion of the police beat in which Mitre-square is included, is patrolled every ten minutes or quarter of an hour, the City beats being much shorter than those of the Metropolitan Police.

Police-constable Watkins 881 passed through the square at about 1.30 or 1.35, and is quite certain that it was then in its normal condition. Within a quarter of an hour he patrolled it again, and then found a woman lying in the corner with her throat cut from ear to ear.

On closer examination he found that her clothes had been raised up to her chest, and that the lower portion of the body had been ripped completely open from the pelvis to the sternum, and disembowelled, just as were Mrs. Nichols and Annie Chapman. Indeed, this last murder is in its main features an almost exact reproduction of the horrible tragedies of Buck's-row and Hanbury-street, and, humanly speaking, it is absolutely certain that it also was committed by the same man.

There were certain deviations from the murderer's ordinary plan, but they are not inexplicable, or very significant. He gashed her face in several places, but there is evidence to show that the woman at the last moment suspected his design, and struggled with him, and it is not improbably that he stabbed her in the face before cutting her throat and committing the other atrocities.

This brief summary of the facts connected with the two tragedies which startled London, yesterday, brings us then face to face with the almost indubitable fact that there exists somewhere in the East-end at this moment, a fiend in human shape, who has committed at least four murders, if not six.

The two wretched women—Mary Ann Smith

and Annie Tabram, who were done to death in George's-yard, and were the first of the East-end victims, may or may not have been murdered by the slaughterer of Mrs. Nichols, Marie Annie Chapman, and the two unfortunates whose mangled remains were found yesterday in Berner-street and Mitre-square.

In Smith's case the death wound was given by some blunt instrument which was thrust into the lower part of the body, and the woman Tabram was savagely stabbed in thirty-nine places. We may charitably assume that the Whitechapel fiend, whose handiwork we are now describing, had no hand or part in those two crimes; though even on this assumption it is more than probable that the impunity with which these atrocities were committed tempted him to enter upon that more horrible sphere of action in which he is now startling the whole country.

### THE BERNER STREET MURDER.

The first murder discovered was that in the little yard in Berner-street, off Commercial-road.

About a hundred yards down Berner-street, on the right hand side, are the rooms of the International Working Men's Educational Society, a club used principally by Russians, Poles, and Jews generally. Adjoining in the entrance to the yard, where Messrs. Walter Handley and Co., sack manufacturers, and Mr. Arthur Dutfield, van and cart builder, carry on business. The entrance to the yard is by a double gate. The right hand side of the yard is occupied for some distance by the house occupied as the International Society's Club, which has a private entrance to the yard.

In this yard, almost against the International Club house, the body of the first victim was found. She lay within three feet of the public street along which the public must have been passing at the time. Her feet were towards the gate and her head was in the gutter running down along the yard.

### HOW THE BODY WAS DISCOVERED.

The body was discovered by Mr. Diemschitz, the steward of the club, who had driven into the yard about one o'clock on Sunday morning.

The pony he was driving appeared to avoid the north side of the yard, and Mr. Diemschitz imagined there must be some dust heap or something of that sort which his horse was trying to escape. He poked with the butt end of his whip, and found some bulky substance lying near the wall. Striking a match, he saw the body of a woman, and immediately entered the club and gave the alarm.

The concert going on in the club was immediately stopped, and the members flocked out to see whether another "Whitechapel horror" had been committed. Their investigation too plainly discovered the fact, and several members started off to communicate with the police.

It was nearly two o'clock yesterday morning before a constable was found, and he, along with some comrades who were early at the spot, conveyed the body to the mortuary connected with the workhouse of St. George's-in-the-East.

### THE CHARACTER OF THE YARD.

The yard off Berner-street is almost exactly in front of a Board school, and is immediately adjoining the International Society's rooms. Although Messrs. Handley and Co. and Mr. Dutfield carry on their business there it is not entirely devoted to commercial purposes.

The International Club have an entrance to it, and there are in it three cottages, occupied as dwelling houses by foreigners. People were, therefore, likely to be passing in and out about the time the murder was committed, say shortly after midnight.

The inhabitants of these cottages had not then retired to rest. Some of their lights were burning and the International Club were having a concert. The inhabitants of the court, or several of them, were lying awake listening to the German songs. Suddenly the singing was stilled on the announcement made by Mr. Diemschitz.

### POSITION OF THE BODY.

The woman was found lying on her left side face downwards, her position being such that, although the court at that part is only nine feet wide, a person walking up the middle might have passed the recumbent body without notice.

The condition of the corpse, however, and several other circumstances which have come to light, prove pretty conclusively that no considerable period elapsed between the committal of the murder and the discovery of the body.

The gates at the entrance to the court having been closed, and a guard set on all the exits of the club and the cottages, the superintendent of the district and divisional surgeon were sent for. In a few minutes Dr. Phillips was at the scene of the murder, and a brief examination sufficed to show that life had been extinct some minutes.

Careful note having been taken of the position of the body, it was removed to the parish mortuary.

### GRAPES IN HER HANDS.

In her right hand were tightly clasped some grapes, and in her left she held a number of sweetmeats. Both the jacket and the bodice were open towards the top, but in other respects the clothes were not disarranged. The linen was clean and in tolerably good repair.

### THE SKILL OF THE MURDERER.

That anyone should have selected for the commission of a murder such a comparatively frequented spot, at such an hour, shows considerable confidence on the part of the murderer that he was able by his dexterity to preclude all possibility of detection.

### THE MURDERER'S PURPOSE.

That the purpose of the assassin of the woman in Berner-street was to extract the uterus is almost certain despite the opinion of Dr. Phillips given further on. This is deduced from the way in which he went about his operations, so identical with what went before and after. He was disturbed in his fiendish operation, and the corpse of the poor woman escaped the horrible indignity of being eviscerated.

### THE APPEARANCE OF THE WOMAN.

The woman now lying at the mortuary of St. George's-in-the-East appears to have been about 30 years of age. It is difficult to judge of the height of a person in a recumbent position, but she appears to have been about middle height.

Her features are pinched, like those of one who has suffered want, but her expression is not unpleasant. Her cheek bones have a tendency to prominence, and her nose is sharp and well chiselled, with a slight marking at the bridge, far removed, however, from the protuberance of the Roman organ. Her hair is auburn, her lips thick, the upper one especially so, with that sort of double fold often noticed in lascivious women.

She has the appearance of being an Irishwoman, but might be a German.

She lies there on the stone with a smile of her pale face, as if she had died without a struggle. Her right hand, however, is encrusted with blood, as if she had tried to thrust her murderer away.

Her clothing is described by the police as "Black diagonal cloth jacket, feather trimming, black alpaca skirt, black velveteen bodice, black crape bonnet, side-spring boots, white stockings." This seems all right enough except in regard to the "feather" trimmings. The trimming of the short dark jacket is imitation sealskin.

As she lies in the mortuary her dress is open over her bosoms, but her stays have not been undone. The left side of her face is much dirtied and bruised, as if she had been forcibly thrust down into the mud of the Court.

### THE CUT IN THE THROAT.

The cut in the woman's neck is not exactly as has been described by our morning contemporaries. It is not from ear to ear. The knife seems to have been stabbed in deeply at the left side to reach the external carotid, and to have emerged at the carotid on the right side. The superficial length of the wound is from three-and-a-half to four inches.

### INTERVIEWS WITH MEN WHO SAW THE WOMAN.

At the mortuary our reporter saw three men who had their suspicions raised on Saturday night by the conduct of a man and a woman in Settles-street, Commercial Road.

J. Best, 82, Lower Chapman-street, said:—I was in the Bricklayers' Arms, Settles-street, about two hundred yards from the scene of the murder on Saturday night, shortly before eleven, and saw a man and woman in the doorway. They had been served in the public house, and went out when me and my friends came in. It was raining very fast, and they did not appear willing to go out. He was hugging her and kissing her, and as he seemed a respectably dressed man, we were rather astonished at the way he was going on with the woman, who was poorly dressed. We "chipped"[98] him, but he paid no attention. As he

---

[98] **"Chipped"**. I could find no definition of Chip that would fit this context, but if the reporter mis-

stood in the doorway he always threw sidelong glances into the bar, but would look nobody in the face. I said to him, "Why don't you bring the woman in and treat her?" but he made no answer. If he had been a straight fellow he would have told us to mind our own business, or he would have gone away. I was so certain that there was something up that I would have charged him if I could have seen a policeman. When the man could not stand the chaffing[99] any longer he and the woman went off like a shot soon after eleven.

I had been to the mortuary, and am almost certain the woman there is the one we saw at the Bricklayers' Arms. She is the same slight woman, and seems the same height. The face looks the same, but a little paler, and the bridge of the nose does not look so prominent.

## THE MAN.

The man was about 5ft. 5in. in height. He was well dressed in a black morning suit with a morning coat. He had rather weak eyes. I mean he had sore eyes without any eyelashes. I should know the man again amongst a hundred. He had a thick black moustache and no beard. He wore a black billycock hat, rather tall, and had on a collar. I don't know the colour of his tie. I said to the woman "that's Leather Apron getting round you." The man was no foreigner; he was an Englishman right enough.

John Gardner, labourer, 11, Chapman-street, corroborated all that Best said respecting the conduct of the man and the woman at the Bricklayers' Arms, adding "before I got to the mortuary to-day (Sunday) I told you the woman had a flower in her jacket, and that she had a short jacket. Well, I have been to the mortuary, and there she was with the dahlias on the right side of her jacket.

## I COULD SWEAR

She is the same woman I saw at the Bricklayers' Arms, and she has the same smile of her face now that she had then.

---

understood Mr. Best the word used could have been: **Chi-ike** (or **Chy-ack**). A street salute, a word of praise (1869). Also as verb, to salute or hail, and (tailors') to chaff unmercifully. *To give chi-ike with the chill off*, to scold. (Farmer)

[99] **Chaff**. 1. Ironical or sarcastic banter, fooling, humbug, ridicule. As verb, to banter, jest, gammon, or quiz (1821). Chaffy, full of banter. (ibid)

## THE TWO MURDERS NOT BY THE SAME HAND.

The idea has got abroad that in some way it is sought to advance medical science by human vivisection, but however likely or unlikely the theory may be, it must not too readily be assumed that the two murders of yesterday morning had the same object.

Dr. Phillips who was called to Berner-street shortly after the discovery of the woman's body, gives (so says Dr. Gordon, who has made a post-mortem examination of the other body) it as his opinion that the two murders were not committed by the same man.

Upon this point Dr. Phillips is an authority. He it was who examined Annie Chapman and discovered the purpose of the murder. Since that he has been to Newcastle to investigate the brutal murder there, and he is qualified in some measure to speak of the manner of the assassin's workmanship.

## A LUNATIC AT WORK.

Dr. Gordon (Brown), speaking of the Mitre-square murder, assured our representative that he was sure it was the work of a lunatic. Dr. Gordon has made his post-mortem of the Mitre-square body without waiting for the coroner's order. He knows that is out of the rule, but he thought under the circumstances that it was necessary, and he hopes he will be backed up by public opinion.

## THE SILENCE OF THE MURDERER.

When the alarm of murder was raised a young girl had been standing in a bisecting thoroughfare not fifty yards from the spot where the body was found. She had, she said, been standing there for about twenty minutes, talking with her sweetheart, but neither of them heard any unusual noises.

A woman who lives two doors from the club has made an important statement. It appears that shortly before a quarter to one o'clock she heard the measured, heavy tramp of a policeman passing the house on his beat. Immediately afterwards she went to the street-door, with the intention of shooting the bolts, though she remained standing there ten minutes before she did so. During the ten minutes she saw no one enter or leave the neighbouring yard, and she feels sure that had any one done so she could not have overlooked the fact. The quiet and deserted character of the street appears even to have struck her at the time. Locking the door, she prepared to retire to bed, in the front room on the ground floor, and it so happened that in about four minutes' time she heard Diemschitz's pony cart pass the house, and remarked upon the circumstance to her husband.

### DISTURBING THE MURDERER.

Presuming that the body did not lie in the yard when the policeman passed—and it could hardly, it is thought, have escaped his notice—and presuming also that the assassin and his victim did not enter the yard while the woman stood at the door, it follows that they must have entered it within a minute or two before the arrival of the pony trap.

If this be a correct surmise, it is easy to understand that the criminal may have been interrupted at his work. Diemschitz says he thinks it quite possible that after he had entered the yard the assassin may have fled out of it, having lurked in the gloom until a favourable moment arrived.

### IDENTIFICATION OF THE WOMAN.

Files of people were allowed to pass through the mortuary, yesterday, in the hope that some clue would be obtained of the woman's identity. It was late in the afternoon, however, before any one was able to say they knew her. Eventually she was identified as Elizabeth Stride, familiarly known as Long Lizzie, who had been living at a common lodging-house, No. 32, Flower and Dean-street and who plied her painful trade in the neighbourhood. She is said to have a sister in Holborn. She was a married woman separated from her husband, who resides in Bath.

Another account says: She left Flower-and-Dean-street between six and seven o'clock on Saturday night. She then said that she was not going to meet any one in particular. Stride is believed to be a Swedish woman from Stockholm. According to her associates, she was of calm temperament, rarely quarrelling with any one; in fact, she was so good-natured that she would "do a good turn for any one."

Her occupation was that of a charwoman. She had the misfortune to lose her husband in the Princess Alice disaster on the Thames some years ago. She had lost her teeth, and suffered from a throat infection. It appears that she was identified at the mortuary, yesterday morning,

by John Arundel and Charles Preston, who reside at 32, Flower-and-Dean-street.

A third account says the victim was an unfortunate, named "Wally" Warden, who had lived in Brick-lane.

### STATEMENT BY THE CLUB STEWARD.

Lewis Diemschitz, who is a steward of the International Working Men's Educational Society, has made the following statement:—"I am a traveller in the common jewellery trade, and work only for myself. I have also been the steward for the International Working Men's Club for between six and seven years, and I live on the premises of the club.

For some time I have been in the habit of going to Westow Hill, at the Crystal Palace, every Saturday, in order to sell my goods at the market which is there.

I got back this Sunday morning about one o'clock, and drove up to our club-room gate in my pony cart. My pony is frisky and apt to shy, though not much, and it struck me when I was passing through the double gates into the yard that he wanted to keep too much to the left side against the wall. I could not make out what was the matter, so I bent my head to see if there were anything to frighten him. Then I noticed there was something unusual about the ground, but I could not tell what it was, except that it was not level. I mean there was something there like a little heap; but I thought it was only mud, or something of the kind, and I did not take much notice of it; still I touched it with my whip, and then I was able to tell it was not mud.

I wanted to see what it was, so jumped out of the trap and struck a match. Then I saw there was a woman lying there. At that time I took no notice, and I didn't know whether she was drunk or dead. What I did was to run indoors, and ask where my missus was, because she is of weak constitution, and I didn't want to frighten her.

I found my wife was sitting downstairs, and I then told some of the members of the club that something had happened in the yard, but I did not give any opinion as to whether the woman was dead or only drunk. I did not say that she had been murdered. One of the members named Isaacs came out with me.

We struck a match, and then a horrible sight came before our eyes: we saw a stream of blood flowing right down to the door of the club. We sent for the police without delay, but it was some time before an officer arrived; in fact we had some difficulty in finding one. A man called Eagle, also a member of the club, went out to find a policeman; and going in a different direction to what we did, found a couple in Commercial-road. One of them was 252 H.

One of the constables blew a whistle. Several policemen immediately came on the spot, and one of them went for a doctor. Two surgeons were soon with us, namely, Dr. Phillips, the police surgeon, of Spital-square and Dr. Kaye, of Blackwall. After that the police took the names of all the members of the club, and told us that we should all be ordered to give evidence. The police left about five in the morning.

Diemschitz being then asked to describe the body as well as he could, said:—"In my opinion the woman was about 27 or 28 years old. Her skin and complexion were fair. (This is not correct, according to the latest accounts that we have received, but the man was evidently too frightened at the time to be able to remember.) Her clothes were in decent order, but her neck and throat had been fearfully gashed and presented a frightful spectacle. There was a cut between two and three inches wide in it.

All her clothes were black, even to the bonnet, which had crape on it. Her hands were tightly clenched, and when they were opened by the doctor I saw immediately that one had been holding sweetmeats and the other grapes.

I should not like to say whether or not she had been knocked about at all in the face; but speaking roughly, she seemed to me to be a more respectable sort of woman than we generally see about these parts. I conclude this because it appears that nobody about here had ever seen or heard anything about her before.

The police removed the body to the mortuary at Cable-street. When I first of all came across the woman, she was lying on her left side, her left hand was on the ground, while the right was lying across her breast. Her head was on the ground of the yard, while her feet pointed towards the entrance. The body was only a yard or so within the entrance.

I keep my pony and trap in Cable-street, but I am in the habit of going to the club first to leave my goods there."

The above is an accurate statement of what Diemschitz told our representative. Diemschitz is a Russian Jew, but he speaks English perfectly. He is a man with more intelligence than is usually to be found amongst men of his class, and in every way is a credit to the neighbourhood in which he resides. This may not seem to be a compliment; but we mean it as such, for our informant is, so far as we are able to judge, an honest, truth-speaking man, on whose evidence we feel that we are able to rely.

## OTHER IMPORTANT STATEMENTS.

The next person whose information we intend to place before our readers in Morris Eagle. He is likewise a member of this club, which has attained a notoriety hardly enviable.

His evidence is shortly this:—I frequent the club. I went into it about 12.40 on this night that you are asking me about, which was about 20 minutes before the body was discovered. I had been in the club before that evening, and had left the premises at midnight in order to see my girl home, with whom I was keeping company. I saw my sweetheart to the door of the house where she was living, and then walked back to the club through little small streets.

On my way I saw nothing to excite my attention. There were numbers of persons about of both sexes, and several prostitutes; but there are always a lot of people in the streets, and they are generally very lively at this time of night. I can swear that there was nothing in the streets to arouse my suspicions or the suspicions of any other man in his senses.

After seeing my girl home, I went back to the club in Berner-street. The front door was closed, so I went round to the back door on the left-hand side. Later on I went over the same ground with Diemschitz. There is nothing unusual in members of the club going in to the club by the side door; in fact, we often do so, when we go in to the club late at night, so as to prevent the knocking at the door, which might be a nuisance to the neighbours. There is no light of any sort in the yard, though there are lights in the street, as there are in every other street.

In the club we had a rare good time. We were singing songs and all that sort of thing. Then there was a sudden scare among us; Diemschitz came in and said a woman had been murdered outside. I ran into the yard immediately and I saw in the yard a stream of blood.

# Monday, 1 October, 1888

There was a general hue and cry for the police. I and others went off to find the officers, so I had no opportunity of seeing the body. Besides, I did not want to look at it, as those sights make me feel ill.

The next person in importance to Eagle, on whose information we may look forward to getting a clue to the perpetrator of these outrageous crimes is Isaac M. Kozebrodsky. Kozebrodsky was born in Warsaw, and can only speak English very imperfectly.

His information, which we are obliged to give very shortly, is this:—"I came into the club about which you are asking me at half-past twelve o'clock. Shortly after I came in Diemschitz asked me to come out into the yard, as he saw there was something unusual had taken place there. So I came out with him, and he then pointed out to me a stream of blood, which was running down the gutter in the direction of the gate, and flowed from the gate to the back-door. The blood in the gutter extended to between six and seven yards.

I immediately went for a policeman, and ran in the direction of Grove-street, but could not find one. Then I went into the Commercial-road, where I found two policemen. I brought them back with me, and they sent for a doctor. The doctor arrived shortly afterwards, and with him came an inspector. While the doctor examined the body I saw that there were some grapes in her right hand and some sweets in her left hand.

To the best of my recollection, she had on a dark jacket and a black dress, and in her bosom she had a small bunch of flowers."

Our next informant was Joseph Lave, a man just arrived in England from the United States. Lave is now living at the club, till such time as he can find permanent lodgings.

What he tells us is this:—"I was in the yard of the club this morning about twenty minutes to one. At half-past twelve I had come out into the street to get a breath of fresh air. There was nothing unusual in the street. So far as I could see I was out in the street about half an hour, and while I was out nobody came into the yard, nor did I see anybody moving about there in a way to excite my suspicions."

So far as we can gather from the information we have collected, and from the persons we have interviewed, there is not the slightest tittle of evidence to show that the yard in question has been habitually used for immoral purposes. In fact, the traffic there is too great and too constant to allow of that secrecy, which is the companion of immorality.

We trust, further, that we shall not be accused of catering to the tabloid tastes of our readers if we describe more fully the geography of the place where this fatal tragedy has taken place. The yard in which the body was found is about ten feet wide. This width is continued for a distance of eight or ten yards at which point there occurs on the left-hand side a row of houses which are set back a little, at which point the width is increased by two feet or more. The extreme length of the court is thirty yards, and it terminates in a workshop, which is now used as a dwelling-house.

The exact spot, then, where this horrible murder was committed is overlooked on three sides, and as the gates were open it seems to the ordinary mind that it would be impossible for this fiend in human form to have committed his diabolical crime without having been detected. The windows of the club are within ten feet of the spot, while the cottages stand about opposite, and command a complete view of the spot where the murderous act was committed.

Abraham Heshburg, a young fellow, living at 28, Berner-street, said:—"Yes, I was one of those who first saw the murdered woman. It was about a quarter to one o'clock, I should think, when I heard a policeman's whistle blown, and came down to see what was the matter.

In the gateway two or three people had collected, and when I got there I saw a short, dark young woman lying on the ground with a gash between four and five inches long in her throat. I should say she was from 25 to 28 years of age. Her head was towards the north wall, against which she was lying. She had a black dress on, with a bunch of flowers pinned on the breast. In her hand there was a small piece of paper containing five or six cachous.

The body was found by a man whose name I do not know—a man who goes out with a pony and barrow, and lives up the archway, where he was going, I believe, to put up his barrow on coming home from market. He thought it was his wife at first, but when be found her safe at home he got a candle and found this woman. He never touched it till the doctors had been sent for.

# Monday, 1 October, 1888

The little gate is always open, or, at all events, always unfastened. There are some stables up there—Messrs. Duncan, Woollatt, and Co.'s, I believe and there is a place to which a lot of girls take home sacks which they have engaged in making. None of them would be there, though, after about one on Saturday afternoon.

None of us recognised the woman, and I do not think she belonged to this neighbourhood. She was dressed very respectably. There seemed to be no wounds on the body."

The house which adjoins the yard on the south side, No. 38, is tenanted by Barnett Kentorrich, who, as to whether he heard any disturbance during the night, said:—"I went to bed early, and slept till about three o'clock, during which time I heard no unusual sound of any description. At three o'clock some people were talking loudly outside my door, so I went out to see what was the matter, and learned that a woman had been murdered. I did not stay out long though, and know nothing more about it. I do not think the yard bear a very good character at night, but I do not interfere with any of the people about here. I know that the gate is not kept fastened."

Mrs. Mortimer, living at 36, Berner-street, four doors from the scene of the tragedy, says:—"I was standing at the door of my house nearly the whole time between half-past twelve and one o'clock this (Sunday) morning, and did not notice anything unusual. I had just gone indoors, and was preparing to go to bed, when I heard a commotion outside, and immediately ran out, thinking that there was another row at the Socialists' Club close by.

I went to see what was the matter, and was informed that another dreadful murder had been committed in the yard adjoining the club-house, and on going inside I saw the body of a woman lying huddled up just inside the gate with her throat cut from ear to ear. A man touched her face, and said it was quite warm, so that the deed must have been done while I was standing at the door of my house.

There was certainly no noise made, and I did not observe any one enter the gates. It was soon after one o'clock when I went out, and the only man whom I had seen pass through the street previously was a young man carrying a black shiny bag, who walked very fast down the street from the Commercial-road. He looked up at the club, and then went around the corner by the Board School.

I was told that the manager or steward of the club had discovered the woman on his return home in his pony cart. He drove through the gates, and my opinion is that he interrupted the murderer, who must have made his escape immediately under cover of the cart. If a man had come out of the yard before one o'clock I must have seen him.

It was almost incredible to me that the thing could have been done without the steward's wife hearing a noise, for she was sitting in the kitchen, from which a window opens four yards from the spot where the woman was found.

The body was lying slightly on one side, with the legs a little drawn up as if in pain, the clothes being slightly disarranged, so that the legs were partly visible. The woman appeared to me to be respectable, judging by her clothes, and in her hand were found a bunch of grapes and some sweets.

A young man and his sweetheart were standing at the corner of the street, about twenty yards away, before and after the time the woman must have been murdered, but they told me they did not hear a sound."

Charles Letchford, living at 30, Berner-street, says:—"I passed through the street at half-past 12 and everything seemed to me to be going on as usual, and my sister was standing at the door at ten minutes to one, but did not see any one pass by. I heard the commotion when the body was found, and heard the policeman's whistles, but did not take any notice of the matter, as disturbances are very frequent at the club, and I thought it was only another row."

—

## THE MITRE SQUARE MURDER
## DESCRIPTION OF THE SQUARE

The scene of yesterday's second murder is a partially enclosed space, about thirty yards square, lying behind Mitre-street, a thoroughfare running off from the western end of Aldgate, within a few yards of the junction of Fenchurch-street and Leadenhall-street.

The entrance to the square from mitre-street is some 15 yards wide, and perhaps eight yards long. The square then widens some seven or eight yards on each side, forming secluded corners on the north-west and south-west.

# Monday, 1 October, 1888

Running from the north-east corner of the square is a covered passage leading to St. James's-place, otherwise known as the "Orange Market," where three men of the Metropolitan Fire Brigade are always on duty at a fire escape station until daybreak.

From the north-west corner another passage runs into Duke-street, so that there are in all three entrances to the square.

The east and part of the north sides of the square are occupied by the warehouses of Messrs. Kearley and Tonge, tea and coffee merchants, and on the north side there is also a private house, occupied by a city policeman named Pierce. On the south side there is the warehouse of Messrs. Horner and Sons drug merchants. On the fourth side, where the roadway leads into Mitre-street, one corner is occupied by Messrs. Walter Williams and Co., and the opposite corner is used as a workshop, and is locked up at night. Next to it are three empty houses, the backs of which look into the square.

During business hours the square is extensively used, but after six o'clock it is comparatively deserted, and, according to people in the vicinity, it is about a quiet place as could be found in the City of London.

It may be added that the square is well lighted, there being one standard lamp in the square itself, another fixed to the wall at the left hand entrance from Mitre-street, a third at the corner of the court at the St. James's-place end, one being placed at each end, so that altogether there are five lamps showing their light into the square.

## DISCOVERY OF THE BODY

It was in the south-west corner of this little square that the murder was committed. Police-constable Watkins, whose duty it is to pass through the square every quarter of an hour or so, was on the spot shortly after 1.30, and then found everything in its ordinary condition. A quarter of an hour later he passed through the square again, and then saw a woman's corpse lying in the south-west corner. The body was lying on its back, on the footway, with the head towards a boarding and the feet towards the kerbstones.

## A FEARFUL SIGHT

The corpse was that of a woman, and it was lying on its back, in the south-west corner, on the footway, with the head towards a boarding, and her feet to the carriage-way. The head was inclined on the left, and both the arms were extended outwards. The left leg was extended straight out, and right leg was bent away from the body. After the first shock of the discovery, the constable bent down and felt the body, which he found to be quite warm. Blood was all around and on the body, but it had not congealed.

Watkins immediately ran across to George James Norris, a night watchman in the employ of Messrs. Kearley, and sent him to Dr. Sequeira, at 34, Jewry-street, and then proceeded to call up Constable Pearce, who lives in one of the houses in the square itself.

The constables then returned to the south-west corner, and throwing the light of their lanterns full upon it, found to their horror that the woman's throat was cut from ear to ear and half-way round the head. The clothes had been raised up to the chest, and, more horrible still, the body had been completely ripped up from the pelvis right up to the chest, the flaps of flesh being turned back and revealing the intestines.

All the viscera were cut out, and the lower part of the abdomen lifted up bodily towards the breast; in fact, a more fearful case of mutilation cannot be imagined.

In addition to these fearful injuries a portion of the right ear was also cut off, and the nose was slashed half-way through. The face was also slashed and cut about in the most brutal fashion, and a portion of the intestines was also placed on the neck.

## A WOMAN OF FINE PHYSIQUE

From various descriptions she is said to be a woman of fine physique, though undoubtedly debauched beyond all respectability.

Dr. Brown, of Finsbury-circus, was immediately summoned, and ordered the body to be removed to the mortuary in Golden-lane, where it lies at present. No minute examination has as yet been made of the body, and it lies as it was found.

To show how mysteriously and quietly the murder must have been committed a watchman was on duty in the square in a counting-house all the morning, and saw nothing. Besides this,

# Monday, 1 October, 1888

in St. James's-place, as we have said, there was a fire-station, where the firemen are on duty all night, and on being closely questioned they affirm that they heard no sound of a scuffle, nor anything to indicate that such a diabolical deed was taking place.

Dr. Sequeira arrived at five minutes to two o'clock and shortly after that time Major Smith, assistant chief commissioner of the City Police; Detective-inspector M William, chief of the City Detective Department; Superintendent Foster and Inspector Collard, of Bishopsgate-street Station were on the spot. They had been preceded, however, by Dr. Brown, surgeon to the City Police Force, while Dr. Phillips, of Spital-square, surgeon to the H division of Metropolitan Police, who had previously examined the body of the woman found in Berner-street, was also present.

As soon as the corpse had been removed from Mitre-square the south-west corner was carefully washed down, in order to disappoint morbid sightseers, and it was not long before all traces of the awful crime had been removed. A sketch of the place was also made, under the direction of the police in charge of the case.

## DESCRIPTION OF THE BODY AND CLOTHING

The following is the official description of the body and clothing:

Age about 40, length five feet, dark auburn hair, hazel eyes. Dress—black jacket with imitation fur collar, three large metal buttons, brown bodice, dark green chintz[100] (with Michaelmas daisy and Gordon lily pattern), skirt (three flounces), thin white vest, light drab linsey underskirt, dark green alpaca petticoat, white chemise, brown ribbed stockings, mended at feet with piece of white stocking, black straw bonnet trimmed with black beads and green and black velvet, large white handkerchief round neck, a pair of men's old laced boots, and a piece of coarse white apron. The deceased had T. C. on left forearm tattooed in blue ink.

## INTERVIEW WITH SUPERINTENDENT FOSTER

Mr. Foster, the superintendent of the City Police, upon being called upon last night by a representative of the Press, expressed his willingness to afford any information it would be safe to publish.

Shortly before three o'clock on Sunday morning, he was called up from bed by a report that a most terrible murder had been committed just inside the City boundary on the eastern side. Measures had already been taken to detect if possible, the murderer, and these he supplemented by sending out a force of detectives and uniform men.

He stated the Police-constable Watkins, No. 881, who is an old and steady and careful officer, was on night duty in the neighbourhood of Houndsditch, Mitre-square, being part of the beat. At half-past one he passed through the square and looked well round, but the space seemed to be positively empty. The square is well lighted with two lamps, but the corner in which the woman was found is over-shadowed by two empty houses, but still the officer feels certain there was nothing in the corner at that time. It is part of his duty to look into this corner, and he is certain he did look in.

A quarter of an hour later he again passed through the square, and then was horrified to see a woman with her throat fearfully gashed lying there in a pool of blood. On turning his light full on he further found that she had been disembowelled. Parts of her entrails were lying on the pavement and another portion was twisted round her throat.

He blew his whistle, and in a few seconds other officers came running up, and medical aid was summoned, but the woman was, of course quite dead.

Two sides of the square are formed by the extensive warehouses of Messrs. Kearly and Tonge, and Superintendent Foster says the watchman who was on duty in these buildings avers that the square was very quiet at the time, and he did not hear the slightest sound of anything unusual. Near the scene of the murder there is also a night fire-station, and the several men who were on duty also state that they heard nothing to attract their attention. A number of persons living within a few yards have also been questioned with a similar result, and they further say they saw nothing of a man and woman about the place.

The superintendent further said that Constable Watkins is a most reliable man and is no doubt correct about the time.

---

[100] **Chintz.** A printed, usually glazed, cotton fabric. (Morehead)

# Monday, 1 October, 1888

## ARRESTS

Shortly before midnight a man, whose name has not yet become known, was arrested in the Borough on suspicion of being the perpetrator of the murders in the East-end yesterday morning.

A tall, dark man, wearing an American hat, entered a lodging-house in Union-street, known as Albert Chambers. He stayed there throughout the day, and his peculiar manner riveted the attention of his fellow-lodgers. He displayed great willingness to converse with them, and certain observations he made regarding the topic of the day aroused their suspicions. Last night this mysterious individual attracted the notice of the deputy-keeper of the lodging-house, whose suspicions became so strong that he sent for a policeman.

On the arrival of the officer the stranger was questioned as to his recent wanderings, but he could give no intelligible account of them, though he said he had spent the previous night on Blackfriars Bridge. He was conveyed to Stones'-end Police-station, Blackman-street, Borough.

Two men at present detained at Leman-street Police-station in connection with the Commercial-road murder. One was arrested late last night, and the other this morning. They are now waiting for the arrival of detectives from Scotland-yard for identification.

The police are extraordinarily reticent with reference to the Mitre-square tragedy. The articles pledged at Jones, the pawnbroker, in Church-street, have been taken away by Detective-inspector M William, who has charged of the case. The pawnbroker states that the articles must have been pledged by a woman, as it is against the rule to receive goods from a man pledged in a woman's name. She cannot have been a regular customer, and he is doubtful whether he could identify her.

The Central News says: A man was arrested, last night, at a coffee-shop opposite the Thurlow Arms public-house at West Norwood, on suspicion of being connected with the Whitechapel murders. Suspicion appears to have been excited by his face being much scratched and by marks apparently of blood upon his clothes. No guilt either of complicity or of actual commission of the crime has, however, yet been proved against him.

—

## EXTRAORDINARY LETTERS THROUGH THE POST
## A BLOOD SMEARED POST CARD
## FROM
## "JACK THE RIPPER"

The Central News gives us the following information, namely, that on Thursday last a letter bearing the E.C. post mark,[101] directed in red ink, was delivered at their agency.

"September 25, 1888.

"Dear Boss—I keep on hearing the police have caught me, but they won't fix[102] me just yet. I have laughed when they look so clever and talk about being on the right track. That joke about Leather Apron gave me rare fits. I am down on whores, and I shan't quit ripping them till I do get buckled.[103] Grand work the last job was. I gave the lady no time to squeal. How can they catch me now? I love my work. I want to start again. You will soon hear from me with my funny little games. I saved some of the proper stuff in a ginger-beer bottle over the last job. I did write with it, but it went thick like glue and I couldn't use it. Red ink is fit enough, ha, ha, ha! The next job I do I shall clip the lady's ears and send them to the police-officers just for folly.[104] Wouldn't you keep this letter back till I do a bit more work; then give it out straight? My knife is so nice and sharp, I want to get to work right away, if I get the chance. Good, luck.

"Yours truly,
"JACK THE RIPPER."

"Don't mind me giving the trade name. Wasn't good enough to post this before I got all the red ink off my hands, curse it. They say I'm a doctor. Ha! ha! ha! ha!

The whole of this extraordinary epistle is written in red ink, in a free bold clerkly hand. It

---

[101] **E.C. Post Code**. East Central London. The city post codes were based on compass directions, W.C., West Central, then N, E, S.E., S.W., W and N.W. for the outlying areas. (PAF)

[102] **Fix**. As verb, (1) to arrest (1789). (Farmer)

[103] **Buckled**. Arrested, scragged. (ibid)

[104] **Folly**. Is folly being used here as a transliteration of *Folle*, French adj. for mad, insane? (Dubois)

220

was of course, treated as the work of a practical joker, but it is singular to note that the latest murders have been committed within a few days of the receipt of the letter, and that also in the case of the last victim the murderer made an attempt to cut off the ears, and did actually mutilate the face in a manner which has never before been attempted.

The letter has been placed in the hands of the Scotland yard authorities.

—

The Central News says: A post-card bearing the stamp "London, E., October 1," was received this morning, addressed to the Central News Office, the address and subject matter being written in red, and undoubtedly by the same person from whom the sensational letter already published, was received on Thursday last. Like the previous missive, this also has reference to the horrible tragedies in East London, forming, indeed, a sequel to the first letter. It runs as follows:

"I was not codding, dear old Boss, when I gave you the tip. You'll hear about saucy Jacky's work tomorrow. Double event this time. Number one squealed a bit. Couldn't finish straight off. Had not time to get ears for police. Thanks for keeping last letter back till I got to work again.

"JACK THE RIPPER.""

The card is smeared on both sides with blood, which has evidently been impressed thereon by the thumb or finger of the writer, the corrugated surface of the skin being plainly shown. Upon the back of the card some words are nearly obliterated by a bloody smear.

It is not, necessarily, assumed that this has been the work of the murderer, the idea that naturally occurs being that the whole thing is a practical joke. At the same time the writing of the previous letter immediately before the commission of the murders of yesterday was so singular a coincidence that it does not seem unreasonable to suppose that the cool, calculating villain who is responsible for the crimes has chosen to make the post as medium through which to convey to the Press his grimly diabolical humour.

—

## INTERVIEW WITH
## SIR JAMES RISDON BENNETT
## HIS VIEW OF THE ATTROCITIES

This morning a representative of the Central News interviewed two eminent London physicians for the purpose of ascertaining whether they could throw any scientific light on the East-end murders.

Sir James Risdon Bennett, of Cavendish-square, West, in the course of a conversation with the reporter said:—"I have no desire to promulgate any theory in reference to these murders. My purpose in writing to the Times the other day was simply to demonstrate the absurdity of the theory that the crimes were being committed for the purpose of supplying an American physiologist with uteruses.

I cannot believe for a moment that any commission has been given out for the collection of uteruses. It would be extremely easy here, or in America either, for a physiologist to secure this portion of the intestines. All he would have to do would be to apply to the public hospitals where there are always many paupers or unclaimed persons who are made the subjects of experiments, and his demands would be easily met.

Supposing, for instance, that a specialist proposed to lecture in the theatre of his institution upon the uterus, he would communicate with the surgeon, who would have no difficulty in providing him with sufficient number of specimens for all his purposes.

The notion that the uteruses were wanted in order that they might be sent out along with copies of a medical publication is ridiculous; not only ridiculous, indeed, but absolutely impossible of realization. I attach no importance whatever to that. If one sane man had instructed another sane man to procure a number of specimens of the uterus, the modus operandi would have been very different from that which has been pursued in these cases. The murderer has run a fearful and a quite unnecessary risk. The mutilations which he committed were to a great extent wanton, and did not assist him in the accomplishment of his intention.

My impression is that the miscreant is a homicidal maniac. He has a specific delusion, and that delusion is chronic. Of course we have at this moment very little evidence indeed, in fact I may say no evidence at all, as to the state

# Monday, 1 October, 1888

of the man's mind except so far as it is suggested by the character of the injuries which he has inflicted upon his victims.

I repeat that my impression is that he is a religious fanatic. It is possible that he is labouring under the delusion that he has a mandate from the Almighty to purge the world of prostitutes, and in the prosecution of his mad theory he has determined upon a crusade against the unfortunates of London, whom he seeks to mutilate by deprivation of the uterus.

There are, on the other hand, a number of theories which might be speculated upon as to the particular form that his mania takes; but inasmuch as we have no knowledge of the man himself, but only of the characteristics which surround the commission of his crimes wherewith to guide us; I come to the conclusion that his delusion has reference to matters of a sexual character.

The two crimes which were perpetrated, yesterday morning, do not lead me to modify my opinion that the assassin is a lunatic. Even if it should transpire that in the case of the Mitresquare victim the uterus is missing I should not be disposed to favour what I may call the American theory in the slightest degree, and I must confess that it was with considerable surprise that I noticed in certain newspapers a disposition to readily accept the theory which the coroner who investigated the circumstances attending the murder of the woman Chapman first suggested.

It is my opinion that if any person wanted a number of specimens of the uterus, and was himself a man possessed of surgical skill he would himself undertake to secure them rather than employ an agent. No love of gain could possibly induce a sane man to commit such atrocities as these, and besides this there is the circumstance remaining, as I have previously said, that they might all be secured at the medical institutions either of England or America—that is to say if they were needed for legitimate purposes—practically without any consideration at all.

It has been said—and it is a very natural observation—that if the murderer were a lunatic he could not commit these crimes and escape with impunity. That is a comment which any person not fully acquainted with the peculiarities of lunatic subjects might very well make.

In my view, however, the extraordinary cunning which is evinced by the homicide is a convincing proof of his insanity. No sane man could have escaped in just the same fashion as this man seems to have done. He must almost necessarily have betrayed himself.

It is a matter of common knowledge, however, amongst "mad doctors," that lunatics display a wonderful intelligence—if it may be called so—in their criminal operations, and I have little doubt that if the murderer were other than a madman he would ere this have been captured by the police. In many instances a madman's delusion is directed to only one subject, and he is mad upon that subject alone.

I doubt, however, that the murderer of these women is other than a man suffering from acute mania, and that being so, his infirmity would be obvious to almost every person with whom he came into contact. That is to say, if he were in the presence of either of us, we should probably say, "Oh, he's a madman."

There are many instances in which the common test is for the doctor to enter into conversation with the subject, to touch upon a variety of topics, and then, as if by accident, to mention the matter in regard to which the patient has a specific delusion, when the person's madness is manifested, although upon every other point he converses rationally. But here the disease is acute and I should say that those persons with whom he comes into daily contact, cannot regard him as a sane person.

Dr. Phillips has stated that the injuries inflicted upon these women have been apparently performed by a person possessing some anatomical knowledge. That is likely enough; but would not a butcher be quite capable of treating the body in this way?

Since I wrote my letter to the Times I have received several communications in support of my view. One of these comes from the Bishop of Bedford, who agrees with me that the theory of the American physiologist has no claim to credit. I wish to have it understood that my only desire is to remove from the public mind the evil impression which has been made by the suggestion that a member of the medical profession is more or less responsible for these murders.

I, however, believed in that theory, and these two last murders confirm me in the opinion that they are the work of a man suffering from acute mania to whom the ordinary rules of motive and procedure do not apply."

## DR. FORBES WINSLOW'S OPINION

Dr. Forbes Winslow, the eminent specialist in lunacy cases, said to our representative:—"I am more certain than even that these murders are being committed by a homicidal maniac, and there is no moral doubt in my mind that the assassin in each case is the same man. I have carefully read the reports in the morning papers, and they confirm me in the opinion which I had previously formed.

While I am clearly of opinion that the murderer is a homicidal maniac, I also believe him to be a mono-maniac, no I see no reason why he should not, excepting, at the periods when the fit is upon him, exhibit a cool and rational exterior. I have here, in my book—a work on psychology—a case in which a man had a lust for blood, as in this case, and he was generally a person of bland and pleasant exterior.

In all probability the whole of the murders had been committed by the same hand, but I may point out that the imitative faculty is very strong in persons of unsound mind, and that is the reason why there has been a sort of epidemic of these crimes. We shall probably find that a good many knives will be displayed to people within the next few weeks.

Still all the evidence that is forthcoming up to the present moment shows clearly enough that the Whitechapel crimes have been perpetrated by the same hand. My idea is that under the circumstances the police ought to employ, for the protection of the neigbourhood, and with the view of detecting the criminal, a number of officers who have been in the habit of guarding lunatics—that is to say, warders from asylums and other persons who have had charge of the insane. These men, if properly disposed in the neighbourhood, would assuredly note any person who was of unsound mind.

I have sent a letter embodying this suggestion to Sir Charles Warren, but I have received only a formal communication acknowledging its receipt. It is not easy to prevail upon the police to accept a suggestion from outside sources. This I discovered the other day when a man in emulation of the Whitechapel murder drew a knife and sharpened it in the presence of a relative of mine at Brighton under circumstances which have been published in the newspapers. When I made a statement to the police on that occasion they thought very little of it indeed.

I attach not the least importance to the American physiologist story. It is a theory which is utterly untenable, and I should think there were very few medical men who ever entertained it seriously.

All that has recently happened appears to me to be a strong confirmation of the views which I have previously given expression to upon the subject. The murderer is a homicidal mono-maniac of infinite cunning, and I fear he will not be brought to justice unless he be caught while engaging in the consummation of one of his awful crimes."

—

## POSSIBLE CLUES
## A FRAGMENT OF APRON

The police have made an important discovery, which they are of opinion affords a clue to the direction in which the murderer made his escape. Yesterday afternoon a portion of an apron was found in Goldstein-street, and when the body of the woman found in Mitre-square as searched, it was discovered that she was wearing the upper portion of the apron to which the piece found belonged. It is therefore concluded that the murderer made his way into Whitechapel.

—

## A KNIFE FOUND IN
## WHITECHAPEL-ROAD

Early this morning a police-constable was passing on his beat in the Whitechapel-road, when he came upon a black-handled knife, keen as a razor, and pointed like a carving-knife. The blade was ten inches long, about the length of weapon assumed by Dr. Phillips to have been used by the Hanbury-street murderer. It is looked upon by the police as supplying a link in the "man from Southampton arrest".

—

## THE BERNER STREET MURDER
## INQUEST THIS DAY

At the Vestry Hall, Cable-street, St. George's-in-the-East, this morning, Mr. Wayne Baxter, coroner for East Middlesex, opened the inquest on the remains of Elizabeth Stride, alias "Long Liz," the unfortunate woman who was so foully murdered in Berner-street early yesterday morning.

The room in which the inquiry was held is extremely spacious, and afforded ample accommodations for the jury, the representatives of the Press, who mustered in strong force, and members of the general public, who, however, were only sparingly admitted. The most intense excitement naturally reigns, this morning, throughout the whole district of St. George's-in-the-East, but the coroner's arrangements for preventing anything like over-crowding in the Vestry Hall were admirable.

The jury having been sworn, they accompanied the coroner to the mortuary, where the dead woman was lying, and many of them shuddered with horror as they viewed the ghastly sight. The corpse still lies in the condition in which it was taken to the mortuary, fully dressed, with the gaping wound in the throat unclosed, and with the bloodstains still on the face. It will be remembered that in previous cases the bodies had been washed and laid out before the jury had an opportunity of viewing them, but the coroner has wisely prevented this premature interference with the remains in the present case.

The first witness called was William West, who said:—I live at 40, Berner-street, Commercial-road, and am a printer. I live in one of the houses on the right hand side of the yard where the murder was committed. At No. 40 there is an International Working Men's club. Facing the street there is one window and a door on the ground floor. The door leads into a passage. At the side of the house there is another passage into the yard. There are two wooden gates at the entrance from the street into the yard. In the right had side gate there is a little doorway. The gates are sometimes left open all night. Sometimes the small door is also locked. There is no particular person to lock the gates so far as I know. In the yard, on the left hand side, there is only one house, but it is arranged into three small tenements, which have separate doors. There is no other way out of the yard except through the gate. Opposite the gate on the first floor there is a workshop occupied by Messrs. Hindley, sack manufacturers, but I do not think there is any way out through these premises. After Hindley's place there is a stable, which I think is unoccupied. Next to the stable are the

premises of the Club, which run back a considerable distance from the street into the yard. The front room on the ground floor is occupied as a room for meals. In the middle of the passage there is a staircase leading to the first floor. At the back of the dinning room there is a kitchen, between which and the yard there is a passage. There is a window from this kitchen into the passage, from which there is a doorway leading to the yard. The passage is only lit by a small window above this door. At the back of this kitchen there is a printing office, consisting of two rooms. The room adjoining the kitchen is a composing room, and the room behind that is used for the editor. As far as I remember, the compositors finished their work about 2 p.m. on Saturday. The editor was on the premises all day, either in his office or in the club, of which he is a member. He was there at the time of the discovery.

The Coroner: How many members are there of the club?

—About 75-80.

Is there any particular qualification for membership? Any working-man can be a member, of any nationality?

—Yes. It is a Socialist Club, and no one is supposed to be a member unless he professes Socialist principles. I had been to work in the printing-office until 2 p.m., on Saturday, and remained in the club until 9 p.m. I returned about 10.30, and remained there until a short time before the discovery of the deceased. When I returned at 10.30, I entered the club through the street door. A discussion was going on upstairs on the first floor where there is a large room for lectures and entertainments. There are here windows from this room into the yard. There would be about a hundred people in the room on Saturday night. The discussion cased between 11.30 and 12, when he bulk of the people left the premises through the street door as that is the most convenient exit. About 30 members remain behind, about 20 being upstairs and the rest downstairs. Some of those upstairs were discussing amongst themselves and others were singing.

(Inquest proceeding.)

# The Times

## THE MURDERS AT THE EAST-END.

Yesterday, Mr. Wynne E. Baxter, Coroner for the South-Eastern Division of Middlesex, opened an inquiry at the Vestry-hall, Cable-street, St. George's-in-the-East, respecting the death of Elizabeth Stride, who was found murdered in a yard in Berner-street on Sunday morning.

Detective-inspector E. Reid, H Division, watched the case on behalf of the Criminal Investigation Department.

The jury having viewed the body, the following evidence was taken:—

William West, who claimed to affirm, said he lived at 40, Berner-street, Commercial-road, and was a printer by occupation. He lived in one of the houses on the right hand side of the gateway. No. 40, Berner-street was the International Working Men's Club. On the ground floor, facing the street, was a window and a door—the latter leading into a passage. At the side of the house was a passage leading into a yard, and at the entrance to the passage were two wooden gates.

The Foreman.—Is that right?

The CORONER.—There is a passage before you get to the yard.

Witness, continuing, said the passage had two wooden gates folding backwards from the street. In the northern gate there was a little door. The gates were sometimes closed, and at other times left open all night. When the gates were closed the doorway was usually locked. They were seldom closed until late at night, when all the tenants had retired. As far as witness knew no particular person looked after the gates. In the yard on the left hand side there was only one house, which was occupied by two or three tenants. That house contained three doors leading to the yard, but there was no other exit from the yard except through the gates. Opposite the gate there was a workshop, in the occupation of Messrs. Hindley, sack manu-facturers. Witness did not believe there was any exit through that workshop. The manufacturing was on the ground floor, and he believed the ground floor of the premises was unoccupied. Adjoining Messrs. Hindley's premises there was a stable, which he believed was unoccupied. Passing this stable a person would come to the premises forming the club.

At this point the Coroner examined a parish map of Berner-street, which showed the yard referred to by the witness.

The witness, continuing, said he was not sure that the gardens of the houses in Batty-street faced the yard. The club premises ran back a long way into the yard. The front room on the ground floor of the club was occupied as a dining-room. At the middle of the passage there was a staircase leading to the first floor. At the back of the dining-room was a kitchen. In this room there was a small window over the door which faced the one leading into the yard. The remainder of the passage lead into the yard. Over the door in the passage was a small window, through which daylight came. At the back of the kitchen, but in no way connected with it, was a printing office. This office consisted of two rooms. The one adjoining the kitchen was used as a composing-room and the other one was for the editor. The compositors, on Saturday last, left off work at 2 o'clock in the afternoon, but the editor was there during the day. He was also a member of the club, and was either there or in his office until he went home. Opposite the doorway of the kitchen, and in the yard, were two closets. The club consisted of from 75 to 80 members. Any working man of any nationality could be a member of the club. It was a Socialist club.

The CORONER.—Have they to agree to any special principles?

Witness.—No person is supposed to be proposed as a member unless he was known to be a supporter of the Socialist movement.

By the CORONER.—Witness worked in the printing office. He remained in the club until about 9 o'clock on Saturday night. He then went out and returned about half-past 10. He then remained in the club until the discovery of the deceased. On the first floor of the club was a large room for entertainments, and from that room three windows faced the yard. On Saturday night a discussion was held in the large room among some 90 or 100 persons. The discussion ceased between 11:30 and 12 o'clock. The bulk of the people present then left the premises by the street door entrance, while between 20 and 30 members remained behind in the large room, and about a dozen were downstairs. Some of those upstairs had a discussion among themselves, while others were singing. The windows of the hall were partly open. Witness left the club about half-past 12. He slept at 2, William-street, and gave as his address 40, Berner-street, as he worked there all day. The distance from his lodgings to Berner-street was about five minutes' walk. Before leaving the club he had occasion to go to the printing office to put some literature there, and he went into the yard by the passage door, thence to the printing office. He then returned to the club by the same way. As he passed from the printing office to the club he noticed the yard gates were open, and went towards them, but did not actually go up to them. There was no lamp or light whatever in the yard. There were no lamps in Berner-street that could light the yard. The only light that could penetrate into the yard was from the windows of the club or the house that was let out in tenements. He noticed lights in one or two windows of the latter house, and they were on the first floor. When he went into the printing office the editor was there reading. Noises from the club could be heard in the yard, but there was not much noise on Saturday night. When he went into the yard and looked towards the gates there was nothing unusual that attracted his attention.

The CORONER.—Can you say there was any object on the ground?

Witness.—I cannot say that an object might have been there, and I not have seen it. I am rather shortsighted, but believe that, if anything had been there I should have seen it.

The CORONER.—What made you look towards the gates?

Witness.—Because they were open.

In further examination, witness said after he returned to the club he called his brother and they both left by the street door and went together home. Another member of the club, named Louis Stansley, left the club at the same time and accompanied them as far as James-street. Witness did not see any one in the yard, and as far as he could remember did not see any one in Berner-street. They went by way of Fairclough-street, Grove-street, and then to James's-street. Witness generally went home from Berner-street between 12 and 1 a.m. On some occasions he had noticed low women and men together in Fairclough-street, but had not seen any in Berner-street. He had never seen

any of these women against his club. About 12 months ago he happened to go into the yard and heard some conversation between a man and a woman at the gates. He went to shut the gates, and then saw a man and woman leave the entrance. That was the only occasion he had ever noticed anything.

By the Jury.—Witness was the overseer of the printing office.

Morris Eagle, who also claimed to affirm, stated that he lived at 4, New-road, Commercial-road, and was a traveller in jewelry. He was a member of the International Working Men's Club, and was there several times during the day. In the evening he occupied the chair and opened the discussion. About a quarter to 12 he left the club for the purpose of taking his young lady home. They left by the front door. He returned to the club about 25 minutes to 1. As he found the front door closed he went through the gateway leading into the yard, and through the back door leading into the club. As he passed through the yard he did not notice anything on the ground by the gates. He believed he passed along about the middle of the gateway, which was about 9ft. 2in. wide.

The CORONER.—Can you say if deceased was lying there when you went in?

Witness.—It was rather dark and I cannot say for certain if anything was there or not. I do not remember whether I met any one in Berner-street when I returned to the yard, neither do I remember seeing any one in the yard.

The CORONER.—Supposing you saw a man and woman in the yard, would you have remembered it?

Witness—I am sure I would.

The CORONER.—Did you notice if there were any lights in the house on the left-hand side?

Witness.—I do not remember.

The CORONER.—Are you often late at night at the club, and do you often go into the yard?

Witness.—I often am there until late, but have seldom gone into the yard. In fact, I have never seen a man or woman in the yard. On the same side as the club is a beershop and I have seen men and women coming from there.

A Juryman.

—That is always closed about 9 o'clock.

The CORONER.—What were you doing at

# Tuesday, 2 October, 1888

the club?

Witness.—As soon as I entered the club I went to see a friend, who was in the upstairs room, and who was singing a song in the Russian language. Afterwards I joined my friend, and we sang together. I had been there about 20 minutes, when a member named Gilleman came upstairs and said, "There is a dead woman lying in the yard." I went down in a second, and struck a match. I could then see a woman lying on the ground, near the gateway, and in a pool of blood. Her feet were about six or seven feet from the gate, and she was lying by the side of the club wall, her head being towards the yard. Another member, named Isaac, was with me at the time. As soon as I saw the blood I got very excited and ran away for the police. I did not touch her.

The CORONER.—Did you see if her clothes were disturbed?

Witness.—I could not say. When I got outside I saw Jacobs and another going for the police in the direction of Fairclough-street, and I then went to the Commercial-road, all the time shouting "Police!" On getting to the corner of Grove-street I saw two constables, and told them that a woman had been murdered in Berner-street. They returned with me to the yard. I then noticed several members of the club and some strangers were there. A constable threw his light on the body, and then told the other officer to go for a doctor, and sent me to the station for the inspector.

The CORONER.—Did you see any one touch the body?

Witness.—I think the policeman touched it, but the other persons appeared afraid to go near it. When I first saw the body of deceased, I should say it was about 1 o'clock, although I did not look at the clock.

In answer to the foreman of the jury, the witness further said he could not remember how far from the wall the body was lying.

On Saturday evening there were free discussions at the club for both men and women. Anyone could go in. On Saturday night there were some women there, but those he knew. He should say there were not more than six or eight women present. Saturday was not a dancing night, although after the discussion was ended some dancing might have been carried on. Had a cry of "Murder" been raised he

believed they would have heard it, or even any other cry of distress. Witness had never been in the stable or in Hindley's workshop, and could not say for certain whether there was any other exit from the yard except from the gateway.

Louis Diemschütz deposed that he lived at 40, Berner-street, and was steward of the club. The correct title of the club was International Working Men's Educational Club. Witness was a married man, and his wife assisted in the management of the club. Witness left home about half-past 11 on Saturday morning, and he returned home exactly at 1 o'clock on Sunday morning. He was certain about the time. Witness had with him a costermonger's barrow, and it was drawn by a pony. The pony was not kept in the yard of the club, but in George-yard, Cable-street. He drove home for the purpose of leaving his goods. He drove into the yard, and saw that both gates were wide open. It was rather dark there. He drove in as usual, and as he entered the gate his pony shied to the left. Witness looked to the ground on his right, and then saw something lying there, but was unable to distinguish what it was. Witness tried to feel the object with his whip before he got down. He then jumped down and struck a match. It was rather windy, but he was able to get a light sufficient to tell it was a woman lying there. He then went into the club, and saw his wife in the front room on the ground floor. He left his pony in the yard, just outside the club door, by itself. He told his wife, and several members who were in the room, that a woman was lying in the yard, but that he was unable to say whether she was drunk or dead. He then got a candle and went out into the yard. By the candlelight he could see that there was blood. He did not touch the body, but at once went off for the police. He passed several streets without seeing a policeman, and returned without one, although he called out "Police" as loud as he could. A young man whom he had met in Grove-street and told about the murder, returned with him. This young man lifted the woman's head up, and witness for the first time saw that her throat was cut. At the same moment the last witness and the constables arrived. When he first approached the club he did not notice anything unusual, and came from the Commercial-road end of the street.

By the CORONER.—The doctor arrived

about ten minutes after the police came. No one was then allowed to leave the place until their names and addresses were taken, and they had been searched. The clothes of the deceased, as far as he remembered, were in order. Deceased was lying on her side with her face towards the wall of the club. He could not say how much of the body was lying on the side. As soon as the police came witness went into the club and remained there.

The CORONER.—Did you notice her hands?

Witness.—I did not notice what position her hands were in. I only noticed that the dress buttons of her dress were undone. I saw the doctor put his hand inside and tell the police that the body was quite warm. The doctor also told one of the constables to feel the body, and he did so.

The CORONER.—Did you notice the quantity of blood about?

Witness.—The blood ran in the direction of the house from the neck of the woman. I should say there were quite two quarts of blood on the ground. The body was lying about one foot from the wall. In the yard were a few paving stones, which were very irregularly fixed.

The CORONER.—Have you ever seen men and women in the yard?

Witness.—I have not.

The CORONER.—Have you ever heard of their being found there?

Witness.—Not to my knowledge.

The Foreman.—Was there sufficient room for you to pass the body when you went into the yard?

Witness.—Yes; and I did so. When my pony shied I was passing the body, and was right by when I got down.

The CORONER.—Did the blood run down as far as the door of the club?

Witness.—Yes.

The Foreman.—When you went for the police, who was in charge of the body?

Witness.—I cannot say. As soon as I saw the blood I ran off.

In answer to Inspector Reid, the witness said everyone who was in the yard was detained. This included the strangers. Their names and addresses were taken, and they were questioned as to their presence there. They were also searched, and their hands and clothes examined by Dr. Phillips. It would have been possible for

any person to have escaped while he went into the club. Had any person run up the yard witness would have seen him.

The CORONER.—Is the body identified yet?

Inspector Reid.—Not yet.

The Foreman.—I cannot understand that, as she is called Elizabeth Stride.

The CORONER.—That has not yet been sworn to, but something is known of her. It is known where she lived. You had better leave that point until tomorrow.

At this stage the inquiry was adjourned until this afternoon.

—

The excitement caused by the murders committed early on Sunday morning in Berner-street, Commercial-road, and Mitre-square, Aldgate, has in no way abated. In the East-end statements and rumours of the most extra-ordinary nature were in circulation yesterday respecting conversations which certain persons, male and female, had had with two or three suspicious-looking men an hour or so before the crimes were committed, the purport of the statements in question being to connect the latter individuals with the outrages.

Nothing, however, can be extracted from these statements of sufficient importance to form any clue. A few arrests have been made by the Metropolitan Police, but none had been made by the City Police up to a late hour last night. The authorities are now fully on the alert in the localities of the murders, and, as stated below, it has been decided by the City Police to offer a reward for the discovery of the assassin.

It is satisfactory to announce that one discovery at least has been made which, in the hands of efficient detectives, should prove an important clue to the lurking-place of the murderer—for the belief is now generally entertained in official quarters that to one person alone is attributable the series of crimes which in the last few weeks have horrified and alarmed the public.

It appears after perpetrating his foul work in Mitre-square the miscreant retraced his steps towards the scene of the crime which he had committed an hour or so earlier. As stated in the particulars given in *The Times* of yesterday, part of the attire of the unfortunate woman who was butchered in Mitre-square consisted of a portion

# Tuesday, 2 October, 1888

of a coarse white apron, which was found loosely hanging about the neck.

A piece of this apron had been torn away by the villain, who, in proceeding to his destination further east after leaving the City boundary, presumably used it to wipe his hands or his knife on, and then threw it away. It was picked up in Goulston-street very shortly after the second murder had been committed, and it was brought to the mortuary by Dr. Phillips soon after the body had been removed there. It was covered with blood, and was found to fit in with the portion of apron which had been left by the murderer on his victim.

Goulston-street, it may be stated, is a broad thoroughfare running parallel with the Commercial-road and is off the main White-chapel-road, and the spot where the piece of apron was picked up is about a third of a mile from Mitre-square. By the direct and open route it is 1,550 feet, but it can be approached through several small streets, making the distance about 1,600 feet. These measurements were taken yesterday.

The only other clues in the possession of the police are two pawnbrokers' tickets which were found lying close to the spot where the Mitre-square murder was discovered, and a knife which was picked up by a police-constable in the Whitechapel-road early yesterday morning. It is described as black-handled, 10 inches long, keen as a razor, and pointed like a carving knife. The pawn-tickets are believed to have belonged to the woman. They were in a small tin box and related to pledges which had been made in August of a pair of boots and a man's shirt. The tickets had been made out in two names— Emily Birrell and Anne Kelly—and the articles had been pawned for 1s. and 6d. respectively with Mr. Jones, of Church-street, Spitalfields, who, however, cannot identify the woman as having made the pledges.

Photographs of the ill-fated creature were taken at the City Mortuary in Golden-lane both before and after the post-mortem examination, after which the features—which, as already reported in *The Times*, had been brutally cut about—were rendered more life-like by the doctors. Up to a late hour last night, however, the body had not been identified, though several persons, having missed relatives or friends have been taken to see it by the police.

Yesterday morning, shortly after 10 o'clock, an interview respecting the Mitre-square murder took place between Mr. M'William (the inspector of the City Detective Department), Superintendent Foster, and Inspector Collard and the City Coroner, who has arranged to hold the inquest on Thursday morning, it being hoped that the woman may be identified in the meantime. The plans taken by Mr. F.W. Foster, of Old Jewry, of the scene of this outrage immediately after it was discovered were submitted to the Coroner, and Mr. Foster will be one of the witnesses as the inquest.

The following is a description of a man seen in company with a woman who is supposed to be the victim of the murderer in the City. The man was observed in a court in Duke-street, leading to Mitre-square, about 1:40 a.m. on Sunday. He is described as of shabby appearance, about 30 years of age and 5ft. 9in. in height, of fair complexion, having a small fair moustache, and wearing a red neckerchief and a cap with a peak.

Two communications of an extraordinary nature, both signed "Jack the Ripper," have been received by the Central News Agency, the one on Thursday last and the other yesterday morning. The first—the original of which has been seen by Major Smith, the Assistant Commissioner of the City Police—was a letter, bearing the E.C. postmark, in which reference was made to the atrocious murders previously committed in the East-end, which the writer confessed, in a brutally jocular vein, to have committed; stating that in the "next job" he did he would "clip the lady's ears off" and send them to the police, and also asking that the letter might be kept back until he had done "a bit more work."

The second communication was a postcard, and as above stated, it was received yesterday morning. It bore the date, "London, E., October 1," and was as follows:—

"I was not codding, dear old Boss, when I gave you the tip. You'll hear about Saucy Jacky's work to-morrow. Double event this time. Number One squealed a bit; couldn't finish straight off. Had not time to get ears for police. Thanks for keeping the last letter back till I got to work again."

The postcard was sent to Scotland Yard. No doubt is entertained that the writer of both communications, whoever he may be, is the same person.

Many adverse remarks have been made concerning the want of vigilance on the part of the police in connexion with the outrages; but it should be remembered, as urged by them, that the women are of a class who know that they are liable to punishment if detected, and who, therefore, go alone to the places where they agree to meet their male companions.

Shortly after the first horrible murders were committed some weeks ago, special precautions were taken by the City Police authorities with a view to detect the criminal or criminals, several plain-clothes constables being ordered on the beats in the district which has now become so notorious.

Instructions were given to the constables to watch any man and woman seen together in suspicious circumstances, and especially to observe any woman who might be seen alone in circumstances of a similar nature.

At about the time when the Mitre-square murder was being committed two of the extra men who had been put on duty were in Windsor-street, a thoroughfare about 300 yards off, engaged, pursuant to their instructions, in watching certain houses, it being thought possible that the premises might be resorted to at some time by the murderer.

Five minutes after the discovery of the murder in Mitre-square, the two officers referred to heard of it, and the neighbourhood was at once searched by them, unfortunately without result. It is believed that had any man and woman been in company with each other going to Mitre-square they must have been observed, and that the man in that case would have been detected and captured. The supposition of the police is that the murderer and the ill-fated woman went to the place separately, having made an appointment.

The general impression is that no man in his right senses could have perpetrated such a series of dreadful crimes. Some of the doctors who have been engaged in the examination of the bodies believe it quite possible that the murders may have been committed in from three to five minutes.

—

At a late hour last night it was decided by the City Police to offer a reward for the discovery and conviction of the criminal, and the following notice was forwarded to us:—

"Murder - £500 Reward.

"Whereas, at 1:45 a.m. on Sunday, the 30th of September last, a woman, name unknown, was found brutally murdered in Mitre-square, Aldgate, in this City, a reward of £500 will be paid by the Commissioner of Police of the City of London to any person (other than a person belonging to a police force in the United Kingdom), who shall give such information as shall lead to the discovery and conviction of the murderer or murderers.

"Information to be given to the Inspector of the Detective Department, 26, Old Jewry, or at any police-station.

"JAMES FRASER. Colonel,
Commissioner.
"City of London Police Office,
26, Old Jewry,
October 1, 1888."

The Lord Mayor, acting upon the advice of Colonel Sir James Fraser, K.C.B., the Commissioner of City Police, will, in the name of the Corporation of London, offer a reward of £500 for the detection of the Whitechapel murderer, the last crime having been committed within the jurisdiction of the City. The Common Council on Thursday will confirm the action of his lordship.

—

During yesterday three persons were detained at the Leman-street Police-station on suspicion of being connected with the murder in Berner-street, but no evidence of a serious nature was obtained against them.

—

The report of the arrest of a man on Sunday night at the Albert-chambers, Gravel-lane, Southwark, was not strictly correct. The man was not taken into custody at all, but was merely requested to go to Stones-end police-station by a detective in order that he might give an account of himself. After a detention of half-an-hour he was allowed to go back to the lodging-house.

—

Police-sergeant Dudman had his attention drawn yesterday afternoon to No. 36, Mitre-Street, a house a short distance from where the

# Tuesday, 2 October, 1888

second murder was committed, and there he found what appeared to be bloodstains upon the doorway and underneath the window, as if a person had wiped his fingers on the window ledge and drawn a bloodstained knife down part of the doorway. Mr. Hurtig, who lives on the premises, said he had only just before noticed the stains. Almost immediately afterwards the same police officer had his attention drawn to similar marks on the plate-glass window of a shop at the corner of Mitre-square; but the occupier ridiculed the idea that they could have anything to do with the murders, as the windows were covered at night by shutters.

—

With reference to the murder in Berner-street, Mrs. Diemschütz, the stewardess of the Socialist Club in that thoroughfare, has made the following statement:—"Just about 1 o'clock on Sunday morning I was in the kitchen on the ground floor of the club and close to the side entrance. I am positive I did not hear any screams or sound of any kind."

The servant at the club strongly corroborates the statement made by her mistress, and is equally convinced that there were no sounds coming from the yard between 20 minutes to 1 and 1 o'clock.

—

Yesterday evening a singular discovery, which is supposed to afford an important clue to the murderer, was being investigated by the police at Kentish-town. At about 9 o'clock in the morning the proprietor of the Nelson Tavern, Victoria-road, Kentish-town, entered a place of convenience[105] adjoining his premises for the purpose of pointing out to a builder some alterations which he desired executed, when a paper parcel was noticed behind the door.

No particular importance was attached to the discovery until an hour later, when Mr. Chinn, the publican, while reading the newspaper, was struck with the similarity of this bundle to the one of which the police have issued a description as having been seen in the possession of a man last seen in company with the woman Stride.

The police at the Kentish-town-road Police-station were told of the discovery, and a detective officer was at once sent to make inquiries. It was then found that the parcel, which had been kicked into the roadway, contained a pair of dark trousers.

The description of the man wanted on suspicion of having committed the murders gives the colour of the trousers he wore as dark. The paper which contained the trousers was stained with blood.

—

Albert Backert, of 13, Newnham-street, White-chapel, made a further statement yesterday in amplification of that which has already been published. He said:—On Saturday night, at about seven minutes to 12, I entered the Three Nuns Hotel, Aldgate. While in there an elderly woman, very shabbily dressed, came in and asked me to buy some matches. I refused and she went out.

A man who had been standing by me remarked that those persons were a nuisance, to which I responded "Yes." He then asked me if I knew how old some of the women were who were in the habit of soliciting outside. I replied that I knew, or thought, that some of them who looked about 25 were over 35. He then asked me whether I thought a woman would go with him down Northumberland-alley—a dark and lonely court in Fenchurch-street. I said I did not know, but supposed she would.

He then went outside and spoke to the woman who was selling matches and gave her something. He returned, and I bid him good-night at about ten minutes past 12. I believe the woman was waiting for him. I do not think I could identify the woman, as I did not take particular notice of her; but I should know the man again.

He was a dark man, about 38 years of age, about 5ft. 6in. or 5ft. 7in. He wore a black felt hat, a dark morning coat, a black tie, and a carried a black shiny bag.

—

The following correspondence has passed between the editor of the *Financial News* and the Home Office:—

"11, Abchurch-lane, London, E.C.,

Oct. 1.

"Sir,—In view of your refusal to offer a reward out of Government funds for the discovery of the perpetrator or perpetrators of the recent murders in the East-end of London, I am instructed on

---

[105] **Place of Convenience.** Privy, water-closet, toilet.

231

behalf of several readers of the *Financial News*, whose names and addresses I enclose, to forward you the accompanying cheque for £300, and to request you to offer that sum for this purpose in the name of the Government.

"Awaiting the favour of your reply,

I have the honour to be
your obedient servant;
"HARRY H. MARKS.
"The Right Hon. Henry Matthews, M.P.,
Secretary of State for the
Home Department."

"Oct. 1.

"My dear Sir,—I am directed by Mr. Matthews to acknowledge the receipt of your letter of this date containing a cheque for £300, which you say has been contributed on behalf of several readers of the Financial News, and which you are desirous should be offered as a reward for the discovery of the recent murders in the East-end of London.

"If Mr. Matthews had been of opinion that the offer of a reward in these cases would have been attended by any useful result he would himself have at once made such an offer, but he is not of that opinion.

"Under these circumstances, I am directed to return you the cheque (which I enclose), and to thank you, and the gentlemen whose names you have forwarded, for the liberality of their offer, which Mr. Matthews much regrets he is unable to accept.

"I am, Sir, your obedient servant,
"E. LEIGH PEMBERTON."

Colonel Sir Alfred Kirby, J.P., the officer commanding the Tower Hamlets Battalion, Royal Engineers, has offered, on behalf of his officers, a reward of £100, to be paid to anyone who will give information that would lead to the discovery and conviction of the perpetrator or perpetrators of the murders.

Sir A. Kirby is ready to place the services of 50 members of his corps at the disposal of the authorities, to be utilized in assisting them in any way they may consider desirable, either for the protection of the public or finding out the criminals. Of course, the Volunteers would have to be made use of as citizens, and not in a quasi-military capacity.

—

At a meeting of the Whitechapel District Board of Works, held yesterday evening, Mr. Robert Gladding presiding, Mr. Catmur said he thought that the board, as the local authority, should express their horror and abhorrence of the crimes which had been perpetrated in the district, and that, although it was not within their province to suggest anything, it would be right that they should address the authorities really responsible.

Proceeding, Mr. Catmur spoke of the evil effect which had resulted in the district in the loss of trade. Evening business had become practically extinct in many trades, women finding themselves unable to pass through the streets without an escort. Moreover, the inefficiency of the police was shown in the striking circumstance that but an hour or two later than the murders in Berner-street and Mitre-square the post-office in the immediate vicinity was broken into and property of the value of £100 taken from it.

Mr. Nicholson said that, while the local authority might not be responsible for the efficiency of the police, they were responsible for the proper lighting of the district. In one instance, which he mentioned, a court had been absolutely without light for nearly a week.

Mr. Abrahams said he could not agree with the wholesale condemnation of the police.

The Rev. Daniel Greatorex, said that the panic caused by the crimes was so great that emigrants refused now to stay in Whitechapel even temporarily.

The new system of police duties, under which constables were frequently changed from one district to another, kept the policemen ignorant of their beats. This was one great cause of police inefficiency. Formerly constables were acquainted, not only with the streets in their district, but also with all the houses.

The chairman said that local bodies had no responsibility in these matters, as the management of the police had been taken away from them.

Mr. Telfer hoped that the recent crimes would result in a reversion to the old system, under which constables were acquainted with

# Tuesday, 2 October, 1888

every corner of their beats.

Mr. G. T. Brown said that the weak point in the London police system was the want of a proper detective service to deal with the criminal portion of the community.

After further discussion the following resolution was carried, on the motion of Mr. Catmur, seconded by Mr. Barham:—"That this board regards with horror and alarm, the several atrocious murders recently perpetrated within the district of Whitechapel and its vicinity, and calls upon Sir Charles Warren so to locate and strengthen the police force in the neighbourhood as to guard against any repetition of such atrocities, and that the Home Secretary be addressed in the same terms."

———

A meeting of the Vigilance Committee which has for some time been formed in Whitechapel, was held yesterday at Mile-end, and a resolution passed calling upon the Home Office to issue a substantial Government reward for the capture and conviction of the murderer.

———

A correspondent writes:—"There are most remarkable coincidences with regard to the times at which all these murders have been committed which demand particular attention. The first and third of the murders, those of Martha Turner and Mrs. Chapman, were committed on exactly the same date of two separate months—namely, the 7th of August and September, while the second and fourth murders had the same relative coincidence, both being perpetrated on the last days of August and September. If the same hand carried out these crimes, these facts seem to point to the idea that the criminal was one who had to be absent from the scene of his crimes for regular periods."

A correspondent writes, October 1:—"Your leading article of to-day recalls the successful employment of a bloodhound in the detection of a barbarous murder at Blackburn 12 years ago. It may be noted that in this case two days at least had elapsed between the commission of the crime and its detection by means of the dog.

Another relevant case is thus related in Jesse's 'Anecdotes of Dogs':—'A servant, discharged by a sporting country gentleman, broke into his stables by night, and cut off the ears and tail of a favourite hunter. As soon as it was discovered, a bloodhound was bought into

the stable, who at once detected the scent of the miscreant, and traced it more than 20 miles. He then stopped at a door, whence no power could move him. Being at length admitted, he ran to the top of the house, and, bursting open the door of a garret, found the object that he sought in bed, and would have torn him to pieces had not the huntsman, who had followed him on a fleet horse, rushed up after him.'

Bewick, after mentioning the detective qualities of the bloodhound, observes, rather unfortunately, that 'as the arm of justice is now extended over every part of the country, and there are no secret recesses where villainy may lay concealed, these services are no longer necessary.'"

———

## TO THE EDITOR OF THE TIMES.

Sir,—Paying my daily visit to my church this afternoon I was surprised to find the caretaker in a semi-stupified state.

Asking her what was the matter, she told me that a man had just entered the church, and finding her all alone inquired whether I was in the vestry. On receiving a reply in the negative he said, "I see you are alone," and immediately took out a pocket-handkerchief and dashed it in her face. The strong smell of whatever liquid it had been steeped in dazed and stupefied her, and she for a moment or two lost her consciousness. The noise of some of the workmen on the roof seemed to have alarmed this scoundrel, and he bolted out of the church.

This incident, Sir, perhaps might afford a clue. At any rate, it will warn solitary women who are in charge of churches.

I am Sir, your obedient servant,
J. M. S. BROOKE.
Vestry of
St. Mary Woolnoth
and St. Mary Woolchurch Haw,
Lombard-street, E.C.

———

## THE WHITECHAPEL MURDERS.
VIENNA, OCT. 1.

With reference to the recent atrocious murders in London, attention may be called to a crime of an exactly similar kind which preoccupied the public in this country for nearly three years. A Galician Jew named Ritter was accused in 1884 of having murdered and mutilated a Christian woman in a village near

233

# Tuesday, 2 October, 1888

Cracow. The mutilation was like that perpetrated on the body of the woman Chapman, and at the trial numbers of witnesses deposed that among certain fanatical Jews there existed a superstition to the effect that if a Jew became intimate with a Christian woman he would atone for his offence by slaying and mutilating the object of his passion. Sundry passages of the Talmud were quoted which, according to the witnesses, expressly sanctioned this form of atonement. The trial caused an immense sensation, and Ritter, being found guilty, was sentenced to death.

The Judges of the Court of Appeal, however, feeling that the man was the victim of popular error and anti-Semitic prejudice, ordered a new trial upon some technicality. Again a jury pronounced against Ritter, and once more the Court of Appeal found a flaw in the proceedings. A third trial took place, and for the third time Ritter was condemned to be hanged, but upon this the Court of Appeal quashed the sentence altogether, and Ritter was released, after having been in prison 37 months. There is no doubt that the man was innocent, but the evidence touching the superstitions prevailing among some of the ignorant and degraded of his co-religionists remains on record and was never wholly disproved.[106]

~

## The Star
### THE MURDERS.
### POINTS FROM THE PUBLIC.
### We Give the Pith of Some of the Hundreds of Letters Received by "The Star."
### Suggestions for Detection.

"Lex," writing from Oxford, favours the idea of having the East-end patrolled by detectives disguised as "unfortunates," and armed.

"Greek" thinks about two dozen of the oldest of the loose women in the district should be entrusted with police whistles, pawn brokers in the vicinity being notified not to receive the whistles. The same correspondent suggests that some well-known clever members of the criminal class should be employed for a month at a small salary to endeavour to catch the murderer on their own account, the offered reward being, of course, their great inducement.

"A.J.F." contends that after, say, two a.m. until daylight the number of street-walkers in Whitechapel is so small that even with the present staff of police a vigilant watch should be kept upon their movements.

Mr. Robert E. King, of 1, St. Agnes-terrace, Victoria-park-road, writes:— Referring to the latter portion of your editorial headed "The Conduct of the Police," I shall be pleased to form one of a vigilance committee, such as you suggest. I will freely give my services in such a cause without fee or reward.

"W.A.G." writes:—Let the criminal authorities who are investigating the mystery compel every slaughterman to submit himself to medical examination, and those men where homicidal tendencies are found to be abnormally developed, let them be compelled to prove an *alibi* for any one of the dates on which the murders were committed.

Mr. N. T. Mooney asks:—"Where are the bloodhounds?" Ugh! Matthews!

Sir Charles Warren is advised by "Tie" to issue an edict prohibiting slaughterers or butchers to wear their gory clothing in the street after dark or before dawn. The murderer would not then so easily escape in repeating his crimes. (But Warren is not yet sole dictator.)

Charles Hambleton writes from Burslem to remind us that the discovery of Fish, the

---

[106] See **The Ritter Trial**, p.398.

234

# Tuesday, 2 October, 1888

Blackburn murderer, was brought about by the aid of bloodhounds, and suggests that the police keep a couple where they can be got at at a moment's notice.

Hugh Hillhouse would like to see started a national subscription to a fund as a reward to the capturer of the miscreant.

"Frangipanni" believes that if every inhabitant of the metropolis made the detection and capture of the murderer a matter of personal interest, he could not escape for long.

"R.W." says:—May we hope that, after a few more of these leisurely-executed crimes have been perpetrated in our midst, Sir Charles Warren, Mr. Matthews, or both, will sanction the use of trained bloodhounds and the offer of a substantial reward?

"One Ready to Act" suggests that the authorities enrol a number of prominent East-end tradesmen willing to supplement our detectives, and act in conjunction with our police.

W. H. Spencer-Howell writes:—I would suggest that a few young men of somewhat feminine appearance should be got up disguised as females. They should wear around their necks steel collars made after the style of a ladies' collaret, coming well down the breast, and likewise well down the back. My reason for this is owing to the fact that the assassin first severs his victim's windpipe, thereby preventing her raising any alarm.

## Quite Another Matter.

"J.S.," writing from Bath, says:—I just fancy to myself what would the cry be if half the dastardly crimes had occurred in poor Ireland! The Government would be called upon to send more soldiers over; so I think it would be better for the country if the Government would order the soldiers from Ireland to London, as the police seem so inefficient there.

From the Dulwich Reform Club[107] Mr. Francis Grannell writes:—As Warren and his baton men have proved conclusively to be totally inadequate to perform their duties as a police force, I would suggest that Balfour recall some of the military force from Ireland to assist in detecting the monster. The men might receive pay for this "special" duty from the Secret

Service fund instead of employing it in "shadowing" John Dillon and William O'Brien.

I should like to ask Sir Charles Warren, writes Mr. Joseph Walker, from 13, Dante-road, S.E., if—supposing the police had been provided with bloodhounds which had been put on the track directly the body was discovered in Mitre-square, whether they do not think the murderer would have been tracked before he had cleansed himself. There is no doubt he walked away, as no vehicle was seen. I venture to say that if half of these atrocities had been committed in the West-end upon ladies London would have been placarded with a reward of not less than £1,000.

"Withdraw the Irish Constabulary from Ireland, let them be the guardians of Trafalgar-square and Scotland-yard, and reinstate the London policeman in his old position, and," says H. A. Morris, "the two burning problems of the day will be solved."

## Who the Murderer May Be.

"A Labourer" suggests that the perpetrator of the murders may be a woman, a Kate Webster[108] who has gained anatomical knowledge while learning midwifery.

Fred W. Ley suggests that the murderer is a religious fanatic.

Mr. T. Barry thinks that the man must be one who, having been ruined by dissipation, is having his revenge.

"A Reader" thinks the murderer will be found among a class well known to the unfortunates themselves, as he escapes so easily.

C. J. Solomons, of Hanbury-street, Spitalfields, has come to the conclusion that the murders cannot have been done by any person in a common lodging-house. Signs of blood on such a man would certainly be noticed. It must be some person who has a room where he can go at any time unnoticed and have a change of

---

[107] **The Dulwich Reform Club** affiliated with the Home Rule Union, which promoted Irish self-governance, in 1888. (Home Rule Union)

[108] **"Richmond Murder"**. Kate Webster was the 30 year old Irish maid who murdered the widow Julia Martha Thomas on 2 March, 1879, dismembered the body, boiled the flesh from the bones then disposed of most of them in the Thames. It was rumoured that she gave the fat rendered from the body to neighbours, telling them it was lard. After posing as Mrs. Thomas for two weeks, Webster fled to Ireland, where she was captured 29 March. She was tried in the Old Bailey, condemned and executed at Wandsworth Prison 29 July, 1879.

# Tuesday, 2 October, 1888

clothing.

"Justice" thinks the perpetrator might be a fanatic among the members of the Society for the Suppression of Prostitution,[109] or of a vigilance committee, who is murdering to frighten prostitutes from the streets.

—

### Matthews Unchanged.

The editor of the *Financial News* has received the following letter:—

1 Oct., 1888.

My Dear Sir,—I am directed by Mr. Matthews to acknowledge the receipt of your letter of this date, containing a cheque for £300, which you say has been contributed on behalf of several readers of the *Financial News*, and which you are desirous should be offered as a reward for the discovery of the recent murders in the East-end of London.

If Mr. Matthews had been of opinion that the offer of a reward in these cases would have been attended by any useful result he would himself have at once made such an offer, but he is not of that opinion.

Under these circumstances, I am directed to return you the cheque (which I enclose), and to thank you and the gentlemen whose names you have forwarded for the liberality of their offer, which Mr. Matthews much regrets he is unable to accept.—I am, Sir, your very obedient servant,

E. LEIGH PEMBERTON.

Harry H. Marks, Esq.

---

[109] The writer is probably referring to the **Society for the Suppression of Vice**, founded in 1802 by William Wilberforce. It succeeded the 1691 Society for the Reformation of Manners (Morals). The goals of the Society were to stamp out "profanation of the Lord's Day and profane swearing; publication of blasphemous, licentious and obscene books and prints; selling by false weights and measures; keeping of disorderly public houses, brothels and gaming houses; procuring; illegal lotteries; cruelty to animals."
In August, 1885 the Society for the Suppression of Vice merged with the National Vigilance Association, which stood "for the enforcement and improvement of the laws for the repression of criminal vice and public immorality."

### The Man From Texas.

The New York correspondent of the *Daily News* cables the suggestion of a theory that the perpetrator of the Whitechapel murders may be a man who a few months ago committed a series of remarkably brutal murders in Texas.[110] The crimes caused great local excitement, but aroused less interest than would otherwise have been the case because the victims were chiefly negro women. A leading Southern paper thus puts the argument:

"In our recent annals of crime there has been no other man capable of committing such deeds. The mysterious crimes in Texas have ceased. They have just commenced in London. Is the man from Texas at the bottom of them all? The fact that he is no longer at work in Texas argues his presence somewhere else. His peculiar line of work was executed in precisely the same manner as is now going on in London. Why should he not be there?"[111]

The Superintendent of the New York Police admits the possibility of this theory being correct, but he does not think it probable.

—

### Fourteen More to Come.

The following letter, evidently the work of someone who tried to disguise his style and handwriting, was received this morning. We are not, however, inclined to believe that the actual murderer has favoured us with his plan of campaign:—

Oct 1st 1888

MR STAR

as you take great interest in the Murders i am the one that that did it wouldent you like to see me but you shant just yet i mean to do some more yet i have done 6 i am going to do 14 More then go back to america the next time i shall do 3 in one night i dont live a

---

[110] See Appendix M, The Texas Axe Murders. *The Atlanta Constitution,* 21 July, 1887, **A Texan Mr. Hyde**, p. 577.
[111] See Appendix M, The Texas Axe Murders. *The Atlanta Constitution*, 26 September, 1888, **Is It the Man from Texas?**, p. 577.

236

thousand miles from the spot not in a common lodging house

Yours in luck
THE BUTCHER.

—

**FIFTH EDITION.**
**WHITECHAPEL.**
**MORE SCARES AND ARRESTS,**
**BUT NO CLUE OF VALUE.**
**MATTHEWS WILL NOT BUDGE.**
**The Mitre-square Victim Still Unidentified**
**Clues Disappear or Become Worthless**

The police have made no visible progress toward the discovery of the master-murderer of the age. The denizens of that portion of London where he has thus far pursued his career of crime continue to live in fear of their lives, and the rest of the city is in momentary expectation of fresh evidence of his fiendish cunning. Such an adept in the art of assassination need never run short of victims nor of opportunities for their annihilation.

The labyrinths of the Whitechapel district are far too dense and extensive for every dark corner to be constantly under the eye of the police, however greatly their number may be augmented, and

**A RED-HANDED MANIAC**

who appears and disappears as if through a trap door in the earth would seem to run small risk of capture. Indeed, it is the knowledge of his supreme success that it is feared will nerve him to a speedy reappearance in the same character. There is scarcely one person who has taken more than ordinary interest in these so-called Whitechapel murder cases who believes that the murders will cease till the murderer is captured. Such appetites as his are not so easily satisfied.

He covers his tracks so well that there seems to be little hope of his ever being captured except in the actual commission of or flight from the scene of a fresh outrage. So general is this idea becoming, even in the minds of the police, that their operations partake quite as much, if not more, of the character of a guard against the reappearance of the assassin, as of an investigation of his past deeds of violence. All their efforts to get a tangible clue on which to work have been futile. Inquiry at the Bishops-gate and Leman-street police-stations this morning developed the fact that there was
**NO CLUE WHATEVER.**

The threads that had been taken up on the possible chance of their leading to something tangible have been laid down again. It is but fair to say that the police have clutched eagerly at every straw that promised to help them out, but there is nothing left to work on. People have come forward by scores to furnish the description of a man they had seen with some woman near the scene, and not a great while before the commission of one or the other of
**SUNDAY MORNING'S CRIMES,**
but no two of the descriptions are alike, and none of the accompanying information has thus far been able to bear investigation.

In the matter of the Hungarian who said he saw a struggle between a man and a woman in the passage where the Stride body was afterwards found, the Leman-street police have reason to doubt the truth of the story. They arrested one man on the description thus obtained, and a second on that furnished from another source, but they are not likely to act further on the same information without additional facts. If every man should be arrested who was known to have been seen in company with an abandoned woman in that locality on last Saturday night, the police-stations would not hold them.

There are many people in that district who volunteer information to the police on the principle of securing lenient treatment for their own offences, and there are others who turn in descriptions on the chance of coming near enough the mark to claim a portion of the reward if the man should be caught, just as one buys a ticket in a lottery. Even where such information is given in good faith, it can rarely be looked upon in the light of a clue.
**SUPERINTENDENT FORSTER**
stated to a *Star* reporter this morning that he believed they had to deal with a man who was far too clever to go about boasting of what he was going to do.

Every drunken man was more or less liable to seek a temporary notoriety by proclaiming himself the Whitechapel murderer. Very many of these reports are taken in hand by the detectives at once, not so much because they expect to get a clue out of them as because it might be unsafe to neglect anything of that character, but at the time when the *Star* man made the rounds of the police stations this morning the detectives had come to a standstill. The reported

## BLOODSTAINS ON THE WINDOW SILL

of No. 36, Mitre-street, turned out to be nothing but candle-grease, and if it had been blood it would have indicated nothing but what was already made plain by the finding of the apron in Goldstein-street.

The police are well satisfied that the murderer, having finished the mutilation of the body in Mitre-square, heard footsteps approaching, and had to make an exit before he could remove any of the personal evidences of his crime. He tore a piece off his victim's apron, wiped his hands and his knife on it as he went along, and dropped the bloodstained rag when he was sure he would not be observed. That he did this in Goldstein-street does not occasion any surprise. The police have never doubted that this midnight murderer lived in the midst of the community he has been terrorising.

## THE PAWNTICKETS

afford no clue. The articles that were pawned have been secured by the police, but the pawn-broker can only say that they must have been offered by a woman, since it is his rule not to take a woman's name from a man. It is not to be expected that he can identify a mutilated dead body as a casual customer, and there is no good reason why the Mitre-square woman may not have given the names on the tickets as well as that Elizabeth Stride should have given a wrong name. The police are trying to trace the unidentified woman by the names on the tickets, and also to learn if Stride was ever known by either of the names, but they have not yet been successful.

Superintendent Forster stated this morning that it was untrue that two shirt studs were found by the body in Mitre-square. The only articles of that kind were a couple of buttons that had been torn off the dead woman's dress.

## A WOMAN FROM ROTHERHITHE,

accompanied by her son-in-law and another man, called at the Bishopsgate-street Police-station yesterday to get permission to see the body. She had read a description of the murdered woman and feared it was her sister. Her attention had been particularly attracted by the statement that the letters "T.C." were tattooed upon the left forearm in blue ink. The woman said she had for many years lost sight of her sister, who was living she understood, with a man named Kelly, in a street leading from Bishopsgate. This sister had had "T.C." tattooed upon her arm by her husband, whose initials they were. Kelly was the name, it will be remembered, which figured on one of the pawntickets supposed to belong to the deceased.

The party were taken to the mortuary, and recognised the body as that of the relation they were in search of. The woman said she knew it from the forehead (the only part of the face that was recognisable) as well as from the marks on the arms, and also from some peculiarity of the body. There seemed to be no doubt of the identification, and an officer went with the visitors to make inquiries at the place where the missing woman was said to have lived.

The door of the house was opened by the woman herself. Her sister nearly fainted at the sight. The officer brought the news back to the police station, where his story was barely credited, so positive had the woman been in her identification. This is the only occasion thus far that any one has thought they recognised the body, and the authorities are very doubtful if it is ever to be identified.

## THE REWARD OF £500

offered by the City of London is worded as follows:—

Whereas at 1.45 a.m. on Sunday, the 30th of September last, a Woman, name unknown, was found brutally murdered in Mitre-square, Aldgate, in this City, a Reward of £500 will be paid by the Commissioner of Police of the City of London to any person (other than a person belonging to a police force in the United Kingdom) who shall give such information as shall lead to the discovery and conviction of the murderer or murderers. Information to be given to the Inspector of the Detective Department, 26, Old Jewry, or at any police-station.

JAMES FRASER,
Colonel, Commissioner.
City of London Police Office.
26, Old Jewry, 1 Oct., 1888.

It will be noticed that a point is made of the exclusion from the benefits of the reward of members of any police force in the kingdom. It is

# Tuesday, 2 October, 1888

believed in some quarters that this clause was inserted to avoid the contingency of the City paying over a reward to any member of the Metropolitan Police Force. A prominent police official stated to-day, however, that it was inserted on the general principle that no police officer needed the prospect of a reward to incite him to do his duty, and because, moreover, there was little fear that any police officer who might capture such a criminal as this would fail of due recognition.

It was noticeable to those who frequent East London after midnight that—possibly as an effect of the offer of rewards—there were a good many more people about the streets early this morning than yesterday. Men whose faces were strange there were to be seen strolling about in pairs, peering into dark corners, and patrolling the back streets like amateur detectives.

—

## Time Table of the Murders.

A correspondent writes:—"There are most remarkable coincidences with regard to the times at which all these murders have been committed which demand particular attention. The first and third of the murders, those of Martha Turner and Mrs. Chapman, were committed on exactly the same date of two separate months—namely, the 7th August and September, while the second and fourth murders had the same relative coincidence, both being perpetrated on the last days of August and September. If the same hand carried out these crimes, these facts seem to point to the idea that the criminal was one who had to be absent from the scene of his crimes for regular periods."

—

## Ludwig Released.

This morning, at the Thames Police-court, Charles Ludwig, too, was brought up on remand charged with threatening to stab Elizabeth Burns, an unfortunate, of 55, Flower and Dean-street, Spitalfields, and also with threatening to stab Alexandra Finlay.

Mrs. Burns stated that about half-past three on the morning of Monday week she was in the Whitechapel-road. Ludwig accosted her, and they went up Butcher's-row. Ludwig put his arm round her neck. When she saw an open knife in his hand she screamed, and two policemen walked up. Prisoner did not say anything at the time, but before that he had been talking to her in English. She heard him tell the police he was a barber.

Prisoner, who says he cannot speak English, said, through the medium of an interpreter, "In the name of all that's good why should I wish to do it? Why did the police not take me?"

The evidence of Finlay showed that at three o'clock on the morning of Tuesday fortnight Ludwig came to a coffee-stall in the Whitechapel-road intoxicated. The man in charge of the stall refused to serve him. Ludwig seemed much annoyed, and said to witness, "What are you looking at?" He then pulled out a long-bladed knife and threatened to stab witness with it. Ludwig followed him round the stall, and made several attempts to stab him, until witness threatened to knock a dish on his head. A constable came up, and witness gave the accused into custody.

Constable 221 H said that when he took Ludwig into custody he was very excited. Witness had previously received information that Ludwig was wanted for attempting to cut a woman's throat. On the way to the station he dropped a long-bladed knife, which was open; and when he was searched a razor and a long-bladed pair of scissors were found on him.

Inspector Pimley, H Division, stated that the prisoner had fully accounted for his whereabouts on the nights of the recent murders.

Mr. Saunders taking into consideration that prisoner had been in custody a fortnight, now discharged him.

~

# Tuesday, 2 October, 1888

## 𝔈𝔳𝔢𝔫𝔦𝔫𝔤 𝔑𝔢𝔴𝔰
### OUR DETECTIVE FORCE
### TO THE EDITOR OF
### "THE EVENING NEWS."

Sir—Whoever has had any special intercourse with our detective force must have been struck with its great inferiority in the detection of crime and search after criminals as compared with the French. Nor is the reason far to seek which explains this deficiency. The requirements and the remuneration of an English policeman preclude the likelihood of obtaining any large number of efficient detectives.

The first consideration in the selection of a French detective is a marked manifestation of intelligence. Secondly, a capability of a metamorphism so complete that the very mother who bore him should hardly recognise her own son, when such a disguise is found necessary. Beside this there is always a willingness to obtain, if possible, a man specially acquainted with the haunts and habits of the class under surveillance; whilst, wherever it is practicable, the incognito is preserved, and when the criminal is fairly run to earth, the final act of arrest is consummated by an officer in uniform.

Here everything which prevails in Paris is ignored. The first consideration in the selection of a policeman is height, size, and weight. The nearer six feet the better. This sine quid non[112] secured, the next thing demanded is, "Is he sound in wind and limb, and about fit for a boxing competition, or fitted to play the part of a gladiator?"

As for any special intelligence, that cannot be expected at the wages of a country waggoner, little more than half the money paid to a decent blacksmith, carpenter, or bricklayer. There is not a gamin[113] in any of our large towns who estimates the nous[114] of our police as much above the amount possessed by a tailor's dummy.

The miserable fiasco which has been displayed in connection with the search into the four murders in the East end, is just what might have been expected by anyone who will look at the mode of procedure. A man known to be a policeman puts in an appearance, this puts every one of the original herd upon the alert, and at once it is game of chess between a few fourteen stone raw country men in livery (for the detective is well known to every prig[115] in London) pitted against the intellect of the keenest blades[116] in the criminal world.

We have seen the detective hidden, as he thought, beneath the garb of an impenetrable disguise. Trousers cut to the regulation pattern, a shooting jacket or office coat (into which one hand is permanently glued), a billycock hat,[117] and often a bright necktie, shoes with thick, heavy soles and broad ponderous heels, with a switch or cane carried much after the fashion of a market drover; whilst, if a pair of gloves are mounted, they are worn as though they were a curiosity which had just been picked up.

Add to this the strut and country look of official importance, and you have the average detective just as he appeared on several occasions to the writer, notably on one where a high class of intelligence was demanded, when a gigantic forgery was committed upon the Imperial Bank of Austria, in which some of the noblest houses in Vienna were implicated, including Count Buol, the then Chancellor of the Exchequer, and who, in consequence, committed suicide.

The agents in this matter were aristocrats, and tried to get their false notes and coins made in Paris; but soon found France too hot. London was next tried—warning had been forwarded from Paris; but it is infra dig[118] to receive suggestions here from any one not on the official staff, and the warning was disregarded. At last, through the representations made to the Foreign Office, a movement was made, and the sort of man described above put upon the trail of accomplished gentlemen who kept a splendid equipage of livery servants.

Six months after the whole had been made and were out of the country, our brilliant ath-

---

[112] **Sine qua non**. Lat. Without which nothing (an absolute necessity). (Morehead)

[113] **Gamin**. Fr. Urchin. (Dubois)

[114] **Nous**. Sense, shrewdness. [From the Greek nous]. (1678). (Farmer)

[115] **Prig**. 1. A thief: also prigger and prigman. As verb, to steal. (ibid)

[116] **Blade**. A roysterer, gallant, sharp, keen, free-and-easy man, good fellow (1595). (ibid)

[117] **Billy-cock**. A round, low-crowned hat generally of soft felt, and with a broad brim. (ibid)

[118] **Infra-dig**. Scornful, proud. (ibid)

letes awoke to a sense that there was something to do, and they commenced by looking for some poor wretch out at elbows, half starved and vegetating in a common lodging house. The real criminals at the same time having the entree to the saloons of the great. This experience does not stand alone.

That a reform is wanted the fact that nearly every great crime remains undetected must prove to the meanest capacity. If permitted to do so through your columns, I will suggest such alterations as will satisfy most that the chances of detection can be indefinitely multiplied.

I am, &c.,
Geo. Savage,
Die Sinker.
Greenleaf lane, Walthamstow
September 28

—

## DISSECTING ROOM PORTERS
## TO THE EDITOR OF
## "THE EVENING NEWS"

Sir—Much has been said concerning the Whitechapel murders. Might I venture to offer a few remarks on the subject.

When I was a student it was the practice to employ porters, one for the dissecting room, and one for the post mortem room. Now these men, with constant association of the internal organs of the human body, had a good chance of picking up a little knowledge. We also know that these men are very illiterate, and that they have to do a deal of dirty work for a small wage, and perhaps a wife and family to keep at home, especially the post mortem porter who generally has to return all organs of the body back to their place and sew the body up.

Now, sir, we have heard the coroner's statement regarding the offer of £20 for certain portions of the human body. Might not this offer have reached the ears of one of these porters? Possibly he may have been discharged, and be in urgent need of money. In any case, no doubt, £20 would be a Godsend to such a man.

Would it not be well for the police to inquire at the two hospitals—whichever they are —respecting such porters, find out if one of them has been discharged, or if not make inquiries respecting the character of them, whether they were at their post at the times of the murders, or if not where they were and what they were doing.

I should be sorry to injure any one branch of industry, but I think at the present time it is necessary to think of all things possible in order to elucidate such horrible crimes.

Apologising for troubling you,
I am, &c.,
MEDICUS

—

### NOTES.

Up till the time of writing we are unable to gratify our readers with the information that the Whitechapel fiend has fallen under the clutches of the police. The air is heavy with theories as to what manner of man the assassin is, but scientific reasoning tends to the adoption of the one we suggested on September 10 last.

To the medical faculty it is a well known fact that epilepsy is often induced by erotic desires and of course no convulsions are necessary to constitute an attack. During the epileptic seizure instead of convulsions there may be a substitution of suicidal or homicidal impulse.

All this does not of course account for the apparent cunning shown by the murderer, but it is possible that when he is discovered his methods are more open and simple than the difficulty of finding him leads the public to suppose. It is presumed that a bloodstained person perambulating the streets would not escape detection, and it will be remembered that the murder of Annie Chapman was committed at the dawn of day.

To account for the immunity of the assassin, it is supposed he must have some private dwelling near the scene of his operations, but as is pointed out by a correspondent of ours today he might easily wear dissecting gloves and a black mackintosh, and both could be taken off and wrapped up in a few seconds.

Again there is a chance that the murderer may cut the woman's throat first from behind and thereby escape the great spurt of blood which rushes forth when the carotid is severed. The throat wounds are all from left to right, and could easily be inflicted by a man fondling a woman, having his left arm round her neck, and suddenly bringing up his knife to her throat with a stab and drawing the blade towards him. This theory exactly accounts for the nature of all the throat wounds, and would be accordant with the supposition that the murderer has no blood on his clothes.

But again there is a difficulty, and that is that at least on the front of the body of the woman murder in Berner-street, there is no blood which might be expected to be found had she been standing when the wound was inflicted. If she were on the ground when first struck, the wound must have been made by a lefthanded person or by an awkward thrust of the right hand in a direction across the breast of the murderer. In the meantime all cases of persons, and especially of butchers and slaughtermen, who have been treated for epilepsy or homicidal mania should be investigated by the police.

Apropos of the Whitechapel murders we are getting all the old tales of Burke and Hare and Bishop and Williams[119] retold. No morning paper has yet reprinted De Quincy's essay on murder, but we may expect it any day now, and indeed, we have already seen large slices from it somewhat disguised and palmed off as original matter. That by the way. When the Whitechapel murderer is found—if he be ever found—he will probably enrich our language with his name. Burke,[120] and Boycott[121] have both pro-

vided us with a verb, though the first is rather hard upon a certain Edmund.[122]

We cannot congratulate Mr. Horace Smith, the magistrate presiding over Dalston Police Court, yesterday, upon his views as regards the due adjustment of punishment to offence. A young man named Henderson was charged before him with assaulting an unfortunate woman named Rosa Goldstein, and threatening to "rip her up, the same as a few more had been done." The prosecutrix, "who appeared with surgical bandages about her head and seemed weak from loss of blood," stated that on Saturday night she was going home when the prisoner made proposals to her, which she refused, when he struck her three times on the head with the buckhorn handle of his stick, causing blood to flow freely, and rendering her partially insensible.

So far as can be gathered from the published report of the case there was practically no defence, save that the prisoner was under the influence of liquor at the time, and Mr. Smith proceeded to give his sentence: "If it had not been that you were drunk," he told the prisoner, "and may not have known exactly what you were doing, I should have dealt very severely with you." As it was, however, the merciful magistrate considered that the offence was not "wilful wickedness," and contented himself with imposing a fine of forty shillings, or a month's imprisonment. If this misplaced leniency does not prove a direct incentive to others to go and do likewise, it will be surprising.

—

## SIDE LIGHTS OF THE WHITECHAPEL TRAGEDY

We were told yesterday in *The Evening News* that on Sunday afternoon delicately reared women daintily picked their way through the crowded streets leading to the spots of the latest murders. They were escorted by men probably as carefully bred as they were themselves, men who have unflinchingly faced the tiger in the jungle, braved the swarthy foe in treacherous Indian

[119] **John Bishop** and **Thomas Head** (alias Williams). Members of the London gang of body snatchers nicknamed the "London Burkers". Hanged before a crowd of 30,000 at Newgate Prison on 5 December, 1831 for the murder of a youth, believed to be a 14 year old Italian beggar named Carlo Ferrari, in order to sell his body to King's College School of Anatomy. In his confession Bishop claimed that the body was actually that of a Lincolnshire cattle drover, and that he and Head had drugged the boy with whiskey laced with laudanum. After he had passed out, they took him outside, tied a rope around his ankles and threw the boy headfirst down a well, pulling him out after he drowned. They then stripped him, shoved his body in a bag, and went off to peddle his remains for 9 Guineas (adjusted for income differential and inflation, app. £13,770 in 2015, $20,655, according to http://www.measuringworth.com.).

[120] **Burke**. 1. To murder by strangulation: as Burke did for the purpose of selling the bodies for dissection. 2. To hush up, smother a matter. (Farmer)

[121] **Boycott**. To combine in refusing to hold relations of any kind, social or commercial, public or private, with a person, on account of political or other differences, so as to punish or coerce him. The word arose in the autumn of 1880. Capt. Boycott, an Irish landlord, was the original victim to describe the

action instituted by the Irish Land League toward those who incurred its hostility. It was speedily adopted into every European language. (ibid)

[122] **Edmund Burke**. (1729-1797) Irish orator, author, statesman and philosopher. Considered to be the father of modern conservatism.

mountain passes, carried the Gospel at the risk of their lives to the benighted brethren, or help to win and keep that greater Britain which excites the wonder and envy of other nations.

Well, we know that history repeats itself not only in its most salient political facts, but in its minor social incidentals. "Pepys,"[123] "The London Spy,"[124] *The Tatler* and the "Rake's Progress"[125] give us vivid pictures of a noisy rout[126] of Pall Mall beaus and belles, country fly catchers,[127] and London scamps[128] passing up and down the corridors of Bethlehem,[129] mocking its unhappy inmates with brutal jests or investigating and gossiping about their delusions and extrava-gances with unfeeling curiosity.

Sir Richard Steele[130] took three schoolboy friends out for a frolic and did not think the junk-

etings complete unless he showed them, in addition to the lions, the tombs, and other sights, Bedlam, "which are entertainments to raw minds because they strike forcibly on the fancy."[131] Carey's hero of "Sally in our Alley"[132] takes his sweetheart to Bedlam, and Carey himself, who watches them through the livelong day, manages to extract from the doings of the shoemaker's apprentice and Sally one of the sweetest of love songs in the English language—one of the most perfect pictures of humble life.

I at once absolve the visitors mentioned by my colleague of the intention of indulging in brutal jests about what they saw, but I am by no means prepared to credit them with the intention of extracting poetry from the scenes through which they passed. Least of all do I suspect their minds of being so raw as to have their fancy forcibly struck by the pictures of squalid poverty of utter degradation that form the backgrounds to the sensation scenes they came to inspect. And yet there is poetry enough in these to move the most callous; unfortunately it happens to be the poetry of Dante's "Inferno," and Dante's "Inferno" is much too strong for modern squeamish mental digestions.

We have, however, improved upon the wisdom of the ostrich, we do not bury our heads in the sand lest we should see and hear, but we look and listen, and, apparently awe stricken, raise our hands to Heaven in supplication as if we did not know that Heaven will only help those that help themselves.

Well may the cynic laugh at seeing such a play as that which I saw last night at the Pavilion Theatre in the Whitechapel road. It is called "The Golden Ladder,"[133] and is from the pens of

---

[123] **Samuel Pepys** (1633-1709). Chief Secretary to the Admiralty under Charles II and James II and MP for Harwich 1679-1689. Best known for his diary, which he kept from 1660-1669, which detailed daily life in Restoration England with astonishing frankness.

[124] **The London Spy**. Written by Edward Ward (1667-1731) and published in 1703, *The London Spy* is his eyewitness account of the seedy side of London.

[125] **A Rake's Progress**. 1733 series of eight morality paintings by William Hogarth (1697-1764) detailing the descent into poverty and madness of Tom Rakewell, a young heir that squanders his fortune on drink and whores, ends up in debtors prison and finishes his days in Bedlam lunatic asylum. Engravings of the paintings were prepared in 1735, and the resulting prints were popular through the 19th Century.

[126] **Rout**. A fashionable party. As verb, to assemble in company (1775). (Farmer)

[127] **Fly-catcher**. An open-mouthed ignoramus, a Gapeseed (q.v.): Fr., *gobe-mouche*. (ibid)

[128] **Scamp**. 1. A highway robber (also *scampsman*); and, 2. Highway robbery (also *scampery*): whence as verb, to rob on the highway; *royal-scamp*, a highwayman who robs civilly; *royal-foot-scamp*, a footpad behaving in like manner; *done for a scamp*, convicted. 3. A rogue; an arrant rascal; sometimes (colloquial) in jest : hence *scampish*, roguish, tricky; *scampery*, roguery. As verb, to do carelessly and ill, give bad work or short measure. (ibid)

[129] **Bethelehem Hospital**. Better known as Bedlam.

[130] **Sir Richard Steele** (1672-1729). Dublin born English essayist, playwright and politician. With his friend and fellow essayist Joseph Addison, published the social/political newspapers *The Tatler,* from

1709-1711, and the *Spectator*, which ran 555 daily issues from 1 March, 1711 to 6 December, 1712. As spokesman for the Whig party in print, his chief nemesis was his Tory counterpart, Jonathan Swift.

[131] Sir Richard Steele, From my own Apartment, June 16. *The Tattler; Or, Lucubrations of Isaac Bickerstaff, Esq., Volume the First. No. 30, Saturday, June 18, 1709*. London, 1774. P. 178.

[132] **Henry Carey** (1687-1743). "Sally in our Alley" appeared in Carey's 1737 collection of his poems set to music, *The Musical Century*.

[133] **The Golden Ladder**. A play by Wilson Barrett and Geo R. Sims, first performed at the Globe Theatre, London, December 22, 1887, with W. Barrett as the

# Tuesday, 2 October, 1888

Messrs. George Sims[134] and Wilson Barrett.[135] It deals with the heroism of a clergyman who sacrifices health and comfort, who incurs a hundred dangers to convert, to save a handful of Polynesians, when, forsooth, there are within a stone's throw of that playhouse thousands and thousands of our white brethren and sisters more degraded by far than the objects of the missionary's care; thousands and thousands leading lives compared with which those of the blacks must be holy and cleanly.

If the latter herd like cattle it is because they know no better, or would not have known better but for the European's interference. The denizens of Osborne place, of Flower and Dean street, of half a dozen other thoroughfares I could mention in that locality, have the difference between their wretchedness and the affluence of their fellow men thrust upon their notice every hour, every minute of the day.

With the battle of life hopelessly lost almost before the first effort is made—for the babe at the mother's breast in that neighbourhood sucks in despair as well as vice—is it a wonder that they get reckless, though not so reckless as to barter their lives—if they barter their honour—for a

---

Rev. Frank Thornhill, Miss Eastlake as Lillian Grant, and other parts by George Barrett, Austin Melford, H. Cooper Cliffe, T.W. Percival, C. Fulton, S. Murray Carson, H. Dana, J. Welch, Mrs. Hemnry Leigh, Miss Alice Belmore, Miss Lillie Belmore, and Miss Phoebe Carlo; first acted in America at the New Park Theatre, New York, April 4, 1892. (Adams)

[134] **George Robert Sims** (1847-1922), prolific author who began his career writing humour but turned to showing the plight of the poor in such works as *The Theatre of Life* (1881), *How the Poor Live* (1883) and *Horrible London* (1889). Co-founded the Refugee Children's Free Breakfast and Dinner Fund in 1880.

[135] **Wilson Barrett** (1846-1904). Son of an Essex farmer, Barrett began his stage career in Halifax in 1864, branching out into producing and writing after having achieved great success in melo-dramatic plays such as "The Silver King" in 1882. "The Sign of the Cross", his most famous, and most lucrative, work, was first performed at the Broadway Knickerbocker Theatre in 1895. A hit in Britain and America, it was an unofficial adaption of Polish author Henryk Sienkiewicz's 1895 novel *Quo Vadis*. "The Sign of the Cross" was adapted to the screen in 1932 by Hollywood director Cecil B. DeMille in a film starring Fredric March, Elissa Landi, Claudette Colbert and Charles Laughton.

meal and for a shelter?

For it has come to this, that these unfortunates do not even dare ply their revolting trade any longer, that the dread of the murderer's knife keeps them huddled together within the quasi protecting shadow of the unspeakable home. During my eight hours perambulation, yesterday, I heard not once, but half a dozen times the terrible wail of "Who knows but what it may be my turn next?"

They know that more of them are doomed, knowing that the pittance required to keep body and soul together can only be obtained in one way, knowing furthermore that in default of this pittance they will be turned out in the chill autumnal night to wander hither and thither—perchance to return no more.

Does this mean that the owners of these lodging houses are altogether merciless? I think not. But they also have liabilities, and to meet these they must be firm. Where and how are they to draw the line? Consideration for one must mean in their care consideration for many, and such consideration must eventually end in ruin.

Meanwhile, those who have this wretched fourpence wherewith to stave off —if only for one night—the attack of the fiend that stalks abroad, appear to be merry, but the gaiety, to him who listens carefully, appears hollow. It sounds like the "Let us eat and drink, for tomorrow we die."[136]

As one passes through the whitewashed dormitories, with nothing but the faint flicker of the farthing rushlight[137]—cut into three for economy's sake—to guide one, the heartrending picture has its comic side also. The profane jest is, of course, not wanting, but, for all that, the homely humour of the people pierces through now and then.

In one of the houses in Flower and Dean street we were shown into a women's dormitory containing about eighteen very narrow beds arranged in two rows. It was too dark to distinguish the sex of the sleepers covered up to the

---

[136] Isaiah 22:13.

[137] **Farthing Rushlight.** A cheap form of artificial light used by the very poor. A rushlight was, literally, a rush dipped in tallow and used like a candle. These could burn, dimly, for up to five and a half hours. Sometimes a burning splinter of wood was also called a rushlight. (Rushlights)

# Tuesday, 2 October, 1888

neck, and as I was under the impression that we were in a men's dormitory I expressed myself to that effect. "There is a gentleman who can only distinguish man from woman when both are dressed," came the remark. I apologised for my mistake and intrusion and retired.

In fact it is highly advisable just now to be profuse in apologies to the fairer sex in the neighbourhood of Whitechapel and Commercial road. More advisable still to give them a wide berth, if possible, for propinquity[138]—let alone juxtaposition—intentional or not, is sure to raise an outcry, and Robert is very much on his mettle. He is evidently resolved to do some-thing, and that something means clapping the "darbies"[139] on.

In less than seven minutes, and along a distance of about a hundred yards, I witnessed two captures last night. The first prisoner had done nothing, and the second had, as far as I could gather, had done less.

A woman was standing outside a shop when a young man, apparently well dressed, came up to her, the woman asserted, stealthily. She gave a piercing yell, and followed it up by the statement that she had seen him loiter in Berner street during yesterday. That was enough. There and then the young man was marched to the police station. Nothing is more likely than "the accused" having been in Berner street, but why his presence should expose him to summary arrest is possibly patent only to Robert's method of deduction.

The second victim of another Robert's zealousness was upon the face of it a tramp. He had retired to a secluded court and alley, and there changed his inexpressibles[140]—that is if we may

believe half a dozen children who raised a cry that there was blood on his clothes. He also paid the penalty of the panic. In fact it appears to be not only a reign of terror but a reign of error.

I will deal with the terror first as manifested by the haunted looks of the women as they pass dark corner. They are evidently under the impression that impunity had made the miscreant bolder, which no doubt is the case. But bold as he may have become he is not likely to make an attempt in a crowded thoroughfare without any preliminary courtship—save the mark[141]—which he has hitherto deemed essential to the execution of his designs. Least of all is he likely to accost those who while yielding to his solicitations would seem a cut above al fresco amamtiveness.[142]

He has marked out a certain class, and the poorest of this class, as his prey; there is no reason as yet to think that he will deviate from his deep laid plan. Nevertheless the less poverty stricken seem to go in fear and trembling also. The others have absolutely deserted their dark haunts. The streets and lanes are deserted, and when at eleven o'clock last night I visited two lodging houses, more than half of the beds were already occupied, an unprecedented occurrence, according to the testimony of the deputy.

The error is the corollary of the terror, or, to put it in plain words, the wish is the father to the thought. It is hoped and believed that after the latest exploits the murderer will forsake the East and approach the West. He may abandon the scene of his former crimes; but for reasons already mentioned he will not venture into less squalid neighbourhoods.

The theory which was broached when Mary Nicholls was done to death, namely, that the deed was committed in a house and that her body

---

[138] **Propinquity**. Nearness, in time, place, or blood. (Morehead)

[139] **Darbies**. 1. Handcuffs. English synonyms: black-bracelets, buckles, Father Derbie's bands, ruffles, wife, snitchers, clinkers, government securities, twisters, darbies and Joans (=fetters coupling two persons). 2. Sausages, bags of mystery, chambers of horrors (q.v.). (Farmer)

[140] **Inexpressibles**. Trousers (1790). English synonyms: arse-rug, bum-bags, bell-bottoms, bum-curtain, bags, calf-clingers, canvasseens, continuations, don't-name-'ems, ducks, gam-cases, hams, indescribables (1835), ineffables, inimitables, kicks, kickseys, moles, mustn't-mention-'ems, peg-tops, pants, rice-bags, sit-upons,

skilts, slacks, strides, trolly-wags, trucks, trunks, unhintables, unmentionables, unutterables, unwhisperables, whistling breeches (1696). (Farmer)

[141] **Mark**. 5. A victim. 6. A street-walker. As verb, to watch, pick out a victim. (ibid)

[142] **Al fresco amamtiveness**. It. and Med. Lat.? The It. term al fresco means "in the cool (air), outside", although it is also Italian slang for being incarcerated. Amativeness, not amamtiveness, is a Medieval Latin adjective meaning "disposed to love, amorous." The nearest translation I can come up with is "outdoor sex."

was removed subsequently, may be at once dismissed as untenable. Mary Nicholls and Annie Chapman were despatched where they were found. The first and foremost guarantee against detection is the accomplishment of the crime in the open air or, at any rate, not within four walls in the ordinary sense of the word. We may safely presume that such victims as the murderer would approach in the better class neighbourhoods would indignantly repulse his advances under the conditions he would hint at. Consequently one may take it for granted that at least one quarter of the metropolis is safe.

This is but poor consolation, and is scarcely improved by the improbability of the criminal being a vagrant or even in poor circumstances. It makes detection all the more difficult. Dr. Forbes Winslow expressed himself to the above effect three weeks ago in an interview with a representative of *The Evening News.*

Subsequent events have given more than a mere colour to the theory of the eminent specialist. Hence there will be little use in Robert's laying hands upon every outcast in or about the neighbourhood of Whitechapel. He must be looked for elsewhere. Mr. Louis Stevenson's book, "Dr. Jekyl and Mr. Hyde," appeared too far-fetched. One is gradually coming to the conclusion that the perpetrator of the East end crimes, if he cannot change his personality as did the hero of the story, can at least disguise it so as to baffle discovery of his terrible doings by the inmates of his own home.

We go further still, we maintain that the relations or friends of this scourge to humanity have no suspicion of having so accursed a creature near them. For we cannot, and will not, believe that they would not throw all other feelings to the wind in order to render this scourge harmless for the future, because we cannot, and will not, believe that this scourge is other than a homicidal maniac. As such no judge would inflict the utmost penalty of the law, and the disgrace of the scaffold would be spared the innocent relations.

A.D.V.

—

## LOOK FOR A MAN WITH A BLACK BAG!

Below will be found "A Plausible Suggestion," signed "Medicus." The writer apparently had no knowledge at the time he despatched his letter of the statement made by a young man named Albert Baskert, of 13 Newnham street, Whitechapel, and therefore the coincidence is, to say the least, peculiar.

"Medicus" says that if the murderer wore a pair of dissecting gloves and an ordinary glazed mackintosh, his work could be accomplished, and the gloves and mackintosh wrapped up in a brief bag, and the man would immediately appear a respectable clerk returning late from the City.

It is a remarkable fact that the only man Mrs. Mortimer observed in Berner street, early on Sunday morning, carried a shiny black bag.

## A PLAUSIBLE SUGGESTION TO THE EDITOR OF "THE EVENING NEWS."

Sir—All the accounts that I have read as yet about the Whitechapel murders describe the murderer as leaving the pot "reeking with blood," "soaked with blood," &c. Now, Sir, this is not at all necessary, neither is it likely, for if the perpetrator is familiar with dissecting or post mortem rooms, he will also be familiar with indiarubber dissecting gloves. If, therefore, he wore a pair of these, and also an ordinary black glazed mackintosh, his work could be accomplished, gloves and mackintosh doffed, rolled up, placed in a small brief bag, and behold! we have a respectable looking clerk returning late from the City. Both gloves and mackintosh are easily washed, and all traces of blood thus removed. I think, therefore, that the police may give up wandering about looking for man "reeking with blood."

I am, &c., Medicus.

—

## BASKERT'S STATEMENT

On Saturday night, about seven minutes to 12, I entered the Three Nuns Hotel, Aldgate. While in there an elderly woman, very shabbily dressed, came in and asked me to buy some matches. I refused and she went out. A man who had been standing by me remarked that these persons were a nuisance, to which I responded, "Yes." He then asked me to have a glass with him, but I refused, as I had just called for one myself.

He then asked me if I knew how old some of the women were who were in the habit of soliciting outside. replied that I thought some of them who looked about 25 were over 35, the reason they looked younger being on account of the powder and paint. He asked if I could tell him where they usually went with men, and I replied that I had heard that some went to places in Oxford street, Whitechapel, others to some houses in Whitechapel road, and others to Bishopsgate street. He then asked whether I thought they would go with him down Northumberland alley—a dark, lonely court in Fenchurch street. I said that I did not know, but supposed they would.

He then went outside and spoke to the woman who was selling matches, and gave her something I believe. He returned to me, and I bid him good night at about ten minutes past twelve. I believe the woman was waiting for him. I do not think I could identify the woman, as I did not take particular notice of her, but I should know the man again.

He was a dark man, about 35 years of age, height about 5ft 6in or 7in. He wore a black felt hat, dark clothes (morning coat) and black tie, and carried a black shiny bag.

—

## THE MURDERER'S DIARY.

A correspondent writes: There are most remarkable coincidences with regard to the times at which all the murders have been committed which demand particular attention. The first and third of the murders, those of Martha Turner and Mrs. Chapman, were committed on exactly the same date of two separate months—namely, the 7th of August and September, while the second and fourth murders had the same relative coincidence, both being perpetrated on the last days of August and September. If the same hand carried out these crimes, these facts seem to point to the idea that the criminal was one who had to be absent from the scene of his crimes for regular periods.

—

## WHY WAS NOT A BLOODHOUND USED?

A correspondent recalls the successful employment of a blood hound in the detection of a barbarous murder at Blackburn twelve years ago. In this case two days at least had elapsed between the commission of the crime and its detection by means of the dog.

Another relevant case is thus related in Jesse's "Anecdotes of Dogs": "A servant, discharged by a sporting country gentleman broke into his stables by night, and cut off the ears and tail of his favourite hunter. As soon as it was discovered a bloodhound was brought into the stable, who at once detected the scent of the miscreant, and traced it more than 20 miles. He then stopped at a door, whence no power could move him. Being at length admitted, he ran to the top of the house, and bursting open the door of a garret, found the object that he caught in bed, and would have torn him to pieces had not the huntsman, who had followed him on a fleet horse, rushed up after him."

Bewick, after mentioning the detective qualities of the bloodhound, observes, rather unfortunately, that "as the arm of justice is now extended over every part of the country, and there are no secret recesses where villainy may lay concealed, these services are no longer necessary."

Mr. Perry Lindley writes: With regard to the suggestion that blood-hounds might assist in tracking the East end murderer, as a breeder of bloodhounds, and knowing their power, I have little doubt that, had a hound been put upon the scent of the murderer while fresh, it might have done what the police have failed in. But now, when all trace of the scene has been trodden out, it would be quite useless.

Meanwhile, as no means of detection should be left untried, it would be well if a couple or so of trained bloodhounds—unless trained they are worthless—were kept for a time at one of the police headquarters ready for immediate use in case their services should be called for. There are, doubtless, owners of bloodhounds willing to lend them, if any of the police, which I fear is improbable, know how to use them.

—

## LATEST DETAILS

The Press Association states that all the men who have, so far, been arrested on the suspicion of having murdered Mrs. Stride and the woman whose remains are still unidentified, were released in the course of yesterday. Up to the present no further arrests have been made, and despite the strenuous efforts that are being made by the police authorities, they seem as far off as ever from getting on the track of the murderer.

Exhaustive inquiries made in the neighbourhood of Bow and Stratford at a late hour last night failed to elicit any reliable information as to the movements of "Long Liz" on Saturday

# Tuesday, 2 October, 1888

night, and so far as is at present known she was last seen when leaving the common lodging house in Flower and Dean street at seven o'clock that evening.

The mutilated remains of the poor woman who was first murdered and then violated with such atrocity in Mitre square still lie at the Golden lane mortuary awaiting identification. The body was viewed in the course of yesterday by a large number of persons, and considering the fact that there are marks which should render identification quite easy to those who were personally acquainted with the deceased, it is singular that so far she should continue unrecognised. Hopes, however, are entertained by the police that before today has elapsed, the identity will be established.

This is a most important matter, as a belief is entertained by the authorities, that when once the name has become known it may afford an important clue in securing a description of the miscreant who still defies all efforts to track him to his lair.

In the early hours of the morning a rumour was afloat in the East end, to the effect that cries of "Murder" and "Police" had been distinctly heard as though proceeding from a woman, in the immediate neighbourhood of the International Working Men's Club, in Berner street, the scene of the murder of "Long Liz." The story, however, was contradicted by the night inspector in charge at Leman street, and our representative was unable to obtain any positive evidence in corroboration. Indeed, the report was contradicted by all the constables on duty in the vicinity at the time specified.

Down to as late an hour as ten o'clock, last night, large crowds of people continued to assemble around the spots where the murders of Sunday were perpetrated, and so great was the crush at Mitre square that until a late hour it was found requisite to keep a considerable number of extra constables on duty.

Towards midnight the streets in the district within the limits of which six murders have now been successively perpetrated without detection began to assume a most deserted appearance.

The one exception, perhaps, was the main thoroughfares, which were thronged with people as usual until the hour dictated by law for the closing of the public houses.

The night air, it is true, was keen and cutting, but this alone did not account for the remarkable absence of anything in the shape of pedestrian traffic, which heretofore has invariably continued until and advanced hour in the evening. The appearance of the whole district conveyed the only too palpable fact that at the present moment the East end—and Whitechapel in particular—is panic stricken.

By one o'clock the streets were absolutely denuded of the unfortunate women who are accustomed to roam about throughout the night, while revellers of the sterner sex were almost equally scarce. Wherever one went he had to listen to the same perpetual growl of the coffee stall keepers that their trade had gone; and when asked how they accounted for the fact, the invariable reply was "The murders." The answer was as brief as it was significant.

In the small hours of the morning our representative plodded through street after street, and still street after street without coming across a living soul of any kind beyond the solitary policeman on his monotonous round. The heavy, regular tramp of the valiant custodian of the peace alone disturbed the stillness of the night. It was, in all truth, a weary round, this perambulation of Whitechapel, its main thoroughfares, its back slums, and its environs, and the heavy showers which fell at intermittent periods did not tend to enhance the pleasures of the night.

There is, however, one fact that cannot fail to strike most forcibly even the most casual observer who cares to make an early evening survey of Whitechapel, with its multitudinous streets, alleys, and dark and tortuous passages. That is the convenient nooks and crannies, well in the shade, which almost at every turn seem to suggest themselves to an evil minded person as fit and suitable places for the perpetration of crimes such as those which within the last day or two horrified the metropolis.

There is no mistaking the fact that if the East end is to be protected in the future against such outrages—for Whitechapel is but a duplicate of that vast area—the police force stationed there for that purpose ought at least to be doubled in strength.

In the course of a night's wanderings in these slums and backways, our representative conversed with not a few of the men whom he found on duty. Almost to a man, when questioned on the subject, they pointed out the impossibility of adequately performing all that was asked of them in the way of protecting the public from outrages such as those that are now disgracing the East end. Again and again attention was called to open staircases in huge piles of modern dwellings erected for the artisan, to dark secluded corners in every direction, and to this, that and the other in the way of affording scope for crime, until one's eyes become almost dazed from perpetually peering into veritable Cimmerian darkness.

It was a positive relief to at length again emerge into broad, well lighted thoroughfares, and finally seek the welcome shelter of the Leman street police station and the pleasant company of the courteous officers in charge.

—

## ANOTHER KNIFE FOUND.

A knife was picked up, last night, at the corner of Endell street, Long Acre. It was taken to Bow street Police station and examined. It measures about 12 inches in length, and about two inches wide at the haft, tapering off to a point.

—

## PARIS, Monday night.

A surgical theory which is advanced here about the Whitechapel murders is that the murderer is a fanatical vivisectionist and disciple of Hoeckel,[143] the German naturalist, who followed in the steps of Darwin in studying the origin of species and who advanced some startling ideas that have not yet been established. A naturalist's aim is visible in the way in which the knife was applied to the two unfortunate

---

[143] **Ernst Haeckel** (1834-1919). Controversial German biologist and early follower of Charles Darwin, best known for developing the Recapitulation Theory. This theory claims that "ontogeny recapitulates phylogeny", in other words, an organisms biological development in the womb or egg parallels its evolutionary development.

This was illustrated in a series of drawings of foetuses of various species, including human, that show them to be very similar in appearance and were claimed to be proof of Evolution.

These illustrations have since been proven to be so inaccurate that it is almost impossible that a biologist as knowledgeable as Haeckel could have accidentally made so many mistakes.

beings at Whitechapel. Perhaps there was not time to operate in an exactly like manner in the second series of murder.

—

## RECENT MURDERS OF WOMEN IN TEXAS.
## IS IT THE SAME MAN?

The correspondent of the Daily News in New York telegraphs: Not a great many months ago a series of remarkably brutal murders of women occurred in Texas. The matter caused great local excitement, but aroused less interest than would otherwise have been the case because the victims were chiefly negro women. The crimes were characterised by the same brutal methods as those of the Whitechapel murders. The theory has been suggested that the perpetrator of the latter may be the Texas criminal, who was never discovered.

*The Atlanta Constitution*, a leading southern newspaper, thus puts the argument:

"In our recent annals of crime there has been no other man capable of committing such deeds. The mysterious crimes in Texas have ceased. They have just commenced in London. Is the man from Texas at the bottom of them all? If he is the monster or lunatic he may be expected to appear anywhere. The fact that he is no longer at work in Texas argues his presence somewhere else. His peculiar line of work was executed in precisely the same manner as is now going on in London. Why should he not be there? The more one thinks of it the more irresistible becomes the conviction that it is the man from Texas. In these days of steam and cheap travel distance is nothing. The man who would kill a dozen women in Texas would not mind the inconvenience of a trip across the water, and once there he would not have any scruples about killing more women."

The Superintendent of the New York police admits the possibility of this theory being correct, but he does not think it probable. "There is," he says, "the same brutality and mutilation, the same suspicion that the criminal is a monster or lunatic who has declared war literally to the knife against all womankind, but I hardly believe it is the same individual."[144]

~

---

[144] See Appendix M, The Texas Axe Murders, p. 577.

# Wednesday, 3 October, 1888

## The Times
### THE EAST-END MURDERS.

Yesterday afternoon Mr. Wynne E. Baxter, coroner for the South-Eastern Division of Middlesex, resumed his inquiry at the Vestry-hall, Cable-street, St. George's-in-the-East, respecting the death of Elizabeth Stride, who was found murdered in Berner-street on Sunday morning last.

Detective-inspector E. Reid, H Division, watched the case on behalf of the Criminal Investigation Department.

Police-constable Henry Lamb, 252 H, deposed as follows:—About 1 o'clock, as near as I can tell, on Sunday morning I was in the Commercial-road, between Christian-street and Batty-street. Two men came running towards me. I went towards them and heard them say, "Come on! There has been another murder." I said, "Where?" As they got to the corner of Berner-street they pointed down the street. Seeing people moving about some distance down Berner-street, I ran down that street followed by Constable 426 H. I went into the gateway of No. 40, Berner-street and saw something dark lying on the right-hand side, close to the gates. I turned my light on and found it was a woman. I saw that her throat was cut, and she appeared to be dead. I at once sent the other constable for the nearest doctor, and I sent a young man that was standing by to the police-station to inform the inspector that a woman was lying in Berner-street with her throat cut, and apparently dead.

The CORONER.—How many people were there in the yard?

Witness.—I should think 20 or 30. Some of that number had followed me in.

The CORONER.—Was any one touching the body when you arrived?

Witness.—No. There was no one within a yard of it. As I was examining the body some crowded round. I begged them to keep back, and told them they might get some of the blood on their clothing, and by that means get themselves into trouble. I then blew my whistle. I put my hand on the face and found it slightly warm. I then felt the wrist, but could not feel the pulse.

The CORONER.—Did you do anything else to the body?

Witness.—I did not, and would not allow anyone to get near the body. Deceased was lying on her side, and her left arm was lying under her.

The CORONER.—Did you examine her hands?

Witness.—I did not; but I saw that her right arm was across the breast.

The CORONER.—How near was her head to the wall?

Witness.—I should say her face was about five or six inches way.

The CORONER.—Were her clothes disturbed?

Witness.—No. I scarcely could see her boots. She looked as if she had been laid quietly down. Her clothes were not in the least rumpled.

The CORONER.—Was the blood in a liquid state?

Witness.—Some was, and some was congealed. It extended close to the door. The part nearest to her throat was congealed.

The CORONER.—Was any blood coming from the throat at that time?

Witness.—I hardly like to say that, Sir. If there was it must have been a very small quantity. Dr. Blackwell, about ten minutes after I got there, was the first doctor to arrive.

The CORONER.—Did anyone say whether the body had been touched?

Witness.—No. Dr. Blackwell examined the body, and afterwards the surrounding ground. Dr. Phillips arrived about 20 minutes afterwards; but at that time I was at another part of the ground. Inspector Pinhorn arrived directly after the doctor arrived. When I got there I had the gates shut.

The CORONER.—But did not the feet of the deceased touch the gate?

Witness.—No; they went just behind it, and I was able to close the gates without disturbing the body. I put a constable at the gate and told him not to let anyone in or out. I then entered the club and, starting from the front door, examined the place. I turned my light on and had a look at the different persons there, and examined a number of their hands and also their clothing to see if I could detect any marks of blood. I did not take up each one's hand. I should say there were from 15 to 20 persons in the club-room on the ground floor. I then went into every room, including the one in which there was a stage, and I went behind it. A person was there who informed me he was the steward.

The CORONER.—You did not think to put

250

him in charge of the front door?

Witness.—No, I did not. When further assistance came a constable was put in charge of the front door. I did not see anyone leave by that entrance, and could not say if it was locked. After I examined the club, I went into the yard and examined the cottages. I also went into the water-closets. The occupiers of the cottages were all in bed when I knocked. A man came down partly dressed to let me in. Everyone I saw, except this one, was undressed.

The CORONER.—There is a recess in the yard, is there not? Did you go there?

Witness.—Yes; and I afterwards went there with Dr. Phillips. I examined the dust-bin and dung-heap. I noticed there was a hoarding,[145] but I do not recollect looking over it. After that I went and examined the steps and outside of Messrs. Hindley's premises. I also looked through the windows, as the doors were fastened.

The CORONER.—How long was it before the cottage doors were opened?

Witness.—Not long. The people seemed very much frightened and wanted to know what was the matter. I told them nothing much, as I did not want to frighten them. When I returned from there Dr. Phillips and Chief Inspector West had arrived.

The CORONER.—Was there anything to prevent any one escaping while you were examining the body?

Witness.—It was quite possible, as I was then there by myself. There was a lot of confusion, and everyone was looking towards the body.

The CORONER.—A person might have escaped before you arrived?

Witness.—That is quite possible. I should think he got away before I got there, and not afterwards.

Inspector Reid.—How long was it before you passed that spot?

Witness.—I was not on the beat; but I passed the Commercial-road end of the street some six or seven minutes before I was called. When I was fetched I was going in the direction of Berner-street. Constable Smith is on the Berner-street beat. The constable who followed

me down is on fixed-point duty from 9 to 5 at the end of Grove-street. All the fixed-point men ceased their duty at 1 a.m., and then the men on the beats did the whole duty.

Inspector Reid.—These men are fixed at certain places, so if a person wanted a constable he would not have to go all the way to the station for one.

The CORONER.—Did you see anything suspicious?

Witness.—No, I saw lots of squabbles and rows such as one sees on Saturday nights. I think I should have seen any one running from the gate of 40, Berner-street if I had been standing at the Commercial-road end of it. I could not tell if the lamps on the plan are correct.

The CORONER.—I may mention there are four lamps between Commercial-road and Fairclough-street. Is the street as well lit as others in the neighbourhood?

Witness.—It is lit about as well as side streets generally are, but some I know are better lighted.

A Juryman.—I think that street is lighted quite as well as any other.

In further examination, witness said,—I remained in the yard the remainder of the night. I started to help convey the body to the mortuary, but I was fetched back.

Edward Spooner said,—I live at 26, Fairclough-street, and am a horse-keeper at Messrs. Meredith's. Between half-past 12 and 1 o'clock on Sunday morning I was standing outside the Bee Hive publichouse, at the corner of Christian-street and Fairclough-street, along with a young woman. I had previously been in another beer-shop at the top of the street, and afterwards walked down. After talking for about 25 minutes I saw two Jews come running along and shouting out "Murder" and "Police." They then ran as far as Grove-street and turned back. I stopped them and asked what was the matter. They replied, "A woman has been murdered." I then went round with them to Berner-street, and into Dutfield's yard, adjoining No. 40, Berner-street. I saw a woman lying just inside the gate. At that time there were about 15 people in the yard, and they were all standing round the body. The majority of them appeared to be Jews. No one touched the body. One of them struck a match, and I lifted up the chin of the deceased

---

[145] **Hoarding**. A temporary wooden fence erected round a building or demolition site. (Collins English Dictionary-Complete and Unabridged)

with my hand. The chin was slightly warm. Blood was still flowing from the throat. I could see that she had a piece of paper doubled up in her right hand, and a red and white flower pinned on to her jacket. The body was lying on one side, with the face turned towards the wall. I noticed that blood was running down the gutter. I stood there about five minutes before a constable came. It was the last witness who first arrived. I did not notice any one leave while I was there, but there were a lot of people there, and a person might have got away unnoticed. The only means I had of fixing the time was by the closing of the publichouses. I stood at the top of the street for about five minutes, and then 25 minutes outside the publichouse. I should say it was about 25 minutes to 1 when I first went to the yard. I could not form any opinion about the body having been moved. Several persons stood around. I noticed that the legs of the deceased were drawn up, but the clothes were not disturbed. As soon as the policeman came I stepped back, and afterwards helped to fasten the gates. When I left it was by the front door of the club. Before that I was searched, and gave my name and address. I was also examined by Dr. Phillips.

By the CORONER.—There was no blood on the chin of the deceased, and I did not get any on my hands. Directly I got inside the yard I could see that it was a woman lying on the ground.

By the jury.—As I was going to Berner-street I did not meet anyone except Mr. Harris, who came out of his house in Tiger Bay (Brunswick-street). Mr. Harris told me he had heard the policeman's whistle blowing.

Mary Malcolm said,—I live at 50, Eagle-street, Red Lion-square. I am married to Andrew Malcolm, a tailor. I have seen the body in the mortuary. I saw it on Sunday and twice yesterday. It is the body of my sister, Elizabeth Watts.

The CORONER.—You have no doubt about that?

Witness.—Not the slightest.

The CORONER.—You had some doubts at first?

Witness.—I had, but not now. I last saw her alive at a quarter to 7 last Thursday evening. She came to me where I worked at the tailoring, at 59, Red Lion-street. She came to me to ask me to give her a little assistance, which I have

been in the habit of doing off and on for the last five years. I gave her 1s. and a little short jacket. The latter is not the one she had on when found in Berner-street. She only remained with me for a few moments, and she did not say where she was going. I could not say where she was living except that it was somewhere in the neighbourhood of the tailors and Jews at the East-end. I understood she was living in lodging-houses.

The CORONER.—Did you know what she was doing for a living?

Witness.—I had my doubts.

The CORONER.—Was she the worse for drink when she came to you?

Witness.—She was sober, but unfortunately drink was a failing with her.

The CORONER.—How old was she?

Witness.—37.

The CORONER.—Was she married?

Witness.—Yes, to Mr. Watts, wine and spirit merchant, of Walton-street, Bath. I think his name is Edward Watts, and he is in partnership with his father, and they are in a large way of business. My sister left her home because she brought disgrace on her husband. Her husband left her because he caught her with a porter. Her husband sent her home to her poor mother, who is now dead. She took her two children with her, but I believe the boy has since been sent to a boarding school by his aunt, Miss Watts. The other child, a girl, was dead. I have never seen my sister in an epileptic fit—only in drunken fits. I believe she has been before the Thames Police-court magistrate on charges of drunkenness. I believe she has been let off on the ground that she was subject to epileptic fits, but I do not believe she was subject to them. I believe she lived with a man who kept a coffee house at Poplar. His name was not Stride, but I could find out by to-morrow. She had ceased to live with him for some time, for he went to sea and was wrecked on the Isle of St. Paul. That was about three years ago. Since then she had not lived with anyone to my knowledge.

The CORONER.—Have you ever heard she has been in trouble with any man?

Witness.—No, but she has been locked up several times. I have never heard of any one threatening her, or that she was afraid of any one. I know of no man with whom she had any relations, and I did not know she lived in

# Wednesday, 3 October, 1888

Flower and Dean-street. I knew that she was called "Long Liz."

The CORONER.—Have you ever heard the name of Stride?

Witness.—She never mentioned that name to me. If she had lived with any one of that name I am sure she would have told me. She used to come to me every Saturday, and I always gave her 2s.

The CORONER.—Did she come last Saturday?

Witness.—No; her visit on Thursday was an unusual one. Before that she had not missed a Saturday for between two and three years. She always came at 4 o'clock in the afternoon, and we used to meet at the corner of Chancery-lane. On Saturday afternoon I went there at half-past 3 and remained there until 5, but deceased did not turn up. On Sunday morning, when I read the paper, I wondered whether it was my sister. I had a presentiment that it was. I then went to Whitechapel and spoke to a policeman about my sister. I afterwards went to the St. George's mortuary. When I first saw the body I did not at first recognize it, as I only saw it by gas light; but the next day I recognized it.

The CORONER.—Did not you have some special presentiment about your sister?

Witness.—About 1:20 a.m. on Sunday morning I was lying on my bed when I felt a kind of pressure on my breast, and then I felt three kisses on my cheek. I also heard the kisses, and they were quite distinct.

A Juryman.—Did your sister have any special mark about her?

Witness.—Yes; a black mark on her leg, and I saw it there yesterday. I told the police I could recognize her by this particular mark. The mark was caused by my sister being bitten by an adder some years ago, and I was bitten on the finger at the same time. Here is the mark (showing it to the Coroner).

The CORONER.—Has your husband seen your sister?

Witness.—He has seen her once or twice some three years ago. I have another sister and a brother who are alive, but they have not seen her for years.

The CORONER.—I hear at one time you said it was your sister, and at another time you said it was not.

Witness.—I am sure it was.

The CORONER.—Have you any one that can corroborate you?

Witness.—Only my brother and my sister. This disgrace will kill my sister. The best thing will be for her brother to come up. I have kept this shame from every one.

(Here the witness sobbed bitterly.)

The CORONER.—Was there any special mark on your sister's feet?

Witness.—I know she had a hollow at the bottom of one of her feet, which was the result of an accident.

The CORONER.—Did you recognize the clothes she wore?

Witness.—No, I did not. I never took notice of what she wore, for I was always grateful to get rid of her. Once she left a baby naked outside my door, and I had to keep it until she fetched it away. It was not one of the two children already mentioned, but was by some policeman or another. I do not know any one that would do her harm, for she was a girl everyone liked.

The CORONER.—Would your brother recognize her?

Witness.—I am positive he could, although he has not seen her for years. I can now recognize her by the hair.

The CORONER.—I think you ought to go again to the spot where you have been in the habit of meeting your sister to see if she comes again. You say she has not missed a single Saturday for two and a half years. How about the Saturday when she was in prison?

Witness.—She has always been fined, and the money has been paid.

Mr. Frederick William Blackwell said,—I live at 100, Commercial-road, and am a surgeon. At 10 minutes past 1 on Sunday morning I was called to 40, Berner-street. I was called by a policeman, and my assistant, Mr. Johnson, went back with him. I followed immediately I had dressed. I consulted my watch on my arrival, and it was just 1:10. The deceased was lying on her left side completely across the yard. Her legs were drawn up, her feet against the wall of the right side of the yard passage. Her head was resting almost in the line of the carriage way, and her feet were about three yards from the gateway. The feet almost touched the wall, and the face was completely towards the wall. The neck and chest were quite warm; also the legs and face

253

were slightly warm. The hands were cold. The right hand was lying on the chest, and was smeared inside and out with blood. It was quite open. The left hand was lying on the ground and was partially closed, and contained a small packet of cachous[146] wrapped in tissue paper. There were no rings or marks of rings on the fingers. The appearance of the face was quite placid, and the mouth was slightly open. There was a check silk scarf round the neck, the bow of which was turned to the left side and pulled tightly. There was a long incision in the neck, which exactly corresponded with the lower border of the scarf. The lower edge of the scarf was slightly frayed, as if by a sharp knife. The incision in the neck commenced on the left side, 2½ in. below the angle of the jaw, and almost in a direct line with it. It nearly severed the vessels on the left side, cut the windpipe completely in two, and terminated on the opposite side 1½in. below the angle of the right jaw, but without severing the vessels on that side. The post-mortem appearances will be given subsequently.

By the CORONER.—I did not ascertain if the bloody hand had been moved. The blood was running down in the gutter into the drain. It was running in an opposite direction to the feet. There was a quantity of clotted blood just under the body.

The CORONER.—Were there no spots of blood anywhere?

Witness.—No. Some of the blood had been trodden about near to where the body was lying.

The CORONER.—Was there any blood on the side of the house, or splashes on the wall?

Witness.—No. It was very dark at the time, and I only examined it by the policeman's lamp. I have not since examined the place.

The CORONER.—Did you examine the clothing?

Witness.—Yes. There was no blood on any portion of it. The bonnet was lying on the ground, a few inches from the head. The dress was undone at the top. I know about what deceased had on, but could not give an accurate description of them. I noticed she had a bunch of flowers in her jacket. The injuries were beyond the possibility of self-infliction.

The CORONER.—How long had the deceased been dead when you saw her?

Witness.—From 20 minutes to half an hour when I arrived. It was a very mild night and was not raining at the time. There was no wet on deceased's clothing. Deceased would have bled to death comparatively slowly, on account of the vessels on one side only being severed, and the artery not completely severed. Deceased could not have cried out after the injuries were inflicted as the windpipe was severed. I felt the heart and found it quite warm. My assistant was present all the time. Dr. Phillips arrived from 20 minutes to half an hour after my arrival, but I did not notice the exact time.

The CORONER.—Could you see there was a woman there when you went in?

Witness.—Yes. The doors were closed when I arrived. I formed the opinion that the murderer first took hold of the silk scarf, at the back of it, and then pulled the deceased backwards, but I cannot say whether the throat was cut while the woman was standing or after she was pulled backwards. Deceased would take about a minute and a half to bleed to death. I cannot say whether the scarf would be tightened sufficiently to prevent deceased calling out.

At this stage the inquiry was adjourned until today.

~

---

[146] **Cachou.** Breath sweetener. (Morehead)

# Wednesday, 3 October, 1888

## The Star

### IN WHITEHALL NOW.
### THE PIMLICO MYSTERY DEEPENED BY ANOTHER DISCOVERY.
### THE WEST-END SHOCKED TO-DAY.
### The Murderer Selects the New Police Offices on the Embankment to Deposit the Trunk of His Victim—How the Mutilation was Effected—The Difficulties He Overcame.

As announced in a second extra special of *The Star* last night, the accumulation of horrors in London has not yet ceased. The locale of the latest ghastliness is in Westminster, within a couple of hundred yards of both Scotland-yard and the Houses of Parliament. The horrible "find" was made yesterday afternoon in the new police buildings between Parliament-street and the Embankment. Shortly after one o'clock several workmen, on opening a bundle which they found hidden in one of the darkest archways of the vaulted foundations of the structure referred to,

### LAID BARE THE REMAINS OF A WOMAN.

The corpse was a mere trunk, both head and limbs having been severed in an apparently brutal and unskilful manner. Evidently the trunk was that of a young and healthy woman. The arm found on 11 Sept. in the Thames, near Grosvenor Railway Bridge, and probably that found in Lambeth a few days ago, were cut from the mutilated trunk. Chief Superintendent Dunlap and Chief Inspector Wren viewed the remains, and took steps to collect all the evidence bearing on the case.

A superficial examination of the trunk indicates conclusively that the dismemberment was effected by means of a saw; at any rate, in the case of the head and legs. It is by no means so certain yet that

### THE ARMS WERE SAWN FROM THE BODY,

and this point is of importance in connection with the bearing the discovery has on the Pimlico mystery. Dr. Neville, after examining the arm recently found in Grosvenor-road, was decidedly of opinion that it had been cut from the body rather than sawn. However, the head has undoubtedly been sawn off in this case, and the same instrument was apparently used in taking off the legs. The body was sawn through just above the abdomen. The difficulty and danger which the murderer must have encountered on bearing the body to its hiding-place, increase the mystery. It is on the site of what was intended for the National Opera House that the new central police buildings are being erected. Their exact location is between Parliament-street and the Embankment, or immediately eastward of the Clock Tower and St. Stephen's Club. The place is surrounded by a high hoarding. The ground structure consists of a vast labyrinth of brick passages, archways, and vaulted chambers. As was pointed out by the foreman of the works, there are really

### BUT TWO POSSIBLE MODES OF INGRESS

to the archway where the body was found, either over the high hoarding from the Embankment side, or from a little alley-way called Cannon-row, almost opposite the Home Office in Parliament-street. The difficulties of access to the ground are so great from the side facing the Embankment to a person loaded with so heavy a bundle are regarded as almost insuperable. But one avenue of approach therefore practically existed, and that was from the obscure corner at the north end of Cannon-row over a seven-foot hoarding. The man must then have conveyed his burden almost 50 yards, through a network of partly underground passages, to a remote corner of the building.

The place in which the trunk was found was such an out-of-the-way kind that one is led to the conclusion that it was deposited there by some party acquainted with the building. No night-watchman is kept at the place, and anyone once within the hoarding after working hours could move about at leisure free from observation. That it was

### PLACED THERE QUITE RECENTLY

seems to be beyond question. The workmen, while making measurements on Friday, passed right over the spot, and are confident the body was not there then. They go so far as to say that it could not have been there when they left at twenty minutes to five o'clock on Saturday. Yet it was there on Monday, for it was seen by the carpenter, Frederick Wildbore, who imagined the object to be nothing but an old coat. The obvious inference is that the parcel was left either on Saturday night or during Sunday. The

# Wednesday, 3 October, 1888

corpse is that of a mature, well-formed, and perhaps an unmarried woman, not over 40 years of age, and who was probably alive about 20 days ago. The man in whose breast the explanation of the mystery lies concealed

### CANNOT LIVE VERY FAR OFF

the scene, it is thought, for several reasons. In the first place, the trunk being that of a broad, well-developed person, it would be a very heavy and clumsy parcel to carry for any distance, and in the second place it seems doubtful whether it was sufficiently concealed to have been carried far without incurring great risk. The skirt in which it was wrapped appeared to have been brought up as far as it would go, but the breasts apparently had never been covered by the skirt. It could never have been carried far through the streets in that partially covered manner, and the theory is advanced that it was brought in a sack and shot out into the place in which it was found. It was impossible to hold an inquest upon the arm found in Grosvenor-road. The law requires that a "vital part" can only form the subject of a coroner's inquiry. This will now take place at once. One of the breasts (the left) of the body appeared either to have been surgically operated upon at some period of the woman's lifetime, or else the process of decomposition at that part of the body became abnormally active. It is intended by the police to

### PHOTOGRAPH THE REMAINS.

The present discovery recalls the somewhat similar dismemberment of the remains of the woman Harriet Lane, killed by the Wainwright brothers. A few years ago also there was the case of Kate Webster, who at Richmond murdered her mistress, and cut the body up piecemeal, and tried to dispose of it in small portions.

The arm recently found in Pimlico has been preserved in the usual way, and will be compared with the trunk.

Detective Inspector Marshall is this morning superintending the search which is being made over the premises in the event of other members having been hidden thereabouts.

The police and medical men were early astir this morning to continue their investigations. Dr. Bond and Dr. Hebbert, the divisional police surgeon and his assistant, arrived at seven o'clock at the mortuary in Millbank-street, where the trunk now lies. They were engaged for an hour and a half on the post mortem examination, and at the conclusion immediately reported the result of their researches to the police. Meanwhile the police themselves were equally busy thoroughly searching the premises.

The night watchman at the Red Lion public-house in Cannon-row explained to a *Star* reporter how it was possible for a man to get into the new police buildings at night. He applied to the clerk of the works for the post of night-watchman, and was told that one would not be appointed, but he is about the neighborhood every night until after twelve. He has, he says, frequently seen men going into the buildings at night to sleep—he supposes in the vaults. A large iron pillar stands at the corner of the kerb-stone in Cannon-row just against the hoarding. It is quite easy for anyone to mount on the top of the pillar, and then to

### SCALE THE HOARDING.

He has seen several people enter this way. He has never seen any females go over, but a man once in could easily open a door from the inside and admit a female. It would be difficult, although not impossible, to get a heavy parcel over the hoarding at the place to which the waterman referred.

### The Discovery of the Arm.

Dr. Neville's opinions on the arm found at Pimlico, which as divisional police surgeon he then examined, are in the light of this subsequent discovery, worth exhuming. As he told a *Star* reporter at the time, he inferred that the arm was not that of a woman of refinement, as the nails were not neatly trimmed, as those of a lady would have been. The murdered woman would be of fair complexion, the hair on the arm being light. Judging from the freshness of the skin and the tension of the muscles and sinews, the arm was considered to be that of

### A YOUNG WOMAN UNDER 30 YEARS.

Dr. Neville's opinion was that the person must have been dead only an hour, or two at the outside, when the limb was severed from the trunk, as the muscles were contracted, and the ccontraction and retraction also of the muscles would indicate that death had occurred not long before, *rigor mortis* not having set in. The proportions of the limb indicated to the doctor that the woman was about 5ft. 8in. in height, stout, well-built, well-proportioned and well nour-

256

ished, with which description, it is important to note, this body just found tallies as far as can be ascertained. When the doctor examined the arm he believed it had not been removed from the body beyond two days before, which would give the date of the dismemberment as about 9 Sept.

—

## WHITECHAPEL.
## THE MITRE-SQUARE VICTIM IS NOW FULLY IDENTIFIED.
### THE SIMPLE STORY OF HER "MATE."
**Though Warned by Him of the Dangers of the Streets—She Fell a Victim to the Wiles and Fury of the Monster—The Presence of the Pawntickets and the Tattoo Marks Explained.**

Both of the latest victims of the master-murderer have now been identified. The recognition of the body of the Berner-street victim by Mary Malcolm, of 50, Eagle-street, Red Lion-square, Holborn, as her sister, Elizabeth Watts, does not contradict the identification by "One-armed Liz" and other frequenters of the Flower and Dean-street lodging-house. Mrs. Malcolm had lost sight of her sister for a long time, and it transpires that it was she who was known in the lodging-house district by the name of Stride and familiarly called "Long Liz." The body that was found in Mitre-square has been positively identified as that of

### A WOMAN NAMED KELLY,

who, strangely enough, lived in a lodging-house in the same street as the one frequented by her fellow victim. There can be no possible doubt of the identity. The body was identified at a late hour last night by a man who has been living with her for seven years, and all the mystery connected with the pawn-tickets and with the India-ink marks on her arm are cleared up. The man's name is John Kelly, and

### THE STORY HE TELLS

is one of very great interest, throwing no light on the probable authorship of the crime, but illustrating in a very pathetic manner the mode of life in those low lodging-houses. A *Star* reporter had a long conversation with Kelly this morning at the lodging-house, No. 55, Flower and Dean-street.

He is about 40 years of age, and, to all appearance, is a poor hard-working man. He told his story in a manner that carried with it an unmistakable stamp of genuineness. At times he almost broke down with emotion, for, as he expressed it, "I have lived with that girl a long while, and we never quarrelled." We will give his story as nearly as possible in his own words:—

"It is nigh on to seven years since I met Kate, and it was in this very lodging-house I first set eyes on her. We got throwed together a good bit, and the result was that we made a regular bargain. We have lived here ever since, as the people here will tell you, and have never left here except when we've gone to the country together hopping. I don't pretend that she was my wife. She was not. She told me long ago that she had a husband, and told me what his name was. It was

### TOM CONWAY.

She said he was a pensioner from the Royal Irish Artillery. She had had several children by him, but I don't know that I ever heard where they were except one daughter, who is married to a gunmaker and lives in King-street, Bermondsey. She told me all about her husband one night, when I spoke about the letters "T. C." being pricked in her arm. It was Conway that did that years and years ago, and it was by them letters partly that I recognised her last night. But she had a falling out with her husband and

### THEY PARTED.

She used to tell me she never wanted to see him again, but I remember her saying once or twice that she had met him in the street. The last time she spoke of him was a good while ago. She never said anything about his trying to cause her any trouble, or that she was in any way afraid of him. I don't believe he ever bothered her at all.

Well, Kate and me lived on here as best we could. She got a job of charing now an then, and I picked up all the odd jobs I could in the Spitalfields Market. The people here were very kind to us. If Kate ever went with other men I never knew it. She would take a drop to drink, but she was never troublesome. I remember once she was up at the police station, and I suppose the police officers were right who thought they recognised her by that.

We went hopping together mostly every year. We went down this year as usual. We didn't get on any too well, and started to hoof it home. We came along in company with another man and woman who had worked in the same fields, but who parted with us to go to Chatham when we

# Wednesday, 3 October, 1888

turned off towards Maidstone. The woman said to Kate, "I have got

### A PAWNTICKET

for a flannel shirt. I wish you'd take it, since you're going up to town. It is only in for 9d., and it may fit your old man. So Kate took it and we trudged along. It was in at Jones's, Church-street, in the name of Emily Burrell. She put the ticket back in our box and we moved on. We did not have money enough to keep us going till we got to town, but we did get there and came straight to this house. Luck was dead against us.

On last Saturday morning we were both done up for cash. I had nothing but a pair of boots that would bring anything, and I says to her, "We'll pop[147] the boots and have a bite to eat anyway." "Oh, no," says she, "don't do that;" but I told her I'd pawn the shirt off my back to keep her out of the street, for she had had only a few odd jobs for a goodish spell back But she said she'd go and see what her daughter could do. Howsomever, we popped the boots, and sat in this 'ere kitchen and had what turned out to be

### OUR LAST MEAL TOGETHER.

She told me she had made up her mind to go to her daughter's in Bermondsey. I begged her to be back early, for we had been talking about the Whitechapel murders, and I said I did not want to have that knife get at her. "Don't you fear for me," said she, "I'll take care of myself, and I shan't fall into his hands." With that she went out. I went with her to the street corner below, and I never laid eyes on her again till I saw her down at the mortuary last night. I was out in the market all day, but did no good.

When she did not come home at night I didn't worry, for I thought her daughter might have asked her to stay over Sunday with her. So on Sunday morning I wandered round in the crowds that had been gathered by the talk about the two fresh murders. I stood and looked at the very spot where my poor old gal had laid with her body all cut to pieces and I never knew it. I never thought of her in connection with it, for I thought she was safe at her daughter's.

Yesterday morning I began to be worried a bit, but I did not guess the truth until after I had come back from another bad day in the market. I came in here and asked for Kate, she had not

been in. I sat down on that bench by the table and carelessly picked up a *Star* paper. I read down the page a bit, and

### MY EYE CAUGHT THE NAME OF "BURRILL."

It looked familiar, but I didn't think where I had seen it until I came to the word "pawnticket." Then it came over me all at once. The tin box, the two pawn-tickets, the one for that flannel shirt, and the other for my boots. But could Kate have lost them? I read a little further. "The woman had the letters 'T.C.,' in India ink, on her arm." Man, you could have knocked me down with a feather. It was my Kate, and no other. I don't know how I braced up to go to the police, but I did.

They took me down to see the body, and

### I KNEW IT WAS HER.

I knew it before I saw it, and I knew her for all the way she was cut. I told the police all I have told you, and I suppose I will tell it again to the Coroner. I never knew if she went to her daughters at all. I only wish to God she had, for we had lived together a long while and never had a quarrel.

The keeper of the lodging-house fully confirms Kelly's statements as to the recent history of the murdered woman. Kelly himself bears a good character, both at the lodging-house and among the butchers in the market. None of the frequenters of the lodging-houses in the neighbourhood seem to have ever seen any man but Jack Kelly in company with the woman, and no one knows of any other relations of the deceased further than the daughter she talked of visiting, except a sister who was said to be the wife of a farthing book seller living in Thrawl-street, Spitalfields. The police will look up this sister, and both she and Kelly will be at the inquest.

The identification of the bodies does not seem to throw any light upon the authorship of the atrocities. The police have found that

### NONE OF THOSE ARRESTED YESTERDAY

are connected with the crimes. The arrest that is reported to have been made in Chingford is said to have had the same result. The man with a black shiny bag who was wanted for having been seen in Berner-street under suspicious circumstances just before the murder turns out to be a respectable man who fully explains his

---

[147] **Pop.** (5) To pawn, to put away: whence pop-shop, a pawnbroker (1823). (Farmer)

# Wednesday, 3 October, 1888

conduct. The only new feature in the way of possible clues comes from the discovery of a pair of trousers at the Nelson Tavern, Victoria-road, Kentish Town, on Monday, lying behind the door in an outbuilding. The trousers, however, were picked up and carried away by a tramp. The fragments of paper in which they had been wrapped were collected and found to be stained with blood.

Kelly has gone, in company with Sergeant Outram and other officers, to find the victim's two daughters and her sister.

—

## FIFTH EDITION.
## THE MITRE-SQUARE VICTIM.
### The Police Seek Out Her Relatives—Hints and Hoaxes.

The police are proceeding with the task of securing a complete identification of the woman Kelly. Her sister was found at her home in Thrawl-street, and had no difficulty in identifying the body. She said she had not seen the deceased for a long time, and did not know where she was living. She had no knowledge that she was known by the name of Kelly, and had no idea that it was her sister who had been murdered until the police came after her. It is expected that the daughters will be found during the day.

### LETTERS OF ADVICE.

The numbers of letters received by the police offering advice or suggestions as to the best way of catching the murderer is something enormous. They come from all over the world. America sends quite as many as all other countries outside of England, and even Australia has been heard from. Practical jokers of the same school as "Jack the Ripper" try to crack their nuts on the police as well as through the Press, but the detectives have yet to learn that they are in possession of a specimen of the way the genuine expert knife handler can use a pen.

—

### A Confession and a Contradiction.

This morning at the Guildhall William Bull, describing himself as a medical student of the London Hospital, and giving an address at Stannard-road, Dalston, was charged on his own confession with having committed the Aldgate murder. He appeared to have been drinking heavily.

Inspector Izzard said that last night, at twenty minutes to eleven, the prisoner went to Bishops-gate-street Station and made the following statement, which he took down:—

**"I WISH TO GIVE MYSELF UP**
for the murder in Aldgate. On Saturday night or Sunday morning, about two o'clock, I think, I met the woman in Aldgate. I went with her up a narrow street not far from the main road for an immoral purpose. I promised to give her half-a-crown, which I did. While walking along together there was a second man, who came up and took the half-crown from her. I cannot endure this any longer. My poor head! (He put his hands to his head and cried, or pretended to cry.) I shall go mad. I have done it and I must put up with it." The inspector asked what had become of the clothing he had on when the murder was committed? The prisoner said, "If you wish to know, they are in the Lea, and

### THE KNIFE I THREW AWAY."

At this point the prisoner declined to say any more. He was drunk, and apparently had been drinking heavily. Part of the statement was made in the presence of Major Smith. The prisoner gave a correct address, but is not known at the London Hospital. His parents are very respectable, and the prisoner has been out of employ. The inspector asked for a few days to make enquiries.

The prisoner, in answer to the Alderman, said he was mad drunk when he made the statement. It was impossible for the murder to have been committed by him.

Inspector Izzard said that when searched the prisoner had on him a very small knife, a halfpenny, and a wheel from a watch.

Prisoner was remanded, Alderman Stone refusing to grant bail.

The police, after investigation, are inclined to believe that the murderer avoids common lodging-houses. Detection would be too easy there, and they have searched every common lodging-house in the neighbourhood, and made inquiries as to the persons who entered them last Saturday morning after one o'clock.

—

### A Scare at Lowestoft.

In Lowestoft during the past few days a man has been going into different shops and threatening to serve females behind the counter

259

in the same way as the murderers did at White-chapel. The man has left the town.

—

## OUR POLICE AND DETECTIVE SYSTEM.

In *The Star* of 18 Sept. we pointed out some of the shortcomings of our existing detective system. We now supplement our remarks with other facts bearing on the detective as well as the police system generally, which are within our knowledge.

The present head of the Criminal Investigation Department is Mr. Anderson, who succeeded Mr. Monro. The actual working chief of the department is Superintendent Williamson, who has had some 40 years experience in the detective force, and is generally allowed to be a very capable officer.

Possibly neither of these officials is responsible for the unsatisfactory system that prevails. The names of those really responsible, if not for its inception, at least for its continuance, are pretty well known; but more responsible than either of these offenders is the perverse Tory Government that persists in retaining them in office while everybody is crying out for their dismissal.

Our police as a body are merely machines, and they know it. As an illustration of this let us take the system of

## "FIXED POINTS."

At the principal points of all the great thoroughfares—for instance, at the Elephant and Castle—one or more constables are always stationed ready for emergencies; but they are not allowed to move away any distance under any pretext whatever, even though it might be to follow suspicious characters whom they might observe plotting "a job."

The police are so fenced in by rules and regulations that they seem to be afraid to act on their own responsibility in a grave emergency. If a deadly fight is taking place in a house they will not enter unless they hear cries of "Murder." If a lodger calls a policeman's attention to the fact that murder is being committed he is asked if he is the landlord, and if he says no, then he is told that the policeman has no authority to enter the house unless invited to do so by the landlord or his deputy. It is quite common in low neighbourhoods for a woman to come up to a policeman in the dead of the night and ask him to

come with her to her lodgings because her husband, or so-called husband, is there, mad drunk, threatening to murder her. The policeman looks at her, mentally studies his code-book, and tells her to go back, and that no doubt it will be all right.

A few words here as to the general system adopted in setting about

## THE INVESTIGATION OF A MURDER MYSTERY,

such as the latest Whitechapel one and the others that have preceded it, may not be out of place.

The detectives from Scotland-yard go down to the station in the locality of the crime, and they and the chiefs and detectives of the police whom they have come to assist have a consultation. Each suggests what is the best way to set to work, and finally a theory is adopted and acted upon. People who are supposed to know something bearing on the case are invited to give evidence, and everything they say is taken down—sometimes openly, sometimes by a concealed shorthand writer. If they are suspected of knowing more than they care to disclose, they are treated in a friendly manner, and pleasantly invited to come again. Meanwhile their movements are closely watched.

The services of "noses"—that is to say, people who are hand in glove with persons of indifferent character, are frequently called into play, and they are deputed to go to the low lodging-houses and other places that are the resort of low characters, and keep their eyes and ears open for anything likely to give a clue to the individual or individuals wanted. Women often act as "noses."[148]

In investigating a crime,

## DETECTIVES PROCEED VERY QUIETLY—

often too quietly, it might be thought—and frequently through the agency of too credulous reporters lead the really suspected person to believe that the scent lies quite in another quarter, while in reality his every movement is being closely watched. In some instances, the reluctance of witnesses to come forward with

---

[148] **Nose.** 1. An informer (1789). 2. A paid spy, shadow (q.v.), nark (q.v.): also noser (1819). As verb, (1) to smell, scent ; (2) to pry, suspect, discover (1651) ; (3) to inform (1821) (Farmer)

evidence is a great stumbling block in the way of success.

The police are generally held responsible for the particular kind of evidence that is brought against a person charged with committing a crime when the case goes for trial, but it seems they are not responsible for the line adopted by the prosecution.

The duties of detectives sometimes cast their lines in pleasant places. At noblemen's balls helmeted policemen keep the doors, but the detective, in dress coat and kid gloves, enters with the company. It is not generally known that even at

## BALLS GIVEN BY THE HIGHEST NOBILITY,

by Ambassadors, and the most exclusive of the "Upper Ten," a detective in evening dress, with a bland smile on his face, and his moustache curled in the most aggravating fashion, stalks about and makes a note of divers things.

—

## EAST-END LODGING-HOUSES.
### Montagu Williams Denounces Them as the Haunt of the Burglar and the Prostitute.

Mary M'Carthy, a powerful young woman well-known to the police, was charged at Worship-street yesterday with stabbing Ann Neason, deputy of a lodging-house in Spitalfields.

Mr. Montagu Williams immediately became interested on hearing this, and asked Neason, How many beds do you make up there?

—Witness: Twenty-eight singles and 24 doubles.

Mr. Williams: By "doubles," you mean for a man and a woman. Can the woman take any man she likes? You don't know if the couples are married or not?

—Witness: No, sir; we don't ask them.

Mr. Williams: Precisely what I thought. And the sooner these lodging-houses are put down the better. They are the haunt of the burglar, the home of the pick-pocket, and the hotbed of prostitution. I don't think I can put it stronger than that. It is time the owners of these places, who reap large profits from them, were looked after.

It subsequently transpired that the "missus" was a Mrs. Wilmot, a baker, of Brick-lane.

Mr. Williams: Has she any more of these common lodging-houses?

—Witness: Yes, sir, two in Wentworth-street, close by where I am in George-yard.

Mr. Williams: And how many beds does she provide there?

—The Prisoner: Sixty or seventy, sir.

Mr. Williams: What is the price of a bed?

—Witness: Fourpence and eightpence.

Mr. Williams: Eightpence for a double. Was M'Carthy a double or single?

—Witness: Double.

Mr. Williams: Is she married?

—Witness: No; I don't think so.

Mr. Williams: Then the place is a brothel?

Mr. Enoch Walker, vestry clerk of Shoreditch, said such places could only be touched by one section of the Criminal Law Amendment Act.

Mr. Williams: Then I hope they will not be exempt from future legislation. They are places where, according to the witness, the thief or the criminal can hide all day for the payment of 4d. or 8d. for a bed each night. As a magistrate I have made it my business to go over some of these places, and I say that the sooner they are put down the better. In my humble judgement they are about as unwholesome and unhealthy, as well as dangerous to the community, as can well be. There are places among them where the police dare not enter, and where the criminal hides all day long. I have seen so much that I hope what I have said will do something to call attention to them.

The prisoner was sentenced to a month's hard labour, and left the dock threatening the prosecutrix.

~

# Wednesday, 3 October, 1888

## Evening News
### EAST END ATROCITIES
### TO THE EDITOR OF
### "THE EVENING NEWS."

Sir—The excitement which the murders in the East end of London has caused throughout the country is very strange. Equally atrocious crimes are of daily occurrence in our very midst, and yet no one is particularly perturbed. And why?

Firstly, because the ordinary atrocity to which we are accustomed lacks the sensational element which is so richly provided in the Whitechapel horrors; and secondly, because most people are either utterly ignorant of the villainies which daily take place, or else shut their eyes to them. Wives are beaten and murdered, children are starved and tortured to death, and robberies with violence are committed every day of the week; but these little eccentricities of our fellow citizens are too commonplace to attract public attention.

That the perpetrator of the Whitechapel outrages should still be at large is anything but surprising. One has only to inspect the streets of London at night to see how easy it is to commit a crime and yet escape detection; in fact, these protégés of the law, the criminals, may do as they like, but respectable citizens must be very careful how they protect themselves.

Another great reason why such "artists in crime" as the Whitechapel demon escape is to be found in that utterly idiotic institution, the coroner's inquest, by means of which every detail which should be kept secret is made public property, and to no purpose, except to put the criminal on his guard.

In Germany all cases of suspicious death are taken in hand by the Untersuchungerichter[149] (a law officer), who institutes a private inquiry, and calls in the Kreisphysikus[150] (a specially trained medical man) to examine the case from a medical point of view, and to perform, in conjunction with another medical man, a post mortem examination of the body, according to the hard and fast rules laid down in the "Regulatio fur der verfahren des Gerichtsarzte,

&c."[151]

The medical description of each portion of the body is taken down in writing by the Richter,[152] and then each of the medical men sends in his opinion as to the cause of the conditions observed.

Perfectly reliable scientific knowledge of the case being thus acquired, the Richter and his colleagues then carry on the case. All unnecessary publicity is thus avoided, the relations of suicides are spared from having their family affairs made vulgar gossip, and the police are better enabled to carry out their investigations than would be the case if any other system were employed.

One word more, Sir. Every penny a liner,[153] butcher boy, and pseudo psychopathologist has his theory on the cases in question. The value of such theories may be judged from the fact that poor rational medical men can only bring forward hypotheses.

I am, &c.,
A.F.H., M.D.

### TO THE EDITOR OF
### "THE EVENING NEWS."

Sir—Will you allow me to offer the suggestion that the series of terrible murders lately perpetrated may be the work of a fanatic, possessed with the belief that he has received a mission to put an end to that particular vice practised by his victim? They are all of the same class, and all the murders of the same fiendish nature, no doubt accomplished by the same hand.

I am, &c.,
S.F.L.
October 1.

### TO THE EDITOR OF
### "THE EVENING NEWS."

Sir—With reference to the two recent, hideous and brutal murders committed on Saturday night or Sunday morning, it has struck me that precious time was lost in not at once placing a cordon of police or military, if the

---

[149] **Untersuchungsrichter.** Ger. An examining judge. (Glucksman)

[150] **Kreisphysikus.** District doctor. (ibid)

[151] This is slightly garbled, but appears to be: "Regulations for the proceedings of the Doctor's Court."

[152] **Richter.** Judge. (ibid)

[153] **Penny-a-liner.** A writer of paragraphs at the rate of a penny a line (or some such small sum), a literary hack. Hence, penny-a-linerism (1840). (Farmer)

# Wednesday, 3 October, 1888

latter could have been procured from the Tower barracks, round the locality where the bodies were found for, say, a square mile in extent, and allow no ingress or egress through this cordon until an exhaustive search had been made at every house habited or uninhabited within the radius of the cordon. The murderer or murderers could not have got away very far; the night was cold, and the bodies were found warm; moreover, it is unlikely the fiend or fiends would go any distance without endeavouring to wash or cleanse themselves from the blood of their hapless victims.

I am, &c.,
SPAHL.

—

## MR. MONTAGU WILLIAMS ON EAST END LODGING HOUSES.

At the Worship street Police court, yesterday, Mary McCarthy, a powerful young woman, well known at this court, was charged at the close of the day's business with stabbing Ann Neason in the face. The prosecutrix said she was deputy of a lodging house in Spitalfields, and the prisoner was a lodger.

The Magistrate (Mr. Montagu Williams Q.C.): Is it one of the common lodging houses one hears of?

Witness:—Yes, sir.

Mr. Williams: Then tell me this. How many beds do you make up there?

Witness:—Twenty-eight singles and twenty-four doubles.

Mr. Williams: By "doubles" you mean for a man and a woman?

Witness:—Yes, sir.

Mr. Williams: And the woman can take any man she likes? You don't know if the couples are married or not?

Witness:—No, sir. We don't ask them.

## THE SOONER THEY ARE PUT DOWN THE BETTER.

Mr. Williams: Precisely what I thought. And the sooner these lodging houses are put down the better. They are the haunt of the burglar, the home of the pickpocket, and the hotbed of prostitution. I don't think I can put it stronger than that. It is time the owners of these places who reap large profits from them were looked after.

Witness than continued her evidence, and said that because the prisoner had become quarrelsome the "missus" told her (witness) to refuse the prisoner's money for the future, and the prisoner out of spite stabbed witness in the face with a piece of a skewer.

Mr. Williams: Who's the "missus" you mention?

Witness:—Mrs. Wilmot.

Mr. William: Oh, a woman. She is the owner, then. But she doesn't live there?

Witness:—No, sir, in Brick lane.

Mr. Williams: What is she?

Witness:—A baker.

Mr. Williams: Has she any more of these common lodging houses?

Witness:—Yes, sir, two in Wentworth street, close by where I am in George yard.

Mr. Williams: And how many beds does she provide there?

The prisoner:—Sixty or seventy, sir.

Mr. Williams: What is the price of a bed?

Witness:—Fourpence and eightpence.

Mr. Williams: Eightpence for a double. Was she a double or single?

Witness:—Double.

Mr. Williams: Is she married?

Witness:—No, I don't think so.

Mr. Williams: Then the place is a brothel?

The inspector on duty in the Court said that the beds were let for the night.

Mr. Williams: That makes no difference. The witness says that any woman can take any man in there and so long as eightpence is paid no question is asked. What is that but a house carried on for immoral accommodation.

## THE LAW CANNOT TOUCH THEM.

Mr. Enoch Walker, vestry clerk of Shoreditch, said that he had had a good deal of experience with such places, but they could only be touched by one section of the Criminal Law Amendment Act.

Mr. Williams: Then I hope they will not be exempt from future legislation. They are places where, according to the witness, the thief or the criminal can hide all day for the payment of 4d. or 8d. for a bed each night. As a magistrate I have made it my business to go over some of these places, and I say that the sooner they are put down the better. In my humble judgement they are about as unwholesome and unhealthy, as well as dangerous to the community, as can well be. There are places among them where the police dare not enter, and where the criminal

263

hides all day long. I have seen so much that I hope what I have said will do something to call attention to them.

The prisoner, after the evidence of a police constable had corroborated that of the lodging house deputy, was sentenced to a month's hard labour. She left the dock threatening the prosecutrix.

—

### FOREIGN PAUPERS.

The East end of London is very much in men's minds and mouths at the present moment, for ghastly reasons—reasons upon which we may as well say at once we do not intend to enter now. The murders that have been committed in this unfortunate region will take their own place—and a unique place it will be—in the history of the last quarter of the nineteenth century. But there are other things belonging to the same period and the same district which will have to be noted by the historian of the future —things which the present horrors may press aside for the moment, but which are intrinsically of much greater importance and will leave a more lasting impression upon our destinies.

"Ye have the poor with you always,"[154] is a mournful truth, applicable in some form or another to every part of the globe; but there is probably no spot in the world to which it is so peculiarly and directly applicable as the eastern side of our great Metropolis. For years past the *Evening News* has directed attention to some of the principal causes of this chronic poverty of the East end, and it has always placed to the forefront the free and unregulated importation of foreign paupers.

These wretched men and women can exist in apparent comfort under conditions which are simply intolerable to any one born and bred in these islands; but their presence amongst us in such overwhelming numbers leaves the native born workman no option but to sink down to their degraded standard of wages and comfort, or else starve.

Now this is not fair; it is not worthy of the name of competition; it helps no one, it profits no one, but a few un-worthy sweaters[155] and greedy vampires of that class. But as yet we have done nothing to stop or discourage this baleful importation. It is going on today as freely as ever, and will apparently go on tomorrow and the next day with increasing force.

We have not even the assurance that when Lord Dunraven's[156] committee has exhausted its apparently exhaustless inquiries we shall arrive at any definite scheme of prohibition or even regulation.

France is suffering from a somewhat similar evil; but, fortunately for herself, France is not dominated by a set of doctrinaire Dry as dusts who call themselves political economists, and therefore her action is somewhat different from our own. The President has signed a decree in reference to the importation of foreigners into France, and, as a consequence, that importation will be very seriously hampered for the future. The preamble of the decree recognises the evils arising from the number of foreigners residing in France, "which is already considerable, and is being constantly increased by emigration," and then President Carnot[157] goes on to lay down some very stringent conditions and regulations.

Every foreigner going to France must, within a fortnight of his arrival, declare to the mayor of the commune in which he proposes to settle the names of his parents, his nationality, the place and date of his birth, his last place of residence, his profession and means of subsistence, and the names, ages, and nationality of his wife and children, if any such accompany him.

These declarations must be supported by all necessary vouchers, and in cases of changes of domicile fresh declarations must be made to the mayor of the new residence. Disregard of any of these formalities will involve police penalties,

---

[154] Matthew 14:7.

[155] **Sweater**. An employer of underpaid labour: usually a middleman between the actual employer and employed; a grinding taskmaster; whence sweating-system, sweater, sweated, etc. (1850). (Farmer)

[156] **Windham Wyndham-Quin** (1841-1926), 4th Earl of Dunraven and Mount-Earl. Irish Conservative politician, founded the Irish Reform Association and championed the cause of limited Irish self-rule under the British crown. After the creation of the Irish Free State in 1922 he became a member of its first Senate.

[157] **Marie François Sadi Carnot** (1837-1894). The 5th President of France (1887-1894), he was assass-inated by anarchist after attending a banquet in Lyon, 24 June, 1894.

"without prejudice," as the decree significantly adds, "to the right of expulsion appertaining to the Minister of the Interior."

It is easy to see how these minute regulations will in themselves check the evil of foreign immigration from which France is suffering equally with ourselves; but of still greater importance is the knowledge which will be placed at the disposal of the Minister of the Interior as to the means of subsistence possessed by the unwelcome intruders, and the power which this knowledge will give him of exercising his "right of expulsion" with unerring precision and effect. So much for the latest move of the French President.

We all know how stringent are the regulations against the landing of alien paupers in the United States, and how jealously Germany and Russia regard the incursion of undesirable foreigners into their respective spheres. In fact, look where we will, apart from home, we find a steady movement in the direction of self preservation from one dominant evil. England is the only country which remains heedlessly and supinely idle, and the result is that England is becoming more and more the dumping ground for foreign refuse of every description.

John Bull is a patient animal; but our rulers will do well to consider with themselves whether he is likely to remain so long under existing conditions.

—

The East end mysteries, instead of being cleared up, tend to become more mysterious. Everything connected with them is extraordinary, and not the least so was the evidence given yesterday before Mr. Coroner Baxter by Mrs. Malcolm. She identified the body of the woman found in Berner street as that of her sister Elizabeth Watts, whose career from respectability to prostitution, she detailed with painful minuteness. Then came more mystery.

She said: "I was in my bed at twenty minutes past one on Sunday. I had a presentiment. I felt the pressure of three kisses on me, and heard them." This is a matter upon which the Psychical Society might have something to say.

Mrs. Malcolm is, no doubt, impressionable, and probably she often has presentiments which lead to nothing.

The strange thing in this case is that her presentiment brought her to the mortuary, where she whom she claims as her sister lay dead. There appears little doubt as to the identification, although the coroner wants further inquiry and although one of the news agencies says Mrs. Malcolm is mistaken.

The East end having supped full of horrors recently, the West is now visited by a crime of the most brutal and, happily, unusual character.

Yesterday afternoon the trunk of a woman was found in a parcel at the site of the new Metropolitan Police Headquarters on the Embankment. The head and limbs are gone, but the object of the mutilation appears here to have been to facilitate disposal of the corpse. There is a belief that the discovery of human limbs in Pimlico and Newington is connected with this latest tragedy.

The police, of course, are making every effort to "get on the track" of the person or persons implicated in the crime, and there is just a possibility that they may succeed better in this case than they have done in the Whitechapel ones. There are the wrappings of the body to help, but they unfortunately afford only a very fragile clue. Murder in London threatens to become so common as to pall upon even the morbidity of our populations.

—

In the midst of all the horrible details of life as lived in the poorer districts of London which are coming to light just now it is some comfort to learn that an energetic committee of ladies is carrying on a successful work in the establishment and management of safe and respectable homes for working girls in the Metropolis.

The scant salaries earned by the major portion of these toilers will not enable them to make sure of respectable lodgings without some such assistance as that provided by the subscriptions of the philanthropically disposed at the instance of the managing committee. The official report of the work done by the eight homes already established, has just been published, and a very interesting document it is in many respects.

For a weekly sum of money very little in excess of what is charged for "dossing" in the common lodging houses of the East end, these girls are secured all the comfort, cleanliness, and safety of a respectable home. The first of these homes was only opened ten years ago, and yet over nine thousand working girls have availed themselves of the advantages offered, and the cry is "still they come." The committee want to be able to apply the same cry to the subscriptions.

—

Mr. Montagu Williams grows epigrammatic. A case was heard before him, yesterday, in the course of which evidence relating to the system on which common lodging houses are managed in the East end, and Mr. Williams expressed himself in considerable force on the subject.

"The sooner these lodging houses are put down the better," he said. Then came the epigram: "They are the haunt of the burglar, the home of the pickpocket, and the hot bed of prostitution."

Very undesirable places, evidently, but even prostitutes and burglars (in the intervals of their "bits o' time"[158]) must sleep somewhere, and they are less likely to beat and murder each other on a common lodging house than anywhere else.

—

The vegetarians are responsible for one of the most ingenious theories yet broached in reference to the Whitechapel atrocities.

According to the men of the pea soup and lentils, the crimes are directly traceable to the brutal and abominable practice of eating the flesh of animals. The Rev. S. Barnett first broached the theory in a letter to *The Times*, and it has been followed up and expanded by the orators of the vegetable cause.

Let us hope that the fathers of British families will henceforth banish the brutalising beef and murderous mutton from their dinner tables, lest they unawares breed up a race of moral lepers, who will want to wallow in the blood of their kind.

But why don't the vegetable ones go a little farther, and prove that the national practice of eating meat will, if persisted in, lead to the revival of cannibalism in the British Isles?

—

## THE WHITECHAPEL HORRORS.
## WHAT A BLOODHOUND EXPERT SAYS.

Professor J. Wentley Axe, principal of the Royal Veterinary College, London, has favoured a representative of the Central News with his views upon the employment of bloodhounds in the detection of murderers. Professor Axe stated that no doubt a leash of bloodhounds might be a useful police auxiliary, but its successful employment would depend upon the efficient training of the dogs and the promptitude with which they were put upon the track. All dogs have a natural instinct for blood odours, but this instinct requires development by training, and in the case of the bloodhound it is necessary to make it an expert at the business.

The dog must in the first phase be familiarised with the odour of blood. The incriminating element of the murder, so far as the dog is concerned, would, of course, be the blood carried in the clothes or upon the boots of the murderer. It is, in fact, a condition precedent of the hunt that some of the blood of the victim should be upon the person of the fugitive. In the country, where the ground and atmosphere may remain undisturbed for a longer period, this system of pursuit would work fairly well. But, said Professor Axe, when you come to deal with the streets of large towns, the ground surface of which must necessarily be impregnated with a number of odours, I apprehend that this fact would materially operate against your success in tracking the murderer with bloodhounds.

The pavements of our own city, for instance, may possibly be stained with the blood of carcases such as sheep in transit, as well, indeed, as with human blood, the result of natural deposit. This would tend to confuse the scent which you desired to follow up unless it were very fresh and strong. Again, the air in large towns is always shifting, or may have been shifted by the ordinary traffic of the street, so that the odours left by the fugitive would not be suffered to abide long without obliteration. Hence, it comes to this, that if you resort to bloodhounds for the tracking of bloodstained fugitives, your dogs must be perfectly trained, must be experts at the business, and next, the condition of the ground must be favourable to the retention of the odour forming the clue. In large towns the latter presents a serious difficulty.

## THE MITRE SQUARE VICTIM IDENTIFIED.

Last night, between nine and ten o'clock, a labouring man, giving the name of John Kelly, 55 Flower and Dean street—a common

---

[158] **Time.** To do (or serve) time, to go to prison; hence *timer*, a convict. (Farmer)

lodging house—entered the Bishopsgate street Police station, and stated that from what he had been reading in the newspapers he believed that the woman who had been murdered in Mitre square was "his wife." He was at once taken by Sergeant Miles to the mortuary in Golden lane, and there identified her as the woman, to whom he subsequently admitted he was not married, but with whom he had cohabited for seven years.

Kelly gave a full statement as to his own movements and those of the ill fated woman, as to whose identity he was quite positive. In this statement he was borne out by the deputy of the lodging house, Frederick Wilkinson, who knew the poor woman quite well, and who had just seen the body.

Kelly, in answer to questions, stated that the last time he saw her—referring to her as "Kate" —was on Saturday afternoon. The last meal she had with him was a breakfast which had been obtained by the pledging of his boots for 2s 6d. Asked if he could explain how it was she was out so late on Saturday night, he replied that he could not say. He left her in the afternoon, believing that she would return to him at the lodging house in Flower and Dean street. He had told her to go and see her daughter, and try to get "the price of a bed for the night." "Who is her daughter?" he was asked, to which he replied, "A married woman. She is married to a gun maker, and they live somewhere in Bermondsey, in King street, I think it is called; but I never went there."

### "T.C.—THOMAS CONWAY."

He was then asked if he knew the murdered woman's name, and if he could explain the meaning of the initials "T.C." on her arm. He at once replied that Thomas Conway was the name of her husband, but he could not state whether Conway was dead or alive, or how long, in the latter case, she had been living away from him. being asked why he had not made inquiries before relative to her absence on Saturday night and since, he replied that he thought she had got into some trouble and had been locked up, and he thought he had better wait. She was given to drinking. He had cautioned her not to stay out late at night on account of the previous murders.

The reason which had induced him at length to call at the police station was his

having read about pawn tickets being found near the murdered woman relating to pledges in the names of Kelly and Birrell. Further questioned on this point, he repeated the reference to the pledging of his boots with a pawnbroker named Jones, of Church street, and stated that the ticket for the other article (a flannel shirt), pledged in the name of Emily Birrell, had been given to them by the latter, who had been with them hopping, and who had slept in the same barn as them.

### SHE HAD JUST RETURNED FROM HOPPING.

He further stated that he and the murdered woman were "both Londoners" and that the latter was born at Bermondsey. They had just returned from hopping at a place which he was understood to call Hunton, adding that it was about two miles from Coxheath in Kent. To the question how he obtained his living, he replied, "I job about the markets now." He added that he had worked pretty constantly for a fruit salesman named Lander for over 12 years. He and "Kate" had, he said, gone through many hardships together, but while she was with him he "would not let her do anything bad." He was asked if he knew whether the woman had any relatives besides the daughter mentioned, to which he replied that "Kate's" sister was living in Thrawl street, Spitalfields, with a man who sold farthing books in Liverpool street.

### ANOTHER COMMUNICATION SIGNED "JACK THE RIPPER."

Wood Green inhabitants were intensely excited on Tuesday evening by the report that a postcard had been received at Barrett's sweetstuff[159] factory (abutting upon Mayes road, Wood Green), signed "Jack the Ripper," and asserting that the writer intended to pay a visit to Wood Green and "do" for[160] six of the girls employed at the factory. Some people suppose the postcard is the work of a practical joker; but many persons in the locality fear that it is a postcard from the actual murderer. Great consternation reigns in the neighbourhood of Wood Green, and already people talk of carrying deadly

---

[159] **Sweetstuff**. Sweetmeats, also **Sweeties** (1758). (Farmer)
[160] **To do for**. (1) to ruin: also to kill (1650). (2) To attend on (as landladies on lodgers). (ibid)

# Wednesday, 3 October, 1888

weapons to be prepared for a sudden attack.

## STREET SCENES LAST NIGHT.

There was nothing unusual about the appearance of the streets in Whitechapel and adjoining district last night, unless it be in the fact that there were fewer women parading the foot ways after a late hour.

In the evening, from eight o'clock onwards, there was the usual busy current of foot passengers, some returning from work, others promenading for pleasure. In the course of the evening the rumour spread rapidly that another terrible murder had been committed, the body, too, being horribly mutilated. This caused the liveliest excitement, every one asking everyone else, "Where was it?"

The arrival of evening papers, however, had the effect of subduing the alarm, for on finding that, to use the common pronunciation of the pavement, the tragedy was "down Westminster way," the sting was taken out of the news, and when it was further learnt that there was really nothing to indicate that the Westminster affair was the work of the East end fiend, the matter hardly obtained any attention.

An enterprising show proprietor in the Mile end road displayed a highly coloured and sensetional picture of a murderous tragedy which was introduced to the public as "The Murder in Berner street." This attracted the attention of vast crowds, many of whom evidently placed implicit reliance upon the accuracy of the representations.

As the evening wore on, and closing time for the "houses" came, the streets were more and more deserted, the "ladies of the pavement,"[161] most of them, withdrawing earlier than usual. One of those who stayed on till the small hours of the morning was asked, "Aren't you afraid to be out at this time of the morning?" She replied, "No." She said the murders were shocking. "But we have no place to go, so we're compelled to be out looking for our lodgings." Another woman, in reply to a similar question, said, "Afraid? No. I'm armed. Look here," and she drew a knife from her pocket. She further declared, "I'm not the only one armed. There's plenty more carry knives now."

---

[161] Var. of **Nymph of the Pavement** (or **of Darkness**). A prostitute. (Farmer)

The coffee stall keepers are grumbling that their trade has been much injured by the terror in the district, for although the condition of the thoroughfares is as usual up to "closing time," there is a great diminution in the number of their customers after midnight. Indeed, some of them say the trade they get is not worth coming out for.

There is no lack of constables in the streets. They are to be met everywhere. Detectives parade the alleys and courts in twos and threes. It is impossible to be many minutes out of their sight or hearing.

Shortly after four o'clock this morning, a man came up to a coffee stall in Commercial street, and as he drank a cup of coffee it was noticed that his hand was covered with blood. A constable was called, and examined the man, but the cause of the blood stain being obvious he was not detained in custody. The sight of blood upon any person or thing in the district just now is as the proverbial red rag to a bull.

## A FALSE RUMOUR.

An alarming rumour got abroad this morning that another atrocious murder had been committed in the East end—Bishopsgate street being the locality fixed upon. A representative of *The Evening News* at once made inquiries at the Bishopsgate Police station, but was informed by the sergeant in charge that nothing whatever had been heard there of the alleged crime. On driving to the Leman street police station he met with similarly negative results, as he did also at the Commercial street Police station. So that it may be safely assumed that there is no foundation for the report.

## THE MITRE SQUARE VICTIM.

There is no doubt in the minds of the police that the man Kelly's identification of the woman murdered in Mitre square as Kate Conway is correct. In order that the matter may be fully cleared up, however, it has been deemed advisable to send the man Kelly, in company with Sergeant Outram and other officers, to find the victim's two daughters and her sister.

## THE BERNER STREET VICTIM.

The Press Association's Bath correspondent telegraphs corroborating the statement of Mrs. Malcolm at the inquest yesterday, as to the history and habits of the woman Elizabeth

# Wednesday, 3 October, 1888

Watts. She married about 27 or 28 years ago, William Watts, son of a wine merchant in Bath, her husband, being then only about 20 years of age. She was a servant at his father's house. They only lived together two years, when the deceased left her husband, who went to America, but he returned from that country four years ago.

### THE MITRE SQUARE MURDER.
### ANOTHER CONFESSION.
### PRISONER BEFORE THE
### MAGISTRATE.

This morning, at the Guildhall Police court, before Mr. Alderman Stone, William Bull, describeing himself as a medical student, of the London Hospital, and giving an address at Stannard road, Dalston, was placed in the dock, charged, on his own admission, with having committed the Aldgate murder. The prisoner appeared to have been drinking heavily.

Inspector Izzard said: Last night, at twenty minutes to eleven, the prisoner came into the room at Bishopsgate street Station and made the following statement, which I took down after cautioning him. He said: "My name is William Bull, and I live at Dalston. I am a medical student at the London Hospital, and I wish to give myself up for the murder in Aldgate.

On Saturday night, or Sunday morning, about two o'clock, I think, I met the woman in Aldgate. I went with her up a narrow street not far from the main road, for an immoral purpose. I promised to give her half a crown, which I did. While walking along together there was a second man who came up and took the half crown from her. I cannot endure this any longer. My poor head! (He put his hands to his head and cried, or pretended to cry.) I shall go mad. I have done it, and I must up with it."

The inspector asked what had become of the clothes he had on when the murder was committed. The prisoner said, "If you wish to know, they are in the Lea, and the knife I threw away." At this point the prisoner declined to say any more. He was drunk, and apparently had been drinking heavily. Part of the statement was made in the presence of Major Smith.

The prisoner gave a correct address, but is not known at the London Hospital. His parents are very respectable, and the prisoner has been out of employ. The inspector asked for a few days to make inquiries.

The prisoner, in answer to the Alderman, said he was mad drunk when he made the statement. As for the murder to have been committed by him it was impossible. Inspector Izzard said that when searched the prisoner had on him a very small knife, a halfpenny, and a wheel from a watch.

Prisoner was remanded, the Alderman refusing to grant bail.

# Thursday, 4 October, 1888

## The Times

### THE EAST-END MURDERS.

Yesterday afternoon Mr. Wynne E. Baxter, Coroner for the South-Eastern Division of Middlesex, resumed his inquiry at the Vestry-hall, Cable-street, St. George's-in-the-East, respecting the death of Elizabeth Stride, who was found murdered in Berner-street on Sunday morning last.

Detective-Inspector E. Reid, H Division, again watched the case on behalf of the Criminal Investigation Department.

Elizabeth Tanner stated:—I live at 32, Flower and Dean-street, Spitalfields, and am a widow. I am the deputy of No. 32, which is a common lodginghouse. I have seen the body in the mortuary, and recognize the features of the deceased as a woman who had lodged off and on at the lodginghouse for six years. I knew her by the name of "Long Liz." I do not know her right name. She told me she was a Swedish woman, but never told me where she was born. She told me she was a married woman, and her husband and children went down in the ship Princess Alice.

The CORONER.—When did you last see her alive?

Witness.—About 6:30 on Saturday afternoon. I do not know the name of her husband, or what occupation he had followed. When I last saw deceased she was in the Queen's Head publichouse, Commercial-street. I went back to the lodginghouse, and did not see any more of her. At that time deceased had no hat or coat on. I saw her in the kitchen of the lodginghouse, and then I went to another part of the building, and never saw her again until I saw her dead body in the mortuary this afternoon.

The CORONER.—Are you sure it is her?

Witness.—I am quite sure. I recognize the features, and by the fact that she had lost the roof of her mouth. She told me that happened when the Princess Alice went down.

The CORONER.—Was she on board the ship at that time?

Witness.—Yes; and it was during that time her mouth was injured.

The CORONER.—Was she at the lodging-house on Friday night?

Witness.—Yes; on Thursday and Friday nights; but on no other night during the week.

She did not pay for her bed on Saturday night.

The CORONER.—Do you know her male acquaintances?

Witness—Only one, and I do not know his name. She left the man she was living with on Thursday to come and stay at my lodginghouse. That is what she told me.

The CORONER.—Have you seen this man?

Witness.—Yes; I saw him on Sunday evening.

The CORONER.—Do you know if she has ever been up at the Thames Police-court?

Witness.—I do not.

The CORONER.—Do you know any other place she has lived?

Witness.—Only Fashion-street.

The CORONER.—Do you know if she had a sister living in Red Lion-square?

Witness.—I do not.

The CORONER.—What sort of woman was she?

Witness.—She was a very quiet and sober woman.

The CORONER.—Did she stay out late at night?

Witness.—Sometimes.

The CORONER.—Do you know if she had any money?

Witness.—I do not. On Saturday she cleaned the rooms for me, and I gave her 6d.

The CORONER.—Have you seen her clothes?

Witness.—Yes. I cannot say if the two handkerchiefs belonged to her. The clothes she was wearing were the ones she usually wore, and they were the same she had on on Saturday. I recognized the long jacket as belonging to her.

The CORONER.—Did she ever tell you she was afraid of any one?

Witness.—No; and I never heard her say that anyone had threatened to injure her.

The CORONER.—Is it a common thing for people who have been lodging in your place not to come back?

Witness.—Yes; I took no notice of it. I was sent for to go to the mortuary.

A Juryman.—Do you remember the hour she came to the lodginghouse?

Witness.—I do not, although I saw her and took 4d. from her for her lodging. At that time she was wearing the long jacket I have seen in the mortuary. I did not see her bring any parcel with her.

Inspector Reid.—Have you ever heard the name of Stride mentioned in connexion with her?

Witness.—No.

A Juryman.—How long had deceased been away from your house before last Thursday?

Witness.—About three months; but I have seen her during that time—sometimes once a week and sometimes nearly every day.

The CORONER.—Did you understand what she was doing?

Witness.—She told me she worked among the Jews, and was living with a man in Fashion-street.

The CORONER.—Could she speak English well?

Witness.—Yes; and Swedish as well.

The CORONER.—When she spoke English could you tell she was a foreigner?

Witness.—No.

The CORONER.—Was there much association between her and her country people?

Witness.—No.

The CORONER.—Have you ever heard of her having in childhood broken a limb?

Witness.—I have not heard her say. I have never heard her carry on a conversation in the Swedish language; but she told me herself she was a Swede.

Catherine Lane, 32 Flower and Dean-street, said:—I am a charwoman and am married to Patrick Lane, a dock-labourer. We live together at the lodginghouse and have been living there since the 11th of February of this year. I have seen the body of deceased in the mortuary and recognize it as "Long Liz," who lived in the same lodginghouse. Lately she had only been there since Thursday last. I have known her for six or seven years. During the time she was away she called at the lodginghouse, and I used frequently to see her in Fashion-street where she was living. I spoke to the deceased on Thursday between 10 and 11 in the morning. She told me she had a few words with the man she was living with and left him. I saw her on Saturday afternoon when she was cleaning the deputy's rooms. I last saw her between 7 and 8 o'clock on Saturday evening. She was then in the kitchen, and had a long jacket and black hat on.

The CORONER.—Did she tell you where she was going?

Witness.—She did not. When she left the kitchen she gave me a piece of velvet and asked me to mind it until she came back. The deputy would always mind things for the lodgers, and I do not know why she asked me to mind the velvet for her. Deceased showed me the piece of velvet on the previous day. I know deceased had 6d. when she left, as she showed me the money, but I cannot say that she had any money besides that. Deceased did not tell me she was coming back. I do not think she had been drinking.

The CORONER.—Do you know anyone who is likely to have injured her?

Witness.—No. I have heard her say she was a foreign woman, and she told me that at one time she lived in Devonshire-street, Commercial-road. I have never heard her say that at one time she lived at Poplar. She told me she had had a husband and that he was dead. Deceased never told me she had been threatened, or that she was afraid of any one. I know nothing about her history beyond what I have stated. I am satisfied it is she. I could tell by her actions that she was a foreign woman and did not bring all her words out plainly. I have heard her speaking to persons in her own language.

A juryman.—Did you ever hear her say she had a sister?

Witness.—No; never.

The CORONER.—Do you know what she had been doing lately?

Witness.—I do not.

Charles Preston stated:—I live at 32, Flower and Dean-street, Spitalfields, and am a barber by occupation. I have been lodging there for about 18 months. I have seen the deceased there and identified her body on Sunday afternoon at the mortuary. I am quite sure the body is that of "Long Liz." I last saw her alive on Saturday evening, between 6 and 7 o'clock. At that time she was in the kitchen of the lodginghouse and was dressed ready to go out. She asked me for the loan of a clothes-brush. At that time she had on a black jacket trimmed with fur, and it is the same one I have seen in the mortuary. She wore a coloured striped silk handkerchief round her neck, and it was the same as I saw in the mortuary. I have not seen her with a pocket-handkerchief, and am unable to say if she had two. I always understood from the deceased that she was a Swede by birth and was born at

Stockholm; that she came to England in the service of a foreign gentleman. I think she told me she was about 35 years of age. She told me she had been married, and that her husband was drowned at the foundering of the Princess Alice. I have some recollection that deceased told me her husband was a seafaring man. I have heard her say she had a coffeehouse at Chrisp-street, Poplar; but she did not say she had often been at the Thames Police-court. I have known her to be in custody on one Saturday afternoon for being drunk and disorderly at the Queen's Head publichouse, Commercial-road. She was let out on her own bail on the Sunday morning. That was some four or five months ago. I have never heard her say she had met with an accident. She did not tell me where she was going on Saturday evening, and never mentioned what time she was coming back. At times the lodgers did not pay for their beds until just before going to bed. When deceased was locked up it was late in the afternoon or towards the evening time. She has always given me to understand her name was Elizabeth Stride, and that her mother was still living in Sweden. I have heard her speaking fluently in a foreign language to persons in the lodginghouse.

Michael Kidney stated:—I live at 38, Dorset-street, Spitalfields, and am a waterside labourer. I have seen the body in the mortuary and it is that of a woman whom I lived with. I have no doubt whatever about it.

The CORONER.—Do you know what her name was?

Witness.—Elizabeth Stride. I have known her for about three years, and she has been living with me nearly all that time.

The CORONER.—Do you know what her age was?

Witness.—Between 36 and 38. She told me she was a Swede and that she was born at Stockholm; that her father was a farmer, and that she came to England for the purpose of seeing the country. She afterwards told me she had come to England as servant to a family.

The CORONER.—Had she any relatives in England?

Witness.—Only some of her mother's friends. She told me she was a widow, and that her husband had been a ship's carpenter belonging to Sheerness. She also told me her husband had kept a coffeehouse at Chrisp-street, Poplar,

and that he was drowned on the Princess Alice.

The CORONER.—You had a quarrel with her on Thursday?

Witness.—No. I last saw the deceased alive on Tuesday week.

The CORONER.—Did you quarrel then?

Witness.—No; I left her in Commercial-street as I was going to work.

The CORONER.—Did you expect her to meet you later on?

Witness.—I expected her to be at home. When I got home I found that she had been in and gone out. I did not again see her until I identified the body in the mortuary. She was perfectly sober when I last saw her. She was subject to going away whenever she thought she would. During the three years I have known her she has been away from me altogether about five months. I have cautioned her the same as I would a wife.

The CORONER.—Do you know any one she has picked up with?

Witness.—I have seen the address of some-one with the family she was living with at Hyde Park; but I cannot find it.

The CORONER.—That is not what I asked you. Do you think she went away with anyone else?

Witness.—I do not think that, for she liked me better than anyone else. It was drink that made her go away, and she always returned without my going after her. I do not believe she left me on Tuesday to go with any other man.

The CORONER.—Had she money at that time?

Witness.—I do not think she was without a 1s. considering the money I gave her to keep the house.

The CORONER.—Do you know of anyone that was likely to have run foul of her?

Witness.—On Monday night I went to Leman-street Police-station for a detective to act on my information, but I could not get one.

The CORONER.—It is not too late yet; can you give us any information now?

Witness.—I have heard something said that leads me to believe, that had I been able to act the same as a detective I could have got a lot more information. When I went to the station I was intoxicated. I asked for a young detective. I told the inspector at the station that if the murder occurred on my beat I would shoot myself. I have been in the Army.

Inspector Reid.—Will you give me any information now?

Witness.—I believe I could catch the man, if I had the proper force at my command. If I was to place the men myself I could capture the murderer. He would be caught in the act.

Inspector Reid.—Then you have no information to give?

Witness.—No.

The CORONER.—Have you heard of a sister of deceased giving her money?

Witness.—No, but Mrs. Malcolm, who stated she was sister to the deceased, is very much like her.

The CORONER.—Did deceased ever have a child by you?

Witness.—No. She told me a policeman used to see her at Hyde Park before she was married to Stride. I never heard her say she had a child by a policeman. Deceased told me she was the mother of nine children. Two were drowned on the Princess Alice with her husband, and the remainder are in a school belonging to the Swedish Church. The school is somewhere on the other side of the Thames. I have also heard her say that some friend of her husband had two of the children. I thoroughly believe the deceased was a Swede, and came from a superior class. She could also speak Yiddish. Both the deceased and her husband were employed on board the Princess Alice.

Edward Johnston said:—I live at 100, Commercial-road, and am assistant to Drs. Kay and Blackwell. About five or ten minutes past 1 on Sunday morning, I received a call from constable 436 H. After informing Dr. Blackwell, who was in bed, of the nature of the case, I accompanied the constable to Berner-street. In a courtyard, adjoining 40, Berner-street, I was shown the figure of a woman lying on her left side. There was a crowd of people in the yard and some policemen. No one was touching the deceased and there was very little light. What there was came from the police-men's lanterns. I examined the woman and found an incision in the throat. The wound appeared to have stopped bleeding. I also felt the body to see if it was warm, and found it was all warm with the exception of the hands, which were quite cold. The dress was not undone, and I undid it to see if the chest was warm. I did not move the head

at all, and left it exactly as I found it. The body was not moved while I was there. The knees were nearer to the wall than the head. There was a stream of blood reaching down to the gutter. It was all clotted blood. There was very little blood near the neck, as nearly all of it had run away in the direction away from the legs. As soon as Dr. Blackwell arrived I handed the case over to him.

The CORONER.—Did you look at the hands?

Witness.—No. I saw the left hand was lying away from the body, and the arm was bent. The right arm was also bent. The left hand might have been on the ground.

The CORONER.—Was there any mark of a footstep on the stream of blood?

Witness.—No. I was looking at the body and not at those around me. As soon as Dr. Blackwell came he looked at his watch. It was then 1:16. I was there three or four minutes before Dr. Blackwell.

The CORONER.—Did you notice the bonnet of deceased?

Witness.—Yes, it was lying on the ground, beyond the head of deceased to the distance of three or four inches. I did not notice the paper in the left hand. The gates were not closed when I got there, but they were shortly afterwards.

Thomas Coram said:—I live at 67, Plummer's-road, Mile-end, and am employed at a cocoanut warehouse. On Sunday night I was coming away from a friends at 16, Bath-gardens, Brady-street. I was walking on the right hand side of the Whitechapel-road towards Aldgate. When opposite No. 253 I crossed over, and saw a knife lying on the doorstep. No. 252 was a laundry business, and there were two steps leading to the front door. I found the knife on the bottom step. That is the knife I found (witness being shown a long-bladed knife). The handkerchief produced was wrapped round the handle. It was folded, and then twisted round the handle. The handkerchief was blood-stained. I did not touch them. A policeman came towards me, and I called his attention to them.

The CORONER.—The blade of the knife is dagger-shaped and is sharpened on one side. The blade is about 9in. or 10in. long, I should say.

Witness.—The policeman took the knife to the Leman-street Police-station, and I went with him.

# Thursday, 4 October, 1888

The CORONER.—Were there many people passing at the time?

Witness.—I should think I passed about a dozen between Brady-street and where I found the knife.

The CORONER.—Could it easily be seen?

Witness.—Yes; and it was light.

The CORONER.—Did you pass a policeman before you got to the spot?

Witness.—Yes, I passed three. It was about half-past 12 at night.

Constable Joseph Drage, 282 H, stated: —At 12:30 on Monday morning I was on fixed-point duty in the Whitechapel-road, opposite Great Garden-street. I saw the last witness stooping down at a doorway opposite No. 253. I was going towards him when he rose up and beckoned me with his finger. He then said, "Policeman, there is a knife down here." I turned on my light and saw a long-bladed knife lying on the doorstep. I picked up the knife and found it was smothered with blood. The blood was dry. There was a handkerchief bound round the handle and tied with string. The handkerchief also had blood-stains on it. I asked the last witness how he came to see it. He said, "I was looking down, when I saw something white." I then asked him what he did out so late, and he replied, "I have been to a friend's in Bath-gardens." He then gave me his name and address, and we went to the police-station together. The knife and handkerchief produced are the same.

The CORONER.—Was the last witness sober?

Witness.—Yes. His manner was natural, and he said when he saw the knife it made his blood run cold, and added that nowadays they heard of such funny things. When I passed I should have undoubtedly seen the knife. I was passing there continually. Some little time before a horse fell down opposite the place where the knife was found. I assisted in getting the horse up, and during that time a person might have laid the knife down on the step. I would not be positive that the knife was not there a quarter of an hour previously, but I think not. About an hour previously the landlady let out some woman, and the knife was not there then. I handed the knife to Dr. Phillips on the Monday afternoon. It was then sealed and secured.

Dr. George Baxter Phillips said:—I live at 2, Spital-square. I was called at 1:20 Sunday morn-ing to Leman-street Police-station, and from there sent on to Berner-street to a yard at the side of a club-house. I found Chief-Inspector West and Inspector Pinhorn in possession of a body, which had already been seen by Dr. Blackwell, who arrived some time before me. The body was lying on the near side, with the face turned towards the wall, the head up the yard and the feet towards the street. The left arm was extended, and there was a packet of cachous in the left hand. A number of these were in the gutter. I took them from the hand and handed them to Dr. Blackwell. The right arm was over the belly. The back of the hand and wrist had on it clotted blood. The legs were drawn up, with the feet close to the wall. The body and the face were warm and the hand cold. The legs were quite warm. Deceased had a silk handkerchief round her neck, and it appeared to be slightly torn. I have since ascertained it was cut. This corresponded with the right angle of the jaw. The throat was deeply gashed, and there was an abrasion of the skin about 1¼ in. in diameter, apparently stained with blood, under her right brow. At 3 p.m. on Monday at St. George's Mortuary, in the presence of Dr. Rygate and Mr. Johnston, Dr. Blackwell and I made a post-mortem examination. Dr. Blackwell kindly consented to make the dissection. Rigor Mortis was still thoroughly marked. There was mud on the left side of the face and it was matted in the head. We then removed the clothes. The body was fairly nourished. Over both shoulders, especially the right, and under the collar-bone and in front of the chest there was a bluish discolouration, which I have watched and seen on two occasions since. There was a clean cut incision on the neck. It was 6in. in length and commenced 2½ in. in a straight line below the angle of the jaw, ¾ in. over an undivided muscle, and then, becoming deeper, dividing the sheath. The cut was very clean, and deviated a little downwards. The artery and other vessels contained in the sheath were all cut through. The cut through the tissues on the right side was more superficial, and tailed off to about 2 in. below the right angle of the jaw. The deep vessels on that side were uninjured. From this it was evident that the haemorrhage was caused through the partial severance of the left carotid artery. Decomposition had commenced in the skin. Dark brown spots were on the anterior surface of the left chin.

# Thursday, 4 October, 1888

There was a deformity in the bones of the right leg, which was not straight, but bowed forwards. There was no recent external injury save to the neck. The body being washed more thoroughly, I could see some healing sores. The lobe of the left ear was torn as if from the removal or wearing through of an earring, but it was thoroughly healed. On removing the scalp there was no sign of bruising or extravasation[162] of blood. The skull was about a sixth of an inch in thickness, and the brain was fairly normal. The left lung had old adhesions to the chest wall, the right slightly. Both lungs were unusually pale. There was no fluid in the pericardium. The heart was small, the left ventricle firmly contracted, and the right slightly so. There was no clot in the pulmonary artery, but the right ventricle was full of dark clot. The left was firmly contracted so as to be absolutely empty. The stomach was large, and the mucous membrane only congested. It contained partly-digested food, apparently consisting of cheese, potato, and farinaceous[163] powder. All the teeth on the left lower jaw were absent. On Tuesday I again went to the mortuary to observe the marks on the shoulder. I found in the pocket of the underskirt of the deceased the following articles—key as if belonging to a padlock, a small piece of a pencil, a pocket comb, a broken piece of a comb, a metal spoon, some buttons, and a hook. Examining her jacket, I found that, while there was a small amount of mud on the right side, the left was well plastered with mud. I have not seen the two pocket handkerchiefs. I will answer any questions put to me, but as there is another case pending I think I had better stop here.

The CORONER.—What is the cause of death?

Witness.—It is undoubtedly from the loss of blood from the left carotid artery and the division of the windpipe.

The CORONER.—Did you examine the blood at Berner-street?

Witness.—I did. The blood had run down the waterway to within a few inches of the side entrance of the club.

The CORONER.—Were there any spots of blood on the wall?

Witness.—I could trace none. Roughly estimating it I should say there was an unusual flow of blood considering the stature and nourishment of the body.

At this point the inquiry was adjourned until Friday morning.

———

The following correspondence has been sent to us for publication:—

"Office of the Board of Works, Whitechapel District, 15, Great Alie-street,
Whitechapel, Oct. 2.

"Sir,—At a meeting of the Board of Works for the Whitechapel District a resolution was passed, of which the following is a copy:—

'That this Board regards with horror and alarm the several atrocious murders recently perpetrated within the district of Whitechapel and its vicinity and calls upon Sir Charles Warren so to regulate and strengthen the police force in the neighbourhood as to guard against any repetition of such atrocities.'

"And by direction of the Board the copy resolution is forwarded to you in the hope that it will receive your favourable consideration

"I am, &c.,
"ALFRED TURNER, Clerk.
"Colonel Sir Charles Warren, G.C.M.G."

———

"POLICE NOTICE.
"TO THE OCCUPIER.

"On the mornings of Friday, 31st August, Saturday 8th, and Sunday, 30th September, 1888, women were murdered in or near Whitechapel, supposed by someone residing in the immediate neighbourhood. Should you know of any person to whom suspicion is attached, you are earnestly requested to communicate at once with the nearest police-station.

"Metropolitan Police Office,
30th September, 1888."

———

"4, Whitehall-place, S.W., Oct. 3.

"Sir,—In reply to a letter of the 2nd inst. from the Clerk of the Board of Works for the Whitechapel District transmitting a resolution of the Board with regard to the recent atrocious murders perpetrated in and about Whitechapel, I

---

[162] **Extravasation**. A discharge or escape, as of blood, from a vessel into the tissues; blood or other substance so discharged. (Miller)

[163] **Farina**. Meal or flour made from cereal grains.— **farinaceous** adj. (Morehead)

have to point out that the carrying out of your proposals as to regulating and strengthening the police force in your district cannot possibly do more than guard or take precautions against any repetition of such atrocities so long as the victims actually, but unwittingly, connive at their own destruction.

"Statistics show that London, in comparison to its population, is the safest city in the world to live in. The prevention of murder directly cannot be effected by any strength of the police force; but it is reduced and brought to a *minimum* by rendering it most difficult to escape detection. In the particular class of murder now confronting us, however, the unfortunate victims appear to take the murderer to some retired spot and to place themselves in such a position that they can be slaughtered without a sound being heard; the murder, therefore, takes place without any clue to the criminal being left.

"I have to request and call upon your Board, as popular representatives, to do all in your power to dissuade the unfortunate women about Whitechapel from going into lonely places in the dark with any persons—whether acquaintances or strangers.

"I have also to point out that the purlieus about Whitechapel are most imperfectly lighted, and that darkness is an important assistant to crime.

"I can assure you, for the information of your Board, that every nerve has been strained to detect the criminal or criminals, and to render more difficult further atrocities.

"You will agree with me that it not desirable that I should enter into particulars as to what the police are doing in the matter. It is most important for good results that our proceedings should not be published, and the very fact you may be unaware of what the Detective Department is doing is only the stronger proof that it is doing its work with secrecy and efficiency.

"A large force of police has been drafted into the Whitechapel district to assist those already there to the full extent necessary to meet the requirements; but I have to observe that the Metropolitan police have not large reserves doing nothing and ready to meet emergencies, but every man has his duty assigned to him; and I can only strengthen the Whitechapel district by drawing men from duty in other parts of the metropolis.

"You will be aware that the whole of the police work of the metropolis has to be done as usual while this extra work is going on, and that at such a time as this extra precautions have to be taken to prevent the commission of other classes of crime being facilitated through the attention of the police being diverted to one special place or object.

"I trust your Board will assist the police by persuading the inhabitants to give them every information in their power concerning any suspicious characters in the various dwellings, for which object 10,000 handbills, a copy of which I enclose, have been distributed.

"I have read the reported proceedings of your meeting, and I regret to see that the greatest misconceptions appear to have arisen in the public mind as to the recent action in the administration of the police. I beg you will dismiss from your minds, as utterly fallacious, the numerous anonymous statements as to the recent changes stated to have been made in the police force, of a character not conducive to efficiency.

"It is stated that the Rev. Daniel Greatorex announced to you that one great cause of police inefficiency was a new system of police whereby constables were constantly changed from one district to another, keeping the ignorant of their beats.

"I have seen this statement made frequently in the newspapers lately, but it entirely without fountain. The system at present in use has existed for the last 20 years, and constables are seldom or never drafted from their districts except for promotion or from some particular cause.

"Notwithstanding the many good reasons why constables should be changed on their beats, I have considered the reasons on the other side to be more cogent, and have felt that they should be thoroughly acquainted with the districts in which they serve.

"And with regard to the Detective Department—a department relative to which reticence is always most desirable—I may say that a short time ago I made arrangements which still further reduced the necessity for transferring officers from districts which they knew thoroughly.

"I have to call attention to the statement of

# Thursday, 4 October, 1888

one of your members that in consequence of the change in the condition of Whitechapel in recent years a thorough revision of the police arrangements is necessary, and I shall be very glad to ascertain from you what changes your Board consider advisable; and I may assure you that your proposals will receive from me every consideration.

"I am, Sir, your obedient servant,
"CHARLES WARREN.
"The Chairman, Board of Works,
Whitechapel District."

———

An American, who refuses to give his name or any account of himself, was arrested last night on suspicion of being the East-end murderer. He is well dressed, rather tall, of slight build, and clean shaven. He accosted a woman in Cable-street, asked for her to go with him, and threatened that if she refused he would "rip her up." The woman screamed, and the man rushed to a cab. The police gave chase, got upon the cab, seized the man, and took him to Leman-street Police-station, where he asked the inspector in charge, "Are you the boss?" The man is detained at the police-station as well as two others who were conveyed there during the evening.

———

Most of the detectives belonging to the City and Metropolitan forces were busily engaged yesterday in investigating suggestions and information conveyed in letters addressed to the authorities by the general public.

———

The statement made by the man Kelly on Tuesday night at the Bishopsgate-street Police-station identifying the Mitre-square victim as Kate Conway, a married woman, with whom he had cohabited for seven years, was confirmed yesterday. A sister of the murdered woman, to whom Kelly alluded in his statement, was inquired for at the address mentioned by him in Thrawl-street, Spitalfields, Sergeant Outram, accompanied by Kelly, conducting the investigations. Her name, it seems, is Mrs. Frost, and on being taken to the mortuary in Golden-lane she at once identified the body as that of her sister, Mrs. Conway. She stated that there is another sister, a Mrs. Jones, who lives in the neighbourhood of Clothfair; but the latter has not yet been traced, nor have the son or daughter of the murdered woman.

———

At a very largely attended meeting of the Whitechapel Vestry last night, a discussion took place on the recent murders which had taken place within the district. On the motion of Mr. J. A. Teller, it was resolved "That this Vestry expresses its sorrow at the diabolical murders that have been lately committed in East London, and urges Her Majesty's Government to use their utmost efforts to discover the criminals."

———

At the Shoreditch Vestry, yesterday, presided over by Mr. F. M. Wenborn, Metropolitan Board of Works, Mr. Barham called attention to the insufficient lighting of the parish, making special mention of certain sequestered places where the want of light would greatly facilitate the commission of some foul deed of robbery or even of murder.

He asked that the General Purposes Committee should be empowered to inspect the places he had mentioned, and to take immediate steps to fix additional lamps where they were thus imperatively needed. An objection was raised to the taking of summary action, the objecting vestryman preferring that the matter should be dealt with with the usual routine of notice of motion and the like. Mr. Barham, however, and Mr. Waynforth showed the great urgency of vesting the committee with immediate powers.

The Vestry finally agreed to Mr. Barham's suggestion, and afterward ordered the fixing of new lamps in certain dark parts of Commercial-street (the thoroughfare which runs from Shoreditch through Spitalfields into Whitechapel and which is not far from the scene of the recent murders), Scrutton-street, and other roads within the parish.

———

## TO THE EDITOR OF THE TIMES.

Sir,—In the absence of any definite clue to the perpetrator of the recent dreadful atrocities at the East-end of London, it seems desirable to consider the question from the point of view of what, for want of a better word, I may call speculative jurisprudence.

It will be admitted that if suspicion can be, with even reasonable conclusiveness, focused on a particular and, if possible, small class of persons, there may be a greater probability of the speedy detection of the perpetrator than by a more or less vague inquiry directed over a large and densely populated area. At the same time, assuming my hypothesis to be fallacious, there is no reason why, while investigating it within its own narrow limits, the wider inquiries now being pursued should be diminished.

There is, I think, a reasonably general consensus of educated opinion that the late several murders, with their exceptionally concomitant horrors, are the work of one and the same person.

Inquiry has also fairly established that the theory suggested that the murders and mutilation where to secure a particular organ of the victim's body is untenable.

Robbery, or the gratification of animal passion, or revenge in its ordinary personal acceptation being beyond the question, the solution of motive may have to be sought in some form of mania arising from one or other, possibly, of the following causes—viz., some wrong, real or imaginary, sustained at the hands of the class to which the poor murdered women belonged; or an insane belief as to the good to result to society by their extermination.

It is to be observed that homicidal mania, in the sense of an unrestrainable desire to kill merely, is not here present, the tendency being directed against a particular class exclusively.

These questions are, however, for the moment comparatively unimportant beside the more pressing one as to the direction in which the murderer or homicidal maniac is to be sought.

For reasons which I shall state concisely, I venture to suggest that the perpetrator of these several outrages is a man of foreign character.

The grounds for this conclusion are:—

(a) That in the whole record of criminal trials there is, I believe, no instance of a series of crimes of murder and mutilation of the particular character here involved committed by a person of English origin; whereas there are instances in some foreign countries of crimes of this peculiarly horrible character.

(b) The celerity with which the crimes were committed is inconsistent with the ordinary English phlegmatic nature; but entirely consistent with the evidence given in some more or less similar cases abroad.

(c) The mutilation and removal of certain organs involved a degree of anatomical knowledge and skill which, according to high medical opinion, would not be likely to be possessed by

an English slaughterman (to whom at first suspicion pointed); whereas this special skill is possessed, to a not inconsiderable degree, by foreigners engaged in the charcuterie[164] and other kindred trades abroad.

(d) The character of the knife used, as suggested by the medical evidence at the inquests, is similar in kind to the instrument known as a French "cook's knife," or at least is, in the circumstances, most consistent with its use by a foreigner than an Englishman.

In offering these opinions I do not desire to suggest what indeed my experience negatives, that a foreigner, as such, has any monopoly of brutality over an Englishman. There are forms of brutality which are committed by Englishmen which a Frenchman or an Italian, for instance, would never dream of. But there are also idiosyncrasies of crime which are, as it were, peculiar to particular countries, both in their conception and mode of execution.

I am, Sir, your obedient servant,
EDWARD DILLON LEWIS[165]
8, Bow-street, Covent-garden, W.C.,
Oct. 3.

—

## TO THE EDITOR OF THE TIMES.

Sir,—Another remarkable letter has been written by some bad fellow who signs himself, "Jack the Ripper." The letter is said to be smeared with blood, and there is on it the print in blood of the corrugated surface of a thumb. This may be that of a man or a woman.

It is inconceivable that a woman has written or smeared such a letter, and therefore it may be accepted as a fact that the impression in blood is that of a man's thumb.

The surface of a thumb so printed is as clearly indicated as are the printed letters from any kind of type. Thus there is a possibility of identifying the blood print on the letter with the

---

[164] **Charcutier.** Pork butcher. (Dubois)

[165] **Edward Dillon Lewis** (1848-1897). Solicitor and businessman noted for his Radical Labour politics and 1880 proposal for reformation of criminal law and procedure. His paternal grandfather was the notorious sheriff's bailiff, extortionist, loanshark and keeper of a Cavendish Court Disorderly House (brothel) William Levy, AKA Levy the Bum (Bumbailiff). Edward died at the age of 49 from Cirrhosis of the Liver. (Ward)

# Thursday, 4 October, 1888

thumb that made it, because the surface markings on no two thumbs are alike, and this a low power used in a microscope could reveal.[166]

I would suggest—(1) That it be proved if it is human blood, though this may not be material; (2) that the thumbs of every suspected man be compared by an expert with the blood-print of a thumb on the letter; (3) that it be ascertained whether the print of a thumb is that of a man who works hard and has rough, coarse hands, or whether that of one whose hands have not been roughened by labour; (4) whether the thumb was large or small; (5) whether the thumb print shows signs of any shakiness or tremor in the doing of it.

All this the microscope could reveal. The print of a thumb would give as good evidence as that of a boot or shoe.

I am , yours, &c.,<br>FRED. W. P. JAGO.[167]<br>Plymouth.

—

## TO THE EDITOR OF THE TIMES.

Sir,—Having been long in India and, therefore, acquainted with the methods of Eastern criminals, it has struck me in reading the accounts of these Whitechapel murders that they have probably been committed by a Malay, or other low-class Asiatic coming under the general term of Lascar, of whom, I believe, there are large numbers in that part of London. The mutilations, cutting off the nose and ears, ripping up the body, and cutting out certain organs—the heart, &c.—are all peculiarly Eastern methods and universally recognized, and intended by the criminal classes to express insult, hatred, and contempt; whereas, here the public and police are quite at a loss to attach any meaning to them, and so they are described as the mere senseless fury of a maniac.

My theory would be that some man of this class has been hocussed[168] and then robbed of his savings (often large), or, as he considers, been in some way greatly injured by a prostitute—perhaps one of the earlier victims; and then has been led by fury and revenge to take the lives of as many of the same class as he can. This also is entirely in consonance with Eastern ideas and the practices of the criminal classes.

Hundreds of these men have resided long in that part of London, speak English well—although when necessary they cannot understand a word—and dress in ordinary English clothes.

The victims have been the poorest and most miserable, and probably only such would consort with the class of man I speak of.

Such a man would be quite safe in the haunts occupied by his fellow-countrymen, or, should he wish to escape, he could join a crew of Lascars on the first steamer leaving London.

Unless caught red-handed, such a man in ordinary life would be harmless enough, polite, not to say obsequious, in his manners, and about the last a British policeman would suspect.

But when the villain is primed with his opium, or bang,[169] or gin, and inspired with his lust for slaughter and blood, he would destroy his defenceless victim with the ferocity and cunning of the tiger; and past impunity and success would only have rendered him the more daring and reckless.

Your obedient servant,<br>NEMO.[170]<br>October 2.

---

[166] Although Cuneiform tablets from the time of the Babylonian King Hammurabi (1792-1750 B.C.) indicate that individuals arrested would have their fingerprints taken by impressing them into wet clay, it was not until 1892 that fingerprints were first used to identify a murderer, or, in this first case, a murderess. After her bloody thumbprint was found at the murder scene, Francesca Rojas of Necochea, Argentina,confessed to murdering her own children because her boyfriend did not want to have any of his own, or raise those of another man. (FindLaw)

[167] **Frederick W. P. Yago.** Scholar and physician best known for two works, The Ancient Language and the Dialect of Cornwall, 1882, and his Cornish dictionary, published in 1887.

[168] **Hocus.** 1. A cheat, impostor: see Hocus-pocus (1654). 2. Drugged liquor (1823). As adj., drunk. As verb, (1) to cheat, impose upon; (2) to drug, snuff (q.v.) (1836).
**Hocus-pocus.** 1. A juggler's phrase: hence a juggler's (or impostor's) stock in trade: also **Hocustrade** (1639). 2. A trickster, juggler, impostor (1625). 3. A cheat, imposition, juggler's trick (1713). As adj., cheating, fraudulent (1715). As verb, to cheat, trick. (Farmer)

[169] **Bhang.** Indian psychoactive beverage made from finely ground cannabis leaves and buds, milk, ghee (clarified butter) and spices. (Breslin)

[170] **Nemo.** Lat. No one, nobody. (Simpson)

# Thursday, 4 October, 1888

—

At Bow street, Henry Taylor, an Army Reserve man, was charged with assaulting Mary Ann Perry, and threatening to stab her. The prosecutrix accused the prisoner of indecent behaviour in her presence in the Clare Market. He pulled out a knife and threatened to stab her. He afterwards knocked her down and ran away. He was followed by a large crowd calling out "Leather Apron". He ran into Catherine street, where he asked Police constable Betts, 190E, who stopped him, to keep the crowd off, or he would rip them up. He had an open knife in his hand, which Betts took away from him. On the way to the station the crowd increased, and an attempt was made to get at and assault the prisoner. It was with difficulty that Betts and another constable kept the crowd back. At the station a razor was found in the prisoner's pocket. Mr. Vaughan sentenced the prisoner to two months' imprisonment, with hard labour, and ordered him to find surety in £5 to keep the peace for the following three months.

—

## POLICE

At the Guildhall, William Bull, 27, was charged on his own confession with having committed the murder in Mitre square, Aldgate. Inspector George Izzard said at 20 minutes to 11 on Tuesday night the prisoner came into the charge room at Bishopsgate Police station and made the following statement:—

"William Bull, No 6 Stannard road, Dalston. I am a medical student. I wish to give myself up for the murder in Aldgate on Saturday night last or Sunday morning. About 2, I think, I met the woman in Aldgate, I went with her up a narrow street, not far from the main road. I gave her half a crown. While walking along together a second man came up, and he took the half crown from her." The prisoner then said, "My poor head. I shall go mad. I have done it. I must put up with it." The inspector then said to him, "What has become of your clothing that you had on when you committed the murder?" He replied, "If you wish to know, they are in the Lea, and the knife I threw away." At this point he declined to say anything more. He was drunk. Inquiries had been made at the London Hospital. No such person as the prisoner was known there. He was out of employment. The prisoner's parents appeared to be most respect-

able people. His father stated that the accused was at home on Saturday night.

The prisoner—I said this when I was mad drunk. I never committed a murder; I could not commit such an act.

The magistrate—I shall remand you; and you have yourself to thank for the position you are in.

The prisoner was then removed to the cells.

~

280

# Thursday, 4 October, 1888

## 𝕿𝖍𝖊 𝕾𝖙𝖆𝖗
### WHAT WE THINK.

SIR CHARLES WARREN'S letter to the Whitechapel Board of Works is a confession of helplessness pitiful to read in the present crisis. What suggestions has our dictator of the streets to offer in this emergency? That the Board should improve the lighting of the Whitechapel slums, and use its influence with the Whitechapel street-walkers (really Sir Charles is very kind; why does he not use his own well-known abilities as a missionary?) to keep them out of the path of danger. Beyond this, we are asked to believe that because we hear nothing of discoveries by detectives, that only shows that the detectives are specially active and energetic; and we are told for the thousandth time that the Metropolitan Police are hopelessly handicapped in dealing with a situation like this for want of reserves to draw on in the emergency.

UP to the present, therefore, the only practical moral to be drawn from the wholesale massacre which is now horrifying the world, is the inadequacy of the police force from top to bottom, apparently in point of intelligence, and certainly in point of numbers. If it does nothing else the Whitechapel mystery should force the question of the control and administration of the London police to the foremost place in metropolitan politics. We are glad to see that the Finsbury Radicals are setting the example in using the occasion for this purpose, and we hope to see them backed up promptly by every political organisation in London.

LOOK at this question of the offer of a reward. At this moment the City proper is placarded with notices of a £500 reward, offered by the municipal authorities. Outside that magic area, the authorities believe that such an offer is useless, or worse than useless, and are so strong in that belief that they reject all proffers of private aid in the matter. Whether the City is right or the Home Office is right, what more convincing demonstration could be offered of the necessity of placing the whole police of the metropolis under the control of a genuine municipal authority?

IN our opinion the City is right. The very fact that the City police believe in the possible efficacy of a reward shows that there is room for doubt on the subject, and where there is room for doubt the benefit ought to be given in the direction of long-established and well-tried practice. It is the duty of Mr. Matthews and his subordinates, as we said the other day, to show that they have left no stone unturned, no resource enexhausted.[171] But there is a special reason for offering a reward in this present case. London is in daily danger of a repetition of the recent butchery. Ordinarily, a reward is merely designed to bring the perpetrator of a past crime to justice; but here it may have the effect of preventing a repetition of the crime. The prospect of a reward is enough in a district like the East-end to convert every other resident into an amateur detective. The criminal must know that it increases his risk a hundredfold, and who knows how many a life may be saved by that knowledge alone? Have our red-tape bound officials in Whitehall looked at this special feature of the present case?

BY the way, why does our friend, the *D.T.*, print facsimiles of the ghastly but very silly letters from "Jack the Ripper?" We were offered them by the "Central News," and declined to print them. They were clearly written in red pencil, not in blood, the obvious reason being that the writer was one of those foolish but bad people who delight in an unholy notoriety. Now, the murderer is not a man of this kind. His own love of publicity is tempered by a very peculiar and remarkable desire for privacy and by a singular ability to secure what he wants. Nor is there any proof of any pre-knowledge of the Mitre-square crimes, beyond the prediction that they were going to happen, which anybody might have made. The reference to ear-clipping may be a curious coincidence, but there is nothing in the posting of the letter on Sunday. Thousand of Londoners had details of the crimes supplied in the Sunday papers.

THERE are one or two fresh additions this morning to the stock of speculative theories of the crime. One of the least extravagant of them is that the fiend may be a foreign butcher gone mad. The character of the work is said to resemble the manipulation of the Parisian charcutier. We have always favoured the "slaughter-man" theory, and this variation of it strikes us as more likely than the idea that the miscreant is a maniac Malay or Lascar. The

---

[171] Variant of *Unexhausted.*

281

# Thursday, 4 October, 1888

neighbourhood of the docks, however, is sufficient to give some support to the theory that some form of Oriental demoniacal possession is at the bottom of the crime. But theorising on such slender materials is not very profitable work.

MRS. FENWICK MILLER'S[172] accusation against our Courts of making "woman-killing no murder" is a vigorous and startling piece of special pleading; but it really proves nothing. Those who have been impressed by it would do well to study a curious article published some time ago on the same subject by Mr. Belfort Bax,[173] whose contention, exactly contrary to that of Mrs. Fenwick Miller, is that women enjoy a sentimental exemption from punishment to the extent of being able to commit atrocious crimes against men with impunity. And he was able to bring forward cases, including acquittals of female murderers and vitriol[174] throwers, quite as startling as any adduced by Mrs. Fenwick Miller. The truth is, as usual, between the two special pleaders. Our vicious system of giving to property the protection, the sanctity, and even the Parliamentary franchise which we deny to humanity, has led to the anomaly that it is safer to kick a human being to death's door than to steal a turnip. But this disregard of life is by no means peculiar to one sex. If scandalously light sentences are passed for assaults on women, even lighter ones are passed for assaults on men. The only difference is that as women are weaker they get much the worst of the bouts of violence which are encouraged by the law's indifference. Consequently poor women get kicked oftener than poor men. If the balance was on the other side, the punishment would be equally inadequate. It is the class question rather than the sex question that is at issue in this matter.[175]

---

[172] **Florence Fenwick Miller** (1854-1936). An early suffragette leader, lecturer and journalist. Co-founded Women's Franchise League.

[173] **Ernest Belfort Bax** (1854-1926). British writer philosopher, socialist and Men's Rights activist. The article referred to is "Some Bourgeois Idols; Or Ideals, Reals, and Shams." Commonweal, April, 1886, p. 25-26.

[174] **Vitriol**. Sulphuric acid. (Morehead)

[175] Victorian era police records made available on Ancestry.co.uk bear out the statements made here by the writer regarding the inequity of the penalties

---

—

## WHITECHAPEL.
## WHAT THE POLICE ARE DOING TO SECURE THE CRIMINAL.
### A Sketch of the Leading Lines of their Energetic Investigations—Warren breaks Silence—What a Smart American would have Done.

The failure of the police to discover the Whitechapel murderer is certainly not due to inactivity. No one who has had occasion to visit the police offices whence the investigations are being conducted can escape the impression that everybody is on the move, and it is probably a fact that very few of the chief officials and detectives have had their regular rest since last Sunday morning. One hears no complaint against the demand for extra duty, except in instances where the pressure is unevenly applied, for the police are individually

**MORE INTERESTED IN THE CAPTURE**
of the murderer than anyone else. The City police, though there has been but one of the series of murders committed within their bailiwick, are no less active in their exertions than the metropolitan, and it is a mistake to suppose that there is too much friction between the two organisations for them to pool issues in this matter. Each office pursues its work according to its own methods, but there is a constant interchange of information, and a constant comparison of views on points affecting more than one case. In conversation with different officials a *Star* reporter has gathered some interesting facts as to the amount of work the police are doing. One prominent feature is in connection with

### THE SLAUGHTERHOUSES.

It appears that the investigation of these establishments has been most thorough. Everyone in the whole East-end district, and some others, have practically been turned inside out. The proprietors and managers have in most cases heartily co-operated with the police, and every

---

imposed. For example, in 1883 Dorcas Mary Snell, 45, was sentenced to five years hard labour for stealing a slice of bacon. That same year 40 year old Mary Morrison also received five years hard labour. Her crime? She threw sulphuric acid on her estranged husband after he missed his alimony payment. (The Telegraph)

# Thursday, 4 October, 1888

employee has been personally "pumped."[176] Each man has been called upon to give an account of himself and his whereabouts not only on last Saturday night, but during the entire period over which the series of crimes extends. Every peculiar circumstance is made note of, and no one to whom the slightest suspicion attaches is lost sight of until the suspicion is completely allayed. Nor has the man's own word been accepted as conclusive. Each man has been asked if he knows of anyone who has not been regular at his work or has played tricks on the timekeeper, for the time-book in each establishment plays an important part in the investigation. More than all this, in some cases, all men who can write have been called upon to make a statement in writing and sign their names, so that any possible question of hand-writing may be more easily compared. The same thoroughness has characterised what has been done in

## THE LODGING HOUSES.

Deputies were required to make a showing of all their regular lodgers, to point out their habits, their peculiarities, and their associates, and to furnish descriptions of all casual visitors who had attracted special attention.

Frequenters of lodging-houses have been interviewed by hundreds, and detectives have been scattered all over the district disguised as men down on their luck in the hope of their picking up some information. But the police have pretty well made up their minds that the man they want is not to be found through the lodging-house channel. The fact that so many of the victims were themselves frequenters of these caravansaries[177] has quickened the in-stinct, and aroused the spirit of the class, and it would be almost impossible for a murderer to be in their midst without someone giving him away. The attention that has been paid to

## THE HOSPITALS,

has been quite as close, but the police have not always found the hospital authorities too eager to assist them. The ethics of medical etiquette

---

[176] **Pump**. Verb, to question artfully, make one tell without knowing he's telling, sound (q.v.): hence, an indirect question: *Your pump is good but the sucker's dry!* A retort on an attempt to pump. (1633) (Farmer)

[177] **Caravansary**. Inn. (Morehead)

appear to stand in the way of full and free investigation among medical students at least, for they are slow to tell what they know or suspect when it may affect one of their number. One police inspector told the *Star* man that he supposed there were over a hundred men who were being individually shadowed in his district alone, and if the same system is in vogue all over the East-end the number of detectives on the job must be something enormous. There is not a vacant building in the East that has not been thoroughly searched lest it might afford a hiding-place for the murderer; and in at least two instances the drain-pipes have been taken up for a long distance where suspicious matter was thought to have been deposited.

## EVERY VESSEL

that has left the harbour since the hour of the commission of the last crime has been thoroughly overhauled, the workhouses have been visited for the examination of all new inmates, and even the prison authorities have been enlisted in the cause for the sake of keeping a close eye on prisoners who may have been glad to get put away for a time for trivial offences. It is estimated, roughly speaking, that there are at least 500 men engaged in these investigations who are not police officers, but who are directly instructed by the police officials.

### Letter from Sir Charles Warren.

Sir Charles Warren, replying to a resolution forwarded to him from the Whitechapel Board of Works, says:—

"The prevention of murder directly cannot be effected by any strength of the police force; but it is reduced and brought to a minimum by rendering it most difficult to escape detection. In the particular class of murder now confronting us, however, the unfortunate victims appear to take the murderer to some retired spot and to place themselves in such a position that they can be slaughtered without a sound being heard; the murder, therefore, takes place without any clue to the criminal being left. I have to request and call upon your Board, as popular representatives, to do all in your power to **DISSAUDE THE UNFORTUNATE WOMEN** about Whitechapel from going into lonely places in the dark with any persons—whether acquaintances or strangers. I have also to point out that the purlieus about Whitechapel are most imperfectly lighted, and that darkness is an important assistant to crime.

I can assure you, for the information of your Board, that every nerve has been strained to detect the criminal or criminals, and to render more difficult further atrocities. You will agree with me that it is not desirable that I should enter into particulars as to what the police are doing in the matter. It is most important for good results that our proceedings should not be published, and the very fact that you may be unaware of what the Detective Department is doing is only the stronger proof that it is doing its work with

## SECRECY AND EFFICIENCY.

I trust that your Board will assist the police by persuading the inhabitants to give them every information in their power concerning any suspicious characters in the various dwellings, for which object 10,000 handbills, a copy of which I enclose, have been distributed." In conclusion, he denies the frequently-made statement that police are transferred from districts they know thoroughly to those with which they are unacquainted, and invites the Board to suggest any changes in the system they think desirable, assuring them that their proposals will receive every consideration.

### Only Twenty Yards Away.

In connection with the Mitre-square murder, the foreman of the sewer hands who are engaged at Aldgate in sweeping the streets in the early hours of the morning has stated most positively that at the time when the murder is supposed to have been perpetrated he was standing not more than 20 yards away from the spot where the body was found. He never heard any woman's cries for help, nor any sounds of a struggle.

### Citizen Police with Noiseless Boots.

Under the supervision of the local vigilance committee, upwards of a score of citizen detectives went out on duty at twelve o'clock last night. The locality is divided into "beats," and by pre-arrangement those who have undertaken the assistance of the regular police meet periodically at central points during the night to report themselves. Noiseless boots,[178] as from

time to time suggested for the force, have been provided for the amateur policemen.

### An American Detective's Opinion.

The Whitechapel murders are attracting widespread attention throughout America. Inspector Byrnes,[179] of New York, was asked how he would proceed to solve the London mystery. He said:—"I should have gone right to work in a commonsense way, and not believed in mere theories. With the great power of the London police I should have manufactured victims for the murderer. I would have taken 50 female *habitués* of Whitechapel and covered the ground with them. Even if one fell a victim, I should get the murderer. Men un-uniformed should be scattered over the district so nothing could escape them. The crimes are all of the same class, and I would have determined the class to which the murderer belonged. But— pshaw! What's the good of talking? The murderer would have been caught long ago."

—

### A Theory from a Coroner.
### TO THE EDITOR OF "THE STAR."

SIR,—A remarkable incident in connection with the recent murders is that in no one instance has it been found that the victim made any noise or cry while being done to death.

My assistant suggests a theory in reference to this very remarkable fact, which strikes me as having something in it, and as such ought to be made public.

The theory is that the murderer goes about with a vial of rum or brandy in his pocket drugged with an opiate—, if not quite tasteless— that he offers a swig of it to his victims (which they would all be likely to greedily accept)

---

[178] **Noiseless Boots**. Boots with vulcanized rubber soles and heels. (Routledge)

[179] **Thomas Byrnes** (1842-1910). Chief of the New York City Detective Bureau, 1880–1895. Born in Dublin, Byrnes emigrated as a child with his parents to New York. Joining the Police Department as a patrolman in 1863 after a stint in the Union Army, Byrnes rose through the ranks, was named as the NYPD's first Chief of Detectives in 1880, and promoted to Superintendent of Police in 1892, retiring in 1895. He is remembered for expanding the NYPD's photographic record of criminals, the "Rogues Gallery", and for coining the term "the third degree" for the brutal methods used for extracting information from prisoners. (N.L.E.M.)

# Thursday, 4 October, 1888

when he meets them, that in about ten to twenty minutes, the poison begins to do its work on constitutions well soaked with alcohol, and that then they are easily dispatched without fear of making any noise or call for assistance.

Having been out of town lately for my holidays I have not closely followed the evidence at the inquests; but there are two questions which would require clearing up if there is anything in this theory. 1st. Have the stomachs or most of them been ripped open to do away with the evidence of poisoning in this manner, and (2nd), has any analysis of the contents of the stomachs been made.—Yours, &c.,

R. MACDONALD,
Coroner for North-East Middlesex

—

**FIFTH EDITION.**
**MITRE-SQUARE INQUEST.**
**The Story of the Gruesome Discovery Told by One of the Witnesses.**

The inquest upon the body of the unfortunate woman who was found murdered in Mitre-square, Aldgate, in the early hours of Sunday morning, and who has since been identified as Kate Eddows or Conway or Kenny, was opened this morning by Coroner Langham, at the City Mortuary, Golden-lane, Barbican. The room is a fairly large one, but accommodation was at a premium, so enormous was the interest which centred in this attempt to ascertain by what means and at whose hands deceased came by her death.

Before proceeding to the mortuary the coroner went and made a personal inspection of the scene of the crime, with a view to the better appreciation of the evidence bearing on the position of the body. The City police were represented by Major Smith, the Acting Commissioner, Superintendent Foster, and Detective-inspector McWilliam; while Mr. Crawford, the City Solicitor, was also present in the interests of the police.

**ELIZA GOLD**

was the first witness. She said:—I live at 6, Thrawl-street, Spitalfields, and am a widow. I identify the deceased as my poor sister. Her name was Catherine Eddows. She was not married, and was not single, but was living with a gentleman named Mr. Kelly. She had been with him for some years. I last saw her alive four or five months ago.

The Coroner: How did she get her living?
—She used to go out hawking things.
Was she a woman of sober habits?
—Yes, sir.
Before she went to live with Kelly had she lived with anyone else?
—Yes, a man named Conway some years, and had two children by him, both of whom are alive.
Is Conway still living?
—I do not know. He was in the army, and was a pensioner who use to go out hawking things.
Did they part on good or bad terms?
—I could not tell you, sir.
Has she been in the habit of seeing him since they parted?
—I don't know. I have never heard her say.
By Mr. Crawford:
—It was seven or eight years since I saw Conway. I could not exactly say whether she was living on friendly terms with Kelly. They were living in Flower and Dean-street at a common lodging-house.

**JOHN KELLY,**

of 55, Flower and Dean-street, said:—I am a labourer jobbing about the markets. I have seen the body of deceased, and I recognise it as that of Catherine Conway. I had been living with her for seven years. She used to sell things about the streets for a living.

When were you last in her company?
—On Saturday, at two in the afternoon in Houndsditch.
Did you part on good terms?
—Yes; on very good terms. She said she was going over to try and see her daughter Annie, in Bermondsey. Those were her last words to me.
Was Annie her daughter by Conway?
—Yes, I believe so.
What time did she say she should return?
—She promised me to be back by four and no later.
She did not return?
—No, sir.
Did you make any inquiries?
—I heard she had been locked up at Bishopsgate-street. I was told so by an old woman, who said she saw her in custody of two policemen.
Did you make further inquiries?
—I did not, sir, feeling sure she would be out

Sunday morning.

Did you hear what she was locked up for?

—A drop of drink, sir.

Did you ever know she went out for an immoral purpose?

—No, sir. I never suffered her to do so.

Was she in the habit of drinking to excess?

—Oh, no, sir, only slightly. Occasionally she might drink to excess.

When you left her had she any money about her?

—No, sir.

What was her object of going to see her daughter?

—With a view of

## GETTING A TRIFLE,

so as I should not see her walking the streets at night without shelter.

Then was she in the habit of walking the streets?

—No, sir; but there's been many a night we have not had the money to pay for our lodging.

Do you know of anyone with whom she was at variance—anyone likely to injure her?

—No, sir, not in the least.

Have you ever seen Conway of late?

—I have never seen him in my existence.

Do you know if she has?

—I don't.

Do you know if he is living?

—I cannot say.

Did you ascertain what time she was discharged from the police-station?

—No, sir.

A Juror: What time did she usually return to your lodgings?

—About eight or nine.

By Mr. Crawford: You say she had no money. Do you know who paid for her drink on Saturday afternoon?

—No, sir.

Is this last time the first occasion on which she has not returned when she has left you?

—Yes, for months. Some months ago she left me in consequence of a few words, but only remained away a few hours.

Had you had any angry conversation on this Saturday afternoon?

—No, sir.

On Friday night did deceased sleep with you?

—No.

Was she walking the streets?

—No, she went into the casual ward[180] at Mile-end.

Did you sleep with deceased at all during last week at a lodging-house?

—No, sir; we were hop-picking at Kent.

Where did she procure the tea and sugar found on her?

—She

## PAWNED MY BOOTS

on Saturday morning for half-a-crown.

And when she left you was she perfectly sober?

—Yes.

Had you any money?

—No; we had spent the half-crown on drink and food.

---

[180] **Casual Ward**. The section of a Workhouse set aside for the shelter of vagrants for a short period of time, usually a night and a day. A poor supper and breakfast were provided, and the inmates were usually required to do hard labour in return for their fare. The following description of the Casual Ward regimen is from Salvation Army founder William Booth's 1890 book In Darkest England and the Way Out:

" J. C. knows Casual Wards pretty well. Has been in St. Giles, Whitechapel, St. George's, Paddington, Marylebone, Mile End. They vary a little in detail, but as a rule the doors open at 6; you walk in; they tell you what the work is, and that if you fail to do it, you will be liable to imprisonment. Then you bathe. Some places the water is dirty. Three persons as a rule wash in one water. At Whitechapel (been there three times) it has always been dirty; also at St. George's. I had no bath at Mile End; they were short of water. If you complain they take no notice. You then tie your clothes in a bundle, and they give you a nightshirt. At most places they serve supper to the men, who have to go to bed and eat it there. Some beds are in cells; some in large rooms. You get up at 6 a.m. and do the task. The amount of stone-breaking is too much; and the oakum-picking is also heavy. The food differs. At St. Giles, the gruel left over-night is boiled up for breakfast, and is consequently sour; the bread is puffy, full of holes, and don't weigh the regulation amount. Dinner is only 8 ounces of bread and 1½ ounce of cheese, and if that's short, how can anybody do their work? They will give you water to drink if you ring the cell bell for it, that is, they will tell you to wait, and bring it in about half an hour. There are a good lot of "moochers" go to Casual Wards, but there are large numbers of men who only want work."

Do you know why she left Conway?

—No, I could not say.

She has never brought you money that she has earned during the night?

—Never, sir.

A Juror: Where were you on Saturday night?

—In the lodging-house.

### FREDERICK WILKINSON,

the deputy of the lodging-house, 55, Flower and Dean-street, said:—I have known the deceased and Kelly for the last seven or eight years. They passed as man and wife, and lived on very good terms. They had a quarrel now and again through drink, but nothing violent happened. Deceased got her living by hawking and by charing amongst the Jews, from what I have heard her say. I do not think I have ever seen Kelly drunk in my life, but deceased I have sometimes. She was not in the habit of walking the streets to my knowledge. She said her name was Kate Conway, "bought and paid for," meaning that she had married Conway.

By Mr. Crawford:

—The last time Kelly and deceased slept together at my lodging house was five or six weeks ago. When deceased did not come home with Kelly on Saturday night I asked him where she was, and he said she was locked up. I am quite positive Kelly did not go out again on Saturday evening after coming in at about ten.

Did Kelly ever quarrel with any man about the woman?

—No, I never saw any such quarrel.

Can you tell me whether when you saw deceased on Saturday she was wearing an apron?

—I believe she was.

What is the distance from your lodging-house to the scene of the murder?

—Five or six hundred yards.

Several of the Jury:

—More than that.

Can you tell me whether any one came into your lodging-house, either a stranger or anyone you knew, and took a bed between one and two?

—No, I don't think so. Two detectives came about three.

Can you by referring to your books see if any one came in between one and two?

—Yes, by my books.

Then I think, Mr. Coroner, the further examination of this witness had better be postponed.

The witness then left to fetch his book.

### POLICE-CONSTABLE WATKINS,

examined by Mr. Crawford, said:—I have been in the City police force for 17 years. On Saturday night last I went on duty at a quarter to ten on my regular beat, which extends from the corner of Duke-street, Aldgate, into Leadenhall-street, along Leadenhall-street eastward into Mitre-street, then into Mitre-square, and round the square again into Mitre-street, back again to my starting place at Duke-street. That takes me 12 or 14 minutes. I had been continuously patrolling that beat from ten till one in the morning.

Had anything excited your attention?

—No, sir.

Or any person?

—No, sir.

Did you pass through Mitre-square at half-past one on Sunday morning?

—Yes, sir.

Had you your lantern alight and fixed on your belt?

—Yes.

And did you in accordance with your usual practice look at the various passages and warehouses?

—Yes, sir.

At half-past one did anything excite your attention?

—No, sir.

Could anyone have been in any portion of the square without your seeing them?

—No, sir.

When did you next come into Mitre-square?

—About sixteen minutes to two, a time I fix by the reference I subsequently made to my watch.

Then something attracted your attention?

—Yes. I turned to the right as I entered the square and I saw the body of a woman lying there.

How was she lying?

—On her back, with her feet facing the square. Her clothes were up above her waist, and I saw her throat was cut, and her bowels protruding.

The stomach was ripped up, then?

—Yes, sir.

Was she lying in a pool of blood?

—Yes, sir.

Did you touch the body?

—No, sir. I ran across the road to Messrs.

Kearley and Tonge's warehouse and called the watchman inside, a man named Morris. He came out, and I sent him for assistance.

Did you remain by the side of the body till the arrival of Police-constable Holland?

—I did.

Was there anyone about but yourself?

—No one till Holland arrived. He was followed by Dr. Sequeira, and Inspector Collard arrived about two.

### DR. GORDON BROWN,

the police surgeon, followed.

As you had entered the square had you heard of any footsteps as of anyone running away?

—No, not a sound.

And to the best of your belief you were the only person in the square except that unfor-tunate woman?

—Yes, sir.

### FREDERICK WILLIAM FOSTER,

of 26, Old Jewry, produced plans of the scene of the murder. The probable route from Berner-street, Commercial-street, to Mitre-square was marked.

Mr. Crawford: Would Gouldstone-street be on the direct route from the lodging-house in Flower and Dean-street to Mitre-square?

—Yes, sir.

What time would it take to go from Mitre-square to this lodging-house, passing through Gouldstone-street?

—Within a quarter of an hour.

And how long would it take to go from Berner-street to Mitre-square?

—About a quarter of an hour at a fair pace.

Mr. Crawford said the importance of this evidence consisted in the fact that a portion of this woman's apron was found in Gouldstone-street.

### WILKINSON,

the lodging-house deputy, had by this time returned. Further examined by Mr. Crawford, he said:—Kelly slept at my lodging-house on Friday and Saturday.

Does your book enable you to say whether any person came in about two on Sunday morning?

—It does not indicate what time anyone would come in.

Is there nothing that you can refresh your memory by?

—I had six strange men sleeping there on Saturday night.

And cannot you tell me if any one of them came in about two on Sunday morning?

—I cannot.

Do you remember any stranger going out soon after twelve?

—I could hardly tell if any one went out at that time. I should be so busy then.

A Juror: Is it usual to have your house open at two in the morning?

—Yes, till about half-past two.

No register is kept of names of any kind?

—No, sir. It's all done by crosses and numbers.

You ask no questions?

—No, sir.

(Proceeding.)

—

### FALSE REPORTS.
#### A Circumstantial Story of the Arrest of the Murderer Proves to be Worthless.

An evening contemporary publishes the following:—

"This morning at half-past four a man was seen to go behind a hoarding in High-street, Shadwell, with a woman. The watchman on duty, having his suspicions, followed them and called the police. The man killed the watchman with a knife, but was secured by several constables who had hurried up. It is believed that the man is the Whitechapel murderer."

Our reporter saw the inspector on duty at Leman-street Police-station with reference to this report. "No one," said the officer, "has been arrested at Shadwell."

Has a watchman or anyone been killed?

—No.

Then you think there is no truth in the report?

—"Think!" he answered. "I am sure of it."

This report proves to be false in two very important particulars. No arrests have been made by the Shadwell police to-day, and no watchman has been killed. The watchman who was said to have fallen a victim to the knife of the murderer was on duty at a building in process of demolition at No. 191, High-street, opposite St. Paul's Church, Shadwell. A *Star* reporter found the watchman alive, though not lively, at No. 6, New Gravel-lane. His name is James McNaughten. He did not look like a man who had undergone an encounter with a desperado, and he assured the *Star* man that his experience did not belie his looks. He was utterly ignorant of the fact that he had awoke

### TO FIND HIMSELF DEAD,

and it was with difficulty that he could recall any incident of the night that could have given rise to the story. At length, however, he remembered that he had seen a man and woman pass him soon after midnight, and noticing a moment later that they had disappeared, he walked up to the other end of the hoarding, and found them in its shadow. "I asked them what they were doing there," said he, "and the woman asked what business it was of mine. I told her I didn't want no game[181] played there, and then the man said something about my wanting to get ripped up." "Of course," continued the watchman, "I didn't want to get ripped up, and I was glad to see 'em move on." The watchman added that he may have men-tioned the circumstance to some of his acquaintances before he went to bed this morning, but he attached no importance to the fact, as similar occurrences took place nightly in that neighbourhood, and something about "ripping up" and "Leather Apron" was in everybody's mouth.

The Central News says:—Passengers to the City from stations north and east of London were this morning greatly excited by the intelligence that "Jack the Ripper" had been captured. The story ran that at an early hour this morning a mounted patrol observed a suspicious-looking character, and challenged him. The man immediately attacked him with a knife, slashing him in a dreadful manner, but after a desperate struggle the constable succeeded in capturing him. A similar account was communicated to the police, but after telegraphing to all the stations in London it was found the story was an entire fabrication.

The police most emphatically deny the truth of the story that has been published as to the discovery of a shopkeeper who had talked with the murderer and his Berner-street victim, had sold them grapes, and had seen them at the entrance to the fatal alley ten minutes before the deed was done. The fact is, that the alleged informant contradicts himself, and there is no evidence that there were any grapes in the possession of the woman.

---

[181] **Game**. 2. A company of harlots. A *game-pullet*, a young prostitute. (Farmer)

### "A Long-Bladed Knife."

Late last night a man entered a coffee-shop in Kilburn-lane, and talked in an incoherent manner about the Whitechapel tragedies. He produced what appeared to be a long-bladed knife. He was subsequently taken into custody, and gave the name of Philip Hurst. On being searched, a bright steel rule was found on him, but no weapon. He had been drinking heavily.

### A Scare at Norwood.

The Whitechapel craze has extended to the genteel neighbourhood lying between Upper Norwood and Croydon, and a belief is held by many persons that the murderer, whoever he may be, finds concealment in a dense wood which skirts Leather Bottle-lane, and leads on to Croydon. The gardeners in the employ of Mr. Horne, to whom the wood belongs, have seen a person dressed as a woman, but whom they assert is a man lurking about the wood at night. On each of the nights that the murders have been committed since August the person has been seen to enter the wood. The gardeners who have charge of the wood by night have armed themselves.

### An American Arrested.

An American, who refuses to give his name or any account of himself, was arrested last night on suspicion of being the East-end murderer. He is well dressed, rather tall, of slight build, and clean shaven. He accosted a woman in Cable-street, asked her to go with him, and threatened that if she refused he would "rip her up." The woman screamed, and the man rushed to a cab. The police gave chase, got upon the cab, seized the man, and took him to Leman-street Police-station, where he asked the inspector in charge, "Are you the boss?" The man is detained at the police-station, as well as two others who were conveyed there during the evening. In one case a man went up to an officer in the street, and said he "had assisted in the Mitre-square job." The constable took him to the Leman-street police-station, where it was found that he was suffering from delirium tremens. He was detained in order that further inquiries might be made.

The man was released at ten o'clock this morning, inquiries having shown that his account of himself was entirely satisfactory.

At the present moment there is no one in custody.

# Thursday, 4 October, 1888

## 𝕰𝖛𝖊𝖓𝖎𝖓𝖌 𝕹𝖊𝖜𝖘
### DOWN WHITECHAPEL WAY.

The contemporary who averred yesterday that the majority of the inhabitants of West and Central London know about as much of the neighbourhood of Whitechapel as they do of the Hindoo Koosh or the Northern Territory of South Australia considerably understated the case. When a moderately intelligent traveller returns from either of these regions he will be "lionised" in drawing rooms; should his return happen to coincide with the annual meeting of the British Association, he will be enthusiastically invited to recount his experiences and be eagerly listened to; should Messrs. Mudie and Smith[182] put into circulation a book of his on the subject, the fair denizens of West and Central London will, at any rate, pretend to have read it and canvass its merits at their "at homes," the men will be genuinely interested. Mayhew, Hollingshead, James Greenwood,[183] and George Sims, after them, had first of all to cut their narrative about "poor and ragged London" into slices and even then it may be doubted whether the instalments were exceedingly palatable to Society, with a big capital, whatever they may have been to the rest of the world.

Of course, there were, and are, a great many good and philanthropic people who read these accounts, but they did not and do not pretend to derive much amusement from them. With the most laudable intentions possible they perused and shook their heads over them, bewailing the depravity and poverty, the lack of cleanliness and the improvidence of these "stepchildren of civilisation." They probably formed themselves into one or more committees to make them morally and physically comfortable, to at least inculcate the elementary principles of domestic hygiene and sanitation, to impress upon them the necessity of saving for a rainy day, &c., &c.

To this end they departed—not unprovided with tracts—to the purlieus[184] of Mile End, Stepney, Bethnal Green, Lambeth, &c. and those that saw them depart lauded their heroism and spoke with bated breath of their expeditions. They were interested for a little while, perhaps, but amused they were not. Nor were those that went. They only saw the serious side of the business, and in their endeavour to impress that serious side upon their so called protégés, they bored them to death.

They applied pretty much the same tactics everywhere, and everywhere they succeeded in being tolerated for the sake of the material benefits they bestowed, except in the East of London. The East of London, I have in my mind's eye, is bounded on the east by the Mile End Gate, to the South by Cable street, to the North by Finsbury Pavement, to the West by Aldgate Pump. If the reader will take a moderately large map of London, he will be able to judge for himself the extent of the tract of ground, the occupants of which have almost to a man remained refractory to the exhortations of well meaning, but essentially impolitic reformers, to mend their ways.

---

[182] **Charles Edward Mudie** (1818-1890) founded Mudie's Lending Library in 1842. Here patrons paid a set fee per year and could borrow one book at a time. Although the Public Libraries Act 1850 allowed the use of public funds to create municipal libraries open to all, the act did not mandate that these facilities be created. So Mudie's Libraries remained in operation until government funded public libraries finally became common in the 1930's. **W.H. Smith & Son** ran a similar service from 1860 to 1961.

[183] **Henry Mayhew** (1812-1887), noted journalist, author, co-founder and editor of <u>Punch</u>. An advocate for social reform, he authored the book series <u>London Labour and the London Poor</u> (1851).

**John Hollingshead** (1827-1904), London journalist that began his career in 1854 with Charles Dickens as his editor. Wrote for the magazines <u>Household Words</u>, <u>Cornhill Magazine</u>, <u>Punch</u> and <u>The Morning Post</u> newspaper, mostly on the topics of social reform, politics and dramatic criticism. He also authored <u>Ragged London</u> (1861). In the 1860's Hollingshead left journalism and helped found the Alhambra Theatre, there he was the stage manager from 1865-68, and introduced the Can-Can to London. After taking over management of the Gaiety Theatre in 1868, Hollingshead brought Gilbert and Sullivan together for their first collaboration, *Thespis*, in 1871.

---

**James Greenwood** (1862-1929), writer concerned with social reform. Authored <u>The True Story of a Little Ragamuffin</u> (1866) and <u>Low-Life Deep (1876)</u>.

[184] **Purlieus.** Outskirts, environs. (Morehead)

Does this mean that they are poorer, more degraded, more uncleanly, or greater spend-thrifts than the denizens of the back slums in the Old Kent road, Marylebone, Westminster, and Lambeth? Does it mean that increasing natural civilisation and its more or less consequent mental development have had no effect upon them? Not at all. If anything the majority of the lower class inhabitants of Whitechapel and Commercial roads are not as poor as the lower classes of other quarters. If anything, notwithstanding the recent revelations, they are not as degraded. Their cleanliness leaves perhaps as much to desire as elsewhere, though this bodily neglect is in many cases not so apparent as there, because of the better kind of clothing—not entirely lacking in ornament—worn by all but the most destitute. As regards their improvidence, I cannot say much though, on the issue of it, I should imagine that of saving less they are more provident than their fellow townsmen of the same category.

Lest the above should appear a paradox I explain. The Whitechapel population spend their money as freely, if not more so, than the proletariat of other districts, but they get better value for it. Their love of personal finery extends to their homes, and I will undertake to say that one will find a considerably greater quantity of decently, sometimes even prettily, furnished apartments and small houses belonging to the humbler classes round about the Commercial, Whitechapel, New and Cambridge Heath roads than in any other part of the metropolis. Of course I repeat that I am strictly speaking of the very humblest.

Are these differences due to what, for want of a better term, I may call preaching on the part of amateur missionaries, lady district visitors, and the like? By no means. They are due in a great measure, perhaps entirely, to the example of the non-Christian population by which this Christian population is, as it were, hemmed in.

In order to make this clear, let us watch the Jew, the poorer as well as the more fortunate one, in his habit as he lives down Whitechapel way, which is still, notwithstanding the many migrations of his co-religionists, the Jewish headquarters. Let us look at him with all his virtues, and all his faults upon him at home, at work, at play. Let us endeavour to find out the

things his Christian brother unconsciously adopts from him.

I have said unconsciously, I might have said unwillingly; for, not to mince matters, the latter has undisguised contempt for him. I know beforehand that this will be denied by persons who in their heart of hearts are as convinced of the truth of this statement as the writer of these lines, but who will think it necessary to jump into the breach for the sake, as they would probably express it, of that religious tolerance which is commonly supposed to be the inheritance of the nineteenth century.

Let me add at the outset that the dislike inspired by the Jews in Whitechapel in the majority of their Christian neighbours does not spring from divergent religious opinions. It springs from different causes which it would take too long to explain at the end of this article, but upon which I will comment in the next when I take the reader "Down Whitechapel Way." A.D.V.

—

## LETTER FROM
## SIR CHARLES WARREN.

At a recent meeting of the Whitechapel District Board of Works, the following resolution was passed: "That this board regards with horror and alarm the several atrocious murders recently perpetrated within the district of Whitechapel and its vicinity, and calls upon Sir Charles Warren so to regulate and strengthen the police force in the neighbourhood as to guard against any repetition of such atrocities." In reply thereto Sir Charles Warren has sent the following letter:

### LONDON IS THE SAFEST CITY IN THE WORLD.

Sir—In reply to a letter of the 2nd inst. from the clerk to the Board of Works for the Whitechapel district, transmitting a resolution of the Board with regard to the recent atrocious murders perpetrated in and about Whitechapel, I have to point out that the carrying out of your proposal as to regulating and strengthening the police force in your district cannot possibly do more than guard or take precautions against any repetition of such atrocities so long as the victims actually but unwittingly connive at their own destruction.

Statistics show that London, in comparison to its population, is the safest city in the world to live in. The prevention of murder cannot be effected by any strength of the police force, but it is reduced and brought to a minimum by rendering it most difficult to escape detection.

In the particular class of murders now confronting us, however, the unfortunate victims appear to take the murderer to some retired spot and place themselves in such a position that they can be slaughtered without a sound being heard. The murder, therefore, takes place without any clue to the criminal being left. I have to request and call upon your Board, as popular representatives, to do all in your power to dissuade the unfortunate women about Whitechapel from going into lonely places in the dark with any persons, whether acquaintances or strangers.

## THE DARKNESS IN WHITECHAPEL.

I have also to point out that the purlieus about Whitechapel are most imperfectly lighted, and the darkness is an important assistant to crime. I can assure you, for the information of your Board, that every nerve has been strained to detect the criminal or criminals, and to render more difficult further atrocities. You will agree with me that it is not desirable that I should enter into particulars as to what the police are doing in the matter.

## SECRECY REQUIRED BY THE DETECTIVE POLICE.

It is most important for good results that our proceedings should not be published, and the very fact that you may be unaware of what the Detective Department is doing is the stronger proof that it is doing its work with secrecy and efficiency. A large force of police has been drafted into the Whitechapel district to assist those already there to the full extent necessary to meet the requirements; but I have to observe that the Metropolitan Police have not large reserves doing nothing and ready to meet emergencies, but every man has his duty assigned, and I can only strengthen the Whitechapel district by drawing men from duty in other parts of the metropolis.

You will be aware that the whole of the police work of the metropolis has to be done, as usual, while this extra work is going on, and that at such times as this extra precautions have to be taken to prevent the commission of other classes of crime being facilitated through the attention of the police being diverted to one special place and object.

## 10,000 HANDBILLS DISTRIBUTED.

I trust that your Board will assist the police by persuading the inhabitants to give them every information in their power concerning any suspicious character in the various dwellings, for which object 10,000 handbills, a copy of which I enclose, have been distributed.

I have read the reported proceedings of your meeting, and I regret to see that the greatest misconceptions appear to have arisen in the public mind as to recent action in the administration of the police. I beg you will dismiss from your minds as utterly fallacious the numerous anonymous statements as to recent changes stated to have been made in the police force of a character not conducive to efficiency.

## THERE IS NO NEW SYSTEM OF POLICE.

It is stated that the Rev. Daniel Greatrex announced to you that one great cause of police inefficiency was a new system of police, whereby constables were constantly changed from one district to another, keeping them ignorant of their beats.

I have seen this statement made frequently in the newspapers lately, but it is entirely without foundation. The system at present in use has existed for the last 20 years, and constables are seldom or never drafted from their districts, except for promotion, or for some particular cause.

Notwithstanding the many good reasons why constables should be changed on their beats, I have considered the reasons on the other side to be more cogent, and have felt that they should be thoroughly acquainted with the districts in which they serve.

## NEW REGULATIONS FOR THE DETECTIVES.

And with regard to the detective department —a department relative to which reticence is always most desirable—I may say that a short time ago I made arrangements which still further reduced the necessity for transferring officers from districts which they know thoroughly.

I have to call attention to the statement of one of your members, that in consequence of the change in the condition of Whitechapel in recent years, a thorough revision of the police arrangements is necessary, and I shall be very glad to ascertain from you what changes your Board consider advisable, and I may assure you that your proposals will receive from me every consideration.

I am, sir, your obedient servant,
(Signed)
Charles Warren.
Metropolitan Police Office,
4 Whitehall place, S.W., Oct. 3.

—

## THE COMMUNICATIONS FROM "JACK THE RIPPER."

A letter appears in *The Times* today,[185] in the above subject, of which the following is a copy:

Sir—Another remarkable letter has been written by some bad fellow who signs himself "Jack the Ripper." The letter is said to be smeared with blood, and there is on it the print in blood of the corrugated surface of a thumb. This may be that of a man or a woman. It is inconceivable that a woman has written or smeared such a letter, and therefore it may accepted as a fact that the impression in blood is that of a man's thumb.

The surface of a thumb so printed is as clearly indicated as are the printed letters from any kind of type. Thus there is a possibility of identifying the blood print on the letter with the thumb that made it, because the surface markings on no two thumbs are alike, and this is a low power used in a microscope could reveal.

I would suggest—

(1) That it be proved if it is human blood, though this may not be material;

(2) that the thumbs of every suspected man be compared by an expert with the blood print of a thumb on the letter;

(3) that it be ascertained whether the print of a thumb is that of a man who works hard and has rough, coarse hands or whether that of one whose hands have not been roughened by labour;

(4) whether the thumb was large or small;

(5) whether the thumb print shows signs of any shakiness or tremor in the doing of it.

All this the microscope could reveal. The print of a thumb would give as good evidence as that of a boot or shoe.

---

[185] *See* **TO THE EDITOR OF THE TIMES**, p. 277.

—

## THE WHITECHAPEL MURDERS.
## TWO PRIVATE DETECTIVES ON THE TRACK OF THE ASSASSIN.
## HIS PERSONAL APPEARANCE.
## WHERE HE BOUGHT THE GRAPES FOUND BESIDE THE MURDERED WOMAN.
## MATTHEW PACKER'S STORY.
## INTERVIEW WITH THE MAN WHO SPOKE TO THE MURDERER.

We are enabled to present our readers this morning in the columns of the *Evening News* with the most startling information that has yet been made public in relation to the Whitechapel murderer, and the first real clue that has been obtained to his identity. The chain of evidence in our possession has been pieced together by two gentlemen connected with the business of private inquiries, who, starting on the track of the assassin without any pet "theory" to substantiate, and contenting themselves with ascertaining and connecting a series of the simplest facts, have succeeded in arriving at a result of the utmost importance. There are no suppositions or probabilities in the story we have to tell; we put forward nothing but simple facts, each substantiated by the evidence of credible witnesses. What they go to establish is that the perpetrator of the Berner street crime was seen and spoken to whilst in the company of his victim, within forty minutes of the commission of the crime and only passed from the sight of a witness

**TEN MINUTES BEFORE THE MURDER** and within ten yards of the scene of the awful deed. We proceed to have hereunder the story of the two detectives, Messrs. Grand and J.H. Batchelor, of 283 Strand: When they began their quest, almost from the first place at which they sought evidence from No. 44 Berner street, the second house from the spot at which the body was found. This is the residence of a man named Mathew Packer, who carries on a small business as a greengrocer and fruiterer. His shop is an insignificant place, with a half window in front, and most of his dealings are carried on through the lower part of the window case, in which his fruit is exposed for sale. Mathew Packer had valuable information to give, and after two or three interviews on the subject, made and signed a statement in writing, the substance of which is as follows:

On the 29th ult., about 11.45 p.m., a man and woman came to his shop window, and asked for some fruit.

## DESCRIPTION OF THE MURDERER.

The man was middle aged, perhaps 35 years; about five feet seven inches in height; was stout, square built; wore a wideawake hat[186] and dark clothes; had the appearance of a clerk; had a rough voice and a quick, sharp way of talking.

## THE WHITE FLOWER.

The woman was middle aged, wore a dark dress and jacket, and had a white flower in her bosom. It was a dark night and the only light was afforded by an oil lamp which Packer had burning inside his window, but he obtained a sufficiently clear view of the faces of the two people as they stood talking close in front of the window, and his attention was particularly caught by the white flower which the woman wore, and which showed out distinctly against the dark material of her jacket. The importance attached to this flower will be seen afterwards.

## BUYING THE GRAPES.

The man asked his companion whether she would have black or white grapes; she replied "black."

"Well, what's the price of the black grapes, old man?" he inquired.

"The black are sixpence and the white fourpence," replied Packer.

"Well then, old man, give us half a pound of the black," said the man. Packer served him with the grapes, which he handed to the woman. They then crossed the road and stood on the pavement almost directly opposite to the shop for a long time more than half an hour. It will be remembered that the night was very wet, and Packer naturally noticed the peculiarity of the couple's standing so long in the rain. He observed to his wife, "What fools those people are to be standing in the rain like that."

At last the couple moved from their position, and Packer saw them cross the road again and come over to the club, standing for a moment in front of it as though listening to the music inside. Then he lost sight of them. It was then ten or fifteen minutes past twelve o'clock, Packer, who was about to close his shop, noting the time by the fact that the public houses had been closed.

With a view of testing the accuracy and honesty of Packer's testimony, the detectives obtained an order to view the body of the woman murdered in Mitre square, and took Packer to see it, leaving him under the impression that they were taking him to see the Berner street victim. On seeing the body he at once declared that it was not the woman for whom the grapes had been bought, and not a bit like her.

The next evidence gleaned by the detectives was that of a Mrs. Rosenfield and her sister, Miss Eva Harstein, both residing at 14 Berner street. Mrs. Rosenfield deposes that early on Sunday morning she passed the spot on which the body had lain, and observed on the ground close by a grape stalk stained with blood. Miss Eva Harstein gave corroborative evidence as to the finding of the grape stalk close to where the body lay. She also stated that, after the removal of the body of the murdered woman she saw a few small petals of a white natural flower lying quite close to the spot where the body had rested.

It will be remembered by those who have read the accounts of the murder and the proceedings of the police subsequent to it, that the passage in which the crime had been committed was washed down by the police as soon as the body was removed. The detectives, reasoning that the grape stalk had probably been washed away with the blood and dirt removed by the police, next proceeded to search the sink down which the results of the police washing had been put, and amidst a heap of heterogeneous filth, discovered a grape stalk.

It is a matter of common knowledge that some grapes were found in one hand of the murdered woman, so that the finding of this fragment of grape stalk, though important as binding the links of the evidence closer together, was scarcely necessary to establish the fact that the victim had been eating the fruit immediately before her death.

There is one seeming discrepancy between the story of Packer and the facts as published; it

---

[186] **Wide-awake**. A soft felt hat with a broad brim. So called because it never had a nap and never wants one. (Farmer)

has been reported that a red flower was found in the murdered woman's bosom, and Packer states that she wore a white flower. This is sufficiently easy of explanation since Packer does not say that the woman wore only a white flower, but that the attention was particularly drawn to the white flower from its standing out against the black of her dress, and the absence of the flower from her jacket when found by the police is unimportant in view of the evidence of Miss Harstein who subsequently saw fragments of it in the passage.

### WHERE THE MURDERER BOUGHT THE GRAPES.
### INTERVIEW WITH THE MAN WHO TALKED WITH HIM.
### (BY OUR SPECIAL COMMISSIONER.)

Last evening was far advanced when I walked into the greengrocer's little shop where the murdered woman was "treated" to some grapes, late on Saturday night, by the inhuman monster who shortly afterwards shed her blood with that revolting brutality peculiar to those now notorious murders. This shop is at No. 44 Berner street, and is kept by a quiet intelligent fruiterer named Matthew Packer, and his wife. They are both a little past the prime of life, and are known as respectable, hard working people. Their unpretending premises are situated just two doors from the scene of the murder, and the presumption of any mind of ordinary intelligence would be that it was the very first place at which the detectives and the police would have made their inquiries. They did nothing of the sort, as the man's simple, straightforward narrative will show.

### MATHEW PACKER'S STORY.

"Now, Mr. Packer, I want you to tell me all that you know about the events of Saturday night last," I said as I took the seat he offered me.

"Well, that's soon told," was his answer.

"I had been out with my barrow most of the day, but hadn't done much business; and as the night came on wet I went home and took the place of the 'missus' in the shop here."

### THE MURDERER AT THE WINDOW.

"Some time between half past eleven and twelve a man and woman came up Berner street from the direction of Ellen street, and stopped outside my window looking at the fruit. The man was about thirty to thirty five years of age, medium height, and with rather a dark complexion. He wore a black coat and a black, soft felt hat. He looked to me like a clerk or something of that sort. I am certain he wasn't what I should call a working man or anything like us folks that live around here."

### WHAT THE WOMAN WAS LIKE.

"Did you notice the woman so that you would know her again?"

"Yes. I saw that she was dressed in dark clothes, looked a middle aged woman, and carried a white flower in her hand. I saw that as plain as anything could be, and I am sure I should know the woman again. I was taken today to the see the dead body of a woman lying in Golden lane mortuary, but I can swear that wasn't the woman that stood at my shop window on Saturday night."

### THE SOUND OF THE ASSASSIN'S VOICE.

"Well, they hadn't stood there more than a minute when the man stepped a bit forward, and said, 'I say, old man, how do you sell your grapes.'"

"I answered, 'Sixpence a pound the black 'uns, sir, and fourpence a pound the white 'uns.'" Then he turned to the woman and said, 'Which will you have, my dear, black or white? You shall have whichever you like best.'"

"The woman said, 'Oh, then I'll have the black 'uns, 'cos they look the nicest.'"

"'Give us half a pound of the black ones, then,' said the man. I put the grapes in a paper bag and handed them to him."

"Did you observe anything peculiar about his voice or manner, as he spoke to you?"

"He spoke like an educated man, but he had a loud, sharp sort of voice, and a quick commanding way with him."

"But did he speak like an Englishman or more in this style?" I asked, imitating as well as I could the Yankee twang.

"Yes, now you mention it, there was a sound of that sort about it," was the instantaneous reply.

### THE MURDERER LAYING HIS PLANS.

"And what became of them after that?"

"First of all, they stood near the gateway leading into the club for a minute or two, and then they crossed the road and stood right opposite."

"For how long?"

"More than half an hour, I should say; so long that I said to my missus, 'Why, them people must be a couple o' fools to stand out there in the rain eating grapes they bought here, when they might just as well have had shelter! In fact, sir, me and my missus left 'em standing there when we went to bed."

"And what time was that?"

"I couldn't say exactly, but it must have been past midnight a little bit, for the public houses was shut up."

"And that was positively the last you saw of them?"

"Yes. Standing opposite the yard where the murdered woman was found."

"Well, Mr. Packer, I suppose the police came at once to ask you and your wife what you knew about the affair, as soon as ever the body was discovered."

"The police? No. They haven't asked me a word about it yet!!! A young man in plain clothes came in here on Monday and asked if he might look at the yard at the back of our house, so as to see if anybody had climbed over. My missus lent him some steps. But he didn't put any questions to us about the man and the woman."

"I am afraid you don't quite understand my question, Mr. Packer. Do you actually mean to say that no detective or policeman came to inquire whether you had sold grapes to any one that night? Now, please be very careful in your answer, for this may prove a serious business for the London police."

"I've only got one answer," said the man "because it's the truth. except a gentleman who is a private detective. No detective or policeman has ever asked me a single question nor come near my shop to find out if I knew anything about the grapes the murdered woman had been eating before her throat was cut!!!"

## MATTHEW PACKER
## THE BERNER STREET FRUITERER
## IDENTIFIES LIZZIE STRIDE.

This afternoon Matthew Packer, the fruiterer, of 44 Berner street, referred to in the above narrative, visited the mortuary of St. George's in the East, and identified the body of Elizabeth Stride as that of the woman for whom the grapes were purchased on the night of the murder.

In our next edition we shall give full details of this most important matter.

## AN EXCITING RUMOUR.

The Central News says: Passengers to the City from stations north and east of London were this morning greatly excited by the intelligence that "Jack the Ripper" had been captured. The story ran that at an early hour this morning a mounted patrol observed a suspicious looking character, and challenged him. The man immediately attacked him with a knife, slashing him in a dreadful manner but after a desperate struggle the constable succeeded in capturing him. A similar account was communicated to the police, but after telegraphing to all the stations in London, it was found that the story was an entire fabrication.

The rumour as to the arrest of the alleged murderer and the killing of a watchman no doubt originated in the same source as that which has been furnished by the Central News, namely, in the excited and panic stricken state of the public mind which nothing but the arrest of the murderer will calm. The immense services rendered by *The Evening News* today to the cause of justice, in placing before the authorities the information of we had exclusive knowledge, as regards the Berner street fruiterer, the selling of the grapes, and the identification of Lizzie Stride will, we do not doubt, be fully appreciated by our readers and, we may add, the London police.

———

## THE MITRE SQUARE MURDER.
## INQUEST THIS DAY.

At the City Mortuary, Golden lane, this morning, before Dr. Langham, the City Coroner, the inquest was opened on the body of the woman who was found murdered and horribly mutilated on Mitre square, Aldgate, at an early hour on Sunday morning. The deceased has been identified as an unmarried woman named Kate Eddowes, but she also passed by the names of Mrs. Conway and Mrs. Kelly.

The proceedings were watched on behalf of the authorities by Major Smith, Acting Commissioner of Police, Superintendent Forster, Detective Inspector McWilliams, and Mr. Crawford, the City solicitor.

The body of the Court was crowded.

Mr. Crawford: In this inquest I appear as the

# Thursday, 4 October, 1888

representative of the City for the purpose of rendering to you possible assistance, and if I consider it desirable to put any questions probably I shall have your permission.

The Coroner: By all means.

Eliza Gold, of No. 6 Thrall street, Spitalfields, widow, said:—I recognise the deceased as my poor sister. Her name was Catherine Eddowes, and she had never been married. Her age would be about 43. She had been living with a man named Kelly for some years. I last saw her alive about four or five months ago. She got her living by hawking, and was a woman of sober habits. Before living with Kelly she had lived with a man named Conway for some years, and had four children by him. I cannot say whether Conway is still living. He was an army pensioner, and used to go out hawking. I cannot say whether they parted on good or bad terms, and I can't say whether she has been in the habit of seeing him since. I have no doubt whatever that the deceased is my sister.

Mr. Crawford: When did you last see Conway?

—About seven or eight years ago.

Was she then on friendly terms with him?

—I believe so.

Did she live on friendly terms with Kelly?

—I believe so.

When did you last see them together?

—About a month or five weeks ago.

Did they then appear to be going on happily?

—Quite.

Where did you see them?

—At a common lodging house in Flower and Dean street.

And that was the last time you saw your sister?

—Yes.

The Coroner: You said before that you had not seen your sister for four or five months, and now you say you saw her three or four weeks ago. Which is right?

—I saw her about a month ago.

John Kelly said:—I live at 55 Flower and Dean street, and am a labourer, jobbing[187] about the markets. I have seen the body of the deceased, and recognise it as that of Catherine Conway. I have lived with her for the last seven years. She used to go about hawking in the streets. 55 Flower and Dean street is a common lodging house. I last saw her on Saturday afternoon, in Houndsditch. We parted there on very good terms. She said she was going to try and find a daughter in Bermondsey. I believe this was a daughter she had had by Conway. She promised me to be back not later than four o'clock, but she did not return. I heard afterwards that she had been locked up on the Saturday night. A woman who works in "the Lane"[188] told me this, and said she had seen her being taken to the station. I made no inquiries, as I supposed she had been locked up for taking a drop of drink.

The Coroner: Have you ever known her to go out for an immoral purpose?

—No, sir. I never knew her to do so.

Was she in the habit of drinking to excess?

—No, only slightly.

Then she was occasionally?

—Yes.

When you left her had she any money about her?

—No, sir.

Why did she go to see her daughter? Did she want to get money from her?

—Yes. I did not want to see her walking the streets all night.

What do you mean by "walking the street"?[189]

—Several times we have had to walk the streets all night together because we had not money to pay for our lodgings.

Were you without money at that time?

—Yes.

Do you know of anyone with whom she was at variance or was likely to injure her?

—No.

Do you know if she has seen Conway lately?

—No. I have never seen him.

Do you know if he is living?

—I cannot say.

---

[187] **Jobber.** 1. One who purchases goods in bulk and is the medium of their distribution, a middleman (1662). 2. One who does piece or occasional work (1658). (Farmer)

[188] **The Lane.** (1) Drury Lane Theatre; (2) Mincing Lane; (3) Mark Lane; (4) Chancery Lane; (5) Petticoat Lane, and (6) the old Horsemonger Lane Jail, now demolished: cf. Cade, House, Garden, etc. (ibid)

[189] **To walk the streets.** To frequent the streets for the purpose of prostitution; to make public quest for men. (ibid)

# Thursday, 4 October, 1888

Mr. Crawford: You say she had no money. Do you know with whom she had been drinking?

—No.

Has she on any recent occasion absented herself?

—No.

Saturday night was the first time for a long time?

—Yes.

When did she last leave you?

—Some months ago.

Why did she leave you?

—We had a few words.

How long did she remain away?

—Only a few hours.

Had you any angry conversation with her on Saturday?

—No.

Do you know where her daughter lived?

—She used to tell me that it was King street, Bermondsey.

When did she last ask her daughter for money?

—A year ago.

How long have you been living in this lodging house?

—Seven years.

On Friday night did you and deceased sleep together in this lodging house?

—No.

Was she walking the streets?

—No, she went into the casual ward in Mile End.

Did you sleep with deceased at the lodging house on any one night last week?

—No.

Where did you sleep on Monday night?

—I was hop picking in Kent, and deceased was with me on Monday, Tuesday and Wednesday. On Thursday night we both slept at Shoe lane Casual Ward.

The Coroner: Had you not earned any money?

—No, sir.

Mr. Crawford: What time did you part on Friday?

—About three or four in the afternoon.

Why did you part?

—She said she would go to Mile End Casual Ward, as we had not money for both our lodgings.

Have you heard that some tea and sugar were found upon her?

—Yes.

Where did she get that from?

—With some money which we got from pawning my boots.

When did you pawn them?

—On Saturday morning, for 2s 6d.

When she left you was she sober?

—Quite sober. We had a little drink, but I am positive she was sober.

During the last seven years do you know of anyone she has lived with beside yourself?

—No.

You never knew her indulge in immoral practices?

—Never.

She never brought money to you in the morning after being out all night?

—Never, sir.

Mr. Crawford called attention to the fact that, according to the pawn ticket, the boots were pawned on the Friday.

Witness said he was so muddled that he could not say whether the pawning took place on Friday or Saturday. It was one of those days. His "missus" pawned the boots and he stood outside in his bare feet. A juryman said if the pawning took place on the Friday it rather upset the theory that the deceased had to go to the casual ward on the Friday night because they had not money for a lodging.

Frederick William Wilkinson, deputy at 55 Flower and Dean street, said he had known the deceased as Mrs. Kelly for the last seven or eight years. She and the last witness passed as man and wife, and they always appeared on very good terms. They have had words occasionally when she had had a little drink, but they were never violent. He believed deceased got her living by hawking and cleaning amongst the Jews. Kelly paid for his lodgings pretty regularly. Deceased was not in the habit of drinking to excess, but she was a very jolly woman. He did not think he had ever seen Kelly drunk in his life. Last week he saw her for the first time on the Friday when they came back from hopping. She went away and he saw her again between ten and eleven on Saturday morning, along with Kelly. He had never heard of deceased walking the streets for an immoral purpose. She generally came to the lodging

298

house between 9 and 10 at night. He had never heard of her being intimate with any individual besides Kelly. She used to say that she had been married and that her proper name was Conway. He never knew her to be at variance with anyone. When Kelly paid for his own bed on Saturday night witness asked him,

"Where's Kate?" and Kelly said, "I hear she is locked up." He then took a single bed. A single bed is fourpence and a double bed eightpence.

By Mr. Crawford:

—I should think Kelly and deceased had not slept together at 55 Flower and Dean street for the last four or five weeks. I believe deceased was wearing an apron when I saw her on Saturday morning.

Did anyone come into your lodging house between one and two?

—I only remember two detectives coming about three o'clock.

Did not a stranger take a bed about two o'clock?

—I cannot recollect. I can tell from my books.

Mr. Crawford said he thought further examination of the witness ought to be postponed until the book was produced.

A Juryman (to witness)—Would you have trusted Kelly and deceased for their lodging on Friday night?

—Certainly.

Police constable Edward Watkins (881) said: —I was on duty at Mitre square on Saturday night. I have been in the City police for seventeen years. On Saturday night I went on duty at 9.45. My beat included Mitre square, and it took me about 12 or 14 minutes to cover the beat. I had continuously patrolled the beat from 10 on Saturday night until 1.44 o'clock on Sunday morning, and nothing had excited my attention. I passed through Mitre square at 1.30 on Sunday morning. I had my lamp fixed on my belt, and looked in the different corners, passages, and warehouses. At 1.30 nothing excited my attention, and I saw no one about. No one could have been in the square at that hour without my seeing them. I next went into Mitre square about 1.44, and entered it from the right from Mitre street. My attention was first attracted by the body of a woman, which was lying on its back. It was lying in the south west

corner. The feet faced the square. The clothes were up above the waist. Her throat was cut, and her bowels were protruding. The stomach was ripped up. She was lying in a pool of blood. I did not touch the body, but ran across the road to Messrs. Kearley and Tonge's warehouse and pushed the yard door open, and called for the watchman, a man named Morris. He came out and I sent him for assistance. I remained beside the body until the arrival of Police constable Holland. He was followed by Dr. Sequeira. Inspector Collard arrived about two with Dr. Browne, the police surgeon. When I entered Mitre square, at 1.44, I did not hear any sound of footsteps, and to the best of my belief when I entered the square I was the only person in it except for the unfortunate woman.

Mr. Frederick William Foster, of 26 Old Jewry, said he had made the plans produced. The direct route from Mitre square to the lodging house, 55 Flower and Dean street, would be by Gouldstone street, and the distance could be walked within a quarter of an hour. It would also take about a quarter of an hour from Berner street to Mitre square. Mr. Crawford, in answer to one of the jurymen, said evidence would be given later on that a portion of the deceased's apron was found in Gouldstone street.

The deputy (Wilkinson) recalled, said:—I have now got my lodging house book. It shows that on last Friday and Saturday nights Kelly slept in No. 52 bed. It does not show whether or not any one came in about two o'clock last Sunday morning. It would only show whether a bed was let at that time. There were six strange men sleeping in the house on Saturday night, but I cannot say whether any of them came in about two on Sunday morning. I cannot remember whether any stranger left the house about twelve on Saturday night. Nothing occurred to excite my suspicion.

By a Juryman:

—We never register the names of the lodgers, and we ask no questions. The house is closed about three in the morning.

(Inquest proceeding.)

# The Times

## THE EAST-END MURDERS.

Yesterday morning Mr. S. F. Langham, the City Coroner, opened the inquest at the mortuary in Golden-lane respecting the death of Catherine Eddows, otherwise Conway or Kelly, who was found murdered in Mitre-square, City, last Sunday morning.

Dr. Sedgwick Saunders, medical officer of health for the City; Mr. Crawford, the City Solicitor; Mr. M'William, the Inspector of the City Detective Department; and Mr. Superintendent Foster were present during the inquiry.

Mr. Crawford at the opening of the proceedings, stated that he was present as representing the City police, for the purpose of rendering the Coroner and the jury every possible assistance. If, when the witnesses were giving evidence, he thought it desirable to put any question, probably he would have the Coroner's permission to do so.

THE CORONER.—By all means.

Eliza Gold was the first witness. She stated that she lived at No. 6 Thrawl-street, Spitalfields, and was a widow. She recognized the deceased as her sister, whose name was Catherine Eddows. She was not married, but was living with a man named Kelly. Her sister had not been married. Her age last birthday was 43, as well as witness could remember. She had been living for some years with Kelly. Witness last saw her alive four or five months ago. She used to get her living by going out hawking. She was a woman of sober habits. Before she went to live with Kelly she had lived with a man named Conway for some years. She had had two children by him, who were married. Witness could not say whether Conway was still living; she had not seen him. Conway was a pensioner in the Army, who used to go out hawking things. Witness could not say whether her sister and Conway had parted on good or bad terms; nor could she say whether her sister had seen Conway since they parted. Witness was quite certain that the deceased was her sister.

By Mr. Crawford.—She had not seen Conway for seven or eight years, and she could not say on what terms her sister had lived with Kelly. She had not seen them together for three or four weeks. They were then living together quite happily. Witness could not exactly fix the time when she saw them. They were living at the time at 55, Flower and Dean-street, a common lodging-house kept by a man named Smith. The last time she saw her sister alive was when the latter visited witness, who was ill at the time.

A discrepancy in her evidence was pointed out to the witness, who had stated in one part that the last time she saw her sister alive was four or five months ago, whilst in another portion of her evidence she had stated that it was three or four weeks ago. The witness said it must have been three or four weeks ago.

John Kelly was the next witness called. He stated that he lived at 55, Flower & Dean-street, Spitalfields. He was a labourer and jobbed about the markets. He had seen and recognized the body of the deceased as Catherine Conway. Witness had known her seven years, and had lived with her the whole of that time. She used to sell things in the streets, and had lived with witness at the lodging-house in Flower and Dean-street. Witness was last with the deceased at 2 o'clock on Saturday afternoon in Houndsditch. They parted there on very good terms. She said she was going to see if she could find her daughter Annie in Bermondsey. He believed Annie was a daughter the deceased had had by Conway. She promised to be back at 4 o'clock and no later. She did not return, but witness heard that she was locked up on Saturday night at Bishopsgate. He was told by a woman that she had seen deceased in Houndsditch with two policemen. He could not say what time it was when he heard that statement. He did not make inquiries about her, feeling sure that she would return on Sunday morning. He heard that she had been locked up because she had had "a drop to drink." He did not know that she ever went out for immoral purposes; he had never allowed her to do so. She was not in the habit of drinking to excess, but occasionally she did so. She had no money about her when witness parted from her. Her object in going to Bermondsey was to see if she could find her daughter and get a little money from her, so that she did not need to walk the streets.

Mr. Crawford.—You were asked before if she walked the streets, and you said she did not.

—Sometimes we were without money to pay for our lodging, and we were at the time I speak of. Witness did not know of anyone with whom the deceased was at variance, or who would be

# Friday, 5 October, 1888

likely to do her an injury. He did not know whether the deceased had seen Conway of late; he had never seen Conway himself. He did not know when the deceased was discharged from custody.

By a Juryman.—She was in the habit of returning to her lodging at 8 or 9 o'clock. He had not inquired about her because he had felt sure that she would return on Sunday morning.

By Mr. Crawford.—He did not know with whom the deceased had been drinking on Saturday afternoon. She had not on any recent occasion absented herself at night time. Some time ago—a few months or weeks—she left witness; he supposed it was in consequence of their having had a few words, but she returned to him a few hours afterwards. He had had no angry words with the deceased on the Saturday afternoon. She had told him that her daughter lived in King-street, Bermondsey.

They had been living together for seven years in Flower and Dean-street. On Friday night she did not sleep with witness. She had no money and went to the casual ward at Mile-end. He slept that night at the lodging-house mentioned.

On the previous Monday night they slept in Kent, where they were hopping. They came up from Kent on Thursday, he believed. They had no money and they went to the casual ward in Shoe-lane.

They were together all Friday until the afternoon, when he earned 6d. She said to him, "You take 4d and go to the lodging-house, and give me 2d and I will go to the casual ward." He wanted to spend the money in food and he told her that, "Fred"—the deputy of the lodging-house—would not turn them away if they had no money. She said she would go to the casual ward at Mile-end, and would see him the following morning, when he met her acci-dentally. She left him at 4 o'clock on Friday afternoon to go to Mile-end for a lodging. He saw her the next morning about 8 o'clock, as well as he could remember, and was surprised to see her so soon.

The tea and sugar found on her had been bought out of the 2s. 6d. for which he had pawned his boots. When she left witness she was, he was sure, quite sober. They had spent the greater part of the 2s. 6d. in food and drink. They parted on good terms. He could not say why she separated from Conway. She had lived with witness for seven years.

When he saw her so early on the Saturday morning she told him that there had been some bother at the casual ward, and that that was why she had been turned out so soon. He did not know the regulations of the casual ward at Mile-end, and whether she could discharge herself when she liked.

By Mr. Crawford.—The boots were pawned on Friday or Saturday by the deceased. Witness remained outside the shop. He slept at the lodging-house in Flower and Dean-street on Saturday night. Mr. Crawford produced the pawn ticket, and stated that the boots were pledged last Friday.

Frederick William Wilkinson, living in Brick-lane, Spitalfields, was next examined.

He said he was deputy of the lodginghouse in Flower and Dean-street. He had known Kelly and the deceased for the last seven or eight years, and they passed as man and wife. They lived on very good terms, but they had a few words occasionally when "Kate was in drink".

Witness believed that deceased obtained her living by hawking things in the streets, and by charring. Whenever she and Kelly were at the lodginghouse they were pretty regular in paying. She was not often in drink, and was "a very jolly woman," often singing. Witness had never seen Kelly in drink since he had known him.

He saw the deceased on her return from hopping at the lodginghouse on Friday afternoon, but he did not see Kelly at the time. She went out on Friday night, and witness saw her on the following morning between 10 and 11 o'clock with Kelly. Witness did not see her again until he saw her in the mortuary.

To witness' knowledge the deceased had not been in the habit of walking the streets.

When she and Kelly stopped at the lodging-house they came in generally between 9 and 10.

He had never known or heard of her being intimate with anyone but Kelly. She used to say that her name was Kate Conway, and that it had been "bought and paid for," meaning that she was married to Conway.

So far as witness knew she was not at variance with anyone. She was quite sober when he saw her with Kelly on Saturday morning between 10 and 11. He asked Kelly when the latter came to pay for his lodging on Saturday where "Kate" was, and Kelly replied that he had heard that she had been locked up.

301

Kelly called between 7:30 and 8 on Saturday night and took a single bed. A single bed was 4d. and a double bed was 8d.

A juryman.—Do you not take the names of those who sleep at the lodginghouse?

—No.

By Mr. Crawford.

—He believed the last time the deceased and Kelly slept together at the lodginghouse was five or six weeks ago; before they went hopping. Kelly was there on Friday and Saturday nights. Deceased was not there on Friday or Saturday. He did not ask Kelly where she was on the Friday, and the reason why he asked the question on the Saturday night was because he had seen them together on that morning. Kelly went to bed at 10 o'clock on Saturday night, and witness was quite positive that he did not go out again. He could not say at what hour Kelly went out on Saturday, but he saw him at the lodginghouse at dinner-time. So far as he was aware, Kelly had had no quarrel with any man about the deceased. He believed she was wearing an apron on Saturday morning.

Mr. Crawford.—Did anyone come to your lodginghouse on the Sunday morning between 1 and 2 o'clock and take a bed; a stranger?

Witness.—I had no stranger there between 1 and 2.

Mr. Crawford.—Can you tell me who entered your lodginghouse on Sunday morning between 1 and 2?

Witness.—Two detectives came and asked if I had any female out.

Mr. Crawford.—Did any one come in before that, between 1 and 2 whom you did not recognize, and take a bed?

Witness.—I cannot remember. I can refer to my book and tell you whether any stranger was there.

By the jury.—I saw the deceased and Kelly together on Saturday morning between 10 and 11 at breakfast.

The examination of the witness was then adjourned to enable him to obtain the book referred to from the lodginghouse.

Edward Watkins, City Police-constable 881, was the next witness, and, in answer to Mr. Crawford, he stated that he had been in the City Police force for 17 years.

On the night of Saturday, September 29, he went on duty at a quarter to 10—on his regular beat. His beat extended from Duke-street, Aldgate, through Heneage-lane, a portion of Bury-street, through Cree Church-lane, into Leadenhall-street, along Leadenhall-street eastward into Mitre-street, into Mitre-square, round the square, and again into Mitre-street, then into and along King-street to St. James'-place, round St. James'-place and thence into Duke-street, the starting point. The beat took 12 or 14 minutes.

He had been continually patrolling that beat from 10 o'clock on Saturday night until 1:30 on Sunday morning without anything exciting his attention. He had passed through Mitre-square at about 1:30 on Sunday morning. He had his lantern fixed in his belt, and in accordance with his usual practice, he looked into the different corners, passages and warehouses. Nothing excited his attention at 1:30 nor did he see any one about. No one could have been in any portion of the square at that hour without the cognizance of the witness.

He next came into Mitre-square about 1:44. He fixed the time by reference to his watch after he had called the watchman. He entered the square from the right, near the corner, where something attracted his attention.

[Plans of the square made by Mr. F.W. Foster, of Old Jewry, were at this point handed in and referred to by Mr. Crawford in his examination.]

About 1:44 witness came into the square, at the right, and he then saw the body of the woman lying there. She was lying on her back, with her feet facing the square. He did not touch the body. The first thing he did was to go across to Messrs. Kearley and Tonge's warehouse. The door was ajar. He pushed it open and called to the watchman Morris. Morris came out, and witness sent him for assistance. Witness remained by the side of the body till the arrival of Police-constable Holland. No one was there with witness till Holland arrived, and he was followed by Dr. Sequeira. Inspector Collard arrived about 2, and Dr. Gordon Brown, surgeon to the City police force, followed.

When witness entered the square at 1:44 he heard nothing—no sound as of the footsteps of someone running away; and to the best of his belief no one was there but the murdered woman.

By the CORONER.

—The door of the warehouse of Messrs. Kearley and Tonge was open, as the watchman was working inside. It was not an unusual thing for the warehouse door to be open at that time.

By the Jury.

—He did not sound a whistle, because they did not carry whistles. The watchman did whistle. Witness's beat was a single beat; no other policeman entered Mitre-square.

Frederick William Foster, of 26, Old Jewry, stated that he was an architect and surveyor, and he had made the plans (produced) according to scale. He had them in three scales—one 8 ft. to an inch, another 200 ft. to an inch, from an Ordnance map of the City; and he had marked on an Ordnance map of the same scale round from Berner-street to Mitre-street. That would be a distance of about three-quarters of a mile; and it would take from 12 to 15 minutes to walk it.

By Mr. Crawford.

—The route described between Berner-street and Mitre-street was the nearest way. It was a direct line.

Mr. Crawford.—Assuming that a person was in Mitre-square, I want to know what route he would probably take, assuming that he passed by way of Goulston-street?

Witness.—There are two routes. There is only 10 ft. difference between them. One route is from Church-passage through Duke-street, crossing Houndsditch, through Gravel-lane, Stoney-lane, crossing Petticoat-lane, and through to Goulston-street. I know Flower and Dean-street.

Mr. Crawford.—Would a person, to get to the lodginghouse there from Mitre-square, go by Goulston-street?

Witness.—He might do so. It is the most direct course he could take if he knew the neighbourhood. He could do the distance in a quarter of an hour; and the distance from Berner-street to Mitre-street would be within a quarter of an hour.

Mr. Crawford, to the Coroner.—You will have evidence later on that a portion of this woman's apron was found in Goulston-street.

The witness Wilkinson was then re-called, and in answer to Mr. Crawford stated, referring to his book, that Kelly slept at the lodginghouse on Friday and Saturday night in "No. 52, single." Witness could not say at what time any stranger entered the place. He found that there were six male strangers there on the Sunday morning. He could not tell whether any of these men came in

about 2 o'clock on the Sunday morning, nor could he remember any one going out of the place soon after 12 o'clock, as that was a very busy time. He took the money and allotted the beds. Nothing excited his suspicion between the hours of 12 a.m. and 2. He recoll-ected the police calling at 3 o'clock on Sunday morning.

By a juryman.

—It was usual for the place to be open at 2 o'clock in the morning. They generally closed at 2:30 or 3. He had no means of remembering any person coming in. He would recognize a regular customer. He did not book the times they came in.

By Mr. Crawford.

—There was no register kept of the names of those sleeping there.

By the jury.

—We take the money of those who come. No questions are asked, and they are shown their beds. I dare say I have over 100 sleeping there now of a night.

Inspector Edward Collard (City Police) was the next witness called. He stated that at five minutes before 2 o'clock on Sunday morning last he received information at Bishopsgate-street Police-station that a woman had been murdered in Mitre-square. The information was at once telegraphed to headquarters, and he dispatched a constable at once to Dr. Gordon Brown.

Witness then proceeded himself to Mitre-square, arriving there at two or three minutes past 2. He there found Dr. Sequeira, several police-officers, and the deceased lying in the south-west corner of the square in the position described by Constable Watkins. The body was not touched until the arrival of Dr. Brown, who came shortly afterwards. The medical gentle-men then examined the body, and remained until the arrival of the ambulance, when the body was taken to the mortuary.

No money was found on the deceased. A portion of the apron produced was found on her, and the other portion, which was picked up in Goulston-street, would also be produced.

When witness arrived at the square he took immediate steps to have the neighbourhood searched for the person who had committed the murder. Mr. M'William, the chief of the detectives, on his arrival shortly afterwards with a number of detectives, sent them to make search in all directions in Spitalfields, both in the streets and the lodging-houses. Several men were stopped and searched in the streets, but without any good result. Witness had a house-to-house inquiry made in the vicinity of Mitre-square, but could find out nothing beyond what would be stated by two witnesses who would be called.

By Mr. Crawford.

—There was no appearance of any struggle having taken place, and there was no blood anywhere except what had come from the deceased's neck. There was nothing whatever in the appearance of the deceased or her clothing to lead him to suppose that there had been a struggle. The blood flowing from her was in a liquid state, not congealed, and from his experience he should say that the body had not been there for more than a quarter of an hour. They endeavoured to find footmarks, but they could discover no trace whatever. A search was made at the back of the empty houses adjoining the square.

Dr. Frederick Gordon Brown, of 17, Finsbury-circus, examined, said he was surgeon of the City of London Police Force. He was called on Sunday morning shortly after 2 o'clock, and reached Mitre-square about 18 minutes after 2, when his attention was called to the body of the deceased.

It was lying in the position described by Constable Watkins. The body was on its back, the head turned towards the left shoulder, and the arms were by the side of the body, as if they had fallen there. Both palms were upwards and the fingers were slightly bent. A thimble was lying on the ground near the right hand. The clothes were drawn up, the left leg was extended straight down, in a line with the body, and the right leg was bent at the thigh and knee.

There was great disfigurement of the face. The throat was cut across, and below the cut was a neckerchief. The upper part of the dress had been pulled open a little way.

The abdomen was all exposed; the intestines were drawn out to a large extent and placed over the right shoulder; a piece of the intestines was quite detached from the body and placed between the left arm and the body.

Mr. Crawford.—By "placed," do you mean put there by design?

Witness.—Yes.

Mr. Crawford.—Would that also apply to the intestines that were over the right shoulder?

Witness.—Yes.

Examination continued.—The lobe of the right ear was cut obliquely through; there was a quantity of clotted blood on the pavement, on the left side of the neck and upper part of the arm. The body was quite warm, and no death-stiffening had taken place. The body had been there only a few minutes.[190]

By Mr. Crawford.

—Certainly within 30 or 40 minutes.

Examination continued.—We looked for superficial bruises and saw none. There were no marks of blood below the middle of the body.

By Mr. Crawford.

—There was no blood on the front of the clothes. Before they removed the body he suggested that Dr. Phillips should be sent for, and that gentleman, who had seen some recent cases, came to the mortuary.

A post mortem examination was made at 2:30 on Sunday afternoon. The temperature of the room was 55 deg. Rigor mortis was well marked.[191]

After careful washing of the left hand a recent bruise, the size of a sixpence,[192] was discovered on the back of the hand between the thumb and the first finger. There were a few small bruises on the right shin of older date. The hands and arms were bronzed as if by sunburning. There were no bruises on the scalp, back of the body, or elbows.

The witness then described in detail the cuts on the face, which, he stated, was very much mutilated. The throat was cut across to the extent of about 6 in. or 7 in. The sterno cleido mastoid

---

[190] The morning low of 30 September was 43.5°F. (Casebook)

[191] According to forensic pathologist Dr. D. Rao, "In ... violent death as by cut-throat, firearms or by electrocution, the onset of rigor is early and duration is short. ... In deaths from asphyxia, severe haemorrhage, ... the onset is delayed. The onset is slow and duration long in cold weather. The onset is rapid due to heat, because of the increased breakdown of ATP (Adenosine Triphosphate) but the duration is short. If the body is in an extremely hot environment and decomposition begins, rigor mortis may disappear in 12 hours after death. it may persist for 3 to 4 days in refrigerated conditions." (Rao)

[192] My 1890 six-pence is .76 in. (19.31mm) in diameter.

# Friday, 5 October, 1888

muscle[193] was divided; the cricoid cartilage[194] below the vocal chords was severed through the middle; the large vessels on the left side of the neck were severed to the bone, the knife marking the intervertebral[195] cartilage. The sheath of the vessels on the right side was just open; the carotid artery had a pin-hole opening; the internal jugular vein was open to the extent of an inch and a half—not divided.

All the injuries were caused by some very sharp instrument, like a knife, and pointed. The cause of death was haemorrhage from the left common carotid artery. The death was immediate. The mutilations were inflicted after death.

They examined the injuries to the abdomen. The walls of the abdomen were laid open, from the breast downwards. The cut commenced opposite the ensiform cartilage,[196] in the centre of the body. The incision went upwards, not penetrating the skin that was over the sternum; it then divided the ensiform cartilage, and being gristle they could tell how the knife had made the cut.

It was held so that the point was towards the left side and the handle towards the right. The cut was made obliquely.

The liver was stabbed as if by the point of a sharp knife. There was another incision in the liver, about 2½ in., and below, the left lobe of the liver was slit through by a vertical cut. Two cuts were shown by a jag of the skin on the left side.

The abdominal walls were divided vertically in the middle line to within a quarter of an inch of the navel; the cut then took a horizontal course for 2½ in. to the right side; it then divided the navel on the left side—round it—and then made an incision parallel to the former horizontal incision, leaving the navel on a tongue of skin. Attached to the navel was 2½ in. of the lower

part of the rectus muscle[197] of the left side of the abdomen. The incision then took an oblique course to the right.

There was a stab of about an inch in the left groin, penetrating the skin in superficial fashion. Below that was a cut of 3 in., going through all tissues, wounding the peritoneum[198] to about the same extent. There had not been any appreciable bleeding from the vessels.

Mr. Crawford.—What conclusion do you draw from that?

Witness.—That the cut in the abdomen was made after death, and that there would not be much blood left to escape on the hands of the murderer. The way in which the mutilation had been effected showed that the perpetrator of the crime possessed some anatomical knowledge.

Mr. Crawford.—I think I understood you to say that in your opinion the cause of death was the cut in the throat?

Witness.—Loss of blood from the throat, caused by the cut. That was the first wound inflicted.

Mr. Crawford.—Have you formed any opinion that the woman was standing when that wound was inflicted?

Witness.—My opinion is that she was on the ground.

Mr. Crawford.—Does the nature of the wounds lead you to any conclusion as to the kind of instrument with which they were inflicted?

Witness.—With a sharp knife, and it must have been pointed; and from the cut in the abdomen I should say the knife was at least six inches long.

Mr. Crawford.—Would you consider that the person who inflicted these wounds possessed great anatomical skill?

Witness.—A good deal of knowledge as to the position of the organs in the abdominal cavity and the way of removing them.

Mr. Crawford.—Could the organs removed be used for any professional purpose?

Witness. —They would be of no use for a

---

[193] **Sternocleidomastoid Muscles**. Located on each side of the throat, they are anchored to the top of the Sternum and to each side of the Mandible, forming a V shape. (Miller)

[194] **Cricoid Cartilage.** A ringlike cartilage forming the lower and back part of the Larynx. (ibid)

[195] **Intervertebral**. Between two vertebrae. (ibid)

[196] **Ensiform Cartilage**. The Xiphoid (sword-shaped) Process is "the pointed process of cartilage, supported by a core of bone, connected with the lower end of the body of the sternum." (ibid)

[197] **Rectus Abdominis**. Straight (Rectus) muscle of the abdomen. The "Abs." (ibid)

[198] **Peritoneum**. The serous membrane lining the walls of the abdominal and pelvic cavities (Parietal Peritoneum) and investing contained viscera (Visceral Peritoneum), the two layers enclosing a potential space, the Peritoneal Cavity. (ibid)

professional purpose.

Mr. Crawford.—You have spoken of the extraction of the left kidney. Would it require great skill and knowledge to remove it?

Witness.—It would require a great deal of knowledge as to its position to remove it. It is easily overlooked. It is covered by a membrane.

Mr. Crawford.—Would not such knowledge be likely to be possessed by one accustomed to cutting up animals?

Witness.—Yes.

Mr. Crawford.—Have you been able to form any opinion as to whether the perpetrator of this act was disturbed when performing it?

Witness.—I think he had sufficient time. My reason is that he would not have nicked the lower eyelids if he had been in a great hurry.

Mr. Crawford.—About how long do you think it would take to inflict all these wounds, and perpetrate such a deed?

Witness.—At least five minutes would be required.

Mr. Crawford.—Can you as a professional man assign any reason for the removal of certain organs from the body?

Witness.—I cannot.

Mr. Crawford.—Have you any doubt in your mind that there was no struggle?

Witness.—I feel sure that there was no struggle.

Mr. Crawford.—Are you equally of the opinion that the act would be that of one man, one person, only?

Witness.—I think so; I see no reason for any other opinion.

Mr. Crawford.—Can you as a professional man account for the fact of no noise being heard by those in the immediate neighbourhood?

Witness.—The throat would be so instantaneously severed that I do not suppose there would be any time for the least sound being emitted.

Mr. Crawford.—Would you expect to find much blood on the person who inflicted the wounds?

Witness.—No, I should not.

Mr. Crawford.—Could you say whether the blood spots on the piece of apron produced were of recent origin?

Witness.—They are of recent origin. Dr. Phillips brought on a piece of apron which had been found by a policeman in Goulston-street.

Mr. Crawford.—Is it impossible to assert that it is human blood?

Witness.—Yes; it is blood. On the piece of apron brought on there were smears of blood on one side as if a hand or a knife had been wiped on it. It fitted the piece of apron in evidence.

Mr. Crawford.—Have you formed any opinion as to the purpose for which the face was mutilated?

Witness.—Simply to disfigure the corpse, I should think.

Mr. Crawford.—Not much violence was required to inflict these injuries?

Witness.—A sharp knife was used, and not very much force would be required.

By a juryman.

—He did not think any drug was administered to the woman, judging from the breath; but he had not yet examined the contents of the stomach.

At this point the inquiry was adjourned for a week.

Mr. Crawford said that it might be of interest for the jury to know that the Court of Common Council had unanimously adopted the suggestion of the Lord Mayor that a reward of £500 should be offered for the detection and conviction of the murderer.

The jury expressed satisfaction at the announcement.

—

## TO THE EDITOR OF THE TIMES.

Sir,—Perhaps you will allow me to suggest that the murderer's object may be—first, by his crimes to cause a reward to be offered, and then by the accusation of an innocent man, and by the manufacture of apparent tokens of guilt against him (as by staining his clothes with blood), to win that reward. A second Titus Oates is not impossible.[199] I remain, Sir, your obedient servant,                                        H.P.B.

40, Mostyn-road, Brixton, S.W., Oct. 3.

---

[199] **Titus Oates** (1649-1705). English clergyman that fabricated the Popish Plot, an imaginary plan by the Jesuits to assassinate Charles II, which resulted in the execution of 22, or more, innocent men between 1678 and 1681. Oates was finally convicted of perjury in 1685, whipped publicly and imprisoned for three years. The presiding judge, George Jeffreys, 1st Baron of Wem, stated that he regretted he could not have Oates executed.

# Friday, 5 October, 1888

## 𝔗𝔥𝔢 𝔖𝔱𝔞𝔯

**POINTS ABOUT THE MURDERS.**
**Letters to the "Star" from People with Theories about the Murders.**

H. Thomas thinks the murderer may be a seafaring man, employed in a coasting or short journey boat, living and sleeping on board. The intervals between the murders are just about the time a collier or trading boat takes for a trip. And how easy for a sailor man to get on board his boat at any time during the night unseen, and remove with a bucket of water all traces of his guilt! Could it not be ascertained by reference to a shipping paper what boats were in London on all the dates of the murders, and if a boat was in port on each of those days, and away in the interval?

"E.A.V.," who favours the police theory, remarks:—After the first three murders these wretched women would probably have thought twice before going up a dark passage or into a dark yard with a perfect stranger. But this man they know, they follow him willingly and unsuspectingly; possibly they are anxious even to court his good graces and tolerance; for if not a member of, he is at least allied to the great army of order, and could have them "run in" if they did not prove compliant. May there not be some obscure police agent—hardly a plain clothes constable—but rather some needy detective, some "nose," as people of the kind are called—who is domiciled in or about Whitechapel, who is physically circumstanced in the manner described by Mr. Forbes?

It is the belief of "R. J. B." that the murderer goes down sewer manholes.

"Perplexed One" asks:—Is it possible that the murderer carries slips for putting on his arms like the waiters, and an apron to get all the splashes on?

"Success" thinks all persons who let lodgings to single men should be asked to take notice of the time their lodgers come home of a night, and their general habits.

"J.B.P." advises the police to look to the West, not to the East. With an experience of Bohemian life in Chambers, he knows how easy it is to isolate oneself from observation.

"A.W." thinks the French secret police system should be immediately adopted here.

"E.L.G.M." advises that detectives, disguised as women and protected with steel, should traverse the streets watched all through the night by police from house windows.

J.P. Vooght[200] suggests that the books in which every house and family is scheduled by the officers of the School Board for London should be utilised in the search for suspicious characters.

E. Hunt thinks the authorities are tempting the murderer to commit a crime in another district by drawing off all the police to Whitechapel.

"Primrose League,"[201] who says he is "a strong Tory," complains of the disgraceful apathy of the Home Secretary.

Robert Walker has come to the conclusion that the murderer is either a police-constable out of uniform, or is an ex-policeman, who has had some surgical education and has a grievance, and that the motive is to bring the present police system into disrepute.

William Douglas says pigs resemble inwardly the human race, and are slaughtered quickly, the first cut being made at the throat and the next at the abdomen. He thinks no one but a pig-killer could have perpetrated these murders.

"A Labourer" fancies the murderer as much likely to be a woman as a man, jealousy being the motive.

"J.P.F.," a butcher of 30 years' standing, protests against the slaughterman theory. He declares that thorough butchers are most humane men.

### What Can Be Done?

The suggestion of Edwin J. Wells, of Brixton, is that the police should be provided with some

---

[200] According to the 21 February, 1889 entry in the <u>Minutes of Proceedings</u>, Volume 30 of the London School Board., "Mr. J.P. Vooght, 99, Grayshott-road, Lavender Hill, S.W., be, and he is hereby, appointed an additional Manager of the Battersea Group of Evening Classes." He is also named in <u>The India List and India Office List</u> as being a 2nd Class Messenger for the India Audit Office in 1898 and as a 1st Class Messenger for the same department in 1905.

[201] **Primrose League.** Founded in 1883 by admirers of Benjamin Disraeli, whose favourite flower was the primrose, the league promoted conservative values and backed the Tory Party. It was disbanded in December, 2004. The motto of the Primrose league was "Imperium et Libertas".

# Friday, 5 October, 1888

sort of magnesium light, by which, on any alarm, they could flash a bright light on the dark places where the murderer walks.

"J. M.," who lives in Whitechapel, urges that the police authorities should take a census of all private houses in London that take in lodgers, with as near a description and occupation of the lodgers as possible, and then should thoroughly investigate every case where there is the least resemblance to the description of the man that is wanted.

Samuel Julius suggests a house-to-house visitation over an area of six or seven miles.

"H.F.," who has often had to walk from Stratford to the City between two a.m. and four a.m., says that from Bow Church to Houndsditch the road has been deserted except by an occasional tramp and by five or six couples—not more. Surely such a limited number of couples could be closely watched.

The regularity of a policeman's round and the heaviness of his tread are pointed out by Henry Knott, of Stamford, as likely to assist the murderer, and he suggests the wearing of indiarubber soles, and the variation of the policeman's beat.

"One who is Shocked" considers there cannot be a better opportunity than is now offered for the use of bloodhounds. Let the dogs take the scent of the piece of apron and trace the man.

When the Queen[202] opened the People's Palace (writes a correspondent) hundreds of Army Reserve men were sworn in to act as special constables. Why should there not be a quantity put on duty in the murder area?

"Trafalgar Square" thinks a public meeting should press on the Government the absolute necessity of replacing our present military Chief Commissioner by a police officer who can think of something besides Trafalgar-square.

From Wiesbaden, Ned Hay writes:—It is morally certain that there are living women who

have escaped after having been completely in the power of the murderer, owing to the sudden appearance of the police or some other person upon the scene. The women who have been accosted and escaped certainly ought to be able to give some clue to the murderer's identity.

### What the Police Do.
P. James, of Bolivia House, Wandsworth, was stopped in Commercial-street, yesterday afternoon by two policemen, who told him their suspicions had been aroused by the fact that he had been looking down courts and alleys. They questioned him, and he purposely answered them in a hesitating manner, saying he was looking for a firm of glass writers. Finally one constable said to the other, "I suppose it's all right, come along." P. James says: "The Whitechapel fiend need not fear capture if they do 'business' like this."

### Matthews' Bumps.
Because the victims are lost sheep, writes F. Thornburn, from Airdrie, Scotland, the Government are slumbering, while London, and even the provinces, are in a panic. How long are we going to stand this imbecility? If Matthews were to get his head examined, I fear the phrenologist[203] would pronounce "causality" very deficient, and "stubbornness" as large as it is on the head of the mule.

### Bringing the Moral Home.
"An Observer" writes from Southampton: —In the lives and positions in the social scale of the victims we have a heartrending picture of a vain struggle to act honestly and uprightly, and the ultimate sacrifice of the body in order to earn its right to shelter from the cold and pitiless night. Whose fault is it that the people are herded and packed in loathsome dens? Who builds and furnishes the flaring gin palaces which beckon and lure the cold and shivering wretch at every step? Who are the seducers of women, and why should women bear the sole blame of that which they equally share with their male accomplices? What a nation of hypocrites we are!

### A Sham Drunkard.
The correspondent who advanced the slaughterman theory, and defended it with much sagacity, declares that it is now strengthened.

---

[202] Although the Queen's Hall concert venue of the **People's Palace** on Mile-End Road was officially opened by Queen Victoria 14 May, 1887, the complex as a whole was not finished until 1892. When completed, the people of East London could now enjoy facilities for education, culture, sport, training and recreation. The original People's Palace burned in 1931 and a replacement was built nearby in 1936. In 1954 it was integrated into Queen Mary College. (Theatres Trust)

[203] **Phrenology.** Study of the faculties and qualities of the mind from the shape of the skull. (Miller)

308

# Friday, 5 October, 1888

Doctors do their work in the dissecting room with minuteness and care; slaughtermen theirs with expedition. They are paid for their quickness, and one slaughterman can dress a sheep, *i.e.*, skin, disembowel, and remove the heart, liver, and lungs in a quarter of an hour; a quick man in 10 minutes. Our correspondent adds:—It is suggested, but it is more than probable that

**THE MURDERER APES DRUNKENNESS**
when in search of his victims. For these reasons:

1. To induce the women to make advances to him, as such women consider drunken men their legitimate prey as they are their most lucrative customers.

2. To lull suspicion and fear in the woman.

3. To lull the suspicion of the police and passengers.

4. To lull the suspicion of his friends and those in whose house he lives.

It is absolutely clear that the man who commits these crimes is perfectly sober when he commits them. He has probably always been sober, and if he has put on the habit of frequent drinking (as he would have to be "on the drink" on other nights than just those of the murder) this would have been done at some time directly after or shortly before the first murder. The time of such a change in a man's apparent habits is a factor in identification.

The man we want is not a slinking peculiar, solitary, un-genial person. To such a one suspicion would have attached before now. The man is of quiet if not amiable manners, and even probably a jolly companion.

While the weak eyes of the police are fixed on Texas villains and American millionaires, let the people of Whitechapel turn the eyes of their minds on their closest and most intimate friends, and in their own circle look for a man who unites in himself the following qualifications:—

1. A man who is a slaughterman.
2. Who lives in Whitechapel.
3. Who is a Volunteer.[204]

4. Who was in uniform, and carrying a bayonet on 7 Aug.

5. Who was not in uniform on 3 April.

6. Who was a sober man till the beginning of these crimes, but then apparently took to drink and to being "out on the booze."

7. Who is respectable, and the "last man one would suspect."

One of these facts would count for nothing. Two or three in conjunction would be worth consideration—but we venture to think there are not many men in London to whom all these will apply.

—

### The Persecution of Pizer.

At Thames Police-court, yesterday, John Pizer, who was arrested on suspicion of being connected with the murder of Annie Chapman in Hanbury-street, and who gave—as the Coroner said—a perfectly satisfactory account of himself, complained to Mr. Lushington that since he was released from custody he had been subjected to great annoyance. Only that morning a woman accosted him in the street, and after calling him "Old Leather Apron" and other insulting expressions, struck him three blows in the face. Mr. Lushington told Pizer he could have a summons against the person who had assaulted him.

### The Grape Story.

The grape story is effectually disposed of by

---

[204] **Volunteer Force.** Formed in 1859, the Volunteer Force was a response to the war scare that had developed after the attempted assassination of French Emperor Napoleon III on 14 January, 1858 with a bomb that had been made in Birmingham. Organized into 100 man corps under the command of a captain, the first groups were rifle companies formed by enthusiast that had been affiliated with local shooting clubs. Later artillery and engineer corps were formed. Members purchased their own uniforms and weapons, but received military pay when on duty. In 1861 the company sized corps were consolidated and reorganized into battalions. Until 1872 the Volunteer's were under the control of the county lord-lieutenants, in that year they passed under control of the Secretary of State for War. The Childers Reforms of 1881 attached the Volunteer Battalion to the new County Regiments These ne Volunteer Battalions usually adopted the distinctive uniform of their parent regiments, further integrating them into the British Army. The Volunteer Force and the Yeomanry (volunteer cavalry) were combined to form the Territorial Force in 1908, which became the Territorial Army in 1920. According to the *Territorial Year Book 1909,* the Volunteer Force had a total strength of 224,012 in 1885.

the statement of the authorities at Leman-street to a *Star* reporter. In the first place the police have no evidence that any grapes were found on the site of the Berners-street murder, and, moreover, Dr. Phillip's post mortem disclosed no trace of grapes or grapestones in Elizabeth Stride's stomach.

~

## Evening News
### THE EDITOR'S DRAWER.
### THE WHITECHAPL MURDERS.
### TO THE EDITOR OF
### "THE EVENING NEWS."

Sir—Having resided for nearly ten years in America, and having carefully examined the facsimile letters you published this afternoon from "Jack the Ripper," I have not the slightest hesitation in saying they are written by an American, or by a person who had resided many years in the States. They are full of Americanisms from beginning to the end, such as boss, fix me, right track, real fits, shan't quit, squeal, fit enough, give it out straight, right away. Many of these expressions are in constant use by all classes of Americans, but never by Englishmen. This fact might become important in tracing the assassin.

I am, &c.,
S.F.G.
October 4.

### TO THE EDITOR OF
### "THE EVENING NEWS."

Sir—Having read the story of Messrs. Grand and Batchelor, published in your columns last evening, with reference to the interview with Matthew Packer, I beg to state that I have very carefully perused and compared the remarks to him by the man who bought the grapes for the Mitre square victim with the facsimile of the letter and postcard from "Jack the Ripper," and I can trace without a doubt a perfect sequence between the alleged murderer's utterances and the bloodstained missive. I observe strong features of Americanism both in the phraseology of the man seen by Packer and the calligraphy of "Jack the Ripper." The spasmodic style of the letters, and the sound and general delivery of the assassin's voice, as described by Packer, appear to me to be identical. Although at first I viewed

with incredulity the theory that the bloodstained communications were the work of the assassin, I am now completely satisfied in my own mind that the self designated "Jack the Ripper" is the perpetrator of the murderous deeds assigned to him, and, moreover, I consider, after examining the matter in every possible phase, that the culprit is a monomaniac of a homicidal tendency. Your publication of last evening has one good service, and will afford graphologists[205] an opportunity of expressing their opinions.

I am, &c.,
C.H.L.
October 4.

—

### THE MITRE SQUARE MURDER.
### A NIGHT IN THE VICTIM'S DOSS HOUSE.
### (BY OUR SPECIAL CORRESPONDENT.)

Cold and rain were venting their combined discomforts upon my scantily protected frame, as I turned out of Whitechapel road into Commercial street about nine o'clock last night. The severity of the weather was such as to force even the most miserable outcast to seek some sort of shelter, but my quest was in the particular direction of the lodging house in Flower and Dean street, where the unfortunate victim of the Mitre square tragedy had been used to put up. In a short time I reached Flower and Dean street, and shuddered from other sensations than cold as I looked down its long, narrow, dingy looking precincts, wrapped, as they appeared to be, in an atmosphere of notorious and murky mystery. There is little light in the street save that thrown from the windows of the houses. At the south west end of the thoroughfare is a large block of model dwellings whose plain, but well ordered archi-tecture lends a welcome sense of relief to the shamble like structures around.

With the exception of the model dwellings almost if not every house in Flower and Dean street is given up to accommodation of the lodging house order, and above the doors are inscriptions setting forth the licensed authority of the proprietors to let "good beds" or "well aired beds" to "single men and travellers." I had some difficulty in finding the particular house I

---

[205] **Graphologist**. A Practitioner of **Graphology**, the study of handwriting as an expression of indication of character. (Miller)

# Friday, 5 October, 1888

was in search of—No. 55—as there were either no numbers on the doors, or they were invisible in the darkness. At last, however, I struck a number 48, and by counting the houses in succession, I came to what was certainly the most commodious place of the kind in the street—my uncertain movements, by the way, being the subject of the attention of several denizens of the unsavoury quarter. On inquiring of an unkempt, bedraggled looking young woman who was standing at the door whether that was No. 55, I received an answer in the affirmative, and, telling her that I wanted a bed for the night, she conducted me to the "deputy" with the invitation, "All right, guv'nor, this way." Opening the half side of the folding doors, I found myself immediately in a capacious kitchen filled with men, women and children of all ages, and redolent with the fumes of cooked dishes and boiling tea. The deputy sat in a pay box at the entrance, and without any questions booked me a single bed at the modest sum of fourpence. Having paid my coppers, I walked up the large square-built kitchen to one of the two glowing coke fires at the top of the room. Turning to survey the surroundings, I found that divested, even as I was, of all the chief habiliments of respectability, I was regarded as an object of interest. But, after a time, the curiosity of my companions soon exhausted itself, and I was able to enter into conversation with several of the men and women standing around the fire. Naturally the main subject of interest among the lodgers was the murders. Newspapers were being read aloud by several of the occupants to eagerly listening knots, and conspicuous among this class of literature was the pink "extra special" of the *Evening News*. The details of the paper were enthusiastically discussed and various theories were advanced as to the personality and motive of the perpetrator of the outrages. There was, of course, a general chorus of denunciations against the unknown criminal in language more expressive than refined.

Occasionally, for the sake of controversy only, I suppose, some cynical member of the company would interpolate a note of dissent to the observations of the revenge party, but he was speedily silenced by howls of indignation or ridicule. One frivolous individual desired that the subject should be changed to something more lively, and proposed that they should discuss "the play." Another declared that "it would be a crying sin to capture the murderer, who was doing a good work in putting so many women out of the way. He reckoned the murderer was a toff[206] and deserved to get off." But he was told by what appeared to be the smart man of the place that "they all knew he was balmy, and that his brains had gone out for an excursion." As the evening wore on and newcomers entered the kitchen, the conversation drifted in various directions, but it all hinged on the one great question of the moment. I ventured to ask for Kelly, the man with whom the murdered woman had been living, but I was told that he had retired to bed early in the evening, being greatly upset at the events of the past few days. Kelly and the woman seem to have had a sincere attachment for each other, and one young fellow told me that since had viewed the body at the mortuary—when he fainted away—Kelly had seemed quite "off his head" and shown signs of an inclination "to do away with himself."

"Kate" herself was undoubtedly a universal favourite among her acquaintances at the lodging house. "Ah, she was a good sort, I know," said one man, "and often gave me the price of my kip[207] when I was short of a night." "Yes, she was a good sort," agreed a burly looking matron standing by, "and I wish she were 'ere now a-putting down her teapot, as she used to do, along wi' us." Kate's friends in Flower and Dean street strongly resented the idea that she was woman of immoral character, and claimed that she was as true as any wife could be to Kelly. "Kate was a decent woman," said one of the females, "and worked for the Jews; that's how she got her living; she never did any harm in her life." And this apparently was the general opinion entertained of the unfortunate woman's character.

An old woman, who was known by the

---

[206] **Toff.** 1. A gentleman, a fop, a swell (q.v.) : ct Toft and Tuft. 2. A superior, a man of grit. Hence toffer, a fashionable whore; tofficky, dressy, showy, gritty (q.v.): toffishness, side (q.v.). (Farmer)

[207] **Kip.** A brothel. *To tatter a kip*, to wreck a house of ill-fame (1766). 2. A bed. As verb, (1) to play truant, do dolly ; (2) to sleep, lodge. (ibid)

sobriquet of "Mother Crack'em"[208] rather startled me by rushing up as I stood at the fireplace and demanding to know if I was "Jack the Ripper." The awkwardness of answering this question I was happily relieved of by the old dame herself assuring me that she did not think I was. "I know you ain't him," she said, "you wouldn't rip me up, would you now? You'd rather give me the fourpence for my doss, but I don't want it, and if you want a cup of tea I'll go and get a farthing's worth of tea and a farthing's worth of sugar, and you shall have a cup." And so the old woman went on with her meaningless but innocent jabber, and I was spared any further attention at her hands by the interference of a number of the other lodgers, who seemed to make her a butt for hilarious horseplay and ridicule, all of which she took in the most good natured way.

A striking evidence of the effect of the murders upon the women of this district was shown in the fact that every one of them in the house declared that they would not venture out in the streets at night after dark. "I ain't going out at night," said one of them who informed that she was the mother of a family. "God knows, it might be my fate to meet him if I was to go out tonight, and I don't want to go just yet. I want to see my boy who is in the 60th's on the rock of Gibraltar before I die, and then to die a natural death." There was one woman amongst them more daring than the rest. She was a dishevelled and dilapidated looking spectacle wrapped in what seemed to be but a bundle of rags. It was evident that she had no money, as she was wishing to Heaven someone would stand her half a pint of beer. As the desire was not gratified, she resolutely tied up her boots, and saying "she would risk it," walked hurriedly out of the kitchen into the street, regarded with something like awe by those who stayed behind.

By and by, the proceedings in the kitchen became more lively. There was very little drunkenness visible. I only saw one man the worse for liquor, and even he would not have been noticed but for his falling from his reclining position on a seat to the floor with a thud. Girls commenced singing songs, and the "poet of the company" entertained the room with quotations from Shakespeare and from his own composition, the latter bearing chiefly upon the horrible murder of the day. This is the chorus of what he called his latest:

"'As any one seen him,
can you tell us where he is,
If you meet him
you must take away his knife,
Then give him to the women,
they'll spoil his pretty phiz,[209]
And I wouldn't give him twopence
for his life."

As the time wore on the place became quieter, and one by one or in couples the lodgers retired to their beds in the rooms above where about perhaps a hundred of the most degraded and poverty stricken people in the great Metropolis sleep upon the deeds—more or less honest—of the day.

—

## THE MURDERS.
## STARTLING NEWS FROM NEW YORK.
## AN ENGLISH SAILOR'S STORY.
## ALASKA, THE MALAY COOK.
## (CENTRAL NEWS TELEGRAM.)

New York, Friday morning.

The atrocious crimes committed in Whitechapel have raised intense interest here. The following statement has been made here by an English sailor named Dodge:

He says he arrived in London from China on August 13, by the steamship Glenorlie.[210] He met at the Queen's Music hall, Poplar, a Malay cook, named Alaska.

The Malay said he had been robbed by women of bad character in Whitechapel of two years' savings, and he said that unless he found the woman and recovered his money, he would murder and mutilate every Whitechapel woman he met.

He showed Dodge a double edged knife, which he always carried with him.

He was about five feet seven in height, one hundred and thirty pounds in weight, and

---

[208] **Crack**. 1. A crazy person: softhead (1609). Verb, 1. To talk to, boast. [The verb was once good English, and in the sense of to talk or gossip is still good Scots. The modern form to crack up, is well within the borderland between literary and colloquial English (1597). (Farmer)

---

[209] **Phiz** (Phyz, or Physog). The face (1693).
[210] I could find no ship named Glenorlie, but see footnote #215, p. 324.

apparently thirty five years of age. Of course he was very dark.

It is a remarkable fact that in yesterday's Times there was a letter signed "Nemo," in which this very theory of the murders was proposed. The coincidence is so curious that we print the letter hereunder:

Sir—Having been long in India and, therefore, acquainted with the methods of Eastern criminals, it has struck me, in reading the accounts of these White-chapel murders, that they have probably been committed by a Malay, or other low class Asiatic coming under the general term of Lascar, of whom, I believe, there are large numbers in that part of London. The mutilations, cutting off the nose and ears, ripping up the body, and cutting out certain organs—the heart, &c.—are all peculiarly Eastern methods, and univer-sally recognised and intended by the criminal classes to express insult, hatred, and contempt; where here the public and police are quite at a loss to attach any meaning to them, and so they are described as the mere senseless fury of a maniac.

My theory would be that some man of this class has been hocussed and then robbed of his savings (often large), or, as he considers, been in some way greatly injured by a prostitute—perhaps one of the earlier victims; and then has been led by fury and revenge to take the lives of as many of the same class as he can. This also is entirely in consonance with Eastern ideas and the practices of the criminal classes.

Hundreds of these men have resided long in that part of London, speak English well—although when necessary they cannot understand a word—and dress in ordinary English clothes.

The victims have been the poorest and most miserable, and probably only such would consort with the class of man I speak of.

Such a man would be quite safe in the haunts occupied by his yellow country-men, or, should he wish to escape, he could join a crew of Lascars on the first steamer leaving London.

Unless caught redhanded, such a man in ordinary life would be harmless enough, polite, not to say obsequious in his manners, and about the last a British policeman would suspect.

But when the villain is primed with his opium, or bang, or gin, and inspired with his lust for slaughter and blood, he would destroy his defenceless victim with the ferocity and cunning of the tiger; and past impunity and success would only have rendered him the more daring and reckless.

Your obedient servant,
NEMO.
October 2.

—

## AN ARREST AT BISHOP STORTFORD.

The Press Association's Bishop Stortford correspondent telegraphs:

A man has been arrested at Tiptree Heath on suspicion of being concerned with the White-chapel murders. He was met by Police Sergeant Cresswell, of whom he asked alms. He objected to be searched and insisted on keeping his hand in his pocket. He was taken to Kelvedon, and it was seen that the appearance of the man answered to the description circulated by the Metropolitan police of the Whitechapel murd-erer in almost every particular. He was detained in custody.

Upon inquiry at the Leman street Police station at nine o'clock this morning, a repre-sentative of the Central News was informed that no further arrest had been made in connection with the Whitechapel murders, and that nothing new had transpired in relation to the matter. At the Bishopsgate Police station a similar reply was given by the City police.

—

## ANOTHER SISTER OF THE
## MITRE SQUARE VICTIM FOUND.

The Central News learns that another sister of Catherine Eddowes has been found by the police, and has also identified the body, notwithstanding its mutilated condition. She saw it yesterday and at once recognised it. She is a married woman, and lives in the South of London.

The City Police have no one in custody, and up to the present have not obtained a tangible clue.

—

## LETTERS AND THEORIES.

As a proof of the widespread excitement which has taken place over the horrible trage-dies which have occurred in East London, it may be mentioned that Mr. Wynne. E. Baxter, the coroner for south east Middlesex, has daily received about 50 letters from all parts of the united Kingdom, and from all classes of the community suggesting theories by which the murderer may be brought to justice.

One letter received by that gentleman cov-ered eight pages of paper, and stated that the writer was acquainted with the murderer, and knew his name and address, but that of course has been proved to be false. Another was from a clergyman, who stated that he had had a large experience amongst the East London poor and upheld the coroner's theory. A third was from a doctor, stating that the murderer must be a butcher. This was handed to the police, as the coroner states that he saw no reason why the doctor should be so anxious to fix the crime on a butcher.

Mr. Baxter at first handed all the communi-cations to the police, but latterly he has only given them those to which he attaches any importance.

—

## FUNERAL OF THE
## MITRE SQUARE VICTIM.

The Central News says: The date of the funeral of the woman Catherine Eddowes or Kate Eddowes is not yet fixed. The relatives of the deceased have not yet decided whether they will bear the expenses of the funeral themselves or whether the body shall be buried by the City authorities, who are willing to do so. A gentleman in the City has also expressed his willingness to bear the expenses of the funeral, if the relatives should so desire.

—

## THE MITRE SQUARE MURDER.
## THE BODY IDENTIFIED.
## THE DOCTOR'S STARTLING
## EVIDENCE.

...

On resuming after luncheon.[211]

Inspector Edward Collard of the City Police said:—At five minutes to two on Sunday morning I received information at Bishopsgate Police station that a woman had been murdered in Mitre square. The information was at once telegraphed to headquarters, and I despatched a constable at once for Dr. Gordon Brown. I also went to Mitre square myself; arriving a few minutes past two, I there found Dr. Sequeira, several police officers, and the deceased person lying in the southwest corner of the square, in the position described by Constable Watkins. The body was not touched until Dr. Brown arrived shortly afterwards. The medical gentlemen examined the body in my presence. Sergeant Jones picked upon the footway on the left side of the deceased three small black buttons generally used for women's boots, a small metal button, a common metal thimble, a small mustard tin containing two pawn tickets. They were handed to me. The doctors remained until the arrival of the ambulance, and saw the body placed in it. It was then taken to the mortuary and stripped by the mortuary keeper in the presence of the two doctors and myself. There was no money whatever about the clothes.

Witness here produced a portion of de-ceased's apron found on the body after the murder, which he said corresponded with another piece found in Gouldstone street later on. Both pieces had been examined by the doctors.

He continued:—I took immediate steps to have the neighbourhood searched for the murderer. Inspector McWilliams, chief of the detective department, on his arrival shortly afterwards with a number of detectives, sent them to search in all directions in Spitalfields, both in the streets and at lodging houses. Several men were stopped and searched in the streets without any good result. I have had a house to house inquiry made in the vicinity of Mitre square, as to whether any noises had been

---

[211] The first half of this article, deleted here, is a duplicate of the 4 October Inquest report. For this, see p. 296.

heard at the time of the murder, or if any persons had seen, but can find nothing.

Examined by Mr. Crawford:

—When I first saw the corpse, her neck and shoulders were lying in blood. I did not touch the body. There were no signs whatever of any struggle having taken place. There was no blood, except that which had flowed from the neck. The blood was not congealed, and I should not think that the body had been there more than a quarter of an hour. I tried to trace footsteps, but could not do so. A search was made at the back of the adjoining empty houses.

## THE DOCTOR'S EVIDENCE.
## A STARTLING, BLOOD CURDLING STORY.

Dr. F. Gordon Brown, surgeon to the City of London police authorities, said:—I was called up shortly after two o'clock on Sunday morning. I left home at 2.18, and at Mitre square my attention was called to a woman lying there. The body was lying in the position that the constable has already described. It was on its back, the hand turned to the left shoulder, the arms by the side of the body, as if they had fallen there, the palms turned upwards the fingers slightly bent, a thimble was lying on the ground near the right hand. The clothes were drawn up above the abdomen. The bonnet was at the back of the head. There was great disfigurement of the face which I will mention presently. The throat was cut across. Below the cut was a neckerchief. The upper part of the dress was open as if it had been pulled open. The abdomen was all exposed, the intestines drawn out to a large extent and placed over the right shoulder. A piece of the intestines about two feet long was quite detached from the body, and placed between the left arm and the body, apparently by design. The lobe of the right ear cut obliquely through, there was a quantity of clotted blood on the left side of the body, on the pavement, above the shoulder, and fluid blood coloured with serum which had flown under the neck to the right shoulder, the pavement sloping in that direction. The body was quite warm, and there was no rigor mortis. She must have been dead but a few minutes, less than half an hour. We looked for superficial bruises then and saw none. There was no blood on the abdomen, There was no spurting of blood on the bricks or pavement around. No marks of blood below the middle of the body. The buttons were found in the clotted blood after the body was removed. When the body arrived at Golden lane the clothes were more covered with blood than when I first saw them, but that was in consequence of the removal. The clothes were carefully taken off the body as described by Inspector Collard. We made a post mortem examination at 2.30 on Sunday afternoon. Rigor mortis was well marked; body not quite cold; green discoloration near the abdomen, post mortem. On washing the left hand carefully, a recent bruise, the size of a sixpence, was discovered on the back of the left hand between the thumb and first finger. There were a few small bruises on the right shin of older date, and a slight graze on the scalp. The hands and arms were browned, as if from exposure to the sun. There were no bruises on the scalp, or the elbows, or the back of the body. The face was very much mutilated.

## FEARFUL MUTILATION OF THE FACE.

There was a cut about a quarter of an inch long below the left eyelid dividing the structures completely through. On the upper eyelid on that side there was a scratch through the skin near to the angle of the nose. The right eyelid was cut through to about half an inch in extent—a similar cut. There was a clean cut over the bridge of the nose, extending from the left border of the nasal bone down near to the angle of the jaw on the right side, across the chin. This cut went into the nasal bone and divided all the structures of the cheek, except the mucous membrane of the mouth. The tip of the nose was quite detached from the nose by an oblique cut from the bottom of the nasal bone to where the wings of the noise join on to the face. A cut from this divided the upper lip and extended through the substance of the gums from the right upper lateral incisor tooth. About half an inch from the tip of the nose was another oblique cut. There was a cut at the right angle of the mouth, as if by the point of a knife, through the mucous membrane, and a cut extended for an inch and a half over the upper lip. There was, on each side of the cheek, a cut which peeled up the skin, forming a triangular flap of an inch and a half. On the left cheek there were two abrasions of the epithelium.[212] There were also similar abrasions under the left ear. The throat was cut, of course, to the extent of about six or seven inches. The superficial cut commenced about an inch and a half behind the lobe of the left ear, and about two and a half inches below the ear, and it extended across the throat to about three inches below the lobe of the right ear. The sterno mastoid muscle was divided, and the large vessels of the left side of the neck was severed. The larynx was severed at the middle of the cricoid cartilage. All the deep structures were severed to the bone, the knife marking the vertebral cartilage. The sheath of the vessels on the right side was just opened. The left carotid artery had a pin hole opening, and the left jugular vein was opened to the extent of an inch and a half. The anterior fibres of the sterno mastoid were cut to the extent of half an inch. The cause of death was haemorrhage from the left carotid artery. The other injuries were inflicted after death. We examined the injuries to the abdomen. The front walls were laid open from the sternum to the pubes. The cut commenced opposite the ensiform cartilage. The incision went upwards and did not penetrate the skin that was over the sternum; it was then divided the ensiform cartilage. The knife must have been held so that the point was towards the left side and the handle to the right. Behind this the liver was stabbed as if by the point of a knife; below this was another incision into the liver about two and a half inches deep; and below this again the left lobe of the liver was cut through about three or four inches. The cuts were shown by a jagging of the skin as if the knife had been drawn and stabbed in again. The abdominal walls were divided vertically in the middle line to within a quarter of an inch of the navel. The cut then took a horizontal course of two and a half inches to the right side, and then divided the navel on the left side, and made a parallel incision to the former horizontal one, leaving the navel on a tongue of skin. The incision then took an oblique course to the right. It divided the lower part of the abdomen, and went down to half an inch behind the rectum. There

was a cut which wounded the peritoneum. At the top of the thigh was another cut.

After describing various other wounds, the witness continued:—There was little or no bleeding from the abdominal injuries, showing that they were inflicted after death. The cuts were probably made by someone on the side of the body, kneeling below the middle of the body.

## CERTAIN ORGANS COMPLETELY CUT OUT.

Examination showed that there was very little in the stomach in the way of food or fluid. After describing the condition of the various organs, and the nature of other wounds discovered by post mortem examination, witness said:—The left kidney was completely cut out and taken away. The renal artery was cut through about three quarters of an inch. This must have been done by someone who knew the position of the kidney and how to take it out. The membrane over the uterus was cut through, and the womb was cut through, leaving a stump of about three quarters of an inch. The rest of the womb was absent —taken completely away from the body, together with some of the ligaments.

Mr. Crawford: have you formed any opinion as to whether the woman was standing when the wounds were inflicted?

—I believe she was lying on the ground. The wounds were inflicted with a sharp pointed knife, with a blade at least six inches long.

Do you consider that the person who inflicted the wounds had a great deal of anatomical knowledge and skill?

—A great deal of knowledge of the position of the abdominal organs.

Could the parts removed be used for professional purposes?

—They would be of no use for professional purposes.

Would the extraction of the left kidney show great anatomical knowledge and skill?

—Great knowledge of its position, for it is very easily overlooked.

Would not such a knowledge be possessed by one accustomed to cutting up animals?

—Yes.

Have you been able to form any opinion as to whether the perpetrator of this act was disturbed during the performance of it?

—I should think he had sufficient time as he

---

[212] **Epithelium**. The cellular covering of internal and external surfaces of the body, including the lining of vessels and other small cavities. (Miller)

# Friday, 5 October, 1888

would not have nicked the eyelids unless he had.

How long would the whole thing take to do?

—It could be done in five minutes. I may say that a man who is accustomed to removing the womb was asked to take one out, and it took him three minutes.

Can you, as a professional man, assign any reason for these parts being taken away?

—I cannot.

Have you any doubts in your own mind that there was no struggle?

—I am sure there was no struggle.

Are you equally of opinion that the act is that of one man?

—I think so.

Can you, as a medical man, account for the fact of no noise being heard by those in the immediate neighbourhood?

—The throat had been so instantly severed that I do not suppose there would be any time for the least sound to be uttered.

Would you expect to find much blood on the person who inflicted those wounds?

—No, I should not.

Was your attention called to this portion of an apron which was found upon the woman?

—It was. There were stains of blood upon the apron.

Are the stains of recent origin?

—They are. Dr. Phillips afterwards brought me a piece of apron which had been found in Goldstone street by a policeman. The stains are those of blood, but it is impossible to say that it is human blood.

On the piece of apron brought in by Dr. Phillips were there smears of blood as if someone had wiped bloodstained hands upon it?

—Yes. There were also what appeared to be stains of faecal matter.

With regard to the mutilation of the face, can you form any opinion as to why it was done?

—I suppose to disfigure the corpse.

The inquiry was adjourned until next Thursday.

—

## A MAN IN FEMALE COSTUME WITH A KNIFE.

At the Hampstead Police court, yesterday, William Webb, 43, a labourer and army pensioner, living at New End square, Hampstead, was charged, before Mr. B.W. Smith and Mr. G.H. Powell, with appearing in Heath street in female costume, with a carving knife in his possession, supposed for an unlawful purpose.

Mackenzie, 591S, deposed that on Wednesday night, about a quarter to eight, he was on fixed point duty near the Metropolitan Fire Brigade Station, when he saw a crowd outside the Horse and Groom public house, Heath street. Witness went to ascertain the cause, and saw the prisoner in the midst of a crowd dressed up in the woman's clothes now produced—hat, skirt, petticoat, and jacket—and with a hand-kerchief round his neck.

Witness thought prisoner was a man, and told him to go away. The prisoner would not go, but drew the knife produced (about a foot long with the blade) from up his sleeve, and acting about with it, said he was going to Whitechapel to catch the murderer.

Witness did not know prisoner, but he was known in Hampstead. He did not seem to be the worse for drink. Witness took him to the station.

The prisoner said he was drunk in the morning, and had some more drink in the evening. Some of his companions had told him that he had not got the pluck to go down to Whitechapel to look after the murderer, and so he went home and put his wife's clothes on, in which he came out, but with no intention of going to Whitechapel. It was only a joke.

Inspector Sly, S division, said that prisoner had shaved off his moustache. Witness thought it right to detain him when he was brought to the station, but now believed that prisoner's conduct was nothing but a joke. Prisoner admitted that he had shaved off his moustache.

The bench said the constable had acted properly in taking the prisoner into custody, and fined the accused 10s., or in default seven days' imprisonment, for disorderly conduct. Prisoner was locked up in default.

317

# Saturday, 6 October, 1888

## The Times
### THE EAST-END MURDERS.

Yesterday afternoon Mr. Wynne E. Baxter, Coroner for the South-Eastern Division of Middlesex, resumed his inquiry at the Vestry-hall, Cable-street, St. George's-in-the-East, respecting the death of Elizabeth Stride, who was found murdered in Berner-street, St. George's, on the early morning of Sunday last. Superintendent T. Arnold and Detective-inspector Reid, H Division, watched the case on behalf of the Criminal Investigation Department.

Dr. Phillips was re-called and said:—After the last examination, in company with Dr. Blackwell and Dr. Brown, I went to the mortuary and examined more carefully the roof of the mouth. I could not find any injury to or absence of anything from the mouth.

I have also carefully examined the two handkerchiefs, and have not found any blood on them. I believe the stains on the larger one were fruit stains. I am convinced that the deceased had not swallowed either skin or seed of a grape within many hours of her death.[213]

The abrasion which I spoke of on the right side of the neck was only apparently an abrasion, for on washing it the staining was removed and the skin was found to be uninjured.

The knife that was produced on the last occasion was submitted to me by Constable 282 H. On examination I found it to be such a knife as would be used in a chandler's shop, called a slicing knife. It had blood upon it, which was similar to that of a warm-blooded being. It has been recently blunted and the edge turned by apparently rubbing on a stone. It evidently was before that a very sharp knife. Such a knife could have produced the incision and injuries to the neck of the deceased; but it was not such a weapon as I would have chosen to inflict injuries in this particular place; and if my opinion as regards the position of the body is correct, the knife in question would become an improbable instrument as having caused the incision.

---

[213] As Dr. Phillips thought fruit stains were on the larger handkerchief, did she peel and pit the grapes as she ate them? Many varieties of grapes have thick, bitter skins, and popping out the meat of the grape into your mouth and spitting out the seeds is a common practice even today.

The CORONER.—Could you give us any idea of the position of the victim?

Witness.—I have come to the conclusion that the deceased was seized by the shoulders, placed on the ground, and that the perpetrator of the deed was on her right side when he inflicted the cut. I am of the opinion that the cut was made from the left to right side of the deceased, and therefore arises the unlikelihood of such a long knife having inflicted the wound described in the neck, taking into account the position of the incision.

The CORONER.—Was there anything in the cut that showed the incision first made was done with a pointed knife?

Witness.—No.

The CORONER.—Have you formed any opinion how the right hand of the deceased was covered with blood?

Witness.—No; that is a mystery. I may say I am taking it as a fact that the hand always remained the same position in which he found it resting across the body.

The CORONER.—How long had the deceased been dead when you arrived?

Witness.—Within an hour she was alive.

The CORONER.—Would the injury take long to inflict?

Witness.—Only a few seconds. It might be done in two seconds.

The CORONER.—Does the presence of the cachous in her hand show that it was done suddenly or would it simply show a muscular grasp?

Witness.—No; I cannot say. You will remember some of the cachous were found in the gutter. I have seen several self-inflicted wounds more extensive than this one, but then they have not divided the carotid artery. You will see by that, as in the other cases, there appears to have been a knowledge where to cut the throat.

The CORONER.—Was there any other similarity between this and Chapman's case?

Witness.—There is a great dissimilarity. In Chapman's case the neck was severed all around down to the vertebral column, the vertical bone being marked, and there had been an evident attempt to separate the bones.

The CORONER.—Would the murderer be likely to get bloodstained?

318

Witness.—Not necessarily, for the comm-encement of the wound and the injury to the vessels would be away from him, and the stream of blood, for stream it would be, would be directed away from him, and towards the waterway already mentioned. There was no perceptible sign of an anaesthetic having been used. The absence of noise is a difficult question in this case, and under the circum-stances, to account for, but it must not be taken for granted that I assumed there was no noise. If there was an absence of noise, there was nothing in this case that I can account for. She might have called out and not have been heard. As I said before, if there was a noise I cannot account for it.

The Foreman.—Was the wound caused by drawing the knife across the throat?

Witness.—Undoubtedly. My reason for sup-posing deceased was injured when on the ground was partly on account of the absence of blood anywhere but on the left side of the body, and between that side and the wall.

The CORONER.—Was there any sign of liquor in the stomach?

Witness.—There was no trace of it.

Dr. Blackwell, recalled, said:—I have little to say except to confirm Dr. Phillip's statement. I removed the cachous from the left hand, which was nearly open. The packet was lodged between the thumb and fourth finger, and had become almost hidden. That accounted for its not having been seen by several of those around. I believe the hand relaxed after the injury was inflicted, as death would arise from fainting owing to the rapid loss of blood. I wish to say that, taking into consideration the absence of any instrument it was impossible that the deceased could have committed suicide. With respect to the knife which was found, I should say I concur with Dr. Phillips in his opinion that although it might have possibly inflicted the injury it was extremely unlikely that such an instrument was used. The murderer using a sharp, round-pointed instru-ment would have severely handicap himself, as he could only use it in one way. He was informed that slaughterers always used round-pointed instruments.

The CORONER.—No one suggested anything about a slaughterer. Is it your suggestion that this was done by a slaughterer?

Witness.—No, I concur with Dr. Phillips as to the post mortem appearances. There were some

pressure marks on the shoulders. These were not regular bruises, and there was no abrasion of the skin.

A juryman.—Do you know how these marks were likely to have been caused?

Witness.—By two hands pressing on the shoulders.

Did you see any grapes in the yard?

—No I did not.

Sven Olsson said:—I live at 36, Prince's-square, and am clerk to the Swedish Church in that square. I saw the body of the deceased in the mortuary on Tuesday morning. I have known deceased about 17 years.

The CORONER.—Was she a Swede?

—Yes.

What was her name?

—Elizabeth Gustafsdotter was her maiden name. Elizabeth Stride was her married name, and she was the wife of John Thomas Stride, a ship's carpenter. She was born on the 27th of November, 1843 at Forslander, near Gotten-burg, in Sweden.

The CORONER.—Was she married in your church?

Witness.—No. We register those who come to this country bringing with them a certificate and desiring to be registered.

The CORONER.—When was she registered?

Witness.—Our register is dated July 10, 1866. She was registered as an unmarried woman.

The CORONER.—How do you know she was the wife of John Thomas Stride?

Witness.—I suppose she gave it to the clergyman, as it is written here. In the registry I find a memorandum, undated, in the handwriting of the Rev. Mr. Palmar, in abbreviated Swedish. It means, "married to an Englishman, John Thomas Stride." I do not know when this entry was made.

The CORONER.—How long has Mr. Palmar been at the church?

Witness.—About a year. This registry is a new one and copied from an older book. I have seen the original entry, and it was written many years ago.

The CORONER.—Would you mind looking at the entry in the older book, and see in whose handwriting it is?

Witness.—I will.

Inspector Reid.—Do you know this hymn-book?

Witness.—Yes.

The CORONER.—Is there any name in it?

Witness.—No; I gave it to the deceased last winter.

The CORONER.—Do you know when she was married to Stride?

Witness.—I think it was in 1869. She told me her husband was drowned in the Princess Alice.

The CORONER.—Have you any schools connected with the Swedish Church?

Witness.—No; I do not remember hearing she ever had any children. She told me her husband went down in the Princess Alice.

The CORONER.—Have you ever seen her husband?

Witness.—No; I think we gave the deceased some assistance before we knew her husband was dead. I forget where she was living at the time, but two years ago she gave her address as Devonshire-street, Commercial-road. She said she was doing a little work—sewing. Deceased could speak English pretty well.

The CORONER.—Do you know when deceased came to England?

Witness.—I cannot say, but I think a little before the name was registered.

William Marshall said:—I live at 64 Berner-street, Commercial-road, and am a labourer. On Sunday last I saw the body of deceased in the mortuary. I recognize it as that of a woman I saw on Saturday evening about three doors off from where I am living in Berner-street. That was about a quarter to 12. She was on the pavement opposite No. 63,[214] and between Christian-street and Boyd-street. She was standing talking to a man. I recognize her both by her face and dress.

The CORONER.—Was she wearing a flower when you saw her?

—No.

The CORONER.—Were they talking quietly?

—Yes.

The CORONER.—Can you describe the man?

—There was no lamp near and I did not see

the face of the man she was talking to. He had on a small black coat and dark trousers. He seemed to be a middle-aged man.

The CORONER.—What sort of cap was he wearing?

—A round cap with a sort of peak to it; something like what a sailor would wear.

The CORONER.—What height was he?

—About 5ft. 6in., and he was rather stout. He was decently dressed, and I should say he worked at some light business, and had more the appearance of a clerk than anything else.

The CORONER.—Did you see whether he had any whiskers?

—From what I saw of his face I do not think he had. He was not wearing gloves, and he had no stick or anything in his hand.

The CORONER. —What sort of coat was it?

—A cut-away one.

The CORONER.—You are quite sure this is the woman?

—Yes, I am. I did not take much notice of them. I was standing at my door and what attracted my attention first was her standing there some time, and he was kissing her. I heard the man say to deceased. "You would say anything but your prayers." He was mild speaking, and appeared to be an educated man. They went down the street.

The CORONER.—Would they pass the club?

—They had done so.

The CORONER.—How was she dressed?

—In a black jacket and black skirt.

The CORONER.—Were either of them worse for drink?

—They did not appear to be so. I went in about 12 o'clock and heard nothing more until I heard "Murder" being called in the street. It had then just gone 1 o'clock.

A juryman.—How long were you standing at the door?

—From 11:30 to 12.

A juryman.—Did it rain then?

—No, it did not rain until nearly 3 o'clock.

The Foreman.—What sort of bonnet had she on?

—I believe it was a small black crape one.

Inspector Reid.—When you saw them first they were standing between your house and the club?

---

[214] The *Daily Telegraph*, 6 October, gave a slightly different account of this part of Marshall's testimony: "She was on the pavement, opposite **No. 58**, between **Fairclough-street** and Boyd-street."

—Yes, and they remained there for about 10 minutes. They passed me once, and I could not see the man's face, as it was turned towards the deceased. There was a lamp over No. 70.

Inspector Reid.—Were they hurrying along?

—No.

Was it raining at the time?

—No, it was not.

Mr. Olsson, recalled, said,—I find that the original entry of the marriage of the deceased is in the handwriting of Mr. Frost, who was the pastor for about 18 years until two years ago.

James Brown stated,—I live at 35, Fairclough-street. I saw the deceased about a quarter to 1 on Sunday morning. At that time I was going from my house to get some supper from a chandler's shop at the corner of Berner-street and Fairclough-street. As I was going across the road I saw a man and woman standing by the Board School in Fairclough-street. They were standing against the wall. As I passed them I heard the woman say, "No, not to-night, some other night." That made me turn round, and I looked at them. I am certain the woman was the deceased. I did not notice any flowers in her dress. The man had his arm up against the wall, and the woman had her back to the wall facing him. I noticed the man had a long coat on, which came very nearly down to his heels. I believe it was an overcoat. I could not say what kind of cap he had on. The place where they were standing was rather dark. I saw nothing light in colour about either of them. I then went on and went indoors. I had nearly finished my supper when I heard screams of "Police" and "Murder." That was about a quarter of an hour after I got in. I do not think it was raining at the time. I should say the man was about 5ft. 7in. in height. He appeared to be stoutish built. Both the man and woman appeared to be sober. I did not notice any foreign accent about the woman's voice. When I heard screams of "Police" and "Murder" I opened the window, but could not see any one and the screams ceased. The cries were those of moving persons, and appeared to be going in the direction of Grove-street. Shortly afterwards I saw a policeman standing at the corner of Christian-street. I heard a man opposite call out to the constable that he was wanted. I then saw the policeman run along to Berner-street.

By the CORONER.

—I am almost certain it was the deceased.

Police-constable William Smith, 452 H, said that on Saturday night his beat was past Berner-street. It went from the corner of Jower's-walk, Commercial-road, as far as Christian-street, down Christian-street and Fairclough-street as far as Grove-street, then back along Fairclough-street as far as Backchurch-lane, up there as far as the Commercial-road, taking all the interior streets, including Berner-street and Batty-street.

The witness continued,—It takes me from 25 minutes to half an hour to go round my beat. I was last in Berner-street about half-past 12 or 12:35. At 1 o'clock I went to Berner-street in my ordinary round. I saw a crowd of people outside the gates of No. 40. I did not hear any cries of "Police." When I got there I saw constables 12 H R and 252 H. I then saw the deceased, and, on looking at her, found she was dead. I then went to the station for the ambulance. Dr. Blackwell's assistant came just as I was going away.

The CORONER.—Did you go up Berner-street into Commercial-road?

—No I turned up Fairclough-street.

Did you see any one?

—No, sir.

When you were in Berner-street the previous time did you see any one?

—Yes, a man and a woman.

Was the latter anything like the deceased?

—Yes, I saw her face. I have seen the deceased in the mortuary, and I feel certain it is the same person.

Was she on the pavement?

—Yes, a few yards up Berner-street on the opposite side to where she was found.

Did you see the man who was talking to her?

—Yes; I noticed he had a newspaper parcel in his hand. It was about 18in. in length and 6in. or 8in. in width. He was about 5ft. 7in. as near as I could say. He had on a hard felt deerstalker hat of dark colour and dark clothes.

What kind of coat was it?

—An overcoat. He wore dark trousers.

Did you overhear any conversation?

—No.

Did he seem sober?

—Yes. I did not see much of the face of the man except that he had no whiskers.

Can you form any idea as to his age?

—About 28 years.

Can you give any idea as to what he was?

—No, sir, I cannot. He was of respectable appearance. I noticed the woman had a flower in her jacket.

When you saw them talking, which way did you go?

—Straight up Berner-street into the Commercial-road. In the centre of Berner-street were some courts which led into Backchurch-lane.

When did it last rain before 1 o'clock?

—To the best of my recollection, it rained very little after 11 o'clock.

The Foreman.—Was the man or the woman acting in a suspicious manner?

—No.

Did you see many prostitutes or people hanging about Berner-street?

—No, very few.

Inspector Reid.—Did you see these people more than once?

—No. When I saw deceased lying on the ground I recognized her at once and made a report of what I had seen.

The witness Kidney was recalled, and the CORONER said,—Have you ever seen that hymn-book before?

—Yes; I recognize it as one belonging to the deceased. It used to be in my place. I found it in Mrs. Smith's room, next to my own. Mrs. Smith said deceased gave it to her to take care of when she left on Tuesday.

Inspector Reid.—When you and the deceased lived together I believe you had a padlock on the door?

—Yes; there was only one key, which I had, but she got in and out somehow. The hymn-book was taken from the room on Wednesday week, the day after she went away. That was done during my absence.

The CORONER.—What makes you think there was anything the matter with the roof of her mouth?

—She told me she was kicked when the Princess Alice went down.

Philip Krantz, who claimed to affirm, said,—I live at 40, Berner-street, and am the editor of a Hebrew paper called the Workers' Friend. I work in the room at the back of the printing office on the ground floor, and the entrance is from the yard. I was in the back room from 9 o'clock on Saturday night until one of the members of the club came and told me there was a woman lying in the yard.

The CORONER.—Had you heard any cry or scream?

—None.

Was your window or door open?

—No.

Is it a wooden structure?

—No; brick.

Supposing a woman had screamed, would you have heard it?

—I do not know. They were singing upstairs.

When you went out into the yard was there any one round deceased?

—Yes, members of the club were near the woman, but there was no one there I did not know.

Were you on the look out to see if there was any stranger there?

—No. I went out into the street to look for a policeman.

Do you think it possible for anyone to escape without being noticed after you arrived there?

—I do not think it was, but he might have done so before.

Did you see the face of the deceased?

—No; my name and address was taken, and I was examined and searched by the police.

Constable 12 HR said,—At half-past 5 on Sunday morning I washed all traces of blood away. That was after the doctors had left. There were no traces of blood on the wall.

Detective-inspector Edmund Reid, H Division, stated,—I received a telegram at 1:25 a.m. on Sunday morning at the Commercial-street police office. I at once proceeded to 40, Berner-street. I saw there Chief Inspector West, Inspector Pinhorn, several sergeants and constables, Drs. Phillips and Blackwell, a number of residents in the yard, and club members, with persons who had come into the yard and had been shut in by the police. At that time Dr. Phillips, with Dr. Blackwell, was examining the throat of the deceased woman. Superintendent Arnold followed in, as well as several other officers.

When it was found a murder had been committed a thorough search was made of the yard, houses, and buildings, but no trace could be found of any person likely to have committed the deed.

As soon as the search was over the whole of the persons who had come into the yard and the

# Saturday, 6 October, 1888

members of the club were interrogated, their names and addresses taken, their pockets searched, and their clothes and hands examined. There were 28 of them. Each person was dealt with separately. They properly accounted for themselves, and were then allowed to leave.

The houses were then visited a second time and the names of the people therein taken, and they were also examined and their rooms searched. The door of the loft was found locked on the inside, and it was forced. The loft was searched, but no trace of the murderer could be found.

A description was taken of the body and circulated round the surrounding stations by wire. Inquiries were made in the street at the different houses, and no person could be found who heard any disturbance during the night. I minutely examined the wall near where the body was found, but could find no spots of blood.

About 4:30 the body was removed to the mortuary. I then informed you (the coroner) verbally at your residence, and then returned to the yard and made another examination. It being daylight, I searched the walls thoroughly, but could find no marks of any person having scaled them. I then proceeded to the mortuary and took a correct description of the body and clothing, which is as follows:—

I guessed her age at 42, length 5ft. 2in. complexion pale, hair dark brown and curly. I raised an eyelid and found that her eyes were light grey; I parted her lips and found that she had lost her upper teeth in front. She had an old black skirt and an old black jacket trimmed with fur. Fastened on the right side was a small bunch of flowers, consisting of maidenhair fern and a red rose. She had two light serge petticoats, white stockings, white chemise with insertion in front, side-spring boots, and black crape bonnet. In her jacket pocket I found two pocket-handkerchiefs, a thimble, and a piece of wool on a card. That description was then circulated. Since then the police engaged in the inquiry had made house to house inquiry in the immediate neighbourhood, with the result that we have been able to produce the witnesses which have appeared before you. The inquiry is still going on. Every endeavour is being made to arrest the assassin, but up to the present with success.

At this stage the inquiry was adjourned to Tuesday week.

———

We are requested to state that Sir Charles Warren has been making inquiries as to the practicability of employing trained bloodhounds for use in special cases in the streets of London; and having ascertained that dogs can be procured that have been accustomed to work a town, he is making immediate arrangements for their use in London.

———

The police authorities of Whitehall have had reproduced in facsimile and published on the walls of London the letter and post-card sent to the Central News agency. The language of the card and letter is of a brutal character, and is full of Americanisms. The handwriting, which is clear and plain; and disguised in part, is that of a person accustomed to write a round hand like that employed by clerks in offices. The exact colour of the ink and smears of blood are reproduced in the placard, and information is asked in identification of the handwriting. The post-card bears a tolerably clear imprint of a bloody thumb or finger-mark.

———

Yesterday afternoon, shortly after 3 o'clock, information was given at the police-station in Moor-lane, City, as to a man who had been seen in Liverpool-street at 20 minutes past 1 o'clock, and who had been followed to a publichouse in Chiswell-street. His conduct was stated to have been suspicious, and he was said to resemble the description given of the East-end murderer.

———

The daughter of the woman who was murdered in Mitre-square has been found. Her age is 19, and she is married. She states that her father, Thomas Conway, with whom the deceased cohabited for some time before she met with Kelly, is still living, but he has not yet been traced. It will be remembered that Kelly stated in the course of his evidence on Thursday, before the coroner, that when the deceased left him early last Saturday afternoon she told him she was going to try to find her daughter Annie. The latter, however, now states that she did not see her mother that day.

———

The funeral of the Mitre-square victim will take place next Monday, at Ilford.

———

A news agency has received a telegram from New York with respect to a statement alleged to have been made in that city by an English sailor bearing the peculiar name of Dodge. The statement is that he arrived in London from China on August 13, by the steamship Glenorchy,[215] that he met at the Queen's Music-hall, Poplar, a Malay cook, and that the Malay said he had been robbed by a woman of bad character, and that unless he found the woman and recovered his money he would murder and mutilate every Whitechapel woman he met.

The statement also includes the following description of the Malay:—"He was about 5ft. 7in. in height, 130lb. in weight, and apparently 35 years of age."

Judging from these precise figures relating to the Malay's appearance, it is evident that Dodge must have scrutinized him very closely. Inquiries have been made by the news agency in London, but no information has been obtained in verification of the sailor's story. It appears that the Glenorchy returned to London from China on August 14.

—

Yesterday, at the Guildhall Police-court, before Mr. Alderman Stone, William Bull, 27, living at Stannard-road, Dalston, was charged on remand with having committed the murder in Mitre-square, Aldgate, on Sunday morning. The facts were given in *The Times* of Thursday.

Mr. Savill (chief clerk) asked Inspector Izzard if he had made inquiries during the remand.

Inspector Izzard.—I have, and the result is perfectly satisfactory. The prisoner for several years was engaged at Messrs. Rylands's and bore an irreproachable character. Recently he has given away to drink, and this is the result. His family are highly respectable.

The Alderman.—Have you ascertained where he was on Saturday night?

Inspector Izzard.—Yes; I have a gentleman in Court, a Mr. Day with whom the prisoner was on Saturday night till 12 o'clock.

The Alderman.—It is with great regret that I

find the law does not permit me to punish you for your conduct. The statement you made to the inspector on Tuesday night was without the least foundation in fact. At a time like this your acts are perfectly inexcusable. I must discharge you, and I hope you will be thoroughly ashamed of your bad behaviour.

Prisoner.—Since I have been in prison I have signed the pledge.

The Alderman.—And I hope you will keep it.

Accused was then discharged.

—

## "UNFORTUNATES."
## TO THE EDITOR OF THE TIMES.

Sir,—Now twice again are we confronted with the atrocious work of this assassin who chooses his poor victims from a class whose lives at the best are, of all known classes, every way the most pitiable—a struggle for daily sustenance only to be purchased by the basest physical abasement.

There will be, nay, there is already, a panic on the pavement; those who have to tread it in their sad midnight calling, one to which they had served an early apprenticeship, must be content to starve; or seeking foul lodgings—trade—as sought, not seeking, and this with scarce the chance of earning the cost of lodging, much less that of the food to sustain life in it.

It has been no writing on the wall which has thus warned the "unfortunates;" the order to depart is writ in crimson on that pavement, in those secluded spots, to which the wearied feet of the midnight seeker of the harlot's hire, by force of necessity, are but too willingly led.

When all the coroner's work is done, the sickening detail published for our whole Christian nation's perusal, then come the texts from which so many sermons will be preached, and now in ordinary pauper form these mangled remains will be committed to the earth, the fully ripened, but decayed fruit of "unfortunate" humanity; packed in the parish shells, scant covering of the shells which but lately clothed immortal souls. Then will be heard the voice of the cemetery chaplain—"It is sown in corruption; it is sown in dishonour."[216] Had such graves echo

---

[215] The only **Glenorchy** I have been able to find for this time period was a 2,229 gross tons, iron hulled, four-masted barque, constructed in 1882 by Sunderland Shipbuilding Co., Ltd. for L.H. MacIntyre & Co. of Liverpool. Renamed Italia after being sold in 1911, in 1915 she collided with SS Atlantide off Cabo de Gata, Spain and sank. (Bruzekius)

---

[216] 1st Corinthians 15:42-43 KJV.
42. So also is the resurrection of the dead. It is sown in corruption; it is raised in incorruption:

# Saturday, 6 October, 1888

power, how fitting would here be its effect! "God has taken to Himself the souls of our dear sisters here departed."[217] Yes, ye of society, its upper class, ye, the dwellers in all attainable luxury, the fortunate of the earth, let your rank be what it may, your wealth a tale of millions, the Godward life of many of you ever in evidence, or the Godless life not less so; the Established Church of your nation proclaims in that solemn hour in which your own graves will be open, that these—the society labelled "unfort-unates"—are before the God to whom you have been taken— your sisters. You may seek to ignore their existence. To speak of them at all is in bad taste; if forced to do so, it is as if they were a sort of human vermin, unclean parasites, a humanity affliction admitted in its existence, but so existent to be held as a matter of course; fortunately scattered where their presence does not intrude on that of those, the made of the same Creator, who dwell in all that the "fortunate" of this life can obtain of this life's enjoyment.

We seem to be on the verge of a creed that, as this state of things has so long existed, it is to be viewed as preordained, and therefore beyond human power to alleviate; it lies in our road of life, but we systematically pass by on the other side, and yet as Christians we affect to be taught of Christ.

The question, to me, seems now to be forced upon us. Is the arm of the Lord shortened, or are the hands which assume to be those by whom He would have his deeds of mercy done paralyzed? Is the axe to strike at the root of evil double-bladed, one edge fitted and sharp to deal with it in heathen lands, the other blunt and ill-adapted for home use? Are we to believe that tens of thousands of those our National Church proclaims to be our brothers and sisters, when dead, are living disgospelized, so born and reared as to be of a race the Gospel tidings and teachings cannot touch?

There is one crumb of comfort in the method by which these poor outcasts were done to death. There can have been little bodily suffering, yet who can say what that one instant feeling may have been, when the clutch of the murderer's hand on the throat of his victim flashed on her sense? This is he whose fell work had formed the theme of the "unfortunates'" talk for many an hour. How many hundreds of this class reach their graves, on the other hand, by a path of utter torment to mind and body, under all the suffering of the loathsome disease, the re-sult of their foul lives? The "pavement"[218] is a thing of the past, changed for the filthy bed from which they will never rise; no wages can now be earned.

Those who still earn such, in compassion may help to stave off actual famine; may find the lodging-money. These can feel for a sister; every surrounding of these last days just such as that on which the life of sin has been spent. The end comes, scant preparation for removal to the contracting undertaker's premises, to wait a sufficient supply of such dead to remove to the cemetery— mere waste material of lodging-house life.

After all, some will say, is there anything novel in all this? Is it not just an everyday tale of the termination of the life of such sinners? Why force it on our attention? Why not confine all reading of this foul page of humanity to those whose official duty may force them to study it, or to those who have taken voluntarily on themselves the unsavoury task of trying to purify it; it is insulting to society that it should be written where society reads? I answer it is in society's own interest that I write. I wish to open eyes wilfully closed to dangers not less danger-ous because thus shut out from sight.

It is well that the fact should be pressed that all rank, wealth, high position is held in trust, has its duties as well as its privileges. The deeds may not be engrossed, the breach penalty may not be open to the eye, the day of its enforcement may be delayed; but come it will, and that often when least expected. Long sufferance may seem to have indicated impunity, but such sufferance has its limits. Wealth and station in its embodiment may at one moment be inclined to cry "Ah, ha, I am warm." It may be the moment in which the warmth only precedes an eruption volcanic which brings destruction. In my poor opinion these are just the days when apathy to the condition of the lowest classes is most fraught with danger to all other classes.

Lewes.
S.G.O.

---

43. It is sown in dishonour; it is raised in glory: it is sown in weakness; it is raised in power:

[217] The Order for the Burial of the Dead. 1559 Book of Common Prayer.

[218] **Nymph of the Pavement**. A prostitute. (Farmer)

325

# Saturday, 6 October, 1888

## WHITECHAPEL.
### TO THE EDITOR OF THE TIMES.

Sir,—It seems desirable, although it ought to be unnecessary, to point out, amid the general demand for further police action, that the citizens themselves of any city are the ultimate constabulary force of that city; that with them rests the final responsibility for the maintenance of order and decency in its streets; that without their support, readily and freely given under all circumstances, but specially organized in times of special danger, the Executive alone cannot fulfil its duties.

After some experience of what may be done in the back streets of Whitechapel and Spitalfields by a few citizens who are prepared to guard the privileges they enjoy, we would urge Londoners to resume for a time their share of those functions which they have in part entrusted to the police, to lend their active and persistent support to that body, and to use the opportunity thus given for studying how our police force may be better fitted for its difficult task.

Members of the Streets Committee established in this neighbourhood for the maintenance of these principles are about in the streets every night under a systematic plan. They report every week in writing on the disturbances that have occurred, the action they or the police have taken, the state of the neighbourhood, &c. The materials thus accumulating will one day form the substance of a report which will be submitted to the public; but in the meantime the committee make representations, where it appears desirable, to the local and police authorities.

When the lovers of order have asserted their right to possess highway and byway alike in the face of those who brawl, when the owners of the houses that disgrace our byways have been obliged by the force of public opinion to perform their duties as landlords, when our local authorities have been roused by their masters, the people, to suppress disorderly houses, to cleanse and widen the streets, to pave and light the courts and alleys, the chief external conditions that favour murder will have been removed. But these things will never be accomplished so long as it is thought that the service of the State can be finally commuted by the payment of policemen, or that a public disaster like this series of murders is to be met by the offer of £1,000 reward.

Those of us who know Whitechapel know that the impulse that makes for murder is abroad in our streets every night; we are aware that these symptoms of unrighteousness can be made to disappear only by the salvation of individual character; but we feel that for this the action of the community must prepare the way. "Only the collected strength of the whole people, organized and (morally) armed to take the initiative—only it, is in a position to cope effectually with social misery. Well for us if we succeed in organizing our people in this sense."

We are, Sir, your obedient servants,
THOMAS HANCOCK NUNN.
THOMAS G. GARDINER.
Toynbee-hall. Whitechapel, Oct. 3.[219]

## A FRENCH CHAPTER OF WHITECHAPEL HORRORS.
### TO THE EDITOR OF THE TIMES.

Sir,—The terror which has naturally been so widespread among the masses in the districts where the recent shocking murders were committed was intense enough without its being aggravated by the gratuitous theory of the Coroner, that these horrible outrages were not the act of a maniac, but had been coolly committed by a sane person, who wished to earn a few pounds by gratifying the whims of an eccentric American anatomist. It will, no doubt, be found that the idea that Yankee enterprise gave a stimulus to these terrible atrocities is utterly baseless.

For weeks I have been expecting that someone would draw attention to the fact that precisely the same crimes were many years ago committed in Paris, and were ultimately found to have been the acts of a monomaniac.

Last summer, while travelling in France, I picked up and glanced over a French work resembling "Hone's Every Day Book,"[220] which

---

[219] **Toynbee Hall** was established as the first University Settlement in 1885 by St. Jude's Curate Samuel Augustus Barnett and his wife Henrietta. Named in honour of Oxford historian and social reformer Arnold Toynbee, it was intended to allow students from Oxford and Cambridge to work to improve the lives of the poor by providing training, legal aid, childrens clubs and educational opportunities.

[220] **The Every-Day Book.** Published by William Hone (1780-1842), best known as a political satirist and

gave an account of a remarkable criminal who must have strongly resembled the fiend who has created such consternation in the East-end of London. For months women of the lowest class of "unfortunates" were found murdered and mutilated in a shocking manner. In the poorest districts of the city a "reign of terror" prevailed. The police seemed powerless to afford any help or protection, and in spite of all their watchfulness fresh cases were from time to time reported, all the victims belonging to the same class, and all having been mutilated in the same fiendish way.

At last a girl one night was accosted in the street by a workman, who asked her to take a walk with him. When, by the light of a lamp, she saw his face, it inspired her with a strange feeling of fear and aversion; and it instantly flashed upon her that he must be the murderer. She therefore gave him in charge of the police, who, on inquiry, found that her woman's instinct had accomplished what had baffled the skill and the exertions of all their detectives. The long-sought criminal had been at last found.

It subsequently came to light that he had been impelled to commit these crimes by a brutal form of homicidal monomania. He had sense enough to know that from this class of women being out late at night, and being friendless and unprotected, he could indulge his horrible craze on them with comparative safety and impunity, and he therefore avoided selecting his victims from a more respectable class.

He was convicted and executed, to the great relief of the public; and if any persons were afterwards tempted to imitate him, his prompt punishment effectually deterred them.

This notorious case must be well known to the Parisian police and to thousands of persons in France, and if inquiry is made its history can be easily procured.

No doubt a ruffian like him has turned up in East London, and will be also detected. When

he is, we must trust that he will meet with the same stern justice that was meted out to his French prototype.[221]

Yours obediently,
MICHAEL MACK
—

## FRIENDLESS AND FALLEN IN WHITECHAPEL.
## TO THE EDITOR OF THE TIMES.

Sir,—While the public are aghast at the atrocities against women of a certain class at the East-end of London is it not possible that out of this appalling evil some good may come if only suitable and prompt action be taken?

Great fear has come upon these unfortunate women, and for a time they avoid their accustomed haunts, though to many of them the loss of the wages of shame brings instantly the want of the barest necessities of life. Now is the opportunity to offer to these poor people, who at all times deserve our sympathy and help, a specially open invitation to forsake their evil lives and to return to the paths of virtue. The various societies which are constantly at work in this direction could not bear the strain of a sudden and large influx of refugees from the streets without large additional funds, and if the panic continues it might be needful to strengthen the organization as well as the finances of these societies. Among these who thus fly from the horrors of the streets, some no doubt would return to their old life when the panic was past, but if only a small proportion of the tens of thousands of London street walkers were rescued this crisis would not have occurred in vain.

If such a fund can be raised, I shall be willing to contribute £50 towards it, and many others will doubtless do much more than this.

Yours truly,
WALTER HAZELL.[222]
15, Russell-square, Oct 2.

---

advocate for the freedom of the press, The Every-Day Book is a two volume, each of about 800 pages, collection of weekly essays that appeared in 1825 and 1826 and gave pertinent information for each day of the year regarding history, horticulture, religion, biography and popular culture. First published in book form in 1826-27, The Every-Day Book remained in print for the next 40 years. (Grimes)

[221] See *Evening News*, 12 October, 1888, **"Jack the Ripper's" Predecessor**, p. 388.
[222] **Walter Hazell** (1843-1919). Head of Hazell, Watson & Viney, Ltd., printers and bookbinders, publisher of Hazell's Annual, Co-founder and treasurer of Children's Fresh Air Mission and Self-help Emigration Society and elected Liberal M.P. for Leicester in 1895. He set up a system where workers could buy shares in the company at a discounted rate by having a portion of the cost deducted from their wages.

# Saturday, 6 October, 1888

## THE HOMES OF THE CRIMINAL CLASS.
### TO THE EDITOR OF THE TIMES.

Sir,—In the *Fortnightly* of last January I ventured to recommend certain remedies for "distress in London." It was impossible in writing on that subject to omit reference to the lowest class of our population; and at this moment, when the veil that hung over the lives of that class has been rudely torn away, I beg that you will kindly allow me to repeat what I then suggested. My words were:—

"That some agency, official and voluntary, be formed to explore the haunts and lairs of the criminals and dangerous refuse of the population. It would need local authorities, detectives, laymen, and ministers of religion acting together. Such a raid might be tried on one district at first. We need knowledge in order to cope with the evil. Police facilities granted by Government to a volunteer committee would help in any organized effort to discover how deep the disease may penetrate. We must make a determined effort to deal with paupers and criminals, instead of, as at present, winking at their existence in our midst."

We have it on the authority of the Rev. S. Barnett, who, at all events, knows Whitechapel thoroughly, that the infected area there is not large. This may also be the case in other parts of London; but this will make the matter easier to deal with.

If the above suggestion is not considered feasible, I hope that the member for White-chapel will, when Parliament meets, move for a Select Committee to inquire into the number of plague-spots, into the "dossing," or lodging-house system, and into the amount of supervision exercised by our police.

Faithfully yours,
COMPTON.
Oct. 4.

~

## The Star
### WHAT WE THINK.

"S.G.O." has written another of his powerful and pathetic letters to the *Times*. The Rev. Lord SIDNEY GODOLPHIN OSBORNE does not spare the society to which he belongs, and so faithful is his sermon that we will not ask whether the preacher has consistently minded his text. It is useful to point out that the Christianity which rejects the doctrine of human brotherhood in life only to confess it by its formularies in death is not precisely the kind of doctrine which its Founder taught:—

"Yes, ye of society, its upper class, ye, the dwellers in all attainable luxury, the fortunate of the earth, let your rank be what it may, your wealth a tale of millions, the Godward life of many of you ever in evidence, or the Godless life not less so; the Established Church of your nation proclaims in that solemn hour in which your own graves will be open, that these—the society labelled 'unfortunates' are before the God to whom you have been taken—your sisters. You may seek to ignore their existence. To speak of them at all is in bad taste; if forced to do so, it is as if they were a sort of human vermin, unclean parasites, a humanity affliction admitted in its existence, but so existent to be held as a matter of course; fortunately scattered where their presence does not intrude on that of those, the made of the same Creator, who dwell in all that the 'fortunate' of this life can obtain of this life's enjoyment."

This is excellent writing, but what does the Rev. Lord SIDNEY GODOLPHIN OSBORNE propose to do? A good many practical consequences flow from the admission that London swarms with men and women who live daily on the very edge of the margin of subsistence, men who are never out of the workhouse for more than a few months at a time, women who sell souls and bodies to get the price of bread and bed. We have been accused of unduly sensationalising these Whitechapel horrors. The charge comes with a good grace from the journal which has carried the policy of sensation to heights undreamed of

# Saturday, 6 October, 1888

by *The Star*, and which has lately been dabbling with rather puerile pleasure in the "blood-baths" of realistic romance. As a matter of fact our withers are unwrung. We have published no bloodstained facsimiles. We have given no unnecessary details. We have aimed throughout at definite social and political ends—the sounding of the chapel bell in the ears of the "classes," the doing the work which "S.G.O." is doing in the *Times* with a fervour of rhetorical energy to which we do not pretend. The fault of modern society is that it does not know the things that belong to its peace, that it is able to conceal, beneath the plausible shows, the conventional charities, and all the well-oiled machinery of selfish upper class and middle class life, the awful reality of the gulf that lies beneath. Society, as "S.G.O." says, cries "Aha! I am warm," when the warmth is that of the gathering volcano.

And now the whole thing is astir. The Press is alive with "the moral of the murders." Scores and hundreds of correspondents deluge us with letters "Is Christianity a Failure?" answering their own question as a rule with the pathetic *non sequitur* that Archbishops at £15,000 a year are. Mr. BARNETT sounds clearly, though a trifle mournfully, the note of the Gospel of Humanity which he and Toynbee Hall have so bravely and so unostentatiously preached year in and year out in the East End. In a few brief days we have got to know exactly what is the measure of our neglect of social duties; and what machinery is available for setting things right. These are great gains, and they have been bought at a not too costly price.

Of course, behind the immediate morals, the problems of practical politics which we all can help to solve, lie the larger facts on which the economist must keep his eye. Nothing can be more appropriate, for instance, than the appearance at such a time of Professor ROGERS'S "Economic Interpretation of History."[223] The title itself strikes a key-note of modern thought, which no man has sounded more emphatically than the late member for Bermondsey. All sensible men have given up treating history as if it were the record of the crimes and follies of kings and queens; and now most of our historians are beginning to learn the lesson that wages, and prices, and poor laws are the great tap-root facts of society, by following which we can delve down, down to its very foundations. Professor ROGERS, for instance, draws attention to the vital point, which he has himself proved to demonstration, that the means of life were more abundant in the Middle Ages than they are now. This is a sufficiently startling comment on the smooth optimism of disciples of "progress." If, as Canon SHUTTLEWORTH[224] said admirably at the Church Congress, the aim of Christianity should be to secure a decent environment for every human being, how far are we from the goal! But there is always hope for a society which knows the worst of itself, and admits it; and after certain realistic performances in Mitre-square and Hanbury-street, no one can any longer pretend ignorance of the tendency of such economic systems as that of unrestricted competition, backed by the devil's gospel of *laissez faire*, and working its disastrous will on a people divorced from the land, and stripped bare of the old labour-rights which held in the Middle Ages. Our duty, then, as a Radical journal is plain. It is, first, not to blink the truth. We have got to take the cotton wool out of Society' ears, and clap an ear-trumpet in instead. But it is also our duty to point other morals than that which the majority of the Press seem inclined to preach, viz., that our only part in this business is to catch the murderer, hang, and possibly torture him. Cursed as we are with Warrenism, we may not even accomplish the two first, but we can at least see that if some of GOD'S poor are dying horrible, but painless, deaths in Whitechapel, we will not forever condemn their brothers and sisters to the living

---

[223] **James Edward Thorold Rogers** (1823-1890). English historian and economist. Educated at King's College London and Magdalen Hall, Oxford, he was ordained into the Church of England after receiving his MA in 1849. He left the Church in 1870 under the provisions of the Clerical Disabilities Relief Act, which he had lobbied to have passed. First Tooke professor of Statistics and Economic Science, King's College

London, 1859 until his death. Liberal M.P. for Southwark from 1880-85, then for Bermondsey 1885-86. A champion free trade and social justice, his Economic Interpretation of History was published in 1888.

[224] **Henry Cary Shuttleworth** (1850-1900). Hymnist, Minor Canon of St. Paul's (1876-1884) and Rector of St. Nicholas, Cole Abbey, London until his death.

death of poverty.

THE *Daily News* has a timely article this morning on the lighting of Whitechapel. The real point of this matter is, not that the highways and byways of the East are worse lighted than those of many other parts of London, but that in the East there are facilities for crime in many ways. For these reasons the district ruled by the Whitechapel Board of Works ought to be better lighted than any other part of the metropolis. But this is a hard saying so long as the rateable value remains abnormally low, and every street lamp represents a capital outlay of £100.

HERE, again, then, it is the old story— something wrong in the government of London. If darkness be, as no one can doubt it is, the best friend of the criminal, this is a matter in which all London is concerned every bit as much as Whitechapel. Is it for the interest of the wealthy West-end that the pickpocket, the burglar, and the murderer should find secure and impenetrable hiding places in the East? The welfare of every part of the metropolis is bound up with that of every other part, and the cost of promoting that welfare ought to be evenly distributed over the whole, as it is in every other city in Christendom. Our want of appreciation of this "corporate unity" is at the bottom of half the evils of London municipal life, and to remedy it is one of the first works that awaits our coming London Council.

NOTHING better illustrates the need for a strong central government of London than the condition of the block of ruined tenements on the south side of King's College Hospital. Here, within a stone's throw of the magnificent pile of the Law Courts, and actually adjoining a large hospital, is a festering mass of rubbish and ruins, so foul in its unsanitary condition that the pathway through it has to be daily watered with carbolic acid to protect the unfortunate wayfarer. The idea will naturally arise in the minds of those who are new to these facts that this property must be part of some estate in Chancery, or belong to some cross-grained old miser who refuses to deal with it. Nothing of the sort; this patch of decaying squalor in the very centre of the largest city in the world, is the freehold property of the richest Government in the world.

THE Government of England bought this plot of ground years ago as a site for a new Bankruptcy Court. For years they did nothing to

it, but a few months ago one of these houses fell down with a crash, and Mr. Plunket was frightened. In consequence of this fright half a dozen labourers appeared on the scene, and took the roof off one of the remaining houses and expelled the inhabitants of those which were still habitable. Having done thus much, the labourers disappeared again, and have not been heard of more. But the London gamin[225] saw his chance of a fling, and there is not a whole window left in the houses which still stand, so that the place is infinitely more gruesome and disreputable than before Mr. Plunket touched it. There is absolutely no excuse for this gross neglect. It would have been perfectly easy to clear the site years ago of its ruins, level the ground, and allow the children of the district to use it as a playground until the time came for building the Bankruptcy Court. But the Chief Commissioner of Works, be he Liberal or Conservative, is much too exalted a personage to care about the children of Clare Market, or the sightliness of Carey-street.

—

### SPECIAL EDITION.
### A DOCTOR'S CLUE.
### HE GIVES INFORMATION OF A MAD MEDICAL ASSISTANT.
### Just Such a Man as Archibald Forbes Described—The Practical Joker Threatens Another Murder—A Night of Comparative Quiet.

A medical gentleman called at *The Star* office yesterday to give us some important information regarding a suspicion which he entertains as to the murderer. But his first words were of protest against the manner he was received at Scotland-yard. He went there in company with another medical gentleman and announced that he had some important information to communicate. He was shown into an underground room where two or three police clerks were standing about. He was not attended to, and after waiting some minutes he said to his friend, "Well, if this is the way we are to be treated I am going." There-upon one of the subalterns said, "Beg pardon, sir, but we are very busy." This came from one of the men who was busy talking to his colleagues. At last the doctor received some, but not too polite, attention. He was conducted

---

[225] **Gamin.** Street urchin. (Morehead)

# Saturday, 6 October, 1888

upstairs to see

**"SOMEONE IN AUTHORITY,"**

but that "someone" refused to see him. His statement was then taken down in a perfunctory manner. "The man," he says, "didn't put down half that I told him, and I was disgusted at the manner we were received and at the careless way Scotland-yard does its duty." The only explanation they gave to his protests was that "There's so many people call here, you know." Having extricated himself from Scotland-yard red tape and Warrenism, the gentleman came with his story to the *Star* office, not because he sympathises with the paper politically, for he is a "rank Conservative," but because of the importance he attaches to the news.

It has been more than once suggested that the murderer is a

**MONOMANIAC WITH MEDICAL KNOWLEDGE.**

The doctor had an assistant who has gone mad recently, and who is exactly the sort of man Mr. Archibald Forbes[226] had in his mind in his diagnosis of the murders. "Clearly," said Mr. Forbes, "the murderer is a man familiar with the geography of the Whitechapel purlieus. Clearly he is a man not unaccustomed in the manner of accosting these poor women as they are wont to be accosted. Clearly he is a man to whom the methods of the policeman are not unknown— the measured pace, the regular methodic round, the tendency to woodenness and unalertness of perception which are the characteristics of that well-meaning individual.

"Probably, a dissolute man, he fell a victim to a specific contagion, and so seriously that in the

---

[226] **Archibald Forbes** (1838-1900). *Daily News* war correspondent and author of books on contemporary military subjects. Some of the conflicts he covered were; the 1870-71 Franco-Prussian War, the 1872-76 3rd Carlist War in Spain, the 1876 Serbian Campaign, the 1877-78 Russo-Turkish War, the 1878 Afghanistan Expedition, and the 1879 Anglo-Zulu War. After the Battle of Ulundi (4 July, 1879), which concluded the Zulu War, he set out from the battlefield on horseback, and, only stopping to change horses, covered the 280 miles to Pietermaritzburg in 55 hours, beating the army despatch rider. His wire of the story to London allowed the *Daily News* to break the story of the British victory before the War Office received word of it.

sequel he lost his career. What shape the deterioration may have taken, yet left him with a strong, steady hand, a brain of devilish coolness, and an active step, is not to be defined."

"The man's physical health ruined," continues Mr. Forbes, "and his career broken, he has possibly suffered specific brain damage as well. At this moment—I cannot use exact professional terms—there may be mischief to one of the lobes of the brain. Or he may have become insane simply from anguish of body and distress of mind. Anyhow, he is mad, and his mania, rising from the particular to the general, takes

**THE FELL FORM OF REVENGE**

against the class, a member of which has wrought him his blighting hurt, against, too, the persons of that class plying in Whitechapel, since it was from a Whitechapel loose woman that he took his scathe."

Now this exactly describes the man whom the doctor suspects. He is a man of about 35. He was not a fully qualified surgeon, but had a certain amount of anatomical knowledge, and had assisted at operations, including ovariotomy.[227] He was the assistant to a doctor in Whitechapel, and

**KNOWS EVERY ALLEY AND COURT**

in the neighbourhood of the places where the murders were committed. He has been the victim of "a specific contagion,"[228] and since then has been animated by feelings of hate, not to say revenge, against the lower class of women who haunt the streets. When seen about eight months ago he was mad. "What man," said the doctor, in concluding his story, "is more likely to have committed the crime than this maniac?" The matter is certainly one which should be sifted by the police, but Scotland-yard is perhaps too busy to attend to it, because forsooth "There's so many call here, you know."

Extreme vigilance is now being exercised by the police in Whitechapel. The whole place swarms with detectives and men in uniform. Last night there was a great force abroad. It was feared that the murderer would again select Saturday morning for the perpetration of another crime, and they knew that unless he was caught red-handed they would have no evidence against him.

---

[227] **Ovariotomy.** Surgical removal of an ovary, or of an ovarian tumour. (Miller)

[228] Venereal Disease.

331

# Saturday, 6 October, 1888

A correspondent who was in Whitechapel last night says that detectives were walking in Commercial-road in couples, being followed by men in uniform. Some of the detectives were dressed up as dock labourers, and the disguise according to this observer was clumsy. These detectives follow every suspicious-looking person. Two of them noticed a man and woman drinking coffee at a stall. They followed the couple, arrested the man, took him to Angel-alley, and searched him, and then let him off. This correspondent while going through the streets was importuned by several women. One begged twopence of him to make up her night's lodging. Another seems to have been one of the decoy women which a private firm of detectives have out in order to try and catch the murderer.

—

### Telegram from "Jack the Ripper."

The Press Association says:—The following postal telegram was received by the Metropolitan Police at 11.55 p.m. last night. It was handed in at an office in the Eastern District at 8 p.m.:—

"Charles Warren, Head of the Police
New Central Office.
Dear Boss,

If are willing enough to catch me I am now in City-road lodging, but number you will have to find out, and I mean to do another murder to night in Whitechapel.

Yours,
JACK THE RIPPER."

The telegram has been proved to have been handed in at the chief office of the Eastern District in Commercial-road, but no information is forthcoming as to how it came to be accepted by the telegraphic authorities, or by whom it was handed in.

A letter was also received at the Commercial-street Police-station by the first post this morning. It was written in black lead pencil and signed "Jack Ripper." It is couched in ridiculous language, and the police believe it to be the work of a lunatic.

—

### Rewards to Catch Murderers.

The Whitechapel murderer, if such there be (says the extremely cautious *Law Journal*), has by invading the City boundary given rise to a curious illustration of the anomalies of local government which are now in process of being reformed. By slightly widening the circle of his crimes he has had brought to bear upon him a resource of barbarism of late years relegated to the past. The Home Secretary, in spite of clamour, has been steadfast in maintaining the practice inherited from his predecessors of refusing to try to catch criminals by offering large rewards. This is a policy which has now been adopted for the whole country, and it is obvious that if once broken in upon the whole mischief of information being held back by those who are waiting for the offer of a reward is revived. Unfortunately, the understanding which has prevailed has only the sanction of the comity of the police authorities throughout the country, and has no legal force. The City authorities, having the control of their own police, can revert to exploded expedients by dealing with crime from the commercial point of view with some show of right, but in point of law every private person may offer a reward for information leading to the detection of crime, and would be held to his promise in a court of law. An Act of Parliament is necessary to save the administration of the law from the periodical reversion to quack remedies to which it is exposed.

—

### The Mitre-square Victim.

The body of the deceased woman Kate Eddowes has been placed in a handsome polished coffin with oak mouldings. It has a block plate with gold letters with the following inscription:—

KATHERINE EDDOWES,
Died Sept. 30th, 1888,
Aged 43 years,

All the expenses in connection with the funeral will be borne by Mr. Hawks, Banner-street, St. Luke's. The City authorities, to whom the cemetery at Ilford belongs, have arranged to remit the usual fees.

—

### A MAN OF DISGUISES.
### The Police Believe the Murderer is in the Habit of Frequently Changing His Clothes.

The police have reason to believe that the Whitechapel murderer is a man of several disguises. They do not care to make public all the information they have on this point, but they will be very pleased to have any information as to

# Saturday, 6 October, 1888

what may be known about anyone changing their clothing under peculiar circumstances near or about the time of any of the murders. The first information on this point came to hand immediately after the Buck's-row murder, and there is a strong probability that facts then ascertained have a direct bearing on subsequent events. It will be remembered that Ann Nichols was murdered on the night of 30 August. On the following night it was reported that a woman was set upon by a gang of roughs[229] in Cambridge-heath-road, one of whom had attempted to force her into an alley way. This report proved to be false as far as the gang were concerned. The police ascertained, however, that

### A WOMAN HAD BEEN SET UPON

by a man, and that her cries had attracted a number of others, whose efforts to capture her assailant led to the gang story. The miscreant escaped in the direction of Commercial-road. That was about eleven o'clock. Not later than a quarter-past eleven a man stepped hurriedly into a yard entrance at No. 2, Little Turner-street, Commercial-road. On one side of the yard is a milk stand. The man asked for a glass of milk, and, when served, drank it hurriedly, then, looking about in a frightened manner, asked if he might step back into the yard. The proprietor, Henry Birch, did not object, but presently, his suspicions being aroused, he stepped towards the man and found him drawing on a suit of new overalls over his ordinary clothes. The pants were already on, and he was stooping to take a jacket from

### A BLACK SHINY BAG

that lay at his feet when Birch stepped up to him. He seemed to be very much upset by the interruption, and for a moment could not speak. Presently he said, "That was a terrible murder last night, was'nt it?" and before Birch could answer he had added, "I think I've got a clue," and, snatching up his bag, he disappeared down the street. Mr. Birch then thought he might be a detective, adopting a disguise for some purpose, but the police believe he was the man who assaulted the woman in Cambridge Heath-road, and that he donned the overalls to mislead anyone who might be tracing him. They have the name of the woman referred to, and her

---

[229] **Rough**. A ruffian. (Farmer)

333

description tallies with that given by Birch of his mysterious caller. The clothing was described as a blue serge suit, and a stiff but low hat. He wore a stand-up collar and a watch-chain. He wore no beard, but

### A SLIGHT DARK MOUSTACHE,

and his face was evidently sunburnt. Birch says he thought he was a seafaring man, or one who had recently made a long voyage. When he got the overalls on he had the appearance of an engineer. Many points of this description correspond so well to that given of the man who made such pointed inquiries about women at the Nuns Head Tavern, Aldgate, last Saturday night, and also to another description the police have received, that they are inclined to connect the man with the latest murders.

### THE ONLY QUESTIONABLE POINT

appears to be in regard to the hat, and it is just there that the theory of his frequent disguises comes in. It is deemed possible also that what a neighbour in Mitre-square thought was a light paper parcel may have been a black shiny bag, which with the light of the street lamp upon its glazed surface might easily have misled one. It is from a combination of the descriptions above referred to that the police have formed a pretty good idea of one man they would like to find.

—

### MEN WHO SAW THE MURDERER.
### Three People Describe a Man Seen with Stride Just Before her Murder.

The most important evidence given at the inquest yesterday on the Berner-street victim of the Whitechapel murderer was that bearing on the personal appearance of a man, supposed to be the culprit, who was seen standing in Berner-street with the woman by three people.

### WILLIAM MARSHALL,

of 64, Berner-street, a warehouse labourer about 50 years of age, said he saw the deceased on Saturday evening at about a quarter to twelve in Berner-street, about three or four doors from where he was living. She was standing talking to a man, and was not then wearing a flower in her bosom, so far as witness noticed. The two were talking together quietly.

The Coroner: Can you describe the man at all?

—He was of middling height, but I did not see his face clearly.

How was he dressed?

—He had a black coat on (not an overcoat), and wore light trousers.

Was he young, old, or middle-aged?

—He seemed to me to be middle-aged.

Was he wearing a hat?

—No; a round cap, with a small peak to it.

Such as a sailor would wear?

—Something of that sort.

Was he thin or stout?

—Rather stout.

Did he look well dressed?

—Yes, very decent.

What class of man did he appear to be?

—I thought he might work at some respectable business, not hard work.

Like a clerk?

—He had that appearance.

Did he have any whiskers?

—I don't think he did from what little I saw of his face.

Did he have any stick?

—No; nothing in his hands.

Did deceased have anything in her hands?

—I did not notice. I took more notice seeing him "a-kissing her and cuddling her." I was standing in my doorway.

Did you hear anything said?

—I heard him say to her, "You would say anything but your prayers."

Different people talk in a different way. Did his voice give you the idea of a clerk?

—Yes; he was mild speaking.

Did he speak like an educated man?

—Yes. I think he was.

### JAMES BROWN,

of 35, Fairclough-street, said that at about a quarter to one on Sunday morning he went out to get some supper at the corner of Berner-street, where there is a chandler's shop. He was gone three or four minutes, and as he returned he saw a man and woman standing by the Board School (which is just opposite the scene of the murder). They were up against the wall. As witness went past them he heard the woman say, "No, not to-night, some other night." That made him turn round and look at them. He was almost certain deceased was the woman, but did not notice any flowers in her bosom. The man had his hand on the wall, and the woman with her back against the wall was facing him.

The Coroner: Did you notice the man at all?

—I saw he had a long coat on, and that is all I noticed. It came very nearly down to his heels. It was an overcoat.

What sort of hat did he have on?

—I did not notice.

What height was the man?

—About the same as myself, 5ft. 7in.

Thin or stout?

—Not so very stout.

Did either seem the worse for drink?

—No.

### POLICE-CONSTABLE SMITH,

the constable on whose beat the murder occurred, said he noticed a man and woman in Berner-street talking together.

Was the woman anything like the deceased?

—Yes. I saw her face, and I think the body at the mortuary is that of the same woman.

Did you look at the man at all?

—Yes.

What did you notice about him?

—He had a parcel wrapped in a newspaper in his hand. The parcel was about 18in long and 6in. to 8in. broad.

Did you notice his height?

—He was about 5ft. 7in.

His hat?

—He wore a dark felt deerstalker's hat.

Clothes?

—His clothes were dark. The coat was a cutaway coat.

Did you overhear any conversation?

—No.

Did they seem to be sober?

—Yes, both.

Did you see the man's face?

—He had no whiskers, but I did not notice him much. I should say he was 28 years of age. He was of respectable appearance, but I could not state what he was. The woman had a flower in her breast. It rained very little after eleven o'clock. There were but few people in the bye streets. When I saw the body in the mortuary, I recognised it at once.

The inquiry was adjourned to Tuesday fortnight, at two o'clock.

~

# Saturday, 6 October, 1888

## Evening News
### DOWN WHITECHAPEL WAY

A clever though somewhat superficial Frenchman, writing about our Sunday observances, opined that the English, who were the most sensible people on the face of the earth for six days of the week, took leave of their senses on the seventh. The East end Christian, watching his Jewish brother, is almost bound to come to the conclusion that the latter, while by no means a fool from Sunday morning till Friday night, is more sensible still on his Sabbath day. The lower class Jew, of whom I am speaking here, not only abstains more strictly from work on his day of rest than his equally humble Christian neighbour does on his, but spends it differently.

As a rule the Jew is not addicted to drunkenness, though his mode of living, less exclusive now than formerly, has made a considerable alteration in that respect. This does not mean that he gets "blind roaring drunk" but he is not a tee-totaller by a long way. But even when he exceeds the bounds of moderation at ordinary times he will leave off swilling on Friday at sunset.

His Christian brother keeps up the game till midnight on Saturday, and as a matter of course, sleeps off his bout on Sunday morning; consequently the ushering in the day of rest—not from a religious, but merely from a family point of view—does not exist for this Christian brother, except perhaps on Christmas Eve. The Jew, on the other hand, unless he is actually destitute, has a very comfortable time of it on Friday night.

Whatever good or bad luck the previous six days may have brought, there has been actual or attempted provision for the seventh. The housewife has been to market on Friday morning according to her means, the homely board is spread at dusk that same evening, and whatever else may be lacking in the way of table appointments that board is sure to be graced by a clean white cloth. If the head of the family be not exactly orthodox, but simply observant of his religion, there will be the blessing of the wine and of the bread, albeit that the former commodity owes nothing to the vineyards of France or elsewhere, and is only a decoction of grocers' raisins and water. After which the whole of the household sit down to their meal—not a very sumptuous one, but carefully cooked. The chances are ten to one—remember I am speaking of the poorer classes—that the repast merely consists of fried fish, bread and butter and tea, but it is good of its kind, for the Jewish housewife is essentially a clever cook.

The girls and boys have "cleaned themselves" and, after supper, their young friends of both sexes will come in and spend the evening with them and their parents. If it will run to it, there will be during the evening such homely delicacies as roasted chestnuts or baked apples in the winter, in the summer cheap raw fruit.

In former days Jewish lads and lasses scarcely ever left their parents' homes, unless it were to go to a near neighbour. Things have changed somewhat, still even now they rarely go on that night to the play or music hall, which outing is reserved for Saturday night. The Jew is especially fond of music, and above all of florid Italian music. When cheap opera in English used to flourish at the Standard Theatre, half of the audience was composed of Hebrews. It is no unfrequent thing, therefore, for the belated wayfarer through the dark alleys in the purlieus of Petticoat lane and Goulston street to be attracted by operatic choruses, nay even solos, sung very decently indeed. Should his curiosity lead him to have a peep through the chinks of the shutters he will be gratified by a family picture such as that described by George Eliot in "Daniel Deronda," a little more lowly, perhaps, in texture, but essentially the same in outline.

As with his Friday night so with his Saturday morning and throughout that day. The poorer Jew must be poor indeed to have no Sabbath suit of clothes. The poorer Jew must be poor indeed not to have superior food on his day of rest.

The Christian brother in his immediate proximity has observed all this, and asked himself how the Jew manages on earnings probably not superior to his own. His wife (the Christian's) is probably engaged in the same workshop with the Jew's daughter, for umbrella making, waistcoat and trouser making is not confined to the Jewess down Whitechapel way. The Christian goes out with the "glass basket," the Jew goes out with his old clothes bag. By the glass basket I mean the men who go from house to house bartering cheap Bohemian glass

335

ornaments, artificial waxen flowers on stands, sets of jugs, &c., &c., for left off clothing. The Jew, instead of giving the latter, gives hard cash. The Christian, therefore, knows that he has as much chance of a windfall as the other.

How, then, does the Jew manage to do more with his money than the Christian? That is what the Christian asks himself, and if he be not altogether a ginsodden brute, he is not very long in arriving at a solution. "The Jew," he says, "tries to buy and sell, in however small a way, instead of doing manual work. So for the old men; the women work with their needle, as do my wife and daughter. The sons do not take to carpentering, smith's, or upholsterer's work. If they toil with their hands at all, they take to cigar making, boot rivetting, and tailoring—trades, in which, if they are steady at all, they can start on their own account with a very small capital indeed. Why should I not do the same?" And he does the same.

If authentic statistics could be arrived at, it would be found that in the area mentioned by me in my former article, there are fewer artisans in proportion to the population than elsewhere, except tailors, boot rivetters, &c., &c. If all the proprietors of the attractive fruit shops in the various populous quarters of London were to be canvassed, and if they were prepared to tell the truth, it would be found that their first start at shopkeeping was due to emulation of the Jew.

The fried fish and potato shops, the fumes of whose pans greet our nostrils in the transpontine and other regions, are due to the initiative of the Jew. The sale of sewing machines, perambulators, mangles, &c., by weekly payments—not an unmixed blessing, perhaps—was inaugurated by a Jew.

In Whitechapel, and in the adjacent roads, the Jew's influence on his Christian brethren is plainly visible for good and evil. The good I have endeavoured to point out, I now come to the evil.

Such businesses as the Jew engages in at starting require, first and foremost, not only assiduous application, but hardheadedness and in the beginning careful husbanding of the first gains. Whether the Jew excels in all these qualities, it would be difficult to say off hand; certain it is that those with whom he deals give him, as a rule, credit for such, chiefly because he has a reputation for sobriety. The Christian is

reputed not to be so sober. But if he be as temperate as the Jew, he is not so daring, especially if he have spring from the humbler orders. With the Jew's example so very close to him, he, however, catches some of it, and it would be easy enough to point out scores and scores of prosperous shops in Whitechapel whose proprietors, Christians, launched into business with a mere nothing.

But to return to my theme. The Jew, as I have already hinted, is fond of finery, but frugal and hard working though he be when needs must, he is also very indolent the moment the first pressure is removed. He then begins to work with his head, while he lets the others do the laborious physical toil. There are down Whitechapel half a dozen coffee shops—not public houses—from which he directs his operations, whatever they may be.

In one case he may have a score of men out for him buying job lots in the City. The humbler ones buy the leather cuttings of the boot and shoe manufacturers, others buy waste paper, and so forth. But one and all, while not pretending to work, work. The Christian who is not in the secret begins by imitating the Jew in not working. By some process of his own he thinks that what the Jew can do at his leisure he can do. And the Christian goes to the wall, and ends in a lodging house in Flower and Dean street, while the Jew migrates to Maida Vale or Canonbury, or Westbourne Park in the end. This is the evil part.

I have left the most delicate matter to the last, and I am very reluctant to tackle it now, lest I be suspected of wishing to prove too much. The police will tell any careful inquirer that there is "not a single Jewess among the class of unfortunates who have lately become the victims of the murderer's knife." Let not the reader infer from this that there are no Jewesses leading immoral lives. At the risk of being contradictory, I can answer that there are. But they are all more or less prosperous. Like their brethren in trade, they began with the intention of throwing the burden on others, and so well have they succeeded that they are the mistresses of establishments, the threshold of which the fiend that stalks abroad would not dare to approach.

In short, the Jew is the Yankee of Europe—acute, scrupulous—because afraid of the law.

Those who come in daily contact with him at his headquarters do equally well, provided they penetrate the secret of his success; but if they only guess part they are submerged. That is why the lower classes in Whitechapel are less poor, less degraded, less unclean, at least outwardly, than elsewhere in the metropolis, unless they are poorer, more degraded, and more unspeakably filthy than any of the lower classes anywhere in the world. The latter are, however, the exception.

A.D.V.

—

## THE MURDERS.
## LETTERS FROM
## "JACK THE RIPPER"
## TO THE POLICE.

The Press Association said the following postal telegram was received by metropolitan police at 11.55 last night. It was handed in at an office in the Eastern District at 8 p.m.

"Charles Warren, head of the Police, New Central Office.

Dear Boss—If you are willing enough to catch me, I am now in City road lodging, but number you will have to find out, and I mean to do another murder tonight in Whitechapel.

Yours, Jack the Ripper."

A letter was also received at the Commercial street police station, by the first post, this morning. It was addressed to the "Commercial street Police Station" in blacklead pencil, and the contents was also written in pencil, and couched in ridiculous language. The police believe it to be the work of a lunatic. It was signed "Jack the Ripper," and said he was "going to work" in Whitechapel last night. He added that he was going to commit another murder in the Goswell road, tonight, and spoke of having "several bottles of blood under ground in Epping Forest," and frequently referred to "Jack the Ripper under the ground."

Detective Inspector Aberline has been informed of the correspondence, and the police of the G division have been communicated with.

—

### ON THE MURDERER'S TRACK.

The police have as yet practically no clue, but they are confident that the murderer is still in the East end, and certain suspected neighbourhoods are under observation. It is pointed out that the murderer, after the commission of his last crime, undoubtedly proceeded from Mitre square by way of Church passage, Duke street, Houndsditch, Gravel lane, Stoney lane, to Goulston street, at which spot a clue appears to have been lost of him.

In this neighbourhood he evidently entered one of the notorious houses, which cannot be entered without elaborate arrangements by and a certain amount of danger to the police. It would take about ten minutes for a person to get from Mitre square to the neighbourhood, so that the murderer was well away from the scene, and perhaps safely under cover before Constable Watkins obtained even medical assistance after the discovery of the body.

This is a point put forward by the police in favour of bloodhounds being employed, as it is suggested had one of the hounds been brought on the scene immediately there would have been little, if any, chance of the murderer evading justice so long as he has.

The prevailing opinion among the police now although the daring which has characterised his previous acts, shake their theories, is that he will keep in hiding for some time until the excitement abates, or the precautions are relaxed; or that he will find a new field for his operations in another part of the town.

—

### SIR CHARLES WARREN WILL USE
### BLOODHOUNDS.

The Central News is authorised to state that Sir Charles Warren has been making inquiries as to the practicability of employing trained bloodhounds in the streets of London; and, having ascertained that dogs, which have been accustomed to work in a town, can be procured, he is making immediate arrangements for their use in London.

—

### ONE OF THE FALSE CONFESSIONS.

Yesterday, at the Guildhall Police court, before Sir Alderman Stone, William Bull, 27, living at Stannard road, Dalston, was charged on remand with having committed the murder in Mitre square, Aldgate, on Sunday morning.

The facts were given in *The Times* of Thursday.

Mr. Savill (chief clerk) asked Inspector Izzard if he had made inquiries during the remand.

Inspector Izzard:—I have, and the result is perfectly satisfactory. The prisoner for several

# Saturday, 6 October, 1888

years was engaged at Messrs. Ryland's, and bore an irreproachable character. Recently he has given way to drink, and this is the result. His family are highly respectable.

The Alderman: Have you ascertained where he was on Saturday night?

Inspector Izzard:—yes; I have a gentleman in Court, a Mr. Day, with whom the prisoner was on Saturday night till 12 o'clock.

The Alderman: It is with great regret that I find the law does not permit me to punish you for your conduct. The statement you made to the Inspector on Tuesday night was without the least foundation in fact. At a time like this your acts are perfectly inexcusable. I must discharge you and I hope you will be thoroughly ashamed of your bad behaviour.

Prisoner:—Since I have been in prison I have signed the pledge.

The Alderman: And I hope you will keep it.

Accused was discharged.

—

## THE DAUGHTER OF THE MITRE SQUARE VICTIM.

The daughter of the woman who was murdered in Mitre square has been found. Her age is 19, and she is married. She states that her father, Thomas Conway, with whom the deceased cohabited for some time before she met with Kelly, is still living, but he has not yet been traced. It will be remembered that Kelly stated in the course of his evidence on Thursday, before the Coroner, that when the deceased left him early last Saturday afternoon she told him she was going to try and find her daughter Annie. The latter, however, now states that she did not see her mother that day.

—

## THE DATE OF THE FUNERAL FIXED.

The funeral of the Mitre square victim will take place next Monday. The remains will leave the City mortuary between two and three o'clock, and will be interred in the cemetery at Ilford. The relatives have accepted the offer of Mr. Hawkes, of Banner street, St. Luke's, to bear the expenses of the funeral.

—

## TO THE EDITOR OF "THE EVENING NEWS."

Sir—You publish in your special edition of the 4th a facsimile of the letter and postcard supposed to have been written by the murderer. Now, having been in America and mixed with American people, I am quite certain that the above have been written either by an American or one who has been in America for some time. The whole of the letter is full of American words and phrases: for instance, boss, fix, right track, real fits, down on, ripping, buckled, give it out straight, and right away are very common expressions used in America. Hoping some hint of this sort might lead to a clue.

I am, &c.,
WHITECHAPEL.
London, E., October 4.

—

## THE BERNER STREET MURDER. RESUMED INQUEST.

Mr. Wynne Baxter resumed the inquest, yesterday, at the St. George's Vestry Hall, Cable street, St. George's in the East, into the circumstances attending the death of Elizabeth Watts or Stride, who was found with her throat cut behind the building at 40 Berner street, on Sunday morning last.

## DR.PHILLIPS GIVES MORE EVIDENCE.

Dr. Phillips, re-examined, said that as requested at the last sitting of the inquiry, he had made a re-examination with regard to the missing palate, and from very careful examination of the roof of the mouth he found that there was no injury to either the hard or the soft palate.

He had also carefully examined the handkerchiefs, and had come to the conclusion that the stains on the larger handkerchief were those of fruit.

He was convinced that the deceased had not swallowed the skin or inside of a grape within many hours of her death. The apparent abrasion which was found on washing the flesh was not an abrasion at all, as the skin was entire underneath.

The knife produced on the last occasion he found to be such as was used in a joiner's shop, and was what was called a "slicing knife." It had been recently blunted, and its edge was turned by continued rubbing on a stone such as a kerb stone; it evidently had been before a very sharp knife, and was such a knife as could have produced the injuries and incision to the neck, but it was not such a weapon as he should have used for inflicting the injuries in this particular case. If his opinion with regard to the position of the body was correct, the knife would become a very improbable instrument as having caused the incision.

He found that the deceased was seized by the shoulders, pressed on the ground, and that the perpetrator of the deed was on the left side when he inflicted the wound. He was of opinion that the cut was made from the left to the right of the deceased and from that, therefore, arose the unlikelihood of such a long knife having inflicted the wound described in the neck. The knife was not sharp pointed; but round and an inch across. There was nothing in the cut to show an incision of the point of any weapon.

## HOW DID HER RIGHT HAND GET COVERED WITH BLOOD?

In reply to the Coroner, witness said that he could not form any account of how the deceased's right hand became covered with blood. It was a mystery. He was taking it as a fact that the hand always remained in the position he found it resting across the body.

Deceased must have been alive within an hour of his seeing her. The injuries would only take a few seconds to inflict, it might have been done in two seconds. He could not say with certainty whether the sweets being found in her hands would indicate that the deed had been done suddenly.

He had seen several self inflicted wounds more extensive than that on the deceased, but they had not generally included the carotid artery.

There was a great dissimilarity between this case and Chapman's. In the latter the neck was severed all round down to the vertebral column, the vertebral bone being enlarged by two sharp cuts, and there being an evident attempt to separate the bones. He would rather say that the assassin would not get necessarily bloodstained as the commencement of the wound and the injury to the vessels would be away from him, and the stream of blood would also be entirely away from him and towards the water course near where she lay.

There was no perceptible trace of any anaesthetic or narcotic in the viscera or stomach. It was difficult to account for the absence of

noise in this case, but it must not be taken for granted that there was no noise. If there was no noise it was impossible to account for.

In reply to the jury, Dr. Phillips stated that in a yard like that where the deed occurred the deceased might cry out and not be heard, but he would rather not interfere with the other evidence on this point.

He had reason to believe that the deceased was lying on the ground when the wound was inflicted.

There was no trace of malt liquor in the stomach.

## DR. BLACKWELL RECALLED.

Dr. Blackwell, recalled, said there was one point on which he was not quite clear. He had removed the cachou from the left hand, which was nearly open; in fact, it was between the thumb and the first finger, which accounted for the police not seeing it, and it was he who spilled the cachous on the ground. The hand would gradually relax while on the ground, while life ceased.

He had seen many more severe wounds which were suicidal, but he agreed with Dr. Phillips that the knife found, although it might have inflicted the injury, was a most unlikely instrument. A murderer would severely handicap himself by using such a knife. It was not such an instrument as slaughterers would use.

There were pressure marks on the shoulders, as if the victim had struggled.

## IDENTIFIED BY A SWEDISH PASTOR.

Sven Ollsen, pastor of the Swedish Church, Princes square, stated that he saw the body of the deceased in the mortuary. Deceased was a Swede, and he had known her for the last seventeen years. Her name was Elizabeth Stride, carpenter, and she was the wife of John Thomas Stride. Her maiden name was Elizabeth Gustafstotger[230], and she was born near Gottenberg, November 27, 1843.

Witness obtained these facts from his church register. All Swedes coming to this country gave in a certificate to the church. Deceased was registered on July 10, 1866. There was also an entry in abbreviated Swedish to the effect that she was married to an Englishman named John Thomas Stride. Witness said he knew the

---

[230] Gustafsdotter.

hymnbook produced, dated 1821, and he mentioned it as one he had given to the deceased last winter. He thought she was married to Stride about 1869, but could not say when the latter died. Deceased was not in good circumstances when her husband died, but was very poor and would have been glad of any assistance. Witness gave her some assistance at that time.

Coroner: Do you know that there was a subscription raised for the friends of those who went down in the Princess Alice?

—No.

Well, I can tell you there was, and I can tell you more, that no one of the name of Stride made any application.

Witness said he had never heard of deceased having had any children, or having made any application to the Princess Alice Fund. He had never seen her husband. Some years ago she gave him her address as Devonshire street, Commercial road. She said she was doing a little sewing. She could speak English pretty well. He thought deceased came to England a little before she was registered in the church books.

## HE SAW LIZZIE STRIDE TALKING WITH THE MURDERER.

William Marshall, 64 Berner street, Commercial road, labourer, was the next witness. He said he had seen the body on Sunday in the mortuary. He had seen the deceased on the Saturday evening before in Berner street, about three doors from the house of witness—that would be at No. 58. She was on the pavement opposite No. 58, between Christian street and Boyd street. She was standing talking to a man on the pavement. He recognised the deceased as the same woman he had seen, both by her face and her dress. He did not notice that she had any flower.

He did not see the man's face distinctly, but he noticed that he was dressed in a black cutaway coat and dark trousers, and was wearing a brown cap with a small peak, somewhat like what a sailor would wear.

The man's height was about 5ft 6in; he was middle aged, rather stout, and appeared decently dressed. He was not like a man who did hard work, nor was he like a sailor, but he had more the appearance of a clerk than anything else witness could suggest. Could not say whether the man had any whiskers, as he did not see his face. He was not wearing gloves; he had no stick or umbrella.

Witness was quite sure that the deceased was the woman he saw. He did not notice that the woman had anything in her hand. he was standing at his own door at the time, and what first attracted his attention was the man "a-kissing and a-cuddling of her."

## "YOU WOULD SAY ANYTHING BUT YOUR PRAYERS."

He heard the man say to the deceased, "You would say anything but your prayers."

Coroner: Did his voice give you the idea of a clerk?

—He was mild spoken.

Did he speak like an educated man?

—Yes. I did not hear him say any more, nor did the woman say anything. She only laughed, and they went away together, down Ellen street, in the middle of the road. They did not pass No. 40 on their way. The deceased was dressed in a black jacket and a black skirt. neither of them appeared to witness to be the worse for drink. He afterwards heard of the murder; that would be after one o'clock. He stayed at his door from 11.30 till 12, and it did not rain then. It did not rain until three. as witness stood at his door the man and woman passed him in the road. There is a gas lamp over the baker's shop at 70 Berner street, at the corner of Boyd street.

Mr. Ollsen, recalled, said he found that the entry of the marriage of the deceased was in the handwriting of Mr. Frost, who was the pastor of the Swedish Church until two years ago.

James Brown, 39 Fairclough street, said he had seen the body of the deceased in the mortuary. He saw her on Sunday morning last, about 12.45, as he was going into his own house at the corner of Berner street and Fairclough street, to get some supper. There was a man and woman standing together at the corner of Board Schools, in Fairclough street. He was in the road just by the kerb, and they were against the wall.

## "NOT TONIGHT, NOT TONIGHT."

He heard the woman say, "Not tonight, some other night." That made him turn round and look at her, and he saw sufficient of her to make him almost certain that the deceased was that woman. He noticed no flower on her dress.

The man was standing, leaning with his arm on the wall; the woman was facing the street with her back against the wall. Witness noticed that the man had a long coat on—it seemed to be an overcoat. He was sure it was not the woman's dress he noticed.

There was no light—it was all dark at the place. It was not raining at the time.

Witness went on into his house, and when nearly finished with his supper he heard cries of "Police!" and "Murder!" That would be about a quarter of an hour after he got home. He did not look at any clock after ten minutes past twelve.

The man's height would be about 5ft 7in, of average build. Neither the man nor the woman appeared to be the worse for drink. Witness did not notice any foreign accent.

He could not say who raised the cries "Murder" and "Police." He went to the window and opened it, but could not see anybody. Shortly afterwards he saw a policeman standing at the corner of Christian street.

## THE POLICEMAN ON THE BEAT CALLED.

Police constable Smith, 452, said that on Saturday, September 29, he went on duty at 10 p.m. His beat was past Berner street, and went as far as Gower walk, along the Commercial road, round Christian street and Fairclough street to Grove street, then along Grove street as far as Backchurch lane, and up the latter into Commercial road again, taking all the interior streets, including Berner street. It would take him from 25 minutes to half an hour to go round his beat.

He was in Berner street about half past 12 or 20 minutes to one. He arrived at 40 Berner street about 1 o'clock on his ordinary round. He was not called.

He found a crowd of people outside the gates of No. 40. The gates were closed. He did not remember passing any one on his way down Berner street. When he saw the deceased he found she was dead, and went to the police station for the ambulance, leaving other constables in charge. Dr. Blackwell's assistant had just arrived about that time.

When he was in Berner street he saw a man and a woman talking together. The woman resembled the deceased. He had seen her face and had seen the body in the mortuary. He was

absolutely certain that the deceased was the woman he had seen. She stood on the pavement a few yards on the opposite side of Berner street from where she was found.

He noticed the man who was talking to her. He had a newspaper parcel in his hand about a foot and a half long, and six or eight inches wide. He was man of about 5ft 7in, and had a dark deerstalker hat on. He was wearing plain dark clothes, with a cut away coat, and dark trousers.

Witness overheard no conversation, and did not see much of the man's face. He had no whiskers; he was respectably dressed. The woman had a flower in her dress.

The inquiry was afterwards adjourned.

—

## IDENTITY OF LIZZIE STRIDE.

On the question of the identity of the woman stated Elizabeth Stride, a Greenwich correspondent writes:

At the inquest at the Vestry hall, Cable street, before Mr. Wynne Baxter, on Wednesday, Elizabeth Turner, deputy at the common lodging house at 32 Flower and Dean street, said she did not know the name of the deceased, but recognised the body as that of "Long Liz" who had lodged in her house on and off for about six years, and added, "She told me she was a married woman, and that her husband went down in the Princess Alice ship."

Michael Kidney, of 35 Dorset street, Spitalfields, who identified the body as that of Elizabeth Stride, said the woman told him she was a widow, and that her husband, who was drowned in the Princess Alice disaster, was a ship's carpenter belonging to Sheerness, and added, "She said she had nine children, and that two were drowned in the Princes Alice." Now, the Bywell Castle, steam collier, ran down the Princess Alice off Tripcock Point, just below Woolwich Arsenal, on the evening of September 3, 1878, and consequently at that time Elizabeth Stride as 25 years of age, and could not have had children over the age of ten years. Mr. C.J. Carttar, late coroner for West Kent, held an inquiry, extending over six weeks, on the bodies of 527 persons drowned by the disaster, at the Town Hall, Woolwich, the majority of whom were identified, and caused an alphabetical list of those identified, above 500, to be made by his clerk.

# Saturday, 6 October, 1888

An inspection of the list, which is in the possession of Mr. E.A. Carter, the present coroner, and son of the late coroner, does not disclose the name of Stride. Whole families were drowned, but the only instance of a father and two children being drowned where the children were under the age of 12 years was in the case of an accountant named Bell, aged 38, his two sons being aged respectively ten and seven years. It is true that Mr. Lewis, the Essex coroner, held inquests on a few of the bodies cast ashore in Essex, but it is extremely improbable that the three bodies of Mr. Stride and his two children were cast ashore on that side of the river, or that they were all driven out to sea and lost. If the bodies were picked up and taken to Woolwich they must have been identified by Mrs. Stride.

It is therefore possible that the body upon which the inquest is now being held is not that of Elizabeth Stride, but of some unknown woman.

# Monday, 8 October, 1888

## The Times
### THE EAST-END MURDERS.

Fears were expressed among the police on Saturday that the night would not pass without some startling occurrence, and the most extraordinary precautions were taken in consequence. It must not be supposed that the precautions taken apply only to the East-end of London. It is fully understood that the murderer, finding his favourite haunts too hot for him, may transfer his operations to another district, and arrangements have been made accordingly. The parks are specially patrolled, and the police, even in the most outlying districts, are keenly alive to the necessities of the situation. Having efficiently provided for the safeguarding of other portions of the large area under his jurisdiction, Sir Charles Warren has sent every available man into the East-end district. These, together with a large body of City detectives, are now on duty, and will remain in the streets throughout the night. Most of the men were on duty all last night, and the work has been found very harassing. But every man has entered heartily into the work, and not a murmur has been heard from any of the officers. They are on their metal, and if zeal were the only thing needed to hunt down the murderer, his capture would be assured.

Yesterday evening all was quiet in the district, and the excitement had somewhat subsided. Nevertheless, the police and the local Vigilance Committee have by no means relaxed their watchfulness, and the inhabitants of the district, disregarding the improbability of the murderer risking his freedom under those circumstances, still appear to expect the early commission of a new crime. During Saturday night and the early hours of Sunday morning several persons were arrested and detained at local police-stations until all the circumstances in connexion with their apprehension were thoroughly sifted. Several of these were given into custody on grounds which proved in inquiry to be flimsy and even foolish, and the police have in consequence been put to a good deal of trouble without any corresponding result. It seemed at times as if every person in the streets were suspicious of everyone else he met, and as if it were a race between them who should first inform against his neighbour.

Alfred Napier Blanchard, who described himself as a canvasser,[231] residing at Handsworth, was charged at Birmingham on Saturday, on his own confession, with having committed the Whitechapel atrocities. He had been arrested in consequence of a circumstantial statement which he made in a publichouse of the manner in which he had effected the murders. He now denied all knowledge of the matter, and said he had spoken under excitement, caused by reading about the murders, and heavy drinking. The Bench declined to release him, however, till to-day, in order to allow time for inquiries.

Up to a late hour last night no important arrest had been reported in connexion with the murders at the East-end at any of the City police-stations. Many communications continue to be received at Scotland-yard and by the City police, describing persons who have been seen in various parts of the country whose conduct is suspicious or who are supposed to resemble the man seen talking to the victim of the Berner-street murder on the night of her assassination.

---

In answer to the petition to Her Majesty, presented by Mr. George Lusk on behalf of his Vigilance Committee and the inhabitants of Whitechapel generally, the following letter was received late on Saturday night:—

Whitehall, Oct. 6, 1888.

"Sir—The Secretary of State for the Home Department has had the honour to lay before the Queen the petition signed by you praying that a reward may be offered by the Government for the discovery of the perpetrator of the recent murders in Whitechapel, and he desires me to inform you that though he has given directions that no effort or expense should be spared in endeavouring to discover the person guilty of the murders, he has not been able to advise Her Majesty that in his belief the ends of justice would be promoted by any departure from the decision already announced with regard to the proposal that a reward should be offered by Government.

"I am, Sir, your obedient servant,
"E. LEIGH PEMBERTON.

---

[231] **Canvasser.** A Canvas maker. (Census1891.com)

343

# Monday, 8 October, 1888

"George Lusk, Esq.,
1, 2, and 3, Alderney-road,
Mile-end road, E."

In reference to the great interest taken by Mr. Lusk in the welfare of the inhabitants of the district, there seems to be no doubt that he has been marked down, for on Saturday evening it became necessary to call in the police for the purpose of keeping a look-out for a mysterious stranger who has been prowling round his premises and his son's house with the object, it is believed, of striking through Mr. Lusk at the Vigilance Committee. After an interview with a constable and a detective-sergeant, the matter was deemed of sufficient importance to warrant the attendance of an inspector from Bethnal-green, and at 10:30 waited on Mr. Lusk and heard his statement on the matter.

The description given of this man is as follows:—Height, 5ft. 9in., aged 38 to 40, full beard and moustache, matted and untrimmed, dent on the bridge of the nose, florid complexion, wide nostrils, eyes sunken, dressed in a rusty frock coat, white turn-down collar, black tie, no watchchain, deerstalker hat, and the left boot broken out on the left side; carried a brown stick with round top.

According to a Reuter telegram from New York, the *New York Herald* declares that the seaman named Dodge, who recently stated that a Malay, whom he met in London, threatened to murder a number of Whitechapel women for robbing him, said he knew the street where the Malay stayed, but that he would not divulge the name until he learnt what chance there was of a reward. He stated, however, that the street was not far from the East India Dock-road; but he was not certain about the house where the man lived. Another seaman said he thought the Malay was now on a vessel plying in the North Sea.

~

## The Star
### WHAT WE THINK.

MR. HENRY MATTHEWS appears to have what lawyers call a "common form" for expressing his views on the Whitechapel atrocities. He has been approached from half a dozen different directions on the subject of a reward, but all that can be got out of him is that he "does not believe," occasionally varied by "he is unable to perceive," that the ends of justice will be served by offering a reward. We have given Mr. Matthews a dozen reasons why a reward should be offered even though the ends of justice were not served by it; but, to adapt a famous repartee of Dr. Johnson, it is no use giving a Tory Minister a reason unless you can at the same time supply him with an understanding.[232]

FORTUNATELY no artificial stimulus is required to awaken the population of East London to their duties in the present emergency. In every direction committees of working men and other residents are taking up the work which the police are unable to do, and for the last night or two the streets of Whitechapel have been patrolled so effectually that the miscreant has had a very slender chance of renewing his operations. The danger now is that these precautions will be relaxed as the excitement dies down, which it is sure to do after a very few days' immunity. All hope of working out any clue from the last crimes is now at an end. The only chance is to catch the murderer in the act of repeating, or on the point of repeating his butchery, and this can only be done by incessant vigilance maintained, it may be, for weeks and weeks.

WE observe that Messrs. Kelly and Peters have persuaded the *Financial News* to start a subscription for the purpose of providing funds, to be expanded by Messrs. Peters and Kelly, and some others in patrolling Whitechapel and Mile-end. Some seventy men, "full of courage and endurance" are to patrol these districts from ten o'clock at night until seven o'clock in the

---

[232] '(Dr. Samuel) Johnson having argued for some time with a pertinacious gentleman; his opponent, who had talked in a very puzzling manner, happened to say, "I don't understand you, Sir;" upon which Johnson observed, "Sir, I have found you an argument; but I am not obliged to find you an understanding."' (Boswell)

# Monday, 8 October, 1888

morning, and by their means Messrs. Peters and Kelly expect to capture the Whitechapel murderer. We regret that our contemporary should have lent its aid to this project. The people of the districts concerned have already taken the necessary steps to help the police, they are helping them, as becomes good citizens, without making any appeal to the public for funds, and they do not require the assistance of Messrs. Peters and Kelly—unless they choose to give that assistance without pay.

THE snuffling *Spectator* is always eager to draw a moral against the poor, but it has not often done a crueller thing than when, by way of meeting our point that prostitution and poverty broadly stand to each other in the relation of cause and effect, it urged that the slaughtered women took to bad ways because they liked vice, drink, and foulness better than virtue, temperance, and decent habits. Now it was proved in the case of the women Stride and Eddowes that they were driven on the streets, not that they went there of their own accord; and the same thing applied in a less conspicuous degree to the woman Chapman. Mrs Stride lost her breadwinner, and drifted on to the streets. The woman Eddowes did honest work when she could get it; when she could not she went wrong. Mrs. Chapman lost her annuity; and it was said of her that she lived honestly as long as the pittance was paid her.

In any case these women sold their persons for board and bed; while fine ladies who read the *Spectator* sell theirs every day in Mayfair for a "position," a carriage, a rent-roll, and a box at the opera. The other difference is that the one kind of union is legalised and solemnised by Christian bishops and ministers; the other is not.

———

### The Police Down on Newsboys.

A constable ordered a newsboy selling papers in Ludgate-circus on Saturday evening to move on. No reason was given, and the lad moved away somewhat reluctantly. While he was crossing the road, the policeman suddenly seized his arm and marched him off to the station. There he was charged with three specific offences:—Causing obstruction; Refusing to go away when ordered; And refusing to give his name and address.

The first offence was of so trivial a nature that to base a charge of breaking the law was of course farcical. The lad did not refuse to go away

when ordered; he was not, for all the spectators could see, asked his name and address. The sergeant heard these two last facts from Mr. Rowe, of 11, Northwood-road, Highgate, who followed the policeman and the newsboy to the station. The charge was not pressed, and the lad was released.

[Several cases of the police interfering with the sale of evening papers have recently been brought to our notice. We shall be glad if those who observe other instances will notify the facts to us, to prevent oppression and injustice. *Send the number of the policeman.*]

———

### FIFTH EDITION.
### WHITECHAPEL.
### One or Two Arrests,
### but None of Any Importance.

Upon inquiry at the East-end police-stations this morning, a reporter was informed that no further arrests had been made in connection with the Whitechapel murders. A man arrested last night has been released, it having been ascertained that he is a Sunday-school teacher occupying a most respectable position. The razor found in his bag was that which he used for the ordinary purpose.

———

### Revival of a Discredited Rumour.

The Central News Agency, which first gave publicity to the original "Jack the Ripper" letter and postcard now resuscitates the rumour—which has already been dismissed as false—that on a wall, within a few yards of the spot where the blood-stained part of an apron was found, were written the words, "The Jews shall not be blamed for nothing." The Agency adds that those who saw this writing recognised the same hand in the letter and postcard. The Agency declares that a third communication has been received, which it is deemed prudent to withhold for the present.

———

### A Spiritualist's "Clue."

At another spiritualistic séance held at Bolton yesterday a medium claims to have had revealed the Whitechapel murderer. She describes him as having the appearance of a farmer, though dressed like a navvy, with a strap round his waist, and peculiar pockets. He wears a dark moustache and bears scars behind the ear and in other places. He will, says the medium, be caught in the act of committing another murder.

# Monday, 8 October, 1888

Evening News

## THE MURDERS.
### A STARTLING DISCOVERY.
### "JACK THE RIPPER" WRITES UPON THE WALL.
### STUPIDITY OF A POLICE OFFICER.
### "THE JEWS SHALL NOT BE BLAMED FOR NOTHING."
### WHITECHAPEL PATROLLED.
### THE VIGILANCE COMMITTEES.
### BLOODHOUNDS READY FOR THE NEXT MURDER.
### LATEST DETAILS.

The Central News says: A startling fact has just come to light in reference to the recent Whitechapel murders, which goes somewhat towards clearing up the mystery with which the crimes have been surrounded. After killing Katherine Eddowes in Mitre square, the murderer, it is now known, walked to Goulstone street, where he threw away the portion of the deceased woman's apron upon which he had wiped his bloody hand and knife. Within a few feet of this spot he had written upon the wall, "The Jews shall not be blamed for nothing."

### SPONGED OUT.

Most unfortunately one of the police officers gave orders for this writing to be immediately sponged out, probably with a view of stifling the morbid curiosity which it would certainly have aroused. But in so doing a very important link was destroyed, for, had the writing been photographed, a certain clue would have been in the hands of the authorities. The witnesses who saw the writing, however, state that it as similar in character to the letters sent to the Central News and signed "Jack the Ripper," and though it would have been far better to have clearly demonstrated this by photography, there is now every reason to believe that the writer of the letter and postcard sent to the Central News (facsimiles of which are now to be seen outside every police station) is the actual murderer.

The police, consequently, are very anxious that any citizen who can identify the handwriting should without delay communicate with the authorities.

The Central News, since the original letter and postcard of "Jack the Ripper" was published, has received from 30 to 40 communications daily, signed "Jack the Ripper," evidently the concoction of silly notoriety hunters.

### ANOTHER COMMUNICATION KEPT SECRET.

A third communication, however, has been received from the writer of the original "Jack the Ripper" letter and postcard, which acting upon official advice, it has been deemed prudent to withhold for the present. It may be stated, however, that although the miscreant avows his intention of committing further crimes shortly, it is only against prostitutes that his threats are directed, his desire being to respect and protect honest women.

In view of the interest and importance of the above news, we think it well to state that back numbers of our issue of Thursday, October 4, containing complete facsimiles of the letter and postcard may be obtained at our office.

—

### A SPIRITUALIST VIEW OF THE WHITECHAPEL MURDERS.

Yesterday, a Bolton spiritualist held a séance with the special object of discovering the Whitechapel murderer. The medium was successful, as the spirits revealed a vision of a man having the appearance of a farmer, but dressed like a navvy with a strap wound his waist and peculiar pockets. He had a dark moustache and scars behind his ears, besides other marks. He will commit one more murder and be caught red-handed.

—

### LATEST
### NOT THE SHADOW OF A CLUE.

The Central News says that at noon no one was in custody in connection with the murders at any of the East end stations. The police have searched all the lodging houses in Limehouse, Shadwell, St. George's in the East, Spitalfields, and the Borough, as well as others at Hoxton and Islington, but nothing which will afford them a clue, has been discovered. Inquiries, too, have been made amongst local butchers, and at all slaughterhouses, to find out whether any one, recently employed in this capacity, has lately become deranged. These inquiries, too, have been fruitless.

It is pointed out as a singular coincidence that all the murdered women have at one time or another lodged in houses in Flower and Dean street, and from this it is thought likely that the murderer has known his victims personally before taking their lives.

—

## THE BLOODHOUNDS ARE READY FOR THE NEXT MURDER.

The police throughout the metropolis have received instructions from Sir Charles Warren, the Chief Commissioner, that in the event of any further persons being found murdered similar to those cases that have recently occurred in Whitechapel, strict instructions are to be given that the body of the victim is not to be removed, but notice at once sent to a veterinary surgeon living in the southwest district who has some bloodhounds properly trained, and that the bloodhounds will, without delay, be taken to the place and placed on the scent with the view of tracing the murderer or murderers.

—

## POLICE PRECAUTIONS.

Extraordinary precautions had been adopted by the police to prevent or detect any repetition of the horrors of last week. Not only are members of the regular force displaying the utmost activity, but in their arduous labours they are receiving valuable aid from the volunteer police of the Vigilance Committee. Last night, and on Saturday every nook and corner of the district was watched, and persons of at all suspicious appearance were tracked until reason for suspicion had been cleared away. The police and the men employed by the Vigilance Committee work very well together. As a proof of the thorough way in which they have respectively been carrying out their duties, it may be mentioned that in several instances some of the plain clothes men who were strange to the neighbourhood were watched by members of the Vigilance Committee, while they in their turn came under the scrutiny of the detectives.

—

## LETTER FROM THE HOME SECRETARY.

A letter from the Home Secretary has been received by the president of the Whitechapel Vigilance Committee, as under:

"Whitehall, October 6, 1888.

Sir—The Secretary of State for the Home Department has had the honour to lay before the Queen the petition signed by you, praying that a reward may be offered by the Government for the discovery of the perpetrator of the recent murders in Whitechapel, and he desires me to inform you that though he has given directions that no effort or expense should be spared in endeavouring to discover the person guilty of the murders, he has not been able to advise Her Majesty that in his belief the ends of justice would be promoted by any departure from the direction already announced with regard to the proposal that a reward should be offered by Government.

I am, Sir, your obedient servant,
E. Leigh Pemberton."

—

The Working Men's Vigilance and Patrol Committee have been augmented by some thirty able bodied men well acquainted with the locality. These were selected by a special meeting of representative working men connected with the dock industries, who assembled at Bow Common on Saturday night.

—

The following may be taken as a sample of the many letters concerning which rumours were current on Saturday. Information was given to the City police on Saturday that Messrs. Bryant and May had received a letter from a person signing himself J. Ripper, couched in the following terms:

"I hereby notify that I am going to pay your girls a visit. I hear that they are beginning to say what they will do with me. I am going to see what a few of them have in their stomachs, and I will take it out of them. so that they can have no more to do on the quiet. (Signed) John Ripper. P.S. I am in Poplar today."

—

## IDENTITY OF LIZZIE STRIDE.

With reference to the identity of Elizabeth Stride, the Woolwich newspapers of the time of the Princess Alice disaster have been referred to, and it is stated that a woman of that name was a witness at the inquest, and identified the body of a man as her husband, and of two children then lying in Woolwich Dockyard. She said she was on board and saw them drowned,

# Monday, 8 October, 1888

her husband picking up one of the children, and being drowned with it in his arms. She was saved by climbing the funnel, where she was accidentally kicked in the mouth by a retired Arsenal police inspector, who was also clinging to the funnel. The husband and two children are buried in Woolwich Cemetery.[233]

—

## A SUSPICIOUS INCIDENT.

Mr. George Lusk, of Alderney street, Globe street, Mile End, the president of the Vigilance Committee, has given information of a suspicious incident which befell him on Thursday afternoon last.

A stranger, who called at his private residence shortly after four o'clock, and who was informed that Mr. Lusk was not at home, appears to have traced the President of the Vigilance Committee to an adjacent tavern. Having manifested great interest in the movements of the volunteer police, he sought an interview in a private room, but owing to the forbidding appearance of the visitor Mr. Lusk seems to have preferred the comparative publicity of the bar parlour.

The conversation had scarcely begun, when Mr. Lusk, who was about to pick up a pencil which had dropped from the table, says he noticed the stranger "make a swift though silent movement with his right hand towards his side pocket." Fearing that his conduct was observed, it is added, the man asked to be directed to the nearest coffee house, and forthwith proceeded to an address in the Mile End road with which he was supplied. Although Mr. Lusk followed without loss of time, he was not quick enough for his visitor, who abstained from visiting the coffee house, and has not been heard of since.

The man is described as between thirty and forty years of age, about 5ft 9in in height, of a florid complexion, with bushy brown beard, whiskers, and moustache.

In the absence of further evidence it is impossible to say whether any personal injury

was actually in store for the head of the "Vigilants," but the ease with which the man escaped has awakened the members of the committee and their colleagues to an increased sense of the difficulty of the task they have in hand."

—

## THE
## CENTRAL VIGILANCE SOCIETY.
## AN IMPORTANT CIRCULAR.

The following circular has been addressed to the members of all the municipal bodies in the kingdom:

"Central Vigilance Committee for the Repression of Immorality, 15 York buildings, Adelphi, W.C., October 6:

Sir—The period of the year at which most of the elections to municipal offices take place appears to be a fitting one for asking your attention to the open provocation to immorality with which so many of our cities and towns abound.

It is to the electors we must look for the use they make of the franchise in selecting those only who will manfully strive for the protection of their property and the security of their own families and the public morals.

In the metropolis and many other centres of population certain streets swarm at night with those whose life is one of shame, and the boldness with which they ply their trade is greatly on the increase. The places in which they reside or to which they resort are rapidly multiplying. The knowledge of evil is thus spread out before the young of both sexes, and the downward path rendered both easy and attractive. Public decency is outraged and proceedings tolerated which are a disgrace to our moral character and our Christian profession.

Much, if not all, this display of profligacy it is in the power of civic, municipal, and parochial bodies to prevent. The law may and does require strengthening, but it is useless to cry out for more power while that which we have is not used, and it is in vain to expect that it will be used unless those having authority or influence are alive to the necessity. The purpose of this society is not to usurp the functions of those in which the power resides, but to so raise the tone of public opinion as to encourage and enforce its exercise. It is ready, however, to aid

---

[233] Although I do not have access to the Woolwich newspapers containing reports on the inquests into the Princess Alice sinking, I have read the transcripts published 7-29 September, 1878 in the London *Daily News*, *The Week's News* and *Lloyd's Weekly News*. In none of these have I been able to find testimony matching that given in this article.

348

in preventing, repressing, and rescuing, through the instrumentality of local associations, and if necessary by direct appeals to the law as circumstances may dictate. It would also point out that any two ratepayers may insist upon proceedings being taken, and, under provisions of the law expressly devised for that purpose, to prosecute to conviction at the expense of the locality in which the mischief exists.

The suppression of houses of ill fame and the restraint of street solicitation probably fall within the province of town authorities, overseers of the poor, &c. the police authorities come in to aid the local officers.

Proceedings in the first instance ought to be taken by those who suffer inconvenience from the presence of persons and places devoted to immorality; and the overseers, municipal authorities, and police should be ready to respond most vigorously to the calls of the public, and ought themselves to search out and proceed against this vice. Prostitutes, brothel keepers, and owners of premises rented for their purposes are alike subject to prosecution.

Hitherto there has not been any general effort for repression and prevention, and interference has been too often limited to the abatement of the nuisance, where it had become too open, by simply driving the perpetrators out of the district, rather than extended to such a

punishment as may deter them from a repetition of the offence elsewhere. Thus, by leaving them to renew their misconduct in other localities, the authorities have incurred a tedious repetition of the process, oftentimes ending in the return of the offenders to their original haunts.

Our desire on the present occasion is to gain your attention to the serious nature of the evil which prevails in our midst, and to express our hope that, in seeking election to positions of local power, you will bring this matter prominently to the notice of those whom you are preparing to represent, and in so doing receive their mandate that it shall not continue. The records of our Courts of Justice, the diaries of our clergymen and district visitors, the facts to which none can shut their eyes, all unite in testifying that immorality is so rife as to be eating out the nation's life, sapping the sources of our greatness, and provoking the indignation of that Power which may either preserve our prosperity or pronounce our destruction, according as we are found honouring the purity in which He delights, or practising the profligacy which He abhors.

We have the honour to be yours faithfully,

Westminster.
Meath.
R.N. Fowler.

~

# Tuesday, 9 October, 1888

## The Times

### THE EAST-END MURDERS.

No arrest in connexion with the atrocious murders at the East-end had been reported up to a late hour last night either at Scotland-yard or at any of the City police-stations, and although elaborate investigations have been made no further clue has yet been discovered.

The funeral of Catherine Eddowes, the victim of the Mitre-square murder, took place yesterday at Ilford Cemetery. The body was removed shortly after 1 o'clock from the mortuary in Golden-lane, where a vast concourse of people had assembled. A strong force of the City Police, under Mr. Superintendent Foster, was present, and conducted the *cortége* to the City boundary. At Old-street a large number of the Metropolitan Police were present under Inspector Barnham. The *cortége* passed Whitechapel parish church, and along Mile-end-road, through Bow and Stratford to the cemetery. The sisters of the ill-fated woman and the man Kelly, with whom she had lived for seven years, attended the funeral. Along the whole route great sympathy was expressed for the relatives.

It is stated by a news agency that definite instructions have been issued to the police that in the event of any person being found murdered under circumstances similar to those of the recent crimes, they are not to remove the body of the victim, but to send notice immediately to a veterinary surgeon in the South-west District, who holds several trained bloodhounds in readiness to be taken to the spot where the body may be found, and to be at once put on the scent.

---

### THE CHILDREN OF THE COMMON LODGING-HOUSES.
### TO THE EDITOR OF THE TIMES.

Sir,—Stimulated by the recently revealed Whitechapel horrors many voices are daily heard suggesting as many different schemes to remedy degraded social conditions, all of which doubtless contain some practical elements. I trust you will allow one other voice to be raised on behalf of the children. For the saddest feature of the common lodging-houses in Whitechapel and other parts of London is that so many of their inmates are children. Indeed, it is impossible to describe the state in which myriads of young people live who were brought up in these abodes of poverty and of crime.

I and others are at work almost day and night rescuing boys and girls from the foul contamination of these human sewers; but while the law permits children to herd in these places, there is little that can be done except to snatch a few here and there from ruin and await patiently those slower changes which many have advocated. Meanwhile, a new generation is actually growing up in them. We want to make it illegal for the keepers of licensed lodging-houses to which adults resort to admit young children upon any pretext whatever. It is also desirable that the existing laws relating to the custody and companionship of the children should be more rigidly enforced.

At the same time some provision is urgently required for the shelter of young children of the casual or tramp class, something between the casual wards of the workhouse and the lodging-house itself, places where only young people under 16 would be admitted, where they would be free to enter and as free to depart, and which could be made self-supporting, or nearly so. A few enterprising efforts to open lodging-houses of this class for the young only would do immense good.

Only four days before the recent murders I visited No. 32, Flower and Dean-street, the house in which the unhappy woman Stride occasionally lodged. I had been examining many of the common lodging-houses in Bethnal-green that night, endeavouring to elicit from the inmates their opinions upon a certain aspect of the subject. In the kitchen of No. 32 there were many persons, some of them being girls and women of the same unhappy class as that to which poor Elizabeth Stride belonged.

The company soon recognized me, and the conversation turned upon the previous murders. The female inmates of the kitchen seemed thoroughly frightened at the dangers to which they were presumably exposed. In an explanatory fashion I put before them the scheme which had suggested itself to my mind, by which children at all events could be saved from the contamination of the common lodging-houses and the streets, and so to some extent the supply cut off which feeds the vast ocean of misery in this great city.

The pathetic part of my story is that my remarks were manifestly followed with deep interest by all the women. Not a single scoffing voice was raised in ridicule or opposition. One poor creature, who had evidently been drinking, exclaimed somewhat bitterly to the following effect:—"We're all up to no good, and no one cares what becomes of us. Perhaps some of us will be killed next!" And then she added, " If anybody had helped the likes of us long ago we would never have come to this!"

Impressed by the unusual manner of the people, I could not help noticing their appearance somewhat closely, and I saw how evidently some of them were moved. I have since visited the mortuary in which were lying the remains of the poor woman Stride, and I at once recognized her as one of those who stood around me in the kitchen of the common lodging-house on the occasion of my visit last Wednesday week.

In all the wretched dens where such unhappy creatures live are to be found hundreds, if not thousands, of poor children who breathe from their very birth an atmosphere fatal to all goodness. They are so heavily handicapped at the start in the race of life that the future is to most of them absolutely hopeless. They are continually surrounded by influences so vile that decency is outraged and virtue becomes impossible.

Surely the awful revelations consequent upon the recent tragedies should stir the whole community up to action and to the resolve to deliver the children of to-day who will be the men and women of to-morrow from so evil an environment.

I am, Sir, your obedient servant,
THOS. J. BARNARDO.[234]
18 to 26, Stepney-causeway, E., Oct. 6.

[234] **Thomas John Barnardo** (1845-1905). Born in Dublin to a German father and English mother, Barnardo's early dream was to be an Evangelical medical missionary to China. In 1866, after receiving training as a missionary, he travelled to the empire's capital to begin medical training at the London Hospital in Whitechapel and soon became aware, through his Christian education work in the East-End, of the unimaginable squalor endured by the poor. He opened his first childrens home at Stepney Causeway in 1870 for the purpose of training boys in carpentry, metal work and shoemaking, giving them the means to make a decent living and have a better life. He later opened homes for girls and younger

### THE DUTIES OF THE POLICE.
### TO THE EDITOR OF THE TIMES.

Sir,—The following incident in some way illustrates the manifold duties of the police.

On Sunday afternoon, close to the Albert-gate, a little girl was run over by a hansom cab. The wheel passed over her body, and I think over her head. She got up and staggered a few paces, moaning pitifully. A policeman dashed at her and caught her up in his arms. He then jumped into the hansom, summarily ejecting the passenger, and was driven to St. George's Hospital.

I should think that the whole occurrence took only a quarter of a minute. The amazing promptitude of the constable and the tender way in which he laid the poor child's bleeding head on his breast seemed a strange commentary on the abuse which some people are pleased to levy at the police for their supposed "brutal conduct" on other occasions.

I am, Sir, your obedient servant,
T. WENTWORTH GRANT.
6, Westbourne-crescent, Hyde Park, W., Oct. 8.

At the THAMES Police-court, HANS BURE, a well-dressed German; was charged with assaulting Elizabeth Jennings, of 37, Duckett-street, Stepney. Prosecutrix[235] said that about 12:30 on Saturday night she was walking along Harford-street, on an errand, when the accused came up, caught hold of her arm, which he pinched, and said, "Come along with me."

Witness was frightened and screamed. She

children, and by the time of his death in 1905, his organization, "The National Association for the Reclamation of Destitute Waif Children", had 96 homes taking care of more than 8,500 children. It is thought that through his work Dr. Bernardo helped at least 60,000 children out of poverty during his life. Renamed "Dr. Bernardo's" after his death, his institute is still carrying on his work of helping children. (Barnardo's, 2014)

[235] **Prosecutrix** and **Prosecutor**. The tenets of English Common Law required that the victim of a criminal or civil offence had to either personally bring charges against the offender, or hire a lawyer to do it for them. Although the position of Director of Public Prosecutions had been created in 1880, most prosecutions for crimes in 1888 were still conducted by the victim.

stood by a young man whom she knew, when prisoner followed and she ran into the road. Prisoner ran after her, but saw another lady coming, and then caught hold of her shawl. Several men caught hold of the accused and detained him until a constable came, when he was given into custody.

Mrs. Matilda Beck said the accused caught hold of her shawl, but she released herself and ran away. He followed, but some men stopped him. Witness was very much frightened.

Constable 150 E said when he arrested the accused he said he did not mean anything. He was under the influence of drink. Prisoner, through an interpreter, said he took the prosecutrix to be a prostitute and did accost her. She screamed and ran away, and he followed to give an explanation, when he was detained. He did the same to the other woman.

A witness for the defence, named Webb, said he saw the prisoner just touch the women. They screamed, and a mob of men got round the prisoner calling him "Jack the Ripper." Mr. Saunders said the accused had frightened the women and at a time when they would easily be frightened. He would be fined 40s. or undergo one month's hard labour.[236]

~

## The Star
### A Suggestion from Vienna.

A Vienna correspondent states that Dr. Bloch,[237] a member of the Austrian Reichsrath,[238] has called his attention to certain facts which may throw a new light on the Whitechapel murders.

In various German criminal codes of the seventeenth and eighteenth centuries, as also in statutes of a more recent date, punishments are prescribed for the mutilation of female corpses, with the object of making from the uterus and other organs "thieves' candles" or "soporitic candles."

According to an old superstition, still rife in various parts of Germany, the light from such candles will throw those upon whom it falls into the deepest slumbers, and they may, consequently, become a valuable instrument to the thieving profession.

At the trial of the notorious German robber Theodor Unger, surnamed "the handsome Charley," who was executed at Magdeburg, in 1810, it transpired that a regular manufactory had been established by gangs of thieves, for the production of such candles.[239]

---

[236] See Appendix O, Hard Labour, p. 584.

[237] **Rabbi Josef Samuel Bloch** (1850-1923). Deputy to the Reichsrath from Kolomea, now part of western Ukraine, from 1884-c.1897.

[238] **Reichsrath**. Ger. Imperial Council. The Vienna based parliament of Cisleithania, the Austrian portion of the Austro-Hungarian Empire. Transleithania, Hungary and Croatia-Slavonia, had its own parliament in Budapest. Formed in 1861, the bicameral Reichsrath consisted of the Herrenhaus (House of Lords) and the Abgeordnetenhaus (House of Deputies). The Imperial Reichsrath was disbanded 12 November, 1918 at the close of the First World War.

[239] A.F. Thiele, "Die Judischen Gauner in Deutschland," Be., 1848, 7: "The handsome Karl made the wives and concubines belonging to his band swear by the prince of darkness, and by everything evil, to deliver up unhesitatingly for that ghastly purpose [thieves' candles] the fruit of their wombs, if they were required so to do by himself or any other graduate of the band. The foetus was then, before it had reached maturity, expelled and roasted!" Theodor Unger (that was "handsome Karl's" real name), who was executed at Mageburg in 1810, was not a Jew, and there is no proof discoverable that the Jews concerned in the robbery disorders of that

# Tuesday, 9 October, 1888

That this superstition has survived amongst German thieves to the present day was proved in a case tried at Biala, in Galicia, as recently as 1875.

—

## THE PEOPLE'S POST BOX.
### Audi Alteram Partem.[240]

SIR,—The "East-end atrocities" have certainly been an ill-wind that has blown grist to the mill of the votaries of the modern woman-cultus. To the unsophisticated mind it would be difficult to see how the murder of a few women by an obviously unique kind of maniac could possibly raise any general point respecting the "woman question" any more than the murder of, say, two or three City clerks by an ex-principal whose mind was affected by losses occasioned through the negligence of penmen he had employed should raise the general question of the social position of City clerks. But there is no one like your woman's rights advocate for making capital out of everything that comes to hand, and nothing like the modern English Press for giving him or her a one-sided hearing.

Accordingly we find Mrs. Fenwick Miller and her allies in the *Daily News* all athirst for the blood of men, seeking to raise the wind in favour of barbarous judicial sentences. The truly bestial howl for the torture of the lash which comes with the regularity of an intermittent fever, is again heard in our midst. The Rev. Mr. Barnett moralises in *The Star*, the general drift of his remarks being that the working man is a kind of semi-monster and his wife a wingless angel let loose from Paradise. Mr. Barnett has, of course, never come across women whom have wrecked the lives of working men—oh, dear, no! If there is one thing that might make a working-man hesitate before contracting a legal marriage, it is that nowadays law and middle-class public opinion place him entirely at the mercy of his wife. As a recent correspondent (a barrister) of the *Daily Telegraph* observed, the whole legislation of the past quarter of a century has been entirely in favour of women at the expense of men.

And now as to these sentences so much talked about. No one who reads his newspaper can deny the extreme reluctance of juries to convict women of any serious offence and the excessive leniency of sentences passed upon them. Only the other day (on the north-west circuit, I think) a big powerful woman was convicted of the murder of her husband, a poor, feeble, paralytic old man, by battering his head in, a continued course of ill-usage having been proved, and was recommended to mercy! Imagine the howl that would have arisen had the cases been reversed. Again, every one must have noticed the growing tendency to twist what would formerly have been regarded as manslaughter cases into murder cases where women are the victims.

Then as to mere brutality, who shall deny that in many of the worst instances of cruelty to children women are the culprits? Only a short time ago a woman tortured her stepson, a little boy of three years old, by burning him with a red-hot iron. Does anyone propose that a brute like this should have the lash? Oh, no; divine woman must not be subjected to degrading punishments!

I write, sir, as an advocate of equality between the sexes. At the present time, apart from mere political rights, which are, after all, only a means to an end, women constitute a privileged class, and the aims of their advocates is to give them a still more privileged position. They are virtually freed from the criminal punishments to which men are liable, and they can compel men to support them on pain of imprisonment. It is all very well to talk about women being economically dependent on men. The feudal lord was also economically dependent on his serfs; that is to say, he would have been in a sorry plight if his vassals and serfs had suddenly deserted him, and would then probably have had to have taken to what used to be euphemistically known as the "road;"[241] much as "deserted" women now sometimes take to the streets. Yet the feudal lord is none the less usually deemed to have belonged to a privileged class.

period had the superstition here under notice. (Strack)

[240] **Audi Alteram Partem**. Lat. *Listen to the other side.* The legal principle that no one will be judged without being given the opportunity to defend themselves by telling their side of the story.

[241] **Road**. To take to the road, to turn highwayman (*the road* also, highway robbery). (Farmer)

# Tuesday, 9 October, 1888

The desperate and glorious inconsistency of your woman advocate is aptly shown in his criticism of seduction cases, where the man is always painted as the malignant scoundrel and the woman as the innocent young person who does not know her right hand from her left, and yet we are told in the same breath this simple young innocent, unable to protect herself against the wiles of wicked man, is the equal of man in all respects, and fit to be entrusted with every political and social function.

Mr. Barnett admonishes the working-man to regard his wife as his equal. Now do let us put aside cant on this subject for once. How can the working-man regard a woman as his equal when she is obviously not his equal. Apart from mere intellectual inequality, most working men know that the greatest obstacle in the way of their political work for the emancipation of their class is precisely the "drab" at home who is perpetually nagging and browbeating him.— Yours, &c.,

"JUSTICE AND EQUALITY."

—

### The Poverty of the East-end of London.

SIR,—In a leading article commenting on the Rev. Mr. Barnett's letter in your issue of 5 Oct., you say truly that "it is poverty which lies at the root of what we, perhaps rightly, call the social evil, and it is by aiming at the abolition of poverty that we shall cure a variety of woes which we usually set down to an entirely different set of causes." I entirely concur with you in this statement; and, as I have had a very long practical acquaintance with the poorer classes of the East-end of London in my capacity as physician to the Metropolitan Free Hospital, which was once situated close to Whitechapel Church, I claim to speak with some experience. To me, then, the extreme squalor and hopelessness of Whitechapel, St. George's-in-the-East, and Bethnal-green are due to the two causes so well pointed out by the Archbishop of Canterbury, in a lecture in Bethnal-green this year, viz., to over-population and drink. The birth-rate of Bethnal-green last year, 1887, was nearly 40 per 1,000 as compared with that of Kensington, which was only 19.5; and as a consequence of this poor families are compelled to crowd together in these sad haunts of the poor about which we have heard so much during the last few weeks. I found on inquiry from out-patients attending at the Metropolitan Free Hospital a few years back, that the average number of children to a family was 7.2—i.e., 100 married women over 45 had had 720 children on an average of many hundreds I questioned. The average of children to a family in prudent France is now 3.2, and although naturally we, with our colonies, could afford to support more children than the French, yet the average of 7.2 is utterly beyond the powers of the poor of the East-end. Alcohol, too, is another of the causes of misery in the East-end; and these two causes combined are quite enough to account for the terrible misery of Bethnal-green, Whitechapel, and St. George's-in-the-East. So that it is not so much of importance that the West-end should give alms to the East-end. What is wanted is that West-end people should teach East-end people to have smaller families, and thus escape from early death and lifelong destitution.—Yours, &c.,

C. R. DRYSDALE, M.D.[242]
23, Sackville-street,
London, W., 6 Oct.

~

---

[242] **Dr. Charles Robert Drysdale** (1829-1907), was a physician at the Metropolitan Hospital and North London Hospital for Consumption, first president of the British Malthusian League and author of *The Life and Writings of Thomas R. Malthus* in 1892. He, his wife Dr. Alice Drysdale-Vickery, and brother Dr. George Drysdale, were Freethinkers (basically atheist) and early proponents of birth-control and eugenics. They were also associated with Margaret Sanger. He was a prolific writer on birth-control, venereal disease, and the harmful effects of tobacco and alcohol, frequently speaking to mens groups and secular organizations on these subjects. (Drysdale-Vickery)

# Tuesday, 9 October, 1888

## Evening News
### THE EDITOR'S DRAWER.
### EAST END ATROCITIES.
### TO THE EDITOR OF
### "THE EVENING NEWS."

Sir—You kindly inserted a letter from me ("Medicus," Chelsea), on October 1,[243] in reference to the Whitechapel murders. Perhaps you would be kind enough now to find space for the following remarks.

It is not very long since I was professionally engaged for a few months in the very district where these murders have been perpetrated. And on many a dark night, accompanied by some poor shivering Jew, have I gone through narrow streets and alleys, that were badly lighted, or with no light at all. Here and there in corners and on doorsteps I could see the dim outlines of forms huddled up apparently in sleep, and, what between the almost total darkness of some spots, and the absence of police everywhere, I felt myself completely at the mercy of the murderer, should he care to work his fell deeds on me.

In my last letter I said that the knowledge of the position of the organs in the body manifested by the Whitechapel murderer would be found outside the medical profession, among butchers, porters in dissection halls, and attendants in post mortem halls. I would now suggest that the butchers and slaughterhouse men of Whitechapel make strict inquiries among themselves as to any individual or individuals of their set who are known, or have been known to be afflicted with epilepsy.

Secondly, the staffs in connection with the various dissection rooms throughout the city should make similar inquiries, and ascertain the whereabouts of any suspicious character who may have left their service within the past year or two.

I am, &c.,
Medicus.

—

### TO THE EDITOR OF
### "THE EVENING NEWS."

Sir—Having thought a good deal about the recent Whitechapel murders, I think that had Constable Watkins india rubber bottoms on his boots he would have captured that fiend in human form. For it is possible for a person doing such a deed to hear the approach of a constable at least five minutes, in the still of the night, before his arrival on the spot, in such a place as Mitre square, where there are exits by which the murderer might easily escape.

I am, &c.,
A Working Man.

—

### TO THE EDITOR OF
### "THE EVENING NEWS."

Sir—I cannot help thinking that the horrible atrocities which have been perpetrated lately upon unprotected females, at present without any detection, reflects discredit upon our detective force. In saying this I do not mean to imply that the men themselves are at fault, but that the whole organisation of the department is carried on in such an absurd and confined manner.

As an instance of this I may inform you that a client of mine who had reasons to suspect that some men had been systematically trespassing on, and stealing from his garden in one of our suburbs requested the inspector of police to have the premises specially watched. The result was that the following day a gorgeous police-man in full uniform was patrolling about in broad daylight, which course of action, I need scarcely state, gave the offenders all the information they wanted with respect to their having been discovered.

On another occasion, also on which a friend of mine (who is a J.P.) had occasion to complain at the same police station of the destruction of his hedges in a lane adjoining his premises by a horde of gipsies, who made it a regular halting place, a constable in full uniform was placed on special duty in the aforesaid lane with the result, of course, that the gipsies, being fully aware that the place was watched, did not come near it.

Now, Sir, would it not be possible to increase the efficacy of our detective force in a very simple manner? There are, no doubt, hundreds of gentlemen, like myself, who would be only too glad to give their services, when required, to act as what I will term "special detectives." These persons, who, being entirely unknown and would could, if necessary, effectually disguise themselves, would surely do a great deal more towards the discovery of

---

[243] Actually 2 Oct. p 246.

the offenders than a man who, in nine cases out of ten, is known to the person he is attempting to find, or if this is not so, can easily be detected by his general deportment and carriage. Of course this plan would entail a special detective being empowered with the same authority for the time being as a real detective, and they must also be furnished with some sort of authority which will immediately enlist the aid of an ordinary constable to their assistance, the reason for such assistance not being questioned.

I am very glad to see that the respectable inhabitants of the neighbourhood of Whitechapel have formed themselves into a committee to assist the police. But, of course, unless they are vested with the necessary powers, this assistance will be of little avail. My system, if practicable (as I venture to say it is), would also put a stop to a great deal of illegality which is carried on in several places openly, and winked at by the police because they wish to keep themselves in good favour with the neighbourhood.

Apologising for trespassing on your valuable space, my only excuse for so doing being that I feel, as an Englishman, the need of drastic reform in this quarter, I enclose my card.

I am, &c.,
An Ex-Superintendent of
Special Constables and a Volunteer Officer.

—

Strange things happen in the Whitechapel "doss houses," but how strange we had no idea until this morning. Yesterday it seems two young people, a man and a woman, were charged at Worship street Police court, with a theft committed in one of the "doss houses." They were accused, a contemporary says, of having robbed one Carl Edwin Hillman of "a purse containing £4 and a pair of trousers." It is only in Whitechapel that purses are to be found with such a miscellaneous assortment of contents.

—

## ANOTHER SUPPOSED CLUE.
## WERE THE MUTILATIONS
## PERFORMED IN DARKNESS?
## A SUPPOSED CLUE.

In Deeke street, opposite Mitre square, there is a club called the Imperial, the members of which are exclusively Jews. On the Sunday morning of the murder, between 1.30 and 1.40,

three of the members named respectively Joseph Levy, butcher, 1 Middlesex street, Aldgate; Joseph Levander, commercial traveller in or manufacturer of cigarettes, whose business premises are in St. Mary Axe, corner of Bury street; and Mr. Henry Harris, furniture dealer, of Castle street, Whitechapel, left the club. They then noticed a couple—man and woman—standing by the iron post of the small passage that leads to Mitre square. They have no doubt themselves that this was the murdered woman and her murderer. And on the first blush of it the fact is borne out by the police having taken exclusive care of Mr. Joseph Levander, to a certain extent having sequestrated him and having imposed a pledge on him of secrecy. They are paying all his expenses, and one if not two detectives are taking him about. One of the two detectives is Foster. Mr. Henry Harris, of the two gentlemen our representative interviewed, is the more communicative. He is of opinion that neither Mr. Levander nor Mr. Levy saw anything more than he did, and that was only the back of the man. Mr. Joseph Levy is absolutely obstinate and refuses to give us the slightest information. He leaves one to infer that he knows something, but that he is afraid to be called on the inquest. Hence he assumes a knowing air. The fact remains, however, that the police, in imposing their idiotic secrecy, have a allowed a certain time to elapse before making the partial description these three witnesses have been able to give public, and thus prevent others from acting upon the information in the event of the murderer coming under their notice.

—

## WERE THE MUTILATIONS
## PERFORMED IN DARKNESS?

A correspondent, writing from Birkenhead, says:

There is one point about the Whitechapel murders which has not yet been commented upon—viz., that the murderer must have had light of some kind by which to carry out the ghastly mutilations, and at the same time avoid stepping in the blood. At the inquest on Annie Chapman the coroner laid stress upon the fact that the missing organ had been removed with considerable skill, and without one unnecessary cut, and the surgical evidence in the case of the Mitre square victim was to the same effect. Would any surgeon living undertake to perform

# Tuesday, 9 October, 1888

a like operation in darkness, and with desperate haste?

—

## STRIDE OR WATTS?

The Central News says: Notwithstanding the apparently conclusive evidence given at the inquest by Michael Kidney as to the identity of the Berner street victim, many people have continued to believe that the poor creature was really Elizabeth Watts, wife of a former wine merchant at Bath. It will be remembered that Mrs. Mary Malcolm, of Red Lion square, swore positively that the deceased was her sister, Elizabeth Watts, whom she had last seen on the Thursday evening preceding the murder. The Central News caused inquiries to be made with a view to settle the question of identity beyond doubt, and as the result has succeeded in finding Elizabeth Watts alive and well in the person of Mrs. Stokes, the hard working, respectable wife of a brickyard labourer living at Tottenham.

—

## DOSS HOUSE FREQUENTERS.

A reporter had some conversation, yesterday, with an old frequenter of lodging houses in the East end, whose experience may be worth relating in view of the theory that the series of murders is the work of a man with anatomical knowledge. The informant stated that during a period of several years spent in "doss houses" he has come in personal contact with men in reduced circumstances who have spent the earlier years of life in far different surroundings. Not only has he known resident in lodging houses those who were formerly prosperous tradesmen but professional men—in two or three instances surgeons, who from drink or misfortune had been compelled to seek such refuges as the "doss house" deputy could offer to them. The informant, moreover, considers that it would be a comparatively easy matter for an astute man to commit crimes such as those now under investigation, and to return to his lodging without exhibiting the slightest trace of his work. He thinks that the carrying of some kind of handbag by the supposed murderer is of some importance, and confirms the suspicions that the culprit is really in hiding within a very short distance of the scene of the murders.

—

## A HIDEOUS SUPERSTITION.

A Vienna correspondent, telegraphing last night, states that Dr. Bloch, a member of the Austrian Reichsrath for the Galician constituency of Kokomes, has called his attention to certain facts which may throw a new light on the Whitechapel murders, and, perhaps, afford some assistance in tracing the murderer. In various German criminal codes of the seventeenth and eighteenth centuries, as also in statutes of a more recent date, punishments are prescribed for the mutilation of female corpses, with the object of making from the uterus and other organs the so called Dieblichter or Schlafslichter, respectively "thieves' candles" and "soporific candles." According to an old superstition still rife in various parts of Germany, the light from such candles will throw those upon whom it falls into the deepest slumbers, and they may, consequently, become a valuable instrument to the thieving profession. Hence their name.

In regard to these Schlafslichter quite a literature might be cited. They are referred to by Ave Lallement in his "Das Deutsche Gaunerthumm" published at Leipsic in 1858; by Loffler in "Die Mangelhafte Justiz";by Thiele, and numerous others. They also played an important part in the trials of robber bands at Odenwald and in Westphalia, in the years 1812 and 1841 respectively. The Schlafslichter were heard of, too, at the trial of the notorious German robber, Theodor Unger, surnamed "the handsome Charley," who was executed at Magdeburg, in 1810. It was on that occasion discovered that a regular manufactury had been established by gangs of thieves for the production of such candles. That this superstition has survived amongst German thieves to the present day was proved by a case tried at Biala, in Galicia, as recently as 1875. In this the body of a woman had been found mutilated in precisely the same way as were the victims of the Whitechapel murderer. At that trial, as at one which took place subsequently at Zeszow which is also in Galicia, and in which the accused were a certain Ritter and his wife, the prevalence amongst thieves of the superstition was alluded to by the Public Prosecutor. In the Ritter case, however, the Court preferred harping on another alleged superstition of a ritual character amongst the Jews of Galicia, which, however, was shown to be a pure

# Tuesday, 9 October, 1888

invention of the Judenhetzer. Dr. Bloch, who, for ten years, was a Rabbi in Galicia, and has made the superstitions of the Province his special study, affirms that the "thieves' candle" superstition still exists among robbers of every confession, and, as he believes, also of every nationality. He considers, however, that it prevails most amongst German thieves. Amongst other German laws, where the crime in question is dealt with, the Code Theresiana, chap. XXII, clause 59, may be referred to.

—

### IS THE WHITECHAPEL MURDERER A JEW?
### IMPORTANT LETTER.

"Shall the Jews be blamed for nothing," was the inscription alleged to have been written on the wall in Goulston street by the perpetrator of the Mitre square murder. In view of this the following letter, received by us from a correspondent with a long experience of metropolitan slaughter houses, seems of peculiar interest.

### To the Editor of "The Evening News."

Sir—Of the many theories that have been put forward as to the probable perpetrator of the East end tragedies, hardly any, to my mind, suggest the likeliest class of man to be capable of working in the silent, quick, and skilful manner that he evidently does, according to the medical evidence given at the various inquests. Having read the many letters in the "dailies" I feel that my views as to the manner of the committal and person committing them may be of some interest to you and your readers.

1. The person likely to commit an act of this description and in the peculiar manner, is a man who is thoroughly acquainted with and is practical in the Jewish method of slaughtering animals for human consumption, a business which is carried on in the immediate neighbourhood of the murders, and at the market in Deptford, which is in constant communication by rail or van with this locality at all hours day and night. My reasons for assuming this is that only a man having a perfect knowledge of how to deliver a cut so effectually and with such certainty as in these cases must know exactly the kind of knife to use, and I know of no more suitable instrument than the knife used by a "Jewish cutter" when slaughtering sheep or oxen. These knives are from twelve to eighteen inches long in the blade, about one and a half to two inches wide, with square end, very rigid, strong back, and made of finest steel, sharpened upon a hone to a razor edge.

The mode of using it is as follows: The sheep or ox is cast turned on its back, the head drawn back to render the skin tense, the cutter is then called upon to do his work which is to cut the animal's throat with one heavy downward drawing cut, using the knife from heel to point so as to divide the whole of the vessels, windpipe and muscles, down to the vertebral column, the animal dying quickly and noiselessly from such a wound—a wound requiring to inflict upon so large an animal as an ox a perfectly suitable knife, skill and force to use it.

2. After the animal is dead the skin being removed by assistants from the abdomen of the carcass, a second person, called a "searcher," steps in and makes a longitudinal incision in the abdomen, immediately below the base of the chest, in this case a razor is used as a cutting instrument. The hand is passed through this opening, and two incisions are made in the diaphragm in order to pass the hand entirely round the cavity of the chest on either side, and feel for any attachment of the lungs to the walls of the chest. The organs of the abdominal cavity are examined by touch in a similar manner, and if it passes the examination as fit for Jewish consumption, it is marked by the searcher, and afterwards a sealer seals it with a small leaden seal.

In my opinion a man who has seen or carried out these functions has committed these crimes, from the fact of the certainty, cleanness, and depth of the cuts in the throats of the victims, the mutilations being so extensive, and evidently carried out by the sense of touch, for it is evident no light could have been used.

Should you publish this letter, I will conclude my argument in a second one tomorrow.

I am, &c.,
A Butcher.

# Wednesday, 10 October, 1888

## The Times
### THE EAST END MURDERS.

Sir Charles Warren witnessed a private trial of bloodhounds in one of the London parks at an early hour yesterday morning.

The hounds are the property of Mr. Edwin Brough, of Wyndyate, near Scarborough, who for years past has devoted himself to bloodhound breeding. It has been Mr. Brough's practice not only to breed for bench points, but to train his animals to exercise those peculiar faculties with which they have been endowed by nature.

On the 4th of October Mr. Brough was communicated with by the Metropolitan Police as to the utility of employing bloodhounds to track criminals, and negotiations followed which resulted in that gentleman coming to London on Saturday evening, bringing with him two magnificent animals named Champion Barnaby and Burgho.

Of the two Barnaby is better known on the show benches, but Burgho, in body, feet, and legs, is as nearly perfect as possible. Burgho is nearly two years younger than his kennel companion. He is a black and tan, and is a rare stamp of hound, powerful, well formed, and exceedingly well-grown. His head measures 12in. in length, and he is one of the fastest hounds Mr. Brough has ever bred. Burgho has been trained from a puppy to hunt "the clean shoe," that is to say, follow the trail of a man whose shoes have not been prepared in any way by the application of blood or aniseed, so as to leave a strongly marked trail.

Barnaby has been similarly taught, but his training was not commenced until he was at least 12 months old. The hounds have been accustomed to working together, which is a considerable advantage in following a trail.

Mr. Brough stated that his system of training the hounds is as follows:—

When they are puppies, four or five months old, he gives them short runs of about 100 yards to begin with on grass and up wind. To encourage the young dogs everything is made as easy for them as possible. The man whom they are going to run is always someone whom they know, and he caresses and fondles the puppies before he starts.

The dogs are allowed to see him start, and the quarry gets out of sight as quickly as possible and conceals himself. The trainer, who must know the exact course the man has taken, puts the puppies on the line, and encourages them by voice and gesture to follow up the trail.

It is quite likely at first that some of the litter, perhaps all of them, will not put their noses down or understand what is required of them, but the trainer takes them along until they reach the man, and he rewards them with some dainty. This is repeated, until very soon the hounds know what is required of them, and once started on the trail work for themselves.

The difficulties are gradually increased, but not until they are 12 months old can the animals be taught to go across country. Eventually, they can be trained to cross roads and brooks, and when they are at fault, say by over-running the line, they will make their own casts and recover the track.

Mr. Brough tried Barnaby and Burgho in Regent's Park at 7 o'clock on Monday morning. The ground was thickly coated with hoar frost, but they did their work well, successfully tracking for nearly a mile a young man, who was given about 15 minutes start.

They were tried again in Hyde Park on Monday night. It was, of course, dark, and the dogs were hunted on a leash, as would be the case if they were employed in Whitechapel. They were again successful in performing their allotted task, and at 7 o'clock yesterday morning a trial took place before Sir Charles Warren.

To all appearances the morning was a much better one for scenting purposes than was Monday, though the contrary proved to be the fact. In all, half a dozen runs were made, Sir Charles Warren in two instances acting as the hunted man.

In every instance the dogs hunted persons who were complete strangers to them, and occasionally the trail would be crossed. When this happened the hounds were temporarily checked, but either one or the other would pick up the trail again.

In one of the longest courses the hounds were checked at half the distance. Burgho ran back, but Barnaby, making a fresh cast forward, recovered the trail and ran the quarry home. The hound did this entirely unaided by his master, who thought that he was on the wrong track, but left him to his own devices.

# Wednesday, 10 October, 1888

In consequence of the coldness of the scent yesterday morning, the hounds worked very slowly, but they demonstrated the possibility of tracking complete strangers on to whose trail they had been laid.[244]

The dogs have been purchased by Sir C. Warren for the use of the police in the detection of crime should occasion arise.

—

GEORGE RICHARD HENDERSON, of rather singular appearance, was charged before Mr. Vaughan with being a suspicious person loitering about the streets.

Police-constable 411 E said that about 3.30 a.m. there was considerable excitement in Covent-garden-market, where it was rumoured that Jack the Ripper was going about threatening people.

He saw the prisoner wandering about aimlessly. He carried a black bag, and his actions were very strange. Several persons appeared to be alarmed, and witness took the prisoner to the station.

There he was searched, and as 54 pawn-tickets were found in his possession, and he could give no proper account of himself, he was detained.

Among other things found on him was a rough draft of a letter which had appeared in print suggesting to the Home Secretary that those who were harbouring the Whitechapel murderer felt that they were equally guilty with him as accomplices after the act and could not come forward and give him up, no matter for what reward, until a free pardon was offered to them.

Witnesses were called for the prisoner, who explained that he was a respectable man, and Mr. Vaughan discharged him, at the same time advising him not to go about the streets in a similar way again.

~

---

[244] See Appendix M, The Texas Axe Murders. *The Atlanta Constitution*, 26 September, 1888, **Is It the Man from Texas?**, for an account of blood-hounds being used to track a murderer in Texas, p. 577.

## The Star
### WHITECHAPEL.
#### Warrenism Still a Failure—Unfortunates Say They Know the Murderer.

Contrary to the usual custom, there were no arrests last night in Whitechapel. A man seized in Haggerston was released later on. The police think Whitechapel is now too closely watched for anything like a murder to take place undetected. If heard of again the man will commit a crime in another quarter of London. It seems as though this would be comparatively easy. The south-western suburbs are almost denuded of police at night to supply White-chapel, and the murderer has given the burglars a good chance of making a living.

In the Whitechapel district detectives and policemen were within easy hail of each other, and the amateur policemen paraded about in gangs.

The following printed bill is posted up in Hanbury-street, nearly opposite the house where the body of Annie Chapman was discovered:—

"MURDER

"Men who are not curs do your duty. Protect the defenceless from the knife of the assassin. I will direct you."

Then follow the name and address.

#### The Blackmailing Theory.

A reporter, who visited some of the wards of the infirmary of St. George's-in-the-East yesterday, found the unfortunate women inmates in a state of great excitement over the Whitechapel murders. Not one of them would entertain fanciful theories respecting the identity and objects of the murderer. They were positive the recent crimes have been the work of one man, who, by the descriptions given and anecdotes related, appears to be a street bully of a somewhat superior type. One woman named Jenny stated to Dr. Saunders that if she were well enough to get about she would soon find and identify the man who she is certain is the murderer. He frequently maltreated the women of the streets, and extorted money from them under threats of "ripping them up." They had sometimes appealed to the police, with the only result of a terrible beating from the scoundrel the very next night. Jenny said every woman in the ward would be able to pick the man out of a thousand. She described him as a foreigner about 40 years of age. She believed he had been a doctor. He dressed fairly well and generally carried a big heavy stick. The police have received more than one statement of this character from women of the street.

~

## Evening News
### CHIT-CHAT

We may fairly claim that *The Evening News* maintains the reputation which it has made for itself in connection with the hunt after the Whitechapel murderer. On Thursday last *The Evening News* was the first and only paper to give to the world the important evidence of Mathew Packer, which has since supplied the police with valuable material to work upon, and the substance of which was republished two or three days late by morning contemporaries. Yesterday we were the first in the field with a special account of the police experiments with bloodhounds in Hyde Park, the first intelligence of which our contemporaries received through the Central News some hours later.

———

### SOME INSTANCES OF HOMICIDAL MANIA.

According to their own account—but very reluctantly supplied—the police are scouring the highways and by-ways of the metropolis for the Whitechapel murder. At risk of casting one more stone at these wonderful myrmidons[245] of Sir Charles Warren, one might ask with Cowper[246]

"How much a dunce that's sent to roam
Excels a dunce that stays at home?"

The police are like Polly Eccles's[247] neighbours, who, according to that damsel, could not think, because they had not been brought up to it.

---

[245] **Myrmidon**. The Myrmidones were the Thessalian warriors led by Achilles in the siege of Troy. It Later came to mean a follower so loyal he would obey an order without question or scruple.

[246] From the poem The Progress of Error (1782), by William Cowper (1731-1800):

"Returning, he proclaims by many a grace,
By shrugs and strange contortions of his face,
How much a dunce that has been sent to roam
Excels a dunce that has been kept at home."

[247] **Polly Eccles**. Main character in T.W. Robertson's popular three act comedy Caste, which debuted at the Prince of Wales's Theatre in April, 1867. (Adams)

So far they are to be pitied, not blamed, ablest that on the face of it they appear as little disposed to accept commiseration as censure. Moreover, their self-confidence prevents them from listening to the suggestions, not of the world at large, but of men whom the world at large considers capable of applying a consistent theory to the homicidal phenomenon that is disturbing the community. Four weeks ago Dr. Forbes Winslow repaired to Scotland-yard, if not by invitation, at least with the concurrence of Sir Charles Warren. The following morning a representative of *The Evening News* interviewed he eminent specialist. Two points stood out clearly from this conversation. According to Dr. Winslow, the murderer was a homicidal maniac, and in a position of life which enabled him to defy detection by a rapid transit from the scene of his crimes, and by an equally rapid change of garments. Dr. Winslow at the time recommended careful inquiry at every public and private lunatic asylum throughout the country as to the names of patients that had escaped and had been discharged as cured. His principle contention, as may be remembered, was that homicidal mania was incurable and consequently that the murderer might be found among the sufferers from that terrible affliction, queasily-restored to reason. Have the police acted upon this advice? Have they interrogated the night cabmen on the ranks in or about Whitechapel? We think not. They have treated those and other suggestions with the indifference characteristic of men of inferior intelligence who resent the imputation of that inferiority. They have pooh-poohed the theory of homicidal mania, and pursued their researches in places where the criminal could not possibly be—namely, in low lodging-houses—as if, forsooth, these dens could harbour a man with bloodstained garments without the suspicion of the other inmates being aroused.

I repeat they have pooh-poohed the theory, not knowing and not caring to know what is common talk among students that have applied themselves to the elucidation of similar mysteries. To them the murderer has a motive, and to them the motive that springs solely from homicidal mania is not one. Nay, they are almost prepared to deny homicidal mania per se. It is revenge—intended or accomplished—upon one person, and transferred upon a greater or lesser number of persons belonging to the same class.

The sanity of the maniac, if that be not a blunder, is according to them, in favour of their theory. For that insanity should sharpen the wits of the maniac before his crimes, in order to devise the best possible means to execute his design, and afterwards to baffle research, is not dreamt of in their philosophy.

This being so, there is no apology needed for recording a few of the many murders induced by homicidal mania, pure and simple. On November 23, 1824, there was tried at the Assize Courts of Versailles one Antoine Leger, for the murder of Constance Debully, aged 12. The murderer had never seen his victim until a few moments before his crime. The medical examination proved that no outrage had been committed, cupidity could not have been the object, for the child belonged to the poorest class of field labourers. She was even barefooted. The public interrogatory brought to light the following facts: The prisoner was provided with a sum of money, amply sufficient for his wants, seeing that for three weeks previous to the deed he had lived on herbs, roots, &c. He was prompted to the murder by the irresistible desire of eating human flesh and drinking human-blood. Medical science was not as far advanced as it is now, albeit that Dr. Georget,[248] one of the shining lights of medicine, conclusively proved Leger not to have been responsible for his actions. Leger was executed on December 1, 1824.

*The Evening News* has already more than once hinted at the possibility of homicidal-maniacal epidemy, either as the result of imitation in the same locality, or springing up in different parts of a country without any apparently connecting causes. Two months after Leger's terrible crime a young woman belonging, to judge by her appearance, to the working classes, was taking a stroll with her two little boys in the Forest of Vincennes. Attracted by the lad's handsome faces, a woman in the same station of life stopped to kiss them. On looking up she noticed that she was watched with a great deal of interest by a man of superior station. She took little or no heed, and scarcely answered the questions he addressed of her. The mother had also noticed the man who immediately afterwards disappeared.

Half an hour later she was confronted by the same individual who, stooping down as if to kiss her boys, plunged a knife into their hearts. The interval between his first and second appearance had been utilized to procure himself a knife. In order to do this he had to leave the wood and make the round of several shops, whose owners refused to sell one of a dozen unless he paid a proportionately large price for it. Undeterred by the obstacle he consented. Papovoine was executed on March 25, 1825, in spite of the doubt thrown upon his sanity, for though the prosecution endeavoured to establish a reason, no reason for the deed could be accepted. The children of Charlotte Herin were illegitimate, and the theory of the prosecution was that Papovoine had been the instrument of Gerbod, their paternal grandfather, who at all risks wished to prevent a marriage between the girl and his son.

(To be continued.)[249]

—

## IS THE MURDERER A JEW?
## TO THE EDITOR OF
## "THE EVENING NEWS."

Sir—In reference to the letter signed "A Butcher," if, as your correspondent seems to think, that it might have been a cutter or searcher belonging to the Jewish community, or an onlooker at such operations, do you not think it might be possible to trace the murderer, providing such was the case? Let each of the cutters or searchers (as there are not many of them, and they can easily be found by inquiry at all slaughterhouses where Jewish meat is killed) be called upon to forward a specimen of their writing to an authority, to be examined to see if it corresponds with the writing of the letters and post card believed to be that of the murderer, and, if corresponding, be made to give an account of himself for the days on which the murders were committed. As for any onlookers, I do not think anyone could perform on a body so skillfully as medical gentlemen say has been performed on the bodies of these unfortunate women by mere onlooking.

I am, & co.,
A JEW.

---

[248] **Étienne-Jean Georget** (1795-1828). Pioneering French forensic psychiatrist who did early studies on monomania. He was also the first to suggest that insanity was a valid defence in criminal cases.

[249] See **Some More Instances of Homicida Mania**, 11 October, p. 373.

Mr. A. Levy writes us, in reference to the above, that the persons who are engaged in slaughtering food for the Jewish public are brought up to be Rabbis, and all are members of the Skeater Board[250] (a council of Rabbis), recognised by the Jewish community, and are men of unblemished character, who could not hold the position if there was the least stain on their reputation.

—

## A NIGHT IN WHITECHAPEL.
## WITH THE
## MURDERED WOMAN'S FRIENDS.
## (BY OUR SPECIAL COMMISSIONER.)

Following up my recent visit to Flower and Dean-street, I returned another night to the district. It had been told to me that I would find the streets in the same quarter all equally disreputable and forbidding. Fashion-street—the next street to Flower and Dean-street—was especially mentioned to me as one of the worst in London, and to it, therefore, I first directed my attention. It was an agreeable surprise, however, to find that after parading this particular thoroughfare for half an hour there was nothing to be seen to indicate that it was at all a place of either an objectionable or repulsive character. Instead of the dirty, dingy, dwellings of the adjacent streets, Fashion-street was well illuminated, and presented all the appearances of a lively busy community.

Decently-dressed children were playing about on the pavement and in the roadway with all the blitheness and freedom of country urchins. Women, in costumes that would have done no discredit to the most respectable promenade of the West-end, stood at the doorways talking to their neighbours, or passed up and down with baskets and parcels in their hands going or returning on their shopping expeditions. This abnormal respectability in the midst of such a hotbed of poverty and destitution, is, perhaps, to be accounted for by the fact that Fashion-street is principally inhabited by Jews, as most of the persons seen had the Israelitish cast of countenance and "Yiddish" announce-ments were visible on several of the shop-keepers'

windows.

Fashion-street is full of courts. They are, however, all well-lighted, and the interiors are remarkably clean, and even respectable looking. The houses are such as might be seen any day on a London suburban roadside. New-court, off Fashion-street, is comparatively an exceptionally attractive place. There are in it 13 well-constructed houses, and almost every windowsill has its flower pot with some green plant or creepers. It is a remarkable circumstance that in this small court there are two Jewish syna-gogues—one on each side of the entry. Turning out of the court into the street again my ears were greeted by the shrill treble voices of a band of children singing "God Save the Queen," and it was with some reluctance that I left this scene for the less congenial atmosphere of Flower and Dean-street again.

There was no change in the aspect of the place since I had been there before, and save that there were a few more signs of life about it, the street looked a veritable valley of the shadow of death. Ghoulish-like figures stalked forth from the doorways into the bleakness of the street or disappeared amongst the recesses of the walls. Crouching and distorted creatures lurched noiselessly about as if waiting for a spring upon some unsuspecting victim. I entered with my artist friend one of the first of the row of lodging-houses at the west end of the street, and tendered eightpence with the request for a couple of beds. The surly looking deputy looked surlier still, and his suspicious glances bespoke his reluctance to accept our money, but he booked us the beds without a word except to tell us our numbers.

The house was one of the smallest of the class. The low-roofed kitchen was fitted up after the general style, with wooden tables and benches, and the fumes of the great coke fire had a stifling and drowsy effect. The occupants at the time were principally women—old, middle-aged, and young—and several poorly-clad, but sharp featured, children were playing about the floor. A group of abject, miserable-looking men stood round the fire-place, and regarded us with a furtive interest as we approached them. Very little conversation was to be had out of the people here. The women proceeded with their cooking or the repairing of some old garments, and the men lazily engaged in the occupation of relighting pipes which they had been too indolent

---

[250] **Shechita Board.** The organization overseeing the Jewish ritual slaughterers, the Shochetim. Shechita is a Hebrew word denoting the slaughtering of kashér animals for food.

to keep in. Of course the murders were a general theme, but so far as any practical suggestion for the elucidation of the mysteries were forthcoming the talk was worthless.

At another house that we went to a brisk passage of arms was proceeding between two half-drunken women, the subject of dispute being the particular position to which the teapots and saucepans of those ladies were entitled before the fire. The women's voices were raised in strident and angry argument, and a challenge to mortal combat was only prevented from being carried into effect by the interference of the Deputy, whose demand for order commended instant obedience.

Mr. Deputy is a power and an authority in these houses. He may be a puny individual, half a dozen of whose like could easily be pulverised and demolished by any one of the inmates, but his position ensures him respect and the summary powers which he possesses in the treatment of refractory lodgers are a certain safeguard against intimidation.

In the next house that we went to we found the same order of things obtain and the same Bohemian tatterdemalion company, with however, just a flavour of the last remnants of bygone respectability in the persons of two old women. These latter had evidently seen much better days, and their faces were marked by intelligence and refinement.

On revisiting No. 55 we were able to see and speak to Kelly, the man who stayed with Kate Eddowes, and a number of other friends and acquaintances of the deceased.

Kelly is an interesting character from the fact that he is in some degree above the class which surrounds him. He is quiet and inoffensive in manner, and has fine features, with sharp and intelligent eyes. He spoke to use freely of Kate, but confessed to being very much "cut up." "I hope to Almighty God her soul's at rest," he said, fervently. "Many's the time I have said to her, 'Well, Kate, you are my wife, and I'll keep you as well as I can,' but when we had not the eightpence I took her to the casual ward—where there has been many a good mother's son—and which is better than the streets, because I thought it kept her out of immoral ways." Speaking of the probability of capturing the murderer, Kelly said, "It's my belief it won't be long before he's taken, and a very good job too." Kelly is not a strong man, as he suffers from an affection of the kidneys and a bad cough. These ailments have prevented him from doing much hard work, and he has earned his living by doing odd jobs about Spitalfields Market and running errands for the Jews. Kate also used to do similar work, as well as going out charing.

While speaking to Kelly we were joined by a couple of female lodgers who garrulously expatiated on the virtues of her late friend Kate. "Ah, she was well and hearty this time last week," moralised one of the two, and then suddenly fell on her knees, and with clasped hands raised aloft she prayed "that the Lord Almighty would deliver the murderer into their hands that night." "If I meet Jack the Ripper to-night," she continued, "it will be Oh, Dolly Daisy, up this way." Then, turning fiercely upon me she cried, "If I thought you were any confederate of him, do you know what I'd do? I'd cut you open with this pot," and she flourished a pewter tankard, from which she had been drinking, in such dangerous proximity to my face that I thought it advisable to get beyond the reach of her arm. I soon succeeded in pacifying Dolly Daisy, and dispelling her suspicions by replenishing the pot and giving her the money for her doss—an act of philanthropy which got speedily bruited abroad and involved several repetitions.

Mrs. Gold, Kate's "Sister Liza," appeared on the scene in the course of the evening.

She, however, was very lachrymose, and between her sobs could only bewail the fate of her poor sister.

A turn round the streets of the district shortly before midnight gave us an insight into Saturday night life in Whitechapel. The public-houses did a roaring trade, and the streets were filled with the cries of the tradesmen's "buy, buy," the shrieks of some drunken woman or the blatant bellowing of some more drunken man. Bands of half tipsy youths indulged in their favourite amusement of hustling everybody else off the pavement, and rolling forth, with fiendish energy, the chorus of the latest popular ditty. Detectives swarmed in every direction, and the activity of the police was unquestionable. But in the wee, small hours after twelve all was quiet and still, and in the morning an anxious public awoke to find, with relief, that the night had passed over without another atrocity having been added to the ghastly list.

## 𝕿𝖍𝖊 𝕿𝖎𝖒𝖊𝖘

### THE EAST-END MURDERS

A good deal of fresh evidence will be given at the adjourned inquest, which will be held to-day at the City Coroner's Court, Golden-lane, upon the body of the Mitre-square victim. Since the adjournment, Shelton, the coroner's officer, has, with the assistance of the City police authorities, discovered several new witnesses, including the daughter of the deceased, who was found to be occupying a respectable situation as a domestic in the neighbourhood of Kensington. She states that she had not seen her mother for some time, and certainly did not see her on the night she met her death. Two witnesses have also been found who state that they saw the deceased standing at the corner of Duke-street, Aldgate, a few minutes' walk from Mitre-square. This was as near as they can recollect about half-past 1 o'clock, and she was then alone. They recognized her on account of the white apron she was wearing. The contents of the deceased's stomach have been analysed, but no trace of a narcotic can be discovered. Ten witnesses will be called to-day, and the coroner hopes to conclude the inquiry this sitting.

Sir Alfred Kirby, colonel of the Tower Hamlets Engineers, recently made an offer to provide 30 or 50 men belonging to that regiment for service in connexion with tracking the perpetrator of the Whitechapel and Aldgate tragedies. The Home Secretary has just written to Sir Alfred saying that, having consulted Sir Charles Warren, he had come to the conclusion that it would not be advisable to put the men on for service. It is thought that several consid-erations have pointed to this deter-mination, the principal being that in the event of any injury happening to the men the question of compensation might be attended with some difficulty.

---

### TO THE EDITOR OF THE TIMES.

Sir,—There is one statement in your other-wise very exact account of the trials of blood-hounds in Hyde Park which I shall be glad to be allowed to correct. My hounds Barnaby and Burgho have not been purchased by Sir Charles Warren for the use of the police.

Yours truly,

October 10.                               EDWIN BROUGH.

---

### THE DETECTION OF CRIME
#### To the Editor of The Times

Sir,—It is to be hoped that the excellent letter of Sir Charles Warren, which was given to your readers on the 4th, will have had the effect of somewhat allaying the misgivings as to the efficiency of the police force which recent events in the east of London appear to have roused among Londoners.

To my mind there is not, and never has been, any substantial cause for apprehension on that score. It is always easy to jump from a minor premise to a foregone conclusion, provided that the major premise be dispensed with and by this process of reasoning, the fact that the perpetrator of the Whitechapel murders has hitherto escaped detection may be held to prove that the police force is, as regards its detective element, inefficient, but by this process only. Those who thus hastily form their judgement of course assume that the police have opportunities which they are not turning to the best account. But where is the evidence of this?

A detective, be it remembered, can no more get on the track of a criminal without a clue than a hound can hunt a fox without a scent; but — and here we come to the gist of the matter — while a fox cannot travel without leaving a scent behind him, a criminal may, although he seldom does, succeed in escaping from the scene of his crime without leaving the slightest trace of his route or indication of his personality. As a rule, either from want of education, from natural dullness, from carelessness or forgetfulness, some small thing is done or left undone which starts as the starting point of pursuit—it may be a bit of gravel in a horse's foot, a smear of brown paint on a lady's dress, or even a single straw. The slip of the tongue by which Houseman, the confederate of Eugene Aram, proclaimed his guilt will occur to many, "That is no more Dan Clark's bone than it is mine."[251]

---

[251] **Eugene Aram** (1704-1759). Gifted English self-taught philogist who recognized the structural similarities between the Celtic languages and other languages of Europe, including Greek and Latin, thus anticipating the work of J. C. Pritchard on the Indo-European families of language in 1831. He is best known, however, for being hanged for the murder of his friend, Daniel Clark, and becoming the subject

# Thursday, 11 October, 1888

Something, I say, there generally is, and something there must be for guidance if a crime is to be detected, so long a detectives are but human, whatever may be their skill and experience. But there is no reason why a particular criminal should not combine in himself the various qualifications requisite for eluding discovery. That these six murders have been the work of the same hand we are all, I think, pretty well agreed; and on this hypothesis the accumulated experience of the criminal tells in his favour and against detection on the very ratio of iteration. Now Sir Charles Warren has forcibly pointed out that the Whitechapel murders were so arranged as to leave no clue whatever; and it appears to be beyond question that in the present instance we are concerned with one who is a consummate master of his art and as wide awake to contingencies as any detective.

Sir Charles Warren has hit the right nail on the head in telling the Whitechapel District Board of Works that "the very fact that you (they) be unaware of what the Detective Department is doing is only the stronger proof that it is doing its work with secrecy and efficiency." There are apparently some wise-acres who cannot be satisfied unless they see everything, detectives included, with their own eyes, and hear everything with their own ears. If we all really knew exactly what detectives are doing and where they are working, then woe betide us.

The detective for our wise friends would be the gentleman in the "House in the Marsh,"[252] who solemnly reports himself to another gentleman who proves to be the very man "wanted", and who forthwith proceeds to drug his interviewer in the most effective manner. Readers of Gaboriau may remember by way of contrast the interview between the Mayor of Corbeil and M. Lecoq. A terrible murder has

been committed, and as a matter of course the great detective is summoned from Paris. The civic dignitary, who is much scandalized by Lecoq's very ordinary dress, instead of the tightly buttoned frock coat with military stock collar, that he had expected, and by his somewhat late arrival in court, offers to explain what has occurred. "Oh, that's quite useless," retorted Lecoq..."I've been here the last two hours." In fact, he had been quietly poking about among the crowd, and had learned all that there was to know.[253]

It would be with some sense of humiliation that we should read the exciting tales of Gaboriac, of A.K. Green,[254] and of Laurence Lynch (E. Murdoch),[255] if we were obliged to believe that, whatever may be the case in France and America, we have at home no match for M. Lecoq, Dick Stanhope, Van Vernet and Mr. Gryce. I have little or no knowledge personally of our present detective staff; but if the history of the dynamite outrages is to be taken as a criterion I do not think that we have much cause for misgivings.

I remain, Sir, your obedient servant,

D.

---

[252] of Thomas Hood's ballad "The Dream of Eugene Aram" and Edward Bulwer-Lytton's novel Eugene Aram. (Encyclopaedia Britannica)

[252] **The House on the Marsh: A Romance.** Published in 1877, it was one of the best known work penned by prolific Victorian and Edwardian writer Florence Warden, pen-name of Florence Alice Price James (1857-1929). The House on the Marsh was produced on the London stage, starring the authoress, in 1885. In 1920 it was adapted to film.

[253] **The Mystery of Orcival (Le Crime d'Orcival).** Émile Gaboriau, 1867.

[254] **Anna Katherine (A.K.) Green** (1846-1935). This Brooklyn born novelist and poet was noted for her well crafted detective fiction. Her first novel, The Leavenworth Case: A Lawyer's Story (1878), became a bestseller and led to the publishing of two dozen more well received who-done-its. Most of these stories featured the characters Ebenezer Gryse, New York Metropolitan Police, and the ancestress of Miss Marple and Miss Silver, Amelia Butterworth, society scion and busy-body. A. K. Green married furniture designer Charles Rohlfs in 1884 and bore three children, Rosamund, Roland and Sterling. Roland and Sterling both became test pilots for Glenn Curtiss, and Roland broke both the airspeed world record (163.1 mph) in 1918 and the altitude world record (34,610 feet) in 1919.

[255] **Lawrence L. Lynch.** Nom de plume of Oswego, Illinois housewife and authoress Emma Murdock Van Deventer (1853-1914). Uninterested in fame or notoriety, she is little known today even though she is credited with at least seven detective novels that were well received in her time. Van Vernet and Dick Stanhope are rival detectives that were the heroes of several of her novels.

# Thursday, 11 October, 1888

—

### DETECTIVES
### To the Editor of The Times.

Sir,—Allow me to ask a question a propos of Sir Charles Warren's announcement published in your issue of this morning. Why should such a thing as a female detective be unheard of in the land? A clever woman of unobtrusive dress and appearance (she need not be 5ft 7in) would possess over her masculine rivals not a few advantages. She would pass unsuspected where a man would be instantly noticed; she could extract gossip from other women much more freely; she would move through the streets and courts without waking the echoes of the pavement by a sonorous military tread; and, lastly, she would be in a position to employ for whatsoever it may be worth that gift of intuitive quickness and "mother wit" with which her sex is commonly credited.

Your readers who may be familiar with the "History of the Crimean War"[256] will remember the splendid chapter wherein Mr. Kinglake sets forth how the masculine minds of all the generals and War Office dignitaries together failed to grapple with the problem of the hospitals, and how the feminine mind, impersonated in Miss Nightingale and her little band of nurses, came to the rescue and out of chaos and indescribable misery brought order and relief.[257] Is it not worth trying now in another public difficulty whether womanly faculties may not again be useful?

A keen eyed woman might do as well in her way as those keen nosed bloodhounds (of whose official engagement I rejoice to hear) may, we hope, do in their peculiar line. Should it so fall out that the demon of Whitechapel prove really to be, as Mr. Baxter seems to suspect, a physiologist delirious with cruelty, and should the hounds be the means of his capture, poetic justice will be complete.

I am, Sir, &c.,
Frances Power Cobbe.[258]
No 1, Victoria street, S.W., Oct. 10.

—

WILLIAM GRIFFITHS, a young man, described as a general dealer,[259] of 1, Mildmay-avenue, Islington, was charged before Mr. Bros with being drunk and disorderly at Essex-road, at 1 o'clock yesterday morning. Police-constable 200 J deposed that he was on duty in Essex-road, when the prisoner came to him and said, "I want to be taken to the police-station. If you do not take me I shall murder somebody to-night. I am Jack the Ripper." Prisoner at the same time produced a rough looking pocket-knife. He did not open it, but made an attempt to do so. Witness told prisoner to go home, but he went into a neighbouring publichouse and came out again and fell down. Witness, thinking he was in a fit, picked him up, and then, finding he was drunk, got assistance and took him to the police-station. In reply to the magistrate prisoner said he was very sorry. It was a drunken freak,[260] and he had no intention of injuring any one. The magistrate said it was a very foolish freak, and prisoner must find one surety in £5 to keep the peace for three months, or go to prison for 21 days.

---

[256] Produced using the personal notes of the British commander in the Crimea, Field Marshal FitzRoy Somerset (1788-1855), 1st Baron Raglan, this minutely detailed history of the first half of the Crimean War, **Invasion of the Crimea** by Alexander William Kinglake, was published in nine volumes between 1863 and 1887, and contains 4,000 pages covering the war from the invasion of Crimea in September, 1854 to the death of Lord Raglan on 29 June, 1855.

[257] The deathrate at the barrack hospital in Scutari, under the control of **Florence Nightingale**, was 42% in February, 1855, and Nightingale herself may be partly responsible for that horrendous statistic. When she and her nurses arrived in the Autumn of 1854, she failed to notice that the hospital had been sited over a sewage dump and that the drinking water was being drawn from a source contaminated by a dead horse. Although it can be said that nurses are not responsible for the poor siting of a facility and the condition of its water supply, Nightingale was there to put into action her theories on the value of cleanliness and sanitation, and, in this instance, she clearly failed. (Gill)

[258] **Frances Power Cobbe** (1822-1904). Anglo-Irish feminist, writer, suffragette, and founder of the Society for the Protection of Animals Liable to Vivisection and the British Union for the Abolition of Vivisection. Entered into a sham marriage with the Welsh sculptress Mary Lloyd in 1864. (Prochaska)

[259] **General Dealer**. A shop that would sell almost anything. (Census1891.com)

[260] **Freak**. 2. A whim, vagary. (Morehead)

# Thursday, 11 October, 1888

---

## RATCLIFF HIGHWAY REFUGE
### To the Editor of The Times

Sir,—My attention has just been called to Mr. Walter Hazell's letter in Saturday's issue of *The Times*.

Nine years ago I came to live in Ratcliff Highway with the simple determination to find out how best to help that class of poor, miserable women whose mode of living has been so prominently brought forward by the horrible events of the past few weeks. During all this time I have been able to keep an open door for them, and with my fellow helpers have been learning, as we could only learn by experience, how most wisely and effectively to help those who come to us. The work has been very quietly carried on, but our houses have always been full to overflowing, and while hundreds of young girls and children have been rescued from the most dangerous surroundings, trained as little servants, emigrated to the colonies, and in other ways given a fair start in life, still many more from among the fallen have found our home a "bridge of hope" by which they have passed on to better things.

The revelation of existence in Whitechapel lodging houses and in the streets of our great city must not simply evoke words of commiseration or be allowed to die out as a nine days' wonder, but must surely result in very practical measures being adopted for perma-nently benefitting those at least who are willing to be helped. Hundreds of women in this sad East end lead their degraded lives of sin for daily bread, or to secure a night's shelter in a fourpenny lodging house, a fact of which none can now plead ignorance, for the horrors of a few weeks (to our shame as a nation be it said) have brought out in awful relief the conditions under which so many of our fellow creatures exist, and which, though told persistently and without exaggeration by East end workers, have made but little impression.

Finding that the missing link in the work in Ratcliff Highway was a night shelter, we have, during the past year, built one as a wing to our new refuge, and this will be opened on the 30th inst. by the Bishop of Bedford, although circumstances have compelled us already to give shelter in it to many who needed immediate help. Night shelters, answering only the purposes of a casual ward, may be the means of as much harm as good, but, managed with judicious discrimination and constant personal supervision, I believe that our "bridge of hope" night shelter will be an effectual means of helping not only those who have fallen but of saving very many friendless young girls from utter despair, when they come to their last resources. At this moment the strain of the work is very great. While people are devising, and very rightly so, how best to organise new methods and larger schemes, it sometimes appears that those who have been plodding on in the midst of the misery, and who have to bear the brunt of sudden emergencies, are apt to be forgotten, and however unwillingly we do so, it seems right to call attention to our present need of financial help. We are always thankful to see visitors, or to send reports if desired.

Apologising for taking up so much of your valuable space,

I am, Sir, yours faithfully,
Mary H. Steer,[261] Hon. Supt.,
Ratcliff Highway Refuge,
St. George's in the East, London, E.
October 8.

~

---

[261] **Mary Hannah Steer** (1846-1930). Cornish born daughter of a Congregational Minister, the devoutly religious Mary Steer, along with her younger sister Helen, never married and both dedicated their lives to helping the poor. In 1888 she and a group of other middle and upper class women opened a night shelter in Stepney for women and girls. She was also Director of Bridge of Hope Mission. This organization sent over 100,000 poor children to Canada and 7,000 to Australia for resettlement, sometimes without the parents knowledge or permission. (Bayliss)

## The Star
### FIFTH EDITION.
### MITRE SQUARE.
### THE INQUEST ON THE VICTIM RESUMES TO-DAY.
### The Medical Evidence Discredits the Theory of Anatomical Motive on the Part of the Murderer—The Daughter Gives Evidence—Production of the Apron.

The inquest upon the body of Catherine Eddowes, the victim of the murder in Mitre-square, Aldgate, was continued this morning by Coroner Langham at the City Mortuary, Golden-lane, Barbican. As before, Mr. Crawford, the solicitor to the City Corporation, watched the proceedings on behalf of the police, and again demonstrated the additional facility and completeness with which facts can be elicited at an inquiry of this sort by the assistance of a legal man. Detective-Inspector McWilliam, head of the City Detective Department, listened closely to the whole of the evidence, while Major Smith, the City Acting Commissioner, and Superintendent Foster were also present.

### DR. SEQUEIRA,

of 34, Jury-street, Aldgate, said:—I was the first medical man to arrive after the discovery of the murder, reaching the scene at five minutes to two. I entirely agree with Dr. Gordon Browne in the evidence he gave last week.

Mr. Crawford: You are acquainted with this locality, are you not?

—Yes, very well, where the body was found would be the darkest corner. There would have been sufficient light, though, to admit of the infliction of the injuries without the aid of any additional light.

From what you saw have you formed any opinion as to whether the perpetrator of the deed had any particular design on any part of the body?

—I have formed the opinion that he had no particular design on any organ.

Judging from the injuries inflicted do you think he must have possessed great anatomical skill?

—No, I do not.

Can you account in any way for the absence of noise?

—Death must have been instantaneous after the severance of the windpipe.

Would you have expected to find the clothes of the murderer bespattered with blood?

—Not necessarily.

For how long had life been extinct when you arrived?

—In my opinion but a very few minutes, and positively not more than a quarter of an hour.

The doctor, who was a smart little gentleman, looking more like a curate than a medical man, then left the witness stand, and was followed by another gentleman of his own profession. This was

### DR. SAUNDERS,

the Medical Officer of Health for the City, who was called at the wish of Mr. Crawford. He occupied some little time in the recital of his list of titles and qualifications, and then proceeded to give evidence bearing upon the murder. "I received," he said, "from Dr. Gordon Browne the stomach of the deceased, carefully sealed, the contents not having been disturbed in any way. I made a careful examination of the contents of the stomach, more particularly for poison of the narcotic class, with negative results, there not being the faintest trace of that class or any other sort of poison.

This cleared up a point upon which a question had previously been put by the jury, and upon which many questions have been written by the general public to the newspapers, namely, as to whether the murderer first drugged his victim to get her more effectually in his inhuman power.

Examined by Mr. Crawford, the doctor added:—I agree with Dr. Browne and Dr. Sequeira that the wounds were not inflicted by anyone who necessarily possessed great anatomical skill, and I equally agree that the perpetrator of the deed had no particular design upon any particular internal organ.

### THEN ANNIE PHILLIPS

was called, and many an inquiring glance was thrown upon her while she was being sworn. She was dressed entirely in black, with much crape on her hat, and proved to be the daughter of deceased. She was a young woman, about 21, married to a lampblack packer, living at 12, Dilston-grove, Southwark.

She said:—My mother always told me she was married to my father, whose name was

Thomas Conway. He was a hawker, but I do not know what has become of him since he left living with me and my husband. He left without giving any reason, but we were not on very good terms with him. He was a teetotaller, and lived on bad terms with my mother because she used to drink. I have not the least idea where he is now living. He was once a soldier, but had been pensioned. It is seven or eight years since he separated from my mother. The last time I saw my mother was two years and a month ago.

The Coroner: Then you did not see her on Saturday, the day previous to her death?

—No, sir. We used to live at King-street, Bermondsey, and when we left there, my mother did not know our address. I have two brothers, but mother did not know where to find them. They purposely kept from her to prevent her applying for money.

By the jury:

—My father knew my mother was living with a man named Kelly.

By Mr. Crawford:

—I believe it was the 18th Royal Irish that my father was a pensioner of, but I am not sure.

Mr. Crawford: It so happens that there is a man named Conway who is a pensioner of the 18th Royal Irish, but he is not the man.

Witness proceeding, in answer to Mr. Crawford, said:—My father is, I believe, living with my two brothers; but I cannot say where they are, and I cannot assist the police to find them. They are 15 and 20 years old, respectively. I have not seen them for 18 months.

You can't give the police the slightest clue where to find then?

—No, sir.

Do you know whether your mother had been intimate with anyone else recently?

—I do not.

The Coroner: I suppose every effort has been made to trace the deceased's relatives?

Mr. Crawford: Yes, Sergeant Mitchell will prove that.

**DETECTIVE-SERGEANT MITCHELL**
thereupon came forward, and said: I have under instruction made every endeavour to find the father and brothers of the last witness, but without success. I have found a pensioner named Conway belonging to the 18th Royal Irish, but he is not identified as the man supposed to have been married to deceased.

Detective Hunt had confronted the pensioner Conway with two of deceased's sisters, and they had failed to recognise him. This Conway is a quartermaster-sergeant.

Dr. Gordon Browne was then re-called, in order that a point might be cleared up by Mr. Crawford. A theory has been put forward, said Mr. Crawford, that the deceased was brought to the square in a murdered state?

—"Oh, there is not the least doubt about it," said the doctor, "that the murder was committed where the body was found. The blood on the left side was clotted, and must have flowed from the wound in the throat at the time it was inflicted, and I don't think deceased moved the least bit after her throat was cut."

Police-constable Robinson proved arresting the deceased for drunkenness on the Saturday afternoon before her death and locking her up in a cell. She was wearing an apron.

**THE APRON**
was here produced by the police, in two pieces, covered with blood, and witness identified it. The ghastly reminder of the crime quite upset Mrs. Phillips, the deceased's daughter, who sobbed bitterly on seeing the blood-smeared rag.

**SERGEANT BYFIELD**
said deceased was detained at the police-station till one o'clock on Sunday morning, which was within an hour of her death. She was then discharged after giving her name and address as Mary Ann Kelly, 6, Fashion-street, Spitalfields. Before going she said, in answer to witness's questions, that she had been hopping.

The Foreman: Was she perfectly sober when released?

—Yes, I believe so.

**POLICE-CONSTABLE HUNT,**
the gaoler at Bishopsgate-street station, corroborated, adding that as deceased left the cell she said to him, "Good night, old cock." She went in the direction of Houndsditch, but said nothing as to where she was going. When being brought out of the cell she had asked what time it was, whereupon witness said, "Too late for you to get any more drink." "What time is it?" she persisted. "Just on one," said witness. "Then I shall get a d— fine hiding when I get home," she said. "Serve you right," said witness; "for

# Thursday, 11 October, 1888

you've no business to go getting drunk." Witness believed the apron produced was the one deceased was wearing. The distance from the police station to Mitre-square was about eight minutes' walk.

### GEORGE JAMES MORRIS,

watchman at Messrs. Kearley and Tonge's tea warehouse, in Mitre-square, said:—I went on duty on the evening of the murder at seven o'clock. I occupied myself in cleaning the offices. At a quarter to two Police-constable Watkins knocked at my door. It was slightly on the jar at the time. I was sweeping the steps down towards the door when the door was knocked, I being then about two yards from the door. I opened it widely immediately, and Watkins said, "For God's sake, mate, come to my assistance." Seeing the constable was agitated, I thought he was ill. Taking my lamp I went outside and said, "What's the matter?" "Oh, dear," he said, "There's another woman cut up." I threw my light on the body, and then ran into Aldgate blowing my whistle.

The Coroner: Did you see any suspicious person about at the time?

—No, sir. Two constables came up, and I directed them to the scene of the murder, following them down, and taking charge of my own premises again.

Had you heard any noise in the square before being called by Watkins?

—No, sir.

If there had been any cry of distress would you have heard it from where you were?

—Yes.

Mr. Crawford: Before you were called by Watkins had you occasion to go into the square, or look into it?

—No, sir.

Not between twelve and one?

—No, sir.

Was there anything unusual in your door being open?

—No.

A juror: How long had your door been ajar before Watkins knocked?

—Only about two minutes, while I was sweeping.

This evidence deepened the feeling of many present at the inquest of

### THE WONDERFUL LUCK OF THE MISCREANT

in effecting his crimes. Had the watchman been sweeping a few minutes earlier he must have opened the door while the murderer was engaged on his horrible mutilations.

(Proceeding.)

—

### The Edge of the Terror Blunted.

More women were in the streets of Whitechapel last night than have been seen for weeks past, and there were no signs of special police precautions. About ten o'clock last night a middle-aged man of stout build walked into the Leman-street Police-station and accused himself of the murders. The man was obviously under the influence of drink, but it was thought desirable to detain him while inquiries were made at the address given. The police found that his name was Geary, that he lived in the neighbourhood, and that he had been an inmate of an asylum. He was released shortly after eleven o'clock. At all the police-stations in the Eastern district the night was reported to have been a quiet one.

—

### Bloodhounds.

Mr. Edwin Brough denies the statement that his hounds Barnaby and Burgho have been purchased by Sir Charles Warren for the use of the police.

—

### Futile Arrests.

A man gave himself up at Kilburn, and was taken to Leman-street Police-station, but after being questioned there by Inspector Abberline he was discharged.

Shortly before closing time yesterday morning three men in the Black Swan public-house, Hanbury-street, struck by the appearance of a stranger present, submitted him to interrogation and a search. They say they took from him a large clasp-knife, and that with assistance of a constable they conveyed him to Commercial-street Police-station, where two more knives, four rings, hairpins, and money were found upon him. After inquiries had been made, the man was liberated.

# Thursday, 11 October, 1888

## Evening News
### THE WESTMINSTER MURDER.
### DESCRIPTION OF THE VICTIM.

The medical evidence given at the inquest held on Monday on the headless and limbless body found at Whitehall, has placed the police in possession of a description of the woman who was the subject of the horrible crime thus committed. A great many cases of missing women have been brought before the police, and the number has caused some embarrassment. Now, however, the police have before them the fact that the deceased woman was a plump woman, of about 5ft. 8in. or 5ft. 9in. high; that she had suffered from pleurisy; that she was from 24 years of age upwards; that she had fair skin and dark hair; and that her hand, found with the arm at Pimlico, showed that she had not been used to hard work. Moreover, the police have the fact that the death may have been from six weeks to two months prior to October 2, which would bring the end of her life to about August 20, and the death, moreover, is defined as having been one which drained the body of blood. This last point means that wherever the woman met her death- and it was not in the water- the place would be marked with blood. Anxious search is being made for the missing head.

---

### CAPTURE OF A SUSPICIOUS CHARACTER.
### To The Editor of "THE EVENING NEWS."

SIR—I beg to correct a report in your issue of to-day, under the heading of "Capture of a Suspicious Character." It is stated that the man was stopped by and inspector of the P division. After an exciting chase up the Old Kent-road the man was apprehended at my instigation, and was taken to the Peckham Police-station. Also, the tramcar incident was on Monday.—

I am, &c.,
W.H. BEHENNA
October 10.

---

### THE BLOODHOUND AS A TRACKER.
### To The Editor Of "THE EVENING NEWS."

SIR—Allow me to contribute my little experience to the discussion now current as to the value of the bloodhound (or sleuth-hound, as I prefer to call it) as a detective. Some years ago I owned a dog of the best strain, a son of Mr. Holford's famous Regent.[262] I took great interest in training Reveller to follow the lightest scent, which he soon learned to do admirably. One instance will suffice. A very little time after I took him in hand, I one day showed him a dry bone, quite free from blood, and unprepared by any artificial scent. I then started a lad with the bone, giving him instructions to conceal it a few miles away, the route and hiding place being both unknown to me. An hour after, I myself started with the dog, and with unfaltering and unerring scent he led me from Upper Norwood, over Streatham Common, to Tooting Beck Common, and to a bush at the later place, wherein the bone, which I had previously marked, was found. The distance was over three miles. But the sleuth-hound's scent is merely the high development of a faculty common to all dogs. As a humourist recently remarked, when two dogs meet and converse, they do not say, "Where have you been?" or "What have you seen?" but "What have you smelt?" I am daily reminded of this by the conduct of a New-foundland dog, used as a yard dog at Messrs. C.T. Brock and Co.'s great firework factory, where I am engaged. At the present time, owning to the pressure of the November business, many fresh hands are temporarily employed. These are always introduced to and smelt by the dog. After this introduction, he invariably scents them every day as they enter the gate, until his sight is as accustomed to them as his nose, and they can go to their work unmolested as soon as the latter organ has satisfied him as to their bona fides.—

I am. &c.,
W. GRIST
South Norwood. London. S.E.,
October 10.

---

[262] **Regent**. Owned by the noted dog breeder C. R. Holford of Ware, Hertfordshire, Regent took first prize in the 1869 National Dog Show.

## SOME MORE INSTANCES OF HOMICIDAL MANIA.

As I told the reader yesterday,[263] both Antoine Leger and Papavoine were guillotined. Through their crimes left no doubt in the minds of experts as having been committed by homicidal maniacs, though Dr. Georget's pamphlet—also mentioned yesterday—was followed by still more luminous treatises on the same subject by even more eminent authorities than he—namely, Esquirol and Orfila, many years had to elapse before the tribunals were to be influenced by the theory of moral irresponsibility in their verdicts against a certain class of homicides.

And yet if Leger's and Papavoine's deeds could and did leave a doubt as to motive with both judges and jury, a case which happened less than a twelve-month after ought to have dispelled such doubt for ever. I am writing from memory, and may be mistaken in some minor details, but am absolutely certain of the main facts of the tragedy. In one of the most populous quarters of Paris there lived a woman keeping a green-grocer's and fruiterer's shop. Frugal and hard-working, all her exertions seemed to tend to the welfare of her only child, a little girl between four and five. A few doors further down the street there was an establishment, half café, half public-house, of the kind still to be seen in the humbler thoroughfares of the French capital. The servant of the publican bought her provisions at the fruiterer's just named, and, if I remember rightly, had been recommended to the situation by its owner. At any rate, though she had not been there more than fortnight a friendly feeling had sprung up between the two women. One afternoon in the end of the summer the servant, Henriette Cournier, came in, and in the course of a conversation told the fruiterer that she was not very comfortable in her new place. The widow happened to mention that she was going to take her little daughter for a walk, and Henriette Cournier by her conduct or manners, either to herself (the witness) or her child, had ever justified such reluctance, the witness frankly answered in the negative, adding that on the contrary Henriette was considered by her a very honest girl, and had been uniformly kind to her,

and appeared to be exceedingly fond of her little daughter.

Nevertheless, the child went with Henriette Cournier, who, after passing through the shop of her employers, who were both absent, took it up to her attic, laid it on the bed, method-ically cut its throat, and as methodically proceeded to disembowel. As she was about to lock her door, "in order," as she confessed, "to escape from the horrible sight," she heard the mother coming up the stairs. Without leaving her time to ascend, she shouted out to her, "It's no use coming up, your little daughter is dead." The mother thought at first that the girl was perpetrating a ghastly joke; in another moment she was convinced of the horrible reality. I do not know whether Henriette Cournier was executed or not, but if her sentence was commuted, her sex rather than her mental condition, about which, however, there could be no doubt, must have influenced her judges, because more than a cycle afterwards Orfila[264] had to explain again and again to magist-rates as well as to juries that homicidal mania is the madness of an hour or a minute, as the case may be, and perfectly consistent with precedent and subsequent sanity of mind. He went further still. He cited the case of a journalist, well known at the time, who was confined in a lunatic asylum as a homicidal maniac. One day his attendant, being alone with him, notices that he is hiding a formidable life preserver[265] under his coat. "I suppose you mean

---

[263] See **Some Instances of Monomania**, p. 361.

[264] **Mathieu Joseph Bonaventure Orfila** (1787-1853). Spanish born, naturalized French, chemist, physician and physiologist. Authored the ground-breaking two volume work on toxicology Traité des poisons, tires des reégnes minéral vegetal et animal; ou toxicologie générale, considérée sous les rapports de la physio-logie, de la pathologie et de la médicine légale in 1814. Because of his expertise served as an expert witness in several high profile legal proceedings.

[265] **Life Preserver** or **Life-preserver**. A short, weighted club, or a slung shot. A slung shot is a weight on the end of a heavy cord, with the other end of the cord looped to fit around the wrist. This was originally a tool used by sailors to throw lines by tying the slung shot cord, which is longer than on the weaponized version, to the end of the heavy line, cast the weight and cord to where you wanted the line to go, where it is picked up and the line is pulled across the space. (Farmer)

to kill me with this," says the keeper, not leaving his patient time to attack. "Remember that if you do," he continues, "you'll be guillotined." "No, I won't," comes the reply. "I have thought it out, the doctors will say I am mad." "Not this time," replies the keeper, "because it will be proved that you premeditated it." "I'll lay you a wager that Orfila will get me off, for I have been looking at his book lately;" retorts the madman. The keeper never loses his presence of mind. "Where's the book?" he asks, "I should like to have a look at it myself." It's downstairs in the doctor's library; go and get it, and I'll show you the passage." There is no need to state that the keeper failed to keep the appointment when once out of the room.

Here, then, we have not only absolute premeditation, but a perfect consciousness on the part of the maniac of the legal bearings of his premeditated act at the very moment of its execution. Orfila lived to see his theory at least accepted partially, though he was too old to take share in the debates, for the celebrated trial in which Drs. Gromier and Tavernier successfully advanced this theory took place but a few months before Orfila's death. On the evening of September 15, 1851, the Celestins Theatre at Lyons was crowded from floor to ceiling. Suddenly the performance of "Adrienne Lecouvreur"[266] was interrupted by a terrific cry, a young matron had been stabbed to the heart by a stranger standing behind her in the ampitheatre. The murderer, Antoine Emmanuel Jobard, not even endeavoured to escape. "I am a miserable wretch," he exclaimed, "do with me what you like." He was taken to the town-hall, and when the examining magistrate entered the cell a few hours afterwards he found the prisoner praying, but thoroughly calm and composed. He did not know Madame Ricard, he confessed that any other victim would have suited him quite as well, that in fact he had at first selected a woman with whom he had passed the previous night in a house of ill-fame, but that he was first of all afraid that her companions would lynch him, and

that secondly she was too handsome. "I wish to have the time to repent before I die," he said, "else I should have committed suicide long ago, but I was afraid to appear before my Maker with this horrible sin upon me without confession." Everything went to prove that Jobard was fully cognizant of the consequences of his act; that he had carefully shifted from one part of the theatre to another in order to get a victim which he might not miss. He had calmly awaited his opportunity until the box-keeper, whom he thought was watching him, had departed; nay, he had tried to avert what he thought suspicion by assuming a great interest in the play, smiling every now and then, to said attendant in order to convince him that the play, and the play only, had brought him to the theatre. He had quietly drawn his knife from his breast and pretended to pare his nails with it when he deemed himself too much observed. He had even shifted between whiles, on perceiving a little girl on the opposite side of the theatre, whom he thought within easier reach; in one word, his presence of mind had never left him for a single instant. Nevertheless, this man was a homicidal maniac, but it was difficult to persuade the jury, perhaps the judges. The verdict of twenty years penal servitude (not detention in a madhouse, or, as we should call it, "during the Queen's pleasure") was based not upon the absence of moral responsibility. Orfila had only conquered partially.

I might quote a dozen similar cases; I will not weary the reader, and conclude to-morrow with the biography and trial of Philippe, the only precedent in criminal annals of the Whitechapel murders; of Philippe, whose exploits were known under the title of "the St. Bartholomew of Unfortunates." A.D.V.[267]

—

## THE MITRE SQUARE VICTIM.
## RESUMED INQUEST ON
## CATHERINE EDDOWES.
## IMPORTANT EVIDENCE.

The inquest into the death of Catherine Eddowes (or Conway), who was found murdered and mutilated in Mitre-square on the morning of the 30th ult. was resumed to-day at the city mortuary in Golden-lane by the City Coroner and a jury.

---

[266] **Adrienne Lecouvreur.** Tragedy by Ernest Legouvé and Eugène Scribe dramatizing the life of celebrated 18th Century French actress Adrienne Lecouvreur (1692-1730). First produced in 1849, it was adapted as the libretto of an opera in 1902 and became the basis for several motions pictures, including *Dream of Love* (1928) starring a young Joan Crawford.

[267] See *Evening News*, 12 October, 1888, **"Jack the Ripper's" Predecessor**, p. 388.

Dr. Sequeira was the first witness. He said that he was the first medical man called to the place of the murder. He corroborated previous witnesses that the murderer had no special design on any part of the woman's body, and showed no great anatomical skill.

Dr. Sidgwick Saunders, the Medical Officer of Health for the City, said he had analysed the stomach, with special reference to narcotic poisoning, but with negative results.

Annie Phillips, a married woman, said she was the daughter of the deceased. Her father, Thomas Conway, was the husband of the deceased. He did not live with her. He had left home suddenly, but on good terms, and she had never seen or heard of him since. He was a teetotaller. She had no idea where her father was living. He did not live with her mother because of her drunken habits. He was a pensioner, she thought, for life. He had been a pensioner in the 18th Royal Irish since witness was eight years old. She was now 23. It was between seven and eight years since he left her mother. She was not in the habit of seeing anything of him after he left witness, about fifteen or eighteen months ago. Her mother used to apply to him for money very frequently. She had not applied to witness for two years and one month. Witness had in the meantime moved, and did not leave her new address. She never saw her mother's marriage lines, but her mother always told her she was married to her father.

By Mr. Crawford (City Solicitor):—She was not quite sure that her father was a pensioner in the 18th Royal Irish. Her mother had not received money from witness for two years and two months. She never had a letter from her mother. She had seen Kelly and her mother in the lodging-house in Flower and Dean-street. The last time was about three years ago. She knew they were living as man and wife. Her father was living with her two brothers. She did not know where they were living. She knew her father was with them because he always lived with them. She had not seen them for 18 months. She had lost all trace of her father, her mother, and her two brothers for at least 18 months, and could not give the police the slightest clue where to find them. She did not know whether her mother had been living recently with anybody but Kelly.

The Coroner said it would be well to call some one to prove that every effort had been made to find Conway and his sons.

Sergeant John Mitchell, of the City Detective Force, was then called, and said he had done everything to find the father and brothers of last witness, without success. He had found a pensioner named Conway, belonging to the 18th Royal Irish. He is not identified as the father of the last witness. Every endeavour and every inquiry has been made to find the man.

Detective Baxter Hunt said he had discovered Conway, of the 18th Royal Irish. He had confronted him with two of the deceased's sisters, and they failed to recognise him as the man who used to live with the deceased. He had made every endeavour to trace the Thomas Conway and the brothers referred to by the witness Phillips.

A Juryman: Why did you not take the daughter?

Witness:—At that time the daughter had not been found.

Mr. Crawford: It shall be done.

Another Juryman: Is it possible for a pensioner to be in the army without your knowing his address?

Mr. Crawford: It is just possible he may not be drawing a pension in the name of Conway. They take such various names, but everything is still being done to find him.

Dr. Brown, City police surgeon, recalled, said that from the way the blood had flowed he did not think the deceased moved in the least bit after the injury to the throat. The murder was undoubtedly committed where the body was found.

Police-constable Robinson, 931, said he was called to 29, High-street, on Saturday night, 29th ult., and found a woman lying outside drunk. He had since identified her as the deceased. There was a crowd, and he asked if there was anybody there who knew her and got no answer. He then picked her up and carried her to the side by the shutters. He tried to lean her against the shutters, and she fell sideways down again. He got assistance and took her to the police-station, where she was locked up.

By Mr. Crawford:

—It was about nine o'clock on the Saturday evening when the deceased was put in the police cell. She was then wearing an apron [The bloody apron was here produced, torn and tattered, and the deceased's daughter, Mrs. Phillips, burst into tears.]

Witness (continuing):—Yes, that is the apron.

Station-Sergeant Byfield said he remembered the deceased being brought to Bishopgate-street station on Saturday, September 29, at about a quarter to nine o'clock. She was drunk and put into a police cell, where she remained till one o'clock in the morning. She was then discharged. She gave the name Mary Ann Kelly, 6, Fashion-street, Spitalfields. She said on being liberated that she had been hopping.

By a juryman: Had she food in the cell?

Witness:—No.

Would it be possible for a person locked up very drunk at nine o'clock to be sober at one o'clock in the morning?

—Yes.

Police-constable John Hutton, 968 City, said that on Saturday, the 29th ult., at a quarter to 10 p.m., he took over the care of the prisoners at Bishopgate Station, among them the deceased. He visited her several times till five minutes to one the following morning. The inspector was out visiting, and he was directed by Sergeant Byfield to see if there were any prisoners fitted to be discharged. He reported the deceased sober, took her to the office, where, after giving the name of Mary Ann Kelly she was discharged. When told to pull the outer door to she said, "All right, old cock." The door was closed to about half a foot, and saw her turn to the left.

By a Juryman: Was it left entirely to your discretion to decide whether the woman was sober or not?

Witness:—No, that is left to the inspector or the acting-inspector. I brought out the deceased for the sergeant to decide. About 12:30 she asked witness when she was to be discharged, and he replied, "When you are able to take care of yourself." She replied, "I am quite capable, now."

By Mr. Crawford: At two minutes before one in the Station-yard, she asked what time it was , and he replied, "Too late for you to get any more drink"; telling her it was just on one. She replied, "Then I shall get a — fine hiding when I get home." Witness said, "Serve you right, you've no right to get drunk." He noticed she was wearing an apron. The apron produced to the last witness, was, to the best of his belief, the apron. The distance from the station to Mitre-square was

about 600 yards. With ordinary walking, it would take a person eight minutes to go to Mitre-square.

Mr. George James Morris, watchman to Messrs. Kearley and Tonge, tea merchants, Mitre-square, said he went on duty at six o'clock on the evening of Saturday, 29th ultimo. About a quarter to two o'clock in the morning he was called by Police-constable Watkins. The door was "on the jar," and he (witness) was then sweeping the steps towards the door. Watkins said, "For God's sake, mate, come to my assistance." Seeing the constable rather agitated he thought him very ill, so taking his lamp went outside, when the constable said, "Oh, dear, here's another woman cut in pieces." Witness having seen the woman, ran up into Aldgate, blowing his whistle. Two police-constables soon appeared. He saw no "suspicious" persons. He had heard no noise in the square previous to being called by Police-constable Watkins.

(The inquiry is proceeding).

—

## THE MURDERS.
## FRESH EVIDENCE EXPECTED AT TODAY'S INQUEST.
## A "WANTED" MAN.
## WHITECHAPEL QUIETER NOW.

A reporter who patrolled the East-end districts, last evening, states that the popular excitement has almost entirely subsided. More women were in the streets than have been for weeks past, and there were no signs of special police precautions. It is understood, however, that the police have in no degree relaxed their vigilance, and that the number of plain-clothes men and amateur patrols has not been reduced.

—

## THE MURDERER COMES FROM A FASHIONABLE PART OF LONDON.

The authorities are greatly harassed by the multitudinous letters pointing to "clues" in this or that locality. Sometimes 70 or 80 written communications and telegrams from all parts of the country arrive at the East-end District Police Office in one day. Certain of the writers have boldly incriminated individuals, and have offered to give full information, with the addendum that they hope to share in the reward. Every item of authenticated private information is eagerly investigated, and, even at the risk of being trifled with, anonymous communications as supposed clues receive due attention.

Yesterday afternoon, for instance, the police at Leman-street, acting on evidence believed to be of a highly important character, took steps to keep under observation a man believed to be guilty of these horrible murders. It is thought that this last clue will lead to elucidating the crime in some measure, even if it does not result in the immediate apprehension of the criminal. The police have strong reasons to believe that the perpetrator of the East-end murders is not now in Whitechapel. His quarters are said to be in a far more fashionable part of the metropolis.

—

## ANOTHER "SUSPECT."

Shortly before closing time yesterday morning three men in the Black Swan public-house, Hanbury-street, being struck by the demeanour of a stranger who was present, submitted him to interrogation, and finally to a search. The three men assert that they took from him a large clasp knife, and that, with the assistance of a constable, they conveyed him to Commercial-street Police-station, where two more knives, four rings, hairpins, and money were found upon him. After inquiries had been made, however, the man was liberated.

—

## DESCRIPTION OF A MAN "WANTED."

Some time ago a man is stated to have landed from a ship at Deptford, who declared that if he could find her he would "do" for a certain woman, who, he conceived, had injured him. He further alleged that he would "do" for any other woman of her class. Yesterday the police gave the man's description as follows:

Age, 28; height, 5ft. 5in. or 5ft. 6in.; complexion fair; whiskers about a month's growth; dressed in dark clothes.

—

## FRESH EVIDENCE AS TO THE MITRE-SQUARE MURDER

A great deal of fresh evidence will be given to the adjourned inquest, which will be held to-day, at the City Coroner's Court, Golden-lane, upon the body of the Mitre-square victim. Since the adjournment, Shelton, the Coroner's officer, has, with the assistance of the City Police authorities, discovered several new witnesses, including the daughter of the deceased, who was found to be occupying a respectable situation as a domestic in the neighbourhood of Kennington. She states that they saw the deceased standing at the corner of Duke-street, Aldgate, a few minutes' walk from Mitre-square. This was as near as they can recollect about half-post one o'clock, and she was then alone. They recognized her on account of the white apron she was wearing. The contents of deceased's stomach has been analysed, but no trace of a narcotic can be discovered. Ten witnesses will be called to-day, and the coroner hopes to conclude the inquiry this sitting.

—

## IS THE MURDERER IN LIVERPOOL?

During yesterday frequent inquiries were made of the Liverpool head constable, Captain Bower, as well as at the detective office, with reference to the action of the Liverpool police in regard to tracing the person or persons supposed to be concerned in the recent atrocities in Whitechapel. A statement has been widely circulated to the effect that one of the supposed criminals was traced to Liverpool, that he had left the city, and that the police had lost sight of him. As a matter of fact, the head constable and the detective department knew nothing of the circumstance until the statements in the newspapers were brought under their notice. The head constable has given instructions for the various railway stations and the departing steamships to be closely watched, and an efficient staff of detectives are endeavouring to give every possible assistance to the London police, but up to last night no trace, so far as Liverpool is concerned, has been found of the criminal. The reward offered for the discovery of the assassin is posted up outside the police stations, and during the day it was eagerly perused by a large number of persons. The Liverpool police do not profess to have any distinct theory as to the identity of the murderer, or any tangible information likely to lead to an arrest. They are, however, deluged with suggestions from various quarters as to the solution of the mystery, but none of these have been found to be of any practical value.

# Friday, 12 October, 1888

## The Times
### THE EAST-END MURDERS.

Yesterday morning Mr. S. F. Langham, the City Coroner, resumed the inquest at the mortuary in Golden-lane respecting the death of Catherine Eddows, otherwise Conway or Kelly, who was found murdered in Mitre-square on the morning of Sunday, 30th ult.

During the inquiry, Major Henry Smith, the Assistant Commissioner of the City Police, Mr. M'William, the Inspector of the City Detective Department, Mr. Superintendent Foster, and Mr. F. W. Foster, architect and surveyor, of Old Jewry, who produced plans of the square were present.

The first witness examined was Dr. George William Sequeira, of 34 Jewry-street, Aldgate, who stated that he was called on Sunday, the 30th ult., to Mitre-square, and was the first medical man to arrive, being on the scene of the murder at five minutes to 2. He saw the position of the body, and he entirely agreed with Dr. Gordon Brown's evidence given on the opening of the inquest.

By Mr. Crawford (the City Solicitor).— He was acquainted with the locality and knew the position of the square. It would probably be the darkest corner of the square where the body was found. There would have been sufficient light to enable the murderer to commit his crime without the aid of any additional light.

Mr. Crawford.—Have you formed any opinion that the murderer had any design with respect to any particular part?

—I have formed the opinion that he had no particular design on any particular organ.

Mr. Crawford.—Judging from the injuries inflicted, do you think he was possessed of great anatomical skill?

—No, I do not.

Mr. Crawford.—Can you account for the absence of any noise?

—The death must have been so instantaneous after the severance of the blood vessels and the windpipe.

Mr. Crawford.—He did not think that the clothes of the assassin would necessarily be bespattered with blood. When witness arrived life had been extinct probably not more than a quarter of an hour, judging from the condition of the blood.

Dr. William Sedgwick Saunders, of 13, Queen-street, Cheapside, examined, said he was doctor of medicine, Fellow of the Institute of Chemistry, Fellow of the Chemical Society, and public analyst of the City of London. He received the stomach of the deceased from Dr. Gordon Brown, carefully sealed, and the contents had not been interfered with in any way. He had carefully examined the stomach and its contents, more particularly for poisons of a narcotic class, with negative results, there not being the faintest trace of any of these, or any other poison.

By Mr. Crawford.—He was present during the whole of the post mortem examination. Having had ample opportunity of seeing the wounds inflicted, he agreed with Dr. Brown and Dr. Sequeira that they were not inflicted by a person with great anatomical skill. He equally agreed that the murderer had no particular design on any particular internal organ.

Annie Phillips, living at 12, Dilston-grove, Southwark-park-road, was the next witness. She stated that she was married, and that her husband was a lamp-black packer. She was the daughter of the deceased, who had always told witness that she was married to Thomas Conway, witness's father. She had not seen him for 15 or 18 months. The last time she saw him was when he was living with witness and her husband at 15, Anchor-street, Southwark-park. Her father was a hawker. She did not know what became of him after he left. He left without giving any particular reason for going, but he did not leave witness on very good terms. He did not say that he would never see her again. He was a teetotaller. He and her mother did not live on good terms after the latter took to drink. She had not the least idea where her father was living. He had no ill will against the deceased, so far as witness knew. She was told that her father had been in the 18th Royal Irish. He left her mother solely because of her drinking habits. He was a pensioner and had had a pension since witness was eight years old. She was now 23. It was seven or eight years ago since her father lived with her mother. Witness frequently saw her mother after they separated; her mother applied to her for money. The last time she saw her mother alive was two years and one month ago. She did not see her on the Saturday, the day previous to her death. Witness used to live in King-street, Bermondsey—that was about two

378

years ago. On removing from there witness did not leave any address. She had two brothers, Conway being their father. Her mother did not know where to find either of them; the information was purposefully kept from her. She supposed that that was in order to prevent her mother from applying to them for money.

By a juryman.

—It was between 15 and 18 months ago since her father lived with witness and her husband. Her father knew at the time that her mother was living with Kelly.

By Mr. Crawford.

—She was not sure that her father was a pensioner of the 18th Royal Irish. It might have been the Connaught Rangers. [Mr. Crawford observed that there was a pensioner of the 18th Royal Irish named Conway, but he was not the Conway who was wanted.] The deceased last received money from witness about two years and two months ago, when she waited upon witness in the latter's confinement. Witness had never had a letter from her mother. She had seen Kelly and her mother together in the lodging-house in Flower and Dean-street; that was about 3½ years ago. Witness knew that they lived together. Her father was living with her two brothers, but she could not say where. She could not give the slightest clue as to their whereabouts. Her brothers were aged 15 and 20. Witness did not know that her mother had recently been intimate with anyone besides Kelly in the lodging house.

Detective-sergeant John Mitchell (City Police), the next witness, replying to Mr. Crawford, said that he had made every effort, acting under instructions, to find the father and the brothers of the last witness, but without success. He had found a pensioner named Conway belonging to the 18th Royal Irish, but he was not identified as the Thomas Conway in question.

To the CORONER.—Every endeavour possible has been made with a view to tracing the murderer.

Mr. Crawford.—Do not go into that. I am sure that the jury believe that, and that the City Police are doing everything they can with that object.

Detective Baxter Hunt (City Police), replying to Mr. Crawford, stated that acting under instructions he had discovered the pensioner

Conway belonging to the 18th Royal Irish. Witness had confronted the man with two of the deceased's sisters, who had failed to recognize him as the man who used to live with the deceased. Witness had made every effort to trace the Thomas Conway and the brothers referred to, but without result.

By a juryman.

—The reason the daughter had not seen the man Conway, whom witness had traced, was that she had not at the time been discovered.

Mr. Crawford intimated that the daughter should see the man.

Witness, in reply to a juryman, stated that the Conway whom he had discovered last received his pension on the 1st inst.

By Mr. Crawford.—He is quartermaster-sergeant.

Dr. Gordon Brown at this point was recalled.

Mr. Crawford.—The theory has been put forward that it is possible for the deceased to have been taken to Mitre-square after the murder. What is your opinion about that?

Dr. Brown.—I think there is no doubt on the point. The blood at the left side of the deceased was clotted, and must have flowed from her at the time of the injury to the throat. I do not believe the deceased moved in the slightest way after her throat was cut.

Mr. Crawford.—You have no doubt that the murder was committed on that spot?

—I feel quite sure it was.

Police Constable Lewis Robinson stated that about half-past 8 o'clock on the night of the 29th ult. he was on duty in High-street, Aldgate, where he saw a crowd of persons. He then saw a woman, who was drunk, and who had since been recognized as the deceased. She was lying on the footway. Witness asked if any one in the crowd knew her or where she lived, but he received no answer. On the arrival of another constable they took her to Bishopsgate Police-station, where she was placed in a cell.

Mr. Crawford.—No one in the crowd appeared to know the woman. Witness last saw her on the same evening at about 10 minutes to 9 o'clock in the police cell.

Mr. Crawford.—Do you recollect whether she was wearing an apron?

—Yes, she was.

Mr. Crawford.—Could you identify it?

—I could if I saw the whole of it.

A brown paper parcel was produced, from which two pieces of apron were taken and shown to the witness, who said,—To the best of my knowledge and belief that is the apron.

By a juryman.

—The woman smelt very strongly of drink.

James Byfield said he was station sergeant at Bishopsgate Police-station. He remembered the woman referred to by the last witness being brought to the station at a quarter to 9 on the evening of the 29th ult. She was very drunk. She was placed in a cell, and was kept there until 1 o'clock the next morning. She was then sober, and was discharged after giving her name as Mary Ann Kelly and her address as 6, Fashion-street. In answer to questions put to her by witness, she stated that she had been hopping.

By a juryman.

—He believed that nothing was given to her while she was in the cell.

By Mr. Crawford.

—He did not notice that she was wearing an apron.

Constable George Henry Hutt, 968, said he was gaoler at Bishopsgate Police-station. On Saturday night, the 29th ult., at a quarter to 10 he took over the prisoners, among whom was the deceased. He visited her several times in the cell until five minutes to 1 o'clock, when he was directed by Sergeant Byfield to see whether any of the prisoners were fit to be discharged. The deceased was found to be sober, and was brought from the cell to the office; and after giving the name of Mary Ann Kelly she was discharged. He saw her turn to the left after getting outside the station.

By a juryman.

—It was left to the discretion of the inspector, or acting inspector, to decide when a person who had been drunk was in a fit condition to be discharged.

By another juryman.

—He visited the woman in the cell about every half-hour from 5 minutes to 10 o'clock until 1 o'clock. She was sleeping when he took over the prisoners. At a quarter past 12 o'clock she was awake, and singing a song to herself. At half-past 12, when he went to her, she asked him when she was going to be let out, and he replied, "When you are capable of taking care of yourself". She answered that she was capable of taking care of herself then.

By Mr. Crawford.—It was not witness, but Sergeant Byfield who discharged her. She left the station about 1 o'clock. In witness's opinion she was then quite capable of taking care of herself. She said nothing to witness as to where she was going. About two minutes before 1 o'clock, when bringing her out of the cell, she asked witness the time, and he replied, "Too late for you to get any more drink." She asked him again what time it was and he replied, "Just on 1." She then said, "I shall get a d— fine hiding when I get home." Witness gathered from that that she was going home. He noticed that she was wearing an apron, and to the best of his belief the apron shown to the last witness was the one.

By Mr. Crawford.

—It would take about eight minutes to walk from the police-station to Mitre-square—ordinary walking.

By a juryman.

—Prisoners were not searched who were brought into the station drunk. Handkerchiefs or anything with which they could injure themselves would be taken from them.

George James Morris, the next witness called, said he was watchman at Messrs. Kearley and Tonge's tea merchants, in Mitre-square. He went on duty there at 7 o'clock in the evening.

THE CORONER.—What happened at a quarter to 2 o'clock?

—Police-constable Watkins, who was on the Mitre-square beat, knocked at the door of the warehouse. It was slightly "on the jar." He was then sweeping the steps down towards the door, and as he was doing so the door was pushed. He opened it wide and he saw Watkins who said, "For God's sake, mate, come to my assistance." The constable was agitated, and witness thought he was ill. He had his lamp by his side lighted, and asked Watkins what was the matter. Watkins replied, "There is another woman cut to pieces." Witness asked where she was, and Watkins replied, "In the corner." Having been a police constable himself he knew what assistance was required. He went over to the spot indicated and turned his lamp on the body. He immediately ran up Mitre-street into Aldgate, blowing his whistle. He saw no suspicious person about at the time. He was soon joined by two police-constables, and he told them to go into Mitre-square, where there had been another terrible murder. He followed the constables there and took charge of his premises again. He had heard no noise in the square before he was called by Watkins. Had there been any cry of distress he would have heard it.

By a juryman.

—He had charge of the two warehouses of Messrs. Kearley and Tonge. At the time in question he was at the one where the counting-house was; it faced the square.

By Mr. Crawford.

—Before being called by Watkins he had had no occasion to go out of the offices or into the square. He was sure he had not quitted the premises before Watkins called him. There was nothing unusual in his door being open or in his being at work at a quarter to 2 o'clock on Sunday morning.

By a juryman.

—His door had not been on the jar more than two or three minutes before Watkins called him.

Constable James Harvey (964 City police) stated that at a quarter to 10 o'clock on the night of the 29th ult., he went on his beat, which he described, and which took in Mitre-street. He saw no suspicious person about while on his beat, and he heard no cry or any noise. When he got into Aldgate, returning towards Duke-street, he heard a whistle, and saw the witness Morris with a lamp. The latter, in answer to witness, said that a woman had been ripped up in Mitre-square. Witness saw a constable on the other side of the street. They went to Mitre-square, where they saw Watkins with the body of the deceased. The constable who followed witness went for Dr. Sequeira, and private persons were dispatched for other constables, who arrived almost immediately, having heard the whistle. Witness waited there with Watkins, and information was at once sent to the inspector. As witness passed the post-office clock at Aldgate on his beat it was between one and two minutes to half-past 1 o'clock.

By a juryman.

—His beat took him down Church-passage to the end. He was there three or four minutes before he heard the whistle; it was then about 18 or 19 minutes to 2 o'clock.

George Clapp said he lived at 5, Mitre-street, Aldgate, of which he was the caretaker. The back part of the house looked into Mitre-square. On the night of the 29th ult., he and his wife went to bed at 11 o'clock. They slept in a back room on the second floor. During the night he heard no disturbance or noise of any kind. The first he heard of the murder in the square was between 5 and 6 o'clock on the following morning.

By Mr. Crawford.

—The only other person in the house that night was a woman, a nurse, who slept at the top of the house on the third-floor.

Constable Richard Pearse, 922 City Police, said he lived at No. 3 Mitre-square. He went to bed on the night of the 29th ult. at about 20 minutes after 12 o'clock. He heard no noise or disturbance of any kind. He first heard of the murder at 20 minutes past 2 o'clock, when he was called by a police-constable. From his window he could plainly see the spot where the murder was committed.

By Mr. Crawford.—He was the only tenant of No. 3, Mitre-square, where he lived with his wife and family.

Joseph Lawende said that he lived at 45, Norfolk-road, Dalston. He was a commercial traveller.[268] On the night of the murder he was at the Imperial Club in Duke-street, with Joseph Levy and Harry Harris. They went out of the club at half-past 1, and left the place about five minutes later. They saw a man and a woman standing together at a corner in Church-passage, in Duke-street, which led into Mitre-square. The woman was standing with her face towards the man. Witness could not see the woman's face; the man was taller than she. She had on a black jacket and bonnet. He saw her put her hand on the man's chest. Witness had seen some clothing at the police-station, and he believed the articles were the same that the woman he referred to was wearing.

The CORONER.—Can you tell us what sort of man it was with whom she was speaking?

—He had on a cloth cap with a peak.

Mr. Crawford.—Unless the jury wish it I have a special reason why no further description of this man should be given now.

The jury assented to Mr. Crawford's wish.

The CORONER.—You have given a description of the man to the police, I suppose?

---

[268] **Commercial Traveller.** An alternate name for a travelling salesman. (Census1891.com)

# Friday, 12 October, 1888

—Yes.

The CORONER.—Would you know him again.

—I doubt it.

By Mr. Crawford.—The distance between the Imperial Club and the top of Church-passage, where he saw the man and the woman standing together, was about nine or ten yards. He fixed the time of leaving the club at half-past 1 by reference to the club clock and to his own watch, and it would have been about 25 minutes to 2 o'clock when he saw the man and woman standing together. He heard not a word of their conversation. They did not appear to be in an angry mood. The woman did not appear to have put her hand on the man's chest as if she were pushing him away. Witness did not look back to see where they went.

Joseph Hyam Levy, of 1, Hutchinson-street, Aldgate, said he was a butcher. He was in the Imperial Club with the last witness, and the time when they rose to leave was half-past 1 by the club clock. It was about three or four minutes after the half-hour when they left. He noticed a man and a woman standing together at the corner of Church-passage, but he passed on without taking any further notice of them. He did not look at them. From what he saw, the man might have been three inches taller than the woman. He could not give any description of either of them. He went on down Duke-street, into Aldgate, leaving the man and woman speaking together. He only fixed the time by the club clock.

By the juryman.

—His suspicions were not aroused by the two persons. He thought the spot was very badly lighted. It was now much better lighted than it was on the night of the murder. He did not take much notice of the man and woman.

By Mr. Crawford.—He was on the opposite pavement to the man and woman. There was nothing that he saw to induce him to think that the man was doing any harm to her.

Police-constable Alfred Long, 254 A, stated that he was on duty in Goulston-street, White-chapel, on the morning of the 30th ult. At about 2:55 he found a portion of an apron (produced as before). There were recent stains of blood on it. It was lying in the passage leading to a staircase of 118 and 119, ordinary model dwelling-houses. Above it on the wall was written in chalk, "The Jews are the men that will not be blamed for nothing." He at once searched the staircases and areas of the building, but he found nothing. He then took the piece of apron to the Commercial-road Police-station, and reported to the inspector on duty. He had previously passed the spot where he found the apron at 20 minutes after 2, but it was not there then.

By Mr. Crawford.—

Witness repeated as before the words which he saw written on the wall.

Mr. Crawford.—Have you not put the word "not" in the wrong place? Is it not, "The Jews are not the men that will be blamed for nothing"?

Witness repeated the words as he had previously read them.

Mr. Crawford.—How do you spell "Jews"?

Witness.—J-e-w-s.

Mr. Crawford.—Now, was it not on the wall J-u-w-e-s?[269] Is it not possible you are wrong?

—It may be as to the spelling.

Mr. Crawford.—And as to the place where the word "not" was put?

Witness again read the words as before.

By Mr. Crawford.—He had not noticed the wall before. He noticed the piece of apron first, and then the words on the wall. One corner of the apron was wet with blood. His light was on at the time. His attention was attracted to the writing on the wall while he was searching. He could not form an opinion as to whether the writing was recent. He went on to the staircase of the dwelling, but made no inquires in the house itself.

By a juryman.

—The pocket-book in which he entered the words written on the wall at the time he noticed them was at Westminster.

The witness's examination was postponed,

---

[269] **Juwes.** Iuwes is the Middle English spelling of Jews. The letter J was used as a variant of the letter I before the 17th Century, usually in Roman numerals as the final I in a number, such as XIIJ for XIII. An example of Iuwes can be found as the second word of the first line on page 401 of the third volume of Rev. William Skeats 1873 edition of William Langlands *Piers Plowman,* written between 1370 and 1390. Another variant, Iewes, was used in the original 1611 edition of the King James Bible. (Langland)

and the pocket-book was ordered to be produced.

Detective Daniel Halse (City Police) stated that on Saturday, the 29th ult., from instructions received at the Detective Office, Old Jewry, he told a number of police officers in plain clothes to patrol the City all night. At about two minutes to 2 on the Sunday morning he was at the corner of Houndsditch, by Aldgate Church, in company with Detectives Outram and Marryat, of the City Police. They heard that a woman had been murdered in Mitre-square, and they all ran there and saw the body of the murdered woman. He gave instructions to have the neighbourhood searched, and every man to be stopped and examined. He himself went by way of Middlesex-street, at the east end of the City, into Wentworth-street, where he stopped two men, who gave a satisfactory account of themselves, and he allowed them to depart. He came through Goulston-street about 20 minutes past 2, at the spot where the apron was found, and he then went back to Mitre-square and accompanied Inspector Collard to the mortuary. He there saw the deceased undressed, noticing that a portion of the apron she wore was missing. He accompanied Major Smith back to Mitre-square, where they heard that a piece of apron had been found in Goulston-street. He then went with Detective Hunt to Leman-street Police-station, where he heard that the piece of apron that had been picked up had been handed to Dr. Phillips. Witness and Hunt then went back to Goulston-street, to the spot where the apron had been discovered. He saw some chalk writing on the wall. He remained there, and Hunt went for Mr. M'William for instructions to have the writing photographed. Directions were given for that to be done. Some of the Metropolitan Police thought it might cause a riot if the writing were seen, and an outbreak against the Jews. It was decided to have the writing rubbed out. The people were at that time bringing out their stalls, which they did very early on the Sunday morning. When Hunt returned inquiry was made at every tenement in the dwelling referred to in Goulston-street, but no tidings could be obtained as to any one having gone in who was likely to be the murderer.

By Mr. Crawford.—At about 20 minutes after 2 he passed over the spot where the piece of apron was found. If it was there then he would not necessarily have seen it, for it was in the building.

Mr. Crawford.—Did any one suggest that it would be possible to take out the word "Juwes", and leave the rest of the writing there?

—I suggested that the top line might be rubbed out and the Metropolitan Police suggested the word "Juwes." The fear on the part of the Metropolitan Police of a riot was the sole cause of the writing on the wall being rubbed out.

Mr. Crawford.—Read out the exact words you took down in your book at the time.

—"The Juwes are not the men that will be blamed for nothing."

By Mr. Crawford.—The writing appeared to have been recently done. It was done with white chalk on the black facia of the wall.

By a juryman.

—The spot where the writing was is the ground of the Metropolitan Police, and they insisted on having it rubbed out.

By Mr. Crawford.—Witness protested against it being rubbed out, and wanted it to be left until Major Smith had seen it.

By a juryman.

—He assumed that the writing was recent, because from the number of persons living in the tenement he believed it would have been rubbed out had it been there for any time. There were about three lines of writing, which was in a good schoolboy hand.

By another juryman.

—The writing was in the passage of the building itself, and was on the black dado of the wall.

A juryman.—It seems to me strange that a police constable would have found this piece of apron, and then for no inquiries to have been made in the building. There is a clue up to that point, and then it is altogether lost.

Mr. Crawford.—I have evidence that the City Police did make a careful search in the tenement, but that was not until after the fact had come to their knowledge. I am afraid that that will not meet the point raised by you (to the juryman). There is the delay that took place. The man who found the piece of apron is a member of the Metropolitan Police.

The witness Long having returned with the pocket-book referred to, stated, in reply to Mr. Crawford, that the book contained the entry which he made at the time as to the words written on the wall. They were, "The Jews are the men that will not be blamed for nothing." The inspector made the remark that on the wall the word was "Jeuws." Witness entered in his book what he believed was an exact copy of the words.

Mr. Crawford.—At all events there was a discrepancy between what you wrote down and what was actually written on the wall, so far as regards the spelling of the word "Jews."

Witness replied that the only remark the inspector made was as to the spelling of the word "Jews."

By Mr. Crawford.—The moment he found the piece of apron he searched the staircases leading to the building. He did make any inquiry of the inmates in the tenements. There were either six or seven staircases, one leading down, and the others upstairs. He searched every staircase, and could find no trace of blood or any recent footmarks. He found the apron at five minutes to 3, and when he searched the staircases it would be about 3 o'clock. Having searched the staircases he at once proceeded to the police-station. Before proceeding to the station he had heard that a murder had been committed in Mitre-square. When he started for the police-station he left Police-constable 190 H in charge of the building. He did not know the constable's name; he was a member of the Metropolitan Police. Witness told him to keep observation on the dwelling, to see whether any one left or entered it. Witness next returned to the building at 5 o'clock. The writing was rubbed out in witness's presence at half-past 5, or thereabouts. He heard no one object to the writing being rubbed out.

A juryman.—Having heard of the murder, and having afterwards found the piece of apron with blood on it and the writing on the wall, did it not strike you that it would be well to make some examination of the rooms in the building? You say you searched all the passages, but you would not expect that the man who had committed the murder would hide himself there.

Witness.—Seeing the blood there, I thought that the murder had been committed, and that the body might be placed in the building.

The juryman.—You did not search the rooms, but left a man to watch the building, and the whole clue seems to have passed away. I do not wish to say anything harsh, as I consider that the evidence of yourself and of the other members of the police redounds to the credit of all of you; but this does seem a point that requires a little investigation. You find a piece of apron wet with blood; you search all the passages, and then you leave the building in the care of a man to watch the front.

Witness.—I thought the best thing I could do was to go to the station and report the matter to the inspector on duty.

The juryman.—I feel sure you did your best.

Mr. Crawford.—May we take it that you thought you would be more likely to find the body of the murdered person there than the assassin?

Witness.—Yes.

By a juryman. —Witness was a stranger in the neighbourhood. No one could have gone out of the front part of the building without being seen by the constable left on the spot by witness.

The CORONER, in summing up, observed that the evidence had been of the most exhaustive character. He thought it would be far better now to leave the matter in the hands of the police, to follow it up with any further clues they might obtain, and for the jury to return a verdict of wilful murder against some person or persons unknown.

It had been shown by the evidence of Dr. Gordon Brown that the murderer must have taken hold of the deceased woman and cut her throat, and by severing the vocal chords, prevented her from making any cry. All the evidence showed that no sound had been heard in connexion with the crime.

The assassin had not only murdered the woman, defenceless as she was, but had so mangled the corpse as to render it almost impossible for the body to be identified.

He thought they would agree that the evidence clearly showed that the woman was taken to the police-station for being drunk, and that she was discharged about 1 o'clock on the morning of the murder.

After that two persons—a man and a woman—were seen talking together at the corner of Church-passage by the witnesses from the Imperial Club, and one of those witnesses had expressed his opinion that the articles of clothing which he had seen at the police-station were the same as those worn by the woman.

She was discharged from the station at about five minutes after 1 o'clock. At half-past one a police-constable went round Mitre-square, and turned his lamp on to the corner, but saw nothing there. Just 14 minutes afterwards he found there the body of a woman who had been murdered, the evidence of the doctor showing that it must have taken five minutes to commit the murder and to have inflicted the injuries on the body.

The murder must have been committed between 1:30 and 1:44, and, allowing five minutes for the crime to be committed, only nine minutes were left to be accounted for.

The history of the case was a very painful one. It appeared that the deceased had been living first with Thomas Conway for seven or eight years. Her drinking habits had induced him to part from her, and the sister of the deceased had stated that she was not married to him.

There was nothing to suggest that either Conway or Kelly had had anything to do with the murder, both of them seeming to be totally inoffensive men. It had been clearly proved that Kelly was in bed at the lodging-house at the time of the murder. He had heard that the deceased had been taken up by the police, and knowing what the custom was in the City, he assumed that she would return to him in the morning.

They had, it appeared, been out hopping for some weeks, and had returned home on the Thursday, (the 27th ult.), taking a lodging for that night in Shoe-lane; and on the Saturday —the last time Kelly saw anything of her—she stated that she was going to see whether she could find her daughter. Something might turn on the fact that she did not see her daughter.

According to the evidence, the deceased was going to Bermondsey to see her, but the daughter had left the address there without mentioning any other address to which she was going. It was possible that the deceased had gone to Bermondsey. What became of her in the interval between that and her being taken in charge there was nothing to show, but she had evidently been drinking.

There could be no doubt that a most vile murder had been committed by some person or persons unknown, and he thought he might say by some person unknown. Dr. Brown believed

that only one person was implicated. Unless the jury wished him to refer to any point in the evidence, there was nothing that need detain them further as far as that inquiry was concerned, and the police could be left with a free hand to follow up the investigation.

A munificent reward had been offered by the Corporation, and it might be hoped that that would set persons on the track and cause the apprehension of the murderer.

Mr. Crawford.—Dr. Brown in his evidence expressed his belief as a medical man that only one person had committed the murder.

The Foreman (the jury having consulted for about a couple of minutes).—Our verdict is "Wilful murder by some person unknown."

The CORONER.—That is the verdict of all of you?

The Foreman.—Yes.

The CORONER afterwards stated that the jury desired him to thank Mr. Crawford and the police for the assistance which they had rendered in the inquiry, and he also wished to add his own thanks.

—

An arrest was made yesterday at Eltham, near Hythe. The master of the workhouse had his suspicions excited over a casual who answered the description of the man wanted. He was dressed in genteel style, with black coat, trousers and hat. Blood was found on the trousers and shirt, the cuffs of which had been ripped off. He gave three or four different names and most contradictory statements as to where he came from. Superintendent Maxted took the matter in hand, but it is expected that as a result of the inquiries then made the man will be released.

—

The revelations made at the inquest on the Mitre-square victim have caused a profound sensation in the East-end of London. It is stated that the order to erase the words on the wall was given by an officer in the Metropolitan Police Force, with the humane intention of averting an increase of the anti-Jewish feeling which is unfortunately but undoubtedly very general in the East-end of London. So real were the apprehensions of the police authorities in this way that on the Sunday night of the murders the chief police-stations in the East-end were reinforced by 50 constables each.

# Friday, 12 October, 1888

## The Star

### A PARALLEL TO WHITECHAPEL.
### A Texan Gentleman Tells a Story of Twelve Similar Crimes in the State.

Frequent allusions having been made to the murders in Texas which bear a close resemblance to the Whitechapel horrors, a representative of *The Star* dug out a Texan gentleman at present on a visit to London, and got from him details of the occurrences in his native State.

The gentleman came from the town of Austen, the capital of Texas.

How many persons were killed in your town?" asked the reporter:

—Twelve; all women, and all, or nearly all, of questionable character. Ten of them were negresses and two white women. They mostly belonged to the servant class, who were of loose reputation. The two white women moved in fairly good circles; but they were also women who had not the highest character. A curious fact about one of the white women was that her husband was found greatly bruised on the night of her death. For some reason or other, however, it was thought that he himself was the murderer, and that he had taken advantage of the prevalent scare to get rid of an unloved wife. He was tried for murder, and was once convicted, but on an appeal he was acquitted.

Was there any resemblance between the *modus operandi* of your Texan murderer and the plan of the Whitechapel fiend?

—No except that both selected women and women of a certain class.

Was the method of murder the same. Had any of the women their throats cut?

—No; not one. They were all killed with a blunt instrument; their skulls in most cases were battered in. They were also very much bruised and slashed about the body; but again with a blunt instrument.

Were the murders periodical, as in the Whitechapel cases?

—Yes; but the intervals were longer. They took place usually at a month's interval, though sometimes a couple of months intervened. It was curious, too, that they always took place when the moon was full. The idea was that they were the work of a madman who became more intensely insane under the influence of the full moon.

What course was taken to put the murders down?

—Two murders were committed on a Christmas Eve. The next day there was a meeting of the citizens, and patrols were arranged. These patrols of the citizens went about for months, and often caused great inconvenience and annoyance. I myself have been stopped several times when coming home with a lady from the theatre, and have been asked my name, destination, &c. These inconveniences, however, we were all willing to put up with.

Did this intimidate the murderer?

—Apparently, for we never had any others. I may add that the effect upon the city was somewhat the same as in the East-end with you. Our houses are differently constructed. The room in which the servant sleeps is usually in the yard apart from the house. For a long time after the murders servants refused to sleep in these rooms, and had to be taken into the house. In some cases they slept in the halls, there being no room elsewhere.

Has there ever been a trace or a suspicion of anybody?

—Never; the secret remains as impenetrable to-day as at the time when they were in full scare.[270]

—

### WHITECHAPEL.

A pensioner from the Hussars named Conway asked a barman at the Duke of York in Clerkenwell this morning to sign some paper to Captain Milne about his having lost his pension papers. Conway was at first supposed to be the man the Mitre-square victim lived with before she lived with Kelly, but at the police office in Old Jewry he proved he was not the man.

—

### Dangerous Errors.

A News Agency says:—The police authorities attach a great deal of importance to the spelling of the word "Jews" in the writing on the wall. The language of the Jews in the East-end is a hybrid dialect, known as Yiddish, and their mode of spelling the word Jews would be "Juwes."

This is absolutely incorrect. A representative

---

[270] See Appendix M, The Texas Axe Murders, p. 577.

of *The Star* called at the *Jewish Chronicle* office, and was informed by the editor, and by a responsible member of the staff whose father is a Polish Jew, that the Yiddish word for Jew is Yiddin, the word "Yiddish" meaning, of course, the language of the Yiddins.

Much indignation is felt amongst the Jews at these repeated and unjustifiable attempts to fasten the responsibility for the dastardly crimes on them.

The *Jewish Chronicle* says:—"We are authorised by Dr. Gordon Browne, the City divisional surgeon, to state, with reference to a suggestion that the City and Whitechapel murders were the work of a Jewish slaughterer, that he has examined the knives used by the Jewish slaughterers, all of which have been submitted to him by the City detectives, and he is thoroughly satisfied that none of them could have been used.

—

### A Suspicious Infirmary Patient.

A report was current late last night that the police suspect a man who is at present a patient in an East-end infirmary. He has been admitted since the commission of the last murder. Owing to his suspicious behaviour their attention was directed to him. Detectives are making inquiries, and he is kept under surveillance.

—

### Has the "Times" Done This?

A man known in Spitalfields by the name of "Parnell" has been arrested on suspicion of connection with the Whitechapel murders. He had long been a regular lodger at the Beehive Chambers corner of Brick-lane and Prince-street, but absented himself on the night of the last murders, and also on the following night, and he has been very irregular in his attendance there since that time. The deputy of the lodging-house thought it his duty to report the circumstances to the police, and the fellow was arrested when he got up this morning. At the Commercial-street Police-station he said his right name was Andrews, and that he was a book hawker. He explained that he had slept at another house on the nights in question, and gave such a fair account of himself that the police believe him innocent, though he will be detained until further inquiries have been made. The prisoner is not more than 22 years of age, and very boyish in his appearance.

## Evening News
### NOTES.

The inquest on the body of the woman known variously as Catherine Eddowes, Catherine Conway, and Mary Ann Kelly, who was murdered in Mitre-square on the 30th ult., was concluded yesterday, the jury returning a verdict of wilful murder against some person unknown.

The evidence given yesterday was in many ways painful. Painful as showing the utterly crapulous atmosphere in which everybody connected with the murdered woman lived, and painful in showing a want of grasp on the part of some person in position in the Metropolitan Police Force. Catherine Conway's husband left her seven or eight years ago owing to her habits and since then she seemed to have cohabitated principally with the witness Kelly. Conway kept up communication for some time with his daughter, as also did his two sons, who are supposed to be living with him, but father and sons have disappeared and left no trace behind. The daughter, who is a respectable married woman, has no knowledge of their whereabouts, not, perhaps, that it would assist the police much to know where they are.

With regard to the handwriting on the wall in Goulston-street, Police-constable Alfred Long, 254 A, who first saw it, appears to have acted with discretion. He copied the words, and, leaving a comrade on guard, reported the matter at the Commercial-road Police Station. The words, "The Jews are not the men that will be blamed for nothing," were almost certainly written by the murderer, who left at the spot the bloody portion of the woman's apron as a sort of warranty of authenticity. On Police-constable Long's report, consultation was held, and the decision taken to rub out the words. Detective Halse, of the City police, who was present, protested. A brother officer of the City had gone to make arrangements for having the words photographed, but the zeal of the Metropolitans could not rest. They feared a riot against the Jews, and out the words must come.

Halse then suggested to rub out the word "Jew" and leave the rest, but this did not correspond with Dogberry's[271] instructions from

---

[271] Sir Charles Warren, comparing him to the incompetent chief of police in Shakespeare's *Much Ado About Nothing*.

headquarters. Off the writing came accordingly, and the only clue to the murderer was destroyed calmly and deliberately, on the authority of those in high places who make it their business to detect criminals. We cannot blame the inferior police. They seem to have acted with caution and discretion; but the public have a right to know who gave the order to efface the murderer's traces. His proper place is not in the Criminal Inquiry Department, and to this Mr. Mathews must look if he values his portfolio.

—

## THE WRITING ON THE WALL.

The Central News learns that the police authorities attach a great deal of importance to the spelling of the word "Jews" in the writing on the wall at the spot where the Mitre-square murderer threw away a portion of the murdered woman's apron. The language of the Jews in the East-end is a hybrid dialect, known as Yiddish, and their mode of spelling the word "Jews" would be "Juwes." This the police consider a strong indication that the crime was committed by one of the numerous foreigners by whom the East-end is infested.

—

The army pensioner who was invited, this morning, to attend at Bishopgate-street Police-station, to see if he resembled the missing husband, Conway, of the murdered woman Catherine Eddowes, was taken to the Old Jewry, but as it was found that he was much younger than the woman's husband must have been the police did not think it necessary to send for Mrs. Phillips, the murdered woman's sister, to see him, so the man went away.

═

## "JACK THE RIPPER'S" PREDECESSOR.
## THE LIFE AND TRIAL OF PHILIPPE,
## THE WAREHOUSE PORTER.

On the morning of January 9, 1866, the inhabitants of the French capital were thrown into a state of consternation by the report of a crime, which was the tenth of its kind committed within the space of the previous three years.

The murder of Marie Bodeux, closing the series of ten, had been perpetrated with a boldness that became appalling. The public for the last few days have been under the impression that the challenge flung by the so-called "Jack the Ripper" to the London police in the shape of postcards and letters is the *ne plus ultra* of con-

temptuous sarcasm. The slayer of Marie Bodeux had gone much further.

He had selected a victim in the very premises the ground-floor of which was occupied by the police-station, and this, notwithstanding his knowledge of the police being in possession of a detailed description of his appearance, which had been furnished more than eighteen months before by a girl who, by a singular instance of presence of mind, had escaped his clutches. Nor was his appearance such as to pass unnoticed in a crowd. Without laying much stress on the thick black hair and beard—the later of which he might have shaved if he had wished—Joseph Philippe, as he turned out to be, was deeply pitted with small-pox, and had in addition a tattoo mark on the right arm, impossible to be effaced.

Nevertheless, he had managed to baffle the police for three years during which at least ten human beings had been done to death by him; for, as the judge presiding at the trial remarked, "We can only proceed upon the evidence of the bodies found, though I am not exceeding the prerogatives of my office in considering these but a part of the slaughter committed by the prisoner in the dock."

The president of the Court was alluding to a number of mutilated and truncated corpses found during that time in various out-of-the-way places of the metropolis. For unlike "Jack the Ripper," Philippe neither confined himself to one particular neighbourhood, nor to one particular mode of procedure.

His lust for blood was induced by what has already been termed "erotic catalepsy" and complicated by cupidity, though the latter was merely a means to an end; in other words, to obtain the wherewithal to indulge in his debauches and in his craving for intoxicants. There is, however, no doubt that the height of his fiendish lasci-viousness was the agony of his victims as they weltered in their blood. Consequently he did not disdain to track his prey among the better class of "unfortunates," but, to use a vulgar expression, "everything was fish that came to his net." Home or no home to which to take him was a matter of indifference as long as he saw his way to accom-plish his all-pervading idea, murder under the pretext of caressing. As such the terror inspired by him was not confined to the poorer category of "girls" only. None felt safe but the very "tip-top" ones, and the newspapers of the time had to record a panic throughout the whole of Paris similar to that which I have already mentioned as prevailing in the neighbourhood of Whitechapel.

No wonder, then, that Paris was awe-stricken at the latest exploit, which, I repeat, surpassed in daring all that had gone before, not only because it occurred in the very house tenanted by the police, but on account of other circumstances connected with it. Marie Bodeux was on most intimate terms with an old man of 73, living on the floor above her. The later never failed to wish her good-night when coming home.

On the night of January 8, after having spent part of it with his relations, he found the outer door of Marie Bodeux's apartment open, and, when getting as far as her bedroom, perceived, by the flickering light of a candle, a stranger arranging his necktie and brushing his hair before the looking-glass. Of course, the old man discreetly retired, with the intention of returning in a few minutes, seeing that the stranger was preparing to depart. When he did return the stranger brushed past him in the room, muttering a hurried good night. It was the old man who gave the first alarm to the police. The latter had no difficulty in arriving at the conclusion that they were once more in the presence of a victim of the mysterious demon that had slain the girl Robert, the woman Mage, and her baby son, eighteen months ago, who had murdered so many others, who had planned the destruction of the girl Foucher. It was she who had supplied the police with the description on the morning of the assassination of Julie Mage and her child. It was she who had related her providential escape when by a ruse she had inveigled him into the street again after he was closeted with her that same night. It was she who had given the particulars of the tattoo-mark on his right arm: "I am born under an unlucky star," the last word of the sentence being replaced by a coarsely-executed drawing of the thing itself. It was that which roused her suspicions, besides his sinister figure. She thought him a convict escaped from the hulks. "Jack the Ripper" being frustrated in Berner-street in the complete execution of his hellish design, loses no time in tracking another quarry. His French predecessor being frustrated by the girl Foucher, loses no time in accosting Julie Mage. He does not even take the trouble of putting some distance between his intended victim and the one that succumbs. They both live

in the same street, the Rue St. Marguerite, which is famed in modern history as having witnessed the death of Baudoir on the second morning after the coup d' etat, which is notorious as the headquarters of the intra-mural Paris ragpickers. The girl Foucher watches him from behind her door entering the house where Julie Mage lives, next morning, when the crime is discovered, she tenders her evidence at once.

Eighteen months have elapsed since then, and notwithstanding the very valuable clue thus provided, notwithstanding the presence at their head of one of the cleaverest detectives of modern times, "monsieur Claude," the police are as puzzled as ever. They have no doubt as to the identity of the murderer of Marie Bodeux with the murderer of so many other "unfortunates," but at the same time they despair of capturing him. The blood-stained water on the washing stand tells them that he has taken his precautions as before. True, the razor with which he has committed the deed has by an oversight been left behind, but it bears not the maker's name, nothing but an English trade-mark, which may or may not be forged. Marie Bodeux's purse, containing all the money she possessed, is gone, her wardrobe has been searched, but as it held no valuables, nothing has been abstracted. The purse has been given her by the old acquaintance already mentioned. Even "monsieur Claude" shakes his head in despair. It is no good use trying the lodging-houses, high or low, the thing has been tried before; the murderer evidently occupies rooms furnished by himself, and thus avoids registration at the Prefecture of Police. They have a very elaborate description, but at a time when vaccination was still not so much practiced as now pockmarked people were too numerous to be all tracked. "Monsieur Claude" opines that, barring an accident, they will be as unsuccessful now as they have been hitherto.

That accident is provided by the murderer himself on the third morning after his crime in the Rue Ville-Levèque. Emboldened by his success he flies at higher game than the ordinary street-walker whether rich or poor. During his five years stay in Paris he has been employed by a carver, gilder, and frame maker in the Faubourg St. Germain, one of whose customers is a Madame Midy, an artist, living in the Rue d'Erfurth.

On January 11, he presents himself at the

# Friday, 12 October, 1888

lady's apartment to inquire for a tool he pretends to have left the last time he was at work there. When the lady replies that she has seen no such tool, he draws from beneath his blouse a pillow case, asking whether she can identify this as her property. The lady, wearied of his importunities, turns her head, and the intruder flings the pillow case over it, intending to set to work in his usual manner- namely, to strangle her partially before cutting her throat. (Note: In view of the reiterated testimony of witnesses at the various inquests as to the absence of cries on the part of "Jack the Ripper's" victims, the coincidence is worthy of consideration.)

In her desperate efforts to free herself from her assailant's grip, Madame Midy firmly sets her teeth in the hand which was endeavouring to stifle her cries. Fortunately her studio is only divided by a thin partition from another one, and the neighbour hearing the noise of struggle rushes to the rescue. He knocks at the door, and receiving no answer, flings open the window on the landing overlooking the courtyard and shouts for the concierge, after which he knocks again. This time the door is opened by an individual who in the coolest way imaginable tells him : "Madame Midy has suddenly taken ill; I am going for the doctor; I don't think it is much." With apparent calmness he proceeds down stairs, until he hears the cries of Madame Midy, "Stop him, stop him," as he is crossing the courtyard. Then he takes to his heels; but in vain, because before he has reached the Rue Jacob he is arrested. A tremendously long-bladed knife is found upon him, and the search in his room reveals, besides many bloodstained garments, the purse of Marie Bodeux and the empty razor case. The rest is plain sailing. Not only the girl Foucher, but the girl Helenè Meurand identify him, the first as the man who accosted Julie Mage on the night she (Foucher) managed to give him the slip, the second as the man who tried to strangle her while he was in her room nearly two years ago. She warned several acquaintances to this effect. In addition, another unfortunate, Alice Cirot, comes forward and swears to Joseph Philippe having said in her presence in a wine shop on the Place de la Bourse, "I am very fond of women, and I accommodate them in my own way. I first strangle them, then I cut their throats."

On Monday, June 25, 1866, Joseph Philippe is tried for the murders of the girl Robert, Julie Mage and her child, and Marie Bodeux. The prosecution confines itself to these four counts, seeing that the evidence gathered in support of them is absolutely overwhelming.

According to eye-witnesses the prisoner, notwithstanding his scarred face, is by no means repulsive. His features, when unmoved by passion or drink, betray nothing of the fiendish, bloodthirsty manis that sways him at his dangerous moments. Their opinion agrees with the evidence of his former employers, all of whom testify to his invariable good temper, honesty, and activity, when not under the influence of drink.

They are further borne out by the military authorities who state that until drunkenness set its seal upon him he served with credit to himself and to the satisfaction of his superiors. But a year after his admission to the ranks he began to misconduct himself, was sentenced to one year's imprison- ment, and after his liberation was transferred to the "punishment battalion in Algeria." He remained there until his final discharge in 1860.

A twelvemonth after he came to Paris, and in a short time took to evil ways. The defence pleads "homicidal mania," the result of erotic epilepsy, the force of bad example and the conse-quent impulse to the imitation of two other murders of "unfortunates," who were, however, prompted by different motives, the one by greed, pure and simple, the other by a kind of revenge on the whole of the sex too horrid to be mentioned.

The jury refuses to be influenced by the plea, and in giving their verdict omit any and every mention of extenuating circumstances. Joseph Philippe was but thirty-four when he was guillotined. He met his death like a man, in fact, psychologists have since declared that the reaction which set in after his capture was tantamount to the wish of having done with life as soon as possible. He knew that if even his life was spared, there would be no chance of indulging the fiendish cravings that during the latter years had been the sole incentive to live. Drink was necessary to him to drown the frightful apparitions that, according to some of his employers, haunted him already before his arrest; and he knew that drink could not be obtained. There was, it appears, nothing in his life that became him so well as the leaving of it.

A.D.V.

390

# Saturday, 13 October, 1888

## The Star
### WHAT WE THINK.

THE very worst bit of evidence against Sir Charles Warren is given in the letter of a provincial chief constable to the editor of the *Pall Mall Gazette*, by way of comment on the Robber's Record of that journal. *"I would not,"* says this gentleman, *"be allowed to hold my place another day if such a state of things existed under my jurisdiction."* This is simply damning, but it is not too strong when one discovers that in noted "E." and "E.C." thoroughfares there is an average of more than one robbery for every house in the street—most of them dating within the last two years. It is now time to insist that Sir Charles Warren shall go, and Mr. Matthews, too, if he backs up the Chief Commissioner.

NOW it will be necessary to keep a sharp eye on this matter. It is no longer a question of party politics, and every shopkeeper in London should press his member to vote for an inquiry into the monstrous system, or want of system, which leaves London a prey to its freebooters, and into the conduct of the man under whose rule Alsatia after Alsatia has sprung up in our midst. It is highly promising that the Vestries are moving, and are one by one addressing remonstrances and suggestions to the Chief Commissioner. The thing to do now is to bring such pressure to bear on the London Tory members that they will not dare to resist the demand for inquiry. We dismissed Sir Edmund Henderson[272] for an isolated act of bad judgement; are we going to let Sir Charles Warren go free for a series of follies unexampled—as the anonymous "Chief Constable" evidently thinks—in the history of police administration in any civilised country in the world?

ON the particular point of the obliteration of the handwriting on the wall we are not disposed to blame Sir Charles Warren so heavily as some of our friends in the press. The point is not so important as it at first appeared to be. It is, we believe, quite untrue to say that "Juwes" is Yiddish for "Jews." "Jews" in Yiddish is Yiddin, the ordinary Hebrew plural, so that the supposition that the writer is a Jew falls to the ground. The only other point that could be proved from the inspection of the handwriting was that the writer was identical with "Jack the Ripper," which would no doubt be valuable. Of course, Sir Charles acted with blundering haste and military rashness; but his motive seems to have been just a trifle more creditable than usual. The real gravamen of the charge against him is his general failure to protect the lives and property of the poor. For instance, every one of the murders of which we gave a list the other day were committed on the persons of the poor; and every one of the ransacked neighbourhoods mentioned in the *Pall Mall Gazette* were poor districts. That is why we want one united effort to hurl the usurper from his place.

THE best clerical comment on the "moral of the murders" is Mr. Chapman's, which we publish on page 4. Mr. Chapman says that the rich must give up luxuries, or there will be a revolution. Of course, this is only a non-scientific, non-economic way of saying that the rich must give up appropriating the surplus value of what the poor produce. Root remedies for root evils. affiliate

WHEN Mr. Herbert Burrows[273] wrote a mock sermon for the Bishop of London he did more for the people's cause than he anticipated. The sermon is still going the round of the Press

---

[272] **Lt.Col. Sir Edmund Yeamans Walcott Henderson, KCB** (1821-1896). Commissioner of Police of the Metropolis from 1869-1886. Although he had been an officer in the Royal Engineers, Henderson had also been the Western Australia Comptroller of Convicts from 1850-63 and the Home Office Surveyor-General of Prisons 1863-69. Because of this combination of military and civil service he was considered the ideal choice to head the London Metropolitan Police. Improved morale by allowing policemen to vote and have beards and mustaches, and fought to have their pay increased. By the 1880's however, he had begun to pay less and less attention to the day to day operation of the police force, leaving it to his subordinates. Resigned after the 8 February, 1886 "Black Monday" Trafalgar Square Riot revealed how disorganized the police department had become.

[273] **Herbert Burrows** (1845-1922). English Socialist, helped organize the London Matchgirls Strike of 1888. A member of many leftist organizations, such as the National Secular Society, Aristotelian Society, and the Social Democratic Federation, he, along with fellow strike organizer Annie Besant, also belonged to Helena Blavatsky's occultic Theosophical Society.

# Saturday, 13 October, 1888

in America. The Bishop was made to give a valedictory sermon from the text, "Go to now, ye rich men, weep and howl for your miseries that shall come upon you." He addressed his people as "Fellow citizens," he arraigned the Church, declared that he had been living in a fool's paradise, and announced his determination to abandon his bishopric, his palace, his seat in the Lords, his ten thousand a year, and devote his life to the cause of suffering humanity. This burlesque sermon was reproduced in all seriousness some months ago by the *Journal of United Labour*, the official organ of the Knights of Labour in America, which has a million readers. It continued Westward, and we notice it has now reached British Columbia, where it is naturally regarded as a "startling Christmas sermon," and spoken of as "terrible denunciation from the pulpit." It occupies the most prominent place in the *Victoria Daily Times* of 8 Sept., and is introduced with rows of startling headlines. Mr. Burrows may congratulate himself on having fooled a continent and at the same time advanced the cause he has at heart.

—

### WHITECHAPEL.
### Extra Police Activity Last Night—
### Feeling Among the Jews.

The force of police and detectives on duty in the Whitechapel district was strengthened somewhat last night, as the murders have generally been committed on the Friday and Saturday nights. The number of amateur policemen on the look-out for the murderer was also greater than usual, but up to the hour named their vigilance had not been crowned with any success. During the evening a number of domiciliary visits were made by the detectives, but no arrests were made.

Statements made to our representatives, and correspondence we have received, show that the Jews strongly resent the attempts which have been made to connect a member of their community with the murders through the handwriting on the wall. They urge very reasonably that nothing is more probable, supposing the writing to have been the handiwork of the murderer, than that its object was to divert suspicion from himself to some member of the community against whom prejudice already exists. They also strongly resent the attempt to bolster up the theory by the assertions made yesterday that anyone acquainted with the German-Hebraic lingo spoken by the foreign Jews, and called Yiddish, would be likely to spell "Jews" "Juwes," as it appeared on the wall. The statement is not only ridiculous, but dangerous, as tending to excite race hatred.

—

### The Man with the Knives at Belfast.

The *Belfast Evening Telegraph*, which received a "Jack the Ripper" letter before the arrest of the man Foster, gives this description of the prisoner as he appeared in the dock. He did not bear that low-class criminal appearance which might be supposed to characterise a murderer. He had quite a tradesman-like aspect. He has flaxen hair, crispy and hedgehog-like, ruddy complexion, and short-cut sandy moustache, his hands being somewhat bronzed and not too clean. His ears project, and might be described as somewhat "cocked," while his eyes —his most characteristic trait—appear to look somewhat outwards. He has a wrinkled brow, and his head, which he slightly inclined to the right while he was standing in the dock, is remarkable for length rather than breadth or height. He was attired in a black frock coat and black vest, and his shirt, several inches of which could be seen, was of much the same colour. He wore a dickey and a large black breast tie. His white turned-down collar has apparently a spot of blood, but this might be the result of a mishap in shaving, and stress need not be laid upon it. He was not particularly anxious-looking as he leaned on the front rail of the dock with his arms folded during the progress of the trial. It may be added that the prisoner speaks with an English accent.

The man was apprehended at 11, Memel-street, on the strength of "information received." He was in bed when the police made their visit. He gave the name of William John Foster, and said he came from Greenock, at which place he stopped two days, he couldn't say with whom. Previously, he said, he had been four days at Glasgow, and that he had been in Edinburgh, but didn't know how long. The police found in his possession a large clasp knife, a table-knife, a chisel, a small knife, and some watchmaker's tools. There was a bag into which these things could be put. Foster said he was a watchmaker by trade, but didn't work as he had an income from his father, a brewer in London. In his pockets were found a watch and chain and a piece of a lady's necklace.

—

## Middle-Life Prostitution in the East-end.

Rev. F. Adamson, vicar of Old Ford, writes to the *Times* this morning on the subject of the prevention of prostitution among women in middle-life. He says sheer necessity has to do with middle-life prostitution. Drink produces this necessity. He says the drink traffic of East London will have to be grappled with. Legislative restrictions of a drastic character will have to be introduced. The whole public-house system demands reform. The police should be freed from the supervision of the public-house system, and a separate force of detectives in plain clothes constituted to supervise and to prosecute, both for drink offences and acts of prostitution. Steps must also be taken to punish the men as well as the women. At present the law is unfair and oppressive to one sex. Let the balance be adjusted, and considerable improvement will appear in the morals of the masses. One thing is worthy of notice. These middle-life women, who are said to be driven from downright starvation to vice, can find a home in the unions. Why do they not? Many loathe the honest existence within unions because they love license (or, as they term it, liberty) and strong drink. It is better to face facts than to ignore them. How is this to be grappled with? I have long thought that there should be two grades of unions: one for the lazy, vicious, and criminal, and the other for the honest distressed and industrious. They should not be required to herd together under one stigma of reproach."

—

## A West-end Woman's Story.

An unfortunate told the police last week that a man, who she declared had a knife, accosted her in Great Portland-street, and said he had just come from the Whitechapel murders. Yesterday she informed the police that the same man had accosted her again, and that when she told him she would give him up to the police he ran away.

~

# Monday, 15 October, 1888

## 𝔗𝔥𝔢 𝔗𝔦𝔪𝔢𝔰
### THE EAST-END MURDERS.

In reference to the writing on the wall of a house in Goulston-street, we are requested by Sir Charles Warren to state that his attention having been called to a paragraph in several daily journals mentioning that in the Yiddish dialect the words "Jews" is spelt "Juwes", he has made inquiries on the subject and finds that this is not a fact. He learns that the equivalent in the Judeo-German (Yiddish) jargon is "Yidden."

It has not been ascertained that there is any dialect or language in which the word "Jews" is spelt "Juwes."[274]

—

Mr. Lusk of 1, Alderney-road, Mile-end, has received the following communication from the Home Office, Whitehall, in answer to suggestions with regard to the proclamation of a reward by the Government, with a free pardon for an accomplice of the murderer:—

"October 12.

Sir,—I am desired by the Secretary of State to thank you for the suggestions in your letter of the 7th inst. on the subject of the recent Whitechapel murders, and to say in reply that, from the first, the Secretary of State has had under consideration the question of granting a pardon to accomplices. It is obvious that not only must such grant be limited to persons who have not been concerned in contriving or in actually committing the murders, but the expediency and propriety of making the offer must largely depend on the nature of the information received from day to day, which is being carefully watched, with a view to determining that question.

"With regard to the offer of a reward, Mr. Matthews has, under the existing circumstances, nothing to add to his former letter.

"I am, Sir, your obedient servant,
"GODFREY LUSHINGTON."

Last Friday Mr. George Lusk, who is a member of the Whitechapel Vigilance Committee, received the following letter:—

"I write you a letter in black ink, as I have no more of the right stuff. I think you are all asleep in Scotland-yard with your bloodhounds, as I will show you to-morrow night (Saturday). I am going to do a double event, but not in Whitechapel. Got rather too warm there. Had to shift. No more till you hear me again.

"JACK THE RIPPER."

This letter was shown to the police. It bears a Kilburn postmark, and the handwriting is very similar to that of the post-card sent to a news agency, which had been copied and posted on the hoardings throughout the East-end by the police.

—

### THE WHITECHAPEL MURDERS
#### To the Editor of The Times

Sir,— I have been a good deal about England of late, and have been a witness of the strong interest and widespread excitement which the Whitechapel murders have caused and are causing. Everywhere I have been asked about them; especially by working folk, and more especially by working women. Last week, for instance, in an agricultural county I shared my umbrella during heavy rain with a maid servant, who was going home. "Is it true, Sir," said she, "that they're a-cutting down the feminine seck in London?" And she explained herself to mean that "they was a'murdering of 'em by ones and twos." This is but one of many examples, and my own main interest in the matter is, that I myself have been taken for the murderer. And if I, why not any other elderly gentleman of quiet habits? It may therefore be well to record the fact by way of warning.

Two days ago I was in one of the mining districts, I had just called on my friend the parson of the parish, and was walking back in the twilight, alone, across certain lonely, grimy fields among the pits and forges. Suddenly I was approached from behind by a party of seven stout collier lads, each of them about 18 years old, except their leader, who was a stalwart young fellow of 23 or so, more than 6ft high. He rudely demanded my name, which, of course, I refused to give. "Then," said he, "You are Jack the Ripper, and you will come along wi' us to the police at _____;" naming the nearest town, two miles off. I inquired what authority he had for proposing this arrangement. He hesitated a moment, and then replied that he

---

[274] See footnote 269, p. 382.

# Monday, 15 October, 1888

was himself a constable, and had a warrant (against me, I suppose), but had left it at home. "And," he added fiercely, "if you don't come quietly at once, I'll draw my revolver and blow your brains out." "Draw it, then," I said, feeling pretty sure that he had no revolver. He did not draw it; and I told him that I should certainly not go with him.

All this time I noticed that, though the whole seven stood around me, gesticulating and threatening, not one of them attempted to touch me. And, while I was considering how to accomplish my negative purpose, I saw a forgeman coming across the field from his work. Him I hailed; and, when he came up, I explained that these fellows were insulting me, and that, as the odds were seven to one, he ought to stand by me. He was a dull, quiet man, elderly like myself, and (as he justly remarked) quite ready for his tea. But, being an honest workman, he agreed to stand by me; and he and I moved away in spite of the leader of the gang, who vowed that he would take my ally in charge as well as me. The enemy, however, were not yet routed. They consulted together, and very soon pursued and overtook us; for we took care not to seem as fugitives.

But, meanwhile, I had decided what to do, and had told my friend that I would walk with him as far as our ways lay together, and then I would trouble him to turn aside with me up to the cottage of a certain stout and worthy pitman whom I knew. Thus, then, we walked on over barren fields and slag heaps for half a mile, surrounded by the seven colliers, who pressed in upon me, but still never touched me, though their leader continued his threats, and freely observed that, whatever I might do, I should certainly go with him to the town. At last we came into the road at a lonesome and murderous looking spot, commanded on all sides by the mountainous shale hills of disused pits. Up among these ran the path that led to the pitman's dwellings which I was making for.

When we reached it, I said to my friend the forgeman, "This is our way," and turned towards the path. "That's not your way," shouted the tall man, "you'll come along the road with us," and he laid his hand on my collar. I shook him off, and informed him that he had now committed an assault, for which I could myself give him in charge. Perhaps it was only

post hoc ergo propter hoc,[275] but, an any rate, he made no further attempt to prevent me and my friend from ascending the byway. He stuck to us, however, he and his mates; swearing that he would follow me all the night, if need were. We were soon on the top of the col, if I may so call it, from which the pitmen's cottages, lighted within, were visible in the darkness against a starry sky.

"That is where I am going," I said aloud. To my surprise, the tall man answered in a somewhat altered tone, "How long shall you be?" "That depends," I replied, "you had better come to the house with me." "No," said he, "I shall wait for you here;" and the forgeman and I walked up to the cottage together. At its door I dismissed my ally with thanks and a grateful coin; and, entering in, I told my tale to my friend the stout pitman and his hearty wife, who heard it with indignation. In less than a minute, he and I sallied from his dwelling in search of the fellows who had dogged me. But they had vanished. Seeing me received and welcomed by people whom they knew, they doubtless felt that pursuit was futile and suspicion vain.

Now, I do not object to adventures, even in the decline of life; nor do I much blame my antagonists, whether their motive were right-eous indignation, or, as is more likely, the hope of reward. But I think them guilty of a serious and even dangerous error of judgement in not distinguishing between the appearance of Jack the Ripper and that of your obedient servant,

An Elderly Gentleman.

—

At Worship Street, three children, named Albert Bentley, 11 years of age; Florence Bentley, aged five; and William Shepherd, aged eight, were charged by Mr. Stevenson, an officer of the Reformatory and Refuge Union, Charing cross, with being found living in the company of prostitutes in a common lodging house, 8 White's row, Spitalfields.

The rescue officer deposed to going to the place mentioned at about midday on Saturday and to finding the children in the kitchen of the house among a number of men and women, some of the latter being undoubtedly prostitutes, as he had seen them at all hours of the night

---

[275] **Post hoc ergo propter hoc.** Lat. After this, therefore because of this.

395

# Monday, 15 October, 1888

about the street corners of Spitalfields and Whitechapel.

The house was registered to accommodate 102 persons in 51 double beds. The house was usually a quiet one, where cohabitation was, he thought, the normal condition between the inhabitants rather than active prostitution.

The boy Shepherd was in care of his father, a hawker, who had told witness that he was parted from his wife and that the boy occupied the bed with him. At the same time the boy was left to pass his time in the lodging house or the streets during the day, the father being away.

The children Albert and Florence Bentley were in the lodging house with their mother. She was willing to part with them, so that they could go to industrial schools. The boy witness proposed to get admitted to Feltham if he passed the doctor.

Mr. Montagu Williams said he supposed the kitchen of the lodging house was where the women passed the day, the children being among them and the men. The officer said that was so, and there were some other children even still younger.

The magistrate said he would like to see the parents, and to enable them to attend he remanded the children to the workhouse.

~

## Evening News
### THE EAST END MURDERS.
### JACK THE RIPPER'S
### HANDWRITING IDENTIFIED.
### A CLUE WORTH ACTING ON.

Superintendent Farmer, of the River Tyne Police, has received information which, it is considered, may form a clue to the Whitechapel murders. An Austrian seaman signed articles on board a Faversham vessel in the Tyne, on Saturday, and sailed for a French port. Afterwards it was found that his signature corresponded with the facsimile letters signed "Jack the Ripper," and that the description of the man also corresponded with that of the Whitechapel murderer circulated by the Metropolitan police. Superintendent Farmer will, to-day, telegraph the result of his inquiries to the Criminal Investigation Department.

—

### AN ARREST IN CHORLEY.

This morning, at Chorley, a stranger, giving the name of John Williams, was brought before the magistrates under singular circumstances. On Saturday night he went into a public-house, drew a long sharp knife from a sheath, boasted that he was "Jack the Ripper," and had polished four off, and meant to do another. A paper was found on him, showing that he had recently travelled in the neighbourhood of London.

The Chief Commissioner of Police has caused the following statement to be circulated: "With reference to a statement in various journals that the word "Jews" is spelt "Juwes," in the Yiddish jargon, the Commissioner of Police has ascertained that this is incorrect. It is not known that there is any dialect or language in which the word "Jews" is spelt "Juwes."[276]

—

### SELF-ACCUSED OF MURDER.

A man giving the name of William Russell, and stating that he was discharged a week ago from an American ship, the National Eagle, at the Victoria Docks, Liverpool, has given himself up to the police at Maidenhead, accusing himself of having committed a murder in London on Tuesday night last. He says that on the night in question he had been drinking with a prostitute, whom he calls

---

[276] See footnote 269, p. 382.

# Monday, 15 October, 1888

"Annie." They subsequently quarrelled, and he threw the woman over the parapet of Westminster Bridge into the Thames. He then ran away, and has since been hiding at Kew and Windsor. Haunted, however by the belief that he was being hunted down, he became so uneasy that he could get no rest, and consequently surrendered himself to the police. He describes the woman as rather good looking, of dark complexion, and rather stout—"the type," he says, "of a London girl."

Russell was detained by the police, and late last night the attention of Sergeant Meade was attracted by a strange gurgling sound, as of some one suffocating. The officer went to the room where the prisoner was confined, and found him black in the face from an attempt to strangle himself. He had tied a silk handkerchief tightly round his throat, the sergeant arriving just in time to remove it and save the man's life. He was charged before the magistrates, to-day, with attempting suicide, and remanded for a week for inquiries to be made.

~

# Tuesday, 16 October, 1888

## The Times

### THE EAST-END MURDERS.

The City Police have succeeded in discovering Thomas Conway, who some years ago lived with Catherine Eddowes, the woman murdered in Mitre-square. Up to yesterday the efforts of the detectives had been at fault, owing, as was suggested by the City Solicitor at the inquest, to the fact that Conway had drawn his pension from the 18th Royal Irish Regiment under a false name, that of Thomas Quinn. Apparently he had not read the papers, for he was ignorant till the last few days that he was being sought for. Then, however, he learned that the City detectives were inquiring for him, and yesterday afternoon he and his two sons went to the detective offices of the City Police in Old Jewry and explained who they were. Conway was at once taken to see Mrs. Annie Phillips, Eddowes's daughter, who recognized him as her father. He states that he left Eddowes in 1880 in consequence of her intemperate habits. He knew that she had since been living with Kelly, and had once or twice seen her in the streets, but had, as far as possible, kept out of her way, as he did not wish to have any further communication with her.

—

Superintendent Farmer, of the River Tyne Police, has received information which, it is considered, may form a clue to the East-end murders. An Austrian seaman signed articles on board a Faversham vessel in the Tyne on Saturday, and sailed for a French port. Afterwards it was found that his signature corresponded with the facsimile letters signed "Jack the Ripper," and that the description of the man also corresponded with that of the Whitechapel murderer circulated by the Metropolitan police. A man, wearing a slouched hat, carrying a black leather bag, speaking with a slightly American accent, and presenting a travel-stained appearance, was arrested at Limavady, near Londonderry, yesterday morning by Constable Walsh, on suspicion of being the man who committed the recent murders in the East-end of London. The arrest was made as a result of the police description of the man wanted. The prisoner refused to give his name or any information whatever about himself. A woman and child who were with him were also taken into custody.

### THE RITTER TRIAL.

We have received from Dr. Josef S. Bloch, member of the Austrian Parliament, a letter recounting the circumstances of the Ritter trial, which was referred to by our Vienna Correspondent on the 2nd inst. in connexion with the Whitechapel murders and mutilations.[277] Ritter and his wife were tried in 1882 at Rzezow, in Galicia, for the murder and mutilation of a young woman named Frances Mnich, and were sentenced to death. The High Court of Justice quashed the sentence and ordered a new trial, the result of which was also quashed in 1884. A third trial took place, and the High Court, in 1886, unanimously resolved to release the prisoners. According to our Vienna Correspondent, at the trial numbers of witnesses deposed that among certain fanatical Jews there existed a superstition to the effect that if a Jew became intimate with a Christian woman he could atone for his offence by slaying and mutilating the object of his passion, and sundry passages of the Talmud were quoted which, according to the witnesses, expressly sanctioned the form of the atonement. In his detailed comments on the facts of the case, Dr. Bloch observes, in the first place, that the surgical evidence as to the mutilations was insufficient, and that there was no actual evidence of Ritter's intimacy with the murdered woman. There was, on the other hand, evidence to show that she was intimate with a notorious thief, in whose lodging she was seen for the last time. In the second place, there are in the Talmud no passages sanctioning such a form of atonement as has been described, and none such were quoted at the trial. Dr. Bloch, himself a native of Galicia, born and educated in an exceedingly Orthodox family, "having been Rabbi of Orthodox communities for many years, and Deputy of a Polish elective district in which the Orthodox Jews have a majority, solemnly asserts that among these spheres there exists not the least trace of such a superstition" as is mentioned by our Correspondent. In his postscript Dr. Bloch points out that the probability of the guilt of the thief at whose lodging the murdered woman was last seen is strengthened by the fact that countless trials have shown the existence among professional thieves

---

[277] See **The Whitechapel Murders**, p. 233.

of a superstition which has often been the cause of the mutilation of corpses.

Another correspondent, however, who also writes from Vienna, affirms, as a lawyer of more than 20 years' standing, that our Vienna Correspondent was virtually correct in his statement of the case. He declares that, whatever may be the reading of the Talmud, the superstition in question was clearly proved at the trial as existing among the low-class Jews of Galicia. The Ritters, he says, were acquitted because the only witness against them died in prison, and the rest of the evidence was meagre and incomplete.

~

## The Star
### WHITECHAPEL.
### The Real Conway Found
### A Guy Got Up for the Police.

The City police have succeeded in discovering Thomas Conway, who some years ago lived with Catherine Eddowes, the woman murdered in Mitre-square. Up to yesterday, the efforts of the detectives had been at fault owing, as now suggested by the City Solicitor at the inquest, to the fact that Conway has drawn his pension from the 18th Royal Irish Regiment under a false name—that of Thomas Quinn. Apparently he has not read the papers, for he was ignorant till the last few days that he was being sought for. Then, however, he learned that the City detectives were inquiring after him, and yesterday afternoon he and his two sons went to the detective office of the City Police in Old Jewry and explained who they were. Conway was at once taken to see Mrs. Annie Phillips, Eddowes's daughter, who recognised him as her father. He states that he left Eddowes in 1880 in consequence of her intemperate habits. He knew that she had since been living with Kelly, and had once or twice seen her in the streets, but had as far as possible kept out of her way.

—

### A Pail and Some Old Clothes.

Two detectives passing through Back Church-lane (near Berner-street), shortly before two o'clock this morning, noticed a dark object lying in a doorway. One struck a light, and found it to be some old female attire and a pail made to resemble a body crouched up in the corner.

—

### A Poor Joke.

Early this morning some "Jack the Ripper" writing in chalk was found on the gate of a stable at Lewisham-road, near Blackheath Railway Station. "Dear Boss," it says, "if you wish to find the head of the body on the Embankment it is in a sack on the water. I have done another to-night. Jack the Ripper. Revenge." A policeman is guarding the gate, though in all probability the writing is only that of someone playing a stupid joke.

—

# Tuesday, 16 October, 1888

## THE PEOPLE'S POST BOX.
### Shelters for the Homeless.

SIR,—Up to last night we sheltered 609 men, women, and children, and fed them, for we now give them food as well as shelter, and help them on to a better road afterwards. Funds are needed; every penny shall be honestly applied and accounted for.—Yours, &c.

SAM HAYWARD.

212, Devonshire-road, Forest-hill,
13 Oct.

—

SIR,—A shelter for outcast females will be opened in a few days at Harlow House, 34, Mile-end-road.

Such poor creatures as are without home, food, friends, or money will be given a warm shelter, with a supper of a pint of coffee and bread, but the same applicants will not be admitted more than three nights in any week. Convenience will be provided for washing, &c. Applicants will be received from ten p.m. until two a.m. every night, and those admitted can leave from five to eight o'clock in the morning to enable them to obtain the casual employment that requires early applications. The only condition will be abject poverty, and decorous conduct while in the shelter. Applicants will be able to obtain an order from the police-station or any constable in the district.

Any donation, however small, will be thankfully received, and duly accounted for. We shall also be glad of the assistance of ladies and gentlemen.—Yours, &c.

R. H. WINTER, J. L. DALE, }Hon. Secs.

Office, 94, Mile-end-road, E.

[The competition in night refuges is becoming severe, but we are informed that the above is a perfectly genuine undertaking. —ED. *The Star*.]

~

## Evening News
## THE EDITOR'S DRAWER.
## THE WHITECHAPEL MURDERS.
### To The Editor of
### "THE EVENING NEWS."

Sir—May I be allowed a small space in your esteemed journal to make a suggestion in reference to the Whitechapel murders? The fiend who has perpetrated these atrocities is supposed to be a man of the shabby-genteel class who carries a shiny black bag, and many individuals of this description, therefore, are objects of suspicion. Arrests have been made, and several shabby folk, no doubt, are included in these arrests, yet to no effect. My theory is, Sir, the murders may have been committed by a woman, and I think that the fact a woman has not been looked for supports my theory. If it is a woman she is doubtless a maniac. The idea is not to be laughed at. A woman accustomed to midwifery I think is more capable and likely to inflict the dreadful mutilation which has attended these murders (when thirsting for blood) than a man of the shabby genteel cut, who perhaps is even unmarried. The woman may have influence over her fellow sex, or might easily have by mixing amongst them as "pals."—I am, &c., J.O. October 15.

—

### THE MURDERS.
### CONWAY DISCOVERED.

The City police have succeeded in discovering Thomas Conway, who for some years ago lived with Catherine Eddowes, the woman murdered in Mitre-square.

Up to yesterday the efforts of the detectives had been at fault, owing, as was suggested by the City solicitor at the inquest, to the fact that Conway has drawn his pension from the 18th Royal Irish Regiment under a false name, that of Thomas Quinn. Apparently he has not read the papers, for he was ignorant till the last few days that he was being sought for. Then, however, he learned that the City detectives were inquiring after him went to the detective office of the City police in Old Jewry, and explained who they were. Conway was at once taken to see Mrs. Annie Phillips, Eddowes's daughter, who recognized him as her father. He states that he left Eddowes in 1880, in consequence of her intemperate habits, which prevented them from

# Tuesday, 16 October, 1888

living comfortably together. He knew that she had since been living with Kelly, and has once or twice seen her in the streets, but has, as far as possible, kept out of her way, as he did not wish to have any further communication with her.

—

## THE TUNBRIDGE WELLS MURDER.
## A STRANGE CONFESSION.

The following letter was left at the office of the *Tunbridge Wells Advertiser* on September 27:

"Sir—Two months having now passed, I venture to ask you to be kind enough to allow me a small space in your valuable paper for a few facts concerning the death of the late Mr. Lawrence. In the first place I beg to state that all the evidence given at the inquest and afterwhers as been utterly false, with the exception of the two lads in the timber. I beg to correct the wrong statement that Mrs. Lawrence gave, for I, the murderer, did not summose (summons) him from his house at all, as it was outside the backdoor when I first spoke to him, or my intension was to have shot him on the spot. Lawrence was very talkative when he was out of doors, little thinking of the death he had so shortly got to die. The last words he spoke when in my company was when he caught sight of the pistol sticking out of my pocket. He said, 'What do you carry them there sort of things about with you for?' My answer was, 'To shoot down dogs and curs like you.' (What, would you shoot a ----). Bang! and once more Tunbridge Wells was startled by another mistery which is never likely to be found out. I might here state that the key which was found on the spot is likely to lead to no clue whatever, as it is as much a mystery to me as the murder is to you. I also wish to threaten Mr. Edwards if he has any more to say concerning Mr. Martin, who is as inosent of the crime as he is.—I remain, yours truly,

## "ANOTHER WHITECHAPEL
## MURDERER.

"Another letter, giving the whole of the particulars from beginning to end, will follow on shortly."

It was naturally thought the letter, which was illiterately worded, and apparently in a disguised handwriting, was a hoax, but it was put in the hands of the police, who placed no reliance upon it. From the opening statement, yesterday, of Mr. W. C. Cripps, the town clerk, who prosecuted, it appeared that on the 9th inst. Dobell was in conversation with a fellow workman, named Page, about the Whitechapel murders, and said, "I have shot a man," the remark being looked upon as an empty boast. Two days afterwards both men went to the local Salvation Army services, where they appear to have been striken by remorse.

When the matter was put into the hands of the police authorities Superintendent Embery proceeded to the sawmills, and saw Gower, stating that he should charge him with being concerned, with another man, in murdering Lawrence, detailing also what the Salvation Army captain had told him. Gower replied, "Yes, that is right. Dobell is a mate of mine, and as true as steel." The superintendent, on searching him, found a key, and this the prisoner said belonged to an outhouse where he kept rabbits, and where the pistol would be found in a box on the top of a rabbit hutch. The superintendent found these things as described, the revolver being loaded in all six chambers. Dobell had been arrested I the meantime by Police-constable Bennett at his house.

## AT FIRST HE DECLARES HIS
## INNOCENCE.

On the road to the police-station he said, "I know nothing about the murder. I am quite innocent of it." Later he asked, "Where is my mate—is he at the police-station?" The detective said, "Who do you mean?" and the prisoner replied, "William Gower." At the police-station Dobell volunteered the statement: "There is only one thing I know of the murder. At the inquest Mrs. Lawrence said a man came to the door and called her husband out. That is wrong. Lawrence was already outside the door when I got there. My intention was to have shot him on the spot, but I heard someone in the passage."

## HOW MR. LAWRENCE WAS COAXED
## ACROSS THE YARD.

Subsequently Dobell added: "A good many people have wondered how it was that Lawrence was on the timber side of the yard. I coaxed him across, telling him we should be able the better to see Mr. Potter coming down the road. The only persons to speak the truth were the two lads in the yard, and everything they said was correct." This statement was not made in answer to questions, but of the prisoner's own free will. The superintendent of police charged him with the

401

murder, and informed Dobell that Gower had declared that he (Dobell) had fired the shot. Prisoner said, in reply, "You are right, you have got the murderer." When searched, a letter was found on him from Gower, commencing, "My dear Mate: I believe the Holy Ghost entered your heart last night; God only knows I wish it had mine. There seems to be something I cannot give up, but I am still believing. I went to see the captain this morning, and had an hour with him and confessed all. He wants to see us both to-night, so please come down to my home at six o'clock instead of 5.30.—Yours, Mate."

### A FRESH DISCLOSURE.

A fresh disclosure was made on Saturday morning, and which, when repeated in the police-court, yesterday, created marked sensation.

Police constable Bennett said Mr. Cripps was passing Dobell's cell when he put his head through the door and remarked, "It is a wonder you did not hear of another murder." Upon the constable replying, "What do you mean?" Dobell answered that on the previous Wednesday week, September 26, he and Gower had sent a letter to a man named Langridge, who worked at the saw mills, telling him to meet them in Clarence-road, where they were going to bring a girl for him. "I and Gower," he continued, "went to Clarence-road and saw Langridge, and we were going to pop him off, only a policeman was there. We thought to finish one more off, and that was Edwards, and ten we should have stopped." The latter, Mr. Cripps explained, gave evidence at the Police-court, on September 14, to the effect that one day a short time preciously he met a man named Martin, who said he had broken into the Baltic Saw Mills some years ago.

Edwards informed the police, and Martin was consequently taken into custody, and committed for trial on a charge of breaking into the mills. These facts having been given at yesterday's proceedings, which lasted nearly six hours, both prisoners were committed for trial. The young fellows appeared very cool and self-possessed. They are respectably connected, and the case has created a painful sensation in the town. On one of the prisoners was found a copy of an illustrated paper whose contents are devoted to stories of a blood-curdling character.

~

# Wednesday, 17 October, 1888

## The Star

### WHITECHAPEL.

### A House to House Search Among the Jews.

The police are making a house to house visit amongst the Jews at the East-end. They demand admission to every room, look underneath the beds, and peer into the smallest cupboards. They ask for the production of knives, and examine them. In some cases they have been refused admittance until proof was produced of authority.

The police commence their work a early as ten o'clock in the morning. In some cases the police remain outside, and

### ASK THE FOLLOWING QUESTIONS:

Have you any lodgers?

How many?

What are their names?

How long have they been living with you?

Are they your friends, relatives, or assistants in your work?

Are they respectable?

Can you give the names of lodgers that left you, and the cause of leaving?

Did they leave friendly or otherwise?

Were they respectable?

All the answers to these questions are entered in a small note-book.

A *Star* reporter interviewed a Mrs. Andleman, of 7, Spellman-street, Whitechapel. She said: I came home from work yesterday, and as soon as I opened the street door, two men came up and said, "Do you live in this front room?" "Yes," I said. "We want to have a look at it." "Who are you, and what do you want?" "We are police officers, and we come to look for the murderer." "Do you think I keep the murderer here, or do you suggest that I associate with him?" I replied. They answered that it was their duty to inspect the rooms. I showed them into my room. They

### LOOKED UNDER THE BED,

and asked me to open the cupboards. I opened a small cupboard, where I keep plates and things. It is not more than two feet wide and about one in depth. They made an inspection of that also. "Do you think," I said, "that it is possible for a man, or even a child, to be hidden in that small place?" They made no answer, and walked out. Then they went next door and inspected those premises.

### The Stabbing of a Detective.

At Clerkenwell Police-court yesterday, James Phillips and William Jarvis, cab washers, were charged on remand with cutting and wounding Detective-sergeant Robinson in Phoenix-place, and Jarvis also with assaulting and wounding Henry Doncaster. Michael Rainole, an Italian ice cream vendor, said he was with the detectives on the morning of the 9th watching "the man who was supposed to be the man who killed all the women" when the two prisoners came up and asked what they were doing. Robison took off the woman's hat which he was wearing and said "I am a police officer." Witness saw Jarvis strike Robinson in the face and cause it to bleed, and he also saw Jarvis, who had something in his hand, deal Doncaster a side blow in the face. Witness denied that the disturbance had begun by the prisoners asking Robinson and the others what they were doing near the cabs, and by Robinson replying, "Mind your own business," and thrusting Jarvis back by putting his fist against his chin. It was Jarvis who struck the first blow. He saw Jarvis on the ground, and heard some men cry out to Robinson, "Shame! Leave off hitting him." Jarvis was in a fainting condition, and was bleeding when taken to the police-station.—Giuseppe Molinari gave corroborative evidence.

Detective Charles Mather said he heard Robinson say, "I am a police constable; you know me. We are watching something." A voice then said, "Why, it's Robinson." The witness then described the assault, corroborating the previous witnesses. Witness admitted, in cross-examination, that none of the plain-clothes officers had shown their warrant cards to prove themselves detectives. They had, he said, no opportunity of doing so. The prisoners were committed for trial.

~

## Evening News

### EDITOR'S DRAWER.
### JACK THE RIPPER'S
### HANDWRITING AND STYLE.
### TO THE EDITOR OF THE
### "EVENING NEWS."

SIR—The formation of the letters strikes me as resembling in many aspects corresponding letters in German handwriting—e.g., the capitals J. G. I., the small zig-zag w (in "want to get to work"), ff, and g, &c. "I have laughed" and "till I do get buckled" are specimens of very questionable English. "Buckled" is not, I think, English idiom, though it readily conveys the idea of being pinioned. It may be worthy of remark that the first two letters in "Juwes"—so written, it is said, in the writing on the wall—are the first two letters in the same word in German. In the collocation of those words the relative positions in German and English of the negative not may also be matter for careful observation. The writer may not necessarily be a German, but I cannot help thinking that German or some kindred patois must be his mother tongue—that he is not, in other words, to the English manner born.—I am, &c.,

A. B. C.
October 15.

—

### THE HOUSE TO HOUSE SEARCH.

The Central News further says that certain statements, to the effect that the police are conducting indiscriminate search among Jews' houses in the East-end, is an entire misrepresentation. It is well-known that ten days ago a body of fifty police were told off to visit and systematically inspect houses of all inhabitants, entirely regardless of nationality in the neighbourhood of the crimes. This was done, the officers doing their work in plain clothes, and being met, in almost every instance, with the willing co-operation of the householders.

—

### THE EAST-END MURDERS.
### LATER NEWS ABOUT THE
### BLOOD-STAINED SHIRT.

With regards to statements current as to the finding of a blood-stained shirt at a lodging-house in Whitechapel, the Central News says the story is founded on some matters which occurred more than a fortnight ago. It appears that a man, apparently a foreigner, visited the house of a German laundress, at Batty-street, and left four shirts tied in a bundle to be washed. The bundle was not opened at the time, but when the shirts were afterwards taken out one was found considerably blood-stained.

The woman communicated with the police, who placed the house under observation, detectives at the same time being lodged there, to arrest the man should he return. This he did last Saturday, and he was taken to the Leman-street Police-station, where he was questioned, and within an hour or two released, his statements being proved correct.

# Thursday, 18 October, 1888

## The Times
### THE EAST-END MURDERS.

We are requested to publish the following:—

Sir Charles Warren wishes to say that the marked desire evinced by the inhabitants of the Whitechapel district to aid the police in the pursuit of the author of the recent crimes has enabled him to direct that, subject to the consent of occupiers, a thorough house-to-house search should be made within a defined area. With few exceptions the inhabitants of all classes and creeds have freely fallen in with the proposal, and have materially assisted the officers engaged in carrying it out.

Sir Charles Warren feels that some acknowledgment is due on all sides for the cordial co-operation of the inhabitants, and he is much gratified that the police officers have carried out so delicate a duty with the marked good will of all those with whom they have come in contact.

Sir Charles Warren takes this opportunity of acknowledging the receipt of an immense volume of correspondence of a semi-private character on the subject of the Whitechapel murders, which he has been quite unable to respond to in a great number of instances; and he trusts that the writers will accept this acknowledgment in lieu of individual replies. They may be assured that their letters have received every consideration.

—

A large number of conflicting rumours in connexion with the murders in the East-end are spread abroad from day to day with reference to the movements of suspicious characters who are stated to be under the close supervision of the police. There is little, however, in all these stories which indicates that the police have succeeded to any appreciable extent in tracking the author of the crimes. The net result, indeed, seems to be that a really genuine clue has yet to be obtained. Some importance has been attached by the police to the arrest made at King-street Police-station on Tuesday morning. The man arrested entered the police-station about 9 o'clock and complained of having lost a black bag. While the officials were taking note of the case he began to talk about the women murdered in Whitechapel, and offered to cut off the sergeant's head, and spoke in a rambling, non-sensical manner. In answer to a question as to what his business was, he said he had studied some years for the medical profession, but gave it up for engineering, and that he had been staying for some nights in coffee-houses. His talk became of such a rambling character that Dr. Bond, the divisional surgeon, was sent for, who examined him, and pronounced him to be a very dangerous lunatic with a homicidal tendency. The man is described as resembling the description of the person last seen with the women at the East-end on different occasions. He was dressed in a serge suit, with a hard felt hat, and is of a very strong build. Although he gave his age as 67, he looks much younger. Before his removal to Bow-street photographs were taken of him. He was also asked to write his name, and it is stated the writing is somewhat similar to that of letters received by the police and others. The detectives have been tracing the man's antecedents and his recent movements. The latest inquires seem to show that there is no evidence forthcoming likely to connect him with these crimes. In July last the man was brought up at Lambeth Police-court on a charge of being abroad as a person of unsound mind, and the magistrate ordered his removal to Lambeth Infirmary. He subsequently left that institution, and since August 15 he has lodged at a coffee-house in the Westminster-bridge-road. The keeper of the house states that the man has slept there every night without exception up to Monday of the present week.

~

405

# Thursday, 18 October, 1888

## Evening News

## THE WHITECHAPEL MURDERS.
## TO THE EDITORS OF
## "THE EVENING NEWS."

SIR—I have read "English Sailor's" letter relating to theory of Whitechapel murders. "Alaska" could not have murdered the first of the poor victims, as he arrived not till August —(see paper of 5th, letter from *The Times* taken, signed "Nemo.") The taking out the heart and hanging it round the neck is not purely Eastern. It is a custom of other nations also. I happen (unfortunately) to be the wife of a native of West India, not a "low class" man either, but fairly educated and intelligent, not drinking or smoking. His great-grandmother was a North American Indian. What the great-grandfather was I know not, but of another country, so that my husband is but little coloured.

Some years back he deliberately wrote to a man that he should like to take his heart out and hang it round his neck. The said letter was put into police detectives' hands, and no doubt is on police records for that year. I am of opinion that the method is one of revenge. My husband is a tall, dark man, and often wears a long coat, but was not in London till after the murders were committed.

You are at liberty to insert this if you wish.—I am, &c.,

A. B.

P.S.—I should have added that the ship's stewards having to cut up animals for their own consumption on board (where they kill their own oftentimes), would know a little about dissecting, as well as would some of the others mentioned. Also what kind of knife to use for such purpose. Seafaring men are "Jacks," so the Malay cook may have done the latter ones.

# The Times
## THE MURDERS IN LONDON.

Mr. George Lusk, builder, of Alderney-road, Globe-road, Mile-end has received several letters purporting to be from the perpetrator of the Whitechapel murders, but believing them to have been the production of some practical joker, he had regarded them as of no consequence. It is stated that a letter delivered shortly after 5 o'clock on Tuesday evening was accompanied by a cardboard box, containing what appeared to be a portion of a kidney. The letter was in the following terms:—

"From Hell.
Mr. Lusk. Sir,
I send you half the kidne I took from one woman, prasarved it for you, tother piece I fried and ate it; was very nice. I may send you the bloody knif that took it out if you only wate while longer.
(Signed)
'Catch me when you can.' Mr. Lusk."

The receiver was at first disposed to think that another hoax had been perpetrated, but even-tually decided to take the opinion of the Vigilance Committee. They could, of course, give no opinion as to whether the kidney was human or not, but they decided to take the contents of the cardboard box to a medical man whose surgery is near. The substance was declared by the assistant to be the half of a human kidney, which had been divided longitu-dinally; but in order to remove any reason for doubt, he conveyed it to Dr. Openshaw, who is pathological curator of the London Hospital Museum. The doctor examined it, and pronoun-ced it to be a portion of a human kidney—a "ginny" kidney, that is to say, one that had belonged to a person who had drunk heavily. He was further of opinion that it was the organ of a woman of about 45 years of age, and that it had been taken from the body within the last three weeks. It will be within public recollection that the left kidney was missing from the woman Eddowes, who was murdered and mutilated in Mitre-square.

Mr. Lusk states that a day or two before receiving the box he had sent to him a postcard, which he now considers of sufficient importance to make public. It is in the following words:—

"Say Boss,—You seem rare frightened. Guess I'd like to give you fits, but can't stop time enough to let you box of toys[278] play copper games with me, but hope to see you when I don't hurry too much.— Goodbye, Boss.
Mr. Lusk, Head Vigilance Committee, Alderney-street, Mile-end."

The letter and postcard are in the hands of the police.

—

It is stated that Sir Charles Warren's bloodhounds were out for practice at Tooting yesterday morning and were lost. Telegrams have been despatched to all the metropolitan police stations stating that, if seen anywhere, information is to be immediately sent to Scotland-yard.

—

Another arrest has just been made in Whitechapel by the police. The man arrested is about 35 years of age, and has recently been living in Whitechapel. He is somewhat confused in his statements respecting his whereabouts lately, and will be detained pending inquiries.

—

The force of police in private clothes specially selected to make the house-to-house search in the neighbourhoods of Hanbury-street, Commercial-street, Dorset-street, Goulston-street, Buck's Row, Brick-Lane, Osborn-street, &c., completed their labours yesterday. They have distributed many thousands of handbills, leaving them in every room in the lodging-houses. The greatest good feeling prevails towards the police, and noticeably in the most squalid dwellings the police had no difficulty in getting information; but not the slightest clue to the murderer has been obtained.

—

A memorial, signed by upwards of 200 traders of Whitechapel, has been sent to the Home Secretary through Mr. S. Montagu, M.P. It states that the traders in Whitechapel have for some years past been painfully aware that the protection afforded by the police has not kept pace with the increase of population in White-chapel. Acts of violence and robbery have been committed in this neighbourhood almost with

---

[278] **Box of Toys**. Noise, Cockney rhyming slang.

# Friday, 19 October, 1888

impunity, owing to the existing police regulations and the insufficiency of the number of officers. The universal feeling prevalent in their midst is that the Government no longer insures the security of life and property in the East of London, and that in consequence respectable people fear to go out shopping, thus depriving the traders of their means of livelihood. They ask that the police in this district may be largely increased, in order to remove the feeling of insecurity which is destroying the trade of Whitechapel.

—

At the Guildhall before Mr. Alderman Renals, Benjamin Graham, 42, described as a glass blower, of 14 Fletcher's row, Clerkenwell, was charged on his own confession with having committed the Whitechapel murders. Detective Constable Rackley deposed that on Wednesday afternoon he was at Snow hill Police station, when the prisoner was brought in by a man who made a statement to the effect that the accused had told him that he was the assassin who was wanted for the recent atrocities in the East end. The witness asked the prisoner if he had anything to say. He replied, "I did kill the woman in Whitechapel and I shall have to suffer for it with a bit of rope." The accused was under the influence of drink. He was seen by a doctor, and then removed to the City of London Infirmary, at Bow. Detective Sergeant Bownes asked for a remand in order that the antecedents of the accused might be inquired into. The Alderman consented, and the prisoner was remanded.

~

## The Star
### WHITECHAPEL
### TRAGEDY OR JOKE?
#### Half of a Human Kidney
#### Sent Through the Post.

Mr. George Lusk, the chairman of the Whitechapel Vigilance Committee, has been the recipient of an extraordinary parcel. It reached him through the post on Tuesday evening, and on examination it was found to contain a meaty substance that gave off a very offensive odour. A closer inspection showed that the article was a portion of a kidney. Enclosed in the box with it was a letter, worded in these revolting terms:—

"From Hell—Mr. Lusk.

Sir, I send you half the kidne I took from one woman. Prasarved it for you. Tother piece I fried and ate; it was very nice. I may send you the bloody knife that took it out, if you only wate whil longer.—

(Signed)
CATCH ME WHEN YOU CAN,
MR. LUSK."

Mr. Lusk decided to bring the matter before the Vigilance Committee, which met at the Crown, Mile-end-road, on Wednesday evening. It was then agreed to investigate the subject next day, and yesterday morning Mr. J. Aarons, the treasurer; Mr. W. Harris, the secretary; and Messrs. Reeves and Lawton, members of the Vigilance Committee, proceeded to Mr. Lusk's house to inspect the strange parcel.

As no definite conclusion could be arrived at, it was decided to call upon Dr. Wiles, of 56, Mile-end-road. In his absence Mr. F. S. Reed, his assistant, examined the contents of the box, and at once expressed an opinion that the article formed the half of a human kidney, which had been divided longitudinally. He thought it best, however, to submit the kidney to Dr. Openshaw, the pathological curator at the London Hospital, and this was at once done.

By the use of the microscope Dr. Openshaw was able to determine that the kidney had been taken from a full-grown human being, and that the portion before him was
#### PART OF THE LEFT KIDNEY.
It at once occurred to the Vigilance Committee that at the inquest on the body of the woman

Eddowes who was murdered at Mitre-square, Aldgate, it was stated that the left kidney was missing, and in view of this circumstance it was deemed advisable to at once communicate with the police. Accordingly the parcel and the accompanying letter and postcard were at once taken to Leman-street Police-station, and the matter placed in the hands of Inspector Abberline.

Subsequently the City police were communicated with, as the discovery relates to a crime occurring within their jurisdiction. The cardboard box which Mr. Lusk received is about 3½in. square, and was wrapped in paper. The cover bears a London post-mark, but the stamping is not sufficiently clear to enable it to be stated from what postal district of the metropolis the article was sent. On this point it is expected that the assistance of the Post Office officials will be invoked. The portion of the kidney which it enclosed has, according to the medical experts, been preserved for some time in spirits of wine. The person from whom it was taken was probably

**ALIVE THREE WEEKS SINCE,**

a circumstance which fits in with the suggestion that the organ may have been taken from the body of the deceased woman Eddowes, murdered in Mitre-square. Another fact is that the kidney is evidently that of a person who had been a considerable drinker, as there were distinct marks of disease.

The handwriting of the letter differs altogether from that of "Jack the Ripper," specimens of whose calligraphy were recently published. The writing is of an inferior character, evidently disguised, while the spelling, as will be seen, is indifferent. A few days before he received the parcel Mr. Lusk received a postcard supposed to come from the same source. It reads:—

Say Boss

You seem rare frightened, guess I'd like to give you *fits*, but can't stop time enough to let you box of toys play copper games with me, but hope to see you when I don't hurry too much.

Bye-bye, Boss.

There seems to be no room for doubt that what has been sent to Mr. Lusk is part of a human kidney, but nevertheless it may be doubted whether it has any serious bearing on the Mitre-square murder. The whole thing may possibly turn out to be a medical student's gruesome joke.

**It Had Been Preserved in Spirits.**

Dr. Openshaw told a *Star* reporter to-day that after having examined the piece of kidney under the microscope he was of opinion that it was half of a left human kidney. He couldn't say, however, whether it was that of a woman, nor how long ago it had been removed from the body, as it had been preserved in spirits.

It is believed that the "revolting parcel" is not from the murderer, but is merely a medical student's practical joke.

The Metropolitan Police last night handed the piece of kidney over to the City Police on the assumption that if the whole thing is not, as is most likely, the disgusting trick of some practical joker, it relates to the Mitre-square crime.

—

**False Reports of an Arrest.**

The Central News is informed, upon inquiry, that the statement that the City Police have arrested in Bermondsey a man, supposed to be an American and concerned in the Whitechapel murders, is quite incorrect. No such arrest, say the police, has been made, and at present they have no one in custody.

~

# Friday, 19 October, 1888

𝕰𝖛𝖊𝖓𝖎𝖓𝖌 𝕹𝖊𝖜𝖘

**FIFTH EDITION.**
**MITRE SQUARE MURDER.**
**STARTLING NEWS.**
**HALF THE VICTIM'S MISSING**
**KIDNEY RESTORED.**
**THE OTHER HALF EATEN BY THE**
**CANNIBAL ASSASSIN.**

Mr. George Lusk, builder, of 1, 2 and 3, Alderney-road, Globe-road, Mile End, E., who is chairman of the Whitechapel Vigilance Committee, called at our office yesterday afternoon, accompanied by Mr. Harris, of 83, Whitehorse-lane, Mile End, secretary to the Committee; Mr. Aarons, treasurer, and Messrs. Lawton, Reeves, G. Lusk and Dr. F. S. Reed. They brought with them a small cardboard box containing half a human kidney, which had been delivered by Parcels' Post at Mr. George Lusk's residence on Tuesday evening.

Mr. Lusk stated that the box was delivered at his house by the postman about eight o'clock in the evening. Upon opening it he discovered a meaty substance, which smelt very strongly, and which he judged to be half a kidney belonging to some animal. Enclosed in the box was a letter. At first he regarded the affair as a practical joke, in the nature of a hoax, but afterwards he decided to bring the matter before the committee and a meeting was accordingly held on Wednesday evening.

Mr. Harris stated that the meeting was hastily held at the Crown, there being a quorum of the Vigilance Committee present, consisting of Messrs. Lusk, Harris, Aarons, S. Lawton, and Reeves. Mr. Lusk communicated to the committee that he had received a strange parcel, and they went to his house and viewed it. The article inside the box smelt very strongly of spirits, as though it had been immersed therein, and it looked like part of a kidney, but the committee could not determine what it was. They, therefore, called upon Mr. F. S. Reed, assistant to Dr. F. W. Wiles, of 56, Mile End-road, to help them to form a conclusion.

Mr. F. S. Reed stated that he examined the contents of the box. It appeared to him that the article was half of a human kidney, which had been divided longitudinally; but in order to make sure he at once conveyed it to Dr. Openshaw, pathological curator at the London Hospital Museum. Dr. Openshaw examined it, and pronounced it to be the half of the left kidney of a full-grown human being. Remembering the fact that it was the left kidney which was missing from the body of the woman Eddowes, who was murdered and mutilated in Mitre-square, Mr. Reed thinks it probable that the ghastly relic is genuine.

We need only add that the contents of the box and the letters were shown to us by Mr. Lusk, who allowed one of our staff to copy the letters. Mr. Lusk and his friends then left our office, en route for Scotland-yard.

The handwriting of the letter and post-card are the same. They bear no resemblance to the letters received by the Central News, signed "Jack the Ripper." The following are copies of the documents.

The post-card, which was received a day or two before the box, was as follows:

SAY BOSS—
You seem rare frightened, guess I'd like to give you fits, but can't stop time enough to let you box of toys play copper games with me, but hope to see you when I don't hurry to much. Bye-bye, Boss.

MR. LUSK,
Head Vigilance Committee,
Alderney-street, Mile-end.

The letter which was enclosed in the box, was as follows:

From Hell
Mr. Lusk
Sir
I send you half the kidne I took from one woman prasarved it for you tother piece I fried and ate it was very nice I may send you the bloody knif that took it out if you only wate whil longer

Signed
Catch me when you can
Mishter Lusk.[279]

---

[279] **Mishter.** In popular literature of the time, S in many words was replaced with Sh to imitate the speech patterns of Jewish immigrants, as in the following extract from "George St. George Julian— The Prince, Part 7.", Henry Cockton. Roberts' Semi-monthly Magazine for Town and Country, Vol. I, 1 May, 1841, p. 285:

# Friday, 19 October, 1888

---

## MR. AARON'S STATEMENT.

Mr. J. Aarons, the treasurer of the White-chapel Vigilance Association, made the following statement, last evening: "Mr. Lusk, our chairman, came over to me last (Wednesday) night in a state of considerable excitement. I asked him what was the matter, when he replied, 'I suppose you will laugh at what I am going to tell you, but you must know that I had a little parcel come to me on Tuesday evening, and to my surprise it contains half a kidney and a letter from "Jack the Ripper."' To tell you the truth, I did not believe in it, and I laughed and said I thought that somebody had been trying to frighten him. Mr. Lusk, however, said it was no laughing matter to him. I then suggested that as it was late, we should leave the matter over till the morning, when I and other members of the committee would come round. This morning, at about half-past nine, Mr. Harris, our secretary, Mr. Reeves, Mr. Lawton, and myself went across to see Mr. Lusk, who opened his desk and pulled out a small square box, wrapped in brown paper. Mr. Lusk said, 'Throw it away; I hate the sight of it.' I examined the box and its contents, and being sure that it was not a sheep's kidney, I advised that, instead of throwing it away, we should see Dr. Wills, of 56, Mile End-road. We did not, however, find him in, but Mr. Reed, his assistant, was. He gave an opinion that it was a portion of a human kidney which had been preserved in spirits of wine; but to make sure, he would go over to the London Hospital, where it could be microscopically examined. On his return Mr. Reed said that Dr.

Openshaw, at the Pathological Museum, stated that the kidney belonged to a female, that it was part of the left kidney, and that the woman had been in the habit of drinking. He should think that the person had died about the same time the Mitre-square murder was committed. It was then agreed that we should take the parcel and the letter to the Leman-street Police-station, where we saw Inspector Abberline. Afterwards some of us went to Scotland-yard, where we were told that we had done quite right in putting the matter into Mr. Abberline's hands. Our committee will meet again tonight, but Mr. Lusk, our chairman, has naturally been much upset."

The parcel and the accompanying letter and post-card were at once taken to Leman-street Police-station, and the matter placed in the hands of Inspector Abberline. Subsequently the City police were communicated with, as the discovery relates to a crime occurring within their jurisdiction.

The Central News says: It is stated that the man called Lardy attended at the City Police Office in Old Jewry, yesterday, but that no importance is attached to his statements. With regard to the half kidney received by Mr. Lusk, Chairman of the Whitechapel Vigilance Committee it is ascertained that the Metropolitan Police last night handed it over to the City Police on the assumption that if the whole thing is not, as is most likely, a disgusting trick of some practical joker, it relates to the Mitre-square crime. Dr. Brown, surgeon to the City Police, who saw the organ yesterday, will again examine it to-day.

~

---

'Vy,' returned the Jew, 'arl I vantsh to explain, Mishter Pull, ish ash thish, that I've cot arf a note, I advanched a hundred and fifty poundsh on, and vantsh for to get the other.'

411

# Saturday, 20 October, 1888

## The Times
### THE EAST-END MURDERS.

No person is under detention at either of the police stations. The house-to-house search is completed, and has led to no discovery of any value. The householders have offered the fullest assistance to the police throughout the work of inspection. Intelligence was received by the detectives that yesterday afternoon in Islington a strange man was observed to write on a wall the words "I am Jack the Ripper." He was pursued for some distance, but got clear away. The horrible incident of the box containing a portion of a kidney sent to Mr. Lusk, of the Whitechapel Vigilance Committee, is not generally regarded as a practical joke in view of the opinion given by two medical gentlemen, Dr. Openshaw and Mr. Reed. The box and its contents were taken from Leman-street to the City Police Office in Old Jewry, and Dr. Gordon Browne, police-surgeon, will examine and make a report in due course. The extra police precautions are still in force.

As Saturday and Sunday—the days which the Whitechapel murderer has hitherto chosen for his work—come round week by week, special precautions are taken by the police as well as by the self-constituted vigilance committee. Last night, when the policemen on night duty were drawn up in their respective station-yards, preparatory to going on their beats, the last letter sent by "Jack the Ripper" was read over to them. It was pointed out that the writer intimated his intention of committing further murders last night, and the necessity for special vigilance was impressed on the police.

Yesterday the police were engaged in an exhaustive search of the ground between the Victoria Embankment and Cannon-row—the site of the new police offices. The purpose of the search was an endeavour to find other parts of the mutilated remains already discovered, and those engaged were assisted by a blood-hound. There is a well on the ground, probably one of ancient date, and this was drained, but without any result. Other investigations are being made with unremitting care.

~

## The Star
### WHITECHAPEL.
#### Easy to Hoax the Police -The Kidney Story.

As Saturday and Sunday—the days which the Whitechapel murderer has hitherto chosen for his work—come round week by week, special precautions are taken by the police as well as by the self-constituted vigilance committee. Last night the last letter sent by "Jack the Ripper" was read over to the night police before starting to their beats. It was pointed out that the writer intimated his intention of committing further murders last night, and the necessity for special vigilance was impressed on the police.

As a motive for the disgusting hoax of the kidney, it is suggested that the person who sent it to its recipient desired to keep up the excitement about the crimes. We are now informed that the information of the receipt of the parcel was sold at a high figure, so that the hoax does not appear so stupid as it seemed at first.

—

#### A Jack the Ripper Arrested.

The Bradford police this morning apprehended a young woman named Maria Coroner on the charge of sending letters signed "Jack the Ripper" to the local press and the chief constable. The girl is good-looking, respectably dressed, and in regular work at one of the leading drapery esta-blishments in Bradford. Several written references to Jackson, the Manchester murderer, and a card of Berry, the hangman,[280] carefully wrapped in silk paper, were found in her possession. She was remanded on a charge of inciting to a breach of the peace.

A Bradford correspondent adds:—She says she wanted to make a sensation. In her boxes at her lodgings were found exact copies of the two letters which she wrote, as well as others which were apparently intended to be issued.

---

[280]**James Berry** (1852-1913). Public executioner 1884-1891. Helped perfect the "Long Drop" method of hanging, but not before decapitating one prisoner and nearly decapitating another by using too long a rope. Executed 126 men and five women. Included in this number is William Henry Bury, who strangled his wife Ellen, then stabbed her to death with a penknife. Berry, and some members of the press, suspected that Bury could have been Jack the Ripper. After resigning his position as executioner, James Berry became an evangelist.

# Saturday, 20 October, 1888

## Evening News
### MITRE SQUARE MURDER.
### THE POLICE HAVE SERIOUS SUSPICIONS.
### GRAVE POLICE SUSPICIONS.

The half kidney sent to the Whitechapel Vigilance Committee, is now in the hands of the City police surgeon, but only a cursory examination has yet been made of it. A small portion only of the renal artery adheres to the kidney, and it will be remembered that in the Mitre-square victim a large portion of the renal artery adhered to the body. This leads the police to attach more importance to the matter than they otherwise would. The half kidney has been preserved in spirits for some time.

As we have already stated, the cardboard box which the chairman received is about 3½ in. square, and was wrapped in paper. The cover bears a London post-mark, but the stamping is not sufficiently clear to enable it to be stated from what postal district of the metropolis the article was sent. On this point it is expected that the assistance of the Post Office officials will be invoked. The portion of the kidney which is enclosed has, according to the medical experts, been preserved for some time in spirits of wine.

### REGARDED AS A HOAX BY THE POLICE.

The incident of the box containing a portion of a kidney sent to Mr. Lusk of the Whitechapel Vigilance Committee was yesterday the subject of much comment in the East-end. It is regarded by the police as a hoax. Even if the kidney forwarded to Mr. Lusk, the chairman of the Vigilance Committee, would prove to be the half of a human organ—and there is medical discrepancy on this point—it could not have been the one extracted from the body of the murdered woman Eddowes. A medical man is said to have ventured to assert—relying upon a microscopic examination—that the organ showed indications of disease from drink. Dr. Sedgwick Saunders, medical officer of the City of London, says this at once disproves the theory that the organ could have belonged to Eddowes, by stating that the right kidney of the woman was perfectly healthy, and presumably the left would be in a similar condition.

### DR. SAUNDERS IS INTERVIEWED.

Dr. Saunders, alluding to the report that a medical man declared the half kidney had belonged to a female, remarked to a reporter who interviewed him: "It is a pity some people have not the courage to say they don't know. You may take it that there is no difference whatever between the male and female kidney. As for those in animals, they are similar. The cortical substance is the same, and the structure only differs in shape.

### MIGHT BE MISTAKEN FOR A PIG'S.

I think it would be quite possible to mistake it for a pig's. You may take it that the right kidney of the woman Eddowes was perfectly normal in its structure and healthy, and by parity of reasoning, you would not get much disease in the left. The liver was healthy, and gave no indications that the woman drank. Taking the discovery of the half of a kidney, and supposing it to be human, my opinion is that it was a student's antic. It is quite possible for any student to obtain a kidney for the purpose.

### INTERVIEW WITH THE CURATOR OF THE PATHOLOGICAL MUSEUM.

A Press representative had an interview, yesterday afternoon, with the Curator of the Pathological Museum at the London Hospital. In the course of the conversation that gentleman stated that the microscopical examination of the article proved it to be the anterior of the left human kidney. It has been preserved, in his opinion, in spirit for about 10 days. The Curator further added that all other statements which had been made were entirely erroneous. Until the portion of the kidney has undergone a more minute examination it is almost impossible to say whether it has been extracted from the body of a male or female. The idea of its being a practical joke is not generally endorsed, especially as so pronounced an opinion has been given by two medical gentlemen, Dr. Openshaw and Mr. Reed. The box and its contents were taken from Leman-street to the City Police office in Old Jewry, and Dr. Gordon Browne, police-surgeon, will examine and make a report in due course. The extra police precautions are still in force.

### A POSSIBLE CLUE AS TO THE SENDER.

A statement which apparently gives a clue to the sender of the strange package received by

Mr. Lusk was made last night by Miss Emily Marsh whose father carries on business in the leather trade at 218, Jubilee-street, Mile End-road. In Mr. Marsh's absence Miss Marsh was in the front shop, shortly after one o'clock on Monday last, when a stranger, dressed in clerical costume, entered, and, referring to the reward bill in the window, asked for the address of Mr. Lusk, described therein as the president of the Vigilance Committee. Miss Marsh at once referred the man to Mr. J. Aarons, the treasurer of the committee, who resides at the corner of Jubilee-street and Mile End-road, a distance of about thirty yards. The man, however, said he did not wish to go there, and Miss Marsh thereupon produced a newspaper in which Mr. Lusk's address was given as Alderney-road, Globe-road, no number being mentioned. She requested the stranger to read the address, but he declined, saying, "Read it out," and proceeded to write something in his pocketbook, keeping his head down meanwhile. He subsequently left the shop, after thanking the young lady for the information, but not before Miss Marsh, alarmed by the man's appearance, had sent the shop-boy, John Cormack, to see that all was right. This lad, as well as Miss Marsh, gives a full description of the man, while Mr. Marsh, who happened to come along at the time, also encountered him on the pavement outside.

## DESCRIPTION OF THE MAN.

The stranger is described as a man some forty-five years of age, fully six feet in height, and slimly built. He wore a soft felt black hat, drawn over his forehead, a stand-up collar, and a very long black single-breasted overcoat, with a Prussian or clerical collar partly turned up. His face was of a sallow type, and he had a dark beard and moustache. This man spoke with what was taken to be an Irish accent. No importance was attached to the incident until Miss Marsh read of the receipt by Mr. Lusk of a strange parcel, and then it occurred to her that the stranger might be the person who had dispatched it. His inquiry was made at one o'clock on Monday afternoon, and Mr. Lusk received the package at eight p.m. the next day. The address on the package, curiously enough, gives no number in Alderney-road, a piece of information which Miss Marsh could not supply. It appears that on leaving the shop the man went right to Mr. Aaron's house, but did not call. Mr. Lusk has been informed of the circumstances, and states that no person answering the description has called on him, nor does he know any one at all like the man in question.

## COMPLAINT BY THE POLICE.

The police complain that their work is increased and morbid excitement created, by the statements made as to alleged arrests of an important character. Both the Metropolitan and City police deny that there was any American or any other man suspected at Bermondsey, whose apprehension was reported to have taken place. There is a clue upon which the authorities have bean zealously working for some time. This is in Whitechapel, not far from the scene of the Berner-street tragedy, and the man is, indeed, himself aware that he is being watched; so much so, that, as far as observation has gone at present, he has scarcely ventured out of doors.

~

# Monday, 22 October, 1888

## The Times

At the Bradford Borough Court on Saturday, a respectable looking young woman, named Maria Coroner, 21 years of age, employed in a mantlemaker's[281] establishment, was brought up on the charge of having "written certain letters tending to cause a breach of the peace." These letters, as stated by the chief constable, purported to be written by "Jack the Ripper," whose object in visiting Bradford, as was stated, was to do a little business before starting for some other place on the same errand. She had written two letters of this character, as she admitted when apprehended, one being addressed to the chief constable and the other to a local newspaper. On searching the girl's lodging the police found copies of the letters. The prisoner excused her foolish conduct on the ground that "she had done it in a joke." She was stated to be a very respectable young woman. The prisoner was remanded until to-morrow, the Bench declining to accept bail.

~

## The Star
### WHAT WE THINK.

AS week after week goes by without a repetition of the Whitechapel murders it is necessary somewhat to modify our theories of the man who committed them. If he is a homicidal maniac, he is obviously not one in the ordinary sense of the term—*i.e.*, a person who indulges his desire to slay whenever it takes him, and regardless of consequences. The murderer waits till the coast is clear, till public interest slackens down, and apparently neglects no precaution to ensure his own safety. All this is conduct usually described as sane; and all the less likely, therefore, is it that we have to deal with the writer of "Jack the Ripper" letters, or with morbid, vicious boys like the Tunbridge Wells criminals.[282]

YET, on the other hand, we cannot assume that the man is sane in the larger sense—his very coolness and ironness of nerve are unnatural, and bespeak that subtler kind of criminal insanity which apes sanity in all its outer aspects, and enables its victim to go about his daily business with a Jekyll-like indifference to his recreations in Hanbury-street and Mitre-square. Nor is it reasonable to suppose that we shall ever catch him unless he commits a fresh crime. All the precautions, such as bloodhounds and house-to-house searches, were taken weeks too late. But it is just possible that the bloodhound experiments may have frightened the man, and that he will stay his hand. In which case, again, it will be clear that we have no maniac, in the vulgar sense, to deal with.

—

### AN EARLY RISER CALLER,
### Who Calls at the "Star" Office to Complain
### of Opposition from the Police.

He was a strong sturdy fellow of some forty years, and as soon as he popped his head into the interviewer's sanctum in Stonecutter-street it was evident that he had a grievance which weighed heavily on him.

"You want to tell us something?" queried *The Star* man.

"Yes," he replied promptly, "I want to tell yer 'ow the police 'ave been annoyin' me in

---

[281] **Mantle Maker.** Maker of mantles for gas lamps. (Farmer)

[282] See *The Evening News*, 16 Oct., **The Turnbridge Wells Murder, A Strange Confession**, p. 401.

# Monday, 22 October, 1888

Commercial-street, instead of trying to catch this 'ere Jack the Ripper. They treat me in a most shameful way, and as I haint much of an edicated man myself, I wanted you to make some correspondences about it."

"How do the police annoy you?"

"By shoutin', hissin', and hollerin' at me as I am a going round my calls of a mornin'. The're jealous, don't you see, mister, 'cause they want to do it theirselves, but as I understands—"

At this point the interviewer thought well to interrupt his visitor, and to find out what this complaint was all about. The caller's card threw some light on the subject. It (the card) was as follows:—

**J. WILKINSON,**
**EARLY RISER CALLER,**
**18, THOROLD-STREET, TURIN-STREET,**
**(Back of "The Bladebone Public-house")**
**BETHNAL GREEN-ROAD, E.**
Persons called at any hour—from twelve till seven o'clock.
J. W. will oblige if only for one morning.

"That's my business," proceeded Mr. Wilkinson. "I call people as wants to get up of a morning, and the police they're on the job too, don't you see? And they want to do all the calls and take the money."

"But the police are not allowed to take money for calling people?"

"Ain't they though? What do you think? All I knows is that they do it, and when they see me going round hiss, shout, and whistle the Dead March in 'Saul,'[283] and go tramping along so," and Mr. Wilkinson stamped heavily on the floor; "and they cry names at me and call me a —! —! and a —! —!! and all that sort of thing, incitin' me to commit a breach of the peace. 'I'll put a stop to this 'ere callin' o' yours,' said one the other day. 'Will yer, tho',' says I. 'Two can play at that game.' I've been 14 years at this 'ere work now, and I ain't been walkin' the streets of London five-an'-twenty years there for nuthin'. An' the police, they're bound to go their rounds in a quiet and orderly manner. But 'ow can they be goin' in a quiet and orderly manner when they whistle the Dead March in 'Saul' at me?"

"Do you know the number of any policeman who annoys you in this way?"

Yes, 223 haitch is the worst 'un. He's allus at it in Commercial-street. And when he begins

---

[283] **"Dead March" from Saul.** Funeral march for Saul and Jonathan from George Friederic Handel's 1738 three act oratio.

hissin' and whistlin' the 'Dead March,' I takes out this 'ere whistle"—and he produced a whistle something like a policeman's—"and does so"—and he blew a gentle solo—"and then so"—and he made the room ring. "That fetches 'em," he said, with a merry twinkle in his eye.

"Why don't you complain that the police take money for calls and annoy you?"

"Aven't I complained hover and hover and hover again? Told the inspector, and gone to the station, but they take no notice. 'Where's your witnesses?' they ask, and I ain't got none. 'Cause the police don't do anythink if there's some 'un with me."

"Are you sure the police receive money for calling people?"

"'Aven't I seen 'em knockin' people up and going round makin' a regler collection on Saturdays? I watch 'em, don't you see. They don't call for the money if they see I'm a-watchin' on 'em. But am up to their tricks. And when they leave I goes and tries to get the call away from them, and I get 'em too. That's why the police have been annoying me for years."

"Are there more callers than you in the neighbourhood?"

"Lots on 'em. But they don't get much. I've been in the business now for 14 years, and go everywhere all round, from Commercial-street to Mare-street. My two boys help me, and my missus sometimes also."

"Do you do anything else."

"No. Live and let live, is what I says. Each 'un to their work. And the police, who get their 27s. and 30s. a week, should stick to their work and not take the bread out of a poor man's mouth. If they only called to oblige I could't object. But catch 'em knocking any one up for nuthin'. No fear, they want bein' paid for it."

"What are your charges, Mr. Wilkinson?"

"Generally sixpence a week. That's a penny a call, but sometimes round Commercial-street way I only gets fourpence. That comes 60 calls for a pound; which sometimes means a lot of trampin'. When does the callin' begin? About one, but there ain't much to do until after three."

"Who are the people who want calling?"

"Market men first. Then firemen, bakers, and all sorts."

"How do you wake them?"

"Knock at the door sometimes, and wait till I get an answer. I have keys, too, and go into courts and yards and upstairs. I even go up and knock at the bedroom door sometimes, and I have a pea-shooter, to fire these 'ere peas (producing some) at the windows. Am as good as a policeman in some ways, for I frighten away burglars and 'ave given the alarm about fires."

Mr. Wilkinson, who seems to be a thoroughly reliable man, and one who may be depended upon to call you punctually, as he rose to go, remarked—

"You put this in your own way, as I ain't much of a scholar. They won't like it, I know. Warren's sure to hear of it. And (this with a pleasant chuckle) then, don't you see, they won't know where it comes from."

~

## Evening News

"Jack the Ripper" has been arrested at Bradford—one of him, at least. He turns out to be in this particular instance anything but a formidable individual. In fact, he is of the softer sex, and apparently a nice-spoken and respecttable young woman. He, or she, declares that her only object in writing the letters was to make a sensation. She has succeeded in experiencing a new sensation, at all events.

—

### THE MITRE-SQUARE MURDER.
### TO THE EDITOR OF
### "THE EVENING NEWS."

SIR—If not encroaching too much on your valuable space, I would beg to offer a few suggestions with regard to tracing the origin of the revolting package stated to have been received by Parcels Post to Mr. Lusk, of Mile End. It may not be generally known, but if the box in question was sent by Parcels Post (unless it was posted out of course, *i.e.*, placed in a pillar or other posting box), it must have been handed in at a post-office by some one, and the printed label of that office would be affixed thereto. The necessary postage in stamps would most probably be attached by the sender, it being against the regulations for the postmaster to do it himself. Doubtless if application were made to the secretary of the General Post Office, he would furnish the police authorities with the time of handling in which, with the other points before-mentioned, might assist them in clearing up the matter.—I am, &c.,

PARCEL POST.
October 20.

# Tuesday, 23 October, 1888

## The Star

### FIFTH EDITION.

The number of the policeman mentioned in the case of J. Wilkinson in the article on the "Early Riser" yesterday is 233, not 223.

—

### WHITECHAPEL.
### A Man Taken Out of Bed at a Lodging House at Bow.

A middle-aged man was arrested early this morning at Gordon-chambers, a lodging-house, near Bow Church, on suspicion, in connection with the East-end murders. His first visit to the lodging-house was yesterday morning, when he went there and asked to be allowed to wash. He had on a pair of white overalls, which he took off and offered to sell for 3d. He washed a stain out of his waistcoat and dried it by the fire, and went away. When he came back at night he was dressed in different clothes. These things seemed so extraordinary that the police were communicated with, and an hour after the man had gone to bed he was arrested. He was lying on the bed fully dressed. Although he had never slept at the lodging-house before, he told the police he had stayed there for 13 nights. He was taken to the Bow-road Station.

—

### The Lady "Jack the Ripper."

There was an extraordinary scene in Bradford Borough Court this morning, when Maria Coroner, mantle hand, was brought up for writing letters under the signature of "Jack the Ripper." A dense crowd fought for admission to the court. The prisoner listened to the proceedings with an amused expression. After an interesting legal argument as to whether she had committed a breach of the peace she was bound over for six months in £20, being told that if she again transgressed she would go to gaol.

A man was to-day arrested near the Tower of London who answers a published description.

418

# Wednesday, 24 October, 1888

## The Times

### THE EAST-END MURDERS.

Yesterday afternoon Mr. Wynne E. Baxter, Coroner for the South-Eastern Division of Middlesex, resumed his adjourned inquiry at the Vestry-hall, Cable-street, St. George's-in-the-East, respecting the death of Elizabeth Stride, who was found murdered in Berner-street, St. George's, on the 30th ult.

Detective-Inspector Reid, H Division, watched the case on behalf of the Criminal Investigation Department.

Detective-Inspector Edmund Reid, recalled, said,—I have examined the books of the Poplar and Stepney Sick Asylum, and find therein the entry of the death of John Thomas William Stride, a carpenter, of Poplar. His death took place on the 24th day of October, 1884. Witness then said that he had found Mrs. Watts, who would give evidence.

Constable Walter Stride stated that he recognized the deceased by the photograph as the person who married his uncle, John Thomas Stride, in 1872 or 1873. His uncle was a carpenter, and the last time witness saw him he was living in the East India Dock-road, Poplar.

Elizabeth Stokes, 5, Charles-street, Tottenham, said,—My husband's name is Joseph Stokes, and he is a brickmaker. My first husband's name was Watts, a wine merchant of Bath. Mrs. Mary Malcolm, of 15, Eagle-street, Red Lion-square, Holborn, is my sister. I have received an anonymous letter from Shepton Mallet, saying my first husband is alive. I want to clear my character. My sister I have not seen for years. She has given me a dreadful character. Her evidence is all false. I have five brothers and sisters.

A juryman.—Perhaps she refers to another sister.

Inspector Reid.—She identified the deceased person as her sister, and said she had a crippled foot. This witness has a crippled foot.

Witness.—This has put me to a dreadful trouble and trial. I have only a poor crippled husband, who is now outside. It is a shame my sister should say what she has said about me, and that the innocent should suffer for the guilty.

The CORONER.—Is Mrs. Malcolm here?

Inspector Reid.—No, Sir.

The CORONER, in summing up, said the jury would probably agree with him that it would be unreasonable to adjourn this inquiry again on the chance of something further being ascertained to elucidate the mysterious case on which they had devoted so much time. The first difficulty which presented itself was the identification of the deceased. That was not an unimportant matter. Their trouble was principally occasioned by Mrs. Malcolm, who, after some hesitation, and after having had two further opportunities of viewing again the body, positively swore that the deceased was her sister—Mrs. Elizabeth Watts, of Bath. It had since been clearly proved that she was mistaken, notwithstanding the visions which were simultaneously vouchsafed at the hour of the death to her and her husband. If her evidence was correct, there were points of resemblance between the deceased and Elizabeth Watts which almost reminded one of the *Comedy of Errors.*

Both had been courted by policemen; they both bore the same Christian name, and were of the same age; both lived with sailors; both at one time kept coffee-houses at Poplar; both were nick-named "Long Liz;" both were said to have had children in charge of their husbands' friends; both were given to drink; both lived in East-end common lodging-houses; both had been charged at the Thames Police-court; both had escaped punishment on the ground that they were subject to epileptic fits, although the friends of both were certain that this was a fraud; both had lost their front teeth, and both had been leading very questionable lives.

Whatever might be the true explanation of this marvellous similarity, it appeared to be pretty satisfactorily proved that the deceased was Elizabeth Stride, and that about the year 1869 she was married to a carpenter named John Thomas Stride.

Unlike the other victims in the series of crimes in this neighbourhood—a district teeming with representatives of all nations—she was not an Englishwoman. She was born in Sweden in the year 1843, but having resided in this country for upwards of 22 years, she could speak English fluently and without much foreign accent.

At one time the deceased and her husband kept a coffee-house in Poplar. At another time she was staying in Devonshire-street, Comm-

# Wednesday, 24 October, 1888

ercial-road, supporting herself, it was said, by sewing and charing. On and off for the last six years she lived in a common lodging-house in the notorious lane called Flower and Dean-street.

She was there known only by the nick-name of "Long Liz," and often told a tale, which might have been apocryphal, of her husband and children having gone down with the Princess Alice.

The deputy of the lodging-house stated that while with her she was a quiet and sober woman, although she used at times to stay out late at night—an offence very venial, he suspected, among those who frequented the establishment.

For the last two years the deceased had been living at a common lodging-house in Dorset-street, Spitalfields, with Michael Kidney, a waterside labourer, belonging to the Army Reserve. But at intervals during that period, amounting altogether to about five months, she left him without any apparent reason, except a desire to be free from the restraint even of that connexion, and to obtain greater opportunity of indulging her drinking habits.

She was last seen alive by Kidney in Commercial-street on the evening of Tuesday, September 25. She was sober, but never returned home that night. She alleged that she had some words with her paramour, but this he denied. The next day she called during his absence, and took away some things, but, with this exception, they did not know what became of her until the following Thursday, when she made her appearance at her old quarters in Flower and Dean-street. Here she remained until Saturday, September 29.

On that day she cleaned the deputy's rooms, and received a small remuneration for her trouble. Between 6 and 7 o'clock on that evening she was in the kitchen wearing the jacket, bonnet, and striped silk neckerchief which were afterwards found on her. She had at least 6d. in her possession, which was possibly spent during the evening. Before leaving she gave a piece of velvet to a friend to take care of until her return, but she said neither where she was going nor when she would return. She had not paid for her lodgings, although she was in a position to do so.

They knew nothing of her movements during the next four or five hours at least—possibly not till the finding of her lifeless body. But three witnesses spoke to having seen a woman that they identified as the deceased with more or less certainty, and at times within an hour and a-quarter of the period when, and at places within 100 yards of the spot where she was ultimately found.

William Marshall, who lived at 64, Berner-street, was standing at his doorway from half-past 11 till midnight. About a quarter to 12 o'clock he saw the deceased talking to a man between Fairclough-street and Boyd-street. There was every demonstration of affection by the man during the ten minutes they stood together, and when last seen, strolling down the road towards Ellen-street, his arms were around her neck.

At 12:30 p.m. the constable on the beat (William Smith) saw the deceased in Berner-street standing on the pavement a few yards from Commercial-street, and he observed she was wearing a flower in her dress.

A quarter of an hour afterwards James Brown, of Fairclough-street, passed the deceased close to the Board school. A man was at her side leaning against the wall, and the deceased was heard to say, "Not to-night, but some other night."

Now, if this evidence was to be relied on, it would appear that the deceased was in the company of a man for upwards of an hour immediately before her death, and that within a quarter of an hour of her being found a corpse she was refusing her companion something in the immediate neighbourhood of where she met her death.

But was this the deceased? And even if it were, was it one and the same man who was seen in her company on three different occasions?

With regard to the identity of the woman, Marshall had the opportunity of watching her for ten minutes while standing talking in the street at a short distance from him, and she afterwards passed close to him. The constable feels certain that the woman he observed was the deceased, and when he afterwards was called to the scene of the crime he at once recognized her and made a statement; while Brown was almost certain that the deceased was the woman to whom his attention was attracted.

It might be thought that the frequency of the occurrence of men and women being seen together under similar circumstances might have led to mistaken identity; but the police stated, and several of the witnesses corroborated the statement, that although many couples are to be seen at night in the Commercial-road, it was exceptional to meet them in Berner-street.

With regard to the man seen, there were many points of similarity, but some of dissimilarity, in the descriptions of the three witnesses; but these discrepancies did not conclusively prove that there was more than one man in the company of the deceased, for every day's experience showed how facts were differently observed and differently described by honest and intelligent witnesses.

Brown, who saw least in consequence of the darkness of the spot at which the two were standing, agreed with Smith that his clothes were dark and that his height was about 5ft. 7in., but he appeared to him to be wearing an overcoat nearly down to his heels; while the description of Marshall accorded with that of Smith in every respect but two. They agreed that he was respectably dressed in a black cut away coat and dark trousers, and that he was of middle age and without whiskers.

On the other hand, they differed with regard to what he was wearing on his head. Smith stated he wore a hard felt deer stalker of dark colour; Marshall that he was wearing a round cap with a small peak, like a sailor's.

They also differed as to whether he had anything in his hand. Marshall stated that he observed nothing. Smith was very precise, and stated that he was carrying a parcel, done up in a newspaper, about 18in. in length and 6in. to 8in. in width.

These differences suggested either that the woman was, during the evening, in the company of more than one man—a not very improbable supposition—or that the witnesses had been mistaken in detail.

If they were correct in assuming that the man seen in the company of deceased by the three was one and the same person it followed that he must have spent much time and trouble to induce her to place herself in his diabolical clutches.

They last saw her alive at the corner of Fairclough-street and Berner-street, saying "Not to-night, but some other night." Within a quarter of an hour her lifeless body was found at a spot only a few yards from where she was last seen alive.

It was late, and there were few people about, but the place to which the two repaired could not have been selected on account of its being quiet or unfrequented. It had only the merit of darkness. It was the passage-way leading into a court in which several families resided. Adjoining the passage and court there was a club of Socialists, who, finished their debate, were singing and making merry.

The deceased and her companion must have seen the lights of the clubroom and the kitchen, and of the printing office. They must have heard the music and dancing, for the windows were open. There were persons in the yard but a short time previous to their arrival. At 40 minutes past 12, one of the members of the club, named Morris Eagle, passed the spot where the deceased drew her last breath, passing through the gateway to the back door, which opened into the yard.

At 1 o'clock the body was found by the manager of the club. He had been out all day, and returned at the time. He was in a two-wheeled barrow drawn by a pony, and as he entered the gateway his pony shied at some object on his right. There was no lamp in the yard, and having just come out of the street it was too dark to see what the object was and he passed on further down the yard. He returned on foot, and on searching found the body of deceased with her throat cut.

If he had not actually disturbed the wretch in the very act, at least he must have been close on his heels; possibly the man was alarmed by the sound of the approaching cart, for the death had only just taken place.

He did not inspect the body himself with any care, but blood was flowing from the throat, even when Spooner reached the spot some few minutes afterwards, and although the bleeding had stopped when Dr. Blackwell's assistant arrived, the whole of her body and the limbs, except her hands, were warm, and even at 16 minutes past 1 a.m. Dr. Blackwell found her face slightly warm, and her chest and legs quite warm.

In this case, as in other similar cases which had occurred in this neighbourhood, no call for assistance was noticed. Although there might have been some noise in the club, it seemed very unlikely that any cry could have been raised without its being heard by some one of those near. The editor of a Socialist paper was quietly at work in a shed down the yard, which was used as a printing office. There were several families in the cottages in the court only a few yards distant, and there were 20 persons in the different rooms of the club.

But if there was no cry, how did the deceased meet her death? The appearance of the injury to her throat was not in itself inconsistent with that of a self-inflicted wound. Both Dr. Phillips and Dr. Blackwell have seen self-inflicted wounds more extensive and severe, but those have not usually involved the carotid artery. Had some sharp instrument been found near the right hand of the deceased this case might have had very much the appearance of a determined suicide. But no such instrument was found, and its absence made suicide an impossibility.

The death was, therefore, one by homicide, and it seemed impossible to imagine circumstances which would fit in with the known facts of the case, and which would reduce the crime to manslaughter.

There were no signs of any struggle; the clothes were neither torn nor disturbed. It was true that there were marks over both shoulders, produced by pressure of two hands, but the position of the body suggested either that she was willingly placed or placed herself where she was found. Only the soles of her boots were visible. She was still holding in her left hand a packet of cachous, and there was a bunch of flowers still pinned to her dress front.

If she had been forcibly placed on the ground, as Dr. Phillips opines, it was difficult to understand how she failed to attract attention, as it was clear from the appearance of the blood on the ground that the throat was not cut until after she was actually on her back. There were no marks of gagging, no bruises on the face, and no trace of any anaesthetic or narcotic in the stomach; while the presence of the cachous in her hand showed that she did not make use of it in self-defence. Possibly the pressure marks may have had a less tragical origin, as Dr. Blackwell says it was difficult to say how recently they were produced.

There was one particular which was not easy to explain. When seen by Dr. Blackwell her right hand was lying on the chest, smeared inside and out with blood. Dr. Phillips was unable to make any suggestion how the hand became soiled. There was no injury to the hand, such as they would expect if it had been raised in self-defence while her throat was being cut. Was it done intentionally by her assassin, or accidentally by those who were early on the spot? The evidence afforded no clue.

Unfortunately the murderer had disappeared without leaving the slightest trace. Even the cachous were wrapped up in unmarked paper, so that there was nothing to show where they were bought.

The cut in the throat might have been effected in such a manner that bloodstains on the hands and clothes of the operator were avoided, while the domestic history of the dead suggested the strong probability that her destroyer was a stranger to her.

There was no one among her associates to whom any suspicion had attached. They had not heard that she had had a quarrel with any one—unless they magnified the fact that she had recently left the man with whom she generally cohabited; but this diversion was of so frequent an occurrence that neither a breach of the peace ensued, nor, so far as they knew, even hard words. There was therefore in the evidence no clue to the murderer and no suggested motive for the murder.

The deceased was not in possession of any valuables. She was only known to have had a few pence in her pocket at the beginning of the evening.

Those who knew her best were unaware of any one likely to injure her. She never accused any one of having threatened her. She never expressed any fear of any one, and, although she had outbursts of drunkenness, she was generally a quiet woman. The ordinary motives of murder—revenge, jealousy, theft, and passion—appeared, therefore, to be absent from this case; while it was clear from the accounts of all who saw her that night, as well as from the post-mortem examination, that she was not otherwise than sober at the time of her death.

In the absence of motive, the age and class of woman selected as victim, and the place and time of the crime, there was a similarity between this case and those mysteries which had recently occurred in that neighbourhood. There had been no skilful mutilation as in the cases of Nichols and Chapman, and no unskilful injuries as in the case in Mitre-square—possibly the work of an imitator; but there had been the same skill exhibited in the way in which the victim had been entrapped, and the injuries inflicted, so as to cause instant death and prevent blood from soiling the operator, and the same daring defiance of immediate detection, which, unfortunately for the peace of the inhabitants and trade of the neighbourhood, had hitherto been only too successful.

He himself was sorry that the time and attention which the jury had given to the case had not produced a result that would be a perceptible relief to the metropolis—the detection of the criminal; but he was sure that all had used their utmost effort to accomplish this object, and while he desired to thank the gentlemen of the jury for their kind assistance, he was bound to acknowledge the great attention which Inspector Reid and the police had given to the case.

He left it to the jury to say, how, when, and by what means the deceased came by her death.

The jury, after a short deliberation, returned a verdict of "Wilful murder against some person or persons unknown."

# Thursday, 25 October, 1888

## The Times
### THE RITTER TRIAL.

On October 16 we published a summary of two letters on the Ritter trial, one from Dr. Josef S. Bloch, member of the Austrian Parliament, and the other, also from Vienna, from a "Lawyer of 20 Years Standing."[284] Dr. Bloch denied, and our other correspondent affirmed the existence among the low-class Jews of Galicia of a superstition such as would account for the mutilation of the body of the woman for whose murder the Ritters were tried, and, it has been suggested, for the mutilations in the case of the Whitechapel murders.

Dr. Adolf Stein, of Vienna, who acted as counsel for Ritter and his wife, now writes strongly corroborating Dr. Bloch's view of the case, and adding that, though the superstitions of thieves were mentioned at the trial, it was never asserted that the superstition was Jewish. Dr. Gotthelf Carl Mayor also writes from Vienna to the same effect, and states that the superstition in question was never proved at the trial as existing among the low-class Jews of Galicia, and that the Ritters were finally acquitted by the Supreme Tribunal on the merits of the case, and not because the only witness against them had died in prison.

(We cannot allow this subject to be discussed any further in our columns.)

~

## Evening News
### THE QUEEN AND THE EAST END MURDERS.

During the three days of the week following the Sunday on which the two murders were committed the following petition to the Queen was freely circulated among the women of the labouring classes of East London through some of the religious agencies and educations centres:

"To our Most Gracious Sovereign Lady Queen Victoria.

"Madam—We, the women of East London, feel horror at the dreadful sings that have been lately committed in our midst and grief because of the shame that has fallen on our neighbourhood.

"By the facts which have come out in the inquests, we have learnt much of the lives of those of our sisters who have lost a firm hold on goodness and who are living sad and degraded lives.

"While each woman of us will do all she can to make men feel with horror the sins of impurity which cause such wicked lives to be led, we would also beg that your Majesty will call on your servants in authority and bid them put the law which already exists in motion to close bad houses within whose walls such wickedness is done and men and women are ruined in body and soul.

"We are, Madam, your loyal and humble servants."

The petition, which received between 4,000 and 5,000 signatures, was presented in due form and the following reply has been received:

"Whitehall.

"Madam—I am directed by the Secretary of State to inform you that he has had the honour to lay before the Queen the petition of women inhabitants of Whitechapel praying that steps may be taken with a view to suppress the moral disorders in that neighbourhood, and that Her Majesty has been graciously pleased to receive the same.

"I am to add that the Secretary of State looks with hope to the influence for good that the petitioners can exercise, each in her own neigh-bourhood, and he is in communication with the Commissioners of Police with a view to taking such action as may be desirable in order to assist the efforts of the petitioners and to mitigate the evils of which they complain.

"I am, Madam, your obedient servant,
"GODFREY LUSHINGTON.
"Mrs. Barnett,
St. Jude's Vicarage,
Commercial-street, E."

# Friday, 26 October, 1888

## The Times
### POLICE

At the Guildhall, yesterday, before Mr. Alderman Renals, Benjamin Graham was charged on remand on his own confession with having committed the Whitechapel murders. The first hearing was reported in *The Times*. It was now shown that the prisoner had no traces of insanity, but it was stated that he drank heavily. The Alderman said he only regretted that he had not the power to send the accused—and all such persons—to prison. It was a mania that should be stopped. As, however, he had not that power, the prisoner must be discharged.

## The Times

An interesting paper on the history and duties of the police of the metropolis is contributed by the Commissioner, SIR CHARLES WARREN, to the November number of *Murray's Magazine*.

SIR CHARLES WARREN has been put on the defensive. He finds himself and the force under his control made the frequent objects of misdirected and misinformed criticism. It is the aim of his paper to clear away some prevailing misconceptions, and to present to the public a correct view of the real facts of the case, and of the essential conditions under which alone the police can be kept level with their work.

These conditions are shown to depend not only on the police, but vary largely, too, on the temper and attitude of the whole body of the citizens. It is not enough for the London police to be under good discipline, and to be ready and capable of discharging their duty as guardians of the public peace. Their efforts must be seconded and supported by the general good will of Londoners. The maintenance of law and order must be felt to be everybody's concern, or at least the concern of all who have not avowedly and permanently declared themselves on the enemy's side. But this is far from being the state of things which SIR CHARLES WARREN discovers.

The London police do not, he declares, receive the outside support which they may justly claim as their due, and without which they are, comparatively speaking, powerless. He assumes, as a matter of course, the exist-ence of a disorderly mob ready at all times to break out into acts of open mischief, and in standing hostility to the police. With these and with their natural allies, the criminal classes, he has, so to say, no quarrel. They act after their kind, and he understands how to deal with them. His complaint is that this whole heterogeneous mass of criminals and semi-criminals and would-be criminals and criminals' friends obtains from time to time a genuine public sympathy which is denied to himself and to his force.

The London temper varies. If there is danger in the air and if a mob outburst seems imminent, the police are the public favourites. But in the quiet intervals between one riot and another, and while there is nothing to disturb the sense of general security, the police are marked down for wide and indiscriminate abuse. Then comes a reaction. The rabble gathers courage, and soon begins to display itself in its old form. Peaceful and law-abiding citizens then take alarm and turn to the police for help against the attack which they apprehend, forgetful meanwhile that they themselves have been doing their best to promote and encourage the movement which they now dread.

It is this oscillation of public feeling, this withholding of steady and regular sympathy from the police, which is the great difficulty in SIR CHARLES WARREN's way. He has no fear of the disorderly classes as long as they are left to themselves, but when he sees persons of influence, ex-Ministers among the rest, taking the side of the rabble, and forward and eager in finding fault with the police, he claims a right to protest against the embarrassment thus created.

The present moment is a critical one. Lord Mayor's Day is near, and it is coming after a quiet time in which the London mob has been kept under due restraint, and Trafalgar-square has not been suffered to be the general rendezvous for mob orators and roughs. SIR CHARLES WARREN scents danger accordingly. There has, he perceives, been something like an organized preparation made for a new outburst and for crippling the power of the Executive, but he sees with pleasure that he is not alone in the discovery and that the citizens of London are beginning to rally to the side of law and order. The strange thing is that they should ever be in a different mind.

The fact is proof of the great need for care and delicacy on the part of the police in the discharge of their appointed work. It is quite right that they should be watched, and that their mistakes and offences and shortcomings should be brought to light and should receive the comments they deserve. But how this is done makes all the difference in the world. There is a right and a wrong way, and when we find endeavours made to hold the police up to public opprobrium, and to bring the whole array of Liberal clap-trap to bear against them, we may with good reason suspect the motives of their critics. They probably mean mischief, or, if not, it can only be because they have no notion whatever of the natural and necessary tendency of their words.

The London police are, as SIR CHARLES

WARREN points out, not a body dangerous in the least to the proper liberty of the subject. Their powers are far less than those enjoyed by the police in other countries. If they exceed their duty in the most minute particular, they are open to rebuke and punishment from the Metropolitan magistrates—an entirely independent body. This separation of the executive and judicial functions is regarded by SIR CHARLES WARREN as the most important step ever taken in the interests of justice. It gives to both orders, to the executive and to the judicial alike, a claim on the public confidence which they could not otherwise possess.

The decisions of the magistrates in police cases are received with a trust which would not be felt if the police force were under their direct control; and the police are well aware that they must not look to the magistrates for the support and countenance in wrong-doing which their own officers would be at least suspected of granting them if it were by them alone that the final verdict could be pronounced.

It is, we fear, inevitable, even so, that some of the multifarious duties cast upon the London police should bring them into a disfavour not wholly undeserved. It is a part of their business to maintain public decency in the streets, and in nothing has their conduct been more open to unfavourable comment than in this. They have made mistakes in some cases.

In every case public sentiment is apt to be with the weaker, with the woman rather than with the policeman. The clamorous brawler who has been disturbing the peace overnight, who has been molesting passers-by, and has been dragged off after a most determined resistance, appears the next morning in quite a different character in court, a modest, down-cast personage, strong only in the weakness of her sex, more like a victim than an offender, and not in the least to be recognized for what she was twelve hours before and will be twelve hours

afterwards if she escapes with a bare reprimand.

But there have been instances, too, in which real mistakes have been made, deplorable on every account, for the misery which they cause to the victim, and for the opportunity which they give to those in search of it for raising a general clamour against the police and discrediting the whole body for the fault of a single member. If caution must be a watchword of the police at all times and in all duties, it is more than ever needful in the discharge of a duty more delicate than any other, and more likely to expose them to hostile remark, with or without cause.

On the constitution and method of the detective force SIR CHARLES WARREN does not tell us much. It is a secret order, told off for special and secret work, on the particulars of which the criminal classes and their friends and abettors would very gladly be informed. But it is no part of SIR CHARLES WARREN's purpose to gratify them. He tells us what he can tell with safety, and he points with satisfaction to results as the best proof possible that the detective service is well organized and efficient.

He has a curious argument in support of his laudatory words. With a perfect detective system there would be no murders but those of so exceptional a character as to elude inquiry. We may expect, therefore, with a detective system so good as our own, that there will be a preponderance of undetected murders, and this the more certainly in the degree in which the proportion of murders per thousand of population approaches a *minimum*.

Detectives are not, SIR CHARLES WARREN says, as well known to the criminal classes as they are thought to be. He quotes a remark of his own—"You know all you know, but you do not know those you do not know." The public, he adds, do not know the detectives as a body, and they often assume that they are not present when they are actually standing at their side.

# Wednesday, 31 October, 1888

## Evening News
### THE EAST END MURDERS.
### SUPPOSED REAPPEARANCE OF
### THE ASSASSIN.

Last night, Mr. Matthew Packer, who keeps a fruitshop next to the gateway where the Berner-street murder was committed, stated that this last night or two he has felt greatly alarmed owing to his having seen a man exactly like the one who bought the grapes off him for the unfortunate murdered woman, Elizabeth Stride, a short time before the murder was committed. He alleges that he had often seen the man before the murder, as well as the woman who was murdered in Berner-street, but he had not seen any one resembling the man since the murder till he saw him again last Saturday night.

He was then standing with his fruit stall in the Commercial-road when he caught sight of him staring him full in the face. He kept calm and collected for a little time, hoping that a police-man would come by, but not one came. After passing and repassing him several times, the man then came behind him in the horse road looking in a very evil and menacing manner at him. He was so terrified that he left his stall and ran to a shoeblack that was near, and, pointing to the man, asked him to keep his eye on him and watch him.

His great fear was that the fellow was going to stab him to prevent him from identifying him, should anything be brought against him, or his arrest take place. No sooner, however, had he called the shoeblack's attention to him, than he ran away as fast as he could and succeeded in getting on a passing tram. He would have followed the tram had he been able to run, or if he could have left his stall, but he could not has he had several pounds of fruit on it. He has little doubt about him being the man, as he knew him again in a moment.

As a coincidence it may be remarked that there have again been several complaints from women who have been accosted by a well-dressed man, supposed to answer the description of the assassin, during the last several nights. One woman so accosted blew a whistle and in a very short time about twenty policemen were on the scene, and the man was taken to Leman-street police-station, but he was liberated on Saturday morning, as he succeeded in giving a satisfactory account of himself.

—

### THREATS OF MORE MURDERS.

By the last post last night a letter, purporting to come from the assassin, was received by the police at the Poplar Police Station, in which the writer said he was going to commit three more murders. The following is said to be the wording:

"Oct. 30, 1888.—Dear Boss—I am going to commit three more murders, two women and a child, and I shall take their hearts this time.—Yours truly, (signed) JACK THE RIPPER."

The letter was enclosed in an envelope which, in addition to the Poplar post-mark, also bore the Ealing post-mark, and was directed to the sergeant.

Though the police do not attach serious importance to it, a copy was sent to the Commissioner of Police. The information, with accompanying instructions, were at once tele-graphed to the different stations, ordering every possible vigilance to be used in case of an attempted repetition of the crimes. It is stated that an endeavour will be made at Ealing to discover the sender, and already various inquiries are going on to-day.

—

### "A LUCID INTERVAL."

The Central News is informed that Dr. Forbes Winslow and other leading authorities on mental disorders are still of opinion that the murders in Whitechapel were committed by a homicidal lunatic, notwithstanding that an opinion to the contrary has been expressed by one lunacy specialist whose views were sought by the police authorities. Dr. Forbes Winslow believes that the murderer has lately been in a "lucid interval." In that condition he would be comparatively rational, and also forgetful of what he had done. As soon as this passes off he will resume his terrible work.

—

### WHAT MATTHEW PACKER SAYS.

A representative of *The Evening News* this morning had an interview with Mr. Matthew Packer, at 44, Berner-street, with reference to the rumour that the supposed Whitechapel assassin had been seen by him again on Saturday last. Packer made the following statement:

"Between seven and eight o'clock, on Saturday evening last, I was standing with my

# Wednesday, 31 October, 1888

barrow at the corner of Greenfield-street, Commercial-road, when I saw a man pass by on the opposite side of Greenfield-street, near the watchmaker's shop. I recognized him in a minute as the man I had seen outside my shop on the night when Elizabeth Stride was murdered in Berner-street. It was the man who bought the grapes and gave them to the woman that was afterwards found murdered in the yard. I shall never forget his face, and should know him again amongst a thousand men."

"I can tell you what it was. I was pretty night knocked over with fright. It gave me such a turn as I have never had in my life. I was too frightened and staggered to know what I was about, and I saw in a minute that the man knew me as well. He looked hard at me as he passed, and then turned round and passed again, with a most vicious look on his face, that made me think I should not have liked to have been with him in any quiet corner. I'm sure he'd have killed me. He walked by four times altogether, and I thought he wanted to get close to me, so I kept moving round to the north side of my barrow. I then called to a young chap that I knew who was standing at the corner of the street, and asked him to keep an eye on the man, as I was afraid he meant mischief. There were no policemen in sight, and I was afraid to lose sight of the man. I sent the young chap for a policeman, and the man seeing there was something up jumped into a tram that was going to Blackwall.

# Thursday, 1 November, 1888

## The Star
**FIFTH EDITION.**
**THE MURDERS.**

### A Policeman Finds Two Knives in Kensington—One Bloodstained.

Plain-clothes officers have recently been watching certain houses in Kensington. A discovery they made while engaged in making investigations has just leaked out. On Sunday night, 21 Oct., the policeman on duty in Harrington-gardens observed something bright upon the ground in the front garden of one of the houses. Entering to satisfy himself, he discovered a case containing a couple of

**HUGE "GHOORKA" KNIVES,**

which had been deposited near some shrubs. One of the knives was much stained with blood, but the other had evidently not been used. The case also had bloodstains upon it. The knives are of the best make and quality, and as sharp as a razor, but the manufacturer's name does not appear. Opinions differ as to whether they are known as the "kreese"[285] or Malay knife, or the "Ghoorka"[286] knife called "korokee."[287] The shape of the blade favours the latter.

A Paddington doctor has expressed the opinion that

**THE BLOOD STAINS**

are a month or two months old.

Whether this is in any way connected with the East-end remains to be seen, but the police are said to be following up a clue to a suspected clerical-looking gentleman, of whom strange things are said. The popular theory is that a murder was contemplated in Harrington-gardens, but the would-be assassin was disturbed, and flung the knives away.

---

[285] Kris.
[286] Gurkha.
[287] Kukri.

# Monday, 5 November, 1888

## Evening News
### THE EAST END MURDERS.
### MORE CORRESPONDENCE FROM "JACK THE RIPPER."

At a late hour on Saturday night the following notice was read out to the police, as printed in the formations at Whitechapel:

"To-day a piece of paper was picked up in Spitalfields on which was written:

Dear Bos—

In spite of all your Police precautions, and in spite of all the efforts of the Vigilance committee, I committed another murder last night, and have hid the body away in Osborne-street, headless, legless, armless, and naked.—

Yours truly, JACK THE RIPPER."

Though the matter is looked upon as a hoax, all constables were ordered to make every inquiry in the neighbourhood to see if anything had been found or whether any one was missing. They were, however, specially enjoined to use their utmost endeavours to try and trace the author of the writing. Special instructions were also ordered to be given to all the auxiliary detectives and officers who went on duty at midnight.

## The Star

### WHITECHAPEL.
### ANOTHER CRIME BY THE MURDER-MANIAC.
### MORE REVOLTING THAN EVER.
### THIS DEMONIACAL DEED DONE IN A HOUSE.

### A Woman is Found in a House in Dorset-street Decapitated and with Her Body Mutilated in a Manner that Passes Description.

At a quarter to eleven this morning a woman was found murdered, with her head nearly cut off, in a room in a house in McCarthy's-court, a turning out of Dorset-street—the street in which the lodging-house is situated where the Hanbury-street victim slept occasionally. Whitechapel is seething with excitement. Cordons of police are drawn up at all the entrances to Dorset-street, and no one is allowed to enter it. A *Star* man went to Commercial-street Police station to learn some further particulars, but was politely but firmly referred to Scotland-yard.

**THE SCENE OF THE LATEST WORK**

of the fiend—from the daring manner in which the murder has been committed, there seems little doubt that the murderer is the man who has given Whitechapel a regular succession of horrors—is a tiny little court with an entrance only permitting one to walk through at a time. The narrow entry terminates in a diminutive square, formed by three sides of little half-whitewashed houses. It was in the room of one of these that the foul deed was done. From the police, who, in uniform and plain clothes, simply swarm all over the place, nothing whatever can be gleaned. But from the startled inhabitants of the lodging-houses in Dorset-street a *Star* man got a few details. The victim is a woman who went by

**THE NAME OF "MARY JANE"**

and she lived in the room in which she has been murdered, with a man and her little son—about 10 or 11 years old. The story of the crime current among the neighbours is that this morning —what time cannot at present be precisely ascertained, but at any rate after daylight, she took a man home to her own room, presumably for an immoral purpose. At a quarter to eleven the landlady of the house went up for the rent, and found her murdered.

Details in respect of the mutilation of the body reveal a

**MORE HORRIBLE**

state of things than anything which has yet been recorded in this series of crimes. The thick flesh has been literally stripped from the thighs of the victim, and placed upon the table in the room. The woman's breasts have also been roughly sliced off. The fleshy parts of the cheeks have also been hacked away, and the corpse presents a spectacle more hideous than anything which has presented itself to even the oldest and most experienced of the police officers who are engaged in the case. Everyone's feelings are revolted, and it is absolute truth to say that the horrors revealed by the case are simply inexpressible.

Another of our reporters writes:—The murder was not discovered till about half past eleven. The excitement arose in the neighbourhood the instant the report was spread. All kinds of reports are flying as to the nature of the crime. It is certain that the woman's head was nearly severed from the body, and others state that the body has been disembowelled. The police, however, refuse to supply information of any kind to certain of the reporters, and guard the entrance to the court where the crime was committed as carefully as if the murderer were still confined within its precincts.

The court itself, which our reporter and artist got an opportunity of viewing from the roof, is one of those miserable little alleys where none but those compelled to live in its stifling atmosphere ever enter. The house where the woman spent her last night is in keeping with its surroundings. The woman appears to have

**LIVED IN THE HOUSE**

where she slept last night with her mother and a man who passed as her husband. She had one child.

A woman named Mrs. Hewitt, living at 25, Dorset-street, supplied our reporter with some information. She said she was up till twelve o'clock last night. She heard nothing. Her husband was up at four o'clock each morning, and he heard nothing of a disturbing character. At eleven o'clock this morning she had occasion to look out of the window which affords a view of the court; but she could see nothing. At about half-past eleven she heard the shouts of a mob,

# Friday, 9 November, 1888

and she then discovered that a horrible murder—it makes me shiver to think of it, she said—had been committed. She also stated that a man—a drover—called on her some time ago. He asked her if a summons came in

## THE NAME OF LAWRENCE

to accept it. This man Lawrence, she says, she believes lived with the dead woman. He was off and on in London, sometimes being absent for five or six weeks.

—

## WARREN SNUBBED.
### His Veracious Reply to Matthews' Mild Remonstrance.

Mr. Atherley Jones asked the Home Secretary in the House of Commons yesterday whether his attention had been called to an article by the Chief Commissioner of Metropolitan Police, published in *Murray's Magazine* of this month, in which the Commissioner discusses the management and discipline of the police under his control, and made disparaging remarks upon members of the late Government; and whether it was in accordance with the usage and discipline of the Civil Service that a salaried official should be permitted to publicly discuss matters relating to his department and disparage the conduct of ex-Ministers of the Crown; and, if not, whether he had seen fit to take any action in the matter.

Mr. Matthews replied: My attention has been called to the article in question. I am assured by the Commissioner that his statements are made without reference to party, and he points out that one of the passages referred to by the hon. member applies on the face of it to successive Governments, and not to any one Government in particular. With regard to the usages of the Civil Service as to the public discussion by salaried officials of matters which touch upon politics, I cannot do better than refer the hon. member to an answer given by the First Lord of the Treasury in this House on 15 March of this year, where he will find the subject fully dealt with. In 1879 the then Home Secretary issued a rule by which officers attached to the department were precluded from publishing works relating to the department without permission, and a copy was sent to the then Commissioner of Police. The present Commissioner, however, informs me that he was not aware of the existence of this rule. I

have accordingly drawn his attention to it, and have requested him to comply with it in future.

Below is the passage referred to which Sir Charles Warren says was made "without reference to party":—

"It is to be deplored that successive Governments have not had the courage to make a stand against the more noisy section of the people representing a small minority, and have given way before tumultuous proceedings which have exercised a terrorism over peaceful and law-abiding citizens, and it is still more to be regretted that ex-Ministers, while in opposition, have not hesitated to embarrass those in power by smiling on the insurgent mob."

The London correspondent of the *Manchester Guardian* says there can be no question as to the very strong feelings entertained among a number of Conservative members with regard to Sir Charles Warren's administration at Scotland-yard. If these members obtain no earlier opportunity, they will take care to express their views in the debate which will be raised upon the Estimates. It is now improbable that there will be any formal meeting upon the subject, but informal communications have passed between the London Liberal members, with the result that they have agreed to take a full night for the discussion of the conduct of the London police.

The London correspondent of the *Manchester Courier* (Tory) says:—There is to be a very animated discussion on the Police Vote, and Sir Charles Warren, is, I believe, to be vigorously attacked. I find that even on the Conservative side there is some disposition to question the wisdom of Sir Charles Warren's administration in some of its details; but the Government will resist the attack which is made on the Chief Commissioner of Police.

~

## The Times
### ANOTHER WHITECHAPEL MURDER.

During the early hours of yesterday morning another murder of a most revolting and fiendish character took place in Spitalfields. This is the seventh which has occurred in this immediate neighbourhood, and the character of the mutilations leaves very little doubt that the murderer in this instance is the same person who has committed the previous ones, with which the public are fully acquainted.

The scene of this last crime is at No 26 Dorset-street, Spitalfields, which is about 200 yards distant from 35 Hanbury-street, where the unfortunate woman, Mary Ann Nicholls, was so foully murdered. Although the victim, whose name is Mary Ann (or Mary Jane) Kelly, resides at the above number, the entrance to the room she occupied is up a narrow court, in which are some half-a-dozen houses, and which is known as Miller's Court; it is entirely separated from the other portion of the house, and has an entrance leading into the court. The room is known by the title of No 13.

The house is rented by John M'Carthy, who keeps a small general shop at No 27 Dorset-street, and the whole of the rooms are let out to tenants of a very poor class. As an instance of the poverty of the neighbourhood, it may be mentioned that nearly the whole of the houses in this street are common lodging-houses, and the one opposite where the murder was enacted has accommodation for some 300 men, and is fully occupied every night.

About 12 months ago Kelly, who was about 24 years of age, and who was considered a good-looking woman, of fair and fresh complexion, came to Mr M'Carthy, with a man named Joseph Kelly, who she stated was her husband, and who was a porter employed at Spitalfields Market. They rented a room on the ground floor, the same in which the poor woman was murdered, at a rental of 4s a week. It had been noticed that the deceased woman was somewhat addicted to drink, but Mr M'Carthy denied having any knowledge that she had been leading a loose or immoral life. That this was so, however, there can be no doubt, for about a fortnight ago she had a quarrel with Kelly, and after blows had been exchanged, the man left the house, or rather room, and did not return. It has since been ascertained that he went to live at Buller's common lodging-house in Bishopsgate-street. Since then the woman has supported herself as best as she could, and the police have ascertained that she has been walking the streets.

None of those living at the court or at 26 Dorset-street, saw anything of the unfortunate creature after about 8 o'clock on Thursday evening, but she was seen in Commercial-street, shortly before the closing of the public house, and then had the appearance of being the worse for drink. About 1 o'clock yesterday morning a person living in the court opposite to the room occupied by the woman heard her singing the song "Sweet Violets," but this person is unable to say whether any one else was with her at that time. Nothing more was seen or heard of her until her dead body was found.

At a quarter to 11 yesterday morning, as the woman was 35s in arrears with her rent, Mr M'Carthy said to a man employed by him in his shop, John Bowyer, "Go to No 13 (meaning the room occupied by Kelly) and try and get some rent." Bowyer did as he was directed, and on knocking at the door was unable to obtain an answer. He then turned the handle of the door, and found it was locked. On looking through the keyhole he found the key was missing. The left-hand side of the room faced the court, and in it were two large windows. Bowyer, knowing that when the man Kelly and the dead woman had their quarrel a pane of glass in one of the windows was broken, went round the side in question. He put his hand through the aperture and pulled aside the muslin curtain which covered it. On his looking into the room a shocking sight presented itself. He could see the woman lying on the bed entirely naked, covered with blood and apparently dead.

Without waiting to make a closer examination he ran to his employer and told him he believed the woman Kelly had been murdered. M'Carthy at once went and looked through the broken window, and, satisfying himself that something was wrong, despatched Bowyer to the Commercial-street Police-station, at the same time enjoining him not to tell any of the neighbours what he had discovered.

Inspector Back, H Division, who was in charge of the station at the time, accompanied

434

# Saturday, 10 November, 1888

Bowyer back, and on finding that a murder had been committed at once sent for assistance. Dr Phillips, the divisional surgeon of police, and Superintendent Arnold were also sent for. During this time the door had not been touched. On the arrival of the Superintendent Arnold he caused a telegram to be sent direct to Sir Charles Warren, informing him what had happened.

Mr Arnold, having satisfied himself that the woman was dead, ordered one of the windows to be entirely removed. A horrible and sickening sight then presented itself. The poor woman lay on her back on the bed, entirely naked. Her throat was cut from ear to ear, right down to the spinal column. The ears and nose had been cut clean off. The breasts had also been cleanly cut off and placed on a table which was by the side of the bed. The stomach and abdomen had been ripped open, while the face was slashed about, so that the features of the poor creature were beyond all recognition. The kidneys and heart had also been removed from the body, and placed on the table by the side of the breasts. The liver had likewise been removed, and laid on the right thigh The lower portion of the body and the uterus had been cut out, and these appeared to be missing. The thighs had been cut. A more horrible or sickening sight could not be imagined. The clothes of the woman were lying by the side of the bed, as though they had been taken off and laid down in the ordinary manner.

While this examination was being made a photographer, who, in the meantime, had been sent for, arrived and took photographs of the body, the organs, the room, and its contents.

Superintendent Arnold then had the door of the room forced. It was a very poorly furnished apartment, about 12 ft. square, there being only an old bedstead, two old tables and a chair in it. The bedclothes had been turned down, and this was probably done by the murderer after he had cut his victim's throat. There was no appearance of a struggle having taken place, and, although a careful search of the room was made, no knife or instrument of any kind was found.

Dr Phillips, on his arrival, carefully examined the body of the dead woman, and later on made a second examination in company with Dr Bond, from Westminster, Dr Gordon Brown, from the City, Dr Duke from Spitalfields, and Dr Phillip's assistant. Mr Anderson, the new Commissioner of Police, Detective-Inspectors Reid and Abberline (Scotland Yard), Chief Inspector West, H Division, and other officers were quickly on the spot. After the examination of the body it was placed in a shell, which was put into a van and conveyed to the Shoreditch mortuary to await an inquest.

From enquiries made among person living in the houses adjoining the court, and also those residing in rooms in No 26 it appears clear that no noise of any kind was heard. No suspicious or strange-looking man was seen to enter or leave the murdered woman's room, and up to the present time the occurrence is enveloped in as much mystery as were the previous murders. The man Kelly was quickly found, and his statement ascertained to be correct.

After the examination the windows were boarded up, and the door padlocked by direction of the police, who have considerable difficulty in keeping the street clear of persons.

Dr M'Donald, coroner in whose district the murder has happened has fixed Monday morning for the opening of the inquest, which will be held at Shoreditch Town-hall.

It was reported that bloodhounds would be laid on to endeavour to trace the murderer, but for some reason this project was not carried out, and, of course, after the streets had became thronged with people that would have had no practical result. The street being principally composed of common lodging houses, persons are walking along it during all hours of the night, so that little notice is taken of any ordinarily attired men, the murderer, therefore, had a good chance of getting away unobserved.

With regard to Kelly's movements just before the murder, a report says that she was seen as usual in the neighbourhood about 10 o'clock on Thursday evening in company with a man of whom, however, no description can be obtained. She was last seen, as far as can be ascertained, in Commercial-street about half-past 11. She was then alone, and was probably making her way home. It is supposed that she met the murderer in Commercial-street, and he probably induced her to take him home without indulging in more drink. At any rate, nothing more was seen of the couple in the neighbouring public-houses, nor in the beerhouse at the corner of Dorset-street.

The pair reached Millers-court about midnight, but they were not seen to enter the house.

# Saturday, 10 November, 1888

The street door was closed, but the woman had a latchkey, and, as she must have been fairly sober, she and her companion would have been able to enter the house and enter the woman's room without making a noise. A light was seen shining through the window of the room for some time after the couple must have entered it, and one person asserts positively that the woman was heard singing the refrain of a popular song as late as 1 o'clock yesterday morning, but here again there is a conflict of testimony which the police are now engaged in endeavouring to reconcile.

The same reports, describing the removal of the mutilated body, says at 10 minutes to 4 o'clock a one-horse carrier's cart, with the ordinary tarpaulin cover was driven into Dorset-street, and halted opposite Millers-court. From the cart was taken a long shell or coffin, dirty and scratched with constant use. This was taken into the death chamber, and there the remains were temporarily coffined.

The news that the body was about to be removed caused a great rush of people from the courts running out of Dorset-street, and there was a determined effort to break the police cordon at the Commercial-street end. The crowd, which pressed round the van, was of the humblest class, but the demeanour of the poor people was all that could be described. Ragged caps were doffed and slatternly-looking women shed tears as the shell, covered with a ragged-looking cloth, was placed in the van. The remains were taken to the Shoreditch Mortuary, where they will remain until they have been viewed by the coroner's jury.

Mr John M'Carthy, the owner of the houses in Millers-court, who keeps a chandler's shop in Dorset-street, has made the following statement as to the murdered woman:—

"The victim of this terrible murder was about 23 or 24 years of age, and lived with a coal porter named Kelly, passing as his wife. They, however, quarrelled sometime back and separated. A woman named Harvey slept with her several nights since Kelly separated from her, but she was not with her last night.

The deceased's Christian name was Mary Jane, and since her murder I have discovered that she walked the streets in the neighbourhood of Aldgate. Her habits were irregular, and she often came home at night the worse for drink.

Her mother lives in Ireland, but in what county I do not know. Deceased used to receive letters from her occasionally.

The unfortunate woman had not paid her rent for several weeks; in fact she owed 30s altogether, so this morning I sent my man to ask if she could pay the money. He knocked at the door, but received no answer. Thinking this very strange he looked in at the window, and to his horror he saw the body of Kelly lying on the bed covered with blood. He immediately came back to me, and told me what he had seen.

I was, of course, as horrified as he was, and I went with him to the house and looked in at the window. The sight I saw was more ghastly even than I had prepared myself for. On the bed lay the body as my man had told me, while the table was covered with what seemed to me to be lumps of flesh. I said to my main "Go at once to the police-station and fetch some one here."

He went off at once and brought back Inspector Back who looked through the window as we had done. He then despatched a telegram to Superintendent Arnold, but before Superintendent Arnold arrived, Inspector Abberline came and gave orders that no one should be allowed to enter or leave the court. The Inspector waited a little while and then sent a telegram to Sir Charles Warren to bring the bloodhounds, so as to trace the murderer if possible.

So soon as Superintendent Arnold arrived he gave instructions for the door to be burst open. I at once forced the door with a pickaxe, and we entered the room. The sight we saw I cannot drive away from my mind. It looked more like the work of a devil than of a man.

The poor woman's body was lying on the bed, undressed. She had been completely disembowelled, and her entrails has been taken out and placed on the table. It was those that I had seen when I looked through the window and took to be lumps of flesh. The woman's nose had been cut off, and her face gashed beyond recognition. Both her breasts too had been cut clean away and placed by the side of her liver and other entrails on the table. I had heard a great deal about the Whitechapel murders, but I declare to God I had never expected to see such a sight as this. The body was, of course, covered with blood, and so was the bed. The whole scene is more than I can describe. I hope I may never see such a sight again.

It is most extraordinary that nothing should have been heard by the neighbours, as there are people passing backwards and forwards at all hours of the night, but no one heard so much as a scream. One woman heard Kelly singing "Sweet Violets"[288] at 1 o'clock this morning. So up to that time, at all events, she was alive and well. So far as I can ascertain no one saw her take a man into the house with her last night."

A correspondent who last night saw the room in which the murder was committed, says it was a tenement by itself, having formerly been the back parlour of No 26, Dorset-street. A partition had been erected, cutting it off from the house, and the entrance door opened into Miller's-court. The two windows also faced the court, and, as the body could be seen from the court yesterday morning, it is evident that, unless the murderer perpetrated his crime with the light turned out, any person passing by could have witnessed the deed. The lock of the door was a spring one, and the murderer apparently took the key away with him when he left, as it cannot be found.

The more the facts are investigated, the more

_____

[288] *Sweet Violets* from **Fritz Among the Gypsies**, 1882. Composed and sung by J.K. Emmet. (Emmet)
1. Sweet violets,
Sweeter than all the roses;
Ladened with fragrance.
Sparkling like the dew.
Sweet violets...
From mossy dell and rivulet, Zillah, darling one,
I plucked them and brought them to you...

CHORUS: Oh, Zillah, stay,
Go not away...
Violets are blooming,
Love, for you alone; Oh!
Sweet violets,
Sweeter than all the roses, Zillah,darling one,
I plucked them and bro't them to you...
(Yodel)
La, la, la, la, la, la, la, la, la, la, la, la, la, la, la, la, la,

2. Sweet violets,
Resting in Beauty's bower,
Crouched all un-noticed,
I did pluck that flower;
Sweet violets...
Still looking up to heaven; Zillah, darling one,
I plucked them , my darling for you...

apparent becomes the cool daring of the murderer. There are six houses in the court besides the tenement occupied by the deceased. The door of Kelly's room is just on the right-hand side on entering from the street, and other houses—three on either side—are higher up the passage.

The young woman Harvey, who had slept with the deceased on several occasions has made a statement to the effect that she had been on good terms with the deceased, whose education was much superior to that of most persons in her position in life. Harvey, however, took a room in New-court, off the same street, but remained friendly with the unfortunate woman, who visited her in New-court on Thursday night. After drinking together they parted at half past 7 o'clock, Kelly going off in the direction of Leman-street which she was in the habit of frequenting. She was perfectly sober at the time. Harvey never saw her alive afterwards.

Joseph Barnett (called in other reports Kelly), an Irishman, at present residing in a common lodging-house in New-street, Bishops-gate, informed a reporter last evening that he had occupied his present lodgings since Tuesday week. Previously to that he had lived in Miller's-court, Dorset-street for eight or nine months with the murdered woman Mary Jane Kelly. They were very happy and comfortable together until another woman came to sleep in the room, to which he strongly objected. Finally, after the woman had been there two or three nights he quarrelled with the woman whom he called his wife and left her. The next day, however, he returned and gave Kelly money. He called several other days and gave her money when he had it. On Thursday night he visited her between half past 7 and 8 and told her he was sorry he had no money to give her. He saw nothing more of her. She used occasionally to go to the Elephant and Castle district to visit a friend who was in the same position as herself.

Another account gives the following details: Kelly had a little boy, aged about 6 or 7 years living with her, and latterly she had been in narrow straits, so much so that she is reported to have stated to a companion that she would make away with herself, as she could not bear to see her boy starving.

There are conflicting statements as to when

the woman was last seen alive, but that upon which most reliance appears to be placed is that of a young woman, an associate of the deceased, who states that at about half-past 10 o'clock on Thursday night she met the murdered woman at the corner of Dorset-street, who said to her that she had no money and, if she could not get any, would never go out any more but would do away with herself. Soon afterwards they parted, and a man, who is described as respectably dressed, came up, and spoke to the murdered woman Kelly and offered her some money. The man then accompanied the woman to her lodgings, which are on the second floor, and the little boy was removed from the room and taken to a neighbour's house. Nothing more was seen of the woman until yesterday morning, when it is stated that the little boy was sent back into the house, and the report goes, he was sent out subsequently on an errand by the man who was in the house with his mother. There is no direct confirmation of this statement. A tailor named Lewis says he saw Kelly come out about 8 o'clock yesterday morning and go back.

Another statement is to the effect that Kelly was seen in a public-house known as the Ringers at the corner of Dorset-street and Commercial-street, about 10 o'clock yesterday morning, and that she met there her lover, Barnet and had a glass of beer with him. This statement is also not substantiated.

A somewhat important fact has been pointed out, which puts a fresh complexion on the theory of the murders. It appears that cattle-boats bringing in live freight to London are in the habit of coming into the Thames on Thursdays or Fridays, and leave for the continent on Sundays or Mondays. It has already been a matter of comment that the recent revolting crimes have been committed at the week's end, and an opinion has been formed among some of the detectives that the murderer is a drover or butcher employed on one of these boats—of which there are many—and that he periodically appears and disappears with one of the steamers. This theory is held to be of much importance by those engaged in this investigation, who believe that the murderer does not reside either in the locality or even in the country at all. It is thought that he may be either a person employed upon one of these boats or one who is allowed to travel by them, and

inquiries have been directed to follow up the theory. It is pointed out that at the inquests on the previous victims the coroners have expressed the opinion that the knowledge of anatomy possessed by a butcher would have been sufficient to enable him to find and cut out the parts of the body which in several cases were abstracted.

The Whitechapel Vigilance Committee who have recently relaxed their efforts to find the murderer, have called a meeting for Tuesday evening next, at the Paul's Head Tavern, Crispin-street, Spitalfields, to consider what steps they can take to assist the police.

A Mrs Paumier, a young woman who sells roasted chestnuts at the corner of Widegate-street, a narrow thoroughfare about two minutes' walk from the scene of the murder, told a reporter yesterday afternoon a story which appears to afford a clue to the murderer. She said that about 12 o'clock that morning a man dressed like a gentleman came up to her and said, "I suppose you have heard about the murder in Dorset-street?" She replied that she had, whereupon the man grinned and said, "I know more about it than you." He then stared into her face and went down Sandy's-row, another narrow thoroughfare which cuts across Widegate-street. Whence he had got some way off, however, he vanished. Mrs Paumier said the man had a black moustache, was about 5ft 6in, high, and wore a black silk hat, a black coat, and speckled trousers. He also carried a black shiny bag about a foot in depth and a foot and a half in length. Mrs Paumier stated further that the same man accosted three young women, whom she knew, on Thursday night, and they chaffed him and asked him what he had in the bag, and he replied, "Something that the ladies don't like."

One of the three young women she named, Sarah Roney, a girl about 20 years of age, states that she was with two other girls on Thursday night in Brushfield-street which is near Dorset-street, when a man wearing a tall hat and a black coat, and carrying a black bag, came up to her and said, "Will you come with me?" She told him that she would not, and asked him what he had in the bag, and he said, "Something the ladies don't like." He then walked away.

A further report received late last night says:—"Not the slightest doubt appears to be

# Saturday, 10 November, 1888

entertained in official headquarters that this fresh crime is by the same hand which committed the others. There is also, it is to be noted, a striking similarity of the month in which the crime has been committed, for while two of the most atrocious of the other murders in the same district were committed on the 7th of the month of September and August, this was committed on the 8th—approximately the same period in the month. This would seem to indicate that the murderer was absent from the scene of these horrors for fixed periods, and that his return was always about the same time. The late storms might account for the crime on this occasion being a day later, the suggestion, of course, being that the murderer journeys across the sea on some of the short passages.

"Last night nothing further was known at Scotland-yard. In fact, all the enquiries centre in the east of London, whither have been sent some of the keenest investigators of the country. The murders, so cunningly continued, are carried out with a completeness which altogether baffles investigators. Not a trace is left of the murderer, and there is no purpose in the crime to afford the slightest clue, such as would be afforded in other crimes almost without exception. All that the police can hope is that some accidental circumstance will lead to a trace which may be followed to a successful conclusion."

The latest account states upon what professes to be indisputable authority that no portion of the woman's body was taken away by the murderer. As already stated, the *post-mortem* examination was of the most exhaustive character, and surgeons did not quit their work until every organ had been accounted for and placed as closely as possible in its natural position.

A man's pilot coat has been found in the murdered woman's room, but whether it belonged to one of her paramours or to the murderer has not been ascertained.

Late yesterday evening a man was arrested near Dorset-street on suspicion of being concerned in the murder. He was taken to Commercial-street police-station, followed by a howling mob, and is still detained there.

Another man, respectably dressed, wearing a slouch hat and carrying a black bag was arrested and taken to Leman-street station. The bag was examined, but its contents were perfectly harmless, and the man was at once released.

—

Another murder, if possible of a more hideous character than the atrocities already committed in Whitechapel, has taken place in the same neighbourhood. No revolting circumstance is wanting to the crime, which has manifestly been committed by one who took a demoniac pleasure in his ghastly work. The victim is again a woman, and of the same class as that to which the miserable creatures foully murdered last August and September belonged, and her body has been mutilated even more hideously than those of the former victims. It would be impossible to describe literally the scene before those who discovered yesterday morning her remains in Dorset-street. No imagination could conceive the effects of the malign and depraved fury of the murderer.

A man, going yesterday forenoon to 26, Dorset-street, Spitalfields, tenanted by MARY ANN KELLY, for arrears of rent, found the door locked. Looking through a broken window, he saw her mutilated remains on the bed. Examination showed that a murder had recently been committed with every circumstance of atrocity. All had apparently been done with frightful celerity and completeness; and the murderer seems to have vanished, leaving no trace of his identity, no clue to his whereabouts, with even greater mystery hanging over his last deed than that which shrouds the former Whitechapel murders.

KELLY was seen, it appears, about 11 o'clock on Thursday night with a man of whom nothing definite is known. It is also stated that she was seen yesterday morning. But as to this there is some conflict of evidence, and it is unfortunate that little can be told of her until she was found, about 11 o'clock in the forenoon yesterday, dead and frightfully mutilated. There is the best possible desire to assist the police, and no pains will be spared to discover the murderer. But we must not be surprised if justice is again baffled.

The maniac, if such the murderer be, combines cunning with his madness; and he had time to make his escape. If he was seen in the company of his victim, the description of him is very vague and uncertain, and the surroundings of Dorset-street are such as to make it easy for him to elude detection in a few minutes. But it

439

# Saturday, 10 November, 1888

can scarcely be doubted that the same person who murdered several poor women in August and September in Whitechapel has returned to his old haunts, and been again at his hideous work. Two such monsters in human form there cannot be. The murderer of Mitre-square is, no doubt, the murderer of Dorset-street.

When evidence is not to be had, theories abound. Even the most plausible of them do not carry conviction; but enough is known to justify search being made in certain specific directions. In this, as in the other crimes of the same character, ordinary motives are out of the question. No hope of plunder could have induced the murderer to kill one who, it is clear, was reduced to such extremity of want that she thought of destroying herself. The body bore the marks of the frenzy and fury that characterized the previous murders. An appetite for blood, a love of carnage for itself, could only explain what has been done. And there are the same indications of dexterity, if not anatomical skill, such as would be possessed only by one accustomed to handle a knife. It will be remembered that in the case of the woman CHAPMAN, murdered in Mitre-square, the face was so disfigured as to make identification very difficult. The same treatment befell KELLY, whose features were barely recognizable.

When the former murders were under discussion, it was noted as a curious fact that they occurred about the end of the week, and this and other circumstances suggested the theory that the assassin did not habitually live in London, but visited it at intervals—that he came, to state one form of this theory, in one of the cattle boats which weekly call here. Some circumstances attending this latest crime give more plausibility to this suggestion. But, whoever he may be, it is plain that some wild beast in human shape haunts the resorts of the outcasts of the East-end to lure them to a terrible death.

Indignation and alarm will prompt, we may be sure, all sorts of wild and foolish suggestions, and blame will be cast, very much at random, in many directions. Some people think that it speaks well for their hearts to lose their heads in such circumstances; and it is possible that MR. MATTHEWS and SIR CHARLES WARREN will not escape some sweeping censure in Parliament. Might we ask those who have reproofs on their lips to formulate before they utter them the precise means and devices which they say should have been resorted to? There is no lack of police in Whitechapel, and they have had the assistance of a private Vigilance Committee. It is true a Government reward has not been offered; but does anyone, reflecting upon the circumstances of the seven murders committed in Whitechapel since last Christmas, believe that a reward of £1,000 or more would have elicited one fact now unknown, or that it might not have fostered a multitude of bewildering fictions? Excellent sometimes in breaking up a confederacy of vice, rewards are useless if the crime be committed, as the crime at Dorset-street no doubt was, in secrecy and silence by one man. It is, of course, open to any one to say that if the Home Office or Scotland Yard employed detectives of superlative acuteness, such as exist only in the pages of novelists, all would have been made clear. But such a theory can be put forward, not to be believed, but only as a pretext for noisy abuse. Of all forms of superstition, few are more abject than the notion that anything, no matter what, can be done by a Government Department. The savage smashes his idol if an earthquake overturns his hut or a high tide carries away his canoe; the modern fashion is in similar circumstances to assail the Home Office. It will be the paramount duty of the HOME SECRETARY and SIR CHARLES WARREN to leave no stone unturned, and they will be assisted as far as possible in their inquiries by the whole community. But there is much more profitable occupation than vague windy abuse of people who cannot create evidence. Deep searching of hearts, humiliation of spirit, and sorrowful reflection over the causes which make these unspeakable atrocities possible, would be more seemly than cheap declamation about the shortcomings of the police.

~

440

# The Star

## WHAT WE THINK.

ANOTHER murder—committed, as we said it would be, when public interest had slackened down, and the Vigilance Committee had ceased to work. For the time being, we must leave our theories as to the moral of the murders and stick to facts which bear on the detection of the fiend who commits them. Thanks to Messrs. WARREN and MATT-HEWS, they are slender enough.

The police did nothing. They lost the blood-hounds at the moment when they wanted them. They neglected—after repeated warnings—to draw a cordon and search the neighbouring houses. Sir CHARLES WARREN, so far as all information at our disposal goes, was away; Mr. MATTHEWS—"heedless and helpless," as the *Daily Telegraph* calls him to-day—was busy with a deputation. Mr. STUART-WORTLEY, Under-Secretary of the Home Department, could not be found. The Detective Department, being deprived of its natural head and in the hands of a clumsy, wilful, and at the same time ignorant martinet, was helpless and disorganised. The police had orders to refuse the newspapers every information, for Sir CHARLES WARREN'S spite against the newspapers who discover crime is only equalled by his own incapacity as a detective. Meanwhile, we must advise, if the WARREN-MATTHEWS coalition cannot. What is the best thing for the detectives to do, wretchedly incapable as they appear to be, or as the organisation which has been crippled for them appears to be, for the detection of crime?

Possibly the man will never be caught unless red-handed. We have only probabilities to go upon, and we must piece these together as best we may. To begin with, it is clear that the murderer has knowledge of the Whitechapel district in which he perpetrates his crimes.

Then he is probably a man of bad character, who, as Mr. ARCHIBALD FORBES suggests, is acquainted with the customary and most taking methods of accosting the women whom he selects as his victims. He is probably a maniac, so far as the prosecution of one single murderous purpose is an indication of mania; but, on the other hand, he is not so much a maniac as to be indifferent to detection, and he watches to strike his blow with unfailing and remorseless cunning at the moment most favourable to his designs. Again, he is probably able to secure solitude whenever he wants it; but, on the other hand, he is not likely to be a man of forbidding appearance, solitary manners, or distinguished by one trait marking him out for notice by his fellows.

In a city like London, where the isolation of life is so complete, it is quite possible that even a man of this character might escape detection among the thousand and one persons who have comparatively innocent reasons of their own for keeping quiet and avoiding the public. But, going on the lines of the greatest probability, we must assume that the murderer is a man not open to ordinary suspicion, and that although he lays his plots with devilish ingenuity, and carries them out with unsurpassed cunning and ferocity, he is a gentleman who is accepted absolutely in his own rank of society, possibly adorning a pew, occupying a clerk's stool, or doing a little business, in leisure moments not devoted to the main purpose of his life, in stocks and shares. Finally, he may assume drunkenness, or a "boozing" fit, for the treble purpose of putting his victims, the police, and his acquaintances off the scent.

It follows, therefore, that in the absence of immediate motive, which means the absence of clue, we must keep our eyes on points of character rather than on such manifestly unsatisfactory and inadequate work as the searching of lodging-houses, which in all probability the murderer does not frequent. The questions for every man to ask himself are:—

1. Has he, among his acquaintance, any man whose movements have been suspicious, and not to be accounted for during the period of the murders?

2. Has he a man in his acquaintance whose history or habits have made him a likely enemy of the class of unfortunates—who, be it noticed, are the most abandoned of the whole prostitute class—against whom the murderer's efforts are directed?

3. Does he know a man who has had attacks of mania of a homicidal kind, and who has been under confinement?

4. Who knows Whitechapel?

5. Who has a certain amount of anatomical knowledge, whether acquired in a dissecting

room or in a doctor's practice, or a slaughter-yard, or in any other rough-and-ready school of anatomy?

6. Who has indulged in any suspicious action, such as washing his own clothes, or has otherwise acted suspiciously in his own house at hours preceding or following the murders?

These are all points on which the eyes of the community should be fixed. It is quite clear that nothing can be expected from the police, and that we may have 20 murders, as well as seven or eight, without their doing a single thing or making a single effort which will be fruitful for the public good.

Meanwhile this seventh murder ought to rid us of Mr. MATTHEWS, and also of Sir CHARLES WARREN. The proclamation of a reward by the City authorities shows that the criminal apathy and indifference of the HOME SECRETARY have not been echoed even in quarters where interest in the lives and welfare of the people is small indeed. What effect the issue of a reward may ultimately have on the capture of the murderer it is impossible to say, but there cannot be the slightest doubt of the result which the withholding of all tangible Ministerial sympathy has had in the poor quarters of London.

We have heard the wildest stories as to the reasons which popular opinion in Whitechapel assigns for Mr. MATTHEWS'S obstinate refusal to offer a reward. It is believed by people who pass among their neighbours as sensible folk that the Government do not want the murderer to be convicted, that they are interested in concealing his identity, that, in fact, they know it, and will not divulge it. Of course this is rank nonsense, but it is nonsense which may end in a panic, while for the Government it is particularly dangerous nonsense. Already the folly of Lord SALISBURY, in sticking to his discredited colleague, will cost the Government every seat which they hold in the East-end of London.

For our part, if it were not for higher considerations even than the winning of two or three seats for Mr. GLADSTONE, we should say—By all means let Mr. MATTHEWS go on and fill the cup of his follies full to the brim. But we remember Trafalgar-square, and the danger of fresh assaults on the unemployed this winter. Therefore, we say MATTHEWS and

WARREN must go, and the sooner the better.

The first is a pitiful creature, a poor and spiritless specimen of the race of smart adventurers who creep into politics by back doors. Above all, he is a tactless, heartless red-tapeist, and probably nine out of ten of the clerks at the Home Office would be better fitted to look after the lives and property of the citizens of London than the right hon. gentleman who takes £5,000 a year for doing nothing. As for the second, there is but one cry from Tory and Liberal—"WARREN must go." At the Show yesterday his name was execrated from Aldgate to Pall Mall. He has become impossible. He is doomed.

One word more. The murderer chose his time well. There is a theory—not an impossible one—that he is one of those diseased creatures who, drunk with an insane love of notoriety, are determined to be the sensation of the hour. So he decided to get up a counter-demonstration to the LORD MAYOR'S Show. If that was his intention he succeeded beyond all expectation. He got his sensation.

While the well-stuffed calves of the City footmen were being paraded for the laughter of London, his victim was lying cold in a foul, dimly-lighted court in Whitechapel.

Whitechapel is once more to the fore—a grim spectre at our shows and banquets. And there Whitechapel will remain—till modern society alters and there are no more White-chapels—and no more Pall Malls.

—

### WHITECHAPEL.
### DETAILS OF THE SEVENTH CRIME OF THE MURDER MANIAC.
### THE POLICE AGAIN COMPLETELY BAFFLED.
### THE BRISK MANUFACTURE OF DETAILS BY LOCAL RESIDENTS.
### WHERE IS SIR CHARLES WARREN?
**In the Face of Strong Police Opposition the Reporters Gather the Leading Facts—Various Statements from Neighbours, but None of Them Worthy of Implicit Credence—The Bloodhounds Have Not Appeared on the Scene.**

A reporter who was prosecuting inquiries in Spitalfields throughout the night says:—Between the hours of one and four nothing which may be termed unusual occurred. Women of the unfor-

# Saturday, 10 November, 1888

tunate class paraded the several highways with an unconcernedness which may be termed remarkable considering the recent hideous crimes. The drafts of auxiliary detectives which have been requisitioned since the perpetration of the Mitre-square and Berner-street tragedies from the suburban districts performed their unenviable duties in the regulation manner, and to a casual pedestrian who may have passed through the district after midnight nothing whatever existed to denote the commission of such a crime as that of the morning. Everyone seems to be perfectly certain that the police possess no clue, and will discover no clue to the identity of the murderer. The only reason for thinking that the popular impression is not correct is that it is confirmed by the statements of the police themselves. They confess themselves to be

## WHOLLY IN THE DARK.

"We know no more than you do," they say, in answer to inquiries, and the reply is given in so mournful a manner that one is almost constrained to accept it for truth. But, however much or little they know, the police have devoted themselves energetically to the task of preventing other people from knowing anything. The row of policemen who during the greater part of yesterday blocked Dorset-street had been withdrawn last night, but the entrance to the court—which is variously known as Miller's-court or McCarthy's-court—was vigilantly kept by two constables, who allowed no one to pass except by special favour, and showed especial zeal in the exclusion of reporters. The desire to be interesting has had its effect on the people who live in the Dorset-street-court and lodging-houses, and for whoever cares to listen there are

## A HUNDRED HIGHLY CIRCUMSTANTIAL STORIES,

which, when carefully sifted, prove to be totally devoid of truth. One woman (as reported below) who lives in the court stated that at about two o'clock she heard a cry of "Murder." This story soon became popular, until at last half a dozen women were retailing it as their own personal experience. Each story contradicted the others with respect to the time at which the cry was heard. A *Star* reporter who inquired into the matter extracted from one of the women the confession that the story was, as far as she was

concerned, a fabrication; and he came to the conclusion that it was to be disregarded.

As far as has been at present ascertained, the murdered woman was last seen alive shortly after eleven o'clock on Thursday night by Mrs. Harvey, a young woman who was on intimate terms with her, and who lives in New-court, Dorset-street. Mrs. Harvey says Kelly was at that time going home alone.

Elizabeth Prater, a married woman, who has been deserted by her husband, knew Kelly well, she told a *Star* reporter, "She lived in No. 13 room, and mine is No. 20, which

## IS ALMOST OVER HERS.

She was about 23 years old. I have known her since July—since I came to lodge here. She was tall and pretty, and as fair as a lily. I saw her go out in the shell this afternoon, but the last time I saw her alive was at about nine o'clock on Thursday night. I stood down at the bottom of the entry, and she came down. We both stood talking a bit, thinking what we were going to do, and then she went one way and I went another. I went to see if I could see anybody." Mrs. Prater adds with frankness, "She had got her hat and jacket on, but I had not. I haven't got a hat or a jacket. We stood talking a bit about what we were going to do, and then I said, 'Good night, old dear,' and she said 'Good night, my pretty.' She always called me that. That," said Mrs. Prater, "was the last I saw of her." Then Mrs. Prater breaks down, and commences to sob violently. "I'm a woman myself," she says, "and I've got to sleep in that place to-night right over where it happened." Mrs. Prater saw the dead and mutilated body through the window of Kelly's room, which it is to be remembered, was on the ground floor. The pump stands just by there, and Mrs. Prater took advantage of a journey for some water to peep through the window for which, when the door was broken open, the curtains were torn down. She says, "I could not bear to look at it only for a second, but I can

## NEVER FORGET THE SIGHT

of it if I live to be a hundred."

"Who was her man?" the reporter asked. "He was a man named Joe Barnett, who worked in Billingsgate-market." "Where had he gone to live?" "To Buller's lodging-house, 25, New-street, close by Bishopsgate Police-station.

# Saturday, 10 November, 1888

**JOE BARNETT'S STATEMENT.**

In a public-house close by Buller's the reporter succeded later on in finding Barnett, who is an Irishman by parentage and a Londoner by birth. He had lived with her for a year and a half, he said, and should not have left her except for her violent habits. She was a Limerick woman by birth, he says, but had lived in Dublin for some time. She went by the name of Mary Jane, but her real name was Marie Jeanette.

He knew nothing about her proceedings since he left her, except that his brother met her on the Thursday evening and spoke to her. He himself had been taken by the police down to Dorset-street, and had been kept there for two hours and a half. He saw the body by peeping through the window.

To our reporter Barnett said he and the deceased were very happy and comfortable together until another woman came to sleep in their room, to which he strongly objected. Finally, after the woman had been there two or three nights he quarrelled with the woman whom he called his wife and left her. The next day, however, he returned and gave Kelly money. He called several other days and gave her money when he had it. On Thursday night he visited her between half-past seven and eight, and told her he was sorry he had no money to give her. He saw nothing more of her.

She used occasionally to go to the Elephant and Castle district to visit a friend who was in the same position of life as herself. Kelly had a little boy, aged about six or seven years, living with her.

**LAST SEEN ALIVE**

There are conflicting statements as to when the woman was last seen alive, but that upon which most reliance appears to be placed is that of a young woman, an associate of the deceased, who states that about half-past ten o'clock on Thursday night she met the murdered woman at the corner of Dorset-street, who said to her that she had no money and, if she could not get any, would never go out any more, but would do away with herself. Soon afterwards they parted, and

**A MAN, RESPECTABLY DRESSED,**

came up and spoke to the murdered woman Kelly and offered her some money. The man then accompanied the woman home to her lodgings, and the little boy was removed from the room and taken to a neighbour's house.

About one o'clock in the morning a person living in the court opposite to the room occupied by the murdered woman heard her singing the song, "Sweet violets," but this person is unable to say whether any one else was with her at that time.

Nothing more was seen of the woman until yesterday morning, when, it is stated, the little boy was sent back into the house, and, the report goes, he was sent out subsequently on an errand by the man who was in the house with his mother. There is no direct confirmation of this statement. A tailor named Lewis says he saw Kelly come out about eight o'clock yesterday morning and go back.

Another statement is to the effect that Kelly was seen in a public-house known as the "Ringers," at the corner of Dorset-street and Commercial-street, about ten o'clock yesterday morning, and that she there met her lover Barnett, and had a glass of beer with him. This statement also is not substantiated.

**A MAN WITH A BLACK BAG.**

Sarah Roney, a girl about 20 years of age, states that she was with two other girls on Thursday night in Brushfield-street, which is near Dorset-street, when a man wearing a tall hat and a black coat, and carrying a black bag, came up to her and said, "Will you come with me?" She told him she would not, and asked him what he had in the bag, and he said, "Something the ladies don't like." He then walked away.

—

**A NEIGHBOR'S DOUBTFUL STORY.**

A woman named Kennedy was on the night of the murder staying with her parents at a house situate in the court immediately opposite the room in which the body of Mary Kelly was found. This woman's statement, if true, establishes the time at which the

**MURDERER COMMENCED HIS OPERATIONS**

upon his victim. She states that about three o'clock on Friday morning she entered Dorset-street on her way to her parent's house, which is situate immediately opposite that in which the murder was committed. She noticed three persons at the corner of the street near the

Britannia public house. There was a man—a young man, respectably dressed, and with a dark moustache—talking to a woman whom she did not know, and also a female poorly clad, and without any headgear. The man and woman appeared to be the worse for liquor, and she heard the man ask, "Are you coming." Whereupon the woman, who appeared to be obstinate, turned in an opposite direction to which the man apparently wished her to go. Mrs. Kennedy went on her way and nothing unusual occurred until about half an hour later. She states that she did not retire to rest immediately she reached her parents' abode, but sat up, and between half-past three and a quarter to four she

## HEARD A CRY OF "MURDER"

in a woman's voice proceed from the direction in which Mary Kelly's room was situated. As the cry was not repeated she took no further notice of the circumstance until this morning, when she found the police in possession of the place, preventing all egress to the occupants of the small houses in this court. When questioned by the police as to what she had heard throughout the night, she made a statement to the above effect.

## A STORY OF LITTLE VALUE.

Mrs. Kennedy has since supplemented the above statement by the following:—

"On Wednesday evening, about eight o'clock, me and my sister were in the neighbourhood of Bethnal-green-road when we were accosted by a very suspicious man about 40 years of age. He was about 6ft. high, and wore a short jacket, over which he had a long top-coat. He had a black moustache, and wore a billycock hat. He invited me to accompany him into a lonely spot, "as he was known about here and there was a policeman looking at him." She asserts that no policeman was in sight. He was very white in the face, and made every endeavour to prevent them looking him straight in the face. He carried a black bag. He avoided walking with them, and led the way into

## A VERY DARK THOROUGHFARE,

at the back of the warehouse," inviting them to follow, which they did. He then pushed open a small door in a pair of large gates, and requested one of them to follow him, remarking, "I only want one of you." Whereupon the women became suspicious. He acted in a very strange

and suspicious manner, and refused to leave his bag in the possession of one of the females. Both women became alarmed at his actions, and escaped, at the same time raising an alarm of "Jack the Ripper." Mrs. Kennedy asserts that the man whom she saw on Friday morning with the woman at the corner of Dorset-street resembled very closely the individual who caused such alarm on the night in question, and that she would recognise him again if confronted with him.

## THIS DESCRIPTION OF THE MAN

suspected of the murder tallies exactly with that in the possession of the police, and there is very little to doubt that the murderer entered the murdered woman's house late on Thursday night or early on Friday morning.

## THE DISCOVERY OF THE BODY.

This is how the discovery of the murder was made. The house in which Kelly was a lodger is owned by a man named McCarthy, who keeps a general shop at the corner of the court. At a quarter to eleven yesterday morning, as the woman was 35s. in arrears with her rent, McCarthy said to a man employed by him in his shop, John Bowyer, "Go to No. 13 (meaning the room occupied by Kelly) and try and get some rent." Bowyer did as he was directed, and on knocking at the door was unable to obtain an answer. He then tried the handle of the door and found it was locked. On looking through the keyhole he found

## THE KEY WAS MISSING.

The left hand side of the room faced the court, and in it were two large windows. Bowyer, knowing that a pane of glass in one of the windows was broken, put his hand through the aperture and pulled aside the muslin curtain which covered it. He looked into the room, and saw the woman lying on the bed, entirely naked, covered with blood and apparently dead. Without waiting to make a closer examination, he ran to his employer and told him he believed the woman Kelly had been murdered.

McCarthy at once went and looked through the broken window, and, satisfying himself that something was wrong, despatched Bowyer to the Commercial-street Police-station. Inspector Back accompanied Bowyer back, and on finding that a murder had been committed at once sent for assistance. Dr. Phillips, the divisional surgeon of police, and Superintendent Arnold, were also sent for. During this time the door had not been touched. Superintendent Arnold caused a telegram to be sent direct to Sir Charles Warren, informing him what had happened, and ordered one of the windows to be entirely removed.

A horrible and sickening sight then presented itself. The poor woman lay on her back on the bed, entirely naked. Her throat was

## CUT FROM EAR TO EAR,

right down to the spinal column. The ears and nose had been cut clean off; the breasts had also been cleanly cut off and placed on a table which was by the side of the bed. The stomach and abdomen had been ripped open, while the face was slashed about, so that the features of the poor creature were beyond all recognition. The kidneys and heart had also been removed from the body and placed on the table by the side of the breasts. The liver had likewise been removed and laid on the right thigh. The lower portion of the body and the uterus had been cut out, and these appeared to be missing. The thighs had been cut. The clothes of the woman were lying by the side of the bed, as though they had been taken off and laid down in the ordinary manner.

While this examination was being made a photographer, who, in the meantime, had been sent for, arrived and

## TOOK PHOTOGRAPHS OF THE BODY,

the organs, the room, and its contents. Superintendent Arnold then had the door of the room forced.

It was a very poorly furnished apartment, about 12ft. square, there being only an old bedstead, two old tables, and a chair in it. The bedclothes had been turned down, and this was probably done by the murderer after he had cut his victim's throat. There was no appearance of a struggle having taken place, and although a careful search of the room was made, no knife or instrument of any kind was found.

Dr. Phillips, on his arrival, carefully examined the body of the dead woman, and later on again made a second examination in company with Dr. Bond, from Westminster, Dr. Gordon Brown, from the City, Dr. Duke, from Spitalfields, and Dr. Phillips's assistant. Mr. Anderson, the new Commissioner of Police, Detective-Inspectors Reid and Abberline (Scot-

land-yard), Chief Inspector West, and other officers were quickly on the spot. After the examination of the body it was placed in a shell, which was put into a van and conveyed to the Shoreditch mortuary to await an inquest.

Mr. John McCarthy, the owner of the house in Miller's-court, has given the following

## FACTS AS TO THE MURDERED WOMAN.

"She was about 23 or 24 years of age, and lived with a coal porter named Kelly, passing as his wife. They, however, quarrelled some time back and separated. A woman named Harvey slept with her several nights since Kelly separated from her, but she was not with her last night. The deceased's Christian name was Mary Jane, and since her murder I have discovered that she walked the streets in the neighbourhood of Aldgate. Her habits were irregular, and she often came home at night the worse for drink. Her mother lives in Ireland, but in what county I do not know. Deceased used to receive letters from her occasionally." McCarthy adds that when he looked through the window, after Bowyer called him, he saw on the table what seemed to be lumps of flesh. When the police inspector came he sent a telegram to Sir Charles Warren

## TO BRING THE BLOODHOUNDS.

Superintendent Arnold gave instructions for the door to be burst open, and McCarthy forced the door with a pickaxe. "The sight we saw," he says, "I cannot drive away from my mind. It looked more like the work of a devil than of a man. I had heard a great deal about the Whitechapel murders, but I declare to God I had never expected to see such a sight as this. The whole scene is more than I can describe. I hope I may never see such a sight again."

It is stated that a man's pilot coat has been found in the murdered woman's room, but whether it belonged to one of her paramours or to the murderer has not been ascertained.

—

## THE DROVER THEORY.

There is, it is to be noted, a striking similarity in the period of the month in which the crime has been committed, for while two of the most atrocious of the other murders in the same district were committed on the 7th of the months of September and August, this was commenced or committed on the 8th—approximately the same period of the month. This would seem to indicate that the murderer was absent from the scene of these horrors for fixed periods, and that his return was always about the same time. The murders, too, have been committed on the later days of the week, and in this connection a somewhat important fact has been pointed out. It appears that the cattle boats bringing live freight to London are in the habit of coming into the Thames on Thursdays or Fridays, and leave again for the Continent on Sundays or Mondays. An opinion has been formed among some of the detectives that the murderer is a drover or butcher employed on one of these boats—of which there are many—and that he periodically appears and disappears with one of the steamers.

—

## WHO WILL HOLD THE INQUEST?

The removal of Kelly's body to the Shoreditch mortuary is likely to lead to some complications through the intersection of the local boundaries and the jurisdiction of the two coroners for the newly-formed divisions of Eastern Middlesex.

Spitalfields, although within the Whitechapel district for all local purposes, is within the North Eastern Division of Middlesex, and is therefore under the jurisdiction of Dr. Macdonald. All the other portions of Whitechapel remain under the jurisdiction of Mr. Baxter, so far as coroner's inquests are concerned.

The Hanbury-street murder, which occurred in Spitalfields, took place in the open air, and it being incumbent on the police to remove the body, they naturally conveyed it to the local mortuary in Old Montague-street. But in the Dorset-street case, there was no duty cast upon the police to remove the body from the house where it was found, and the coroner's officer for the district being communicated with, he was obliged to take it where he could. If he had taken it to Old Montague-street, it would have gone from his control, so he took it to Shoreditch, which is within his district.

It remains to be seen whether the Shoreditch Vestry will be content to afford mortuary accommodation in such instances of a neighbouring district not within their parish, to oblige the coroner or his officer, but it is pretty certain when it comes to a question of parochial burial, the relieving officer will be found in a difficulty as to whether he is justified in incurring the expense for the Shoreditch ratepayers.

This difficulty may be got over by removing the body back again to Whitechapel, and placing it in the Old Montague-street mortuary, so as to throw the cost of the burial upon the Whitechapel Board of Guardians. Here again another difficulty arises, because the body will come into Mr. Baxter's district, who, according to the state of the "Coroner's Quest Law," will be obliged to hold another inquest, if only a formal one.

The inquest on the body has been definitely fixed for Monday next, at eleven a.m., at the Shoreditch Town Hall, before Mr. Macdonald, the coroner for the district.

## HOW THE MURDERER ESCAPED.

The murderer must have got out of the window, as the door was barricaded from the inside with the bedstead.

## THE POST-MORTEM.

Dr. Bond, of Westminster Hospital, Dr. Gordon Brown, City Surgeon, and Dr. Phillips held a post-mortem on the body this morning. The ears are cut off, but are not missing.

The opinion is entertained by some of the Scotland-yard officers that the missing organ has been burnt in the fireplace in the murdered woman's room. There is a mass of ash and rubbish under the grate, among which are portions of a coat and hat; and the police intend

## EXAMINING THE ASHES

with the assistance of Dr. Phillips and Dr. Bond, for the presence of any fatty matter, or any trace of burnt flesh. The whole of the rubbish, in fact, will be carefully sifted and scrutinised, because if the burnt coat should happen to be part of the murderer's clothing a clue of some sort, meagre enough, perhaps, but better than nothing at all, would be supplied.

The uninjured coat which was found in the room will also be examined, and the pockets turned inside out, this important step not having yet been taken, because the article was locked up in the room while the police were making their external investigations. The investigation of the ashes is expected to take place during the course of this afternoon.

# Saturday, 10 November, 1888

## THE VICTIM.

The woman murdered in Spitalfields yesterday was born in Limerick, her name being Marie Jeanette Kelly. Her parents removed from Limerick to Carmarthen, and here the deceased married a collier[289] whose name is believed to be Davies. He, however, was killed in a colliery explosion, and the deceased woman then lived an ill life at Cardiff, afterwards removing to London. Her parents are still living in Wales.

—

## A REMARKABLE PROPHECY.

*London and Brighton*, a paper published on Wednesday, contains the following:—

On Sunday the new moon came in. If Jack the Ripper is a lunatic and if there is any truth in the theory of the susceptibility of lunatics to lunar influence we ought to hear from him in the course of a few days.

~

## Evening News
### THE WHITECHAPEL ATROCITY.

Again the East end fiend has been at work, and this time the insane love of mutilation is more apparent than ever. The victim in this case, Mary Ann Kelly, has been cut, eviscerated, and disfigured as none of her unfortunate predecessors sacrificed by the "Lust Morder" have been. Still the manner of the handicraft shows, we believe, that the same artist has been engaged. We call him an artist not in ridicule, but in very seriousness, from the evident fact that he loves his diabolical work, and endeavours to excite in ever increasing degree the attention of the world. His art is horror and he seeks ever to intensify it.

On September 10 we ventured to suggest that the murderer was a monomaniac, and also possibly an epileptic. We did not then condemn the police, as many of our contemporaries did, for their failure to trace the assassin, recognising as we did the obscurity that surrounds the acts of the insane. We did, however, recommend that as the ordinary methods of criminal investigation had proved inadequate to the emergency a divergence should be made in face of the unusual circumstances. We hoped that inquiries would be made at various hospitals to discover what cases of epilepsy had been treated there, and the names of persons discharged as cured say within the last two years. We have not learned that our hint was accepted. The medical men of East London have, as far as we know, not been consulted. our theory, however, has been adopted by Dr. Forbes Winslow and every other eminent alienist qualified to judge.

Most of our contemporaries have also —without acknowledgement—come round to our view. We still adhere to what we then wrote. Everything tends to the belief that one man and one man only is responsible for the series of murders, though fashion in murder as in suicide exerts potent influence on ill regulated minds. The atrocity of yesterday, a special and graphic account of which appears in other columns, shows, as in the other cases, that the murderer while revelling in mutilation is not a skilful anatomist. His knowledge, whatever it may be, is not that of a school bred man. He was proved in the Mitre square instance to have bungled his work, and if in the present case he

---

[289] **Collier**. Coal miner, coal merchant or someone who worked on coal barges. (Census1891.com)

# Saturday, 10 November, 1888

has proceeded to greater lengths of horror, the more advantageous conditions of seclusion in a house amply explain it.

Much was made by Sir Charles Warren of the use to which bloodhounds could be turned. Yesterday they were sent for, but they were not forthcoming. Perhaps there is no great loss in this. The proper bloodhounds in this matter must be the police, and in order to succeed in their search, they must abandon their time honoured traditions.

—

**ANOTHER EAST END MURDER**
**A SEVENTH VICTIM SLAUGHTERED**
**HORRIBLE MUTILATION OF A WOMAN**
**ON HORROR'S HEAD HORRORS**
**ACCUMULATE**
**THE VICTIM'S CRY OF "MURDER"**
**MRS. KENNEDY'S STATEMENT**
**SPITALFIELDS LAST NIGHT**
**SIGHTS AND SCENES**
**GREAT EXCITEMENT IN THE**
**DISTRICT**
**THE SUPPOSED MURDERER SEEN AT**
**KENNINGTON**

A representative of *The Evening News*, who spent the night on the scene of the murders attributed to the revengeful knife of Jack the Ripper, states that down to a late hour, last night, the utmost excitement—if not terror—pervaded all classes of the population in the East End. The Dorset street murder, with all its revolting details, was the one topic of conversation, and as the closing hour of half past twelve approached there was an obvious renewal of the panic that ensued on the occasion of the recent double murder in Whitechapel. As then, so now, the thoroughfares which constitute the main arteries of traffic in the East End were deserted shortly after one o'clock—a strange scene to those accustomed to the bustle and turmoil of the Whitechapel streets far into the early morn. Ere an hour had passed after the midnight stroke, festive revellers had disappeared from the scene, while females of the unfortunate class were conspicuous chiefly by their absence.

## THE VIGILANCE COMMITTEE AT WORK.

But peaceful though the appearance of the streets may have been, the sturdy burghers of the East end were not unmindful of the duties voluntarily undertaken by them a few weeks back. The members of the Vigilance Committee were everywhere to be seen peering into dark and shady nooks that would afford even a suggestion for a crime, while detectives in plain clothes—and in overwhelming numbers—were ever on the alert. But in the small hours of the morning it must be confessed that Whitechapel looked dreariness itself. As the hours stole by plain clothes detectives, both amateur and professional, left the scene of their monotonous perambulations and once again the streets resounded only to the heavy mechanical tread of the blue coated guardians of the night.

Even the coffee stalls were deserted, and their owners, enraged at the long continued paucity of nocturnal customers, did not hesitate to give free vent to their vocabulary of indignation. Jack the Ripper may, from his peculiar and monomaniacal point of view, be having a merry time of it, but coffee stall keepers think otherwise. This latest tragedy makes their prospects look even more gloomy than before, and the sullenness that comes of despair is rapidly stealing into the face of many an East end distributor of the cup that is said to cheer but not inebriate.

Throughout yesterday Dorset street was the scene of intense excitement, and the strong cordon of police drawn around the approaches to the street only with the utmost difficulty prevented the ever increasing throng from breaking through. The search for the perpetrator of this the most revolting of all the East end tragedies has been kept up with the most persistent zeal, though so far without success. Yesterday, a man was arrested and taken to Commercial street, on the suspicion of being Jack the ripper, but subsequent infor-mation that came to hand led to his release. Late at night a further arrest was made at the same station. Here again it is anticipated by the authorities that the inquiries will fail to establish the identity of the prisoner with Jack the Ripper, and his speedy release is anticipated.

The authorities themselves readily admit that up to the present they have not the slightest clue as to the perpetrator of this atrocious murder. The audacity of the deed has startled every one, and none more so than the police.

449

## THE HOUSE AND ITS INHABITANTS

The actual scene of the murder is Miller's court, Dorset street—though the locality if known to residents in the neighbourhood as McCarthy's court. This is owing to the fact that a man named McCarthy is the chief owner or occupier of the houses there. Information has come to hand which tends to throw a strong light on the much disputed point as to when the tragedy was actually perpetrated. Immediately opposite the house in which Mary Jane Kelly was murdered is a tenement occupied by an Irishman, named Gallagher, and his family. On Thursday night Gallagher and his wife retired to rest at a fairly early hour. Their married daughter, a woman named Mrs. Kennedy, came home, however, at a late hour. Passing the Britannia, commonly known as Ringer's, at the top of Dorset street, at three o'clock on the Friday morning, she saw the deceased talking to a respectably dressed man, whom she identified as having accosted her a night or two before.

## THE CRY OF "MURDER"

She passed them without taking any notice, and went home to bed. Between half past three and four o'clock in the morning Mrs. Kennedy, who passed a very restless night, heard a cry of "Murder" that seemed to come from the opposite side of the court, but according to her, she little thought of the awful tragedy that was then being enacted. She went to sleep, and it was not until eleven o'clock in the morning that she heard of the murder. So far as can be ascertained, Mrs. Kennedy is the only person who heard the cry of "Murder" that came from the unfortunate woman. In connection with Mrs. Kennedy, it may be mentioned that she and her sister, a widow, were, on Wednesday night last, accosted by a man when they were walking down the Bethnal Green road. It was about eight o'clock when this occurred.

## THE MAN WITH THE BLACK BAG

The man is described by Mrs. Kennedy as having on a pair of dark mixture trousers and a long dark overcoat. He wore a low crowned brown hat and carried a shiny black bag in his hand. Further, it was stated that he was a man of medium stature, with dark moustache, and that he had an extremely awkward gait, which could at once be recognised. The stranger refused to stand Mrs. Kennedy and her sister a drink, but invited them to go with him down a dark sideway off the main road.

They accompanied him as far as a gateway with a small door in it, but when he stepped through and left his bag on the ground, saying he would take either of them with him, a feeling of distrust seized the women. Mrs. Kennedy picked up the bag, whereupon the stranger exclaimed that he was not Jack the Ripper. Just then the woman noticed the unnatural glare of the man's eyes, and instinctively fled from the spot leaving him behind. They subsequently ascertained that the same man accosted other women the same night.

Mrs. Kennedy is confident that the man whom she noticed speaking to the woman Kelly at three o'clock on Friday morning is identical with the person who accosted her on the previous Wednesday. Both she and her sister are most positive in their assertion that they could at once identify the man if they saw him. This evidence as to the cry of "Murder" is extremely important in view of the fact that a number of witnesses have come forward and stated that they saw the deceased woman Kelly as late as ten o'clock on the morning that the murder occurred.

The entrance to Miller's court is guarded by constables night and day, and the public are rigidly excluded. It was at first erroneously stated that the body was found on a bed in the second floor front room. In reality the remains were found on the ground floor, and the windows have since been barricaded by the police. The body was in the course of yesterday removed to the Shoreditch Mortuary. It is currently reported that in the course of yesterday afternoon and evening a large number of arrests were made the police, but that in each case it was found necessary to discharge the prisoners through lack of sufficient evidence as to identity.

## A GOOD THEORY OF THESE MURDERS

A somewhat important fact has been pointed out, which puts a fresh complexion on the theory of the murders. It appears that the cattle boats bringing live freight to London are in the habit of coming into the Thames on Thursdays or Fridays, and leave again for the Continent on Sundays or Mondays. It has already been a matter of comment that the recent revolting crimes have been committed at the week's end, and an opinion has been formed among some of the detectives that the murderer is a drover or butcher employed on one of these boats—of which there are many—and that he periodically appears and disappears with one of the steamers. This theory is held to be of much importance by those involved in the investigation, who believe that the murderer does not reside either in the locality or even in this country at all. It is thought that he may be either a person employed upon one of these boats, or one who is allowed to travel by them, and inquiries have for some time been directed in following up the theory. It is pointed out that at the inquests on the previous victims the coroners had expressed the opinion that the knowledge of anatomy possessed by a butcher would have been sufficient to enable him to find and cut out the parts of the body which in several cases were abstracted.

### THE VIGILANCE COMMITTEE

The Whitechapel Vigilance Committee, who have recently relaxed their efforts to find the murderer, have called a meeting for Tuesday evening next, at the Paul's Head Tavern, Crispin street, Spitalfields, to consider what steps they can take to assist the police.

### NO PARTS OF THE BODY
### ARE MISSING

The Central News states, upon indisputable authority, that no portion of the murdered woman's body was taken away. A post mortem examination was held by the medical authorities summoned by the police, and the surgeons did not quit their work until every organ had been accounted for, and placed as closely as possible in its natural position.[290]

### MR. MCCARTHY'S STORY

John McCarthy, a provision dealer, residing at 27 Dorset street, and who is the landlord of No 26 in the same thoroughfare as the house in which the murder was committed, said: "Mary Jane Kelly, the murdered woman, was a person about 25 years of age. She was an unfortunate. The last that was heard of her was at one o'clock this (Friday) morning, when she was singing in her room and appeared to be very happy. At eleven o'clock last night she was seen in the Britannia public house at the corner of this thoroughfare, with a young man with a dark moustache. She was then intoxicated. The young man appeared to be very respectable and well dressed. About half past ten this morning I saw a man named Henry Bower go to Mary Jane Kelly's room and ask for the rent she owed me. Bower went to the house but failed to get any answer to his knocks. He then peered through one of the windows and saw the woman lying cut up on the bed. The bed was saturated with blood. Bower came and called me, telling me what he had seen, and we went and looked through the window.

### THE SIGHT WAS TOO MUCH FOR HIM

"I cannot fully describe her injuries, for the sight was too much for me. I noticed that both her breasts were cut off, and that she was ripped up. he intestines were laid on the table; both ears were cut off, as was also the nose. The legs were cut to such an extent that the bones could be seen. Her face was one mass of cuts. We ran to the Commercial street Police station, and gave information."

In answer to questions as to whether the woman was married, McCarthy said deceased's husband was a fish porter, employed in Billingsgate, but in consequence of a quarrel between them four nights' ago, the man was now lodging in a boarding house in Bishopsgate street.

### INTERVIEW WITH MRS. MAPWELL

Mrs. Caroline Mapwell, of 14 Dorset street, the wife of a night watchman at Commercial Chambers, a common lodging house able to shelter 244 persons, and which is opposite the scene of the murder, said: "I have known the murdered woman well for the past six months. This (Friday) morning, as near as possible about half past eight, I saw Mary Jane (the murdered woman) standing outside the court. I said, "What brings you out so early, Mary Jane," and she answered, "I feel very queer. I cannot sleep. I have the horrors of the drink on me, as I have been drinking this last day or two." I said, "Well, I pity you, " and passed on. I then went to Bishopsgate; and on my return, just after nine o'clock, I saw Mary Jane talking to a man at the end of the street. Who he was I do not know. He was a short, stout man, about fifty years of age.

---

[290] See Appendix P, Mary Jane Kelly Post Mortem.

I did not notice what he had on, but I saw that he wore a kind of plaid coat. I then went indoors to go to bed, as I had been on duty all night. Mary Jane (I only know her by that name) was a pleasant little woman, rather stout, fair complexion, and rather pale. I should say her age was about 23. I had no idea she was an unfortunate, for I never saw her with any one, nor have I ever seen her drunk. She was a very quiet young woman, and had been in the neighbourhood about two years. She spoke with a kind of impediment. She belonged, I think, to Limerick, and had evidently been well connected.

## THE TIME OF THE MURDER

Another important statement was made this morning to a representative of the Central News, by Mrs. Maxwell (or Mapwell) the wife of the deputy of a lodging house in Dorset street, situate just opposite the court in which the crime was committed. From the circumstantial character of Mrs. Maxwell's statement there is little doubt of its accuracy, and the police are now working on it in all directions. As Mrs. Maxwell saw the deceased woman at nine o'clock yesterday morning the crime must have been perpetrated in the broad light of day.

Mrs. Maxwell's statement (which practically coincides with her previous statement given above) is as follows: "I assist my husband in his duties but we live next door, at No. 26 Dorset street. We stay up all night, and yesterday morning as I was going home, carrying my lantern and other things with me, I saw the woman Kelly standing at the entrance of the court. It was then about half past eight, and as it was unusual for her to be seen at that hour, I said to her, "Hallo, what are you doing up so early?" She said, "Oh, I'm very bad this morning. I have had the horrors. I have been drinking so much lately." I said to her, "Why don't you go and have half a pint of beer, it will put you right." She replied, "I've just had one, but I'm so bad I couldn't keep it down." I didn't know then that she had separated from the man she had been living with, and I thought he had been "paying" her. I then went out in the direction of Bishopsgate to do some errands, and on my return I saw Kelly standing outside the public house, talking to a man. That was the last I saw of her.

## THE TWO MEN ARRESTED RELEASED

The two men arrested during the night on suspicion of being concerned in the murder in Dorset street, yesterday, have been released.

## THE YOUNG WOMAN HARVEY

A young woman named Harvey, who had slept with the deceased on several occasions, has also made a statement. She said she had been on good terms with the deceased, whose education was much superior to that of most persons in her position of life. Harvey, however, took a room in New court, off the same street, but remained friendly with the unfortunate woman, who visited her in New court on Thursday night. After drinking together, they parted at half past seven o'clock, Kelly going off in the direction of Leman street, which she was in the habit of frequenting. She was perfectly sober at the time. Harvey never saw her alive afterwards. Hearing in the morning that a murder had been committed, she said, "I'll go and see if it is any one I know," and, to her horror, found it was her friend.

## THE SUPPOSED MURDERER SEEN AT KENNINGTON

A reliable correspondent informs us that yesterday morning, about 11.45, a respectably dressed man, a stranger to the locality, was observed to stoop and wash his hands in a puddle at the corner of Clayton street, nearest to the Kennington Oval. He wore a dark suit, black coat, black billycock hat, and had a small black leather bag with him. He was about 5ft 6in in height, under 30 years of age, broad shouldered, and wore a thick, dark brown moustache. The person who saw him wash his hands in this singular place declares that he noticed marks of blood upon one hand. This, of course, occurred at a time when the news of the murder in Dorset street had not reached Kennington. He further describes this mysterious individual as having a sallow complexion and a thin, clean shaved face.

## JOSEPH BARNET'S STATEMENT

Joseph Barnet, an Irishman, at present residing in a common lodging house in New street, Bishopsgate, stated that he had occupied his present lodgings since Tuesday week. Previous to that he had lived in Miller's court, Dorset street, for eight or nine months with the murdered woman, Mary Jane Kelly. They were very happy and comfortable until another woman came to sleep in their room, to which he strongly objected. Finally, after the woman had been there two or three nights, he quarrelled with Kelly, and left her. The next day, however, he returned, and have her money. He called several other days, and gave her money when he had it. On Thursday night he visited her between half past seven and eight, and told her he was sorry he had no money to give her. He saw nothing more of her. He was indoors when he heard that a woman had been murdered in Dorset street, but voluntarily went to the police, who after questioning him, satisfied themselves that his statements were correct, and therefore released him. Barnet believed Kelly was an Irishwoman.

## THE AUDACITY OF THE ASSASSIN

The audacity of the assassin seemed to be a very general theme among the crowds last night, and on all hands could be heard expressions of opinion that the probability was he was then among them, listening to their denunciations of him with diabolical enjoyment. This disposition of the crowd to look at each other for the criminal constituted a real peril for any stranger among them, the women especially making no secret of the longing they felt to lynch somebody, and it looked as though in one or two cases the police were compelled to make arrests to prevent something of the kind being attempted.

## A FUNNY INCIDENT

One unfortunate foreigner, whose physiognomy was certainly not prepossessing, was taken into Commercial street Police station, when it turned out that that was the third time he had been arrested on suspicion of being Jack the Ripper, in the course of these murders. What with his odd face, his deprecatory shrugs and posturings, and his broken English as he tried to answer the interrogatories put to him, his examination was irresistibly comic. "How d'ye manage to get into trouble like this, then?" demanded an officer.

## "DAT IS ZE ZING"

"What do you do? What makes people pounce on you?" "Dat is ze zing," said the unlucky fellow spreading the palms of his hands and shrugging his shoulders. "Zat is what I like

to know. Why do zey?" He had given a false name at his lodging house, but that, he tried to explain, was because "it eez not grand to leave in a lodging house."

## THE POLICE NON PLUSSED

It is generally admitted by the police that a murder attended by such hideous circumstances has never before been known. The deliberate manner in which the murderer has slain and mutilated his last victim has completely nonplussed the authorities. They state that they have adopted every possible precaution to entrap the fiend, without success, and now that he has adopted the precaution of dissecting his unfortunate victims in their own houses, their ends are completely defeated.

Notwithstanding every effort, the police assert that they failed to establish the time at which, or about which, the crime was committed. Many persons who have been interviewed state that the unfortunate woman never left the house at 26 Dorset court after she entered it on Thursday midnight, while on the other hand numerous persons who declare that they were companions of the deceased, and knew her well, state that she came out of her house at eight o'clock on Friday morning for provisions, and, furthermore, that they were drinking with her in the Britannia, a local tavern, at ten o'clock on the same morning as her mutilated body was found at eleven. In view of these conflicting statements, the hour at which the murder was committed is of course the all important point in connection with the crime.

A representative of the Press Association has interviewed a woman named Kennedy, who was on the night of the murder staying with her parents at a house situate in the court immediately opposite the room in which the body of Mary Kelly was found. This woman's statement, if true—and there is very little reason for doubting its veracity—establishes the time at which the murderer commenced his operations.

She states that about three o'clock on Friday morning she entered Dorset street on her way to her parents' house, which is immediately opposite that in which the murder was committed. She noticed three persons at the corner of the street, near the Britannia public house. There was a man—a young man, respectably dressed, and with a dark moustache, talking to a woman whom she did not know, and also a female poorly clad and without any headgear. The man and woman appeared to be the worse for liquor, and she heard the man ask, "Are you coming," whereupon the woman, who appeared to be obstinate turned in an opposite direction to which the man apparently wished her to go.

Mrs. Kennedy went on her way, and nothing unusual occurred until about half an hour later. She states that she did not retire to rest immediately she reached her parents' abode, but sat up, and between half past three and a quarter to four she heard a cry of "Murder" in a woman's voice proceed from the direction in which Mary Kelly's room was situated. As the cry was not repeated she took no further notice of the circumstance until the morning, when she found the police in possession of the place, preventing all egress to the occupants of the small house in this court. When questioned by the police as to what she had heard throughout the night, she made a statement to the above effect.

She has since supplemented that statement by the following: On Wednesday evening, about eight o'clock, me and my sister were in the neighbourhood of Bethnal Green road when we were accosted by a very suspicious man about forty years of age. He wore a short jacket, over which he had a long top coat. He had a black moustache, and wore a billycock hat. He invited us to accompany him into a lonely spot "As he was known about here, and there was a policeman looking at him." She asserts that no policeman was in sight. He made several strange remarks, and appeared to be agitated. He was very white in the face and made every endeavour to prevent them looking him straight in the face. He carried a black bag. He avoided walking with them, and led the way into a very dark thoroughfare "at the back of the workhouse," inviting them to follow, which they did. He then pushed open a small door in a pair of large gates, and requested one of them to follow him, remarking "I only want one of you," whereupon the women became suspicious. He acted in a very strange and suspicious manner, and refused to leave his bag in the possession of one of the females. Both women became alarmed at his actions and escaped, at the same time raising an alarm of Jack the Ripper. A

gentleman, who was passing, is stated to have intercepted the man while the women made their escape.

Mrs. Kennedy asserts that the man whom she saw on Friday morning with the woman at the corner of Dorset street resembles very closely the individual who caused such alarm on the night in question, and that she would recognise him again if confronted with him.

This description of the man suspected of the murder tallies exactly with that in the possession of the police, and there is very little doubt that the murderer entered the murdered woman's house late on Thursday night, or early on Friday morning.

The non appearance of the bloodhounds, yesterday, is accounted for by the fact that during recent trials in Surrey the animals bolted, and, it is understood, have not been recovered.

## DATES OF THE FORMER CRIMES

Seven women have now been murdered in the East end under mysterious circumstances, five of them within a period of eight weeks. The following are the dates of the crimes and names of the victims so far as known:

1}Last Christmas week—An unknown woman found murdered near Osborne and Wentworth streets, Whitechapel.

2}August 7—Martha Turner, found stabbed in 39 places on a landing in model dwellings known as George Yard buildings, Commercial street, Spitalfields.

3}August 31—Mrs. Nicholls, murdered and mutilated in Buck's row, Whitechapel.

4}September 7—Mrs. Chapman, murdered and mutilated in Hanbury street, Whitechapel.

5}September 30—Elizabeth Stride, found with her throat cut in Berner street, Whitechapel.

6}September 30—Mrs. Eddowes, murdered and mutilated in Mitre square, Aldgate.

7}November 9—Woman murdered and mutilated in Dorset street, Spitalfields.

~

# Monday, 12 November, 1888

## The Times

### THE WHITECHAPEL MURDER.

The two arrests made on Friday night in connexion with the recent murder in Dorset-street, Spitalfields, were found after a short investigation to have nothing to do with it, and consequently the unfortunate persons were liberated by the police, with many apologies for their temporary detention.

Since the murders in Berner-street, St. George's, and Mitre-square, Aldgate, on September 30, Detective-Inspectors Reid, Moore, and Nairn, and Sergeants Thicke, Godley, M'Carthy, and Pearce have been constantly engaged, under the direction of Inspector Abberline (Scotland-yard), in prosecuting inquiries, but, unfortunately, up to the present time without any practical result. As an instance of the magnitude of their labours, each officer has had, on average, during the last six weeks to make some 30 separate inquiries weekly, and these have had to be made in different portions of the metropolis and suburbs.

Since the two above-mentioned murders no fewer that 1,400 letters relating to the tragedies have been received by the police, and although the greater portion of these gratuitous communications were found to be of a trivial or even ridiculous character, still each one was thoroughly investigated. On Saturday many more letters were received, and these are now being inquired into. The detective officers, who are now subjected to a great amount of harassing work, complain that the authorities do not allow them sufficient means with which to carry on their investigations.

Great difference of opinion exists as to the exact time, or about the time, the murder of Mary Jane Kelly took place. Mrs. Maxwell, the deputy of the Commercial lodging-house, which is situated exactly opposite Miller's-court, the place in which the room of the murdered woman is situated, gave positive information that she saw Mary Jane Kelly standing at the entrance to Miller's-court at half-past 8 on Friday morning. She stated that she expressed surprise at seeing Kelly at that early hour, and asked why she was not in bed. Kelly replied, "I can't sleep. I have the horrors from drink". Mrs. Maxwell further stated that after that she went into Bishopsgate-street to make some purch-ases, and on her return saw Kelly talking to a short, dark man at the top of the court. When asked by the police how she could fix the time of the morning, Mrs. Maxwell replied, "Because I went to the milkshop for some milk, and I had not before been there for a long time, and that she was wearing a woollen cross-over that I had not seen her wear for a considerable time". On inquiries being made at the milkshop indicated by the woman her statement was found to be correct, and the cross-over was also found in Kelly's room. Another young woman, whose name is known, has also informed the police that she is positive she saw Kelly between half-past 8 and a quarter to 9 on Friday morning.

Against these statements is the opinion of Dr. George Bagster Phillips, the divisional surgeon of the H Division, that when he was called to the deceased (at a quarter to 11) she had been dead some five or six hours. There is no doubt that the body of a person who, to use Dr. Phillip's own words, was "cut all to pieces" would get cold far more quickly than that of one who had died simply from the cutting of the throat; and the room would have been very cold, as there were two broken panes of glass in the windows. Again, the body being entirely uncovered would very quickly get cold.[291]

It is the opinion of Mr. M'Carthy, the landlord of 26, Dorset-street, that the woman was murdered at a much earlier hour than 8 o'clock, and that Mrs. Maxwell and the other person must have been mistaken.

The police, on making a more minute search of the room in which the body was found, on Saturday morning discovered in the fireplace the charred rim and wirework of a woman's felt hat, as well as a piece of burnt velvet. These, no doubt, formed a portion of a hat and velvet jacket belonging to and worn by Kelly, which are missing. A woman, who is known by the name of Julia and who was in the habit of continually visiting Kelly's room, states she knew that she had two cotton shirts there. These the police are unable to find, and believe they were consumed with the hat and jacket. As a proof that the fierce fire must have been made in the fireplace, there was found a large quantity of ashes, and the rim, the handle, and spout of

---

[291] The high temperature on 9 November was 46.3° F. The low was 38.9° F. (Casebook Productions)

the kettle had been burnt away from the remaining portion of the vessel.[292] The police are of the opinion that the murderer did his fiendish work in daylight, and burnt the above-named articles probably because they were blood-stained. In support of that theory, they have ascertained that on Wednesday night the dead woman purchased a halfpenny candle at the neighbouring chandler's shop, and on the room being searched this candle was barely half consumed.[293] Detective-Inspector Abberline has interviewed a girl named Kennedy, who states that about half-past 3 on the morning of the murder she went to her parent's house, which is opposite the room occupied by Mary Jane Kelly, and on reaching the court she saw a woman talking to two men. Shortly afterwards, when inside her father's house she heard a cry of "Murder" in a woman's voice, and she alleges the sound came from the direction of Kelly's room.

After the discovery of the murder on Friday morning, great curiosity was expressed as to whether bloodhounds would be used to endeavour to trace the murderer to his hiding-place, but these much-talked-of animals were not forthcoming. In fact, no one seemed to know for certain where they were kept. Some officers believed they were at Thornton-heath, others that they were at the Portland-road Station.

As early as half past 7 on Saturday morning, Dr. Phillips, assisted by Dr. Bond (Westminster), Dr. Gordon Brown (City), Dr. Duke (Spital-fields) and his (Dr. Phillips') assistant, made an exhaustive post-mortem examination of the body at the mortuary adjoining Whitechapel Church.[294] It is known that after Dr. Phillips "fitted" the cut portions of the body into their proper places no portion was missing. At the first examination which was only of a cursory character, it was thought that a portion of the body had gone, but this is not the case. The examination was most minutely made, and

lasted upwards of 2½ hours after which the mutilated portions were sewn to the body, and therefore the coroner's jury will be spared the unpleasant duty of witnessing the horrible spectacle presented to those who discovered the murder. The ashes found in the fireplace of the room rented by the deceased woman were also submitted to a searching examination, but nothing likely to throw any light on this shocking case could be gleaned from them.

Joseph Barnett, who for about 20 months lived with the murdered woman, and was separated from her on Tuesday week, and who is now residing in a common lodging-house in New-street, Bishopsgate, gives her an excellent character for generosity of disposition, and says he lived happily with her until she brought another woman, whom he called Julia, to stay in the house. Through this quarrels arose, which eventually led to Barnett leaving her. He had seen her once or twice since that time and had on each occasion given her money. Kelly was an Irishwoman. She was in the habit of going nightly to a publichouse at Fish-street-hill; but Sergeant Bradshaw, on making inquiry at the house in question, found that she had not been there for upwards of a month past.

During the whole of yesterday Sergeant Thicke, with other officers, was busily engaged in writing down the names, statements, and full particulars of persons staying at the various lodging-houses in Dorset-street. That this was no easy task will be imagined when it is known that in one house alone there are upwards of 260 persons, and that several houses accommodate over 200.

The inquest will be opened at 11 o'clock this morning by Dr. Macdonald, Coroner for the North-Eastern Division of Middlesex, at the Shoreditch Town-hall. On Saturday, both Dr. Macdonald and Mr. Wynne Baxter, the coroner for the other portion of the district, visited Dorset-street, and each gentleman maintains that the murder occurred in his district; but removing the body to the Shoreditch mortuary settled the point as to who was to hold in inquiry, as that building is in Dr. Macdonald's district. After the inquiry is over, or when the coroner signs the certificate of burial, a question will probably arise as to which parish will have to defray the cost of the burial of the deceased, as, although the inquest will be held in Shore-

---

[292] According to Hasluck's 1904 edition of Metal-working the 4,4,1 lead, tin, bismuth soft solder used on tin teapots has a melting point of 320° F. (Hasluck)

[293] A Halfpenny Candle would usually burn about two hours. (Royal Commission)

[294] See Appendix P, Mary Jane Kelly Post Mortem, p. 585.

ditch, the murder took place in Whitechapel.

—

The following notice of pardon to accomplices who may give information leading to conviction, has been issued by Sir C. Warren:—

MURDER.—PARDON.—Whereas on November 8 or 9, in Miller-court, Dorset-street, Spitalfields, Mary Janet Kelly was murdered by some person or persons unknown: the Secretary of State will advise the grant of Her Majesty's gracious pardon to any accomplice, not being a person who contrived or actually committed the murder, who shall give such information and evidence as shall lead to the discovery and conviction of the person or persons who committed the murder.

CHARLES WARREN,
The Commissioner of Police of the Metropolis.
Metropolitan Police-office,
4, Whitehall-place, S.W.,
Nov. 10, 1888.

—

The public excitement has abated to hardly any appreciable extent, as was shown by the crowded state of the streets in the neighbourhood of Whitechapel yesterday. There was a report that a woman had been found murdered in Jubilee-street, but this turned out to be untrue.

—

Great excitement was caused shortly before 10 o'clock last night by the arrest of a man with a blackened face who publicly proclaimed himself to be "Jack the Ripper." This was at the corner of Wentworth-street, Commercial-street, near the scene of the latest crime.

Two young men, one a discharged soldier, immediately seized him, and the great crowd, which always on a Sunday night parades this neighbourhood, raise a cry of "Lynch him." Sticks were raised, the man was furiously attacked, and but for the timely arrival of the police he would have been seriously injured.

The police took him to Leman-street station, when the prisoner proved to be a very remarkable person. He refused to give any name, but asserted that he was a doctor at St. George's Hospital. He is about 35 years of age, 5ft. 7in. in height, of dark complexion, with dark moustache, and was wearing spectacles. He wore no waistcoat, but had an ordinary jersey vest beneath his coat. In his pocket he had a double-peaked, light check cap, and at the time of his arrest was bareheaded.

It took four constables and four other persons to take him to the station and protect him from the infuriated crowd. He is detained in custody, and it seems that the police attach importance to the arrest, as his appearance answers to the police description of the man who is wanted.

—

Shortly after 10 o'clock last night as a woman named Humphreys was passing George-yard, Whitechapel, she met in the darkness and almost on the identical spot where Martha Tabram was murdered, a powerful-looking man wearing large spectacles.

Trembling with agitation she asked, "What do you want?" The man made no answer, but laughed and made a hasty retreat. The woman shouted "Murder" several times and soon alarmed the neighbours.

Uniformed policemen and detectives ran to the yard from all directions. They entered a house into which the man had retreated, and he was apprehended. A crowd of people quickly collected, who exhibited an almost unanimous inclination to lynch the mysterious person, but the police were fortunately able to protect him.

Being taken to Leman-street Police-station, he accounted for his presence in the yard by the fact that he was paying a visit to a friend who is an inhabitant of it. He referred the police to a well-known gentleman at the London Hospital, and in the result he was set at liberty.

Other men who were in custody yesterday on account of suspicious movements have been released, all of them having given satisfactory explanations.

—

## The Star
### FIFTH EDITION.
### WHITECHAPEL.
### IMPORTANT EVIDENCE AT THE INQUEST TO-DAY.
### A DESCRIPTION OF THE MURDERER.
**A Witness who Resides in the Same House Describes a Man whom She Saw Enter the Room with the Deceased on the Night of the Murder.**

Vague rumors and contradictory stories have been more prevalent in connection with this most recent horror, the murder of Mary Janet Kelly, than perhaps has been the case with any of the preceding East-end crimes. The police, expecting all possible assistance from the public, have handicapped their capacity for rendering any aid by doing all in their power to suppress information of the crime without which information help cannot be very judiciously given. The result of the police reticence has been the creation of a market for false news, and the actual facts of this latest horror differ with each narrator of the revolting details. Consequently the inquest, and the sworn testimony which it would produce, could not but be

### ANTICIPATED WITH EXCEPTIONAL EAGERNESS.

This inquiry was opened this morning by Coroner Macdonald at the Shoreditch Town Hall, in a small but well-ventilated and well-furnished room on the ground floor. With the accommodation so limited, the Coroner's officer had to be careful to prevent overcrowding. He was at first satisfied with holding the door shut, but as the crush outside threatened to overmaster his strength he locked the door, and stationed an inspector on duty there. Inquiries went round as to why a larger room was not requisitioned, and it then transpired that the council chamber could not be used, because it was being repaired. At length those with business at the inquest were all accommodated, but by that time the place was literally packed. Inspector Abberline and Inspector Nairn watched the proceedings on behalf of the police.

The inquiry did not open auspiciously, for the jury had a grievance, and the Coroner did not apparently feel in a compromising mood. The coroner's officer was asking the jurors to select a foreman, when several of them complained that their services ought not to have been required to investigate a death which occurred out of their parish. "Don't argue with me, gentlemen," said the coroner's officer, "but speak to the Coroner." "What's the matter?" asked Dr. Macdonald. "The woman did not die in this parish," said a juror, "and therefore we think we ought not to have been summoned on the jury." "Do you think we don't know what we are doing?" asked the Coroner, warmly. "Do you think we don't know our own district? The jury have no business to object. They are summoned in the usual way and can't object. If they persist in their objections

**I KNOW HOW TO DEAL WITH THEM,**

that is all." There were several murmurs among the jurors that Mr. Baxter was their Coroner, and so on, when the Coroner challenged the mutineers in the following words:—"If any juryman says he distinctly objects, let him say so." Whatever the penalties would have been (and they would have been severe, judging from Dr. Macdonald's tone), no juror thought fit to incur them by answering, and the Coroner went on, "I may tell you that jurisdiction lies where the body lies, and not where it was found."[295]

The jurors then all submitted to be sworn and proceeded to view the body. It was lying in

---

[295] According to Richard Sewell's <u>A Treatise on Law of Coroner</u> (1843), p. 27:
"That the coroner only within whose jurisdiction the body of any person upon whose death an inquest ought to be holden shall be lying dead shall hold the inquest, notwithstanding that the cause of death did not arise within the jurisdiction of such coroner..."
And on p. 30:
"When the Coroner receives notice of a violent death, casualty or misadventure, which regularly ought to be from the proper or peace officer of the parish, place, or precinct where the body lies dead, having satisfied himself that it is within his jurisdiction, he is then to issue his precept or warrant to summon a jury to appear at a particular time and place named, to inquire when, how, and by what means the deceased came by his death; which warrant is directed to the peace officers of the parish, place, or precinct "where the party lies dead," and to others of the next adjoining parishes... (Sewell)

# Monday, 12 November, 1888

the Shoreditch mortuary, the effect of the horrible mutilations being lessened in the eyes of the inspecting jurors by the fact that the pieces cut from the body had been replaced and sewn up. The sight even then was ghastly and sickening enough, in all conscience.

By the coroner's directions the jury were taken from the mortuary to the scene of the crime in order that they might acquaint themselves with the appearance of the room. It contained two very old tables, a broken chair, an ancient wooden bedstead, and a dilapidated fender.[296] In a corner there was a pail, and these few articles exhausted the catalogue of the furniture. The walls were papered, but the pattern could hardly be traced for the dirt which covered it, and the floor boards were bare and filthy. There were two windows, both on the same side of the passage, and in one of the windows were the two broken panes of glass, which admitted of the drawing back of the curtain and the revealing of the traces of the terrible crime. It was thus close upon twelve o'clock before any evidence was taken. The first witness was

### JAMES BARNET,

but when he had been sworn the coroner interposed for a few moments to say that the papers had been making a great fuss as to the jurisdiction under which this inquest came, but there was no need for any fuss at all. He had had no communication with Mr. Baxter at all.

Then the witness Barnet told his story. He was a fish porter, about six and twenty years old, and looking very respectable for one of his class.

He said:—To my calculation deceased has lived with me for the last year and eight months. I have seen the body and I identify Mary Kelly by the ears and the eyes. I am positive about it. We used to live in 13 room, Miller's-court, Dorset-street, and had been there for over eight months. On the 30th of last month I separated from her, because she had a prostitute with her in her room, having taken her in out of compassion. Being out of work had nothing to do with my leaving her, he added, in answer to a question from the Coroner. I last saw her alive, continued witness, between half-past seven and a quarter to eight on the night she was supposed to have been murdered. I had

called to see after her welfare, and stayed there a quarter of an hour. We were on friendly terms, but I told her I was out of work and had nothing to give her, for which I was very sorry.

Did you have any drink together there?
—No, sir.
Was she quite sober?
—Yes, quite.
Was she generally of sober habits?
—I always found her so, but she has been drunk several times in my presence.
Was anyone else there on the Thursday evening you were there?
—Yes; a female living in the court. She left first and I left very shortly afterwards.
Did she ever tell you where she was born and brought up?
—Yes; she said she was

### BORN IN LIMERICK,

and was taken to Wales when very young. She came to London about four years ago. Her father was a foreman in some ironworks in Wales. She said she had one sister who was respectable, and who followed her aunt's occupation of travelling from market place to market place with materials. She said she had six or seven brothers, six at home, I think, and one in the army. I never saw one of them to speak to.

Was she ever married, did she say?
—Yes, when very young, about 16, in Wales, to a colliery owner or a collier, but I have never been in those parts and don't know which. She said her husband's name was Davis, and that he was killed in an explosion. After her husband's death she went to Cardiff, and was in an infirmary there between eight and nine months. She followed a bad life at her cousin's in Cardiff, and I have often told her that was the cause of her downfall. After leaving Cardiff she came to London, and was in a gay house[297] in the West-end. There a gentleman came to her and asked her if she would like to go to France, so she described to me. She went to France, as she told me, but did not stop there long, as she did not like the part. After her return to England she went to

### THE RATCLIFF HIGHWAY,

and lived opposite the gasworks with a man named Morganstone. I have never seen that man in my life. Then she went to Pennington-street, I

---

[296] **Fender.** Fireplace guard. (Morehead)

[297] **Gay House.** Brothel. (Farmer)

believe, and lived in a bad house there. In connection with that house she mentioned the name of Joseph Flemming, a mason's plasterer, of whom she said she was very fond. He used to often visit her. I picked up with her in Commercial-street one night when we had a drink together, and I made arrangements to see her on the following day, which was a Saturday. We then agreed to live together, and I took lodgings in a place in George-street, not far from where the George-yard murder was committed. I then lived with her up to when I left her, just recently.

Did you ever hear her say she was afraid of anyone?

—Yes, she used to get me to bring her evening papers and see if there was another murder. Beyond that she was not afraid of anyone that I know of.

Here a note was handed into the court from Dr. Phillips asking if he should attend to-day to give his evidence.

The Coroner thought he should just give them roughly an idea of the cause of death, leaving the details of his evidence for a future day, and dispatched a message to that effect.

### THE MAN WHO FOUND THE BODY.

Thomas Bowyer, of 37, Dorset-street, Spital-fields, said:—I am servant to Mr. McCarthy, the landlord of deceased's room. At a quarter to eleven on Friday morning I was ordered to go to her room, No. 13, to collect her rent. I knocked at the door and got no answer. I knocked again, and then still getting no answer went to her window.

Here Inspector Ledger put in a plan of the place, to enable the witness the better to explain exactly where he went. It was the window nearest the entrance, the smaller one of the two, to which he went.

Proceeding, Bowyer said:—There was a curtain covering the window, but putting my hand through the broken pane I pulled it on one side and looked in. I saw two

### LUMPS OF FLESH LYING ON THE TABLE,

which was close against the front of the bed. The second time I looked I saw the body of someone lying on the bed, and blood on the floor. I at once went very quietly back to Mr. McCarthy, who stood in the shop which he keeps in Dorset-street. I told him what I had seen, and he said, "Good God! do you mean to say this, Harry?" We both went down to the police station, Mr. McCarthy having first been with me and looked through the window to satisfy himself. We gave information of what we had seen to the police, and the inspector on duty came back with us.

Did you see this woman in and out there?

—Yes, sir, often. I know Barnet through seeing him go in often, and have never seen him drunk. I have seen deceased drunk once.

### JOHN M'CARTHY,

a gentlemanly-looking man, describing himself as a grocer and lodging-house keeper, said:—At about half-past ten or a quarter to eleven on Friday morning, I sent my man Bowyer to collect the rent at room 13, in Miller's-court. He came back, and from the information he gave me, I went with him. I saw the woman's body lying on the bed, and for the moment I could say nothing. Then I said, "Harry, don't tell anyone; go and fetch the police." As he was going I recovered myself, and thought I had better go with him, and followed him down the court, and we both saw Inspector Back, who returned with us at once. Deceased has lived in this room for over 10 months, and Barnet with her. The rent of the room was 4s. 6d. weekly. Deceased was about 29s. in arrears. I have very often seen deceased the worse for drink. She was an exceptionally quiet woman when sober, but when she had drink she had a little more to say. I never saw her helpless.

### THE MURDERER DESCRIBED.

Mary Ann Cox, a wretched looking specimen of East-end womanhood, said:—I live at No. 5 room, Miller's-court. I am a widow, and having been unfortunate lately, I have had to get my living on the streets. I have known the deceased between eight and nine months. On Thursday night at a quarter to twelve I saw her very much intoxicated in Dorset-street. There was with her a short, stout man, shabbily dressed, who went with her up the court. He had a longish dark coat on, not an overcoat, and he had a pot of ale in his hand. He had a round felt hat on. He wore a full carroty moustache, and had a blotchy face. He had a clean-shaved chin, and very slight whiskers. He went with the deceased into her room, and I said "Good night,

# Monday, 12 November, 1888

Mary." Thereupon the man turned round and banged the door, the deceased having answered me, in a drunken voice, "Good night, I'm going to have a song." She thereupon sang "A violet I plucked from my mother's grave when a boy."[298] I remained in my room a quarter of an hour to warm my hands, and when I went out again

**DECEASED WAS STILL SINGING.**

I then remained out till three, and when I returned all was quiet, and deceased's light was out. I did not sleep that night, and should have heard any noise if there had been any after that, but there was not. At a quarter past six in the morning, I heard a man go out of the court, but from which house I could not say. I heard no door bang. The man I saw go in with deceased was about 36. There was no noise from his tread as he went up the court with deceased.

The Coroner: So that his boots must have been dilapidated?

—I suppose so.

A Juror: Should you know the man again if you saw him?

—Oh, yes, I should.

Could you see her through the window?

—No, the blinds were down.

---

[298] *A Violet From Mother's Grave*
Words and music by Will H. Fox.
Philadelphia: J. W. Pepper. (Andrews)

1. Scenes of my childhood arise before my gaze,
Bringing recollections of bygone happy days.
When down in the meadow in childhood I would roam,
No one's left to cheer me now within that good old home,
Father and Mother, they have pass'd away;
Sister and brother, now lay beneath the clay,
But while life does remain to cheer me, I'll retain
This small violet I pluck'd from mother's grave.

CHORUS: Only a violet I pluck'd when but a boy,
And oft'times when I am sad at heart this flow'r
has giv'n me joy;
But while life does remain in memoriam I'll retain,
This small violet I pluck'd from mother's grave.

2. Well I remember my dear old mother's smile,
As she used to greet me when I returned from toil,
Always knitting in the old arm chair,
Father used to sit and read for all us children there,
But now all is silent around the good old home;
They all have left me in sorrow here to roam,
But while life does remain, in memoriam I'll retain
This small violet I pluck'd from mother's grave.

**ELIZABETH PRATER,**

a young married woman living apart from her husband, in 20 Room, Miller's-court, said:—My room is just over that of the deceased. On Thursday night I slept in my clothes, having barricaded the door with two tables, as I generally did. My kitten disturbed me by putting its cold nose on my mouth, and as I turned over I heard a cry, "Oh, murder!" the first ejaculation being one of surprise, and the second a rather faint cry. Being used to cries of alarm in that neighbourhood, I did not take much notice, but dropped off to sleep.

(Proceeding.)

—

Nothing has yet been discovered which seems likely to lead to the capture of the Whitechapel murder fiend. The clue on which the police on the first discovery of the crime founded their strongest hopes of discovering the criminal—the finding of a pilot coat in the victim's room—seems to have utterly broken down, as it is now pretty certain that the garment in question was the woman's own property, or at any rate left in her charge by one of her many acquaintances. Yesterday afternoon a man's shirt covered with blood was found in the area of some schools in Russell-street, opposite the side entrance of Drury-lane Theatre. This garment has been submitted to Dr. Mills, divisional surgeon, for examination, but does not promise much. The key of the murdered woman's door has been found, so that her murderer did not carry it away with him, as was at first supposed.

Another point which has been cleared up is that

**NO PART OF THE BODY IS MISSING.**

There have been many conflicting statements as to the time at which Kelly was last seen. Some women have said they saw her between half-past eight and nine on Friday morning. But medical opinion goes against this. Dr. Bagster Phillips, divisional surgeon, says that when he was called (at a quarter to eleven) Kelly had been dead some five or six hours. Owing to the loss of blood the body would have got cold quickly, but a big fire seems to have been kept up, and the police say that when they entered the room it was quite warm. As a proof that a fierce fire must have been made in the fireplace, there was found a large quantity of ashes, and the rim, the handle,

461

and spout of the kettle had been burnt away from the remaining portion of the vessel. This led the police to believe that

**THE MURDERER BURNED SOMETHING,**
and they searched the ashes. In the fireplace was found the charred rim and wirework of a woman's felt hat, as well as a piece of burnt velvet. These, no doubt, formed a portion of a hat and velvet jacket belonging to and worn by Kelly, which are missing. A woman, who is known by the name of Julia, and who was in the habit of continually visiting Kelly's room, states that she knew that she had two cotton shirts there. These the police are unable to find, and believe they were consumed with the hat and jacket. The police are of opinion that the murderer did his fiendish work in daylight, and burned the above-named articles probably because they were bloodstained. In support of that theory, they have ascertained that on Wednesday night the dead woman purchased a halfpenny candle at the neighboring chandler's shop, and on the room being searched this candle was found, barely half consumed.

Some further details as to the woman's antecedents are coming out. Joseph Barnett, the man she lived with in the room in which she was murdered said:—"When she was but little over 16 years of age she married a collier, but I do not remember his name. He was killed in an explosion in the mine, and then Marie went to Cardiff with her cousin. Thence she went to France, but remained only a short time. Afterwards she

**LIVED IN A FASHIONABLE HOUSE**
in the West-end of London; but drifted from the West-end to the East-end, where she took lodgings in Pennington-street. Her father came from Wales, and tried to find her there; but, hearing from her companions that he was looking for her, Marie kept out of the way. A brother in the Second Battalion Scots Guards came to see her once, but beyond that she saw none of her relations, nor did she correspond with them. When she was in Pennington-street a man named Morganstone lived with her, and subsequently a man named Joseph Fleming passed as her husband."

The authorities have been making inquiries concerning the soldier who, according to Barnett, was in the second battalion of the Scots Guards. That regiment is now in Dublin, and it

is understood that inquiries will be immediately prosecuted there.

Mrs. Elizabeth Phoenix, residing at 157, Bow Common-lane, Burdett-road, Bow, called at the Leman-street Police-station last evening and made a statement to the officers on duty which it is thought will satisfactorily establish the identity of the murdered woman. She stated that about three years ago a woman, apparently the deceased from the description given of her, resided at her brother-in-law's house at Breezer's-hill, Pennington-street, near the London Docks. She describes this lodger as a woman about 5ft. 7in. in height, and of rather stout build, with blue eyes and a very fine head of hair, which reached nearly to her waist. At that time she gave her name as Mary Jane Kelly, and stated that she was about 22 years of age, so that her age at the present time would be about 25. There was, it seems, some difficulty in establishing her nationality.

**SHE STATED FIRST THAT SHE WAS WELSH,**
and that her parents, who had discarded her, still resided at Cardiff, whence she came to London. On other occasions, however, she declared that she was Irish. She is described as being very quarrelsome and abusive when intoxicated, but "one of the most decent and nicest girls you could meet" when sober. About two years ago she left Breezer's-hill and removed to Commercial-road, from which quarter she had been reported to Mrs. Phoenix as leading a loose life. It has been stated more than once that Kelly was a native of Limerick, but a telegram received from that place last night says that inquiries made in that city have failed to identify the latest Whitechapel victim as a native of the town.

There is little doubt that Kelly came to London from Cardiff some five or six years ago, leaving in that town her friends, whom she has described as being well to do. She is stated to have been an excellent scholar and an artist. It would appear that on her arrival in London she made the acquaintance of a French lady residing in the neighborhood of Knightsbridge, who, she informed her friends, led her into the degraded life which has brought about her untimely end. She made no secret of the fact that while she was with this lady she

**DROVE ABOUT IN A CARRIAGE,**
and made several journeys to the French capital,

and in fact led the life of a lady. By some means, however, at present not exactly clear, she suddenly drifted into the East-end. Her first experiences of the East-end appear to have commenced with Mrs. Buki, who resided in one of the thoroughfares off Ratcliff-highway, now known as St. George's-street. Both women went to the French lady's residence, and demanded Kelly's box, which contained numerous costly dresses. From Mrs. Buki's place, Kelly went to lodge with Mrs. Carthy, at Breezer's-hill, Pennington-street. This place she left about 18 months or two years ago, and took up her quarters in Dorset-street. As to her ever having a child, the testimony is conflicting. Mrs. Carthy declares positively that she never had one. Mrs. Carthy states that the deceased when she left her place went to live with a man who was apparently in the building trade, and who she (Mrs. Carthy) believed would have married her.

It appears from inquiries made at Carmarthen and Swansea, that after leaving the former place for the latter, Kelly, who was then only 17 years of age, entered the service of a Mrs. Rees, who stands committed to the next assizes on a charge of procuring abortion, and who is the daughter of a medical man formerly resident at Carmarthen.

### SEVERAL ARRESTS

were made yesterday, but every suspect, after a short detention, was allowed to go free. The arrest which was productive of most excitement was that of a doctor turned amateur detective. About ten o'clock last night the idle and inquisitive crowd, who since the ghastly discovery was made have infested Dorset-street and its immediate neighborhood, had their attention attracted to the extraordinary behaviour of a man who for some short time before had been officiously making inquiries and generally conducting himself in an unusual manner. Over a pair of good trousers he wore a jersey in place of a coat, and his face was most papably artificially blacked. His manner led to considerable remark and at last a cry was raised that he was "Jack the Ripper." In the prevailing state of the public mind in the district this was quite enough to inflame the anger of those in the street, and he was at once roughly seized. Fortunately for him, there was a large number of policemen about, both in uniform and plain clothes, by whom he was at once surrounded on the first alarm being given.

### HE AT FIRST RESISTED CAPTURE,

but, happily for himself, soon realised his position, and consented to go quietly to Leman-street Police-station. Meanwhile, the officers who had him in charge had the greatest difficulty in saving their prisoner from the fury of the mod, who amid the wildest excitement made the most desperate endeavors to lynch him. As it was, he was very roughly handled and considerably bruised by the time he reached the police-station, where he gave his name and address, which are withheld by the police authorities. He stated that he was a medical man, and had disguised himself in the absurd manner above described in order to endeavor by what he thought were detective means to discover and apprehend the perpetrator of the Whitechapel horrors. He gave such particulars of himself as enabled the police to quickly substantiate their accuracy, and to discharge him.

While the police have been working zealously in the hope of making some discovery of value, the public themselves appear to have been conscious that the responsibility of the officers of the law is in a measure shared by them. This is seen by

### AN EXCITING INCIDENT

which occurred yesterday, and which resulted in the arrest and detention of a strange man at Bishopsgate-street Police-station. Some men were drinking at a beerhouse in Fish-street-hill. One of them began conversing about the Whitechapel murder, and a man named Brown, living at 9, Dorset-street, thought he detected a blood mark on the coat of the stranger. On the latter's attention being called to it he said the mark was merely paint, but Brown took out a pocket-knife, and, rubbing the dried stain with the blade, pronounced it to be blood. The coat being loose, similar stains were seen on the man's shirt, and he then admitted that they were bloodstains. Leaving the house at once, Brown followed, and when the suspicious stranger had got opposite to Bishopsgate Police-station Brown gave him into custody. The prisoner gave the name of George Compton. On being brought before the inspector on duty he excitedly protested against being arrested in the public street, alleging that in the present state of public feeling he might have been lynched. The man had been arrested at Shadwell on Saturday by a police-constable, who considered his beha-viour suspicious, but he had been discharged.

Another arrest was effected at an early hour in the morning through the exertions of two young men living in the neighborhood of Dorset-street. They had their attention drawn to two men in Dorset-street who were loitering about. The two men separated, and one of them was followed by the two youths into Hounds-ditch. They carefully observed his appearance, which was that of a foreigner. He was about 5ft. 8in. in height, had a long pointed moustache, was dressed in a long black overcoat, and wore, also, a cloth deerstalker hat. When near Bishopsgate-street the young men spoke to a policeman, who at once stopped the stranger and took him to Bishopsgate Police-station. Here he was detained pending inquiries, but afterwards allowed to go.

Another man was detained at Commercial-street Station on account of his suspicious movements. A man named Peter Maguire says that about eleven o'clock on Saturday night he was drinking at the public-house kept by Mrs. Fiddymont, in Brushfield-street, which is known as the Clean House, when he noticed a man talking very earnestly to a young woman. He asked her to accompany him up a neighboring court, but she refused, and afterwards left the bar. Maguire followed the man, who, noticing this, commenced running. He ran into Spitalfields Market, Maguire following all the while. The man then stopped, went up a court,

### TOOK OFF A PAIR OF GLOVES

he was wearing and put on another pair. By a roundabout route he proceeded into Shoreditch, and got into an omnibus, which Maguire still followed. A policeman was asked by Maguire to stop this vehicle, but he refused, and Maguire continued his pursuit until he met another constable, who stopped the omnibus. The man was inside huddled up in a corner. Maguire explained his suspicions, and the man was taken to Commercial-street Station, where he was detained pending inquiries.

In the excited nervous state of the people living in the district in which the crimes have been committed there are naturally

### MANY SCARES.

Great excitement was created last night about a quarter past nine in Wentworth-street, Commercial-street, close to Dorset-street, by loud cries of "Murder" and "Police" which proceeded from George-yard-buildings. Police-sergeant Irving and Police-constable 22 H R were quickly on the spot, and at once rushed into the buildings, which are a large set of model dwellings. In the meantime the street rapidly filled with persons from the adjoining houses, while some of those who lived in the top storey of the buildings clambered on to the roof in order to intercept any person who might attempt to make his escape by that means. After a little inquiry, however, by the officers the truth came out. It seems that a Mrs. Humphries, who is nearly blind, lives with her daughter on the second floor of the buildings, and about the time mentioned went to an outhouse for the purpose of emptying some slops. As she went in a young man, who is courting her daughter, and was on his way to visit her, slipped out of the place past her. Mrs. Humphries at once asked who it was. The young man, who, it is said, stutters very badly, made some unintelligible answer and the old lady, who, like her neighbors, was haunted with the terror of "Jack the Ripper," at once gave the alarm, which was promptly responded to. The mistake, however, was soon explained, and quiet restored in the vicinity.

—

### ARREST THIS MORNING.

The police at Commercial-street station made another arrest at three o'clock this morning in Dorset-street at the scene of the murder. The man refused to satisfy the officers as to his recent movements. At eight o'clock he was still in custody.

### IN WOMAN'S CLOTHES.

A man dressed in woman's clothing was arrested on suspicion in Goswell-road on Saturday night. He proved he could have had nothing to do with the murder, and said he put female attire on only "for a lark," but he will be brought before the magistrate charged with having done it for an unlawful purpose.

### BRAVO BROS!

Charles Thomas was charged at Clerkenwell with being drunk in Crowndale-road, St Pancras.

Constable 550 Y saw the man drunk and surrounded by a crowd of persons early on

# Monday, 12 November, 1888

Sunday morning. He kept shouting out "I'm Jack the Ripper."

Mr. Bros sentenced Thomas to 14 days' imprisonment, with hard labour, and said he should send every man to prison, without the option of a fine, who was brought before him for shouting out in the street that he was the Whitechapel murderer.

### WHAT WOMEN SAY.

The *Women's Gazette* says:—"In the name of the women of England we demand that some steps be taken for the protection of our unfortunate sisters in the East-end. First and foremost we demand the dismissal of those two conspicuous monuments of failure, Mr. Home Secretary Matthews and Sir Charles Warren. We expect little consideration from the present Government. We are, after all, only women— and women have no votes. We are, however, confident that our demand will be backed by everything that is chivalrous in the manhood of our country.

—

### WARREN GONE!

The Press Association says:—The report is current at Scotland-yard to-day that Sir Charles Warren has sent in his resignation. No official confirmation or denial can be obtained.

Information has been brought to *The Star* office tending strongly to confirm this rumour.

~

## Evening News
### HE LATEST HORROR
### THE SUPPOSED MURDERER SEEN AT KENNINGTON
### THE MURDERED WOMAN'S HISTORY
### ARREST THIS MORNING
### THE INQUEST TODAY
### REPORTED LETTER FROM THE MURDERER

It is reported this morning, from Spitalfields, that Mrs. McCarthy, the wife of the landlord of No. 26 Dorset street, this morning received by post a letter signed Jack the Ripper, saying that they were not to worry themselves, because he meant to "do" two more in the neighbourhood, a mother and daughter. The letter was taken immediately to Commercial street Police station and handed to the Inspector on duty.

A Press Association, on inquiring at Commercial street Police station, subsequently was assured that no such letter had been received there.

A reliable correspondent informs us that on Friday morning, about 11.45, a respectably dressed man, a stranger to the locality, was observed to stoop and wash his hands in a puddle at the corner of Clayton street, nearest to the Kennington Oval. He wore a dark suit, black coat, black billycock hat, and had a small black leather bag with him. He was about 5ft 6in in height, under 30 years of age, broad shouldered, and wore a thick brown moustache. The person who saw him wash his hands in this singular place declares that he noticed marks of blood upon one hand. This, of course, occurred at a time when the news of the murder in Dorset street had not reached Kennington. He further describes this mysterious individual as having a sallow complexion and a thin, clean shaved face.

—

### THE AUDACITY OF THE ASSASSIN

The audacity of the assassin seemed to be a very general theme among the crowds on Friday night, and on all hands could be heard expressions of opinion that the probability was he was then among them, listening to their denunciations of him with diabolical enjoyment. This disposition of the crowd to look at each other for the criminal constituted a real peril for any stranger among them, the women especially making no secret of the longing they felt to lynch somebody, and it looked as though in one or two cases the police were compelled to make arrests to prevent something of the kind being attempted.

—

## WHO THE MURDERED WOMAN WAS.

The Central News says: The woman murdered in Spitalfields, on Friday, was born in Limerick, her name being Marie Jeanette Kelly. Her parents moved from Limerick to Carmarthen, and here the deceased married a collier whose name is believed to be Davies. He, however, was killed in a colliery explosion and the deceased woman then lived an ill life at Cardiff, afterwards removing to London. Her parents are still living in Wales.

Some statements have appeared respecting the deceased's antecedents, and as to her having formerly lived for some time in a fashionable house in the West end. There is reason to believe that not only are these statements as to her antecedents well founded, but that she still maintained some sort of communication with the companions of her prosperous days. Seeing that it was contrary to Kelly's custom for her to bring strangers to her room, it is believed that her destroyer, whoever he may be, offered her some exceptional inducement to take him there.

—

## THE HOME SECRETARY OFFERS A FREE PARDON

Whereas, on November the 8th or 9th, in Miller court, Dorset street, Spitalfields, Mary Janet Kelly was murdered by some person or persons unknown, the Secretary of State will advise the grant of Her Majesty's gracious pardon to any accomplice not being a person who contrived or actually committed the murder, who shall give such information and evidence as shall lead to the discovery and conviction of the person or persons who committed the murder.

(Signed) Charles Warren
The Commissioner of
Police of the Metropolis
Metropolitan Police Office:
4 Whitehall place, S.W.
10th November 1888

—

"*London and Brighton*", a paper published on Wednesday, contains the following:

On Sunday the new moon came in. If Jack the Ripper is a lunatic, and if there is any truth in the theory of the susceptibility of lunatics to lunar influence we ought to hear from him in the course of a few days.

—

## ATTEMPT TO LYNCH AN AMATEUR DETECTIVE

About ten o'clock last night, the idle and inquisitive crowd, who since the ghastly discovery was made have infested Dorset street and its immediate neighbourhood, had their attention attracted to the extraordinary behaviour of a man who for some short time before had been officiously making inquiries and generally conducting himself in an unusual manner. Over a pair of good trousers he wore a jersey in place of a coat, and his face was most palpably artificially blacked. His manner led to considerable remark, and at last a cry was raised that he was Jack the Ripper. In the prevailing state of the public mind in the district this was quite enough to inflame the anger of those in the street, and he was at once roughly seized. Fortunately for him, there were a large number of policemen about, both in uniform and plain clothes, by whom he was at once surrounded on the first alarm being given. He at first resisted capture, but, happily for himself, soon realised his position and consented to go quietly to Leman street Police station.

—

## VERY NEARLY LYNCHED

Meanwhile, the officers who had him in charge had the greatest difficulty in saving their prisoner from the fury of the mob, who amid the wildest excitement made the most desperate endeavours to lynch him. As it was, he was very roughly handled and considerably bruised by the time he reached the police station, where he gave name and address which are withheld by the police authorities. He stated that he was a medical man, and had disguised himself in the absurd manner above described in order to endeavour by what he thought were detective means to discover and apprehend the perpetrator of the Whitechapel horrors. He also gave such particulars of himself as enabled the police to quickly substantiate their accuracy, and to discharge him after a short detention in the cells.

466

# Monday, 12 November, 1888

## THE WORK OF THE POLICE

Since the murders in Berner street, St. George's, and Mitre square, Aldgate, Detective Inspectors Reid, Moore, and Nairn, and Sergeants Thicke, Godley, M'Carthy, and Pearce have been constantly engaged, under the direction of Inspector Abberline (Scotland yard), in prosecuting inquiries, but, unfortunately, up to the present time without any practical result. As an instance of the magnitude of their labours, each officer has had, on an average, during the last six weeks to make some 30 separate inquiries weekly, and these have had to be made in different portions of the metropolis and suburbs. Since the two above mentioned murders no fewer than 1400 letters relating to the tragedies have been received by the police, and although the greater portion of those gratuitous communications were found to be of a trivial and even ridiculous character, still each one was thoroughly investigated. On Saturday many more letters were received, and these are now being inquired into. *The Times* says that the detective officers, who are now subjected to a great amount of harassing work, complain that the authorities do not allow them sufficient means with which to carry on their investigations.

—

## A POSSIBLE CLUE

On Saturday afternoon a gentleman engaged in business in the vicinity of the murder gave what is the only approach to a possible clue that has yet been brought to light. He states that he was walking through Mitre square at about ten minutes past ten on Friday morning, when a tall, well dressed man, carrying a parcel under his arm, and rushing along in a very excited manner, ran plump into him. The man's face was covered with blood splashes, and his collar and shirt were also bloodstained. The gentleman did not at the time know anything of the murder.

—

## THE SEARCH FOR A CLUE IN THE ROOM

A somewhat important investigation was made on Saturday in the room in Miller's court in which the woman was murdered. The police had reason to believe that the murderer had burnt something before leaving the room after the crime, and accordingly the ashes and other matter in the grate were carefully preserved. Dr. Phillips and Dr. Macdonald, M.P., the coroner for the district, visited Miller's court, and after the refuse had been passed through a sieve it was subjected to the closest scrutiny by the medical gentlemen. Nothing, however, was found at the examination which is likely to afford any assistance or clues to the police.

—

## WHAT A CITY MISSIONARY SAYS

It seems as though every few paces in this neighbourhood of Spitalfields street singers and preachers are doing their best to take full advantage of the solemnising effect of the successive tragedies. "There is no doubt," said a City missionary, "that the impression has been very profound among these unhappy women. We have had special meetings for them, and at the very outset of our efforts we got 34 of them away to homes, and we have had a good many others since. I knew the poor girl who has just been killed, and to look at, at all events, she was one of the smartest, nicest looking women in the neighbourhood. We have had her at some of our meetings, and a companion of hers was one we rescued. I know that she has been in correspondence with her mother, It is not true, as it has been stated, that she is a Welshwoman. She is of Irish parentage, and her mother, I believe, lives in Limerick. I used to hear a good deal about the letters from her mother there. You would not have supposed if you had met her in the street that she belonged to the miserable class she did, as she was always neatly and decently dressed, and looked quite nice and respectable."

"You have been at this work for a good many years?"

"Seven years in this neighbourhood."

"And do you find the state of things improving in any degree?"

"Well, I think there is a little improvement—some little improvement. I have been out and about the streets at all hours, and have sometimes found a shocking state of things. I remember a year or two back going out one night and finding 11 women who had crept for shelter into the staircase of one house. They were quite destitute, and were sleeping there. The opening of the refuges of one sort and another has done something to reduce the numbers found in this way, but there is still a deplorable state of things."

# Monday, 12 November, 1888

## 1500 MEN SLEEP IN DORSET STREET

It may be stated that although Dorset street is only a very short thoroughfare no less than 1500 men sleep every night in the common lodging houses with which it abounds. In Miller's court quite a panic has occurred, and Mr. McCarthy, the landlord of the house, states that the result of the alarm engendered by the murder has already been the loss of four tenants who, presumably, are too frightened to remain in the immediate vicinity of the scene of so terrible a tragedy.

—

## STATEMENT BY A FLOWER GIRL

A flower girl, named Catherine Pickell, residing in Dorset street, states that at about 7.30 on Friday morning she called at Kelly's house to borrow a shawl, and that, though she knocked several times, she got no answer.

—

## ARREST THIS MORNING

The Press Association says: The police at Commercial street Station made another arrest at three o'clock this morning, in Dorset street, at the scene of the murder. The man, who does not answer the description of the supposed murderer, was acting very suspiciously, and refused to satisfy the officers as to his recent movements. Inquiries are being made, but at eight o'clock he was still in custody.

—

## ELIZABETH FOSTER'S STATEMENT

Elizabeth Foster, who lives in a lodging house in Dorset street, and whose whereabouts were difficult to ascertain, made the following statement to a Press Association reporter:

"I have known Mary Jane Kelly for the last eighteen months, and we were always good friends. She used to tell me she came from Limerick. She was as nice a woman as one could find, and although she was an unfortunate, I don't think she went on the streets whilst she lived with Barnet. On Wednesday night I was in her lodgings with her, and the next evening I met her in the Ten Bells public house near Spitalfields Church. We were drinking together, and she went out about five minutes past seven o'clock. I never saw her after that."

—

## KELLY'S WELSH ANTECEDENTS

The statements of the man Barnet, connecting the murdered woman Kelly with South Wales have had the effect of creating considerable additional excitement in this part of the country. Up to the present, however, the investigations by local Press representatives have not resulted in the discovery of Kelly's parents or other relatives. It appears, from inquiries made at Carmarthen and Swansea, that after leaving the former place for the latter, Kelly, who was then only seventeen years of age, entered the service of a Mrs. Rees, who stands committed to the next Assizes on a charge of procuring abortion, and who is the daughter of a medical man formerly resident at Carmarthen. From Swansea it is said that Kelly went to Cardiff, but no trace of her in that town can be discovered.

—

## THE INQUEST
## OBJECTIONS BY THE JURYMEN

At the Shoreditch Town Hall, this morning, before Dr. Macdonald, coroner for North east Middlesex, an inquest was opened upon the remains of the unfortunate woman, Mary Jeanette Kelly, who was found brutally murdered in a house in Miller's court, Dorset street, Spital-fields, on Friday morning, and whose body was afterwards mutilated in the most horrible manner.

The Court room was inconveniently small, and was overcrowded.

Before the jurymen were sworn, one of the men who had been summoned said he did not understand why he should be summoned on a jury in Shoreditch when the murder occurred in Whitechapel.

The Coroner: Do you think we do not know what we are doing?

The Juryman: I object.

The Coroner: You have no right to object. You are summoned here and must do your duty. If any of the jurymen persist in objecting, I shall know how to deal with them.

The Juryman: The murder occurred in the Whitechapel district. I am in the list for Shore-ditch, and I do not see why I should be summoned about the matter.

The Coroner (impatiently): I shall not argue with the jury. If any juryman has any distinct objection, let him say so.

Two other jurymen also objected.

The Coroner: I may tell you that jurisdiction

lies where the body lies, and not where the murder was committed; and the body lies in Shoreditch.

The Coroner's officer then asked the jury to select a foreman, but several who were selected refused to fill the post, and some difficulty was experienced before a foreman could be sworn.

### THE JURY VIEW THE BODY

After the jury had been sworn, they viewed the body in the neighbouring mortuary, and afterwards went to inspect the scene of the murder. Nearly three quarters of an hour elapsed before their return, and the inquest then proceeded.

The police were represented by Inspectors Abberline and Nairn.

### THE CORONER ON THE NEWSPAPERS

The coroner said he thought the newspapers had made a great deal of unnecessary fuss about the question of jurisdiction. He had had no communication with Mr. Baxter about the matter. The body was removed to the Shoreditch mortuary and therefore came under his (the coroner's) jurisdiction.

### THE MAN WHO LIVED WITH THE MURDERED WOMAN

Joseph Barnet was the first witness. He said: —I used to be a fish porter and afterwards became a labourer. Up to last Saturday I lived at 24 New street. Since Saturday I have stayed with my sister in Portpool lane, Gray's Inn road. I lived with the deceased a year and eight months.

### MARIE JEANETTE KELLY

Her name was Marie Jeanette Kelly; at least, so she always told me. I have seen the body and I identify it by the ear and eyes. I am positive it is the same woman. I lived with her in Miller's court for eight months, I believe, but the landlord says it was longer than that. I separated from her on the 30th of last month, because she took a prostitute into her room out of compassion. My being out of work had nothing to do with my leaving her.

### ON THE NIGHT BEFORE THE MURDER

I last saw her alive between 7.30 and 7.45 on the night on which she was supposed to be murdered. I went to call upon her and ask after her welfare. I remained with her a quarter of an hour. We were on very friendly terms, but I had nothing to give her and told her so, at the same time saying how sorry I was it was so. We did not have a drink together whilst I was there.

### GENERALLY A SOBER WOMAN

She was quite sober. She was a sober woman generally whilst she was with me, though I have occasionally seen her drunk. When I went there on Thursday evening a female who lived in the court was present whilst I was visiting the deceased. I have had many conversations with deceased about her parents.

### KELLY'S STORY OF HER OWN LIFE

She said she was born in Limerick but went to Wales when very young, and came to London about four years ago. Her father's name, she told me, was John Kelly, a "gaffer"[299] at an ironworks in Wales—Caernarvonshire or Carmarthenshire. She also said she had a sister, who was a respectable woman, and that she had seven brothers, six of them at home and one in the Army. I never saw any of these brothers to my knowledge. She said she was married when very young in Wales.

### HER HUSBAND KILLED IN AN EXPLOSION

Her husband was a collier named David or Davies, and she lived with him until he was killed in an explosion. I cannot say how long the accident was after the marriage. She said she was about 16 when she married. After her husband's death she went to Cardiff to meet a cousin, and stayed there a long time, being in the infirmary there for eight or nine months. She was living a bad life with her cousin, who was the cause of her downfall.

### FOR SOME TIME AT THE WEST END

After leaving Cardiff she came to London, and lived in a fast house in the West end. Whilst there she said a gentleman asked her if she would like to go to France.

### A TRIP TO FRANCE

She went there with him, but soon returned, as she did not like the place. She did not say what part of France she went to. On returning to London she walked the streets in Ratcliff Highway. She stayed there some time, and lived with a man named Morganstone, who worked at

---

[299] **Gaffer.** Workcrew foreman. (Farmer)

the Stepney Gas Works. She also lived in Pennington street with a man named Joseph Fleming. She said she was very fond of this man, who was a mason's plasterer, but I do not know what she left him for. I first picked up with her in Commercial street, Spitalfields.

### HOW HE FIRST MET KELLY

We had a drink together, and I arranged to see her on the following day—a Saturday. On that day we agreed that we should remain together, and I took lodgings in George street, Commercial street, where I was known. From that time I lived with her until we parted the other day.

### A FATAL PRESENTIMENT

On several occasions she has expressed fear of the Whitechapel murderer. I read all the details to her from the papers. She never expressed fear of any particular individual. We have had quarrels, but they were always soon over, and usually we were on the best of terms.

### HOW THE DISCOVERY WAS MADE

Thomas Boyer, 47, Dorset street, Spitalfields, servant to Mr. McCarthy, the landlord of No. 13 Miller's court, said:—

On Friday morning last about a quarter to eleven I was ordered by Mr. McCarthy to go to Mary Jane's room. I only knew her as Mary Jane. He told me to get the rent. I knocked at the door and got no answer, and knocked again, with a similar result. I then went round the corner by the gutter spout where there is a broken window.

Inspector Ledger, G Division, was sworn, and proved that a plan produced was a correct plan of the premises.

### WHAT HE SAW THROUGH THE BROKEN WINDOW

Boyer's examination was resumed, and he described from the plan the position of the window he went to.

Continuing, he said:—There was a curtain on the window, and I put my hand through the broken pane, pulled the curtain on one side and looked in.

### TWO LUMPS OF FLESH ON THE TABLE

I saw two lumps of flesh lying on the table, close against the front of the bed. I looked a second time, and saw a body lying on the bed and blood on the floor. I at once went very quietly back to my master and told him what I had seen. "Good God," he said, "Do you mean to say this?" We both went to the police station at once after my master had had a look through the window. We told the police what we had seen. Only my master and myself knew of the murder before we informed the police. The inspector on duty returned with us to Miller's court. I had often seen the woman in and out of the court whilst she lived there. I also knew the last witness, Joseph Barnet. I saw deceased under the influence of drink once, but I never saw Barnet drunk. I last saw deceased alive on Wednesday afternoon. Mr. McCarthy's shop is at the corner of the court.

### THE OWNER OF THE HOUSE CALLED

Mr. John McCarthy said:—

I am a grocer and lodging house keeper at 27 Dorset street. On Friday morning last, about 10.30, I sent my man Boyer to No. 13, Miller's court, for the rent. He went there and came back in about five minutes, saying, "Governor, I knocked at the door and could not make anybody answer. I looked through the window and saw a lot of blood." I went out with him, looked through the window, and saw the blood and the body lying on the bed. For a moment I could not say anything, but afterwards said, "Harry, don't tell anyone; go and fetch the police." I knew deceased as Mary Jane Kelly. I have seen both alive and dead, and have no doubt about her identity. I followed Boyer to the police station in Commercial street and saw Inspector Beck. I inquired first for Inspectors Reid and Abberline. I saw the inspector on duty and told him what I had seen. He put on his coat and hat and came with me at once. Deceased had lived at No. 13 about ten months with Barnet. I did not know whether they were married or not. They lived on comfortable terms. They had rows occasionally, but nothing of any consequence. Some time ago they broke two windows during a row. The furniture in the room belonged to me—the bed linen and everything. The rent of the room was 4s 6d per week, but deceased was 29s in arrears. I was supposed to get the rent weekly.

(Inquest proceeding.)

~

## The Times

### THE WHITECHAPEL MURDER.

During yesterday several arrests were made, but after a short examination in all cases the persons were set at liberty, as it was felt certain they had no connexion with the crime. Dorset-street still continues to be a thoroughfare of great interest, and during the whole of the day people, who were evidently drawn thither solely out of curiosity, passed up and down the street, while before the entrance of Miller's-court a crowd collected. They were not, however, allowed to enter the court, which was guarded by two police constables.

Some surprise was created among those present at the inquest in Shoreditch Townhall by the abrupt termination of the inquiry, as it was well known that further evidence would be forthcoming. The Coroner himself distinctly told the jury that he was only going to take the preliminary portion of Dr. G. B. Phillips's evidence, the remainder of which would be more fully given at the adjourned inquiry. No question was put to Dr. Phillips as to the mutilated remains of the body, and the Coroner did not think fit to ask the doctor whether any portions of the body were missing. The doctor stated to the jury during the inquiry that his examination was not yet completed. His idea was that by at once making public every fact brought to light in connexion with this terrible murder, the ends of justice might be retarded. The examination of the body by Dr. Phillips on Saturday lasted upwards of six-and-a-half hours. Notwithstanding reports to the contrary, it is still confidently asserted that some portions of the body of the deceased woman are missing.

The explanation given of why the bloodhounds were not used is that they would be of no use whatever in the locality in which this murder took place. Had it occurred in an open, unfrequented part, the dogs might have had some chance of success.

The police yesterday evening received an important piece of information. A man, apparently of the labouring class, with a military appearance, who knew the deceased, stated that on the morning of the 9th inst. he saw her in Commercial-street, Spitalfields (near where the murder was committed), in company with a man of respectable appearance. He was about 5 ft. 6 in. in height, and 34 or 35 years of age, with dark complexion and dark moustache turned up at the ends. He was wearing a long, dark coat, trimmed with astrachan, a white collar with a black necktie, in which was affixed a horse-shoe pin. He wore a pair of dark gaiters with light buttons, over button boots, and displayed from his waistcoat a massive gold chain. His appearance contrasted so markedly with that of the woman that few people could have failed to remark them at that hour of the morning. This description, which confirms that given by others of the person seen in company with the deceased on the morning she was killed, is much fuller in detail than that hitherto in the possession of the police.

—

Yesterday morning Dr. Roderick M'Donald, M.P., coroner for North-East Middlesex, opened the inquiry into the cause of death of Mary Jane Kelly, the young woman who was found dead and horribly mutilated on Friday morning last, at a house in Miller's-court, Dorset-street, Whitechapel. The inquiry took place at the Shoreditch Town-hall. Great interest was manifested in the proceedings by the crowds which had assembled both inside and outside the hall. Some little difficulty arose at the outset, one of the jurymen objecting to be summoned, as, he contended, the death did not take place in Shoreditch, but in the adjoining parish of Whitechapel. The CORONER said he was quite aware what jurisdiction he had. The jury had no business to object on the ground mentioned, and if the objection was persisted in, he should know how to act. He was not going to discuss the matter of jurisdiction with the jury at all. The body lay in his district, and he should have to conduct the inquiry.

The jury proceeded to the mortuary at the rear of Shoreditch Church to view the body, afterwards, by the coroner's directions, visiting the scene of the crime. They were absent nearly an hour.

Superintendent Arnold and Inspectors F. G. Abberline and Nairn watched the proceedings on behalf of the authorities.

Before the first witness was called the CORONER said he should like to state that it was not correct, as had been asserted, that he had had any communication with Mr. Wynne Baxter on the question of jurisdiction. There was no question whatever as to his right to hold the inquiry. One

# Tuesday, 13 November, 1888

of the previous murders had taken place in his district, but the body was removed into Mr. Baxter's district, and that gentleman, of course, conducted the inquiry.

Joseph Barnett was then called, and said he was a labourer working by the riverside, and up to Saturday last he lived at 24 New-street, Bishopsgate, having been staying at 21, Ponpool-lane since then. He had lived with the deceased Marie Jeanette Kelly for a year and eight months, and had seen the body in the mortuary, which he identified. He was quite positive the body was that of the woman he lived with. Kelly was her maiden name. He had lived with her at 13 room in Miller's Court about eight months, and ceased to live with her on October 30, because she insisted on taking in a woman of immoral character. It was not because he was out of work that he ceased to live with her. He last saw her alive about 7:30 on Thursday evening, when they were on friendly terms. She was quite sober at the time and did not have anything to drink with witness. Deceased occasionally got drunk, but generally speaking she was sober when she lived with him. She had told him several times that she was born in Limerick, but removed to Wales when quite young. Witness could not say whether it was at Carnarvon or Carmarthen that she lived, but her father was employed at some ironworks. She also told witness that she had a sister who resided with her aunt and followed a respectable calling. She had six brothers and sisters, one of the former being in the army. She told him she had married a collier named Davis in Wales when she was 16 years of age, and lived with him until he was killed in an explosion a year or two afterwards. After her husband's death she went to Cardiff with a cousin and came to London about four years ago. She lived at a gay house in the West-end for a short time, and then went to France with a gentleman, but did not like it and soon returned to London, living in Ratcliff-highway, near the gasworks, with a man named Morganstone. She afterwards lived with a mason named Joseph Fleming somewhere in Bethnal Green. Deceased told witness all her history while she lived with him. Witness picked her up in Spitalfields on a Friday night and made an appointment to meet her the next day, when they agreed to live together, and they had done

so ever since. He did not think deceased feared anyone in particular, but she used to ask witness to read to her about the murders. She occasionally quarrelled with witness, but not often, and seldom with anybody else.

Thomas Bowyer said he resided at 37, Dorset-street and acted as servant to Mr. M'Carthy, the owner of a chandler's shop at 27, Dorset-street. About 10:45 on Friday morning he was directed by M'Carthy to go to deceased's room for the rent. Witness knew the deceased only as Mary Jane. He knocked at the door, but did not receive an answer. He knocked again, but still no answer was returned, and he then went round the corner where there was a broken pane of glass in the window.

Inspector Ledger, G Division, here handed in a plan of the premises, which was shown to the witness, who indicated the window he referred to.

Continuing his evidence, the witness said there was a curtain before the window, which he pulled aside and looked in. The first thing he observed was what appeared to be two pieces of flesh lying on the table in front of the bedstead. The second time he looked in he saw a body lying on the bed and blood on the floor. He immediately returned to Mr. M'Carthy and told him what he had seen. Mr. M'Carthy exclaimed "Good God, do you mean that Harry?" Mr. M'Carthy went and looked through the window, and then they both went to the police-station and told what they had seen. At that time no other persons in the court knew what had occurred. He returned to the room with Inspector Beck. He last saw deceased alive on Wednesday last in the court and spoke to her. He had seen deceased under the influence of drink once; and he was acquainted with the last witness, Joe Barnett.

John M'Carthy said he was a grocer and lodging-house keeper at 27, Dorset-street. On Friday morning about half-past 10 he sent the last witness to No. 13 room in Miller's-court to call for the rent. He returned in about five minutes and told witness that as he could not get an answer to his knock he looked through the window and saw a lot of blood. Witness went to the room and looked through the window and saw the body. When he recovered from the shock the sight gave him he went for the police. He knew the deceased, and, having seen the body, he had no doubt about her identity. At the police-station he saw Inspector Beck, who went back to the house with him. Deceased had lived in that room for about 10 months with the man Joe. He did not know whether they were married or not. A short time ago they had a row and the windows were broken. Deceased was supposed to pay 4s. 6d. per week for the room, but she was £1 9s. in arrear. Everything in the room, including the bed clothing, belonged to witness. He had often seen the deceased the worse for drink, and when she was in liquor she was very noisy; otherwise she was a very quiet woman.

Mary Ann Cox said she resided at the last house at the top of Miller's-court. She was a widow and got her living on the streets. She last saw deceased alive about a quarter to 12 on Thursday night. Deceased was very much intoxicated at the time and was with a short, stout man, shabbily dressed, with a round billycock hat on. He had a can of beer in his hand. He had a blotchy face and a heavy carrotty moustache. Witness followed them into the court and said goodnight to the deceased, who replied, "Good night; I am going to sing." The door was shut and witness heard the deceased singing, "Only a violet I plucked from mother's grave." Witness went to her room and remained there about a quarter of an hour, and then went out. Deceased was still singing at that time. It was raining, and witness returned home at 3:10 a.m., and the light in deceased's room was then out and there was no noise. Witness could not sleep, and heard a man go out of the court about a quarter past 6. It might have been a policeman for all witness knew. The man she saw with the deceased was short and stout. All his clothes were dark and he appeared to be between 35 and 36 years of age. She would know the man again if she saw him.

Elizabeth Prater, a married woman, living apart from her husband, said she occupied No. 20 room, Miller's-court, her room being just over that occupied by the deceased. If deceased moved about in her room much witness could hear her. Witness lay down on her bed on Thursday night or Friday morning about 1:30 with her clothes on, and fell asleep directly. She was disturbed during the night by a kitten in the room. That would be about half-past 3 or 4 o'clock. She then distinctly heard in a low tone

and in a woman's voice a cry of "Oh! murder." The sound appeared to proceed from the court and near where witness was. She did not take much notice of it, however, as they were continually hearing cries of murder in the court. She did not hear it a second time, neither did she hear a sound of falling, and she dropped off to sleep again and did not wake until 5 o'clock. She then got up and went to the Five Bells publichouse and had some rum. She did not see any strangers in the publichouse. She was quite sure there was no singing in deceased's room after 1:30 that morning, or she would have heard it.

Caroline Maxwell, of 14, Dorset-street, wife of Henry Maxwell, a lodging-house deputy, said she had known the deceased about four months, and she also knew Joe Barnett. The deceased was a young woman who did not associate much with strangers, and witness had only spoken to her twice. On Friday morning between 8 and 8:30 she saw the deceased at the corner of Miller's-court. She was quite sure it was the deceased, and was certain about the time because it was the time her husband left off work. It being an unusual thing to see the deceased about so early, witness spoke to her and asked her to have a drink. Deceased refused, saying she was very ill and had just had a half-pint of ale, which she brought up again. Witness left her saying she could pity her feeling. On returning half an hour later witness saw the deceased standing outside the Britannia publichouse, talking to a man. That would be between 8 and 9 o'clock on Friday morning. She could not give any description of the man deceased was with because they were some distance off. She did not pass them, as she came from the other end of the court. She was quite positive it was the deceased, but could not describe the man. He was not a tall man. Deceased had on a dark skirt, velvet bodice, and maroon shawl.

Sarah Lewis, a laundress, of 24, Great Pearl-street, Spitalfields, said she went to the house of Mrs. Keyler, in Miller's-court, on Friday morning about 2:30, and saw a man standing at the lodging-house door by himself. He was stout, but not very tall, and had on a wideawake hat. Witness did not take any notice of his clothes. She did not hear any noise as she went down the court, but about 3:30, when she was in Mrs.

# Tuesday, 13 November, 1888

Keyler's house, she heard a woman cry "Murder." As it was not repeated, she did not take any further notice of it. On Wednesday evening, as she was going along Bethnal-green-road with another woman, they were accosted by a man who was carrying a black bag, and who asked one of them to follow him into a court. They became alarmed and refused to do so. He was not a tall man. He had a black moustache and was very pale. He had on a round hat, a brown overcoat, a black undercoat, and "pepper and salt" trousers. Witness could not say where he went to, but on Friday morning about 2:30 she saw him again, speaking to a woman in Commercial-street, but he was dressed a little differently.

The CORONER said he proposed at that stage to take, briefly, the evidence of the doctor. They could not go into all the particulars at that stage.

Dr. George Bagster Phillips said,—I reside at 2, Spital-square, and am divisional surgeon to the H Division of police. I was called by the police on Friday morning about 11 o'clock and proceeded to Miller's-court, which I entered at 11:15. I went to the room door leading out of the passage running at the side of 26, Dorset-street. There were two windows to the room. I produce a photograph which will enable you to see exactly the position. Two panes in the window nearest to the passage were broken, and finding the door locked I looked through the lower of the broken panes and satisfied myself that the mutilated corpse lying on the bed was not in need of any immediate attention from me. I also came to the conclusion that there was nobody else upon the bed or within view to whom I could render any professional assistance. Having ascertained that probably it was advisable that no entrance should be made into the room at that time, I remained until about 1:30, when the door was broken open, by M'Carthy I believe. I know he was waiting with a pickaxe to break open the door, and I believe he did it. The direction to break open the door was given by Superintendent Arnold. I prevented its being opened before. I may mention that when I arrived in the yard the premises were in charge of Inspector Beck. On the door's being forced open it knocked against the table. The table I found close to the left-hand side of the bedstead, and the bedstead was close up against the wooden partition. The mutilated remains of a female were lying two-thirds over towards the bedstead nearest to the door. She had only her chemise on, or some under linen garment. I am sure the body had been removed subsequent to the injury which caused her death from that side of the bedstead which was nearest to the wooden partition, because of the large quantity of blood under the bedstead and the saturated condition of the palliasse and the sheet at the corner nearest the partition. The blood was produced by the severance of the carotid artery, which was the immediate cause of death. This injury was inflicted while deceased was lying at the right side of the bedstead.

The CORONER said it would not be necessary for the doctor to go into any further particulars then. If it was necessary they could recall him at a subsequent period.

After a short adjournment, Julia van Teurney, a laundress, of No. 1 room, Miller's-court, was called, and said she knew the deceased and Joseph Barnett. They appeared to live together very quietly, and Joe would not allow the deceased to go on the streets. She occasionally got too much to drink. She told witness that she had another man, named Joe also, of whom she appeared to be very fond. Witness believed this second Joe was a costermonger. She last saw the deceased alive about 10 o'clock on Thursday morning. Witness slept in the court that night, retiring to bed about 8 o'clock. She could not sleep, but did not hear any noise in the court during the night. She did not hear the deceased singing during the night.

Maria Harvey, No. 3, New-court, Dorset-street, said she knew the deceased, Mary Jane Kelly. Witness slept with the deceased on Monday and Tuesday nights. They were together on Thursday afternoon, and witness was in the deceased's room when Joe Barnett called. Witness left the house on Thursday evening, leaving several articles in the deceased's care, including sheets, an overcoat and a bonnet. She had not seen any of the articles except the overcoat since. The deceased and witness were great friends, but the deceased never said anything to witness about being afraid of a man.

Inspector Walter Beck, H Division, said on Friday morning he was called to the house and

# Tuesday, 13 November, 1888

ascertained what had occurred. He did not give orders to force the door, but sent for the doctor, and gave orders that no one should be allowed to leave the court. He did not know whether the deceased was known to the police.

Frederick G. Abberline, detective-inspector, Scotland-yard, having charge of this case, said he arrived at Miller's-court about 11:30 on Friday. He did not break open the door as Inspector Beck told him that the bloodhounds had been sent for and were on the way, and Dr. Phillips said it would be better not to break open the door until the dogs arrived. At 1:30 Superintendent Arnold arrived, and said the order for the dogs had been countermanded, and he gave orders to force the door. Witness had seen the condition of the room through the window. He examined the room after the door had been forced. From the appearance of the grate it was evident a very large fire had been kept up. The ashes had since been examined, and it was evident that portions of a woman's clothing had been burnt. It was his opinion that the clothes had been burnt to enable the murderer to see what he was about. There were portions of a woman's skirt and the rim of a hat in the grate. An impression had got abroad that the murderer had taken the key of the room away, but that was not so, as Barnett had stated that the key had been lost some time ago, and when they desired to get into the room they pushed back the bolt though the broken window.

The CORONER said that was all the evidence he proposed to take that day. He did not know whether the jury considered they had had enough evidence to enable them to return a verdict. All they had to do was to ascertain the cause of death, leaving the other matters in the hands of the police.

The Foreman said the jury considered they had heard enough to guide them to a decision, and they desired to return a verdict of "Wilful murder against some person or persons unknown."

—

It will be remembered that, at Sir Charles Warren's request, Mr. Brough, the well-known bloodhound breeder of Scarborough, was communicated with shortly after the Mitre-square and Berner-street tragedies, and asked to bring a couple of trained hounds up to London for the purpose of testing their capabilities in the way of following the scent of a man. The hounds were name Burgho and Barnaby, and in one of the trials Sir Charles Warren himself acted as the quarry and expressed satisfaction at the result.

Arrangements were made for the immediate conveyance of the animals to the spot in the event of another murder occurring, and in order to facilitate matters Mr. Brough, who was compelled to return to Scarborough, left the hounds in the care of Mr. Taunton of 8, Doughty-street, who is a friend of his. Mr. Taunton, who is a high authority on matters appertaining to the larger breeds of dogs, has ample accommodation in the rear of his residence for kennelling such valuable animals, and he was accordingly entrusted with their custody pending the conclusion of the negotiations which had been opened for the ultimate purchase of the dogs. Sir Charles Warren, however, it is said, would not give any definite assurance on the point, and the result was Mr. Brough insisted on resuming possession of the animals.

Mr. Taunton has made the following statement:—

After the trial in Regent's Park Burgho was sent to Brighton, where he had been entered for the show, which lasted three days. In the meantime Barnaby remained in my care. Burgho would have been sent back to me, but as Mr. Brough could not get anything definite from Sir Charles Warren, he declined to do so, and wrote asking me to return Barnaby. I did not do so at first, but, acting on my own responsibility, retained possession of the dog for some time longer.

About a fortnight ago I received a telegram from Leman-street Police-station asking me to bring up the hounds. It was then shortly after noon, and I took Barnaby at once. On arrival at the station I was told by the superintendent that a burglary had been committed about 5 o'clock that morning in Commercial-street, and I was asked to attempt to track the thief by means of the dog. The police admitted that since the burglary they had been all over the premises. I pointed out the stupidity of expecting a dog to accomplish anything under such circumstances and after such a length of time had been allowed to elapse, and took the animal home.

# Tuesday, 13 November, 1888

I wrote telling Mr. Brough of this and he wired insisting that the dog should be sent back at once, as the danger of its being poisoned, if it were known that the police were trying to track burglars by its aid, was very great, and Mr. Brough had no guarantee against any pecuniary loss he might suffer in the event of the animal's being maltreated. Therefore, there has not been a "police bloodhound"—that is to say, a trained hound, in London for the past fortnight.

The origin of the tale regarding the hounds being lost at Tooting while being practiced in tracking a man I can only account for in the following way. I had arranged to take Barnaby out to Hemel Hempstead to give the hound some practice. The same day a sheep was maliciously killed on Tooting-common, and the police wired to London asking that the hounds might be sent down. I was then some miles away from London with Barnaby, and did not get the telegram until my return, late in the evening. Somebody doubtless remarked that the hounds were missing, meaning that they did not arrive when sent for, and this was magnified into a report that they had been lost. At the time Burgho was at Scarborough.

Under the circumstances in which the body of Mary Ann Kelly was found I do not think bloodhounds would have been of any use. It was then broad daylight and the streets crowded with people. The only chance the hounds would have would be in the event of a murdered body being discovered, as the others were, in the small hours of the morning, and being put on the trail before many people were about.

—

## RESIGNATION OF
## SIR CHARLES WARREN.

As will be seen from our Parliamentary report, Sir Charles Warren tendered his resignation on Thursday last.

A News Agency learns on the highest authority that the relations between Sir Charles Warren and the Home Office have for some time been strained. The action of the department in reference to the resignation of Mr. Monro caused the first serious difference of opinion. Sir Charles took exception to certain of the methods of the Assistant-Commissioner, and he intimated to Mr. Matthews that either he or Mr. Monro must resign. A few days afterwards Mr. Monro's resignation was announced.

Sir Charles complains that this was accepted without consultation with him, and that prior to the Home Secretary's statement in the House of Commons last evening he was not even aware of the reason assigned by his subordinate for severing his connexion with Scotland-yard. Since Mr. Monro's transference to the Home Office matters have become worse. Sir Charles complains that, whereas he has been saddled with all the responsibility, he has had no freedom of action, and in consequence his position has become daily more unbearable.

Although Mr. Monro has been no longer in evidence at Whitehall-place, he has to all intents and purposes retained control of the Criminal Investigation Department. Indeed, it was added, Mr. Matthews last evening admitted that he was deriving the benefit of the advice of Mr. Monro in matters relating to crime, and was in communication with him at the present time on the subject of the organization of the detective staff. This division of authority Sir Charles Warren has strenuously fought against.

He maintains that if the Commissioner is to be responsible for the discipline of the force, instructions should be given to no department without his concurrence. Latterly, in spite of the remonstrances of Sir Charles Warren, the control of the Criminal Investigation Department has been withdrawn more and more from Whitehall-place. Every morning for the last few weeks there has been a protracted conference at the Home Office between Mr. Monro, Mr. Anderson, and the principal detective inspectors, and the information furnished to the Commissioner in regard to these conferences has been, he states, of the scantiest character.

These facts will explain how, apart from any other consideration, it was impossible for Sir Charles Warren, holding the views he did in regard to the functions of the Commissioner, to continue in command. The reproof of the Home Secretary last week in reference to the article in *Murray's Magazine* completed the rupture.

Sir Charles thereupon took counsel with his friends and immediately tendered his resignation to the Home Secretary. Yesterday morning his books and papers were removed from the Commissioner's office, and this was the first intimation in Whitehall-place that he had relinquished the position.

In the lobby last evening Mr. Monro was

looked upon as the most likely person to be selected to succeed Sir C. Warren. It was pointed out that the resignation of Sir Charles Warren practically arose out of a difference of opinion with Mr. Monro, and that, inasmuch as Mr. Monro, though nominally shelved, had really gained the day, therefore it was only natural that he should resume control of the force, and develop the system of administration, the proposition of which led to his transference to the Home Office.

On the other hand, it is believed in some quarters that the present opportunity will be seized to emphasize the distinction between the Criminal Investigation Department and the ordinary members of the force to which Sir Charles Warren takes exception, in which case a provincial chief constable, who has attracted much notice for his successful organization and disciplinary tact, is mentioned as the probable head of the "uniform" police, with Mr. Monro at the head of the detective branch, as an independent branch of the force.

—

In reply to a question, the HOME SECRETARY announced yesterday, in the House of Commons, that SIR CHARLES WARREN tendered his resignation on Thursday last, and that it has been accepted by the Government. The loud Opposition cheers that followed this announcement were undoubtedly prompted by a recollection of the important services rendered by SIR CHARLES WARREN to the Government upon a critical occasion, rather than by dispassionate solicitude for the efficiency of the police. They may serve to remind Ministers that, whatever may be the merits of the disputes that have involved SIR CHARLES WARREN'S retirement, the net result to them is the loss of a valuable servant.

It has been tolerably well known for some time that the relations between SIR CHARLES WARREN and his official chief have not been of an entirely pleasant or harmonious nature. For the beginning of discord we should probably have to go back to the Trafalgar-square riots, when SIR CHARLES WARREN clearly knew his own mind, and how to carry out a definite policy, while MR. MATTHEWS as evidently did not know his own mind and showed no capacity for action.

A rupture might, however, have been avoided had nothing occurred to throw an exceptional strain upon the department. But the series of brutal and mysterious murders in Whitechapel concentrated public attention upon the constitution and management of the police and detective forces. The defects of a faulty organization were dragged into daylight, and the men responsible for the time being came in for the severe criticism which ought in justice to have been bestowed upon their predecessors and upon the public which had long acquiesced in what is now unsparingly condemned.

SIR CHARLES WARREN in particular was held responsible for the failures of the Criminal Investigation Department, which he did not construct and which he found himself powerless to reorganize. That department is largely, if not exclusively, manned by the ordinary police, but appears to be, nevertheless, provided with a chief who has direct relations with the Home Office, behind the back of the man actually responsible for the discipline, organization, and efficiency of the whole police force. In such circumstances friction is inevitable as soon as the Chief Commissioner, either from choice or necessity, makes any sort of energetic and thoroughgoing effort after efficiency.

The resignation of MR. MONRO showed that the situation had become acute, but it now turns out that he continued after resignation to advise the HOME SECRETARY, and that the control of the detective arrangements was withheld from the Chief Commissioner as completely as before. The reproof administered to SIR CHARLES WARREN by the HOME SECRETARY for defending himself in the pages of a magazine was merely the accident which determined a resignation sooner or later inevitable.

MR. MATTHEWS says that he is considering the whole system of the Criminal Investigation Department with a view to introducing any improvements that experience may suggest. This is a very lame and feeble announcement to put forth in the circumstances. The public will not rest satisfied with what amounts to nothing more than a promise of languid tinkering at details. Some new chief will have to be found for the police force.

If MR. MONRO is promoted, as some seem to expect, he will either retain the control of the detective department or he will hand it over to

# Tuesday, 13 November, 1888

another. In the first case, the reform on which SIR CHARLES WARREN insisted will be made the excuse for shelving him, and will be carried out for the benefit of another man who was a party to opposing it. In the second case, the ineffective system now in operation will be perpetuated, and although MR. MONRO may acquiesce in the division of authority to which SIR CHARLES WARREN objected, he will do it at the expense of the public interest.

Exactly the same thing will happen if MR. MONRO retains control of the detective department while some new man is put in SIR CHARLES WARREN'S place. Most of our detectives are ordinary policemen detailed for special duties, and they cannot serve two masters. There is plenty to be said for entirely separating the detective branch from the ordinary constabulary, giving it an independent head and making him directly responsible to a Secretary of State.

There is much to be said in favour of placing detectives and constabulary alike under the control of a single official who should work the two branches together. But there is nothing at all to be said for what seems to be the present system of dividing authority without making any clear separation of functions. The detectives are a part of the ordinary constabulary, but they are under the orders of a special officer who reports direct to the Home Office.

This arrangement is destructive of all discipline and all real efficiency among the men, while at the same time it reduces the responsibility of the chiefs to a farce. For once in a way we may throw all the resulting inconvenience upon a public servant. But we cannot permanently carry on our business with any success by making believe that a Chief Commissioner is responsible for that over which he has no authority.

We do not know whether MR. MATT-HEWS really imagines that he can stop inquiry with the answer he gave last night—that MR. MONRO resigned because differences of opinion had arisen between the Chief Commissioner and himself. If he does he is preparing a serious disappointment for himself; and if his colleagues wish to escape discredit they will endeavour too convince him that the whole matter will really have to be dealt with in a very difference spirit.

The inquest on the last victim of the Whitechapel murderer has terminated like its predecessors. There is no clue to the perpetrator of an outrage which in deliberate and cold-blooded brutality outdoes even the previous ghastly murders by the same hand. Nor is there any very good ground for hoping that the miscreant will be discovered so long as he retains his diabolical cunning and nerve. His victims are so far accessory to their own deaths, and his operations are conducted amid a population so utterly careless of what goes on at its very doors that most of the conditions are wanting upon which the efficiency of ordinary protective arrange-ments depends.

Great as are the terror and excitement in the district, they do not seem to affect the class from which the murderer chooses his victims. It might have been supposed that they would have organized some system of mutual supervision and companionship in their dreadful trade, but instinct and habit are apparently too strong, and in spite of warnings they place themselves in the power of any stranger. It is quite unreasonable to blame the police in such circumstances for failing to give protection, and hardly less unreasonable to condemn them for failing to detect the murderer.

With certain qualities and certain external advantages the doer of evil deeds has little difficulty in so managing matters as to leave no trace of his identity. In this case he is evidently very minutely acquainted with his ground, he chooses spots where there is a population so dense as to render identification next to impossible, and he is endowed with exceptional coolness and cunning. It is rather remarkable that accident has not effected what is beyond the reach of calculation. In all cases of secret crime and its detection accident plays a very large part. It constitutes the permanent odds on the side of society. But nothing has occurred to disturb the calculations of this Whitechapel fiend, and so to redress the heavy disadvantages under which justice labours. The demand for the offering of a reward will probably be silenced by the explanation given last night by the HOME SECRETARY.

SIR WILLIAM HARCOURT[300] seems to

[300] **Sir William Vernon Harcourt** (1827-1904). Liberal MP, served as Home Secretary and Chancellor of the

have thought the matter out, and arrived at the conclusion that except where a confederacy exists, or where search is made for a known individual, the offering of rewards does no good and may do much harm. The Home Office has acted on that view ever since, and although it is received with impatience by the people who are given to exclaiming that "something must be done", we believe it will commend itself to the common sense of the community at large.

—

## THE EAST-END MURDERS AND WHAT IS TO BE DONE.
## TO THE EDITOR OF THE TIMES.

Sir,—Occupying as I do the rectory-house of St. Botolph, Bishopsgate, which is agreeably situated, with Mitre-square within easy access at the back and Dorset-street in the front, flanked by Petticoat-lane on the east and Liverpool-street, which is the focus of harlotry, on the west, I confess that at this crisis I share with my neighbours in the horror of the situation. "Our hearts are disquieted within us, and the fear of death is fallen upon us,"[301] and we ask, What is to be done? Murder succeeds to murder, and for a time we are staggered. A number of people are arrested who ought to have been let alone, but gradually the excitement passes off, the faithful bloodhounds are sent back to their kennels, the tide of business flows on, and the murders seem to be forgotten; but I really do hope that the event of Lord Mayor's day will not be allowed to pass off so quietly, and that some measures will be adopted to assure our disquietude. But what is to be done? It is not so much the murders, ghastly as they are, that sadden and appall us, but it is the awful state of things which these murders reveal—the disorderly and depraved lives which these poor people lead. What is to be done to remedy this state of things? That is the problem to be solved. Having had some experience in these matters, and having lived among these people for nearly half a century, I venture to think that I speak with some authority, and I offer two suggestions. The first is that all those women

who ply the meretricious[302] trade should be registered, and if need be licensed. I know the cry that will be raised against this, but I ask, Are the interests of society to be sacrificed to a blatant prudery? Secondly, there should be a house to house visitation, which would throw light into these bleak dwellings. As a Christian minister I should like to see this carried out by devoted men living in these districts, and by their self-sacrifice and sympathy gaining the confidence of the inhabitants. This, however, would require organization and some leader to set it on foot. I should like to do it myself, but non sum qualis eram,[303] and I cannot undertake it. Failing this, the work should be carried out by the police-police dressed as the "new police" were when they were first introduced by Sir Robert Peel, in the dress of civilians-men set apart for the work, going in and out among the people and mingling with them. As friends they would be in correspondence with the various philanthropic societies who would render assistance for rescue and relief. Of course there will be a cry raised against such a movement, which would be said to interfere with the rights of the Englishman. Every man's house is his castle, &c. What was poor Mary Ann Kelly's castle?

However, if judiciously carried out it would, I am sure, eventually become popular; at all events the plague would be stayed.

Your faithful servant,
WILLIAM ROGERS.[304]
Rectory, Bishopsgate, E.,
Nov. 12.

—

At MARLBOROUGH-STREET, WILL-IAM AVENELL, 26, chimney sweep, Adam and Eve-court Oxford-street; and FREDERICK W. MOORE, 28, carver and gilder, Carlisle-street, Soho, were charged with being disorderly and with assaulting Henry Edward Leeke, an oil

---

Exchequer under Gladstone, later as Leader of the Opposition in Parliement.
[301] Variant of Psalm 55:4 used in the *Book of Common Prayer*, here changed from singular to plural.

[302] **Meretricious.** 1. Superficially or garishly attractive. 2. Insincere. 3. (*Archaic*) Of, like, or relating to a prostitute. (Collins Dictionary)
[303] **Non sum qualis eram.** Lat. I am not what I used to be. Horace, Odes, Book IV.
[304] **Rev. William Rogers** (1819-1896). Rector of St. Botolph's. Advocate for education reform and free public libraries. One of the founders of Bishopsgate Institute in 1895.

and colour man, of Gilbert-street, Oxford-street, on Saturday night.

Leeke said that on Saturday evening about 5 o'clock he went into a publichouse at the corner of a street when several persons accosted him. The prisoners accused him of being "Jack the Ripper," and told him that they were detectives in private clothes, and that they should arrest him as the Whitechapl murderer.

They took him outside and dragged him in a brutal manner through Castle-street as far as Newman-passage. They struck him with a stick, and he implored them not to be so brutal. They would not let him go, they said, until they knew who he was and where he had been. He told them he had just delivered two gallons of oil at 62, Berners-street, whereupon they said they would take him back and ascertain whether his statement was true. He resisted as well as he could, and they struggled in the streets together for about three quarters of an hour. Many persons stopped and looked at them, and when the prisoners called out "He is Jack the Ripper, we are detectives," they walked away and did not attempt to render him assistance. He therefore got no protection, and was shaken and bruised until he felt quite disabled.

When he got near 62, Berners-street, he managed to get away from his assailants, and sprang down the steps of that house into the basement, got into the kitchen, and lost sight of his pursuers for a few moments. A number of young women were at tea in the room, and when Avenell followed and told them they had a strange man in the house, and that he (Avenell) was a private detective, they became very much frightened and screamed for the police. Avenell finding the prosecutor dragged him up the stairs, exclaiming, "He's Jack the Ripper."

Madame Muntz, the landlady of 62, Berners-street, deposed that the man Leeke had been in the habit of bringing oil, soap, wood, and other articles to the house, and she therefore knew him. She sent for a constable, and Avenell was taken into custody. Leeke became so unwell after the affair that he had to take to his bed.

In defence, Avenell said that he and his friends were in the publichouse when they saw Leeke sitting in a corner. He had his head down, and was mumbling something to himself. As he seemed strange in his manner they asked him what was the matter, and he replied, "Do not bother me; I am in serious trouble." They asked him whether they should see him home, and when he told them he lived at 62, Berners-street, he (Avenell) doubted it, as he did the chimney-sweeping there, and knew that it was only occupied by women. He therefore expressed his intention of taking Leeke to the house to ascertain whether that statement was correct. On reaching the house Leeke ran down the steps into the basement and shouted to the inmates, "There's a strange man in the house." He (Avenell) followed, and finding Leeke crouching in the cellar, dragged him out. Madame Muntz and all the young women began to scream, until one of them, recognizing the prosecutor, exclaimed, "Why it is our little oilman," and then they became less excited.

The prisoner Moore said that when he descended the steps he tried to pacify the young women by telling them that the affair was only a foolish joke.

Constable Downey, 364 D, said that he saw Avenell holding the prosecutor outside the house in Berners-street. Avenell called out, "Here he is; I have got him. This is Jack the Ripper; I mean to take him to the police-station," adding, with a coarse expression, "If the police cannot do their duty I can." Being asked who he was, Avenell said he was a private detective. The prisoner Moore ran out of the house, and was pursued and taken into custody.

The prosecutor was sober, but the prisoner Avenell had been drinking. A witness for the defence was called who stated that when the prosecutor entered the publichouse some one exclaimed, "Here is a funny little man; perhaps he is Jack the Ripper." On being questioned Leeke said his name was Smith, and that he was a tin plate worker. That statement being doubted it was resolved to ascertain who and what he was; and in this way the affair began.

Mr. Hannay said it was a very dangerous thing for people to personate detectives, and directed Inspector Ettridge to see whether the prisoners could not be further charged with that offence. Very serious results might have arisen out of the affair, which required further inquiry, and he would therefore adjourn the case for a week, allowing bail in the sum of £10 for each of the prisoners.

~

# Tuesday, 13 November, 1888

## The Star

### WHAT WE THINK.

LONDON democracy has won its greatest victory since the fall of Hyde-park railings. It is "triumphant democracy" with a vengeance. On the anniversary of the day on which we write these lines Sir CHARLES WARREN met the people of London in Trafalgar-square and drove them violently out of it, Pall Mallism applauding with both hands, and crowning the champion of law and order with never-fading laurels. To-day Sir CHARLES WARREN is a defeated and discredited man, deserted by the Minister who is responsible for his mistakes, betrayed by the party which supported him, snubbed by the Press which made the welkin ring[305] with his praise. The long steady cheers which greeted the news of his resignation in the House of Commons were ominous of much.

They were the death-knell of militarism, Trafalgar-squareism, and generally of that mysterious order of disease known as Warrenitis. Sir CHARLES WARREN was the sincere victim of a delusion. He thought London was in the hands of a violent and disorderly "mob." He said so with his usual frankness. Then the Minister who had all along been acting as if Sir CHARLES were right—who, as long as political credit was to be got from the "law and order" cry, backed it with all his might—seized the opportunity afforded by a breach of official etiquette—a breach committed, and rightly committed, by Sir THOMAS FARRER and many another Civil Servant—and threw the unpopular agent overboard. When the Hyde-park railings fell, WALPOLE wept. When the Whitechapel murders occurred, and Warrenism, apt for the bludgeoning of the people, incapable of detecting crime, began to stink in the nostrils of the men of London, MATTHEWS ran away. A more contemptible episode in the career of the weakest of politicians and the meanest of men was never on record. King DEMOS may well laugh "Aha!" when he sees that these are his masters.

Sir CHARLES WARREN is gone after twelve months' ineffectual struggle with popular opinion. We do not regret him, but we say firmly that a worse offender remains. Mr. MATTHEWS is the Minister who is responsible for Sir CHARLES WARREN'S administration. It was he who gave and broke the pledge about "*bona fide* meetings." It was he who defended from his place in Parliament the savage treatment of London Radicals by the official who simply carried out his orders with military promptitude and severity.

It is true that Mr. MATTHEWS gives the Press and the House of Commons to understand that he accepted Sir CHARLES WARREN'S resignation on account of differences of opinion as to the organisation of the Detective Department. That is true, but it is not the whole truth. Sir CHARLES WARREN, having succeeded in a flank movement in Trafalgar-square, thought he could succeed as a detective. In the attempt he came into sharp conflict with Mr. MONRO, and eventually with Mr. MATTHEWS. But no man with the smallest acquaintance with such natures as Mr. MATTHEWS'S doubts the real reason for the Chief Commissioner's supersession. And, that being so, it behoves the people of London to say whether they will sacrifice the agent and let the director go free. Sir CHARLES had at least the courage of his mischievous opinions. Mr. MATTHEWS has neither courage nor opinions, but only the base instinct of self-preservation.

MATTHEWS then must go. But that is not the immediate moral of last night's victory. The pressing question is the appointment of a successor to Sir CHARLES WARREN. Now we invite the London Liberal members to make two demands on the Government. The first is that the new CHIEF COMMISSIONER shall be a policeman, and not a military man. The reign of the HENDERSONS and the WARRENS is over. Both parties are to blame for the militarising of the police, and one party at least must confess its error in sackcloth and ashes before it is too late.

The best Chief Commissioner which London ever had was Sir RICHARD MAYNE, who was a lawyer. Either a lawyer or a policeman like the excellent Chief Constable of Birmingham should be chosen to succeed the Major-General who has been happily restored to the profession which we suppose he adorns.

---

[305] **Make the Welkin Ring**. To make a loud noise. Welkin. (*Archaic*) The sky, firmament. From Middle English Welken, which was from Old English Wolcen, Weolcen, cloud. (Morehead)

# Tuesday, 13 November, 1888

But that is not all; indeed it is only half of the popular demand. We are not at all sure that the time has not come for the total abolition of the office of Chief Commissioner and the decentralisation of the police. But most emphatically the time has come for placing the Chief Constable of London under popular control. The Radicals, therefore, should press for a purely temporary appointment, made with the express understanding that as soon as the County Council is called into existence its holder shall be at the service of the people's representatives. That should, we think, be a sine qua non[306] of the popular demand inside Parliament.

And outside? What is to be done about Trafalgar-square? Well, the main point on which to insist is that nothing shall be done in a hurry. Within the last two weeks the policy of Parliamentary pressure has won two startling and significant victories. *The Star* programme has been acknowledged and partly incorporated by the Liberal party; and the people have struck down military government in London.

Do not let us lose the moral of these events. Sir CHARLES WARREN called us a mob. The answer to that must be that we are not a mob, but an army marching on to assured and speedy victory. Our policy is to watch with lynx-like vigilance the next step taken by her MAJESTY'S Government, jealously to canvass the new appointment, and then to ask the new official whether he will make terms for a responsible and properly-organised meeting to be held in the Square. In other words, the policy of "rushes" has not succeeded; the policy of Parliamentary attack has and will. The first was magnificent, but it was war at long odds; the second is hum-drum, but it is the winning game. We can play it now with the assurance that no power on earth can stand against the united voice of an emancipated people, speaking through its chosen representatives.

WE are sorry to see a small section of London democrats mixing themselves up with the cause of Anarchism. We have only to point the moral of our leader with an emphatic condemnation of such a gratuitous piece of folly, and what is worse, such rank treason to the popular cause. Anarchism is tyranny's best friend. It is the negation of progress; the destruction of rational society; the last miserable resort of intellectual and moral pessimism. Away with it! We will have no part or lot in it; and the sooner our friends the Socialists understand that, the better. Let them look to the lesson of Birmingham and the lesson of Trafalgar-square, as against the lesson of Chicago. There is the true moral of the situation in London to-day.

SIR CHARLES WARREN may now be reconciled to his bloodhounds. These animals, it will be remembered, mysteriously disappeared, and there is no doubt that, finding they could not get on with the Chief commissioner, they resigned.

The inquest on Mary Janet Kelly has closed, like its predecessors, without throwing any useful light on the crime. Light of a certain sort there is, but it is so confused and shifting as to be almost worse than useless. We have at least three descriptions of an individual who may be the man wanted.

There is Mrs. Cox's account of a man who went with the deceased into her room about midnight on Thursday—"a short stout man, shabbily dressed," with "a blotchy face and a full carrotty moustache."

There is Sarah Lewis's description of the man who accosted her on Wednesday in Bethnal-green-road, which varies slightly from the preceding, but might fit the same man.

Finally, we have the statement by an anonymous witness which has found its way into the morning papers, and which makes the suspected individual an elegantly-dressed gentleman about 5ft. 6in. in height, "with a dark complexion, and a dark moustache curled up at the ends."

Why this statement has been made public at this particular juncture is one of those mysteries in the police management of the case which no one out of Scotland-yard can understand.

—

---

[306] **Sine qua non**. Lat. Without which nothing. This was originally a legal term for an absolute necessity. (Morehead)

## THE MILLER'S-COURT MURDER.
## THE TWO DESCRIPTIONS OF THE SUPPOSED ASSASSIN.
### That Given by the Widow Cox Tallies With the Man Followed on the Morning of the Hanbury-street Murder—The Deed Done in the Dark—The Mystery of the Bloodhounds Explained.

The most important point which has yet transpired in connection with the Miller's-court murder is the fact that Mary Ann Cox, who lives in the house where the dreadful deed was done, saw Kelly go into her room at midnight on Thursday with a man who was

### SHORT, STOUT, AND SHABBILY DRESSED.

He had on a long dark coat, a black billycock hat, and carried a pot of ale, and had a blotchy face, shaven chin, and a full carrotty moustache. The first care of the police on receiving this statement on Friday was to compare it with the descriptions given by various people and at various times of men supposed to have been seen in company of the murderer's previous victims. Unfortunately the accounts do not harmonise. The Berner-street suspect was described as a very dark man. The Hanbury-street victim was seen in company with a dark, foreign-looking man, and a similar description was given of a suspected individual at the time of the Buck's-row murder. It is noteworthy, however, that there were two descriptions given of the suspected Mitre-square and Hanbury-street murderers which agree in some respects with that furnished by the witness Cox. About 10 minutes before the body of Catherine Eddowes was found in Mitre-square a man about 30 years of age, of fair complexion, and with a fair moustache, was said to have been seen talking to her in the covered passage leading to the square. On the morning of the Hanbury-street murder a suspicious-looking man entered a public-house in Brushfield-street, and was afterwards

### FOLLOWED INTO BISHOPSGATE-STREET.

He was of shabby-genteel appearance, was stoutish, and had a sandy moustache. He was suspected because he was bloodstained.

It is said that a man who knew Kelly has stated to the police that on the morning of the 9th inst. he saw her in Commercial-street, Spitalfields (near where the murder was committed) in company with a man of respectable appearance, about 5ft. 6in. in height, and 34 or 35 years of age, with dark complexion, and dark moustache turned up at the ends, wearing a long, dark coat, trimmed with astrachan, a white collar with black necktie (in which was affixed a horseshoe pin), a pair of dark gaiters with light buttons over button boots, and displaying from his waistcoat a massive gold chain. Strangely enough, since it

### DIFFERS SO COMPLETELY

from the description given by Cox, the police are said to attach a good deal of importance to the man's statement.

A point in Cox's evidence which seemed likely to afford some clue was the statement that the man was carrying a pot of beer. The can or pot which contained the liquor was not found in the room, and a careful examination of the fireplace and ashes showed that it had not been melted down, as was at first considered probable. If, therefore, the beer was actually taken into the house as described, the murderer must have taken the can away. This would seem to show that the murderer

### FEARED THE CAN MIGHT FORM A LINK

in a possible chain of evidence against him. As far as inquiries have gone, no man answering the description given by Cox entered any tavern in the immediate neighbourhood and took away beer.

As to the time of the murder, it is now generally admitted that Kelly could not, as some have stated, have been alive on Friday morning. The police have come to the conclusion that the woman who made the most positive statement to this effect must have been mistaken as to the day. Dr. Phillips's evidence, together with that of Mary Ann Cox, Elizabeth Prater, and others, proves that the murder was committed

### SHORTLY AFTER THREE O'CLOCK

—a fact which brings into startling relief the murderer's coolness, caution, and tenacity of purpose. The woman's drunken merriment lasted until shortly after one o'clock, by which time doubtless the liquor taken in had been consumed, and the couple must have sat up talking for half an hour or more before they retired for the night, because it is now known that the light was not extinguished until about two o'clock. The murderer must have restrained his impulse for nearly another hour, probably waiting until all fear of the return of late revellers and others had passed. Long before the murderer began his deadly work the victim must have been in a deep sleep, from which she was awakened by the murderer's onslaught, but only for a moment, as she was able to utter only one cry of murder, as said to have been heard by several dwellers in the court.

Some surprise was created among those present at the inquest yesterday by the abrupt termination of the inquiry. No question was put to Dr. Phillips as to the mutilated portions of the body, and the coroner did not think fit to ask the doctor whether any portions of the body were missing. The idea was that by at once making public every fact brought to light in connection with this terrible murder, the ends of justice might be retarded. Notwithstanding reports to the contrary, it is still confidently asserted that

**SOME PORTIONS OF THE BODY ARE MISSING.**

During yesterday several arrests were made, but after a short examination in all cases the persons were set at liberty, as it was felt certain they had no connection with the crime.

—

### Decent Burial.

The threatened dispute as to who should bear the cost of the burial of the latest victim of the murder-maniac has been settled by several private persons coming forward to pay the expense. A local undertaker has offered to make the coffin and superintend the arrangements without fee, and two of the jurors are prepared to pay for a hearse and coach if the undertaker's offer is accepted.

~

## Evening News
### ANOTHER SUPPOSED MURDER AT THE EAST END
### MYSTERIOUS AFFAIR

On Friday last, William Wood, a waterman, was in his boat off Wapping Stairs, when he noticed the body of a woman, dressed in superior clothing, floating down the river. He secured the body and took it ashore. The police were then communicated with and the body was removed to the mortuary. It was fully dressed with the exception of the hat and boots, which were missing. Inquiries were at once set on foot by the police, and it was found that the body was that of Frances Annie Hancock, who had been missing since October 21. On that day she was seen walking along the Strand, in company with a tall, fair gentleman with a heavy moustache. She was then wearing a gold necklace, and that was the last time she was seen alive. When the body was recovered the necklace was missing. Deceased resided at Prusom street, Brixton, where it is stated she was supported by some gentleman at present unknown. At an inquiry held by Mr. Wynne E. Baxter, Coroner for the South eastern Division of Middlesex, last evening, on the body of the deceased, only evidence of identification was taken, and, owing to the mysterious nature of the case and supposition that the deceased woman has met her death by foul means, the coroner adjourned the inquiry in order that a post mortem examination might be made on the body, and to give police an opportunity of full inquiry into the facts of the case, which, it is stated, will be of a startling and sensational character, owing to the relations formerly existing between the deceased woman and some gentleman of distinction.

—

### RESIGNATION OF
### SIR CHARLES WARREN

The Press Association, in reference to Sir Charles Warren's resignation, learns on the highest authority that the relations between Sir Charles Warren and the Home Office have for some time been strained. The action of the department in reference to the resignation of Mr. Monro caused the first serious difference of opinion. Sir Charles took exception to certain of the methods of the Assistant Commissioner, and he intimated to Mr. Matthews that either he or Mr. Monro must resign. A few days afterwards Mr. Monro's resignation was announced. Sir Charles Warren complains that Mr. Monro's resignation was accepted without consultation with him, and that prior to the Home Secretary's statement in the House of Commons last evening he (Sir Charles Warren) was not even aware of the reason assigned by his subordinate for severing his connection with Scotland yard. Since Mr. Monro's transference to the Home Office, matters have become worse.

Sir Charles complains that, whereas he has been saddled with all the responsibility, he has had no freedom of action, and in consequence his position has become daily more unbearable. Although Mr. Monro has been no longer in evidence at Whitehall place, he has to all intents and purposes retained control of the Criminal Investigation Department.

Indeed, Mr. Matthews last evening admitted that he was deriving the benefit of the advice of Mr. Monro in matters relating to crime, and was in communication with him at the present time on the subject of the organisation of the detective staff. This division of authority Sir Charles Warren has strenuously fought against. He maintains that if the Commissioner is to be responsible for the discipline of the force, instructions should be given to no department without his concurrence.

Latterly, in spite of the remonstrances of Sir Charles Warren, the control of the Criminal Investigation Department has been withdrawn more and more from Whitehall Place. Every morning for the last few weeks there has been a protracted conference at the Home Office between Mr. Monro, Mr. Anderson, and the principal detective inspectors, and the information furnished to the Commissioner in regard to these conferences has been, he states, of the scantiest character.

These facts will explain how, apart from any other consideration, it was impossible for Sir Charles Warren, holding the views he did in regard to the function of the Commissioner, to continue in command. The reproof of the Home Secretary last week in reference to the article in "Murray's Magazine" completed the rupture. Sir Charles thereupon took counsel with his friends, and immediately tendered his resignation to the Home Secretary.

Yesterday morning his books and papers were removed from the Commissioner's office, and this was the first intimation in Whitehall place that he had relinquished his position.

## THE PROBABLE SUCCESSOR

The names of Mr. Monro, late Assistant Commissioner of Metropolitan Police; Mr. Malcolm Wood, Chief Constable of Manchester; and Mr. Farndale, the Chief of the Birmingham Police Force, are mentioned in connection with the vacant Chief Commissionership.

—

## THE DORSET STREET MURDER
## IMPORTANT STATEMENT
## DESCRIPTION OF THE PROBABLE MURDERER

The police, yesterday evening, received an important piece of information. A man, apparently of the labouring class, with a military appearance, who knew the deceased, stated that on the morning of the 9th inst. he saw her in Commercial street, Spitalfields (near where the murder was committed), in company with a man of respectable appearance. He was about 5ft 6in in height, and 34 or 35 years of age, with dark complexion and dark moustache turned up at the ends. He was wearing a long, dark coat, trimmed with astrachan, a white collar with black necktie, in which was affixed a horseshoe pin. He wore a pair of dark gaiters with light buttons, over button boots, and displayed from his waistcoat a massive gold chain. His appearance contrasted so markedly with that of the woman that few people could have failed to remark them at that hour of the morning. This description, which confirms that given by others of the person seen in company with the deceased on the morning she was killed, is much fuller in detail than that hitherto in the possession of the police.

—

## YESTERDAY'S ARRESTS

During yesterday several arrests were made, but after a short examination in all cases the persons were set at liberty, as it was felt certain that they had connection with the crime. Dorset street still continues to be a thoroughfare of great interest, and during the whole of the day people, who were evidently drawn thither solely out of curiosity, passed up and down the street while before the entrance to Miller's court a crowd collected. They were not, however, allowed to enter the court, which was guarded by two police constables.

—

## THE TRUTH ABOUT THE BLOODHOUNDS

In order to arrive at the truth of the conflicting statements which have appeared as to the use or non use of bloodhounds in the attempts to track the murderer of Marie Janet Kelly, the last Whitechapel victim, a representative of the Central News had an interview with Mr. K W Taunton on the subject yesterday evening.

It will be remembered that at Sir Charles Warren's request Mr. Brough, the well known bloodhound breeder, of Scarborough, was communicated with shortly after the Mitre square and Berner street tragedies, and asked to bring a couple of trained hounds to London for the purpose of testing their capabilities in the way of following the scent of a man. The hounds were named Burgho and Barnaby, and in one of the trials Sir Charles Warren himself acted as the quarry, and expressed satisfaction at the result. Arrangements were made for the immediate conveyance of the animals to the spot in the event of another murder occurring, and in order to facilitate matters Mr. Brough, who was compelled to return to Scarborough, left the hounds in the care of Mr. Taunton of 8 Doughty street.

Mr. Taunton said: After the trial in Regent's Park, Burgho was sent to Brighton, where he had been entered for the show, which lasted three days. In the meantime Barnaby remained in my care. Burgho would have been sent back to me, but as Brough could not get anything definite from the police he declined to send the dog, and wrote asking me to return Barnaby. I did not do so at first, but acting on my own responsibility, retained possession of the dog for some time longer.

About a fortnight ago I received a telegram from Leman street Police station asking me to bring up the hounds. It was then shortly after noon, and I took Barnaby at once. On arriving at the station, I was told by the superintendent that a burglary had been committed about five o'clock that morning in Commercial street, and I was asked to attempt to track the thief by means of the dog. The police admitted that since the burglary they had been all over the premises. I pointed out the stupidity of expecting a dog to accomplish anything under such circumstances and after such a length of time had been allowed to elapse, and took the animal home.

I wrote telling Mr. Brough of this, and he wired insisting that the dog should be sent back at once, as the danger of its being poisoned if it were known that the police were trying to trace burglars by its aid was very great, and Mr. Brough had no guarantee against any pecuniary loss in the event of the animal being maltreated. Therefore there has not been a "police blood-hound"—that is to say, a trained hound—in London for the past fortnight.

The origin of the tale regarding the hounds being lost at Tooting whilst being practised in tracing a man I can only account for in the following way: I had arranged to take Barnaby out to Hemel Hempstead to give the hound some practice. The same day a sheep was maliciously killed on Tooting Common, and the police wired to London asking that the hounds might be sent down. I was then some miles away from London with Barnaby, and did not get the telegram until my return late in the evening. Somebody, doubtless, remarked that the hounds were missing, meaning that they did not arrive when sent for, and this was magnified into a report that they had been lost. At the time Burgho was at Scarborough.

Under the circumstances in which the body of Marie Janet Kelly was found I don't think bloodhounds would have been of any use. It was then broad daylight and the streets crowded with people. The only chance the hounds would have would be in the event of a murdered body being discovered, as the others were, in the small hours of the morning and being put on the trail before many people were about.

—

## THE ABRUPT TERMINATION OF THE INQUEST

Some surprise was created among those present at the inquest in the Shoreditch Town Hall by the abrupt termination of the inquiry, as it was well known that further evidence would be forthcoming. The coroner himself distinctly told the jury that he was only going to take the preliminary portion of Dr. G. B. Phillips's evidence, the remainder of which would be more fully given at the adjourned inquiry. No question was put to Dr. Philips as to the mutilated portions of the body, and the coroner did not think fit to ask the doctor whether any portions of the body were missing. The doctor stated to the coroner during the inquiry that his examination was not yet completed. His idea was that by at once making public every fact brought to light in connection with this terrible murder, the ends of justice might be retarded.

—

## SOME PORTIONS OF THE BODY ARE MISSING

The examination of the body by Dr. Phillips, on Saturday, lasted upwards of six and a half hours. Notwithstanding reports to the contrary, it is still confidently asserted that some portions of the body of the deceased woman are missing.

—

## ANOTHER LETTER TO THE POLICE

Another letter, signed Jack the Ripper, of which the following is a copy, was received by post last night by the Metropolitan Police, and was published by them today:

"Dear Boss—I am now in Queen's Park estate in the Third Avenue. I am out of red ink at present, but it won't matter for once. I intend doing another here next Tuesday night about ten o'clock. I will give you a chance now to catch me. I shall have check trousers on and a black coat and vest, so look out. I have done one not yet found out, so keep your eyes open.

Yours, Jack the Ripper."

The police are receiving a very large number of letters on the subject of the murder.

—

The Central News learns that the police now have no one in custody. All has been quiet in the district during night, and there is very little excitement apparent. The police are as busily engaged as ever, and are now actively following up fresh information gathered from yesterday's inquest. So conflicting, however, are various descriptions of the supposed criminal, that there is but slight ground for anticipating successful investigation.

—

The Central News says: Last night the police made a careful inspection of all the casual wards, and at one of three places near Holborn a man was arrested, who had a knife of formidable proportions in his possession. His account of himself was very confused, and he was arrested. The excitement in the East end has materially abated.

—

Miller's court, this morning, is still guarded by two police constables, but persons having business to transact are allowed to enter the court. The room in which the murder was committed is still closed. There is a considerable crowd in Dorset street. Nothing has yet been definitely settled respecting the funeral, but it is expected that all details in connection with it will be settled in the course of today.

—

## THE JACK THE RIPPER MANIA

Several drunken men were brought up at the Metropolitan police courts today, each charged with shouting out "I'm Jack the Ripper," or words to the same effect. At Westminster Police court an individual, who was seen between one and two o'clock this morning to climb some railings and try to open the ground floor window of a private house, explained his action by assuring the policeman who took him into custody that he "was looking for Jack the Ripper."

# Wednesday, 14 November, 1888

## The Times
### THE WHITECHAPEL MURDERS.

In the Holborn casual ward yesterday the police arrested a man who gave the name of Thomas Murphy. He was taken to the police station at Frederick-street, King's-cross-road, where, on being searched, he was found to have in his possession a somewhat formidable looking knife with a blade about ten inches long. He was therefore detained in custody on suspicion, and the police proceeded to make inquiries into the truth of his statements. The task was rendered very difficult by the confused and contradictory accounts which Murphy gave of himself, and the man was still in custody at 6 o'clock yesterday evening. Murphy is about 5ft. 6in. in height, and has the general appearance of a sailor. His hair and complexion are fair. He is dressed in a blue jersey tucked underneath his trousers, and his coat and trousers are of a check pattern.

Another man was arrested late yesterday afternoon in the neighbourhood of Dorset-street, but was released on inquiries being satisfactorily answered.

The funeral of the murdered woman Kelly will not take place until after the arrival from Wales of some of her relatives and friends, who are expected to reach London this evening. If they be unable to provide the necessary funeral expenses, Mr. H. Wilton, of 119, High-street, Shoreditch, has guaranteed that the unfortunate woman shall not be buried in a pauper's grave. Any person, however, who may be desirous of sharing the expense with Mr. Wilton can communicate with him. The remains, according to present arrangements, will be interred either on Thursday or Friday at the new Chingford Cemetery.

The following statement was made yesterday evening by George Hutchinson, a labourer:—"At 2 o'clock on Friday morning I came down Whitechapel-road into Commercial-street. As I passed Thrawl-street I passed a man standing at the corner of the street, and as I went towards Flower and Dean-street I met the woman Kelly, whom I knew very well, having been in her company a number of times. She said, 'Mr. Hutchinson, can you lend me sixpence?' I said I could not. She then walked on towards Thrawl-Street, saying she must go and look for some money. The man, who was standing at the corner of Thrawl-street then came towards her and put his hand on her shoulder and said something to her, which I did not hear, and they both burst out laughing. He put his hand again on her shoulder, and they both walked slowly towards me. I walked on to the corner of Fashion-street near the public-house. As they came by me his arm was still on her shoulder. He had a soft felt hat on, and this was drawn down somewhat over his eyes. I put down my head to look him in the face, and he turned and looked at me very sternly, and they walked across the road to Dorset-street. I followed them across and stood at the corner of Dorset-street. They stood at the corner of Miller's-court for about three minutes. Kelly spoke to the man in a loud voice, saying, 'I have lost my handkerchief.' He pulled a red handkerchief out of his pocket and gave it to Kelly, and they both went up the court together. I went to look up the court to see if I could see them, but could not. I stood there for three-quarters of an hour, to see if they came down again, but they did not, and so I went away. My suspicions were aroused by seeing the man so well dressed, but I had no suspicion that he was the murderer. The man was about 5ft. 6in. in height, and 34 or 35 years of age, with dark complexion and dark moustache turned up at the ends. He was wearing a long dark coat trimmed with astrachan, a white collar with black necktie, in which was affixed a horse-shoe pin. He wore a pair of dark spats with light buttons over buttoned boots, and displayed from his waistcoat a massive gold chain. His watch chain had a big seal with a red stone hanging from it. He had a heavy moustache curled up, and dark eyes and bushy eyebrows. He had no side whiskers, and his chin was clean shaven. He looked like a foreigner. I went up the court and stayed there a couple of minutes, but did not see any light in the house or hear any noise. I was out last night until 3 o'clock looking for him. I could swear to the man anywhere. The man I saw carried a small parcel in his hand about 8in. long and it had a strap round it. He had it tightly grasped in his left hand. It looked as though it was covered with dark American cloth. He carried in his right hand, which he laid upon the woman's shoulder, a pair of brown kid gloves. He walked very softly. I believe that he

# Wednesday, 14 November, 1888

lives in the neighbourhood, and I fancied that I saw him in Petticoat-lane on Sunday morning, but I was not certain. I went down to the Shoreditch mortuary to-day and recognized the body as being that of the woman Kelly, whom I saw at 2 o'clock on Friday morning. Kelly did not seem to me to be drunk, but was a little bit spreeish. After I left the court I walked about all night, as the place where I usually sleep was closed. I am able to fix the time, as it was between 10 and 5 minutes to 2 o'clock as I came by Whitechapel Church. When I left the corner of Miller's-court the clock struck 3 o'clock. One policeman went by the Commercial-street end of Dorset-street while I was standing there, but no one came down Dorset-street. I saw one man go into a lodging-house in Dorset-street, and no one else. I have been looking for the man all day."

The description of the murderer given by Hutchinson agrees in every particular with that already furnished by the police and published yesterday morning.

At a late hour last night the man Murphy was still in custody, and he will be detained until the result of police inquiries into his antecedents, which are being conducted at Gravesend, Woolwich, and other places, is known.

~

## The Star
### WHITECHAPEL.
### STORY OF THE MAN WHO SAW KELLY WITH A "GENTLEMAN."
### He Fixes the Time at Two o'Clock on Friday Morning, and Says the Stranger Carried a Parcel, Wore Gloves, and Walked with Noiseless Tread.

This morning we have a fuller statement respecting the well-dressed man said to have been seen with Kelly early on Friday morning. The story is told by George Hutchinson, a groom by trade, but now working as a laborer. He says:—"On Thursday last I had been to Romford, in Essex, and I returned from there about two o'clock on Friday morning, having walked all the way. I came down Whitechapel-road into Commercial-street. As I passed Thrawl-street I saw a man standing at the corner of the street, and as I went towards Flower-and-Dean-street I met the woman Kelly, whom I knew very well, having been in her company a number of times. She said, 'Mr. Hutchinson, can you lend me sixpence?' I said, 'I cannot, as I am spent out going down to Romford.' She then walked on towards Thrawl-street, saying, 'I must go and look for some money.' The man who was standing at the corner of Thrawl-street then came towards her and

### PUT HIS HAND ON HER SHOULDER

and said something to her, which I did not hear, and they both burst out laughing. He put his hand again on her shoulder, and they both walked slowly towards me. I walked on to the corner of Fashion-street, near the public-house. As they came by me his arm was still on her shoulder. He had a soft felt hat on, and this was drawn down somewhat over his eyes. I put down my head to look him in the face, and he turned and looked at me very sternly, and they walked across the road to Dorset-street. I followed them across, and stood at the corner of Dorset-street. They stood at the corner of Miller's-court for about three minutes. Kelly spoke to the man in a loud voice, saying, 'I have lost my handkerchief.' He pulled

### A RED HANDKERCHIEF

out of his pocket, and gave it to Kelly, and they both went up the court together. I went to look up the court to see if I could see them, but could not. I stood there for threequarters of an hour to see if they came down again, but they did not, and so I went away. My suspicions were aroused by seeing the man so well-dressed, but I had no suspicion that he was the murderer. The man was about 5ft. 6in. in height, and 34 or 35 years of age, with dark complexion and dark moustache, turned up at the ends. He was wearing a long dark coat, trimmed with astrachan, a white collar, with black necktie, in which was affixed a horseshoe pin. He wore a pair of dark 'spats' with light buttons over button boots, and displayed from his waistcoat a massive gold chain. His watch chain had a big seal, with a red stone, hanging from it. He had a heavy moustache curled up and dark eyes and bushy eyebrows. He had no side whiskers, and his chin was clean-shaven. He

## LOOKED LIKE A FOREIGNER.

I went up the court and stayed there a couple of minutes, but did not see any light in the house or hear any noise. I was out last night until three o'clock looking for him. I could swear to the man anywhere. I told one policeman on Sunday morning what I had seen, but did not go to the police-station. I told one of the lodgers here about it yesterday, and he advised me to go to the police-station, which I did last night. The man I saw did not look as though he would attack another one. He carried a small parcel in his hand about 8in. long, and it had a strap round it. He had it tightly grasped in his left hand. It looked as though it was covered with dark American cloth.[307] He carried in his right hand, which he laid upon the woman's shoulder, a pair of brown kid gloves. One thing I noticed, and that was that

## HE WALKED VERY SOFTLY.

I believe that he lives in the neighbourhood, and I fancied that I saw him in Petticoat-lane on Sunday morning, but I was not certain. Kelly did not seem to me to be drunk, but was a little bit spreeish.[308] After I left the court I walked about all night, as the place where I usually sleep was closed. I am able to fix the time, as it was between ten and five minutes to two o'clock

as I came by Whitechapel Church. When I left the corner of Miller's-court the clock struck three o'clock. One policeman went by the Commercial-street end of Dorset-street while I was standing there, but not one came down Dorset-street. I saw one man go into a lodging-house in Dorset-street, and no one else. I have been looking for the man all day."

The police have received from Mr. Samuel Osborne, wireworker, 20, Garden-row, London-road, a statement to the effect that he was walking along St. Paul's Churchyard yesterday behind a respectably-dressed man, when a parcel wrapped in a newspaper fell from the man's coat. Osborne told him that he had dropped something, but the man denied the parcel belonged to him. Osborne picked up the parcel and found that it contained

## A KNIFE WITH A PECULIARLY SHAPED HANDLE,

and a thick blade 6in. or 7in. long, with stains upon it resembling blood; the parcel also contained a brown kid glove, smeared with similar stains on both sides. Osborne found a constable, and together they searched for the mysterious individual, but without success. The parcel was handed over to the City police authorities, who, however, attach not the slightest importance to the matter, as the knife proved to be a table knife, eaten with rust, and so blunt that it could not possibly have been used in connection with the late murders.

A second inquest would have been held on Kelly's body had it been removed into the Whitechapel district for burial. But the double inquiry has been averted by the action of Mr. H. Wilton, parish clerk and keeper of the Shoreditch mortuary. He has undertaken to inter the body at his own expense, assisted by contributions which may be received, and yesterday he obtained from the coroner's officer an order to prepare a coffin. In

## SUDDENLY CLOSING THE INQUEST,

Dr. Macdonald stated that the duty of the jury was merely to ascertain the cause of death, but the common law, since Edward I., has declared that in the language of the declaratory statute, "all the injuries of the body, also all wounds, ought to be viewed; and the length, breadth, and deepness, with what weapon, and in what part of the body the wound or hurt is; and how many be culpable, and how many wounds there be,

---

[307] **American Cloth.** Cotton cloth with a waterproof coating, Oilcloth. (Collins Dictionary)

[308] **Spree.** A frolic. As verb, to carouse; **spreeish,** drunkish : see **Screwed** (1821).

**Screwed (or Screwy).** Drunk, tight (q.v.). (Farmer)

and who gave the wounds—all which things must be enrolled in the roll of the coroner's." No question was put as to any of these points.

—

## This Morning's Scares and Arrests.

Soon after three o'clock this morning screams of "Police! Murder!" were heard in the neighbourhood of Commercial-street. Several policemen ran to the spot, and found a young woman lying on the pavement insensible and bleeding from an ugly wound in the head. After she recovered she said she was accosted by a man who, when she refused to go with him, drew a large knife. She gave the alarm and the man knocked her down. The woman was sober, and gave the police a description of the man which tallies with that published.

At five o'clock this morning there were three persons in custody at Commercial-street Police-station. One tried to persuade two women to accompany him into one of the small streets adjoining Spitalfields Market. He was watched, and ultimately handed over to a policeman. At the police-station the man refused to give an account of himself or where he lived, on the ground that he did not wish his parents to be alarmed by the police inquiries regarding him. Questioned as to his whereabouts on Thursday night, and Friday morning last he gave various explanations, and contradicted himself so frequently that it was considered advisable to detain him until his identity and antecedents were thoroughly investigated.

At Leman-street Station no fewer than 10 persons were brought in the course of the morning; but of this number only two were detained at half-past five.

—

## The Night Watch.

A correspondent writes:—Between twelve and two o'clock this morning I and a friend perambulated the murder district. Except in the main thoroughfares, there was not a woman to be seen; for the terror has struck so deeply that they will not venture out of Whitechapel-road. There were a few, seemingly quite destitute, here and in Commercial-road, but in the network of lanes and alleys lying north of Cable-street, and the maze of winding courts about Osborne-street there was not a soul but policemen, mostly in plain clothes. There were several easily distinguishable people got up as amateur detectives, one ingenious young man feigning drunkenness in a most unnatural fashion. It struck me as strange that most of the police confined their attention to the main streets, and gave but scanty attention to the more dangerous bye-lanes. In order to test the much talked-of ubiquity of the police in Whitechapel at present my friend and I halted under the bridge in Christian-street, determining to see how long we would remain undisturbed. It was seventeen minutes before anyone appeared, and then the arrival was not a policeman, but a young man who entered a house near by. There was plenty of time for the undisturbed performance of another tragedy. We tried the same experiment in several of the dark courts of the district, and in the majority of cases it was over ten minutes before we were observed. My experience did not by any means bear out the idea that the police are particularly vigilant in the district, except, of course, in the main streets, where there are police every few yards apart."

Thomas Murphy, arrested in a Holborn lodging-house and found in possession of a knife, has been discharged.

~

# Wednesday, 14 November, 1888

## Evening News

### THE DORSET STREET MURDER
### ANOTHER IMPORTANT STATEMENT
### YESTERDAY'S ARREST IN HOLBORN
### ANOTHER ARREST THIS MORNING

At an early hour this morning a Press Association reporter was informed that between midnight and four o'clock this morning three arrests were made in the eastern district in connection with the recent terrible murders. About one o'clock some young men had their suspicions aroused by the peculiar behaviour of a man in the vicinity of the Spitalfields Flower Market. He accosted two women, and after remaining conversing with them for a considerable time, tried to persuade them to accompany him into one of the small streets adjoining the market. These thoroughfares are in general gloomy and badly lighted, and the women, being suspicious, refused to go with the man. He was followed for some distance by the watchers, and ultimately handed over to a policeman, who took him to Commercial street Police station. Here the man refused to give an account of himself or where he lived, on the ground that he did not wish his parents to be alarmed by police inquiries regarding him. Questioned as to his whereabouts on Thursday night and Friday morning last, the man gave various explanations, and contradicted himself so frequently that it was considered advisable to detain him until his identity and antecedents were thoroughly investigated.

In the Holborn casual ward, yesterday, the police arrested a man who gave his name as Thomas Murphy. He was taken to the police station at Frederick street, King's Cross road, where, on being searched, he was found to have in his possession a somewhat formidable looking knife with a blade about ten inches long. He was therefore detained in custody on suspicion, and the police proceeded to make inquiries into the truth of his statements. The task was rendered very difficult by the confused and contradictory accounts which Murphy gave of himself, and the man was still in custody at six o'clock yesterday evening. Murphy is about 5ft 6in in height, and has the general appearance of a sailor. His hair and complexion are fair. He is dressed in a blue jersey tucked underneath his trousers, and his coat and trousers are of a check pattern.

At a late hour last night the man Murphy was still in custody, and he will be detained until the result of police inquiries into his antecedents, which are being conducted at Gravesend, Woolwich, and other places, is known.

—

### ANOTHER STATEMENT CONFIRMING ONE MADE ON MONDAY

The following statement was made yesterday evening by George Hutchinson, a labourer:

"At 2 o'clock on Friday morning I came down Whitechapel road into Commercial street. As I passed Thrawl street, I passed a man standing at the corner of the street, and as I went towards Flower and Dean street I met the woman Kelly, whom I knew every well, having been in her company a number of times. She said, "Mr. Hutchinson, can you lend me sixpence?" I said I could not. She then walked on towards Thrawl street, saying she must go and look for some money. The man who was standing at the corner of Thrawl street then came towards her and put his hand on her shoulder and said something to her, which I did not hear, and they both burst out laughing. He put his hand again on her shoulder, and they both walked slowly towards me. I waited on the corner of Fashion street, near the public house. As they came by me his arm was still on her shoulder. He had a soft felt hat on, and this was drawn down somewhat over his eyes. I put down my head to look him in the face, and he turned and looked at me very sternly, and they walked across the road to Dorset street. I followed them across and stood at the corner of Dorset street. They stood at the corner of Miller's court for about three minutes. Kelly spoke to the man in a loud voice, saying, 'I have lost my handkerchief.'

### HE GAVE HER A RED HANDKERCHIEF

"He pulled a red handkerchief out of his pocket and gave it to Kelly, and they both went up the court together. I went to look up the court to see if I could see them, but I could not. I stood there for three quarters of an hour, to see if they came down again, but they did not, so I went away. My suspicions were aroused by seeing the man so well dressed, but I had no suspicion that he was the murderer. The man was about 5ft 6in in height, and 34 or 35 years of age, with dark complexion and dark moustache turned up at the ends. He was wearing a long, dark coat trimmed with astrachan, a white collar with black necktie, in which was affixed a horseshoe pin. He wore a pair of darks spats with light buttons, over button boots, and displayed from his waistcoat a massive gold chain.

## HIS WATCH CHAIN AND SEAL

"His watch chain had a big seal with a red stone hanging from it. He had a heavy moustache curled up, and dark eyes and bushy eyebrows. He had no side whiskers, and his chin was clean shaven. He looked like a foreigner. I went up the court and stayed there for a couple of minutes, but did not see any light in the house or hear any noise. I was out last night until 3 o'clock looking for him. I could swear to the man anywhere. The man I saw carried a small parcel in his hand about 8in long, and it had a strap round it. He had it tightly grasped in his left hand.

## DARK AMERICAN CLOTH

"It looked as though it was covered with dark American cloth. He carried in his right hand, which he laid upon the woman's shoulder, a pair of brown kid gloves. He walked very softly. I believe that he lives in the neighbourhood, and I fancied that I saw him in Petticoat lane on Sunday morning, but I was not certain. I went down to the Shoreditch mortuary today and recognised the body as being that of the woman Kelly, whom I saw at two o'clock on Friday morning.

## KELLY WAS SOBER

"Kelly did not seem to me to be drunk, but was a little bit spreeish. After I left the court I walked about all night, as the place where I usually sleep was closed. I am able to fix the time, as it was between ten and five minutes to two o'clock as I came by Whitechapel Church. When I left the corner of Miller's court the clock struck three o'clock. One policeman went by the Commercial street end of Dorset street while I was standing there, but no one came down Dorset street. I saw one man go into a lodging house in Dorset street, and no one else. I have been looking for the man all day."

The description of the murderer given by Hutchinson agrees in every particular with that already furnished by the police and published yesterday morning.

—

## THE VIENNA PAPERS ON THE SUBJECT

The Vienna newspapers reproduce, almost in extenso, the accounts of the Whitechapel murder. That atrocious crime has made a profound sensation in Vienna, but there can be no doubt that had such a series of crimes been perpetrated in this country without detection the highest officials of State would have been called to account. The announcement that bloodhounds would be used on the next occasion to track the assassin has excited considerable interest in Austria, where the opinion amongst fanciers is that the experiment would probably prove successful.

Although several persons have been detained at Commercial street and Leman street police stations for inquiries, they had all been released at noon today. Dorset street is quieter this morning than it has been for some days, but the police still guard Miller's court.

—

## ANOTHER SHAM JACK THE RIPPER

John Avery, a ticket writer, of Willesden, was charged with being drunk and disorderly in York road, the previous night. John Carvell, a private in the 11th Hussars, said that on Monday night he was standing at the corner of York road, Islington, when the prisoner came up to him, caught hold of him, and said, "I'm Jack the Ripper: I'll show you how I do all the lot." The witness told him to go away, but Avery, who was intoxicated, followed him, and threw his right arm round his neck. A scuffle ensued between them, and the witness's nose was scratched. He soon, however, shook off the prisoner, who said, "Come and have a glass of beer, and I will tell you a secret, and you can make some money." They accordingly went into the Duke of York public house, Caledonian street, and there, in the bar, Avery repeated two or three times that "he was Jack the Ripper." Tommy Atkins then thought it best to give the prisoner into custody, and accordingly dragged him outside, and gave him in charge of a policeman, who was on duty near by.

## The Star
### WHITECHAPEL.
### Worthless Stories Lead the Police on False Scents
### Scares also Keep Them Busy.

The only new thing to report this morning in connection with the Miller's-court murder —except the arrest of more innocent men—is another story told by Matthew Packer, the man on whose statement with respect to the Berner-street crime, the discredited "grape story" was built up. Now he says that two men came to him the other day and asked him to describe the man who bought the grapes, and that after he had done so one of the strangers expressed the conviction that the murderer was his cousin, who had come from America, termed everybody "boss," and one day referring to some Whitechapel women said he meant to

### "CUT THEIR THROATS AND RIP THEM UP"

as they had been accustomed to do "where he came from." The reporter to whom Packer made his statement sent off a copy of it to the Home Secretary, and also to the Chief Commissioner of the City Police. This morning it was officially stated that the information has not led to any result.

Another story now discredited is that of the man Hutchinson, who said that on Friday morning last he saw Kelly with a dark-complexioned, middle-aged, foreign-looking, bushy-eyebrowed gentleman, with the dark moustache turned up at the ends, who wore the soft felt hat, the long dark coat, trimmed with astrachan, the black necktie, with horseshoe pin, and the button boots, and displayed a massive gold watch-chain, with large seal and a red stone attached.

As we have already said, the only piece of information of any value which has yet transpired is the description given by the widow Cox of a man—short, stout, with a blotchy face and a carroty moustache—who at midnight on Thursday went with the murdered woman into her room.

Mr. A. Eubule-Evans writes to the *Standard* pointing out that a month ago, with only reason to guide him, he gave

### AN EXACTLY SIMILAR DESCRIPTION

of the man he supposed had committed the murders. He adds:—In this latest murder we have fresh data for calculating the personal equation of the assassin. Finding that it is no longer so easy as before to murder his victims in the open street, he does the deed of horror in a room; and these altered circumstances enable him to carry out to a fuller extent than before the work of butchery. Two things are clear from this—the man is not only cunning, he is original also. He has struck out a new line in crime, and he is capable of changing its method to meet specific exigencies as they arise. It is this originality of mind, far more than his cunning, which has rendered him such a baffling study to the detective police, who are very clever in working along traditional grooves, but are powerless before the unexpected. Another proof of the originality which mingles with this man's cunning is to be found in the curious limitation of the area within which he commits his crimes. In this way, he induced the police to believe that he must have his *habitat* in Whitechapel, and he succeeded in confining the search after him almost entirely to that district. Living, however, as he does, elsewhere,

### HE NEEDS ONLY A QUARTER OF AN HOUR'S START

to get out of this district, and practically to place himself beyond suspicion. Every man must act in accordance with the law of his specific nature, and the Whitechapel murderer, cunning though he be, is no exception to the rule. For instance, he betrayed himself, to some extent, by the periodicity which he suffered to mark his crimes. They were committed at certain definite times in the month. A detective of original character would have noticed this and have turned it to good account. He would have felt a moral certainty that between 7 and 10 Nov. another attempt at murder would be made, and he would have organised for those nights a special service of decoys. No doubt such a service has its dangers, but these dangers might be reduced to a minimum. In fact, the assassin is hardly dangerous except to the unsuspecting and unwary. His terrible procedure cannot be carried out against those on their guard. What is wanted is a man in authority possessing originality and imagination. Such a man would divine beforehand when the next attempt will be made—the cycle will be changed now—and he would devise a trap for the assassin.

# Thursday, 15 November, 1888

The "scares" are getting almost laughable. Yesterday while a City constable was walking along the Commercial-road in mufti and a low broad brim hat of rather singular appearance, somebody called out that he was "Jack the Ripper." Hundreds of people surrounded him, and the results might have been serious had not some constables come up. The officer made known his identity to them, and was got away from the mob. Another arrest caused more than usual excitement. A man stared into the face of a woman in the Whitechapel-road, and she at once screamed out that he was "Jack the Ripper." The man was immediately surrounded by an excited and threatening crowd, from which he was rescued with some difficulty by the police. He was taken under a strong escort to the Commercial-street Police-station,

**FOLLOWED BY AN ENORMOUS MOB,**

howling and screaming at him. He proved to be a German, and explained through an interpreter that he arrived in London from Germany on Tuesday, and was to leave for America to-day. Confirmation of this statement having been obtained, he was set at liberty.

An arrest was made in the Old Kent-road yesterday evening. A man left a shiny black bag at the Thomas a Becket public-house. The police were communicated with, and on the bag's being examined it was found to contain a very sharp dagger, a clasp knife, two pairs of very long and curious looking scissors, and two life preservers. The man was afterwards taken into custody.

—

### This Morning's Arrests.

About half-past one this morning, several young men watching some premises in Spital-square, noticed a man talking to a young woman, and overheard him ask her to accompany him. She consented. As they were walking away a constable stopped them and took the man to the Commercial-street Police-station. He refused to state where he was on Thursday night last or give any information whatever, and he was detained.

At a quarter past three a man was arrested in the Mile-end-road and taken to Leman-street Police-station.

—

### An Arrest at Dover.

An arrest has been made at Dover in connection with the Whitechapel murders. A suspicious-looking character was seen near the railway station, and as he answered the description given of the murderer he was taken into custody, but was afterwards released.

—

### THE PEOPLE'S POST BOX.
#### Whitechapel.

SIR,—May I trouble you with a few words as to the conduct of the Home Secretary with regard to the East-end murders, speaking from a working-man's point of view? Could Mr. Matthews only hear what working-men generally think about his refusal to offer a reward, he would be able to form some idea of the injury he is doing his party, and which they will feel at the next election. The working class think, and rightly think, if a reward is offered and it does not lead to the conviction of the murderer no harm can have been done, and no money will have to be paid; on the other hand, it might lead to the man's conviction; and more, they argue that if the victim was some person of high standing in society a reward would have been offered long since. But life is life, and it is as much to the poor degraded victims of this fiend as it is to the highest in the land. A reward might bring forward evidence of the conduct of the murderer at his lodgings or in a hundred different ways.

With regard to the notice of pardon to anybody not the actual murderer, in the last case, it is childish. Degraded as the poor victim was, does Mr. Matthews think she would take a third person to witness her immorality?—Yours, &c.,
C. THOMAS.
Canterbury-place, Lambeth, S.E., 12 Nov.

~

# Thursday, 15 November, 1888

## Evening News
### THE EAST END MURDERS
### EXTRAORDINARY STATEMENT
### THE MURDERER IS BELIEVED TO
### BE KNOWN

Mr. Matthew Packer, of Berner street, the fruiterer who sold some grapes to a man who just before the Berner street murder was in company with the murdered woman, vouches for the following extraordinary statement. He says: "On Tuesday evening two men came to my house and bought twelve shillings' worth of rabbits off me. They then asked me if I could give an exact description of the man to whom I sold the grapes, and who was supposed to have committed the Berner street and Mitre square murders, as they were convinced they knew him, and where to find him.

### "IT IS MY OWN COUSIN"

"In reply to some questions by Packer, one of the men then said, 'Well, I am sorry to say that I firmly believe it is my own cousin. He is an Englishman by birth, but some time ago he went to America, stayed there a few years, and then came back to London about seven or eight months ago. On his return he came to see me, and his first words were, 'Well, Boss, how are you?' He asked me to have some walks out with him, and I did round Commercial street and Whitechapel. I found that he had very much altered on his return, for he was thoroughly harem scarem.[309]

### "WE USED TO RIP THEM UP"

"'We met a lot of Whitechapel women, and when we passed them he used to say to me, 'How do you think we used to serve them where I came from? Why, we used to cut their throats and rip them up. I could rip one of them up and get her inside out in no time.' He said, 'We Jack Rippers killed lots of women over there. You will hear of some of it being done over here soon, for I am going to turn a London Jack Ripper.'" The man then said, 'I did not take much notice then of what he said, and I thought it was only his swagger and bounce of what he had been doing in America,' at some place which Packer says he

mentioned, but he forgets the name. 'But,' continued the man, 'When I heard of the first woman being murdered and stabbed all over, I then began to be very uneasy, and to wonder whether he really was carrying out his threats. I did not, however, like to say anything about him, as he is my own cousin. Then, as one murder followed another, I felt that I could scarcely rest.

### "A MONSTER TOWARDS WOMEN"

"'He is a perfect monster towards women, especially when he has had a drop of drink. But, in addition to what he said to me about these murders in America, and what was going to be done here, I feel certain it is him, because of the way these Jack Ripper letters which have appeared in the papers begin. They all begin 'Dear Boss,' and that is just the way he begins his letters. He calls everybody 'Boss' when he speaks to them. I did not want to say anything about him if I could help it, so I wrote to him, but he did not answer my letter. Since this last murder I have felt that I could not remain silent any longer, for at least something ought to be done to put him under restraint.'"

### PACKER THINKS THEY SPOKE
### THE TRUTH

Packer states he feels sure the men are speaking the truth, as they seemed very much concerned and hardly knew what to do in the matter. He says he knows where to find the men; one works at some ironworks and the other at the West India Docks, and the man they allude to lives somewhere in the neighbourhood of Whitechapel. The reporter to whom the above statement was made at once sent off a copy of it to the Home Secretary, and also to Sir J Fraser, the Chief Commissioner of the City Police.

### THE POLICE TAKE IT UP

Sir William Fraser immediately acted on the information and sent Detective sergeants White and Mitchell to investigate it. They read the letter to Packer, who said it was true, and then took the detectives to the man's house. On being questioned by the police he stated where his cousin was generally to be found. It transpired that he is sometimes engaged on the Thames, and late, last night, a search was, it is said, being made for him upon the river.

—

---

[309] **Harum-scarum.** 1. Giddy, careless, wild, a reckless or thoughtless fellow (1740). 2. Four horses driven in a line, suicide. (Farmer)

# Thursday, 15 November, 1888

## AN ARREST IN THE OLD KENT ROAD

An arrest was made in the Old Kent road, yesterday evening, but the man, whose movements excited suspicion, does not answer to the description of the person who is wanted. Attention was drawn to him by his leaving a shiny black bag at the Thomas a Becket public house. The police were communicated with, and on the bag's being examined it was found to contain a very sharp dagger, a clasp knife, two pairs of very long and curious looking scissors, and two life preservers. Meanwhile the man had gone to a pawnbroker's, and on emerging from the shop was taken into custody in order that inquiries might be made.

—

## ANOTHER JACK THE RIPPER LETTER

Last night a letter was received by post at Camberwell Green Police station, and the writer, who signed himself jack the Ripper, stated that it had been written in the blood of the last Whitechapel victim. He added that it was his intention to carry on operations in Camberwell during the next night or so.

—

## ARREST AT DOVER

An arrest has been made at Dover in connection with the Whitechapel murders. A suspicious looking character was seen near the railway station, and, as he answered the description given of the murderer, he was taken into custody. He made a statement to the police, and two constables were sent in charge of the man to verify it. It proved accurate, and he was released. The affair has caused some sensation in the town. The railways and Channel steamers are being watched by the police.

—

## THE FUNERAL POSTPONED

The relatives of the murdered woman, who were expected yesterday, have not yet arrived. The funeral has been again postponed, and may not take place until Monday. Yesterday afternoon the remains were removed from the temporary coffin in which they have been lying at the Shoreditch Mortuary, and placed in a coffin of French polished elm and oak, with brass handles, in which they will be interred. Mr. McCarthy, the landlord of the deceased, offered to defray part of the cost of the funeral, but his offer was declined, sufficient funds for the purpose having already been subscribed.

## ANOTHER THEORY OF THE MURDERS

The correspondent of the *Independace Belge* at Berne sends the following remarkable communication: "A curious coincidence taken in connection with the London murders is now the topic of conversation at Lucerne. A possible author for the Whitechapel horrors has been discovered. It appears that some 16 years ago the population of Paris was greatly excited by the murderous exploits of a mysterious assassin who chose his victims amongst the class of demi-mondaines.[310] He was finally discovered, and turned out to be a certain Nicolas Wassili, of Russian origin, who was born at Uraspol[311] in 1847. He had received an excellent education at the University of Odessa. The murderer was examined by a council of physicians, who declared him insane. He had committed his horrible crimes under the influence of religious fanaticism. Wassili was consequently placed in an insane asylum, from which he received his discharge only last January. The question is whether this religious maniac has gone to London and recommenced his curious method of saving souls."

—

## A SOCIAL PURITY MANIAC

There is, it stated, no fresh intelligence upon which the police can work; while among the numerous written suggestions that the police authorities have recently received is one that the assassin has at one time been connected with the "social purity craze," and possibly is suffering from a peculiar and acute form of mania in consequence. There is nobody now under detention on suspicion of being connected with the East end murders, the man who was detained last night having been released at about two o'clock this morning. The police authorities, though bound to investigate the story of the fruiterer Matthew Packer, attach no importance whatever to his statement. The police had ample opportunity before this of testing the value of Packer's assertions, with the result that they have been put to great trouble without any tangible result.

---

[310] **Demi-Mondaines.** Fr. demi-monde, half-world, from the 1855 comedy *Le Demi-Monde* by Alexander Dumas fils. Demimondaines originally denoted the members of what would later be called the bohemian lifestyle. By the 1880's a demi-monde was a mistress or high class prostitute. (Hickman)

[311] Tiraspol, Transnistria, Moldova.

## The Star

### WHITECHAPEL.
### A Man who Tallys with Kelly's Murderer Seen to Accost Women.

Mr. Galloway, a clerk employed in the City, and living at Stepney, has made the following statement:—"As I was going down the White-chapel-road in the early hours of Wednesday morning, on my way home, I saw a man coming in the opposite direction, about fifty yards away. We both crossed the road simultaneously, and came face to face. The man had a very frightened appearance, and glared at me as he passed. I was very much struck with his appearance, especially as he corresponded, in almost every particular, with the man described by Mary Ann Cox. He was short, stout, about 35 to 40 years of age. His moustache, not a particularly heavy one, was of

### A CARROTY COLOUR, AND HIS FACE BLOTCHY

through drink and dissipation. He wore a long, dirty brown overcoat, and altogether presented a most villainous appearance. I stood still and watched him. He darted back almost imme-diately to the other side of the road, and then, apparently to avoid a group of women a little further on, crossed the road again. I determined to follow him, and just before reaching the coffee-stall past the church he again crossed the road. On nearing George-yard he crossed over and entered a small court. He reappeared in a couple of minutes, crossed Whitechapel-road for the sixth time, and proceeded up Commercial-street. Up to this time he had walked along briskly, but directly he got into Commercial-street, he slackened speed and

### ACCOSTED THE FIRST WOMAN

whom he met alone, but was repulsed. On approaching Thrawl-street a policeman on point duty suddenly appeared. The man was evidently startled, and for a moment it looked as though he would turn back or cross the road. He recovered himself, however, and went on. I then informed the constable of what I had seen, and pointed out the man's extraordinary resem-blance to the individual described by Cox. The constable declined to arrest the man, saying that he was looking for a man of a very different appearance."

—

### Fourteen Captures Last Night.

No fewer than 14 people were taken to the East-end police-stations last night and early this morning on suspicion, but they were all released after a short detention.

—

### A Dark Foreigner Arrested.

A man was arrested at Market Harborough last night on suspicion of being the Whitechapel murderer. He has been lodging in the neigh-bourhood two months, but has been frequently absent. He is a very dark, swarthy-looking man, and speaks with a slightly foreign accent. His behaviour at Harborough has been always very quiet, but he has no occupation or apparent means of subsistence.

—

### Turning the Scare to Account.

Because Wolff Leviohne, a Polish Jew, who went to Whitechapel on business, refused the solicitations of two women named Johnson and De Grasse, they shouted out, "You are Jack the Ripper," and drew an excited crowd about him. He had to take refuge in the Commercial-street Police-station the people became so threatening. The women were brought before the Worship-street magistrate to-day. They said they only remarked to Leviohne that he "looked like Jack the Ripper," as he had a shining bag.—Mr. Bushby said the public must be protected from this kind of molestation, and he fined the prisoners 20s. each. In default they were committed for 14 days.

—

### THE PEOPLE'S POST BOX.
### Another Protest.

SIR,—While willing to bow to superior judgement on this matter, I, too, would support Mrs. Langworthy by my protest against the wholesale publication of the details of White-chapel. I have been asking myself over and over again what possible good can result from such publication. That harm does follow, as a consequence, we know from the horrid Newcastle imitation, and who can say for a certainty that the same fiend has been guilty of the whole series?

I quite agree that the detective department has totally collapsed; but although the press must to some extent fill the gap, yet is it necessary to fill our children's minds (for even children read newspapers now-a-days) with all

# Friday, 16 November, 1888

the bestial details of these crimes? My reason for writing is that this very evening a child of mine called out to his sister "I am Jack the Ripper. Look out!" and I learn that even the street Arabs[312] are making a game of it. We object to a "Zola" and tolerate an "Ouida,"[313] we allow in Ireland what we object to in Russia, and we tolerate a Hughes-Hallett[314] under the very roof that rings with the eloquence of a Gladstone. Where is our consistency? Only the other day there was a huge outcry against the *Pall Mall Gazette* for publishing prurient details in which the welfare of our children was vitally concerned, and now the very papers (yours excepted, because it was not in existence then) which called out the loudest are publishing broadcast details which makes the *Pall Mall Gazette* take a back seat altogether. There is not the slightest doubt that murder begets murder, and horror begets horror; for weak minds brood over disgusting and vicious details until the frail thread of reason becomes too slight for the tension exercised, and the balance is unhinged.

For God's sake, sir, use your powerful influence to overcome the morbid tendencies of the age, or ere long we shall revert to the dark periods when human torture was rampant and the stake a potent force for the inculcation of ideas of a higher civilisation.

Yours, &c.,
J. ARTHUR ELLIOTT.
Liberal Club, Wood-green, 12 Nov.

~

## Evening News
### TO-DAY'S POLICE
### THE "JACK THE RIPPER" SCARE

Mary Ann Johnson, 30, and Christine de Grasse, 33, both women of ill repute, were charged, at Worship-street, with the offence of solicitation, a Polish Jew, named Wolf Leviehne being the prosecutor.—The prosecutor said that on the previous night he had occasion in pursuit of his occupation as traveller[315] to go to White-chapel. He completed his business, and at 11.30 he was on his way home to St. Ann's-road, Tottenham, when he was accosted by Johnson, who made a proposition to him which he declined. The woman then called out "You are Jack the Ripper," and the other woman, who had also accosted him, joined in the cry. An excited crowd soon collected, and fearing that the consequences might be very unpleasant for himself, witness took refuge in the Commercial-street Police-station, and then the police took the women into custody. The prisoners both said that they simply said that the prisoner "looked like Jack the Ripper" as he had a shining bag.—Mr. Bushby said the public must be protected from this kind of molestation, and he fined the prisoners 2£s. each. In default they were committed for 14 days.

—

A man named Edward Shannon, aged 44, a bricklayer, was charged, at Bow-street, with being a suspected person loitering for the supposed purpose of committing a felony.

Mr. Church, a job-master,[316] of Kappel-street, stated that on Thursday night, at ten o'clock, he saw the prisoner in the neighbour-hood dressed in woman's clothes. He followed him into Bedford-place, and owing to his suspicious manner in which he entered a doorway witness gave information to the police, and the accused was taken into custody.

Police-constable 299 E deposed that he touched the prisoner on the shoulder, and really thought he was a woman until he spoke and said, "I am here on a bit of business." At the station he said he was looking out for "Jack the Ripper." He was wearing a hat and veil and a

---

[312] **Arab**. (1) A young street vagrant: also street arab and city arab. (2) An outcast (1848.) (Farmer)

[313] **Ouida**. Nom-de-plume of Anglo-French writer, social commentator and animal lover Maria Louise Ramé (1839-1908).

[314] **Colonel Francis Hughes-Hallett** (1838-1903). Royal Artillery officer and MP for Rochester 1885-89. Stood down in 1889 after divorce scandal involving affair with step-daughter. On committee that investigated Martha Tabram murder.

[315] **Traveller**: Travelling salesman. (Census1891.com)

[316] **Job-Master**. A supplier of carriages, horses and drivers for hire. (ibid)

skirt.

Mr. Bridge remanded him for inquiries.

—

## SYMPATHY IN LONDON

As an instance of the widespread sympathy with the unfortunate victims in the East-end which prevails throughout this great metropolis of strangers, it may be stated that last evening a young lady took to Mr. M'Carthy a beautiful floral wreath which she had made for this the purpose, and desired to place it personally on the coffin of the deceased. In consequence of the funeral arrangements not having been completed, this, she was informed, she could not do.

—

## A SUSPECTED INDIVIDUAL

Mr. Galloway, a clerk employed in the C**** and living at Stepney, has made the following statement: "As I was going down the Whitechapel-road in the early hours of Wednesday morning, on my way home, I saw a man coming in the opposite direction, about fifty yards away. We both crossed the road simultaneously, and came face to face. The man had a very frightened appearance, and glared at me as he passed. I was very much struck with his appearance, especially as he corresponded, in almost every particular, with the man described by Mary Ann Cox. He was short, stout, about 35 to 40 years of age. His moustache, not a particular heavy one, was of a carroty colour, and his face was blotchy through drink and dissipation. He wore a long, dirty, brown overcoat, and altogether presented a most villainous Appearance. I stood still and watched him. He darted back almost immediately to the other side of the road, and then, apparently to avoid a group of women a little further on, crossed the road again. I determined to follow him, and just before reaching the coffee-stall past the church he again crossed the road. On nearing George-yard he crossed over and entered a small court. He reappeared in a couple of minutes, crossed Whitechapel-road for the sixth time, and proceeded up Commercial-street. Up to this point he had walked along briskly, but directly he got into Commercial-street he slackened speed and accosted the first woman whom he met alone, but was repulsed. On approaching Thrawl-street, a policeman on point duty suddenly appeared. The man was evidently startled, and for a moment it looked as though he would turn back or cross the road. He recovered himself, however, and went on. I then informed the constable of what I had seen, and pointed out the man's extraordinary resemblance to the individual described by Cox. The constable declined to arrest the man, saying that he was looking for a man of a very different appearance.

—

## HUMAN BLOOD AND HAIR.

The police at Battersea are in search of a man who is stated to answer to the description of the man wanted for the murder of Mary Jane Kelly. He was seen under somewhat singular circumstances yesterday afternoon. He entered a coffee-house in that neighbourhood, and displayed some hair, which is stated to have been human, with congealed blood attached. No one thought to detain him, but information was subsequently given to the police. It is understood that he left the hair behind him.

—

## ANOTHER ARREST

The Central News says that a man was arrested at Market Harborough, last night, on suspicion of being the Whitechapel murderer. He has been lodging in the neighbourhood for two months, but has been frequently absent. He is a very dark, swarthy-looking man, and speaks with a slightly foreign accent. His behaviour at Harborough has been always very quiet, but he has no occupation nor apparent means of subsistence. The account he has given of himself to the police is not satisfactory.

500

# Monday, 19 November, 1888

## The Times
### THE WHITECHAPEL MURDER.

On Saturday afternoon the police arrested at Euston Station a man who had just arrived from Birmingham, and who described himself as a doctor. Upon being questioned the suspect made certain statements as to his whereabouts at the times of the murders which the police are now investigating. The man was subsequently released.

The funeral of the murdered woman Kelly will take place to-day, when her remains will be buried in the Roman Catholic Cemetery at Leytonstone. The hearse will leave the Shoreditch Mortuary at half-past 12.

———

At WORSHIP-STREET, shortly before Mr. Bushby left the bench at the close of the day's business, a Swede named NIKANER A. BENELIUS, 27 years of age, and described as a traveller, living in Great Eastern-street, Shoreditch, was placed in the dock charged with entering a dwelling-house in Buxton-street, Mile-end, for an unlawful purpose and with refusing to give any account of himself. The prisoner is a man of decidedly foreign appearance, with a moustache, but otherwise cannot be said to resemble any of the published descriptions of men suspected in connexion with the Whitechapel murders. Detective-sergeant Dew attended from Commercial-street Station, and stated that the prisoner had been arrested that morning under circumstances which made it desirable to have the fullest inquiries made as to him. Before the last murder —of Mary Kelly, in Miller's-court—the prisoner had been arrested by the police and detained in connexion with the Berner-street murder, but was eventually released. He had, however, remained about the neighbourhood, lodging in a German lodging-house, but having, the officer said, no apparent means of subsistence. The landlord said that the prisoner was 25s. in debt to him. Harriet Rowe, a married woman, living in Buxton-street, Mile-end, then deposed that at about 10:30 that morning she had left the street door open, and while sitting in the parlour the prisoner, a stranger to her, opened the door and walked in. She asked him what he wanted, but he only grinned in reply. She was greatly alarmed, being alone, and ran to the window.

The prisoner then opened the parlour door and left. She followed him into the street until she saw a constable; but the prisoner first stopped the officer and spoke to him. Witness ran up and told the constable what the prisoner had done, and he was thereupon taken to the station. The police-constable, Imhoff, 211 H, said that the prisoner was asking him the way to Fenchurch-street when the witness Rowe ran up. After hearing her complaint he asked the prisoner what he wanted to go to Fenchurch-street for, and the prisoner said he expected some letters at the post-office. The prisoner was searched at the station, but nothing was found on him. In answer to the charge he said he only went into the house to ask his way to Fenchurch-street. Mr. Bushby said he should follow the usual course and remand the prisoner for inquiries. The prisoner was remanded till Friday. Two men, one of whom was stated to be the prisoner's landlord, subsequently called about him and said that he had been preaching in the streets at times and acting of late very strangely.

~

## The Star
### FIFTH EDITION.
### Kelly Followed to the Grave.

At half-past twelve to-day the remains of Mary Janet Kelly, were removed from the Shoreditch Mortuary to the burial-ground at Leytonstone, followed by Joseph Barnett, the man who lived with her. Thousands of people saw the remains taken from the mortuary.

—

### WHITECHAPEL
### The London Police Blunder Over a Birmingham Suspect.

Considerable excitement was caused in London yesterday by the circulation of a report that a medical man had been arrested at Euston, upon arrival from Birmingham, on a charge of suspected complicity in the Whitechapel murders. It was stated that the accused had been staying at a common lodging-house in Birmingham since Monday last, and the theory was that if, as was supposed by the police, he was connected with the East-end crimes, he left the metropolis by an early train on the morning of the tragedies. The suspected man was of gentlemanly appearance and manners, and somewhat resembled the description of the person declared by witnesses at the inquest to have been

### SEEN IN COMPANY WITH KELLY

early on the morning that she was murdered. Upon being minutely questioned as to his whereabouts at the time of the murders, the suspect was able to furnish a satisfactory account of himself, and was accordingly liberated. It has since transpired that he has been watched by Birmingham police for the last five days, and when he left that town on Saturday the Metropolitan police were advised to continue to "watch" him, not to arrest him. But, in spite of this warning, the London police seem to have stupidly warned the man that he was suspected.

A *Star* man made a round of the police-stations this morning, and received everywhere the report of a very quiet night. Neither at Commercial-street nor Leman-street was any-one detained. Expectation of another murder being discovered this morning was the only cause of stir, and the detectives were mustered at the stations in readiness for any emergency. Up to twelve o'clock, however, nothing had turned up. Late last night there was some little excitement consequent on the arrest in a Flower and Dean-street tenement house of a young man named Charles Akehurst, of Canterbury-road, Ball's Pond-road, N. He accompanied a woman to her room, and there had the misfortune to make use of expressions which caused her to jump to the conclusion that

### SHE WAS IN THE HANDS OF THE MURDERER.

She ran trembling to a policeman, who arrested the man. He satisfied the detective, however, and was released after a short detention.

Full inquiries have been made into the movements of the Swede Nikaner A. Benelius, remanded by Mr. Bushby on a charge of being on private premises for an unlawful purpose. Inspector Reid states that the man's innocence of any hand in the murders has been fully established. The man, who has been lodging at a German lodging-house at 90, Great Eastern-street, has been preaching in the streets, and behaving in a manner which suggests that he is not so fully responsible for his actions as he might be. It was therefore thought advisable to make the fullest inquiries, which, however, have quite cleared him. He was arrested on suspicion in connection with the Berners-street murder, and is likely to be arrested every time the public attention is strained to the point of suspecting every man of odd behaviour. Dorset-street has still its knot of loungers, although it is more than a week since it achieved notoriety.

—

### A "Unionist" Theory.

We are on the track of the murderer at last! No one will be surprised to hear that all those who ought to know—police, journalists, doctors, and the rest—are on a false scent. It has been reserved for a lowly Scotch "Meenister" to evolve the truly new and the newly true theory from his inspired cranium.

### "The EMISSARIES OF THE IRISH-AMERICAN SECRET SOCIETIES,"

says this ingenious scribe, "were thwarted in all their efforts to terrorise London with dynamite, &c., but no one who knows their creed and aims is likely to believe that they have abandoned their fiendish schemes. May it not be possible that one of their most dare-devil agents has taken this plan to annoy and engross the Metropolis? By waging war on a class of practically helpless and unknown waifs, he is more likely to accomplish his work with impunity, needing only the inevitable knife, which can be easily concealed." This worth Scotch cleric considers the fact that "Jack the Ripper" carries a black bag, wears a black moustache and a wideawake hat (if it be a fact), suspicious, and triumphantly declares that there are several Americanisms in the letters attributed to him. Here is some ground for Warren's successor to work on, and if he wants the name of the author of the theory the editor of the (of course) Unionist *Scotsman* will no doubt give it him.

~

## Evening News
### THE EAST END MURDERS
### FUNERAL OF KELLY.

The funeral of the murdered woman Kelly took place, at the Roman Catholic Cemetery, Leytonstone, this afternoon, the remains being removed thither from the Shoreditch mortuary. Large crowds were present.

Three large wreaths were on the coffin, which bore the inscription, "Marie Jeanette Kelly, died November 9, 1888, aged 25 years." The car was followed by two mourning coaches.

~

# Tuesday, 20 November, 1888

## The Times

### THE WHITECHAPEL MURDER.

The funeral of Marie Jeannette Kelly took place yesterday at Leytonstone Cemetery. Several thousand persons had gathered outside Shoreditch Church. Shortly after half-past 12 the coffin was borne from the mortuary to the car. Three large wreaths were on the coffin, which bore the inscription, "Marie Jeannette Kelly, died November 9, 1888, aged 25 years." The car was followed by two coaches containing mourners, among whom was Joseph Barnett. Shortly after 12:30 the funeral procession left Shoreditch, and proceeded by way of Hackney-road to Leytonstone. The Rev. H. Wilson Robinson calls attention to the fact that Mr. Henry Wilton, who has been clerk of St. Leonard's Shoreditch, for 50 years, is bearing the cost of the interment. If the public wish to bear any share in the expense they can send their subscriptions to Mr. Wilton, at the church. Should there be a surplus a tombstone would be erected.

## Evening News
### ATTEMPTED MURDER IN THE EAST END.
### A WOMAN ATTACKED IN A LODGING HOUSE.
### THE ASSAILANT SEEN AND FOLLOWED.
### HIS DESCRIPTION

As we were about to go to press this morning news reached us from several sources that another murder and mutilation, similar to those which have already been perpetrated, had been committed at the East-end.

We immediately dispatched two of our staff to the spot to report and obtain confirmation. Meanwhile several inhabitants of the locality arrived at our office confirming the first rumour, which, however, we decided not to publish pending the return of our own reporters. Before they had returned we received from the Central News the intelligence which we printed in our Second Edition. In addition to what appeared in that edition, we received also from the same source a detailed description of the supposed murder and mutilation. Almost immediately came the Press Association with news of the crime to the same effect.

Relying as we naturally do upon the news agencies for accurate information, the reports first given by them were of course taken by us as confirming those brought in by persons from the East-end, and we did not hesitate to go to press with the intelligence as furnished to us.

All of this we publish below. When our reporter returned it appeared that the woman had not been killed but only wounded, and it was only subsequent to his return with this important intelligence that we received the messages of the Central News and Press Association, confirming his statement, viz., that the murderer had not succeeded in dispatching his victim.

We make these observations to show our own bona fides in the matter.

The information first supplied to us by the Central News is as follows:

The Central News learns that another terrible murder was committed, last night, near Flower and Dean-street, Spitalfields. The murder took place in a lodging house, the unfortunate woman having her throat cut, and being otherwise shockingly mutilated. The murderer again escaped, leaving no trace behind.

The following was delivered to us but not published:

The Central News says the news that another terrible murder was committed in the East-end of London, last night, has caused another thrill of horror through London.

The news flew like wildfire throughout the whole of East end district, and in a short time hundreds of people were rushing in the direction of the scene, and the building is now surrounded by an excited throng.

It was only when the room occupied by the poor woman was opened, shortly after nine this morning, that the terrible fact was discovered.

The police were hastily summoned, and at once took possession of the building, making a thorough search in the house itself and in the surrounding district. No one is now allowed to enter or to leave the house.

It is conjectured that the victim took her companion home with her last night, and that, as in the last case, the crime was committed during the early hours of the morning.

The mutilations in this case were again of a most shocking character: but the full extent of these have not even yet transpired. Up to the moment of telegraphing there are not the slightest traces of the assassin, and it is doubtful whether even in this case the police will secure any tangible clue. The excitement is growing momentarily throughout the district.

### THE TRUE ACCOUNT

Our first reporter says that the first report which was received by the police stated that a woman named Farmer, was murdered, but that was found not to be so. About eight o'clock, a man and Farmer engaged a bed at a common lodging-house, 19, George-street, Spitalfields. At about 9.30 screams were heard, and a man rushed out. Farmer was seen bleeding profusely from a wound in the throat. She was taken to Commercial-street station after the wound had been dressed.

The description of the assailant is as follows: Thirty years of age: height, 6ft. 6in.: fair moustache: he wore a black diagonal coat, and hard felt hat. He is known, and his capture is confidently anticipated by Superintendent

# Wednesday, 21 November, 1888

Arnold, Inspector Ferrett and Detective officers Thicke, Dew, Pearse, Record and Macguire, who have this case in hand.

Another of our men reports: The woman is not dead, only severely wounded. The scene of this miscarried crime is within a few yards of Flower and Dean-street. Crowds are blocking the throughfare, but I was fortunate enough to see "Jack the Ripper's" intended victim, though no thanks to the police. It is difficult to guess her age, for want and sordidness have left their mark upon her to such an extent that even the most experienced would be baffled. We met the stretcher as it was borne along Commercial-street, and by the greatest accident managed to be in the station as she walked in, for she seems to be able to walk, if not to speak, unless she has already on the way been forbidden to open her lips to anyone but the constituted authorities. This much we know, the rest must be all conjecture. We frankly confess to not indulging in hopes of being able to inform the public as to the real story, for no doubt the clever guardians of our lives and property will sequestrate the latest intended victim of "Jack the Ripper." As it is at present they look at you, smile, and assume an important demeanour. One might as well try to obtain information from a sphinx.

A third representation of *The Evening News*, on calling at the Commercial-street Police Station just before noon found a large crowd of people collected in front of the entrance to the station. All efforts made to gain admission, however, proved to be unavailing. A sergeant who was posted at the door, firmly, but courteously, declined to let our representative enter. Questioned as to the cause of this reticence, he stated that the superintendent was inside, and that the strictest orders had been given that under no consideration should any member of the Press be admitted. He further declined to state whether the woman had been brought to the station alive or dead.

Enormous crowds block Flower and Dean-street, Thrawl-street, and George-street, and the most intense excitement prevails in the East-end generally.

The woman was found with her throat badly cut, but still alive, and was taken to the Commercial-street Station, which is close by.

It is stated, though at present we are not able to say precisely with what foundation, that the woman has rallied sufficiently to place most important clues as to the identity of her would-be murderer in the possession of the police.

The authorities are making extraordinary preparations for carrying out an effective search of the whole district, and many of the members of the Vigilance Committee are already on the spot at work.

Later on we received the following from the Central News:

The Central News says: Later intelligence shows that the woman attacked by a man in a lodging-house in Flower and Dean-street, was not killed but merely wounded.

The police are extremely reticent, and prevent any one entering the house, while an excited crowd surrounds the place, but from one of the residents in the house the Central News learns that a woman, whose name has not yet transpired, was drinking in a public house with a man in Spitalfields. At ten o'clock, he accompanied her home to her lodgings in George-street, Spitalfields, and directly after that appears to have suddenly made an attempt to cut her throat. The woman, however, became aware of his design before he could carry it out, and struggled with the man, at the same time screaming loudly. The throat was wounded but slightly, and the woman was thus able to exert all her strength to cope with her assailant. The man, seeing the alarm was given, sought at once to make good his escape, and, relinquishing his victim, fled from the house. A few persons, attracted by the screams, and seeing the man running, pursued him for 300 yards, but he was then lost sight of. The police were on the spot within a few minutes, and were able to get from the woman a full description of the would-be murderer. The victim is between 40 and 50 years of age, and is now carefully guarded by police. In the district the belief is universal from all the facts surrounding the case that the work is that of Jack the Ripper, and the excitement consequently is intense. If this surmise be correct it is the first of his victims who has escaped. The woman's description of the man, however, will be invaluable to the police, and he should be apprehended within the next few hours. There is, of course, a possibility that after all this may not be the fiend who has already committed so many fearful deeds, but no one in the district entertains this idea.

## WHAT THE PRESS ASSOCIATION SAYS.

The Press Association says a report from Spitalfields this morning states that another murder of a woman was discovered about 10 o'clock, at 19, George-street—a street running from Flower and Dean-street to Thrawl-street. The woman's throat had been cut, and it is stated there were a number of stabs on the body. The police were at once informed, and took possession of the premises. The house is a small two-storied building fronting on to George-street, and the right opposite the Loiesworth Model Dwellings, and is within a few hundred yards of Miller-court, Dorset-street, where the last murder occurred. The houses in George-street are mostly let out as lodging-houses, some of them being used by the woman of the streets.

Another report states that the woman whose throat was cut in Spitalfields this morning is generally known as Tilly, and that she went by the name of Mrs. Smith whenever she went into the Casual Ward. A shoeblack, who carries on his vocation outside Shoreditch Church, states that the woman is about 34 years of age. She usually walks about in this neighbourhood of Shoreditch Church, and is believed to be the wife of a flower and feather dyer. It was about half-past nine this morning when he saw a woman from the lodging-house.

The Press Association's reporter had an interview with a woman who professed to have some knowledge of the circumstances. The informant states the woman, who is now at the police station, is called Matilda. She lodges in various common lodging-houses in the locality, and as far as personal appearance is concerned she is very good looking, and altogether appears to have been brought up in far-better surroundings than she now occupies. I believe she has known the man who attacked her for about twelve months. From what I hear it is not true that the couple slept in Dorset-street last night. It was about eleven o'clock in the morning when the woman met the man near to Spitalfield church. He asked her what she was doing at such an early hour, and she said she had not been able to pay for a bed, as the charge was 8d. He gave the woman 8d., and they went to the house together. They had not been long in the room when the woman shouted out, "He has cut my throat," and she followed the man down stairs. He made off, but some men in the lodging-house hearing the cry of the woman pursued the man, but they lost sight of him, and he got away.

It has further been ascertained that a man stood opposite the lodging-house door at the very moment when the fugitive was escaping, but he made no effort to arrest him, thinking that it was perhaps a petty theft of some kind that he had committed. He is not able to describe the man now sought for. The injured woman told the police that she was willing to walk to the station, but the police insisted on taking her there on a stretcher, which, of course, aroused a great deal of excitement, especially as a cover was thrown over the woman.

The Press association says the following telegraphic communication has been circulated among the police this morning:

"Wanted, for attempted murder, on the 21st inst., a man, aged 36 years; height, 5ft. 6in.; complexion dark, no whiskers, dark moustache; dress, black jacket, vest, and trousers, round black felt hat. Respectable appearance. Can be identified."

## WHAT SARAH TURNER SAW.

Sarah Turner, of 27, Thrawl-street, has made the following statement to a Central News reporter:

"About a quarter to ten, this morning, I was standing at my door in Thrawl-street when I saw a man come running round from George-street and three or four men running after him. I saw him turn the corner, and afterwards heard that he had disappeared. He was a short, thick fellow, about five feet four, with no whiskers. I could not see if he had any moustache as his hand was held up to his mouth. He wore a rough blue overcoat, and had a round billycock hat. He did not seem to be carrying anything."

~

# Thursday, 22 November, 1888

## The Times
### MURDEROUS OUTRAGE in WHITECHAPEL.

Considerable excitement was caused throughout the East-end yesterday morning by a report that another woman had been brutally murdered and mutilated in a common lodging-house in George-street, Spitalfields, and in consequence of the reticence of the police authorities all sorts of rumours prevailed.

Although it was soon ascertained that there had been no murder, it was said that an attempt had been made to murder a woman, of the class to which the other unfortunate creatures belonged, by cutting her throat, and the excitement in the neighbourhood for some time was intense. Whether the woman's assailant is the man wanted for the seven recent murders committed in the district of Whitechapel is, of course, not known, although his description tallies somewhat with that given by one of the witnesses at the last inquest; but, should he be, the police are sanguine of his speedy capture, as a good and accurate description of him is now obtained, and if arrested he could be identified by more than one person.

The victim of this last occurrence, fortunately, is but slightly injured, and was at once able to furnish the detectives with a full description of her assailant.

Her name is Annie Farmer, and she is a woman about 40 years of age, who lately resided with her husband, a tradesman, in Featherstone-street, City-road, but, on account of her dissolute habits, was separated from him.

On Monday night the woman had no money, and, being unable to obtain any, walked the streets until about half-past 7 yesterday morning. At that time she got into conversation, in Commercial-street, with a man, whom she describes as about 36 years of age, about 5ft. 6in. in height, with a dark moustache, and wearing a shabby black diagonal suit and hard felt hat. He treated her to several drinks until she became partially intoxicated.

At his suggestion they went to the common lodging-house, 19, George-street, and paid the deputy 8d. for a bed. That was about 8 o'clock, and nothing was heard to cause alarm or suspicion until half-past 9, when screams were heard proceeding from the room occupied by the man and Farmer. Some men who were in the kitchen of the house at the time rushed upstairs and met the woman coming down.

She was partially undressed, and was bleeding profusely from a wound in the throat. She was asked what was the matter, and simply said "He's done it," at the same time pointing to the door leading into the street. The men rushed outside, but saw no one, except a man in charge of a horse and cart. He was asked if he had noticed any person running away, and said he had seen a man, who he thought had a scar at the back of the neck, run down George-street and turn into Thrawl-street, but, not thinking much of the occurrence, had not taken particular notice of the man and had made no attempt to detain him.

By this time a considerable number of people had assembled, and these ran into Thrawl-street and searched the courts leading out of that thoroughfare, but without any success. While this was being done the police were communicated with and quickly arrived on the scene. In the meantime the deputy of the lodging-house had wrapped a piece of rag over the woman's wound, and, seeing that it did not appear to be a dangerous cut, got her to dress herself.

Dr. George Bagster Phillips, divisional surgeon of the H Division, together with his assistant, quickly arrived, and the former gentleman stitched up the wound. Seeing that it was not a dangerous one, and in order to get the woman away from the crowd of inmates, who pressed round, he suggested that she should be removed to the Commercial-street Police-station, and that was quickly done on the ambulance.

Although none but police officers were allowed to interview her with regard to the attack, and consequently nothing definite is known as to the cause, it has transpired that she had previously met her assailant some 12 months since, and owing to this fact the officers are doubtful whether the man had anything to do with the murders. Owing to the excellent description given they are sanguine of securing the man's arrest within a very short space of time.

Superintendent T. Arnold, who was quickly apprised of what had happened, at once ordered Detective-officers Thicke, New, M'Guire, and others to endeavour to capture the man, and by about 10:30 a full description of him was

# Thursday, 22 November, 1888

telegraphed to all the police-stations throughout the metropolitan police district.

It is stated that Farmer is able to converse freely, and that lodgings will be found for her by the police until the person who attacked her is captured. Directly the police arrived at the house in George-street a constable was stationed at the door, and no person was allowed to leave until his or her statement and full particulars concerning each one had been written down.

During the whole of the day a crowd collected in front of 19, George-street, apparently drawn thither merely out of curiosity to view the house, but none not belonging to it were allowed to enter.

—

## AN ARREST IN WHITECHAPEL

It is reported that a man was arrested in the East end early this morning under very suspicious circumstances. Between 1 and 2 o'clock a woman, who was in company with a man in a narrow thoroughfare near Brick lane, was heard to call "Murder" and "Police" loudly. At the same moment the man was seen making off at a rapid pace. He was pursued through several streets by the police and detectives who have lately been concentrated in considerable numbers in the neighbourhood, and was captured near Truman, Hanbury, and Buxton's Brewery. The man is reported to have drawn a knife and made a desperate resistance, but he was eventually overpowered and conveyed to Commercial street station.

# Friday, 23 November, 1888

## The Times
### THE WHITECHAPEL OUTRAGE.

The man who committed the assault on Annie Farmer on Wednesday morning at a common lodging-house in George-street, Spitalfields, has not yet been captured.

It is now believed that the wound to Farmer's throat was not made with a sharp instrument; also, that a quarrel arose between the pair respecting money, as, when the woman was at the station, some coins were found concealed in her mouth.

The authorities appear to be satisfied that the man has no connexion with the recent murders, and expect that he will shortly surrender himself into their hands.

~

## The Star
### Arrests in Whitechapel.

Shortly before six o'clock this morning, Mr. McCarthy, the landlord of the house where Kelly was murdered, seized a suspicious man in Dorset-street. A police-constable searched the man, and found a long knife on him. The man said he used it in his business. He was allowed to go.

Several were taken to the stations during the night, but at six this morning no one was in custody.

—

### THE PEOPLE'S POST BOX.
#### Whitechapel.

SIR,—I trust you will allow me, now that public attention is again aroused by another Whitechapel horror, to say I hope something will be done to reach those who are second only in criminality to the murderer himself—namely, the class of infamous scoundrels who are commonly known as "bullies."

These are the wretches who live on the earnings of these poor women, and who in the midst of all this terror have driven them out to their awful doom that they may eat the bread of idleness and sink themselves still deeper with drink.

Only a little while ago a young girl only 15 years of age came to us for protection from one of these fellows, and after we had placed her in charge of the matron of our home for fallen girls, she informed us that she had been decoyed into a house of ill-fame, and they threatened her (with an uplifted knife over her head) with murder if she dared try to escape. Now, I was only able to get this man and his wife six months' hard labour each on another indictment—namely, for harbouring a girl under 16 years of age for immoral purposes, as they were the keepers of the house.

Happily, the law does now reach those who keep the houses, but I do hope before these horrors are forgotten as a nine days' wonder some member of Parliament will be led to press for a short Act of Parliament as an addition to the Criminal Law Amendment Act so that these scoundrels may be reached, as at present the police are utterly powerless, although these fellows are as well known as the public-houses, at the corners of which they are continually loafing and looking out for fresh victims to entrap, and where they may be seen at all hours of the day, and, if questioned, will pretend to be labourers out of work.

Hoping that we shall at least have this one reform in our law, though others are also greatly needed.—Yours, &c.,

FREDERICK N. CHARRINGTON.[317]

Great Assembly Hall,
Mile-end, E.

~

## Evening News
### THE EAST END MURDERS

No person was in custody last evening in connection with the latest East-end outrage. The detention of a man early yesterday morning on suspicion of being the woman Farmer's assailant was due to the cries of a woman, who said the man had drawn a knife, but it appears that the occurrence was an ordinary drunken quarrel, to which the police attached no importance. Several men have been brought to the police-station in the district on suspicion, but have been released after inquiries. There was an absence of crowds in the streets yesterday, but the district remains in a very excited state.

---

[317] **Frederick Nicholas Charrington** (1850-1936). English Evangelical Christian social reformer. Founded the Tower Hamlets Mission. He renounced a £1.25 million family fortune made from brewing beer to devote his life to helping the poor of London and advancing the Temperance Movement.

# Monday, 26 November, 1888

## Evening News

### THE NEW COMMISSIONER OF POLICE.

The Press Association says: It was reported in Scotland-yard, yesterday, that Mr. Monroe had been appointed Commissioner of Police, in the stead of Sir Charles Warren.

The official announcement of the name of the new Commissioner of Police cannot be received until to-day. After the Cabinet Council, on Saturday, a communication was made to the Queen by special messenger at Windsor. Her Majesty's reply will not be received at the Home Office until to-day.

—

### THE EAST END MURDERS.
### AN EXTRORDINARY LETTER.

An extraordinary letter, of considerable length, and signed, "Jack the Ripper's Pal," has been received by an old gentleman, Mr. Robert Porter, residing at Hucknall Torkard, Notts. The envelope bears the London East Central post-mark, and the writer states that he is a Notts man, has been in America some years, and since leaving Colorado has been carrying on "a deadly game" in the East-end. Most people thought that there was only one in the affair, but there are two, and the other taught him how to do it: but he was as bad as he was now, if not worse, for he never felt frightened in cutting a woman up now. When they went into a public-house and heard someone reading about the Whitechapel affairs he had many a laugh. His "pal" was a wild wretch. There was not one soul in Nottingham who thought that a man who had lived in Huckall some years ago was doing all this. His "pal" was a Bavarian; they met on board a steamship, and he was mesmerized. When he found out his hideous calling they had become very intimate, and his "pal" cast a sort of spell over him. It was amusing to see the police arresting "Leather Aprons" every day. His "pal" was a great magician, and a very clever man. The letter has been handed over to the police authorities.

—

### AN ARREST LAST NIGHT.

Another abortive arrest in connection with the East-end murders was made last night. A man observed to enter Angel-alley, White-chapel, with a woman, and his resemblance to the man whose description has been circulated caused some men to follow him. He ran out of the other end of the alley and entered a public-house, where he was arrested. He was taken to Commercial-street Police-station, but succeeded in establishing his innocence, and was liberated.

—

### LAST WEDNESDAY'S OUTRAGE

As regards the assault made upon Annie Farmer in a common lodging-house at George-street, Flower-and-Dean-street, by a man who afterwards made his escape, nothing further of him has been seen, and the police are inclined to believe that the affair was only an ordinary brawl, and that the woman is acquainted with the man who assailed her, but will not give information which will lead to his detection.

511

# Wednesday, 28 November, 1888

## Evening News
### NOTES

Sir Charles Warren has at last been replaced. Mr. James Monroe, formerly Assistant Commissioner of Police, who was obliged to retire from Scotland-yard on account of disagreement with Sir Charles Warren, now takes the vacant post, and his appointment has received the Royal sanction. It will be remembered that on Mr. Monroe's resignation from his police duties he was taken into the Home Office, where Mr. Matthews continually accepted his advice upon matters of police organization. Mr. Monroe is well acquainted with the police, their organization, and their duties, and will probably make as good a Commissioner as could be found. His influence with the Home Office will prevent or render less likely any conflict between the Comm-issioner and the Minister. It will also tend to sweeten official relations if Mr. Matthews does not call in any discontented colleague of Mr. Monroe's to be his private director. The position of Commissioner is not an easy one, so that every one must wish Mr. Monroe success in the execution of the many tasks he is called upon to accomplish.

—

### BEFORE THE "BREAKS."
### (BY A LOAFER).
### THAMES COURT.

A well known versifier has remarked that "Hope springs eternal in the human breast," and I have no doubt there is some warrant for the observation, which is more than can be said for a good many of the ideas which poets have thought fit or found profitable to put upon paper. I am inclined o think that one of the constables who frequently hangs about the police-court at Arbour-square, Stephney, is a perpetual victim oF the most delusive of the three Christian graces. At least he has been ever since a substantial reward was offered for the apprehension of the Whitechapel murderer, for which inhuman monster he is continually on the look-out. It is the officer with whom I had a conversation some little while ago on the gruesome subject. At that time his chief enjoyment appeared to be the prospect of that fiendish slaughterer being brought before the "beak" at the Thames Court. But since then my friend "Robert"—like many a man in a higher rank of life—as allowed personal ambition to get the better of official loyalty, until he is now all agog to lay his hands upon the most notorious character of the age (not even excepting the Grand Old Man) and win for himself a deathless fame in the force.

### HE HAS GOT AN IMPRESSION

A little judicious flattery will generally set the craftiest tongue wagging, and in this respect a "bobby" is about as weak as a woman, which is saying a good deal. In the incident of yesterday I found this weakness available for a good deal of quiet fun.

"I don't mind tellin' you, sir, as we've talked this yere matter over afore now, that I've got a sort of impression as it's me that'll ketch 'Jack the Ripper' whenever 'e is caught. You might hask me why I think so, and a very reasonable question it would be, too. But the funny part of it is that I could not tell you for the life o' me! It 'ave been borne in upon my mind, so to speak, and there it is.

As I had no means of disputing the permanent whereabouts of this particular idea, I wisely held my peace. I should think any idea ought to feel comfortable on that man's mind; there is so little chance of its being crowded.

"I suppose you are calculating upon the kudos that such an arrest would bring you," I ventured to remark in the most velvety tones I could command.

A shy, half-guilty look broke over his homely and expansive features as he answered:

"Well, sir, if that foreign word you've just used means 'quids,' I ain't ashamed to confess that I 'ave thought a bit about it in that there light, and so 'ave the missus, too. You see, it ain't alius as a man can make good money and a good job in one shot, like that would be. Yes, I've got that impression, and I can't shake it off."

And so I left him anticipating his celebrity and his competency with a pleasantly divided affection.

## The Times

### DRUITT, APPELLANT-GOSLING, RESPONDENT.

This case, reserved from Christchurch, Hampshire, raised a question as to joint occupation of a dwellinghouse. The case stated that two claimants of the name of Hake claimed in respect of "a house and land joint." It turned out that they occupied a dwellinghouse, St. Michael's vicarage, and there was no land except the garden. The vicarage was let to both of them (the vicar residing elsewhere), and the value was far over £20, the rateable value being £72; but only one of them was rated. It was contended that the case came within the definition of a £10 qualification, a house being a tenement. It was objected that use of the claimants was already on the overseers' occupiers' list for the same house, and that the alleged joint occupation was in respect of the same house, and that two persons could not have a joint occupation qualification under 30 and 31 Vic., e. 102, a. 3. The Barrister was of that opinion and disallowed the claims. The claimants appealed.

Mr. M.J. Druitt appeared for the appellants and argued on their behalf that both were entitled to be registered, not, indeed, for a "dwellinghouse," but for a house or "tenement," if the value is sufficient. The main objection, he said, was as to the joint occupation of the dwellinghouse, though there were two subsidiary objections-one as to misdescription of the qualification and the other as to one of the claimants being already on the overseers' list of occupiers for the same house. He urged that the claimants came within the definition of the borough household qualifications in the Reform Act, the value being amply sufficient for both claims.

{MR JUSTICE MANISTY.—One only of the claimants was rated.}

That is not material; the rating of one is sufficient, the rates being paid by either of them; and that is not an objection taken.

{LORD COLERIDGE.—What is the objection?}

It is difficult to say.

Mr. ROBSON, who appeared for the respondent, said it was certainly difficult to make out from the case as stated.

{LORD COLERIDGE.—What objection can you suggest?}

It is impossible to rely upon the objection taken as to joint occupation. That qualification exists.

{LORD COLERIDGE.—I should say so.}

There is no doubt an enactment that no one shall claim is respect of the joint occupation of a dwellinghouse.

{LORD COLERIDGE.—The claimants do not claim for a "dwellinghouse."}

That is so, no doubt; but section 27 of the Reform Act is repealed.

Mr. DRUITT pointed out that in the 48 Vic., e. 3, a. 5, it was in substance re-enacted. {LORD COLERIDGE.—Subject to the like conditions, i.e. MR. JUSTICE MANISTY.— That would require rating, would it not?} Then in section 7 it is enacted that the borough occupation franchise shall be doomed to be that defined in section 27 of the Reform Act. And that section, coupled with section 29, confers the occupation franchise for the joint occupation. {LORD COLERIDGE.—So it should seem, certainly, what can be said against it?}

Mr. ROBSON said he confessed he hardly knew that anything could be said against it.

{LORD COLERIDGE assented and asked what other objections there were?}

Mr. ROBSON urged that one of the claimants being already on the overseers' list of occupiers, both could set claim for the same qualification.

{LORD COLERIDGE.—He did not put himself on the list, the overseers put him there; and that does not preclude them from making a joint claim.}

There would be duplicate entries for the same qualification.

{LORD COLERIDGE.—The Barrister should have struck out the entry in the overseers' list.}

There is a misdescription of the qualification.

{LORD COLERIDGE.—There is nothing in any of these objections. Appeal dismissed with costs.}

The Case sent to be amended, will, his Lordship said, be taken on Saturday.

~

# Friday, 30 November, 1888

## The Times

### DRUITT, APPELLANT-GOSLING, RESPONDENT.

In this case, which was heard on Tuesday before Lord Coleridge, Mr. Justice Hawkins, and Mr. Justice Manisty, the appellant was successful, and the Revising Barrister's decision reversed.

~

## Evening News

### MISSION WORK IN WHITECHAPEL.

A large number of members and workers of the East London Evangelisation Society and Lodging-house Mission, met, last night, at the Gospel Hall, Osbourne-place, Brick-lane, White-chapel, for the purpose of giving a hearty welcome to the new president, John Lobb, Esq., C.C., M.L.S.B.

Mr. J. Harvey, honorary secretary, in reading the report, said the most important feature of the society's work was to carry the gospel to the men, women, and children residing in the common lodging-houses. The members of the society, therefore, on each recurring Sabbath, hold services in the kitchens of the various lodging-houses, both at the East and West-end of London.

The society had been the means of re-instating many men who had seen better days. During the last six months no less than 26 men had been permanently removed from their evil surroundings and were now occupying respectable positions n life, and this had been done at a cost of 6s. 8d.

Mr. John Lobb, in responding to the hearty welcome accorded him, said never had any society such a glorious future before it. They aimed at reaching the lowest members of society, and uplifting them from their baneful surroundings. That was the sort of pioneer work that was wanted in the metropolis to counteract the demoralising influences of Socialism and Secularism with which, unfortunately, London was honeycombed. The whole funds of the society were devoted to the work, and no officer, from the president downwards was paid. Messrs. Gordon, Paynter, Maysmith, Shepherd, Nicholls, and others afterwards

~

## Evening News
### THE EAST END
### ARREST OF THE SUPPOSED
### ASSASSIN IN BURDETT ROAD.

A man was arrested last night at the Crystal Tavern, Burdett road, Mile End, on suspicion of being the Whitechapel murderer. He got into conversation with a woman, whom he asked to accompany him, but she refused. He afterwards addressed a photographer who was soliciting orders, asking him if he could take some photographs, and using expressions which excited suspicion. He was given in charge. He has given the address "Mr. Stewart, 305 Mile End road," but at the Bow Police station he gave his name as "Ever." He appears to be a Polish Jew.

~

## Evening News
### EAST LONDON AND CRIME
### WHAT MRS. S.A. BARNETT HAS TO SAY.

It is always gratifying, and generally instructive, to listen to what a good and clever woman has to say upon any huge and troublesome moral problem. The instinctive faculty for getting at or very near the truth in such cases is a peculiarity of the educated and sympathetic female mind, and there is no one familiar with the strange and tragical phases of social life in the East of London who is entitled to be heard with more respectful attention than the amiable and observant wife of the indefatigable vicar of St. Jude's, Whitechapel.[318]

There are periods in the social and moral history of this great metropolis when public attention is, for the time, rivetted upon some particular district, and when an exceptional, albeit a generally painful, interest is awakened in its inhabitants. Such a one is upon us now in consequence of the fiendish tragedies which have darkened the very name of the East end by their horrors, and it is only at such periods that the public conscience is awakened to the contemplation of the grim horrors of poverty, degradation, and crime which are of daily occurrence in our midst, and to which these more notable tragedies may be almost said to form the natural sequel. Mrs. S.A. Barnett's has taken advantage of this fact to call a closer attention to the lives lived from day to day, and from year to year, by those whose claim to human brotherhood and sisterhood Society is too apt to ignore. This appeal, and a thoroughly touching and womanly one it is, appears in the current number of the *National Review*, under the title of "East London and Crime," forming one of a series of articles on "The Social Problem."

---

[318] **Dame Henrietta Octavia Barnett, DBE** (1851-1936). Author and social reformer. She and her husband, Anglican priest and fellow reformer Samuel Augustus Barnett, moved to Whitechapel after Rev. Barnett was assigned to the parish of St. Jude's in 1873. Here they devoted their lives to helping the poor of the district, with Mrs. Barnett focusing on the destitute women and children. Their work also included improving the conditions found in the workhouses and founding the Children's Country Holiday Fund.

### A DEFENCE OF THE EAST END.

The writer complains, and with very good reason too, that "people speak and write as if the inhabitants of East London were all degraded and crime stained, as if the streets were not safe for the passage of respectable people; as if its denizens had the monopoly of vice; and as if in its houses virtue were unloved, and right-eousness unpursued." Against these ignorant assumptions, Mrs. Barnett protests on the strongest grounds, and pleads that people, instead of allowing their minds to be swayed by these prejudices, should endeavour to seek out the simple, unadulterated truth upon the question. "The majority of East London inhabitants," she maintains, "are well intentioned citizens, often with a low standard of life and principle, but generally law abiding; with narrow interests and limited outlooks, but with consciences which they keep alive, and a moral which, if low, is nevertheless obeyed."

### THE STATE OF THE TOWER HAMLETS.

Here are some statistics quoted by the writer, which are of more than ordinary interest at the present time. "The people of the Tower Hamlets number, roughly, 456,000 people, and of these only some 71,000 belong to the class of unskilful labour from which, as a rule, in East London the criminal classes are recruited; or, to put the same fact in another form, out of nearly 90,000 heads of families, some 15,000 earn their living by irregular work, or work paid for, owing to its poorness of execution, at a lower than the market rate of payment. If the matter is reduced to percentages it will show that 65 per cent of the East London people are above the line of poverty, 22 per cent on the line, while those who fall chronically below it into the region of distress are 13 per cent."

### A PLEA FOR THE POOR.

In the face of thee figures, and of the recent events which have made that part of the metropolis so notorious Mrs. Barnett holds that much of the misunderstanding which prevails with respect to the denizens of that district is due to the entire ignorance which the rich and poor of London have of each other. Upon this point she remarks: "With some knowledge both of rich and poor, I have learned to think that the rich people's ignorance of the poor is most to be regretted; the circumstances of the poor develop beauties of character which with difficulty grow apart from the atmosphere of labour, sacrifice, effort, and obedience. Such lives and characters it is almost impossible to describe. They must be loved and lived with before they can be really known; but the knowledge of them makes 'the bliss of solitude' even more surely than Wordsworth's daffodils."[319] Then follow a number of illustrations of filial affection and family solicitude, which, though in most cases roughly expressed, are very beautiful in their innate tenderness and loyalty.

## MUZZLING THE PRESS.

Mrs. Barnett is deeply and somewhat unreasonably indignant at the attitude of the daily Press with respect to the recent murders. She maintains that the publication of such details as have come to light is a disgrace to our humanity, and an unmitigated evil to the rising generation. This, however, is a point upon which a great many people will entirely disagree with her. This is certainly not the age for hushing up the particulars of great crimes, and it is this important factor of a public demand which Mrs. Barnett unfortunately omits from the calculation upon which her protest is based.

"But these Whitechapel horrors," continues the writer, "disgraceful as they, injurious as has been their effect on the public mind, and painful as it is to live through them, will not be in vain of the thinkers and the responsible are awakened to the condition of the poor quarters of London, their police supervision, and their local boards; or if the gentle and refined are aroused, until conscience struck, they are compelled to sacrifice some of their happiness and ease, and to give and share with the rough and the ignorant all that males life gentle and refined to themselves. That the kindly have already been awakened there can be no doubt, and large sums of money have been offered and raised to meet the evil."

We regret that we have not the space to quote more extensively from this truly important and interesting article.

—

---

[319] **I Wandered Lonely as a Cloud**, 1807 poem by William Wordsworth.

## ANOTHER ATTEMPTED MURDER OF A WOMAN.
## THIS TIME AT KING'S CROSS.
## THE VICTIM TAKEN TO THE HOSPITAL.
## NO TRACE OF THE MAN.

This morning, at about one o'clock, intense excitement was caused in the district of King's Cross by a report that another attempt had been made to murder a woman. It appeared that Harriet North, an unfortunate, residing at 12 Wood street, Cromer street, Gray's Inn road, was accosted in the Euston road by a young man, with a black moustache. After some conversation she accompanied him up Belgrave street, King's Cross, and a few minutes afterwards she found that she had been stabbed with some sharp instrument in the abdomen. She exclaimed, "Oh, my God, what have you done?" and the man, without replying, ran off. The woman called out, and Sarah Ann Masters, a companion of hers, went to her assistance. Police constables Hy. Stone, 273E, and Chas. Palmer, 871E, also went to her and, finding she was bleeding profusely from the wound, they removed her to the Royal Free Hospital, Gray's Inn road, where she was seen by Dr. Henry Tonks, one of the house surgeons, and was by him admitted into the Milne Ward. Whether the wound is serious or not, has not yet been ascertained. The man made good his escape. The woman North states that he was apparently a foreigner, and that he wore a heavy black moustache.

On inquiry at the Royal Free Hospital, Gray's Inn road, this morning, respecting the woman Harriett North, reported to have been stabbed at King's Cross, this morning, the Central News was informed that she was in no danger whatever. The matter had been much exaggerated, as it is doubtful of she had been stabbed at all. There are some scratches on the were (sic) part of the body but these might have been caused by sharp fingernails, in a struggle. The woman will most likely leave the hospital today. No importance is attached to the matter.

The Press Association says: The injury discovered on examination is in the nature of an abrasion, and could not have been inflicted by any sharp instrument, such as a knife. So strong is Mr. Tonks's opinion that it is not a case of premeditated assault, that he thinks the man probably was as much alarmed at the appear-

# Monday, 3 December, 1888

ance of blood as the woman herself, and so made his escape. A woman named Sarah Ann Masters, who lives in the same house as North, was with her for a few minutes before the occurrence, Masters having been accosted by the same man. From a statement of Masters it would appear that the woman Worth was herself under the impression that she had been stabbed with a knife, and that in her alarm she called Masters to her assistance. the woman's fears as to the nature of her injury are not, however, borne out by the surgeon in whose temporary charge she has been placed.

———

## THE NEW CHIEF COMMISSIONER.

Mr. James Monro, the new Chief Commissioner, who today enters upon his duties at Whitehall, is the subject of the above sketch. He is the son of the late Mr. George Monro, a solicitor, practising before the Supreme Courts, Edinburgh, and was born on November 25, 1838. He has consequently just completed his 50th year. Mr. Monro is a graduate of the University in his native city, and like many a Scotchman, early in life went out to India, where he was destined to have a distinguished official career. This was in or about the year 1860. His first appointment, if we are not mistaken, was in the Bengal Presidency. The reputation of the young official for administrative capacity soon grew, and we find him in rapid succession filling the posts of assistant magistrate and collector, district judge, and, finally, inspector general of police in the Presidency. In the latter position he had a very large body of men under his control, and the admirable way in which he handles the force was universally admired. Mr. Monro served with a distinction during the Wahabi conspiracy that gained him the thanks of the Indian Executive of the period. A curious turn of events a few years ago changed entirely the current of Mr. Monro's life and led him to severing his connection with India. It so happened that at the time when Mr. Howard Vincent resigned his appointment as head of the Central Criminal Investigation Department, Mr. Monro was in London on leave of absence, and although he had no friends in commanding positions at the Home Office, yet he did not hesitate to make application for the vacancy. His career in the far East was one that immediately commended itself to the authorities, and his appointment as Assistant Commissioner of Police soon followed. At the time when he assumed his new duties London was demoralised by the series of dynamite outrages perpetrated by Gallagher and his fellow conspirators; and how well, and with what success, Mr. Monro directed the operations of the detective department during the crucial period, is now a matter of history. His recent differences with Sir Charles Warren are too recent to need recapitulation. At all events, for a time he withdrew from Whitehall, though he continued to be one of the Home Secretary's confidential advisers at the Home Office. Now again he had been reinstated with increased authority, and there is every reason to believe that the appointment will be a good one. Mr. Monro, we may state, is a very popular man in the detective department, and enjoys the thorough confidence of his subordinates. A stiffly built, middle height man, with short side whiskers, firmly chiselled face and a head that is rapidly getting bald, Mr. Monro unfortunately suffers from one great physical disability. He is very lame, and can only with difficulty mount on horseback. When in India some years ago he met with a serious accident while in pursuit of an offender whom he was endeavouring to arrest. In attempting a wall over which the culprit had disappeared, his horse fell, and it was discovered by the doctors that the gallant official's hip joint had been permanently disabled. This is a physical infirmity that we believe will not debar the new Chief Commissioner from a thorough and efficient discharge of duties that must inevitably tax even his superabundant energies.

~

# Friday, 7 December, 1888

## The Times
### THE WHITECHAPEL MURDERS.

A news agency states that the police yesterday made a singular arrest, which was reported to be in connexion with the White-chapel murders. It appears that during the afternoon a man, described as a Polish Jew, was arrested near Drury-lane, but for what offence is not exactly clear. The man, who is of short stature, with a black moustache, was taken to the Bow-street Police-station, where he was detained for a time.

In the meantime a telegraphic comm-unication was forwarded to Leman-street Police-station, which is the head-quarters of the Whitechapel division, requesting the attendance of one of the inspectors. Detective-Inspector Aberline immediately proceeded to Bow-street, and subsequently brought away the prisoner in a cab, which was strongly escorted. The man, who is well known to the local force of police and detectives, is stated to have been absent from the neighbourhood of Whitechapel lately

~

## Evening News
### THE EAST END MURDERS.
### ARREST OF A MAN ANSWERING THE DESCRIPTION OF THE SUPPOSED MURDERER.

The police yesterday made a singular arrest, which was reported to be in connection with the Whitechapel murders. It appears that during the afternoon a man, described as a Polish Jew, was arrested near Drury lane, but for what offence is not exactly clear. The individual, who is of short stature with a black moustache, was taken to the Bow street Police station, where he was detained for a time. In the meantime, a telegraphic communication was forwarded to Leman street Police station, which is the headquarters of the Whitechapel division, requesting the attendance of one of the inspectors. Detective Inspector Abberline immediately proceeded to Bow street, and subsequently took away the prisoner in a cab, which was strongly escorted. While on the one hand he is stated to have stolen a watch for which he is detained, it is believed that, beyond that fact, he corresponds to the description of the supposed Whitechapel murderer, and there are other circumstances which are causing the detective force in the East end to make further inquiry concerning the prisoner. He is well known to the local police and detectives, although he is stated to have been absent from the neighbourhood lately.

Another account says: It was subsequently ascertained that the man was apprehended for stealing a watch, with which offence he has been charged; but the police were led to believe that he was connected, not with the mutilations, but with the recent attempt to murder a woman in George street, Spitalfields. Exhaustive inquiries were made, but as far as can be ascertained the man could in no way be connected with that outrage.

—

The current number of the *British Medical Journal* introduces to the public the theory of "an eminent surgeon" about the Whitechapel murders. This superior person prefaces his theory with a little sneer at the theories and speculations of other people who are not eminent surgeons, which, he suggests, "are prompted rather by a desire to account for them (the murders)—that is to say, to find some motive for them—than by any knowledge of the subject." Most writers on the point, says the eminent surgeon, have treated the occurrences as though they were unprecedented in the annals of crime, and therefore he considers "it seems desirable to point out that such is by no means the case."

Thereupon our eminent one goes on to explain that "a certain horrible perversion of the sexual instinct is the one motive and cause of such apparently aimless acts," to quote the German authority, Von Krafft Ebing, and to discourse learnedly on "Psycopathia Sexualis," adding a few examples of previous cases of the same class. This is doubtless a valuable contribution to the literature of the Whitechapel murders, but its value is considerably discounted by the fact that the suggestion as to a "Lustmord," the quotation of Von Kraft Ebing, the dissertation on "Psycopathia Sexualis," and the examples of previous cases, were all given in *The Evening News* of October 15th, and given much more fully and clearly than the eminent surgeon of the *B.M.J.* gives them. Yet we do not profess to be a medical journal.

# Saturday, 8 December, 1888

## Evening News

### THE WHITECHAPEL MURDERS.

Joseph Isaacs, 30, who said he had no fixed abode, and described himself as a cigar maker, was charged at Worship street, yesterday, with having stolen a watch, value 30s., the goods of Julius Levenson.

The prisoner, who was brought up in the custody of Detective sergeant Record, H division, is the man who was arrested in Drury lane on Thursday afternoon on suspicion of being connected with the Whitechapel murders. It transpired during the hearing of this charge that it was committed at the very time the prisoner was being watched as a person "wanted."

The prosecutor, Levenson, said that the prisoner entered his shop on the 5th instant, with a violin bow, and asked him to repair it. Whilst discussing the matter, the prisoner bolted out of the shop, and witness missed a gold watch belonging to a customer. The watch had been found at a pawn shop.

To prove that the prisoner was the man who entered the shop, a woman named Mary Cusins was called. She is deputy of a lodging house in Paternoster row, Spitalfields, and said that the prisoner had lodged in the house, as a single lodger, for three or four nights before the Dorset street murder—the murder of Mary Janet Kelly, in Miller's court. He disappeared after that murder, leaving the violin bow behind. The witness on the house to house inspection gave information to the police, and said she remembered that on the night of the murder she heard the prisoner walk about his room.

After her statement a look out was kept for the prisoner, whose appearance certainly answered the published description of a man with an astrachan trimming to his coat. He visited the lodging house on the 5th, and asked for the violin bow. It was given to him and the witness Cusins followed him to give him into custody as requested. She saw him enter Levenson's shop, and almost immediately run out, no constable being at hand. Detective Record said that there were some matters alleged against the prisoner, which it was desired to inquire into. Mr. Bushby remanded the prisoner.

~

# Tuesday, 11 December, 1888

## Evening News

There can be little doubt that, as the winter grows upon us, the bitter cry of outcast London will be as loud, as keen, as persistent this season as it has been at all. No substantial improvement has taken place in the condition of the destitute population of the Metropolis since last winter. Indeed, there is every probability that these sufferers will, in many instances, be worse off than they were a year ago, in consequence of the disastrous hopping season through which they had to pass.

Those who, in former years, have been able to put a little on one side to help them and their families through the long and dreary winter, have not had that opportunity this year, and the result will be an increase in the bulk of poverty in our midst. That some special effort will have to be made to meet this emergency goes without saying; but that the means of alleviation should be placed in the hands of General Booth[320] and his noisy host is quite another matter.

The "boss" of the Salvation Army has never shown any embarrassment through excessive modesty, especially when the tapping of the pockets of the public happened to be the question of the hour, which, by the way, it generally has been. But his latest proposal knocks all his other performances in this direction into the shade.

He has presented a memorial to the Home Secretary, in which he coolly proposes that the Government should aid the Salvation Army in what it is pleased to call its rescue work, and in the provision of food and shelter depots, by a grant of £15,000. Mr. Matthews has, of course, promised the matter his careful attention, but he is hardly likely to place such a nice little plum in the General's mouth on the off chance of its being properly distributed.

There are other institutions for the relief of the destitute than the Salvation Army, and until it can be proved to the public satisfaction that these agencies have failed, there is no possible excuse for appointing such a man as General Booth almoner of the Government bounty. If he took the public a little more into his confidence as to the fairness of his own fanatical organisation, the opposition of this last and coolest of his many demands would, possibly, be less strenuous, though equally well founded. As things stand it will not do at any price.

---

[320] **General William Booth** (1829-1912). Founder and first General of the Salvation Army (1878-1912). As can be seen, there was fierce opposition to General Booth and the Salvation Army in its early days, most especially from the makers and sellers of alchohol, who were afraid of losing their customers, the press, which portrayed Booth as a money-hungry charlatan and his followers as fanatics, and even the Church of England, which labelled Booth as "Anti-Christ" because he elevated women "to man's status." By the time of General Booth's death, however, the Salvation Army had become a beloved and respected institution, and Queen Mary attended his funeral, not as royalty, but as an admirer of what he, and his organization, had accomplished in helping the poor and needy all over the World.

## The Times
### INQUEST.

Yesterday Mr. Langham, the City and Southwark Coroner, held an inquest at Guy's Hospital on the body of WILLIAM HALL, aged 32, a Post Office employée lately residing at Royal Naval-place, New-cross, who met with his death under somewhat remarkable circumstances on Friday last, and in connexion with which a man named William James is at present under remand at the Southwark Police-court. Inspector Marriott watched the case on behalf of the Police authorities.

George William Figes, a letter sorter, deposed that he and the deceased were employed at St. Martin's-le-Grand. They went on duty at 5 p.m. on Thursday last and left for the purpose of going home at 12:25 a.m. (midnight) on Friday. They came over Southwark-bridge and passed along Marshalsea-road to get to St. George's Church, so as to go home viá Great Dover-street and Old Kent-road.

When in Marshalsea-road they met a young woman who was crying and who complained that a man who was with her had grossly insulted her. At this moment another man—the accused, William James—came up and struck the man complained of a violent blow in the head, knocking his hat off into the road. The man picked up his hat and made off as fast as he could towards the Borough.

Several other men by this time arrived, and they all, including the young woman, witness, and the deceased, followed in the direction the man complained of had gone. On reaching the Borough a constable was informed of what had taken place, and witness and the deceased passed over to the corner on the opposite side of the road, where they stood watching what became of the young woman and the other man.

Without any warning the deceased all of a sudden received a heavy blow at the side of his head just behind the right ear and fell heavily on the kerb. The man who struck the blow ran away, but was captured by a constable and taken to Stone's-end Police-station, where he was identified by the deceased as the man who had knocked him down. The deceased, who had to be assisted to the station, was removed to Guy's Hospital on the police ambulance.

By the Coroner.—The accused man James appeared to be perfectly sober. There had been no words between the deceased and him, nor did he say anything when he struck the blow.

By Dr. Price, house surgeon at Guy's Hospital.—He could not say if James had a knuckleduster[321] in his hand or anything else. The deceased had his right hand in his pocket at the time, and was smoking. He appeared to have no power to save himself and fell with great force backwards on his head.

By the jury.—Witness thought the woman was a respectable person who had somehow lost her way, and was not in collusion with the accused.

In reply to the Coroner Inspector Marriott said the accused said he was a costermonger, but he was well known to the police.

William Mortimer Sheen, a medical student, deposed to reaching St. George's Church shortly after 1 a.m. and to seeing the accused steal along the outside of the crowd of persons who had assembled at the corner of Marshalsea-road until he came to where the deceased was standing with his back to the people. Immediately afterwards he saw the deceased fall with great force to the ground, striking his head against the kerb-stone. He saw no blow struck. He went and examined the deceased while the police gave chase and arrested the accused.

Police-constable Sutherland, 253 M, deposed to the first witness and the deceased informing him of the complaint by the young woman of having been insulted and to their also telling him they thought the men were trying to take the young woman away, and that they ought to be watched. The accused man James then came up and said he was "Jack the Ripper." (Laughter in Court.) Witness took no notice of this, but went to the young woman and asked her if she was aware in whose company she was. She was then crying and said she was not, and he, finding she lived at Wandsworth, directed her which way to go, and nothing had been seen of her since. By this time he found the deceased had been badly injured and that another constable had arrested the accused man James.

Police-constable Freeman, 327 M, deposed

---

[321] **Knuckle-duster.** 1. A knuckle-guard of iron or brass which, in striking, protects the hand from injury and adds force to a blow. 2. A large, heavy, or over-gaudy ring. (Farmer)

# Wednesday, 12 December, 1888

to hearing cries for the police and to overtaking the accused, who made no resistance, and whose only remark while on the way to the station was an inquiry as to what had become of the woman.

Inspector Marriott deposed to taking the charges at the station, and to the accused, in reply to the charge, calling the deceased a filthy beast and to his having stated on the way to the cells that he had interfered because the men had assaulted the young woman, who was a barmaid.

Mr. Price, house surgeon at Guy's Hospital, deposed to the deceased being both conscious and sober when admitted. There was a scalp wound behind the right ear about half an inch long, but which did not go down to the bone. The symptoms pointed to fracture at the base of the skull. Death ensued the same morning and the post-mortem examination showed it had resulted from an extensive fracture, coupled with a blood clot on the brain, caused by a fall.

The Coroner, in summing, said the circumstances of the case would fully justify the jury in returning a verdict of willful murder against William James, and the jury, after a brief consultation, returned this verdict. The witnesses were then sworn in the usual way to appear against the accused at the Old Bailey.[322]

~

## Evening News

Mr. Berry, public executioner, seems to have had "a high old time" in Kidderminster, which town he visited after a professional engagement in Worcester. "He visited several public houses, and at one was induced to make a speech to a large number of persons. He spoke of various executions carried out by him, and moralised upon his public calling. He freely distributed his visiting cards, bearing his name and profession as public executioner.

One publican offered him five pounds to lecture in the evening on his public duties. He conversed freely with all, and was followed about by a considerable number of persons, members of the Corporation were introduced to him, and he held quite a levee at one hostelry." Thus the accounts of the visit. Mr. Berry should receive a hint to have a little more regard to public decency.

—

### AN EX-MILITARY OFFICER AS "JACK THE RIPPER."

William Moses, 50, of military appearance, giving his address as 229 Mare street, Hackney, was charged before Mr. Horace Smith, at Dalston Police court, today, with being drunk and disorderly, in Dalston lane.

Constable 128J said that he was on duty in Dalston lane, at a quarter to ten on Tuesday night, when he saw the prisoner go up to a number of females and speak to them. When they declined to have anything to do with him, he became very disorderly and shouted out that he was "Jack the Ripper." He was evidently drunk, and witness took him into custody.

The Clerk showed the magistrate the charge sheet on which the prisoner was described as a retired officer from the army, and Mr. Smith remarked that for a man of the prisoner's education and position to be guilty of such conduct was positively disgraceful. He should impose a fine of 40s., with 7s 6d the doctor's fee, or one month, but he was not quite sure that he ought not to send the accused to prison without the option of a fine.

---

[322] See Appendix N, William James, p. 583.

# Thursday, 13 December, 1888

## The Times

### THE HAVANT MURDER.

The inquest was continued yesterday relative to the death of the boy Percy Searle, when some additional evidence was given.

A lad named Charles Clark stated that on the night of the murder he saw Husband near the latter's house, and heard him say in the presence of other lads "Here comes Jack the Ripper," and showed a knife with the blade open. He stopped witness and pointed the knife at him. He had never mentioned the circumstance to anybody but Sergeant Knapton and his grandmother.

Professor Tidy repeated his evidence as to the examination of the blood stains upon the accused's clothes. He could not say whether a boy of the age and size of Husband could have inflicted the wounds.

Robert Husband, the father of the accused, was then examined. He said that about 20 minutes past 6 his son came indoors and said that a man was killing a boy. He did not notice any blood upon his hands. He had not washed his hands at the time, but his mother afterwards told him to wash as his face and hands had got dirty in the coalyard. He remembered Mrs. Searle coming to make a complaint. She said that her little boy had been for coal and that the accused would not serve it. He never allowed his son to serve coal when he himself was not present.

Mrs. Husband gave corroborative evidence.

The jury, after long consideration, eventually brought in a verdict of "Wilful murder against some one unknown."

~

## Evening News

### AN ARM FOUND AT KING'S CROSS.
### MEDICAL STUDENTS' STUPID JOKE.

Yesterday morning, about nine o'clock, a policeman passing along Lavinia grove, King's Cross, had his attention called to a brown paper parcel which had been found in the gutter, and which, on being opened, was found to contain a human arm. He took it to the police station, where it was examined by the divisional police surgeon who found it was the left arm of a woman, and that it had been used for anatomical purposes. From the condition of the limb it was evident that it must have been lying about for some months. It is believed to have been thrown away by some medical student.

~

# Saturday, 15 December, 1888

## Evening News

### BERRY, THE HANGMAN'S, LEVEE.

The High Sheriff of Worcestershire, as directed by the Home Secretary, yesterday, made an official inquiry at Kidderminster respecting the conduct of Berry, the executioner, when he visited that borough on Tuesday last. he High Sheriff received evidence from the chief constable of the borough and others who heard the speech of the executioner and saw members of the Corporation presented to him at the levee held at a public house, and the statements made in the *Evening News* report were fully confirmed. The High Sheriff will at once send his report to the Home Secretary. The episode has created much excitement in the district.

—

## THE WHITECHAPEL SUSPECT.

At Worship street Police court, yesterday, Joseph Isaacs, 30, cigar maker, with no fixed abode, was charged, on remand, with having stolen from the shop of a watchmaker named Levenson a gold watch, value 30s. The prisoner, it may be remembered, had been sought for by the police in consequence of a report of his movements on the night of the murder of Mary Janet Kelly in Dorset street, Spitalfields; and it was aid by the police that they wished the fullest inquiry as to the prisoner's movements on the night of November 8. For that purpose he was remanded, but Detective Sergeant Record, H division, said that so far there was no further charge against the prisoner. The prisoner was then asked if he wished to go for trial, but he pleaded guilty, and was sentenced to three months' hard labour.

~

# Wednesday, 19 December, 1888

## Evening News
### JACK THE RIPPER IN BERLIN.

A person purporting to be "Jack the Ripper has sent the following letter to the Berlin Police President:

"To the Police president of Berlin.

Mr. President, as I am going to spend a short time in Berlin, I will see if the famous Berlin police will catch me. I shall only have fifteen victims. So take warning!

Yours respectfully,
Jack the Ripper."

The letter is in German in a large handwriting, and is a ridiculous fabrication sent by a Berliner as a stupid joke, and therefore of no value whatever as a clue to the London crimes. It is full of Berlinisms, such as the substitution of mich for mir.

—

General Booth is not to be entrusted with the handling of the £15,000 which he modestly requested from the Government the other day. In the House of Commons last night, the Home Secretary, in reply to Professor Stuart, said he had received a memorial from general Booth, of the Salvation Army, respecting the establishment of cheap shelters for the outcast poor in London, and had replied that the Government could not assist a charitable work by private persons by grants of money, buildings, or stores. This decision will, probably, disappoint the enterprising "boss" of the Salvation Army, but it will be a great satisfaction to the general public.

~

## The Times
### THE ASSIZES.

—

### WESTERN CIRCUIT.

At Winchester, yesterday, before Mr. Justice Stephen, ROBERT HUSBAND, 11, was charged with the willful murder of Percy Knight Serle, at Havant, on November 26.

Mr. Temple Cooke and Mr. Rubie prosecuted for the Treasury; Mr. Charles Mathews and Mr. Bovill Smith defended.

This case, the facts of which have recently been before the public, created much interest, and the court was densely crowded.

The prisoner, a boy aged 11 years and 11 months, is the son of a man in charge of a coalyard, living in North-street, Havant. The deceased was eight years old, the son of a labourer living in another part of Havant.

Shortly before 6 p.m. on November 26, which was a dark, cloudy, and rainy night, deceased was sent by his mother to buy some things at a shop at the corner of North-street and the Pallant. A boy named Farnden was in the shop when the deceased was there and noticed the prisoner peeping in at the door. Farnden went out, leaving the deceased in the shop, and the prisoner walked up the Pallant with him, down a lane, and back again to Farnden's home. Farnden went in, leaving the prisoner outside. The deceased would have passed up the Pallant, close by Farnden's house, to reach his house.

About a quarter of an hour later a man named Shirley, who was at Randall's shop, saw the prisoner running down the Pallant in the direction of his home. Seeing Shirley, he crossed the road and told him a man was killing a boy. A man named Platt, living opposite, came out and went with the prisoner and found little Serle lying at a spot in the Pallant, not far from Farnden's home; after gasping twice, the little boy died.

Two scratches were found on the front of the throat, and a deep gash (which must have been inflicted from behind) on the right side of the neck, which was the cause of death. The little boy's cap, and the parcel he had brought from the shop, were found in the road near the body.

The police were fetched, and also a medical man.

The prisoner said to several witnesses that he saw a tall man murder the boy and then run away in the direction of Fairfield. From the description given a man was actually arrested, but was afterwards discharged.

An old knife, covered with blood, was picked up eight yards from the body. This knife had been given to the prisoner's brother a few days previously; he had lost it the day before the murder, and the prisoner had it in his possession, as on the 26th he was offering it for sale to another boy, and was seen sharpening it.

In cross-examination, the prisoner's brother admitted that just before he found he had lost the knife he had walked by the spot where the body was afterwards found.

The other witnesses were cross-examined at some length as to the identity of the knife shown to them by the prisoner and the knife produced. Earlier in the evening of the 26th the prisoner came up to a boy flourishing a knife in his hand, and said he was "Jack the Ripper," but meant no harm.

The prisoner made various statements, said to be inconsistent with each other. To Platt he stated he was standing near a lamp when he saw the murder committed. It was said, owing to the position of the body, it was impossible he could have seen it from the lamp mentioned. Next day he told the police he had gone to Mrs. Farnden's for some money, and when at her door had seen the murder committed. It was untrue that he had been to her at all; nor, again, could he have seen any one from that place, according to the experiments subsequently made by the police and other witnesses.

On the 28th the prisoner was arrested. No blood was found on the clothes which his mother gave to the police as those worn by him on the 26th. A towel was asked for with which the prisoner was seen drying his hands after he had given information of the murder; but this apparently had been washed.

A number of witnesses were called in support of the case for the prosecution, among them Dr. Bond, of Havant, who saw the body of the deceased. Professor Tidy (one of the official analysts of the Home Office), to whom the knife and the various articles of clothing worn by the prisoner were handed by the police on November 30, said the blood on the knife was living blood.

On the right wristband of the shirt there were

# Thursday, 20 December, 1888

a few slight stains of blood which appeared to be at least a month old; he added that if the stains were recent these signs might be produced by washing the shirt, but it did not seem to have been washed. He found no other trace of blood on any of the other clothes.

At the close of the evidence for the prosecution, Mr. Mathews said he confidently hoped the jury would be able in the result to set the prisoner at liberty. He appealed to the facts as showing the charge was unfounded. There was no evidence of malice. No adequate motive had been shown, nor the existence shown of any ill feeling between the prisoner and the deceased. He also urged that the knife found had not been proved to be the prisoner's. The case was adjourned at his request before he had finished his speech and will be resumed to-day.

~

## Evening News
### SUSPICIOUS DEATH AT POPLAR.

The Press Association says that Police sergeant Goldie this morning found the dead body of a woman lying in Clarke's yard, High street, Poplar. Mrs. Thompson, of the East India Arms, High street, states that shortly after three o'clock this morning, she heard the dog barking very loudly, but on looking out of her window she could see nothing. The police are instituting inquiries, and Mr. Chivers, the coroner's officer, sent a special message to the coroner asking his consent to a post mortem examination. There were no distinct marks of violence, but there was great discolouration of the face, neck, and arms. The woman appeared to be about 25 years of age.

~

## The Times
### THE HAVANT MURDER.

At Winchester Assizes, yesterday, before Mr. Justice Stephen, the trial of Robert Husband, 11, for the willful murder of Percy Knight Searle, was resumed. Mr. Temple Cooke and Mr. J.F. Rubie prosecuted for the Treasury; Mr. Charles Mathews and Mr. Bovill Smith defended.

Mr. Mathews proceeded with his address to the jury, and referred first of all to the walk taken just before the murder by the prisoner and Farnden from Randall's shop, which he pointed out must have taken time. During it no knife was seen or referred to by either. Whether the prisoner actually entered Farnden's house or not was, he said, absolutely immaterial, though there was a controversy about it.

He complained that Farnden's sister, who was now at Alton, but who was said to have been at home that night, had not been called to clear up the evidence given on the point by the rest of the family.

He contended the prisoner's account was a truthful one, and that, having seen the occurrence, he ran back towards Randall's shop as fast as he could to give information.

The prosecution not only said the prisoner committed the murder, but also immediately invented the defence about it having been done by a man.

As to the knife, he urged that it was impossible that the prisoner's hands or clothes could have been free from marks of blood immediately afterwards if he had done the act.

He also contended that it was physically impossible, owing to the prisoner and the deceased differing only one inch in height, that the blow which caused the death could have been inflicted by the prisoner, and this, added to the absence of any sign of struggle at the spot, pointed conclusively to the murder having been committed by a man.

The prisoner's whole conduct was inconsistent with guilt, and his story had always been the same, both before and after his arrest. His clothes were handed over to the police without demur, and on them, beyond two small spots of blood a month old, no traces of blood were found by Professor Tidy.

In conclusion, referring to the question as to who was the actual culprit, Mr. Mathews alluded to the tragedies which had occurred in London, in which no culprit had yet been found. He pointed out that several trains left Havant almost directly after the time of the murder, and that thus escape was possible; and, while hoping that the culprit might be discovered, he said the matter must remain, for the present, shrouded in mystery.

His LORDSHIP, in summing up, referred to the prisoner's age, and directed the jury in the words used in his Lordship's "Digest of the Criminal Law," namely, that—"No act done by any person over seven and under 14 is a crime, unless it be shown affirmatively that such person had sufficient capacity to know that the act was wrong." The jury must be satisfied that the boy had some adequate conception of the wickedness of the act and its awful consequences before they could convict him.

Adopting the language he had used in summing up a similar case at Exeter the other day, when a girl of 12 was being tried for the murder of a child of four, he asked the jury to recall to their minds what they themselves were at the age of 11, and the thoughts and feelings which then actuated them, and, in considering the case, to remember that the prisoner was now not unlike what they were then.

After complimenting the counsel on both sides, his Lordship proceeded to deal with the evidence, pointing out that the whole of the events of the evening were fixed as taking place between 6 p.m., when the deceased was at Randall's shop, and 6:23, when Knapton came to the spot where the murder was committed.

Referring to the details, he said the expression used by the prisoner about "Jack the Ripper" would probably be considered by the jury as childish play. It was clear he must either, directly Farnden left him, have at once attacked Searle on seeing him approach, or else his story that he saw a man committing the crime must be true.

It was, no doubt, strange that the crime should have been committed at all, but the question for them was, Did they feel quite sure that the prisoner did it? They were not told why he did not go to Farnden's to give the alarm, and it would perhaps have been better if he had done so, instead of going back again down the Pallant.

Dealing with Platt's evidence, it was impor-

529

tant to remember that he had stated the prisoner's right hand was dry and free from blood; in fact, there was no proof that his hands had any blood on them at all that night.

He agreed with Mr. Mathews that the prisoner had given the same account on each occasion when mentioning the occurrence.

The evidence about the knife was important, assuming it to be the knife with which the murder was committed. But the question was, Were the jury confident that the witnesses were correct as to its identity? Still, there was strong evidence that the deceased was murdered with the knife produced, because it fitted the wound and was found smothered with blood. There was satisfactory evidence that the knife was given to the prisoner's brother, and there was some evidence that the prisoner had a chance of stealing or taking it from him.

Having referred to the paltriness of the motive suggested for the murder by the prisoner, his Lordship concluded by observing that whatever made the prisoner's account of what he had seen improbably acted equally in his favour, but it was far more important for the jury to determine whether or not it was physically impossible that the prisoner's story could be true.

The jury retired, and after a quarter of an hour's deliberation, found a verdict of Not Guilty, and the prisoner was discharged.

His Lordship arranged that on the rising of the Court on Saturday he would adjourn until Thursday, the 27th, at 11 a.m.

—

A singular scene was witnessed at Havant last evening. When Husband reached his home a large number of his former playmates met him and congratulated him on the results of the trial. A public subscription was raised to meet the expenses of the defence, and up to the present over £70 has been received by Mr. George Feltham, of Portsmouth, the boy's solicitor.

~

# The Times

## MURDER AT POPLAR.

Yesterday Mr. Wynne E. Baxter, the Coroner for the South-Eastern Division of Middlesex, opened an inquiry at the Town-hall, Poplar, as to the death of a woman unknown, whose body was found lying in a yard attached to the premises of Mr. Clarke, builder, of High-street, Poplar, early on Thursday morning last. Inspector Parlett, K Division, attended to represent the police authorities.

Police-sergeant Robert Golding, 26 K, deposed that he was patrolling High-street, Poplar, on Thursday morning about 4:15. He was in company with Police-constable Thomas Costella. While passing Mr. Clarke's yard he saw something lying under the wall, and on going close found it to be the body of a woman. She was lying on her left side, her left arm underneath her. The right leg was at full length, and her left leg slightly drawn up. The body was quite warm. Her clothes were not disarranged, nor could he detect any mutilation of the body. She was lying under the wall, with her head away from the street. The witness left the constable in charge of the body while he went for the divisional surgeon. Dr. Harris, the assistant, returned with him and examined the body before it was moved. He at once pronounced life to be extinct. The witness then sent for the ambulance, and the body was taken to the mortuary. He searched it and made an examination of the clothing. Round the neck the deceased was wearing a blue-spotted handker-chief, tied loosely. There was no string round the neck. In the pocket of the dress he found 1s. in silver and 3 1/2d. in bronze, together with a small empty bottle or phial. The woman was about 5ft. 2in. high, had light hair, hazel eyes, and hair frizzed close to the head. She was wearing a black alpaca dress, brown stuff skirt, and red flannel petticoat. She also had on a dark tweed jacket, double-breasted, a lilac print apron, blue and red striped stockings, and side-spring boots. She had no hat on, nor was any found near the spot. The witness said he believed he had seen the woman before, and that she was of loose character. After leaving the mortuary he carefully searched the yard where the body was found, but could not discover any traces of a struggle having taken place.

Thomas Dean, of 159, High-street, Poplar, deposed that he was employed by Mr. Mead at that address. On Wednesday night he left the workshop which was in Mr. Clarke's yard about 10 o'clock. The body was not there then. There were no persons in the yard. The shop was opposite the yard and the witness slept there, but heard no noise during the night.

Mr. Matthew Brownfield, of 170, East India-road, Poplar, deposed that he was divisional surgeon of police. At 4:25 on Thursday morning he was sent for, but his assistant went instead and found the body of a woman lying in Clarke's yard. She was dead. Yesterday morning the witness saw the body in the mortuary and subsequently made a *post-mortem* examination. He found the body to be that of a woman about 30 years of age and well nourished. He noticed marks of mud on the front of the left leg. The eyes were normal and the tongue did not protrude. There were slight marks of blood having escaped from the nostrils, and the right side of the nose showed a slight abrasion, while on the left cheek was an old scar. The mark on the nose might have been caused by any slight violence. On the neck there was the mark apparently of a cord extending from the right side of the spine round the throat to the lobe of the left ear. He had, by experiment, found that a piece of four-fold cord would cause such a mark. On the neck he also found marks as of the thumbs and middle and index fingers. He had tried his thumb and fingers and found that they could cause such abrasions. The marks ran perpendicularly to the line round the neck before described. There were no injuries to the arms or legs as if any violent struggle had taken place. On opening the head he found the brain engorged with blood of a very dark colour. The lungs were normal. In the stomach was some food which had only very recently been eaten. There was no sign of any poison or alcohol in the stomach. From his examination he was of opinion that the cause of death was suffocation by strangulation. The strangulation could not possibly have been done by the woman herself, but must have been caused by a person standing behind and slightly to the left of her. The witness said the person must have wrapped the ends of the cord round his hands and then, from behind, thrown the noose over the deceased's head and pulled tight, crossing both hands. This would account for the mark round the neck not completing the circle. The cord was held round the throat till after death had taken place. At this point the Coroner adjourned the inquiry.

—

The mystery surrounding the murder can only be compared to that which attended the recent series of crimes in the same district. The yard in which the body of this woman was found is a dark and neglected byway. Several small traders in the neighbourhood have workshops in it. No one appears to have passed through the yard from 10 o'clock on Wednesday night until the body was discovered, and no cry of distress was heard. At a late hour last night the body was still unidentified, and the police had no one in custody in connexion with the crime.

~

## Evening News
### THE MURDER AT POPLAR.

Yesterday morning, Mr. Wynne E. Baxter, coroner for South east Middlesex, opened an inquiry at Poplar town Hall into the circumstances attending the death of a woman, unknown, whose body was discovered lying in Clarke's yard, High street, Poplar, on Thursday, under circumstances which lead to the supposition that she was the victim of foul play. Inspector Parlett, K division, attended to watch the case for the Commissioner of Police.

### HOW THE DISCOVERY WAS MADE.

Police sergeant Robert Golding, 26K, stated that at 4.15 a.m. on Thursday, he was on duty in High street, Poplar, in company with Police constable 470K. Whilst passing Mr. Clarke's yard he saw a heap of something lying some distance up the yard. He went up and examined it, and found it to be the body of a woman, apparently dead. She was lying on her left side, with her left arm under her. The right leg was under her, and the left at full length. The body at that time was warm. the clothes were not disarranged. The body was lying parallel with and under the wall. He left the constable in charge, and went for the divisional surgeon, whose assistant came and pronounced life extinct. the body was then removed to the mortuary, where witness searched it and examined the clothing. he found one shilling in silver and two pence in bronze, together with a phial, which was empty. the woman was wearing a black dress made of alpaca, a brown stuff skirt, a red flannel petticoat, and white drawers and chemise. She also had on a dark tweed double breasted jacket, blue striped stockings, and side spring boots. She had no hat on, and her hair was all rough and fell over her face. One earring was on the right ear.

### NO MARKS OF A SCUFFLE.

Witness said that he did not meet anyone in High street while he was patrolling it. He examined the ground but could not find any marks as if a scuffle had taken place there. The features of the woman were familiar to him, and he believed she was a girl of the streets.

Thomas Dean, a blind maker, of 159 High street, Poplar, deposed that he passed through Clarke's yard late on Wednesday night. He did not notice the body then, and he must have done had it been there. Witness knew that women of ill fame were in the habit of frequenting the spot, which was open to nay one, there being no gate. His house was right opposite the yard, but during the night he heard no noise.

## THE DOCTOR WHO EXAMINED THE BODY CALLED.

Mr. Matthew Brownfield, of 170 East India road, Poplar, divisional surgeon of police, deposed that at 4.30 a.m. on Thursday morning he was called by the police to a woman who had been found lying in Clarke's yard. His assistant, Mr. Harris, attended and pronounced her dead. Wit-ness made a post mortem examination yesterday morning. He found the body to be that of a woman about 30 years of age, 5ft 2in high, complexion fair, hazel eyes, and moderately stout. She was well nourished. Blood was oozing from the nostrils, and on the right side was a slight abrasion. On the right cheek was a scar apparently of old standing. The mark on the nose might have been caused by any slight violence. On the neck he found a mark which had evidently been caused by a cord drawn tightly round from the spine on the back to the lobe of the left ear.

## PRODUCED BY CORD.

He had since found that the mark could be produced by a piece of four fold lay cord. Beside that mark the impression of the thumbs and the middle and index fingers were plainly visible on each side of the neck. There were no injuries to the arms and legs. On opening the brain he found the vessels engorged with a dark, almost black fluid blood. The lungs were congested and the heart normal. The kidneys were congested but not diseased. the stomach was full of meat and potatoes which had only recently been eaten. There was a little fluid, and that and the food had been Irish stew. There was no smell or sign of poison in the stomach. The cause of death, in witness's opinion, was suffocation by strang-ulation. There were no signs of a struggle except the mark on the cheek.

The Coroner: Do you think she could have done it herself?

Witness:—No, I don't think so. If she had done it I should have expected to find the cord round the neck, but it was not, nor has any cord been found near the spot.

## WHAT ABOUT THE FINGER MARKS?

The Coroner: To what do you ascribe the finger marks?

Witness:—I think they were made in her efforts to pull off the cord.

The Coroner: I think you said that the string had not gone right round the neck, but only from the spine to beneath the left ear, travelling round by the throat. How do you account for that?

Witness:—I think the murderer must have stood at the left rear of the woman, and, having the ends of the string wrapped round his hands, thrown the cord round her throat, and crossing his hands, so strangled her. Where the hands crossed would be just where the marks of the cord are absent.

The Coroner: Do you think the woman was held like that for any length of time?

Witness:—I think the cord was pulled till after death had ensued. The cord being tight would prevent the woman from calling our for help. I may say that having studied the question as to the position of the man and the force used, I think it quite possible that the cord was run through two holes or rings and then twisted by a turn of the wrist till death ensued.

## THE CORONER TAKES A SERIOUS VIEW OF THE CASE.

The Coroner said that the law only allowed him to call in one doctor, but the jury had the power to summon a second one if they thought it necessary. Now Dr. Harris's evidence was most important to the inquiry, but before that evidence could be got the jury must give him (the Coroner) power to summon Dr. Harris. It seemed very much as if a foul murder had been committed, and all available evidence should be got before the jury concluded the case. Under these circumstances, he thought it would be better to adjourn at this point, and give his officer and police time to make inquiries.

This was agreed to and the inquiry was then adjourned.

## THE NEIGHBOURHOOD OF THE CRIME

High street, Poplar, at the best of times when business is in full swing is not particularly well lighted. It is a dirty, narrow thoroughfare, and in the neighbourhood of Clarke's yard, as there are several private houses facing the street, the illumination is poor. Clarke's yard is a long, narrow lane leading from the main thoroughfare down to some workshops and stables. It is about eight or ten feet wide; it is not lit up; one of the two gates which formerly kept out intruders at night at night time has disappeared, and lately the yard has become a nuisance from a sanitary point of view, while it is much frequented by women of the unfortunate class. The tenants of the workshops and stables are usually passing up and down until close on midnight. But on the night of the murder no one seems to have gone through the yard after ten o'clock. At that hour it was moonlight, and certainly nobody was there then. The discovery was made at four o'clock in the morning, and the outrage had then not long been committed. It may be added that disturbances with abandoned women are of frequent occurrence in the locality, especially soon after midnight. The affair up to a late hour last night was still enshrouded in mystery, one of the chief difficulties of the police arising from the fact that the deceased is totally unknown. Two or three inquiries have already been made of the police by women who have missed companions, but all efforts at identification have proved futile.

## A STARTLING SUGGESTION.

Some colour is given to the suggestion that "Jack the Ripper" has adopted a new style of assassination by a complaint recently made at Dalston Police court by a woman that a man had attempted to strangle her in a somewhat similar manner. The force of detectives in the Poplar district has now been considerably increased, and no efforts are being spared to clear up the mystery.

# Monday, 24 December, 1888

## The Times
### THE POPLAR MURDER.

The mystery surrounding the murder at Poplar has in no way diminished, and the excitement in the neighbourhood has become intense. Up to a late hour last night the police had made no arrests. Only two persons have been able to throw any light on the identity of the unfortunate woman, and one of these is a young woman named Graves, resident in Whitechapel. She called on the coroner's officer, Mr. Chivers, who resides in High-street, Poplar, on Saturday night and made the following statement:—

"My name is Alice Graves. I live at 18, George-street, Spitalfields. I am an unfortunate, and I identify the body as that of another unfortunate whom I had known for some time past and was intimate with. I knew her by the name of 'Lizzie.' I last saw her alive on Thursday morning at 2:30. She was standing outside the George, Commercial-road, and was in the company of two men. She was then the worse for drink. I passed her and went home."

This statement is regarded as of the utmost importance, inasmuch as it leaves only one hour and 45 minutes to be accounted for between the time of her last being seen alive and the discovery of her body by Sergeant Golding. The other person who has identified the body is Mrs. Hill, of Simpson's-row, High-street, Poplar, which address is about 30 or 40 yards from Charles-yard, where the body was found. Her statement corroborates in several particulars that made by Alice Graves. She visited the mortuary yesterday afternoon and recognized the body as that of Alice Downey, *alias* "Fair Alice," *alias* "Drunken Liz." She was, however, unable to say where the deceased had been residing. It was only occasionally that she visited Poplar. Mrs. Hill said that she saw the deceased at half-past 11 on the night preceding the murder. She then complained of being without money, and added that she did not know what to do. Mrs. Hill gave her some coppers and bade her good night. She was then perfectly sober. She had been an inmate of the Bromley Sick Asylum, quitting it about a month ago.

As far as the movements of the deceased can be traced it would appear that she went into the East India Dock-road after leaving Mrs. Hill, and thence walked along until she reached Commercial-road. It is supposed that, after having been seen in the company of two strange men in the Commercial-road by Alice Graves at 2:30 a.m. on Thursday, she walked back to the East India Dock-road, which is the main thoroughfare through Poplar. Late on Wednesday night or early on Thursday morning an engineer, whose name has not been reported, while passing along the East India Dock-road near the Eagle Tavern, noticed a woman's hat within the railings of a garden in front of a private dwelling. He thought nothing of this at the time, but on hearing of the murder he acquainted the police with the incident. There were no indications of a struggle in the yard where the woman was found, and doubts have arisen as to whether her life was taken in the yard or not. The discovery of the hat, which is supposed to have belonged to Downey, in the East India Dock-road, shows that the woman must have been helplessly intoxicated or rendered powerless by her assailant or assailants. It would have been a very easy task to carry her from the spot where her hat was found to the yard in which she was discovered. It is but a few hundred yards from the one place to the other, and the streets just here are very badly lighted.

~

# Monday, 24 December, 1888

## The Star
### IS HE A THUG?
### A STARTLING LIGHT ON THE WHITE-CHAPEL CRIMES.
### THE ROPE BEFORE THE KNIFE.
### The Police Surgeon Theory that the Poplar Murder was the Work of the Whitechapel Fiend Borne Out by Hitherto Inexplicable Evidence—Why the Murdered Women Never Cried Out.

The Poplar murder has developed under inquiry a startling and sensational aspect. So far, it has passed almost unnoticed. The town has supped so full of horrors that mere murder unaccompanied by revolting mutilation passes apparently for common-place, and the discovery on Thursday morning in Clarke's-yard, Poplar, of a woman's dead body with the white mark of a strangler's cord around her throat has failed to create any excitement even in the neighbour-hood. The police themselves appear to have shared the general feeling of non-interest. The swift and silent method of the Thug is a new and terrifying feature in London crime, and this murder is invested with a startling significance by the discovery that it has a possible bearing upon the series of Whitechapel crimes. The suggestion is this:—"Was this Poplar murder another of the series of Whitechapel and the work of the same man? If so, has the murderer changed his methods, or is it not possible that the deed of Clarke's-yard is a new revelation of his old methods—that in the other cases partial strangulation was first of all resorted to, and that when the victims were by this means rendered helpless,

### THE KNIFE WAS USED

in such a manner as to obliterate the traces of the act?"

The theory is no empty speculation of sensationalism. It derives weight from the fact that it originates with Dr. Matthew Brownfield, of 171, East India Dock-road, who, as the divisional police surgeon of Poplar, made the post-mortem examination of the body found in Clarke's-yard, and who gave evidence at the inquest on Friday. Dr. Brownfield put forward the suggestion on Saturday in an interview with a *Star* reporter.

"I have no doubt at all," said Dr. Brownfield, "that death was caused by strangulation, of which the mark round the neck of the body is the evidence."

There was a disposition on the part of the police to believe, or to affect to believe, that the mark round the which was spoken of at the inquest was

### ONLY A COINCIDENCE

that it was not caused by the act which brought about the woman's death, but that it had been previously inflicted. Our reporter, therefore, put the question,

"Is there any doubt that the mark round the neck was quite recent, and was simultaneous with death?"

—"None whatever. It was a white mark, and there were no signs of "sloughing" or of inflammation coming on around it, as there must have been if it had been borne during life."

"The mark could not have been caused on the day before she died?"

—"Impossible! The cord was pulled round her neck, and was kept there until she was dead. Otherwise there must have been signs of inflammation, as I have said."

"And the other post-mortem appearances?"

### "ALL INDICATED DEATH BY SUFFOCATION.

The left side of the heart was full of fluid black blood—particularly filled and particularly black—and the lungs were gorged with the same fluid black blood, meaning that for the space of several respirations she had not breathed before the heart ceased to pulsate. Looking at the condition of all the organs in conjunction with the mark round the throat, my opinion is that death was caused by strangulation by means of a cord being pulled tightly round the neck."

"From the appearance of the mark, you believe it was a thin cord which caused death, doctor?"

—"I experimented, and have come to the conclusion that it was

### A PIECE OF "FOUR-STRAND" CORD

—not thick cord by any means. With such a piece of cord I could produce a facsimile of that mark upon you. I smelt the stomach, and was unable to find any trace of alcohol at all. Neither should I say from the condition of the organs that she was a woman who was much given to drink."

# Monday, 24 December, 1888

"Do you think, doctor, that the woman met her death anywhere else, and that her dead body was carried to the place where it was found?" - "I think it extremely improbable, considering the great difficulty of carrying a dead body about from one place to another. At the time the body was found death had not taken place more than three-quarters of an hour. I think it very probable she was an immoral woman."

All the facts seemed to combine to one suggestion—that this was the work of the Whitechapel murderer. Our reporter put this to Dr. Brownfield, and it was then that he made the

## NEW AND STARTLING SUGGESTION.

"The question is," he said, "whether there is not another and still more striking point of resemblance. If this murder was the work of the same man the question is whether strangulation is not the beginning of all his operations. Does he strangle or partially strangle them first, and then cut their throats afterwards?"

Then Dr. Brownfield went on to explain why this was likely. "If his object is mutilation," "he said, he could cut their throats so much more cleanly and deliberately. And this would explain, too, how the murderer would be able to do his work without getting covered with blood."

"But, if the other victims had been first strangled would there not be post-mortem indications?"

—"If he

## CUT THE THROAT ALONG THE LINE

of the cord he would obliterate the traces of partial strangulation."

"And in the present case?"

—"The question is whether he did not intend to cut the throat as in the other cases, but was disturbed, and had to leave his work half finished."

The evidence given by Dr. Phillips on 18 Sept. at the Hanbury-street inquest is incontrovertible proof that Annie Chapman was partially strangled before her throat was cut. When Dr. Phillips was called to see the body he found that

## THE TONGUE PROTRUDED

between the front teeth, but not beyond the lips. The face was swollen, the finger-nails and lips were turgid, and in the brain, on the head being opened, he found the membranes opaque and

the veins and tissues loaded with black blood. All these appearances are the ordinary signs of suffocation. In Dr. Phillip's own words, "I am of opinion that the breathing was interfered with previous to death, but that death arose from syncope consequent on the loss of blood following the severance of the throat." Subsequently, under cross-examination, the doctor said, "I am clearly of opinion that the person who cut the deceased's throat took hold of her by the chin and then commenced the incision from right to left." The Coroner asked could that be done so instantaneously and a person

## COULD NOT CRY OUT?

Dr. Phillips—By pressure on the throat no doubt it would be possible.

The Foreman—There would probably be suffocation? Dr. Phillips was understood to express assent.

Here there is everything to support Dr. Brownfield's theory. The woman's throat was cut all round in such a manner that the mark of strangulation must have been completely obliterated.

Of the Whitechapel murders this is the only case in which there is actual proof of strangelation so severe as to leave its traces after death. But in all the other cases the facts are perfectly consistent with the supposition that the murderer first of all seized his victims in the grip of strangler's cord, and having thus effectually prevented them from crying out despatched them with the knife. For in all the cases the throat was so cut that the mark of the cord would have been obliterated and in some of the cases there are circumstances which have never been explained, but which are reconcilable with the theory of strangulation. For instance, in the evidence of Dr. Phillips given at the

## BERNERS-STREET

inquest on 8 Oct., there is the following remarkable passage:—

"I have come to the conclusion, both as regards the position of the victim and that of the perpetrator of the deed, that she was seized by the shoulders and placed on the ground. The murderer was on the right side when he inflicted the cut. The absence of noise is a difficult question to account for. She could not cry out after the cut, but why did she not whilst she was being put on the ground.

537

### I CANNOT ACCOUNT FOR THE ABSENCE OF NOISE."

Dr. Phillips qualified this statement by the suggestion that the woman might have cried out, but without her cries being heard. But, on the other hand, is it not much more likely that there was no cry, and that the reason was that the victim, before being laid down, was rendered by partial strangulation incapable of crying out. In Mitre-square Catherine Eddowes was first laid down on the ground and her throat was afterwards cut. If she had been suddenly seized as the victim of Clarke's-yard was seized, and thus forced upon the ground, there would not necessarily be post mortem indications of the fact.

### WHAT DR. PHILLIPS THINKS

is a matter of direct and most important bearing upon the question because Dr. Phillips, of course, knows more of the medical bearings of the murders than any other man. So *The Star* man called upon the doctor at his surgery in Spital-square. Dr. Phillips was disinclined to express any opinion on the matter to a newspaper man, but from another source our reporter ascertained that Dr. Phillips, as soon as he knew of the Poplar discovery, expressed the opinion that it was

### THE WORK OF THE SAME MAN.

He also recalled at once the fact of the strangulation in the Hanbury-street case. With respect to the other murders Dr. Phillips points out that the retraction of the skin following immediately upon severance of the throat would immediately destroy the marks of the cord supposing it to have been first used. But there is also another and a most important point of resemblance which Dr. Phillips is understood to perceive. He has always maintained the opinion that the murderer was a man of considerable surgical knowledge. In this belief the Poplar case confirms him. "The murderer," he says, "must be a man who had

### STUDIED THE THEORY OF STRANGULATION,

for he evidently knew where to place the cord so as to immediately bring his victim under control. It would be necessary to place the cord in the right place. It would be a very lucky stroke for a man at the first attempt to hit upon the proper place."

Here, then, we arrive at this. That in the opinion of the man who is best qualified to judge the Poplar murderer and the Whitechapel murderer are one and the same man, that the method of preliminary strangulation was certainly employed in Hanbury-street, and was possibly employed in the other cases. Does not this new theory open out a vista of probabilities which, being followed, may lead to the identification of the murderer?

One more word as to the practicability of the theory. Dr. Brownfleld most distinctly asserts that by the employment of a cord arranged on the tourniquet principle the victim could be so suddenly seized as to prevent the possibility of a scream.

~

## Evening News
### THE POPLAR MURDER.
### IDENTIFICATION OF THE DECEASED.
### PROBABLE LOCALITY OF THE CRIME.
### IS THE MURDERER A SAILOR?

The body of the woman found murdered at Clarke's yard, Poplar, has been identified as that of Alice Downey, otherwise "Fair Alice," otherwise "Drunken Liz." Alice Graves, a young woman living at Spitalfields, has stated that she was an acquaintance of the deceased, and last saw her alive with two men at 2.30 on Thursday morning—an hour and three quarters before the body was found.

### THE WOMAN'S HAT.

It has transpired that late on the night of Wednesday or early on Thursday morning, an engineer, whose name has not transpired, while passing along the East India Dock road, near the Eagle Tavern, noticed a woman's hat within the railings of a garden in front of a private dwelling. He thought nothing of the matter at the time, but on hearing of the murder the police were told of the incident, and are carefully following up this slight piece of evidence. It will be remembered that the deceased was without her hat when found in Clarke's yard, therefore this curious discovery sets up a new theory. There were no indications of a struggle in the yard where the woman was found, and serious doubts have arisen as to whether the woman's life was taken in the yard or not. The discovery of the hat which is supposed to have belonged to Downey, in the East India Dock road, shows that the woman must have been helplessly intoxicated or rendered powerless by her assailant or assailants.

### THE MURDER COMMITTED ELSEWHERE.

It is pointed out, and with some degree of reason, that the woman's life may have been taken elsewhere than in Clarke's yard, and that, supposing her assailants to be the two men with whom she was last seen it would have been a very easy task to have carried her from the spot where her hat was found to the yard in which she was discovered. With regard to the manner in which the woman's life was taken, it is supposed that it was done by a sailor, actuated by jealousy. This receives support in many ways.

### A "LAID" CORD.

It is thought from the marks on the neck that the cord used was a "laid" cord, which comprises four plaited strings, which when made is about the thickness of a bootlace. In support of the supposition that a seafaring man is responsible for the death of Alice Downey, it is stated that this would be about the thickness of a lanyard, and the peculiar knots, as described by Dr. Brownfield at the inquest, through which the cord was passed in order to produce strangulation, are such as would be found in a lanyard, while, moreover, the loops at the one end and the knife at the other, would have enabled its owner to bring into play force which could not have possibly been acquired with a piece of string. Furthermore, this would account for the cord being taken away. Regarding the phial which was found in the deceased's possession, together with money and other things, which conclusively prove that robbery was not the motive of the person guilty of this murder, some curious facts have transpired which undoubtedly clear or tend to clear up the mystery surrounding it.

### EVIDENCE AS TO THE PHIAL.

Although the phial was quite empty when found, a medical expert, who has since examined it concludes that it had contained sandal wood oil. A chemist residing in the neighbourhood believed the bottle to have been given to a postman who purchased some sandal wood oil at a large chemist's in the East India Dock road some time before Wednesday last.

### THE PURCHASER WILL BE IDENTIFIED.

It is believed the bottle and also its purchaser can be identified. At the forthcoming adjourned inquest, which is fixed for January 2, some further important medical evidence will be adduced. On this occasion Dr. Harris will then be called, and will give his theory of the murder and certain post mortem inferences arrived at by Dr. Brownfield and corroborated by Dr. Harris will, it is expected, give the case a still more mysterious aspect.

# Monday, 24 December, 1888

**THE IDENTITY QUESTIONED.**

Up to noon today, the latest victim of the murder maniac remained unidentified. Yesterday, several persons visited the mortuary, amongst them a woman named Alice Graves, who stated that she knew the deceased and saw her at 2.30 on Thursday morning. This, however, is not credited, as Graves at first said she saw the woman on Friday morning, which of course was impossible. Inquiries are still being prosecuted by the coroner's officer, Mr. Cheevers, and the police, and it is thought that the deceased belonged to the Whitechapel brigade, and had been driven into Poplar by the fear of "Jack the Ripper." In support of this it may be mentioned that two or three women who have seen the body, state that deceased used to walk Baker's row, Whitechapel, but none of them knew her name or address, though from what deceased had told them it would appear that she lived with her mother somewhere in the district.

~

## The Times
### THE POPLAR MURDER.

The police are said to have succeeded in establishing the identity of the unfortunate woman who was murdered on Thursday last in Clarke's-yard, High-street, Poplar. It would appear that she was known in Poplar by the name of Downey or Downe, and in White-chapel, which it has been discovered was the last neighbourhood in which she lived, by the name of Davis. Both these names have, however, been found to be assumed. The police, after some considerable difficulty, secured the attendance at the Poplar mortuary yesterday of Elizabeth Usher, the head nurse at the Bromley sick asylum, where the deceased woman was stated to have been an inmate.

Miss Usher immediately recognized the woman as Rose Milett or Mylett, who had been an inmate of that institution on several occasions.

There can be but little doubt that the name under which Miss Usher recognized her is her real name, for the books of the asylum were referred to, and it was discovered that she last entered the asylum on the 20th of January, 1888, and discharged herself on the 14th of March last. On each occasion she went under the same name and for treatment of the same disease. The police have found that the woman lived in a common lodging-house in George-street-a thoroughfare in Spitalfields made notorious by the recent attempt to murder a woman in a similar establishment.

~

## Evening News
### THE POPLAR MURDER.
### IDENTIFICATION OF THE VICTIM.

The police have succeeded in finding Mrs. Mylett, the mother of the woman found dead in Clarke's yard, Poplar, a few days ago. The deceased woman had frequently spoken of her mother living somewhere near Baker's row, Whitechapel, and it was near this thoroughfare, in Pelham street, that Mrs. Mylett was found to be residing. When the detectives called at the house on Boxing day they found the inmates indulging in Christmas festivities, and upon their stating the object of their visit one of the women in the house had a serious fit. Upon visiting the mortuary Mrs. Mylett stated that she had no doubt that the body shown her was that of her daughter, and added that she last saw the deceased alive on Sunday week, when she called at Pelham street. The mother had frequently remonstrated with her daughter upon her mode of life, but without avail. Mrs. Mylett, who is an Irishwoman, also stated that her daughter was born in London, and some years ago married, unknown to her parents, a man named Davis, whom Mrs. Mylett believed was an upholsterer by trade. The young couple had one child, but as they often disagreed they separated. The child is now in a school at Sutton, and is about seven years of age. A curious fact in reference to the woman having had a child is that Dr. Brownfield, when at the inquest, expressed the opinion that the deceased had never been a mother.

~

# Saturday, 29 December, 1888

## The Times
### THE POPLAR MURDER.

Nothing in the shape of a clue to the identity of the murderer of the woman Mylett had been obtained up to last night. Dr. Brownfield, the divisional surgeon of police, has not the slightest reason to alter the opinion he expressed at the inquest—namely, that the deceased was foully murdered. The medical men who have been concerned in the inquiry are of the opinion not only that the deceased was murdered, but that the deed was the work of a skilful hand. A second examination of the body was made after the inquest, and on the skin of the neck being removed a quantity of congealed blood was found. This proved that considerable pressure must have been applied from without. It is understood that surprising medical evidence may be expected when the coroner's inquiry is resumed on Wednesday next. A strange feature in connexion with the matter is the fact that when the body was found the mouth was shut, whereas in cases of death by strangulation the tongue is generally found to protrude.

~

## Evening News
### THE POPLAR MURDER.
### THE TWO SAILORS CAN BE IDENTIFIED.

Mr. Charles Ptolomey, whose name was mentioned in our columns yesterday, as having seen two seamen accost the woman near where she was discovered dead, has received a visit from some officers of Scotland yard. Mr. Ptolomey, who is a night attendant at the Poplar Union, made the following statement to a reporter, yesterday:

"Last night some detectives from Scotland Yard came to see me about this mysterious affair. They asked me if I could identify the sailors? I told them I could pick the men out of a thousand. How I came to notice them was in this way: It was about five minutes to eight o'clock on Wednesday night, when I was going to my work. Upon going up England row (nearly opposite Clarke's yard) I noticed two sailors. The shorter one was speaking to the deceased, and the tall one was walking up and down. So strange did it seem that I stopped and 'took account' of them. Then I heard the woman say several times "No! No! No!" and the short sailor spoke in a low tone. The tall one was about 5ft 11in. He looked like a Yankee. The shorter one was about 5ft 7in. It struck me that they were there for no purpose, and that was the reason I took so much notice of their movements. I shall always remember their faces, and could, as I say, pick them out of a thousand. I have been to the mortuary, and seen the deceased. She is the same woman, and she was sober when I saw her with the sailors."

### THE MEDICAL EVIDENCE.

It is understood that sensational medical evidence may be expected when the Coroner's inquiry is resumed on Wednesday next.[323]

---

[323] As these continuations of the Inquest occurred in January, 1889, outside the scope of this work, see Appendix Q, Catherine 'Rose' Mylett Murder, p. 586.

# Emma Smith Murder
## Morning Advertiser
### Monday, 9 April, 1888
### THE HORRIBLE MURDER IN WHITECHAPEL

Mr. Wynne Baxter held on Saturday morning, at the London Hospital, an inquiry into the circumstances attending the death of an unfortunate, named Emma Eliza Smith, who was assaulted in the most brutal manner early on Tuesday morning in the neighbourhood of Osborn-street, Whitechapel.

Mary Russell, the deputy-keeper of a common lodging-house in George-street, Spitalfields, stated that the deceased, who had lived eighteen months in the house, left home on Monday evening in her usual health and returned between four and five next morning, suffering from horrible injuries. The woman told witness that she had been shockingly ill-treated by some men and robbed of her money. Her face was bleeding and her ear cut. Witness took her at once to the London Hospital, passing through Osborn-street on the way, near a spot close to a cocoa factory, which Smith pointed out as the place where the outrage had been committed. Smith, who seemed unwilling to go into details, did not describe the men nor give any further account of the occurrence to witness.

Dr. G.H. Hillier, the house surgeon in attendance on Tuesday morning, when the deceased was brought in, said the injuries which the woman had received were horrible. A portion of the right ear was torn, and there was a rupture of the peritoneum and other internal organs, caused by some blunt instrument. The account given of the occurrence, by the unfortunate woman to the doctor, was that about half-past one o'clock on Tuesday morning, when near Whitechapel Church, she crossed over the road to avoid some men, who followed, assaulted her, robbed her of all the money she had, and then committed the outrage. There were two or three men, one of them looking like a youth of about nineteen. The patient died on Wednesday, about nine a.m., of peritonitis. In reply to questions from the coroner and the jury, the doctor said he had no doubt whatever that death had been caused by the wounds. He had found the other organs generally in a normal condition. The deceased stated that she came from the country, but had not seen any of her friends for ten years.

Another woman subsequently examined as a witness deposed to seeing Smith about a quarter-past twelve on Tuesday morning, near the Burdett-road, talking to a man dressed in dark clothes with a white neckerchief round his neck. She had been assaulted a few minutes before seeing Smith, and was getting away from the neighbourhood, where there had been some rough work that night. Two fellows had come up to her, one asking the time and the other striking her on the mouth, and both running away. She did not think the man talking to Smith was one of her assailants.

Mr. John West, chief inspector of police of the H division, said he had no official information of the occurrence. He had questioned the constables on duty in the Whitechapel-road at the time, but none of them had either seen or heard any such disturbance as that indicated in the evidence, nor had seen anyone taken to the hospital. He would make inquiries as to Osborn-street in consequence of what had transpired at the inquest.

The Coroner, in summing up, said that from the medical evidence, which must be true, it was perfectly clear that the poor woman had been murdered, but by whom there was no evidence to show.

After a short consultation, a verdict of "Wilful murder" against some person or persons unknown was returned by the jury.

~

## The Hoxton Murders
## 𝔗𝔥𝔢 𝔗𝔦𝔪𝔢𝔰
### Thursday, 11 July, 1872
### DOUBLE MURDER AT HOXTON

Yesterday afternoon it was found that two murders had been committed at 46, Hyde-road, Hoxton, the victims being a mother and daughter named Squires, aged respectively 76 and 48, who have for some time past carried on business as stationers at the above address.

It seems that the two women lived alone in the house, which was a leasehold property belonging to the mother, and the shutters were taken down as usual yesterday morning by the daughter, who was seen outside the shop at various times between 9 and 11 o'clock, one person stating positively that he saw the mother standing at her door as late as 12.30.

Be that as it may, about 1.30 p.m. a little boy went into the shop to purchase a newspaper, and seeing no one there leant his arms upon the counter waiting till he could be served, when he observed blood and hair upon the counter and sprinkled over the papers. He rushed out of the house into the coffee-shop next door and told the proprietress what he had seen.

The latter forthwith proceeded to the house, and, looking over the counter, saw the bodies of the two women, dreadfully mutilated, lying in a pool of blood. The police were communicated with, and Mr. Hawthorn, a surgeon, pronounced life in each case to be extinct. On arrival of Inspector Ramsay, of the N Division of Metropolitan Police, a minute examination was made of the premises. Mrs. Squires lay behind the counter, with her head frightfully battered, and resting on her right arm; while the daughter was found, with her head dreadfully injured, lying in the shop parlour, her body in the room, and her legs towards the shop. The whole of the drawers and boxes had been broken open and ransacked, evidently with the intention of robbery. In several rooms the furniture was out of place. A clock which stood in the parlour had been knocked down or otherwise moved from the peg on which it usually hung, and as it had stopped at 12 o'clock, and was in good order and wound up, the presumption is that the murders were committed at that time. The murderer evidently used some heavy blunt instrument,

such as a hammer or iron bar, but no trace of the weapon has yet been discovered, notwithstanding a minute search by the police. It was stated in the last night's evening Papers that a lunatic brother of the younger victim was seen at or near 46, Hyde-road yesterday morning. It has been ascertained, however, that this man had been confined in the lunatic ward of the Shoreditch Workhouse, that he had not left the building the whole day, and that he would receive no benefit from the death of his mother. There seems to be little doubt that robbery was the object, but the police stated late last night that they suspected no one as yet, and had no clue. The case has been placed in the hands of two experienced detectives. From the position in which the bodies were found it is believed that the elder woman was first attacked and knocked down, and that as the daughter ran to her mother's assistance she was met on the threshold of the room and instantaneously killed.

Up to a late hour last night no clue, as far as we could learn, had been obtained.

The bodies now lie at the parish mortuary to await the coroner's inquest, which will be hold tomorrow afternoon by Mr. Humphreys.

—

### Saturday, 20 July, 1872

The ghastly story now slowly unravelling itself in the Coroner's Court at Hoxton is rich in horrors. The ferocity of the murderer appears to have been united with a business-like method which appals while it compels attention. In addition, a certain mystery about the life of the victims, hardly less than about their death, exercises an unwholesome fascination over the public mind. A hundred wild theories are being concocted daily to explain the crime; nor can we wonder at the ingenuity which dwells on the details of the murder, and invents emulous and equally illusive interpretations of the facts. At the present moment, the supply of horrors may be thought fully equal to the demand. Some, however, of the most notable are scarcely ripe for consideration. The pitiable condition of the woman accused of poisoning at Chelmsford has caused a sensible feeling of relief at the suspension of the prosecution; while it is still possible that death from his self-inflicted wounds may save the chief actor in the tragedy at Bermondsey from a Criminal Court. But the elements which at once repel and attract in the

# Appendix B, Hoxton Murders

Hoxton Murders may satisfy the most ardent lover of sensation. The audacity of the criminal in attempting a deed of violence so desperate in an open shop, in a public street, and at noon-day, has indeed, sometimes, though but rarely, been paralleled. Nor is the mystery which surrounds the event greater than envelopes some other famous murders. It is the combination of audacity with the apparent success in escaping which gives an exceptional interest to this attack on two lonely and helpless women.

The inquiry before the Coroner was advanced another stage yesterday, but it is still incomplete, and it has hardly succeeded as yet in finding a clue to the criminal. Meanwhile, no doubt, the Police are at work collecting, weighing, and sifting facts. The information which has been made public hitherto respecting the past lives of the murdered women has been meagre, although the evidence of their nearest relatives and most intimate acquaintances has been taken. What is known may be briefly told. SARAH SQUIRES, an aged widow of eccentric habits, with her daughter, CHRISTIANA, a woman of thirty eight, kept a small print-shop in Hyde-road, Hoxton. Both women seem to have been peculiarly averse from society; they had no intimates, few visitors; they hardly ever accepted assistance in their business or in their domestic affairs, and it was rumoured in the neighbourhood that they were saving money.

A little after 1 o'clock in the afternoon of the 10th instant a boy entered Mrs. SQUIRES' shop to make a small purchase of stationary; the door was half open, and the shop seemed empty; he knocked on the counter, but got no answer. It appears he saw a smear of blood, but it did not occur to him that anything was wrong. Presently he was joined by another lad, who, startled at the silence and the blood, called in the wife of a greengrocer living on the opposite side of the street, and this woman discovered behind the counter the corpse of Mrs. SQUIRES stretched on the floor. The Police were summoned, and the house was carefully examined. In the parlour behind the shop was found the body of the younger victim. Beyond, it was apparent that an attempt had been made to rifle the house; cupboards were found opened and beds disturbed, but the search of the murderer, if seriously intended, had been defeated by its haste, for a considerable sum of money had escaped him. A brutal ferocity had distinguished the attack; the skull had been in each case beaten in by repeated blows from a heavy weapon— nine wounds being counted on the head of the elder and fifteen on that of the younger woman. The wounds were such, according to a medical witness, as might have been inflicted with a plasterer's hammer.

The life of seclusion the two women led makes conjecture as to the motive of the crime the more difficult. Was the brutality a mere incident in a common scheme of robbery, such as might enter the head of any burglar, or does some darker explanation of the crime lurk behind the semblance of a hurried search for plunder? The former theory is supported by the evidence of a witness who deposes that the younger woman had a few days before the murder complained of an attempt at burglary, but had declined a suggestion that they should keep a dog for protection, on the ground that "her mother did not "like dogs." On the other hand, there are some painful passages in the lives of both mother and daughter. The latter, it is stated, has a son living, the fruit of an intimacy long ago terminated by the death of the boy's father. The elder woman was twice married, and has two sons living, one of whom, an imbecile in Shoreditch Workhouse, was at first suspected of some connexion with the outrage. In spite, too, of the seclusion in which the deceased lived they had occasional visitors, and it will be the duty of the Police to investigate the relations between these persons and the victims. The evidence of the illegitimate son of CHRISTIANA SQUIRES, which was taken yesterday, disclosed the fact that the most frequent associates of the deceased women were an old man, formerly a sailor, a friend of the elder victim, and a stonemason, supposed to be a suitor of the younger. The latter is represented to be at present seriously ill, which accounts for his absence from the investigation, but both men, of course, will be called upon to give an account of their proceedings on the day of the murder. One or two persons at whom suspicion at first glanced have been able to do this successfully. In some instances the witnesses at the inquest have been severely crossexamined, but as yet the public, if not the Police, have failed to catch even a probable clue to the real history of the crime.

There is, indeed, a possibility that the deed

may have been dictated by a spirit of revenge, rather than merely inspired by greed and perpetrated by an ordinary burglar. It has but few marks of a London burglary, and differs almost as widely from the commonplace character of that class of crimes as the extravagant criminal fictions which the grotesque genius of EDGAR POE used to revel. To walk at mid-day into a shop in a busy thoroughfare, to beat an old woman's brains out behind the counter, and to finish the work by murdering her daughter in the next room, are hardly the acts of a mere burglar, who, as a rule, has not much more daring or deliberate love of violence than an ordinary area-sneak. We do not forget the evidence of the waggoner who happened to be driving along the street about the time when the murder was discovered. His story is corroborated in its most important particulars by a bystander, which goes to show that at the hour in question a person was seen crossing the road in haste and confusion. This evidence, as containing a possible clue to the mystery, will, doubtless, be carefully sifted, but it may very likely turn out to have nothing in it whatever. The man observed by the waggoner was not seen to leave Mrs. SQUIRES' house, and when he crossed the road the two boys, if they noted the time correctly, were waiting in the shop. It appears probable from the medical evidence that the murders were committed nearly an hour before the occurrence observed by the waggoner, and it is unnecessary to point out the improbability of the murderer dallying so long and so idly on the scene of his crime while subject to so tremendous a risk of detection. It should be added, however, that the evidence of all the witnesses examined on Tuesday and Yesterday is vague and conflicting in its indication of time. By all means let this clue, if there be a clue, be followed; but let not the search for clues in other directions be abandoned. We are all of us interested in the detection of criminals. Life in a great city would be intolerable if it were to be overshadowed by the mystery of undetected and unpunished murder. The capture of MARGUERITE DIBLANC was felt to be a necessary guarantee for the safety of our homes, even in the midst of a crowded capital, from the outbreaks of a tigerish ferocity. The discovery and conviction of the Hoxton murderer will not be less eagerly looked for. For many reasons it is desirable that the suggestion of the jury at the close of yesterday's proceedings be adopted, and the amount of the Government reward increased. If the secret of this horrible affair remains unbroken, timid persons will imagine that there is more danger in a London street than in a country village; instead of which we believe the Londoner to be infinitely better protected than his friends in the country.

# Appendix C, Eltham Murder

## The Eltham Murder
## The Times
### Tuesday, 2 May, 1871
### THE ELTHAM MURDER

The young woman found frightfully muti- lated in Kidbrooke-lane, near Eltham, on Wednesday morning last, expired in Guy's Hospital about half past 9 o'clock on Sunday night. At 3 o'clock on the afternoon of the same day, Inspector Mulvany of the Detective department of Scotland-yard took into custody the son of a very respectable tradesman carrying on business in the town of Greenwich, on suspicion of being the murderer.

From information which has been obtained by our reporter, it appears that the body of the murdered girl has been identified as that of Jane Maria Clenson, aged 17 last Friday, and that she had lived as domestic servant in the family of the father of the accused for a period of a year and ten months. She left this situation a fortnight ago, being pregnant at the time. Her identification was brought about in a singular manner.

At a quarter past 9 on Sunday evening her uncle, William Trott, a lighterman, residing at 6, Agnes-place, Old King-street, Deptford, was reading an account of the outrage in the newspaper, when it struck him that the descript- tion resembled the clothes his niece was in the habit of wearing. Trott and his wife accordingly went to the house, 12, Ashburnham-road, Greenwich, where the deceased had lodged since leaving her situation, and thence to the Blackheath-road Police-station, where they saw Mr. Superintendent Griffin and Inspector Mulvany.

The Superintendent, with Trott and his wife and daughter, proceeded to Guy's Hospital yesterday morning, when they identified the clothing first shown to them, producing a piece of lace to match that round the neck of the deceased's jacket. They were then shown the body, which with great difficulty, owing to the disfigurement, they also identified. They then proceeded to the house of her father, James Clenson, who is a watchman employed at Messrs. Dudgeon's ironworks, Millwall, and resides at 6, Strafford-street, Millwall. The father then went to the hospital and identified the body.

Acting upon information obtained that the deceased, on leaving her lodgings on the night previous to her body being found as stated, had remarked that she was going to meet the son of her late master, the accused was taken into custody at his father's place of business. When told the charge, he declared himself innocent.

He will undergo an examination at the Greenwich Police-court to-day.

~

## The
## Illustrated London News
### Saturday, 22 July, 1871
### THE ELTHAM MURDER TRIAL

The trial of Edmund Walter Pook for the murder of Jane Maria Clousen, at Eltham, which terminated in a verdict of acquittal, has furnished material for painful reflection, which may, however, be turned to good account. We do not refer to the fearful crime in relation to which it was held. All that need be said of that is that it remains unpunished and its perpetrator unde- tected. There will be no occasion, therefore, to revive the emotions of horror which the facts connected with it, when first published, stirred in everybody's mind. The few observations which follow concern only the means adopted by the prosecution to bring home the guilt of it to the man who lately stood a "prisoner at the bar." It is hardly too much to say that a portion of the evidence elicited during the progress of the trial touches at a vital point the interests of every member of the English community. Through a momentary, and we may say accidental, rift in the haze which enveloped the subject-matter of the legal investigation at the Old Bailey last week, a glimpse was obtained by the public of the machinery usually resorted to for the purpose of ascertaining the perpetrators of serious, and especially of extraordinary, crimes, which might well excite in us, not merely humiliation, but mistrust and fear.

The fact that all the steps preliminary to the actual trial in court taken in reference to great offences against the law—the search for evidence, the weaving it into a theory consistent in all its parts, the arrangement of information with the object of effectively establishing that theory, the choice and rejection of witnesses, and all matters of a cognate kind—are committed—or we may more correctly say are left—to the responsibility of the police ought to have been no new discovery to any intelligent Englishman in these days; and, perhaps, to a large majority was not. Questioned on the point, most people would probably admit that they were not unaware of the fact, though they had seldom, if ever, considered what it involves. The Eltham murder trial has forced it into notice. The spirit and manner of the police in their attempts to trace the death of Jane Maria Clousen to Edmund Walter Pook, as disclosed in court, and commented upon by the Lord Chief Justice and by the counsel on both sides, show that there is no man's life that may not be jeopardised at some time or other in its ordinary progress by this feature of administering criminal law. Now we disclaim, *in limine*,[324] any suspicion of the police as a body. We willingly credit them with fair, honest, and laudable motives, taking for granted that in so large a number of men there will be an average proportion of individual exceptions. But it by no means follows that because in the exercise of their constabulary functions they come up to a high standard of merit they are qualified to assume the direction of prosecutions for criminal offences. Indeed, when the subject comes to be thought upon, the presumption will be found to lie the other way.

Bodies of men, organised and disciplined as are the police, are actuated strongly by an *esprit de corps*. They emulate each other in the discharge of their official duties, and are jealous of the reputation of their comrades. They are not, however, men of refined culture. They are not conversant with human nature at its best. Their imagination has to manipulate coarse and foul materials; and their prejudices render them extremely sceptical of innocence whenever a public charge has been made. All this, which may very well suit the performance of their pro per work as constables, unfits them to guide with discrimination the conduct of a prosecution which should be as judicial in its character as the trial to which it leads. We do not say that in the case of the accused Walter Pook there was

on the part of the police, regarded as prosecutors, any deliberate and wilful attempt to mislead the Court and the jury—any conscious effort to tamper with the evidence which they had collected, or which had been brought before them. But their bias was most perceptibly in aid of the supposed clue hastily seized hold of by them in the first instance. By its consistency or inconsistency with the theory they had formed of Pook's guilt they judged of the worth or worthlessness of facts as evidence, and gave them prominence or thrust them aside accordingly. Having apprehended their man, they naturally looked about for further evidence in support of their conjecture that he was the criminal; and if they felt a stronger desire than other men would have done to bring out a result in harmony with their first proceedings, the ill-chosen position, rather than the dishonest character, of the men must bear the chief blame. It is an infirmity of nobler minds than theirs to be less anxious to find themselves on the side of truth than to find the truth on their side.

One cannot, however, contemplate the possibilities which might have accrued from this cause in Pook's case without becoming very unpleasantly conscious of the perils to which the reputation and life of Englishmen are exposed. It is not at all an extreme improbability that a man may find himself in contact with a web of circumstances which will throw a shadow of suspicion upon him in relation to some event of which he has not the smallest knowledge. At any time of his life any man may be in the closest proximity to the site upon which a fearful tragedy is being simultaneously enacted, and a little ingenuity, guided by a foregone conclusion, may point him out as the apparent agent in the violation of the law. We need to be assured that, if such a calamity should befall us, we are in no peril of being made the victims of other men's prejudices or of their professional pride. It is of the last importance to us that the facts relating to an event which momentarily clouds our fair name should immediately come under the preliminary consideration of an impartial and judicial mind, and that there should exist no motive on the part of any public authority charged with the collation of those facts, and with the responsibility of drawing from them conjectural inferences, to prefer any imaginable result to another. It is

---

[324] **In Limine**. Lat. At the beginning, on the threshold. In law, a motion made at the beginning of a trial requesting that the judge rule that certain evidence may not be introduced. (Law.com, 2015)

# Appendix C, Eltham Murder

proverbial that human conclusions are generally more or less coloured by human inclinations, and it is not a safe state of things when, in the ordinary motives by which men are actuated, the bias of a prosecutor is towards the establishment of the guilt of the accused, which, without imputing to them any heinous offence, may be generally alleged in the case of prosecutions by the police.

Not a few circumstances have occurred of late to indicate the expediency of appointing officers, unknown as yet to the English law, upon whom should be devolved the responsibility of conducting all prosecutions for public offences. Of all people, perhaps, Englishmen are the most conservative of their particular customs, and they are in no respect more conservative than in whatever relates to the administration of justice.

Doubtless, they have reason to be proud of the machinery and of the rules by which justice is administered in the vast majority of cases; but the proceedings involved in the process are unquestionably capable of improvement. They have but to look around them to become cognisant of many particulars in which they may glean useful hints from the practices of their neighbours. They need not resort to meddlesome methods. They need not give up the maxim of law which assumes every man's innocence until his guilt has been proved. They need do nothing more than open their eyes and use their common-sense, and we think they all but inevitably reach the conclusion that one of the greatest defects of legal procedure in this country is the non-existence of a public prosecutor.

~

# Appendix D, Cannon St. Murder

## The Cannon St. Murder
## The Telegraph
### Friday, 15 June, 1866
### THE CANNON STREET MURDER.

When, after a trial for murder that has lasted two days, a jury, without deliberating for two minutes, return a verdict of Not Guilty, it is tolerably certain that an innocent man has been most unjustly and most wantonly accused. The atrocity in Cannon street will probably be added to the long catalogue of undiscovered crimes; and to-day we have only to congratulate the public that the greatest crime of all—that which is sometimes perpetrated in the name and by the sanction of the law—has happily been foiled. It is sad enough that poor Sarah Milson has been slain by the hand of some desperado; it would have been sadder still had the man Smith[325] perished by the hands of the executioner. Let no one think that we are speaking of a danger which is imaginary. But for the generous aid of a few friends, the fellow would in all probability have been convicted. Had he been a foreigner, or a poor homeless tramp, it would have gone hard with him; his confused protestations of innocence would have been discredited; the written proof of his relations with the victim would have told against him with overwhelming weight; and the direct, absolute, point-blank evidence to his identity given by a nervous woman, would probably have sufficed to send him to the gallows. Smith, however, thought a lazy, graceless, dissipated *vaurien*, seems to have had the fortunate gift of making friends; he came of a hard-working and respectable family; and partly for their sakes, and partly for his own, his neighbours determined that he should not be left without help in his hour of need. The case that seemed so strong against him was carefully sifted—sifted, we may fairly say, until scarcely a grain of it was left. The chain of accusation was tested link by link, and link by link it snapped.

We shall not recapitulate the whole of the story; but there are two little sketches of incident and character which we are bound to place in juxtaposition, Let us first look at Cannon street on the night of Wednesday, April 11.

Business has long been over; and in one of the largest warehouses two women are left by themselves. One of these, Sarah Milsom, the housekeeper, has certain society of her own; has strange relations with men who call for her at night, who threaten her, who send her menacing letters. She has debts, not large in themselves, but considerable for a woman in her position, and contracted for some reason as yet unexplained. At a little after nine o'clock the bell of the front door rings. Milsom tells her companion, Elizabeth Lowes, the cook, that the visit is for her, and she goes down stairs. A whole hour elapses, and at length the cook, growing nervous, takes a candle, and proceeds in search of her companion. At the bottom of the stairs she finds her—senseless. She flings open the door; she sees a woman standing there apparently for shelter from the rain The woman hurries away, Lowes gives the alarm, and a policeman finds that Sarah Milsom is covered with blood, and dead. Five minutes before the cook went down stairs, a Mrs Arabella Robbins, housekeeper at the warehouse next to that of Messrs Bevington, was returning home; as she rang her bell, she heard Bevington' door violently slammed; a man came on and passed her hurriedly. The night was wet and dark, but the light from a lamp fell upon him; he gave her a "side-look" their eyes met; and she has since sworn, solemnly that the man was William Smith.

We shift the scene to Eton and Windsor. At a quarter-past seven on the same evening Smith left off work in the shop of a respectable hatter, who had carried on business there for twenty years. He quitted the shop in company with his master's son; for, lazy and unprincipled as he was, he seems to have had some redeeming qualities which made him popular amongst his associates. When they parted, Smith said he was going to Slough Turnpike, and he set off in that direction. At half-past seven, or a few minutes later, he was met by John Whitehouse, a thoroughly trustworthy witness, who, called for the prosecution, really helped to clinch the defence. At eight o'clock the accused was seen, coming from Slough Turnpike by Gabriel Wood, butler to one of the masters of Eton College. At twenty minutes past eight he was back in Eton, and met young Harris and some of his other associates. They walked into Windsor,

---

[325] William Smith.

551

# Appendix D, Cannon St. Murder

strolled about, and then adjourned to Wheeler's beer shop. There some of them began to play cards for pints of ale; but Smith, saying he had no money, simply looked over young Harris's hand, and gave him advice about his play. At ten minutes past ten, the exact time when Mrs Robbins swears she saw Smith in Cannon-street, young Harris bade him good night at Eton. Smith still remained at Wheeler's. The lads who were with him might have been better engaged, no doubt, than in drinking beer and playing cards; but they were honest-looking English youngsters, fond of playing cricket on the Brocas, and apparently not a jot worse than lads in a little country town are apt to be. Some of them had gone with one Holderness to get a pair of boots mended; and the cobbler, when examined, swore to the time and the night. After Harris's departure, Smith stayed at the beerhouse till eleven, when they all had to leave, and then he walked towards home with Dodner, from whom he borrowed twopence. It was at this time that he most have been seen by a county constable named Clarke, whom we earnestly recommend to the particular attention of his superiors, for a constable with a more convenient and elastic memory never wore a blue coat. With twopence in his pocket, Smith determined to finish his evening at another beershop, which did not close quite so early as Wheeler's. Accordingly, at a quarter past eleven,

he entered Goddard's, and there he met Stone, a baker, with whom he had not lately been on friendly terms. They made up their quarrel, however, and chatted about the City and Suburban race, which was to come off at Epsom next day. That night it so happened that Mrs Goddard had been to some amateur theatricals; on returning she saw Smith, and she served him with a pint of beer. The borrowed twopence being thus spent, and no more liquor forthcoming, Smith walked home, was let in by his sister, and went quietly to bed, little dreaming that his "loafing" propensities would ever stand him in such good stead as they have done. For it should be observed, that if on this rainy night he had stayed with his mother and sisters, *their* evidence would have been fairly viewed with a certain degree of suspicion. But he took a walk in the rain, and he was recognised by a couple of men whose veracity is unimpeachable. He went to a beer-shop, and he was accompanied by lads whose truthfulness there is not the slightest reason to suspect. And finally, to guard (?) against Constable Clarke, it so befell that his thirsty nature led him to take a stirrup cup at Goddard's, in the presence of Mrs Goddard and of Stone. Fifteen witnesses in all were summoned for the defence; and a more conclusive *alibi* was never established in a court of justice.

~

## The Great Coram Street Murder

### The Times

#### Thursday, 26 December, 1872
#### SUPPOSED MURDER

Yesterday afternoon about 3 o'clock, a shocking discovery was made at No.12, Great Coram-street, Russell-square. The second-floor back room was occupied by a girl named Clara Bruton, said to be connected in some way with a theatre. As she did not come downstairs, and as no answer was returned to calls, the landlady had the door broken open. The girl was then found to be quite dead, her thro at having been severely cut. Spots of blood were detected in different parts of the room, the bed exhibiting a dreadful appearance. The door had been locked on the outside and the key removed, but no marks of blood could be seen there. On the forehead of the deceased there was an indentation apparently caused by a thumb and a little further down the print of a hand. It transpired that on the previous night the deceased was visited by a German, who left the house after other occupants had gone to bed. Inquiries are being actively prosecuted by the police.

—

#### Thursday, 27 December, 1872
#### THE CORAM-STREET MURDER

The tragedy in Great Coram-street, mentioned in *The Times* of yesterday, proves beyond doubt to be a most atrocious murder. The facts are given in a few words. The victim appears to have eked out a living on the stage as a member of the *corps de ballet* by aid of prostitution, and her murderer is supposed to be a man described as a "German gentleman" who met her in the street, and accompanied her to her lodgings. The girl's name is Clara Boswell (not Burton or Buswell), and she was 27 years of age. She was a good-looking girl, and what is known is that she came home late on Christmas-eve and went direct to her room on the second-floor back of No.12, Great-Coram-street. She returned to the lower part of the house and said that she had brought a gentleman with her, and gave the landlady a half-sovereign from which to take 9s. rent. She received a shilling change and then went back to her room. Nothing more was heard until the morning, when the man was heard to go out early. The tenant of the room not moving hour after hour, the room was on Christmas afternoon burst open, and the woman was found in the bed with her throat cut. The murderer stabbed the poor girl under the left ear, and there is another wound on the left of the wind-pipe large enough to put a man's fist in. The object of the murderer was evidently to possess himself of what trinkets and money the girl possessed, for earrings which she had borrowed to wear were not to be found; and a purse into which she was seen to put the shilling change was also missing. The murderer might have supposed that a person living in so respectable a locality would have some booty, hence the crime. Superintendent Thomson, who has had much experience as a detective officer, is in charge of the district in which the murder was committed, and he at once set upon the task of tracking out the murderer. It is believed that this will be accomplished, for the man is said to have gone into a fruit shop with the girl, and must have blood upon his garments, for the wounds inflicted are very awful. Death must have quickly followed, for the body is drawn up as from the convulsion of the sinews caused by pain. The murderer washed his hands, and, locking the door after him, took the key. The appearance of the person who left the house after the inmates had gone to bed is thus described:—"He is about 23 years of age, 5ft. 9in. high, with neither beard, whiskers, nor moustache, but not having shaved for two o r three days, his beard when grown would be rather dark. He has a swarthy complexion, and blotches or pimples on his face. He was dressed in dark clothes, and wore a dark brown overcoat down to the knees, billycock hat, and rather heavy boots." The body was yesterday removed to St. Giles's Workhouse, and was identified by the deceased's brother, who comes from Berkshire, of which county it is said the girl was a native. The inquest will be held today.

~

# The 4, Burton-Crescent Murder

## The Times

**Friday, 13 December, 1878**
*MURDER.*

Yesterday morning, between 1 and 2 o'clock, a terrible discovery was made at 4, Burton-crescent, Euston-road. For some time past Mrs. Rachel Samuels, a widow, a Jewess, has lived in that house, letting a portion of it to a Bohemian musician. It was understood that she had amassed a large sum of money and kept it hoarded about the premises, and in the neighbourhood she was said to be excessively parsimonious.

This impression was strengthened by the fact that, notwithstanding the large size of the house, she kept no regular servant. A girl used to come in each morning and leave at night, and the deceased lady closed the door on her and went to bed. Her lodger came home from his professional duties about 1 o'clock in the morning. During the past month the house has been under repair, and it is stated that the workmen finished the job and quitted the house for good at 3 o'clock on Wednesday afternoon last.

The lodger returned as usual at 1 in the morning, bolting the front door and going straight upstairs to his supper. Shortly afterwards he went down into the kitchen, and there found Mrs. Samuels lying dead with frightful wounds on her head and face. He ran out of the house for the police, and Dr. Kendrick, of Woburn-square, and afterwards Dr. Hutchinson of Woburn-place, were called in.

In addition to the wounds on Mrs. Samuels' head and face, there were great bruises on the arms and hands. The wounds had been inflicted with some blunt instrument. Behind a screen in the room was a large billet of wood with nails in it, and upon this billet were found blood and hair. This, no doubt, was the instrument with which the murder was committed.

Chief Inspector Le Maye and some reserve men from Hunter-street then went over to the premises. Blood was found from the kitchen to the fourth or fifth stair leading from the basement, and it is assumed that Mrs. Samuels was struck while on the stairs and dragged into the kitchen. The murderer probably got into the house by means of a skeleton or duplicate key. Mrs. Samuels was a woman of nerve, and it is probable that on hearing the crash of glass she went down to ascertain the cause. Seeing the murderer, she fled, and had reached the fifth stair when she was stuck down. The blow was a careless, clumsy one, and had to be repeated till the breath had been beaten out of the victim's body. The murderer went into the next room to wash his blood-stained hands at the sink (where evidence of such washing was found), and had smeared his blood-stained fingers all over the dresser and sink.

The motive of the crime is supposed to have been plunder, but, so far as could be ascertained after the visit of Superintendent Williamson and other Scotland-yard investigators, nothing is missing.

No particular person is suspected at present, at least so the police say, but there is one fact to which their attention has been drawn. For some days past a man of about 50 years of age has been seen loitering near the house and behaving in so suspicious a manner that he attracted the attention of the police. The murder was committed yesterday morning, and yesterday, for the first time, this man has been absent.

—

**Saturday, 14 December, 1878**
**THE MURDER IN BURTON-CRESCENT.**

Last night Dr. Hardwicke, the Coroner for Central Middlesex, opened an inquiry at the Silver Cup Tavern, Cromer-street, Gray's-inn-road, as to the circumstances attending the death of Mrs. Rachel Samuels, aged 75, who was found murdered at 4, Burton-crescent, Euston-road, on the morning of Thursday last, as already reported.

The first witness was Mr. Judah Samuel, of 32, Store-street, W.C., son of the deceased, who identified the body. The deceased, he said, was the widow of a diamond merchant, who died six years ago. He saw her on Saturday last, when she was in excellent health. He was called on Thursday morning to 4, Burton-crescent, by his mother's lodger, who said, "Your mother has been found murdered in her kitchen." Witness called on his brother, and they all went back to the house. The lodger opened the door with his key, and on going downstairs he saw his mother lying in the kitchen, quite dead, and covered

# Appendix F, 4, Burton-Crescent Murder

with blood. The witness at once obtained a doctor who said, she had been dead about two hours. The time then was 12·30 on the Thursday morning. He noticed that the deceased had no boots on and was very much injured.

John Francis Borschidjki, professor of music, said that he had lodged with the deceased for two years, and had the back parlour and the top back room. He took his breakfast and supper there. On Thursday morning, about 12·5, he went home and found the parlour gas alight, but his supper was not spread as usual. He went downstairs, and in the kitchen found Mrs. Samuels, lying dead. He at once went to the house of the son, as stated.

By the CORONER.—He had left the house on the previous morning as usual. The deceased was generally in bed when he returned home at night. The deceased had a servant, who came in every day. Formerly the deceased had a servant named Mary Donovan, who had been in her service for 10 years. Another lodger, named Cooke, had left the house some time previously.

Fanny White, 136, Ossulston-street, Somerstown, said the deceased told her that "Mary and Kate had been to see her the night before" (the night before the murder). "Mary" was Mary Donovan, now in custody. The deceased said that the lodger had opened the door to Mary on the Tuesday. Kate was the sister of Mary.

The previous witness, recalled, said that on Tuesday night he opened the door to Mary Donovan. She was half intoxicated, and went down to see the deceased. Mrs. Samuels subsequently said to him that Mary was intoxicated. He did not see Kate Donovan, the sister. Mrs. Samuels told the witness that she scolded Mary for coming intoxicated and so late.

William Johns, 468 E, said that he was called to the house by the lodger, who told him that Mrs. Samuels was murdered. They went there with the first witness and his wife, and found the deceased lying on her back, dead. He, however, at once went to Dr. Kendrick, who came to the house immediately.

Dr. Phineas Kendrick, of Tavistock-square, said that he was called by the last witness, and found the deceased lying dead. Her hands were clinched, the face looking as though it had been rubbed over with dirty fingers. The right eye was blackened, and there were two incised wounds at the back of the head, penetrating to the bone. The wounds were five inches in length, and had been inflicted with some blunt instrument. He looked for the instrument, but there was only a knife smeared with blood. The piece of broken wood was discovered subsequently, but he was sure that those pieces of wood could not have inflicted the wounds. A blunt hatchet might have done it.

Mr. Le Maye, Chief Inspector at Hunter-street, said that when called to the househe made a thorough examination, and found that there were traces of blood from the kitchen stairs to the kitchen itself. There was some water and smears as though an attempt had been made to mop up the blood. He found the area door window broken from the inside with marks of blood upon it. There was blood in the sink, and a pail in the sink with blood upon it. He found no trace of any person having escaped from the house by the area door, the roof, or the back. He found the piece of broken wood, a hat rail, and it appeared as though blood had been washed off it. in fact, most of the blood had been washed up with an old house flannel, which was found lying by the side of the body.

The girl White identified the flannel as one which she had used on the Wednesday.

Mr. Le Maye said that he found no evidence of disorder in the house. The boots of the deceased had not been traced. In her pocket was found a handkerchief and her keys, but no money.

By Mr. Samuels.—Some money was supposed to have been taken from her, as about two or three pounds were missing. The boots missing were new felt boots with fur tops and shiny toe-caps.

Dr. Francis Hutchinson, of Woburn-place, he divisional surgeon of police, deposed that he accompanied the last witness to the house and found the body and appearances as described. The scalp wounds had probably been inflicted with the rail. There were punctured wounds on the face and hands, probably inflicted with the nails in the hat rail. The rail had blood upon it and some light coloured hair, tallying with the hair of the deceased. The house flannel had no doubt been used for the purpose described. On making a *post-mortem* examination, he found that there was no fracture of the school, but a considerable effusion of blood beneath the

# Appendix F, 4, Burton-Crescent Murder

whole of the scalp. The lungs, heart, and liver were healthy. He believed that the cause of death was concussion of the brain and haemorrhage. He believed that she had fought for her life, and that the struggle continued so long as she had any life in her. He felt quite certain that the murder was committed with the hat rail.

INSPECTOR Kerley, of the detective department, said that he received information that the woman, Mary Donovan, had been left in the house with the deceased at 8·30, on Wednesday evening, and Mary Donovan had been arrested and taken to Bow-street. He found her at 42, Lancaster-road, Notting-hill, and she admitted that she had been present on the Wednesday night. He found spots of blood on her dress, which she said were ironmould. There were also spots of blood on her petticoat.

Inspector Andrew Landsdowne said that he had ascertained that on the night of the murder Mary Donovan was away all night, and had been drinking to excess since the previous Sunday. No property of the deceased was found on her, and when she was charged with the wilful murder of the deceased she said she was entirely innocent.

At this stage of the proceedings the inquiry was adjourned until Monday next, at 4 o'clock, when the verdict will be given.

Mary Donovan will be charged before the Bow-street magistrate to-day with the wilful murder of Mrs. Samuels.

.~

## The Echo
### Saturday, 14 December, 1878
### THE MURDER AT
### BURTON-CRESCENT.
### EXAMINATION AT BOW-STREET.

Mary Donovan, 40 years of age, an ill-looking woman, was brought up before Mr. Flowers charged with the wilful murder of Rachel Samuels, at 4, Burton-crescent, between eight p.m. on the 11th and one a.m. on the 12th instant. Superintendent Williamson made a statement of the facts of the case afterwards detailed in evidence. Mr. Abrams defended the prisoner.

John Francis Boschedzky deposed—I am a professor of music, living at 4, Burton-crescent. I have lodged there two years. I went home a little after twelve. My supper things were not ready. I went into the kitchen and found Mrs. Samuels lying on the floor. I thought she had fainted. I shook her and found blood on her. I then went to deceased's son at Store-street. He came back with me with a policeman. We found Mrs. Samuels in the same place. I cannot say that she was dead when I first saw her, but I thought she was. I have often seen the prisoner there. She had not been lately. I opened the door for the prisoner on Tuesday last. She used to do the cleaning for Mrs. Samuels. She had been ten years in her service, but had since been married. I cannot say that the deceased had money in her house. I had paid her 3 pounds odd for rent.

Cross-examined by Mr. Abrams—Deceased was much attached to prisoner. The only complaint she made was that prisoner was in the habit of drinking. I went out at a quarter-past ten on Wednesday. I left a servant-girl and Mrs. Samuels in the house. I did not know Mrs. Samuels was going to discharge her.

Francis Hutchinson, F.R.C.S.[326]—I was called on Thursday evening, between two and three o'clock, to 4, Burton-crescent. I found Mrs. Samuels lying on the floor. There was a large quantity of blood on her clothes. I found two scalp wounds. I passed my finger round her head, but there was no fracture. The forehead was much bruised. Her hands were also much bruised, as if they had been pressed to the head to prevent the blows. I examined the house with the

---

[326] **F.R.C.S.**, Fellow of the Royal College of Surgeons.

# Appendix F, 4, Burton-Crescent Murder

inspector, and found blood in the lower part of the house. There were some marks of blood on the staircase, which had been wiped up. I went to the sink and found someone had washed their hands. The two pieces of wood produced were found by the inspector. The wood has been broken in two. The blows might have been inflicted by the wood. There is some blood and human hair on both pieces. I made a post-mortem examination. Beneath the scalp was a quantity of blood. The deceased appeared to be a healthy woman. The blows inflicted upon her would doubtless have caused death. She must have been stunned by the blows, and died afterwards. I should say she had been dead four hours.

Cross-examined by Mr. Abrams—Deceased was in front kitchen, lying on her back. Her head was not pointed to the fire. The kitchen has a stone floor. The wounds were very severe.

Inspector Kerley, E Division—About twelve o'clock yesterday I went to No. 12, Lancaster-street, Borough-road, in company with Inspector Landsdowne. I knocked at the door; it was opened by a woman, who called out, "Mrs. Donovan, you are wanted." The prisoner came downstairs. I said I wished to speak to her privately. We went upstairs to the first floor back room. There was a man in the room. The prisoner said, "Donovan, there is someone wants to speak to you." I said, "No, I want to speak to you. We are two police officers, and we are going to say something to you, and I want you to be very particular in what you say, as it might be given in evidence against you." I told her there had been a murder in Burton-crescent. Mrs. Samuels was murdered on Wednesday night, and I am told you were the last person who was seen in the house that night. She hesitated a moment and said, "Yes, I was there; I went to get the address of my sister. I was also there the night before, and then I went to get the address of my sister. I also cut Mrs. Samuels' toe nails." I said, "Which night?" She replied, "Wednesday night. The lodger let me in on Tuesday night, and it was the next night I cut her nails. I was there about eight or half-past, a gentleman came and knocked at the door, and asked to look at some apartments. Mrs. Samuels gave me some things to wash. She gave me part of the things and said, "If you will wait until the gentleman has gone, I will give you the others." He stopped so long that

Mrs. Samuels said, "You can fetch me a haddock, and I will give you the things another night." I went out to get the haddock, but could not get one, and got a bloater instead, which I gave to Mrs. Samuels. The gentleman was then in the parlour. Mrs. Samuels knew him. He looked like a plasterer or paperhanger. I then came away, leaving the man in the house." I asked her if she had seen anyone in the house besides. She said, "Yes, there were two women came about a situation, but they went before I did." I asked her what shawl she wore that night. She pointed to one at the foot of the bed, and said, "That one." Lansdowne and I examined it, and thought we could see one mark of blood. I then asked what dress she wore that night. She said, "The one I have on." I said, "Let me look." She came up, and I told her to turn round to the window. On the front part of the dress there were stains which I considered to be blood. I said, "What are those stains?" at the same time pointing to the dress. She said, "That's ironmould." I told her I had no doubt it was blood, and took her into custody. I had previously told her that Mrs. Samuels had been murdered. She said, "I am not afraid"—and repeated it several times. Sergeant Fordham was then called in and took charge of the prisoner, while Landsdowne and I searched the premises. I saw Landsdowne find a black skirt on the bed with stains upon it which he thought were blood. Prisoner said, "You will never find any blood on that." She was then brought to Bow-street Police-station in a cab, and handed over to a female searcher to be searched. The charge was read over to her, and she was told she would be charged in the morning. She only replied, "Oh, in the morning."

Mr. Abrams deferred the cross-examination of Inspector Kerley for another occasion.

This being the only evidence proposed to be given at present, the case was adjourned to this day week.

(The *Daily Chronicle*, 11 January, 1879, reported that Mary Donovan was discharged from custody by order of Magistrate Flowers due to lack of evidence.)

# The 12, Burton-Crescent Murder

## The Times

### Tuesday, 11 March, 1884
### MURDER IN BURTON-CRESCENT.

A young woman was found dead in a house in Burton-crescent, Euston-road, on Sunday after-noon, in circumstances which leave little doubt that a deliberate murder had been committed. It appears that the house, No. 12, Burton-crescent, is let out in furnished apart-ments, mostly to young women, and the occupant of the back room on the first floor was a young woman about 24 years of age, known as Annie Yates.

On Saturday night she went out as usual with a fellow lodger, named Annie Ellis, who parted from her in the Euston-road, about 1 o'clock on Sunday morning, when Yates got into conversation with a respectably-dressed man. Shortly before 2 o'clock, as it was believed, Yates was heard to come home and go up to her room by some of the other lodgers, and the footsteps of a man were distinctly heard accompanying her.

Somewhere about 3 o'clock, it is believed, a man and woman who were occupying an adjoining room were roused by hearing screams proceed from the room occupied by Annie Yates, but no notice was taken of the circumstance, as she was subject to fits of hysteria, and frequently made similar noises. A considerable time after-wards the footsteps of a man were heard going downstairs, and he let himself out by the front door, but this was not an uncommon occurrence, and it attracted no particular attention.

As Yates did not come down to get her breakfast as usual, between 12 and 1 o'clock on Sunday afternoon Ellis went up to her room to call her, and, finding the door partly open, went in, but could see nothing of Yates. The bed-clothes appeared to be piled up on something, and on looking more attentively the woman Ellis saw a foot with a boot on protruding from under the clothes at one side of the bed. On her removing the bedclothes a terrible sight pre-sented itself. The young woman Yates, only partially undressed, lay with her head on the pillow in a pool of blood, which had issued from a serious gash on the left side of the head, above the ear, while a towel was tied tightly over her mouth, the knot being at the back of the head.

Ellis immediately raised an alarm, and the landlady of the house, Mrs. Apex, hearing what had occurred, sent at once for medical aid and to the police station of the E Division in Hunter-street. Dr. Richard Paramore, of 18, Hunter-street, was the first to arrive, and was speedily followed by Inspector Blatchford, who also sent for Dr. Murphy, of Brunswick-square, the divisional police surgeon. The unfortunate woman was pronounced to have been dead several hours. The face was very livid, and a severe wound had been inflicted at the back of the left ear. It was the opinion of the medical men that the actual cause of death was suffocation. They considered it impossible that the injuries could have been self-inflicted.

The police made a searching examination of the room to ascertain, if possible, with what sort of instrument the wound to the head had been inflicted, but nothing was found. A gold ring, which Yates was known to have worn Saturday night, was gone, but money was found in her clothes. Inspector Langrish, of Bow-street Station, was subsequently associated with Inspector Blatchford in pursuing the police inquiries.

On Sunday evening the body was removed to St. Pancras mortuary, where it remains to await a coroner's inquest by Dr. Danford Thomas, the Central Middlesex coroner, to whom information has been forwarded. A *post-mortem* examination was made yesterday afternoon, and the medical evidence points to the fact that the blow upon the head of the deceased was not self-inflicted, and it is regarded as certain that suffocation was the cause of death. The inquest will be held to-morrow.

It has been suggested that the case is not one of murder, but that the deceased struck her head against the iron bedstead, causing the wound to the head, that her companion bound the wound up with a towel to stop the bleeding, and that after this the towel slipped down over the deceased's mouth, and thus caused her to be suffocated.

The police, from information in their posse-ssion, have circulated the following description of a man supposed to be the murderer of Annie

Yates.—"A man, age 35, fair, medium height, dressed in black felt hat, brown cutaway coat, respectable appearance, who stole an old dark brown leather purse with clasp, containing 3s. and a 9-carat gold finger ring with three stones, a turquoise in centre and a pearl on each side."

—

**Wednesday, 12 March, 1884**
**THE BURTON-CRESCENT MURDER.**

During yesterday afternoon the St. Pancras mortuary was visited by a large number of persons anxious to view the body of the young woman who was murdered at No. 12, Burton-crescent, in circumstances reported in *The Times* of yesterday, and who was known there by the name of Annie Yates or Yeates, in order to speak to her identity, as it is believed that name was assumed to hide from relatives or friends the life she was leading. One woman was almost certain that the deceased was a young woman named Marshall who had lodged with her two years ago, who had a situation at a West-end dressmaker's, and whose friends reside somewhere in Hertford-shire, but no one could speak positively upon the subject. With the same object a photograph has been taken, but the face is much swollen and so altered that some of her immediate companions say they would hardly recognize her.

It would appear impossible for the deceased to have tied the towel over her mouth with the knots at the back of the head, inasmuch as she was paralyzed in the left arm and side. Up to last evening no clue had been obtained by the police as to the man who accompanied the unfortunate woman to her lodgings, the meagre description obtained rendering her identity exceedingly difficult. Inspectors Langrish and Blatchford have been unremitting in their endeavours to trace out the authors of the letters which were found in the deceased's room, and have been succeeded, but have ample evidence that none of the writers were in the vicinity of Burton-crescent on Saturday night or Sunday morning. Nearly every pawnbroker in the metropolis has been visited, but no trace of the ring the deceased was wearing on Saturday night has been found.

## Leaves of a Life:
### Being the Reminiscences of Montagu Williams,
### Volume 2
### Chapter XVI.
### Fallacis Semita Vita[327]

**Trial of Hannah Dobbs—Habits of the deceased—Evidence of the Bastindoffs—A blood-stain on the carpet—The cash-box, the book of dreams, and the jewellery—Finding the body in the cellar—The relationship between Hannah Dobbs and her master—Bastindoff prosecuted for perjury—The evidence against him—An altered beard—**
**The defence—Verdict and sentence.**

On the 2nd and 3rd of July, 1879, a somewhat extraordinary trial for murder took place in the new Court of the Old Bailey, before Mr. Justice Hawkins. I did not appear in it myself, but as I was counsel in a case at the end of the year arising out of this one, I must briefly review the evidence, in order to place the complete story before the reader. Hannah Dobbs, a girl twenty-four years of age, was indicted for the wilful murder of Matilda Hacker, *alias* Huish, an unmarried lady sixty-six years of age. The case, which was entirely one of circumstantial evidence, occupied the Court two days. Upon the 9th of May, a decomposed body, subsequently identified as that of Miss Hacker, was found in a cellar at 4, Euston Square, under circumstances which clearly indicated that she had been murdered.

Miss Hacker was an eccentric old spinster, of Canterbury, which borough she left in consequence of a quarrel she had with the rating authorities there. She moved from spot to spot and passed under different names, being fearful, it would seem, that she would be traced, recognised, and made answerable for the liabilities she had incurred. After living in a number of houses, she took lodgings, in the name of Huish, at 4, Euston Square.

The proprietors of that house were a Mr. and Mrs. Bastindoff, who, I may mention, were the leading witnesses for the prosecution. It was proved by relatives of the deceased that she was

a woman of means, and evidence was given to the effect that it was her invariable custom to keep a large stock of ready money by her in a cash-box.

It was believed that the murder took place on the 14th of October, 1878. There was no doubt whatever that she was alive on the 10th October, for, on that day, she communicated with her agent respecting some house property she possessed, directing him to reply to "M. B.," at the Post Office, Holborn. It appeared beyond all doubt that, on the 14th, which was a Sunday, Miss Hacker and the servant, Hannah Dobbs, were alone in the house. On the following day, Bastindoff, the landlord, ordered Dobbs to go up to the old lady and get some rent which was due from her. According to Bastindoffs evidence, the accused ran past him saying, "I'll go," and presently returned with a fivepound note. It was changed, and the amount of the rent having been deducted, the balance was handed to Dobbs. Mrs. Bastindoff stated in the witness-box that, on the morning of the 14th, Dobbs told her she thought Miss Hacker was going to leave her lodgings that day, and that she believed she had actually done so.

According to the evidence of the Bastindoffs, they took little notice of the disappearance of the old lady, and did not even trouble themselves to go up into her rooms until two days afterwards, when it was necessary to prepare for the arrival of another lodger. Mrs. Bastindoff saw on the carpet a large stain, which, as an analysis subsequently showed, was a stain of blood. There was, she said, unmistakable evidence that an attempt had been made to wash out the discoloration.

It was proved that, shortly after the old lady's disappearance, Hannah Dobbs showed one of the children a book of dreams, which she stated had belonged to Miss Hacker. She gave to another child, as a plaything, the old lady's cash-box, the lid of which had been broken. Hannah Dobbs was also noticed to be wearing a watch and chain that had never been seen in her possession before. She explained away the circumstance by saying that an uncle of hers having recently died at Bideford, she had inherited from him a little property, including the watch and chain and some rings she was wearing. The watch and chain were subsequently pawned by her in a false name, and it

---
[327] **Fallacis Semita Vita**. Lat. Treacherous path of life. A pun on "fallentia semita vitae", unseen paths of life., from Horace, *Epistle 1.18.103.*

# Appendix H, Euston Square Murder

was afterwards proved that they had belonged to Miss Hacker.

Soon after the disappearance of the old lady, Hannah Dobbs left the house in Euston Square, and took lodgings with a Mrs. Wright. Being unable to pay her rent, she left her box in pawn, and it was discovered that, among the things contained in that box, were several articles that were identified as having been the property of Miss Hacker. Inquiries showed that the story told by the accused as to the death of her uncle at Bideford was completely a fable.

On the 9th of May, 1879, at Bastindoffs request, the cellar at the house in Euston Square was cleared out, so that one of the lodgers might use it for the storage of coal, and it was during the process that the corpse was discovered there. The identification of the body—which was found with a rope round the head—as that of Miss Hacker was complete. The height, the colour of the hair, the deformity of the spine, and other circumstances, left no doubt upon the point. One or two articles of jewellery were found close to the body, and they were identified as having belonged to the unfortunate old woman.

The evidence against the accused was, as I have shown, tolerably strong. The defence relied upon the improbability of a woman twenty-four years of age being able, unassisted, to commit the murder in the short time that could have been at her disposal; to remove the body, which was a heavy one, to the cellar; and to obliterate all traces of the deed. A great deal also was made of the improbability of the Bastindoffs having lost their lady lodger in so sudden and mysterious a manner without their suspicions being aroused that foul play had been resorted to. Counsel for the accused dwelt upon the fact that there was not a particle of direct evidence to show that she committed the murder, or that she was even aware of its commission. The Bastindoffs were most un-satisfactory witnesses. In answer to questions put to Severin Bastindoff by the counsel for Hannah Dobbs (questions no doubt which she instructed him to put), he said that there never had been any immoral intercourse between himself and his servant, that he did not make her acquaintance before she entered their service, and that it was not at his instigation that his wife engaged her. I mention these facts

because they were of considerable importance in relation to the second trial, with which I was myself concerned.

After Mr. Justice Hawkins had elaborately and patiently summed up, the jury came to the conclusion, in which I think they were fairly justified, that, though the greatest suspicion must rest upon the accused, the case against her was not proved beyond all doubt. There was, indeed, an entire absence of legal proof of the guilt of Hannah Dobbs, and in acquitting her, the jury only acted in accordance with the exigencies of the law as administered in this country.

Thus, this murder remained undiscovered, and I may mention as a remarkable circum-stance—and as a remarkably unsatisfactory circumstance—that it was one of three committed within an area of a quarter of a mile, of which the authors had not been apprehended. The others took place, one in Great Coram Street, and the other in Burton Crescent.

The prosecuting counsel in this case were the Attorney-General (Sir John Holker), Mr. Gorst, Q.C., and Mr. A. L. Smith (now one of Her Majesty's Judges); while the prisoner was defended by Mr. Mead.

As so often happens in cases of this sort, the prisoner was, on being discharged, straightway made a heroine by the eccentric portion of the British public.

Among those who took her by the hand was a gentleman of the name of Purkiss, the pro-prietor of *The Police News,* and very soon a pamphlet emanated from the office of that journal, purporting to contain an account of the career of Hannah Dobbs. The publication gave her version of the murder of Miss Hacker in Euston Square, and of the alleged immoralities that had taken place, both before and after she entered service there, between herself and her master, Severin Bastindoff. Attention being drawn to the pamphlet, Bastindoff instructed his solicitors to apply to the High Court for an injunction to prevent its further publication.

In an affidavit, he denied the allegations as to his intimacy with Dobbs; and upon the affidavit being filed, an action for libel was instituted against the publisher. A summons was then taken out against Bastindoff for perjury, and he was brought up before the magistrate, and committed for trial. The charge against

561

# Appendix H, Euston Square Murder

Bastindoff was heard in the identical court in which Hannah Dobbs had been tried, and the same Judge presided in the two cases.

The trial occupied four days. I, with Mr. E. Thomas and Mr. Cavendish-Bentinck, appeared for the prosecution; the prisoner being defended by Mr. Powell, Q.C., Mr. Poland, and Mr. Sims. The principal witness against the accused was, of course, Hannah Dobbs herself, who, I may mention, so far as dress was concerned, cut a much better figure o n this occasion than at her own trial. The pivot on which the case turned was Hannah Dobbs' account of her intimacy with the prisoner.

She swore that that intimacy commenced in the autumn of 1877, when she was a servant in a house in Torrington Square. She said: "It was at Mrs. Pearce's, 42, Torrington Square, that I first met Mr. Severin Bastindoff. He spoke to me and to another servant while we were cleaning windows, and in consequence of that conversation, he and I went out together that night, or a night or two afterwards, and from that time until I entered his service, we frequently went out together. The relationship was kept up during the time I was an inmate of his house."

Those who had been her fellow-servants were called, and gave corroborative evidence. A Mrs. Carpenter was also put into the box, and she swore that, upon a particular day in August, 1877, Dobbs and Bastindoff passed the night together at her inn at Redhill. This woman, who gave her evidence with marvellous intelligence, and, apparently, with perfect truth, was the witness most antagonistic to the accused.

In her cross-examination, Hannah Dobbs was forced to admit that she had once been tried and convicted for theft. The story of her whole life, indeed, as revealed during her cross-examination, was such as to draw from the presiding Judge the remark that she was a "most infamous person." This much was certain, she was remarkably clear-headed and clever, for a most searching and ingenious cross-examination, lasting nearly a whole day, failed to shake her in the smallest particular.

Two of the servants who corroborated her story were Selina Knight and Clara Green. One of the incidents they described undoubtedly had, *prima facie,* the stamp of truth upon it. One night, it appeared, when Dobbs had promised to meet Bastindoff, she and her two fellow-servants fell asleep before the fire, carelessly leaving the area door wide open, a circumstance that attracted the attention of two vigilant policemen, who entered, woke the girls up, and stayed to take coffee with them.

In reference to their evidence against Bastindoff, the question arose, could they have been mistaken in his identity? Bastindoff was pointed out to them in Court, and they swore that he was the man, but added that his appearance was somewhat altered. Explaining that the alteration was in his beard, they minutely described the appearance which that facial adornment had presented at the time of his intimacy with Hannah Dobbs. His lordship at once gave instructions that an old business partner of the accused, who had already given evidence, should be recalled; and, sure enough, this gentleman, on being questioned on the point, gave a description of how Bastindoff had previously worn his beard that fully confirmed the statement of the servant girls.

The defence in this case always struck me as being rather a clumsy one. The theory of it was—and evidence was called in support of that theory—that at the time Severin Bastindoff was said to have been with Hannah Dobbs, he was elsewhere, and that the man who was with Dobbs was his brother Peter, who was very like him in appearance. The principal witness in support of the theory for the defence was Bastindoff's mother-in-law.

Evidence was called to prove that, on the day on which Severin Bastindoff was alleged to have been with Dobbs at Redhill, he was with a fishing party in quite another district. These witnesses, when cross-examined by me, declared that Peter Bastindoff also made one of the fishing party.

This statement, of course, rather upset the theory of the defence, and, naturally, in my reply to the jury, I made a strong point of this admission, and of the fact that Peter Bastindoff was not put into the witness-box.

When Mr. Justice Hawkins had charged the jury, and completely exhausted the evidence on both sides, a verdict of "Guilty" was returned, and the prisoner was sentenced to twelve' months hard labour.

~

# Appendix I, Harley St. Murder

## The Harley St. Murder
## The Times
### Saturday, 5 June, 1880
### *MURDER.*

On Thursday morning a horrible discovery was made at the residence of Mr. Enriques, 139, Harley-street, Cavendish-square. The butler, in clearing out a cellar under the pavement, found the body of a woman in a cask. It was much decomposed, having been covered with quick-lime. The cellar was not kept locked, and it is stated that nobody has been missed from the house. The age of the woman cannot be even conjectured, but it is hoped that by means of a few vestiges of underclothing found in the cask and the remains of hair on the head the body will be identified. The butler had been led to clear out the cellar by noticing an unpleasant smell there. The body was removed to Marylebone Work-house, where it was examined by Drs. Bond and Spurgin. The police have made a thorough search of the cellars, but have made no discovery likely to throw light on the mystery, with the exception of a bundle of clothing supposed to have belonged to the deceased. Mr. Enriques, it may be added, has resided in the house for nearly a quarter of a century, and during the last three years has had three butlers. The inquest will probably be opened on Tuesday.

—

### Monday, 7 June, 1880
### *THE HARLEY-STREET MURDER.*

In connexion with the horrible discovery in Harley-street there are now various indications beyond the evidence afforded by the manner in which the body was concealed to confirm the belief that a murder has been committed. A weapon has been discovered with which the crime may have been committed, and it is a singular fact that chloride of lime, an anti-septic, had been used to cover the body instead of quicklime, which would have destroyed the remains. This points to ignorance on the part of the murderer. There is not wanting evidence which may serve as a clue to the period at which the crime was committed, and even ultimately point to the guilty person.

Mr. Jacob Quixano Henriques has resided in the house, No. 139, Harley-street, for very many years, and the present butler, who made

the discovery, has been with him since the end of 1878. Soon after he entered the service of Mr. Henriques, in the commencement of the winter season, a smell was noticed which was thought to arise from the drains, and workmen were called in to remedy the supposed defect. For a year and a half after the smell has continued until the discovery was made on Thursday.

The police notice respecting the remains states that they are those of a woman apparently between 40 and 50 years of age, and with front teeth unusually short—"as if sawn." The police conclude from the material of the clothes that the deceased was in poor circumstances. The body is that of a short woman with dark brown hair. The cask in which the remains were concealed was one in which it had been usual for the house to receive goods from the city.

The body has been removed from the St. Marylebone Workhouse to the parish mortuary to await an inquest by Dr. Hardwicke, who has meanwhile given orders for an independent medical examination.

—

### Tuesday, 8 June, 1880
### *THE HARLEY-STREET MURDER.*

Yesterday Dr. Hardwicke, the central Middle-sex coroner, opened an inquest at Marylebone upon the body found in the cellar of 139, Harley-street.

After the coroner and jury had viewed the remains, Mr. Jacob Quixano Henriques was called as a witness. He stated that he was a merchant. He had lived at 139, Harley-street, for more than 20 years. On Thursday the butler came to him while he was at breakfast and said that human remains had been found in a barrel in the rear cellar. This was the first he had heard of the matter. He told the butler to send for a police-man. Two policemen came and went into the area, where they saw the barrel, which had been removed from an inner cellar. He left the police to deal with the remains, and they were removed to the workhouse that night. The butler had been with him for 18 months. The police had been furnished with the names of all the servants he had had during the last three years. The family were in the habit of going away for a month or six weeks in the autumn. They had done so two years ago. Each spring that the area had been whitewashed and painting had been done, and in the autumn, also, workmen had been employed. The cellar in which the remains had been found was situated behind another cellar in which boots and knives were clean. It contained a cistern and some lumber. The present butler, when he came into his service, had complained of bad smells, and suggested that they came from the drains. This witness was satisfied could not be the case, and he had the dusthole seen to, regarding that as the cause of the smells. The butler had not told him that the smells had ceased. The persons who had kept the house while the family went into the country were not his own servants, who went with the family. Witness could give no clue to a solution of the mystery.

John Spendlove deposed that he had been butler to Mr. Henriques since the 21st of November, 1878. He usually slept of Hawley-street, but went home occasionally to his wife at Wimbledon. His pantry was in the basement, and when he first went into Mr. Henriques's service he noticed a bad smell from the area. The dustbin was look too, but the smell continued. From the first he had notice the barrel under the cistern in the inner cellar. He had thought it was full of seltzer water bottles, as a number of empty bottles were on the top. On Thursday he happened to go into the cellar, and it occurred to him to see what was in the barrel. He took off some of the seltzer bottles, and found something which look like an effigy in the dim light. He called the footmen to assist him, and they made out that it was a human body. He told Mr. Henriques, on whose order he sent for the police. The name of the butler had been in Mr. Henriques's service previously he believed was Henry Smith. The area gates were locked each night, and that he's taken up to Mr. Henriques.

Arthur Kirkland, footman to Mr. Henriques, said he had been in his service for a year. During this time he had noticed the smell in the cellar, but had not regarded as anything in particular. On Thursday the butler pulled the tub out. Witness saw the limbs of a human being. On the butlers order he brought the police.

Mr. Stephen Lucas, Chief Inspector of the D Division, stated that on being called to 139, Harley-street, on Thursday, he saw the body in a flour barrel, and after it had been seen by Mr. Spurgin, the police divisional surgeon, it was sealed up by an order of the Director of Criminal Investigation and taken to St. Marylebone Work-house, where it was seen by Dr. Bond.

The CORONER here explained to the jury that the police authorities in thus acting had interfered with the duties and responsibilities of the coroner. By his orders the body had been taken to the mortuary for a separate examination by Dr. Pepper, of St. Mary's Hospital. It has now been removed to the parish mortuary in Paddington-street. He had had correspondence with the police authorities, and explanations had been given.

Mr. Lucas, in reply to questions by the jury, said that many things had been found in the cellar. He should be unable at a future time to state fully the results of inquiries which were now being made.

Mr. Spurgin, the police divisional surgeon, deposed.—I was called at 12 o'clock on Thursday morning to 139, Harley-street, where I saw the barrel containing human remains. When I first saw it the barrel had been reversed from the position in which it originally stood, and the original bottom was uppermost, with a board taken out, showing hair to be adhering to the side of the cask. I had the barrel reversed so as to stand in the way it had stood in the cellar, taking care that nothing escaped in the process. I then saw the knees of a human body upper-most. I saw on the legs, after careful looking, the remains of stockings, and both legs were gartered with elastic garters having metal buck-les. The body appeared to be entirely or nearly naked, and decomposition was considerably advanced. I had no time than to continue the investigation, and, placing the barrel and its contents under Inspector Lucas, I returned at 3 o'clock and renewed my examination. The body was removed to the St. Marylebone Workhouse, where Dr. Bond also examined it with me. Since then I have made an examination with Dr. Pepper and with Dr. Bond. When I examined the body with Dr. Bond several other medical man were there—Dr. Randall and Dr. Fuller. I had the body removed from the cask. The head was doubled backwards with the face to the right. On the head was a small portion of hair, which appeared to have been cut off as to leave an inch and a half on the scalp. The hair adher-

# Appendix I, Harley St. Murder

ing to the side of the cask was longer. I found in the flesh of the neck a red coral bead, apparently belonging to a necklace. There were no earrings or rings. There were some portions of garments which had been on the body. I have been able to measure the body, and make it 4 ft. 7 in. I should say that the body had a considerable curvature of the spine, caused by pressure, but not during life. It was covered more or less was chloride of lime and was partially "mummified"—dried, but decayed.

The CORONER.—Can you form an idea of the length of time to which the body has been subject to the action of decomposition?

Witness.—My opinion is that the body has been where it was found for more than a year. It might have been for certain period beyond that. I should limit myself to a year beyond that, supposing that the atmospheric conditions to which it has been exposed here have been unchanged. Part of the left shoulder has rotted away; but, making the examination with Dr. Pepper, a soul and opening on the left side between the fourth and fifth ribs, and the appearance in the tissues surrounding this opening were such as to indicate an infusion of blood.

The CORONER.—Hence you have arrived at the conclusion that the death arose from a stab?

Witness.— I arrived at a strong assumption that such might be the case, but the investigations are still going on. Still, I can say that I have seen things which lead me to the view that the death of this woman was due to violence. I should like to add that the ribs were separated from the cartilages on the left side, and not on the right side.

Dr. A. J. Pepper, of St. Mary's Hospital, said,—When I examined the body on Saturday I found an examination has been made and part of the viscera removed. Yesterday I made an examination, lasting for some hours, in the presence of Dr. Spurgin. I have come to the conclusion that the body found in the barrel is the body of a woman 4ft. 10 in. in height. My reason for taking a different height from that given by Dr. Spurgin is that I allow two inches for the spine curvature, which was certainly a *post mortem* curvature. The woman was certainly as much as 30 years of age, probably 40; she may have been a little over 40. The cause of death I think was probably a stab. The stab

could scarcely have been self-inflicted, and it could hardly have been accidental.(The witness then gave a lengthy history of the dental appearance, and stated that one wisdom tooth had not been cut.) I should say that the body had been in the place where it was found within six months of two years—six months more or less.

The CORONER.—Do think that the person came to her death by violence?

The Witness.—I do, by stabbing with a knife. A table knife with cause the stab.

In reply to the CORONER, Mr. Lucas said the police would be ready to continue the evidence next week, and the inquiry was accordingly adjourned.

—

## Tuesday, 15 June, 1880
### THE HARLEY-STREET MURDER.

The inquest on the body found in the cellar of a house in Harley-street was continued yesterday before Dr. Hardwicke, the coroner for Central Middlesex, assisted by Dr. Thomas, the deputy-coroner. The evidence given was of a serious and significant character. Mr. St. John Wontner represented the police commissioners. The fact brought to light had been traced out by Inspectors Lucas and King, of the Divisional Police, assisted by Inspectors Greenham and Swanson, of Scotland-yard.

The CORONER stated that the police had laid before him the depositions of several persons, who might give some points necessary to be known to the jury; but it would save the time of the Court if only witnesses who could give evidence having a direct relation to the case were called. As the medical evidence was not complete on the last occasion, he would recall the medical gentleman who had examined the body.

Dr. Spurgin, surgeon to the D division of police, recalled, said.—I have examined the body further and more particularly to ascertain the immediate cause of death. I have no doubt death was caused in this case by a stab in the left breast between the fourth and fifth ribs. There was no appearance of injury to the heart, and as the lung had entirely disappeared the injury to that could not be traced; but the evidence of effusion of blood in the region of the stab was abundantly clear, while the right side was free from any such indications. Since the last sitting of this Court casts of the mouth and teeth have been taken, and I now present them to the jury. (The casts were handed to the jury.) I have also formed an opinion as to the manner in which the body had been treated before being placed in the cask. It was either buried in chloride of lime had chloride of lime sprinkle over it before it was put into the cask. I arrived at this conclusion from the fact that the whole of the body was covered with the chloride of lime, while there was none in the cask itself or in the interstices or cracks. Moreover, the action of the chloride of lime was equally distributed over the body.

A juror.—Were there any stains of blood in the cask?

Witness.—Yes, there were stains which answer to the chemical test for blood, but these might have come from the mouth or nose after death. It is important that I should inform you that there were in the cask patches or smears of the lime, as if caused by the body was covered being placed in the cask. Among the other things found in the cellar immediately about the cask were this table-knife, two old pokers, and a quantity of ordinary cording rope (all produced). The knife is covered with rust, but I do not think any conclusion can be drawn from that. The linen found on the body—or rather the remnants of what was linen—showed that the garments were not only of coarse materials, but were coarsely made.

In reply to the jury.—There was literally no lung left in the body. The curvature of the spine, I have no doubt, was made by the body having been forced into the cask. There had been a negative result in the examination of the knife for traces of blood, but after a time these might be lost. That knife would make such a wound as that seen in the body.

A young man in a soldier's uniform was then brought forward as a witness. He deposed.—My name is Henry Smith, and I am in the 3d Surrey (whether the Line or Militia was not stated). I am a married man, and was married when I was in Mr. Henriques's service as butler. I do not know when that was, but it is about three years ago. (It is in evidence that he left in November, 1878.) I was there about 18 months. I cannot give any explanation of this mystery of the cask with the body under the cistern in the inner cellar. I seldom went there. I was discharged by Mr. Henriques for being found

the worse for drink. I used to sleep in the servants' hall. A footman named Tinapp was there while I was butler, and he used to sleep in the pantry. My wife is alive now, but I do not live with her. I knew of no one being brought to the house of a night—no supper parties there. I knew of a case of disorderly conduct on the part of a footman while I was there—his coming home intoxicated. He used to stop out of a night, and I have let him in. The area gate was supposed to be closed of a night, and I was responsible for the closing of it. I have known it not to have been closed. The footman who used to come home drunk has not brought any one home with him.

In reply to Mr. Wontner, the witness said,—I was responsible for locking the gate at night, but it used to be left unlocked three or four times a week. I used to be out at night about three times a week—I used so to be out for some months. The footman, while I was thus away, was the only servant in that part of the house. I was discharged for allowing the footman to be out at night.

Mr. Wontner.—You see that cask; when did you first see that in the cellar?

Witness.—I do not remember seeing it at all.

Mr. Wontner.—Now, do you not know something about an attempt to dig a hole in the cellar?

Witness.—Well, I did have a man to dig a hole in one of the cellars.

Mr. Wontner.—When?

Witness.—Well, this was about three months before I left about the autumn or August of 1878.

Mr. Wontner.—What was your purpose in having a hole dug in the cellar?

Witness.—I had a great accumulation of stale bread at the time, and I thought I should get into trouble, so I thought I would have a hole dug to bury it.

Mr. Wontner.—Was the hole dug?

Witness.—No; the man, who was an old stableman, named Green, came upon some concrete under the bricks, and he replaced the bricks. The man was an "odd man" about. I am certain I never saw the tub before.

The next witness was this "odd man," John Green, of 16, Weymouth-mews, who deposed. —I am living as a jobbing man or coachman. I am 73 years of age, and have lived 40 years in

# Appendix I, Harley St. Murder

Marylebone. I knew 139 Harley-street, and I knew Smith, formerly butler to Mr. Henriques. One day he asked me if I was a paviour,[328] as he had seen me laying some stones in the stable. About three years ago—I cannot remember the date exactly—I went to the house, 139, Harley-street, on being asked by Smith, the butler, and I saw bricks in the cellar all taken up, the hole being about a yard across. I did not dig any hole. I relaid the bricks. I did not ask Smith what he what he took them up for. The hole I had to fill was in the middle cellar, next to the one where the rubbish was—in one of the coal cellars as now used. The next morning Smith said to me, "Come and tidy up a cellar," and I went down to the outer cellar, leading to that in which the cask was found. I tidied up the outer cellar, and put what I cleared into the dust-bin. Another day Smith asked me to carry mould out of the back of the house, and I told him I was not strong enough to carry it away and that I had nowhere to take it—that he had better get the scavengers[329] to do it. I never went beyond the pantry of the house.

By Mr. Wontner.—I did not dig the hole; I only put the bricks down. Smith never said he wanted to bury bread. I thought someone had been digging for a drain. I had to level the stuff about the hole. I hinted to Smith to pay me; but he only gave me a glass of ale, and said he would make it "all right" with me. I made the inner cellar clean. There were no broken pokers there, nor this knife; but there were packing cases. I made a clean sweep of the cellar, but I did not sleep under the cistern. [There was some confusion as to the various cellars, and the Coroner suggested that the witness should go to the house and point out the spots indicated to Inspector King, who accordingly went with the witness.]

William Tinapp, a German, deposed,—I went into Mr. Henriques's Service as a footman, at 139, Harley-street, in August, 1878. Smith was the butler there then, and I believe the barrel was in the cellar when I first went. When I first went the bricks in the middle cellar had been removed and replaced. This had been done just before I went, for Green told me soon after

I went into the service that Smith had had him early one morning to replace the bricks. The dusthole was emptied by the butlers order. The refuse of the kitchen was thrown into the dusthole. I never saw any large quantity of waste bread in the house.

The present butler, Spindlove, was recalled, and said that there never was any such waste of bread in the house as to render it necessary for a man to try and bury it under the bricks in the cellar.

Mrs. Jewry, who was cook in Mr. Henriques's Service from 1874 to 1879, and knew Smith as butler there, said she was not aware of his sleeping away from the house for a period, and with regard to the alleged accumulation of waste bread, she denied that there was ever any waste bread, and in the most emphatic terms denied that it could have been necessary for Smith to have had holes dug to bury it. Moreover, if there had been a waste the dust-man would gladly have taken it. With regard to the mould which Green stated that Smith had desired him to take away, she said that as there was no garden to the house there could be no mould. The only mould there could be would be under paved stones in the yard between the back of the house and the stables, except the small quantity in boxes, in which some ivy grew.

George Campbell, servant at 134, Harley-street, who had lived for five months in 1876-77, deposed that there was no cask in the cellar when he lived at 139, and there was no smell in the place at the time.

John Bortham, a butler, in service at Eccleston-square, and George Minton, a foot-man at Queen's-gate, were called to depose that when they were in Mr. Henriques's service up to 1877 there was no cask in the cellar, and no bad smell.

The witness Green, recalled, said,—It was in the middle cellar where I put down the bricks. I now remember there was a heavy box, a packing box, in the inner cellar, and some old chairs. I never saw the mould Smith spoke about my moving.

Inspector Lucas remarked that the workman had been found who had stood on the heavy box, which was a champagne-case, in order to repair the cistern.

Inspector King, who went with Green, said the place Green had pointed out as the spot

---

[328] **Paviour.** Someone that lays pavement, a road paver. (Census1891.com)

[329] **Scaleraker or Scavenger.** Street cleaners. (ibid.)

567

# Appendix I, Harley St. Murder

where the attempt to dig the hole had been made had been opened, and it was found that two stones had been let in to cover the place where a cesspool had formerly been.

Mr. Woodroffee, who was the caretaker of the house, deposed,—For the last six years I have taken care of Mr. Henriques's house in the autumn, and my wife and son with me. In the autumn of 1878 I went into the cellar to hunt out a rat, and saw the barrel, for I knocked a stick against it. Bottles were on it. Smith was butler at the time, but was with the family in the country. I always kept the area gate locked to prevent hawkers coming down. I saw that bricks had been moved into the cellar.

Henry Charles Goatley, plumber, of Kentish-town, deposed to having done work on the cistern in the second cellar in July, 1878 (his time-sheet giving the date), and to having stood on a champagne-case, which had blocked up the aperture under the cistern where the barrel stood. Witness never noticed any smells—"they were so common." Witness had taken up the bricks which had been moved, and had found that a cesspool still existed under the floor of the cellar.

Inspector King also gave evidence showing that after Smith left the fact of his having the bricks taken up had been talked of, and as there was a valuable piece of jewelry missing the bricks were again taken up to see whether it was concealed there. The barrel, with its contents, was pushed under the cistern at that time, and the way to it was blocked up by champagne-case. There were marks of burning on the wall, accounted for by the footman Tinapp burning some paper to overcome the stench.

Dr. Pepper was recalled, and deposed that he had proved beyond all doubt that the stain-marks on the remnants of the chemise found on the deceased were blood-stains. He substan-tiated the evidence of Dr. Spurgin but there was blood in the cavity of the chest on the left side. The knife produced (that found in the cellar) would cause death.

The CORONER said the jury could hear Mr. Bond, of Westminster Hospital, who had also examined the body.

The CORONER said it was for the jury to say what course they would pursue, whether they would hear all the evidence the police could lay before them, or whether they would adjourn, or whether they would come to a verdict. Their duty was simply to find "the cause of death." This duty performed, if they could add names they were empowered to do so; but he took it from the views which some had expressed that the jury were ready to leave the further investigation and the hands of the police.

The jury at once agreed to a verdict that the body of the woman, name unknown, found in the cellar at 139, Harley-street, was the body of a murdered woman, the criminal being also unknown.

# Unsolved Murder Mysteries
## Charles Pearce
### Chapter VII.
# Mrs. Reville
# Slough's Black Secret

Less terrible but more mysterious than the murder of the Marrs was that of Mrs. Reville, the butcher's wife, at Slough. Nothing could be less suggestive of crime than the unpretending shop in the High Street of a sleepy town, yet within a few minutes the weapon of death descended and the wielder had vanished as though he had never been.

Imagine a shop about 18 feet by 12 feet, in the centre of which stood a chopping block and to the left of the entrance a counter on which the scales were kept. Behind was a fairly large room, between which and the shop was a door and with a window commanding the entire view of the front premises. Immediately beneath this window was a desk at which Mrs. Reville was in the habit of sitting to post and make up the accounts. Behind her and a little to the left in the middle of the room was a table covered by a green ornamental cloth. At the back of the room, also a little to the left, a door led into a yard, which door could be opened from the inside but not from the outside. Close to this door a window looked into the yard. This window was fitted with a blind, but it was not drawn down on the evening in question. A kitchen could be entered from the room just described, the door of communication being just behind where Mrs. Reville would sit. A gas burner was placed close to the small window, immediately to the right of the head of a person sitting at the desk, and a second burner was in the shop; the tap of the latter was half turned down on the evening in question and the light was but dim. There was no access from the back of the house.

It is essential to bear in mind the arrangement of the premises as it shows that no one could enter the room from the rear; while any person coming into the shop from the street would be at once seen by Mrs. Reville. The inmates of the house were Mr. and Mrs. Reville and two children. The assistants in the business were a boy, Frederick Glass, and Augustus Payne, a youth of eighteen. Both had been in the employ of Mr. Reville some two years.

It was the night of April 11th, 1881. Business was over for the day, and at about ten minutes past eight Mr. Reville left the house to pay a few calls and gossip with his cronies after the fashion of the country tradesman. He left his wife sitting in her usual seat at the desk in the room behind the shop posting up her account books, and the lad, Frederick Glass, was helping her. Augustus Payne was in the shop and the two children were upstairs in bed. Mrs. Reville and the boy continued to work until five-and-twenty minutes past eight, when the boy prepared to go. Meanwhile, Payne had come from the shop and had passed through the room into the kitchen. As a rule, Glass and Payne went away together, but on that night Payne told Glass he might be a quarter of an hour later as he had to rub salt into some hams. Mrs. Reville put twopence on the table and Glass and Payne each took a penny. Then Glass took his leave, Payne remaining behind.

The time at which Payne left depends upon his own word. There was no corroborative evidence. He came out of the kitchen, and as he crossed the room Mrs. Reville bade him good night. "I asked her," said Payne, "if I should shut the shop door and she said 'No; turn the gas down and leave it open.' It was 8.32 when I came out of the door. I looked at the clock."

If Payne's word as to the time he left the house is to be depended upon, what happened next must have occupied no more than a couple of minutes or so. Mrs. Beasley, who lived next door to the Revilles, was in the habit of looking in every evening to keep Mrs. Reville company after the boys had left, and on the night of April 11th she went in as usual. The shop door was a little way open and the time was, she thought, about half-past eight, but she could not be sure to five minutes. Mrs. Reville was in her accustomed seat, as Mrs. Beasley could see when she looked through the window. There was something strange about her appearance. Her face was of a leaden pallor. The poise of the head was wrong. Considerably alarmed, the visitor went a little nearer. She at first thought Mrs. Reville had fainted. Then she caught sight of an ominous red streak in her neck and she could not go a step further by herself. She ran out of the shop for assistance.

Either before Mrs. Beasley entered or while she was away other eyes had seen the terrible sight. Those eyes belonged to one of Mrs. Reville's children, a little tot of five years old. She was very thirsty, and not being able to sleep she went downstairs, and while on the staircase heard the sound of a door slamming. She reached the door opening into the room at the back of the shop, peeped in and saw her mother sitting in front of her desk. The child spoke, but getting no answer went a little nearer and then saw blood on her mother's neck. Trembling with fright she ran upstairs and got into bed, where she lay, not daring to utter a sound, until the next morning when she told her father. She also said she heard a noise as of her mother choking. If so, this would fix the time of the child's entrance as *before* the visit of Mrs. Beasley.

In the meantime, Mrs. Beasley had poured a somewhat incoherent tale into the ears of a neighbour, a Mr. Light, who at once started for the Revilles' shop. He could not tell the exact time, but his wife put it at twenty-five minutes past eight, but the clock it turned out was slow. When Light saw Mrs. Reville he knew she was dead. Within a few minutes Police-sergeant Hobbs was on the scene, and it was then a quarter to nine. Hobbs saw a large wound on the side of the neck and two wounds on the front of the head. On the table were some papers, a chopper and some bread and cheese. The handle of the chopper was from the dead woman nearest the back door. Both the back doors were shut, but he could not say whether they were fastened. Seeing no blood on the upper part of the chopper, he took it up and found the underside covered with blood, wet and running and with hair upon it. Some pieces of money—a penny, a halfpenny, and a shilling—were lying partly on Mrs. Reville's dress, and her handkerchief was partly in and partly out of her pocket.

What the surgeon found pretty well told how the murderer went about his work. Mrs. Reville was sitting on the forepart of the chair and leaning back. The two severe wounds on the forepart of the head were probably caused by blows from someone standing behind, and by such an instrument as the chopper. The blows had been delivered from right to left. It is important to note that no blood was found on the floor where anyone would have been standing, so that the assassin might have escaped without having any blood on his clothing.

A singular piece of writing was found on the table. On a half sheet of notepaper was the following:

"Mrs. Reville—You will never sell me any more bad meat like you did on Saturday. I told Mrs. Austin at Chalvey that I should do for her. I have done it for the bad meat she sold me on Saturday.— H. Collins, Colnbrook."

If this paper was intended to throw the police off the scent the method adopted was palpably absurd. Enquiries, of course, were made, but as might be expected they led to nothing. At the same time it was significant that whoever wrote the words must have known something of the Revilles' business. It turned out that though H. Collins was not known at Colnbrook there was a Robert Collins living at Chalvey, and Robert Collins was one of Reville's customers. He, however, had not written the note nor did he know anything of any bad meat. It was true also that at Chalvey lived a Mrs. Elizabeth Austin, but she knew no H. Collins and no one of that name had complained to her of bad meat.

So much for the alleged motive. The police could find out no one who had a grudge against Mrs. Reville, and though it was not proved that Mrs. Reville had much money in her pocket at the time she was attacked, whatever was the amount it was gone. Murder for the sake of robbery was hardly likely, though, of course, it could be urged that a stranger would not know what money the poor woman had about her and might be tempted to take his chance. But there were powerful objections to this supposition. The shop door it is true was open, but no one could enter without being seen by Mrs. Reville from her seat at the desk. Moreover, the murderer when he struck the fatal blows was *behind* his victim. Is it conceivable that a strange man could enter the room without some protest from Mrs. Reville and could swiftly leap behind her and not be seen? If she *did* see him her natural instinct would have prompted her to get up from her chair, either to call for assistance or to escape from some threatened

# Appendix J, Slough Murder

danger. But when discovered dead the attitude of her body was unchanged from that of life. Nor was there the slightest sign of a struggle.

The distinctive features of this singular case are firstly, the amazing swiftness of the murderer, and secondly, that he should have escaped without bloodstained clothing. Payne was the last to leave the shop and he fixed the time at 8.32. Shortly afterwards he was met in the street by one witness who thought the time was about five-and-twenty minutes to nine. Mrs. Beasley went into the shop at half-past eight or thereabouts. Obviously, the difficulty of fixing by the memory alone the exact moment of every particular occurrence is insuperable. All that can be said is that these three times probably ranged within the limit of five minutes, and one is justified in assuming that the entry of the murderer, the attack, the robbery and his escape, did not occupy more than this brief interval. It was probably less, for although the child who crept into the room while outside the door heard a noise as of someone, she saw nothing when she peeped into the room but the sight of her mother and the blood on her neck. By this time the deed was done and the murderer had fled.

The second feature of the crime—the absence of any clue from bloodstained clothing—is equally puzzling. The miscreant had inflicted upon his victim four terrible wounds and one appeared to have received two blows. The surgeon was of opinion that the wounds at the back of the head were first delivered and the effect would be to cause immobility. The head being thrown back the other blows were more consistent with being given from behind than from any other direction. He thought it was quite possible there was not much spurting of blood, but if the person were standing behind he should have expected the person would have been covered with blood. Still he could have rifled the woman's pockets and yet be free from blood had he proceeded *very carefully*.

No doubt, but this presupposes deliberation, and the murder was consummated so rapidly that there could have been no time for deliberation. Considering that the crime was determined upon, it is possible, however, that the murderer, finding the woman was made unconscious by his first blow, robbed her and

finished his appalling work afterwards. The deed was no haphazard one and hence the perpetrator had an eye to the avoidance of bloodstains.

A third puzzle—that relating to the chopper—must not be overlooked.

The weapon used to commit the murder was undoubtedly the butcher's chopper. This chopper was always kept on the block in the shop. How came it into the room? Did the murderer catch sight of it as he passed as a ready instrument for his purpose? Was it by accident, or had he planned out his deed beforehand and noted where the chopper was kept? Frederick Glass did not notice when he left the house at twenty-five minutes past eight whether the chopper was in its place. Alfred Payne, his fellow assistant, told the coroner that when he left at thirty-two minutes past eight the chopper, with other tools, was on the block, except the knife, and that laid against the weights close to the scales. Save Payne's, there was no other evidence relating to the chopper.

For certain reasons which will be gone into presently, the police came to the conclusion that the murder was committed by someone well acquainted with the business. The boy Glass was at once eliminated from their conclusions and so also was Mr. Reville, who was at a neighbouring tavern at the time of the murder. There remained Alfred Augustus Payne. Now, some curious discoveries were made in regard to the note signed "H. Collins" which seem to direct suspicion towards Payne, so much so that, while the coroner's inquest was being held, the police kept the youth under a species of surveillance.

This suspicion rested upon more grounds than one. When Mr. Reville went out at a quarter to eight, he left Payne in a corner of the shop writing on a sheet of paper. On searching the shop and room the police superintendent found a piece of notepaper which, on being compared with the letter addressed to Mrs. Reville left on the table, was found to correspond. A notch on the side of one fitted into the side of the other. This coincidence suggested that, in addition to doing the woman to death, the murderer found time to write the note in question. The watermark also corresponded.

The important point was to establish whose was the handwriting. Asked for specimens of

# Appendix J, Slough Murder

his handwriting Payne gave them willingly, and these specimens, together with the letter signed "H. Collins," were submitted to Mr. Chabot, a well-known writing expert. But the expert's evidence was like the evidence of most experts in such cases, very unsatisfactory. He found more similarities in handwritings which were proved not to be Payne's than in those that were. Before the coroner Mr. Chabot was much more positive that the handwriting of the letter addressed to Mrs. Revile resembled that of Payne than he was at the assizes.

The question of the handwriting was left unsettled at the inquest, and left as it was, it tended to cast a shadow over Payne's protestation of innocence. This shadow was deepened when it was inferred from certain evidence given by Mr. Reville that Payne might have nursed a grudge against Mrs. Reville. The latter, it appeared, had some weeks before told her husband that there was something wrong in regard to some money being missed and that if he did not get rid of Payne she would. "She calculated," said Reville, "that he was robbing us."

Much was made of the superintendent's statement that when Payne was taken to the scene of the murder he showed no emotion, but as every student of psychology knows, the absence of outward emotion proves nothing. In such a case as Payne's it tells as much in favour of innocence as of guilt. However, the cumulative effect of all that told against Payne was that thirteen of the coroner's jury returned a verdict of wilful murder against Payne and he was committed to the assizes.

The trial disclosed nothing more than has already been related. The right of a prisoner to give evidence if he wished to do so had not then been established, and Payne's mouth was closed. What he told the coroner, however, may be quoted, as it tallied exactly with his statement to the police superintendent. It ran: "I am innocent of the crime and knew nothing in the least about it till Mr. Dunham came to my house. He asked me to go to Mr. Reville's to see whereabouts Mrs. Reville was sitting when I left her. From what I left her at thirty-two minutes past eight she did not seem to have moved an inch. Mr. Reville says I had some ill feeling against Mrs. Reville and I had not the least. Two never could agree better than me and Mrs. Reville. Mr. Reville says I have been in the habit of going to public houses for the last two months and I have not. I gave it up ever since he told me. I should not have gone then had it not been for Mr. Reville. I don't see why he should put upon me, calling me such a bad boy after giving me so many presents as he has. That's all I've got to say."

He never went from these words; he was never confused, and throughout the trial he maintained-his self-possession. The police tried to make out that when Payne was taken to the scene of the murder he showed no sign of emotion, but this he strongly denied. He nearly fell down at the sight, he said, and would have done so but for his supporting himself by laying his hand on the block.

The jury were not long in finding Payne not guilty, and it is difficult to see how they could come to any other conclusion. The whole tragedy was so inexplicable and so motiveless—in spite of the self-implicating letter—that one can discover no point to start from even to piece out a theory. The Slough shop murder must in the absence of any belated confession—a most unlikely thing to happen now that over forty years have passed since the deed was committed—forever remain one of the darkest of Unsolved Mysteries.

~

572

## The Kentish Town Dairy Murder

### 𝕻𝖆𝖑𝖑 𝕸𝖆𝖑𝖑 𝕭𝖚𝖉𝖌𝖊𝖙
**Thursday, 17 March, 1887**
*MURDER AND ATTEMPTED ROBBERY IN KENTISH TOWN.*

A DARING murder arising out of an attempted robbery has been perpetrated at a shop in the Bartholomew road, in one of the most secluded parts of Kentish-town. Mr. Samuels, the husband of the unfortunate victim, carries on business as a dairyman at No. 92 in that road, which at this spot is very quiet, and is faced by a dead wall. Adjoining the shop is a small parlour, and from the door of this room any one inside can command a good view of the shop and its entrance. It was at the door of this apartment that Mrs. Samuels received her death blow from the hands of her assailants.

Shortly before four o'clock on Friday afternoon several men were seen driving in a small trap towards the dairy, but before they reached it the horse was brought to a standstill. There is a public-house situated a short distance off, and it would be supposed that the occupants were going there for refreshments. No further notice was taken of the men, whose actions gave rise to no suspicion. It would appear, although there is no witness to prove it, that the men, instead of going to the public-house for refreshment, entered the premises of Mr. Samuels. Everything that followed the arrival of the men in the Bartholomew-road, until the finding of the victim's body, remains a mystery, for up to the present no Witness is forthcoming to explain what took place in the shop, and it is feared that so quick was the action of the gang that no person other than the men implicated witnessed the crime. It is conjectured that on the men entering the shop one man took up his position at the door of the parlour while another crossed the counter to the shelf where an

**The Scene of the Murder.**

iron safe, which weighed nearly 2 cwt., was standing, and the third man waited on the public side of the counter and near the door, so that he could convey the safe away on receiving it from his confederates. This theory is entertained by the police authorities.

It is suggested that Mrs. Samuels, on seeing the men enter, made an effort to enter the shop from the parlour, but was struck down by a blow on the head from a crowbar or some other such instrument by the man who had taken up his position at the door of the parlour to prevent a surprise. There appears to have been no scuffle, for the only things that were moved or out of place were two quart milk cans which were standing on the counter and the iron safe. The safe either proved too heavy for the men, or they were surprised by someone approach-ing, for they had dropped it in the doorway and there left it. It was some minutes afterwards that a person passing the shop noticed the safe. His suspicions being aroused, he entered the shop where a shocking spectacle presented itself.

Lying in the parlour doorway at the end of the counter was the body of Mrs. Samuels, with her head in a pool of blood and fearfully battered in. Much alarmed, the man left the shop and went in search of assistance.

The police authorities at the Kentish-town police-station at once sent several officers and the divisional police surgeon to the scene. Mr. Samuels, who was out on business, was sent for, and on his arrival home at a quarter-past four o'clock he found his unfortunate wife, who is fifty-eight years of age, in an unconscious condition, the back of her head being completely smashed. The medical man ordered the removal of Mrs. Samuels to the hospital, and she was conveyed to University College Hospital where she expired at twenty-five minutes past eight, never having regained consciousness. Much excitement prevailed in the neighbourhood during the evening.

~

## The George St. Murder
## 𝕿𝖍𝖊 𝕿𝖎𝖒𝖊𝖘

### Saturday, 28 January, 1888
### THE MARYLEBONE MURDER

The Coroner for Central Middlesex, Dr. George Danford Thomas, last evening opened an inquiry, at the Marylebone Coroner's Court, into the circumstances attending the death of Lucy Clark, aged 49, who carried on the business of a dressmaker, at 86, George-street, Portman-square, where she was murdered on the evening of Monday last.

Mr. Inspector Robson, of the Detective Department, who has charge of the case, was present.

Francis Clark, stonecutter, of 150, Walworth-road, identified the body as that of his sister. He said that she was a single woman. Her age was 49, and she carried on the business of a dressmaker. He last saw her alive on Monday, January 8, and she then complained of having a cold. He last visited her at her residence on the 31st of December, when she was quite well. She occupied three rooms on the first floor, and had resided there some three years. She earned a good living by her dressmaking and seemed to live most comfortably. There was a shop beneath her front room, and when he last visited his sister other parts of the house were to let. He subsequently wrote a letter to his sister inviting her to dinner on Sunday last, but received no answer. He heard of her death on Monday evening, but he had not been to the house to see her. He was not aware that deceased had a banking account, but he presumed that she had. He was aware that she possessed a gold watch and chain and other articles of jewelry, but he did not know whether she kept any money in the house. The deceased had lately been visited by two nephews. Their ages were 21 and 19 years, and they resided with their mother at Pimlico. The eldest was in an architect's office, and the other was a shop assistant. He understood that the deceased had not a friendly feeling towards them, as she believed that they had taken away some of her property. She said she had lost a few trinkets and her nephews had taken them, and she meant to accuse them of having done so. He did not know whether the trinkets had been recovered or not. On Monday evening he saw the nephews at the station. He gave the police a description of the property, which the deceased told him she had lost. He understood that the deceased's rooms were found in a disordered state.

Sydney Meas, corndealer, said he was deceased's brother-in-law, and resided in the country. Hearing of the death he came to London and went to the mortuary and identified the body. He last saw her in November. She then informed him that she had means, but she did not tell him where she deposited her money. He has since ascertained she had money in the Post-office bank.

William George Betts, clerk to Mr. Walter Holcombe, auctioneer, of 23, Orchard-street, deposed that on Monday evening about a quarter to 5 he went to the house, 86, George-street, for the purpose of showing two ladies the premises, which were to let. One entering the passage he saw the body of a female lying at the foot of the staircase with her head hanging over the kitchen stairs. There was a large quantity of blood about passage.

Police-constable James Greystone, 136 D, stated that he was called by the last witness to the house, and found the woman dead. He went for Dr. Times, who returned to the house with him. They went upstairs, and saw that the first floor front room was in a state of disorder. The drawers had been opened and ransacked, and on the floor found some jewel-cases empty. The adjoining bedroom they found in a similar state of disorder.

Dr. Henry Times, surgeon, of Manchester-square, said he considered that the woman had been dead several days. Her throat was severely cut, and on moving the head he found there was an extensive fracture at the back of the skull. He met with the constable upstairs and found the rooms in great disorder. He came to the conclusion the murder and robbery had been committed. He had since, with Dr. Spurgin, made a *post-mortem* examination. The throat had been cut very extensively, most of the principle arteries being severed. There was also an extensive fracture at the back of the skill and other injuries to the head. It was utterly impossible that the deceased could have inflicted such injuries upon herself. The injuries to the skull were such as might have been inflicted by a heavy mallet or blunt instrument. There was no weapon of any kind discovered, which was another proof of the deceased having been subjected to violence from some other person or persons.

Dr. Frederick William Spurgin, of 14, Henrietta-street, Cavendish-square, divisional police surgeon, gave corroborative evidence, and added that there were also bruises on the arms, which indicated that the deceased had put up her arms to defend their head.

In answer to the Coroner, Dr. Spurgin said that such injuries could not have been inflicted by the deceased falling down stairs. The throat was cut very extensively, and no doubt this was done during life. He should say that the deceased had been dead four or five days when the body was found. There was no weapons of any kind found; but they came to the conclusion that the wound in the throat was not caused by any very sharp instrument, as the edges of the wound were very jagged. There were marks on one of the fingers of the deceased's left hand as if a ring had been violently pulled off.

Inspector Robert French, of the D Division, stated that he had searched the house, but had not found any weapon by which such injury could have been inflicted.

Detective Inspector George Robson, of the D Division, produced the jewel-cases which had been found on the floor of the deceased's front room, and also a small jewel had found on the floor. The drawers appear to have been thoroughly ransacked. The witness produced a letter which he had found, in the deceased's handwriting, addressed to Mr. Harry Chadwick, of Gloucester-street, Belgravia, asking him when he was going to pay for the damage done by him to her chain, and when he was going to return the things which he had taken away from her. She further designated Harry Chadwick as a villain, and added that she had it in her power to make him pay one way or the other. They found another letter, which had been addressed to the deceased on business and evidently opened by her on the 17th, on the evening of which, it was believed, she met her death. On the following day, on making a further search, they found some money in the deceased's room and some Consols[330] and a bank book. If robbery had been

the object, it was the opinion of the witness that it could not have been done by expert thieves. The Harry Chadwick referred to in the letter was one of the nephews to whom the previous reference had been made. He had seen the nephew, Harry Chadwick, at 70, Gloucester-street, and in answer to his questions he said he had never had any quarrel with his aunt. The witness observed, "Not about jewelry?" Chadwick replied, "Surely she has not told you anything about that?" He afterwards said that, about three weeks before, his aunt was staying at their house, and, being unwell, she gave him and his brother her keys to go to George-street and find the cat. They went, and took away two stoppers and three watches they found in the drawers, which his brother Walter sold for 10s. at a pawnbroker's. They did so as they were under the influence of drink at the time. The deceased wrote to their mother, who was her sister, about it, and he went in consequence to see her and asked her to forgive him, which she promised to do. He admitted when at the house that he broke a neck chain, which the deceased said she was going to get repaired. He had not seen the deceased since. The brother, who was with him, said he had not been to the house since he took the stoppers.

Detective Inspector John Tunbridge, of Scotland-yard, deposed to interviewing the nephews Chadwick and searching them at their residence. He took them to Marylebone Police-station. After being detained for some time they were allowed to go. He had had them under surveillance ever since, and he read his diary as to their daily and nightly movements up to the present time. There were no points of any importance elicited, except that they were once or twice in company with the Clarks, brothers and other relatives of the deceased.

Harry Chadwick, one of the nephews, was then examined. He said that he was an architect and surveyor, and resided with his mother at 78, Gloucester-street, Pimlico. His aunt visited them on New Year's Eve. While with them she was too ill to go home, and asked him and his brother to go to her house to find the cat. He admitted breaking the watch-chain and she wrote to his mother about it. On Monday, the 16th, he went to his aunt's house to see her to apologize, to ask her forgiveness for having broken her watch-chain, and to ask her why she did not come on the Monday as she had promised. He saw her on the

---

[330] **Consol**. First issued in 1751, the Consol (Consolidated Annuity), is a British government bond that does not mature and pays perpetual interest.

step of the door. He did not go into the house or upstairs. He also asked her forgiveness on behalf of his brother for having taken the stoppers away. His brother had been out of employment for nearly two years, and that accounted for his taking the things—to get money. He sometimes himself gave his brother money. The last time was on Saturday week, when he let him have four or five shillings. His aunt promised to forgive both him and his brother. After leaving her, he met his brother Walter at the Warwick Arms, Pimlico, but he did not recollect whether he told him what his aunt had said. He then explained their movements up to the time of hearing of the deceased's death. He knew the jewel belonging to his aunt which had been produced, and when he and his brother went to find the cat they left it in the jewel-box, which is brother had opened with some keys they found in a tin box kept under the table. The jewel-box was not broken as it now was when they left it. It had some bracelets in it when they left it. He knew nothing whatever about the death of his aunt till he heard what had taken place.

The Coroner observed that if the witness did know anything it was his bounden duty to inform the court.

The witness said he would readily do so.

Walter James Chadwick, a tall, gentlemanly-looking a youth of about 19, the other nephew, was next examined. He said that he had not been in active employ for the last two years. He had been a clerk at the Army and Navy Stores. He had never visited the deceased at her own home, but he had seen her at his mother's many times, and they were very friendly. He then repeated the story about going with his brother to the deceased's house to find the cat. On the following day he went to Stratford, and he might have spent four or five shillings, but could not exactly say. He knew nothing whatever of his aunt's death till he was informed of it by the police.

Inspector Robson, in answer to the Coroner, said the money found in the deceased's room consisted of gold, silver, notes, and cheques.

There being no further evidence, the Coroner, in summing up, pointed out the prominent features of the case, which he thought were such as to lead to the view that a most brutal murder had taken place, and that a robbery had been committed. He had no doubt that the police would make every endeavour to bring the perpetrators of the crime to justice.

The jury returned a verdict of wilful murder against some person or persons at present unknown.

## The Texas Axe Murders
### The Atlanta Constitution
#### Thursday, 21 July, 1887
#### A TEXAN MR. HYDE
#### An Awful Suspicion as to the Assailant of Two Girls.
#### DETECTIVES COMPLETELY BAFFLED.
#### No Explanation Except That the Butchery is the Work of a Maniac—The Crime Like the Austin Murders.

GAINESVILLE, Tex., July 20.—The memory of one young girl murdered and another still hanging between life and death, acts like a pall on the city. At all churches the services partook of a funeral character. People in assembly seemed to tread more softly and whisper words of sympathy and sorrow for the hearts today bowed down in suffering. The firm tones of the men in talking over the bloody dou-ble butchery showed that the fire of human vengeance still burns, and seems to be fed by time.

As investigation, after five day's analysis of every circumstance attending the murder, utterly fails to find the slightest reasonable clue, hushed conjecture is beginning to connect the assault upon these two girls with the horrible series of murders in Austin two years ago. Nine women were killed in just twelve months' time in that neighboring city, and almost every incident in each of those murders is duplicated in last Wednesday night's tragedy here. There was never a clue found to the perpetrator of the Austin murders. There was never an explanation to them, except that they were the work of one man, and he a maniac. The horrible fear is beginning to spread that he has begun his work here.

The Austin series started on one Christmas eve and closed with a double tragedy on the eve of the next sacred natal day.

The first victim of the bloody line was Mary Smith, a colored servant woman. Her body was found in the yard attached to her house on Christmas morning, 1884. There had been frightful mutilation gashes and cuts so vigorously made that the body fell apart when the neighbors came to lift it into a coffin. It was a bright moonlight night when the murder was committed, and the assassin seemed to take abundance of time for his work. His footsteps were traced here and there around the yard, as though he had lingered long about the spot. There was deliberation marked at every point, and with no slight effort at concealment. It seems incredible that no clue was left leading up to the assassin. Explanation came readily enough. It was a discarded lover, the general opinion agreed, who had done the deed and there was not much talk over it.

#### REPEATING THE CRIME.

But on the night of May 7, 1885, Lizzie Shelley, another colored servant, was killed in precisely the same fashion. It was a bright moonlight night, as before. There was the same dragging out of the victim from her bed to the open air; then the gashing and slashing with some instrument of the hatchet type—not a mere killing or forcing into insensibility, but a repeated use of the weapon, as though the ruffian found delight in hearing the thud upon the bone and flesh of his victims. The same explanation came readily enough—jealously and the gratification of love turned to hate. In June came the third on the list. She, too, was a colored servant girl, Irene Cross. There was the same hacking and muti-lation, the same seeming fiendish delight in mangling the body. In this case it was not dragged out to the open air, but the victim's room showed that the ruffian had been hurried away by an alarm which he imagined had been directed at him.

This crime stirred the community. The negroes were certain that some terrible Voudoo was working out an evil charm, and there was a great sale of all manner of nostrums and queer combinations to fight off the evil one. The white population began to put out some efforts, but the culmination had not yet been reached, and the unknown fiend felt emboldened in his work.

#### THE TERRIBLE RECORD CONTINUED.

On August 30th of that year the same assassin, it now seems clear, visited a cabin on the place of Mr. V.O. Wood, a nephew of the late Thurlow Wood. In the cabin were two colored servants, mother and daughter—Rebecca Ramey, aged forty, and Mary Ramey, aged twelve. It was 4 o'clock in the morning when Mr. Wood heard groans in the cabin. He found the mother bleeding from a gash in the head and the daughter missing. The trail was a hot one, for fresh blood spots led to a stable half a mile away, where the body of the girl was found, assaulted and bashed on the head with the same hatchet

# Appendix M, The Texas Axe Murders

blow. There was not the usual scene of butchery, but there were evidences of haste in the work. The excitement ran up to fever heat, and when the bloodhounds were put on the scent and a ten miles track was made in and out of the city streets, then out into the country and back until the scent was lost in the streets again. This use of the hounds convinced many that the murderer was a negro, for the hounds were thrown off the scent by the old slave methods of baffling the dogs. Others pointed out that the great unknown may have been a white man, thoroughly familiar with negro lore on hounds and the best methods of throwing them off the scent. There were many traces which seemed to lead direct to certain individuals, but in each case innocence was proven. The negroes abandoned their notion that witches were doing the bloody work and insisted that a white man was the wrong-doer, as the whole campaign showed too much method and purpose for a black brain to compass.

Another month swung by, and the people had ceased to sleep with rifle in hand behind double-barred doors. September 29 was the date of the next bloody act. Again the scene was a negro cabin, this time occupied by four people—Mrs. Gracie Vance, Orange Washington, Lucinda Boddy and Patsey Gibson, two mulatto girls. There were two apartments. In one the murderer beat the girls into insensibility, apparently with a sand club.[331] The man was hammered into insensibility, and died the next morning; while Mrs. Vance was dragged out of the cabin through a window, taken along the road some eighty yards and there, after assault, had her brains beaten out. A stone club was the weapon of murder in this case, and the hatchet, or heavy cleaver seemed to have been left at home. In the lifeless fingers of Gracie Vance was a bit of watch chain with broken crystal, but even this carelessly left piece of evidence did not serve to lead to the detection of the criminal.

October brought the next one of the list. It was another colored woman, Alice Davis, and she, too, was dragged from her bed in a cabin, taken some distance away, assaulted and then hacked up far past the limit of ordinary killing. A whirlwind of doubt and dread swept over the city. Whites and blacks alike were in terror, but

---

[331] **Sand Club**. A sand filled sack used as a makeshift Blackjack.

especially the latter, whose superstitious fear was at times most pitiful to see.

## TWO MORE MURDERS TO CLOSE THE YEAR.

The last and bloodiest of the awful series was on Christmas eve, 1885. Mrs. Hancock and her husband lived in a pretty cottage in one of the quiet streets of Austin. He was a mechanic of good standing, a white man. Hearing a slight noise on that night he went to his wife's apartment. He found the bed empty and gory. The trail of blood was short and fresh. It ran to the yard and there on the ground, weltering in her blood and gasping, lay his wife, with two hatchet wounds in the head, not yet dead, but beaten into insensibility; she died the next morning. There was the bright moonlight as before, the apparent invitation to detection, and yet the old time immunity from detection. But the murder of one white woman was not the whole record of that Christmas eve. After midnight Mr. James Phillip heard groaning in a lower room of his house. The room whence the sounds came was occupied by a married son, together with his wife and infant son. The young man lay groaning upon the bed, gashed into the brain above the right ear with the familiar hatchet mark. The sleeping child had its garments saturated with the blood of its parents. The Mother was absent, but there was the open tell tale trail leading out to the yard and there the nude body of Mrs. Phillips lay, assaulted, with the skull cleft almost in two by a blow dealt upon the forehead. A log had been lifted and flung across the chest. There had been no outcry, not the least sound or appeal for help, nothing until the quickly awakened father heard the groaning of his son and hurried down to the ghastly spectacle.

The bloodhounds came in on Christmas morning, took up both trails only to follow them away, and then to bay in acknowledgment of defeat.

## ABSOLUTELY NO CLUE.

Not alone was the instinct of the brute called in to find the criminal, but the best detective talent which money could secure was brought to bear on the case; but today they are as much shrouded in mystery as they were a year and a half ago. The husband of the murdered Eula Phillips was tried for her murder, as was the husband of Mrs. Hancock. In each case long and exhaustive trials were had, but nothing was brought out of a criminating character. The Pinkertons were called upon to aid in unravelling the crime, and given carte blanche as to time and money. Other detectives, too, were employed, but so far not even a remote clue has been unearthed.

Everyone in Austin has read Stevenson's extra-ordinary novel with an intensity of interest known in no other community. Was there a Dr. Jekyll and a Mr. Hyde living there—one who could in a twinkling of a eye change his identity? If so, even how was it that there never was a discovery? Why did not someone meet the assassin, bloody-handed and saturated with blood, as he must have been from head to foot? He took no special pains for concealment. He never made a failure. Was it a conspiracy for murder or was someone playing a lone hand in the fearful game? There was no seeming purpose in some of the murders. Not a penny of gain by the slaughterer, no grudge to gratify, no feud to fight out. He defied alike the brute and the human detective.

## HAS HE APPEARED IN GAINESVILLE?

And the terrible similarity of his methods to the tragedy here, of which these dispatches have given the readers of *The World* full account. Miss Genie Watkins, the daughter of a hotel keeper in Dallas, had been on a visit to Miss Mamie Bostwick, the daughter of a rich cattle dealer in this city. They were aged nineteen and twenty years, respectively. The house was a single story one and, after the Texas fashion, spreading over a good deal of ground. The two young ladies occupied separate beds in a front room. It was about 3 o'clock last Wednesday morning when Mrs. Bostwick heard a slight scuffle in the girl's room. It was just on the first edge of daylight, and when she entered the apartment her glance fell first upon the figure of a man sitting near the window with his feet upon the sill, as though taking a rest after a difficult job. He was thoroughly at ease, and, without extra haste, placed his hand upon the sill, vaulted lightly out and disappeared, leaving only the imprint of his bloody palm upon the woodwork. Mrs. Bostwick turned to the beds where the girls were moaning in insensibility. Mrs. Bostwick screamed and fainted away, but aid came at once. The household was aroused, and all that could be done by medical skill was done for the two young ladies. They were both fearfully gashed,

and the blood flowing turned the room to the appearance of a slaughter house. There had been the struggles of youth and vigor against the assailant, but in each instance the hatchet had been used to give the quietus to the victim. Miss Watkins had received two blows. One had cut through the bones of the forehead from the right temple across to the left. It was given with force, and from the gaping opening the brains were pouring out upon the clotted blood. Another blow had fallen upon the right temple and had forced in the bones of the skull in such a way as to force the eye from its socket. There were bruises upon the arm as though the assailant had clutched her in a strong grip against her struggles to free herself from his hold.

## THE SURVIVING GIRL'S STORY.

Miss Bostwick was three times struck with that active hatchet. One blow on the left temple fractured the skull, another cut was a deep triangular slash on the right cheek, the third opened the face from the corner of the nose to the center of the upper lip. Two upper teeth were knocked out and two lower ones were broken. The wounds were terrible and the pain from them excruciating. Yet the victim lived, and her first inquiry upon becoming conscious was about Genie. She was evidently not aware of what had taken place. From such questions as could be put to the wounded girl it was inferred that the assailant was a white man with a black mustache, but with such wounds it is not surprising that the mind wandered, and little weight was placed upon such information. Here was her almost inarticulate story: When asked if she saw her assailant she said, "Yes."

"Was he colored?"

"No."

"White?"

"Yes, and he had a black mustache."

"Where did you see him first?"

"In the yard."

"What were you struck with?"

She returned no answer.

"With a stick?"

"No."

"With a hatchet?"

"Yes."

"Did the man enter at the window?"

"No."

"At the door?"

"Yes."

# Appendix M, The Texas Axe Murders

"Did he go out through the window?"

"Yes."

She saw him first "in the yard." Did this murderer, as his Austin prototype, drag his victim out of doors after beating her into insensibility, and then perhaps return her mangled body to the bed? Several of the Austin victims must have been beaten into unconsciousness while asleep and then taken away, for their outcry would also have alarmed others in the house. The deliberation of the Gainesville murderer makes it possible that he did so drag the helpless body out and back again. But if so he must be a maniac.

**THE BLOODHOUNDS AGAIN BAFFLED.**

There was bright moonlight the night before—as on each night of the nine Austin murders—and an examination showed that the hard sod outside the windows had failed to take impress of the assassin's foot. But when daylight came, tracks were found in the ploughed ground among the growing corn, in which a large portion of the vacant lot adjoining is planted. Still there was little to indicate that the tracks belonged to the murderer save the fact of their being found near the scene of his assault. The tracks were evidently made by feet incased in socks only, and were of gigantic size, measuring over 12 inches in length. Another track of different size and shape was also found leading towards the house, but neither could be found near the window at which the fiend made his egress.

A meeting of citizens raised $2,000 for use in ferreting out the criminal. Immediately upon being informed of the bloody affair officers telegraphed to several towns for bloodhounds, and a train arrived bringing two of the trailers. They were taken to the house and given the scent, but so great was the crowd about the lot that they failed to strike a trail. The dogs were taken away and the crowd asked to disperse, which it did. Later on the dogs were again given the scent, and, striking the trail, they followed it in a northerly direction to the creek bottom, where it was lost. Once more the dogs were taken back to the house. This time they were kept for some time in the room where the deed was committed, were shown the spots of blood upon the window-sill left by the hand of the assassin and the track found in the garden. Again they gave cry and followed the trail over the same

course as formerly, losing it again at the same place. A third time they were taken back and a third time they went over the same ground and gave up the chase at the same point. The great heat and extreme dryness seemed to have destroyed the scent and the dogs were unable to accomplish anything more.

In the meantime at least five hundred men, divided in twenty or more posses, mounted on horseback, scoured the country in all directions. As they went along they aroused the farmers, who joined in the pursuit. Nine arrests were made and the suspected partie(s) were put under guard to await examination. They were doubly protected by resolute men for fear that the enraged populace would tear them limb from limb even on slight suspicion of guilt.

**YOUNG NORWOOD'S QUEER SUGGESTION.**

The arrested men one by one easily succeeded in proving their innocence, and then came an astonishing suggestion from young Abel Norwood, of Dallas, who was the affianced lover of Miss Watkins and who came on here at once after the murder. Perhaps the young man is somewhat unbalanced by his grief, but here is his story: He met in Dallas some time ago a young lady, whose name he declines to give, who fell in love with him.

At first he thought the murder was the work of a discarded suitor of Miss Watkins, but now he believes it was instigated by the infatuated woman referred to. After meeting this person he says he did not call on her until invited by letter to do so, and "then did not make any advances to indicate that he regarded her in any but the light of a mere friend." She told him she had understood that he was engaged to Miss Watkins, and vowed she did not wish to come between them, but declared that she loved him and that "she could work harder and make more sacrifices for his happiness than Miss Watkins could. He repelled her advances gently but firmly, telling her that Genie loved him and that he loved Genie and must be true to her." This young lady sent for him several times, so he avers, and never wearied of telling him of her devotion, though she saw her case as hopeless. He gave the place of her residence, which is a small Texas city, he said. She never was in Gainesville that he knew of, but he seemed to think, in spite of his disclaimer, that someone might have hired

# Appendix M, The Texas Axe Murders

someone to be a representative here.

## FRUITLESS CLUES.

In fact, there are all manner of reports, besides the conjecture that the murder was the work of a maniac. It is asserted, and the report seems to come from a reliable source, that Captain Watkins stated in an interview that Miss Genie Watkins was a very important witness in a case several years ago, wherein a man was sent to the penitentiary for robbery, and that the man's sentence was out a few days before this murder was committed. The man was heard to vow vengeance at the time of his conviction, and it is possible he may be the guilty party, having committed the crime at the first opportunity he had to secure the vengeance he vowed long ago.

But so strong is the belief here that the murder is the work of a maniac that grave suspicions rested upon the brother of Miss Bost(w)ick a young man some twenty-one or twenty-two years old, who is afflicted with epilepsy. Persons, however, well acquainted with the family and knowing the young man's condition, expressed emphatic disbelief in the theory. His physical condition, they said, was such that he could not climb in and out of the window without assistance. Others expatiated on the ease with which he could have jumped from the window, could have run around the house, throwing the hatchet in the well as he passed, climbed in a back window and crawled into bed. It was even rumoured that the bloodhounds ran around the house from the last window to a back window and tried to climb in the boy's room. This story on investigation proved to be false. A close examination was made of the well, parties going down into it twice, and nothing could be found. The boy's room was carefully searched, and no marks of blood or other traces could be found which would connect him with the awful crime. Besides, some of those who were present early after the alarm was given, declare that he came into the room almost immediately with unmistakable signs upon his face of having just waked up, and that his horror and fright were such as could not be simulated. In short, the matter has been thoroughly sifted, and his connection with the assault seems to be clearly shown to be impossible.

## A BIG REWARD OFFERED.

The officers who held the inquest on Miss Watkins admit that they have absolutely no clues. R.V. Bell, ex-district attorney, said: "It is a horrible thought, for we cannot tell where he may strike next, but it looks like the work of a maniac, a man who considers himself commissioned to kill certain persons, whose diseased mind is unable to resist what he considers his call to duty, and who is yet possessed of that subtle cunning which enables him to cover up his tracks successfully. As to the identity of the maniac, I have no theory and no clue from which to weave one." Hon. J.A. Garnett, one of the leading criminal lawyers at this bar, was found in his office and said in reply to a question: "I think the assassin must have entered the house with the intention of committing an outrage, and that, discovered in his attempt or else frightened by the presence of two young ladies, when he thought to find but one, he struck his murderous blows to enable him to make his escape. It is impossible to conceive of anybody committing such a deed without a motive, and what other motive could be there except that of satisfying a brutal lust?"

Governor Ross has offered a reward of $1,000 for the capture of the murderer. Citizens of Gainesville have raised $2,500 altogether for that purpose, and the *Dallas News* has offered its columns for a popular subscription fund to secure the best detective ability to work up the case. J. Marks, a banker of Texarkana, has sent a check for $250, and is the first to respond to the call for a popular subscription.

Miss Bostwick is slowly recovering. Much hope is expressed that with returning strength her mind will become clearer and that she will remember something so conclusive of the terrible ordeal which she passed as will aid the detectives to track the assassin.

(On 26 December, 1887, William L. Beason forged a check in Luling, about 50 miles southeast of Austin. When Luling policeman Ben Evans questioned Beason's sister-in-law as to his whereabouts she told him that he had fled Texas and gone home to Mississippi. She also told him that Beason had confessed to her that he had attacked the two girls in Gainesville, 300 miles north of Luling, when they woke up as he was burglarizing their room in search of jewellery. Friends of the fugitive had earlier told Evans that Beason "was suffering from a heavy load on his mind, that he could not sleep, and often threatened to kill himself." Beason was captured in Meridian, Mississippi, but committed suicide on 29 February, 1888 by jumping from the train that was carrying him back to Texas. Although W.L. Beason did confess to the killing, how many later confessed to the Ripper crimes? (McQueen))

581

# Appendix M, The Texas Axe Murders

## Wednesday, 26 September, 1888.
### Is It the Man from Texas?

And now it is announced that the mysterious London murderer has killed another woman, his fifth victim within a few weeks.

The five women have all been murdered in the same manner, at about the same hour and in the same locality. Our readers who have followed these remarkable cases will recollect that the assassin always pounced upon the women in the street just about daybreak. After killing them he mutilated their bodies in the most shocking fashion, and then disappeared, leaving no trace behind him. Of course, the police and the people have their theories, and one of them is that this unknown murderer is a monster or a lunatic who has sworn to kill twenty women, and then give himself up to justice.

Suppose we try another theory. In the present generation the London murders have only been matched by the horrible tragedies in Texas nearly two years ago. The Texas man, like the London monster, always selected women for his victims. He assaulted them when they were alone, and mutilated their bodies. He killed several women in Austin, and several in another town. His movements were so secret that the police could find no clew. The women who were murdered were not robbed, and they were not known to have an enemy in the world.

The Texas and the London murders are precisely alike. There is the same absence of a reasonable motive, the same grotesque brutality in the mutilations, the same mystery, and the same suspicion that the criminal is a monster or a lunatic, who has declared war literally to the knife against all womankind.

Is the London assassin the man from Texas?

Why not? In our recent annals of crime there has been no other man capable of committing such deeds. The mysterious crimes in Texas have ceased; they have just commenced in London. Is the man from Texas at the bottom of them all?

If he is a monster or a lunatic, he may be expected to appear anywhere. The fact that he is no longer at work in Texas argues his presence somewhere else. His peculiar line of work, executed in precisely the same manner, is now going on in London—why should he not be there?

The more one thinks of it, the more irresistible becomes the conviction that it is the man from Texas. In these days of steam and cheap travel distance is nothing. A man who would kill a dozen women in Texas, would not mind the inconvenience of a trip across the water, and once there he would not have any scruples about killing more women.

Undoubtedly it must be the man from Texas.

~

## William James

### 𝕿𝖍𝖊 𝕿𝖎𝖒𝖊𝖘

**10 January 1889**

**CENTRAL CRIMINAL COURT, Jan. 9.**

**(Before MR. JUSTICE DENMAN.)**

WILLIAM JAMES, 33, hawker, was indicted for the manslaughter of William Hall.

Mr. Mead and Mr. Charles Mathews conducted the prosecution; Mr. Keith Frith was counsel for the defence.

It seemed that on the night of December 7 the deceased, a sorter in the General Post Office, was walking home along Marshalsea-street, Borough, with a companion, when a woman, who had been in company with a man, came up to them crying and made a statement to them. The prisoner also came up and spoke to the woman, and then left her, and struck the man in whose company she had been. The man walked away, and the deceased subsequently spoke to a constable about the prisoner. The constable questioned the prisoner, who said he was "Jack the Ripper." The deceased and his companions walked away, and the prisoner afterwards followed them and, as it was alleged, struck Hall a blow which knocked him down and caused his head to come into violent contact with the ground, the force being such that the thud of the fall was heard by a constable who was standing some distance away.

The blow rendered the deceased insensible for a time, and he was removed to Guy's Hospital, where he died from the injury he had sustained at half-past 10 on the same morning. The prisoner denied striking the deceased, and said he only pushed him, and he subsequently made a statement to the effect that he heard the man whom he struck in the first instance making improper overtures to the woman, who was a married woman, and that when he returned and pushed the deceased he was under the impression that Hall was the man he had first struck. A witness was called on the part of the defence.

In reply to MR. JUSTICE DENMAN, Mr. KEITH FRITH said he was instructed that the prisoner pushed the deceased in consequence of a threatening gesture, and that was the defence which he proposed to raise.

MR. JUSTICE DENMAN said there was no evidence that the push was given in self-defence. It was extremely uncertain whether the prisoner struck the deceased.

Mr. KEITH FRITH said that after what his Lordship had said he would not contest that the case was one of manslaughter, but it was in circumstances of mitigation.

The prisoner then said he was guilty of manslaughter by a shove.

It was stated that the prisoner had been before convicted of assault.

MR. JUSTICE DENMAN postponed sentence.

~

# Appendix O, Hard Labour

From <u>Forty-Ninth Report of the Inspectors-General of the General State of the Prisons in Ireland, 1870, Carlow County Gaol at Carlow.</u>
*Pp 359-60*

Punitive labour consists chiefly of the tread-wheel and stone-breaking. Male prisoners, sentenced to hard labour, are engaged at the mill during the first part of their imprisonment for six and a quarter hours daily in summer, and five and a quarter hours in winter, with periods of rest regulated according to the number of prisoners engaged. During the latter part of their imprisonment they are only to be put on the tread-wheel for two and a half hours daily in all seasons. Prisoners when at the mill should, during their intervals of relief, be employed by picking oakum, as it frequently happens that the periods of rest are quite as long as the time spent at the mill.

The tread-wheel is now merely utilized for grinding the Indian corn used in the prison.

The industrial labour for males consists of spinning, cording, mat and clog-making, tailoring, carpentry, tinning, and oakum picking. Most of these employments are carried on in a large workshed, in which linen, canvas, frieze, and linsey are made here under the super-intendence of a master tradesman...

The industrial labour carried on by the females, consist chiefly of spinning and sewing. They also make up all their own clothing, and pick oakum; but as I have already stated, these women do not perform a sufficient quantity of either industrial or punitive labour, washing being the most arduous of their occupations. Each female sentenced to hard labour should, in addition to her ordinary day's work, be compelled to pick at least 1½ to 2 lbs. of oakum daily, as it is quite useless for judges and magistrates to pass on prisoners the sentence of hard labour, if such be not carried out in our gaols. (IGPI)

~

From <u>Eighteen Months Imprisonment (With a Remission)</u>, Donald Shaw, 1883:
*Pp 183-84*

Oakum is one of the most tell-tale commodities I ever came across. If merely unravelled, it remains black and juicy; but the more it is picked and pulled the paler it gets, till it is capable of assuming the appearance of Turkish tobacco. An experienced eye can at once detect the amount of labour bestowed on it, and some of the huge bundles I saw my confrères carrying down were works of art as regards finish.

*Pp 278-79*

The tread-wheel is moved by elaborate machinery worked by powerful engines, which, in addition to setting the wheel in motion, grinds corn in an adjoining building for the use of the prison. It is entirely different from the Adelphi one, and may be described as four long cylindrical wheels extending the length of the building on either side and along the gallery. Partitions, of sufficient dimensions to enable a man to stand up, run the entire length of the various wheels, thereby precluding all communication between the several occupants. Two hundred and sixty men can be "on" at once, and the punishment is carried out on the principle of ten minutes "off" and twenty minutes "on." The victims are marched down at 7.30 A.M., and beguile the time thus pleasantly till 11.30. They return at 1.30 p.m., and continue the enjoyment till 5.

I am told this is considered an easy wheel, and men who have experienced the working of others assured me that this one was mere child's play. A great deal depends on the worker, and the experienced jail-bird rises—or, as it was termed to me, "waits for "—the step with little or no exertion. With the novice, however, it is severe labour, and the exertion involved bathes him in perspiration. A supply of warm water is given them on returning to their cells of an evening, to obliterate in a degree the unpleasant consequences of the wheel. But the discomfort—can one estimate it? A poor wretch bathed in perspiration, and having to sleep in the same shirt and work in it for a week! Only prisoners fit for hard labour are put to the wheel, and no man is ever so employed unless passed by the surgeon. (Shaw)

~

# Appendix P, Mary Jane Kelly Post Mortem

## Dr. Thomas Bond's Post Mortem Examination of Mary Jane Kelly

*This post-mortem report, written by Dr. Thomas Bond after he examined the remains of Mary Jane Kelly, was lost until 1987, when it was returned anonymously by mail to Scotland Yard.*

### Position of body

The body was lying naked in the middle of the bed, the shoulders flat, but the axis of the body inclined to the left side of the bed. The head was turned on the left cheek. The left arm was close to the body with the forearm flexed at a right angle & lying across the abdomen. The right arm was slightly abducted from the body & rested on the mattress, the elbow bent & the forearm supine with the fingers clenched.

The legs were wide apart, the left thigh at right angles to the trunk & the right forming an obtuse angle with the pubes.

The whole of the surface of the abdomen & thighs was removed & the abdominal Cavity emptied of its viscera. The breasts were cut off, the arms mutilated by several jagged wounds & the face hacked beyond recognition of the features. The tissues of the neck were severed all round down to the bone.

The viscera were found in various parts viz: the uterus & Kidneys with one breast under the head, the other breast by the Rt foot, the Liver between the feet, the intestines by the right side & the spleen by the left side of the body. The flaps removed from the abdomen and thighs were on a table.

The bed clothing at the right corner was saturated with blood, & on the floor beneath was a pool of blood covering about 2 feet square. The wall by the right side of the bed & in a line with the neck was marked by blood which had struck it in a number of sphearate splashes.

### Postmortem examination

The face was gashed in all directions the nose cheeks, eyebrows and ears being partly removed. The lips were blanched & cut by several incisions running obliquely down to the chin. There were also numerous cuts extending irregularly across all the features.

The neck was cut through the skin & other tissues right down to the vertebrae the 5th & 6th being deeply notched. The skin cuts in the front of the neck showed distinct ecchymosis.

The air passage was cut at the lower part of the larynx through the cricoid cartilage.

Both breasts were removed by more or less circular incisions, the muscles down to the ribs being attached to the breasts. The intercostals between the 4th, 5th & 6th ribs were cut through & the contents of the thorax visible through the openings.

The skin & tissues of the abdomen from the costal arch to the pubes were removed in three large flaps.

The right thigh was denuded in front to the bone, the flap of skin, including the external organs of generation & part of the right buttock. The left thigh was stripped of skin, fascia & muscles as far as the knee.

The left calf showed a long gash through skin & tissues to the deep muscles & reaching from the knee to 5 ins above the ankle.

Both arms & forearms had extensive & jagged wounds.

The right thumb showed a small superficial incision about 1 in long, with extravasation of blood in the skin & there were several abrasions on the back of the hand moreover showing the same condition.

On opening the thorax it was found that the right lung was minimally adherent by old firm adhesions.

The lower part of the lung was broken & torn away.

The left lung was intact: it was adherent at the apex & there were a few adhesions over the side. In the substaces of the lung were several nodules of consolidation.

The Pericardium was open below & the Heart absent.

In the abdominal cavity was some partially digested food of fish & potatoes & similar food was found in the remains of the stomach attached to the intestines. (Casebook Productions)

# Catherine "Rose" Mylett Murder

## The Times

**Thursday, 3 January 1889**

**THE SUPPOSED MURDER AT POPLAR.**

Yesterday Mr. Wynne E. Baxter, the Coroner for the South-Eastern Division of Middlesex, resumed his adjourned inquiry at the Town-hall, Poplar, respecting the death of Catherine Millett, aged 26, whose dead body was found in Clarke's-yard, High-street, Poplar, on the 20th of December.

Mr. St. John Wontner watched the case on behalf of the Treasury.

Mrs. Margaret Millett, widow, of 16, Pelham-street, Whitechapel, stated that deceased was her daughter and was 26 years of age. Her name was Catherine Millett. Witness had been told that deceased was married, but deceased herself never told witness that she was. She once saw a man with deceased and believed him to be her husband. Witness knew deceased had one child, but she could not say whether she had more than that one. Witness last saw her alive on the Monday or Tuesday before her death, when she called at her house. Deceased then arranged to meet witness at the top of Brushfield-street the following Thursday at 4 o'clock. Witness did not get there to time, and did not see her again. She never told witness where she was living. She told her she had been "hopping" with another woman. Deceased also told witness her child was in Surrey. Witness had no idea how she was getting her living. She left witness six years ago to go and live at Bow.

By Mr. St. John Wontner—Witness knew that she was very much given to intemperance.

By the Jury—Deceased's child was born at Bow. Witness did not know that she lived with any other man but her husband.

Mrs. Elizabeth Usher, nurse at the Stepney Sick Asylum, said she had seen the body of deceased in the Poplar mortuary, and recognized it as that of a former inmate. She knew her under the names of Rose Millett and Rose Davis. She had been in the asylum several times. According to the books, her age was about 28. She was admitted as a single woman, and was last in the asylum in March, 1888. She had been there then since January. Witness knew deceased had a child seven years of age, and when she was

discharged she said she was going to get her mother to mind it.

By the Jury—Deceased was in the asylum four times, and witness knew her well.

Sergeant Golding, recalled at the request of the jury, stated that when he found the body there was a spotted handkerchief round the throat, which he now produced, It was not tightly round the throat, and was not tied at all. It did not appear to have been tied or pulled tightly round the throat.

By Mr. St. John Wontner—There was no sign on the handkerchief of there having been a struggle. When witness found the body it was lying parallel with the wall, and the head was about a foot from the wall. Witness's first impression was that deceased had been leaning against some posts near the wall and had fallen down. The yard was not paved, but was composed of earth, and would show signs of a struggle had once taken place.

Mr. George James Harris, 170, East India-road, Poplar, deposed that he was a surgeon and acted as assistant to Dr. Brownfield. On Thursday, December 20, witness was called by the police at 4:30 a.m., and was taken to Clarke's-yard. He there saw deceased, who was dead, and was lying with her left cheek on the ground. There was a little blood-stained mucus issuing from the nostrils. The head was lying over the jacket, but he did not think it was in such a position as to cause strangulation. The collar of the jacket was quite loose. Her lips were livid, the mouth closed, and the eyes were normal. The left arm and leg were stiff. Witness assisted Dr. Brownfield to make the post-mortem examination, and with regard to the internal examination he agreed with Dr. Brownfield's evidence. With regard to the cause of death, witness noticed a mark which commenced at the spine and passed round the neck to the ear. There was a space of two or three inches at the back of the neck which was not marked. That mark might be produced with a piece of string. He did not see any other way by which the mark could be produced. In his opinion it was not possible for the collar of the jacket to have produced it. It was a much finer mark than he thought the collar could have produced. There were five superficial abrasions on the left side of the neck and three on the right side. Witness was of opinion that they were caused by finger nails, resulting from an

# Appendix Q, Catherine "Rose" Mylett Murder

endeavour to remove something from the neck. On the left side of the jaw there was a small bruise. In his opinion the cause of death was asphyxia, from strangulation.

By the Jury—Witness believed the string was crossed over, and used in a way similar to the way used when soap was cut. The marks on the neck could not have been caused by a man's hand.

By the Coroner—Witness examined the windpipe and found no foreign matter in it.

By Mr. St. John Wontner—The mark on the neck was above the necktie. When witness first saw the body he did not notice the mark and did not then suspect foul play. He then thought deceased had died from asphyxia, from drunkenness or natural causes. Death would be brought about very quickly if the string was used in the way he described. The deceased's tongue was not protruding, nor were the eyeballs. He should have expected that the face would have been more disturbed had the strangulation been slow.

Dr. Thomas Bond, 7, Sanctuary, Westminster Abbey, F.R.C.S., stated that he was asked to examine the body by Mr. Anderson, Assistant Commissioner of Police. Witness examined the body on the 24th of December. Mr. Hibbard, Demonstrator of Anatomy at Westminster Hospital, had examined the body on the Saturday with Drs. Brownfield and Harris, and he supplied witness with his notes. On the Monday witness had the body reopened, and compared his notes with his (witness's) observations. He and the other doctors agreed, with the exception of the mark on the throat. At the date of his examination the mark, which had been described as the mark of a cord, had disappeared. The other marks, which were described as finger marks, witness saw. He also saw in front of the larynx three extravasations of blood, where incisions had been made, and found blood effused around the larynx and deep congestion of the mucous membrane of the larynx. Witness took possession of the contents of the stomach and had what remained analysed. Witness could find no injury to the skin where the mark had been. He agreed with the deductions of Drs. Brownfield, Hibbard, and Harris that the deceased died from strangulation, but his opinion was that it was not murder. The amount of violence which would be required to rapidly strangle an able-bodied woman would leave such a mark on the neck that it would not disappear even during the five days that had elapsed. Witness should have expected to find injuries to the skin and tissues under the skin. The woman's skin was of such a nature that it would take a mark like wax, and from previous experience witness knew that strangulation might occur through a tight dress or a collar and leave deep marks. His opinion was that the woman, in a state of drunkenness, fell down and the larynx was compressed against the neck of the jacket, and that the mark described as the mark of a cord must have been produced by the rim of the collar, either while she was dying or while she was dead in the interval between the finding of the body and its being undressed.

By the CORONER—The injury to the larynx must have been caused before death, but the mark above that might be caused before or after death.

By the Jury—The collar of deceased's jacket measured 14 in. Witness did not think the collar of deceased's jacket was stiff enough to strangle her. He thought it was possible that the woman made the finger marks herself. Had it been a case of quick strangulation he should have expected to find more contortion of the face.

Mrs. Mary Smith, of 18, George-street, Spitalfields, deposed that she had had a lodger who went by the name of Lizzie Davis. The photograph produced (that of the deceased) was that of her. She also recognized deceased's clothing. On Wednesday, the 19th of December, between 7:30 and 8 o'clock, deceased left the house and never returned. She was sober when she left, and was wearing the neckerchief produced by the police-sergeant. Witness was not alarmed at deceased not returning, as she believed she was locked up. She had been sentenced to five days' imprisonment during the three months she was with witness. Deceased was more often drunk than sober. When she left witness's house she told her she was going to Poplar, where she went every night.

Lizzie Hanlon, of George-street, Spitalfields, said she had known deceased for three months as a fellow lodger. She last saw her alive on Wednesday, the 19th ult., when she left the house to go to Poplar.

Elizabeth Griffen, of 18, George-street, gave corroborative evidence, and said the deceased had drunk with a man called Ben Goodson, who was present at the court.

The case was again adjourned.

# Appendix Q, Catherine "Rose" Mylett Murder

## The Times
### Thursday, 10 January 1889
### THE POPLAR MURDER.

Yesterday Mr. Wynne E. Baxter, the Coroner for the South-Eastern division of Middlesex, resumed his adjourned inquiry at the Town-hall, Poplar, respecting the death of ROSE MILLETT, aged 26, who was found lying dead in Clarke's-yard, High Street, Poplar, on the early morning of December 20 last.

Mr. St. John Wontner represented Mr. Monro Chief Commissioner of Police; and Superintendent Steed and Detective-Sergeants Bradshaw and Duck, K Division, also represented the police.

Benjamin Payne, of 184, High-Street, Poplar, a grocer's manager, living next door but one to Clarke's-yard, and Richard John Ashby, of 186, High-street, Poplar, whose bedroom looked into Clarke's-yard, both spoke to hearing voices during the night in question down the yard, but no cries of distress.

Dr. Brownfield, in answer to the Coroner, stated that besides Drs. Hibberd and Bond, Dr. MacKellar, chief surgeon of the Metropolitan Police, saw the body. After hearing Dr. Bond's evidence, his own opinion was not at all altered that death was due to homicidal violence. The mark was too straight and too even in witness' opinion to have been caused by the dress or collar of the jacket.

Jane Hill, of 152, High-street, Poplar, said she kept a boarding-house. She had known the deceased five years. She last saw her alive about 12:15 a.m. on Thursday the 20th ult. She was then neither sober nor drunk. Deceased was retching and said she had a touch of the bile. She took her into a public-house and gave her some brandy.

Constable Barrett, 470 K, said he was with Sergeant Golding when the body was found, another officer and himself being left in charge of the body while the Sergeant went for the doctor. He looked for a mark round the neck when he took the body to the mortuary, but could find none.

Mr. Curtain T. Chivers, the Coroner's officer and mortuary keeper, was sworn and said he first saw the body on the morning of the 20th at 9:30. He noticed a mark round the neck and some scratches. The mark was about an eighth of an inch deep, and the scratches were above it. Witness informed Dr. Harris of it; and he said he had not noticed it, but when he made the post mortem examination he would look carefully for it. As the body was lying witness should say the mark could be seen. Witness had seen the body on several occasions. The mark was visible on December 21.

William Randall, assistant to Mr. Chivers, said that when, on January 6, he fastened the body down in the coffin he noticed the mark round the neck. It was about a quarter of an inch deep and there was a bruise on the left of it. He drew the attention of Inspector Bridgeman to it.

Alice Graves, of 18, St. George-street, Spitalfields, deposed that, having seen the body of the deceased in the mortuary, she identified it as that of a fellow lodger who was known by the name of "Drunken Lizzie." Witness last saw her alive at a quarter to 2 on the morning of Thursday, the 20th ult., when she was walking along the Commercial-road with two men, one on each side of her. She was near the George Tavern and was going towards the City. Witness saw that she was wearing a hat. She could not tell whether the men were sober.

By the Jury—The gas was alight in the window of the George publichouse when she saw the time. Deceased was drunk and was staggering. Witness did not speak to Lizzie. She could give no description of the men, and would be unable to recognize them again were she to see them.

By Mr. Wontner—The distance from Clarke's-yard to the George was about one and a half mile.

The CORONER, proceeding to sum up, said that there were two points in connexion with the case which were singular, and which required careful attention.

The first was that one could not help noticing that if this was a case of strangulation the string that produced the strangulation had not been found, and the second was that there was a medical opinion that this was not a case of homicidal strangulation. Therefore, the case would have to be considered very carefully.

With regard to the evidence of identification, it appeared the deceased was about 26 years of age, but the mother did not appear to know whether she was married or not. She may have been married, because she was heard of under

# Appendix Q, Catherine "Rose" Mylett Murder

different names.

One of the witnesses who knew the deceased stated she was more often drunk than sober.

Deceased lived at Spitalfields, and it was a curious fact that whenever they had cases of violence in London they were generally associated with Spitalfields.

The night before her death the deceased appeared to have left the lodging-house where she lived at about 7:30. She was next seen by the witness Hill at 12:15, when she was undoubtedly under the influence of liquor. She was next seen at about a quarter to 2 o'clock on the morning of the 20th ult. near the George public house, which was some considerable distance from the spot where the body was found. Nothing more was seen of her until the body was found at about 4:30.

If the unfortunate woman met her death at the spot where the body was found it might have been done very rapidly, and no serious struggle went on. When the body was found it was in a comparatively natural condition. The usual signs of strangulation, such as protrusion of the tongue and clenching of the hands, were absent, there being nothing at all suggestive of death from violence. It was right to say, as some stress had been laid to the fact, that the police did not discover any mark at the time. The mark was not noticed until the mortuary keeper had the body stripped. The deceased's clothes were not disarranged, so that the violence must have been done with great rapidity.

In connexion with the recent so-called Whitechapel murders, there was not the slightest disarrangement of the clothes. It all depended on the suddenness with which the deceased was attacked and the capability of the deceased to resist the attack. The constable who was on the beat stated that he noticed nothing unusual about the body. After Dr. Brownfield and his assistant, duly qualified men, came to the conclusion that this was a case of homicidal strangulation, some one had a suspicion that that evidence was not satisfactory.

At all events, they heard that doctor after doctor went down to view the body without his knowledge or sanction as coroner. He did not wish to make that a personal matter, but he had never received such treatment before.

Of the five doctors who saw the body, Dr. Bond was the only one who considered the case was not one of murder. Dr. Bond did not see the body until five days after death, and he was, therefore, at a disadvantage. Dr. Bond stated that if this was a case of strangulation he should have expected to find the skin broken, but it was clearly shown, on reference being made to the records of the Indian doctors in the cases of the Thug murders, that there were no marks whatever left. Other eminent authorities agreed with that view. In this case the deceased was completely helpless and would be easily overcome.

In answer to the jury, the CORONER said he did not think any disrespect to him was intended when several doctors were sent to view the body.

The jury returned a verdict of "Wilful murder against some person or persons unknown," and commended the conduct of Sergeant Golding in the matter.

~

589

# GHASTLY MURDER

## IN THE EAST-END.

### DREADFUL MUTILATION OF A WOMAN.

## Capture : Leather Apron

Another murder of a character even more diabolical than that perpetrated in Back's Row, on Friday week, was discovered in the same neighbourhood, on Saturday morning. At about six o'clock a woman was found lying in a back yard at the foot of a passage leading to a lodging-house in a Old Brown's Lane, Spitalfields. The house is occupied by a Mrs. Richardson, who lets it out to lodgers, and the door which admits to this passage, at the foot of which lies the yard where the body was found, is always open for the convenience of lodgers. A lodger named Davis was going down to work at the time mentioned and found the woman lying on her back close to the flight of steps leading into the yard. Her throat was cut in a fearful manner. The woman's body had been completely ripped open and the heart and other organs laying about the place, and portions of the entrails round the victim's neck. An excited crowd gathered in front of Mrs. Richardson's house and also round the mortuary in old Montague Street, whither the body was quickly conveyed. As the body lies in the rough coffin in which it has been placed in the mortuary · the same coffin in which the unfortunate Mrs. Nicholls was first placed · it presents a fearful sight. The body is that of a woman about 45 years of age. The height is exactly five feet. The complexion is fair, with wavy brown hair; the eyes are blue, and two lower teeth have been knocked out. The nose is rather large and prominent.

# Bibliography

Adams, W. Davenport. A Dictionary of the Drama: A Guide to the Plays, Play-wrights, Players, and Playhouses of the United Kingdom aand America, From the Earliest Times to the Present. Vols. 1, A-G. Philadelphia, 1904.

Andrews, Billy. Billy Andrews' Comic Song-ster, Containing a Choice Collec-tion of the Newest Comic Songs. New York: Samuel Booth, Printer, 1873.

Aragon-Yoshida, Amber. Lustmord and Loving the Other: A History of Sexual Murder in Modern Germany and Austria (1873-1932). Ph.D Dissertation. Washington University in St. Louis. St. Louis: Washington University Open Scholarship, 2011.

Attewell, Alex. "Florence Nightingale." Prospects XXVIII.1 (1998).

Bachman. The Early Use of Police and Fire Alarms. 22 Mar 2015. 28 Mar 2015 <http://nrs.harvard.edu/urn-3:FHCL: 14081358>.

Barnardo's. The History of Barnardo's. 2014.

Bayliss, Bill. Miss Steer's Bridge of Hope & The Chingford Cottage Homes For Girls. Chingford, England, 2014.

Ben-Simhon, Coby. World of our (God) fathers. 21 Oct 2004. 15 Jan 2015 <http://www.haaretz.com/mobile/world-of-our-god-fathers-1.137987>.

Booth, William. In Darkest England and the Way Out. London: The Salvation Army, 1890.

Boswell, James. The Life of Samuel Johnson, LL.D. Ed. Christopher Hibbert. New York: Penguin Classics, 1979.

Breslin, Garry, ed. Collins English Dictionary-Complete and Unabridged. New York: HarperCollins Publishers, 2003.

Bruzekius, Lars. Glenorchy. 1996. 20 April 2015 <http://www.bruzelius.info/nautica/ships/Fourmast_ships/Glenorchy%281882%29.html>.

Casebook Productions. 2015 <http://www.casebook.org >.

Census1891.com. Victorian Occupations. 2003. 25 Mar 2015 <http://www.census1891.com/occupations-a.php>.

Cockton, Henry. "George St. George Julian-The Prince, Part 7." Roberts' Semi-monthly Magazine for Town and Country 1 May 1841: 285.

Collins Dictionary. Collins Dictionary. 2015. 20 Mar 2015 <http://www.collinsdictionary.com>.

Cunnington, C. Willett, Phillis Cunnington, A. D Mansfield, and Valerie Mansfield. The History of Underclothes. London: Faber and Faber, 1981.

Dibley, John. Police Rattles and Whistles. 2014. 10 March 2015 <http://www.oldpolicecellsmuseum.org.uk/page_id_434.aspx>.

Drysdale-Vickery, Dr. Alice. "Women's Part in the Malthusian Movement." Birth Control Review V.1 (1921): 11 and 17.

Dubois, Marguerite-Marie. Larousse's French-English, English-French Diction-ary. New York: Pocket Books, 1975.

Electricity. "No Title." Electricity: A Popular Electrical and Financial Journal 3.13 (1892): 170.

Emmet, ]. K. "Sweet Violets." Cincinnati: John Church & Co., 1882.

Encyclopaedia Britannica. Vol. 3. London, 1911.

Evans, Stewart & Paul Gainey. Jack the Ripper: First American Serial Killer. New York: Kodansha International, 1995.

Eveleigh, David J. Candle Lighting. Princes Risborough: Shire Publications Ltd., 2003.

Farmer, John S. and W. E. Henley. A Dic-tionary of Slang and Colloquial English. London: George Routledge & Sons, Ltd., 1905.

Fashion-era.com. Stays to Corsets-Fashion History. 2014. 28 May 2015 <http://www.fashion-era.com/stays_to_corsets.htm#Corsets%20After%201840>.

FindLaw. Fingerprints: The First ID. 2014. 2 April 2015 <http://criminal.findlaw.com/criminal-procedure/fingerprints-the-first-id.html>.

Gill, Christopher J. and Gillian C. Gill. "Nightingale in Scutari: Her Legacy Reexamined." Clinical Infectious Diseases (2005): 1799-1805.

Gilpin, Richard. The Princess Alice Disaster. 25 Aug 2010. 10 Mar 2015 <httpl//www.thamesdiscovery.org/riverpedia/the_princess_alice_disaster>.

Grimes, Kyle. The Every-Day Book (1825-26). 28 December 2003. 1 August 2015 <http://honearchive.org>.

Hasluck, Paul N., ed. Metalworking: A Book of Tools, Materials and Processes for the Handyman. London: Cassell and Company, Ltd., 1904.

Hickman, Katie. Courtesans: Money, Sex and Fame in the Nineteenth Century. New York: Morrow, 2003.

IGPI. Forty-Ninth Report of the Inspectors-General of the General State of the Prisons in Ireland, 1870; with Appendix. Dublin: Alexander Thom, 1871.

Jamieson, John. An Etymological Dictionary of the Scottish Language. Edinburgh: Abernethy & Walker, 1818.

Langland, William. The Vision of William Concerning Piers the Plowman, Together with Vita de Dowel. Dobet, et Dobest. Ed. Rev. Walter W. Skeat. Vol. 3. London: Early English Text Society, 1873. 4 vols.

Law.com. 2015.

Lloyd's. Lloyd's Register for British and Foreign Shipping: From 1st July, 1892 to the 30th of June, 1893. London: Lloyd's Register of Shipping, 1892.

McQueen, Kevin. The Axeman Came from Hell, and Other Southern True Crime Stories. Gretna: Pelican Publishing Co., 2011.

Miller, Benjamin F., MD and Claire Brackman Keane, RN. Encyclopaedia and Dictionary of Medicine, Nursing, and Allied Health. Philadelphia: W.B. Saunders Co., 1978.

Ministry of Labour. The Dictionary of Occupational Terms, Based on the Classification of Occupations used in the Census of Population 1921. London: His Majesty's Stationary Office, 1927.

Morehead, Albert and Loy, ed. The New American Webster Handy College Dic-tionary. Third. New York: Signet, 1995.

MP&C. "Obituary: Dr. Charles Robert Drys-dale." The Medical Press and Circular 135 (1907): 644.

Odell, Robin. Ripperology: A Study of the World's First Serial Killer and a Literary Phenomenon. Kent: The Kent State University Press, 2006.

# Bibliography

PAF. The History of UK Postcodes. 2015. PAF. 10 Mar 2015 <http://www.powered bypaf.com/the-history-of-uk-postcodes/>.

Post Magazine and Insurance Monitor. Vol. 61. W.S.D. Pateman, 1900.

Prochaska, F. K. Women and Philanthropy in Nineteenth-century England. Oxford: Oxford University Press, 1980.

Rao, Dr. Dinesh. Muscular Changes. Ed. Dr. Dinesh Rao. 2013. Forensic Pathology Online. 29 Mar 2015 <http://forensic pathologyonline.com/e-book/post-mortem-changes/muscular-changes>.

Roberts, M.J.D. Making English Morals: Voluntary Association and Moral Reform in England, 1787-1886. Cambridge: Cambridge University Press, 2004.

Routledge, Robert. Discoveries and Inventions of the 19th Century. 12th. London: George Routledge & Sons, Ltd., 1898.

Royal Commission. Reports by the Juries: On the Subjects in the Thirty Classes Into Which the Exhibition was Divided. London: William Clowes & Sons, 1852.

Rumbelow, Donald. Jack the Ripper: The Complete Casebook. Chicago: Contemporary Books, 1988.

Rushlights. 2015. 15 Mar 2015 <http://www.oldandinteresting.com/rushlights.aspx>.

Seccombe, Thomas. "Osborne, Sidney Godolphin." Dictionary of National Biography, 1885-1900. Vol. 42. London: Smith, Elder & Co., 1885. 294-295.

Sewell, Richard Clarke. A Treatise on Law of Coroner; with Copious Precedents of Inquisitions and Practical Forms of Proceedings. London: Owen Richards, Law Bookseller and Publisher, 1843.

Shaw, Donald. Eighteen Months Imprisonment (With a Remission). London: George Routledge and Sons, 1883.

Simpson, D.P., ed. Cassell's Latin and English Dictionary. New York: Collier Books, 1987.

Stewart, Robert W. The Police Signal Box: A 100 Year History. Glasgow: University of Strathclyde, 1994.

Strack, Hermann L. The Jew and Human Sacrifice: Human Blood and Jewish Ritual. Cope & Fenwick: London, 1909.

The Telegraph. Victorian Women Criminals' Records Show Harsh Justice of 19th Century. 25 Feb 2011. 3 April 2015 <http://www.telegraph.co.uk/news/newst opics/howaboutthat.8345046/Victorian-women-criminals-records-show-harsh-justice-of-19th-century.html>.

Theatres Trust. People's Palace (London). 2015. 20 Mar 2015 <http://www.theatres trust.org.uk/resources/theatres/show/3347 -people-s-palace-london>.

Thomas, Joseph. A Complete Pronouncing Medical Dictionary: Embracing the Terminology of Medicine and the Kindred Sciences. London: J.B. Lippincott Co., 1889.

Tortora, Phyllis G., and Keith Eubank. A Survey of Historic Costume. 5. New York: Fairchild Publications, 1989.

Ward, Robert David. Wealth and Notoriety: The Extraordinary Families of William Levy and Charles Lewis of London. Shepley, Huddersfield: Robert David Ward, 2013.

Webster's Revised Unabridged Dictionary. New York: C. & G. Merriam, 1913.

Williams, Montagu Stephen. Leaves of a Life: Being the Reminiscences of Montagu Williams. Vol. 2. Boston: Houghton, Mifflin and Co., 1890. 2 vols.

Yost, Dave. Elizabeth Stride and Jack the Ripper: The Life and Death of the Reputed Third Victim. McFarland, 2008.

Made in the USA
Las Vegas, NV
14 December 2023

82824209R10345